THE OXFORD HAN

SACRAMENTAL
THEOLOGY

THE OXFORD HANDBOOK OF

SACRAMENTAL THEOLOGY

Edited by

HANS BOERSMA

and

MATTHEW LEVERING

OXFORD

UNIVERSITY PRESS

UNIVERSITY PRESS

Great Clarendon Street, Oxford, OX2 6DP,
United Kingdom

Oxford University Press is a department of the University of Oxford.
It furthers the University's objective of excellence in research, scholarship,
and education by publishing worldwide. Oxford is a registered trade mark of
Oxford University Press in the UK and in certain other countries

Published in the United States of America by Oxford University Press
198 Madison Avenue, New York, NY 10016, United States of America

British Library Cataloguing in Publication Data
Data available

Library of Congress Cataloging in Publication Data
Data available

ISBN 978-0-19-965906-7 (Hbk.)
ISBN 978-0-19-881661-4 (Pbk.)

Acknowledgements

We are keenly aware that without the hard and meticulous work of our Research Assistants, this project would not have come to completion. Our warm thanks, therefore, go to David Augustine, Elizabeth Farnsworth, Alex Fogleman, and Matthew Thomas. We are grateful to David Augustine for preparing the Index. Tom Perridge supported this project from the outset, and we thank him and the Oxford University staff, especially Karen Raith, for their help in the process of bringing the volume to publication. Finally, we wish to thank our wives, Linda Boersma and Joy Levering, for their support and encouragement during the years in which this volume was in preparation.

CONTENTS

PART II PATRISTIC SACRAMENTAL THEOLOGY

PART III MEDIEVAL SACRAMENTAL THEOLOGY

PART IV FROM THE REFORMATION THROUGH TODAY

PART V DOGMATIC APPROACHES

PART VI PHILOSOPHICAL AND THEOLOGICAL ISSUES IN SACRAMENTAL DOCTRINE

Notes on Contributors

Anthony Akinwale, O.P. is a Dominican friar of the Nigerian Province. After initial philosophical studies in Ibadan and Kinshasa, he obtained a licentiate in theology at the Dominican University College, Ottawa, Canada, and a doctorate at Boston College. A past President of the Catholic Theological Association of Nigeria, and consultant to the Catholic Bishops' Conference of Nigeria, he is Professor of Systematic Theology at the Dominican Institute, Ibadan, Nigeria.

Michael Allen is Associate Professor of Systematic and Historical Theology at Reformed Theological Seminary in Orlando, Florida. He has written several books including, most recently, *Reformed Catholicity* (with Scott R. Swain).

Khaled Anatolios received his doctorate from Boston College in 1996. He is Professor of Theology at the University of Notre Dame and the author of *Retrieving Nicaea: The Development and Meaning of Trinitarian Doctrine* (2011), *Athanasius* (2004), and *Athanasius: The Coherence of his Thought* (1998).

Yury P. Avvakumov is Assistant Professor of Theology at the University of Notre Dame, USA. Before coming to Notre Dame in 2010, he taught Medieval and Modern Church History and was Dean of Humanities and the founding Chair of the Department of Classical, Byzantine, and Medieval Studies at the Ukrainian Catholic University in Lviv, Ukraine. He is the author of *Die Entstehung des Unionsgedankens: Die lateinische Theologie des Hochmittelalters in der Auseinandersetzung mit dem Ritus der Ostkirche* (2002) and the editor of *Metropolitan Andrei Šeptyc'kyi and Greco-Catholics in Russia, 1899-1917* (2004).

Lewis Ayres is Professor of Catholic and Historical Theology at the University of Durham, UK. His most recent book is *Augustine and the Trinity* (2010/2014).

Richard Bauckham was until 2007 Professor of New Testament Studies and Bishop Wardlaw Professor in the University of St. Andrews, Scotland, and is now Professor Emeritus at St Andrews and Senior Scholar at Ridley Hall, Cambridge. He taught historical and contemporary theology for fifteen years at the University of Manchester, before moving to St Andrews in 1992. His many publications range over many areas of biblical studies and theology.

Hans Boersma holds the J. I. Packer Chair in Theology at Regent College, Vancouver. He has authored several books, including *Embodiment and Virtue in Gregory of Nyssa* (2013); *Heavenly Participation: The Weaving of a Sacramental Tapestry* (2011); and *Nouvelle Théologie and Sacramental Ontology: A Return to Mystery* (2009). Together with Matthew Levering, he edited *Heaven on Earth? Theological Interpretation in Ecumenical Dialogue* (2013).

David Brown has been Wardlaw Professor of Theology, Aesthetics and Culture at the Institute for Theology, Imagination and the Arts in the University of St. Andrews since 2007. Prior to that, he taught first at Oxford and then at Durham where he held the Van Mildert Chair in Divinity. He was elected a Fellow of the British Academy in 2002.

Brian A. Butcher, a subdeacon in the Ukrainian Greco-Catholic Church, is currently Assistant Professor at the Metropolitan Andrey Sheptytsky Institute of Eastern Christian Studies, in Saint Paul University's Faculty of Theology (Ottawa, Canada)—where he also received his doctorate in 2011. His dissertation explored the pertinence of the hermeneutical philosophy of Paul Ricoeur for liturgical theology, as exemplified in the Byzantine Rite's "Great Blessing of Water" for Theophany. Prior to his appointment at Saint Paul, he taught in British Columbia at Redeemer Pacific College/Trinity Western University, Simon Fraser University and the Seminary of Christ the King/ Westminster Abbey.

Peter J. Casarella is an Associate Professor at the University of Notre Dame where he is also a Fellow of the Kellogg Institute of International Studies, the Institute for Latino Studies, and the Medieval Institute. He formerly served as founding Director of the Center for World Catholicism and Intercultural Theology at DePaul University. His publications focus on Nicholas of Cusa, Hans Urs von Balthasar, and U.S. Latino/a Theology.

Boyd Taylor Coolman (Ph.D., University of Notre Dame, 2001) is Associate Professor of Theology at Boston College. His scholarly interests lie in the twelfth and thirteenth centuries, with a particular focus on the Victorines (especially Hugh of St. Victor and Thomas Gallus) and on early thirteenth-century Franciscan theology, especially the theology of Alexander of Hales. He is also interested in such theological topics as Trinity, Christology, Eucharist, and mystical theology.

Adam A. J. DeVille is Associate Professor and Chairman of the Department of Theology-Philosophy at the University of Saint Francis, Fort Wayne, Indiana; editor of *Logos: A Journal of Eastern Christian Studies*; and the author of *Orthodoxy and the Roman Papacy* (2011) as well as of over 100 articles and reviews in journals in Europe and North America. He is currently editing three collections of scholarly articles: one on Orthodox-Muslim relations for Routledge Press; another on the future of Eastern Orthodoxy in North America for the University of Notre Dame Press; and a third on celibacy and marriage among Eastern Catholic priests, also forthcoming from University of Notre Dame Press.

Craig A. Evans received his Ph.D. from Claremont and his D.Habil. from Budapest. He is the Payzant Distinguished Professor of New Testament at Acadia Divinity College and author of numerous publications.

David W. Fagerberg is Associate Professor in the Department of Theology of the University of Notre Dame. He holds an M.Div. from Luther Northwestern Seminary; an M.A. from St. John's University, Collegeville; an S.T.M. from Yale Divinity School; and the Ph.D. from Yale University. His work has focused on the integration of liturgy, theology, and asceticism.

Everett Ferguson is Distinguished Scholar in Residence at Abilene Christian University, Abilene, Texas. He is a past president of the North American Patristics Society and has served on the board of the American Society of Church History and the Association internationale d'études patristiques. His books include *Baptism in the Early Church: History, Theology, and Liturgy in the First Five Centuries* (2013); *Backgrounds of Early Christianity* (1987; 3rd ed., 2003); *Church History*, vol. 1: *From Christ to Pre-Reformation* (2005); and *The Early Church at Work and Worship* (2 vols.; 2013–14). He was editor of *The Encyclopedia of Early Christianity* (1997) and the journal *The Second Century* and co-editor of its successor *Journal of Early Christian Studies*. The library of Abilene Christian University has recently digitized and is making available online his slide collection of nearly 10,000 slides pertaining to the ancient Mediterranean world and early Christian history.

Peter Galadza, an archpriest of the Ukrainian Greco-Catholic Church, is Kule Family Professor of Liturgy at the Sheptytsky Institute of Eastern Christian Studies, Saint Paul University, Ottawa, Canada. He is also managing editor of *Logos: A Journal of Eastern Christian Studies*. In 2003–04 he was a research fellow at Harvard University's Dumbarton Oaks Byzantine Research Center, and in 2010 was elected president of the Society of Oriental Liturgy.

E. Brooks Holifield is the Charles Howard Candler Professor of American Church History, Emeritus. He spent his career at the Candler School of Theology at Emory University in Atlanta. The author of seven books, including the award winning *Theology in America*, he received three fellowships from the National Endowment for the Humanities and one each from the Luce Foundation, the Pew Endowment, and the Louisville Center. He is a fellow of the American Academy of Arts and Sciences.

Edith M. Humphrey is the William F. Orr Professor of Biblical Studies at Pittsburgh Theological Seminary and a member of the Orthodox Church. She has written seven books (*The Ladies and the Cities; (Guide to) Joseph and Aseneth; And I Turned to See the Voice; Ecstasy and Intimacy: When the Holy Spirit Meets the Human Spirit; Grand Entrance: Worship on Earth as in Heaven; Scripture and Tradition: What the Bible Really Says*) as well as numerous scholarly and popular articles on biblical, theological, ecclesial, and contemporary ethical topics.

Thomas Humphries is an Assistant Professor of Philosophy, Theology, and Religion and the Assistant Director of the Honors Program at Saint Leo University in Florida, USA. While his teaching is broad at the undergraduate and graduate levels, his research focuses on fifth- and sixth-century theology and its reception.

George Hunsinger received his degrees from Stanford, Harvard, and Yale. He is currently the Hazel Thompson McCord Professor of Systematic Theology at Princeton Theological Seminary. In 2006 he founded the National Religious Campaign against Torture. He is a delegate to the official Reformed/Roman Catholic International Dialogue (2011–17). Among his books are *The Eucharist and Ecumenism: Let Us Keep the Feast* (2008) and *The Beatitudes* (2014). He is an ordained Presbyterian minister (PCUSA).

Luke Timothy Johnson is the Robert W. Woodruff Distinguished Professor of New Testament and Christian Origins at Candler School of Theology, Emory University. His works include *The Writings of the New Testament: An Interpretation*, 3rd edition (2010), *Among the Gentiles: Greco-Roman Religion and Early Christianity* (2009), and *Hebrews: A Commentary* (2006).

Jeremiah J. Johnston received his Ph.D. from Middlesex University and completed his residency at the Oxford Centre for Mission Studies. He serves as Associate Professor at Houston Baptist University and has published works on early Christianity.

John C. Kasza is a priest of the Archdiocese of Detroit, Michigan (USA). He holds degrees in history, divinity and earned his doctorate in sacramental theology from the Pontifical Athenaeum Sant'Anselmo in Rome, Italy. He has held many positions in parishes, chancery, and seminary, including Vice-Chancellor and Secretary to the Cardinal, assistant professor of liturgy and sacraments, and Academic Dean. Currently, he is pastor of St. James the Greater parish in Novi, Michigan.

Lucas Laborde, S.S.J., a native of Argentina, is pastor of St. Patrick's Catholic Church in Portland, and director of the Portland State University Newman Center, where he teaches philosophy, theology, and apologetics. He is a priest of the Saint John Society.

Gordon W. Lathrop is a Lutheran pastor and a liturgical theologian. From 2004 to 2010, he taught in Yale Divinity School as Visiting Professor of Liturgical Studies. Since 2004, he has been Professor of Liturgy Emeritus at the Lutheran Theological Seminary at Philadelphia, where he taught for twenty years. He is the author of several books, including *Holy Things: A Liturgical Theology* (1993) and *The Four Gospels on Sunday* (Fortress 2012). His doctoral studies, completed in 1969, were at the University of Nijmegen, the Netherlands, under the direction of Bastiaan van Iersel and Edward Schillebeeckx. He lives in Arlington, Virginia.

Peter J. Leithart is President of the Theopolis Institute, a study center and pastoral training program in Birmingham, Alabama. An ordained minister in the Presbyterian Church in America, he also serves as a teacher at Trinity Presbyterian Church, Birmingham, and as an adjunct Senior Fellow of Theology at New Saint Andrews College, Moscow, Idaho. He is author, most recently, of *Gratitude: An Intellectual History* (2014) and *Traces of the Trinity* (2015).

Matthew Levering is James N. and Mary D. Perry Jr Chair of Theology at Mundelein Seminary. He serves as co-editor of two theological quarterlies, *Nova et Vetera* and the *International Journal of Systematic Theology*. He has authored numerous books, including *Sacrifice and Community: Jewish Offering and Christian Eucharist* (2005) and *Christ and the Catholic Priesthood* (2010). With Hans Boersma, he edited *Heaven on Earth? Theological Interpretation in Ecumenical Dialogue* (2013). He and Gilles Emery co-edited *The Oxford Handbook of the Trinity*.

Ian Christopher Levy is Associate Professor of Theology at Providence College in Providence, Rhode Island. His work focuses on medieval sacramental theology, biblical exegesis, and ecclesiology. His most recent book is *Holy Scripture and the Quest for Authority at the End of the Middle Ages* (2012).

David Lincicum is Associate Professor of New Testament Studies at the University of Oxford, and G. B. Caird Fellow in Theology at Mansfield College. He is the author of *Paul and the Early Jewish Encounter with Deuteronomy*, and his research focuses on the intersection of early Jewish, early Christian, and New Testament studies.

Andrew Louth is Professor Emeritus of Patristic and Byzantine Studies, University of Durham, and Visiting Professor of Eastern Orthodox Theology at the Amsterdam Centre of Eastern Orthodox Theology (ACEOT), Vrije Universiteit, Amsterdam, 2010–14. He is also a priest of the Russian Orthodox Diocese of Sourozh (Moscow Patriarchate), serving the parish in Durham. His books include *The Origins of the Christian Mystical Tradition: From Plato to Denys* (1981; revised edition, 2007); *Denys the Areopagite* (1989); *Maximus the Confessor* (1996); *St John Damascene: Tradition and Originality in Byzantine Theology* (2002); *Greek East and Latin West: the Church AD 681–1071* (2007); *Introducing Eastern Orthodox Theology* (2013).

Bruce D. Marshall is Lehman Professor of Christian Doctrine at the Perkins School of Theology, Southern Methodist University. He has also taught at St. Olaf College, and did his graduate work at Yale, following undergraduate work at Northwestern University. He is the author of *Trinity and Truth* and *Christology in Conflict*, and of several articles on Trinitarian theology, Christology, and the relationship between Judaism and Christianity.

Mickey L. Mattox is Associate Professor of Theology at Marquette University, Milwaukee, WI. His recent publications include *Changing Churches: An Orthodox, Catholic, and Lutheran Theological Conversation* (2012), and *Iohannes Oecolampadius: An Exposition of Genesis* (2013).

R. W. L. Moberly is an ordained Anglican who is Professor of Theology and Biblical Interpretation at Durham University. He loves working next door to Durham cathedral. His most recent book is *Old Testament Theology: Reading the Hebrew Bible as Christian Scripture* (2013).

Martha L. Moore-Keish is Associate Professor of Theology at Columbia Theological Seminary in Atlanta, Georgia. She earned her Ph.D. in theology at Emory University and is an ordained minister in the Presbyterian Church (USA). Her primary areas of interest are liturgical, sacramental, and ecumenical theologies, as well as interfaith relations. She has published two books: *Do This in Remembrance of Me: A Ritual Approach to Reformed Eucharistic Theology* (2008), and *Christian Prayer for Today* (2009).

Francesca Aran Murphy is Professor of Systematic Theology at the University of Notre Dame. She is the author of numerous books, including *Christ the Form of Beauty* (1995), *God is Not a Story* (2007) and a theological commentary on *I Samuel* (2010). She is currently editing a new series for Bloomsbury Academic called *Illuminating Modernity*. The first book in the series, of which she is a co-author, is called *Illuminating Faith*.

Dennis T. Olson is the Charles Haley Professor of Old Testament Theology and chair of the Biblical Department at Princeton Theological Seminary in Princeton, New Jersey. His research focus is the Pentateuch and Old Testament theology. Among other books, he has written theological commentaries on the books of Numbers, Deuteronomy, and Judges, and he is currently working on a commentary on the book of Exodus.

Chad C. Pecknold (Ph.D., Cambridge) teaches historical and systematic theology at the Catholic University of America. He is the author of *Transforming Postliberal Theology* (2005), *Christianity and Politics: A Brief Guide to the History* (2010), and has edited several volumes of essays, including *The T&T Clark Companion to Augustine and Modern Theology* (2012) with Tarmo Toom.

Nicholas Perrin (Ph.D., Marquette University) is Dean of the Wheaton Graduate School where he also holds the Franklin S. Dyrness Chair of Biblical Studies. Between 2000 and 2003, he was research assistant for N. T. Wright and has since authored and edited numerous articles and books, including *Thomas and Tatian* (2003); *Thomas: The Other Gospel* (2007); *Lost in Transmission? What We Can Know about the Words of Jesus* (2009); and *Jesus the Temple* (2010), the first of a three-part trilogy on the historical Jesus. He is also co-editor of the recently revised edition of *Dictionary of Jesus and the Gospels* (2013).

Catherine Pickstock is a University Reader in Philosophy and Theology at Cambridge University and a Fellow of Emmanuel College, Cambridge. Her most recent book is *Repetition and Identity* (2013).

Trent Pomplun (M.A., Ph.D., University of Virginia) is the author of *Jesuit on the Roof of the World: Ippolito Desideri's Mission to Tibet* (2010) and co-editor of *The Blackwell Companion to Catholicism* (2007). His articles have appeared in *The Journal of Religion*, *Modern Theology*, and *History of Religions* (among other journals), and his interests include baroque theology, missions history, and Indo-Tibetan religion and culture.

John D. Rempel is a Mennonite minister. He has been active as a pastor, Mennonite liaison for peace and development at the United Nations, and professor of theology. He is the editor of his church's *Minister's Manual* (1998). Currently he is the director of the Mennonite Centre at the Toronto School of Theology. His abiding concern has been the relationship between worship and social change.

Jorge A. Scampini, O.P. (Th.D., University of Fribourg, Switzerland), is Titular Professor of Dogmatic Theology at the Centro de Estudios de Filosofía y Teología de la Orden de Predicadores—Universidad del Norte Santo Tomás de Aquino (Buenos Aires) and Extraordinary Professor of Sacramental Theology and Ecumenism at the Faculty of Theology of the Pontificia Universidad Católica Argentina (Buenos Aires). Previously he was Invited Professor at the Faculty of Theology of the *Angelicum* University (Rome) and Member of the Plenary Commission of Faith and Order (1991–2013); the Baptist–Roman Catholic Conversations (2006-2010); the Reformed–Roman Catholic International Dialogue (2010–); and the Methodist–Roman Catholic International Dialogue (2012–). He also served as President of the Sociedad Argentina de Teología (2010–13).

Benoît-Dominique de La Soujeole, O.P. is a French Dominican who teaches ecclesiology and the sacraments at the University of Fribourg (Switzerland). His main field of research focuses on the sacramentality of salvation, including Christology, ecclesiology, sacramental theology, and ecumenical and interreligious dialogue. He is a member of the editorial board of *La Revue Thomiste* (Toulouse, France). His principal publications include *Le sacrement de la communion: Essai d'ecclésiologie fondamentale* (1998), *Introduction au mystère de l'Église* (2006), and *Prêtre du Seigneur dans son Église* (2009).

Scott R. Swain is Professor of Systematic Theology and Academic Dean at Reformed Theological Seminary in Orlando, Florida. His recent books include *The God of the Gospel: Robert Jenson's Trinitarian Theology* (2013) and *Trinity, Revelation, and Reading: A Theological Introduction to the Bible and its Interpretation* (2011).

Mark G. Vaillancourt is a priest of the Archdiocese of New York and the president of Kennedy Catholic High School, Somers, New York. He holds a doctorate in historical theology from Fordham University and is a member of the North American Patristics Society. Fr. Vaillancourt is both a translator and author of a number of works on the historical development of theology, including *Lanfranc of Canterbury, On the Body and Blood of the Lord, Guitmund of Aversa, On the Truth of the Body and Blood of Christ in the Eucharist* (2009).

Geoffrey Wainwright is an ordained minister of the British Methodist Church, who early served as a missionary teacher and pastor in Cameroon, West Africa (1967–73). From 1976 to 1991 he was a member of the Faith and Order Commission of the World Council of Churches. From 1986 to 2012 he co-chaired the Joint Commission for Dialogue between the World Methodist Council and the Roman Catholic Church. From 1983 to 2012 Professor Wainwright taught Systematic Theology in the Divinity School of Duke University, Durham, North Carolina, where he now holds the title of Cushman Professor Emeritus of Christian Theology.

Peter Walter received his doctorate of Theology in 1980 after his studies in Philosophy and Catholic Theology in Mainz and Rome. After working in pastoral care, he was Research Assistant in Tübingen and earned his *Habilitation* there in 1989. Since 1990, he has been Professor of Dogmatics at the theological faculty of the University of Freiburg in Breisgau and Director of the *Arbeitsbereichs Quellenkunde* of the theology of the Middle Ages (Raimundus–Lullus–Institut). Since 1991, he has been a member of the *Ökumenischer Arbeitskreis* of Evangelical (Lutheran/Reformed) and Catholic theologians, and since 2004 Chairman of the Society for Publication of the Corpus Catholicorum.

Brent Waters, D.Phil., is the Jerre and Mary Joy Professor of Christian Social Ethics, and Director of the Jerre L. and Mary Joy Stead Center for Ethics and Values at Garrett-Evangelical Theological Seminary, Evanston, Illinois. He is the author of *Economic Globalization and Christian Ethics* (forthcoming), *Christian Moral Theology in the Emerging Technoculture: From Posthuman Back to Human* (2014); *This Mortal Flesh: Incarnation and Bioethics* (2009); *The Family in Christian Social and Political Thought* (2007); *From Human to Posthuman: Christian Theology and Technology in a Postmodern World* (2006); *Reproductive Technology: Towards a Theology of Procreative Stewardship* (2001); and *Dying and Death: A Resource for Christian Reflection* (1996). He is a graduate of the University of Redlands (B.A.), School of Theology at Claremont (M.Div., D.Min.), and the University of Oxford (D.Phil.).

Joseph P. Wawrykow teaches in the Theology department at the University of Notre Dame, where he is also a fellow of the Medieval Institute. He is the author of *God's Grace and Human Action* (1995) and *The Westminster Handbook to Thomas Aquinas* (2005), and co-editor of *Christ among the Medieval Dominicans* (1998) and *The Theology of Thomas Aquinas* (2005).

Thomas Joseph White, O.P. is the Director of the Thomistic Institute at the Pontifical Faculty of the Immaculate Conception in Washington, D.C. He is the author of *Wisdom in the Face of Modernity: A Study in Thomistic Natural Theology* (2009) and *The Incarnate Lord: A Thomistic Study in Christology* (2015).

INTRODUCTION

The Handbook's Three Purposes

HANS BOERSMA AND MATTHEW LEVERING

THE vast subject of the sacraments of the Christian churches cannot be exhausted by one Handbook, valuable though we hope it will prove to be. As a multi-faceted introduction to sacramental theology, the purposes of this Handbook are threefold: historical, ecumenical, and missional. In this brief Introduction, therefore, we wish to briefly explain these three purposes.

First, of the 44 chapters that comprise our Handbook, 28 are historical. By devoting two-thirds of the Handbook to historical surveys, we are able to introduce readers to the historical roots and development of Christian sacramental worship. That history is testified to in the various writings of the New Testament, and it has important background both in the Old Testament and in Second Temple literature (some of which finds a place in the Catholic and Orthodox canons of Scripture). The contributors to this Handbook explain the diverse ways in which believers have construed the sacraments, both in inspired Scripture and in the history of the church's practice. In Scripture and the early church, Orthodox, Protestants, and Catholics all find evidence that the first Christian communities celebrated and taught about the sacraments in a manner that Orthodox, Protestants, and Catholics today affirm as the foundation of their own faith and practice.

Over time, the diverse Christian churches have developed their own theological conversations, so that an expert in the sacramental theology of one ecclesial tradition or time period may devote a lifetime to studying a set of figures who may be almost unknown within other ecclesial traditions or time periods. Yet the historical surveys in this volume also show that in the diverse ecclesial traditions, the reception history of the scriptural testimony exhibits strong family resemblances. Furthermore, in each historical period, among Orthodox, Protestants, and Catholics we observe cross-fertilization and mutual indebtedness in the face of the problems and issues common to the historical period. Put simply: historical studies, including historical research into Scripture, exhibit not merely differences but also the seeds and evidence of unity.

Thus, for those who want to understand what has been taught about the sacraments in Scripture and across the generations by the major thinkers of the various Christian traditions, this Handbook provides an introduction. However, the volume also contains 16 chapters that are not classified as historical. These include a chapter on liturgical theology and the sacraments; constructive chapters on each of the sacraments (including the ecumenically contested ones); and theological and philosophical chapters that reflect on the sacraments in light of other theological loci (eschatology, the Trinity, and so forth). Not surprisingly, these chapters, too, reflect the divisions and distinctions that we find in the explicitly historical sections; and these constructive chapters also draw upon and develop the major sources that the historical chapters present to the reader. Not least because the authors of these constructive chapters are ecumenically diverse, the challenge of the historical chapters persists: where is Christian unity in worship to be found? As a second purpose, therefore, this Handbook is intended to be a contribution to Christian ecumenism.

How could it be otherwise, as Christians arrive at the 500th anniversary of the Reformation divisions? And at the same time, how could it be otherwise, given that the Christian gospel is as compelling as ever and Christ calls us to be one (John 17:22)? Ecumenically, the editors of the Unitas Books series—a series that like the present Handbook is a fruit of the great twentieth-century ecumenical movement—remind us that "[d]ivision has become deeply embedded in the everyday life and thought of the churches" (Hjelm, Root, and Rusch 2004: iii). A Handbook on *sacramental* theology, even more than on most other Christian topics, makes poignantly manifest these divisions. They are not "mere" theoretical divisions but divisions at the level of basic Christian practice. Indeed, they involve our very unity with the crucified and risen Lord through the means by which he wills to unite us to his own self-offering to the Father in the Spirit. Yet the present Handbook also exhibits powerful streams and sources of unity in Christian sacramental faith and practice. The ecumenical organization and thrust of this Handbook need not lead us to seek a common denominator, whether found in Scripture or in the histories of the sacramental theologies of particular Christian communities. Rather than taking such an approach, we have sought instead to involve contributors whose sympathies and perspectives lie firmly within a particular Christian community. As a gift of the Holy Spirit, Christian unity requires learning how to perceive each other's gifts, which can be done only when these gifts are fully and faithfully presented.

Experience has also shown that the ecumenical movement falters when it becomes focused upon the churches themselves, rather than upon the Lord and upon bearing witness to his conquest of death, his call to charity in and through his Holy Spirit, and his invitation to everlasting sharing in the life of God. Thus, insofar as our Handbook has an *ecumenical* purpose, it unavoidably also has a *missional* dynamism. We are not suggesting that these chapters, or the volume as a whole, stand in for catechesis or have a catechetical intention. But the task of writing about Christianity, even in a painstakingly objective manner, inevitably invites the sharing of the gospel, the message of joy, and consummation and communion that lurks behind even the driest or most critical description. Moreover, this Handbook has been prepared and published during a time of religious transition and turmoil in the world. On the one hand, there are energetic and growing Christian movements, especially Pentecostal ones, for which many of the structures known to traditional ecumenism have become otiose. These new movements are present in a Christianity that is becoming more global than ever. In this global context—either paradoxically or predictably, depending upon one's perspective—hierarchical structures (not least the papacy) are demonstrating their relevance and their power for energetic intellectual and pastoral renewal. On the other hand, other religions, such as Islam, and the rising popularity of atheism as a counter-religion, are also radically reshaping the landscape, not least in Europe, North America, and the Middle East.

A Handbook with a historical trajectory invites questions about the nature of history, which Christians understand to be guided and unified, in an often mysterious manner, by divine providence. Kevin Vanhoozer observes, "The Christian story—the grand narrative that encompasses the histories of the cosmos, of Israel, of Christ, and the church—has a beginning, middle, and end" (Vanhoozer 2010: 316). Written in the "middle," this Handbook may turn out to be an instrument for the communication of Christian realities to societies and peoples who have turned away from the gospel or who have never truly heard it, or who have embraced the gospel but without historical knowledge of its Spirit-guided reception. In the midst of the Second Vatican Council, Yves Congar wrote, "Two-thirds of the world's population live in Asia. It follows that we must rethink everything in terms of a mission and of a mission that is world-wide" (Congar 1963: 75). Indeed, no Handbook on sacramental theology can be truly historical and ecumenical without having also a missional dimension, a sense of the gospel as something not simply *for the churches* but something to be shared.

The connection between the gospel, sacraments, and mission is made explicit by the Orthodox Archbishop Anastasios Yannoulatos, who like Congar (and not coincidentally) was writing during the Second Vatican Council: "The Resurrection constitutes the backbone of Orthodox worship.... Orthodox hymnology—that of the period of Pentecost, as well as that of the Sunday Vespers and Matins—proclaims it as the very center par excellence of the salvation of all humankind and describes the missionary obligation that arises from this unique historical event" (Yannoulatos 2010: 28). Again, we trust readers will recognize that the Handbook has not been conceived as a labor of catechesis, however laudable such an endeavor may be. The point, rather, is that a work such as this, precisely as conceived with historical and ecumenical purposes, also by its nature has missional implications.

In short, while the divisions in Christian sacramental understanding and practice are certainly evident in this Handbook, the Handbook is not thereby without ecumenical and missional value. Ecumenically, division cannot be the focus, but rather the Lord's gifts must be. In a chapter on the relationship of spirituality and theology, Alejandro García-Rivera offers a conclusion that we can apply to the situation encountered by an ecumenical Handbook on the sacraments, since the sacraments are sites of serious division and disharmony in Christian history that are nonetheless, and simultaneously, markers and instruments of unity and harmony: "We are, in the language of Vatican II, pilgrims, communities of discernment in the midst of a great suffering. Suffering, an ever present reality, is not the foundation of our discernment. Rather, the Glory of the Lord, Beauty itself, charges the world with values as signposts to a vision scarcely imagined" (García-Rivera 1998: 133). The sacraments are such signposts; the Lord, Beauty itself, has indeed charged the world with signposts. Death is not the end of the story. The material cosmos is not a site of endless, meaningless entropy, distance, and annihilation. The story of the Christian sacraments is, despite divisions in interpretation and practice, one of tremendous hope.

Bibliography

Congar, Yves (1963), *Report from Rome: The First Session of the Vatican Council*, trans. A. Manson (London: Geoffrey Chapman, 1963).

García-Rivera, Alejandro (1998), "Wisdom, Beauty, and the Cosmos in Hispanic Spirituality and Theology," in *El Cuerpo de Cristo: The Hispanic Presence in the U.S. Catholic Church*, ed. Peter J. Casarella and Raúl Gómez (New York: Crossroad), 106–133.

Hjelm, Norman A., Michael Root, and William G. Rusch (2004), "Unitas Books," in Ola Tjørhom, *Visible Church—Visible Unity: Ecumenical Ecclesiology and "The Great Tradition of the Church"* (Collegeville, MN: Liturgical Press).

Vanhoozer, Kevin J. (2010), *Remythologizing Theology: Divine Action, Passion, and Authorship* (Cambridge: Cambridge University Press).

Yannoulatos, Archbishop Anastasios (2010), "Orthodoxy and Mission," in Yannoulatos, *Mission in Christ's Way: An Orthodox Understanding of Mission* (Brookline, MA: Holy Cross Orthodox Press), 25–37.

PART I

SACRAMENTAL ROOTS IN SCRIPTURE

CHAPTER 1

···

SACRAMENTALITY AND
THE OLD TESTAMENT

···

R. W. L. MOBERLY

SACRAMENTS are integral to Christian faith and theology in the mainstream churches, and much sacramental theology takes its bearings from the New Testament. The Old Testament, however, although a major part of the Christian Bible, is a collection of writings that are all pre-Christian in origin. It is thus not self-evident how best to bring this material to bear upon a Christian understanding of the sacraments.

Of course, the fact that the church has located these pre-Christian scriptures of Israel within the Christian Bible, as Old Testament alongside the New Testament, implies that they have enduring significance for the understanding of Christian faith. At the very least this can take the form of showing historical antecedents to Christian faith. But Christians have characteristically wanted to do more than this with Israel's scriptures, on the grounds that in important ways they remain both a source and a norm for Christianity. Even so, it is an open and ongoing question how best to understand and appropriate their content for this purpose.

First, a brief comment about the possible sacramental nature of these ancient texts as themselves material objects, especially in a Jewish frame of reference. Within Jewish tradition Torah scrolls are holy objects. They must be prepared according to detailed standards; they are housed in an ark in a central position at the front of a synagogue; when they are transported, it is customary to stand; and they are lovingly held in joyful dance on the festival of *Simchat Torah*. The writing of these scrolls is a hallowed and meticulous responsibility, and these scrolls, if worn out through prolonged usage, are never to be destroyed but rather laid aside in a special store room, a genizah, or given a ceremonial burial. The Torah scrolls both depict and symbolize the LORD's loving call of Israel to be His special people, and they contain the written form of the foundational story of the Jewish people and the commandments they must accordingly observe. There are obvious analogies with some Christian reverential practices with regard to the Bible, and especially certain liturgical handlings of the Gospels as the heart of Christian Scripture as the Torah is the heart of Jewish Scripture. Thus Jewish tradition ascribes to the first five books of Torah, in their material form as sacred scrolls, a significance which Christians might well consider merits the epithet "sacramental." Nonetheless, the focus in this essay will be on the content of Israel's scriptures in relation to sacramentality, rather than these scriptures themselves as possibly sacramental.

I will approach the issue in two ways. First, I will say something about the classic Christian way of relating the Old Testament to Christian sacraments. Secondly, I will make some suggestions as to how the notion of sacramentality might be encountered within Israel's scriptures in terms of their own conceptualities and frame of reference.

CLASSIC CHRISTIAN FIGURAL READING OF THE OLD TESTAMENT

The understanding that the content of the Old Testament in various ways adumbrates and anticipates the New Testament is present already in the New Testament, and is extensively developed by the Church Fathers. A characteristic Christian reading strategy developed in late antiquity, with a particular interest in Old Testament content as in various ways analogical to the content of the New Testament, such that it is appropriately read in a figural manner. A major locus for this understanding of the Old Testament became Christian liturgy, and this understanding can still be seen in many mainstream Christian liturgies today. One of the best accounts of this patristic construal of the Old Testament in relation to liturgy is by Jean Daniélou, S. J. (see especially Daniélou 1960). Recent renewed interest in the possibility of rearticulating and reappropriating this classic approach in the light of modern literary and hermeneutical theory is well represented by the work of John Dawson (2002). If historical accuracy and lack of anachronism is no longer the sole interpretive priority, as it typically has been in mainstream historical-critical biblical scholarship, but imaginatively serious engagement with the world depicted within the biblical texts and with their symbolic and existential dimensions becomes also an acceptable mode of intellectual engagement, then numerous possibilities for re-engagement with those modes of thought characteristic of patristic and premodern approaches can open up afresh.

Christians historically differ on precisely what counts as a sacrament (see e.g. Davison 2013: 66–74). One famous difference is between Protestant churches, which allow only two sacraments, baptism and Eucharist/holy communion/Lord's Supper as instituted by Christ, and the Roman Catholic Church, which recognizes seven sacraments (baptism, Eucharist, confirmation, ordination, marriage, anointing, confession). For simplicity I will in this section solely focus on baptism and Eucharist, as this will provide sufficient opportunity to appreciate the characteristic hermeneutical strategies employed in relating these uncontested sacraments to their Old Testament antecedents, strategies which are not different in kind from those employed in relation to those other Christian practices which have also been considered sacramental.

The basic logic of a figural reading in relation to baptism is to consider significant moments in the Old Testament that involve water in conjunction with two specific concerns: deliverance and purification. Daniélou (1960: 78) notes "the error of certain exegetes [who] try to recognize a type of Baptism wherever water is mentioned in the Old Testament." The most extensive water-and-deliverance narrative is the story of Noah and the flood, and already in the New Testament this is figurally related to baptism (1 Pet 3:18–22). The next most momentous water-related event is Israel's crossing of the Red Sea, which marks the climax of Israel's deliverance from Egypt and the power of the Pharaoh, and this is seen as a figure of baptism by Paul (1 Cor 10:1–4). Both of these are taken up and extensively developed by the Fathers, who also develop the implications of the crossing of the river Jordan, primarily by Israel under Joshua when they enter the promised land (Josh 3–4), but also by Elijah and Elisha when Elijah is taken up to heaven (2 Kgs 2:1–18).

With regard to the Eucharist there are two distinct dimensions in relation to which Old Testament figures are adduced. One is the self-offering of Jesus, which can be related to Old Testament sacrifices, not least in relation to the stories of Abel and Isaac (Gen 4: 22). The other is the participation of believers in what Jesus has done, in which the prime symbol of participation is eating, as figured in various ways in the Paschal meal (Exod 12), the manna (Exod 16), and in certain meals with a divine invitation attached to them (e.g. Isa 25:6, 55:1).

Figural readings are classically understood to be far more than pleasing imaginative exercises. As Daniélou puts it, in the context of discussing types of baptism (1960: 71):

> In the thought of the Fathers, these types are not mere illustrations: the Old Testament figures were meant to authorize Baptism by a showing that it has been announced by a whole tradition: they are *testimonia* ... And, above all, their purpose is also to explain Baptism, a purpose which still holds good today.

Moreover, different Old Testament passages can serve different theological purposes. Daniélou (1960: 75) observes of the Flood narrative that its symbolism "is not primarily that of water as washing, but of water as destroying, and this will allow us to grasp the direct relationship between the rite itself and the theology of Baptism as configuration to the death of Christ." With the crossing of the Jordan, however, "the water here is not water considered as destroying and creating, but rather as purifying and sanctifying" (1960: 100), and it thus relates closely to the baptism of Christ in the Jordan, with the further dimension of Joshua as a type of Jesus.

A figural example worth developing a little, in relation to the Eucharist, is that of Melchizedek, who undoubtedly intrigues the imagination. He is mentioned only twice in the Old Testament, once as someone who is not only king of Salem [probably Jerusalem] but also priest of "God Most High" and who brings bread and wine to Abraham and blesses him (Gen 14:18–20), and once as an exemplar of unending priesthood for the addressee of Psalm 110 (Ps 110:4). In the New Testament the writer to the Hebrews draws on both these passages and develops an extended analogy between the priesthood of Melchizedek and that of Christ (Heb 5–7). His reading is imaginative and seminal. For example, the mysterious abruptness of Melchizedek's appearance and disappearance in Genesis, with the complete lack of conventional narrative markers, is read as depicting him as "without father, without mother, without genealogy, having neither beginning of days nor end of life," and thereby "resembling the Son of God, he remains a priest for ever" (Heb 7:4). Although the writer to the Hebrews does not develop the significance of Melchizedek's bread and wine, which on its own terms in the Genesis narrative might solely signify food and drink to refresh Abraham, others were not slow to see its figural potential. Thus Cyprian says: "For who is more a priest of the most high God than our Lord Jesus Christ, who offered sacrifice to God the Father and offered the very same thing that Melchizedek had offered, bread and wine, that is, actually, his body and blood" (*Letters* 63:4, in Sheridan 2002: 26). In the sixteenth century, however, Calvin uses the silence about the bread and wine in Hebrews as the basis for arguing that a Eucharistic reading of Melchizedek is unwarranted, and is merely "the fictions of the ancients" (Calvin 2005 [1847; 1554]: 390). It is probably this polemical background that makes Daniélou feel the need to make the argument, in itself rather surprising, that Jesus' choice of bread and wine in the Upper Room was made with conscious reference to Melchizedek, and so "the visible matter of the Eucharist was an effective allusion to the sacrifice of Melchisedech, an allusion willed by Christ and not imagined later by the Fathers" (1960: 145).

The figure of Melchizedek could be readily read in polemical mode, not just between Protestants and Catholics, but also between Christians and Jews. The Fathers were able to follow the lead of the writer to the Hebrews, and also the argument of Paul in Romans and Galatians, to read Melchizedek as a figure whose Genesis context gives him particular significance. Not only, like Abraham, is he prior to Moses and Torah and the Levitical priesthood, but also, insofar as he blesses Abraham, he appears to be Abraham's spiritual superior. Ambrose states it sharply:

> Receive what I say, to know that the mysteries of the Christians are anterior to those of the Jews. If the Jews go back to Abraham, the figure of our sacraments came before, when the high priest Melchizedek came before Abraham the victor and offered for him bread and wine. Who had the bread and wine? It was not Abraham, but Melchizedek. He it is, then, who is the author of the sacraments. (*On the Sacraments* 4:10, in Daniélou 1960: 144)

In the late nineteenth century Franz Delitzsch (1888: 412) re-expresses basic elements of this ancient understanding in a more lyrical mode:

> [J]ust where Abraham appears at the most ideal elevation, Melchizedek stands beside and towers above him. Melchizedek is like the setting sun of the primitive revelation made to men before their separation into nations, the last rays of which shine upon the patriarch, from whom the true light of the world is in process of coming. This sun sets to rise again in antitype in Jesus Christ, when the preparatory epoch of Israel shall have passed. In the light of this antitype the gifts of Melchizedek acquire

a typical significance. They foreshadow the gifts which the exalted heavenly Priest-King brings in love for the refreshment of those who are of the faith of Abraham.

Within their own frame of reference such readings of the text can be rich and suggestive. But there are also other frames of reference for reading.

A FIGURAL READING OF NAAMAN

Something of both the strength and the weakness of a classic figural reading of the Old Testament can be seen through a detailed consideration of the story of Naaman in 2 Kings 5. Naaman, an Aramean/Syrian general, is, among other things, healed from "leprosy" when, on Elisha's instructions, he immerses himself seven times in the river Jordan.[1] At least since the time of Origen, Naaman's immersion in the Jordan has been figurally related to baptism. As Daniélou (1960: 110) puts it:

> [T]he aspect of baptism which is brought out by the figure of the bath of Naaman is that of purification—as ordinary water washes stains from the body, so the sacred bath purifies us by the power of God. This power, which was exercised on a physical malady with Naaman, acts on the soul in Baptism: 'The healing and purifying power which, according to the Biblical narrative, the river Jordan had for Naaman, is the image of the purification produced by the water of baptism'. (The citation is from Denzinger, *Ritus Orientalium*, 1863)

A figural reading of Naaman is preserved also in the context of Christian worship in the *Revised Common Lectionary*. In the readings for Epiphany 6 (Year B), 2 Kings 5:1–14, the story of Naaman up to and including his healing immersion in the Jordan, is paired with Mark 1:40–45, in which Jesus heals a man suffering from "leprosy" by touching him. The primary logic is straightforward (though interestingly there is no baptismal resonance in the Gospel passage). Each narrative depicts an astonishing healing of the same disease: Elisha can be seen as a figure of Jesus, and also Naaman prefigures the nameless man in the Gospel whose life is renewed by Jesus.

However, when the prime interest in the Old Testament story is Naaman's healing with its baptismal and Christological resonances, it can be easy to curtail a reading of the narrative at v.14, the point at which Naaman is healed (where the story is curtailed by the lectionary compilers). Although the story is already a fascinating one to this point—through the role of the young slave girl (5:2–4), the misdirection of Naaman to the king of Israel (5:5–7), and Naaman's indignation at Elisha's failure

---

[1] The quotation marks are used because a range of skin diseases is covered by the Hebrew term used. The specific affliction understood as leprosy by modern medicine, Hansen's Disease, is not necessarily envisaged.

to do or say what he expected (5:8–13)—one may not unreasonably observe that the lectionary stops just when the story is reaching its most interesting point. For the story continues:

> Then Naaman returned to the man of God, he and all his company; he came and stood before him and said, 'Now I know that there is no God in all the earth except in Israel; please accept a present from your servant'. But he said, 'As the LORD lives, whom I serve, I will accept nothing!' He urged him to accept, but he refused. Then Naaman said, 'If not, please let two mule-loads of earth be given to your servant; for your servant will no longer offer burnt-offering or sacrifice to any god except the LORD. But may the LORD pardon your servant on one count: when my master goes into the house of Rimmon to worship there, leaning on my arm, and I bow down in the house of Rimmon, when I do bow down in the house of Rimmon, may the LORD pardon your servant on this one count'. He said to him, 'Go in peace'. (2 Kgs 5:15–19, NRSV)

There is an extraordinary richness in this short paragraph. Naaman recognizes the God of Israel as the one true God; such recognition is a basic concern elsewhere in the Old Testament (e.g. Deut 4:35,39; 1 Kgs 18:21,39), and a fundamental component in historic Judaism and Christianity (and, distinctively, Islam). Elisha makes clear that God's gift of healing is given freely (a point which Elisha's servant Gehazi tries to overturn and then cash in on in the final part of the story). Although henceforth Naaman will offer his own worship exclusively to the LORD, he seeks allowance, indeed pardon, for the *prima facie* compromise inherent in his role as a personal aide to the Aramean king back in a temple in Damascus, and Elisha allows this compromise—a vignette of perennial difficult issues over loyalty and compromise which believers regularly face. If the interest is mainly in Naaman's healing and its figural resonances, that which appears to be most important within this narrative itself may recede from view: the recognition of Israel's deity as the true God with the corollary of a practical change of allegiance, both of which are the consequence of Naaman's healing.

To be sure, the writer of a commentary who works through the whole text need not be constrained in the way that a lectionary compiler is. A good example of a contemporary re-presentation of the classic figural reading of Naaman can be seen in Peter Leithart's recent commentary on Kings (Leithart 2006), in a series explicitly designed to reconnect biblical interpretation with the classic Christian doctrinal tradition on the grounds that doctrine should illuminate Scripture.

> The story of Naaman is the richest Old Testament story of baptism and anticipates Christian baptism in a number of specific ways. For starters, it is an important typological witness because the subject of baptism is a Gentile, an Aramean general ... Naaman shows an admirable grasp of the implications of his baptism. Having been baptized, he realizes that he is exclusively devoted to Yahweh and promises to worship no other gods (2 Kgs. 5:17) ... Like Naaman, some Christians doubt what the New Testament says about the power of baptismal water ... God does wonders,

but he promises to do wonders through water ... Baptism is an insult to the wisdom of the world: through the foolishness of water God has chosen to save those who believe ... (Leithart 2006: 192–194)

The rich resonance of Leithart's reading with the New Testament and Christian baptismal theology shows well how an ancient approach to the Old Testament text can be reformulated in a contemporary context.

Naaman's Request for Israelite Soil

In relation to our concern with sacramentality, Naaman's request that he be given two mule-loads of earth to take back to Syria with him deserves further reflection. How is this to be understood? He should hardly be seen as simply "ask[ing] for a souvenir of Israel" (Hobbs 1985: 60)! Naaman presumably has a practical issue in mind. He apparently envisages the earth as the most suitable material for building an altar to the LORD (akin to the specification in Exodus 20:24, "make for me an altar of earth"), which would be the focus of all his own future worship. Since, however, such an altar would be very small, it may be that he envisages spreading out the Israelite earth to provide a base upon which a larger altar could be built. Either way, the fundamental concern would be the same: true sacrifices require holy soil for their appropriate offering. Commentators, especially Protestant commentators, are not infrequently rather dismissive of such an understanding. The great Puritan commentator Matthew Henry says: "he would not only worship the God of Israel, but he would have clods of earth out of the prophet's garden.... He ... over-values the earth of Israel, supposing that an altar of that earth would be most acceptable" (Henry 1960 [1710]: 406). Most commonly in modern commentaries, Naaman is seen to articulate a limited pre-monotheistic theology, of a kind which was widespread in his ancient context, in which the LORD is a "national God" who "can only be worshipped aright upon the soil of Israel's land" (Burney 1903: 280), such that "if Naaman is to worship Yahweh in Damascus then he must take back some of Yahweh's domain with him" (Begg 1989: 176). In theological terms Naaman's request for Israelite soil appears to be "naïvely inconsistent" with his confession of the sole reality of the LORD (Gray 1977: 507), and represents "a splendid earthbound understanding of God, still far removed from the theoretical monotheism of, for instance, Deutero-Isaiah (e.g. Isa 45:5–6)" (Dietrich 2001: 251). Such readings are of course possible; but they all significantly depend upon some form of polarization between the universal and spiritual confession of God and the particular and material request for earth, such that the latter downgrades or diminishes the former in one way or other. They also ignore questions about the role that the narrator sees Naaman performing in relation to his confession of Israel's God, especially given the narrator's own understanding at the outset that the LORD is the one who has given victory to Aram over Israel (2 Kgs 5:1).

In a different vein, Terence Fretheim reads Naaman's request for an altar of Israelite soil as indicating a desire to "provid[e] a tangible and material tie to the community of faith Elisha represents" because his imminent return home and return to duties with his king means that "the life of faith must be lived out in ambiguous situations and away from the community of faith" (Fretheim 1999: 153). This is suggestive, though it arguably transposes the issue of soil into an issue of human community. Of course, it is possible that one should read the logic of Naaman's request simply as akin to that of those who cherish a garment or keepsake from a loved one from whom they are separated—a logic more of the heart than of the head, where a deeply felt action may be hard to rationalize satisfactorily. One further possibility, however, is that one might appropriately read Naaman's request as enabling a sharper differentiation between the sacrifices to the LORD that he will offer himself, and those sacrifices at which he will need to be present in the temple in Damascus. This would be because he recognizes the particular connection between the LORD and Israel, and so the presence of Israelite soil would have a material specificity that would symbolically represent Israel in such a way as to focus his understanding and identify his sacrifice as directed to the LORD, the God of Israel; in other words, it would not be the LORD's limitations but his own that would be assisted by the presence of Israelite earth. The role of Israelite earth within such a logic could arguably be recognized as sacramental.

Readings of the story of Naaman thus usefully illustrate wider issues. On the one hand, a figural reading of an Old Testament narrative in relation to Christian baptism genuinely directs the reader to significant and imaginatively suggestive elements within the pre-Christian text. Yet at the same time, such a reading may (re)direct the reader away from some of the things that are important within the story's own frame of reference. The explicit Christian recontextualization brings both gain and loss. On the other hand, the difficulty of finding the best category for depicting Naaman's request for Israelite soil underlines the intrinsic difficulty of knowing how best to read the pre-Christian text even when one is attempting to stay within its own frame of reference. The exercise of the informed and disciplined imagination, which is intrinsic to good historical work, will necessarily draw on categories that are in some way meaningful to the interpreter; and although some interpretive options can readily be identified as anachronistic, more than one option is still left in play. If the notion of sacramentality is used with some flexibility, I have suggested that it may be appropriate for depicting the nature of Naaman's request.

In any case, this issue of seeking to do justice to the pre-Christian text on its own terms anticipates, and so leads directly into, the second part of this essay.

Sacramentality within the Old Testament: Some Problems of Definition

Thus far I have considered classic Christian use of the Old Testament, where the conceptual starting-point is the New Testament and a Christian frame of reference, from which the Old Testament is re-read for adumbrations and analogies of Christian realities. I will now try to consider Israel's scriptures primarily within their own frame of reference, with regard to that which might be considered sacramental within them on their own terms.

Initially, this makes it important no longer to take the meaning of "sacrament" for granted, but rather to offer a brief account of precisely what it is that we are looking for in the Old Testament. A classic Anglican understanding of a sacrament, as articulated in the Catechism in the *Book of Common Prayer*, is that it is "an outward and visible sign of an inward and spiritual grace." Valuable though this definition has been, it is nonetheless limited as a definition in that it is too broad. For such a definition could depict much that happens within a life of covenant-observance or discipleship: actions of mercy, kindness, and justice could all be said to be the outward and visible signs of an otherwise inward spiritual reality. The "spiritual" realm, in itself intrinsically invisible, is *tested for its reality* and *demonstrated* by "moral" actions that are in principle visible and accessible. Thus, for example, King Jehoiakim's attempt to demonstrate his kingship through the construction of a palace, a prestige building project (in which he also exploited his labor force), is unfavorably contrasted by Jeremiah with the life of moral integrity demonstrated by his father, King Josiah:

> Are you a king
>   because you compete in cedar?
> Did not your father eat and drink
>   and do justice and righteousness?
>   Then it was well with him.
> He judged the cause of the poor and needy;
>   then it was well.
> Is not this to know me?
>   says the LORD. (Jer 22:15–16, NRSV)

Josiah's consistent moral practice (where the likely idiomatic sense is that "doing justice was like meat and drink to him"; see Moberly 2006: 66) displays both the real meaning of kingship and true knowledge of God, unlike the oppressive and attention-seeking practices of Jehoiakim. Josiah's giving justice to the poor and needy is "the outward and visible sign of an inward and spiritual grace," the mark of a living knowledge of God. (Jeremiah's concern here is similar to that of James and 1 John in the New Testament, in both of which letters the issue is what is necessary to show the reality of claims to have faith in, or know, God).

The issue of being able to demonstrate spiritual reality in moral practice, vitally important though it is, is distinct from what is usually indicated by "sacramentality." To be sure, there are various ways in which one can define the distinctively sacramental. In mainstream Christian understanding a sacrament is characteristically a rite which entails certain prescribed actions and makes use of certain material elements, whose core presupposition is the Incarnation, the adoption of bodily reality by God in the person of Jesus. This means that the "material" and the "spiritual" are not opposites to be polarized, but rather are, or at least can be, intrinsically conjoined.

The issue on which I will focus here is the importance of the material, and non-personal, realm as the possible bearer of spiritual reality in the Old Testament. That non-sentient material objects should be spiritually significant, indeed the bearers or conveyors of spiritual reality, is perhaps the prime dimension within Israel's scriptures for reflection on the nature of sacramentality. In terms of an historically oriented reading of Israel's scriptures any notion of sacramentality cannot of course be grounded in the Incarnation, for within their pre-Christian frame of reference the Incarnation is a reality as yet unknown. It is necessary, therefore, to appeal rather to the importance of creation in the Old Testament, and to seek to articulate an understanding of material reality as God's handiwork and the vehicle of His purposes. The Old Testament begins with an account of God's act of creating, and delighting in, all known reality (Gen 1:1–2:3), and the psalmist is representative of the wider canonical collection when he affirms that "The earth is the LORD's and all that is in it" (Ps 24:1). Yet even so, where should one look for sacramentality in the Old Testament?

A particular notion of material objects as potentially spiritual, and so sacramental, needs also some differentiation within the historically attested range of varying conceptions of the material as possibly spiritual. One can, for example, find accounts of premodern conceptions of reality that envisage the sacred as permeating everything in ways that are hard for those in the modern desacralized West to conceive (see e.g. Eliade 1959); and this can be helpful, although the phenomenon took distinctive forms in different cultures. Among the many wide-ranging issues here, in this context we should simply note a certain silence in the Old Testament with regard to such wide-spread religious phenomena as holy springs, trees, stones, or caves. Of course, springs, trees, stones, and caves are sometimes mentioned in religiously significant contexts: the Gihon spring in Jerusalem where Solomon is anointed and proclaimed king (1 Kgs 1:32–40); the oak of Moreh in whose proximity the LORD appeared to Abraham and Abraham built an altar (Gen 12:6–7); the stone set up as a covenant witness by Joshua (Josh 24:26–27); the cave at Horeb where the LORD "passed by" Elijah (1 Kgs 19:9–18). However, the texts do not depict these as "holy" or as significant in their own right. This might be because their sacred significance is so taken for granted that it does not need to be mentioned; earlier generations of scholars readily found self-evident traces of animism here (e.g. Oesterley and Robinson 1937: 23–49). But it might also be because the writers are deliberately refraining from recognizing their sacred quality. Indeed, it is possible that even if the characters within these narratives should be imagined as conceiving these objects/places as holy, the narrator may nonetheless be tacitly directing future readers away from such an understanding. The reason for this could be the significant "aniconic" or "iconoclastic" element within the Old Testament, especially its deuteronomic/deuteronomistic writings. This element develops the striking prohibition of images in the second commandment of the Decalogue, and delegitimizes many religious sites, objects, and practices that were commonplace in Israel's world. On any reckoning, even if the Old Testament has narratives that may occasionally reflect the ascription of holiness to springs, trees, stones, and caves, none of the narratives could be said to promote or prescribe such an understanding. So it is probably not a fruitful avenue for the consideration of sacramentality in the Old Testament.

ARE CIRCUMCISION OR
THE MANNA SACRAMENTAL?

If Christian sacraments are essentially actions, ritual words, and gestures with material elements that carry core meaning for Christian identity, then an obvious approach is to look for rites in Israel's scriptures that are analogous to Christian sacraments. Is circumcision, for example, analogous in this way to baptism? Disappointingly, however, the answer has to be negative, for the simple reason that the Old Testament does not portray such rites. The covenantal significance of circumcision is articulated, and the practice of circumcision is initiated by Abraham (Gen 17), but no ritual action is depicted.

To be sure, circumcision is specified with relation to God's promise to make Abraham "the ancestor of a multitude of nations" (Gen 17:4–8). Presumably this means that at least part of the symbolic significance of circumcision is that the marking of the male organ, which is used in the sexual act that will give rise to the next generation, ties the practice of sexual intercourse to the fulfilment of the divine promise: the particular action has meaning in the context of God's overall purposes for Israel, to whose fulfilment it contributes. In this sense, not as a rite but as a symbol, circumcision might reasonably be considered sacramental. Such symbolic significance would also be at least part of the reason why Paul in the New Testament marginalizes the significance of circumcision, because entry into the Christian community through faith and baptism has a different dynamic; one cannot be born a Christian in the same way that one can be born a Jew.

Alternatively, another obvious approach to considering the material realm as the conveyor of spiritual reality in Israel's scriptures is to look again at some of the passages which are highlighted in a figural reading. The manna, whose story is told in Exodus 16, can, as already noted, be read in relation to John 6, and seen as an anticipation of Jesus as the bread from heaven who gives his flesh and blood to be eaten and drunk by those who believe in him. But what is the significance of the manna in its pentateuchal context?

The exposition of the manna's significance in Deuteronomy 8, where Moses is the speaking voice and is addressing Israel, guides one in a particular direction:

> Remember the long way that the LORD your God has led you these forty years in the wilderness, in order to humble you, testing you to know what was in your heart, whether or not you would keep his commandments. He humbled you by letting you hunger, then by feeding you with manna, with which neither you nor your ancestors were acquainted, in order to make you understand that one [Hebrew *adam* is better rendered 'humanity'] does not live by bread alone, but by every word that comes from the mouth of the LORD. (Deut 8:2–3, NRSV)

The keynote here is the LORD's *humbling* Israel, which in context appears to mean making them cease to be self-reliant (because things were beyond their control) and thereby become teachable. What the LORD taught them through the manna, which was something entirely unprecedented and so beyond their existing frame of reference, was that humanity depends for its existence not only on the material ("bread") but also on the relational and spiritual ("every word that comes from the mouth of the LORD"). In other words, Israel acquired an importantly non-reductive understanding of human life. This understanding is by no means assured, as Moses goes on to warn that this lesson that was learned when life was hard in the desert might be unlearned in the Promised Land when life will be much easier (Deut 8:11–18). Israel might "exalt themselves" (8:14, the opposite of being humbled) and ascribe their well-being solely to themselves and not to the LORD's enabling; that is, they might revert to a reductive understanding of themselves, in which God and God's ways become "unnecessary."

However, Moses's exposition does not draw attention to the intrinsic quality of the manna so much as direct attention to the obedient relationship with the LORD which it engenders. This is in keeping with the emphases of the narrative in Exodus 16, where it is the patterns of obedient daily living, the keeping of divine instruction (*torah*, Exod 16:4)—going out and collecting, and not hoarding, for six days in the week, but not going out or collecting on the seventh day, and being provided for by a special double and durable portion from the sixth day—which are the specified purposes of the manna. In other words, the interest in the manna is less that it is a material provision of an intrinsically spiritual nature than that it is a material reality whose unusual provision teaches the spiritual lesson of trust and obedience. One might perhaps suggest that the manna is open to sacramental understanding more than that it is sacramental as such.

THE ARK AS SACRAMENTAL

Perhaps the object with arguably the most sacramental significance in the Old Testament is the ark of the LORD. For the ark, whose construction is linked with Moses, is closely associated with the presence, and also the power, of the LORD. This is particularly so in the narratives of 1 and 2 Samuel and the Psalms. In 2 Samuel 7, when David proposes to build a house/temple for the LORD, he says to Nathan, "See now, I am living in a house of cedar, but the ark of God stays in a tent" (7:2; compare Ps 132:1–8). When the LORD tells Nathan to decline this offer, the wording is: "Thus says the LORD: Are you the one to build me a house to live in? I have not lived in a house since the day I brought up the people of Israel from Egypt to this day, but I have been moving about in a tent and a tabernacle …" (7:5–6). In a strong but undefined way the LORD's presence and the location of the ark are identified. Similarly, one psalm speaks of God "going up with a shout" and another of gates being opened "that the King of glory may come in" (Ps 47:5, 24:7,9), where probably what is to be imagined is a ceremonial procession with the ark, and its festive acclamation, in the environs of the Jerusalem temple; as also in the wording "Rise up, O LORD, and go to your resting-place, you and the ark of your might" (Ps 132:8).

These assumptions about the close relationship between the LORD's presence and the ark also strikingly characterize the initial account of the ark in 1 Samuel (1 Sam 4:1–7:2). When Israel loses to the Philistines in battle, they suppose that the presence of the ark will bring them victory in the future: "Let us bring the ark of the covenant of the LORD here from Shiloh, so that he may come among us and save us from the power of our enemies" (4:3). When the ark arrives in Israel's camp the Philistines hear of it and are afraid: "Woe to us! … Who can deliver us from the power of these mighty gods?" (4:7–8; the Philistines speak of Israel's deity in the plural, which represents their "pagan" understanding). Nonetheless, they resolve to fight as best they can, and in the event they defeat Israel more crushingly than previously, and also capture the ark (4:9–11). Expectations on both sides are confounded. The reason for this is not the LORD's absence from the ark, but rather the opposite. Because Israel has, by implication, tried to utilize the ark improperly (superstitiously?), without appropriate attitude and practice on their part, it is the LORD's presence that has enhanced their defeat.

More surprises follow. The Philistines place the ark in the temple of Dagon at Ashdod; the next day the statue of Dagon is prostrate on the ground. Although the statue is reinstated, the following day it is not only prostrate again but also mutilated (5:1–4). When plagues also afflict the people of Ashdod, they recognize the hand of the God of Israel, and decide not to keep the ark any longer and send it to their neighbors at Gath. But soon all Philistines, afflicted by plague, want to be rid of the ark and they send it back to Israelite territory, at Beth-shemesh, in a cart with offerings (5:6–6:12). Yet some Israelites who receive the ark themselves die, and the ark finally comes to rest at Kiriah-jearim (6:13–7:2).

It is a strange narrative. Its concern, however, seems to be to show not only that the LORD is intimately connected with the ark, but that the divine presence is dangerous to those who treat the ark complacently in one way or other, be they Israelite or Philistine. In significant ways, the logic of the narrative, especially in relation to Israel's initial loss of the ark, is akin to the logic of Jeremiah's famous temple sermon (Jer 7:1–15). Here people complacently say, "This is the temple of the LORD" (7:4), and correspondingly suppose that "We are safe" (7:10); that is, they are confident that the LORD will preserve

Judah from its enemies. Yet because the people's way of living is faithless and corrupt (7:3,5–7,8–9), Jeremiah pronounces their trust in the LORD's protection to be "false/ deceptive" (7:4,8). On the contrary, the LORD's presence in the temple—where the ark was housed—will mean that He will enable Judah's enemies to defeat them, destroy the temple, and carry them into exile (7:12–15). The divine presence intensifies the moral stakes.

The ark is closely associated with Mount Sinai, where the people of Israel enter into their covenant with the LORD. The fullest accounts of it are in Exodus 25:10–16 and Deuteronomy 10:1–5, where it is depicted as a chest made of acacia wood (a type of wood that is native to the Sinai and other desert regions). The deuteronomic account emphasizes that its role is to house the tablets of stone on which were written the Ten Words/Commandments (and when the ark is brought into Solomon's temple, "there was nothing in the ark except the two tablets of stone that Moses had placed there at Horeb, where the LORD made a covenant with the Israelites," 1 Kgs 8:9). These Words/ Commandments are presented as spoken by the Lord Himself, speaking "face to face" with Israel (Deut 5:4, cf. 5:22–27). Although the locating of the stone tablets in the ark can be seen as analogous to the practice of depositing legal documents in a sacred place, it also means that the ark contains that which expresses the life-giving will of the LORD for His people and symbolically represents the very covenant itself (Deut 4:13).

Thus the ark, as the most "sacramental" object in the Old Testament, has significant affinities with the sacramental understanding of the bread and wine in the New Testament. The bread and wine symbolize the self-giving death of Jesus which institutes the new covenant, while the ark symbolizes the heart of Torah and the divine presence which constitutes Israel as God's covenant people. Even the dangerous dimension of the ark has an analogy in Paul's understanding of the potentially dangerous dimension of partaking improperly in the bread and wine (1 Cor 11:27–32). But the dominant note in, for example, Psalms 24, 47, and 132, which appear to celebrate the ark, is awed joy.

CONCLUSION

A chapter such as this is necessarily preliminary. It can point towards some of the issues involved in considering the notion of sacramentality in Israel's scriptures, both within their own pre-Christian frame of reference and as the Christian Old Testament. But at best it can only be an overture for more sustained engagement with sacramentality and sacraments—which is to be found in the other chapters of this collection.

SUGGESTED READING

Ronald P. Byars (2011); Jean Daniélou, S. J. (1960); J. D. Dawson (2002); Gary Anderson (2009); C. L. Seow (1992).

BIBLIOGRAPHY

Anderson, Gary (2009), "Towards a Theology of the Tabernacle and its Furniture," in Ruth A. Clements and Daniel R. Schwartz (eds.), *Text, Thought, and Practice in Qumran and Early Christianity* (Leiden: Brill), 161–194.

Begg, Christopher T. (1989), "1–2 Kings," in Raymond Brown, S. S., Joseph Fitzmyer, S.J., and Roland Murphy, O.Carm. (eds.), *The New Jerome Biblical Commentary* (London: Geoffrey Chapman), 160–185.

Burney, C. F. (1903), *Notes on the Hebrew Text of the Books of Kings* (Oxford: Clarendon Press).

Byars, Ronald P. (2011), *The Sacraments in Biblical Perspective* (Louisville, Ky.: Westminster John Knox Press).

Calvin, John (2005 [1847; 1554]), *Calvin's Commentaries*, vol. 1: *Genesis*, reprint of translation by John King for Calvin Translation Society, 1847, from Latin original of 1554 (Grand Rapids, Mi.: Baker).

Daniélou, Jean, S. J. (1960), *The Bible and the Liturgy* (London: Darton, Longman & Todd).

Davison, Andrew (2013), *Why Sacraments?* (London: SPCK).

Dawson, J. D. (2002), *Christian Figural Reading and the Fashioning of Identity* (Berkeley and London: University of California Press).

Delitzsch, Franz (1888), *A New Commentary on Genesis*, 5th ed., trans. Sophia Taylor (Edinburgh: T&T Clark).

Dietrich, Walter (2001), "1 and 2 Kings," in John Barton and John Muddiman (eds.), *The Oxford Bible Commentary* (Oxford: Oxford University Press), 232–266.

Eliade, Mircea (1959), *The Sacred and the Profane: The Nature of Religion* (San Diego, Ca.: Harcourt Brace Jovanovich).

Fretheim, Terence E. (1999), *First and Second Kings*, Westminster Bible Companion (Louisville, Ky.: Westminster John Knox Press).

Gray, John (1977), *I & II Kings*, 3rd ed., Old Testament Library (London: SCM).

Henry, Matthew (1960 [1710]), *Matthew Henry's Commentary on the Whole Bible*, ed. Leslie F. Church (London: Marshall, Morgan & Scott).

Hobbs, T. R. (1985), *2 Kings*, Word Biblical Commentary 13 (Waco, TX: Word).

Leithart, Peter, J. (2006), *1 & 2 Kings*, SCM [Brazos] Theological Commentary on the Bible (London: SCM).

Moberly, R. W. L. (2006), *Prophecy and Discernment* (Cambridge: Cambridge University Press).

Oesterley, W. O. E. and Theodore H. Robinson (1937), *Hebrew Religion: Its Origin and Development*, 2nd ed. (New York: Macmillan).

Sheridan, Mark (2002), *Ancient Christian Commentary on Scripture: Old Testament II: Genesis 12–50*, General Editor Thomas C. Oden (Downers Grove, Il.: InterVarsity Press).

Seow, C. L. (1992), "Ark of the Covenant," in David Noel Freedman et al. (eds.), *The Anchor Bible Dictionary*, vol. 1, A–C (New York: Doubleday), 386–393.

CHAPTER 2

SACRAMENTALITY IN THE TORAH

DENNIS T. OLSON

THE five books of the Torah, Genesis to Deuteronomy, provide essential background for understanding the sacraments of the Christian Church. This chapter's exploration of sacramentality in the Torah will keep in mind three possible uses of the term "sacrament" in the Christian tradition. (1) Most Protestant traditions speak narrowly of two sacraments, baptism and the Lord's Supper, that were commanded and instituted by Christ in Scripture (Matt 28:19; Matt 26:26–27; Mark 14:22; Luke 22:19; 1 Cor 11:24). In this interpretation, it is the combination of a divine word of promise joined with a visible sign or element that constitutes the core of what is meant by a sacrament. (2) Another broader and diffuse tradition uses the term "sacramental" to apply to any physical or material event or object through which God is perceived as present, revealing or offering grace or blessing (communing with nature, meditating, enjoying a piece of art, waking from sleep, and the like). (3) For Orthodox and Roman Catholic traditions, baptism and Eucharist are central sacraments, but they are augmented by five other sacraments: ordination to priesthood or holy orders, marriage, anointing of the sick, reconciliation or penance, and confirmation or chrismaton (Thiselton 2007: 521–522). Our survey will focus on parallels and background from Genesis to Deuteronomy that particularly relate to baptism and the Lord's Supper while also noting elements that touch on broader understandings of sacramentality.

THE SACRAMENTS AND GENESIS 1–11

The book of Genesis begins with two different stories of God's creation of the world placed side by side: Genesis 1:1–2:4 and Genesis 2:4b–25. The first creation story in Genesis 1 begins with God's "wind" (*ruach*) hovering over the primeval waters of chaos. God then speaks a powerful word of command, "Let there be light," followed by the word becoming a reality: "and there was light" (Gen 1:2–3; see John 1:1–5). God continues creation by speaking at the beginning of all six days of creation (Smith 2010: 109), joined with verbs of making (Gen 1:7, 16, 25, 26, 31), separating (Gen 1:4, 6, 14), naming (Gen 1:5, 8, 10), assigning co-creative vocations (Gen 1:11, 14–17, 20, 22, 24, 26), blessing (Gen 1:22, 28; 2:3), evaluating as good (Gen 1:4, 10, 12, 18, 21, 25, 31), and delegating authority to rule (Gen 1:16, 18, 26, 27). Humans are uniquely created to "have dominion," in which they are accountable to God and which, by implication, is to be exercised "in the image of God" (Gen 1:26–27) for the flourishing of all creation. The emergence out of water, the divine word spoken, the Spirit of God hovering, the blessing, and the evaluation as good all occurring at the initiation of the world's coming into being echoes a number of elements in the initiating baptism of Jesus at the River Jordan (see Matt 3:16–17). The climax of creation in Genesis 1 is the seventh day which God sets apart and blesses as a sabbath day of rest, a rest from work in which God participates and by which God was refreshed (Gen 2:2–3; see Exod 31:17). This divine participation in sabbath rest in Genesis 1 is the first time in Scripture that God takes an incarnational step toward accommodation and self-limitation in order to dwell within the framework of the created order which God has created. The Christian sacraments, often practiced within Sabbath day worship, may be seen as extensions of God's continuing self-accommodation and resolve to be Immanuel—"God with us"—within God's own created order of time, space, and the material world (Olson 2008: 13–14).

The second creation story, in Genesis 2:4b–25, begins not with a vast ocean of water as in Genesis 1 but with a lack of water, a dry desert. God brings the desert to life with the gift of water in the form of a stream that dampens the ground and creates a lush garden called Eden (the Hebrew meaning "Delight"—Gen 2:8). God forms the human ('adam) from the "dust of the ground" ('adamah) and breathes into the human's nostrils the "breath/spirit of life" (Gen 2:7). God generously offers the human the freedom "to eat from every tree of the garden" except for one, "the tree of the knowledge of good and evil," for "in the day that you eat of it you shall [surely] die." The stage is set for the Bible's first recorded meal in Genesis 3. There the woman and man together, urged on first by hearing the clever words of God's own created serpent, succumb to the temptation to become "like God, knowing good and evil." All they need to do, according to the snake, is simply to disobey God and eat the forbidden fruit. The woman and the man who was "with her" (Gen 3:6) are attracted by the fruit's appeal to their physical senses (smell, taste, and touch), by their aesthetic enjoyment of the fruit's beauty, and their intellectual yearning for its wisdom (Gen 3:6). The temptation is a whole body experience of a modest meal, a piece of fruit.

The unexpected consequences of eating the forbidden fruit are the humans' experience of shame, their estrangement from one another, their fearful hiding from God, the ongoing struggle with serpent and soil, the pain of childbirth, and the inequality of power between the man and the woman (Gen 3:7, 8, 15–19). These unintended consequences escalate into the next generation when Cain kills his own brother Abel (Gen 4:8) and Lamech threatens a seventy-sevenfold vengeance on anyone who would hurt him (Gen 4:23–24). If the first meal of the first humans created such havoc within

God's garden of Delight, then the "Last Supper" on a night involving another garden (Gethsemane) and the move to another definitive act of unjust violence (the cross) promise not a return to Eden (Gen 3:24) but the saving proclamation of "the Lord's death until he comes" (1 Cor 11:26), which orients toward an open future and not a return to a closed past. Already in Genesis 3–4, God's overriding will to be gracious and merciful is evident in the mitigation of the death penalty for Adam and Eve (Gen 2:17), the divine gift of leather clothing to replace scratchy fig leaves (Gen 3:21), and the visible sign of a protective mark on Cain rather than imposing upon him the penalty of death which he deserved under the retributive law of "life for life, eye for eye" (Gen 4:14–15; see Gen 9:5–6; Deut 19:21).

Human violence and corruption continue to escalate into the story of Noah and the flood (Gen 6:11–13). Liturgical prayers associated with the sacrament of baptism often include references to God's rescue of Noah and his family in the ark from floodwaters of judgment that destroy the rest of humanity and other creatures upon the earth. The worldwide flood returns the earth to its pre-creational state of watery chaos as the waters above and the waters below that were separated at creation (Gen 1:2, 6–9) are allowed to rush back in from above and below and inundate the dry land. Noah, his family, and two of every kind of creature are saved through the ark. By association, baptism involves both a judgment of death and drowning of the old as well as a raising up of new life and a new creation (Rom 6:1–11; Col 2:12–15). After the flood subsides, God makes a covenant promise "with every living creature" that God would never again use a flood to destroy the earth. God then places a visible sign of the promise, a rainbow in the sky, that will remind God of "the everlasting covenant between God and every living creature" (Gen 9:12–17).

The Sacraments and God's Covenant with Abraham and Sarah

Genesis 1–11 begins with God's interactions with all of humanity and all creation. That creation-wide concern never disappears from the pages of Scripture (Isa 65:17; Rom 8:19–23; Rev 21:1). In Genesis 12, God chooses a new strategy that focuses special divine attention on one particular human family—the family of Abram and Sarai, later Abraham and Sarah. God calls this family to leave its home in Mesopotamia and to go to another land where God will make of them "a great nation." God reminds this one elected people, however, that his ultimate goal is the blessing not only of this family but of all the world: "in you all the families of the earth shall be blessed" (Gen 12:3).

God's spoken covenant promises of innumerable descendants and a land made to Abraham and Sarah are often attached to visible signs. Sometimes the signs are recurring (the stars of the heavens, the dust of the earth, the sand of the seashore—Gen 13:16; 15:5; 22:17). At other times, the sign involves a dramatic, one-time covenantal ceremony of split animal carcasses, fire, and a smoking pot in which God stakes God's own life on the line as assurance that God will indeed fulfill the promise God has made to Abraham and Sarah (Gen 15:7–21; see Jer 34:17). These covenant promises are made in the face of what seem impossible obstacles: the barrenness of Sarah (Gen 11:30) and the old age of both Abraham and Sarah (Gen 15:2–3; 17:1–2, 17; 18:10–15; 20:7). Even when at long last the son of the promise is born and named Isaac (meaning "He Laughs"), God "tests" Abraham with a command to kill his son Isaac and offer him as a burnt offering to God (Gen 22:1–2). God stops Abraham as he raises his knife to kill the child and provides a ram instead of Isaac for the burnt offering. Thus, the one son Isaac lives and becomes a visible and material sign, a small token of the promise of innumerable descendants. Likewise, when his wife Sarah dies, Abraham ends up buying a small piece of land from native Canaanites as a burial plot for his wife (Gen 23:1–20). The land purchase and Isaac are real but only partial fulfillments of God's promise. The burial plot and the young son are tangible and visible sacramental signs of the faithfulness of God in the past and present and pointers to a blessed future yet to come. In a similar way, the Christian sacraments of baptism and the Lord's Supper reach back to the past, create faith and love in the present, and point to the future with hope.

One Old Testament tributary that feeds into later New Testament understandings of baptism is the ritual practice of circumcision, namely, the removal of the man's foreskin (see Col 2:11–12). A rich set of associations surround the descriptions of circumcision in the Torah, including religious identity, fertility, marriage, entering into a covenant relationship with God, and protection against threats of harm or death. In Genesis 17, God initiates and reaffirms a covenant with Abraham, promising him fertility, many descendants, and an unending covenant with all future generations. The one requirement and sign of this covenant is that every male within the households of Abraham's descendants should be circumcised, both free and slave, when they are eight days old (Gen 17:10–13; see Lev 12:3). Any male descendant of Abraham whose foreskin is not cut off and circumcised "shall be cut off" from God's covenant people since he has broken God's covenant (Gen 17:14). The covenant of circumcision results in a change of identity signified by the change of names (Abram to Abraham, Sarai to Sarah) and the promise of a son named Isaac through Sarah who will be the ancestor of Israel (Gen 17:5, 15, 19, 21). Ishmael, Abraham's older son through the Egyptian slave-maid Hagar, was also circumcised (Gen 17:23), along with Sarah's son Isaac (Gen 21:4). The Passover instructions in Exodus 12 include the strict requirement that all who eat the Passover meal be circumcised, including even slaves and foreigners (Exod 12:44, 48–49) (Goldingay 2000: 3–18; Fleischman 2001: 19–32). The meaning of the enigmatic episode involving God's attack on Moses and Moses's wife Zipporah's rescue of Moses by circumcising their son in Exodus 4:24–26 is much debated. The brief narrative contributes to a sense of mystery and density in understanding the full significance of the ritual of circumcision.

Circumcision of the heart and other metaphorical references occur in Deuteronomy. On the one hand, God commands the Israelites not to be stubborn or rebellious and instead to circumcise the foreskin of their own hearts (Deut 10:16; see Jer 4:4). On the other hand, God promises that after Israel has endured the judgment of exile to a foreign land, He will circumcise the hearts of the Israelites and their descendants so that they will "love the LORD" with all their being (Deut 30:1–6). Other figurative allusions to being "uncircumcised" in the Torah include Exodus 6:30 and Leviticus 19:23; 26:41 (see also Jer 6:10; 9:26; Ezek 44:7, 9; Rom 2:28–29) (Lemke 2003: 299–319).

Another generative site for reflection on sacramentality is the hospitality and meal shared by Abraham and Sarah with the three divine strangers (Gen 18:1–5). The chapter opens with the narrator's aside to the reader: "the LORD appeared to Abraham." All Abraham and Sarah know at the beginning is that three human strangers appear at their tent. Abraham extends hospitality to the strangers, offering the gift of a "little water" to "wash your feet" and a "little bread, that you may refresh yourselves" (Gen 18:4–5). Abraham and Sarah, however, wildly exceed these customary cultural expectations of hospitality and quickly cobble together a lavish feast of floured cakes, tender meat from their best calf, curds, and milk. The generosity of repeated divine promises to Abraham and Sarah in the past (Gen 12:1–3, 7–9; 15:1–20; 17:1–22) have formed their practice of generous hospitality to strangers exemplified in a meal. As with the disciples on the road to Emmaus who offer hospitality to "a stranger" whose true identity is revealed as Jesus in the breaking of bread (Luke 24:13–35), so Abraham and Sarah discern that it is the LORD who has visited them. The LORD affirms the promise to Abraham of an heir and adds the specific promise that Sarah will be the mother of the child (Gen 18:9–15). The promise gives rise to a meal of hospitality that becomes the site for the exchange of gifts and for the renewal and deepening of the promise (Walter 2013: 14–36). As the narrative continues, Abraham intercedes before God on behalf of the wicked people of Sodom whom God is about to destroy, exemplifying his vocation as a blessing to other families of the earth (Gen 18:20–33; see Gen 12:3). As the two angels visit Sodom to assess its wickedness, the men of Sodom show the opposite of hospitality and seek violently to assault the two "strangers." As a result and in spite of Abraham's intercession, God destroyed Sodom in judgment for its long history of hostility toward outsiders (Gen 19:1–29).

THE SACRAMENTS AND EXODUS

The book of Exodus contains some of the most important elements of ancient Israel's story that intersect with Christian understandings of the sacraments. They include the natural elements of fire and cloud associated with God's presence, the Passover meal, the rescue through the waters of the Red Sea, the water from the rock in the wilderness, the manna from heaven, the making of a covenant on Mount Sinai, and the contrast of the golden calf versus the tabernacle as the true sign of the visible presence of God's glory.

God's presence first appears to Moses in the form of fire within a continually burning bush that was not extinguished "at the mountain of God" called Horeb as Moses stood "on holy ground" (Exod 3:1–12). God continues to be present in a pillar of cloud by day and pillar of fire by night as God led Israel out of Egypt and through the wilderness

(Exod 13:21; 14:24; 40:38). God's later appearance on top of Mount Sinai (the alternate name of Mount Horeb) was likewise accompanied by natural elements of fire and smoke that convey power, danger, light, and holiness (Exod 19:18; 24:17; see also Deut 4:12, 15, 24, 33, 36; 5:4, 22–25).

The Passover meal commemorates God's dramatic deliverance of Israelite slaves from bondage in Egypt. The interweaving of the narrative account of the Passover along with instructions for future generations for observing the Passover as an annual festival underscores how future Israelites are to claim the exodus story as the core of their own life story and religious identity. The Passover narrative and instructions appear in the context of the death of all Egypt's first-born sons, which was the last of ten plagues sent by God in order to convince Pharaoh to let the Israelites go (Exod 12–13). All three Synoptic Gospels portray the Lord's Supper as instituted by Jesus in the context of the celebration of this annual Jewish Passover meal (Matt 26:17–30; Mark 14:12–26; Luke 22:7–20; see John 1:29, 36).

Many scholars suggest that the festival of Passover and the feast of Unleavened Bread were originally two separate festivals that came to be joined together as one in the present biblical text. The pre-biblical Passover festival may have focused on the sacrificial offering and eating of a lamb while the festival of Unleavened Bread placed a spotlight on the offering and eating of bread, with a possible link with the celebration of the spring grain harvest in the land of Canaan. The Unleavened Bread festival is mentioned alone without reference to Passover in Exodus 23:15 and 34:18. The law in Leviticus 23:5–6 commands the celebration of Passover to begin on the fourteenth day of the first month of Abib "at twilight," while the feast of Unleavened Bread is to begin on the fifteenth day of the same month, presumably at sunset and thus overlapping with the beginning of Passover (see Num 28:16–17). The most extensive instructions for the feast of Unleavened Bread are provided in Exodus 12–13. The sections concerning the sacrifice of the lamb for Passover (Exod 12:1–13, 43–49) are distinct from the instructions for the festival of Unleavened Bread (Exod 12:15–20; 13:3–10). This lack of full integration of the festival instructions suggests that originally these were probably separate festivals that came to be spliced together. They clearly were celebrated together by the post-exilic period (see Ezek 45:18–25; Ezra 6:19–22; 2 Chr 35:17) (Wagenaar 2004: 250–268).

A central feature of the combined Passover/Unleavened Bread festival was that only unleavened bread could be eaten during the seven days of the festival (Exod 12:8, 15, 17, 20; 13:7; 23:15; 34:18; Lev 23:6; Num 28:17; Deut 16:3, 8). Nothing with yeast could be consumed. On the first day of the festival, the Israelites were commanded to "remove leaven from your houses" (Exod 12:15). Also on the first day of the festival, the roasted lamb was to be eaten with the unleavened bread and the bitter herbs that symbolized the bitterness of Israel's slavery in Egypt (Exod 12:8; Num 9:11). The consequence for eating anything leavened with yeast during the seven days of the festival was severe; the violator would "be cut off from Israel" (Exod 12:15).

The festival's unleavened bread was a remembrance that the Israelites left Egypt in "great haste" and "could not wait" for the rising of bread dough after the death of the Egyptian first-born and Pharaoh's decree that the Israelite slaves should leave Egypt (Exod 12:39; Deut 16:3). The unleavened bread is also remembered as "a bread of affliction" (Deut 16:3). Eating the unleavened bread is commanded for "all the days of your life" so that Israelites may remember their departure from Egypt. Eating bread made without yeast, a bread commonly associated with the diet of the poor in many cultures, is intended to stimulate the communal memory of slavery in Egypt and God's rescue from its suffering and oppression.

The feast of Passover is closely interwoven with the tenth plague, God's killing of all the first-born of Egypt, both humans and animals. The roasted lamb at the center of the meal commemorates the blood of a slaughtered lamb with which the Israelite slaves marked the doorposts of their houses. The angel of death who killed the Egyptian first-born "passed over" the Israelite homes smeared with blood so that no Israelite firstborn would die in the plague (Exod 12:3–14). Earlier in Exodus, God had affirmed that Israel was God's "firstborn son" (Exod 4:21–23) whom God would protect when Egypt's first-born were killed. In the context of the instructions for the Passover, God reminds Moses that all the firstborn among the Israelites are consecrated to God and belong to God, both humans and animals (Exod 13:1–2). While firstborn animals were to be sacrificed as burnt offerings to God in future generations, all human firstborn sons among the Israelites were to be "redeemed" through a payment of money (Exod 13:11–16; see Exod 34:19–20). The individual members of the priestly and landless tribe of the Levites also served as substitutes for the firstborn sons in other Israelite tribes (Num 3:11–13; 8:15–19).

This motif of a deity's right to claim all firstborn of humans or animals seems to reflect an ancient belief in some cultures of the biblical world that the sacrifice of a first-born son as a burnt offering had special power and gravity. Thus, an enigmatic epi-sode in 1 Kings 3:26–27 reports how the king of Moab was losing in a battle against the Israelite army. The Moabite king then offered his firstborn son as a burnt offering to his deity, and "great wrath came upon" the Israelite army so that it was forced to withdraw and go back home. The association of the Passover, the lamb whose blood saved the Israelites, and God's claim upon all human firstborn of the Israelites provided the seedbed for the intimate connection of the annual Passover meal with the story of Abraham's near-sacrifice or binding of his son Isaac in Genesis 22, a connection that emerged in the literature of Second Temple Judaism as well as later Jewish traditions (Levenson 1993: 176–186).

In Genesis 22, God commands Abraham to offer his only son, Isaac, as a burnt offer-ing at Moriah. Abraham obeys. Just as he raises his hand to slay his son with a knife, the angel of God intervenes and prevents Abraham from killing his son. God provides a ram as a substitute burnt offering for Isaac while God also affirms that Abraham has passed his test, trusting God's promise and obeying God's command. The motif of the beloved or firstborn son, the command to offer the son as a burnt offering to God, the lamb or ram whose blood spares the son from death, and the deliverance from death and oppres-sion are elements common to the Passover story and the near-sacrifice of Isaac.

The connection of the Passover story in Exodus 12–13 with the near-sacrifice of Isaac in Genesis 22 is further deepened by the later biblical text of 2 Chronicles 3:1 that linked the place name "Moriah" (the location of Abraham's near-sacrifice of Isaac—Gen 22:2) with the temple in Jerusalem where Israelites brought their burnt offerings of grain and animals. Abraham's willingness to sacrifice his own son may be understood as a one-time, unrepeatable act of faith and obedience that earned for the Israelite people a virtually inexhaustible bank account of merit before God. When Israelites in future generations brought their sacrifices of grain and animals to the Jerusalem temple, their sacrifices in effect drew on the merit of Abraham's unrepeatable act of obedience (Childs 1992: 325–336). The willingness of the father, Abraham, to give up his son and thereby accrue inexhaustible merit for future Israelites was apparently reinterpreted in a New Testament text like Romans 8:32 in which the willingness of God the Father to offer up his own Son created an unlimited reward of promise and assurance for believers in Christ: "He who did not withhold his own Son, but gave him up for all of us, will he not with him also give us everything else" (Dahl 1974: 146–160)? These associations of the Last Supper, the Passover, temple sacrifices, and Abraham's near-sacrifice of Isaac provide a rich nexus of associations and meanings that may enhance the New Testament and later Christian interpretations of the sacrament of the Eucharist.

If the death of the firstborn and Passover illuminate aspects of the Lord's Supper, the story of the crossing of the Red Sea (or Reed Sea) provides a fruitful Old Testament resource for the understanding of baptism. Two versions of the story stand side by side, one narrative and one poetic. The prose narrative recounts how God works through the mediation of Moses and a strong east wind to split the waters of the Red Sea into two, creating a pathway of dry land through which the Israelite slaves walk from bondage into freedom. The Egyptian army pursues the Israelites into the sea, God returns the waters, and Pharaoh and his army drown in the sea (Exod 14:21–31). The narrative echoes God's creational work of a divine "wind" sweeping over the waters and separating the waters above from the waters below, thereby creating dry land (Gen 1:2–11). The poetic version in the Song of the Sea in Exodus 15 portrays more of a direct battle between God as a divine warrior and Pharaoh in which Moses and Israel are more passive observers rather than active agents. God uses the evil waters of chaos to drown and defeat the enemy power of Pharaoh (Exod 15:1–11). The earth also participates along with the sea in swallowing up the enemies of God (Exod 15:12). Moreover, the victories of God extend to the conquest of the land of Canaan and the planting of God's "holy abode" where God's sanctuary is established (Exod 15:13–18). The poetry of Exodus 15 moves the exodus beyond the level of a one-time historical encounter between Israel and Egypt to a paradigm of a recurring cosmic battle in which God will be victorious against the powers and enemies, both historical and cosmic, arrayed against God and God's people. Thus, as in the ritual of baptism, the passage through water in Exodus 14–15 is both judgment and deliverance, both death and life, both freedom from bondage to other powers and freedom for obedient service to the one true Ruler who is the LORD, the God of Israel.

Two wilderness texts in Exodus have special associations with the sacraments: God's provision of manna from heaven in Exodus 16:1–36 and the miracle of water from the rock in Exodus 17:1–7. Both of these sustenance stories in the wilderness occur as the freed Israelite slaves begin their journey through the wilderness toward the promised land of Canaan. Hunger and thirst are basic and legitimate causes for the Israelites to complain to Moses and to God, and God responds positively to the complaints by pro-viding the food and water necessary for their life in the wilderness. In the manna story, the LORD promises, "I am going to rain bread from heaven for you" which the people will receive each day in quantities sufficient for their needs for that day, no matter how long or short a time they work (Exod 16:4, 16–21; see Matt 6:25–34; 20:1–16). On the sev-enth or sabbath day of the week, they are not to go out and work by picking up manna since it is a day of rest (Exod 16:23–30). This story actualizes for the first time the gift of the sabbath day of rest which God first introduced into creation in Genesis 2:1–3. God also instructs future generations of Israelites to keep a portion of the manna in a jar to be placed "before the LORD" and visible during the worship of the community as a kind of public, sacramental reminder of God's gracious provision of the community's basic human needs (Exod 16:33–36), an echo of a petition from the Lord's Prayer: "Give us this day our daily bread" (Matt 6:11; see John 6:30–51), and an echo of the several feeding sto-ries with sacramental overtones in the Gospels (Matt 14:13–31; 15:32–38; Mark 6:34–44; 8:1–9; Luke 9:12–17; John 6:1–14).

The other sustenance story is more baptismal in its nuances with the miraculous pro-vision of water from the rock. God instructs Moses to strike the rock in the wilderness with his staff, the same staff with which Moses struck the Nile River when it turned to blood and parted the waters of the Red Sea so that Israel could escape to freedom on dry ground (Exod 17:1–7). The apostle Paul alludes to this text with a nod to a baptismal and Christological typology:

> I do not want you to be unaware, brothers and sisters, that our ancestors were all under the cloud, and all passed through the sea, and all were baptized into Moses in the cloud and in the sea, and all ate the same spiritual food, and all drank the same spiritual drink. For they drank from the spiritual rock that followed them, and the rock was Christ. (1 Cor 10:1–4)

As baptism is the rite of initiation for individuals in the New Testament, Exodus 19:1–24 and 24:1–18 are the narrative bookends of a communal rite of initiation into the covenant between God and God's people Israel on Mount Sinai. This covenant-making ceremony begins with the story of God's gracious deliverance of Israel: "how I bore you on eagles' wings and brought you to myself" out of the bondage of slavery in Egypt (Exod 19:4). Following from this divine deliverance is Israel's God-given vocation and identity: "you shall be my treasured possession . . . a priestly kingdom and a holy nation" (Exod 19:5–6; see 1 Peter 2:9–10). Exodus 24 provides an additional perspective on the covenant-making ceremony. Although Moses is the primary mediator who goes up Mount Sinai in Exodus 19, Moses is joined on Mount Sinai by the high priest Aaron, his sons Nadab and Abihu, and seventy elders of the people. They all go part way up the mountain, and remarkably, the text reports, they

> went up and they saw the God of Israel. Under his feet there was something like a pavement of sapphire stone, like the very heaven for clearness. God did not lay his

hand on the chief men of the people of Israel; also they beheld God, and they ate and drank. (Exod 24:9–11)

The covenant-making meal of eating and drinking, the "seeing" of God, the beauty associated with the divine, and the participation of priests and elders together provide a rich portrait of covenant-making with sacramental overtones. In other instances in the Old Testament, to "see God" is dangerous and often prohibited (Gen 16:13; 33:20; Judg 6:22–23; 13:22). Along with the leaders of the community, the people participate as well in the covenant ceremony. Moses sets up twelve pillars for the twelve tribes of Israel and then supervises the sacrifice of animals as burnt offerings, setting the blood of the sacrifices aside.

> Moses took half of the blood and put it in basins, and half of the blood he dashed against the altar. Then he took the book of the covenant, and read it in the hearing of the people; and they said, "All that the LORD has spoken we will do, and we will be obedient." Moses took the blood and dashed it on the people, and said, "See the blood of the covenant that the LORD has made with you in accordance with all these words." (Exod 24:6–8; see Matt 26:28; Mark 14:24; Heb 9:20; 12:24)

The covenant-making rituals of Exodus 19 and 24 surround the giving of the Ten Commandments (Exod 21:1–17) and the laws of the Book of the Covenant (Exod 20:22–23:33). These covenant obligations flow out of a prior relationship initiated by God. Before any commandments are given, God affirms: "I am the LORD your God, who brought you out of the land of Egypt, out of the house of slavery" (Exod 20:1). The laws that follow formally instruct the people on how to live more deeply in that already established relationship with God.

The disciples of Jesus swore undying allegiance to Jesus "on the night in which he was betrayed," and yet all his disciples betrayed, denied, or abandoned him on the night of the covenant meal of the Last Supper (Matt 26:21–25, 31–35, 56; Mark 14:19, 29–31, 50; Luke 22:33). Similarly, the Israelites all enthusiastically endorsed their commitment to the covenant and promised to do "all that the LORD has spoken," including the first and most central commandments against worshipping other gods and making no graven images or idols. Yet the Israelites quickly abandoned God and formed an idol of a golden calf which they worshiped, saying, "These are your gods, O Israel, who brought you out of the land of Egypt" (Exod 32:4; see 1 Kgs 12:25–33). God was prepared to destroy all the Israelites except for Moses, and yet Moses interceded and persuaded God to forgive them (Exod 32:9–14). Moses angrily broke the two tables of stone containing the words of the covenant written by God as he came down the mountain (Exod 32:15, 19). Moses returned to intercede further with God, and in the end God made a new covenant grounded in God's mercy and forgiveness, symbolized by two new tablets of stone (Exod 34:1–10; see Jer 31:31; Luke 22:20; 1 Cor 11:25).

Although the golden calf was condemned and destroyed as an idol, the book of Exodus devotes much attention to the plans and construction for the tabernacle or movable tent that functions as a visible sign of God's presence in the midst of Israel as it traveled through the wilderness (Exod 25–31, 35–40). Indeed, the climax of the book of Exodus comes in Exodus 40:34 when the divine "cloud covered the tent of meeting, and the glory of the LORD filled the tabernacle." This settling of the divine presence upon the tabernacle fulfills God's purpose in delivering Israel out of its slavery in Egypt: "that I might dwell among them" (Exod 29:46).

THE SACRAMENTS AND LEVITICUS

In the present shape of the Pentateuch, the laws of Leviticus provide order and structure to the community so that it is protected by radiating zones of holiness and the service of priests who mediate between the intense and dangerous holiness of the divine presence and a sinful and impure community. The death of Nadab and Abihu, sons of Aaron the high priest, illustrate the threat of sinful individuals coming into direct contact with the divine (Lev 10:1–3). Leviticus divides into two parts: (1) laws concerning sacrifices, purity, and the Day of Atonement focused on the holiness of the priests and the tabernacle (Lev 1–16) and (2) laws that concern the holiness of the whole community and the land of Israel (Lev 17–27).

One feature of purity in Leviticus that forms some of the background to New Testament baptism is the repeated reference to cleansing oneself, washing one's clothes, and bathing in water as part of becoming ritually clean after experiencing some ritual impurity or in preparation to coming near the divine presence. Rituals of bathing or cleaning of garments may apply to priests (Lev 8:6; see Exod 30:18–21; 40:12, 30–32; Num 19:7), Levites (Num 8:6, 21), or to all members of the community (Lev 14:7–9; 15:5, 10, 13, 27; see Exod 19:10, 14). In the priestly symbol system of clean and unclean, an individual may become ritually impure through such things as contact with a corpse, the involuntary flow of bodily fluids (for example, blood or semen), certain skin diseases, or the eating of prohibited foods. Becoming impure or unclean from various causes was a common occurrence for most people (simply attending a funeral, unintentionally eating unclean food, menstruation, and the like). Thus rituals of purification were readily available and involved some combination of ritual washings, the passage of time, or specified offerings.

Purity and cleanness often had nothing to do with moral sin; they simply involved a ritual condition of certain boundaries being crossed or confused (boundaries of life and death, bodily fluids that abnormally transgressed boundaries of skin, animals with characteristics that did not fit into their perceived class of animals, and the like). One set of laws in Leviticus does treat both ritual impurity and moral sin in the community on the annual Day of Atonement. This annual ritual had a two-fold purpose. First of all, the purification offerings purge the tabernacle or place of worship from uncleanness (Lev 16:16–19). Secondly, the priestly confession of sin, the blood of the animal sacrifices, the setting free of the scapegoat which carries away the sin of the community, and the people's refraining from work and food all participate in purging the sin of the people (Lev 16:21–31).

The Sacraments and
the Book of Numbers

God's positive and gracious provision of manna earlier in Exodus 16 has a negative counterpart in the later wilderness narrative of Numbers 11. The Israelites continue to receive the manna daily, but they are tired of the same diet of manna day after day and complain to Moses. Moses is extremely frustrated to the point of wanting God to put Moses to death to end his misery as a leader of the Israelites. God ends up punishing the people but also constructively redistributing the burdens of leadership on a group of elders so that Moses remains the chief leader but shares many of the duties with other elders (Num 11:16–17, 24–25). Moses even celebrates the coming of God's Spirit on two individuals who are not officially authorized as leaders but nevertheless "prophesy in the camp" (Num 11:26–30).

One other interesting feature of the Numbers 11 narrative is Moses's implied description of God's provision of food using feminine and maternal imagery for God. Moses asks God why God has placed the burden of leadership of the Israelites on Moses: "Did I conceive all this people? Did I give birth to them, that you should say to me, Carry them in your bosom, as a nurse carries a sucking child" (Num 11:12). The implied answer is that God, not Moses, is the one who has conceived, given birth, and breast fed the people of Israel. One finds similar maternal imagery of divine nourishment in Deuteronomy 32:13–14 (Claassens 2004: 4–9).

How does one discern when a material object or element serves a positive role in a sacrament versus when the object or element becomes an idol and an object of worship? The story of the "serpent of bronze" (Hebrew *nechash nechoshet*) in Numbers 21:4–9 recounts the Israelites complaining about the lack of water and the lack of variety in their diet with only manna every day. The LORD sends poisonous snakes among them in judgment against their murmuring. The people confess their sins to Moses who then intercedes to God on their behalf. God instructs Moses to erect a "serpent of bronze" on a pole. Anyone who had been bitten by a snake and who looked at the bronze serpent would be healed and not die. Later in Israel's history, however, King Hezekiah renovated and reformed the Jerusalem temple. Part of the religious reform of the temple involved tearing down and destroying what was alleged to be Moses's bronze serpent called "Nechustan." The sacred object had become an idolatrous object of worship because "the people of Israel had made offerings to it" (2 Kgs 18:4). One person's sacramental element may become another person's idol.

The Sacraments and Deuteronomy

The laws of Deuteronomy are among the most strongly aniconic of the Torah, strongly resistant to any material object or element being associated with the presence of God on earth. Earlier we noted traditions in Exodus in which certain leaders of the people "saw" God (Exod 24:10–11). Moses saw the back but not the face of God (Exod 33:23). Deuteronomy resists such claims, arguing instead: "Since you saw no form when the LORD spoke to you at Horeb [Deuteronomy's alternate name for Mount Sinai] out of the fire,… do not act corruptly by making an idol for yourselves in the form of any figure." Indeed, God's presence dwells in heaven so Israel experienced God only through the divine fire on Mount Horeb and "his words coming out of the fire" (Deut 4:36). The prayer accompanying the offering in Deut 26:15 asks God to "look down from your holy habitation, from heaven, and bless your holy people Israel." Unlike Exodus where the tabernacle is the site of the visible presence of God on earth and in the midst of the community of Israel, Deuteronomy allows that it is only the "name" of God, not the full presence of God, that dwells in a temple at "the place that the LORD your God will choose" (Deut 12:5; 14:23). At the same time, Deuteronomy affirms the intimacy and closeness of God to God's people: "For what other great nation has a god so near to it as the LORD our God is whenever we call to him?" (Deut 4:7; see Deut 30:11–14).

In Exodus, the "ark of the covenant" is an ornate, gold-plated box with a mercy seat and two statues of cherubim that function as a footstool or throne for the divine presence within the tabernacle: "There I will meet with you" (Exod 25:22). In Deuteronomy, the "ark of the covenant" is an ark made simply of wood and functions only as a container for the covenant tablets of stone with the words of the covenant on them which are to be read aloud to the people at regular intervals (Deut 10:1–5; 31:9, 25). God's presence remains in heaven, and the focus is on the words of God and the name of God with resistance to any material object or element being attached to the presence of God. In this disagreement between Exodus and Deuteronomy on the topic of the presence of God, we see some of the origins for later debates regarding God's presence and action in various Christian theologies of the sacraments.

One other notable feature in Deuteronomy's theology is its commitment to God's name being attached to the one place that God would choose. This centralization of worship in one city and temple (presumably Jerusalem, although the name of the city is never mentioned) is an expression of Deuteronomy's commitment to a unifying vision of one God, one people, one land, and one law for the chosen people of Israel. Thus, for example, Deuteronomy requires all Israelites in the land to celebrate key festivals together in one city that the LORD would choose (Deut 14:22; 16:2, 9–11, 13–16). In contrast, the instructions for the three major annual festivals (including Passover) in Exodus 23:14–17 seem to imply that the festivals could be observed at different local shrines near people's hometowns rather than everyone coming together in the single city of Jerusalem. The Passover law in Exodus 12:3–7 goes further and implies that

Passover should be celebrated by each family in their own home, not even at a local sanctuary. Deuteronomy significantly revises these festival laws, mandating that all Israelites are to come to the one place that the LORD will choose for the three annual festivals. In Deuteronomy's program, the gatherings become national pilgrimage festivals that unite the whole nation as one people in one place. This includes the observance of Passover (Deut 16:1–17; see the centralization program of King Josiah in 2 Kgs 23:21–23). This requirement that all Israelites celebrate Passover together in Jerusalem provides background to Jesus and the disciples being in Jerusalem when they celebrate the Passover where Jesus institutes the Last Supper (see also Luke 2:41; John 2:13, 23; 11:55). Deuteronomy's program resonates with the apostle Paul's concern to maintain the unity of the one body of believers in Christ expressed through the proper celebration of one baptism in Christ (1 Cor 12:12) and the visible unity of the body in the eating of the Lord's Supper (1 Cor 10:17).

CONCLUSION

Our survey of the books of Genesis-Deuteronomy has unearthed a rich tapestry of images, themes, narratives, and laws that provide important background and resonance to Christian understandings and practices of sacraments in the life of the community of faith. Baptism's associations with water, cleansing, initiation into a new covenant relationship, death and resurrection, judgment and new life, vocation and identity, and promises that reach far into the future echo throughout the texts of the Torah: the breath or spirit of God moving over the waters of "the deep" in creation (Gen 1:2), the story of Noah and flood (Gen 6–9), the ritual of circumcision that linked identity and promise (Gen 17:9–14), Israel's crossing through the waters of the Red Sea (Exod 14–15), God's provision of water in the wilderness (Exod 17), the inauguration of the Sinai covenant in which Israel receives both identity and vocation from God (Exod 19:5–6), laws about rituals of bathing and cleansing (Lev 8:6; 14:7–9; 15), and the vision of unity expressed in one people coming together to worship one God, with the "circumcision of the heart" signifying obedience both as divine gift (Deut 30:1–6) and human calling (Deut 10:16).

The sacrament of the Lord's Supper is also deeply rooted in the Pentateuch's story of God and God's people Israel. Abraham and Sarah extend lavish hospitality and a generous meal to "strangers" and receive a gift of divine promise in return (Gen 18). Jesus ate a Passover meal with his disciples on the eve of his death on the cross. He did so in obedience to the Torah's command that all Israelites celebrate the annual Passover meal (Exod 12–13), a meal that includes a story about unleavened bread, the saving blood of the lamb, a connection with the near-sacrifice of the beloved son Isaac (Gen 22), and the remembrance that the story of being slaves in Egypt rescued by God is the defining story of God's people. God's gift of manna or "bread from heaven" in the wilderness (Exod 16:4), the people seeing God as "they ate and drank" at Mount Sinai (Exod 24:11), the maternal images for God's feeding God's people (Num 11:12; Deut 32:13–14), and the forgiveness of sins in the blood sacrifices and other rituals of the Day of Atonement (Lev 16:16–31) all provide essential background to the sacrament of the Lord's Supper. In Christian sacramentality as also throughout the Torah, tangible and material signs are coupled with intimate and divine words of promise, identity and vocation spoken individually and corporately to God's people. Through such sacramental words and signs, the holy and mysterious presence of a powerful, faithful and loving God comes near to God's people (Deut 4:7; 30:14) in order that God "might dwell among them" (Exod 29:46) and so carry God's "blessing to all the families of the earth" (Gen 12:3).

Suggested Reading

Claassens (2004); Levenson (1993); Olson (2008); and Thiselton (2007): 509–40.

See also:

Balentine, S. (1999), *The Torah's Vision of Worship* (Minneapolis, MN: Fortress).
Byars, R. (2011), *The Sacraments in Biblical Perspective* (Louisville, KY: Westminster John Knox).

Bibliography

Childs, B. (1992), *Biblical Theology of the Old and New Testaments: Theological Reflection on the Christian Bible* (Minneapolis, MN: Fortress).
Claassens, J. (2004), *The God Who Provides: Biblical Images of Divine Nourishment* (Nashville, TN: Abingdon).
Dahl, N. (1974), "The Atonement—An Adequate Reward for the Akedah," in *The Crucified Messiah, and Other Essays.* (Minneapolis, MN: Augsburg), 146–160.
Fleischman, J. (2001), "On the Significance of a Name Change and Circumcision in Genesis 17," *Journal of the Ancient Near Eastern Society* 28: 19–32.
Goldingay, J. (2000), "The Significance of Circumcision," *Journal for the Study of the Old Testament* 88: 3–18.
Lemke, W. (2003), "Circumcision of the Heart: The Journey of a Biblical Metaphor," in N. Bowen and B. Strawn (eds.), *A God So Near: Essays on Old Testament Theology in Honor of Patrick Miller* (Winona Lake, IN: Eisenbrauns), 299–319.
Levenson, J. (1993), *The Death and Resurrection of the Beloved Son: The Transformation of Child Sacrifice in Judaism and Christianity* (New Haven, CT: Yale University Press).
Olson, D. T. (2008), "Sacred Time: The Sabbath and Christian Worship," in C. Bechtel (ed.), *Touching the Altar: The Old Testament for Christian Worship* (Grand Rapids, MI: Eerdmans), 1–34.
Smith, M. (2010), *The Priestly Vision of Genesis 1* (Minneapolis, MN: Fortress).
Thiselton, A. (2007), *The Hermeneutics of Doctrine* (Grand Rapids, MI: Eerdmans).
Wagenaar, J. (2004), "Passover and the First Day of the Festival of Unleavened Bread in the Priestly Festival Calendar," *Vetus Testamentum* 54: 250–268.
Walter, G. (2013), *Being Promised: Theology, Gift, and Practice* (Grand Rapids, MI: Eerdmans).

....

CHAPTER 3

INTERTESTAMENTAL BACKGROUND OF THE CHRISTIAN SACRAMENTS

....

CRAIG A. EVANS AND JEREMIAH J. JOHNSTON

THE number of sacraments observed in the Christian church varies. Roman Catholicism and Eastern Orthodoxy recognize seven sacraments: baptism, confirmation (or chrismation), Eucharist, penance, anointing of the sick, holy orders, and matrimony. Anglicans and most other Protestants recognize two sacraments (baptism and Eucharist) though Anglicans, with varying interpretation, recognize five additional "sacramental rites" that are to be distinguished from the two "Sacraments of the Gospel" (*Thirty-Nine Articles* art. 25). Many Protestant groups refer to baptism and Eucharist as ordinances rather than sacraments. Others, such as matrimony, are called institutions. The two ordinances, or sacraments, that are universally recognized, that is, baptism and Eucharist, are deeply rooted in the Old Testament and intertestamental traditions and events.

BAPTISM

....

Christian baptism has its roots in the purity rites prescribed in Israel's ancient scriptures and various practices that emerged in the intertestamental period. In various ways water was used in ancient times to purify people or things, either to remedy a state of uncleanness or to prepare for contact with the sacred. To understand developments in the intertestamental period it is necessary to begin with an overview of law and practice in the Old Testament period.

Immersion and Washing in Israel's History and Scripture

In preparation for meeting God at Mount Sinai the people of Israel were commanded to consecrate themselves and "wash their clothes" (Exod 19:10; cf. 19:14). As part of their consecration to the priesthood Aaron and his sons had to be washed with water (Exod 29:4), which had to be repeated when they approached the newly constructed tabernacle (Exod 40:12, 31). Similarly, going in and out of the tabernacle and handling sacred items required washing (Exod 30:19–21; Lev 11:25, 25, 28, 40). To purify themselves the Levites were required to wash their clothes, cleanse themselves, and be sprinkled with "water of purification" (Num 8:7). Those who sprinkled the water for impurity were required to wash their clothes (Num 19:21; 31:23–24). The one who released the scapegoat was required to wash his clothes and bathe (Lev 16:26). Likewise the one who burned the sacrifice was required to wash his clothes and bathe (Lev 16:28; Num 19:7–10; 2 Chron 4:6).

Washing was often required in matters involving impurity or uncleanness. For example, the suspected leper who was declared clean was required to wash his clothes (Lev 13:6, 34; 14:8–9); so also those who had come in contact with him or his house (Lev 14:47). Those who had had discharges were to wash their clothes; so also those who came into contact with such persons (Lev 15). Anyone who ate something unclean was required to wash his clothes and bathe (Lev 17:15). Anyone who came into contact with a corpse was unclean for seven days and was required to be purified with water (Num 19:11–19).

Although there is no obvious cultic connotation in the story of the healing of Naaman, the Syrian commander (2 Kgs 5:8–14), it is probable that Jewish readers understood Elisha's command that the man wash himself in the Jordan River, in order to be cleansed of his leprosy, as consistent with the Mosaic law of purification.

The laws of washing and cleansing were often employed as metaphor. The Psalmist petitions God that he might be washed and cleansed from sin (Ps 51:2, 7). Similarly, an angry Isaiah enjoins Israel to wash themselves and make themselves clean (Isa 1:16). But the prophet knows that only God will be able wash away Israel's sin (4:4). These expressions are echoed in Jeremiah (2:22; 4:14) and Ezekiel (16:4, 9).

Immersion and Washing in the Intertestamental Period

The laws of washing remained very much in force during the intertestamental period. We hear them echoed in the literature that was written and circulated in this time. For example, the patriarch Levi instructs his sons, who will serve as priests: "before entering into the holy place, bathe; and when you offer sacrifice, wash; and again, when you finish the sacrifice, wash" (*T. Levi* 9:11). This instruction is expanded in the related pseudepigraphal works, the *Ordinance of Levi* (cf. 19, 26, 53) and the *Prayer of Levi* (cf. 1–2).

According to the pseudepigraphal *Letter of Aristeas*, Jews washed their hands before prayer to signify their purity, that they had done no evil (*Aristeas* 305–306). The Essenes, according to Josephus, bathed and said prayers before partaking of food (*Jewish Wars* 2.129–31; cf. 4Q514 frag. 1, col. i, lines 9–10).

When the righteous Tobit returns home, after burying a Jewish exile whose corpse had been thrown into the market square, he washes and then eats (Tob 2:4–5). Although the text does not specify, it is likely that Tobit immersed himself and perhaps even washed his clothes, in keeping with the Mosaic law relating to corpse impurity. Writing at about the same time as the composition of the book of Tobit, the sage Jesus ben Sira speaks of one who bathes, or immerses himself (Greek: *baptizomenos*) after touching a corpse (Sir 34:30).

Later in the story of Tobit his son Tobias washes himself in the Tigris River in preparation for eating his food (Tob 6:3). This is very early attestation of the tradition that required washing the hands before eating, earlier than the attestation found in the practice of the Essenes (noted above). Washing before eating is presupposed in Jesus' dispute with religious authorities (cf. Mark 7:3, "the Pharisees, and all the Jews, do not eat unless they thoroughly wash their hands, thus observing the tradition of the elders") and later codified in the Tosefta (*c.* AD 300), a compendium of legal rulings that supplement the Mishna (cf. *t. Berakot* 4.8, where those reclined at table are given water to wash their hands before eating).

The righteous heroine Judith, who spent time with the gentile commander Holofernes, "went out each night into the ravine of Baityloua and immersed herself [Greek: *ebaptizeto*] at the spring of water" (Jdt 12:7, slightly modified). Evidently she did this to remove any impurity she may have contracted from being in the company of Holofernes.

There are some remarkable elaborations on the older stories and traditions. The angels collected the body of Adam "and carried him off to the Acherusian lake, and washed him three times, in the presence of God" (*Apoc. Moses* 37:3), presumably for purification. The dying Levi recounts to his sons a vision in which seven men (angels?) prepared him and dressed him for the priesthood, including, among other things, washing him with pure water (*T. Levi* 8:1–6). In a very interesting tradition we are told that the angels who buried the body of Moses were not required to wash themselves (contrary to the law of corpse impurity), for the body of Moses was holy and thus conveyed no impurity (*Assumption of Moses* frag. 7). In yet another novel tradition King Solomon is commanded to wash his hands and then sit on his throne (*T. Sol.* 13:2). The washing of his hands no doubt relates to the Jewish laws of purity, but in the context of the *Testament of Solomon* magic is probably involved.

According to the *Sibylline Oracles* the righteous "lift up holy arms toward heaven … always sanctifying their flesh with water" (*Sib. Or.* 5:591–593). One is again reminded of the Essenes, who are said to rise early in the morning and pray, facing the sun, and then "bathe their bodies in cold water" (*Jewish Wars* 2.129).

Josephus claims that as a youth (*c.* 53 AD) he studied with one Bannus, a hermit, perhaps related in some way to the Essenes. Bannus wore simple clothing, ate the food that the wilderness provided (cf. Mark 1:4–6, where John the Baptist, also in the wilderness, was sustained by a diet of locusts and wild honey), and washed frequently, for purification, "with frigid water, day and night" (Josephus, *Life* 11). This description may have had a Roman readership in view, which appreciated daily bathing, including bathing in cold water. Indeed, the philosopher Nigrinus required it of his students, to "toughen them up" (Lucian, *Nigrinus* 27), a feature that Josephus may well have had in mind when he described his wilderness training under Bannus.

The men of Qumran (whose community was founded *c.* 100 BC), thought by most to be the Essenes mentioned by Josephus and other authors of late antiquity, stressed the importance of bathing for purification. Some of their practice reflects a priestly (as opposed to lay) self-understanding. Those who had become impure were to "bathe and wash in water and they shall be clean. Afterwards they may eat their bread according to purity" (4Q514 frag. 1, col. i, lines 9–10). The *Temple Scroll* (11Q19–20) delineates at length rules, sometimes complex, pertaining to ritual bathing (multiple times, over a number of days, until sundown). The sanctity of the temple and city of Jerusalem is especially emphasized (11Q19 cols. 45–47), as a number of purity laws (11Q19 cols. 49–51). Some of the laws and practices of washing and immersion in the scrolls were distinctive of Qumran; others seem to have been part of an emerging general practice, as attested in other sources, including early rabbinic literature.

Archaeology of Ritual Immersion

Although "living water" (i.e. natural, flowing water) was often preferred (cf. Lev 15:13), it was practical for most Jews to immerse themselves in pools designed for this purpose. Archaeological excavations of the last forty years or so have uncovered and identified several public and private immersion pools called *miqva'ot* (singular: *miqveh*).

The best known immersion pools in Jerusalem are found in the vicinity of the temple mount. There are several. Some of these pools have wide divided steps, to separate the impure who descend from the pure who ascend. That this was the intention of the divider is confirmed by an apocryphal story, preserved in a small Greek fragment, in which an indignant priest says to Jesus in the temple precincts: "I am clean, for I washed in the pool of David, and having descended by one set of steps I ascended by another. And I put on white and clean clothes, and then I came and looked upon these holy vessels" (P.Oxy. 840 2.5–6). Archaeologists are uncertain which immersion pool is the "pool of David" (the "King's Pool"? Cf. Neh 2:14), or even if it has in fact been uncovered in the ongoing excavations at the south and west areas outside the temple mount itself.

Other pools, possibly used for immersion (and scholars debate this), have been found in old Jerusalem. These include the pool of Siloam (see John 9:7), whose actual site has only recently been confirmed, and perhaps the pool near the Sheep Gate (see John 5:2). A number of pools are mentioned in Old Testament literature (e.g. 2 Kgs 18:17; Neh 2:14; 3:15–16; Isa 7:3; 22:9, 11), though whether any of them were used for ritual immersion in this period of time is unknown. The mysterious first-century AD *Copper Scroll* describes a treasure "at the edge of the aqueduct, six cubits to the north of the immersion pool" (3Q15 1:11–12). Most interpreters believe this pool was in the vicinity of Jerusalem, though precisely where no one knows.

As many as seven to nine synagogues that date before AD 70 have been identified. Archaeological excavations have uncovered *miqva'ot* alongside or in close proximity to five of these synagogues (Gamla, Herodium, Jericho, Magdala, and Modi'in). Synagogues dating after AD 70 also have *miqva'ot* within or in close proximity. In the lower levels (or basements) of several private homes, at Sepphoris and elsewhere, *miqva'ot* have been found.

The presence of so many ritual immersion pools, in public and private places, suggests that the Jewish people of late antiquity took the Mosaic laws of bathing and immersion for purity very seriously. The physical remains suggest that practice, at least for many, closely followed scriptural mandates.

Immersion, Repentance, and Renewal

During the intertestamental period some of the laws related to washing were expanded and given new applications. One significant feature is the emergence of a close association between washing and repentance. This association is seen in the *Sibylline Oracles*, where the wicked are commanded to repent and "wash your whole bodies in ever-flowing rivers" (4:162–170, here 165). Although *Oracle* 4 has been redacted in later times, most of it dates to the third century BC. The command to wash the "whole body" (Greek: *holon*) is not in reference to ritual, daily washing, but to repentance to avoid judgment. This idea is seen in the Joseph and Aseneth romance. After repenting of her idolatry and vanity, Aseneth "washed her face with pure water" (*Jos. Asen.* 14:17). Her repentance (and washing, presumably) make it possible for Aseneth to "eat the bread of life and drink the cup of immortality" (*Jos. Asen.* 15:4).

The act of washing, often involving full immersion, not only was associated with repentance but also with national renewal and restoration. We may have two examples of first-century movements based on this association. The first involves John, known as the baptizer or baptist, and the second involves a man named Theudas. The first-century Jewish historian and apologist Josephus describes the activities of both men. Of John, whose public activities probably commenced in the late 20s AD, Josephus says:

> Now it seemed to some of the Jews that the destruction of Herod's army was by God, and was certainly well deserved, on account of what he did to John, called the Baptist. For Herod had executed him, though he was a good man and had urged the Jews—if inclined to exercise virtue, to practice justice toward one another and piety toward God—to join in baptism. For baptizing was acceptable to him (God), not for pardon of whatever sins they may have committed, but in purifying the body, as though the soul had beforehand been cleansed in righteousness. And when others gathered (for they were greatly moved by his words), Herod, fearing that John's great influence over the people might result in some form of insurrection (for it seemed that they

did everything by his counsel), thought it much better to put him to death before his work led to an uprising than to await a disturbance, become involved in a problem, and have second thoughts. So the prisoner, because of Herod's suspicion, was sent to Machaerus, the stronghold previously mentioned, and there was executed. But to the Jews it seemed a vindication of John that God willed to do Herod an evil, in the destruction of the army. (*Ant.* 18.116–119)

What prompted Josephus to mention John was the widespread opinion among Jews that the catastrophe that overtook Herod Antipas at the hands of his former father-in-law Aretas the king of Nabatea (and contributed to Rome's eventual removal of Antipas from office) came about because of his treatment of the Baptist. Evidently Josephus agrees with this assessment and so portrays John as a "good man" who urged righteous Jews to join him in baptism. Moreover, Josephus seems to have had a pretty good idea of what John's baptism was all about. He understood that baptism signified repentance and a cleansing of the soul. Alone, baptism could not pardon "whatever sins they may have committed." (We may assume that Josephus has downplayed ideas of national restoration, regime change, and the like.)

Whether Josephus knew more about John's preaching and suppressed it, out of his reluctance to divulge to the Roman public Jewish interest in eschatology and messianism, is difficult to say. But what Josephus tells us does complement in important ways the portrait in the New Testament Gospels, especially when viewed in the context of the activities and promises made by other men of this time.

According to tradition shared by Matthew and Luke (what is usually identified as the Q source) the Baptist warns the Jewish people not to presume upon God's grace by saying, "We have Abraham as our father." No Jew can say this, John asserts, because "God is able from these stones to raise up children to Abraham" (Matt 3:9; cf. Luke 3:8). Reference to "these stones" in the context of the Jordan River may well have alluded to the story of Joshua building a monument of twelve stones when the twelve tribes of Israel crossed the Jordan to enter the Promised Land. On this occasion Joshua says to the people: "When your children ask their parents in time to come, 'What do *these stones* mean?' Then you shall let your children know, 'Israel passed over this Jordan [River] on dry ground'" (Josh 4:21–22 [emphasis added]; cf. Deut 27:4; Josh 4:2–23). The symbolism of twelve stones also appears in the story of Elijah, who led the struggle in Israel against adoption of foreign gods (cf. 1 Kgs 18:31 "Elijah took twelve stones, according to the number of the tribes of the sons of Jacob"), who for a time lived near the Jordan River (cf. 1 Kgs 17:3–5) and even parted its waters (cf. 2 Kgs 2:8), whose disciple Elisha also parted the water (cf. 2 Kgs 2:14) and later ordered the Syrian captain to be baptized in the Jordan River (cf. 2 Kgs 5:10–14). This is significant, for the clothing of John the Baptist resembles that of Elijah (Mark 1:6; cf. 2 Kgs 1:8) and Jesus himself identifies John as the famous prophet of old (Mark 9:11–13).

It seems clear that John's preaching and activities were significantly informed by biblical symbolism, especially the symbolism of the Jordan River and, by inference, the tradition of the twelve stones. Jesus' appointment of twelve disciples (cf. Mark 3:14–19; 6:7) provides significant support for this line of interpretation. Most commentators rightly recognize that the number twelve was intended to symbolize the twelve tribes of Israel, implying that the goal of the ministry of Jesus was the restoration of the whole of the nation.

What is important here is that John's baptism not only signified repentance but also was part of a ministry that apparently called for national renewal. John's baptism, thus, was far more than mere personal washing and purification. It should be added that according to the Gospel of John, the disciples of Jesus also baptized (John 3:22; 4:1–2). This shows that baptism was part of Jesus' ministry from the very beginning and not something that was added on after the resurrection.

Other prophetic figures mentioned in Josephus, invariably in highly negative, prejudicial language, had similar goals and in some instances utilized similar biblical symbolism. One of these figures was a man called Theudas, who in about the year AD 45 summoned all who would heed him to join him at the Jordan River. About this figure Josephus says:

> Now when Fadus was procurator of Judea, a certain pretender named Theudas persuaded the greater part of the mob to take up their possessions and follow him to the Jordan River. For he told them that he was a prophet and that at his command he could divide the river, providing them with easy passage. Saying these things, he deceived many. Fadus, however, did not permit them to take advantage of the madness, but sent a squadron of cavalry against them, which falling upon them unexpectedly killed many and took many alive. Capturing Theudas, they cut off his head and conveyed it to Jerusalem. (*Ant.* 20.97–98)

Theudas' claim to be able to part the Jordan River is an unmistakable allusion either to the crossing of the Red Sea (Exod 14:21–22) or, more likely, to the crossing of the Jordan River (Josh 3:14–17), part of the imagery associated with Israel's redemption (cf. Isa 11:15; 43:16; 51:10; 63:11). In either case, it is probable that Theudas was claiming to be the prophet "like Moses" (Deut 18:15–19; cf. 1 Macc 4:45–46; 14:41; 9:27), who could perform signs like those of Moses's original successor Joshua. That his following could actually carry their possessions on their backs strongly suggests that they were landless poor, understandably desperate for social and economic change. We should imagine that they crossed the Jordan to the east side and there awaited the promised miracle by which they would recross the Jordan in a westerly direction, only this time dryshod.

Admittedly, Josephus says nothing about Theudas baptizing anyone. Perhaps he did, perhaps he did not. But the crossing of the Jordan likely symbolized a baptism of sorts, even as it does for the apostle Paul, in his letter to the Corinthians composed less than a decade after the Theudas debacle. In 1 Corinthians 10:1–2 Paul interprets the passing through the sea (alluding to Exod 14:21–25) as baptism. The analogy is remarkable. The application to Christian baptism is obvious enough, but what accommodated the analogy was the kind of thinking seen in people like John, Jesus, and Theudas, who gathered at the Jordan and proclaimed personal and/or national renewal in one way or another.

The crossing of the Jordan and/or the explicit act of baptizing at the Jordan symbolized national renewal. For Paul this national renewal had been transformed into admission into the church, the new people of God. The washings and ablutions that were part of the purification rituals enunciated in the Law of Moses had developed into ideas of eschatological and national purification, which in turn was understood as necessary for national restoration.

Immersion/Baptism after Easter

When the risen Jesus commanded his apostles to "make disciples of all nations, baptizing them in the name of the Father and of the Son and of the Holy Spirit" (Matt 28:19), the ground had already been laid. In a sense the Great Commission contained little that was new. All that was new was the narrower focus of the baptism. The focus was not simply one of repentance and renewal, it was one of submission to the Lordship and authority of the risen Christ. To be baptized in his name was to become part of his body, the church.

The apostles of Jesus quickly put into practice his command. On the day of Pentecost Peter urged those in Jerusalem, "Repent, and be baptized every one of you in the name of Jesus Christ so that your sins may be forgiven" (Acts 2:38). Some three thousand repented and were baptized (Acts 2:41). Through Philip's preaching a number of Samaritans believed the gospel and were baptized (Acts 8:12–13). When Philip told the Ethiopian official the meaning of Isaiah 53, the latter requested baptism (Acts 8:36–38). Paul was baptized not long after his encounter with the risen Christ (Acts 9:18). Even a Roman centurion and his household were baptized (Acts 10:47–48).

At its first council (Acts 11) the young church recognized that the conversion and baptism of the Samaritans and Gentiles were valid, for the Holy Spirit in every case came upon the new converts. In reaching this decision, which had enormous consequences for the future growth and character of the church, Peter recalled the words of the risen Christ, which in fact echoed the original preaching of John the Baptist: "John baptized with water, but you will be baptized with the Holy Spirit" (Acts 11:16; cf. Acts 1:5; Matt 3:11; Mark 1:8; Luke 3:17).

EUCHARIST

The Eucharist is the holiest of the Christian sacraments. Few words of Jesus are as familiar as those uttered at the Last Supper with his disciples: "Take; this is my body ... This is my blood of the covenant, which is poured out for many" (Mark 14:24; cf. Matt 26:28; Luke 22:20; 1 Cor 11:23–25; *Did.* 9:1–5). According to Paul, Jesus adds: "Do this in remembrance of me" (1 Cor 11:24, 25). This command instituted the Eucharist. The words of Jesus are both startling in their novelty and at the same time redolent of Jewish cultic tradition.

Their cultic echoes are quite obvious. The words of Jesus clearly allude to Exodus 24:8 ("See the blood of the covenant that the Lord has made with you in accordance with all these words"), Jeremiah 31:31 ("The days are surely coming, says the Lord, when I will make a new covenant with the house of Israel and the house of Judah"), and perhaps Zechariah 9:11 ("because of the blood of my covenant with you"). The probability of allusion to Jeremiah 31:31 is increased when we take into account the versions of the eucharistic tradition found in Luke 22:20 ("the new covenant in my blood") and 1 Corinthians 11:25 ("This cup is the new covenant in my blood"), where the adjective "new" appears.

The ratification of the original covenant at Sinai with blood and Jeremiah's prophecy of a new (or renewed) covenant provide the scriptural foundation for Jesus' words. But Jesus speaks of *his* blood and *his* body, not the blood and the body of a sacrificial animal. Clearly underlying his thinking are concepts that have developed beyond the original ideas expressed in the Law of Moses. Jesus' self-application of these scriptural concepts reflects Israel's history of martyrdom, especially as experienced during the intertestamental period and later remembered and idealized. To describe Jewish history as a "history of martyrdom" may perhaps be simplistic, but it contains an element of truth. Of course, the other side of Jewish history is a history of revolt, revolt against pagan neighbors.

Noble Death and Martyrdom

To understand the Words of Institution, from which the ordinance or sacrament of Eucharist is derived, one must appreciate the history of Jewish martyrdom and the broader ideal of what is sometimes termed the noble death.

Old Testament examples of noble death and martyrdom. There are examples of heroic figures in the oldest stories of Old Testament literature. In some cases the protagonist risks his life but is rescued. We see this in the story of Joseph, who is betrayed by his brothers, sold into slavery in Egypt, is falsely accused by his master's wife, is imprisoned, is forgotten by a man he helped in prison, and then finally is vindicated (Gen 37–41). Even Samson, who for the most part brought his misfortune upon himself through his recklessness and immorality, nevertheless died in a manner that could be regarded as heroic (Judg 16:18–31). David, who was threatened and pursued by King Saul, his jealous father-in-law, bravely faced death on behalf of his people and in the service of God. Among other things, David faced Goliath the Philistine champion (1 Sam 17:26–54) and he spared the life of Saul (1 Sam 24:1–7; 26:1–25).

Old Testament prophets sometimes risked death by proclaiming the word of God to monarchs who did not want to hear it. Elijah is forced to flee (1 Kgs 19:1–14), Jeremiah is threatened (Jer 38:4–13), and Zechariah the son of Jehoiada the priest is stoned (2 Chron 24:20–21). The tradition of the persecuted prophet and righteous person is greatly developed in the intertestamental period.

Pagan examples of noble death and martyrdom. There are many pagan stories and traditions of good men who face imprisonment, torture, and death. One of the oldest is the story of Ahiqar, who is betrayed by his adopted nephew. He is imprisoned, sentenced to death, and then is marvelously rescued and vindicated. Although he was not killed, his bravery and dignity in the face of gross injustice and the threat of death made him a model throughout the Middle East in the intertestamental period. Several Greek philosophers and statesmen (e.g. Zeno, Anaxarchus) were recognized as noble men who died with honor and dignity. Best known was Socrates who was forced to commit suicide by drinking hemlock. First-century philosopher Epictetus is remembered to have said: "If you want to be crucified, just wait. The cross will come. If it seems reasonable to comply, and the circumstances are right, then it is to be carried through, and your integrity maintained" (Epictetus, *Dissertations* 2.2.20).

Jewish examples of noble death and martyrdom in the intertestamental period. The old stories of the persecution of some of the prophets were greatly embellished in the intertestamental period. Legends about the persecution and brutal murder of Isaiah emerged in this time. Although there is not a hint in the Hebrew scriptures of the ill-treatment of this prophet, later legends tell us that the wicked king Manasseh had him sawn in two (*Mart. Ascen. Isa.* 5:1–2, 11–14; cf. Heb 11:37). About one third of the prophets whose lives and major prophecies are briefly recounted in the first-century *Lives of the Prophets* are martyred. Daniel's three friends are willing to be cast into the fiery furnace rather than worship the golden image (Dan 3). Daniel himself would rather face hungry lions than cease praying to God (Dan 6). According to the first-century *Testament of Moses* the martyrdom of the righteous priest Taxo and his seven sons sets the stage for the end of evil and the appearance of the kingdom of God.

The belief that the righteous were routinely persecuted becomes widespread in the first century. Even Moses himself, it was believed, was threatened with stoning when the fleeing Israelites were stopped by the sea (cf. Exod 14:10–12, as recounted in Josephus, *Ant.* 2.327). It is hardly a surprise that in his lamentation for the city of Jerusalem Jesus can say: "O Jerusalem, Jerusalem, killing the prophets and stoning those who are sent to you!" (Matt 23:37 = Luke 13:34). Killing and threatening prophets and righteous persons had by the first century become a commonplace.

Noble death and the Maccabean martyrs. Probably the single greatest factor in the creation of the idea of noble death and martyrdom in the intertestamental period was the persecution of the Torah-observant Jews that led up to the Maccabean wars. Antiochus IV Epiphanes (ruled 175–164 BC) not only demanded that the Jewish people worship Zeus, he also demanded that they worship him. The despot imposed restrictions on Jewish traditions and forced Greek customs on the Jewish population. An edict forbade the rite of circumcision and the observance of the Sabbath. A pagan altar dedicated to the worship of Zeus was built in the Jerusalem temple (the "abomination that makes desolate" mentioned in Dan 11:31; 12:11). As a sign of loyalty, Jews were required to offer pagan sacrifices, including the offering of swine flesh. Antiochus placed Seleucid troops in Jerusalem at a citadel known as the Akra to ensure compliance to his edicts. On two occasions Seleucid troops plundered the temple on the orders of the king.

According to Josephus, in the face of suffering and self-sacrifice not even the commitment of the Spartans and Lacedemonians can adequately compare with the Jewish people. In fact, Jews should be "admired" (*Against Apion* 2.226) for unflinching loyalty to their laws despite "ten thousand changes in our fortune" (*Against Apion* 2.228). Josephus' history remembers the Jews' unmatched zeal in their desire to die rather than violate *Torah*, for "we are more courageous in dying for our laws than all other men" (*Against Apion* 2.234).

Martyrdom as atonement for the sin of Israel. 1 Maccabees portrays all five sons of Mattathias as being willing to die for their people: "If our time has come, let us die bravely for our kindred, and leave no cause to question our honor" (1 Macc 9:10). They are willing to die for Torah: "Then there united with them a company of Hasideans, mighty warriors of Israel, every one who offered himself willingly for the law" (1 Macc 2:42). On his deathbed Mattathias exhorts his sons to "show zeal for the law, and give your lives for the covenant of our ancestors" (1 Macc 2:50; cf. 13:4).

The Maccabean martyrs not only established the benchmark of suffering and martyrdom, their suffering came to be viewed as having atoning benefit for Israel itself. According to 1 Macc 6:44, Eleazar, brother of Judas Maccabeus, "gave himself [*edoken auton*] to save his people and to win for himself an everlasting name" (cf. Gal 1:4: "who gave himself [*dontos eauton*] for our sins"; Titus 2:14: "who gave himself [*edoken eauton*] for us").

In the gruesome account of the martyrdom of the mother and her seven sons, the youngest of the sons says to the king: "I, like my brothers, give up body and life for the laws of our ancestors, appealing to God to show mercy soon to our nation ... and *through me and my brothers* to bring to an end the wrath of the Almighty which has justly fallen on our whole nation" (2 Macc 7:33, 37–38; emphasis added).

In 4 Maccabees we hear of the salvific value of the suffering or death of the righteous: "By their endurance they conquered the tyrant, and thus their native land was purified through them" (4 Macc 1:11b). In reference to "those who gave their bodies in suffering for the sake of religion," the author asserts: "Because of them the nation gained peace, and by reviving observance of the law in the homeland they ravaged the enemy" (4 Macc 18:3–4). Even more explicitly, and in language reflecting the cultus itself, the author declares that these martyrs became, "as it were, a ransom for the sin of our nation. And through the blood of these devout ones and their death as an expiation, divine Providence preserved Israel that previously had been afflicted" (4 Macc 17:21b–22).

In the Song of the Three Young Men, a first-century BC addition to the book of Daniel (between Dan 3:23 and 24), Azariah likens himself and his two companions to a burnt offering, "such may our sacrifice be in your sight today" (Song of the Three 16–17).

The shedding of the blood of the righteous will prompt God to act and to make expiation for his people. In another tradition we are told that Isaac's willingness to give his life resulted in God's election of the descendants of Abraham: "And because he did not refuse, his sacrifice was well pleasing to me, and on account of his blood I chose them" (*L.A.B.* 18:5). The already mentioned Palestinian work, *Testament of Moses*, promotes the idea of the benefits of the death of the righteous. The protagonist, the righteous priest Taxo, urges his seven sons to "die rather than transgress the commandments of the Lord of Lords," so that by doing this their "blood will be avenged before the Lord. Then his [God's] kingdom will appear throughout his whole creation. Then the devil will have an end" (*T. Mos.* 9:6b–10:1).

One should also consider the comment in the *Community Rule* scroll from Qumran: "they shall atone for sin by doing justice and by suffering the sorrows of affliction" (1QS 8:3–4; cf. 5:6; 9:4). What is not clear is if the atonement is for the individual who does justice and suffers or if the atonement is for the nation of Israel as a whole.

The deaths of the Masada rebels. One of the most dramatic accounts of martyrdom is provided by Josephus, who recounts for his readers what he believes was the final speech given by the rebel Eleazar, whose followers had seized and occupied Masada during the Jewish revolt against Rome (AD 66–70), but who now prepare to commit mass suicide (AD 73). Eleazar tells his following that they have it in their power "to die nobly and in freedom" (*Jewish Wars* 7.326), preferring "death to slavery" (7.336). Josephus tells us that some of Eleazar's followers were "filled with delight at the thought of a death so noble" (7.337). Others were less certain, requiring further exhortation from Eleazar, "let us hasten to die honorably!" (7.380).

Historians have expressed doubts about the veracity of the account that Josephus has provided. It is possible that most of the Masada rebels committed suicide, fearing capture by the Romans. But the speech credited to Eleazar is very doubtful and may represent an imitation of the speech of Vulteius (first century BC), recounted in Lucan's poetry (*De bello civili* 4.516–17), in which he urged his men to commit suicide. If Josephus intended such an allusion, then he sees nothing noble in the deaths of Eleazar and the rebels. Be that as it may, we can be confident that when Josephus has Eleazar speak of a desire to avoid torture (*Jewish Wars* 7.384–88) he intended to draw a distinction between the rebels, for whom Josephus held contempt, and the Maccabean martyrs, for whom he had admiration.

Rabbinic ideas of noble death and martyrdom. Early rabbinic tradition entertained ideas that linked the death of the righteous and the restoration of Israel. Commenting on 1 Kings 20:42 and 22:34, Simeon ben Yohai (second century CE) is remembered to have said: "That single drop of blood which flowed from that righteous man [the prophet of 1 Kgs 20:37] effected atonement on behalf of all Israel" (*y. Sanh.* 11.5). Two more Tannaitic traditions should be mentioned: "When Israelites are slain by the nations of the world, it serves them as expiation in the world to come" (*Sipre Deut.* §333 [on Deut 32:43]); "you find everywhere that the patriarchs and the prophets gave their lives on behalf of Israel" (*Mek.* on Exod 12:1 [*Pischa* §1]).

Relevance of noble death traditions for Jesus. From these texts and traditions it seems reasonable to conclude that Jesus in all probability did attach atoning and salvific significance to his impending death. The Words of Institution, even if unique in important ways, cohere with ideas of the atoning value of the suffering and death of a righteous man. Facing the probability of death, it would only have been natural for him to conclude that his death would advance God's purposes, just as surely as the deaths of the Maccabean martyrs and other righteous persons atoned for Israel's sin and paved the way for national deliverance. Jesus' death would in fact establish the renewed covenant and guarantee the consummation of the kingdom of God. So assured was Jesus that he vowed not to drink wine again until he would drink it in the kingdom of God (Mark 14:25).

The emergence of the tradition of the Eucharist in itself also attests to the atoning significance that Jesus placed on his death. The solemnity of the occasion, the words of institution with their reference to the "blood of the covenant," and the deep impression made on the disciples gave rise to early Christianity's doctrine of atonement. Apart from Jesus' words at the Last Supper and their connotations of atonement, the doctrine of atonement (as opposed to ideas of simple martyrdom) that emerged cannot be easily explained. Moreover, the mere fact of the institution of the Lord's Supper as something to be commemorated by the church also corroborates the atonement orientation of Jesus' words. Recognizing Jesus' death as atonement and not simply as martyrdom, in combination with the conviction that he was God's Son, would have facilitated the institution of the Eucharist.

CONCLUDING COMMENTS

Baptism and Eucharist, the two major sacraments, or ordinances, are rooted firmly in Israel's ancient scriptures and in the newer writings and interpretations that arose in response to the vicissitudes and developments that took place in the intertestamental period. In important ways eschatological immersion, signifying repentance and a break with the past, was a logical extension of the various purity regulations expressed in the Law of Moses. Immersion as practiced by the followers of Jesus was linked specifically to Jesus as Israel's Messiah and God's Son and not simply to repentance as such. This new association transformed what had been repentance immersion, with eschatological connotations, into the distinctive baptism practiced by the early church.

The Words of Institution, which give meaning to the Eucharist, are also rooted in Israel's ancient scriptures, but again not without further development and new application. Jesus' application of the language of the Sinai covenant to himself is clarified by Israel's recent history of severe persecution and the celebration of martyrs (especially the Maccabean martyrs) who chose noble death over apostasy and violation of God's Law.

SUGGESTED READING

D. Boyarin (1999); M. Hengel (1981); J. Klawans (2000); S. McKnight (2005); L. J. Vander Zee (2004).

BIBLIOGRAPHY

Barth, K. (1963), *The Teaching of the Church Regarding Baptism* (London: SCM Press).

Baumeister, T. (1980), *Die Anfänge der Theologie des Martyriums* (Münster: Aschendorff).

Boyarin, D. (1999), *Dying for God: Martyrdom and the Making of Christianity and Judaism* (Stanford, CA: Stanford University Press).

Chan, S. (2006), *Liturgical Theology: The Church as a Worshipping Community* (Downers Grove, IL: IVP Academic).

Collins, J. J. and G. W. E. Nickelsburg (eds.) (1980), *Ideal Figures in Ancient Judaism: Profiles and Paradigms* (Chico, CA: Scholars Press).

Cullmann, O. (1950), *Baptism in the New Testament* (London: SCM Press).

Cummins, S. A. (2001), *Paul and the Crucified Christ in Antioch: Maccabean Martyrdom and Galatians 1 and 2* (Cambridge: Cambridge University Press).

Evans, C. A. (2006), "Josephus on John the Baptist and Other Jewish Prophets of Deliverance," in D. C. Allison, Jr., J. D. Crossan, and A. J. Levine (eds.), *The Historical Jesus in Context* (Princeton, NJ: Princeton University Press), 55–63.

Frend, W. H. C. (1965), *Martyrdom and Persecution in the Early Church: A Study of a Conflict from the Maccabees to Donatus* (Oxford: Oxford University Press).

Fuhrmann, S. and R. Grundmann (eds.) (2012), *Maryriumsvorstellungen in Antike und Mittelalter: Leben oder sterben für Gott?* (Leiden: Brill).

Hartman, L. (1992), "Baptism," in D. N. Freedman et al. (eds.), *The Anchor Bible Dictionary*, 6 vols. (New York: Doubleday), 1: 583–594.

Hengel, M. (1981), *The Atonement: The Origins of the Doctrine in the New Testament* (London: SCM Press).

Horbury, W. and B. McNeil (eds.) (1981), *Suffering and Martyrdom in the New Testament: Studies Presented to G. M. Styler by the Cambridge New Testament Seminar* (Cambridge: Cambridge University Press).

Kilpatrick, G. D. (1983), *The Eucharist in Bible and Liturgy* (Cambridge: Cambridge University Press; repr. 2008).

Klauck, H.-J. (1992), "Lord's Supper," in D. N. Freedman et al. (eds.), *The Anchor Bible Dictionary*, 6 vols. (New York: Doubleday), 4: 362–372.

Klawans, J. (2000), *Impurity and Sin in Ancient Judaism* (Oxford: Oxford University Press).

Ladouceur, D. J. (1980), "Masada: Consideration of the Literary Evidence," *Greek, Roman, and Byzantine Studies* 21: 245–260.

Lichtenberger, H. (2000), "Baths and Baptism," in L. H. Schiffman and J. C. VanderKam (eds.), *Encyclopedia of the Dead Sea Scrolls*, 2 vols. (Oxford: Oxford University Press), 1:85–89.

McKnight, S. (2005), *Jesus and His Death: Historiography, the Historical Jesus, and Atonement Theory* (Waco, TX: Baylor University Press).

McNeil, B. (1981), "Suffering and Martyrdom in the Odes of Solomon," in W. Horbury and B. McNeil (eds.), *Suffering and Martyrdom in the New Testament: Studies Presented to G. M. Styler by the Cambridge New Testament Seminar* (Cambridge: Cambridge University Press), 136–142.

Middleton, P. (2006), *Radical Martyrdom and Cosmic Conflict in Early Christianity* (London and New York: T & T Clark).

Nickelsburg, G. W. E. (1972), *Resurrection, Immortality and Eternal Life in Intertestamental Judaism* (Cambridge, MA: Harvard University Press).

O'Neill, J. C. (1981), "Did Jesus Teach that His Death would be Vicarious as well as Typical?" in W. Horbury and B. McNeil (eds.), *Suffering and Martyrdom in the New Testament: Studies Presented to G. M. Styler by the Cambridge New Testament Seminar* (Cambridge: Cambridge University Press), 9–27.

O'Toole, R. F. (1992), "Last Supper," in D. N. Freedman et al. (eds.), *The Anchor Bible Dictionary*, 6 vols. (New York: Doubleday), 4: 234–241.

Porter, S. E. and A. R. Cross (eds.) (1999), *Baptism, the New Testament and the Church: Historical and Contemporary Studies in Honour of R. E. O. White* (Sheffield: Sheffield Academic Press).

Porter, S. E. and A. R. Cross (eds.) (2002), *Dimensions of Baptism: Biblical and Theological Studies* (Sheffield: Sheffield Academic Press).

Rajak, T. (1997), "Dying for the Law: The Martyr's Portrait in Jewish-Greek Literature," in M. J. Edwards and S. Swain (eds.), *Portraits: Biographical Representation in the Greek and Latin Literature of the Roman Empire* (Oxford: Clarendon Press), 39–67.

Reich, R. (2000), "Miqva'ot," in L. H. Schiffman and J. C. VanderKam (eds.), *Encyclopedia of the Dead Sea Scrolls*, 2 vols. (Oxford: Oxford University Press), 1: 560–563.

Rutz, W. (1960), "*Amor mortis* bei Lucan," *Hermes* 88: 462–475.

Schwemer, A. M. (1999), "Prophet, Zeuge und Märtyrer: Zur Enstehung des Märtyrerbegriffs im frühesten Christentum," *Zeitschrift für Theologie und Kirche* 96: 320–350.

Seeley, D. (1990), *The Noble Death: Graeco–Roman Martyrology and Paul's Concept of Salvation* (Sheffield: JSOT Press).

Taylor, J. E. (1997), *The Immerser: John the Baptist within Second Temple Judaism* (Grand Rapids, MI: Eerdmans).

Vander Zee, L. J. (2004), *Christ, Baptism and the Lord's Supper: Recovering the Sacraments for Evangelical Worship* (Downers Grove, IL: IVP Academic).

van Henten, J. W. (1997), *The Maccabean Martyrs as Saviours of the Jewish People: A Study of 2 and 4 Maccabees* (Leiden: Brill).

van Henten, J. W. and F. Avemarie (2002), *Martyrdom and Noble Death: Selected Texts from Graeco-Roman, Jewish and Christian Antiquity* (London: Routledge).

Webb, R. L. (1991), *John the Baptizer and Prophet: A Socio-Historical Study* (Sheffield: JSOT Press).

CHAPTER 4

···

SACRAMENTS AND SACRAMENTALITY IN THE NEW TESTAMENT

···

NICHOLAS PERRIN

THE practices of Eucharist and baptism are not only well instantiated in the New Testament canon, but also—already by the mid-first century AD—well developed in theological terms. While the early Christian communities naturally evolved in their understanding of the two sacraments, even as there may have been local differences between liturgical traditions, there is a remarkable consistency throughout the scriptural witness in how both were conceived. Regarding itself as heir to the promises of Israel, the early church embraced the two rites as covenantal signs, standing in fundamental continuity with earlier signs that had not only marked off the people of God but also, in some sense, constituted them as such.

EUCHARIST

The word "Eucharist" is a post-biblical term, derived from the narrative in which Jesus gives thanks (εὐχαριστέω) and/or blesses the bread and cup at the meal traditionally known as the Last Supper (Matt 26:26–27//Mark 14:22–23//Luke 22:19–20). Within the New Testament, the more common nomenclature is "breaking bread" (1 Cor 10:16; Acts 2:42, 46; 20:7, 11), although terms such as "communion" (κοινωνία) (1 Cor 10:16), the "table of the Lord" (1 Cor 10:21), the "Lord's Supper" (1 Cor 11:20), and "love-feast" (Jude 12) also obtain. From all appearances, the sacrament was a fixture from the time of the church's founding (Acts 2:42) and was particularly associated with the Lord's Day (Acts 20:7).

Gospels and Acts

While in the early part of the twentieth century, scholars influenced by the History of Religions School often regarded the Gospel accounts of the Last Supper (Mark 14:22–26//Matt 26:26–29//Luke 22:14–23; John 13–17) as a cultic myth, such skepticism has now generally given way to the conviction that the evangelists are preserving a core of authentic material going back to Jesus' final hours. This is not to say that all the details in the synoptic tradition are equally reflective of the historic meal; much less is there consensus as to its timing and paschal nature. On the basis of various evidence—not least John's indications that Jesus was crucified before the evening of the Passover (John 13:1; 18:28; 19:14)—many scholars maintain that the meal was not a Passover meal at all. At the same time, others (Jeremias 1966: 41–62) are equally insistent that the *seder*-esque nature of the meal is beyond question. Meanwhile, apparent discrepancies between Johannine and the synoptic chronologies have been variously explained, either by pitting one account over and against the other or by adopting a harmonizing solution, which, for example, might admit the possibility that Jesus calculated the date of Passover differently from the temple leadership (Jaubert 1965; Nodet 2010). At a minimum, it is broadly granted that the historic Jesus in his last day(s) did indeed recline with his disciples for a solemn farewell supper, an event at which he ascribed unprecedented symbolic significance to the meal's components.

There is, at any rate, little doubt that the synoptic evangelists intended to convey the supper as a Passover meal. This is most clearly the case for Mark (cf. 14:12–21), who may reflect the earliest account of the meal (so Jeremias 1966: 189–191), even if the primitiveness of Luke's report (22:14–23), which follows Paul's very closely (1 Cor 11:17–26; see "Paul," below), has also been touted (Schürmann 1955: 82–132). Passover was of course one of the three great feasts of Israel's cultic life, celebrating the nation's redemption when Israel's faithful spread lambs' blood on the door lintels shortly before the Exodus. Accordingly, the synoptic writers' tendency to present Jesus as the Moses-like catalyst for the New Exodus supports the conclusion that the early church had from a very early point understood the Eucharist as a recapitulation of Israel's redemptive event par excellence (cf. 1 Cor 5:7). This is further borne out by the so-called words of institution, which—in varying degrees across the triple tradition—invoke significant texts such as Zechariah 9:11 ("the blood of my covenant" [NRSV and throughout]), Exodus 24:8 ("See the blood of the covenant that the LORD has made with you"), and Isaiah 53:12 ("he poured out himself to death"). By preserving these scriptural allusions, the evangelists are concerned to present the Last Supper as a redemptive event (Isa 53), simultaneously rehearsing the inauguration of the Mosaic covenant (Exod 24), and anticipating the eschatological climax envisioned in the prophets (Zech 9–14). As such, both the meal and Jesus' imminent death, to which it points, are ascribed a unique redemptive significance. Drawing on Zechariah's apocalyptic vision and the narrative of the ratification of the Mosaic covenant, Jesus' words of institution, as recorded in the Synoptic Gospels, set the cross and the table into a mutually interpretive relationship, all the while retaining both a prospective (eschatological) and retrospective (redemptive-historical) aspect.

Scholars are also increasingly recognizing the messianic implications of the meal for at least three reasons. First, the phrase "fruit of the vine" (Matt 26:29//Mark 14:25// Luke 22:18), which occurs in the cup-saying, marks a clear allusion to the eschatological messianic feast (Zech 8:12; cf. Isa 25:6–8, 1 Enoch 62.13–16; 2 Baruch 29.5; 1 QSa 2.17– 22; 1QS 6.4–6) and therefore sets off this event as a proleptic messianic repast. Second, given certain indications (discernible in the shared vocabulary of Mark 6:41 par.; 8:6 par.; 14:22 par.) that the evangelists sought to cast the feedings of the five thousand and four thousand as rehearsals for the Last Supper, and given, too, the undeniable messianic overtones of the same miracles, the messianic significance of Jesus' climactic meal all but follows. Finally, it is very possible that in identifying his body with the bread, Jesus is equating himself with the *aphikomen* (that is, the morsel of bread which was set aside for the expected Messiah and indeed symbolized the Messiah) (see Carmichael 1991). In this case, by consuming the bread, the disciples are not only signaling their own participation in Jesus' New Exodus movement (cf. *m. Pesah* 10.5) but also their own confession of Jesus as rightful Messiah. Along these lines, Luke's wording, "Do this in remembrance of me" (Luke 22:20//1 Cor 11:25) constitutes a command not simply to cognitive recall but to a communal praxis which embodies and re-enacts Jesus' self-giving in the life of the community (Senior 1989: 64).

Strikingly, the fourth Gospel omits the words of institution altogether, an omission which has attracted various explanations (for a review, see Perrin 2013: 498–499). While it possible that John consciously suppresses the report of the Last Supper (Bultmann 1959: 174–177), or simply takes it for granted (Petersen 2008: 207–208), perhaps a more promising explanation is that John intended the footwashing of John 13 to be understood as a parabolic reenactment of the Eucharist (so, e.g., Henrici 1985: 148–150). On this theory, if the Eucharist commemorates and gives concrete expression to Jesus's self-giving unto death, the fourth evangelist may well be interpreting sacramental participation as a call to selfless acts of humble service, exemplified iconically in Jesus' washing of the disciples' feet. The absence of the words of institution in John, at any rate, should not be construed as reflecting an anti-sacramental stance. On the contrary, mild allusion to the elements throughout John (2:1–11; 19:34; 20:19–29), together with very strong allusions in 6:51–58, demonstrate that John (perhaps even more so than Matthew and Mark) had a robust eucharistic theology.

Luke the evangelist gives added emphasis to the Eucharist by including narratives of communal meals in his sequel. Shortly after his recounting of Pentecost, the author of Acts narrates that the first believers "devoted themselves to the apostles' teaching and fellowship, to the breaking of bread and the prayers" (Acts 2:42). Closely associated with other early Christian practices, the "breaking of the bread" is almost certainly a technical term for eucharistic practice (Marshall 1981: 126–127). Its presence at the earliest stage of Luke's history speaks not only to its primitiveness (or at least Luke's interest in describing it as primitive) but also to its foundational significance within the church. That eucharistic practice is also in view in Acts 6:1 is possible but nonetheless questionable.

Luke records two other instances of "bread breaking" where sacramental practice is almost certainly in view. The first occurs at Acts 20:7–12, where the church is said to come together on the first day of the week (v. 7), apparently in keeping with habit, for the stated purpose of breaking bread *simpliciter*. Assuming that this datum is an accurate reflection on the church's practice in the early 50s, one surmises that the Eucharist was, at least in that period, *the* central activity of early Christian fellowship. Later in the narrative, aboard the storm-tossed cargo ship, Paul breaks bread much in the fashion of Jesus (Acts 27:35; cf. Luke 22:19). Here it is noteworthy that Paul engages in eucharistic practice in order to bring divinely mediated comfort to his sailing companions (believers and unbelievers) amidst a crisis (27:27–38). The rather public nature of this event, as Luke recounts it, seems to stand apart from later post-apostolic practice, which tended to draw starker lines of exclusion for those outside the believing community.

Paul

If the synoptic accounts of the Lord's Supper together constitute one of two *loci classici* for a New Testament understanding of the Eucharist, the other is contained in 1 Corinthians 11:17–34, a discussion which is anticipated by 1 Corinthians 10:1–22. The two chapters from the Corinthian correspondence attest not only to the antiquity of early Christian practice (Paul's first letter was composed in the early 50s and well before the Gospels) but also to its essential stability (the close parallelism between the Pauline and Lukan words of institution have been noted above). Comparisons between 1 Corinthians and the Gospels also yield insight into a basic theological continuity. Like the later Gospel writers, Paul roots his understanding of communion firmly within the theologically generative soil of redemptive history. This is no innovation on Paul's part. While it is all but certain that the apostle's reflections on the Lord's Supper—not least his deploying the Eucharist as a grounding for practical ethics—marked a historical development in early sacramental thought, it must be recalled that Paul's tradition was something of a theological trust (1 Cor 11:23). Paul's reception of pre-existing eucharistic tradition must have included not simply a rubric for enacted ritual but also a supporting theological logic.

Paul's first letter to the Corinthians is addressed to a church beset by various sins, including divisions (1:10–17; 3:1–15, 18–23), worldly wisdom (1:18–2:16; 4:1–21), sexual immorality (5:1–13; 6:12–20), litigiousness (6:1–8), and the abuse of Christian freedom (8:1–11:1). The church's difficulties also extended to their practice of the Lord's Supper. Having praised the Corinthians for holding faithfully to the apostolic traditions (11:2), Paul is deeply grieved by how believers are conducting their meetings (11:17–22). The believers at Corinth fall short in their failing to wait for one another before partaking of their communal meal and in their neglecting to ensure commensurate portions for the gathered participants (vv. 21–22). Such oversights, unacceptable in Paul's sight, were likely because the Corinthians had uncritically carried over standard cultural practices associated with the Greek symposium, when the well-to-do typically identified themselves as such by coming early and bringing for themselves relatively large quantities of food (Lampe 1994). Ironically, then, in the case of the Corinthians, the very practice which was meant to dramatize the believers' equal co-participation in Christ actually had the unintended consequence of reinforcing hierarchical social divisions, socioeconomic divisions in particular. Interpreting reported cases of sickness and death among the Corinthians as evidence of their eucharistic misconduct (1 Cor 11:29–30), Paul sternly warns of the dire consequences associated with this recurring act of disobedience.

Toward remediating the situation, Paul recounts the words of institution (vv. 23–25). Following a recitation of Jesus' actions on the night of his betrayal, Paul goes on to quote a pre-existing formula in which Jesus (1) identifies his body with the bread ("This is my body …") (v. 24); (2) connects the cup with both his own blood and the New Covenant (v. 25); and (3) commands his disciples to do the same on a recurring basis "in remembrance of me" (v. 24, 25). Following the rehearsal of Jesus' words, the apostle then editorially adds that by celebrating the Eucharist believers are "proclaiming" the Lord's death until his return. For Paul, the practice of the Lord's Supper was an integral (albeit non-verbal) component of the kerygma, as it was to be proclaimed by the believing community. The ritual served to invoke the historic chain of events culminating in Jesus' death and only then to interpret the same death in covenantal terms, more precisely, as the inaugural seal of the New Covenant (Jer 31:31).

The covenantal framework of Paul's eucharistic theology is consistent with an earlier discussion (1 Cor 10), in which the apostle compares the Corinthians to the Sinai generation. Those who had been baptized into Moses through the Exodus, Paul notes, had also partaken of "the same spiritual food" and "the same spiritual drink" (1 Cor 10:3, 4) as the Corinthians. On this analogy, if the eucharistic bread was typified by manna (Exod 16), the cup found its counterpart in the water which issued from the rock (Exod 17:1–7), which, according to both Paul and broader Jewish tradition (Num 21:17; b. Sabbat 35a; b. Avot 5.6), had followed the wandering Israelites through the desert. That rock, Paul declares, "was Christ" (1 Cor 10:4). Assuming that the apostle would have agreed with his first-century contemporaries regarding the life-giving properties of the manna, the "food of angels" (Ps 78:25; Wis 16:20; 4 Ezra 1:19), his positing a basic continuity between wandering Israel, whose apparel did not perish (Deut 29:5), and the communities in Christ, whose members would be raised up imperishable (1 Cor 15:42–50), prompts the question as to whether Paul would have also ascribed manna's unique qualities *a fortiori* to the Eucharist. Scholars who view the typology as entailing a realistic or material continuity (Hanson 1974: 100) tend to affirm as much; others (e.g. Hays 1997: 161), who see the analogy as purely typological, would tend to demur.

As Paul takes pains to stress, consumption of the Eucharist was no guarantee of eschatological salvation. Just as Yahweh did not shrink from judging the disobedient among the manna-consuming Israelites, so too the Corinthian believers were in no position to presume on their place at the Lord's table (1 Cor 11:6–13). On the contrary, Paul assumes that believers' participation in the Eucharist—precisely as the sign and seal of a greater covenant (2 Corinthians 3)—effectively only "raised the stakes" of their ethical choices.

If the church's supper was the climax of that which God's people had earlier and more fleetingly experienced in the desert under Moses, then, so Paul's argument goes, only the grimmest of consequences would await those who had mishandled the Lord's Supper or, indeed, who would partake while falling prey to the catalogue of sins besetting the church at Corinth.

Paul's analogy between Sinai and Corinth again implies that the church's practice of the Lord's Supper was in effect an ongoing reaffirmation of the covenant, much in the way that Israel's enjoyment of manna was itself a repetitively enacted covenantal meal in the Mosaic economy. Furthermore, since to participate in the meal was to affirm one's κοινωνία (association, communion, partnership) in the body of Christ (1 Cor 10:16), Paul can only have regarded the sacrament as a unique ongoing public marker of one's inclusion in and commitment to Christ. In this respect, Paul's interest in the Eucharist can hardly be separated from one of the letter's more prominent concerns: inasmuch as partaking in the *one* bread symbolized the believer's inclusion in the *one* body of Christ (v. 17), the Corinthians' weak grasp of their positional unity in Christ (cf. 1 Cor 12) could effectively be redressed by a more robust sacramentology.

Other New Testament Literature

References to communion in the remainder of the New Testament canon are less developed. Several scholars (Thurén 1973, Brege 2002) have suggested that the Eucharist provides a central backdrop for Hebrews. In this case, the *auctor Hebraeos* is thought to be polemicizing against Jewish fellowship meals (συνδείπνα), since these, precisely as reenactments of the temple peace offering, have been made redundant through the Lord's Supper. While this argument has not garnered broad support as an explanation for Hebrews as a whole, a number of scholars are willing to draw on this background in interpreting Hebrews 13:9–10. Although the statement "we have an altar from which those who officiate in the tent have no right to eat" (v. 10) is notoriously difficult, it may be argued that the "altar" in view is not to be understood figuratively (referring either to the cross or to the altar within the heavenly sanctuary), but more literally as the Lord's table, which is notionally interchangeable with the altar (Ezek 41:22; Mal 1:7, 12; 1 Cor 10:21). On this reading, those who "have no right to eat" are Jewish leaders and others outside the community, including the lapsed who "have tasted the heavenly gift" (Heb 6:4). On this reading, too, the writer of Hebrews regarded ongoing participation in Jewish συνδείπνα as incompatible with the Lord's table (cf. Williamson 1975) exactly because Christ was the true peace offering and the Eucharist was the unique continuation of the fellowship meal associated with that sacrifice. If this interpretation is valid, then the Lord's Supper functioned not only as a boundary marker for the early Christian community but also as catalyst for the parting of ways between early Christianity and mainstream Judaism.

In his extended diatribe, the author of Jude laments that false teachers are "blemishes on your love-feasts (ἀγάπαις) while they feast with you without fear, feeding themselves"

(Jude 12; cf. 2 Pet 2:13). Here Jude represents the earliest instance of the plural abstract of ἀγάπη ("love") functioning as a shorthand term for the Christian sacred feast, a usage which would become standard in subsequent centuries (Jeremias 1966: 116). Here, as elsewhere in the biblical literature, the Eucharist appears to be embedded within larger church-wide celebratory meals. That the meal should be termed a "love-feast" may reflect the distinctive Christian virtues that ideally characterized such meals; alternatively, it may derive from the early church's practice of almsgiving in the context of eucharistic meals (Justin, *1 Apol.* 67). That the author is especially alarmed that the heretics participate in the Eucharist is further corroboration of the meal's especially sacred nature.

In Revelation, the Risen Lord issues an invitation to the believers at Laodicea: "Listen! I am standing at the door, knocking; if you hear my voice and open the door, I will come in to you and *eat* (δειπνήσω) with you, and you with me" (Rev 3:20). Impressed by the fact that cognates of δειπνέω occur in other eucharistic passages (Luke 22:20; John 13:2, 4; 21:20; 1 Cor 11:20, 21, 25), together with the context, a number of scholars have inferred that the sacrament is in view (e.g. Boring 1989: 90; Beale 1999: 309). The Risen Jesus would then be calling the Laodicean believers not so much to conversion but to renewal, symbolized by the Eucharist qua fellowship meal, signifying a restored relationship between the divine and human co-participants. Other allusions to the Lord's Supper in Revelation are less direct. Even if, strictly speaking, Revelation 2:17b ("To everyone who conquers I will give some of the hidden manna") and 19:9b ("Blessed are those who are invited to the marriage supper of the Lamb") refer not to sacramental practice but to the long-awaited eschatological feast, such images undoubtedly had the reinforcing effect of positioning the believers' eucharistic activity within an eschatological framework, circumscribing the meal as a foretaste of the great eschatological banquet.

Baptism

The word "baptize" (βαπτίζω) occurs seventy-seven times in the New Testament; "baptism" (βάπτισμα), a Christian neologism so far as we know, occurs nineteen times, being applied to the ablutions administered by John the Baptist, Jesus' (pre-Easter) disciples, and early Christians. While the cognate terms normally connote immersion or dipping in water (Oepke 1964: 529–530), early Christian appropriation of the term served to extend beyond such specificity, allowing for such notions as "baptism in the Spirit" (e.g. Luke 3:16), baptism into Moses and a cloud (1 Cor 10:2), and more metaphorical usages (e.g. Mark 10:38–39). The shared concept behind the usages of the βαπτίζω word family in the New Testament involves the soaking of individuals (Marshall 2002: 22–23). Certainty regarding the modality of early Christian baptismal practices on the basis of an equivocal New Testament witness is elusive; inferences based on philological grounds are dubious altogether. In the early church, baptism was the basic initiation rite of those seeking entry into the covenant community associated with Jesus Christ.

Gospels and Acts

Within the canonical Gospels, Matthew 28:19 ("Go therefore and make disciples of all nations, baptizing them in the name of the Father and of the Son and of the Holy Spirit") provides the most explicit teaching on baptism. Within the New Testament canon, the same verse not only contains the most elaborate baptismal formula; it is also the only text that speaks of baptism in the name of the Father, Son, and Holy Spirit. As to how the words of Matthew's Jesus are to be understood within the Gospel and against the broader scope of the early church's developing doctrine is an intriguing, if somewhat complex, question.

The text of Matthew 28:19b is a striking expression of early Trinitarian theology, all the more so considering that elsewhere in the New Testament baptism language consistently bears a Christological focus. Thus, for example, we have: baptism "in (ἐπὶ) the name of Jesus Christ" (Acts 2:38), "in (εἰς) the name of the Lord Jesus" (Acts 8:16), "in (ἐν) the name of Jesus Christ" (Acts 10:48), "in (εἰς) the name of the Lord Jesus" (Acts 19:5), "into (εἰς) Christ Jesus" (Rom 6:3), and "into (εἰς) Christ" (Gal 3:27). The historically closest parallel to Matthew 28:19b occurs in the (late first-century or early second-century) *Didache*, where readers are instructed to baptize "in the name of the Father, and of the Son, and of the Holy Spirit" (*Did.* 7.1). The Didachist's reference to baptism in Trinitarian terms, interestingly enough, is no bar to his also speaking of baptizing "into (εἰς) the name of the Lord" (*Did.* 9.5), all of which suggests a certain fluidity in first-century baptismal traditions. Assuming the *Didache*'s dependence on Matthew and a Syrian provenance for both texts, one may posit that the tradition reflected in Matthew 28:19b and *Didache* 7.1 was well established in Syrian Christianity (cf. also Ign. *Magn.* 13.2), if not more broadly.

Whether the evangelist initiated the triune formula or reiterated a pre-existing phraseology is another question. Unconvinced by either of these possibilities, scholars of an earlier generation chalked up Matthew's distinctive wording to an intruding scribe, who was steeped in a later, more developed Trinitarian theology. This hypothesis, however, has been largely discarded. The very fact that a Trinitarian framework already undergirds some of our earliest apostolic texts (1 Cor 12:4–6; 2 Cor 13:13; Gal 4:6), together with the absence of supporting manuscript evidence, renders speculative any hypothesis which call into question the textual stability of Matthew 28:19.

Within the first Gospel itself, Jesus' instructions in Matthew 28:19b must be interpreted in relation to the evangelist's earlier recounting of John's baptism in Matthew 3. Baptism, John announces, was a baptism "for repentance" (3.11). It should not go unobserved that when Jesus himself submits to the Baptizer's baptism (3:13–17), all three members of the Trinity are involved, just as they are all named in 28:19–20. The link could hardly be coincidental. Perhaps it suggests that the very baptism which Jesus received with the full participation of the triune God (3:13–17) provided the basis for his own command, issued in his status as Risen Lord, to baptize in the name of the same triune God (28:19). If the first baptism was open to Israel and was calculated to "fulfill all righteousness" when applied to Jesus (3:16), the second baptism was available for the nations and constituted an extension of the same righteousness.

The Trinitarian formula in Matthew 28:19 is also evidence that the early Christians assigned the rite a covenantal significance. After all, in Greek and Jewish usage, prepositions of entrance ("to" or "into") or location ("in") followed by "the name of X" indicated not simply belonging but also relationship. Moreover, since in Matthew's text there is no mention of circumcision in connection with the nations' conversion, the evangelist may well be assuming that which Colossians 2:11–12 more explicitly asserts, namely, that in the new salvific economy baptism has replaced circumcision as the sign of the covenant. That is, baptism fulfills circumcision as that which marks off those who are in the covenant. It is no surprise then that baptism, as understood by Matthew, is one of the foundational tasks of the church, notionally on par with instruction. Although Matthew accords little space to the topic of baptism within his narrative, its significant positioning in the summative, climactic verses of Matthew 28:19–20 can hardly be discounted.

Of course Matthew, like Luke, carefully distinguishes the baptisms of John and Jesus. For the first evangelist, John the Baptist sees his own baptism as being "with water for repentance," while the Messiah would bring a categorically different baptism involving "the Holy Spirit and fire" (Matt 3:11). While there is considerable debate as to the nature of the later-coming baptism (including whether the phrase refers to one baptism or two), it is plausible enough that Spirit and fire are together alluding to the cleansing function of the baptism announced in Matthew 28:19b (Hui 1999). (This is not to deny a cleansing significance to John's baptism: indeed, water lustrations were inevitably tied to a symbolism of purification.) In any event, John's contrasting his own baptism with the baptism to come drives home his subordinate role vis-à-vis Christ. As Matthew and indeed all the Gospel-writers conceive it, John's baptism served a unique but limited place in the unfolding redemption (Matt 21:15 par.); in identifying his own baptism as being *into the name* of the Father, Son, and Holy Spirit, the Risen Lord reinforces this distinction.

These considerations, however, do not necessarily resolve the question as to how Matthew 28:19b relates *historically*, if at all, to John's baptism. Some have suggested that Matthew's community self-consciously and at a rather late stage retrieved the Baptist's practice as a strategy of self-legitimization (Nepper-Christensen 1985: 195–198). But if John 4:1–2 is historically accurate in its representation of the Jesus movement as carrying on the practice of baptism, initiated by the Baptist, then it hardly strains credulity to suppose that Matthew's Jesus is enjoining a practice that stands in some continuity with the pre-Easter Jesus movement and in turn the Baptist's movement (so France 1994). The very fact that Matthew introduces the baptismal imperative with so little explanation suggests that the evangelist regarded the instruction as no *novum*, but rather as an etiological account for a well-established practice. At precisely what point the Trinitarian formula established itself after the Easter event is impossible to determine.

In Mark, as in Matthew, the majority of references to "baptism" are in connection with John the Baptist (Mark 1:4, 5, 8, 9; 11:30). Jesus also uses the terms in reference to his own impending passion (10:38–39), but here it is unclear what relation, if any, this has with

Christian baptism. In the so-called Longer Ending of Mark, the Risen Jesus promises that "[t]he one who believes and is baptized will be saved; but the one who does not believe will be condemned" (16:16). This reading, typically assigned to *c.* AD 125, is part of a larger passage which shows dependence on all four Gospels and thus is of only secondary importance in establishing a New Testament theology of baptism. Clearly, the text reflects a setting in which baptism was a *sine qua non* of Christian confession, which is consistent with the apostolic period.

In the treatment of baptism in the Gospel of Luke, the evangelist barely moves beyond his sources. However, in his companion volume, Acts, we find numerous instances of baptism associated with the act of conversion (2:38, 41; 8:12–13, 26–40; 9:18; 10:47–48; 16:15, 33; 18:8; 22:16; etc.). Luke also recounts instances in which some adherents of the Way and devotees of John the Baptist had proven ignorant of the necessity of being baptized into the name of Jesus (18:25; 19:1–7). This hardly reflects antipathy between the early Christian circles and a John the Baptist sect (as first argued by Baldensperger 1898); on the contrary, Luke's point is to emphasize that baptism into Christ is the logical and appropriate next step for those who had earlier followed John.

John's Gospel is also spare in *direct* reference to baptism. From John we learn that baptism was an initiation rite associated with entry into the Jesus movement (4:1); the fourth evangelist also takes pains to note that it was not Jesus himself but only his disciples who administered this baptism (4:2). Distancing Jesus from this water baptism probably has to do with the earlier promise that Jesus would administer the Holy Spirit baptism (1:33). The allusion of John's Jesus to water in 3:5 has been linked with Christian baptism since at least the time of Augustine (*Tr. Ev. Jo.* 11.1.2). But even if, in such cases, an Old Testament subtext may more convincingly be adduced, this does not rule out the possibility that the evangelist is enlisting the water imagery in a double duty, namely, to root Jesus' mission in the redemptive-historical context, *and* in turn to link this redemptive-historical narrative with the rite of Christian baptism.

Paul

The apostle Paul's most thoroughgoing elaboration on baptism occurs in Romans 6:1–11. Here, having laid out his teachings on justification by faith, Paul now attempts to preempt possible objections that his doctrine will lead to a wanton disregard for the law (Rom 6:1). Toward explaining why this consequence need not—indeed cannot—follow, the apostle poses a rhetorical question: "Do you not know that all of us who have been baptized into Christ Jesus were baptized into his death?" (Rom 6:3). (The premise must have been broadly accepted, since Paul assumes that his audience will readily grant the point.) This in turn provides the scaffolding for the apostle's further assertion that "we have been buried with him by baptism into death so that (ἵνα) just as Christ was raised from the dead by the glory of the Father, so we too might walk in newness of life" (6:4). On the logic of the comparison, baptism qua burial is straddled on the one side by Christ's death and on the other side by resurrected life.

That baptism symbolized Christ's death for Paul and the broader church is indisputable; precisely how the death of Christ correlates with the believer's baptism remains contested. In this connection, explanations issuing from a *religionsgeschichtliche Schule* appeal to Greek mystery religions must now be discounted (Wedderburn 1987). Two broad approaches present themselves: a subjective and an objective reading. Within the former option, Paul may be seen as interpreting baptism either as a re-enactment of Jesus' death (e.g. Flemington 1948: 59) or, with more directly ethical emphasis, as a powerful symbol for renouncing worldly passions (classically articulated by Rendtorff 1905: 36). In either case, here the shared tendency is to draw a formal analogy between, on the one side, Christ's death and burial, and, on the other side, the believer's participation in baptism and subsequent commitment to a moral life. The other major alternative is to suppose that in the moment of baptism, the believer is objectively and realistically incorporated into Christ's death and resurrection, whereby the sacrament seals an objective mystical co-participation between Christ and those who are baptized into him.

While opinion is broadly divided on the question, two points speak in favor of the objective reading. First, in instances where εἰς follows βαπτίζω, the preposition draws attention to that state which is realized through baptism (Beasley-Murray 1962: 128). Thus, when Paul speaks of believers having been baptized εἰς Χριστὸν Ἰησοῦν (e.g. Rom 6:3) the baptism may be seen as actualizing their realistic incorporation into Christ. (At the same time, if the phrase "into Christ Jesus" is shorthand for "in the name of Christ Jesus," it is also possible that the import is less radical, signifying nothing more than allegiance to Christ—an argument supported by the analogy with the baptism into Moses in 1 Corinthians 10:2.) Second, given the close connection between baptism and being "clothed with Christ" in Galatians 3:27 ("As many of you as were baptized into Christ have clothed yourselves with Christ"), and given, too, the likelihood that Paul's garment metaphor is meant to convey the believer's union with Christ, it virtually follows that, for Paul, baptism betokened the same mystical reality in concrete terms.

In the final analysis, a sharp dichotomy between the objective-mystical and subjective-experiential interpretation is unnecessary, and perhaps ultimately misleading. Having expounded upon humanity's incorporation into the first Adam (Rom 5:12–17), and seeking to provide a rationale for a Spirit-led way of life (6:12–23), Paul is plainly speaking to the objectively wrought transfer from the realm of Adamic flesh to the realm of the Spirit, effective through baptism, as the proper basis for behavior consistent with "newness of life." Baptism is therefore retrospective, inasmuch as it looks back to Jesus' death, and prospective, inasmuch as it anticipates the resurrection, proleptically realized through the giving of the Spirit. It gives concrete expression both to the forgiveness available through Jesus' death and the power of the Spirit-enabled life (8:1–4).

In Galatians 3:23–29, Paul takes the same logic in a slightly different direction by highlighting baptism's social implications. Although baptism here as well may imply co-participation in Christ's death and therefore also death unto the law (Gal 2:20–21), the more emphatic point bears on the believers' membership in "the seed" through baptism (Gal 3:29). This means, in the first place, that baptism serves to validate and bring to fruition the Abrahamic promises (a covenantal notion); in the second place, it means the dissolution of ethnic, social, and gender categories, to the extent that these categories lent fundamental definition to the Galatians' anthropology (cf. 1 Cor 12:13). If in Romans, the close correlation between baptism and mystical union constituted a new humanity *coram Deo*, in Galatians, it marked off a new economy of human relations.

The ecclesiological import of baptism is also teased out in 1 Corinthians. Apparently, the Corinthian believers had been aligning themselves with different apostolic figure-heads and using the baptisms administered by these same individuals (including Paul himself) as a basis for self-differentiation (1 Cor 1:10–17) (but cf. Pascuzzi 2009). Against this posture, Paul insists that their baptismal "washing" had instead marked a break with their sinful past (6:11) and served to incorporate believers into the body of Christ (12:12–13). Again, for Paul, baptism serves as the threshold to participating in a new humanity, one in which prior social distinctions are transcended.

Paul makes a final reference to baptism in the same Epistle: "Otherwise, what will those people do who receive baptism on behalf of the dead? If the dead are not raised at all, why are people baptized on their behalf?" (1 Cor 15:29). This mysterious text has tested the exegetical prowess of Paul's readers down through the centuries, admitting in contemporary scholarship "about forty general hypotheses" (Hull 2005: 8). Some propose that here Paul is referring to a kind of baptism by proxy, others hold that ordinary baptism is in view, and still others explain the verse by providing textual emendation. Perhaps we are best served by agreeing with G. E. Fee when he writes: "The best one can do in terms of particulars is to point out what appear to be the more viable options, but finally to admit ignorance" (Fee 1987: 763).

In the (deutero-)Pauline letter to the Colossians, the author is seeking to combat the lure of vain philosophies by extolling the superiority of Christ. Accordingly, he writes: "In him also you were circumcised with a spiritual circumcision, by putting off the body of the flesh in the circumcision of Christ; when you were buried with him in baptism, you were also raised with him through faith in the power of God, who raised him from the dead" (Col 2:11–12). The author deems baptism to be a kind of "spiritual circumcision," certainly hinting at the shared cleansing symbolism of both rites (Deut 10:6; Jer 4:4). For the author of Colossians, baptism has a sanctifying function (cf. Tit 3:5); it connotes "putting off the body of the flesh," which also lay at the root of false humility and idolatrous angel worship (Col 2:18, 23). On the assumption that "circumcision of Christ" is a subjective genitive (i.e. the circumcision which Christ has wrought), some (e.g. Jeremias 1949: 40–41) have argued that Christ's giving of baptism provides the analogue to and continuation of circumcision, thereby lending support to the notion that paedobaptism was practiced in the early church. Others (e.g. Hunt 1990: 241–244), however, are unconvinced, and remain more convinced that the "circumcision of Christ" is in fact a metaphorical circumcision of Christ's body on the cross (cf. Rom 6:3–4).

Other New Testament Literature

The author of Hebrews exhorts his audience to "leave behind the basic teachings about Christ" (Heb 6:1), including, among various doctrinal matters, "instructions about baptisms" (βαπτισμῶν διδαχῆς) (6:2). The phrase is curious, not least because it employs a plural as opposed to a singular form of βαπτισμός; with the exception of Colossians 2:12 the standard term for baptism is not βαπτισμός but βάπτιϲμα. While it is possible, even likely, that "baptisms" in Hebrews 6:2 includes the notion of Christian-initiatory baptism, it could hardly have *only* this non-repeatable rite in view. It is arguable that the phrase "instructions about baptisms" refers to focused teaching on the differences between Christian baptism and Jewish (and perhaps pagan) lustrations. Meanwhile, a minority position holds that "baptisms" (Heb 6:2) refers to martyrdom (cf. Mark 10:38–39, Luke 12:50) (Lane 1991: 138; Cross 2002). While both options make excellent sense, given the context in which Hebrews was written, the former is preferable. After all, when the *auctor Hebraeos* in short order goes to remark that "it is impossible to restore again to repentance those who have once been enlightened, and have tasted the heavenly gift, and have shared in the Holy Spirit" (Heb 6:4), there are reasons to believe that said "enlightenment" is Christian baptism (Hartman 1997: 125).

Later in the homily, the author exhorts: "[L]et us approach with a true heart in full assurance of faith, with our hearts sprinkled clean from an evil conscience and our bodies washed with pure water" (10:22). To be sure, it is not impossible that the mention of bodily washing is a metaphorical description of Christ's sanctifying work (so Attridge 1989: 288–289), but given the specificity of the language ("pure water"), one suspects a more concrete reality in view, viz. baptism. The text is certainly consistent with sentiments in the Pauline literature that baptism effects an internal change, but the idea is more pointed. Because the concept of "sprinkling" invokes the rite of ordination associated with the Aaronic priesthood (Lev 8:6), the use of similar language in 10:22, in conjunction with mention of penetrating behind the veil (v. 20) which partitions the Holy Place from the Holy of Holies (Heb 6:9), suggests that baptism specifically functions as a rite of ordination (Flemington 1948: 98; Leithart 2000).

Finally, mention should be made of 1 Peter 3:20–21, where the author states that "God waited patiently in the days of Noah, during the building of the ark, in which a few, that is, eight persons, were saved through water. And baptism, which this prefigured, now saves you—not as a removal of dirt from the body, but as an appeal to God for a good conscience, through the resurrection of Jesus Christ." Two points are instructive. First, the analogy between the Noahic flood and baptism implies that just as God used water to rescue the primordial patriarch from impending judgment against an evil generation, so too baptism would have the effect of rescuing believers from the eschatological judgment looming over Asia Minor and beyond. Second, it is interesting to note baptism being identified as an ἐπερώτημα. The word is lexically difficult, liable to such translations as "request" or "appeal." However, if with an increasing number of commentators, we understand the word to mean "pledge" (i.e. in the sense of a contractual obligation), then this implies that baptism, again consistent with its covenantal framework, betokened the believer's public commitment to moral purity. The various ways in which baptism—and Eucharist—are put to theological use only underscores the richness of sacramental theology in the apostolic era.

ABBREVIATIONS

Bib	Biblica
CBQ	Catholic Biblical Quarterly
CTQ	Concordia Theological Quarterly
EvQ	Evangelical Quarterly
IKaZ	Internationale katholische Zeitschrift
Int	Interpretation
JBL	Journal of Biblical Literature
JSNT	Journal for the Study of the New Testament
NICNT	New International Commentary on the New Testament
NIGTC	New International Greek Testament Commentary
NovT	Novum Testamentum
NTS	New Testament Studies
TDNT	Theological Dictionary of the New Testament
TynBul	Tyndale Bulletin
WBC	Word Biblical Commentary
WUNT	Wissenschaftliche Untersuchungen zum Neuen Testaments

SUGGESTED READING

Beasley-Murray (1962); Flemington (1948); Hartman (1997); Jeremias (1966); Marshall (1981).

BIBLIOGRAPHY

Aalen, S. (1963), "Das Abendmahl als Opfermahl im Neuen Testament," *NovT* 6: 128–152.

Attridge, H. W. (1989), *The Epistle to the Hebrews: A Commentary on the Epistle to the Hebrews*, Hermeneia (Philadelphia, PA: Fortress Press).

Baldensperger, W. (1898), *Prolog des vierten Evangeliums: Sein polemisch-apologetischer Zweck* (Freiburg: Mohr Siebeck).

Barth, M. (1951), *Die Taufe—ein Sakrament?: Ein exegetischer Beitrag zum Gespräch über die kirchliche Taufe* (Zollikon-Zürich: Evangelischer Verlag).

Beale, G. K. (1999), *The Book of Revelation*, NIGTC (Grand Rapids, MI: Eerdmans).

Beasley-Murray, G. R. (1962), *Baptism in the New Testament* (London: Macmillan).

Boring, M. E. (1989), *Revelation*, Interpretation (Louisville, KY: Westminster John Knox Press).

Brege, D. J. (2002), "Eucharistic Overtones Created by Sacrificial Concepts in the Epistle to the Hebrews," *CTQ* 66: 61–81.

Bultmann, R. (1959), *Das Evangelium des Johannes* (Göttingen: Vandenhoeck & Ruprecht).

Byars, R. P. (2011), *The Sacraments in Biblical Perspective*, Interpretation (Louisville, KY: Westminster John Knox Press).

Carmichael, D. B. (1991), "David Daube on the Eucharist and the Passover Seder," *JSNT* 42: 45–67.

Cross, A. R. (2002), "The Meaning of 'Baptisms' in Hebrews 6.2," in S. E. Porter and A. R. Cross (eds.), *Dimensions of Baptism: Biblical and Theological Studies*, 163–186.

Dunn, J. D. G. (1970), *Baptism in the Holy Spirit: A Re-Examination of the New Testament Teaching on the Gift of the Spirit in Relation to Pentecostalism Today* (London: SCM Press).

Fape, M. O. (1999), *Paul's Concept of Baptism and its Present Implications for Believers: Walking in the Newness of Life*, Toronto Studies in Theology 78 (Lewiston, NY: Mellen Press).

Fee, G. D. (1987), *The First Epistle to the Corinthians*, NICNT (Grand Rapids, MI: Eerdmans).

Flemington, W. F. (1948), *The New Testament Doctrine of Baptism* (London: SPCK).

France, R. T. (1994), "Jesus of Nazareth," in J. B. Green and M. Turner (eds.), *Jesus of Nazareth: Lord and Christ: Essays on the Historical Jesus and New Testament Christology* (Grand Rapids, MI: Eerdmans).

Hanson, A. T. (1974), *Studies in Paul's Technique and Theology* (Grand Rapids, MI: Eerdmans).

Hartman, L. (1997), *"Into the Name of the Lord Jesus": Baptism in the Early Church*, Studies of the New Testament and its World (Edinburgh: T&T Clark).

Hays, R. B. (1997), *First Corinthians*, Interpretation (Louisville, KY: John Knox Press).

Henrici, P. (1985), "'Do this in Remembrance of Me': The Sacrifice of Christ and the Sacrifice of the Faithful," *IKaZ* 14: 226–235.

Hill, D. (1982), "'To Offer Spiritual Sacrifices' (1 Peter 2:5): Liturgical Formulations and Christian Paraenesis in 1 Peter," *JSNT* 16: 45–63.

Hui, A. (1999), "John the Baptist and Spirit-Baptism," *EvQ* 71: 99–115.

Hull, M. F. (2005), *Baptism on Account of the Dead (1 Cor 15:29): An Act of Faith in the Resurrection*, Academia Biblica 22 (Atlanta, GA: Society of Biblical Literature).

Hunt, J. P. T. (1990), "Colossians 2:11–12, the Circumcision/Baptism Analogy, and Infant Baptism," *TynBul* 41: 227–244.

Jaubert, A. (1965), *Date of the Last Supper* (Staten Island, NY: Alba House).

Jeremias, J. (1949), *Hat die Urkirche die Kindertaufe geübt?* (Göttingen: Vandenhoeck und Ruprecht).

Jeremias, J. (1966), *The Eucharistic Words of Jesus* (New York: Scribner).

Kodell, J. (1988), *The Eucharist in the New Testament* (Wilmington, DE: Glazier).

Lampe, P. (1994), "The Eucharist: Identifying with Christ on the Cross," *Int* 48: 36–49.

Lane, W. L. (1991), *Hebrews 1–8*, WBC 47a Dallas, TX: Word).

Leithart, P. J. (2000), "Womb of the World: Baptism and the Priesthood of the New Covenant in Hebrews 10.19–22," *JSNT* 78: 49–65.

Léon-Dufour, X. (1987), *Sharing the Eucharistic Bread: The Witness of the New Testament* (Mahwah, NJ: Paulist).

Marshall, I. H. (1981), *Last Supper and Lord's Supper* (Grand Rapids, MI: Eerdmans).

Marshall, I. H. (2002), "The Meaning of the Verb 'Baptize,'" in S. E. Porter and A. R. Cross (eds.), *Dimensions of Baptism: Biblical and Theological Studies*, 8–24.

Nepper-Christensen, P. (1985), "Die Taufe im Matthäusevangelium im Lichte der Traditionen über Johannes den Täufer," *NTS* 31: 189–207.

Nodet, E. (2010), "On Jesus' Last Supper," *Bib* 91: 348–369.

Oepke, A. (1964), "βάπτω, βαπτίζω, βαπτισμός, βάπτισμα, βαπτιστής," *TDNT* 1: 529–530.

O'Neill, J. C. (1996), "The Connection between Baptism and the Gift of the Spirit in Acts," *JSNT* 63: 87–103.

Pascuzzi, M. (2009), "Baptism-Based Allegiance and the Divisions in Corinth: A Reexamination of 1 Corinthians 1:13–17," *CBQ* 71: 813–829.

Perrin, N. (2013), "Last Supper," in J. Green, J. Brown, and *idem* (eds.), *Dictionary of Jesus and the Gospels* (Downers Grove, IL: Intervarsity).

Petersen, S. (2008), *Brot, Licht Und Weinstock: Intertextuelle Analysen Johanneischer Ich-Bin-Worte*, Novum Testamentum Supplements 127 (Leiden/Boston: Brill).

Porter, S. E., and A. R. Cross (2002), *Dimensions of Baptism: Biblical and Theological Studies*, Journal for the Study of the New Testament: Supplement Series 234 (London and New York: Sheffield Academic Press).

Rendtorff, F. M. (1905), *Die Taufe im Urchristentum im Lichte der neueren Forschungen: Ein kritischer Bericht* (Leipzig: Hinrichs).

Schnackenburg, R. (1964), *Baptism in the Thought of St. Paul: A Study in Pauline Theology* (New York: Herder and Herder).

Schürmann, H. (1955), *Der Einsetzungsbericht, Lk 22, 19–20: II Teil, Einer Quellenkritischen Untersuchung des lukanischen Abendmahlsberichtes, Lk 22, 7–38*. (Munster, Westf.: Aschendorff).

Senior, D. (1989), *The Passion of Jesus in the Gospel of Luke* (Wilmington, DE: Glazier).

Thurén, J. (1973), *Das Lobopfer der Hebräer: Studien zum Aufbau und Anliegen von Hebräerbrief 13*, Acta Academiae Aboensis 47.1 (Åbo: Åbo akademi).

Wedderburn, A. J. M. (1987), *Baptism and Resurrection: Studies in Pauline Theology against its Graeco-Roman Background*, WUNT 44 (Tübingen: J.C.B. Mohr [P. Siebeck]).

White, J. R. (1997), " 'Baptized on Account of the Dead': The Meaning of 1 Corinthians 15:29 in its Context," *JBL* 116: 487–499.

Williamson, R. (1975), "Eucharist and the Epistle to the Hebrews," *NTS* 21: 300–312.

Witherington, B. (2007), *Troubled Waters: The Real New Testament Theology of Baptism* (Waco, TX: Baylor University Press).

CHAPTER 5

··

SACRIFICE AND SACRAMENT: SACRAMENTAL IMPLICATIONS OF THE DEATH OF CHRIST

··

EDITH M. HUMPHREY

No angel in the sky can fully bear that sight,
But downward bends his burning eye at mysteries so bright.

—"Crown Him with Many Crowns"

WITH these luminous words, Matthew Bridges captures the wonder of our Lord's sacrifice and its implications for heavenly (and earthly!) worship. What angels fear to gaze upon is the focal point of our meditation: the relationship between sacrifice and sacrament, as made clear in the body of Jesus the Christ. Immediately we are confronted with difficulties. What do we mean by "sacrament"? What do we mean by "sacrifice"? How do we understand the energy of the God-Man on our behalf, and that One's relationship to heaven and earth—specifically, to us in the church? These have been topics of debate among those who name Christ, particularly from the time of the Reformation. Further, they are questions that should never be posed simply for the purpose of theological speculation or doctrinal nicety—much less the formulation of denominational shibboleths! Rather, they lead us more fully into worship: here we reach the holy of holies. Our proper posture is that of adoration, though astonishment need not chase away "reasonable" worship.

We will begin by probing the main concepts and offering working definitions, and then proceed to read key scriptural passages (aided by interpretive texts) on sacrifice and sacrament—all along tracing the mutual connections between sacrifice and sacrament, illumining the sacramental nature of Jesus' death, and exploring how his sacrifice interprets the sacraments. We hope to discover a way between those who seize upon

Jesus' death as the sole point of the Son's sacrifice, and those who dismiss such a view as barbaric.

PROBING THE CONCEPTS

We begin by setting down working definitions, and by suggesting connections between sacrifice and sacrament. Etymology may be deceiving; nevertheless, the initial four letters of both English terms, from the Latin *sacer* ("holy"), aptly indicate their interconnection. They deal with what is "holy" or "set apart" for a special purpose: "sacrifice" from *sacer* and *facere*, "to make something holy or separate"; "sacrament" from *sacramentum,* a sacred military oath, or solemn sign of security. For Christians, the link goes beyond etymology. Both sacrifice and sacrament have to do with the physical as well as the spiritual: "sacrifice is a sort of physical prayer" (Vasey 1984: 5); sacraments partake of the physical world and mediate or point to the divine world. Because of these connections, the manner in which theologians connect these concepts signals more general—and sometimes conflicting—understandings of the nature of the world, soteriology, grace, ecclesiology, and God's kingdom.

Some insist that the entire notion of "sacrifice" is so culturally laden that it must be optional for contemporary faith (cf. McGrath 2013). However, as Frances M. Young insists, despite "the trouble that … narrow expositions of the sacrifice of Christ … no longer strike a chord in most people today," the fact remains that "scriptural expression of the Christian gospel … is saturated with sacrificial terminology" (Young 1975: 10). Perhaps the "trouble" is located not in the concept *per se* but in too narrow a horizon. Both in cultural expressions and in the biblical/Christian tradition, "sacrifice" may refer to actions and dispositions that fall short of (or go beyond) the cultic death of a victim. We speak not only of a soldier's sacrifice but also of a mother's sacrificial actions, or a saint's sacrificial life (whether or not that one is martyred). This larger use is borne out by Scripture, where sacrifice may refer to a *living* offering to God (θυσία, Rom 12:1). In the Old Testament traditions there are numerous terms suited to various kinds of cultic offerings, some involving animals (*zebaḥ* as a general term; *'ōlâ* for any burnt offering; *tāmîd* for the daily burnt offering), but others not. Even in the case of animal sacrifice, priestly service is not confined to sacerdotal slaughter, but incorporates three elements: the ritual "oblation," the "immolation" or cleansing by sprinkled blood, and the offering to God, often accompanied by a fellowship meal. (On these, see De la Taille 1940: 10–23.)

Though priestly work is not fully comprehended by sacrificial slaughter, the Old Testament presents oblation as necessary, since inanimate objects of sacrifice (e.g. grain, first-fruits) are "essentially relative" (De la Taille 1940: 15) to animal sacrifice. Thus, neither the Old Testament prophetic critique of *pro forma* sacrifice, nor the supplanting of sacrifice by Jesus' Crucifixion, gives grounds for us to dismiss the typological significance of animal oblation. Romans, which speaks of the "good and holy Torah" (7:12), was recognized as harmonious with the canon of truth, not the *Epistle of Barnabas*, with its sneering attitude towards Old Testament rites (2.9). Oblation played a key part in that first dispensation, and continues, according to New Testament writers, to foreshadow, indicate and explain Jesus' actions. Nevertheless, there is some truth to the declaration: "[T]he root idea of sacrifice … is not *death* … but *transformation*" (Mascall 1953: 99). Perhaps Mascall here has moved beyond the *foundation* of sacrifice to its desired *effect*. We might more accurately say that the root idea of sacrifice is not death, but self-abnegation—of which death is the most graphic representation. Thus, Abraham's "offering" of Isaac is the archetypical sacrifice: though connected with the ram's death, it is not oblation, but Abraham's readiness that emerges as the sacrifice par excellence. Complexity surrounding the notion of sacrifice becomes clearer as we approach the climax of human history, when God the Son willingly comes among us (Heb 10:5–7). "The New Testament connects the idea of sacrifice with the whole earthly life of Jesus … [T]he sacrifice begins in the incarnation.… [I]ncarnation and sacrifice are inseparably connected" (Ramsay 1936: 148).

Sacrament is an even more difficult term to capture than sacrifice, and for many today it is an equally alien concept. Because of the way in which the sacraments have been revered, they are sometimes described as alien to this world, as belonging "to the order of grace, not to that of nature" (Mascall 1953: 41). This depiction highlights a division between Eastern and Western approaches: many Orthodox, in contrast to Mascall and the West generally, speak of the sacraments as revealing the foundational yet hidden nature of the material world, which was created to glorify God and to bring Him near, but which has fallen. (Recall the Anaphora of St. Basil's Divine Liturgy, that the Holy Spirit might "reveal" the eucharistic elements to be the body and blood of Christ.) As Schmemann declares, "[A] sacrament is primarily a revelation of the genuine nature of creation.… [I]n the Orthodox experience, a sacrament is primarily a revelation of the *sacramentality* of creation itself" (Schmemann 2005: 33). Western theologians such as Mascall worry, in light of contemporary moves to downplay the impact of the Fall, that such an approach might devalue the sacraments; Eastern theologians are concerned that Western theology has so accentuated the Fall that it posits a rigid division between the cosmos and the heavenly kingdom, to which the cosmos has been called by God. Both sides, however, recognize that the sacrament includes that which properly belongs to the material world, even while it opens the door to the divine. For example, Aquinas makes a bridge between grace and the material world: "anything that is called sacred may be called *sacramentum*" (*ST* III, q.60, a.5, ad1, cited in James 1962: 15). With the exception of those radical Protestants who understand the sacraments to be merely propaedeutic "symbols" (in the contemporary sense), the sacrament is understood to have a foot in both the seen and unseen worlds, showing that God's kingdom is (or will be!) one, as God is one.

The word "sacrament" does not occur in the New Testament in relation to either Baptism or the Eucharist, though sometimes the Scriptures employ the Greek word μυστήριον in contexts related to Jesus' death (Eph 1:9; Col 1:26–27; 1 Tim 3:16). That word is normally translated by the Latin *sacramentum,* even though μυστήριον has a larger semantic range and comes to be used in Eastern Christianity for the sacraments themselves. In the historic church's understanding, the sacrament is a "sign" that is "effective"—a physical reality that both signifies and confers. This inherent power of sacrament is further emphasized when the Greek term ("mystery") is recalled. The material property of the sacrament is essential, as is its link (however defined) with the divine world: we receive "no longer common bread, but the Eucharist, consisting of two realities, earthly and heavenly" (Irenaeus, *AH* 5.2.3). Thus, the sacrament is analogous to Christ, possessing, as it were, two natures: many in the Reformation tradition and a few in the Catholic tradition have spoken of Jesus as "the quintessential sacrament" (Vander Zee 2004: 45; see also Jungel 1989: 212; Osborne 2005: 205), that place where heaven and earth meet. If the sacraments are mysteries where heaven and earth join, then the God-Man is the mystery of mysteries, the bedrock, cause and substance of these blessed material loci. "He is prior to all things and in him all things cohere" (Col 1:17).

The sacraments retain their mystery, but since they are relative to the One who is the Word, they do not devolve into magic or irrationality. Many in the West, including Calvin and Luther, followed Augustine in insisting that, like Christ, the visible sign must also be a "visible word": *Accedat Verbum ad elementum et fit sacramentum* ("Add the Word to the element and it becomes a sacrament," Augustine, *Tract.80 in Ioh.*). The East has not articulated this connection, perhaps because the Orthodox tradition concentrates more on the incarnate over the written/spoken Word. Yet the Eastern liturgy behaves in such a manner that it shows consent: its mysteries, whether Baptism or Eucharist (or other sacramental acts), are interpreted by an accompanying narrative. The traditional interplay between the kataphatic and apophatic means of revelation makes for a different understanding among Eastern theologians, so that the verbal dimension is not laid down as a *sine qua non*. For example, in the Orthodox wedding liturgy, there is no required performative utterance ("I now pronounce you ... ") or even a human vow, to render the ceremony sacramental. It is interesting, however, that material objects such as icons (which do not require words) are not considered sacraments (see the discussions of the seventh ecumenical council), though they have a mystagogic function.

Protestant ecclesial communities consider that for something to be labeled a "sacrament," it must have originated with a dominical declarative, imperative, or performative word: hence two only have been accepted by most. (Foot-washing is sometimes admitted on the basis on John 13:14.) For Catholics and Orthodox, the living tradition of the church reveals, or perhaps recognizes, the sacraments—whether seven (the typical Western understanding), or an unnumbered host of mysteries, headed by Baptism and Eucharist (the Eastern perspective). Such actions using material means include Baptism, Eucharist, laying on of hands and/or anointing with oil for consecration or healing, wedding rites, ordination, sprinkling with water, foot-washing on Maundy/Holy Thursday, and so on. The Roman Church distinguishes between the seven traditional sacraments and other "sacramentals"; the East neither enumerates nor distinguishes, since "heaven and earth are full of his glory." In both cases, matter remains integral to God's action, and is not merely propaedeutic. "The world … becomes an *epiphany* of God, a means of his revelation, presence, and power.… We *need* water and oil, bread and wine, in order to be in communion with God and to know him" (Schmemann 2005: 120).

READING THE SCRIPTURES
AND THE FATHERS

Let us move on to a select reading of the Scriptures and the Fathers concerning sacrifice and the two major sacraments.

Sacrifice

The earliest church drew her understanding of sacrifice from the Old Testament, though Christians were embedded in Hellenistic culture, itself replete with civic and mystery religions, where sacrifices marked public occasions and even the marketplace. The incorporation of Hebrews into the New Testament collection testifies to the new covenant's continuity with the Old Testament tradition, seen also in the Gospels, Epistles, and Apocalypse. Sacrifices were enacted in many ancient cultures, but took on particular force when commanded by the LORD . Indeed, the meaning of Old Testament sacrifice is pointedly distinguished from that of the surrounding societies, whether contemporaneous with various stages of Israel or with early church history. Arguably, this contrast is foundational to the tragicomic shaped *Aqedah* ("Binding") of Isaac (Gen 22:15–18; cf. Ezek 20:30–31): what pagan gods were believed to require, YHWH does not demand; instead, he provides the necessary sacrifice. Even more insistent are prophetic disclaimers that God does not need sacrifice (Ps 50/LXX 49:7–15; Hos 6:6; Amos 5:21–24; Mic 6:6–11), the repudiation of food offered to idols (Rev 2:14), and the warning that, though all food may be eaten to God's glory, "one cannot drink both the cup of the Lord and the cup of demons" (1 Cor 10:20–21; cf. Baruch 4:7).

Hebrew writers shared vocabulary with pagan cultures in describing sacrificial mystery: the Hebrew *kipper* ("to make atonement") has its cognates in Arabic and Akkadian, and certain passages speak about YHWH receiving an offering as a "pleasant aroma," as though God had an appetite. However, extra-biblical cults served more as cautionary tales than as a thesaurus. Thus the Old Testament is replete with passages forbidding sacrificial theurgy ("strong-arming" God), and mocking those idols who required to be fed (e.g. Ps 50/LXX 49:7–15). When mythological language was used, it was, as Helmut Thielicke puts it, "disarmed" of its pagan connotations in order to speak truly of God, the cosmos and salvation history (1974: 84–114). Similarly, the New Testament's chosen context for understanding sacrifice is the Hebrew Bible rather than the surrounding cultures. Though Hellenistic cultic terms such as "knowledge" (γνῶσις, 1 Cor 8:1, 7) "mystery" (μυστήριον, Eph 1:9) and "appeasement/propitiation" (ἱλασμός, 1 John 2:2) are used, the New Testament authors signal a meaning consonant with the gospel initiated by the sovereign LORD. They remembered that the Torah's foundational moment of holocaust and peace offerings at Sinai (Exodus 24:4–8) was paired with an intimate tableau in which the elders communed with YHWH (24:9–11), and that Moses entered into the very glory of God (24:18). The Old Testament emphasis is as much on covenant, participation and communication as on death, blood and cleansing. When the New Testament writers read the Old Testament, they recognized sacrifice, but also a great mystery where, by physical means—sprinkling, eating, climbing, Moses entering, stone tablets given—the people "afar off" from the LORD were brought near.

This thick meaning is found also in the martyrologies of the deuterocanonical/apocryphal books. At some point in the first century BC, Eleazar's martyrdom, with that of the seven boys, was narrated as a refusal to offer to idols, prefaced and interspersed with assertions of the sovereignty of God (2 Macc 6:12–16; 7:28–30), and finally interpreted as an offering "paid in advance" (7:37) that "bring[s] to an end the wrath of the Almighty God that has justly fallen upon our whole nation" (7:38). This sacrificial aspect of martyrdom was more fully exploited about a century later in the racier 4 Maccabees, where Eleazar offers his blood for purification, his life as an exchange, and his punishment as effective for the whole nation (6:28–29). At the end of all the luridly described torments, the narrator comments that the martyrdom was undertaken by those "consecrated for God ... having become, so to speak, a life-exchange (ἀντίψυχον) for the sin of our nation ... and an atoning sacrifice (τοῦ ἱλαστηρίου) through their blood ... and death" (17:21–22). Even here, where there are no qualms in describing martyrdom as ritual slaughter, this element is advanced with the qualifier ὥσπερ ("so to speak"). After all, the holy martyr is not simply a holocaust to avert God's wrath, but a participant who "dies for the sake of God" and "lives in God." Even where the vicarious aspect of martyrdom is fully registered, God is not finally depicted as a punishing exactor, but as the creating and resurrecting One in whom martyrs retain hope as they engage in a "divine" contest (17:11–16), showing the character of God (might we say "sacramentally"?) by consecrated deaths. Certainly the more reserved story of 2 Maccabees would have been known to the writers of the New Testament; the more developed sacrificial language of the second narrative provides a parallel to language concerning Jesus' death in the Gospels and the Epistles.

Mark 10:45 (//Matt 20:28; cf. Luke 22:27) provides a striking *logion*: "The Son of Man came not to be served but to serve, and to give his life as an ransom in exchange for many (τὴν ψυχὴν αὐτοῦ λύτρον ἀντὶ πολλῶν)." Here the word ransom (λύτρον), often used in the LXX context of ritual holocaust, is combined with the idea of life-exchange (τὴν ψυχὴν ... ἀντὶ) that we noted in 4 Maccabees (ἀντίψυχον). Many scholars also judge that it echoes the language of service and sin-offering in Isaiah 53:10–12, thus heightening the sacrificial implications. Some argue that diaconal service is far removed from sacrifice, and thus the words about ransom must have been patched onto Mark's source, which originally focused upon service alone. However, the imbedded allusion to the Isaianic servant, who suffered for others, already makes this connection. Moreover, the saying arises on the road up to Jerusalem, in a discussion concerning those will-ing to "drink the cup" of the Lord's death (Mark 10:38–39//Matt 20:22–23). Luke does not mention "ransom," but his placement of the saying (Luke 22:27)—between the Last Supper, with its covenantal cup of poured-out blood, and Jesus' prayer in the Garden about his coming cup—has much the same effect. Service and sacrifice commingle in Jesus' teaching.

The contrast between human striving for honor over against Jesus' abject service is also celebrated in Philippians 2:5–11, which may well be a pre-Pauline hymn. If so, the combination of motifs (Servant, self-abnegation, death, being seated in glory) appears in the earliest stratum of Christian worship. Throughout these texts, Jesus demonstrates a lifelong servanthood, which finds its astonishing expression in his willing death, the cup given by the Father: thus the Servant takes his proper place on high. A similar cluster is seen in the fourth Gospel, where Jesus is introduced by the Baptizer as the "Lamb of God who takes away the sin of the world" (1:29), where descending and ascending imagery is prominent, where Jesus washes feet (13:16), and where his humiliation is described as glory. Isaianic servant-language is also coupled with sacrifice in 1 Peter 2:21–25. Similar concepts are depicted in the Apocalypse, where the "standing slaughtered Lamb" (5:6) finds his position both "in the midst of the throne" (ἐν μέσῳ τοῦ θρόνου, 5:6; ἀνὰ μέσον τοῦ θρόνου, 7:17) and "in the midst of" worshippers (ἐν μέσῳ τῶν πρεσβυτέρων, 5:6) who need his service (7:17). Everywhere Jesus, the Servant and the Sacrifice, is exalted and commended to all faithful, martyrs among them.

Yet the New Testament writings also display a contrast with Old Testament ideas of sacrifice. 1 Corinthians 11 links old and new covenant peoples through the motif of bap-tism (verses 1–4), but then comments that the Old Testament narratives stand as *nega-tive* types for us (τυπικῶς, verse 11). We are to contrast the faithlessness of God's chosen people with new covenant worship and life, which are grounded in our sharing the body and blood (verses 14–16) of the Lord. St. Paul aims not simply to emphasize past infidel-ity and God's displeasure with "most of" the old covenant people at Sinai, but also the inherent incompleteness of that covenant (cf. 2 Cor 3:13, where Torah's glory is described as καταργουμένος, something not merely "fading," cf. RSV, but "to be put aside"). This is also central in Hebrews, with its dynamic from the incomplete to the complete. There, Jesus' priesthood is linked to his status as Son in contrast with the "servant" Moses (3:1–4). It is perhaps telling that his high priesthood is prefigured not by Moses but by Melchizedek, who is never connected with the slaughter of animals. Jesus' service is seen not in his daily offering of sacrifices (7:27; 8:3), but in his "once-for-all" offering, which put away sin, cleansed and sanctified those in solidarity with him (10:10), and culmi-nated in his eternal mediation on our behalf (4:14–16).

Moreover, in Hebrews, the blood-and-flesh sacrifice of Christ is stressed, even to the extent that Jesus' blood is sprinkled in the *heavenly* sanctuary. Also detailed is Jesus' suf-fering "outside the camp" like the Old Testament scapegoat (Heb. 13:11–12), and his offer-ing "to bear the sins of many" like the Servant (9:27; cf. Isa 53:12; Mark 10:45; Rom 5:19). The Crucifixion is climactic, but part of a larger picture—Jesus' sharing of our nature (2:14) and his life-long obedient suffering (2:10; 5:7–9). Similarly, Christ's Incarnation and death are illuminated in Hebrews 10:5 by a citation of Psalm 39 (LXX): 6–8, in which the reference to "body" (in contrast with the Hebrew reference to "ear") provides an explicit contrast to the Old Testament offerings, by which it was "impossible" that sins should be removed:

> Now, he has appeared once for all at the end of the age to put away sin by the sacrifice of himself.... Consequently the One coming into the world said "You have not desired sacrifices and offerings, but *you have prepared a body for me*; with holocausts and sin offerings you are neither delighted nor pleased.... Behold, I have come to do your will." (9:26b; 10:5–7)

It is instructive that Hebrews highlights the entire life of Jesus as sacrificial and sacerdotal without downplaying his atoning death. Elements frequently seen as alternatives are placed side-by-side, as is also the case with the high Christology of the book, where Jesus is unabashedly called "God" (1:8), yet must "learn obedience" (5:8). The entire scope of Jesus' holy expedition is kept in view, from the Incarnation through to his session at the right hand of the Father. Hebrews, along with the apostle Paul, sees in this One's person and actions God's own character: Jesus' death "for the ungodly" demonstrates God's justice (Romans 1:16–17; 5:6) and love, giving "hope of sharing the glory of God" (Romans 5:3, 6–7).

This conjunction of atonement and reconciliation, death and life, descent and ascent, obedience and glory, is reflected in many Church Fathers, of whom St. John Chrysostom is representative. In one of his meaty sermons on the Ascension, he ties together Jesus' Incarnation, Crucifixion, resurrection, and Ascension with the theosis of the faithful, echoing Hebrews, and dipping into Genesis, Psalms, Isaiah, Luke, and Romans:

> So that you may learn that he did not hate our nature, but that he was turning away evil ... [remember that] we who appeared to be unworthy of the earth, were this day [through his Ascension] brought up to the heavens. For we, who from the beginning were not even worthy of what was below, have come up to the kingdom on high; we have gone beyond the heavens; we have grasped hold of the royal throne.
>
> Even that very [human] nature, on account of which the Cherubim had to guard Paradise, this day is seated above the Cherubim! But how has this great wonder happened? How did we who were stricken—who appeared unworthy of the earth and were banished below from the earliest ages—how did we come up to such a height? How was the battle destroyed and how was the wrath lifted? How?
>
> For this is the wonderful thing: that it wasn't we who had grown unjustly angry with God who made the appeal, but that One who was justly vexed, who called us to his side, who entreated us, so that there was peace. 'For on Christ's behalf we are ambassadors, as though God were entreating you through us.'
>
> What is this? Is the One who is himself abused the very same One who encourages? Indeed, yes! For he is God and, because of this, our philanthropic Father entreats us. And look what happened! The Son of the One who is making the appeal is the mediator—not a human, nor an angel, nor an archangel, nor anyone of the household slaves.

And what did this mediator do? The work of a mediator! For it is as if two had been turned away from each other and since they were not willing to talk together, another one comes, and, placing himself in the middle, loosened the hostility of each of the two. And this is also what Christ did. God was angry with us, for we were turning away from God, our human-loving Master. Christ, by putting himself in the middle, exchanged and reconciled each nature to the other. And how did he put himself in the middle? He himself took on the punishment that was due to us from the Father and endured both the punishment from there and the reproaches from here.

Do you want to know how he welcomed each? Christ, Paul says, 'redeemed us from the curse of the law, having become a curse for us.' You have seen how he received from on high the punishment that had to be borne! Look how also from below he received the insults that had to be borne: 'The reproaches of those who reproached you,' Scripture says, 'have fallen upon me.' Haven't you seen how he dissolved the enmity, how he did not depart before doing all, both suffering and completing the whole business, until he brought up the one who was both hostile and at war—brought that one up to God himself, and he made him a friend?

And of these good things, this very day is the foundation. Receiving, as it were, the first fruits of our nature, he bore it up in this way to the Master. And indeed just as it happens in the case of plains that bear ears of corn, it happens here. Somebody takes a few ears, and making a little handful, offers it to God, so that because of the little amount, he blesses the whole land. Christ also did this: through that one flesh and 'first-fruits' he made to be blessed our [whole] race.... Therefore he offered up the first-fruits of our nature to the Father, and the Father was so amazed with the offering, both because of the worthiness of the One who offered and because of the blamelessness of the offering, that he received the gift with his hands that belonged, as it were, to the same household as the Son. And he placed the Offering close to himself, saying, 'Sit at my right hand!' (*In Ascensionem D.N.J.C., PG*, 50.444–446, original translation)

In this splendid passage, the Golden-Mouthed preacher describes Christ's sacrifice as representative atonement, as reconciliation, and as triumphant thank-offering. His actions both fulfill the Old Testament sacrifices, and confirm their inadequacy to deal with God's anger over sin. "God was angry with us, the human-loving Lord" so that an "exchange" of natures was necessary, something only the God-Man could accomplish. De la Taille, unfortunately, seems to read Chrysostom's sermon through the lens of Leo's Latin translation (*PL*, 54, 1183), and ascribes to him the concept of "appeasing the Father" (De la Taille 1940: 254) by sacrifice—a crude view of propitiation not enjoined by St. John. Instead, Jesus' priestly nature is connected by the Golden-Mouthed without embarrassment to our Fall, and to his Crucifixion, by which he stood between us and death; it is also intertwined with his entire person, from the Incarnation, which shows the honour afforded human flesh, through to his Ascension, which promises human glory. Sacrificial death appears as the necessary shape that divine priestly service must take if it is to be effective in a fallen world: but the service itself is not something super-added because of the Fall. Rather, it is indicative of the very nature of Christ, the "*totus Christus*" (De la Taille, 1940, *passim*; cf. Aulén 1958: 19), who defers to the Father in eternity and who "will also be subjected to" the Father, that God may be sacramentally present in everything to everyone (1 Cor 15:28).

The Sacraments

A survey of how contemporary theologians trace the relationship between sacrifice and the sacraments seems more instructive of their own debates than of the development of sacramental theology in the early church. In the earliest Christian documents, both Baptism and the Lord's Supper were understood, along with Jesus' life and death (Luke 24:27), to be foreshadowed in the Old Testament. In 1 Peter 3:20–22 Noah's salvation is a type of Baptism; in 1 Corinthians 10:1–4 the sea is the "baptism" of the chosen people, and their spiritual "food" and "drink" are linked to the new covenant supper. With Baptism, the link is obvious from the earliest times: "Do you know that all of us who have been baptized into Christ Jesus were baptized into his death.... We have been united with him in a death like his ... so that we might no longer be enslaved to sin" (Rom 6:3, 5–6). Jesus himself submits to Baptism at the beginning of his ministry, an event that leads to his temptation in the wilderness (cf. also the pattern in Romans 8:14–17); this initial acts bespeaks the entire sacrificial life of Jesus, gloriously expressed in the Crucifixion.

Not as clear to some is a straight line between Jesus' atoning death, the Lord's Supper of the New Testament, and the Eucharist as it developed in the church. While some highlight the Passover sacrifice in explaining the Eucharist, others appeal to the *todah* (thanksgiving sacrifice) and the *berakah* (blessing) of the synagogue meetings (Kereszty 2004: 11). It is maintained that "the New Testament never speaks of the eucharist as a sacrifice" (Vasey 1984: 7) and that in *Didache* 9, the Eucharist is described in terms of vine and broken bread, but without reference to Jesus' death: the link of sacrifice with the sacrament is thus posited as a later development.

A detailed trajectory of eucharistic theology is difficult to trace, since we have so little evidence of the earliest period, and because reality is messy. Yet it is instructive that very soon in the second century we see the deliberate commingling of sacramental and sacrificial language, based on biblical imagery. It seems that those who question first-century connections are, for the most part, intent to distance the earliest church from the notion of sacrificial death as the significant feature of the Son's work among us, and are urging certain contemporary paradigms of Eucharist. Is it the case, however, that the New Testament texts do not make the link between the mysteries and Jesus' sacrifice?

Let us consider the "institution narratives," John's water and manna discourses, Hebrews' sacerdotal passages, and the Apocalypse's visionary glimpses. We begin with a dominical saying: "This is my blood of the [new] covenant poured out for many" (Mark 14:24). Like Mark 10:45, this echoes Isaiah 53:12 ("for many") but also, it seems, Isaiah 42:6 ("I have given you as a covenant") and Exodus 24:8 (the first covenant). Matthew's parallel includes "for the forgiveness of sins" (26:28) and Luke supplies a command for continued remembrance. Some think this is a Lucan innovation, but it is also found in the apostle Paul's earlier handed-on tradition (1 Cor 11:25). Indeed, already by 1 Corinthians 11:20, the phrase κυριακὸν δεῖπνον ("Lord's Supper") has a technical force that the apostle's readers understood. All three Synoptic Gospels stress "blessing" (Paul a "thanksgiving") and breaking of the bread associated with Jesus' body. In Luke's Gospel, this breaking is formalized and extended in a saying that is symmetrical with the words about the cup (Luke 22:19). Such attention makes it probable that Luke's description of the early church as "devoting themselves ... to the breaking of *the* bread and *the* prayers [over the bread]" (Acts 2:46, Humphrey 2011: 48–49) is an explicit reference to the Lord's Supper, not simply to table fellowship. This continuing action attested by Luke and Paul means that at least some of the earliest Christian community saw Jesus' words over bread and wine as more than a one-off prediction concerning his impending death. Though it is possible to read Mark's account of the Lord's Supper in this minimalist way, we might wonder why our Lord speaks of *drinking* blood—something far more internal than the sprinkling of the first covenant. Finally, all four passages include a prospective aspect—Jesus speaks of the coming meal of reunion in the kingdom, Paul of Jesus' parousia ("presence, coming"). The cup and bread signify Jesus' ultimate sacrifice, mysteriously incorporate his followers in this, and represent an ongoing action until he comes.

When we turn to the fourth Gospel, we encounter a paradox: there is no narrative of Jesus' Baptism or of Jesus establishing a meal rite; yet the entire Gospel is imbued with sacramental images and sacramental thinking. With due respect to Rudolph Bultmann (Bultmann 1971: 189–192) and James Dunn, who believe the Gospel to be anti-sacramental, it is hard to imagine that John's discourses could have made sense to a readership unaware of the sacraments. The argument of C. H. Dodd and Joachim Jeremias, that the mysteries are depicted in terms intelligible to those initiated, seems far more likely: the Evangelist's reserve matches the Eastern liturgical prayer, "I will not speak of your mysteries to your enemies!" Our scope in this article embraces the two major sacraments, Baptism and Eucharist, so we will not further the more maximalist interpretations (e.g. Oscar Cullman), which have traced all seven Catholic rites in the Gospel. A brief foray into the water and bread discourses illustrates John's thoroughgoing sacramentalism.

Jesus' offer of living water is both surprisingly specific and general. To the Samaritan woman, an outsider, he explains, "If you knew the gift of God, and who it is that is saying to you, 'Give me a drink,' you would have asked him, and he would have given you living water.... [W]hoever drinks of the water that I give him will never thirst; the water that I shall give him will become in him a spring of water welling up to eternal life" (4:10, 14). To the pilgrims at the Feast of Booths, Jesus proclaims, "If any one is thirsty, let him come to me, and let the one who believes in me drink. As the scripture has said, 'Out of his heart shall flow rivers of living water' (7:37–38). St. John Chrysostom queries, "But where has Scripture said, that 'rivers of living water shall flow from his belly?' Nowhere!" (*In Joannem* 51.1). It would seem that Jesus is alluding to Zechariah 14:8, Ezekiel 47, Baruch 3:12, and Jeremiah 2:13, where the fount of waters both comes *from* God and *is* God himself. The waters partake sacramentally of the divine life, and are on display most dramatically when the centurion pierces Jesus' side, whereupon both blood *and water* are released (19:34), as solemnly attested. Flowing water is thus identified with the crucified Jesus, but also with the Holy Spirit: "this [Jesus] said about the Spirit ... as yet not given" (7:39). Thus the Evangelist implies that the water flowing from Jesus' wounded side would embrace and become internal to others: an image similar in force to St. Paul's "being baptized into Christ" and the Johannine Jesus' own words concerning being "born from above ... of water and the Spirit" (3:3, 5). This language, coupled with the illumination of the man born blind (chapter 9), sitting for healing by the water, but finally illumined by the One who brings true water and true light, surely intimates the importance of Baptism for John's readers.

Chapter 6 is similarly evocative. It is helpful to recall that Jesus has already been introduced as "the Lamb of God" in 1:29 and 1:36. The feeding (6:1–12) occurs during Passover (6:4), and is narrated in eucharistic terms: Jesus "gives thanks" and distributes (6:11), a detail underscored at 6:23 by the narrator when he recaps by saying "they ate the bread after the Lord had eucharized." The narrative moves into a discourse couched in terms that the church recognizes as eucharistic—Jesus' body as bread, his "bread" for the life of the world, the food that is imperishable, the true and living bread from heaven, the people's request that they would have this bread "always," the ability of this bread to confer immortality, and the strangely concrete vocabulary that his disciples must "devour flesh" (ἐὰν μὴ φαγῆτε τὴν σάρκα) and "drink blood" (6:53). The latter is a breach of the most minimal application of the Mosaic code (cf. Acts 15:21, 28–29) and inexplicable without a sacramental connection. Also striking is the gratuitous addition of "blood," following an emphasis upon bread alone. Some have denied a eucharistic context, since the phrase is "flesh and blood" rather than "body and blood"; yet Jeremias argues "flesh" may be closer to Jesus' Aramaic in the institution (Jeremias 1955: 140–141). Finally, the sacramentalism is bound up with the Incarnation as well as the Crucifixion: the Son has taken on "flesh" (1:14) and will "give his flesh" (6:51) on the cross. Sacrifice and sacrament come together.

Hebrews incorporates a similar conjunction of concepts: Jesus shares "flesh and blood" with his siblings (2:14). He is the human priest foreshadowed by Melchizedek, whose appearance in the Old Testament is characterized by an action of "blessing" (7:6–7) and by his bearing of wine and bread. Though Hebrews does not explicitly mention the blessed gifts brought forth by Melchizedek, any informed reader naturally supplies this detail. (Many ancient and modern commentators are unable to avoid a foreshadowing of the sacraments in the Melchizedekian narrative, perhaps with cause.) Moreover, the author is intent on the antitype, the Son, who will "offer himself" once and for all (7:27); his own "flesh and blood" (2:14; 10:19–20), when rent and spilled, prepare a way for us to follow. By his sacrifice, our hearts are sprinkled (10:22) and our own bodies washed with the pure water (of Baptism, 10:22). Thus the new priestly people of God possess a new altar of sacrifice from which they may eat (13:10). The unique sacrifice and sacramental character of the Son, who shares God's nature and our nature, and whose blood speaks more powerfully than that of Abel, makes its mark upon the lives of the Son's siblings, who are called to "offer up a sacrifice" (13:15) and show forth God's mystery in the world. Again, sacrifice and sacrament are conjoined.

The final book of the Bible speaks to those with open imaginations by an astonishing juxtaposition of words and images. In vision-sequences replete with imagery associated with the Divine Liturgy (incense, prayers, hymnody, words of acclamation, feeding like a shepherd, encouragement to "give thanks," cups and supper language, calls for Jesus to "come soon"), we meet the slain Lamb who is the presence of God in the world, the sign of victory, and the center of the great banquet. It is he who "gives the water of the fountain of life" (21:6), who grants "the hidden manna" (2:17), who cleanses his people that they may walk in new white garments (3:4–5; 19:8; 22:14), who joins in communion with the Bride, who fills the great city with his light and presence, and who feeds us eternally. Even the inverse images call attention to Baptism and Eucharist: the great Prostitute mimics the sacramental world by sitting upon many waters, and by sipping a cup of martyrs' blood (17:1–2). Though there is no overt scene of any sacrament, all the language is there, bound up with the body and blood of the Lamb. Again, sacrifice and sacrament come together, connected not only with the death of Jesus, but with his entire person, his coming and walking among the lampstands, the gathering of the entire cosmos around him. From birth through death through resurrection and Ascension, his parousia ("presence, coming") is detailed: this is seen especially in the cosmic worship of chapter 5 and the drama of chapter 12. The Lamb continues to "come" to his own as they join with heaven in worship and, washed and fed (22:14; 22:2), they enter into that life as "priests and kings" (1:6; 3:21; 22:3). So strong is the sacramental character of the Apocalypse that Michael Wilcock describes the entire book as "a word you can see and feel and taste ... [offering] potent images of Christian truth, to use as we use the sacraments" (Wilcock 1975: 24–25).

REFLECTION

All these texts stress not only the sacrificial implications of Jesus' death, but link this with a sacramentality that takes into consideration the entire story of salvation. Some of the current debates concerning the connection of atonement with sacrament in the New Testament are predicated on too narrow a view of the sacrament, which fastens exclusively upon the death of Jesus (though this nadir—or apex—of the God-Man's sacrificial offering should never be dismissed!). Careful attention to how the New Testament documents knit their themes together will prevent three common dangers enumerated by A. M. Ramsay: that we think of Jesus' sacrifice only in terms of his death; that we separate the action of the Son from that of the Father; and that we consider the priest's eucharistic action as separate from the offering of the rest of the church (Ramsay 1936: 117). To this we might add the restriction of Jesus' death to a legal transaction, without reference to his assumption of humanity and its healing effect: Baptism leads to "new life"; the Eucharist is the "medicine of immortality."

We hold all this together without backing away from the scandal of the cross, and the gravity of the altar/table, which even the earliest writing apostle considered perilous if approached in the wrong way (1 Cor 11: 21–22, 29–30). As *De Profundis* reminds us: "there is forgiveness with thee, that thou mayest be feared" (Psalm 130:4, RSV). It is a mistake to confuse our twin topics of sacrifice and sacrament with pagan notions of theurgy and magic; yet even the world's stories glimpse the enormities with which we are dealing. Consider the mythological character in C. S. Lewis's *Till We Have Faces*, who begins with a distorted fear of the anger of "the gods," who recognizes that most holy places are "dark," and who wishes that the gods would "go away and leave us to live our short days to ourselves" (Lewis 1956: 249). In the end she learns, at least partially, what the Gospel declares: that "You [Lord] are yourself the answer." The all-embracing sacrifice, the arch-sacramental mystery of the God-Man on the cross, the immanence of God in baptismal waters and in bread and wine—these are truths that bring the Christian to a deeper amazement than Lewis's Orual-turned-Psyche. Christ's actions are more impenetrable (not less!) than sub-Christian propitiatory rites that contemporary theologians eschew, and infinitely more illuminating. As St. John the Golden-Mouthed put it: "He dissolved the enmity, and did not depart before doing all, both suffering and completing the whole business, until he brought up the hostile one who was at war [with God]— brought that one up to God himself, and made of him a friend!" (*In Ascensionem*, *PG* 50:445)

SUGGESTED READING

C. S. Lewis (1956; 1966); E. L. Mascall (1953); A. Schmemann (2005); F. M. Young (1975).

BIBLIOGRAPHY

Aulén, G. (1958), *Eucharist and Sacrifice,* trans from 1956 *För eder utgiven* (Philadelphia, PA: Muhlenberg Press).

Bultmann, R. (1971), *The Gospel of John* (Oxford: Blackwell).

Cullman, O. (1953), *Worship in the Early Church* (London: SCM).

De la Taille, M. (1940), *The Mystery of Faith: Regarding the Most August Sacrament and Sacrifice of the Body and Blood of Christ,* 2 vols. (New York and London: Sheed and Ward), vol 1.

Dodd, C. H. (1953), *The Interpretation of the Fourth Gospel* (Cambridge: Cambridge University Press).

Dunn, J. (1970–1), "John VI—A Eucharistic Discourse?" *NT Studies* 17, 328–338.

Humphrey, E. M. (2011), *Grand Entrance: Worship on Earth as in Heaven* (Grand Rapids, MI: Brazos).

James, E. O. (1962), *Sacrifice and Sacrament* (New York: Barnes and Noble).

Jeremias, J. (1955), *The Eucharistic Words of Jesus,* trans. N. Perrin (Oxford: Oxford University Press).

Jüngel, E. (1989), *Theological Essays,* trans. J. B. Webster (Edinburgh: T & T Clark).

Kereszty, R. A. (2004), *Wedding Feast of the Lamb: Eucharistic Theology from a Historical, Biblical and Systematic Perspective* (Chicago: Hillenbrand).

Lewis, C. S. (1956; 1966), *Till We Have Faces* (Grand Rapids, MI: Eerdmans).

Mascall, E. L. (1953), *Corpus Christi: Essays on The Church and the Eucharist* (London: Longmans, Green and Co.).

McGrath, J. F. (2013), "Sacrificing Sacrificial Language," July 10. <www.patheos.com/blogs/exploringourmatrix/2013/07/sacrificing-sacrificial-language>. Accessed September 2013.

Osborne, K. B. (2005), "Jesus, Sacrament of God: A Contemporary Franciscan View," in Roger R. Keller and Robert L. Millet (eds.), *Salvation in Christ: Comparative Christian Views*, (Provo, UT: Religious Studies Center, Brigham Young University), 205–235.

Ramsay, M. (1936), *The Gospel and the Catholic Church* (New York: Longmans).

Schmemann, A. (2005), *For the Life of the World* (Crestwood, NY: St. Vladimir's Press)

Thielicke, H. (1974), *The Evangelical Faith*, vol. 1, trans. Bromley (Grand Rapids, MI: Eerdmans).

Vander Zee, L. J. (2004), *Christ, Baptism and the Lord's Supper: Uncovering the Sacraments for Evangelical Worship* (Downers Grove, IL: InterVarsity Press).

Vasey, M. (1984), "Eucharist, Sacrifice and Scripture," in B. Buchanan (ed.), *Essays on Eucharistic Sacrifice in the Early Church* (Bramcote, Notts.: Grove City, Grove Liturgical Study No. 40), 3–9.

Wilcock, M. (1975), *The Message of Revelation: I Saw Heaven Opened* (Downers Grove, IL: InterVarsity Press).

Young, F. M. (1975), *Sacrifice and the Death of Christ* (London: SPCK).

CHAPTER 6

SACRAMENTS AND THE GOSPEL OF JOHN

RICHARD BAUCKHAM

ALTHOUGH many aspects of the interpretation of the Gospel of John are controversial, there can hardly be a topic on which modern scholarship has exhibited such a wide range of views as that of sacraments. The various interpretations of this Gospel's stance on the sacraments have been labeled anti-sacramental, non-sacramental, sacramental, and ultra-sacramental or hyper-sacramental. But greater clarity about the issues can be had by distinguishing two different, though related, areas of disagreement.

First, there is the question: how often, if at all, does John's Gospel allude to sacraments? Rudolf Bultmann's view, which scholars have often taken as a starting point for their own discussions, was that the present text of the Gospel refers to sacraments on three occasions: to Christian baptism in 3:5 (the word "water"), to the Eucharist in 6:51c–58, and to both together in 19:34. But he held that these allusions are late additions to the Gospel text, made by the "ecclesiastical redactor" who edited the Gospel in order to bring it closer to the theology of the mainstream church (Bultmann 1971: 11, 138–139 n.3, 218–220, 677–678). Few contemporary scholars accept Bultmann's view that these passages are interpolations, but in each of the three cases there are scholars who deny any sacramental allusion. Some deny that any of these three passages refer to sacraments and that there are any sacramental references in the Gospel at all (e.g. Michaels 2010: 182–185, 395–396, 969). Others maintain that the Gospel (in these and other passages) uses symbolism drawn from the sacraments, but to refer to other subjects, not to the sacraments themselves (e.g. Paschal 1981).

At the other extreme, Oscar Cullmann (Cullmann 1953) found allusions to baptism or the Eucharist or both in most chapters of the Gospel. As a Protestant, he thought only of baptism and the Eucharist as sacraments, but the Roman Catholic exegete Bruce Vawter (Vawter 1956), extending Cullmann's approach, also found allusions to Christian matrimony (2:1–11), the sacrament of anointing (12:1–11), and the sacrament of penance (20:22–23). Such maximal views of sacramental reference in John have precedents in the literature and art of the early church from the second century onwards, as Cullmann was aware, while Paul Niewalda (Niewalda 1958) regarded such early interpretation of the Gospel as a reliable guide to the meaning intended in the Gospel.

Since water, wine, and bread are prominent in the Gospel of John and often undoubtedly carry symbolic meaning, it is not difficult to find allusions to baptism and the Eucharist if the reader is looking for such allusions. Reacting against what he called "the ultra-sacramental view of John," exemplified by Cullmann, Raymond Brown (Brown 1965) attempted to deploy more rigorous criteria for identifying sacramental symbols in the Gospel. He judged that nine passages meet his criteria, four referring to baptism (3:1–21; 4:1–30; 7:38; 9:1–39), three to the Eucharist (2:1–11; 6:1–3, 26–65; 15:1–8), and one to both (19:34). He judged the probability of these cases variously: in the case of an allusion to baptism in the healing of the blind man in chapter 9, he thought the evidence "reasonably probative", while an allusion to the Eucharist in the miracle at Cana has "good probability," and an allusion to baptism in the story of the footwashing is "solidly probable" (Brown 1965: 66, 70, 63). Brown's view of the extent of sacramental symbolism places him midway between, on the one hand, the "ultra-sacramental" views of Cullmann and Niewalda, and, on the other, not only Bultmann's position but also the views of a significant number of more recent scholars, who judge there to be few if any sacramental allusions. For example, in the case of the healing of the man born blind, most recent commentaries either fail even to mention the possibility of a baptismal allusion or dismiss it very cursorily. The tide of opinion has recently been running strongly in the direction of minimal reference to sacraments in John. Probably only 3:5; 6:52–58, and 19:34, the passages admitted to be sacramental by Bultmann, continue to enjoy much support.

A second area of disagreement among scholars concerns the question: how important does John consider the sacraments to be? Answers to this question do not necessarily correspond closely to answers to the first question. Clearly those who take the 'ultra-sacramental' view of John are likely to think the sacraments were of great importance to him. But those who find minimal reference to the sacraments may well see those few references John does make as indicating their considerable importance. For example, Udo Schnelle thinks that 3:5 treats "baptism as an initiatory rite that is necessary for salvation," and sees in 6:53 an "emphasis on the Eucharist as the indispensable condition for salvation" (Schnelle 1992: 185, 204). He sees this emphasis on the indispensability of the sacraments as a polemic against docetists who deprived the sacraments of significance. James Dunn, on the other hand, while agreeing that John 6 is anti-docetic, finds there also a secondary concern to counter 'sacramentalism' and links this with the absence of an account of the institution of the Eucharist in John 13. Emphasizing 6:63, he holds that "John is concerned lest too much attention be given to the ritual act and lest eternal life be thought somehow dependent on or given through the physical elements" (Dunn 1970–1: 337). Likewise, of 3:5 he remarks that "John seems to be challenging any sacramentalism which he assumes on the part of his readers" (Dunn 1970: 190).

Although the absence of a eucharistic institution narrative in chapter 13 is important for some scholars, for the most part the real issue about the theological status of the sacraments in John's theology is not so much how many references there are as the character of those references. Do they indicate the importance of the material aspect of the rites of baptism and Eucharist, or do they, without altogether rejecting the material rites, play them down in favor of the really important factors: Spirit, Word, and faith?

Finally, even the view that John's Gospel does not refer at all to Christian baptism or the Eucharist need not entail that John attached no importance to these. Brown pertinently asked what sort of reference to sacraments can be expected "in *a gospel*" (Brown 1965: 59). The Synoptic Gospels refer to the Eucharist only in their accounts of the Last Supper. Only Matthew refers to Christian baptism—in a post-resurrection context (Matt 28:19). It has rather often been assumed that John's Gospel, unlike the Synoptics, merges the time of Jesus' earthly ministry with the time after his resurrection, such that subjects of concern to the church or 'the Johannine community' should be expected to be treated within the Gospel even if they were not part of the tradition of the words and acts of Jesus before his death. But this view is mistaken (see, e.g., 2:22; 12:16; 13:7; 16:13, 25). Provided that the absence of 'eucharistic' words and acts of Jesus at the Last Supper can be explained otherwise, a general silence of the Gospel on the subject of the sacraments can be understood as no more than an implication of the Gospel genre.

However, we might also question whether the category "sacraments" is appropriate at all. Barnabas Lindars observes that there can be no "sacramental theology" in the New Testament because its writers had no category "sacraments" with which to classify baptism and the Eucharist as two of the same kind of thing (Lindars 1991: 51–54). 1 Corinthians 10:1–4 is at least evidence that they were seen as the two principal rites of the Christian movement, but we should be wary of supposing that John had a theological concept of "the sacraments". In view of the controversial nature of our topic, it will be best to proceed by examining in detail the passage that has the most scholarly support as a reference to baptism (3:5) and the passage that has the most scholarly support as a reference to the Eucharist (6:52–58). Unless these references can be sustained it is doubtful if any other references to sacraments in John will be plausible. They can also serve as examples to be followed in assessing other possible references.

BORN FROM WATER AND SPIRIT (3:5)

The most likely reference to Christian baptism in John occurs early in Jesus' dialogue with Nicodemus, when Jesus states, as a matter of first importance, what Nicodemus evidently most needs to learn: "Very truly, I tell you, no one can see the kingdom of God without being born from above" (3:3). The word ἄνωθεν, here translated "from above," is understood by Nicodemus in the sense of "again." He takes Jesus to be talking about a second birth of the same sort as the first, and is mystified: "How can anyone be born after having grown old? Can one enter a second time into the mother's womb and be born?" (3:4). Jesus repeats his statement, but with additions designed to make clear that he is speaking of a very different kind of birth: "Very truly, I tell you, no one can enter the kingdom of God without being born of water and the Spirit (ἐξ ὕδατος καὶ πνεύματος). What is born of the flesh is flesh, and what is born of the Spirit is spirit" (3:5–6, NRSV).

The words "born of water and the Spirit" have been variously interpreted, both in support of a baptismal reference and against one. To guide us through this interpretative debate, I suggest a set of criteria for a plausible reading of the phrase in its context:

(1) A plausible interpretation must make sense in its narrative context, i.e. Jesus' conversation with Nicodemus, a Pharisaic member of the Jewish ruling council, at an early stage of Jesus' earthly ministry. This criterion does not entail any assumptions about historicity. Even if the narrative is entirely fictional the criterion applies, because it is required by the literary genre of the text as a narrative set in the past. The criterion does not exclude the possibility of a secondary level of meaning, available to readers of the Gospel but not to the characters within the narrative, but the primary meaning must be one that makes sense within the narrative context.

(2) In this particular narrative context, a plausible interpretation should be one available to Nicodemus. The second person singular pronouns and verbs in vv. 3, 5–8 keep the reader aware that the words are addressed to Nicodemus, while even the plural "you" in v. 7b refers back to Nicodemus' "we" in v. 2. It is true that Jesus in this Gospel often makes enigmatic statements that are not understood by the characters in the story. John sometimes indicates that these riddles could not have been understood until after Jesus' resurrection (2:19; 13:7). Almost all are references to Jesus' coming death and exaltation. However, it is clear that what Jesus says to Nicodemus in 3:3–10 is not of this kind, because Jesus concludes the dialogue with a clear indication that, as "the teacher of Israel," Nicodemus should have understood "these things" (3:10).

(3) Jesus' saying in 3:5, which is a reformulation of the saying in v.3, substituting "of water and the Spirit" for "from above," should function as a clarification in response to Nicodemus' misunderstanding. It is worth noting that Jesus does not blame Nicodemus for this misunderstanding, but proceeds to explain his meaning more fully. Only in response to Nicodemus' subsequent expression of incredulity (3:9) does Jesus speak negatively of his failure to understand. So it would be incongruous if, following v. 4, Jesus did not attempt quite seriously to help Nicodemus reach an understanding of his message. (Readers, of course, may see Nicodemus' misunderstanding as crass, but for them too it functions as the occasion for Jesus to provide a fuller account of his meaning.)

(4) A plausible interpretation must do justice to the close association of the two terms "water" and "Spirit." This pair of anarthrous nouns connected by καί ("and") resembles other pairs in John's Gospel (1:14; 4:23, 24; 6:63). While the relation between the two nouns cannot be quite the same in all these cases, in all four cases the two nouns are closely associated and some kind of conceptual unity is implied. So it would seem unlikely that in 3:5 "water" and "Spirit" are *contrasted*.

With the help of these criteria, we can now assess the main proposals for the significance of "water" in 3:5:

(a) The phrase "born of water and Spirit" refers to Christian baptism; that is, water baptism in close association with the gift of the Spirit (e.g. Lindars 1972: 152; Moloney 1998: 99). This view clearly fails criterion (1).

(b) Some proposals connect "water" with various Jewish ritual uses of water about which Nicodemus could have known: John the Baptist's practice of baptism, proselyte baptism, or other forms of ritual purification (see, e.g., Hoskyns 1947: 214; Burge 1987: 163–164; Koester 1990: 163–164; Keener 2003: 549–552). Often such proposals serve to support a secondary reference to Christian baptism. Their common weakness is that in all these cases the use of water symbolizes cleansing (from impurity or sin), not new birth. None of these Jewish practices is connected with a notion of new birth. Cleansing, on the other hand, is completely absent from Jesus' discussion with Nicodemus. To see a reference to it in the word "water" places too much weight on this one word, especially when the alternative significance of water as life-giving was just as available in the cultural and scriptural context, and in fact predominates in John's Gospel (4:7–15; 7:37–39). Water as life-giving has a much more obvious connection with the context than water as cleansing.

(c) "Water" refers to the amniotic fluid of the womb, and so "water and Spirit" refers to two births, one natural and the other spiritual (e.g. Witherington 1989). In favour of this is the fact that the reference to water in 3:5 immediately follows Nicodemus' reference to birth from "his mother's womb." Moreover, the phrase "water and Spirit" would then parallel the two kinds of birth described in the next verse (3:6). According to Sandra Schneiders (Schneiders 1987: 192), Nicodemus is asked to understand that "it is necessary not only to be born into the Covenant of Israel but also to be born anew in the Spirit because what is born of flesh is fleshly while what is born of the spirit [sic] is spiritual." However, there are two objections to this proposal. First, it fails our criterion (4) because, especially in view of 3:6, "water" and "Spirit" would be in contrast to each other. Secondly, it is difficult to see why natural birth needs mentioning in 3:5. Nicodemus does not need to be told that it is necessary. The phrase "born from water and Spirit" seems naturally to refer to one birth only, in parallel with "born from above" and "born from the Spirit."

(d) Whereas all the proposals discussed so far take "water" and "Spirit" to refer to distinct, even if closely related, entities, this proposal, popular among recent commentators, takes "water and Spirit" as a hendiadys in which both terms refer to the same entity and the καί ("and") is epexegetical (e.g. Carson 1991: 194; Snodgrass 1993: 190–191; ; Keener 2003: 550–551; Lincoln 2005: 150–151; Michaels 2010: 184). The meaning is: "water, that is to say, Spirit." Water functions here as a symbol of the Spirit, as it is explicitly in 7:37–39 and implicitly in 4:7–15.

To explain how Nicodemus could understand this, proponents appeal to biblical prophecies of a future divine gift of the Spirit imaged as water, especially Ezekiel 36:25–27, which predicts that God will "sprinkle clean water" on Israel to purify them (v. 25) and "put my spirit within you" (v. 27). However, there is a difficulty in seeing this text as the scriptural background of John 3:5 in that the water has a purifying, not a life-giving function, and proponents of this view therefore find cleansing as well as renewal in the birth of which John 3:5 speaks. I have already pointed out that cleansing is foreign to this context and imports an unnecessary complication into a text where the obvious symbolism of water in connection with birth is water as lifegiving (as in John 4:7–15; 7:37–39). A remedy for this problem would be to refer instead to a prediction that God will pour his Spirit like water on dry ground so that new life will spring up from it (Isa 32:15; 44:3–4).

(e) Here I offer a new proposal that I suggest combines the strengths of proposals (c) and (d): "Water" refers to the amniotic fluid of the womb, and the phrase is a hendiadys. The phrase should be understood as "the womb-water that is Spirit." Jesus is clarifying his earlier saying in response to Nicodemus' misunderstanding of it in 3:4, which refers to birth from a human mother's womb. Nicodemus' mistake is to think Jesus is speaking of another birth of the same kind as the first. So Jesus clarifies: "to enter the kingdom of God one must be born, not from the womb-water of a human mother, but from the womb-water that is Spirit." This takes up the common symbolism of water for God's life-giving activity (Spirit) and gives it a new twist that incorporates it into the metaphor of birth. To understand "water" Nicodemus has only to see that it picks up his own reference to the womb, while "Spirit" shows him that he has been mistaken in thinking of another birth of the ordinary kind. The phrase "water and Spirit" leads him from natural birth, which is all that has occurred to him so far, to the notion of another sort of birth, stemming directly from the life-giving activity of God. The following verse (3:6) further clarifies the difference. This proposal gives "water" a precise function in connecting 3:4 and 3:5 and so explains why it occurs only at this point in Jesus' exposition of new birth. It also does full justice to the close association of "water" and "Spirit" suggested by the grammatical structure.

This proposal does not require that Nicodemus recall prophecies about "water" as well as "Spirit" in order to understand Jesus' meaning. Biblical prophecies about a new outpouring of the Spirit explain why Nicodemus should have understood Jesus' talk of a birth "from above" or "from the Spirit" (3:6, 8) and justify Jesus' rebuke (3:10). But the word "water" itself need not allude to such prophecies.

A Secondary Reference
to Baptism in 3:5?

Since the phrase "born of water and Spirit" is adequately explained by proposals (d) and (e) above, it is difficult to establish whether a secondary overtone, alluding to baptism, was also intended by the author or likely to have been perceived by early readers. This might seem probable if there were a common association between the idea of new birth and baptism. Such an association is so familiar from the Christian tradition that it may come as a surprise to realize that there is no New Testament text that unambiguously associates baptism with the new birth. The divine act that gives a person a renewed and transformed life is imaged as birth in James 1:18 (ἀποκυέω) and as new begetting in 1 Peter 1:3, 23 (ἀναγεννάω), but in both cases this occurs through the Word of God and there is no explicit allusion to baptism. In Romans 6:3–4 and Colossians 2:11–13 baptism is associated with new life, but the image is of being raised from death, not new birth.

The passage that is most comparable with John 3:5 is Titus 3:5–6, where most, though not all, scholars see a reference to baptism. According to this text, God "saved us through the washing of a new beginning (παλιγγενεσίας) and through renewal (ἀνακαινώσις) by the Holy Spirit which he poured upon us" (my translation). Most English translations render παλιγγενεσίας as "regeneration," but the word is connected with γίνομαι, not γεννάω, and means something more like "new genesis" or re-creation (Ysebaert 1962: 96–107). Its meaning is close to ἀνακαινώσις (renewal). However, this text probably does associate renewal of life with baptism in water and enables one to see how John 3:5 might be read in the same way.

Since baptism was the rite of admission to the new community of life it was easy to see it as including in its symbolism the divine act of giving new life to believers. So it is not surprising that John 3:5, which undoubtedly refers to that divine act, seems, like 1 Peter 1:3, 23 and Titus 3:5–6, to have been universally understood as referring to baptism in the early centuries, from Justin Martyr (1 Apol. 61.3–5), Irenaeus (Dem. 41), and Clement of Alexandria (Eclog. 7–8) onwards (many examples in Ferguson 2009). These three New Testament texts were often associated in discussions of baptism. In this light we might say that John 3:5 was open to a baptismal reading, which we could understand as the sensus plenior, properly discerned in the church's reception of the text. At the same time, however, responsible interpretation today should not allow such a secondary reference to replace the primary meaning of the text. The latter should determine the way in which the text is related to baptism. The water used in baptism may be understood to symbolize the activity of the Spirit, but it is the Spirit who effects rebirth, not the water.

EATING AND DRINKING JESUS (6:31–59)

In an exegetical tradition going back to some of the Fathers (Koester 1990: 420–422), many modern scholars have held that Jesus' whole discourse about the bread of life (6:26–58) is eucharistic, identifying the "bread from heaven" throughout not only with Jesus but with Jesus present in the bread and wine of the Eucharist. However, this view, which usually depends on reading the whole discourse in the light of vv. 53–58, is rarely found in recent scholarship, where the focus of debate has been on vv. 53–58. Some scholars hold that at v. 52 there is a transition from non-eucharistic to eucharistic reference, a view that has often been accompanied by the explanation that vv. 52–58 are a secondary addition to the discourse (which in itself is non-sacramental). The addition can be understood as an interpolation that diverges from the theology of the discourse (as Bultmann held) or as harmonious with the rest of the discourse, added perhaps even by the author himself, developing the thought in an explicitly sacramental way (e.g. Brown 2003: 231–232). Alternatively, an increasing number of scholars maintain that the whole discourse, including vv. 53–58, can be understood without reference to the Eucharist (e.g. Witherington 1995: 162–163; Ridderbos 1997: 235–242; Koester 2005: 94–100, 259–262; Michaels 2010: 395–396). Some think there is reference to the Eucharist, but only at a secondary level (e.g. Lincoln 2005: 232–235). There are also those who think that eucharistic language is used but not with reference to the Eucharist (or perhaps even to warn against unacceptable sacramentalism) (e.g. Dunn 1970–1; Paschal 1981: 161–166; Menken 1993; Anderson 1996: 212–213, 220). A few scholars hold that the whole discourse can be read on two levels, with a non-eucharistic meaning that would have made sense to Jesus' hearers in the narrative context and a eucharistic significance intended for readers of the Gospel (e.g. Léon-Dufour 1958; 1987: 252–272). (For the various positions and the scholars who have held them, see Roberge 1982).

Peder Borgen's (Borgen 1965) argument that vv. 31–58 has a homiletic structure has been widely accepted and is important for establishing that vv. 52–58 are an integral part of the discourse. The main text of the homily is cited in v. 31 (Exod 16:4 + 15) and then expounded step by step: "He gave" (v. 32), then "bread from heaven" (vv. 38–48), then "to eat" (vv. 48–58). There is also a secondary text (Isa 54:9-55:5), quoted in v. 45 (Isa 54:13) and echoed in a series of allusions ("thirst … come … eat … bread … come to me … so that you may live") in vv. 35, 37, 40, 44, 45, 47, 51, 54, 57, 58. The implied reading of this text from Isaiah is that, in contrast to the food and drink that cannot satisfy, God gives to those who come to him food and drink that truly sustain life. Especially important for the thematic coherence of the discourse is 6:23, which is the first and fullest allusion to Isaiah 55:1–3: "I am the bread of life. The one who comes to me will never be hungry, and the one who believes in me will never thirst." Jesus here identifies himself not only with the bread of the Exodus text, but also as the divine speaker in Isaiah 55 who offers both food and drink to those who come to him. Jesus cites the "come to me" of that text and then interprets it as "believes in me," while implicitly equating it also with both eating and drinking. The theme of eating *and drinking* is taken up later in vv. 53–56. For the coherence of the whole discourse it is significant that, while vv. 49–51 and 57–59 take up the motif of "eating bread" from Exodus, vv. 53–56 take up the motif of "eating *and drinking*" from the key saying in v. 35 and its source text in Isaiah 55:1–5.

The theme of "eating bread" is introduced in vv. 49–51 in a way that makes quite clear that it is equivalent to "coming to" Jesus and "believing in" Jesus. The theme returns in vv. 57–58 in very similar terms. Between these passages is the passage that speaks of *eating Jesus' flesh and drinking his blood* (vv. 53–56), the passage that is frequently said to be unmistakably eucharistic. The transitions between this language and that of "eating bread" used before and after it are carefully made. In v. 51 the bread is said to be Jesus' flesh. In v. 57 the language of eating his flesh and drinking his blood gives way to the simple "eat me," which enables a transition back to eating the bread (which readers have known since v. 35 is Jesus himself). So why is the language of *eating Jesus's flesh and drinking his blood* introduced in the four verses 53–56? Since the image of both eating and drinking was already announced in v. 35, why is it not taken up until v. 53, and why is it developed as eating *flesh* and drinking *blood*?

A key to the use of this language lies in v. 51c ("the bread that I will give for [ὑπὲρ] the life of the world is my flesh"). Here Jesus alludes, for the first time in chapter 6 and somewhat cryptically, to his coming sacrificial death. Before chapter 6 Jesus has made a few even more cryptic allusions to his death and exaltation (1:51; 2:19; 3:14, 16). They will become more common after chapter 6 (7:33–34; 8:14, 21, 28; 12:23, 24, 32; 13:3–11, 31–33, 36; 16:16–22, 28) and in a few cases more explicit (10:11, 15, 17–18; 12:7; 15:13). 6:51 is the first of these texts that say that Jesus' death will be "for" (ὑπὲρ) people (also in 10:11, 15:13; cf. 11:52). Thus, within the discourse, v. 51c makes a transition from the Incarnation (Jesus as the bread that came down from heaven) to the cross (Jesus as the bread that he gives for the life of the world). It is the latter theme that is then developed in the following verses, where "flesh" is expanded to "flesh" and "blood." "Flesh" is a reminder of the real and vulnerable humanity of Jesus (1:14), vulnerable to violence and death. The addition of "drinking blood" makes clear that Jesus' violent death has come into view: blood must be shed before it may be drunk. From the context (cf. v. 57: "eat me") it is clear that the flesh and blood are Jesus himself, considered as crucified as well as incarnate. The transition in v. 51c is not from faith to the Eucharist as the means of eternal life, but from believing in Jesus as the incarnate one to believing in Jesus as the one who died a violent death for the life of the world.

Thus, while there is important continuity between the earlier part of the discourse and vv. 51c, 53–56, there is also an advance. The Jesus to whom people are invited to come and in whom they are invited to believe is now the crucified one. But there is simultaneously another advance. Up to v. 55 the gift of God to those who believe in Jesus is characterized as eternal life. But now we learn that this eternal life is an actual participation in Jesus' own life, made available through his death. This is the significance of vv. 56–57. In v. 57 Jesus explains that he himself lives out of the eternal divine life of his Father, and so believers, participating in Jesus' life, are alive with that same divine life. In v. 56 he explains that faith in the crucified Jesus unites the believer with him in a union so intimate and enduring that it can be depicted as mutual indwelling and abiding. John introduces the language of mutual indwelling here as a means of connecting this discourse with the Last Supper discourse, where the image recurs (10:14–23; 15:4–7).

None of this requires reference to the Eucharist. But it is likely that the *language* of eating Jesus' flesh and drinking his blood is drawn from the eucharistic "words of institution." It is true that in Jewish temple sacrifices "flesh" and "blood," the two component parts of a sacrificial animal, were separated (e.g. Lev 1:3–9), and in some cases the flesh was eaten, but drinking blood was specifically forbidden (Gen 9:4; Lev 17:11, 14; Deut 12:23). In the context of the Last Supper in the Synoptic Gospels, Jesus makes wine a symbol of the blood he is about to shed, an innovatory move that may have been aided by the traditional association of blood with red wine (Gen 49:11; Deut 32:14; Isa 63:3, 6;

Sir 39:26; 50:15; 1 Macc 6:34). But in John 6 there is no reference to wine to ease the introduction of the otherwise shocking image of drinking blood. So it seems likely that John had the eucharistic words of Jesus in mind when he wrote vv. 53–56. This is the more likely because already v. 51c seems to use language from the words of institution (cf. Luke 22:19: "my body which is given for you" [ὑπὲρ ὑμῶν]). It might be objected that in all four versions of the words of institution in the New Testament Jesus speaks of his "body" (σῶμα) rather than, as in John 6, his flesh (σάρξ). But Ignatius, writing not long after John's Gospel, uses "flesh" and "blood" in his eucharistic references (*Trall.* 8:1; *Smyrn.* 6:2; *Rom.* 7:3; *Phld.* 4; cf. Justin, *Apol.* 1.66.2). So it may have been an alternative and established usage known to John. In any case, he could well have preferred "flesh" both because it belongs to the biblical language of sacrifice and because of the incarnational association he had already given it in 1:14. The Word became flesh in order to give his flesh for the life of the world.

The use of eucharistic language does not mean that vv. 53–56 are actually *about* participation in the Eucharist. Rather, because John now wishes to stress that the faith that leads to eternal life is faith in the Jesus who gave himself in death, he employs language used in the rite in which Jesus' sacrificial death was symbolically portrayed and its benefits symbolically appropriated. The fact that John uses two different verbs for "to eat"— φαγεῖν (6:49–53, 58) and τρώγειν (6:54, 56–57)—has sometimes been held to show that he moves from a metaphorical sense of eating (i.e. faith) to a literal one (i.e. Eucharist). But that John in fact uses the two words interchangeably seems clear from the strict parallel between v. 53a and v. 54a. In the Greek of the New Testament φαγεῖν is used only in the future and aorist, while ἐσθίειν is normally used in the other tenses, but John never uses ἐσθίειν and always uses τρώγειν instead for the present participle (in 6:54–58 and also 13:18, where LXX uses ἐσθίειν). In this he apparently follows a popular usage and intends no difference of meaning between φαγεῖν and τρώγειν (Barrett 1978: 299; Menken 1990: 65; 1993: 17).

In discussion of John 3:5 I maintained that words of Jesus in the Gospel must be understood in the first place within their narrative context. This must apply also in John 6. However, the fact that Jesus' hearers within the story could not possibly have understood Jesus if he were teaching them about the Eucharist cannot be a reason for denying that the primary meaning of vv. 53–56 is eucharistic. Earlier in the discourse Jesus does respond to objections by explaining more clearly what he means, but after v. 52 this can no longer be his intention, since vv. 53–56 hardly serve to make what "the Jews" have found impossible to believe any more acceptable. On the contrary, they intensify the offence. It is notable that the point at which Jesus appears to give up expecting comprehension is the point at which he begins to speak of his death. As we have already noticed, Jesus' references to his death in this Gospel are regularly cryptic and open to misunderstanding. Similarly, in vv. 53–56 Jesus' language should be understood as deliberately riddling. At this stage of the narrative, even Jesus' disciples lack the Spirit-given ability to understand the riddle. So reference to the Eucharist cannot be excluded on the grounds that it would not have been comprehensible within the narrative context. The reason for excluding it from the primary meaning of the text is rather that, in the context of the discourse, vv. 53–56 are fully intelligible to John's readers without any such reference.

Some scholars have supposed that, in vv. 53–56, John stresses the physical reality either of the Incarnation and death of Jesus as such or of those realities as represented in the Eucharist in order to counter docetic teaching (e.g. Borgen 1965: 183–192; Schnelle 1992: 101–8). But this has no support from the context. The problem "the Jews" have is not with the material reality of Jesus but—quite the opposite—with his divine origin (6:42). Another misconception that needs to be laid to rest is the view that v. 63 is some kind of comment on vv. 53–56, asserting that the mere "flesh" of Jesus is useless apart from the Spirit. This interpretation has sometimes been used to support the view that John is referring to the Eucharist but only in order to counter a form of sacramentalism that ascribed salvific efficacy to the mere consumption of the physical elements. In fact, v. 63 is a comment, not on the Christological or eucharistic content of the discourse, but on the disciples' difficulty in understanding it. As Lincoln (2005: 237) observes, John "employs 'flesh' positively when it is linked with Jesus [as in 1:14; 6:51c, 53–56] and negatively when it is linked with human response to the divine revelation [e.g. 8:15]." In the latter sense, "flesh" "refers to the sphere of merely human existence which, without the activity of the Spirit, is alienated from God.... The flesh is of no avail in evaluating Jesus; merely human categories can only take offence at the claim that the flesh of the divine Son of Man must be offered up in death for the life of the world." What is useless, according to v. 63, is not the flesh of Jesus, but the merely fleshly perspective of the disciples.

A SECONDARY REFERENCE
TO THE EUCHARIST IN 6:51C, 53–56?

John used eucharistic language to speak, not of the Eucharist, but of faith in the crucified Jesus and participation in his life. But the case for a secondary allusion to the Eucharist is certainly stronger than the case for a secondary allusion to baptism in 3:5. Since it is distinctively eucharistic language that appears in 6:53–56, it will almost inevitably call the Eucharist to the minds of Christian readers familiar with that language. We must reckon seriously with this "overtone," but at the same time we should not allow it to replace the primary meaning of the text. Responsible readers who recognize the eucharistic overtone will understand it in a way that is consistent with the primary meaning of the text. There is nothing in the context to support the view that John was actually warning against an unacceptable sacramentalism in which too much importance was attached to the material elements of the rite. But the passage surely does resist any eucharistic reading of it in which the material elements of the rite take the place of the faith in the crucified Jesus that it is primarily about. In other words, the Eucharist can be relevant to a reading of the text only insofar as the Eucharist is understood precisely as an expression of faith in the crucified Jesus and as a symbol of participation in his life. Then the text can function to teach participants in the Eucharist what the sacrament is actually about. At the same time, it is vital to recognize that, while the Eucharist is the communal rite that focuses what this text is about in the life of the church, the meaning of the text exceeds the Eucharist. The primary meaning is both more basic and more extensive than the sacramental overtone.

Were there space here to explore the reception history of this text, we might well find that it confirms this conclusion, for, while this text has often been read as directly eucharistic (among the Fathers, for example, by Cyril of Alexandria and John Chrysostom), there has also been a significant tradition of non-sacramental interpretation (including Clement of Alexandria, Origen, Eusebius, Luther, and Calvin). For Augustine, Thomas Aquinas, and some of those who debated the issue at the Council of Trent, a decisive consideration was that the text promises eternal life to those who eat and drink, whereas this could not be said of mere reception of the sacrament. So, according to Aquinas, the promises refer to those who eat and drink "not only in a sacramental way, but also in a spiritual way" (Koester 1990: 420–425). A sacramental interpretation misleads unless it is allowed only a secondary place.

THE LAST SUPPER

The absence of an account of "the institution of the Eucharist" from John's account of the Last Supper has been variously explained. I suggest two main considerations. (1) I have argued elsewhere (Bauckham 1997) that John presupposes his readers know Mark's Gospel and deliberately does not repeat what could be read in Mark unless he has a specific reason for doing so. (2) To call Mark 14:22–25 and Matthew 26:26–29 accounts of "the institution of the Eucharist" is misleading because, unlike Luke (22:19) and Paul (1 Cor 11:25), they contain no indication that what Jesus does is to be repeated by his disciples. The *function* of these accounts in Mark and Matthew is to provide readers, in advance of the narrative of Jesus' death, with a sacrificial interpretation of that death. John has no need of such an account for this purpose, because his narrative of the death of Jesus itself suggests a sacrificial interpretation (19:34). So, at the Last Supper, he narrates instead another symbolic act of Jesus, the footwashing (13:1–11), which also interprets the death of Jesus, in this case as the culmination of his ministry of loving service in the role of a slave.

CONCLUSION

Johannine soteriology is overwhelmingly concerned with the fundamental aspects: faith in Jesus the Savior and reception of eternal life, which comes from God and through participation in the life of Jesus himself. These realities are represented by baptism and the Eucharist, and the task of sacramental theology is to show that and how they are. My own conclusion from this study of the two passages in John where a sacramental overtone is most plausible is that this Gospel's contribution is to prioritize the soteriological realities that are focused in the sacraments but always exceed the sacraments. There is no reason to see this prioritization as polemical. John is not opposing sacraments or an over-emphasis on sacraments or a mistaken reliance on the outward rite as such. That the Gospel refers to sacraments only in secondary overtones, if at all, should be attributed to its genre as a narrative of the history of Jesus and to its topical selectivity, its concentration on key themes to the exclusion of much that might otherwise be judged important. That it has nevertheless funded sacramental liturgies and spirituality with words and images is not a problem, because the sacraments represent those central realities of salvation in Christ to which this Gospel gives memorable expression.

SUGGESTED READING

Brown (1965); Paschal (1981); Koester (1990); Snodgrass (1993); Moloney (2001).

BIBLIOGRAPHY

Anderson, P. N. (1996), *The Christology of the Fourth Gospel: Its Unity and Diversity in the Light of John 6* (Tübingen: Mohr Siebeck; Valley Forge, PA: Trinity Press International, 1997).

Ashby, G. W. (2002), "Body and Blood in John 6:41–65," *Neotestamentica* 36: 57–61.

Barrett, C. K. (1978), *The Gospel according to St John*, 2nd ed. (London: SPCK).

Bauckham, R. (1997), "John for Readers of Mark," in *idem* (ed.), *The Gospels for All Christians: Rethinking the Gospel Audiences* (Grand Rapids, MI: Eerdmans/Edinburgh: T. & T. Clark), 147–171.

Borgen, P. (1965), *Bread from Heaven: An Exegetical Study of the Concept of Manna in the Gospel of John and the Writings of Philo*, Supplements to Novum Testamentum, 10 (Leiden: Brill).

Brown, R. E. (1965), "The Johannine Sacramentary," in *idem*, *New Testament Essays* (New York: Paulist), 51–76.

Brown, R. E. (2003), *An Introduction to the Gospel of John*, ed. F. J. Moloney (New York: Doubleday).

Bultmann, R. (1971), *The Gospel of John*, trans. G. R. Beasley-Murray (Oxford: Blackwell).

Burge, G. M. (1987), *The Anointed Community: The Holy Spirit in the Johannine Tradition* (Grand Rapids, MI: Eerdmans).

Carson, D. A. (1991), *The Gospel according to John* (Leicester: InterVarsity/Grand Rapids, MI: Eerdmans).

Cullmann, O. (1953), *Early Christian Worship*, trans. A. S. Todd and J. B. Torrance, Studies in Biblical Theology, 10 (London: SCM Press).

Dunn, J. D. G. (1970), *Baptism in the Holy Spirit*, Studies in Biblical Theology, 2/15 (London: SCM Press).

Dunn, J. D. G. (1970–1), "John VI—A Eucharistic Discourse?" *New Testament Studies* 17: 328–338.

Ferguson, E. (2009), *Baptism in the Early Church* (Grand Rapids, MI: Eerdmans).

Hoskyns, E. C. (1947), *The Fourth Gospel*, ed. F. N. Davy (London: Faber & Faber).

Keener, C. S. (2003), *The Gospel of John: A Commentary*, 2 vols. (Peabody, MA: Hendrickson).

Koester, C. R. (1990), "John Six and the Lord's Supper," *Lutheran Quarterly* 40: 418–437.

Koester, C. R. (1995), *Symbolism in the Fourth Gospel* (Minneapolis, MN: Fortress).

Léon-Dufour, X. (1958), "Le Mystère du Pain de Vie (*Jean VI*)," *Recherches de Science Religieuse* 46: 481–523.

Léon-Dufour, X. (1981), "Towards a Symbolic Reading of the Fourth Gospel," *New Testament Studies* 27: 439–456.

Léon-Dufour, X. (1987), *Sharing the Eucharistic Bread: The Witness of the New Testament*, trans. M. J. O'Connell (New York: Paulist).

Lincoln, A. T. (2005), *The Gospel according to St John*, Black's New Testament Commentary (London: Continuum).

Lindars, B. (1972), *The Gospel of John*, New Century Bible (London: Marshall, Morgan & Scott).

Lindars, B. (1991), "Word and Sacrament in the Fourth Gospel" (first published 1976), in *idem*, *Essays on John*, ed. C. M. Tuckett, Studiorum Novi Testamenti Auxilia, 17 (Leuven: Leuven University Press/Peeters, 1992), 51–65.

Menken, M. J. J. (1990), "The Translation of Psalm 41:10 in John 13.18," *Journal for the Study of the New Testament* 40: 61–79.

Menken, M. J. J. (1993), "John 6,51c-58: Eucharist or Christology?" *Biblica* 74: 1–26.

Michaels, J. R. (2010), *The Gospel of John*, New International Commentary on the New Testament (Grand Rapids, MI: Eerdmans).

Moloney, F. J. (1998), *The Gospel of John*, Sacra Pagina, 4 (Collegeville, MI: Liturgical Press).

Moloney, F. J. (2001), "When Is John Talking about Sacraments?" in *idem*, *"A Hard Saying": The Gospel and Culture* (Collegeville, MI: Liturgical Press), 109–130.

Niewalda, P. (1958), *Sakramentssymbolik im Johannesevangelium?* (Limburg: Lahn-Verlag).

Paschal, R. W. (1981), "Sacramental Symbolism and Physical Imagery in the Gospel of John," *Tyndale Bulletin*, 32: 151–176.

Ridderbos, H. N. (1997), *The Gospel according to John: A Theological Commentary* (Grand Rapids, MI: Eerdmans).

Roberge, M. (1982), "Le Discours sur le Pain de Vie Jean 6,22–59: Problèmes d'Interprétation," *Laval Théologique et Philosophique* 38: 265–299.

Schneiders, S. M. (1987), "Born Anew," *Theology Today* 44: 189–196.

Schnelle, U. (1992), *Antidocetic Christology in the Gospel of John*, trans. L. M. Maloney (Minneapolis, MN: Fortress).

Snodgrass, K. R. (1993), "That Which Is Born from ΠΝΕΥΜΑ is ΠΝΕΥΜΑ: Rebirth and Spirit in John 3:5–6," in *Perspectives on John: Method and Interpretation in the Fourth Gospel*, ed. R. B. Sloan and M. C. Parsons (Lewiston, NY: Edwin Mellen), 181–205.

Vawter, B. (1956), "The Johannine Sacramentary," *Theological Studies* 17: 151–166.

Witherington, B. (1989), "The Waters of Birth: John 3.5 and 1 John 5.6–8," *New Testament Studies* 35: 155–160.

Witherington, B. (1995), *John's Wisdom: A Commentary on the Fourth Gospel* (Louisville, KY: Westminster John Knox).

Ysebaert, J. (1962), *Greek Baptismal Terminology: Its Origins and Early Development*, Graecitas Christianorum Primaeva, 1 (Nijmegen: Dekker & Van der Veft).

CHAPTER 7

··

SACRAMENTS IN THE
PAULINE EPISTLES

··

DAVID LINCICUM

INTRODUCTION

THE apostle Paul's thought is preserved for us in a set of scattered pastoral letters responding, on the whole, to concrete situations that arose during his travels around the Mediterranean in his missionary journeys, and remembered in several letters probably written after his death in his name. Rather than sustained treatises on the nature of the sacraments, therefore, we see his sacramental thought in action, brought to bear on discrete situations in which problems of ritual practice had arisen (e.g. 1 Corinthians), or employed as an agreed common experience from which Paul can depart for further theological and pastoral outposts (e.g. Galatians or Romans). The particularity of the Pauline Epistles does not, however, require us to abandon a search for coherence in his thinking about the sacraments, but simply requires us to contextualize his statements in such a way that proper reconstruction of his thought becomes possible.

To do so is not unimportant, as Paul's letters serve as the earliest written records of the Christian sacraments. Although Jesus himself was baptized, the Gospels (composed, it should be recalled, after Paul's letters) nowhere record his teaching on baptism, beyond passing comments that may or may not reflect an actual rite (e.g. Mark 10:38; Luke 12:50). In this light, it is striking that when we consider the evidence in Paul's letters and Acts, baptism seems to be the universally presupposed Christian experience (Holladay 2012: 347). Likewise, when Paul discusses the Lord's Supper, he makes it clear that he is invoking shared tradition from the early Jesus movement rather than inventing something out of whole cloth. Paul's letters firmly attest to an established and widespread tradition of both baptism and the Lord's Supper within two decades of the early Christian movement's beginnings. Paul is no mere traditionalist, however, and his sacramental theology bears the stamp of his eschatological thinking as a whole.

But can we rightly speak of "sacramental theology" in Paul? Paul nowhere uses the term "sacrament." He uses the term "mystery," on the whole, to denote something previously hidden but divinely revealed in the end of days, rather than to adopt the later sacramental usage that probably arose, in some ways, as a response to the mystery cults (the Latin term *sacramentum* first seems to have been used in its Christian sense by Tertullian, *Marc.* 4.34; cf. Köpf n.d.). Nor does the evidence justify speaking of more than two sacraments in Paul's thinking, even if his letters do brim with suggestive theological reflections that open themselves to later sacramental interpretation. This is perhaps nowhere more the case than with his discourse about marriage. In 1 Corinthians Paul suggests that an unbelieving spouse is "sanctified" by the believing partner, and the children of such a mixed union are likewise "holy" (1 Cor 7:12–14). In even stronger terms, the author of Ephesians suggests that marriage functions as a signifier for the mystical relationship between Christ and the church (Eph 5:31–33). Here Ephesians, by hinting at a typological interpretation of Genesis 2:24 in the context of discussing union with Christ, moves toward combining the usual Pauline understanding of mystery with a sacramental impulse, and so the passage lends itself to seeing Christian marriage as a sacrament, even if it remains underdetermined in terms of its original meaning.

Arguably, however, even if one must bracket later and rather more elaborate definitions of a "sacrament," Paul operates with a clear sense of the powerful significance of baptism and the Lord's Supper as vehicles of divine grace. This grace is not automatic, but responds to faith (which, in turn, it helps foster), but Paul nowhere gives the impression that the Lord's Supper or baptism are "mere" symbols. Rather, they appear to be public rituals, and one might draw an analogy to the public nature of a wedding: a wedding is a ritual that does not merely symbolize marriage, but enacts it, even if love and personal commitment are also required for an authentic marriage to exist (cf. Flannery 2008). Similarly, baptism and the Lord's Supper, as ordering rituals that mark the new age and signal participation in Christ, should not be reduced to their merely symbolic freight for Paul.

The Background
of the Pauline Sacraments

Since the rise of the *religionsgeschichtliche Schule* in Göttingen and elsewhere in Germany at the turn of the twentieth century (e.g. Heitmüller 1903), Pauline scholars have debated the extent to which Pauline conceptions of the sacraments may be indebted to the mystery religions, or perhaps better, mystery cults. It is clear that Paul inherits the practices of both the Lord's Supper and baptism from early Jewish Christianity, but Paul's theological unfolding of baptism in particular seems to go beyond his predecessors, and so raises the question of derivation or, less strongly, inspiration. The mystery cults themselves are ancient and vary widely by location and rite (Graf n.d.). Common to these groups, though, is an emphasis on voluntary association, including undergoing an initiation rite whose details were kept secret as a matter for insiders only, thus complicating the efforts of later historians to provide cogent reconstructions of their original forms.

While some scholars early in the twentieth century offered maximalist accounts of Paul's dependence on mystery religions, including borrowing the notion of dying and rising with a god from the rites of Mithras or the soteriology of the Isis-initiation, for example, more recent scholarship has made clear that these accounts are problematic in several ways. On the one hand, they seem to require an *interpretatio Paulina* in which disparate statements in various mystery cults over a long period of time are read together to reconstruct a backstory to Paul's own thinking, rather than being read first on their own terms and only then being interpreted in light of a possible similarity to the phenomena we find in early Christianity. On the other hand, it is prima facie implausible to think that Paul would have consciously borrowed from the mystery cults, though it is likely that early Christian baptism, as an initiation rite, will inevitably share broad commonalities with a range of initiation practices in antiquity, and these points of commonality should not be pressed to make unsupportable judgments about the indebtedness of Paul's thinking to one or another cult (Wedderburn 2005). It is undeniable that later Christian authors, beginning with the apologists of the second century, used the language of the mysteries to facilitate understanding of the new Jesus movement. And it is equally plausible to suggest that some of Paul's first converts would have viewed the experience of baptism as comparable to an initiation into a mystery cult. As A. J. M. Wedderburn rightly suggests, "The analogies presented by the mysteries may often help us to understand the way in which the Christian message was perceived and understood in the non-Jewish world, but offer us rather less help if we are seeking to understand what its Jewish Christian propagators were trying to communicate" (Wedderburn 2005: 268).

Nevertheless, Paul's participationist theology is unparalleled in pre-Christian Judaism, even if it has certain points of contact with early Jewish mysticism. The search for heuristic analogues suggests that Pauline scholars will continue to debate whether the similarities between Pauline baptismal theology and the initiation rites of the mystery cults are superficial (Wedderburn 1987a, 1987b, 2005; Légasse 1996) or more substantive (Betz 1994; Johnson 1998: 69–104), even if outright derivation can now be finally excluded.

THE LORD'S SUPPER

In contrast to baptism, which is discussed in several letters in the *corpus Paulinum*, the Lord's Supper is only directly addressed in 1 Corinthians 10 and 11, and only there because of problems in the Corinthians' observance of the ritual. Paul does not use the term "Eucharist" to denote the rite, but rather speaks of the "Lord's Supper" (*kyriakon deipnon*; 11:20), a phrase designed to contrast with the Corinthian practice of eating "one's own supper" (11:21).

The Lord's Supper begins to come into view while Paul is still discussing the controverted question of whether the Corinthians are permitted to eat meat that has been sacrificed to idols (1 Cor 8–10). In chapter 8, the apostle agrees with the "strong" position that idols have no real existence in the world, and so, he urges, conscience and love should be twin guides in assessing whether and when one should eat food sacrificed to pagan gods. In chapter 10, Paul seems to retreat from this line of argument, identifying idols with demons who do have the power to effect real harm in the world. In 1 Corinthians 10:1–22, Paul draws on the example of Israel in the desert to argue a two-sided case: on the one hand, participation in the sacraments, typologically foreshadowed in Israel's history, did not prevent the Israelites from falling away; on the other, partaking of the sacred food makes one a sharer of the altar and so a participant in the deity standing behind that altar.

First, then, the typological reading. In a somewhat surprising statement, Paul suggests that Israel's forefathers were "baptized into Moses in the cloud and in the sea, and all ate the same spiritual food and all drank the same spiritual drink. For they drank from the spiritual rock that followed them, and the rock was Christ" (1 Cor 10:2–4). This clearly offers a retrospective re-reading of the wilderness tradition which sees the Israelites being led by the cloud and passing through the sea as typifying baptism, and the miraculous provision of manna typifying the Lord's Supper (but see Aitken 1997 for the argument that Exodus 24 is also in view). The precise identification of these midrashic traditions need not detain us, though they have often been discussed (e.g. Watson 2004: 354–411). Significant here is the rhetorical force of Paul's argument: if the Israelites could partake of such divine gifts and still fall away to die in the wilderness, then so too could the Corinthians. Paul thus implicitly urges that baptism and the Lord's Supper, as important as they are, offer no guarantees. Some have seen here, probably rightly, an indication that Paul is walking a fine line in trying to critique Corinthian hyper-sacramentalism without thereby suggesting that the rites of the Lord's Supper and baptism are immaterial. Indeed, a further indication that the Corinthians may have enjoyed a robustly sacramental understanding of baptism can be gained from 1 Corinthians 15:29, where Paul mentions but does not critique an apparent Corinthian practice of baptism on behalf of the dead (for discussion, see Lincicum 2010 and literature there cited). As Hans Freiherr von Soden writes, 1 Corinthians 10 serves as

> the biblical proof that the sacraments do not provide a charm, that they do not provide security insofar as they do not bind God, that the sacramental gift in the present does not eliminate the eschatological reservation and its future. The sacraments are not talismans or magic cloaks that license intercourse with the demons and enjoyment of their gifts with impunity. (von Soden 1972: 260; *pace* Sandelin 2012)

On the other hand, Paul resists any implication that acts of cultic sacrifice are spiritually insignificant. Rather, in 10:16–17, 21, Paul writes, "The cup of blessing that we bless, is it not a sharing in the blood of the Messiah? The bread that we break, is it not a sharing in the body of the Messiah? Because there is one bread, we who are many are one body, for we all partake of the one bread....You cannot drink the cup of the Lord and the cup of demons. You cannot partake of the table of the Lord and the table of demons." To eat food sacrificed to a demon would be to share in the demonic body, and to drink the cup of demons would be to participate in the very essence of the demonic. This is the negative corollary of Paul's robustly sacramental understanding of the bread and cup. To share in these is to participate in the Messiah's body and blood, a sharing that probably presses beyond the mere metaphor of the "body politic" and hints at Paul's more participationist understanding of soteriology that comes most fully to light when discussing baptism in Romans 6.

In 1 Corinthians 11:17–34 Paul comes to address the eating of the Lord's Supper directly. Paul has heard (11:18; cf. 1:11) that there are divisions in the assembly when they come together to eat. Since the 1980s, scholars have increasingly called attention to the social divisions within the Corinthian community and the way in which distinctions in economic and social standing may have contributed to the disunity of the church (Theissen 1982; Meeks 1984). It is important to grasp that early Christian practice, as reflected in 1 Corinthians, was not merely a symbolic morsel of bread and a sip of wine; rather, the memorial ritual took place in the context of a common meal (sometimes called an *agape* or "love feast" under the influence of Jude 12). The fact that 1 Corinthians 11:25 explicitly mentions that Jesus took the cup "after supper" may indicate that the breaking of bread took place to open the meal, and the cup was celebrated after the common meal had concluded, though this is only a possibility.

Shared cultic meals were a common element of Graeco-Roman culture (Lampe 1991), and so the Corinthian participants would have had a horizon of expectation in attending these meals. The precise problem is difficult to specify, but it seems as though some, perhaps wealthier members of the community, were enjoying better fare than others in the meals, even getting drunk in the process, and so inscribing division in the community. To this Paul reacts sternly, since the Lord's Supper should be a uniting rite. Paul's caution against not "discerning the body" in 11:29 probably primarily has in view, then, in light of the social problems to which he calls attention, the communal body of Christ in the corporate gathering of the church, about which he will go on to write in chapters 12–14 (esp. 12:12–31). So serious is the threat of division for Paul that he invokes the risen Jesus as judge, even ascribing ill health and death to the effects of divisive practices. Again we see the rejection of an automatic effectiveness. As Lampe suggests, "in the Eucharist the risen Lord is present not only with his saving power but also as judge (11:27–32), a concept that excludes up front any safeguarding automatism that might be construed in connection with the sacraments (10:1–13)" (1994: 43; cf. 46). To spurn the visible unity of the community but still assume that one could achieve union with the Messiah through partaking in the Lord's Supper is, for Paul, absurd, since "the Lord's Supper, like baptism, unites us with the heavenly Lord by integrating us into his earthly body" (Käsemann 2013: 70).

Finally, we also see clearly the presence of pre-Pauline tradition. While acknowledging the process of *traditio*, Paul does not merely recite a formula but actualizes it to

engage the Corinthians. At first blush, it seems as though by citing the words of institution in 11:23–25 (on which see Schröter 2009), Paul simply recollects for the Corinthians
the past event of a meal that Jesus shared with his disciples:

> For I received from the Lord what I also handed on to you, that the Lord Jesus on the
> night when he was betrayed took a loaf of bread, and when he had given thanks, he
> broke it and said, 'This is my body that is for you. Do this in remembrance of me.' In
> the same way he took the cup also, after supper, saying, 'This cup is the new covenant
> in my blood. Do this, as often as you drink it, in remembrance of me.' For as often as
> you eat this bread and drink the cup, you proclaim the Lord's death until he comes.

Paul does not offer explicit appropriative guidance to the Corinthian church, as for
example if he were to say, "In the same way that Jesus shared this meal with his first
followers, so you also should share it with one another." Rather, in what amounts to a
contemporizing presentation of this scene, Jesus himself is allowed to address the
Corinthians: "This is my body that is for *you*. You do this in remembrance of me." By
transposing Jesus' words to this new context, Paul has effectively actualized them as the
directive of Jesus to the Corinthians. The distance between past and present is collapsed,
or transcended, though it is couched in the language of the transmission of tradition in
v. 23. The enacted practice has the force of proclamation and comprises an act of anamnesis that mediates between past and present, in that it looks to the death of Jesus in the
past repeatedly in a patient waiting for the return of Jesus (of which Paul had already
written in 7:26). So as an act of participation in the Messiah, a means of uniting with
him and his church in the end of the ages, the Lord's Supper is a powerful prefiguration,
though not an irrefragable guarantee, of the ultimate consummation of all things, when
God himself will be all in all (15:24–28).

BAPTISM

In some contrast to his discussion of the Lord's Supper, baptism features more frequently and in multiple letters, with a healthy presence in the Deutero-Pauline Epistles
as well. Paul is overwhelmingly concerned about the meaning of baptism rather than
the practicalities of performing it (rightly Betz 1994), so we are unfortunately lacking
in our ability to answer any number of questions concerning the mode, location, and
specific words used, though the silence has not stopped commentators from suggesting
that certain elements in Paul's letters may preserve pre-Pauline baptismal formulae (see,
e.g., the somewhat maximalist account in Ellis 1999, though more sober estimations are
possible). Nor does Paul offer us explicit testimony about his own baptism (but see Acts
9:18; 22:16). It is also the case that, in the midst of competing claims for party loyalty in
Corinth, Paul explicitly downplays or decentres the role of baptism in his own ministry
(1 Cor 1:16–17). He has baptized a handful of people, but no more, and for this he is glad.

Apparently he did not consider baptizing to be of the same importance as the proclamation of the gospel in his apostolic vocation.

It would, nonetheless, be a mistake to conclude from this that Paul did not have a high view of baptism. His comments in 1 Corinthians are called forth by the threat to the unity of that church, and nowhere does he disparage baptism as such. Moreover, not only does baptism feature a number of times in Paul's letters, but it also seems to occupy a privileged position as the ritual that publicly effects union with the Messiah by faith, and so seems to function as a shared presupposition with his audience.

Paul's terminology to designate baptism and its significance is relatively stable, with a few significant variations. He often uses the term "baptize" and its cognates (Oepke 1964), but can also speak of "being washed" (1 Cor 6:11; cf. Tit 3:4–7). Much discussion has considered the significance of being baptized "in the name of Jesus" or "in the name of Paul" (1 Cor 1:12–13). Probably the formula expresses ownership or allegiance, but it seems equally clear that the shorter formulae "into Christ" (Gal 3:27) or "into Christ Jesus" (Rom 6:3) or even "into one body" (1 Cor 12:13) should not be seen as abbreviations of the longer phrase but arise from an alternative background and are used in order to designate union with Christ (rightly Wedderburn 1987b; cf. Hartman 1997).

In what is probably the earliest reference to Christian baptism, in Paul's letter to the Galatians he connects baptism with belonging to Christ and so being an heir of the promise: "As many of you as were baptised into the Messiah have clothed yourselves with the Messiah. There is no longer Jew or Greek, there is no longer slave or free, there is no longer male and female; for all of you are one in Jesus the Messiah. And if you belong to the Messiah, then you are Abraham's offspring, heirs according to the promise" (3:27–29). The question motivating Paul's dense exegetical discussion in Gal 3:6–29 is precisely that of who counts as valid children of Abraham and so heirs of God's promise to Abraham. Baptism, and explicitly not circumcision, functions as an incorporation into the Messiah and so the promise given to him, as Abraham's singular "seed," comes also to the Gentile Galatians.

Already in this earliest occurrence, we see Paul's participationist theology at work (on which, see Deissmann 1892; Schweitzer 1931). Those who are baptized have been baptized *eis Christon*, and have clothed themselves with the Messiah. The imagery of clothing may recall the baptismal process itself (Beasley-Murray 1993: 62), in which an immersion may have required a change of clothes, although explicit testimony to that practice postdates the Pauline letters by some time. The imagery furthermore implies an ethical correlate of a new life of obedience.

All this hints at a significant dimension of religious experience in baptism, given that Paul also regularly associates the reception of the Spirit with baptism. Peerbolte suggests that "baptism was seen as the ritual manifestation of the presence of the Spirit" (2012: 189; cf. Johnson 1998: 74–78; Flannery 2008). Paul does not describe at length the precise relationship among faith, baptism, and the Spirit, but they are closely enough associated that Paul can apparently prioritize one or another at various points without discomfort. L. T. Johnson goes so far as to suggest that "Paul's allusion to the 'spirit of adoption' received by the baptized certainly seems to support the conclusion that the Holy Spirit was regarded as the medium through which the unique relationship between Jesus and God was transferred to others, so that at baptism this same filial relationship was established" (Johnson 1998: 77).

Arguably the place where Paul thinks in baptismal terms in the most sustained manner is Romans 6:1–11. Commentators who point out that this text is strictly speaking not about baptism per se are not incorrect (e.g. Dunn 1998; Jewett 2007 *ad loc.*), but the fact that Paul thinks about the consequences of the death and resurrection of Jesus for the Roman Church in terms of baptism should not be lost to vision, and this makes a merely metaphorical allusion to baptism without some concrete purchase in the lives of the Romans highly unlikely (*pace* Dunn and Jewett; similarly for Hunn 2004's case for Galatians 3). This would require a metaphorical usage of the term which, though not unknown in early Christian circles, seems clearly secondary to the embodied act.

Romans 6 clearly describes baptism as a "transfer event" (Schnelle 2005: 328–332). Paul portrays the baptized as having been crucified with Christ (v. 6), baptized into the death of Jesus (v. 3), buried with him by baptism into death (v. 4), and thus sharing in some sense in his resurrection (vv. 4–5). Here Paul is more precisely presenting a fusion of two events that belong equally to the past—namely the death of Jesus and the baptism of Roman Christians, though of course from the perspective of one about to be baptized this would appear as an actualization of the death of Christ, a fusion of horizons as it were. Paul's words here go beyond a mere rhetorical strategy to express the reality of his participationist soteriology, but this demonstrates the permeability of the boundary between past and present for Paul, as the ritual of baptism in some sense re-presents the death, burial, and resurrection of Jesus in the sacramental act. The experience of Christ and the Spirit evidently necessitated a significant change in vocabulary, including a large number of *syn*-compound words (here, for example, "buried with him"; cf. Riddle 1928).

We see here clearly once more the ethical implications of baptism, in which a death to sin and resurrection to newness of life entails a change of lordship: death and sin no longer have dominion over the baptized Christian, but the person now owes their allegiance to the crucified Lord (Rom 6:12–23). The baptized body remains "your mortal body" (v. 12), but the baptismal transfer removes one from existence merely "in Adam" and the old age, and relocates one to new existence in the Messiah and the age that is to come. In this sense, it is appropriate to describe baptism as an eschatological rite, a concrete act that, through faith and by the Spirit, effects the transfer from the present evil age to the overlapping new age.

In Colossians, Ephesians, and Titus, treated here as probably Deutero-Pauline, we see a continuation and extension of characteristically Pauline themes. In Colossians 2:11–13, we find a parallel between putting off the body of flesh, the circumcision of Christ, and baptism (Ferguson 2009: 159; cf. 158–160). The schema of death, burial, and resurrection closely parallels that found in Romans 6, though now some of the imagery has changed. The metaphor of circumcision here is unusual, and evidently refers to the cutting off of the Messiah. But does this passage go further in setting up a typological relationship between circumcision and baptism? If so, then we would find here a hint about the question of infant baptism, on which Paul's letters are otherwise silent. Unfortunately the language of spiritual circumcision, or circumcision of the heart, recalls Romans 2:25–29 and the scriptural traditions on which that passage draws, and so seems to function metaphorically for eschatological renewal, rather than to have in view physical circumcision.

Colossians goes on, in chapter 3, to offer paraenesis on the basis of this resurrection—admittedly a somewhat more realized picture of the resurrection than in the undisputed Pauline letters. But this does attest to the Pauline connection between renewed post-baptismal life and the resistance of sin.

Ephesians mentions baptism once explicitly (4:4–6), another time highly probably (5:25–26), and then has a handful of further potential allusions to baptismal practices (Dahl 2000 points to 1:5, 7, 13–14; 2:5–6; 4:21–24). In a creedal confession, Ephesians says, "There is one body and one Spirit, just as you were called to the one hope of your calling, one Lord, one faith, one baptism, one God and Father of all who is above all and through all and in all" (4:4–6). Baptism is here included in a highly selective list of foundational elements of the Christian faith. The unifying function of having "one baptism" recalls also 1 Corinthians 12:13, in which "by one Spirit we were all baptised into one body." In Ephesians 5:25–26, we read, "Husbands, love your wives, just as Christ loved the church and gave himself up for her, in order to make her holy by cleansing her with the washing of water by the word ... " Given the signifying nature of the mystery of marriage for the relationship between Christ and the church, it seems reasonable to understand "cleansing her with the washing of water" to recall baptism, here understood in its purifying function as a removal of impurity and sin. Dahl is thus correct to point out the significance of baptism for Ephesians; as he writes, "In Ephesians baptism marks the entry to a new room, both in terms of a new time and a new world, a universe that has been subordinated to Christ" (Dahl 2000: 416).

Finally, in Titus 3:4–7 we find a hymn-like statement that includes the lines, "he saved us, not because of any works of righteousness that we had done, but according to his mercy, through the washing of rebirth and renewal by the Holy Spirit." The "washing of rebirth," as in Ephesians 5:25–26, most plausibly recalls baptism, and perhaps offers some indication of the growing esteem in which it was held, with a greater emphasis on the effect of baptism than in previous writings.

Conclusion

If the *corpus Paulinum* does not supply us with an exhaustive or systematic discussion of the sacraments, enumerating them and offering practical guidance for their execution, it does preserve powerful instances of sacramental thinking in action. Paul does sometimes think of baptism and the Lord's Supper directly, but even more so does he think with them, arguing from shared premises to new conclusions, pushing the inheritance he received from the early Christian *koine* to deeper and more profound places. It is above all in his participationist soteriology that Paul's sacramental *proprium* becomes most clear. If the Lord's Supper had been handed on to him, perhaps in the guise of early Christian recollection of Jesus' last Passover meal, Paul sees it as indicating participation in the body and blood of Christ, expressed concretely in solidarity with the church. If baptism had come to Paul as a universal Christian practice, following on from its adoption by Jesus' disciples after their master's example, Paul sees in the rite not merely a cleansing or an initiation, but a real participation in the death, burial, and resurrection of the Messiah, and so a public act corresponding to the internal disposition of faith, which together form the stance of receiving from God the promised Spirit as a means of achieving union with Christ.

In this sense, both the Lord's Supper and baptism are eschatological phenomena that signal, and in some sense usher in, the new age. Both belong to the time when the sun is beginning to set on the age of "Adam," and the dawn of the Messianic age is beginning to break the horizon. At the same time, both stand under threat: as the Israelites fell in the wilderness, although they were baptized and had partaken of spiritual food and drink, so Paul's Christian communities could find no magical guarantees by taking refuge in the sacraments. Without the disposition of faith and obedience, expressed concretely in maintaining the unity of the community in love, the sacraments could become fruitless works.

Finally, both baptism and the Lord's Supper mediate between past, present, and future, involved simultaneously in an anamnetic movement of recollection and an anticipatory movement of hope.

SUGGESTED READING

Useful introductory surveys of Paul's baptismal thought can be found in Beasley-Murray (1962): 127–216; Beasley-Murray (1993); Dunn (1998): 442–459; Ferguson (2009): 146–165, on which see Holladay (2012). For the Lord's Supper, see Léon-Dufour (1987): 203–229; Dunn (1998): 599–623; Lampe (1994); Marshall (1993).

BIBLIOGRAPHY

Aitken, Ellen B. (1997), "τὰ δρώμενα καὶ τὰ λεγόμενα: The Eucharistic Memory of Jesus' Words in First Corinthians," *Harvard Theological Review* 90: 359–370.

Beasley-Murray, G. R. (1962), *Baptism in the New Testament* (London: Macmillan).

Beasley-Murray, G. R. (1993), "Baptism," in G. F. Hawthorne and R. P. Martin (eds.), *Dictionary of Paul and His Letters* (Downers Grove, IL: InterVarsity), 60–66.

Betz, Hans Dieter (1994), "Transferring a Ritual: Paul's Interpretation of Baptism in Romans 6," in Troels Engberg-Pedersen (ed.), *Paul in his Hellenistic Context*, SNTW (Edinburgh: T&T Clark), 84–118.

Dahl, N. A. (2000), "The Concept of Baptism in Ephesians," in *idem, Studies in Ephesians*, WUNT 131 (Tübingen: Mohr Siebeck), 413–439.

Deissmann, Adolf (1892), *Die neutestamentliche Formel in Christo Jesu* (Marburg: N. G. Elwert).

Dunn, J. D. G. (1998), *The Theology of Paul the Apostle* (Grand Rapids, MI: Eerdmans).

Ellis, E. Earle (1999), *The Making of the New Testament Documents*, Biblical Interpretation Series 39 (Leiden: Brill).

Ferguson, Everett (2009), *Baptism in the Early Church: History, Theology, and Liturgy in the First Five Centuries* (Grand Rapids, MI: Eerdmans).

Flannery, Frances (2008), "The Body and Ritual Reconsidered, Imagined, and Experienced," in Frances Flannery, Colleen Shantz, and Rodney A. Werline (eds.), *Experientia*, vol. 1: *Inquiry into Religious Experience in Early Judaism and Christianity* (Atlanta, GA: Society of Biblical Literature), 13–18.

Graf, Fritz (n.d.), "Mysteries," *Brill's New Pauly*. Antiquity volumes ed. Hubert Cancik and Helmuth Schneider. Brill Online, 2014. *Reference*. Oxford University libraries. August 17, 2014. <http://referenceworks.brillonline.com/entries/brill-s-new-pauly/mysteries-e814910>.

Hartman, Lars (1997), *"Into the Name of the Lord Jesus": Baptism in the Early Church*, SNTW (Edinburgh: T&T Clark).

Heitmüller, W. (1903), *'Im Namen Jesu'. Eine Sprach- und religionsgeschichtliche Untersuchung zum Neuen Testament, speziell zur altchristlichen Taufe*, FRLANT 2 (Göttingen: Vandenhoeck & Ruprecht).

Holladay, Carl R. (2012), "Baptism in the New Testament and Its Cultural Milieu: A Response to Everett Ferguson, *Baptism in the Early Church*," *Journal of Early Christian Studies* 20.3: 343–369.

Hunn, Debbie (2004), "The Baptism of Galatians 3:27: A Contextual Approach," *Expository Times* 115.11: 372–375.

Jewett, Robert (2007), *Romans: A Commentary*, Hermeneia (Minneapolis, MN: Fortress).

Johnson, Luke Timothy (1998), *Religious Experience in Earliest Christianity: A Missing Dimension in New Testament Studies* (Minneapolis, MN: Augsburg Fortress).

Käsemann, Ernst (2013), "Guests of the Crucified," trans. Frederick J. Gaiser, *Word and World* 33. 1: 62–73.

Köpf, Ulrich (n.d.), "Sacraments, I. Church History," *Religion Past and Present*. Brill Online, 2014. *Reference*. Oxford University libraries. August 17, 2014. <http://referenceworks.brillonline.com/entries/religion-past-and-present/sacraments-COM_024691>.

Lampe, Peter (1991), "Das korinthische Herrenmahl im Schnittpunkt hellenistisch-römischer Mahlpraxis und paulinischer Theologia Crucis (1 Kor 11, 17–34)," *Zeitschrift für die neutestamentliche Wissenschaft* 82: 183–213.

Lampe, Peter (1994), "The Eucharist: Identifying with Christ on the Cross," *Interpretation* 48: 36–49.

Légasse, Simon (1996), "Paul et les mystères," in J. Schlosser (ed.), *Paul de Tarse: Congrès de l'ACFEB (Strasbourg, 1995)*, Lectio Divina 165 (Paris: Cerf), 223–241.

Léon-Dufour, Xavier (1987), *Sharing the Eucharistic Bread: The Witness of the New Testament*, trans. Matthew J. O'Connell (New York: Paulist).

Lincicum, David (2010), "Thecla's Auto-Immersion (*APTh* 4.2–14 [3.27–39]): A Baptism for the Dead?" *Apocrypha* 21: 203–213.

Marshall, I. H. (1993), "Lord's Supper," in G. F. Hawthorne and R. P. Martin (eds.), *Dictionary of Paul and His Letters* (Downers Grove, IL: InterVarsity), 569–575.

Meeks, Wayne A. (1984), *The First Urban Christians: The Social World of the Apostle Paul* (New Haven, CT: Yale University Press).

Oepke, Albrecht (1964), "βάπτω, βαπτίζω, κτλ," in G. Kittel (ed.), *Theological Dictionary of the New Testament*, trans. G. Bromiley (Grand Rapids, MI: Eerdmans), 1:530–535.

Peerbolte, Bert Jan Lietaert (2012), "Paul, Baptism, and Religious Experience," in Colleen Shantz and Rodney Werline (eds.), *Experientia, Volume 2: Linking Text and Experience* (Atlanta, GA: Society of Biblical Literature), 181–204.

Riddle, Donald Wayne (1928), "The Non-Septuagint Element in the Vocabulary of Paul," *Journal of Biblical Literature* 47: 74–90.

Sandelin, Karl-Gustav (2012), "Does Paul argue against Sacramentalism and Over-Confidence in 1 Cor 10:1–13?" in *idem, Attraction and Danger of Alien Religion*, WUNT 290 (Tübingen: Mohr Siebeck), 77–93.

Schnelle, Udo (2005), *Apostle Paul: His Life and Theology*, trans. M. Eugene Boring (Grand Rapids, MI: Baker Academic).

Schröter, Jens (2009), "Die Funktion der Herrenmahlsüberlieferungen im 1. Korintherbrief: zugleich ein Beitrag zur Rolle der 'Einsetzungsworte' in frühchristlichen Mahltexten," *Zeitschrift für die neutestamentliche Wissenschaft* 100: 78–100.

Schweitzer, Albert (1931), *The Mysticism of Paul the Apostle*, trans. William Montgomery (London: A. & C. Black).

Theissen, Gerd (1982), *The Social Setting of Pauline Christianity: Essays on Corinth*, ed. and trans. John H. Schütz (Philadelphia, PA: Fortress).

von Soden, Hans Freiherr (1972), "Sacrament and Ethics in Paul," in Wayne A. Meeks (ed.), *The Writings of St. Paul: A Norton Critical Edition* (New York: Norton), 268–276.

Watson, Francis (2004), *Paul and the Hermeneutics of Faith* (London: T&T Clark).

Wedderburn, A. J. M. (1987a), "The Soteriology of the Mysteries and Pauline Baptismal Theology," *Novum Testamentum* 29: 53–72.

Wedderburn, A. J. M. (1987b), *Baptism and Resurrection: Studies in Pauline Theology against Its Graeco-Roman Background*, WUNT 44 (Tübingen: Mohr Siebeck).

Wedderburn, A. J. M. (2005), "Paul and the Mysteries Revisited," in Christian Strecker (ed.), *Kultur, Politik, Religion, Sprache-Text*, vol. 2 of *Kontexte der Schrift* (Stuttgart: Kohlhammer), 260–269.

CHAPTER 8

SACRAMENTALITY AND SACRAMENTS IN HEBREWS

LUKE TIMOTHY JOHNSON

THE anonymous New Testament composition called *To the Hebrews* is not a true letter but a sermon or exhortation with an epistolary appendage. One of the most stylistically complex and rhetorically sophisticated of Christianity's earliest writings, Hebrews also ranks, with Paul's *Letter to the Romans*, as the longest and most powerful theological argument from the apostolic age. Hebrews has had a profound impact on the shaping of classical Christian worship and spirituality. Before addressing those aspects of Hebrews that are particularly significant for sacramental theology both in the past and the present, it is appropriate to locate the composition in its original context.

THE CHARACTER OF THE COMPOSITION

Hebrews was at first attributed to Paul, but this ascription was eventually abandoned. Since the author is unknown, other standard questions of introduction also are problematic. Hebrews gives rise to many theories and counter-theories concerning the circumstances of its composition. It was certainly written between AD 45– and 90 —it is used by Clement of Rome—and could well be among the New Testament's earliest compositions, contemporaneous with Paul's letters (written between AD 49 and 64). The designation "to the Hebrews" represents a guess concerning the addressees, but there is much in the letter to support the idea that the addressees were Greek-speaking Jewish Christians. There is no indication that any but the "children of Abraham" are being addressed (2:16; 3:9; 4:9; 11:1–12:1); there is certainly no indication of the Jewish people being displaced by Gentiles.

Little can be said about the specific circumstances of the first readers. Despite the many original elements in the author's argument, the composition makes clear that author and readers alike share in the common life of the community brought into existence by the death and resurrection of Jesus: they share in faith, hope, and love (10:22–24); they meet in assemblies (10:25); they practice the hospitality (13:2) and sharing of possessions (13:5, 16) characteristic of the early church; they have local leaders (13:17); they know of signs and wonders and gifts of the Holy Spirit (2:4). Precisely because the author regards all these as among "elementary matters" that can be taken for granted (6:1–2), and because the author wants them to "move forward" to a fuller maturity (5:11–14), we can conclude that some time has passed since the audience's initial conversion (10:32), although it is impossible to say how long they have been Christian.

The readers (or hearers) are assumed to have sufficient knowledge of Koine Greek to grasp the author's intricate citations from the Greek translation of the Jewish Scripture, and sufficient culture to be able to follow the author's rhetoric as he develops his argument. We are told that the readers are experiencing some form of suffering, which is causing them to grow lax in their allegiance to their commitment, signaled by their neglect of the assembly (10:25). The suffering does not take the form of martyrdom (12:4), but involves some physical deprivation (the expropriation of property and imprisonment) that is exacerbated by a sense of shame (10:32–34). In response to the effect such shame is having on his hearers, the author of Hebrews crafts an argument that encourages them to fidelity: they have a better homeland in heaven (11:16; 12:18–24), to which Christ has already gone as the "pioneer and perfecter of faith" (12:1), and like Christ, they should "despise the shame" they are experiencing, because of the joy that lies before them (12:2; 13:13).

Hebrews' exhortation that believers should hold fast to their convictions because of their hope in a better future (6:9–20) relies heavily on the rhetorical argument *a minore ad maius* ("from the lesser to the greater"), which involves a series of comparisons between the lesser blessings of the past and the greater ones of the present, made available through Christ. This argument, in turn, relies heavily on two specific aspects of a symbolic world shared by the author and his readers.

The first is the distinctive way in which the author makes use of Scripture less as a set of written texts and more as a living word spoken by God in the past that continues to address the present. The history of Israel is construed as a pilgrimage of God's people toward God: the wandering of the patriarchs in search of a home (11:8–21), and the wanderings of the desert generation seeking a "rest" in Canaan (3:7–4:10), provide the pattern and the precedent of the progress of the present generation, led by Jesus, toward the city of God, the heavenly Jerusalem (12:22). The image of a people on pilgrimage to God enables Hebrews to assert both continuity and discontinuity between generations. Both seek a place of rest, but Jesus leads believers to what is truly "God's Sabbath rest," the very presence of God (4:9–10). Hebrews also appropriates the language of Israel's ancient cult in a manner unparalleled by other New Testament compositions. The author contrasts the old covenant of God, which was concerned above all with the external, ritual holiness of the people, and the new covenant, which is concerned with the transformation of the conscience (8:6–13). The imagery of Israel's worship carried out in the desert sanctuary through the mortal priesthood of Aaron (9:1–10:21), which served to "sanctify" the people, provides the perfect foil for Hebrews' demonstration that the new covenant established through the death and resurrection of Christ—a high priest not like Aaron, but "according to the order of Melchizedek" (5:6)—can be expressed in cultic terms as well.

The second distinctive aspect of Hebrews' symbolic world is its fundamentally platonic conception of reality. The "Platonism" of Hebrews does not derive from a direct reading of the philosopher, but is an outlook whose basic perceptions and convictions point to the influence of a philosophical school. The outlook is dualistic. A sharp distinction is drawn between the realm of the material and the spiritual at three levels. Ontologically, "things unseen" (that is, the spiritual) are regarded as more real than "things seen" (the material); material things are always in stages of growth and corruption, never stable in their being, whereas spiritual things are eternal. Epistemologically, truth is only possible in the realm of the spiritual, while in the material realm only opinion obtains. Axiologically, the spiritual realm is better and more honorable than the realm of the merely material.

In a manner not uncommon in what is called "middle Platonism," Hebrews joins these dualistic convictions to the biblical cosmology. Like the Alexandrian Jews Aristobolos and Philo, the author of Hebrews finds a deep consonance between Platonism and Scripture, so that it is possible to read Scripture through a platonic lens without distortion. Thus, the biblical "heaven" as the place of divine presence corresponds to the platonic realm of the spirit, while "earth," the place of human activity, corresponds to the platonic realm of the material. There is a causal connection between the realms, whereby material or earthly beings bear the imperfect stamp or impression of the spiritual or heavenly realities. Thus, for Hebrews, humans bear imperfectly the "image of God"; the tent in the wilderness constructed by Moses was made according to the "type" of the spiritual sanctuary shown Moses on the mountain (LXX Exod 25:40; Heb 8:5); and in contrast to mortals who live and die, Christ has been "exalted to the right hand" of God after his mortal death, and has entered into the very presence of God where he lives forever (10:11–13).

Hebrews also modifies a standard platonic worldview (such as we would find it in a Plutarch) in important ways. The contrast between the less-real and the more-real, for example, is applied not only vertically (so that the earthly sanctuary is but a shadow of heavenly worship), but also horizontally, so that the events of Israel's past provide images of what is now being brought to fulfillment; thus, Melchizedek is a "likeness" of the high priest Jesus (7:3). The dualistic contrast works both cosmologically and historically. More significant still, Hebrews' understanding of how God has worked in the past and the present, and above all, how God was at work in the life, death, and exaltation of Jesus, shatters the relatively static worldview of Platonism. God enters into human existence through the true humanity of Christ, and as a consequence, new value is given to bodies, motion, time, and history. The body is not merely a point of contrast to the spiritual; rather, the body becomes a place where the spiritual is revealed. Change is not merely the unfortunate characteristic of materiality; it becomes the positive medium of transformation, indeed the very means by which Christ reaches the fullness of his status as Son, and the means by which humans come to participate more fully in the divine presence.

Consideration of "sacramentality" in Hebrews must recognize how a basically platonic worldview and an engagement with Scripture are fundamentally reshaped by the experience of the life, death, and exaltation of Jesus Christ, and are worked into a powerful new vision of human existence through the exhortation of an unknown first-century preacher with remarkable rhetorical ability and unusual range of theological imagination. It is reasonable to take up first the question of for what "sacraments"—here understood in the widest sense as communal physical actions that involve participation in spiritual realities—Hebrews might provide evidence. Then, the broader question of how Hebrews' theological imagination has served as a resource for thinking sacramentally can be taken up.

HEBREWS AS WITNESS TO EARLY CHRISTIAN SACRAMENTS

Baptism

The most widely attested of early Christian sacraments is baptism, the ritual of initiation (Matt 28:19; Acts 8:12; 1 Cor 1:13–17; 12:13; 15:29; Gal 3:27; Eph 4:5; Col 2:12; 1 Pet 3:21). Passages mentioning baptism elsewhere in the New Testament connect the ritual variously to the death and resurrection of Jesus (Rom 6:3–4), the forgiveness of sins (Acts 2:41), the gift of the Holy Spirit (Acts 10:48; John 3:5), a sanctifying bath (1 Cor 6:11; Tit 3:5; Eph 5:26), a new birth (John 3:3, 7; 1 Pet 1:3; Tit 3:5), and an enlightenment (Eph 5:14). Although the testimony of Hebrews on baptism is complex and not entirely clear, the language used by the composition fits within this cluster of associations.

Part of the complexity in Hebrews' presentation is its odd use of the plural form of *baptismos* ("washing"). In 9:10, where the author speaks of the dispensations of the earlier covenant, he mentions "various washings" (*baptismois*) along with "foods and drinks" as among the "regulations for the flesh" that cannot "perfect the conscience of the worshipper." But when he speaks in 6:2 of the "elementary doctrine of Christ" (*ton tes arches tou christou logon*), the author also uses the plural form for "washings" (*baptismoi*) as among the foundational elements that ought to be assumed for the believer seeking to move to greater maturity. In this case, the "washing" is not that of the old but of the new covenant, and is not a regular ritual practice but is among those "in the beginning" things—like repentance and faith—of Christian existence.

Given that other New Testament texts link baptism and the forgiveness of sins, a second set of associations in Hebrews may be connected to baptism. A major part of Hebrews' argument involves a comparison between the sacrifice carried out in the ancient ritual of the Day of Atonement and that of Christ's death. Thus, Hebrews declares that the shedding of blood is necessary for the forgiveness of sins (9:22), but the ancient cult could not accomplish this through the sacrifice of animals. In contrast, the blood of Christ purifies consciences from dead works to serve the living God (9:14). The reference here must be primarily to the death of Christ, as it is also in 1:3, when Christ is said to have accomplished "purification for sins" before taking his place at God's side, and when Christ is said to "sanctify" (2:11; see 13:12) and "to make expiation" for sins (2:17). Such forgiveness and sanctification touches those who belong to him (2:11): in contrast to those who worshipped year after year, those cleansed/purified by Christ "no longer have any consciousness of sin" (10:2). The connection with baptism is made most directly by 10:22, when the author speaks of his hearers having the full assurance of faith, "with hearts sprinkled clean from an evil conscience and our bodies washed with pure water." While it is possible that the image of "sprinkling" may refer back to the death of Jesus, the phrase "bodies washed with pure water" almost certainly refers to the ritual of baptism (see 1 Cor 6:11; Tit 3:5; Eph 5:26).

Also a reference to baptism as a ritual of initiation is Hebrews' language about enlightenment. In 6:4–5, shortly after mentioning "baptisms" among the elementary things concerning Christ, the author speaks of "having been once enlightened (*photisthentas*), having tasted (*geusamenous*) the heavenly gift and become partakers (*metochoi*) of the Holy Spirit, and having tasted the goodness of the word of God and the powers of the age to come." The image of tasting occurs also in 1 Peter 2:3 in connection with baptism and the word of God, while the image of being enlightened is also found in Ephesians 5:14. The second mention of enlightenment (in Heb 10:32) points equally unmistakably to an experience at the start of the readers' life as believers: "Recall the former days (*tas proteron hemeras*) when, after you were enlightened (*photisthentes*), you endured a hard struggle with suffering." This call to remembrance occurs shortly after the author's speaking of the readers "receiving the recognition of the truth" (10:26).

Ritual Meals

Although the evidence is less abundant than for baptism, the New Testament supports the fact that early Christians shared meals having a more than ordinary significance. Whether designated the breaking of the bread (Acts 2:46; 10:41; 27:35) or love-feasts (Jude 11) or the Lord's Supper (1 Cor 11:20), such meals involved a sense of participation in Christ (John 6:52–58; 1 Cor 10:16–22), and above all a connection to Jesus' death (1 Cor 11:23–32; Mark 14:22–25; Matt 26:26–29; Luke 22:14–20).

Despite its concern for attendance at common assemblies (10:25), Hebrews offers little or no positive evidence for the sharing of such meals among its readers. The reference in 6:4 to "tasting the heavenly gift and participating in the Holy Spirit" seems at first suggestive, but is more easily understood as applying to baptism (compare 1 Pet 2:3), especially when "tasting the goodness of the word of God and the powers of the age to come" occur in the same sentence. "Tasting" does not mean eating but experiencing. Indeed, Hebrews speaks disparagingly of "food and drink" as among those elements of the old covenant that are not efficacious (9:10), and declares, "it is well that the heart be strengthened by grace, not by foods, which have not benefited their adherents" (13:9).

Yet this same injunction is explained in this fashion: "We have an altar from which those who serve in the tent have no right to eat" (13:10). The form of the clause has the unspoken premise "from which we have the right to eat." Does this suggest, perhaps, a Christian ritual meal exclusive to believers? It is possible, but unlikely, for the following sentences point not to rival ritual meals, but to the believers' joining in the shame and suffering of Jesus "outside the camp" (13:13–14). Indeed, the author's conclusion moves away from the question of meals altogether; the readers are urged to "offer a sacrifice of praise to God, that is, the fruit of the lips that acknowledge his name" (13:15), and this is explicated as not to "neglect to do good and to share what you have, for such sacrifices are pleasing to God" (13:16).

THE WORD

In several New Testament compositions, the word of proclamation has a special importance: it is not only a message of good news from and about God (*euangelion tou theou*, Rom 1:1), and good news from and about the Christ (*euangelion tou christou*, 2 Cor 2:12), but it is a message that has intrinsic power for the transformation of humans (Rom 1:16; 16:25; 1 Cor 15:1–2; 2 Cor 4:4; Gal 3:1–5; 1 Thess 1:5–6; 1 Pet 1:23–25). The "hearing" (*akoe*) of this message is the beginning of faith by which humans are saved (Gal 3:1–5; Rom 10:16–17; 1 Thess 2:13). As a material cause from which spiritual realities result, the word of proclamation can be considered "sacramental" in the broadest sense. In Hebrews, the sacramental dimension of the word is particularly noteworthy.

Critical to Hebrews' argument is the proposition that God speaks continually to God's people. In the past, God spoke in many and fragmentary ways, but in the present, God speaks in a singular and comprehensive fashion in God's Son (1:1–2). The Son is, in a real sense, God's word. We note that the world was created by the word (*rhema*) of God (11:3), and that the Son "upholds the universe by his word (*rhema*) of power" (1:3). In Hebrews, moreover, Scripture is not cited as a written text—it is never introduced as "it is written"—but as prophetic words expressed by the Holy Spirit in the past with significance for the present (see 3:7; 9:8; 10:15). As the author's extended explication of Psalm 95 (LXX) makes clear, God's word continually calls humans to faith: "Today if you hear his voice, do not harden your hearts" (3:1–13). The word God spoke to the people in the wilderness "did not meet with faith in the hearers" (4:2); in contrast, the roll-call of the saints in 11:1–12:3 describes all those in Israel's story who heard with faith, culminating in Jesus, the pioneer and perfecter of faith (12:2).

God's word was spoken through angels in the past (2:2), but in the present, it was "declared at first by the Lord and was attested to us by those who heard him" (2:3). In the author's own time, the leaders of the community "speak the word of God" (13:7). In short, although there is a difference in the agents through whom God speaks—angels, Moses, prophets, Christ, followers of Christ—it is the same word of God, "living and active, sharper than any two-edged sword" (4:11–13). In light of this emphasis, the unswervingly *oral* character of Hebrews itself is significant. The author does not write but speaks, using throughout the first person plural "we," and shifting to direct address for emphasis: "... of which we are speaking" (2:5); "... about which we have much to say, which is hard to explain, because you have become dull of hearing" (5:11); "... though we speak thus" (6:9). It is entirely possible that the author conceives of his discourse, which he calls in 13:22 a "word of exhortation" (*logos tes parakleseos*), as itself continuous with the word of God spoken prophetically through the ages, and calling for the same response of faith.

Hebrews as the Source of Sacramental Imagination

Hebrews has shaped sacramental thinking in the church less through what it has to say about specific ritual actions practiced by early believers than through what might be called a "sacramental imagination," a way of envisaging the world in its relation to God that invites the perception of material realities as bearers of significance beyond themselves. Hebrews accomplishes this first through the way it imagines the construction of the world, then through its portrayal of Christ, and finally through its most distinctive contribution, its understanding of Christ as the great high priest.

Construction of the World

Hebrews' merging of a platonic worldview with biblical cosmology creates a sense of the world in which the invisible is made manifest in the visible, and the visible points beyond itself to the invisible. The empirical does not exhaust being; indeed, what is most real and true in reality lies "beyond the veil" (10:20) of appearances. Such a conception lies at the heart of a sacramental imagination. Thus, the wandering of Israel under Moses in the desert in search for a "rest" in the promised land of Canaan and the reaching of that land under Joshua is contrasted to the movement of believers today, led by Jesus, to the true "rest" for the people as participants in "God's Sabbath Rest" (3:1–4:10). Within the platonic framework, this spiritual "rest" is infinitely more real and better than dwelling in Canaan. Yet, at the same time, the ancient seeking of a rest—or in the case of the patriarchs, seeking a homeland (11:14–16)—provides the terms by which the higher reality might be imagined, and serves as a material pointer to the higher goal.

Similarly, at the climax of its argument in 12:18–24, Hebrews draws a sharp contrast between the theophany at Mount Sinai when Moses revealed the law, and the believers' approach to "Mount Zion, the city of the living God, the heavenly Jerusalem." The description of Mount Sinai emphasizes "what can be touched," the material elements of revelation: "a blazing fire, and darkness, and gloom, and a tempest, and a sound of a trumpet, and a voice" (12:18–19), while the description of the heavenly Jerusalem emphasizes spiritual presence: "angels in festal gathering, the assembly of the first-born who are enrolled in heaven … and to the spirits of just men made perfect" (12:22–23). The "better" encounter with God in the spiritual realm does not, however, work to discredit the earlier, more material encounter, which was not only real in its own terms, but continues to point beyond itself to a higher realization.

Most dramatically, in 9:1–10:22, Hebrews takes the image of the tent of the wilderness—with its horizontal distinction between the outer and inner sanctuary—and turns it vertically into an image for the distinction between the outer court that is earth and the inner sanctuary that is heaven, exploiting the passage in Exodus 25:40 (LXX) that declared the tent built by Moses to be "according to the pattern (*typos*)" shown him on the mountain (Heb 8:5). Hebrews understands this in platonic terms as an actual heavenly sanctuary that is superior to the one in which ancient Israelite worship was conducted. In his description of that Mosaic sanctuary, the author of Hebrews pays particular attention to the distinction between the outer tent and the inner tent "behind the veil" that represented the presence of God among the people, and to which access was granted only to the High Priest once a year on the Day of Atonement, when he sprinkled blood on the Ark of the Covenant and thereby sanctified the people. The architectural distinction between "outer" and "inner" is then turned vertically to represent the distinction between the "outer" material worship on earth, which is necessarily transitory and of limited efficacy, and the "inner" spiritual worship in heaven, which is eternal and of full efficacy. This imaginative turn is the necessary basis for the author's development of Christ as high priest (see "Christ as High Priest," below), but it is also the most striking example of how a platonic worldview married to scriptural cosmology yields a "sacramental" vision of reality: what happens on the empirical plane points to and in some sense participates in a deeper reality "behind the veil" of what is visible and can be touched.

Christology

The portrayal of Jesus in Hebrews is extraordinarily rich, holding together an emphasis equally on the divine and human character of Christ. On one side, he is Son of God (4:14; 6:6; 7:3; 10:29), the divine Son through whom the world was created and who upholds the universe by his word, bearing the glory of God and the stamp of God's nature (1:2–3). He is Lord (1:10; 2:3; 7:14; 13:20) who was for a little while made lower than the angels, but with his exaltation to the right hand of the Father has been crowned with honor and glory (2:9), receiving as inheritance the status that was his before he "came into the world" (10:5). Hebrews is one of the few New Testament compositions to ascribe the title "God" (*theos*) to the Son (1:8; 3:4). A number of Hebrews' distinctive titles for Jesus suggest his approaching humans from the side of God: he is apostle (3:1), cause of salvation (5:9), sanctifier (2:11) the great shepherd of souls (13:20), the builder of the house (3:3), the guarantor (7:22).

On the other side, Hebrews places equal emphasis on Jesus' full share in humanity (2:9). He participates fully in the human condition, being tested like other humans (2:11–18) and sharing in the human experience of weakness (5:2). Although he was Son, and although he came into the world with the exclamation that he had come to do God's will (10:5), he nevertheless needed to learn obedience from the things he suffered in order to become the cause of salvation (5:9). By speaking of the prayers and supplications with loud cries and tears that Jesus offered to God "in the days of his flesh," Hebrews provides a vivid description of his participation in human suffering; the author declares as "fitting, that he for whom and by whom all things exist, in bringing many sons to glory, should make the pioneer of their salvation perfect through suffering" (2:10). The emphasis on the humanity can be seen in Hebrews' frequent use of the simple name "Jesus" (2:9; 3:1; 4:14; 6:20; 7:22; 10:19; 12:24; 13:12, 20), as well as the traditional Jewish designation of Messiah (3:6, 14; 5:5; 6:1; 9:11, 14, 24, 28). Only three times, and each with solemn intonation, does Hebrews use the full title "Jesus Christ" (10:10; 13:8, 21).

Just as one set of distinctive titles captured the divine aspect of Jesus, another set of titles unique to Hebrews points to Jesus' role as representative human: he is minister (8:2), heir (1:2); first-born (1:6), pioneer (2:10; 12:2); perfecter (12:2), and forerunner (6:2). Jesus is preeminently the mediator (8:6; 9:15; 12:24), the one who bridges the gap between the human and the divine. Hebrews is a far distance from the Council of Chalcedon, but the ontological categories of classical Christological development can be applied to this composition in a manner matched only by the Gospel of John. In his very being, Jesus is the place of encounter between the human and the divine.

The Christology of Hebrews, however, is not one of static ontology, but one of dynamic function. The distinctive titles ascribed to Jesus in this composition point to what Jesus does, and in this respect, the greater emphasis falls on his human characteristics, undoubtedly because of the impact made by the experience of Jesus' suffering, death, and resurrection (1:3; 2:9; 6:6; 10:19; 12:2; 13:13): "Since, therefore, the children share in flesh and blood, he himself partook of the same nature, so that through his death he might destroy him who has the power of death, and deliver all those who through fear of death were subject to lifelong bondage" (2:14–15), and "because he himself has suffered and been tempted, he is able to help those who are tempted" (2:18). Two aspects of this functional Christology are especially significant: the importance of change, and the importance of the body and will.

The element of change connects Jesus to the realm of materiality. He "came into the world" (kosmos, 10:5), was made for "a little while" lower than the angels (2:9). He spoke God's word of salvation (2:3). He came a first time to bear the sins of many, and will appear a second time to save those who eagerly await him (9:28). He experienced testing and suffering (2:10–18), underwent a shameful death by crucifixion (12:2), and having thereby made purification for sins, was enthroned at the right hand of the majesty on high as the "heir of all things" (1:1–4). These are external changes. More startling is Hebrews' claim that in his human condition, Jesus underwent internal change, as he was transformed through a process of education. Though he was (by status) God's Son, he learned how to be an obedient (faithful) son through the things he suffered (5:9–10; see 12:3–11). In this sense, Jesus was "pioneer and perfecter of [the] faith" (12:2) shown by all the heroes of Israel's past, since his obedient hearing of God's word made him progressively ever more God's Son.

External change is a consequence of somatic existence; internal change is a function of having freedom of the will. Obedient faith is significant only if disobedience or the refusal to hear is an option (3:7–4:13). Hebrews brings the two together in 10:5–10 through its interpretation of Psalm 40:6–8 (LXX): "Consequently, when Christ came into the world, he said, 'Sacrifice and offerings thou hast not desired, but a body thou hast prepared for me; in burnt offerings and sin offerings thou hast taken no pleasure. Then I said, 'Lo, I have come to do thy will, O God,' as it is written of me in the roll of the book." Hebrews notes, "by that will we have been sanctified through the offering of the body of Jesus Christ once for all" (10:10). Such an intense valorization of the body severely stretches Hebrews' platonic framework, but does not eliminate it, for "behind the veil" of the human experience of Jesus (the outer tent), there was implicitly present the "inner tent" of the divine power. Thus, the humanity of Jesus serves as a sacrament of God's effective presence.

Christ as High Priest

Hebrews' presentation of Jesus as the Great High Priest and of his death and resurrection as a priestly offering constitutes the unique contribution of this composition to early Christianity. The image pulls together all that has been said concerning Hebrews' merging of a platonic worldview and biblical symbolism concerning the cult, as well as the manner in which the actual experience of Christ's death and exaltation reshapes its symbolic world. This dimension of Hebrews has also had the most obvious influence on the development of worship and sacramental life within the church, above all with respect to the understanding of the Eucharist as sacrifice.

It should be made clear at once, however, that Hebrews' argument does not in itself offer support for understanding ministry within the church as a form of priesthood; indeed, Hebrews' point seems to be the opposite, namely that the high-priestly act of Jesus eliminates the need for a formal order of priests and sacrifices within the assembly. Although the development of priestly and sacrificial language in connection with Christian ministry becomes a major feature in the second and third centuries through church orders, and the language of Hebrews inevitably becomes attached to this development, it cannot be said that such appropriation is entirely faithful to the logic of Hebrews itself. The interest of the composition is Christological rather than ecclesiastical.

Hebrews is not unique in its understanding of Jesus' death and resurrection in terms of Jewish sacrifice. Paul says that "Christ our Passover lamb (*pascha*) has been sacrificed" (1 Cor 5:7) and uses the image of the sprinkling of blood on the mercy-seat (*hilasterion*) on the Day of Atonement to speak of Jesus' death (Rom 3:25). Peter refers to the precious blood of Christ that is like that of a lamb (1 Pet 1:21). John declares that the blood of Jesus cleanses us from all sins (1 John 1:7). Revelation portrays Jesus as the Lamb who was slain (Rev 5:12). The Synoptic Gospels, moreover, have Jesus speak of the cup at his last meal with his disciples as the blood of the covenant poured out for many (Matt 26:27). That Jesus' death was that of a sacrificial victim, then, is widely shared; Hebrews' originality among the New Testament writings is to portray Jesus also as the priest who carries out the sacrifice.

Hebrews alone calls Jesus "priest" (10:21), "high priest" (3:1; 4:14; 5:5, 10; 6:20; 7:26; 8:1; 9:11), and a "merciful and faithful high priest" (2:17). The priestly title is combined with the imagery of royal enthronement that runs throughout the composition (1:3, 8, 13; 2:5, 7, 9; 4:16; 7:1, 2; 8:1; 10:12; 12:2, 28). The source for both is Psalm 109:1–4 (LXX). The first verse of this psalm, "The Lord said to my Lord, 'Sit at my right hand until I make your enemies a footstool for your feet'" is a favorite New Testament proof text for the exaltation of Jesus (see Matt 22:44; Mark 12:36; Luke 20:42; Acts 2:34; 1 Cor 15:25) and is cited by Hebrews in 1:13. The author of Hebrews alone, however, exploits the implications of Psalm 109:4: "The Lord has sworn and will not change his mind, 'Thou art a priest forever after the order of Melchizedek'" (Heb 7:17, 21). Jesus is priest as the Lord who has taken his seat at the right hand of God (1:3)—he is Priest-King.

Hebrews announces the theme of Christ as high priest in 4:14, immediately following his exposition of the desert generation that failed to reach God's rest because in their case, the living word did not meet with faith (3:19), and his exhortation to his readers that they strive to enter God's Sabbath rest (4:10–11). The one who will lead them to God's rest is Jesus: "We have a great high priest who has passed through the heavens, Jesus, the Son of God." This announcement makes two things clear at once: a) Jesus' priestly act involves not only his death but above all his exaltation to the right hand of God, and b) Jesus secures access to the "throne of grace" for believers, the very presence of God (4:14–16).

The first stage in the development of Hebrews' argument in 5:1–10 focuses on the way he meets the criteria for a high priest. He can represent humans in relation to God because he shares in human weakness, and has "in every respect been tempted as we are, yet without sin" (4:15; 5:2–3). And, he has been appointed by God: in 5:5–6, Hebrews combines citations from Psalm 2:7 ("Thou art my Son, today I have begotten thee") and Psalm 109:4 ("thou art a priest for ever after the order of Melchizedek"). Hebrews follows this divine certification with the remarkable passage describing Jesus' agony "in the days of his flesh" and the way in which he learned obedience as Son from the things he suffered, thus becoming the "cause of eternal salvation" to all who in turn obey him (5:7–10).

The second stage of the argument is the extensive scriptural comparison between the priesthood of Aaron and the priesthood of Christ (7:1–28) grounded in the story of the encounter between Abraham and Melchizedek, King of Salem, recounted in Genesis 14:18–22. Since the name Melchizedek occurs only in this passage and in Psalm 109:4, the author of Hebrews interprets one passage in light of the other; and since Psalm

109:4 clearly applies to Christ, the Genesis passage can be reread in light of the exaltation of Christ to the presence of God. Two main points emerge from the comparison. The first is that Scripture has no report either of Melchizedek's genealogy or his death: "resembling the Son of God, he continues as a priest forever" (7:3). Jesus is priest "by the power of an indestructible life"; he is "holy, blameless, unstained, separated from sin, exalted above the heavens" (7:26). Jesus' priesthood "after the order of Melchizedek" therefore is eternal in virtue of his resurrection it was "once for all" (7:27), in contrast to the mortal priests of Israel who were required to make sacrifices daily (7:27–28). The second point made by the comparison is that when Abraham offered a tenth of his spoils to Melchizedek, he recognized the superiority of the eternal priesthood according to Melchizedek to the levitical priesthood of Israel that would spring from his loins (7:4–10).

The third stage of Hebrews' argument concerning Christ as high priest builds on the contrast between the external cult of the tent in the wilderness and the internal transformation of the human conscience accomplished by the death and exaltation of Christ (8:1–10:22). Hebrews argues that a change of covenant requires a change in cult: just as the former covenant and its cult focused on the external behavior of the people, so the "new covenant" promised by Jeremiah would focus on the internal transformation of persons, bringing the forgiveness of sins and the knowledge of God (8:8–12). And as the Day of Atonement carried out in the earthly sanctuary was able to accomplish an external "sanctification" of the people through the sprinkling of blood, so must the new covenant have a cultic expression that could sanctify the people internally, "purifying the conscience" (9:14). This is how the death and exaltation of Christ should be understood: "When Christ appeared as a high priest of the good things to come, then through the greater and more perfect tent (not made with hands, that is, not of this creation) he entered once for all into the Holy Place, taking not the blood of goats and bulls, but with his own blood, thus securing an eternal redemption" (9:11–12).

In human terms, Christ's death on the cross was shameful, but he "despised the shame of the cross" because of the joy that lay before him (12:2). His death was not a closure but rather an opening to the very presence and power of God. His priesthood is eternal because he lives now with God: "Christ entered, not into a sanctuary made with hands, a copy of the true one, but into heaven itself, now to appear in the presence of God on our behalf" (9:24). Hebrews magnificently pulls together the themes of pilgrimage and cult: "Therefore, brethren, since we have confidence to enter the sanctuary by the blood of Jesus, by the new and living way which he opened for us through the curtain, that is, through his flesh, and since we have a great priest over the house of God, let us draw near with a true heart in full assurance of faith, with our hearts sprinkled clean from an evil conscience and our bodies washed with pure water" (10:19–22). We notice again in this last statement the valorization of the body: it is "through his flesh" that Jesus enters into the divine presence, and the consequence of his action is that believers have both a purified conscience and "bodies washed with pure water."

CONCLUSION

Although Hebrews is a firm witness to the practice of baptism in early Christianity, and offers an understanding of the word of proclamation that suggests a certain sacramental character, it is of the greatest significance for its distinctive fashioning of the symbolic worlds of Platonism and Scripture in light of the death and resurrection of Jesus in a direction that is unmistakably sacramental. If by sacrament, one means a material thing or act that points beyond itself to a spiritual reality, then Hebrews is the New Testament composition par excellence that invites the perception of the empirical world as a veil, behind which lies the invisible but all-powerful presence of the divine.

SUGGESTED READING

H. W. Attridge (1989); L. T. Johnson (2006); B. Lindars (1991).

BIBLIOGRAPHY

Andriessen, P. (1972), "L'Eucharistie dans l'Épitre aux Hébreux," *Nouvelle Revue Théologique* 3: 275–276.

Attridge, H. W. (1989), *The Epistle to the Hebrews: A Commentary on the Epistle to the Hebrews* Hermeneia (Philadelphia, PA: Fortress Press).

Beasley-Murray, G. R. (1973), *Baptism in the New Testament* (Grand Rapids, MI: Eerdmans).

Cody, A. (1960), *Heavenly Sanctuary and Liturgy in the Epistle to the Hebrews* (Saint Meinrad: Grail).

Dahl, N. A. (1951), "'A New and Living Way': The Approach to God according to Hebrews," *Interpretation* 5: 401–412.

Fitzmyer, J. (2000), "Melchizedek in the MT, LXX, and the NT," *Biblica*, 81: 63–69.

Horton, F. L. (1976), *Melchizedek Tradition through the First Five Centuries of the Christian Era and in the Epistle to the Hebrews*, SNTSMS 30 (Cambridge: Cambridge University Press).

Johnson, L. T. (2006), *Hebrews: A Commentary*, New Testament Library (Louisville, KY: Westminster John Knox).

Johnson, L. T. (2003), "Hebrews' Challenge to Christian Christology and Discipleship," in D. Fleer and D. Bland (eds.), *Preaching Hebrews*, Rochester College Lectures on Preaching 4 (Abilene, TX: ACU Press), 11–28.

Johnson, L. T. (2003), "The Scriptural World of Hebrews," *Interpretation* 57: 237–250.

Johnsson, W. G. (1977–1978), "The Cultus of Hebrews in Twentieth-Century Scholarship," *Expository Times* 89: 104–108.

Johnsson, W. G. (1978), "The Pilgrimage Motif in the Book of Hebrews," *Journal of Biblical Literature* 97: 239–251.

Koester, H. (1962), "'Outside the Camp': Hebrews 13:9–14," *Harvard Theological Review* 55: 299–315.

Leithart, P. J. (2000), "Womb of the World: Baptism and the Priesthood of the New Covenant in Hebrews 10:19–22," *Journal for the Study of the New Testament* 78: 49–65.

Lindars, B. (1991), *The Theology of the Letter to the Hebrews* (Cambridge: Cambridge University Press).

Nairne, A. (1913), *The Epistle of the Priesthood: Studies in the Epistle to the Hebrews* (Edinburgh: T&T Clark).

Nairne, A. (1921), *The Epistle to the Hebrews*, rev. ed. (Cambridge: Cambridge University Press).

Nelson, R. D. (2003), "He Offered Himself: Sacrifice in Hebrews," *Interpretation* 57: 251–265.

Owen, H. P. (1956–1957), "Stages of Ascent in Heb 5:11–6:3," *New Testament Studies* 3: 243–253.

Peterson, D. (1982), *Hebrews and Perfection: An Examination of the Concept of Perfection in the "Epistle to the Hebrews,"* SNTSMS 47 (Cambridge: Cambridge University Press).

Spicq, C. (1952–1953), *L'Épitre aux Hébreux*, 2 vols. (Paris: J. Gabalda).

Swetnam, J. (1989), "Christology and Eucharist in the Epistle to the Hebrews," *Biblica* 70: 74–95.

Thompson, J. W. (1982), *The Beginnings of Christian Philosophy: The Epistle to the Hebrews*, CBQMS 13 (Washington: Catholic Biblical Association of America).

Vanhoye, A. (1986), *Old Testament Priests and the New Priest according to the New Testament*, trans. J. B. Orchard (Petersham: St. Bede's Publications).

Williamson, R. (1963), "Platonism and Hebrews," *Scottish Journal of Theology* 16: 415–424.

Williamson, R. (1974–1975), "The Eucharist and the Epistle to the Hebrews," *New Testament Studies* 21: 300–312.

PART II

PATRISTIC SACRAMENTAL THEOLOGY

CHAPTER 9

SACRAMENTS IN THE PRE-NICENE PERIOD

EVERETT FERGUSON

INTRODUCTION

To speak of sacraments in the pre-Nicene period is somewhat anachronistic. The classic definition of a sacrament, "the visible sign of an invisible grace," is a formulation derived from Augustine (354–430; Cutrone 1999: 741–747), who spoke of sacraments as leading "from visible to invisible, from corporeal to spiritual, from temporal to eternal things" (*Ep.* 55.13), for in them "one thing is seen, another is to be understood" (*Serm.* 272). After a survey of word usage we shall examine what we know for the pre-Nicene period of the seven ceremonies later identified by the Western church as sacraments.

WORD USAGE

Sacramentum

The Latin *sacramentum* meant an oath (Varro, *Ling.* 5.180; Cicero, *Rep.* 2.60; *Caec.* 97), especially the oath taken by the military (Julius Caesar, *Gal.* 61.2; Cicero, *Off.* 1.36), and thus could refer to a solemn obligation (Petronius 9.20; Quintillian, *Decl.* 357). It perhaps referred to an initiation found in Apuleius, *Soc.* 22.

In Christian usage, *sacramentum* could refer to a pagan religious rite (Tertullian, *Apol.* 15.8), but it could also keep the sense of a bond (Cyprian, *Unit. eccl.* 6; *Ep.* 59.6) and refer to a rule or law (Cyprian, *Ep.* 45.1). It is used of something that gives a teaching (Cyprian, *Dom. or.* 9; *Ep.* 63.12), particularly of Old Testament types that are referred to Christian practices (Cyprian, *Test.* 2.16; *Ep.* 69.14). In regard to items which relate to the subject of this article Tertullian is the first to use the term "sacrament" in relation to baptism: "Concerning the sacrament [*sacramento*] of our water" (*Bapt.* 1.1). He describes "sacraments" of baptism, anointing with oil, and the bread of the Eucharist in *Against Marcion* 1.14.3. The baptismal confession of faith is the topic of the phrase about one who "interrogates the sacrament" (*sacramentum interrogat*), that is, "asks the sacramental words" (*Sent. epis.* 1). Cyprian seems to allude to baptism in *Demetrianus* 27 (25): "Let us be registered [enrolled?] by his sacrament and sign." He has a clear reference to the Eucharist in the phrase "sacrament of the cup" (*Laps.* 25).

Mysterion

Sacramentum was the Latin translation of the Greek *mysterion* (μυστήριον), which had a much wider range of application. From its principal usage for the secret rites of initiation in the Greek mystery religions *mysterion* came to be applied to many kinds of secrets or unexplained phenomena: a secret medicine, magical formulae, sexual relations, even philosophical teachings (Plato, *Thaetetus* 156a; *Gorgias* 497c). Jewish apocalyptic literature employed the word for divine secrets, especially those related to eschatology. This usage with reference to God's future plans that only he can make known (cf. Dan 2:28–29) prepared for the New Testament usage, especially in Pauline letters for the previously unknown purposes of God now made known in Christ (Rom 16:25–26; Eph 3:3,4, 9; Col 1:26–27).

Early Christian authors outside the New Testament used *mysterion* in a variety of ways for secrets (Lampe 1965: 891–893 for an elaborate classification). These included secrets in general, including reference to the Christian religion ("Do not expect to be able to learn from a human being the mysteries of the religion of Christians"—*Ep. Diog.* 4.6; cf. 7.1; 8.10); a secret purpose or activity (the virginity of Mary, her giving birth, and death of the Lord—Ignatius, *Eph* 19.1); a revealed secret (that Jesus is Son of God and Christ was a mystery made known to Paul by revelation—Irenaeus, *A. H.* 3.12.9); something obscure, as in an interpretation of Scripture ("concerning the mystery of [Jesus'] birth" in Isaiah 53—Justin, *Dial.* 43.3; the Gnostic interpretation of Jesus' age of thirty [Luke 3:23] as the thirty aeons—Irenaeus, *A. H.* 1.1.3); specifically the hidden meaning of Scripture ("things said and done by the blessed prophet with much intelligence and mystery"—Justin, *Dial.* 112.3; cf. 68.6); items in the Old Testament as a symbol or type (the stone cut out without hands [Dan 2:34] proclaimed in mystery the virgin birth—Justin, *Dial.* 76.1); the purpose of God revealed in an event (Deut 28:66 proclaimed the mystery of the Lord's Crucifixion—Melito, *Pasch.* 61; cf. Justin, *Dial.* 131.2).

Within this broad usage occur references to rites of the church. Although Lampe, in *A Patristic Greek Lexicon*, 892–893, cites no references before the fourth century when such references become frequent, as the triumphant church became less reticent to employ terminology from the pagan world, we may note passages referring to baptism: Clement of Alexandria, *Exhortation* 12.120.1–2 (Marsh 1936: 64–80; Echle 1951: 54–65); Origen, *Commentary on Romans* 3.1.11). A fourth-century writer in describing the second-century Ebionites, but perhaps reflecting the terminology of his own day, uses mystery for their observance of the Eucharist (Epiphanius, *Pan.* 2.30.16.1).

Baptism

Baptism received more discussion in the early centuries than the other ceremonies that came to be given sacramental meaning. It was the central rite of admission to the church (Ferguson 2009; Hellholm 2011). The practice was based on the command of the resurrected Jesus recorded in Matthew 28:18–20 and had the precedent of Jesus' own baptism by John the Baptist (Matt 3:13–17).

Action of Baptism

The earliest non-canonical account of baptism is found in the surviving form of the text of *Didache* 7. An immersion in cold (natural) running water is clearly the preferred mode of baptism. The *Didache* is unique in surviving literature in making an exception in the case of a lack of water, when a representative approximation of immersion was allowed by pouring water over the head three times. The *Didache* agrees with other sources in administering baptism in the name of "Father, Son, and Holy Spirit" (for instance Justin, *1 Apol.* 61.3; Irenaeus, *Dem.* 3; Tertullian, *Adv. Prax.* 26; Firmilian in Cyprian, *Ep.* 75.9.1).

The other occasion when an exception to immersion was allowed was in cases of deathbed baptism. Cyprian, bishop of Carthage (248–258), defended pouring or sprinkling, which he designated "divine abridgements," when "necessity compels and God bestows his mercy," on the basis of instances of aspersion in the Old Testament, provided that "the faith both of the receiver and giver is sound" (*Ep.* 69.12.1–3). From the time of Tertullian, *c.* 200, the normal practice was a triple immersion (*Cor.* 3). Contrary to the *Didache*, Tertullian argued that the Holy Spirit sanctified all water for baptism (*Bapt.* 4.3–4).

Subjects of Baptism

The consistent testimony of early Christian writers required repentance and faith for baptism, as in Justin Martyr *1 Apology* 61.2, 10. The repentance became verbalized in a renunciation of Satan and all his works (Tertullian, *Cor.* 3). Faith was confessed, usually in the form of an affirmative response to the question, "Do you believe?" There is a separate interrogation for Father, Son, and Holy Spirit distributed according to the three immersions in the *Apostolic Tradition* 21.14–18.

The earliest certain reference to infant baptism occurs in Tertullian (*Bapt.* 18), the only known author who explicitly opposed the practice. Inscriptions that give the date of a person's baptism and the date of death suggest that child baptism originated in emergency situations where the person's death was imminent and the family did not want the person to die unbaptized (Ferguson 1979: 37–46). The practice spread as a precaution against an unexpected premature death, but not as rapidly as often supposed, becoming more common in the fourth century but not routine until the fifth and sixth centuries, when the liturgy was adapted for parents or sponsors to speak the renunciation and confession (Saxer 1988: *passim*; Wright 1997).

Meaning/Purpose of Baptism

The practices of sickbed baptism and infant baptism testify to the importance, indeed necessity, attached to receiving baptism. The two most frequently mentioned blessings ascribed to baptism were the forgiveness of sins and the gift of the Holy Spirit (cf. Acts 2:38). A number of texts associate the forgiveness of sins with baptism (e.g. *Barn.* 11.1, 11; Hermas, *Mand.* 4.3.1–4 [31.1–4]; Justin, *1 Apol.* 61.9; Irenaeus, *Dem.* 3; Clement of Alexandria, *Paed.* 1.6.32.1; Tertullian, *Adv. Marc.* 1.28.2–3; Origen, *Comm. Mt.* 16.6). The Holy Spirit was active in baptism and was an abiding gift conferred at baptism (Irenaeus, *Dem.* 42; Tertullian, *Bapt.* 11.3–4; Cyprian, *Ep.* 63.8.3; *Didas.* 26).

The most common image for what occurred at baptism was new birth, or birth from above (cf. John 3:3, 5), or more precisely regeneration. Indeed the language of John 3:5 heavily influenced the baptismal theology of the second and third centuries (e.g. Justin, *1 Apol.* 61.4; Clement of Alexandria, *Ecl. Proph.* 7–8; Tertullian, *Bapt.* 12–13; Origen, *Hom. Lk.* 14.5; Cyprian, *Test.* 1.12; Ps. Clem., *Hom.* 11.26). Another common motif was illumination (Justin, *1 Apol.* 61.12). Clement of Alexandria anticipated later authors in giving a list of the names for baptism that expressed its benefits: regeneration, grace-gift, illumination, perfection, and bath (*Paed.* 1.6.26.2).

These blessings conferred at baptism were the basis for designating it a sacrament. In this regard it is important to note that, in spite of the emphasis on water, the power of baptism was not strictly speaking ascribed to the water but to God through his Spirit acting through the water or at the time of its administration to give regeneration (Theophilus, *Autol.* 2.16; Irenaeus, *Adv. haer.* 3.17.2; *Sent. epis.* 5). The blessings of baptism were based on the benefits of the blood of the cross received by faith; as expressed by Justin, "the saving bath" purifies "by faith through the blood of Christ" (*Dial.* 13.1). The water was related to the cross (*Barn.* 11.1; Justin, *Dial.* 138–"water, faith, and wood"). The salvation offered in baptism is given to faith (Irenaeus, *Adv. haer.* 4.2.7; Clement of Alexandria, *Paed.* 1.6.30.2; Origen, *Comm. Rom.* 5.10.2).

CONFIRMATION

The Latin *confirmatio* began to be used in the fifth century for the ceremony in the Western church for the bestowal of the indwelling of the Holy Spirit separate from the baptismal activity of the Spirit. In the pre-Nicene period this ceremony was part of a unified baptismal practice (Neunheuser 1964; Turner 1993; Johnson 1995).

From the third century, at the latest, the baptismal ceremony was concluded by the administrator laying on hands, anointing the head, and making the sign of the cross, followed by the candidate being led into the assembly of Christians for observance of the Eucharist. Theophilus in the second century explained, "We are called Christians because we are anointed with the oil of God" (*Autol.* 1.12). If Theophilus is speaking literally and not metaphorically (oil standing for the Spirit of God?), he is the first orthodox writer to speak of anointing when one became a Christian. Anointing was prominent in the initiatory rites of Gnostic groups (Irenaeus, *Adv. haer.* 1.21.3–4; cf. *Gospel of Philip* 83 [NHC II 74, 12–15] and *Gospel of Truth* [NHC I 3, 36, 19–20] for Valentinians).

Tertullian gives a sequence of unction, signation, and imposition of hands after the triple immersion (*Carn. res.* 8), but the sequence in the *Apostolic Tradition* 21.21–23 is an anointing of the body by a presbyter, then a bishop's laying on of hands accompanied by a prayer, anointing the head, and signing the forehead. A baptismal anointing is attested by Origen (*Comm. Rom.* 5.8.3; *Hom. Lev.* 6.5.2), presumably after the immersion, but it is not associated by him with the conferring of the Holy Spirit. Cyprian is clearer that the anointing followed the immersion: "The one who is baptized" is also to receive "the chrism [*chrisma*], or anointing [*unctio*]" so that as "the anointed of God" he may receive "the grace of Christ" (*Ep.* 70.2.2). The practice of the church in Syria, however, was to have a pre-baptismal anointing (*Acts of Thomas* 121, 132, 152, 157; *Didas.* 16).

The imposition of hands, usually accompanying prayer, could occur at various times in the preparation for baptism and at the immersion itself, but occasion for theological comment was principally the post-baptismal laying on of hands, associated with the imparting of the Holy Spirit. Cyprian said that hands were laid upon the person baptized in the name of Christ "so that he may receive the Holy Spirit" (*Ep.* 74.5.1). The unknown author of the treatise *On Rebaptism* opposed Cyprian's insistence that those who had been baptized in a heretical or schismatic group had to be rebaptized on coming to the catholic church, and instead argued that they could be admitted to the church by the laying on of hands of the bishop to complete the absence of the Holy Spirit in the other group (*Rebapt.* 10). He thus concurred with Cyprian on the association of imposition of hands with the gift of the Holy Spirit. The biblical precedent for this view was the imparting of the Spirit by the laying on of hands by apostles (Acts 8:17).

It is not clear whether making the sign of the cross was a separate act or was included in the anointing or the laying on of hands. Cyprian may treat the signing as distinct in significance, but his statements may also be explanatory of the significance of imparting the Spirit. In arguing for the baptism of those converted from a heretical or schismatic church, Cyprian reasoned if they could receive baptism and forgiveness of sins with a "perverted faith," they could have received the Holy Spirit too and "there is no need for hands to be laid upon him so as to receive the Spirit and be sealed [*signetur*]" (*Ep.* 73.6.2). He adds, "By our prayers and by the laying on of hands those who are baptized in the church receive the Holy Spirit and are perfected with the Lord's seal" (*Ep.* 73.9.2).

In giving a theological meaning to the different aspects of the baptismal ceremony, Tertullian separated the coming of the Spirit from baptism and thereby anticipated the development of confirmation as a separate sacrament in the Western church. "Not that the Holy Spirit is given to us in the water, but that in the water we are made clean by the action of the angel and made ready for the Holy Spirit" (Tertullian, *Bapt.* 6.1). After the anointing "follows the laying on of the hand in benediction, inviting and welcoming the Holy Spirit" (*Bapt.* 8.1).

During the early Middle Ages infant baptism by rural priests was often separated by an extended period of time before urban-based bishops could complete the initiation by anointing, laying on of hands, and signing with the cross. This led to the defining of the latter acts as a separate sacrament of confirmation. The separation of the immersions from the anointing and imposition of hands did not occur in the Eastern churches, where the priest could perform all the actions and a unified rite was maintained.

EUCHARIST

Eucharist (εὐχαριστία, 'thanksgiving'), which is also known as the Lord's Supper (1 Cor 11:20), communion (1 Cor 10:10:16), and breaking of bread (Acts 2:42), was from the second century the common name for the sharing of bread and wine in the weekly assembly of the church (Rordorf 1978; Kilmartin and Daly 1998; Ferguson 1999, 79–132; and Johnson 2012).

Relation to a Meal

The basis for eating bread and drinking from a cup of wine in memory of Jesus (1 Cor 11:23–26) was Jesus' words at his Last Supper with his disciples, in the context of the Jewish Passover (Matt 26:17–30 and *par.*). This meal setting was the occasion for disorders at the observance of the Lord's Supper at Corinth (1 Cor 11:17–34). The earliest non-canonical instructions for the Eucharist in *Didache* 9–10 in its surviving form seemingly preserves its meal context. It gives a prayer over the cup, a prayer for the breaking of bread, a full meal, and a concluding thanksgiving. The last prayer offers thanksgiving to God as the mighty Creator who gives food and drink, both physical and spiritual, and offers a petition for the church and for the coming of the Lord. It is notable that no reference is made to the death and resurrection of Jesus but rather an emphasis on receiving knowledge and immortality. Another unusual feature is the order of the cup preceding the bread.

Very early there was a separation of the partaking of the bread and cup from a meal, for other accounts make no mention of a meal. The meal had a separate development as the *agape* ("love feast"), a fellowship and charity meal, distinct from the commemoration of the Lord in the Eucharist (Ferguson 1999: 125–132).

Frequency

The Eucharist was the central act in the weekly assembly of Christians. It was apparently long since separated from a meal in the account Justin Martyr gave of the worship assembly in the mid-second century: "On the day called Sunday there is a gathering together in the same place of all who live in a city or a rural district." After Scripture reading, sermon, and prayer, bread and wine mixed with water were presented. The president offered thanksgiving according to his ability, and the people responded with "Amen." A distribution and participation of the elements for which thanks had been given was made to each person, and to those who were not present it was sent by the deacons (1 *Apol.* 67). Then there was the collection of the contribution. Justin gives a parallel account of the Eucharist as concluding the baptismal service, itself likely occurring on a Sunday as well. A kiss of peace preceded the taking of the bread and mixed cup. The prayer of thanksgiving offered "praise and glory to the Father of all through the name of his Son and of the Holy Spirit ... for the gifts we were counted worthy to receive from him" (1 Apol. 65).

The early emphasis was on meeting for the Eucharist every Sunday. "Having earlier confessed your sins so that your sacrifice may be pure, come together each Lord's day, break bread, and give thanks" (Did.14.1). Early evidence is slim to non-existent for taking the Eucharist on other days of the week, but from the late third century there seems to have been at places an extension of the Sunday meeting back to Saturday. The taking of the Eucharist on other days of the week and its separation from the assembly of the church are later developments.

Meaning of the Eucharist

From the name itself it is evident that the theme of thanksgiving (verb form in Mark 14:23) was preeminent. The thanksgiving praised God for the gifts of creation and of redemption (Justin, 1 Apol. 13; 65.3; Dial. 41.1; Ap. Trad. 4.4–13). Also prominent was the theme of remembrance, or memorial. This was shown by the incorporation into the eucharistic prayer of the words of institution according to 1 Corinthians 11:24–25 (Ap. Trad. 4.9–10). The Eucharist not only remembered the death and resurrection of Jesus but also had an eschatological aspect (Luke 22:18; 1 Cor 11:26), looking forward to the heavenly kingdom (Did. 9.4; 10.5; cf. Ap. Trad. 4.8).

Ignatius, in opposing schism, emphasized the theme of the unity of the church (1 Cor 10:16–17): "Be careful to employ one eucharist, for there is one flesh of our Lord Jesus Christ and one cup for unity with his blood, one altar" (Philad. 4; cf. Ap. Trad. 4.12). In order to achieve this, Ignatius placed administration of the Eucharist under the bishop: "Let that be considered a dependable eucharist which is done by the bishop or by whomever he appoints" (Smyrn. 8). The concern was for unity, not priestly validity.

Eucharist as Sacrifice

The language of sacrifice was integral to religions of the ancient world, so its application to Christian activities was natural (Ferguson 1980: 1151–1189 and specifically on the Eucharist, Hanson 1979). Malachi 1:11 ("My name has been glorified among the nations, and in every place incense and a pure sacrifice are offered in my name" [old Greek translation]) was the most quoted eucharistic text in the second century. It is cited already in Didache 14 as warrant for requiring reconciliation of those having quarrels "that your sacrifice may not be defiled."

Justin associated the thanksgiving for the bread and cup with a thank-offering: after quoting Malachi 1:10–12, Justin explains, "He speaks beforehand concerning us Gentiles who in every place offer sacrifices to him, that is the bread of the thanksgiving [Eucharist] and the cup similarly of the thanksgiving [Eucharist]" (Dial. 41.3), and again after referring to the Malachi passage he declares, "I also agree that prayers and thanksgivings performed by worthy persons are the only sacrifices perfect and well pleasing to God" and "these alone Christians undertake to make, even at the memorial of their solid and liquid food in which also is brought to mind the sufferings that the Son of God endured" (*Dial.* 117.2–3). Irenaeus, in his polemic against the Gnostic disparagement of material creation, extended the thank-offering motif by applying it to first fruits. The church "in the whole world," by offering the bread and cup, confessed to be the body and blood of Jesus, "offers to God ... the first fruits of his own gifts in the new covenant," followed by a quotation of Malachi 1:10–11 (*A. H.* 4.17.5).

Cyprian, in a bold step anticipating later developments, combined the ideas of a sacrifice of the Eucharist and a real presence of Christ in the elements. In arguing for the necessity of wine, as well as water, in the Eucharist he said, "And because we make mention of his passion in all sacrifices (for the Lord's passion is the sacrifice which we offer), we ought to do nothing else than what he did [offer wine and not water alone]" (*Ep.* 63.17). In the fourth century sacrificial ideas were expanded in some circles from thanksgiving to a sacrifice of propitiation and from offering the elements to offering Christ crucified, ideas that were to have a great development in the medieval West (Ferguson 1999: 115–123, esp. 116–117, 120–121).

Real Presence of Christ in the Elements

The biblical basis for a doctrine of the real presence was Jesus' words of institution, concerning the bread, "This is my body," and concerning the cup, "This is my blood" (Matt 26:27–28), supported by the eucharistic interpretation of Jesus' discourse on the bread of life in John 6 (esp. vv. 48–56) (for contrasting views, see MacDonald 1930; Crockett 1989). At the Last Supper Jesus performed an act of prophetic symbolism in offering the bread and cup to his disciples (Nock 1964: 125). When the gospel moved from a Semitic setting, in which his words had a functional meaning, into a Greek context that thought in terms of substances, early Christian authors struggled with their meaning (Ferguson 1997: 21–45). Ignatius, in opposing those who claimed that Jesus only seemed to have a real human body, made a simple identification of the bread and wine with his flesh and blood and so the conveyers of spiritual health (*Smyrn.* 7; *Eph.* 20). Justin's ambiguous language has been subject to various interpretations:

> We receive these elements not as common bread and common drink. In the same manner as our Savior Jesus Christ was made flesh through the word of God and had flesh and blood for our salvation, even so we were taught that the food for which thanks have been given through the prayer of the word that is from him and from which our blood and flesh are nourished according to the bodily processes is the flesh and blood of that Jesus who was made flesh. (*1 Apol.* 66.2)

Elsewhere Justin does not use such realist language but calls the bread and wine a "memorial" of the body and blood (*Dial.* 70), so his paralleling of the Incarnation may not be intended to convey a comparable change in the substance of the elements and so not go beyond a change in function of the elements that carried a significant benefit. This change in function was effected by the "prayer of the *logos*." Did this refer to the words of institution by Jesus or an invocation of the divine Logos to come on the elements? More likely the phrase refers to a prayer formula that Justin thought derived from Jesus or the pattern of thanksgiving provided by Jesus.

Irenaeus stressed the reality of the physical elements in the Eucharist and the real body and blood of Jesus as a counter to Gnostic depreciation of material creation. He said his opponents were inconsistent to say the bread was the body of the Lord and the cup his blood, if they did not grant that he is the Son of the Creator of the world and if they claimed that the flesh that is nourished from the body of the Lord "comes to corruption and does not partake of life" (*A. H.* 4.18.4; cf. 5.2.2–3). Instead of speaking of a change in regard to the elements, he speaks of the addition of a new reality to them. By the invocation of God, the bread now consists of a heavenly as well as an earthly reality so that those who partake "have the hope of the resurrection to eternity" (*A. H.* 4.18.5). Irenaeus affirmed that the bread and wine remained material elements, but when consecrated they became capable of conveying "the gift of God which is eternal life" (*A. H.* 4.18.5).

Other authors modified the simple equation of the elements with the body and blood. Latin authors used the language of "figure" (*figura*). Tertullian explained that "by saying, 'This is my body,' Jesus meant, 'figure of my body,'" but "there would not have been a figure unless there was a true body" (*Adv. Marc.* 4.40). Cyprian said that by the wine "the blood of Christ is shown forth" (*Ep.* 63.2). Greek authors used the language of "symbol" or "allegory" to present the distinction yet relation between the elements and what they symbolized (Clement of Alexandria, *Paed.* 2.2.19–20; Origen, *Comm. Mt.* 11.14; *Hom. Lev.* 7.5). For the ancients a figure or symbol contained the power of what it represented to a greater extent than modern usage of these words might suggest.

In the fourth century some writers spoke more explicitly of a literal change in the elements, going beyond a change in their purpose or effects (Cyril of Jerusalem, *Cat. mys.*1.7; 4.4; 5.7; Ambrose, *Sacram.* 4.4.14–4.5.23). In the later Middle Ages the Western church developed transubstantiation as the philosophical explanation of how the change was effected.

The idea of a real presence in the bread and wine was a key ingredient in understanding the Eucharist as a sacrament that conveyed or symbolized spiritual nourishment and spiritual benefits.

PENANCE

The word penance derives from the Latin *paenitentia* ("penitence"), itself the translation of the Greek μετάνοια (*metanoia*, repentance, "change of mind"). Penance refers to the rites for discipline leading to forgiveness of sins committed after baptism (Rahner 1982; Ferguson 1994: 81–100; Firey 2008). The New Testament called for repentance, confession of sin, and prayer (Acts 8:22; Jas 5:16; 1 John 1:9) by persons involved in sin after their conversion to Christ.

Forgiveness of Post-Baptismal Sin

The *Shepherd of Hermas* was much concerned with the problem of post-baptismal sins, for some taught that there was no repentance except the baptismal repentance (*Mand.* 4.3.1–2 [31.1–2]). The ideal was to live sinlessly, yet the heavenly Shepherd revealed to

Hermas that there was only one repentance after baptism, and thus one who sinned repeatedly had no recourse (*Mand.* 4.3.6 [31.6]; cf. *Vis.* 2.2.4-5 [6.4–5]). One must demonstrate repentance by being humble and afflicting the soul (*Sim.* 7.4 [66.4]). Clement of Alexandria concurred that there was only one post-baptismal repentance, a "second repentance" (*Str.* 2.13.56.1–58.1). Repentance meant to cease from one's sins, pray, and fast (*Q.D.S.* 39–42). The discipline of the church included being excluded from communion. The common word in Greek for the discipline that secured forgiveness and readmission to the church was ἐξομολόγησις (*exomologesis*, "confession"). This word called attention to the central importance of a public acknowledgement of the sin(s).

Public Humiliation

Irenaeus referred to the public confession accompanied by mourning and weeping that some were ashamed to make (*A.H.* 1.13.5–7). A fuller account is reported by Eusebius about Natalius restored from a heresy:

> [H]e arose early in the morning and put on sackcloth and sprinkled himself with ashes and with much haste and tears he fell down at the feet of Zephyrinus the bishop [of Rome]. Rolling at the feet of the clergy and laity, he moved with his tears the compassionate church of the merciful Christ. Although he made many petitions and showed the wounds from the blows he had received [from angels], he was scarcely admitted to fellowship. (*H.E.* 5.28.10–12)

The fullest account comes from Tertullian, who wrote the earliest treatise *On Repentance*. He explained that the "second plank" of salvation was "most often expressed by the Greek term *exomologēsis*, by which we confess our transgressions to the Lord." He then elaborates on the public humiliation as a behavior that brings mercy by exchanging severe treatment for one's sins: to dress in sackcloth and ashes, to lament night and day, to fast and pray, to fall prostrate before the elders of the church, and to beg the church to make supplications on one's behalf (*Paen.* 9). There are instances in the third century of a private confession before the bishop (Cyprian, *Laps.* 28).

Third-Century Controversies

Tertullian later took the position that there was no forgiveness on earth or reconciliation to the church for those guilty of the mortal sins of murder, idolatry, and adultery (*Pud.* 5; 7; 9; 12; 22). Lesser sins could be pardoned by the bishop, but greater ones were remitted by God alone (*Pud.* 18). Origen listed seven items that bring forgiveness of sins under the gospel, the last of which was repentance and confession to a priest (*Hom. Lev.* 2). Others placed no limits on the sins that the church could forgive (Dionysius of Corinth in Eusebius, *H.E.* 4.23.6). All agreed that martyrdom brought a forgiveness of all sins (Tertullian, *Bapt.* 16.2; Origen, *Mart.* 30; *attr.* Hippolytus, *Ap. Trad.* 1.19).

The church at Rome experienced two schisms related to the reconciliation of penitents. The lenient practice of Callistus in regard to those guilty of sexual sins was one factor in Hippolytus separating from the main body of the church (*Ref. Haer.* 9.7). A more lasting schism was led by Novatian, who opposed reconciling to the church those who offered pagan sacrifice at the command of emperor Decius in contrast to the policy adopted by bishop Cornelius (Eusebius, *H.E.* 6.43).

The persecution under Decius left the church in North Africa in disarray, and in its aftermath Cyprian had to contend with rigorists who denied reconciliation to those who apostatized or compromised in the persecution and with those who readily forgave them. Cyprian took a middle course of adjusting the discipline to the degree of offense. He regularized the process of reconciliation, beginning with acts to demonstrate contrition, public confession before the church, and concluding with restoration to "the peace of the church" by laying on of the bishop's hand and prayer (*Laps.* 16; *Epp.* 4;15–17; 31; cf. *Didas.* 7 and 10 for the church in Syria). He maintained the control of discipline and restoration to the church under the bishop. In the Greek church the process of returning to the communion of the church was regularized in the *Canonical Epistle* 11 attributed to Gregory Thaumaturgus.

Interpretation

The basis for the sacramental interpretation of penance in the Middle Ages was laid by the understanding of the penitential acts as a satisfaction for sins. Forgiveness of sins in baptism was by the grace of God, but one had to make atonement for sins committed after baptism. Clement of Alexandria made the distinction that "the deeds done before baptism are remitted, and those done after are purged" (*Str.* 4.24.154.3). Tertullian especially developed the propitiatory understanding of the acts of repentance and confession. The afflictions of one's public humiliation replaced the punishments for sin in the afterlife:

> All these things *exomologēsis* performs so that it may make repentance acceptable, so that it may honor God by the fear of danger, so that by itself pronouncing judgment on the sinner may act in place of God's wrath and by temporal afflictions may (I do not say frustrate but) expunge eternal punishments.... [W]hen you prostrate yourself at the brethren's knees … you are entreating Christ. Likewise when they shed tears over you, Christ is suffering, Christ is supplicating the Father. (*Paen.* 9; 10)

Tertullian paralleled "second repentance" with baptismal repentance, so the penitential discipline could be described as a "second baptism" that brought forgiveness of sins.

ORDINATION

Ordinatio was the Latin equivalent of the Greek χειροτονία (*cheirotonia*), which from its classical usage for an election by a show of hands came in the Hellenistic age to mean a selection by whatever means and then in Christian usage ordination, particularly the ceremony of installation in a church office (Ferguson 1960–1961; Bradshaw 1990; Patsavos 2007). Various methods of selection were employed in the early church: most often election by the people (*Did.* 15; *1 Clem.* 44; Cyprian, *Ep.* 59.5–6; 67.3), selection by the clergy (Cyprian, *Ep.* 55.8; *Ap. Trad.* 2.2), or appointment by a bishop (*Didas.* 9). Wherever the initiative lay, agreement by the people, clergy, and representative bishops was expected and taken as an indication of the divine choice (Cyprian, *Ep.* 55.8–9, 68.2).

Procedures in Ordination

The *Apostolic Tradition* gave the right of ordination to a bishop, but presbyters joined in giving their blessing (8.1, 9.6, 2.3–4). That document provided for appointment to the order of widows by giving the name (10), a reader by giving him the "book of the apostle" (11), a virgin by her choice (12), a subdeacon by giving the name (13).

For the major orders of bishop, presbyter, and deacon the uniform testimony is to ordination by laying on of hands with an accompanying prayer (*Ap. Trad.* 2–3, 7–8). This practice was already common in New Testament times (Acts 6:6; 13:1–3; 1 Tim 4:14). The earliest non-canonical reference to the imposition of hands in appointment is *Acts of Peter* 10, where Jesus appointed Peter as an apostle by laying on of hands, something not mentioned in the Bible, but indicative that such was so common in ordination that the author could not think of conferring an office in the church without this act (for later references cf. Cyprian, *Ep.* 67.5; Ps. Clem., *Ep. ad Jac.* 19.1).

Significance of Ordination

The ordination prayers praised God as the one who gives leaders to his people, asked for the divine favor upon the recipient in performing the duties for which he was being ordained, and appealed to biblical precedents for the office to which one was appointed (Gy 1979). The laying on of hands signified conferring a blessing, and the accompanying prayer spelled out the blessing intended (Ferguson 1975; Coyle 1989). Since one of the blessings that might be imparted was the Holy Spirit, and the prayer at ordination invoked the Holy Spirit on the one ordained, fourth-century writers saw the special meaning of ordination as the imparting of the Holy Spirit, and thus a sacramental change in the recipient (Gregory of Nazianzus, *Or.* 43.78; Gregory of Nyssa, *Bapt. Chr.* PG 46.581D).

Marriage

Marriage has been the most problematic of the sacraments, since it lacks specific institution by Christ or the apostles and has no commonly recognized outward sign. The reference to a "great mystery" in reference to marriage in Ephesians 5:32 has no sacramental meaning but refers to the secret meaning of man and woman becoming "one flesh" as comparable to the union of Christ and the church.

The church's involvement in marriages between Christians is found early in the instruction of Ignatius: "It is right for men and women who marry to be united with the consent of the bishop that the marriage may be according to the Lord and not according to lust" (*Polyc.* 5.2– Stevenson 1983; Hunter 1992). Athenagoras implies definite Christian regulations for marriage when he speaks of being married "according to the laws we have laid down, with a view to nothing more than procreation" (*Leg.* 33). As was the case in Roman law, presumably for Christians mutual consent constituted marriage.

A nuptial blessing is the most often indicated aspect of a Christian marriage ceremony. Tertullian appears to give a Christianized version of the elements in a Roman wedding:

> How shall we ever be able adequately to describe the happiness of that marriage which the Church arranges, the Sacrifice strengthens, upon which the blessing sets a seal, at which angels are present as witnesses, and to which the Father gives his consent? (*Ad Ux.* 2.8.6; Stevenson 1983: 17).

The church here takes the place of the relative or friend who arranged the marriage. The sacrifice, or oblation, would refer to the Eucharist as a counterpart of the sacrifice offered by the groom and bride on the morning of the wedding, and the blessing replaces the seal placed on the marriage contract. The angels serve the function of the household gods, and the heavenly Father gives the consent given by an earthly father to the marriage (Stevenson 1983: 18).

In other works Tertullian alludes to specific actions at the wedding: wearing a veil, being kissed, and holding hands (*Or.* 22.9–10; *Vel. virg.* 11.5).

In the *Acts of Thomas* the apostle attends a wedding, sings a bridal song, prays for the bridal pair, and lays his hands on them in blessing (4–10).

The development of a Christian wedding liturgy prepared for the sacramental interpretation of marriage, but that had to wait until later in the Middle Ages.

ANOINTING THE SICK 12

Roman Catholics have adopted "Anointing of the Sick" as the title for the rite formerly known as "extreme unction" (last anointing or last rites). The ceremony includes anointing the five senses of the body with oil consecrated by a bishop, laying on of hands, and prayer for healing of body and for forgiveness of sins (Porter 1956; Poschmann 1964).

The biblical basis for the rite is James 5:14–15 (for oil in healing cf. Mark 6:13; Luke 10:34). Origen is the first to quote James 5:14–15, adding the phrase that the presbyters "place their hands on him," but he applies the passage to penance as the seventh means of forgiveness of sins mentioned in New Testament texts (*Hom. Lev.* 2.4). The *Apostolic Tradition* presents a sample prayer of thanks for oil offered to the church: "As, sanctifying this oil, you give, God, health to those using and receiving [it], whence you have anointed kings, priests, and prophets, so also may it afford strengthening to all tasting [it] and health to all using it" (5; trans. in Bradshaw 2002: 50). The document provides for recognition of those with the gift of healing, but no hand is laid on them for ordination (14).

Anointing the sick and dying was first identified as a sacrament in the ninth century and numbered among the seven sacraments by Peter Lombard in the twelfth.

The early church believed that God was active in administering his grace and could use material elements in doing so but would have denied any automatic connection between grace and the means of grace.

SUGGESTED READING

L. J. Johnson (2009); M. E. Johnson (2012); P. F. Palmer (1955); P. F. Palmer (1960).

BIBLIOGRAPHY

Bradshaw P. F. (1990), *Ordination Rites of the Ancient Churches of East and West* (New York: Pueblo).

Bradshaw, P. F. et al. (2002), *The Apostolic Tradition: A Commentary* (Minneapolis, MN: Fortress).

Bradshaw, P. F. and M. E. Johnson (2012), *The Eucharistic Liturgies: Their Evolution and Interpretation* (Collegeville, MN: Liturgical Press).

Coyle, K. (1989), "The Laying on of Hands as Conferral of the Spirit: Some Problems and a Possible Solution," *Studia Patristica* 18.2: 339–353.

Crockett, W. R. (1989), *Eucharist: Symbol of Transformation* (New York: Pueblo).

Cutrone, E. J. (1999), "Sacraments," in Allan D. Fitzgerald (ed.), *Augustine through the Ages* (Grand Rapids, MI: Eerdmans), 741–747.

Echle, H. A. (1951), "Sacramental Initiation as a Christian Mystery Initiation according to Clement of Alexandria," in A. Mayer et al. (eds.), *Vom Christliche Mysterium* (Düsseldorf), 54–65.

Ferguson, E. (1960-1), "Ordination in the Ancient Church, 1–4," *Restoration Quarterly* 4 [1960]: 117–138; 5 [1961]:17–32, 67–82, 130–146.

Ferguson, E. (1975), "The Laying on of Hands: Its Significance in Ordination," *Journal of Theological Studies* 26: 1–12.

Ferguson, E. (1979), "Inscriptions and the Origin of Infant Baptism," *Journal of Theological Studies*, n.s. 30: 37–46.

Ferguson, E. (1980), "Spiritual Sacrifice in Early Christianity and Its Environment," in H. Temporini and W. Haase (eds.), *Aufstieg und Niedergang der römischen Welt* (Berlin: Walter de Gruyter), II.23.1, 1151–1189.

Ferguson, E. (1994), "Early Church Penance," *Restoration Quarterly* 36: 81–100.

Ferguson, E. (1997), "The Lord's Supper in Church History: The Early Church Through the Medieval Period," in Dale Stoffer (ed.), *The Lord's Supper: Believers Church Perspectives* (Scottdale, PA: Herald Press), 21–45.

Ferguson, E. (1999), *Early Christians Speak*, 3rd ed. (Abilene, TX: ACU Press), 79–132.

Ferguson, E. (2009), *Baptism in the Early Church: History, Theology, and Liturgy in the First Five Centuries* (Grand Rapids, MI: Eerdmans).

Firey, A. (ed.) (2008), *A New History of Penance* (Leiden: Brill).

Gy, P.-M. (1979), "Ancient Ordination Prayers," *Studia Liturgica* 13: 70–93.

Hanson, R. P. C. (1979), *Eucharistic Offering in the Early Church* (Bramcote, Notts.: Grove).

Hellholm, D., et al. (eds.) (2011), *Ablution, Initiation, and Baptism* (Berlin: De Gruyter).

Hunter, D. G. (ed. and trans.) (1992), *Marriage in the Early Church* (Minneapolis, MN: Fortress).

Johnson, L. J. (2009), *Worship in the Early Church: An Anthology of Historical Sources*, 4 vols. (Collegeville, MN: Liturgical Press).

Johnson, M. E., ed. (2012), *Sacraments and Worship* (Louisville, KY: Westminster John Knox).

Johnson, M. E. (ed.) (1995), *Living Water, Sealing Spirit: Readings on Christian Initiation* (Collegeville, MN: Liturgical Press).

Kilmartin, E. J. and R. J. Daly (1998), *The Eucharist in the West: History and Theology* (Collegeville. MN: Liturgical Press).

Lampe, G. E. H. (ed.) (1965), *A Patristic Greek Lexicon* (Oxford: Clarendon), 891–893.

MacDonald, A. J. (ed.) (1930), *The Evangelical Doctrine of Holy Communion* (Cambridge: W. Heffer & Sons).

Marsh, H. G. (1936), "The Use of MUSTHRION in the Writings of Clement of Alexandria with Special Reference to His Sacramental Doctrine," *Journal of Theological Studies* 37: 64–80.

Neunheuser, B. (1964), *Baptism and Confirmation* (New York: Herder & Herder).

Nock, A. D. (1964), "Hellenistic Mysteries and Christian Sacraments," in *Early Gentile Christianity and its Hellenistic Background* (New York: Harper Torchbook), 109–145.

Palmer, P. F. (1955), *Sacraments and Worship: Liturgy and Doctrinal Development of Baptism, Confirmation, and Eucharist* (Westminster, MD: Newman).

Palmer, P. F. (1960), *Sacraments and Forgiveness: Historical and Doctrinal Development of Penance, Extreme Unction and Indulgences* (Westminster, MD: Newman).

Patsavos, L. J. (2007), *A Noble Task: Entry into the Clergy in the First Five Centuries* (Brookline, MA: Holy Cross Orthodox Press).

Porter, H. B. (1956), "The Origin of the Medieval Rite for Anointing the Sick or Dying," *Journal of Theological Studies*, n.s. 7: 211–225.

Poschmann, B. (1964), *Penance and Anointing of the Sick* (London: Burns and Oates), 234–257.

Rahner, K. (1982), *Penance in the Early Church* (New York: Crossroad).

Rordorf, W., et al. (1978), *The Eucharist of the Early Christians* (New York: Pueblo).

Saxer, V. (1988), *Les rites de l'initiation chrétienne du IIe au VIe siècle: Esquisse historiqe et signification d'après leur principaux témoins* (Spoleto: Centro italiano di studi sull'alto medioevo).

Stevenson, K. (1983), *Nuptial Blessing: A Study of Christian Marriage Rites* (New York: Oxford University Press).

Turner, P. (1993), *Sources of Confirmation: From the Fathers Through the Reformers* (Collegeville, MN: Liturgical Press).

Wright, D. F. (1997), "At What Ages Were People Baptized in the Early Centuries?" *Studia Patristica* 30: 389–394.

CHAPTER 10

....

SACRAMENTS IN THE FOURTH CENTURY

....

KHALED ANATOLIOS

THE fourth-century church did not analyze its sacramental life by specifying seven sacraments, as would be done later in Western Christianity. To avoid anachronism, an account of sacraments in the fourth century should focus on the two "mysteries" which fourth-century Christians did identify as the foundational events of Christian worship: baptism and Eucharist. Recent scholarship has contributed greatly to our understanding of the forms and interpretation of these mysteries in the early church, and has acknowledged the influence of the doctrinal debates of the fourth century on their content and understanding. Yet, there is still a great need for closer analysis with respect to the mutual influence of *lex orandi* and *lex credendi* in the fourth century, which witnessed a momentous consolidation of both the liturgical and creedal aspects of the Christian life. This chapter will present an overview of both the practice and interpretation of the sacraments of baptism and Eucharist in the fourth century, with special attention to the interaction between sacramental experience and doctrinal debate in this period.

CHRISTIAN WORSHIP IN CONFLICT: THE TRINITARIAN DEBATES OF THE FOURTH CENTURY

....

In the fourth century, as today, Christians interpreted the sacraments as a means of rendering worship to God and of transforming human life by bringing it under the influence of divine salvific agency. But, in the fourth century, both the worship of God and the content of human salvation were directly implicated in the tumultuous conflicts over how the confession of Jesus as Lord and Savior was to be related to the confession of the one God. The eruption of this controversy, in around 318, was instigated by the disagreement between Arius, an Egyptian presbyter, and his bishop, Alexander of Alexandria, over the ontological status of Christ's divinity. Arius asserted that the divine Word was created by the one uncaused God as the first and greatest of creatures. Even though he was graced with the title of "Lord" and "God" and was the agent by which other creatures were brought into being, nevertheless he was still, like other creatures, himself brought into being from nothing. Conversely, Alexander insisted that the Son's being was eternally correlative with that of the Father, and the Father-Son relation itself was constitutive of the perfection of divine being. The Council of Nicaea, in 325, endorsed Alexander's position and anathematized Arius'. While the above cursory summary is likely to be well known to students and scholars of ancient Christianity, it is still not sufficiently appreciated that this was also a disagreement about the character and inner content of Christian worship. In Arius' *Thalia*, there are strong hints that he considers the proper object of Christian worship to be the one God, while the Word is a facilitator of worship to the one God, rather than himself being an object of worship: "We worship the eternal one through the one who came to be in time" (Athanasius, *Syn.* 15). Such an understanding becomes more explicit in the clarification made by one of Arius' supporters, Theognis of Nicaea, who explained that worship is properly directed "to the Father alone," whereas "we reverence (*veneramur*) the Son, because we are certain that his glory ascends to the Father" (Bardy 1936: 212). On the other hand, Alexander justified his excommunication of Arius by asserting that his doctrine is not compatible with "the Church which worships the divinity of Christ" (Opitz 1936: 14:6). Around the middle of the fourth century, these debates also extended to an explicit consideration of the role of the Spirit in Christian worship. In the Council of Constantinople, in 381, the affirmation of the divinity of the Spirit was declared not in the Nicene language of *homoousios* but directly in terms of worship: the Holy Spirit is "co-worshipped and co-glorified with the Father and the Son."

A persistent underlying question in the Trinitarian debates of the fourth century was that of identifying the kind of transformation which the believer can expect in the performance of Christian worship. Defenders of the full divinity of the Son and Spirit tended to extend the notion of the shareability of the divine being among Father, Son, and Spirit to a conception of a graced human participation in divine life, or "deification." Participation in the sacraments of baptism and Eucharist was understood to be a vital and necessary means for this graced deification. On the other hand, those who rejected an ontological continuity within the Trinity also shied from the notion of humanity's sharing in divine life, and characterized sacramental participation in other scriptural terms, such as glorifying God and acquiring knowledge of God. While all these questions were taken up in argumentative treatises, their doctrinal treatment was both informed by and in turn actively transformed both the practice and interpretation of Christian worship. The analysis of the practice and interpretation of the rites of baptism and Eucharist in the remainder of this chapter will be attentive to this dynamic.

THE RITE OF BAPTISM
IN THE FOURTH CENTURY

The event of baptismal celebration in the fourth century began with a usually extensive course of pre-baptismal catechesis, ranging from three years in the environs of Antioch to possibly only forty days in Egypt. The primary content of pre-baptismal instruction was scriptural exposition. The Spanish nun, Egeria, tells us that, during Lent, the bishop of Jerusalem recounted the entire contents of the Scriptures, expounding both its literal and spiritual meaning (*Pilgrimage of Egeria* 46). Catechumens were also given creedal instruction, with the understanding that the church's creed was a summary of Scripture and a guide to its proper interpretation. This was also a time when catechumens would be initiated into the ongoing doctrinal debates and taught to distinguish between orthodoxy and heresy. Creedal instruction was sometimes formalized in rites of transmitting the creed to the baptizand (*traditio symboli*) and the baptizand's handing it back by a recitation to the bishop (*redditio symboli*). There were also rites of exorcism, in some places administered daily during the final Lenten preparations, which culminated in a renunciation of Satan (*apotaxis*) and pledging allegiance to Christ (*syntaxis*). A pre-baptismal anointing was common, but it is one of the distinguishing features of the fourth-century development of baptismal rites that, with East Syria being an important exception, the pre-baptismal anointing was increasingly associated with exorcism and the imagery of athletic training and military combat against the forces of evil, while the granting of the Holy Spirit was aligned with a post-baptismal anointing. In most places, the rite of baptism was performed in conjunction with the celebration of Easter, though we also have allusions to its performance on other feast days, such as Theophany and Pentecost. Baptism was predominantly administered through a threefold immersion, though a number of fourth-century sources report that the anti-Nicene "Eunomians" practiced a single immersion into the death of Christ, apparently in an effort to dissociate the threefold immersion from the invocation of the Trinity. Nevertheless, the recitation of the Trinitarian name was universally practiced, even among these Eunomians. The newly baptized person was often donned with a white garment, symbolizing the new life attained through the sacrament. Eucharistic communion brought the liturgical celebration of baptism to its consummation. Another distinctive feature of the fourth-century development of this rite is the rise of the practice of mystagogy, a detailed explanation and meditation on the inner contents of the rite of baptism conveyed to the participants after the event. This practice likely began with Cyril of Jerusalem and counted among its notable practitioners Ambrose of Milan, John Chrysostom, and Theodore of Mopsuestia. Much of our current knowledge of the baptismal rites themselves comes indirectly from these mystagogic commentaries.

THEOLOGICAL INTERPRETATION
OF BAPTISM IN THE FOURTH CENTURY

Among the various themes and motifs of these mystagogic catecheses, one of the more prominent is the typological interpretation of the baptismal rite as a mystical participation in and recapitulation of the whole economy of divine salvation, from the original act of creation, to the ark of Noah, the Exodus, the crossings of the Red Sea and the Jordan river, Jesus' own baptism, and ultimately, the death and resurrection of Christ. Liturgical historians note a significant development in the fourth-century interpretation of baptism, which shifts from an emphasis on the imagery of "new birth," based on John 3:1–10, to that of a sharing in the death and resurrection of Christ, as we find in Romans 6:1–11. However, this general shift of emphasis should not be exaggerated, since the "new birth" motif persisted and was readily associated with the "Resurrection" part of the Christological paschal interpretation and with the eradication of sin which was considered to result from baptism. Moreover, the understanding of baptism as a sharing in the death and resurrection of Christ was often supplemented by reference to Jesus' own baptism as the foundation of the baptism of Christian believers. Ambrose maintained both that the source of baptism is the cross and death of Christ (*Sacr.* 2.6) and that Jesus instituted the rite of baptism (*formam baptismatis daret*) by his own baptism, through which he vicariously purified human sin (*Sacr.* 1.15). St. John Chrysostom provides a paradigmatic statement of the Christological-Paschal interpretation of baptism, with some overtones of the "new life" motif: "As you know, baptism is a burial and a resurrection: the old self is buried with Christ to sin and the new nature rises from the dead. . . . We are stripped and we are clothed, stripped of the old garment which has been soiled by the multitude of our sins, clothed with the new that is free from all stain. What does this mean? We are clothed in Christ himself. St. Paul remarks, 'As many of you as were baptized into Christ have put on Christ' " (*BH* 2.11; Yarnold 1994: 155–156).

In his *Mystagogic Catechesis*, Cyril of Jerusalem uses the overarching framework of the Paschal understanding of baptism derived from Romans 6 to interpret the different moments within the rite of baptism. In the course of doing so, Cyril devises a sacramental terminology that distinguishes between the literal reality of the originating event in Jesus' own life, its symbolic representation in the performance of the sacrament, and the literal reality of the salvific power communicated by the symbolic representation. The rite as a whole is interpreted as a new Exodus in which Christ liberates those who have been tyrannized by sin. In renouncing Satan, the baptizand confesses the victory of Christ who has defeated death by his own suffering and death. In stripping off his clothing, the baptizand puts aside the old Adam (cf. Col 3:9). The pre-baptismal anointing enables the baptizand to become a sharer in Christ, the true olive, in order to repel the attacks of demons. The triple immersion with the invocation of the Trinitarian name is an imitation of Christ's three days in the tomb. All of this is a "symbolic" imitation insofar as the baptizand does not literally and physically die and rise again, as Jesus was crucified and died in the flesh, and yet the salvific efficacy of Jesus' death and resurrection are really and literally communicated to the baptizand:

> How strange and wonderful! We did not truly (ἀληθῶς) die, we were not truly buried, we did not truly rise after being crucified. All of this was an imitation by way of symbols (ἐν εἰκόνι ἡ μίμησις), but our salvation truly took place. Christ was really crucified and really buried and truly rose again. He bestowed on us all these things, so that by sharing his sufferings in imitation, we might attain salvation in truth. (*Myst. Cat.* 2.5)

While the rite of baptism as a whole was often interpreted as an imitation of and a participation in the death and resurrection of Christ, there was also an increased emphasis in the fourth century on the Spirit's role in transforming both the matter of the sacraments and their human participants. Beyond specific prayers calling on the Spirit to sanctify the baptismal water or the eucharistic gifts, John Chrysostom can say simply that the Spirit's activity accompanies all of the actions of the priest to effect sacramental transformation (*BH* 2.10). As we noted, one of the significant developments in the form of the baptismal rite in the fourth century was a general even if not universal tendency to shift the location of the granting of the Spirit from a pre-baptismal to a post-baptismal anointing. This development is likely at least partly attributable to a focus on Jesus' own baptism in the context of the Trinitarian controversies of the fourth century. In his *Orations against the Arians*, Athanasius mentions as one of the "Arian" prooftexts, Psalm 45:7: "Therefore, the Lord your God has anointed you with the oil of gladness above your fellows" (*Or. Ar.* 1.46). One interpretation of this text, offered by Eusebius of Caesarea, was that it indicated that the "anointed" God is inferior to the God who anoints him: "The Anointer, who is the Supreme God, is far superior to the Anointed, who is God in a different sense" (*Dem.* 4.15). Athanasius' own exegesis of this text insists that Christ's anointing by the Spirit in his humanity did not constitute his own holiness but was rather a receiving of the Spirit for the sake of humanity, so that human beings may henceforth be incorporated into Christ's human reception of the Spirit. The sacramental application of this doctrinal problematic can be discerned in Ambrose's *On the Sacraments*, where he raises the question of why the baptismal water is consecrated before the immersion of the baptizand into it, whereas in Jesus' baptism the descent of the Spirit follows upon the descent of Christ. Ambrose responds that the order in Jesus' baptism indicates that Jesus was not himself in need of the sanctification of the Spirit; rather, Jesus' descent was itself sanctifying while the Spirit's consequent descent upon him indicates that the Spirit too is a sanctifying agent: "But Christ descended first, and the Spirit came after. Why was this? It was in order that the Lord Jesus might not appear to have need of this mystery of sanctification, but that he himself might sanctify, and that the Spirit might also sanctify" (*Sacr.* 1.18; Yarnold 1994: 107). In a similar vein, Cyril of Jerusalem explains the post-baptismal granting of the Spirit as consistent with Jesus' own anointing by the Spirit in his baptism. Citing Ps 45:6–7, Cyril interprets the baptizand's receiving of the Spirit as also a reception of Christ's divinity through the Spirit (*Myst. Cat.* 3.5). It seems reasonable to surmise that the liturgical practice of a shift toward post-baptismal anointing reflected an understanding of Christian baptism as an imitation of Jesus' own baptism. Jesus' baptism was interpreted according to a Christological-Pneumatological pattern in which Jesus vicariously purifies human sin by his descent into the Jordan and then receives the Spirit on our behalf.

Throughout the Trinitarian controversies of the fourth century, defenders of the ontological equality of the Trinity made regular and emphatic appeal to the church's baptismal practice. Jesus' baptism itself provided a framework for speaking of the Trinitarian agency in baptism, as Ambrose pointed out to the newly baptized: "So Christ came down into the water, and the Holy Spirit came down in the likeness of a dove. God the Father also spoke from heaven. So there you have the Trinity present" (*Sacr.* 1.19; Yarnold 1994: 107). In a later mystagogical sermon, Ambrose explains further that there is a "joint causality, a single sanctifying action" of the Trinity in the event of baptism but within that common activity, there are also "individual effects" (*Sacr.* 6.5; Yarnold 1994: 147). The "distinction of Persons" is experienced by the baptizand through being called by the Father, sealed by the anointing of the Spirit, and co-crucified with Christ; thus, "you can see here the distinction of Persons, but the whole mystery of the Trinity is interconnected" (*Sacr.* 6.8; Yarnold 1994: 148). Yet, those who rejected Nicene doctrine could also appeal to baptismal practice and the general structure of liturgical prayer to support their own position. For the latter, who continued to invoke the Trinitarian name in conformity with the dominical command of Matthew 28:19, the ontological hierarchy that obtains between Father, Son, and Spirit was reflected in the very order of the names that constitute Trinitarian invocation, as well as in the pattern of liturgical prayer, which directed prayer to the Father through the mediation of the Son and the Spirit. Both these liturgical givens could be used to support an understanding of Christian worship as enabled by the Son and Spirit but ultimately oriented to the one God, who became the Father of Jesus Christ. One of the many councils that sought an alternative to the Nicene *homoousios*, the Council of Antioch of 341, expressed this subordinationist theology of the Trinitarian name when it interpreted the Trinitarian baptismal invocation as indicating the distinct existences and order among the three, whose unity is that of "agreement" rather than substance. Contrasting Trinitarian conceptions sometimes led to modifications in actual liturgical practice, as in the Eunomian baptism by single immersion or Basil of Caesarea's introduction of a non-hierarchical doxology ("Glory be to the Father and to the Son, with the Holy Spirit," rather than, "Glory be to the Father through the Son in the Holy Spirit"). But, for the most part, advocates of distinct Trinitarian options simply interpreted liturgical practice differently. For those who supported Nicene Trinitarian faith, the activity of the Trinity in the rite of baptism was understood as a single activity that issues from a single nature, as we saw in Ambrose. At the same time, the divine Trinity was posited as the single destination to which the baptismal act transferred the baptizand. This understanding thus also posited the content of the baptismal act as deification, an insertion and "adoption" into the dynamic unity of divine life. Its proponents argued that the failure to confess the ontological equality of the Trinity both violates the agency which makes the rite efficacious, by mixing creaturely with divine agency, and misses the destination of baptism, by making that destination an impossible hybrid of God and creatures. Both in polemical and doctrinal treatises as well as in pre-baptismal instruction, they insisted that these errors rendered the rite of those who did not confess orthodox Trinitarian doctrine inefficacious and invalid.

Form of the Eucharist
in the Fourth Century

The overall shape of the Eucharistic liturgy in the fourth century retained the basic structure reported by Justin Martyr in the second century: Liturgy of the Word; intercessions; kiss of peace; prayers over the gifts; communion (*1 Apology* 65–67). At the same time, there was some variety from one geographical region to another; for example, the Antiochian Church prescribed two readings before the Gospel (from the Old Testament and the Epistles/Acts) whereas other churches had only one, while the East Syrian Church was an exception to the general tendency in the fourth century to have an institution narrative in the eucharistic prayer. Liturgical historians point to the paradigmatic developments of eucharistic practice in the fourth century as including a heightened sense of awe and majesty pervading the eucharistic celebration, which sometimes led to a decrease in the reception of communion; more frequent celebration of the Eucharist; an increase in the use of the institution narrative; a more emphatic stress on the sacrificial character of the eucharist; and an emphasis on the transformation of the eucharistic gifts effected by the consecratory prayers. The prevailing tendency of Christian liturgical life in the fourth century was toward standardization and consolidation, with the result that these fourth-century developments came to be constitutive of subsequent practice. One of the effects of this momentum toward consolidation was that the extemporizing and individual composition of prayers over the bread and wine gave way to standardized eucharistic prayers. As Rowan Williams has remarked, these prayers occupied a crucial place in the eucharistic celebration since they identified the divine recipient of thanksgiving as well as the grounds for rendering such thanksgiving, and thus expressed the rationale for the eucharistic celebration as a whole (Williams 2004). Consequently, they were both primary reference points for evaluating the *lex credendi* on the basis of *lex orandi*, as well as prime targets for the molding of worship for the sake of doctrinal concerns. An analysis of the eucharistic prayers recited in Jerusalem, West Syria, and Alexandria can afford us some insight into the diverse practices of fourth-century eucharistic liturgies and their interplay with doctrinal controversies.

For the eucharistic liturgy of Jerusalem in the fourth century, our main source is the mystagogical catecheses of Cyril of Jerusalem. After the kiss of peace, Cyril's account of the eucharistic prayer begins with the *sursum corda* ("Up with your hearts"), followed by a thanksgiving for creation that merges with the praise of the angels (the triplex *sanctus*). There follows a supplication (*epiclesis*) that God may send forth the Holy Spirit to transform the bread into the body of Christ and the wine into the blood of Christ. This transformation is considered by Cyril as effecting a "spiritual sacrifice" and a "sacrifice of propitiation" (*Myst. Cat.* 5). The eucharistic intercession for the church, the world, and the human protagonists of salvation history is directly linked with the offering of Christ's sacrifice: "[W]e offer Christ who was slain for our sins, propitiating God who is the lover of humanity, for them and for ourselves" (*Myst. Cat.* 5.10). After the recitation of the Lord's Prayer and the invitation to communion ("Holy things for holy people"), the faithful receive communion to the chanting of the psalm verse, "Taste and see that the Lord is good." Cyril's account notably omits an institution narrative, though scholars disagree as to whether that omission indicates a corresponding lacuna in the liturgy upon which he comments. The eucharistic liturgy described by Cyril of Jerusalem exemplifies the typical, if not exceptionless, fourth-century characteristics of an explicit invocation to the Holy Spirit, a clear conception of the transformation of bread and wine into the body and blood of Christ, and the application of the language of sacrifice to the Eucharist which is also linked to liturgical intercession.

The liturgical contestation of Trinitarian doctrine in the fourth century is reflected in two eucharistic liturgies from the environs of Antioch, documented respectively in the *Apostolic Constitutions* and the anaphora of St. Basil. The *Apostolic Constitutions* reflects a liturgy that shows clear traces of the influence of Eunomian doctrine. Eunomius, whose theology became prominent in the 350s, could be understood as a reformer and reviser of Arius' original doctrine that the Logos was a creature who came into being from nothing through the will of the one God. Arius had contended that the Son and the Spirit were "unlike" the Father in substance and that the Son, as a creature, did not fully comprehend the Father or even his own essence. After Arius, those who agreed that the Son was not coeternal with the Father nevertheless modified Arius' language of the Son's unlikeness to the Father. They preferred to speak more positively and scripturally of the Son's likeness and imaging of the Father's power and activity, even while retaining the notion of the Son's ontological inferiority. Eunomius returned to Arius' original language of the Son's unlikeness to the Father with respect to essence, but modified the apophatic emphasis of Arius' doctrine. Whereas Arius stressed the sheer ineffability and incomprehensibility of the essence of the one God, Eunomius asserted that the essence of the "God over all" was available to human knowledge through the concept of "unoriginated" (ἀγέν(ν)ητος). Conversely, the designation of "only-begotten" appropriately signified the distinct essence of the Son which, being caused, was incomparable with the unique uncaused essence. The Anaphora documented in the *Apostolic Constitutions* provides a liturgical implementation of this doctrine. It begins with a Trinitarian invocation: "The grace of almighty God and the love of our Lord Jesus Christ and the fellowship of the Holy Spirit be with you all" (Jasper and Cuming 1987: 104). There follows the *sursum corda*, and then a long section of praise which is directed to God and which exhibits the Eunomian emphases on the self-existence and uniquely uncaused substance of the one God as well as on God as the source of knowledge: "It is truly fitting and right to praise you before all things, essentially existing God … alone unbegotten, without beginning, without lord or master … greater than every cause and origin.… For you are knowledge, without beginning, eternal vision, unbegotten hearing, untaught wisdom" (Jasper and Cuming 1987: 104). Before embarking on a long and detailed thanksgiving for creation, the prayer acknowledges the Son as the agent of creation but carefully qualifies his status as begotten through the will of the one God and as a worshipper of the one God, rather than himself being an object of worship, "the firstborn of all creation, the angel of your great purpose, your high-priest and notable worshipper, king and lord of all rational and sentient nature" (Jasper and Cuming 1987: 105). A recounting of salvation history up to the time of the Old Testament figure of Joshua concludes with a doxology that envisions the inter-Trinitarian worship of God by the Son and the Spirit: "For all things glory be to you, almighty Lord. You are worshipped by every bodiless and holy order, by the Paraclete, and above all by your holy servant Jesus the Christ, our Lord and God, your angel and the chief general of your power, and eternal and unending high priest, by innumerable armies of angels" (Jasper and Cuming 1987: 108; translation altered). This doxology is followed by the *sanctus*, after which there is an elaborate recounting of the ministry and salvific work of Christ, culminating in the institution narrative and an *epiclesis* invoking the Spirit "upon this sacrifice" so that he may "manifest" (ἀποφήνῃ) the bread and wine as the body and blood of Christ. Intercessions follow and then the "holy things for the holy people," followed by communion.

The eucharistic prayer of the Byzantine Liturgy of St. Basil, which was likely redacted by the Cappadocian bishop himself, provides liturgical expression for an altogether different theological approach. Its formal structure closely resembles that of the *Apostolic Constitutions*: Trinitarian greeting; *sursum corda*; praise of God (though without a narrative of creation and salvation at this point); *sanctus*; recounting of creation and salvation history to the point of the appearance of Jesus Christ; institution narrative; *epiclesis* invoking the Spirit to "bless, sanctify, and show (ἀναδεῖξαι)" the bread and wine as the body and blood of Jesus Christ; intercessions; the "holy things for the holy people"; and communion. Despite these structural similarities, however, which evidence a common foundation for both versions, there are also significant contrasts that both reflect and liturgically implement doctrinal differences. Both anaphoras identify God as the "truly existing" one in the opening praises, but whereas the *Apostolic Constitutions* describes this God as "unbegotten" twice before the *sanctus*, the term is altogether missing from the corresponding section in Basil's anaphora. Rather than "unbegotten," God is identified once as "without beginning" (ἄναρχη), a designation which does not automatically exclude the Son, who is scripturally identified as "only-begotten." Conversely, Basil addresses his praises to God as "Father" from the outset ("Existing One, Lord God, Almighty Father"), while the *Apostolic Constitutions* names God as "Father" only when it begins an account of creation. Both anaphoras praise God for granting knowledge of himself to humanity, but Basil's prayer sounds the typically Cappadocian anti-Eunomian stress on divine infinity and incomprehensibility, acclaiming God as "invisible, incomprehensible, infinite, unchangeable, the Father of our Lord Jesus Christ" (Jasper and Cuming 1987: 116). While both prayers recite the scriptural exalted titles of Jesus

Christ (such as only-begotten Son, Word, Wisdom), Basil's prayer borrows from an anti-Arian sermon in order to interpret these titles as expressive of the Father's own being, speaking of Christ as "the image of your goodness, the identical seal, manifesting you the Father in himself" (Jasper and Cuming 1987: 116–117). As we noted, the *Apostolic Constitutions* identifies God as Father at the commencement of its thanksgiving for creation and it is at that point also that it recites the exalted titles of Christ; it thus effectively places the Father–Son relation within God's relation to creation in general. On the other hand, Basil's anaphora separates "doxology" and "thanksgiving" in a way that corresponds with Basil's distinction between theology and economy in his anti-Eunomian treatise *On the Holy Spirit* (7.16). Glory and praise are the contents of the anaphora up to the *sanctus,* at which point the praise of the earthly congregation is aligned with the angelic choir. Beyond acknowledging God as Lord of creation and granter of salvation, there is minimal concrete reference in this section to God's working in history and maximal attention to divine attributes and to God as the object of glorification. The exalted titles of Christ are first recited in this doxological section, as are those of the Spirit, who is identified as "the Spirit of truth, the grace of sonship, the pledge of the inheritance to come, the first fruits of eternal good things, lifegiving power, the fountain of sanctification" (Jasper and Cuming 1987: 117). Whereas the *Apostolic Constitutions* approaches the *sanctus* by describing the Son and Spirit as the first glorifiers of the self-existing God, Basil's anaphora not only makes the praise of Son and Spirit coordinate with that of the Father but also glorifies the Spirit as the one who enables creatures to glorify God: The Spirit is the one "by whose enabling the whole rational and spiritual creation does you service and renders you unending glory" (Jasper and Cuming 1987: 117). After the *sanctus,* Basil's anaphora turns to thanksgiving for the divine economy. When it reaches the point of the appearance of Christ, it draws on contemporary anti-Arian exegesis both to declare the Son's divinity by referring to Hebrews 1:3 and to account for his human self-emptying by reference to Philippians 2: "He thought it not robbery to be equal to you, the God and Father, but he who was God before the ages was seen on earth and lived among people ... he was conformed to the body of our humiliation that he might conform us to the image of his glory" (Jasper and Cuming 1987: 118). Finally, after communion, a concluding doxology addressed to "the all-honorable and magnificent name" of "the Father and the Son and the Holy Spirit" stands in contrast to the hierarchically parsed doxology of the *Apostolic Constitutions,* which gives glory, worship, and thanksgiving to the Father through Christ and "honor and adoration" to the Holy Spirit.

The euchology of the Egyptian bishop, Sarapion of Thmuis (*c.* 359), Athanasius' friend and correspondent, contains a eucharistic prayer that also reflects the Trinitarian controversies of that time. The prayer of offering begins by addressing praise and glory to "the uncreated (ἀγένητον) Father of the only-begotten Jesus Christ." It continues by sounding an apophatic note such as we found in the Basilian anaphora, praising God as "unsearchable, ineffable, incomprehensible by all created being" (Jasper and Cuming 1987: 76). But it immediately qualifies this theistic apophaticism with a Trinitarian cataphatacism. In contrast to Arius' teaching that the Son does not know the Father as well as to Eunomius' teaching that the highest point of human knowledge is to know God as unbegotten, this Alexandrian anaphora conceives of intra-Trinitarian mutual knowledge that is extended to creation through the Son and the Spirit: "We praise you who are known by the only-begotten Son, who were spoken of through him and interpreted and known to created nature. We praise you who know the Son and reveal to the saints the glories about him, who are known by your begotten Word, and seen and interpreted to the saints … Give us Spirit of light, that we may know you, the true one and him whom you have sent, Jesus Christ. Give us holy Spirit that we may be able to speak and expound your holy mysteries" (Jasper and Cuming 1987: 76). The prayer then sounds the distinctly early Egyptian motif of Christ and the Spirit leading the heavenly choir of praise to the Father: "May the Lord Jesus Christ and the Holy Spirit speak in us and hymn you through us" (Jasper and Cuming 1987: 76). The opening doxological section of the anaphora culminates in the *sanctus*, after which comes the institution narrative. Intertwined with a memorial of the institution narrative, the bread is offered as the "likeness (τὸ ὁμοίωμα) of the body of the only-begotten" and the wine as the "likeness of the blood." There follows an *epiclesis* to the Word, rather than to the Spirit, a feature which sometimes has been interpreted as reflective of a stage when Word and Spirit were indistinguishable. It is much more likely, however, that we have here an understanding of the Eucharist as representing the Incarnation, a conception which mirrors Athanasius' use of eucharistic language to speak of the Incarnation and salvific work of Christ as "an offering" (cf. Athanasius, *Inc.* 9–10). It should also be understood in terms of Athanasius' letters to the same Sarapion to whom this prayer is attributed, where the Alexandrian bishop stresses the inseparability, rather than indistinguishability, of the activity of Son and Spirit. The *epiclesis* of Sarapion's eucharistic prayer seems to envision a change in the status of the bread and wine inasmuch as prior to it they are represented as the "likeness" of the body and blood, whereas the epicletic prayer calls for the bread and wine to simply "become" the body and blood: "Let your holy Word come upon this bread, O God of Truth, that the bread may become the body of the Word; and upon this cup, that the cup may become the blood of the Truth" (Jasper and Cuming 1987: 77). The phrase "body of the Word" is also typical of Athanasius' language and his general Christological conception in which the divine Word is the subject of the humanity. It might also bear the resonance of debates about how the embodied Word can be worshipped despite the creatureliness of his undeniable humanity. In a letter written in about 370, Athanasius adverts to the necessity of identifying the body with its direct ownership by the Word: "But those who do not want to worship the Word who has become flesh show no gratitude for his humanization. And those who separate the Word from the flesh negate the belief that there is one redemption from sin and one destruction of death. Just how will these impious ones ever find the flesh assumed by the Savior all by itself, so that they may dare to say: 'We do not worship the Lord with his flesh but we separate the body and worship him alone.' If the flesh then is inseparable from the Lord, must they not altogether cease this error and henceforth worship the Father in the name of our Lord Jesus Christ?" (*Adelph* 5). After the intercessions, the prayer during fraction sounds the Alexandrian stress on the gnosiological aspect of redemption ("make our bodies receive purity, and our souls insight and knowledge") and contains a doxology in which the Father is glorified through the Son and in the Holy Spirit.

Eucharistic Theology
in the Fourth Century

As with baptism, the theological interpretation of the Eucharist in the fourth century hearkened back to Old Testament types of which it was understood to be the fulfillment. Following John 6, the Eucharist was likened to the manna which God fed to the Israelites in the desert (cf. Ex 16), as well as to the sacrificial offering of the "bread of the presence" in the Temple (cf. Ex 25:30; Lev 24:5–9) and understood as the fulfillment of the whole sacrificial order of the Old Testament. Psalm 23, which was probably sung as a communion chant in some fourth-century liturgies, was also understood to be a prophecy referring to the Eucharist. Cyril of Jerusalem explains, in a standard interpretation, that the fifth verse of the psalm ("You prepared a table before me in the face of those who afflict me and how strong is your cup which intoxicates me," LXX) refers to the "spiritual table" which God has prepared in opposition to the demons and the cup which Jesus declared to be his blood in the Last Supper (*Myst Cat* 4.7). Ambrose interpreted both baptism and Eucharist as bringing to fulfillment the love between God and humanity allegorically described in the *Song of Songs*. When the new Christian emerges from the baptismal waters, cleansed from sin and endowed with the Holy Spirit, Christ declares to the church, "Behold, you are beautiful, my beloved, behold you are beautiful. Your eyes are like doves . . . You are beautiful, my beloved, and there is no fault in you" (*Myst.* 7.37). The act of eucharistic communion is an exchange of kisses between Christ and the communicant who represents the church; each says to the other, "Let him kiss me with the kisses of his mouth" (*Sacr.* 5.5–7; cf. Songs 1:2). Most immediately, however, the church's celebration of the Eucharist was understood as representing Jesus' Last Supper with his disciples as well as the subsequent events which were considered to be proleptically signified therein, namely, the Passion, death, and resurrection of Jesus Christ. John Chrysostom is a good example of such a synthetic understanding. He tells his congregation that the altar which they are approaching is "the same table, nothing less" as the one in the Upper Room where Jesus celebrated the Last Supper with his disciples. (*Hom. Matt.* 82.5). The eucharistic bread is also "that same body, stained with blood, pierced by the lance" which hung upon the cross (*Hom. 1 Cor* 24:4). Simultaneously, it is also the Risen Christ: "You should know that those of us who partake of the body and taste that blood partake of that which is not in any way different or separate from that which is enthroned on high" (*Hom. Eph* 3.3).

There was no standard and uniform terminological framework by which fourth-century theologians conceived the liturgical representation and communication of Christ's salvific work in the Eucharist. Nevertheless, underlying a variety of formulations, there was a common conceptual structure which balanced an acknowledgment of the distinction between liturgical symbolization and its referent with an emphatic realism and affirmation of an identity of ultimate content. Awareness of this dialectic can help us avoid simply dismissing its balanced affirmations as merely contradictory. Theodore of Mopsuestia, for example, speaks of the eucharistic liturgy as the "memorial" of Christ's death and resurrection (*BH* 5.18; Yarnold 1994: 236) containing "commemorations and signs" by which the risen Christ is approached (*BH* 5.18; Yarnold 1994: 241). Yet, elsewhere, he seems to reject the language of "symbol": "When he gave his apostles the bread he did not say, 'This is the symbol of my body,' but, 'This is my body.' So too with the chalice, he did not say, 'This is the symbol of my blood,' but, 'This is my blood' – and with good reason. For he wanted us to turn our attention from the nature of the bread and chalice once they received the grace and the presence of the Holy Spirit, and to receive them as the body and blood of our Lord." (*BH* 4.10; Yarnold 1994: 205). Theodore thus simultaneously acknowledges both a distinction of manifestation and an identity of content between liturgical action and its Christological referent. We find a similar dialectic in Cyril of Jerusalem. In his *Mystagogic Catechesis*, he is emphatic in reminding the newly initiated participants in the eucharistic rites of the identity of content between the bread and wine, on the one hand, and the body and blood of Christ, on the other. The bread and wine are not really bread and wine to the precise extent that their reality as bread and wine is conceived as something separate in content from the body and blood of Christ: "You have learnt with full assurance that what looks like bread, despite its taste, is not bread but Christ's body; that what looks like wine is not wine, despite what its taste suggests, but Christ's blood" (*Myst. Cat.* 4.9; Yarnold 2000: 181). Yet, once the identity in ontological content is presupposed, Cyril can speak of the enduring "form" of the bread and wine through which Christ's body and blood are communicated: "For in the form of bread you are given his body, and in the form of wine you are given his blood" (*Myst. Cat.* 4.3). Similarly, Ambrose speaks of the "figure" of the bread and wine which through consecration "become" the real body and blood of Christ (*Sacr.* 4.20, 23).

The realism by which fourth-century theologians spoke of the eucharistic presence of Christ also extended to the efficacy attributed to eucharistic communion. Just as Christ's blood was originally shed "for the remission of sins," so the sinner has regular recourse to this forgiveness through the Eucharist (Ambrose, *Sacr.* 4.28). Just as the bread and wine become the body and blood of Christ, so does the communicant, to the point where she becomes a "Christbearer," and thus a "partaker of the divine nature" (Cyril of Jerusalem, *Myst. Cat.* 4.3; cf. 2 Pet 1.4). The bishop of Jerusalem spoke of the eucharistic communicants as becoming "one body and one blood" with Christ (*Myst. Cat.* 4.1; cf. Eph 3:6), while John Chrysostom typically referred to the "commingling" of Christ and communicant. Theodore of Mopsuestia, quoting Hebrews 10:4 ("By a single offering he has perfected for all time those who are sanctified"), affirmed the unique and unrepeatable sacrifice of Christ (*BH* 4.19) but also claimed that all who partake of the Eucharist themselves not only share in the fruits of Christ's sacrifice but in some way also "perform" the sacrifice in communion with the celebrant: "The most important point to grasp is that the food we take is a kind of sacrifice we perform ... It is clearly a sacrifice, although it is not something that is new or accomplished by the efforts of the bishop: it is a recalling of this true offering" (*BH*; Yarnold 1994: 209). Along with effecting a union with Christ's original and perfect sacrifice and the fruits of that sacrifice, eucharistic communion also creates unity among the members of the church: "[F]or what is the bread? The body of Christ. And what do they become who partake of it? The body of Christ; not many bodies, but one body" (Chrysostom, *Hom. 1 Cor* 24; Sheerin 1986: 210). For Cyril of Jerusalem, eucharistic communion is also the foundation for the intercessory vocation of the church in the world. He explains the standard liturgical sequence of offering and intercession by seeing both as aspects of participation in Christ's sacrificial offering: "Then, after the completion of the spiritual sacrifice, the worship without blood, we call upon God over this sacrifice of propitiation for the peace of all the Churches, the stability of the world, for kings, for our armies and allies, for the sick and suffering, and in short for all who need help, and in intercession we all offer this sacrifice ... for we believe that great benefit will result for the souls for whom prayer is offered when the holy and awesome sacrifice lies on the altar" (*Myst. Cat.* 5.8–9; Yarnold 2000: 183–184).

CONCLUSION: DOCTRINE, SACRAMENTS, ETHICS

Throughout this chapter, I have noted the interplay in the fourth century between sacramental experience and doctrine. It remains to say that fourth-century sacramental experience was also intensely aware of the ethical content of the sacraments. We can find one of the many expressions of the inviolable nexus between doctrine, sacraments, and ethics in fourth-century Christianity in the catechetical and mystagogic instructions of Cyril of Jerusalem. There, he instructs his hearers that a devout Christian life consists in both the assent to true doctrine and in proper moral conduct (*Cat.* 4.2). The sacrament of baptism brings about a marriage between the heavenly Bridegroom and the human being who has committed herself to both the church's faith and its ethics. He exhorts the baptizands to memorize the creed which contains "all the religious knowledge contained in the Old and New Testaments" (*Cat.* 5; Yarnold 2000: 114). But he also reminds his hearers that proper doctrine is useless without moral uprightness. In turn, right conduct is inefficacious for salvation apart from sacramental participation: "[E]ven if your deeds have made you virtuous, you won't enter the kingdom of heaven if through the water you have not received the seal" (*Cat* 3.4; Yarnold 2000: 90). Conversely, sacramental participation is itself voided by unethical behavior: "Do you want to enjoy the grace of the Holy Spirit while not deigning to give material food to the poor?" (*Cat* 3.8; Yarnold 2000: 93). In a similar vein, Gregory of Nyssa goes so far as to say that the validity of the sacrament of baptism is voided by unjust and uncharitable behavior, while John Chrysostom preached that the one who ignores the hungry partakes of the Eucharist unworthily and will incur judgment (*Hom. 1 Cor* 27.5). The general understanding of Christian life as deification, honed in the process of the Trinitarian controversies, stipulated that the authenticity of sacramental participation in divine life be grounded both in a true confession of divine being and a genuine assimilation to the divine mode of acting.

ABBREVIATIONS

Ambrose:
Sacr.   *On the Sacraments (De sacramentis)*
Myst.   *On the Mysteries*

Athanasius:
Or. Ar.   *Orations against the Arians*
Inc.   *On the Incarnation*
Adelph   *Letter to Adelphius*
Syn.   *On the Syndos of Ariminum and Selecuica (De Synodis)*

John Chrysostom:
BH   *Baptismal Homilies*
Hom.   *Matt Homilies on Matthew*
Hom.   *1 Cor Homilies on 1 Corinthians*
Hom.   *Eph Homilies on Ephesians*

Cyril of Jerusalem:
Cat.   *Catecheses*
Myst.   *Cat. Mystagogical Catecheses*

Eusebius of Caesarea:
Dem.   *Demonstration of the Gospel*

SUGGESTED READING

Jasper and Cuming (1987); Johnson (2007); Sheerin (1986); Yarnold (1994).

BIBLIOGRAPHY

Anatolios, K. (2011), *Retrieving Nicaea: The Development and Meaning of Trinitarian Doctrine* (Ann Arbor, MI: Baker Academic).
Bardy, G. (1936), *Recherches sur Saint Lucien d'Antioche et son école* (Paris: Beauchesne).
Bouyer, L. (1968), *Eucharist: Theology and Spirituality of the Eucharistic Prayer* (Notre Dame, IN: University of Notre Dame Press).
Bradshaw, P. F. (2002), *The Search for the Origins of Christian Worship: Sources and Methods for the Study of Early Christian Liturgy*, 2nd ed. (London: S.P.C.K.).

Bradshaw, P. F. (2004), *Eucharistic Origins* (Oxford: Oxford University Press).

Daniélou, J. (1956), *The Bible and the Liturgy* (Notre Dame, IN: University of Notre Dame Press).

Finn, T. (ed.) (1902) *Early Christian Baptism and the Catechumenate: West and East Syria* (Collegeville, MN: Liturgical Press).

Hänggi, A. and I. Pahl (eds.) (1968), *Prex eucharistica: textus e variis liturgiis antiquioribus selecti*. Singularum partium textus paraverunt Louis Ligier [u.a] Spicilegium Friburgense 12 (Fribourg, Éditions universitaires).

Harkins, P. W. (trans.) (1963) *St. John Chrysostom: Baptismal Instructions* (London: Newman Press).

Jasper, R. C. D. and G. J. Cuming (eds.) (1987), *Prayers of the Eucharist: Early and Reformed*, 3rd ed. (Collegeville, MN: Liturgical Press).

Johnson, M. (1995), *The Prayers of Sarapion of Thmuis: A Literary, Liturgical, and Theological Analysis* (Pontificium Institutum Orientalium Studiorum).

Johnson, M. (2007), *The Rites of Christian Initiation: Their Evolution and Interpretation* (Collegeville, MN: Liturgical Press).

Johnson, M. and E. C. Whitaker (2003), *Documents of the Baptismal Liturgy*, 3rd ed. (London: S.P.C.K.).

Jungmann, J. (1965), *The Place of Christ in Liturgical Prayer* (Staten Island, NY: Alba House).

Mazza, E. (1989), *Mystagogy: A Theology of Liturgy in the Patristic Age* (New York: Pueblo).

Mazza, E. (1995), *The Origins of the Eucharistic Prayer* (Collegeville, MI: Liturgical Press, Pueblo).

Opitz, H.-G. (1936), *Athanasius Werke. Band 3. Teil 1. Urkunden zur Geschichte des Arianischen Streites 318–328. 1. Lieferung* (Berlin: De Gruyter).

Ramsey, B. (1997), *Ambrose* (London: Routledge).

Schultz, H-J. (1986), *The Byzantine Liturgy: Symbolic Structure and Faith Expression* (New York: Pueblo)

Sheerin, D. J. (1986), *The Eucharist* (Wilmington, DE: Michael Glazier).

Williams, R. (2004), "'The Creed and the Eucharist in the Fourth and Fifth Centuries," <http://rowanwilliams.archbishopofcanterbury.org/articles.php/1210/the-creed-and-the-eucharist-in-the-fourth-and-fifth-centuries#sthash.9FfiYWYx.dpuf>.

Yarnold, E. (1994), *The Awe-Inspiring Rites of Initiation*, 2nd ed. (Collegeville, MN: Liturgical Press).

Yarnold, E. (2000), *Cyril of Jerusalem* (London: Routledge).

CHAPTER 11

AUGUSTINE AND THE WEST TO AD 650

LEWIS AYRES AND THOMAS HUMPHRIES

AUGUSTINE's rich sacramental theology is highly systematic; he uses a set of basic principles to approach a wide variety of questions. And yet, Augustine inherited a fairly well-established sacramental structure and developing ritual structures. These continued to develop during and after his lifetime, in many places without any great influence from his thought or practice. Augustine's theology was sometimes foundational for later thinkers, and sometimes received only piecemeal or superficially. In what follows, then, we try to give a sense both of Augustine's distinctive emphases, and of the broader tradition within which he was situated. We begin by outlining some of the most basic features of Augustine's view of the sacramental, and then examine in turn a number of Christianity's most basic sacramental actions, the Eucharist, baptism, marriage, and holy orders (in addition to the summary provided in this article see Cutrone 1999 and Macy 2013).

It may be helpful to begin by noting that the Latin word *sacramentum* was used to translate the Greek *mysterion* from a very early date; we find it, for example, in the earliest translations of New Testament Epistles (alongside transliterations of the Greek into Latin). The Latin term has a slightly different range of meaning: whereas the Greek term primarily signifies a religious rite, the Latin signifies an oath (that one swore, for example, when joining the military), or a pledge for the future, or sometimes an initiation. Tertullian uses the term in a wide variety of senses, but he also seems to have been the first to apply the term to what we would recognize as one of the seven sacraments. But, at the same time, the term is also used for a wide range of events, especially events in the history of Israel that foreshadow the future. Tertullian, for example, understood Jacob's blessing of Ephrem as a sacrament that foreshadowed baptism, and Cyprian of Carthage understood Noah and Melchizedek to participate in sacraments that foreshadowed the Eucharist (for a survey see Nocent 2014).

Augustine inherited this broad established usage, but made a distinctive contribution by offering a systematic conception of a sacrament as a sign within which his various discussions can be located. In his early work Augustine uses the term *sacramentum* to refer to a wide variety of symbols that are used within religions as bonds of union (*c. Faust* 19.11; Augustine 2007: 244–245). Not only words and narratives are signs; actions and objects may also be nothing less than "visible speech" (*c. Faust* 19. 16; Augustine 2007: 246–247). All of these events and rituals found in the Old Testament are, he argues, types of Christ, and they pass away once Christ has appeared (*c. Faust*. 19.13; Augustine 2007: 245). Augustine also uses the term to refer to many aspects of Christian practice and ritual, as well as to many aspects of Christ's life and teaching (*doc.* 3.9.13; Augustine 1996: 175).

One of Augustine's most interesting and important discussions of sacraments is to be found in two letters to a Catholic layman, Januarius, written in answer to a series of questions in around AD 400. Augustine begins by invoking a rhetoric that distinguishes between the complexity of the Jewish Law and the relative simplicity of the Christian sacraments (Matt 11:30). He mentions baptism and Eucharist first, but then also a number of feasts, including the Easter triduum, the Ascension and Pentecost. Interestingly Augustine lists Scripture, the apostles, and councils as legitimate sources of these sacraments. Augustine speaks here of Christ "binding together the society of the new people" by means of these sacraments, following his sense of the unifying nature of religious signs found in the roughly contemporary *Against Faustus* (*ep.* 54.1.1; Augustine 2001: 210).

In the second, and more extensive, letter Augustine offers us two themes that take us to the heart of how he views the sacramental. First, he likens the working of the sacramental to the "allegorical" or the "mystical" more widely. Augustine is discussing why the celebration of Easter includes the Sabbath between the Lord's death and his resurrection. There is an oddity here, Augustine argues, because the only true rest comes at the end of labor—as God rested only at the end of creating. But the Sabbath was placed here—and Augustine insists that Christ arranged for his Crucifixion at a time of his choosing—as a sign of our sanctification in the Spirit, as a sign that our movement toward true rest comes through the work of the Spirit within us, the same Spirit who will also be the source of that true rest (*ep.* 55. 10.18–19; Augustine 2001: 224–225). A little later Augustine offers this general comment:

> All these things, however, that are presented to us in figures pertain somehow to nourishing and fanning the fire of love by which we are carried upward or inward to rest as if by a weight. For they arouse and kindle love more than if they were set forth bare without any likenesses of the sacraments. The reason for this fact is difficult to state. But it is, nonetheless, a fact that something presented in an allegorical meaning arouses more, delights more, and is appreciated more than if it were said in full openness with the proper terms. I believe that, as long as it is still involved with the things of earth, the feeling of the soul is set afire rather slowly, but if it is confronted with bodily likenesses and brought from there to spiritual realities that are symbolized by those likenesses, it is strengthened by this passage, and is set aflame like the fire in a coal when stirred up, and is carried with a more ardent love toward rest. (*ep.* 55. 11.21; Augustine 2001: 226)

Augustine's insistence on the value of the figurative here is famously found also in the second book of his *On Christian Teaching*. In that book, as soon as Augustine offers the comment that the figurative stimulates greater delight and thus better rouses the soul towards its true love, he offers us an account of the various stages through which the soul ascends or grows (*doc.* 2. 6.7–7.11; Augustine 1996: 131–133). His list of stages, however, ends not with the direct sight of God but with emphasis on the continuing necessity of recognizing that in this world we walk by faith. Augustine's vision of the sacramental is thus deeply rooted in his doctrine of signs, and particularly in his belief that indirect signification, signification that makes use of the material to lead us to the immaterial, is more effective and more appropriate for reforming minds obsessed with the material (see also his insistence that signs and sacraments are only properly used when we know that to which they refer; cf. *doc.* 3. 5.9; Augustine 1996: 173).

The second theme underlying his account of the sacramental comes out in a closely related section of *Letter* 55 when Augustine explores the symbolism of the cross. The different dimensions of the cross symbolize the different aspects of the Christian life. Overall the cross signifies the present life, the "time of the cross," while the burial and resurrection speak of that which we have only in faith and hope. We are crucified as we work to put to death the desires and practices of the old self (Rom 6:6, 8:13; Gal 6:14) in order that the new and interior self may be renewed day by day. Within this context the transverse beam of the cross, to which Christ's hands are nailed, signifies the works that we should undertake in joy. The height of the cross signifies the expectation of reward at the end of our striving. The length of the cross signifies the patience necessary. But the depth of the cross, hidden in the earth, symbolizes "the secret of the sacrament" (*ep.* 55. 14.25; Augustine 2001: 228). Robert Dodaro has recently explored how Augustine here refers to the foundation of all sacramental work in grace. The Spirit's work undergirds our movement toward rest; thus all sacramental renewal of the inner person is ultimately effected by divine gift (Dodaro 2004: chs. 4–5).

Although, in what follows we discuss Augustine and those who came after him, it is important to bear in mind two general problems with our account. First, it is very difficult to summarize developments after Augustine because our knowledge of the period between his death and the mid-600s is often limited to discussions in particular regions. We sometimes do not know whether the points on the map that are illuminated are exceptional or paradigmatic. Second, because of Augustine's status in Western Christianity, it is easy to assume that later authors are always in dialogue with and dependent upon him. In actual fact, some authors we treat are heavily dependent on Augustine, while others seem to take from him aspects that suit their purposes, but otherwise seem to be dependent on the broader tradition of which Augustine is only a part.

Eucharist

Turning first to the Eucharist will enable us to see with real clarity how the height of the sacramental for Augustine is found in the work through which Christ and the Spirit incorporate Christians into the body of Christ (on this theme in Augustine, see Jackson 1999, Cavadini 2010; on the structure of the eucharistic liturgy in Augustine's church, see Van Der Meer 1961, chs. 10–11; for a broader introduction to Patristic developments, see Mazza 1999). We can understand much about Augustine's eucharistic teaching by spending some time with his short *Sermon* 272, a sermon preached either at Easter or Pentecost, probably in the first decade of the fifth century. Augustine begins this short sermon by commenting on the distinction between what we see and what should be acknowledged in faith:

> So what you can see, then, is bread and a cup; that's what even your eyes tell you; but as for what your faith asks to be instructed about, the bread is the body of Christ, the cup the blood of Christ. (*Serm.* 272; Augustine 1993: 297)

The visible here has its significance only in relation to what cannot be seen and must be believed. He then imagines his audience asking how the actual Jesus whom we know to have lived, died, and risen can be the same as this bread and wine:

> The reason these things, brothers and sisters, are called sacraments is that in them one thing is seen, another is to be understood. What can be seen has a bodily appearance, what is to be understood provides spiritual fruit. (*Serm.* 272; Augustine 1993: 297)

So far, Augustine follows lines we have explored. For Augustine we certainly eat and drink under the forms of bread and wine, but the real "eating" that occurs is not of a different bodily substance hidden within, but a spiritual "eating" that is an accepting of the transforming work of the Spirit reforming us and drawing us into Christ's body. But now the most distinctive features of his eucharistic teaching suddenly appear:

> So if you want to understand the body of Christ, listen to the apostle telling the faithful, You, though, are the body of Christ and its members (1 Cor 12:27). So if it's you that are the body of Christ and its members, it's the mystery meaning you that has been placed on the Lord's table; what you receive is the mystery that means you. It is to what you are that you reply Amen, and by so replying you express your assent. What you hear, you see, is the body of Christ, and you answer, Amen. So be a member of the body of Christ, in order to make that Amen true. (*Serm.* 272; Augustine 1993: 297)

To understand this passage we need to recall Augustine's doctrine of the *totus Christus*, the "whole Christ." Throughout his mature work Augustine speaks of the link between Christ and Christians through invoking the theme of the "whole Christ." In *Sermon* 341 he explains that just as the Word of God is complete in itself, so the Word has chosen to be complete with the human nature he assumed, and now he has chosen also to be complete with his body, the church. The Word can do this because he possesses fully the divine power (*serm.* 341.10–11; Augustine 1995: 25–26). Christians are then taken into the person of Christ; Christ infuses his love and will into us, and we are drawn into the very death and resurrection of Christ. At the same time, being drawn into Christ is a complex relationship; Augustine speaks constantly of the head of the body, Christ, going on before the body, us. The body strains after the head; and yet the head is constantly present in the limbs encouraging, transforming, incorporating. Because of this relationship

Augustine can say that Christ offers himself on the cross and in the sacrifice of the Mass, but he says also that the church itself is offered on the altar. In book 10 of the *City of God* he writes as follows:

> [T]he whole of the redeemed city—that is the congregation and fellowship of the saints—is offered to God as a universal sacrifice for us through the great high priest who, in his passion, offered even himself for us in the form of a servant, so that we might be the body of so great a head ... This is the sacrifice of Christians: 'we being many, are one body in Christ'. And this also, as the faithful know, is the sacrifice which the Church continually celebrates in the sacrament of the altar, by which she demonstrates that she herself is offered in the offering that she makes to God. (*civ.* 10.6)

The phrase "so that we might be" is key here and matches the language of the prior quotation. The body is offered so that we might be drawn ever more fully into the body, so that we might follow and join our head. Returning to *Sermon* 272, Augustine explains a little more of how his doctrine of the church as the body of Christ is also a doctrine of Christians' growth into the body:

> So why in bread? Let's not bring anything of our own to bear here, let's go on listening to the apostle himself, who said, when speaking of this sacrament, One bread, one body, we being many are one body (1 Cor 10:17). Understand and rejoice. Unity, truth, piety, love. One bread; what is this one bread? The one body which we, being many, are. Remember that bread is not made from one grain, but from many. When you were being exorcised, it's as though you were being ground. When you were baptized it's as though you were mixed into dough. When you received the fire of the Holy Spirit, it's as though you were baked. Be what you can see, and receive what you are. (*Serm.* 272; Augustine 1993: 297–298)

Why is bread the appropriate sign here? Because we may share one bread between many—the bread symbolizes the unity of the body. As Augustine writes in *Sermon* 57: "You see, the special property to be understood in it is unity, so that by being digested into his body and turned into his members we may be what we receive" (*Serm.* 57.7; Augustine 1991: 112). The bread is a sign of the unity that the Eucharist effects and to which it calls us. Thus, Augustine sees the Eucharist as signifying and helping to effect that harmonious unity that is ultimately the function of all sacraments, as it is the ultimate shape of the restored human community.

THE EUCHARIST AFTER AUGUSTINE

Augustine's strong emphasis on the Eucharist represents a wide consensus among Latin writers of the period that this sacrament is central to Christianity. The practice of receiving Communion weekly and sometimes daily is reasonably well attested in Christian literature both contemporary with Augustine and later. Some of these references concern the practice among ascetics, but not all (see e.g. de Vogüé 1985).

Against this background, Augustine's sacramental theology was a central if not ubiquitous resource in the centuries that followed his death. Some were heavily dependent on him and able to follow closely the dynamics of his thought. For example, the sixth-century African bishop St. Fulgentius of Ruspe is able to make connections to pneumatology, grace, ecclesiology, personal transformation, and the real presence of Christ without being subject to the naïve position of thinking about the Eucharist, as Thomas Aquinas would later warn, as a corpse. In his reply to Monimus, Fulgentius weaves technical Trinitarian doctrines such as the inseparable operations and irreducible persons with an analysis of the eucharistic prayers.

> Therefore, when the coming of the Holy Spirit is sought for sanctifying the sacrifice of the whole Church, nothing else is sought, it seems to me, than that through the spiritual grace in the Body of Christ (which is the Church) the unity of charity be preserved endlessly unbroken. For this is the principal gift of the Holy Spirit. (*Monim.* 2.9.1; Fulgentius 1997: 246)

As in Augustine's own theology of the Eucharist, love and the Holy Spirit are key: "when the Church asks that the Holy Spirit be sent from heaven upon itself, it is asking that the gift of charity and concord be conferred on it by God" (*Monim.* 2.10.1; Fulgentius 1997: 247). Fulgentius argues that the church does this most appropriately at the consecration of the sacrifice of the body of Christ. The Eucharist, like baptism, causes believers to "become the members of the Lord Jesus Christ and belong to the structure of the body in the unity of the church" so that we both share in and are the holy sacrifice itself (*Ep.* 12.11.24; Fulgentius 1997: 493).

In the three centuries following Augustine's death there was no great and definitive controversy over the eucharistic presence. Most writers simply assume that Christ is present in a unique and transforming way, sometimes struggling to state their positions clearly. For example, Facundus of Hermione, another sixth-century African bishop, argued, "we say that the sacrament of his body and blood, which is in the consecrated bread and cup, is his body and blood, not that the bread is his own body and the cup his blood, but that they contain in them the mystery of his body and blood" (*Def.* 9.5.25; Facundus 2004: 196). Beyond attempts at definition, the period saw extensive expression of eucharistic piety. Gregory the Great, who was well versed in Augustinian theology, is reported to have had a famous vision of Christ bleeding (either a part of Christ or the whole crucified Christ) within the host during the consecration at Mass. Contemporary homilies also teach that the sacrament allows us to be present to the saving mystery of the cross even though we are removed in time from the Incarnate Christ. Eucharistic sacramental communion includes the *sacrifice* of the body and blood of Christ poured out for us on the cross. Thus, Isidore explains, "we believe that it is a tradition from the apostles themselves that the sacrifice is offered for the repose of the faithful departed or to pray for them, because ... the Catholic Church holds this everywhere" (*De Ecc. Off.* 1.18.11;

Isidore 2008: 44). While not all theologians followed Augustine's complex eucharistic theology, there is consensus that the Eucharist is an important sacrament that transforms individual believers, builds the church in unity and love, and makes Christ present through liturgical action.

BAPTISM

Augustine's account of baptism made use of many of the same dynamics that we have seen in the case of the Eucharist (for a broad survey of patristic developments, see Ferguson 2008). In a number of sermons to catechumens Augustine compares the catechumenate to wheat being stored up in a granary. Lent corresponds to the milling of the wheat, which is then moistened by baptism and baked into a loaf by the fire of the Holy Spirit as the candidates are anointed. And yet this is only one of a rich series of traditional images that Augustine uses to describe baptism. At the same time he participates in a long tradition of commentary on Romans 6, identifying baptism with a participation in the death of Christ: "baptism in Christ is nothing but an image of the death of Christ" (*ench.* 14.52; Augustine 2005: 304).

In the same way Augustine inherited and reflected deeply on increasingly well-established traditions of Christian initiation, and traditions of Christian penitential practice. We will come to these after discussing Augustine's theology of baptism itself. This theology was profoundly shaped by his controversy with Donatism in North Africa. Donatists demonstrate a profound concern for ritual purity, to the extent of assuming that the impure could not validly baptize or ordain. But this deep concern was not unique to the Donatist movement, and is also seen in a number of previous Latin writers, in Cyprian for example. Against the challenge of Donatism, Augustine articulated with increasing clarity the principle that Christ is the agent of baptism, that those being baptized are channels for the divine agent, and that the effectiveness of the sacrament does not depend upon their "purity":

> For what does Paul say? 'I have planted, Apollos watered; but God gave the increase. Neither is he that plants anything, nor he who waters; but God who gives the increase.' He who is a proud minister is in a class with the devil; but uncontaminated is the gift of Christ which flows through him undefiled, which passes perfectly clear through him and comes to fertile soil. Suppose that the proud minister is made of stone because he cannot produce fruit from the water. The water passes through the stone conduit, the water passes on to garden plots; in the stone conduit it produced nothing but nevertheless brings forth plentiful fruit in gardens. For the spiritual power of a sacrament is like light in this way: it is both received pure by those to be enlightened, and if it passes through the impure, it is not defiled. Let the ministers be just, indeed, and let them not seek their own glory but his whose ministers they are. Let them not say, 'It is my baptism,' because it is not theirs. (*ev. Io. tr.* 5.15; Augustine 1988: 122–123)

The other conflict that shaped Augustine's views of baptism was his engagement with Pelagius and his associates. This dispute pushed Augustine to argue that the baptism of infants was necessary for their salvation because by the mere fact of being born into the world they have inherited the consequences of Adam's sin. In so doing he developed a theme already present in his predecessor Cyprian of Carthage. Augustine finds the logic of this position inescapable, but the result he often admits to be simply mysterious. He was happy to express both the necessity of the position that infants need baptism for salvation, alongside a hesitancy about what sort of condemnation it is possible to imagine for those who die in infancy, and a confession that an answer could only be found in the mystery of God's will and action (often quoting Rom 11:33). What textbooks call "the Pelagian controversy" was in actuality a series of controversies over interrelated questions, and those controversies continued long after Augustine's death. One fundamental point of reference in our period is the Council of Orange (529). This council reasserted Augustine's insistence on the inescapability of original sin and the consequent necessity of baptism, and these principles became central for later Latin Christianity. At the same time, Orange's complex negotiations between Augustine-inspired accounts of the working of grace and accounts opposed to these views are more complex and represent a stage in a debate that would continue up and through the reformations of the sixteenth century.

At this point we should also note that during this period baptism and confirmation were gradually becoming separated (for a survey of relevant texts and a controversial thesis, see Kavanagh 1988). At the beginning of the fifth century Pope Innocent I decreed that only bishops were to administer confirmation. Isidore of Seville passes this teaching along as the universal norm and separates the anointing that is part of baptism from the anointing which is part of confirmation:

> Although it is permitted to priests either without a bishop or with a bishop present to anoint the baptized with chrism when they baptize, they may do so only with chrism that has been consecrated by the bishop. Nevertheless, they are not to sign the forehead with that oil, because that ought to be done only by bishops when they hand on the Holy Spirit. (*De Ecc. Off.*, 2.27; Isidore 2008: 113)

We can now return for a moment to the traditions of initiation and post-baptismal penance that Augustine inherited and which slowly developed during and after his lifetime (see Johnson 1999; Jensen 2012). By Augustine's time there was a clear process of initiation for adult catechumens that involved several rituals including an exorcism and the gift of the creed, as well as a lengthy process of catechesis in preparation for baptism (see Harmless 1995; Pasquato 2014). This process continues to be witnessed in sources throughout the period, though specific rituals differ. While catechumens express genuine sorrow and repentance for their sins and receive forgiveness in their baptism, a separate penitential process developed for serious and scandalous post-baptismal sin (see Dallen 1986; Favazza 1988). In both contexts Augustine (like other patristic authors) emphasizes that the church has the power to forgive sins (following Matt 16:19, 18:18, John 20:22–23). The length and severity of penance depended on the local church and the gravity of the sins. Prior to the missionary work of St. Columbanus (i.e. through the sixth century), many scholars separate a private ritual of confession of sins in the Irish Church from the public order of penitents in the Mediterranean churches. Those who were enrolled in the order of penitents were not allowed to approach the other sacraments until they had been restored to sacramental communion. Though there are not a great number of texts that discuss anointing of the sick (James 5:24) as a sacrament in this period, there is evidence that penitents were not allowed to receive this anointing.

The practice of penance and readmission to the sacraments developed alongside the rituals of initiation (see Vogel 2014). Pope St. Leo the Great offers a particularly clear teaching of the sacramental parallel between baptism and penance: "The manifold mercy of God assists human beings who have fallen, so that the hope of eternal life is restored not only through the grace of baptism, but also through the medicine of penance ... safeguards were ordained for the divine goodness that God's indulgence cannot be obtained except through the prayers of priests ... The Mediator ... gave this power to those whom he put in charge of his Church" (Leo, *Ep.* 108; Leo 1957: 190–191).

MARRIAGE AS A SACRAMENT

Augustine's own struggles with sexuality were epitomized in his famous prayer, "Grant me chastity and self-control, but ... not yet" (*Conf.* 8.7.17; Augustine 2001: 149). Augustine came to understand that Christian marriage offers grace to help men and women develop their sexuality and even to forgive certain sins. In an age in which there were major debates about whether marriage was a good, Augustine defended not only the practice and bond of marriage, but also that men and women are equal participants in marriage, even though he saw celibacy as a superior good (on the principle that while under the law it was essential for human beings to produce children in preparation for Christ's coming, after Christ this task is no longer essential). In so doing he represents something of a middle way between some of the more extreme voices of his day (see Hunter 1999). Augustine's insistence that Christian marriage is an important good became the universal teaching of the church.

The term *sacramentum* is used in older translations of "mystery" in Ephesians 5:31–32 ("For this reason a man shall leave his father and mother and be joined to his wife, and the two shall become one. This is a great mystery, and I mean in reference to Christ and the Church") as well as in Jerome's Vulgate. For this reason, marriage was almost universally discussed as a sacrament in Latin, though there are different customs and development of thought about what constitutes the sacrament of marriage in this period (see Reynolds 1994: 244–311). The union of Adam and Eve as discussed in Genesis (esp. at Gen 2:18–24) and Jesus' words in Matthew 19:4–12 dominate discussions of marriage. There are contrasting examples of marriage in Scripture that proved difficult to reconcile. Abraham and Sarah's marriage includes intercourse with Hagar, but Joseph and Mary's marriage admits of no intercourse. It was common for theologians of this period to admit that marriage in the Old Testament allowed for polygamy, while Christian marriage does not. The practice of marriage, divorce, and remarriage received a mixed reception, with many Christian writers and councils expressly forbidding it. Nearly two centuries after Augustine, Isidore of Seville summarizes what became standard teaching in the West: marriage "is said to be a sacrament between married people because, as it is not possible that the church be divided from Christ, neither can a wife from the man ... [It] is thereby an inseparable sacrament of union in the individuals who are men and wives" (*De Ecc. Off.* 2.20.11; Isidore 2008: 113).

Augustine's teaching that the bond of husband and wife is "the first natural bond of human society" became a pillar of Catholic understandings of marriage, as did his teaching that sacramental marriage is not dissolved by civil divorce (*Excellence of Marriage*, 1.1–7.7; Augustine 1999: 33–39). His insistence that even within marriage sexual activity does not occur without the fallen desire to possess and dominate was controversial in his lifetime, but was mostly sustained by later tradition (see Cavadini 2005). Augustine also taught that there are three goods of marriage, the procreation of children (*proles*), the mutual fidelity of the spouses (*fides*), and its value as a sacred sign or symbol (*sacramentum*). His attempt to balance these three goods of marriage has been highly influential in Christian understandings of the sacrament of marriage.

> The value of marriage ... for all people lies in the objective of procreation and the faithful observance of chastity. For the people of God ... it lies also in the sanctity of the sacrament, and this has the consequence that it is forbidden for a woman to marry anyone else while her husband is still living ... Although [having children] is the only purpose there can be for a marriage, the bond of matrimony is not broken when its purpose is not achieved, but only by the death of a husband or wife. It is like ordination to the priesthood, which takes place for the purpose of forming a community of the faithful. (*Excellence of Marriage*, 24.32; Augustine 1999: 56)

Once again, sacraments, for Augustine, are about the formation or re-formation of genuine human community under and in God.

Holy Orders

When Augustine was ordained the theology and practice of ordination already constituted a complex and ancient tradition, if one that was still in a process of change (in brief, see Nocent 2014a; Joncas 1999). The terms *ordo* (order) and *ordinatio* (ordination) have their original context not in the church or religious use, but Roman civil organization. The latter term signified the appointment of someone to an official position. In the Christian context, because official positions were liturgical in nature, the term came quickly to signify a rite of consecrating someone to this position. Augustine's conception of church order follows existing North African tradition, which can be traced in his predecessors Cyprian and (in more sketchy fashion) Tertullian. The latter distinguishes between bishops, presbyters, and deacons (he also speaks of subdeacons as ordained, although Cyprian clearly distinguished the minor orders), and speaks of different ranks of bishops—these distinctions probably reflect an increasingly differentiated and subdivided structure in the Christian community's ministerial organization. Unfortunately, we do not know enough to speak with any certainty about the structure of ordination rites in North Africa during this period. After Augustine the process of increasing organization continues. Many Latin sources from this period list more than eight grades that lead to sacramental priesthood. For example, Isidore lists bishops, priests, deacons, and some form of sacristan before discussing subdeacons who, when they "are ordained ... do not receive the imposition of hands, as priests ... do" (*de Ecc. Off.* 2.5–20; Isidore 2008: 81). The list continues with lectors, Psalmists, exorcists, and porters before considering monks, penitents, virgins, widows, and married.

Augustine also parallels baptism and holy orders, speaking of both as sacraments (see the text quoted at the end of the last section of this chapter), and insisting that in both cases the change effected by the sacrament in the person is irreversible. Even as Augustine inherited a fairly stable tradition, the role of priest was undergoing changes. Almost every town of any importance had its own bishop as the ordinary pastor, the priests being very clearly the bishop's helpers. But as the size of the Christian communities grew, the role of the priest increased, and soon some priests were preaching, administering churches and acting as local pastors. This was only the very beginning of the parish system as we know it today; Augustine himself wanted his clergy to live together in a common life, sharing property.

The requirements for ordination found in the Pauline letters dominate the discussion of the requirements for ordination (e.g. 1 Tim 3:1–13; Gaudemet 1962). Married bishops were not prohibited, but seem to have been few in number during these centuries, though married priests seem to have been common. There is discussion about whether the church should prohibit married bishops simply, or whether St. Paul could be understood to prohibit a new marriage or continued sexual activity with one's wife after ordination as a bishop (see Rousseau 1962). Many councils forbade deacons, priests, and bishops to live with a woman, with only a few exceptions. Today there is some discussion among historians about the extent to which women participated in various orders of ministry (e.g. Martimort 1986; Otranto 1991).

The immense importance accorded ordained ministry is seen both in Augustine and the centuries that follow. Leo the Great, for example, teaches that "Those to be ordained are never to receive the blessing except on the day of the Lord's Resurrection ... [Sunday] is a day which has been hallowed by such great mysteries in the divine plan of events that whatever of major importance the Lord decided on was carried out on this honored day." Leo lists the creation of the world, the resurrection, the command to baptize in the name of the Father, Son, and Holy Spirit, the gift of the Holy Spirit (as described by John 20:23), and the descent of the Holy Spirit (as described by Acts 2.1) before he concludes, "Thus we know through some divine plan the custom was introduced and became traditional whereby the rites for the laying of hands on priests are to be celebrated on that day on which all the gifts of grace were conferred" (Leo, *Ep.* 9; Leo 1957: 35).

CONCLUSION

By the fifth century, every aspect of the sacramental and ritual life of the church was taken to be rooted in Scripture, tradition, and inspired by the Holy Spirit. The definition of "sacrament" in particular, while remaining broad enough to include various details within Scripture, events from salvation history prior to the Incarnation, and contemporary liturgical rites, began to be focused on a Christian reading of the ancient Roman oath and a theory of signs. Sacraments were understood as complex rites through which God has promised to offer specific graces and by which Christians promise to remain united to God through the church. In this, later Western tradition followed lines of development that we can trace back to Tertullian and Cyprian, but is also deeply (if not universally) influenced by Augustine's vision of the effect and character of sacramental signs. Augustine's emphases combined with sometimes quite ancient assumptions, such as that a *sacramentum* is most fundamentally a promise. For example, in the seventh century Isidore explains, "A *sacramentum* is a bond given in support of a promise, and it is called a *sacramentum* (lit. 'holy thing') because to violate a promise is a breach of faith" (Isidore, *Etym.* 5.31; Isidore 2006: 121). And yet Isidore also offers us a clear summary that incorporates Augustine and the broader Latin tradition into a synthesis that would be fundamental for Latin Christianity in the centuries that followed:

> A sacrament takes place in a particular liturgical rite when an action is performed in such a way that it is understood to signify something that ought to be received in a holy way. Sacraments, then, are baptism and unction, and the body and blood. These things are called sacraments for this reason, that under the covering of corporeal things the divine virtue very secretly brings about the saving power of those same sacraments—whence from their secret or holy power they are called sacraments. Sacraments are fruitfully performed under the aegis of the Church because the Holy Spirit dwelling in the Church in a hidden way brings about the aforesaid effect of the sacraments. Hence, although they may be dispensed through the Church of God by good or by bad ministers, nevertheless because the Holy Spirit mystically vivifies them ... these gifts are neither enlarged by the merits of good ministers nor diminished by the bad. For this reason in Greek a sacrament is called a 'mystery', because it has a secret and recondite character. (Isidore, *Etym.* 6.39–42; Isidore 2008: 148–149)

SUGGESTED READING

Kelly, J. N. D. (1977), "The Later Doctrine of the Sacraments," in *Early Christian Doctrines* (London: A & C Black), 422–458 is an accessible chapter on sacraments that could be helpful for students, but it is a bit older than some of the newer encyclopedias we cite in the chapter and which can be found below. Those encyclopedias should also be consulted. There is no good and up-to-date one-volume treatment of the sacraments covering Augustine and subsequent Western developments up to 600.

BIBLIOGRAPHY

Anciaux, P. (1962), *The Sacrament of Penance* (London: Sheed & Ward).

Augustine (1988), *Tractates on the Gospel of John 1–10*, trans. John W. Rettig, Fathers of the Church 78 (Washington, DC: Catholic University of America Press).

Augustine (1991), *Sermons* (51–94), Works of Saint Augustine III/3 (Hyde Park, NY: New City).

Augustine (1993), *Sermons* (230–72B), Works of Saint Augustine III/7 (Hyde Park, NY: New City).

Augustine (1995), *Sermons* (341–400), Works of Saint Augustine III/10 (Hyde Park, NY: New City).

Augustine (1996), *Teaching Christianity/De Doctrina Christiana*, Works of Saint Augustine I/11 (Hyde Park, NY: New City).

Augustine (1999), *Marriage and Virginity*, Works of Saint Augustine I/9 (Hyde Park, NY: New City).

Augustine (2001), *Confessions*, Works of Saint Augustine I/1 (Hyde Park, NY: New City).

Augustine (2001), *Letters 1–99*, Works of Saint Augustine II/1 (Hyde Park, NY: New City).

Augustine (2005), *On Christian Belief*, Works of Saint Augustine I/8 (Hyde Park, NY: New City).

Augustine (2007), *Answer to Faustus a Manichean*, Works of Saint Augustine I/20 (Hyde Park, NY: New City).

Cavadini, J. C. (2005), "Feeling Right: Augustine on the Passions and Sexual Desire," *Augustinian Studies* 36: 195–217.

Cavadini, J. C. (2010), "Eucharistic Exegesis in Augustine's *Confessions*," *Augustinian Studies* 41: 87–108.

Cutrone, E. J. (1999), "Sacraments," in Allan Fitzgerald (ed.), *Augustine Through the Ages: An Encyclopedia* (Grand Rapids, MI: Eerdmans).

Dallen, James (1986), *The Reconciling Community: The Rite of Penance* (Collegeville, MN: Liturgical Press).

De Vogue, A. (1985), "Eucharist and Monastic Life," *Worship* 59: 498–510.

Dodaro, R. (2004), *Christ and the Just Society in Augustine* (Cambridge: Cambridge University Press).

Facundus (2004), *Facundus d'Hermiane. Défense des Trois Chapitres (À Justinien), Livres VIII–IX*, Sources Chrétiennes 484 (Paris: Éditions du Cerf).

Favazza, Joseph A. (1988), *The Order of Penitents: Historical Roots and Pastoral Future* (Collegeville, MN: Liturgical Press).

Ferguson, Everett (2008), *Baptism in the Early Church: History, Theology, and Liturgy in the First Five Centuries* (Grand Rapids, MI: Eerdmans).

Fulgentius (1997), *Selected Works*, trans. Robert B. Eno (Washington, DC: Catholic University of America Press).

Gaudemet, J. (1962), "Holy Orders in Early Conciliar Legislation," in *The Sacrament of Orders. Some Papers and Discussions at a Session of the Centre de Pastorale Liturgique* (London: Aquin Press), 181–201.

Gy, P. M. (1962), "Notes on the Early Terminology of the Christian Priesthood", in *The Sacrament of Orders. Some Papers and Discussions at a Session of the Centre de Pastorale Liturgique* (London: Aquin Press), 98–115.

Harmless, W. (1995), *Augustine and the Catechumenate* (Collegeville, MN: Liturgical Press).

Harmless, W. (1999), "Baptism," in Allan Fitzgerald (ed.), *Augustine Through the Ages: An Encyclopedia* (Grand Rapids, MI: Eerdmans).

Hunter, D. G. (1999), "Marriage," in Allan Fitzgerald (ed.), *Augustine Through the Ages: An Encyclopedia* (Grand Rapids, MI: Eerdmans).

Isidore of Seville (2006), *Etymologies*, trans. S. Barney, W. Lewis, J. Beach, and O. Berghof (Cambridge: Cambridge University Press).

Isidore of Seville (2008), *De Ecclesiastics Officiis*, trans. Thomas L. Knoebel (New York: Paulist Press).

Jackson, P. (1999), "Eucharist," in Allan Fitzgerald (ed.), *Augustine Through the Ages: An Encyclopedia* (Grand Rapids, MI: Eerdmans).

Jeanes, G. P. (1988), *The Origins of The Roman Rite* (Cambridge: Grove).

Jensen, R. (2012), *Baptismal Imagery in Early Christianity: Ritual, Visual, and Theological Dimensions* (Grand Rapids, MI: Baker Academic).

Jensen, R. and P. Burns (1999), "Eucharistic Liturgy," in Allan Fitzgerald (ed.), *Augustine Through the Ages: An Encyclopedia* (Grand Rapids, MI: Eerdmans).

Johnson, Maxwell L. (1999), *The Rites of Christian Initiation: Their Evolution and Interpretation* (Collegeville, MN: Liturgical Press).

Joncas, J. M. (1999), "Ordination, Orders," in Allan Fitzgerald (ed.), *Augustine Through the Ages: An Encyclopedia* (Grand Rapids, MI: Eerdmans).

Kavanagh, Aidan (1988), *Confirmation: Origins and Reform* (Collegeville, MN: Liturgical Press).

Lampe, G. W. H. (1951), *The Seal of the Spirit, A Study in the Doctrine of Baptism and Confirmation in the New Testament and the Fathers* (London: SPCK).

St. Leo the Great (1957), *Letters*, trans. E. Hunt (Washington, DC: Catholic University of America Press).

Macy, G. (2013), "Sacramental Theology," in Karla Pollman and Willemein Otten (eds.), *The Oxford Guide to the Historical Reception of Augustine* (Oxford: Oxford University Press).

Martimort, A. G. (1986), *Deaconesses an Historical Study*, trans. K.D. Whitehead (San Francisco, CA: Ignatius Press).

Mathisen, R. (1989), *Ecclesiastical Factionalism and Religious Controversy in Fifth-Century Gaul* (Washington, DC: Catholic University of America Press).

Mazza, Enrico (1999), *The Celebration of the Eucharist: The Origin of the Rite and the Development of Its Interpretation*, trans. Matthew J. O'Connell (Collegeville, MN: Liturgical Press).

Nocent, A. (2014), "Sacraments," in Angelo di Beradino (ed.), *Encyclopedia of Ancient Christianity* (Downers Grove, IL: InterVarsity Press).

Nocent, A. (2014a), "Order—Ordination," in Angelo di Beradino (ed.), *Encyclopedia of Ancient Christianity* (Downers Grove, IL: InterVarsity Press).

Otranto, G. (1991), "Priesthood, Precedent, and Prejudice. On Recovering the Women Priests of Early Christianity," trans. Mary Ann Rossi, *Journal of Feminist Studies in Religion*, 7: 73–93.

Pasquato, O. (2014), "Catechumenate—Discipleship," in Angelo di Beradino (ed.), *Encyclopedia of Ancient Christianity* (Downers Grove, IL: InterVarsity Press).

Reynolds, P. (1994), *Marriage in the Western Church. The Christianization of Marriage during the Patristic and Early Medieval Periods* (Leiden: Brill).

Rousseau, O. (1962), "Priesthood and Monasticism," in *The Sacrament of Orders. Some Papers and Discussions at a Session of the Centre de Pastorale Liturgique* (London: Aquin Press), 168–180.

Van Der Meer, F. (1961), *Augustine the Bishop* (London: Sheed and Ward).

Vogel, C. (2014), "Penance," in Angelo di Beradino (ed.), *Encyclopedia of Ancient Christianity* (Downers Grove, IL: InterVarsity Press).

CHAPTER 12

....

LATE PATRISTIC DEVELOPMENTS IN SACRAMENTAL THEOLOGY IN THE EAST: FIFTH–NINTH CENTURIES

....

ANDREW LOUTH

SACRAMENTAL theology up to the end of the fourth century focuses on the sacrament of baptism: the fundamental incorporation into Christ's death and resurrection through baptism is *the* sacramental event. Reflection on the Eucharist is bound up with this, for the Eucharist was first encountered as the final stage of the process of initiation which included baptism and generally anointing of some kind (with oil or *myron*, or both: local customs varied); this is particularly true of the catecheses that survive from the fourth century (St. Cyril of Jerusalem [?], St. Ambrose, St. John Chrysostom, Theodore of Mopsuestia), that witness to the development of the initiatory rites after the peace of the church (see Yarnold 1972). At the beginning of the fifth century, there seems to be a change; the focus in sacramental theology moves to the Eucharist. Though the reasons for this are doubtless manifold, it is easy to give a brief explanation of this change. Well into the fourth century, very many (maybe, most) Christians adopted the faith as adults; in the course of the fourth century, the rites of initiation, beginning with baptism and concluding with the Eucharist, were made more dramatic to retain a strong sense of turning away from the world to the church. Very soon, more and more Christians were baptized as infants; baptism itself became an unconscious memory, and the focus of sacramental experience turned to the Eucharist, or Divine Liturgy. In the early sixth century, the author of the *Corpus Areopagiticum* (whom we shall refer to as Dionysius the Areopagite) calls the Eucharist (the σύναξις, in his terms) the "rite of rites" (τελετῶν τελετή), and comments that "hardly any of the hierarchic rites can be accomplished without the most divine eucharist at the climax of the celebration" (*EH* 3. 1).

THEOPHILUS OF ALEXANDRIA

The first clear sign of the shift of focus is to be found in a homily, once ascribed to St. Cyril of Alexandria, now restored to his uncle and predecessor in the see, St. Theophilus, "on the Mystical Supper." It was given on Holy Thursday, quite late in Theophilus' life (he died in 412), and therefore refers both to the foot washing and the giving of the commandment to love in imitation of Christ. So far as sacramental theology is concerned, there are several things to notice about this homily. Theophilus begins by recalling the figure of Wisdom in Proverbs 9, who prepares bread and wine for those seeking after wisdom. This, along with other examples from the Old Testament, forms a type, or prefiguration, of what Christ, the personal Wisdom (ἐνυπόστατος Σοφία), does in the Eucharist. The types of the Old Testament are not simply fulfilled in the Incarnate activity of Christ in his lifetime, but in the sacraments of the church. What Christ did in the upper room before his passion, what he achieved on the cross, what he does in the sacraments of the church: all these are assimilated to each other, all are seen as fulfillment of the prophetic types of the Old Testament. This conveys a very strong sense of the presence of Christ, the present activity of Christ, in the sacrament. So he remarks, referring to the fulfillment of the figure of Wisdom in Proverbs:

> The divine gifts are laid out, the mystical table has been prepared, the life-giving cup has been mixed. The King of Glory is summoning, the Son of God accepts, the incarnate Word of God invites. The substantive Wisdom of God the Father, who prepared for herself a temple not made by human hands [that is, the Virgin Mary], distributes her own body as bread, and gives her own life-giving blood as wine. O fearful mystery! ... (Russell 2007: 53–54)

Theophilus' understanding of the Eucharist is informed, too, by his strong sense of the inseparable unity of divinity and humanity in Christ, characteristic of the Alexandrian tradition that he embodies: precisely because of this, in encountering Christ in his human form, we encounter God himself, the second person of the Trinity, and this applies to the Eucharist. "For if it is the body of God that is distributed, then Christ the Lord is true God ... And if the drink is the blood of God, then one of the adorable Trinity, the Son of God, is not unveiled Godhead but God the Word incarnate" (Russell 2007: 59). His nephew Cyril shared this realistic sense of Christ's presence as God in the Eucharist; as Henry Chadwick remarked, "Every eucharist is a reincarnation of the Logos who is there πάλιν ἐν σώματι, and whose ἰδία σάρξ is given to the communicant" (Chadwick 1951: 155). It is hardly surprising that twice in the homily, Theophilus quotes 2 Peter 1:4, about becoming "partakers of the divine nature."

This strong sense of sacramental realism reposes on a robust Christology, in which perfect divinity and perfect humanity are united in Christ. It is both as God and man that Christ is active in the Eucharist, and especially in the offering of the eucharistic sacrifice. In words that were soon to find their way into the Byzantine liturgy, Theophilus affirms that "[w]e should believe that he remains simultaneously priest and victim, that he is both the one who offers and the one who is offered, that he is received and distributed" (Russell 2007: 60). Finally, the fact that Theophilus' words here soon found their way into the Byzantine rite should be noted, for throughout this period there is an overlap, or maybe better symbiosis, between theological reflection and liturgical development.

This link between theological reflection on the sacraments, or mysteries (μυστήρια) as they are designated in the Greek East, and liturgical celebration should be noted, for there is a strong sense in the Greek (and Orthodox) tradition that the sacraments are not isolated rites, but a central aspect of the liturgical activity of the church, so that "sacramental theology" treats the sacraments not as objects, but as activities.

DIONYSIUS THE AREOPAGITE

This is strikingly the case with our next figure, the author of the *Corpus Areopagitum*. Dionysius' influence on the Byzantine theological tradition has been immense, as it has been, though in a rather different way, on the theological tradition of the West. What we might call the "sacramental theology" of Dionysius is but an aspect of a more encompassing vision which draws together visible and invisible aspects of the cosmos, the relationship of the cosmos to God, and the way in which the divine-human community of the church celebrates, and furthers, the activities of the unknowable and transcendent God in the created order, both visible and invisible; there is a fundamental place, too, for the individual ascetic, or monk (μοναχός in Greek, cognate with μόνος, alone or single), who strives for contemplative union with God.

It is a central principle for Dionysius that the invisible expresses itself in the visible, while the visible can only be understood as it discloses the invisible: "truly visible things are manifest images of invisible things" (*Ep.* 10). The human being stands at the interface between the visible and the invisible, for the human itself is composed of both a visible body and an invisible soul; the role of grasping, and articulating, the relationship between the visible and the invisible falls to humankind. This sets up an understanding of the cosmos in which image and symbol are central: visible symbols and images disclose to us something of the invisible. What is to be understood, and participated in, is the way in which God's creative activity is expressed in the cosmos as a way of drawing the cosmos back into union with God. Behind this is the familiar neo-Platonic principle of existence as the meeting point of an outward movement from God, procession, and a movement of response to God on the part of the created order, a movement of return, expressed in a contemplative gaze directed towards God. This movement is a movement from the oneness of God to the multiplicity of the created order, which gathers up the manifold and restores it to its unity in God.

Dionysius' doctrine of the "sacraments" needs to be set against this broader background. This can be seen clearly in his account of the Eucharist, or the assembly (*synaxis*) as he calls it, for the Eucharist is centrally concerned with drawing the manifold together into the unity of God. As we have seen, all, or virtually all, liturgical rites find their fulfillment in the Eucharist, so what is true of the Eucharist applies in some way to the whole sacramental activity of the church. In his account of the Eucharist, Dionysius starts by giving an account of the censing of the church by the bishop, who comes from the sanctuary and encircles the church, censing it and the people, and then returns to the sanctuary. This symbolizes a movement out into multiplicity and back to unity—a movement from the One to the many and back to the One—a movement that enfolds the many and restores them to the One. The two terms, which Dionysius uses to designate the Eucharist, are assembly or gathering together, σύναξις, and communion, κοινωνία, for the gathering together of the community on behalf of the world, indeed the cosmos, leads to communion with, participation in, God's healing and reconciling unity.

Sacraments are, then, an aspect of the drawing together of the visible and the invisible, which is the peculiar business of the human, itself visible and invisible, as part of the restoration of the fragmented and decaying created order to the oneness of God and union with him. Dionysius' account of the Eucharist starts from the liturgical rite as actually performed; it is concerned with movement and ceremony—and song, which he mentions, too—rather than words and concepts. The words of the prayers are only alluded to, and his understanding of the sacramental rite seems to avoid any conceptuality; he rather points to the grand plan of God's saving work, οἰκονομία, so that when he talks about communion, instead of explaining the nature of the eucharistic presence, he speaks of the way in which, through the Incarnation, "out of the kindness of his love for humankind he calls the human race to participation in himself and in his own good things, since we are being united to his most divine life through assimilation of ourselves to him as far as possible, and through this being perfected in truth as participants in God and divine things" (*EH* 3. 13).

Dionysius' *Ecclesiastical Hierarchy* can be (and has been) regarded as a treatise on the sacraments, though it is better regarded as about the activities of "our hierarchy," as he calls it ("ecclesiastical" is only in the title, and is conceivably editorial). It starts with an introductory chapter on the nature and purpose of "our" hierarchy, interposed as it is between the "legal" hierarchy (of the Old Testament) and the purely spiritual "celestial" hierarchy (of the heavenly beings), its purpose being, as with all hierarchy, according to Dionysius, union with God and deification. There follow six chapters, first, on the three "rites" (τελεταί) of Illumination, Assembly, or Communion, and the rite of *myron*, or chrism, and then on priestly ordination, monastic consecration, and the (funeral) service for the holy departed, these latter are not called "rites," but simply "mysteries" (as are the rites themselves). It is misleading to think of the three "rites" as baptism, Eucharist and chrismation, for "Illumination" refers to the whole rite of initiation, including a pre-baptismal anointing with oil, a post-baptismal anointing with *myron*, and eucharistic Communion, while the sacrament of *myron* is mostly concerned with its elaborate ceremony of its consecration, and its use envisages much more than the chrismation that accompanies baptism (cf. *EH* 4. 3. 10).

MAXIMUS THE CONFESSOR

The next stage in the unfolding of sacramental reflection in the East is to be found in commentaries on the eucharistic liturgy, notably the *Mystagogia* of St. Maximus the Confessor and the *Ecclesiastical History and Mystical Contemplation* (perhaps more comprehensibly translated as "What happens in church and its hidden meaning"), ascribed in the manuscript tradition to various of the Fathers, but most likely by St. Germanus, patriarch of Constantinople 715 to 730, when he resigned over Emperor Leo III's introduction of Iconoclasm. Like Dionysius in the *Ecclesiastical Hierarchy* (and Maximus' *Mystagogia* is presented explicitly as a supplement to Dionysius' work), both these works set reflection on the sacraments in the context of the liturgical action, interpreted symbolically. Maximus' *Mystagogia* falls into three parts: first, an account of the symbolism of the church building in which the liturgical action takes place (cc. 1–7); secondly, an account of the liturgical action of the Eucharist (cc. 8–21); thirdly, a summary, which applies the liturgical actions to the life of the soul, and conclusion (cc. 22–24). In the first part, Maximus sets up a series of parallels. The first is between God and the church: between God, who has brought everything into being, and "contains, gathers, and limits them, and in his providence binds both intelligible and sensible beings to himself and one another," and the church, which is

> shown to be active among us in the same way as God, as an image reflects its archetype. For many and of nearly boundless number are the men, women and children who are distinct from one another and vastly different by birth and appearance, by race and language, by way of life and age, by opinions and skills, by manners and customs, by pursuits and studies, and still again by reputation, fortune, characteristics and habits: all are born into the Church and through it are reborn and recreated in the Spirit. To all in equal measures it gives and bestows one divine form and designation: to be Christ's and to bear his name.

The church's essential function is to draw all into unity, in this imitating the activity of God himself in the cosmos. This drawing into unity is continued in a series of other parallels, now between the church building, divided into nave and sanctuary, and the visible and invisible parts of the cosmos (*Myst.* 2); in the division within the visible cosmos between earth and heaven (*Myst.* 3); in the division within the human between body and soul (*Myst.* 4); in the division within the soul between the active and the contemplative functions of the soul (*Myst.* 5). There follow two further chapters outlining how the Scriptures can be said to be a human being (body and soul reflected in the Old and New Testaments, or in the distinction between literal and spiritual exegesis), and how the cosmos itself can be seen as a human being, and vice versa. The importance of this series of parallels is that it frames the liturgical symbolism that Maximus is going to explore in the second part of the *Mystagogia*, and thereby gives the liturgical action resonance from the cosmic to the psychological; what takes place in the church can only be understood by grasping its cosmic dimension, and its dimension that reaches into the depths of the soul. So as the liturgical action celebrates and re-enacts God's activity in the cosmos in creation and redemption, culminating in the mystery of the death and resurrection of Christ, recalled (in the strong sense of *anamnesis*, making present) in the Eucharist, the framing parallels make plain that the eucharistic celebration is effective not just for the gathered community, but for the whole cosmos, both visible and invisible, and for each human soul. The way in which the eucharistic action applies to the spiritual life of each Christian is recapitulated in the summary and conclusion.

It is important to grasp the significance of this framing, as otherwise the detailed symbolism explored in chapters 8–21 can seem arbitrary or, worse, as depriving the eucharistic action of its own significance by making it a cipher for something else— a recapitulation of the life of Christ, for instance. Such a recapitulation does enter the symbolism of the Eucharist as it developed later on, but there is little sign of it in Maximus' exposition. It is true that the entry of the bishop into the church is said to symbolize the Incarnation of the Word of God, and the bishop's entry into the sanctuary the Ascension and the Second Coming; the effect of this, however, is to place the whole action of the Eucharist in an eschatological setting—it all takes place after the second coming, which is, indeed, "remembered" in the eucharistic prayers of both St. Basil and St. John Chrysostom. The liturgical actions of the Eucharist are understood in terms of conversion of the world (the entry of the people into the church following the bishop), participation in God's intentions for us that involve struggle for the Gospel and ultimately martyrdom (the readings, the bishop's greeting "Peace to all"), the end of the world and judgment (the reading of the Gospel and the closing of the doors), union with God and one another, as heaven and earth come together, and deification (the entrance of the gifts, the kiss of peace, the Sanctus, the Lord's Prayer, and exclamation "One is Holy" and communion itself). Maximus' detailed explanation recalls the vivid impression given in the very earliest liturgies we have, such as that sketched in the *Didache*, of the Christian community, celebrating the Eucharist, and standing on the very threshold of the Kingdom. The cosmic dimension of the liturgy, developed by Maximus, influenced the architecture of Byzantine churches, built as miniature representations of the cosmos, with the nave representing the earth, and the dome and the sanctuary with its apse representing heaven. We should remember, too, that in *Myst.* 7, Maximus dwells on the notion of the human as a microcosm: in the church building, mirroring in its structure the cosmos, the human, the microcosm, fulfils his function of holding the cosmos in unity, something the human abandoned at the Fall, but which has been restored through the Incarnation and the Paschal Mystery. Maximus is at pains, too (in *Myst.* 4–5, 23–24), to demonstrate how the rhythms of the spiritual life of the soul are reflected in the structures of the Divine Liturgy.

GERMANUS OF CONSTANTINOPLE

Germanus' *What Happens in the Church and Its Hidden Meaning* develops in a highly condensed form what we have found in Dionysius and Maximus (indeed, many manuscripts of the work have inserted excerpts from Maximus' *Mystagogia* into it). Germanus' work became very influential and was often incorporated into the priest's book (the *Hieratikon*) of the liturgy as a kind of authoritative guide to the interpretation of the liturgy. Here we find the kind of detailed symbolism, mapping the liturgical actions on to the life of Christ, that has been generally deplored by modern liturgical scholars. It is certainly present: the apse corresponds to the cave of the Nativity, the holy table to the place in the tomb where Christ's body was placed, the altar (that is, the sanctuary) to the tomb itself. This is, however, only one strand. This is quite clear in the first chapter, where we are told:

> The church is the temple of God, a holy place, a house of prayer, the assembly of the people, the body of Christ. It is called the bride of Christ . . .
> The church is an earthly heaven in which the God beyond the heavens dwells and walks about. It represents the crucifixion, burial, and resurrection of Christ: it is glorified more than the tabernacle of the witness of Moses, in which are the mercy-seat and the Holy of Holies. It is prefigured in the patriarchs, foretold by the prophets, founded in the apostles, adorned by the hierarchs, and fulfilled in the martyrs. (Meyendorff 1984: 57)

This definition of the church draws together at least five registers of reference: it is a place, a people, heaven on earth, the paschal mystery, the fulfillment, in some way, of the Temple of the Jews (originally the Tabernacle, the tent that was the place of the divine presence after the flight from Egypt). Consequently, the symbolism often operates at several of these levels, there is no simple mapping of the life of Christ on to the liturgical action; that is but one element and evoked quite episodically. The holy table, we have seen, represents the place in the tomb where the body of Jesus was laid. It represents, too, the throne of God, borne by the cherubim, the table at which Christ celebrated the Last Supper, and the table in the tabernacle/temple on which was placed the manna, which itself symbolizes Christ, descended from heaven (cf. John 6:58). The parallel between the historical events of Christ's life and the liturgical action is one among many: the liturgical action fulfils the liturgy of the Temple of the Old Testament, it reflects and joins us to the worship of heaven. The importance of place is recognized (the word translated "place" above represents the Greek τέμενος, a sacred place, a shrine), but the liturgical action is the action of the people of God, a structured community, in which can be discerned various ranks and functions. The meaning of the liturgical action is, therefore, manifold, discerned within a symbolic world that has, as it were, several chambers of resonance.

The question of the real presence of Christ in the Eucharist, so important to Theophilus, might seem to be rather mute in Dionysius, Maximus, and Germanus, and the question of the eucharistic sacrifice rather lost in a host of symbolic references. This perception, I suspect, has more to do with the way in which in the West sacramental theology came to be very sharply defined (as did much else). Symbolism in the Fathers (perhaps especially the Greek Fathers) is not a matter of arbitrary signs, to be interpreted by the mind; instead, symbolism is participatory: to apprehend the symbol is to participate in the reality symbolized. Furthermore, the purpose of the symbolism is made plain: in all three Fathers discussed the purpose of the symbols is to draw the believer, through the world of the senses, into the spiritual world and ultimately to union with God. It is emphasized over and over again that the liturgical rites are means of deification, union with God. Maximus explores this further with his idea that the reality into which the symbolic structures of the liturgical action introduce us are to be assimilated by ascetic activity, pursuit of the virtues, and the extirpation of vices. There are paths through the forest of symbols; it is not a place to get lost. Nevertheless, there is insistence, parallel to what we have found in Theophilus, on a reality that is simply there. In his account of the Holy Gifts, Germanus explores their symbolism: the bread used by the priest represents God's overflowing goodness, and also (presumably because it is leavened bread, though this is not explicit) represents the perfect human nature the Son of God assumed in the Incarnation; the piece, now called the lamb, cut by the priest from the loaf to be consecrated signifies the sheep led to the slaughter (Isa 53:7); the wine and water signify the blood and water that came from Christ's pierced side. And then he comes to the bread and the chalice: these he says are "really and truly [κυρίως καὶ ἀληθῶς], by imitation of the mystical supper, in which Christ took bread and wine ..." (c. 22)—the sentence seems lacunose, but it must mean that the bread and wine become really and truly the body and blood of Christ. This conviction of the utter reality of what is encountered in the Eucharist is manifest, it seems to me, in the very simplicity with which Germanus speaks of Holy Communion: "Partaking of the divine mysteries is called Communion because it bestows on us unity with Christ and makes us partakers of His Kingdom" (Meyendorff 1984: 107).

John of Damascus

The nature and limits of symbolism came to a head in the Byzantine world with the iconoclast controversy. Deeply involved in the Orthodox response to iconoclasm was St. John Damascene. His teaching on sacramental theology, however, probably predates the controversy over icons, and is certainly earlier than the developments in iconoclast theology that provoked clarification among the Orthodox over the nature of the eucharistic presence. We shall, therefore, turn to the Damascene first.

In his *On the Orthodox Faith*, there is a chapter devoted to "The holy and pure mysteries of the Lord" (86; in the Latin enumeration, IV.13). Although the baptism is mentioned in this chapter (there is also a separate chapter on baptism: 82), it is predominantly about the Eucharist, which provides further confirmation of our contention that in our period the Eucharist has become the focus of sacramental reflection. The chapter begins, however, with a paragraph about God's loving concern for his creation with which he intends to share the "wealth of his goodness": the mysteries, or sacraments, in general, and the Eucharist, in particular, are the means by which this is made possible; the mysteries themselves are made possible by the Mystery of Christ, the Paschal Mystery. He emphasizes, too (as he had in the chapter on baptism), that sacraments, involving as they do material things, are appropriate means of God's sharing with us his goodness, because human beings are twofold, with material bodies and spiritual souls, and therefore need to be provided for at both material and spiritual levels. After giving an account of the institution of the Eucharist, he goes on to affirm the reality of the transformation of the eucharistic bread and wine into the pure body and precious blood of Christ, first, by referring to the creative power of the Word of God, who both created everything at the beginning and also formed for himself humanity from the human nature of the Mother of God, and secondly, by invoking "the overshadowing power of the Holy Spirit." The creative Word and the power of the Spirit are sufficient explanation: "I tell you, the Holy Spirit comes down and does these things that are beyond reason and understanding." The use of bread and wine in the Eucharist is a concession to human weakness; as with all sacramental actions, God takes what we are used to—bread, wine, water, oil—"so that through what we are familiar with and in accordance with nature we might come to those things that are above nature." The eucharistic body is "the body truly united to divinity, that which came from the holy Virgin, not that the body that was taken up comes down from heaven, but that the bread itself and the wine are changed into the body and blood of God." We cannot know how this change takes place, but he gives an analogy (drawn from Gregory of Nyssa's *Catechetical Oration*, which John is following closely here) of the way in which food and drink are changed into a human body by the process of digestion, "so the bread of the offering and the wine and water are changed in a way beyond nature through the invocation and descent of the Holy Spirit into the body and blood of Christ."

John goes on to reject the idea (that we shall see was to be dear to the iconoclasts) that the eucharistic bread and wine are a figure, τύπος, of the body and blood of Christ: they are the "deified body of the Lord itself." Similarly, if the sacred elements are spoken of as "antitypes," as they are in the Liturgy of St. Basil, this is so only before the consecration. The Eucharist is also called "participation" (μετάληψις), because through it we participate in the divinity of Christ, and "communion" (κοινωνία), because "through it we have communion with Christ and partake in his flesh and his divinity, and have communion and are united with one another through it. For since we partake of one bread, we all become one body and one blood of Christ and members of each other, having become con-corporate with Christ."

The importance of the bodily and material aspect of the sacraments for John Damascene emerges in a passage in his third *Treatise against the Iconoclasts*, where he argues that, because "the two natures [of Christ] are hypostatically and inseparably united in the Body of Christ, of which we partake ... we share in the two natures, in the body in a bodily manner, and in the divinity spiritually ... through assimilation with the Body and the Blood" (Louth 2003: 103); for this reason, he continues, we are higher than the angels who, with their purely spiritual natures, cannot be united to the Godhead as we human beings are through participation in the body and blood of Christ in the Eucharist.

The clarity with which John Damascene affirms the reality of the presence of Christ in the Eucharist does not at all mean that he fails to recognize the power and importance of symbols and images. On the contrary, in his defense of the making and veneration of icons, he argues that, because we are twofold, both material and spiritual, it is only through recourse to images and symbols that we can come to grasp anything of the spiritual realm of the angels and the uncreated nature of God. God is utterly unknowable in his being, but through symbols and images we can come to some knowledge of God and participation in him; something similar is true of the spiritual world of the heavenly beings.

THE EUCHARIST AND THE ICONOCLAST CONTROVERSY

Iconoclasm, of which John Damascene was the most redoubtable opponent, led to a resounding affirmation of the kind of clarification of the nature of the eucharistic presence that we have found in the Damascene. This was the side effect of the attempt under Constantine V in the 740s, in the preparation of the Synod of Hiereia of 754, that endorsed iconoclasm, to provide a theological justification for iconoclasm. Initially, it seems, in the reign of Leo III, iconoclasm was simply a matter of the rejection of the icons as idols. In the 740s, encouraged (or led) by Constantine V, a more sophisticated argument was adduced. This was contained in the *Inquiries—Peuseis—*written by Constantine V himself, as papers in preparation of the synod he eventually called in 754 to be the Seventh Œcumenical Synod, now known as the Synod of Hiereia, after the palace where it took place. The argument of the *Peuseis* was incorporated in the definition, or *Horos*, of the Synod of Hiereia. Both the *Peuseis* and the *Horos* survive in Orthodox sources: the latter in the acts of the sixth session of Nicaea II, where it was read out paragraph by paragraph and refuted, and the former in the extracts quoted from it by Patriarch Nikephoros in his refutation, the three *Antirrhetici adversus Constantium Copronynum*. From these sources, we can, I think, venture to assemble a carefully constructed argument against icons, both their fashioning and their veneration. First of all, an icon could only function if it were a true icon—an undeceiving icon, ἀψευδὴς εἰκών. There followed two lines of attack arguing that a visual icon was a false, deceptive icon—ψευδὴς εἰκών. First, a true icon would need to be consubstantial (ὁμοούσιος) with the original, as the eternal Son was consubstantial with the Father; this was obviously not the case with a visual icon. As this does not concern sacramental theology, we shall pass over it. Secondly, noting that icons were claimed by the iconodules to recall the memory of some holy person or event, the iconoclasts offered an alternative to the icon by claiming that the real way of remembering Christ was to do what he had asked his followers to do in his memory—that is, to celebrate the holy mystery of the Eucharist. Instead of an icon made by an artist, the true way of remembering Christ, the iconoclasts claimed, was in the Eucharist, which was a true type or figure—τύπος—of Christ, in some sense genuinely ὁμοούσιος with Him. The series of extracts from the *Peuseis* concerning the Eucharist read thus:

> According to his godhead he foresaw his death and resurrection and the ascent into the heavens, and that we who believe in him would preserve a continual memory of his Incarnation day and night ... And he commanded his holy disciples and apostles to pass on a figure of his incarnation [τύπον εἰς σῶμα αὐτοῦ] in a way that pleased him; so that through the priestly service [τῆς ἱερατικῆς ἀναγωγῆς], if we take part according to the ordinance, we receive it as truly and properly his body ... And if we wish to understand the image [εἰκών] of his body as something derived from that [*sc.* the body], we take this as the true form of his body ... For why? The body that we receive is an image [εἰκών] of his body, having the form [μορφάζων] of his flesh, since it has become a figure [τύπος] of his body ... Nor is any bread his body, just as neither is any wine his blood, but only that which has been taken up through the priestly rite from that which is made with hands to that which is not made with hands [διὰ τῆς ἱερατικῆς τελετῆς ἀναφερόμενος ἐκ τοῦ χειροποιήτου πρὸς τὸ ἀχειροποίητον]. (Hennephof 1969: 54–55)

The argument here is: (1) that we should remember Christ in the way he commanded us; (2) that this is through the bread and wine of the Eucharist, which are a τύπος and εἰκών of his body and blood; (3) that here we find the true ἀχειροποίητος icon, the true icon "made without hands"; (4) that this figure and image of Christ is only made through the proper priestly rite (the importance of this underlined by its being affirmed twice).

There are a couple of points worth emphasizing. First, we should recognize that this is intended to be an uncontroversial affirmation of the real presence of Christ in the Eucharist. The language of τύπος, in particular, is taken from the eucharistic texts; the anaphora of St. Basil, the one most commonly used at this time in the liturgy at Hagia Sophia, as is well known, refers to τὰ ἀντίτυπα τοῦ ἁγίου σώματος καὶ αἵματος τοῦ Χριστοῦ σου (the antitypes of the holy body and blood of your Christ). The use of the language of type and antitype is not at all meant to deny that the consecrated bread and wine is truly the body and blood of Christ. What the iconoclasts are saying is that the bread and wine are symbols of the body and blood of Christ made present in the Eucharist, and to express this they are simply using traditional, hallowed language. Secondly, note the claim that the Eucharist is not just an icon, but an icon, "made without hands," ἀχειροποίητος. One argument in favor of icons was surely (though this argument is not important in the justification of icons we find in St. John Damascene) that there are icons "made without hands," miraculous icons like the face of Christ impressed on the *mandylion*, whose very existence demonstrates divine approval and authentication of icons. Finally, and closely related to this iconoclast undermining of claims about icons "made without hands," we should notice the stress on the "priestly rite" that effects the presence. In short, the iconoclast claim—and argument—was that the true "image and type" of Christ is the one he has provided us with, the consecrated bread and wine of the Eucharist; this is the true icon "made without hands"; and it can only be furnished through priestly consecration.

It would, I think, be fair to say that the iconoclast argument that involved the Eucharist was not, in fact, about the Eucharist at all. Their argument was about the nature of the icon. They took for granted that in the Eucharist Christ was truly present under the types or figures of bread and wine, and argued from this that the Eucharist was a—the—true consubstantial image or icon of Christ. It was their orthodox opponents who turned what, for the iconoclasts, was an argument about the nature of the icon into an argument about the nature of Christ's presence in the Eucharist.

The response of the Orthodox defenders of the icons to this argument of the icono-clasts was to dismiss what their opponents thought was uncontroversial eucharistic the-ology and claim that the consecrated elements are *not* types and images, but the very body and blood of Christ. Nikephoros argues that the bread becomes the body "which the Word assumed from the moment he became incarnate" (*antirr.* 2: PG 100: 333C); it is not a matter of form or shape (μόρφωσις: compare the word used in the *Peuseis*), but of truth (διὰ τὴν ἀλήθειαν: 336B). He goes on to argue, as John Damascene had done, about the use of the word ἀντίτυπα of the bread and wine in the anaphora of St. Basil, that "they are called this not after the sanctification, but before being sanctified" (οὐ μετὰ τὸν ἁγιασμόν τοῦτο, ἀλλὰ πρὸ τοῦ ἁγιασθῆναι ἐκλήθησαν: 336C). Similarly, St. Theodore the Stoudite makes this rejoinder to his iconoclast opponent:

> But if they [the consecrated body and blood of Christ] are the truth—as indeed they really are, for we confess that the faithful receive the very body and blood of Christ, according to the voice of God himself—why do you talk nonsense, changing the mysteries of the truth into types? (Roth 1981: 30)

It has been argued that this change in emphasis led to the anaphora of St. Basil, which refers to the eucharistic elements as "antitypes," being dislodged from its position as the normal liturgy of the Great Church to be replaced by the Liturgy of St. John Chrysos-tom with its more unequivocal language (Alexopoulos 2006). It may also have led to a focus-ing on the *epiklesis* as *the* moment of consecration, since the use of the term "antitypes" in the anaphora of St. Basil occurs just before that moment in the prayer.

Conclusion

The iconoclast controversy, therefore, led to a renewed emphasis on the reality of the presence of Christ in the Eucharist that we found affirmed, for Christological reasons, at the beginning of our period. In between, we find the development of a rich symbolism that interpreted the sacraments and provided avenues of participation for those who participated in them. Moreover, the emphasis on symbolism helped to underline the sense, present in the liturgical texts, that the earthly liturgy participates in the heavenly liturgy, for, as we have seen, symbolism is multivalent, so there is no difficulty in the liturgy of the church on earth celebrating the Paschal mystery, finding that interpreted in the Old Testament Temple, and reflecting the perpetual liturgy of the heavens: indeed, bringing all these together helps to emphasize the eschatological nature of Christian worship. As the nature of the eucharistic presence, and the nature of the eucharistic sacrifice, came to be explored more deeply, the relationship between the historical events at the supper and on the cross, on the one hand, and the liturgical action of the church, is in some way "triangulated" by the sense that both this historical past and the liturgical present can only be understood in terms of the eternity of heaven. Perhaps for this reason the East avoided some of the problems in understanding the Eucharist that began to emerge in the West in the ninth century.

SUGGESTED READING

Berthold (1985), 183–225; John Damascene (1973), 354–361; Luibheid (1987), 193–259; Meyendorff (1984); Russell (2007), 52–60.

BIBLIOGRAPHY

Texts

Dionysius the Areopagite (1991), *Ecclesiastical Hierarchy* (*EH*) in Günter Heil and Adolf Martin Ritter (eds.), *Corpus Dionysiacum* II (Berlin: Walter de Gruyter), 61–132; *Epistle* 10 in ibid., 208–210; trans. (not used) Luibheid (1987).

Germanus of Constantinople, *Historia Ecclesiastica et Mystica Contemplatio*, text and trans. Meyendorff (1984).

John Damascene (1973), *On the Orthodox Faith*, ed. B. Kotter, *Die Schriften des Johannes von Damaskos* I, PTS 12 (Berlin: Walter de Gruyter); trans. (not used), St. John of Damascus, trans. Frederic H. Chase, jnr., Fathers of the Church 37, New York: Fathers of the Church Inc. (1958).

John Damascene (1975), *Treatises against the Iconoclasts*, ed. B. Kotter, *Die Schriften des Johannes von Damaskos* III, PTS 17 (Berlin: Walter de Gruyter); trans. Louth (2003).

Iconoclast texts: Hennephof, Herman (1969), *Textus Byzantinos ad Iconomachiam Pertinentes* (Leiden: E.J. Brill).

Maximos the Confessor (2011), *Mystagogia*, ed. Christian Boudignon, CCSG 69 (Turnhout: Brepols); trans. (not used) Berthold (1985), 183–225.

Nikephoros of Constantinople, *Antirrhetici III adv. Constantinum Copronymum*, PG 100: 205–534.

Theodore the Stoudite, *Antirrhetici III adversus Iconomachos*, PG 99: 327–436; trans. Roth (1981).

Theophilus of Antioch, "On the Mystical Supper", PG 77:1016C–1029B; trans. Russell (2007), 52–60.

Studies and translations

Alexopoulos, Stephanos (2006), "The Influence of Iconoclasm on Byzantine Liturgy: A Case Study," in Roberta Ervine (ed.), *Worship Traditions in Armenia and the Neighboring Christian East* (Crestwood, NY: St. Vladimir's Seminary Press), 127–137.

Berthold, George C. (1985), *Maximus the Confessor. Selected Writings* (London: SPCK).

Chadwick, Henry (1951), "Eucharist and Christology in the Nestorian Controversy," *JTS* ns 2: 145–164.

Louth, Andrew (2003), *St John of Damascus, On the Divine Images* (Crestwood, NY: St. Vladimir's Seminary Press).

Louth, Andrew (2009), "The Doctrine of the Eucharist in the Iconoclast Controversy," [in Russian] in Православное учение о церковных таинствах. V Международная Богословская Конференция Русской Православной Церкви. Москва, 13–16 ноября 2007. Vol. 2: Евхаристия: богословие и Священство, Москва: Синодальная Библейско-Богословская комиссия, 124–129.

Luibheid, Colm (1987), *Pseudo-Dionysius: The Complete Works* (New York: Paulist Press).

Meyendorff, Paul (1984), *St Germanus of Constantinople. On the Divine Liturgy* (Crestwood, NY: St. Vladimir's Seminary Press).

Pelikan, Jaroslav (1974), *The Spirit of Eastern Christendom (600–1700)*, vol. 2 of *The Christian Tradition: A History of the Development of Doctrine* (Chicago: University of Chicago Press), 95–145 *passim*.

Roth, Catherine (1981), *St Theodore the Studite: On the Holy Icons* (Crestwood, NY: St. Vladimir's Seminary Press).

Russell, Norman (2007), *Theophilus of Alexandria* (London: Routledge).

Sahas, Daniel (1986), *Icon and Logos. Sources in Eighth-Century Iconoclasm* (Toronto Medieval Texts and Translations 4, University of Toronto Press).

Stone, Darwell (1909), *A History of the Doctrine of the Holy Eucharist*, vol. I (London: Longmans, Green and Co.), 55–156.

Yarnold, Edward (1972), *The Awe Inspiring Rites of Initiation. Baptismal Homilies of the Fourth Century* (Slough: St. Paul Publications).

PART III

MEDIEVAL SACRAMENTAL THEOLOGY

CHAPTER 13

SACRAMENTAL THEOLOGY FROM GOTTSCHALK TO LANFRANC

MARK G. VAILLANCOURT

In sacramental theology from the ninth century to the eleventh, an extended debate on the doctrine of the real presence took place as to whether the body of Christ in the Eucharist was the same as the body born of the Virgin, which suffered and died, and is now risen in glory at the right hand of the Father. This debate began in response to the first ever monograph on the Eucharist, the *De corpore et sanguine Christi* by Paschasius of Corbie. This work formed the basis of a discussion on the sacrament for almost 250 years, spurring doctrinal development and theological speculation on the Eucharist throughout the period. This chapter will address the doctrinal elements of that debate, beginning with an exposition of Paschasius' work, followed by a treatment of both his critics and supporters from Gottschalk of Orbais to Lanfranc of Canterbury, placing special emphasis on the teaching about the presence of Christ, and the substantial change in the elements of bread and wine by which it is brought about.

PASCHASIUS RADBERTUS AND THE NINTH-CENTURY EUCHARISTIC DEBATE

In around 831, Paschasius of Corbie wrote a treatise on the Eucharist for the monks at the new foundation of Corvey (Ganz 1990: 29), the *De corpore et sanguine Christi*. A second edition of the work, written in around 844, was a gift to the Emperor Charles the Bald. The *Epistola ad Frudegardum*, largely an apologetic for the *De corpore*, was written no later than 860 and consisted mostly of patristic sources that supported Paschasius' eucharistic doctrine (Fahey 1951: 4). His theological treatise on the Virgin Birth entitled

De partu virginis, as well as his *Expositio in Matthaeum* further elucidate his eucharistic teachings. Although the works of Paschasius take great care to treat the Eucharist as a sacrament and a sacrifice, his central concern in the *De corpore* was "to show that the Eucharistic flesh of Christ is identical to the historical body of Christ" (Appleby 2005: 18), that is, the "body born of the Virgin Mary, that hung upon the cross, was buried in the tomb, rose from the dead, pierced the heavens and has now been made eternal high priest who daily intercedes for us" (Paschasius, *De corpore* 7: CCCM 16, 38). Paschasius has often been categorized as an ultra-realist because of this; yet his understanding of the sacrament as a mystery and his fidelity to the patristic sources, especially Ambrose and Augustine, as well as his significance in the theological development of eucharistic doctrine, merits a reconsideration of this charge.

Paschasius says "it is in mystery," or that which is secret or hidden, that Christ's "own body [*proprium corpus*]" (Paschasius, *Ad Fred.*: CCCM 16, 145), which was "handed over," and "his own blood that was poured out on behalf of our offenses" (Paschasius, *Ad Fred.*: CCCM 16, 146) is communicated with in the sacrament of the Lord's body and blood (Paschasius, *De corpore* 1: CCCM 16, 15). Present in *reality* or *truth* (*veritas*) (Paschasius, *De corpore* 1: CCCM 16, 18; *De corpore* 2: CCCM 16, 21; *De corpore* 4: CCCM 16, 27), his true flesh and his true blood are immolated daily in the eucharistic sacrifice for the forgiveness of sins. In this sacrament of his flesh, Christ remains "corporally" (Paschasius, *De corpore* 9: CCCM 16, 55) and "whole" (Paschasius, *De corpore* 7: CCCM 16, 39), by a presence that is "powerfully created" (Paschasius, *De corpore* 4: CCCM 16, 27) by God from the substance of the bread and the substance of the wine. This presence is brought about from a secret power by the consecration of the priest and the activity of the Holy Spirit (Paschasius, *De corpore* 4: CCCM 16, 28).

In agreement with Augustine, a sacrament for Paschasius is a sacred sign made up of both figure and truth. The figure is what can be perceived by the senses, the truth on the other hand, is the inner reality contacted only by faith. According to Paschasius, the inner reality of the Eucharist is not perceptible because "God the Father in his wisdom has decided that the bread and wine, which have been changed, should remain in the outward appearance of color and taste, although what should be recognized is none other than the flesh and blood" (Paschasius, *De corpore* 10: CCCM 16, 69). This change, brought about from the pre-existing substances of bread and wine, comes from the will of God (Paschasius, *De corpore* 1: CCCM 16, 13). It is the sacrament of his flesh, confected through the consecration at the altar by the ministry of the priest—Christ's real body that one receives spiritually.

An examination of the text shows that Paschasius is as intent upon stressing the real presence of Christ's historical body in the Eucharist as he is on emphasizing the spiritual nature of Holy Communion. "It is not right," he says, "that Christ should be torn by the teeth" (Paschasius, *De corpore* 4: CCCM 16, 27); one receives "spiritually," therefore, and not "carnally" (Paschasius, *De corpore* 20: CCCM 16, 106). For,

> Although [bread] is converted into flesh, and wine into blood ... nevertheless these
> things should be considered higher, for in no way is the flesh and blood of Christ

converted into our flesh and blood, but rather they raise us up from carnal things and make us spiritual. (Paschasius, *De corpore* 20: CCCM 16, 106)

The body of Christ is eaten, then, in a way that is "totally spiritual" (Paschasius, *De corpore* 10: CCCM 16, 69), where the power of faith and understanding "spiritually tastes and relishes" it (Paschasius, *De corpore* 13: CCCM 16, 83), so that the immaculate flesh of the lamb is "interiorly consumed" (Paschasius, *De corpore* 13: CCCM 16, 84).

In the eucharistic theology of Paschasius, therefore, there is a realism that identifies the historical body of Christ as the inner reality of the sacrament, brought about by a conversion of the elements of bread and wine in the daily sacrifice of the Mass. The outward appearances remain, hiding the internal reality of Christ, who can be perceived only by faith. Starting with Gottschalk, along with other contemporaries of Paschasius, the respondents to his doctrine challenged both the mode of this presence, or how real the real presence was, and what the Rule of Faith held about the same.

Re-discovered in the mid-twentieth century by Dom Germain Morin and edited by Dom Cyril Lambot (Morin 1931: 310–311), the *De corpore et sanguine domini* by Gottschalk of Orbais was probably written in around the year 850 during the time of his confinement in the abbey at Hautvillers. By his own account, Gottschalk became familiar with Paschasius' *De corpore* while in the Balkans (Gottschalk, *De corpore*: 325). What began as a criticism of some aspects of Paschasius by Gottschalk eventually developed into his own treatise on the nature of the real presence.

In agreement with Paschasius, Gottschalk understands the body and blood of the Lord to be his true flesh and blood, "powerfully created from the bread and the wine at the consecration by the power of the Holy Spirit" (Gottschalk, *De corpore*: 325). He could not accept, however, that the body of Christ in the Eucharist was the same body born of the Virgin, which suffered on the cross and rose from the tomb (Gottschalk, *De corpore*: 325), nor could he agree with Paschasius that Ambrose himself taught such realism. The historical body of Christ that walked this earth, he contended, could no longer be present to us in the sacrament. Further, the now glorified body of Christ could not be harmed, that is chewed by teeth, immolated, or sacrificed repeatedly in the daily celebration of the Eucharist (Gottschalk, *De corpore*: 326).

For Gottschalk, all important is the distinction *nec naturaliter sed specialiter* (Gottschalk, *De corpore*: 327) when contrasting the historical body of Christ with the eucharistic one. Christ now in glory is communicated with in a "special way," not a "natural way," in the sacrament. It is the body of Christ, born of the Virgin but now glorified, into which the sacrament is transferred *specialiter*. Furthermore, when one speaks about the church, it is the body of Christ *specialiter*, just as the Eucharist offered and received daily in her is also the body of Christ *specialiter* (Gottschalk, *De corpore*: 327).

Gottschalk views the reception of Holy Communion as a contrast between the body of Christ that *can be consumed*, brought about by the prayer of supplication of the priest, and that body born of the Virgin now in glory that *cannot be consumed* and which remains whole and entire in the sacrament (Gottschalk, *De corpore*: 327–328). The Eucharist is the body of Christ that is in heaven, and also on the altar, but in a special way. To clarify this point, Gottschalk notes that in the Eucharist there are not two bodies, but one. The one on the altar is transferred into the pre-existing one in heaven, so that the former is transferred into the latter in a special way so that, after the consecration, the two become one, just as the two natures divine and human unite in the one person of Christ, or man and wife who are two become one flesh (Gottschalk, *De corpore*: 334). Thus Gottschalk acknowledges that the inner reality of the sacrament is Christ, integral and whole, but present in a special, not a natural way. In this his theology is something quite different from that of Ratramnus of Corbie.

Written as a reply to the Emperor Charles the Bald, the *De corpore* of Ratramnus, (probably written at about the same time as the treatise of Gottschalk, that is, not long after Paschasius' revised 844 edition), was a response to two of the Emperor's questions about the realism of Paschasius: (1) Was the body of Christ visible after the consecration? (2) Is the body of Christ in the Eucharist the same body born of Mary? The reply by Ratramnus was one that moved away from realism toward symbolism, for Ratramnus held that the bread and wine, because they were sacraments, were merely symbols, and as such only a commemoration of Christ (Ratramnus, *De corpore* 97: PL 121,169). Christ, according to Ratramnus, becomes present in the Eucharist only by his power (Ratramnus, *De corpore* 19: PL121,136; *De corpore* 56: PL121,150), which he refers to as an "invisible substance" (Ratramnus, *De corpore* 49: PL121,147). What appear are the figures of the spiritual reality within, a reality or power perceptible only by faith (Ratramnus, *De corpore* 25: PL121,138). It is not Christ's body in truth, that is, the body born of Mary (Ratramnus, *De corpore* 89: PL121,165), but rather only his body in figure (Ratramnus, *De corpore* 92: PL121,167; *De corpore* 97: PL121,169).

Ratramnus came to his conclusions from the perspective that he adopted toward the nature of reality. For Ratramnus no change takes place because no change is perceived in the external reality present to the senses (Ratramnus, *De corpore* 56: PL121,150). It is not the inner reality of the sacrament that he focuses on, therefore, but rather what appears to the senses after the consecration. Like Gottschalk he also makes a distinction. Christ is present, he says, not *corporaliter* but *spiritualiter* (Ratramnus, *De corpore* 60: PL121,152). What happens is spiritual not physical, because of the contrast between truth and figure. Only what appears to the senses is true; a figure on the other hand, points to a more remote reality. Speaking in terms of what seems like a metaphor, Ratramnus employs a primitive form of empiricism in relation to the sacrament. For him there are no distinctions between species and inner reality; the former only points to the latter, which exists on the level of the spiritual, or non-physical.

A key to understanding the difference between the realism of Paschasius and the symbolism of Ratramnus is in their diverse understandings of the divine power of Christ's body over nature. Ratramnus refuses to attribute to the body of Christ a power that subjects the physical laws of nature to itself whereas Paschasius emphatically does. This is evident in the debate between the two on the perpetual virginity of the Virgin Mary (Paschasius, *De partu Virginis*: PL120,1365–1386). According to Paschasius, Christ can be physically present in the Eucharist through mystery because of his divine power—a power that allowed him to leave the womb of the Virgin intact, walk on the water and enter the Upper Room although all the windows and doors were barred and locked. Ratramnus, however, will admit of no such possibility (Ratramnus, *De Nativitate Christi*: PL121, 81–102; see Fahey 1951: 93–94). According to Ratramnus, Christ is in the sacrament only in the spiritual order and not the real because of physical impossibility. Not so for Paschasius; for him, Christ's body is actually present in the Eucharist because of the power that body is able to exercise over nature in general, and the elements of bread and wine in the Eucharist in particular. This same idea also seems to be present in the *specialiter* distinction of Gottschalk, who held that Christ's glorified body in heaven is present in the sacrament by a form of transference with the elements of bread and wine on the altar.

Thus for Ratramnus the conversion is spiritual and the celebration of the sacrament is figurative. The body and blood are figures pointing to an invisible spiritual reality. The visible species feeds the body and the soul is fed by the more powerful invisible spiritual substance, a view apparently held in part by the one-time abbot of Gottschalk and eventual Archbishop of Mainz, Rabanus Maurus.

In Rabanus Maurus, a contemporary of Paschasius, Gottschalk, and Ratramnus, there is an apparent partial rejection of the realism of Paschasius because of some of the earliest known discussions on stercorism—an opinion that held that the body of Christ in the Eucharist could not be the same body born of the Virgin, since it would then be subject to the natural laws of digestion. Rabanus denied, therefore, that the body of Christ could pass into the sewer and criticized those who have "recently written about the sacrament of the body and blood of the Lord," who do not think properly when they say that it is "the same body born of the Virgin, suffered on the cross and rose from the tomb" (Rabanus, *Poenitentiale* 33: PL110,493). Rather, for him, the Eucharist is a principle of unity where the members of the church are made one, joining all to Christ the head. "It is converted into us," he says, "when we eat and drink of it, and we are converted into the body of Christ when we live obediently and piously" (Rabanus, *De clericorum institutione* 31: PL107,318). The change of the bread into the body is real, as is the wine into his blood. What is visible, namely, the species, feeds the body, whereas what is invisible feeds the soul.

Thus, like Paschasius, Rabanus accepts a real presence of Christ; what is different is the mode of that presence. Like Gottschalk, he sees it not simply as a spiritual presence but rather as a real one, yet different from his life here on earth as well as his current one in glory. Unlike Ratramnus, he regards it not as simply a spiritual power, but rather as the real presence of Christ that generates the spirit of Christ in the believer. What are figures or symbols, on the other hand, are only the external appearances that point to the inner reality of Christ himself. With Paschasius and Gottschalk, he believes that the real presence of Christ is brought about by a miraculous change, for: "Who would ever believe," he says, "that bread could be converted into flesh, or wine into blood, unless the Savior himself, who created bread and wine and made all things out of nothing, said it" (Rabanus, *De sacris ordinibus* 19: PL112,1185).

Hincmar of Reims, another contemporary of these men, agreed with the doctrine of the real presence as an identity between the eucharistic and historical bodies of Christ.

In the Eucharist, he says, "the true blood of the immaculate Lamb cleanses us, who, although he sits at the right hand of the Father, nevertheless in the same flesh which he took from the Virgin accomplishes the Sacrament of propitiation" (Hincmar, *De cavendis vitiis et virtutibus exercendis* 10: PL125,928).

Along with Hincmar, Haymo of Halberstadt is another example of the acceptance of Paschasian realism. Haymo, a friend of Rabanus, became the abbot of Hersfeld in 839 and bishop of Halberstadt in 841. Haymo accepted Paschasius' teaching and held that the bread and wine were substantially converted into another substance, that is, into the flesh and blood: "The substance of the bread and the wine that are placed upon the altar become the body and blood of Christ through the mystery of the priest and the work of grace" (Haymo, *De corpore*: PL118,815). The substance of the bread and wine, he says, are converted into another substance through the operation of a divine power. The taste and appearance of bread and wine remain, although "the nature of the substances have been completely converted into the body and blood of Christ" (Haymo, *De corpore*: PL118,816). As to its sacramental character, "it must be observed," he says, "that the consecrated bread and cup are called signs" (Haymo, *De corpore*: PL118,817), but this does not refer to the flesh and blood of the Lord, but rather to "the likeness of the things received" (Haymo, *De corpore*: PL118,817), where the unity of the many grains of wheat in the bread and the many grapes in the wine express the unity of Christians in Christ. Furthermore, as was the case with all who accepted Paschasius' realism, for Haymo, the same Christ is received whole and entire under the forms of bread and wine (Haymo, *De corpore*: PL118,818).

From Haymo onward, a firm acceptance of Paschasian realism continues throughout the latter part of the Carolingian period into the Cluniac reform movement (Pelikan 1978: 85–86; Spinks 2013: 218). Especially in the Benedictine schools at the end of the tenth century, the eucharistic realism of Paschasius was widely and readily received as the tradition of the church, born of the Rule of Faith, and authoritative for interpreting the doctrine of the real presence.

The Era of Berengarius and the Pre-Scholastics

The fonts of theological study during the Carolingian Renaissance were tradition and sacred Scripture. The content of this tradition (*traditio*) was for the most part the decrees of the great ecumenical councils of the fourth and fifth centuries, the writings of the Fathers (especially Ambrose, Jerome, Augustine, and Gregory the Great), and papal pronouncements (utterances, epistles, and decretals). Tradition was used to interpret sacred Scripture, and tradition and Scripture taken together made for *auctoritas*, or "authority," the Rule of Faith by which orthodox theology was measured.

There is a change, however, with the Cluniac revival of the tenth century. A thorough study of the period revealed that the monks "in the cloister industriously collected and preserved costly libraries" (Grabmann 1909: 211–212). Most of these libraries contained two primary sixth-century authorities: the Calabrian Cassidorus (490–583) and the Roman Boethius (480–524) (Pederson 1997: 38), both of whom laid the foundation for monastic study of the classical works of antiquity. It is Boethius, however, to whom is owed the great debt of preserving much of the Aristotelian philosophical corpus for posterity.

The post-Carolingian period of the monastic schools, therefore, preserved a treasury of Aristotelian philosophy alongside the patristic corpus. These works were studied principally to learn the Latin language and the arts of rhetoric, but they also contained the "germ" of Aristotelian metaphysics. This rudimentary collection of Aristotle was in marked contrast with the latent philosophy of the fathers, most notably the early works of Augustine, which were essentially neo-Platonic. This same monastic treasury would also be the source of learning for the developing cathedral schools, and in Gerbert of Aurillac (945–1003), later Pope Sylvester II, there is the earliest shift of scholastic activity away from the monasteries to these cathedral schools.

In the cathedral school of Rheims where Gerbert taught there were many well-worn manuscripts of Boethius. With Gerbert and his own work entitled the *De corpore et sanguine domini*, reason or *ratio* comes to the defense of *auctoritas* as it was articulated in the work of Paschasius. Like the respondents before him, Gerbert was concerned as to whether or not what was received from the altar was that which was born of the Virgin. As a challenge to Rabanus (probably, because of manuscript confusion, Gottschalk) and Ratramnus, Gerbert cited the testimonies of Ambrose, Jerome, and Hilary in defense of Paschasius' realism (Gerbert, *De corpore* 2: PL139,181). Gerbert contended that although Paschasius might have been inaccurate in some of his quotations from the fathers, especially Ambrose (Gerbert, *De corpore* 8: PL139,187), it is the body of Christ both in figure and truth nonetheless: "Simply we confess that it is a figure while bread and wine are seen externally, truth, however, while the body and blood of Christ are believed in interiorly" (Gerbert, *De corpore* 4: PL139,182).

Of significance is Gerbert's citation of Cyril of Alexandria's *Third Letter Against Nestorius*, which refers to the vivifying flesh of Christ that the Word has made his own, as having a life naturally existing as God. This Gerbert sees as resolving all ambiguity implied in Ambrose, since, "naturally" the flesh which is received from the altar would be the same as that born of the Virgin. Here, the *naturaliter* used by Gerbert reflects Hilary's use of the word in his anti-Arian work, *De Trinitate*. The Eucharist, Gerbert says, is the same nature as Christ as Christ himself is the same nature as the Father (Gerbert, *De corpore* 6: PL139,184). This Trinitarian use of *naturaliter* by Gerbert starts a thread of logic which continues into the anti-Berengarian literature of the next century.

Fulbert of Chartres, a student of Gerbert, was the founder of the cathedral school at Chartres and its bishop from 1007 until his death in 1028. The school flowered in the twelfth century and was known all over Europe as a center of study of *artes liberales*. With Fulbert there is a continuation of this same *naturaliter* thread, "for," Fulbert says, "if the Word was made flesh, and we really receive the Word made flesh in the food of the Lord how can we fail to think that Christ abides in us *naturaliter*?" (Fulbert, *Epistola* 5: PL141,202) Christ, he says, dwells in us when we receive him in communion, not through a concordance of wills but "through the truth of a united nature" (Fulbert, *Epistola* 5: PL141, 202).

Fulbert concludes with the very strong assertion that by the power of him who made all things out of nothing, in the spiritual sacraments, transcending the merit of their nature and being, earthly matter is "changed into the substance of Christ" (Fulbert, *Epistola* 5: PL141,203). In another letter, he makes a strong identification between the bread consecrated by the priest and the body of the Lord located now in heaven, which "by an unseen power become one and the same" (Fulbert, *Epistola* 3: PL141,194) by way of mystery. This is the same flesh that we are in communion with at the table of the altar, where the "bread consecrated on earth is called the true body of Christ, since that which was taken from the Virgin and that which is consecrated on earth is called the real body of Christ, and that which is consecrated from the material and the virginal creatures is transformed into the substance of his true flesh by the Spirit who works in an invisible operation ..." (Fulbert, *Epistola* 3: PL141,195).

So Fulbert at the dawn of the eleventh century presents a clear reprise of the realism of Paschasius in the ninth. This realism will see not only criticism, but in fact derision and scorn from one of Fulbert's students—Berengarius of Tours. Berengarius was born in Tours in the year 1000, was educated at Chartres and became the director of the cathedral school at Tours around the year 1031. Sometime around 1040 he began to disseminate his own eucharistic doctrine, which held for a spiritual presence of Christ in opposition to the realism of Paschasius. Highly influenced by the innovations in dialectics of his day, the overly rationalistic views of Berengarius proposed a serious challenge to the orthodox teaching of the church.

The facts about the nature and character of Berengarius' teaching are derived more from his critics and secondary sources of the period than from primary ones. (The known writings of Berengarius are: correspondence with Ansfroi, Ascelin, and Adelmann; short extracts from his little treatise quoted in the *De Corpore et Sanguine Domini* of Lanfranc; the *De Sacra Coena*; the *Acta Concilii Romani* [1078–1079].) Although some aspects of his doctrine are uncertain, what is clear and well founded was the unorthodox nature of that doctrine itself. Directed against the regnant theology of his day, Berengarius responded vehemently against the realism of Paschasius with its origins in the Carolingian renaissance. The core of the Berengarian reaction was an emphasis on the spiritual character of the sacrament as well as a severe criticism of the realism of Paschasius. For him, Paschasius' work was nothing more than the belief of the "common crowd," lacking any theological sophistication. The teachings of John Scotus Eriugena (or in reality Ratramnus—it is well established that it was not any known work of John the Scott, a contemporary of Ratramnus. Most believe that it was actually the work of Ratramnus himself that Berengarius used. See Montclos 1971: 49; also PL122, xx–xxii.), on the other hand, offered a theology of the sacrament, that although it was pure symbolism (O'Connor 2005: 99), was in his view the authentic tradition of the church. And it was this promotion of a purely symbolic interpretation of the sacrament that brought condemnations upon him, first at Rome, then at Vercelli, in councils held in the year 1050, at the instigation of his one-time friend turned nemesis, Lanfranc of Canterbury.

A letter written by Berengarius at this time clearly illustrates his position before the Council of Rome in 1059. Writing to Adelmann, bishop of Liège, Berengarius says: "When I speak of body and blood of Christ, I speak of the reality of the sacrament of the table of the Lord, not the sacrament itself, for you will not find the Scriptures using the words 'figure' or 'likeness.' I use the word sacrament synonymously with the words: sign, figure, likeness and pledge" (Berengarius, *Epistola contra Almannum*: 532). This reality, he goes on to say: "is what the Fathers publicly preached and about which they were not silent, for they spoke of the body and blood as one thing, and the sacrament of the body and blood as another" (Berengarius, *Epistola contra Almannum*: 533). Against any change in substance he declared: "Universal reason and proper authority hold that if what has been said is to stand, namely: 'This bread is my body,' or 'The bread we break is the Body of Christ,' then the bread must remain in all its modes and its substance has not been absorbed" (Berengarius, *Epistola contra Almannum*: 534). About Paschasius, Berengarius said: "However, the position of the common crowd and Paschasius is no position at all, but insanity: that on the altar is a piece of flesh of the Lord, now broken in hands, now his extremities crushed by the teeth of men" (Berengarius, *Epistola contra Almannum*: 534).

What is significant in this letter, furthermore, is the well-articulated contrast between his position and that of Paschasius:

> The opposition, therefore, of the common crowd, and with them the insane Paschasius, Lanfranc and whoever else is of like opinion, holds the following view: Bread and wine present on the altar by virtue of the consecration itself, are somehow driven out, either by consumption or corruption, and are sensually changed into a portion of the flesh and blood of Christ.
>
> My position, or rather that of the Scriptures is this: The bread and wine of the table of the Lord are not sensually but intellectually changed, not by consumption but by assumption, not into a piece of flesh, against the Scriptures, but in accordance with the Scriptures, are converted into the whole body and blood of the Lord. (Berengarius, *Epistola contra Almannum*: 534)

In the Roman synod of 1059 called by Pope Nicholas II, Berengarius was forced to publicly retract the aforesaid views in a profession of faith he signed at the council. In it he professed that the body and blood of Christ in the Eucharist, after the consecration, "are not only the Sacrament but the true Body and Blood of Our Lord Jesus Christ, and that they are in truth [*veritas*] sensibly and not only sacramentally touched by the hands of the priests and broken and chewed by the teeth of the faithful" (Profession of Faith, *Ego Berengarius*, Council of Rome 1059).

From 1059 until 1075 the Berengarian controversy entered a period of protracted literary warfare. One of the early respondents to Berengarius, and someone to whom we owe a great deal for recording the history of the debate, was Durandus of Troarn. With Durandus we find the last open defense of Paschasius and his theology (Durandus, *De corpore* 10: PL149,1389). From Lanfranc forward, the full weight of the theological argument moves away from an explicit defense of Paschasius towards an in-depth treatment of the doctrinal issues that surround the controversy: the distinction between substance and accidents as well as the substantial change in the elements of bread and wine.

Like his predecessors, Durandus continues the patristic thread from Hilary that the body of Christ is "naturally" in the sacrament, complaining that Berengarius holds that it is there, *non naturaliter sed figuraliter*. On the contrary, Durandus says, the visible elements are invisibly and substantially made the real body and blood of Christ, and that the same flesh that is present is what was taken from the Virgin, now glorified in heaven. Communicants receive it spiritually and in so doing, Christ is in them and they are in Christ. The sacrament of the Lord, he says, "is really the body and blood of Christ, not only in effective and spiritual force of power, but also in the complete peculiarity of natural reality, nor is it anything other than that same flesh which the Virgin conceived of the Holy Spirit" (Durandus, *De corpore* 9: PL149,1387). "Rightly," he says, "is the flesh of the body of Christ received under the mystery," who assumed our flesh from the Virgin, and "by way of this mystery no one should have any doubt of communicating with the reality of his flesh and blood" (Durandus, *De corpore* 5: PL149,1383).

Next to Berengarius of Tours, Lanfranc of Canterbury stands out as one the most significant figures in the eucharistic crisis of the eleventh century. Prior of Bec at the onset of the controversy, his theological contribution was an important factor in the theological debate immediately following the Council of Rome in 1059.

The general consensus is that the *De corpore et sanguine domini* was written by Lanfranc at the request of a former student, Theodoric of Paderborn, in 1062 while he was still prior at Bec and just before he became the abbot at Caen. The tract was written to refute Berengarius' polemical pamphlet *Scriptum contra synodum*, an attack on the Roman Synod of 1059 written soon after the council itself; all that survives of the document today are 23 fragments found in Lanfranc's work.

For Lanfranc, the consecration effects a miraculous transformation in the elements of bread and wine on the altar such that they become in "essence" the flesh and blood of Christ. This consecration takes place through the ministry of the priest, and is an action that Lanfranc describes as a blessing (*benedictio*) (Lanfranc, *De corpore* 9: PL150,420). This conversion of the elements which brings about the real presence of Christ upon the altar is supernatural, beyond the ability of the human mind to comprehend, and is accessible to the mind only by faith. The words that describe this change are: *converti, mutari, conversio, commutari, materialis mutatio, transferri, transire,* and *fieri*. The bread and wine placed on the altar are transformed *essentially* in substance into the body and blood of the Lord, where the *nature* of the bread and wine themselves are replaced by the *nature* of the flesh and the blood of Christ. It is a miraculous work of divine power that supplants the reality of the bread and wine with the flesh and blood of Christ.

In the *De corpore*, Lanfranc insists that this change brings about an authentic presence of Christ in the Eucharist, transforming the natures of the bread and wine in such a way that they become essentially, or really, the body and blood of Christ. It is the same body, and yet not the same body, for unlike the glorified body in heaven the body of Christ on the altar appears under the forms of bread and wine. For Lanfranc, therefore, the Eucharist is constituted of two principles—the visible and the invisible, for "the sacrifice of the Church exists in two realities and is confected in two things, that is, in the visible appearance of the elements, and the invisible flesh and blood of Christ, namely in the sacrament and in the reality of the sacrament" (Lanfranc, *De corpore* 10: PL150,421).

For Lanfranc, the flesh and blood of Christ are on the altar, but the body of Christ, that is, Christ's own proper body, is in heaven. The bread and the wine, which are essentially the same reality as the body of Christ, retain their former appearances to veil this mystery. "For we do indeed believe that the Lord Jesus is truly and salubriously eaten on earth by worthy recipients, and we most certainly hold that he exists in heaven uncontaminated, incorruptible and unharmed" (Lanfranc, *De corpore* 17: PL150,427).

This distinction within Lanfranc's understanding of the real presence, though incomplete, will receive a more expanded treatment in the work of one of his former students from Bec: Guitmund of Aversa. Written to address questions on the Eucharist by a certain monk named Roger, the *De corporis et sanguinis Christi veritate in eucharistia* of Guitmund of Aversa was probably written while he was still a monk in Normandy between the years 1073 and 1075. It is clear from the text that the work is a theological defense of the "Ego Berengarius" confession of faith of 1059, where Guitmund's central thesis is that the body of Christ is in fact chewed by the teeth in holy communion, not just sacramentally but sensibly. In this work, along with an extensive description of the nature of the real presence, there is a significant theological advance in his development of the distinction between substance and accidents, along with a unique insight into the quality of the species themselves.

Concerning the real presence, Guitmund accepts the *naturaliter* theme found in the works of his predecessors. For Guitmund, the word *naturaliter*, when applied to the Eucharist, means that just as the Son is of the same nature as the Father, so the Eucharist is "of the same nature as Christ," and through our reception of the Eucharist, Christ is "naturally, that is substantially" in us (Guitmund, *De veritate* 3:14: PL149,1476). Thus the reality of the body of Christ, that is, the body born of the Virgin Mary, becomes present by a substantial change in the bread and wine placed upon the altar during the consecration. "All of that bread," he says, "and all of that wine of the altar of the Lord are therefore substantially [*substantialiter*], by way of divine consecration, changed [*commutentur*] into the flesh and blood of Christ, so that afterwards they can be completely nothing other than, from now unto eternity, the flesh and blood of our Savior, the Lord God Jesus Christ" (Guitmund, *De veritate* 3:57: PL149,1494).

According to Guitmund, the substantial change in the Eucharist involves one reality being transferred into another (*in unum aliud transferatur*) (Guitmund, *De veritate* 1:9: PL149,1431), or, to be more specific, "bread and wine pass over [*transire*] into the flesh and blood of the Lord" (Guitmund, *De veritate* 2:18: PL149,1452). It is a type of change "where that which exists passes [*transit*] into that which already exists," whereby "bread and wine by a unique divine power are changed [*commutari*] into Christ's own body" (Guitmund, *De veritate* 1:39: PL149,1444).

It is a change known only by faith (Guitmund, *De veritate* 1:31: PL149,1440), reserved by God himself for his own body (Guitmund, *De veritate* 1:37: PL149,1442), and has no equal in the created order (Guitmund, *De veritate* 1:34: PL149,1441). It is a change similar to the one where accidents that inhere in a substance themselves change, "for as the accidents recede, just as we have said, either they are annihilated, or, if they are changed [*permutantur*], then they are changed into the arriving ones, which in no small way would approach the matter we are investigating" (Guitmund, *De veritate* 1:38: PL149,1444). Based on this analogy, the eucharistic change is one where the substance of the bread, by means of a conversion, becomes the preexisting body of Christ. For Guitmund, this substantial change is an accidental one in reverse, where the substances of bread and wine change while the accidents remain the same. Thus in Guitmund's doctrine, as in later scholastic theology, the substantial change in the Eucharist is a conversion that takes place on order of reality, where the reality of the bread gives way to the higher reality of Christ's body, and the reality of the wine gives way to the higher reality of Christ's blood. What remains after this change are only the "appearances" of bread and wine, which have retained their "likeness" to the former reality that they once were, for, "the substances [*substantiae*] of things are changed, but on account of horror, the prior taste, color and the rest of certain accidents [*accidentia*], in so far as they pertain to the senses, are retained" (Guitmund, *De veritate* 3:28: PL149,1481).

One of the most fascinating aspects of Guitmund's eucharistic theology is his understanding of the sacrament of the altar as another post-resurrection appearance of the Lord, that is, of a genre like those various appearances of Christ recorded in Scripture where he went unrecognized by his disciples. The notion of the *species domini* (a term that I have coined to classify the scriptural accounts of Christ being unrecognized by his disciples.) is one that sees the real presence as a sacramental continuation of Christ's earthly presence. According to Guitmund, Christ "is wholly in heaven while his whole body is truly eaten upon earth" (Guitmund, *De veritate* 2:51: PL149,1466). What one sees on the altar is another of the many appearances that Christ assumed while he was still in this world, that is, when the disciples, although looking at him, did not recognize him:

> For when Mary Magdalene, weeping at the tomb of the Lord, saw the Lord himself, was it not most certainly Jesus, but, deceived by the eyes, she thought instead that she was looking at a gardener? Or, when the Lord himself, on the day of his own resurrection, as if he were a pilgrim, explained the Scriptures to two of his disciples while they were walking along the way; was it anyone other than Jesus, for it is written: 'Their eyes were held lest they recognize him?' (Guitmund, *De veritate* 2:51: PL149,1437)

According to Guitmund, then, if the eyes could see the true reality of the Sacrament, one would see the Lord Jesus in his own proper form in the glory of heaven.

Conclusion

The final edition of Lanfranc's *De corpore* contained the Profession of Faith of the Roman Synod of 1079. The synod itself brought about the definitive end to the Berengarian crisis, and made it clear that the real presence of Christ in the Eucharist was none other than the same body born of the Virgin, made present on the altar by a substantial conversion (*substantialiter converti*) of the elements at the consecration. A real first step towards the formal definition of the doctrine of transubstantiation, the Profession of 1079 became the touchstone for orthodoxy for future theological discussions on the sacrament until the period of Thomas Aquinas and the high scholastic era.

SUGGESTED READING

Montclos (1971); O'Connor (2005); Pelikan (1978); Vaillancourt (2009).

BIBLIOGRAPHY

Appleby, D. (2005), "Beautiful on the Cross, Beautiful in his Torments: The Place of the Body in the Thought of Paschasius Radbertus," *Traditio* 60: 1–46.

Berengar of Tours (2000), *Serta Mediavalia Textus varii saeculorum X–XIII*, CCCM 171 (Turnhout: Brepols).

Berengar of Tours (1988), *De sacra coena: Rescriptum contra Lanfrannum*, Corpus Christianorum Continuatio Mediavalis (CCCM) 84 (Turnhout: Brepols).

Berengar of Tours (1971), *Epistola contra Almannum*, J. de Montclos (ed.), in *Lanfranc et Bérenger: La controverse Eucharistique du XI siècle* (Louvain: Spicilegium Sacrum Lovaniense), 531–538.

Durandus of Troarn (1882), *De corpore et sanguine Christi contra Berengarium et ejus sectatores*, Patrologiae Cursus Completus: Series Latina (PL) 149 (Paris: Migne), 1375–1424.

Fahey, J. (1951), *The Eucharistic Teaching of Ratramn of Corbie: Dissertationes Ad Lauream Pontificia Facultas Theologica Seminarii Sanctae Mariae Ad Lacum* (Mundelein, IL: St. Mary of the Lake Seminary).

Fulbert of Chartres (1880), *Epistola* 3, PL141, 192–195.

Fulbert of Chartres (1880), *Epistola* 5, PL141, 195–204.

Ganz, D. (1990), *Corbie in the Carolingian Renaissance* (Germany: J. Thorbecke Verlag GmbH & Co.).

Gaudel, A. (1941), "Stercoranisme," *Dictionnaire de théologie catholique* 14 (Paris: Letouzey et Ané), 2590–2612.

Gerbert Aurillac (1880), *De corpore et sanguine Domini*, PL139, 179–88.

Gottschalk of Orbais (1945), *De corpore et sanguine Domini*, ed. Dom Cyril Lambot, *Oeveres Théologiques et Grammaticales de Godescalc D'Orbais* (Louvain: Spicilegium Sacrum Lovaniense), 324–337.

Grabmann, M. (1909), *Die Geschichte der scholastischen Methode nach den gedruckten und ungedruckten Quellen dargestellt* (Freiburg: Herdersche Verlagshandlung).

Guitmund, Archbishop of Aversa (1882), *De corporis et sanguinis Christi veritate in eucharistia libri tres*, PL 149, 1427–1494.

Haymo of Halberstadt (1880), *De corpore et sanguine Domini*, PL118, 815–818.

Hilary of Poitiers (1954), *Saint Hilary of Poitiers: The Trinity*, trans. S. McKenna, FC 25 (New York: Fathers of the Church, Inc.).

Hincmar of Reims (1879), *De cavendis vitiis et virtutibus exercendis*, PL125, 858–930.

Lanfranc of Canterbury (1881), *De corpore et sanguine Domini adversus Berengarium Turonensem*, PL 150, 407–442.

Lienhard, J. (2013), "*Sacramentum* and the Eucharist in St. Augustine," *The Thomist* 77: 173–192.

Montclos, J. de (1971), *Lanfranc et Bérenger: La Controverse eucharistique du XI siècle* (Louvain: Spicilegium Sacrum Lovaniense).

Morin, G. (1931), "Gottschalk Retrouve," *Revue Benedictine* 43: 303–312.

O'Connor, J. T. (2005), *The Hidden Manna: A Theology of the Eucharist* (San Francisco, CA: Ignatius Press).

Paschasius Radbertus (1969), *De corpore et sanguine Domini: cum appendice epistola ad Fredugardum*, CCCM 16 (Turnhout: Brepols).

Paschasius Radbertus (1879), *De partu Virginis,* PL120, 1365–1386.

Pederson, O. (1997), *The First Universities: Studium Generale and the Origins of Education in Europe*, trans. R. North (Cambridge: Cambridge University Press).

Pelikan, J. (1978), *The Growth of Medieval Theology (600–1300): The Christian Tradition 3* (Chicago: University of Chicago Press).

Rabanus Maurus (1864), *De clericorum institutione*, PL107, 297–420.

Rabanus Maurus (1864), *Poenitentiale*, PL110, 467–494.

Rabanus Maurus (1878), *De sacris ordinibus*, PL112, 1165–1192.

Ratramnus of Corbie (1880), *De corpore et sanguine Domini*, PL 121, 103–222.

Ratramnus of Corbie (1954), *De corpore et sanguine Domini: Texte Établi d'aprè les Manuscrits et Notice Bibliographique*, ed. J.N. Bakhuizen van den Brink (Amsterdam: Holland Publishing Co.).

Ratramnus of Corbie (1880), *De Nativitate Christi*, PL121, 81–102.

Spinks, B. (2013), *Do this in Remembrance of Me: The Eucharist from the Early Church to the Present Day* (London: SCM Press).

Stone, D. (1909), *A History of the Doctrine of the Holy Eucharist*, 2 vols. (New York: Longmans, Green and Co.).

Vaillancourt, M. G. (2004), "The Role of Guitmund of Aversa in the Developing Theology of the Eucharist" (Ph.D. diss.; New York: Fordham University).

Vaillancourt, M. G. (2009), Lanfranc of Canterbury, *On the Body and Blood of the Lord,* Guitmund of Aversa, *On the Truth of the Body and Blood of Christ in the Eucharist*, trans. Mark G. Vaillancourt, Fathers of the Church Mediaeval Continuation 10 (Washington, DC: Catholic University of America Press).

Vaillancourt, M. G. (2013), "The Eucharistic Realism of St. Augustine: Did Paschasius Radbertus Get Him Right? An Examination of Recent Scholarship on the Sermons of St. Augustine," *Studia Patristica* 70, v.18 (Leuven: Peeters): 569–576.

CHAPTER 14

THE CHRISTO-PNEUMATIC-ECCLESIAL CHARACTER OF TWELFTH-CENTURY SACRAMENTAL THEOLOGY

BOYD TAYLOR COOLMAN

INTRODUCTION

An adequate summary of the sacramental theology articulated between the death of Gregory VII (1085) and the Fourth Lateran Council (1215), the "long twelfth century" as defined here, cannot be accommodated by the brief compass of this chapter. Many worthy aspects of the topic must remain underdeveloped, even untouched. Instead, a single, though multifaceted claim is here advanced: twelfth-century writers consistently construed the sacraments as salvific mediations of the saving power of Jesus Christ and of the mysteries of his human life. The sacraments were means of grace—that was universally affirmed—but grace understood not as some static "thing," as a quantifiable commodity, produced and purveyed mechanistically to individual consumers through an efficient distribution system. Rather, the very life of Jesus was communicated to embodied believers by the active power of the Holy Spirit, who joined believers to Christ in and through the sacraments. Precisely as conjoined to Christ by the Spirit through the sacraments, finally, believers constituted the church.

In short, twelfth-century theologians conceived of the sacraments within a highly integrated, organic, and dynamic conception of Christian existence. Arguably, the deep theological intuition operative here is that the sacraments mediate a divine action directed toward humanity that reaches its terminus, *not* when grace is communicated to individual believers, but rather when by that communication individual humans are drawn together more deeply and integrated more fully into the mysterious union of Christ and his Church.

PRELIMINARY OBSERVATIONS

At the outset, an all-too-brief sketch of general twelfth-century developments and achievements in sacramental theology is in order. The beginnings of our period witnessed a certain narrowing and refining of the term *sacramentum* to refer to the consecrated material and visible elements in specific rituals of the church. It appears that Berengar of Tours (d. 1088) "was the first to limit the term to the consecrated material and visible element" (Levy 2004: 545). At the same time, in the 1130s Hugh of St. Victor (d. 1141) could still include holy water, the reception of ashes, the sign of the cross, and the invocation of the Trinity as "sacraments" (Levy 2004: 545). By the thirteenth, though, an informal consensus existed regarding the seven sacraments of the Catholic Church, enshrined influentially in Peter Lombard's (d. 1160) *Sentences*, the basis of nearly all scholastic theology for the next several centuries, among other works.

Reflecting the nascent scholastic mentalities of the time, this period also witnessed a concerted effort to define a sacrament. Several candidates, all claiming Augustinian authority, if not his actual words, jostled for ascendancy, until Peter Lombard (d. 1160) influentially synthesized them in his *Sentences*. Hugh of St. Victor offered both a short and a long definition: The first was Augustine's "a sign of a sacred thing"; the second his own elaboration, "a corporeal or material element set before the senses without, representing by similitude and signifying by institution and containing by sanctification some invisible and spiritual grace" (Hugh of St. Victor: *Sacr.*, 1.9.2). Otto of Lucca (fl. 1130s) stressed the sign-quality: "For a sacrament is a sign of a sacred thing (*sacrae rei signum*). But a sign is that which causes something to enter the mind in addition to what the appearance itself produces [in the mind]" (Otto of Lucca: PL 176.140A). Drawing on various twelfth-century authors preceding him (Evans 2010: 213–214), Peter Lombard offered three general Augustinian definitions of a sacrament: "a sacred secret" (cf. Ps-Hugh of St. Victor: PL 177.365C), "a visible form of an invisible grace" and "a sign of a sacred thing" (*Sent.* IV.1.2). He then formulated a more specific definition, his famous "proper definition" of a sacrament: a "sign of God's grace" (cf. Peter Abelard, *Theologia "Scholarium"* 1 [CCM 13:321]) and a "form of invisible grace" (cf. Otto of Lucca: PL 176.140A), but more precisely a sacrament "bears the image of grace" and is the "cause of grace" (cf. Otto of Lucca: PL 176.140A) (*Sent.* IV.1.4.1–2). After the Lombard, Simon of Tournai and following him Radulphus Ardens narrowed the Lombard's generic definition by inserting the word "sacred" to distinguish these signs from all others: "a sacred sign of a sacred thing," allowing a distinction between the sacraments of the Old Testament, which were not sacred, and the New, which are (Evans 2010: 215).

Twelfth-century thinkers also initiated an influential train of thought regarding the composition of the sacraments. All sacraments required both matter and form, the former rather narrowly defined in strictly physical terms, the latter, the ritual words of institution, which made the material to be more than it ordinarily was. Water is just water, for instance; but with the invocation of the Trinity, it can become the sacrament of baptism (Van den Eynde 1950: 1–20).

Lastly, though twelfth-century theologians affirmed that the sacraments conferred salvific grace, they also allowed that God could save human beings without them. Why, then, the sacraments? Influentially, Hugh of St. Victor espied an oft-repeated, three-fold rationale: first, they foster humility; second, they instruct; and third, they provide a salutary exercise (Hugh of St. Victor: PL 176.320C). The deep Victorine intuition behind these was that in the sacramental economy—indeed, in the whole economy of creation and salvation—the visible mediates the invisible: *Per visibilia ad invisibilia*. Accordingly, the sacramental life in this century was viewed as a kind of theological pedagogy that fostered a certain symbolic mode of thought and multilayered way of seeing reality, an ability, as the Lombard put it, "to recognize the invisible within the visible" (*Sent.* IV.1.5.3). The sacraments fostered a "depth-grammar" in which the truest is always the deepest, the most important is always the least apparent, while the most apparent, though least important, is a fitting and appropriate and therefore a truly mediating sign (*sacramentum*), leading to the deepest, most important reality.

THE EUCHARIST AS PARADIGM

In the wide context of the development of Christian sacramental theology from its beginnings to the present, one of the most significant contributions of the twelfth-century is the creation, consolidation, and then successful deployment of a tripartite framework for conceiving of the nature and the effects of the sacraments. This framework governs much twelfth-century reflection on the sacraments and enables the sophisticated and complex, though ultimately unified and coherent account of the sacraments and their place in the Christian life, noted at the outset.

Like much in the Middle Ages, this framework is "Augustinian" in inspiration and even content (its terms and concepts), but is not as such found in the African bishop's writings. In discussing the Eucharist, Augustine had stressed the invisible effect, the grace, signified and wrought by the visible sacrament, which joined believers to each other and to Christ their Head in the unity of his mystical body—"be what you see and receive what you are" (Augustine, *Sermon* 272, in Jackson 1999: 331–332). This approach distinguished the sacrament (*sacramentum*) from the power of the sacrament (*virtus sacramenti*), a power and grace which brought about the reality of the sacrament (*res sacramentum*), namely, its salvific effect (Jackson 1999: 330–334; Wawrykow 2012: 74–75). Twelfth-century writers seized upon and systematized this set of distinctions.

With the eleventh-century eucharistic controversy over Berengar acting as a catalyst, twelfth-century thinkers elaborated this Augustinian distinction by distinguishing three dimensions in the Eucharist—"three elements, as it were ... three stages of depth, all three of them essential to its integrity" (de Lubac 1988: 96). They distinguished, on one hand, between the visible appearance or "species" of bread and wine and the invisible reality of Christ's body and blood, the former being the sign of the latter. At the same time, they distinguished the reality of Christ's bodily presence from the reality of its saving effect (*virtus*) or benefit, of which Christ's true presence was both sign and cause. This latter reality was not itself a sign of anything else. In the words of Alger of Liege (d. 1131): "The sacrament, namely, that species which is seen; the reality of the sacrament, that is, the truth of the Lord's substance, which, as it was truly born of a virgin, is believed to be truly in the sacrament; the effect of the sacrament, just as it is eaten by some unto life, to others unto judgment" (Alger of Liege: PL 180.885A–C). Hugh of St. Victor put it with characteristic simplicity: "For although the sacrament is one, three distinct things are set forth there, namely, visible appearance, truth of body, and virtue of spiritual grace" (Hugh of St. Victor: *Sacr.,* 2.8.7). Toward the mid-twelfth century, these three aspects were commonly referred to, respectively, as (1) the *sacramentum tantum*, the appearance of bread and wine, which was a sign only and not the reality it seemed to be; (2) the *res et sacramentum*, the reality or real presence of the Incarnate Christ's body and blood, which was itself also a sign of something else, namely (3) the *res tantum*, the effect or benefit associated with and derived from Christ's presence, which was a reality only, not a sign of anything else (Goering 1991: 151; van den Eynde 1950: 70; Macy 1984: 51–53). Apparently, the Victorine *Summa sententiarum*, likely written in the second quarter of the century and attributed to Otto of Lucca, first employed this terminology (Goering 1991: 151): "It is necessary to consider three things here: one which is only a sacrament (*sacramentum tantum*), another which is a reality and also a sacrament (*sacramentum et res*), and third what is a reality alone (*res tantum*)" (Otto of Lucca: PL 176.140A). Despite its debt to Augustine—de Lubac called it "structurally Augustinian" (de Lubac 1988: 96)—this tripartite framework and its terminology is a uniquely twelfth-century development; it would become standard for subsequent medieval discussion of the Eucharist (de Lubac 1988: 97–8). Peter Lombard adopted it in his *Sentences* and so transmitted it to later scholastic thinkers (Macy 1984: 85, n. 15); it was employed by Innocent III in his decretal, *Cum Marthae*, of 1202 (Levy 2003b: 171).

With respect to the *sacramentum tantum*, Otto of Lucca spoke for the consensus when he defined it as "the visible species (*species visibiles*), that is, the bread and the wine; and those things which here are visibly celebrated, such as the fraction, the deposition, and elevation" (Otto of Lucca: PL 176.140A). In light of the sign-quality of the species, a rich tradition of eucharistic symbolism would develop regarding the manner in which these signified their corresponding realities (as described below).

Regarding the first reality, the *res et sacramentum*, there had been strong insistence on Christ's "true" and "substantial" presence in the Eucharist since the eleventh-century controversy between Lanfranc and Berengar. Throughout the twelfth century thinkers increasingly denied the remnance of the bread and wine after consecration. Gratian's *Decretum* gave the position a status that would become canonical in the following century, by stating: "After consecration it is not the substance, but the species that remain" (Levy 2003b: 178). This ruled out some versions of "consubstantiation" as well as "impanation" as viable options for understanding the relation between Christ's presence and the bread and wine. (Generally speaking, "consubstantiation" refers to any view that affirms the continuing, substantial reality of bread and wine, *along with* ("con") the substantial presence of Christ's body and blood. Impanation not only affirms the ongoing substantial presence of bread and wine along with body and blood, but also specifies a relationship between them, on analogy with the Incarnation (lit. "being enfleshed"). Just as a fully divine person assumes a complete human nature, so in the Eucharist, Christ assumes into his person the bread and wine, without causing them to cease to exist. Guitmund of Aversa (d. 1099) referred to "*impanatores*," who affirm that "the Lord's body and blood are truly contained there, but in a hidden way, and they are impanated—if I may say it in that way—so that they may be consumed" (Guitmund of Aversa: PL 149.1430C–D). This, he claimed, was Berengar's view.) In 1215, the Fourth Lateran Council officially invoked (without defining) the term "transubstantiation" to describe how Christ came to be present in the sacrament: the bread and wine "having been transubstantiated" (*transubstantiatis*) into the body and blood by divine power (Friedberg 1959: 2:5). As Levy notes, in an effort "to promote pastoral care and lay piety, and to solidify matters of doctrine in the face of Cathar and Waldensian threats," the Council included a pronouncement regarding the Eucharist within a "general affirmation of fundamental Catholic trinitarianism, Christology and ecclesiology," reflecting the important place the sacrament had come to occupy, both doctrinally and devotionally, by the later Middle Ages. The Council's opening chapter, *Firmiter*, was quickly incorporated into canon law and was published in Gregory IX's *Liber Extra*, compiled by Raymond of Penafort and published in 1234 (Levy 2003b: 172–173). But "the term 'transubstantiation' '*transubstantio*' (a precursor to '*transubstantiatio*') was first introduced at Paris around 1140," most likely by Robert Pullen, to explain an affirmation about Christ's presence in the sacrament that was already assumed and taken for granted (Goering 1991: 147; cf. de Ghellinck 1924: 1290–1293; Macy 1983: 1–17). By the end of the century, accordingly, the notion that "the very body and blood of Christ" (Otto of Lucca: PL 176.140B), "the flesh of Christ, which he took from the Virgin, and the blood, which he shed for us" (Master Bandini: PL 192.1095B), was present on the altar by a transubstantiation of bread and wine was the prevailing "theory of presence" and a lasting legacy of this period.

Regarding the second reality, the *res tantum*, a wider range of terms and notions came into play, though nearly all revolved around the notion of the ecclesial unity of believers, through faith and charity, with Christ their head and with one another, through the Holy Spirit. It was called the "spiritual grace" and "power" (Ps-Hugh of St. Victor: PL 175.530B), the "efficacy" (Otto of Lucca: PL 176.140D), and the "invisible grace" (Ps-Hugh of St. Victor: PL 177.365C) of the sacrament. Upon elaboration, though, a pronounced ecclesial dimension emerged: This deeper reality is the "unity of the Church" (Ps-Hugh of St. Victor: PL 175.530B), the "unity of the head with its members" (Otto of Lucca: PL 176.140C), "the union of the head and the members" (Ps-Hugh of St. Victor: PL 177.365C). But, succinctly emphasizing both the Christological and the pneumatological aspects, it could be called simply "the spiritual flesh of the Lord" (Master Bandini:

PL 192.1095B) or "the spiritual flesh of Christ," eaten by whomever "is joined and conformed to Christ through faith" (Otto of Lucca: PL 176.140C).

At this juncture, several observations are in order. First, this framework explicitly insisted on two distinct realities (*res*) in the Eucharist: Christ himself and some saving benefit. As a Victorine commentator on First Corinthians put it: "The first sacrament therefore has two realities, one that it signifies and contains, namely, the true body and blood of Christ; the other that it signifies and does not contain, namely, the unity of the Church" (Ps-Hugh of St. Victor: PL 175.530B). Second, these were genuinely distinct, but crucially related. For that "spiritual grace is invisibly and spiritually received along with the body and blood" (Ps-Hugh of St. Victor: PL 177.365C–D). That is, the substantial presence of Christ was the necessary (though not sufficient, as will be seen) condition for the possibility of receiving the spiritual grace. Third, the goal or purpose, so to speak, of the first reality was to communicate the second reality available. As the *Speculum de mysteriis ecclesiae* declared, the real and substantial presence of Christ, the *res et sacramentum*, was by itself "of no benefit" (*non prodest*) without the *res tantum*, the "spiritual grace," namely "the spiritual flesh of Christ" (Ps-Hugh of St. Victor: PL 177.365C–D). Fourth, and most importantly, this paradigm located or positioned, as it were, the Incarnate Christ as the active agent and effective distributor of sacramental grace. As an anonymous Victorine writer put it, in the Eucharist "there is not only an increase of power and grace, but that very One is received, who is the font and origin (*fons et origo*) of all power and grace" (Ps-Hugh of St. Victor: PL 175.530A–B). This last point should be stressed. The triadic structure created a "space" for the living Christ to be present, not as an inert "thing," not as a miraculous but static *factum* of his true body and blood, but as the active personal agent of salvation, the direct and immediate source of saving power and spiritual life. Not only that but the sacramental "space," as it were, that opened up between the presence of Christ himself (*res et sacramentum*) and the salvific effect (*res tantum*) of his saving activity becomes the sacramental "theatre" of the dramatic encounter between believers and Christ through the power of the Spirit; it becomes the ecclesial incubator and generator, the place within the body of Christ where the body of Christ is being newly formed and intensified.

This threefold framework emerged initially and most fully in relation to the Eucharist, but it was gradually applied to the other sacraments as well, thus becoming the basic sacramental paradigm of the twelfth century. In this period, then, if it were not already so, the Eucharist became the sacramental "center of gravity," the sacramental center point, in relation to which all other sacraments were conceived and oriented. The foundation is thus here laid for what will emerge in the following century, for example, in the sacramental theology of Thomas Aquinas, namely, that the sacrament of the Eucharist "perfects or consummates the other six."

The hierarchy of the sacraments is the result of the degree of their participation in the power of Christ's humanity. The other six sacraments also participate in something of the instrumental power of that humanity. The Eucharist is the model sacrament whose efficacy is found in the other six sacraments to a lesser degree, mainly because Christ's presence is not as intense (Blankenhorn 2006: 273). All the twelfth-century sacraments are thus sacraments *of Christ*, deriving their saving power in relation to his saving mysteries made present in his person in the Eucharist.

THE OTHER SACRAMENTS

Twelfth-century thinkers frequently saw a profound and particular link between the Incarnation, the Eucharist, and the other sacraments, as expressed by Hugh of St. Victor:

> The sacrament of the body and blood of Christ is the one of those upon which salvation principally depends and is peculiar among all, since from it is all sanctification. For that victim who was offered once for the salvation of the world gave power to all preceding and subsequent sacraments, so that from it they sanctify all who are to be freed through it. (Hugh of St. Victor, *Sacr.*, 2.8.1)

Though Hugh's understanding of the sacraments that chronologically preceded the Incarnation is rather unique to him, his conviction that all the other sacraments find the source of their sanctifying power in the incarnate Christ made present in the Eucharist was widely shared. Peter Damian argued that in his post-resurrection appearance in the upper room, Jesus "poured forth the sacraments through the in-breathing of the Holy Spirit (*insufflationem sancti Spiritus*)" (Peter Damian: PL 145.421B). Peter Lombard noted that Christ "is often called the Redeemer with respect to his humanity, since according to the humanity and in the humanity he assumed, he filled those sacraments which are the cause of our redemption" (Peter Lombard, *Sent.*, III.19.5).

BAPTISM

Throughout the Middle Ages, baptism was the rite of Christian initiation typically received in infancy. It was the pre-condition for all the others, since it removed both original and actual sin and conferred grace. Its material component was water, of course; its form was the invocation of the Trinity over the material element with the intention to baptize (Levy 2003a: 546).

Twelfth-century treatments of baptism consistently illustrate the organic integration of Christological, pneumatic, ecclesial dimensions, often through that use of scriptural symbols and allegorical interpretations so characteristic of the medieval "sacramental imagination." As often the case, Hugh of St. Victor (d. 1141) provides a framework and the tone. In his *On the Sacraments*, he grounds the detailed discussion of the individual sacraments, first in an extended treatment of the Incarnation and then a short but highly significant discussion of the church, stressing its essential nature as the one body of Christ, vivified by the one Spirit of Christ. He then situates baptism as the point of incorporation: "Now in the sacrament through baptism we are united ... Through baptism we are made members of the body ..." (Hugh of St. Victor: *Sacr.*, 2.2.1). Writers throughout the century insisted Christ himself was the active agent of baptism, in which he gives the Holy Spirit to those being baptized for their justification/sanctification. So, Eckebert of Schönau (d. 1184) states:

> ... the Lord Jesus Christ himself is the common baptizer of all those who are baptized in the catholic church in the name of the holy Trinity, so that namely he himself invisibly sanctifies their spirit by the Holy Spirit, and cleanses them from all sin ... Every spiritual grace, which is conferred in baptism, that highest priest, the Lord Jesus Christ, gives to them through the power of the Holy Spirit. (Eckebert of Schönau: PL 195.48D–49A)

Accordingly, Geoffrey of Vendôme (d. 1132) could claim: "Christ daily gives birth to Christians spiritually in baptism. Hence, we are Christians, are so-called and are such, from Christ" (Geoffrey of Vendôme: PL 157.247D). And "since it is Christ alone who baptizes, an equally good baptism is given by whomever, whether given by a good or bad [priest]" (Master Bandini: PL 192.1094C). Peter Damian (d. 1073) accentuated the pneumatic dimension by inserting the Spirit right into the Augustinian definition of a sacrament: "what is water, except water? But add the word to the element, *and by the descent of the Spirit* it becomes a sacrament (*descendente Spiritu, fit sacramentum*)" (Peter Damian: PL 145.102C), while Peter Lombard stressed the work of the entire Trinity in baptism: "so it was then [at Christ's own baptism in the Jordan] that Christ's baptism was instituted, in which the Trinity ... baptizes a person inwardly" (Peter Lombard, *Sent.*, IV.3.5.3) even "as [the Trinity] operates outwardly and visibly through the minister" (Peter Lombard, *Sent.*, IV.3.4.5).

Not surprisingly, many authors emphasized the notion that through baptism believers were incorporated into Christ's own life. In his *Speculum ecclesiae*, Honorius of Autun (d. 1154) depicts the baptizand as experiencing all of Christ's paschal mysteries:

> On the Sabbath the people are baptized, since Christ is said to have rested in the tomb [on the Sabbath], since through baptism the death of Christ is imitated. For by renouncing the world, we are co-crucified with Christ, and we are buried with him in his death through baptism. We are crucified with vices and desires, while we are submerged in baptism in the mode of the cross. For three days we are buried with the Lord when we are taken under the water three times as if under the earth. When we ascend from the font of baptism, we are, as it were, resurrected with Christ unto glory. Signed with chrism they are vested in white, since clothed with immortality through the death of Christ, they will be crowned kings and priests in the kingdom of God. By the candle, which is consecrated that day, is designated the pillar of fire which led the children of Israel through the Red Sea to the promised land; and it was Christ, who as that paschal lamb was sacrificed for us, whose blood broke the bond of heavy tyranny, who carried us away from its dominion through baptism, by whose fire, namely the Holy Spirit, all faithful souls are illumined and are rejoiced to go to his supernal fatherland led in the way of charity. (Honorius of Autun: PL 172.928B–D)

As Peter Lombard put it: "[T]hose who are baptized *in Christ* (that is, in conformity with Christ, so that they die to the ancientness of sin, as Christ did to the ancientness of pain) put on Christ, whom they have dwelling in them through grace" (Peter Lombard, *Sent.*, IV.4.3.1). In short, the result of baptism is union with Christ.

This insistence on the active presence of Christ giving the Spirit in baptism fostered the appropriation of the eucharistic threefold framework. Comparing baptism to the entrance of a church, Gerhoh Reichersberg (d. 1169) likened "the gate" to "the visible sacrament" and "the door of this gate" to "Christ, who is not only the institutor but also the reality of the sacrament (*res est sacramenti*)," while the "lock of this door is the hidden mystery." In Gerhoh's analogy, without precisely the same terminology, baptismal water clearly corresponds to the *sacramentum tantum*, the reality of Christ himself to the *res et sacramentum*, and the hidden mystery to the *res tantum*. For as he explains, those who receive in faith receive two realities, "the reality, as much of the mystery as of the sacrament." For "the reality [of Christ] is a sacrament, since there is salvation and sanctification, which is conferred through him, because [baptism] is received for the obtaining of salvation and for sanctification ..." So, Christ himself is the "reality and the cause of baptism," without which the "reality of the mystery" (*res mysterii*) is not available. That latter reality is "the hidden sanctification of the visible sacrament." Aptly completing the analogy, he observes: "The key of this lock or of this door, is [turned] by none other than Christ, because it is the Spirit of Christ. Christ therefore by the finger or key of his Spirit deigns to open for us the lock of this mystery" (Gerhoh of Reichersberg: PL 193.300A–D). Though Peter Lombard does not quite implement the threefold structure in his *Sentences*, he summarizes much of the preceding tradition regarding what he calls the "*res sacramenti*" or the *res tantum* of baptism: "renewal of the mind," "inner cleanness," and the conferral of the beauty of the possession of the virtues (Peter Lombard, *Sent.*, IV.3.9.1); all of which he sums up in the term "justification" (Peter Lombard, *Sent.*, IV.3.9.2). Writers less scholastic were often more poetic. Bruno the Carthusian (d. 1101), for example, could note simply that Christ "bestows the Holy Spirit in baptism for justification" (Bruno the Carthusian: PL 153.494C). But he could also say: "Flour combined with water and without yeast is called paste. Our humanity, which by itself is sterile and dry, is understood as dry flour, which is conglutinized with the water of the Holy Spirit in baptism (*rore Spiritus sancti in baptismo conglutinatur*), so that, with the aridity dispersed, it might bear fruit ... *You are*, he says, *a new paste*, that is, you have been made members of the new Adam, namely, Christ, you who have been renewed by the Holy Spirit" (Bruno the Carthusian: PL 153.147C).

ANOINTINGS: CONFIRMATION AND UNCTION

Frequently, twelfth-century writers treated both confirmation and extreme unction/last rites together, under the general rubric of anointing. "There are three kinds of anointing," said Peter Lombard. "For there is an anointing which is done with chrism which is called the principal anointing, because in it principally the Paraclete is given ... There is also another anointing, by which catechumens and neophytes are anointed on the breast and between the shoulders at the reception of baptism. But there is a third anointing, which called the oil of the sick" (Peter Lombard, *Sent.*, IV.23.2).

The sacrament of confirmation had become separated from baptism by the fourth century, and from that time hence its administration was reserved for bishops. Its matter was chrism oil—oil mixed with balsam and consecrated for its sacramental use; its form was the words spoken by the bishop as he applied the chrism to the forehead of the baptized person (Levy 2003a: 547).

The notion of confirmation as an anointing accentuated the link with Jesus, the Christ, that is, "the anointed one," as Hugh of St. Victor pointed out with respect to the sacrament of confirmation: "For Christ is so called from chrism and the Christian is named from Christ"; so this sacrament makes us "sharers in his unction" (Hugh of St. Victor, *Sacr.*, 2.7.1). Radulphus Ardens (fl. 1190s) noted that "in confirmation there is an anointing in the sign of the cross ..." (Radulphus Ardens: PL 155.1472C). Others emphasized the reception of the Spirit: "bishops ... mark the Christian and hand down the Spirit Paraclete ... " (Hugh of St. Victor, *Sacr.*, 2.7.2). Ivo of Chartres (d. 1115) claimed that "all the faithful ought to receive the Holy Spirit after baptism through the imposition of the hands of the bishop so that they may be found to be fully Christians" (Ivo of Chartres: PL 161.1069C), while Bruno of Segni (d. 1123) praised confirmation "in which the fullness of the mystery of the whole Christian religion is completed" (Bruno of Segni: PL 165.1102ᵃ). For his part, Anselm of Laon (d. 1117) noted that the Holy Spirit is received in the "fire" of confirmation for "strengthening and inflammation" and for "the fortification of good works" (Anselm of Laon: PL 162.1266A–B).

The giving of the Spirit in confirmation enabled his active agency in the distributions of his grace. So, again without quite the terminology, a threefold structure emerges in this sacrament: the exterior anointing, which is the sacrament; the reality given, namely, the Holy Spirit; and the further reality of the graces of the Spirit, "who brings his seven gifts" (Hugh of St. Victor: *Sacr.*, 2.7.6). So Master Bandinus: "the sacrament is the exterior anointing of the person, but the reality of the sacrament is the interior fecundity which is then given to us by the Holy Spirit" (Bandinus: PL 192.1102D–3A). Or again, the Lombard: "The power of this sacrament is the giving of the Holy Spirit for strengthening, who in baptism was given for remission" (Peter Lombard: *Sent.*, IV.7.3).

By the Middle Ages, the ancient practice of anointing the sick typically by the laity had become the domain of the clergy. By the twelfth century it was seen to have both physical and spiritual benefits, namely, alleviation of illness and remission of sins. During this period it also came to be known as "extreme unction" (Levy 2003a: 550–1).

Though with less elaboration, this other sacrament of anointing, namely, unction, was treated similarly to confirmation. So, Zachary of Besançon (d. 1155) claimed that "the visible anointing is the sacrament; but the reality of the sacrament is the remission which is conferred on the soul by the spiritual anointing of grace" (Zachary of Besançon: PL 186.167B). Similarly, Peter Lombard wrote that "the sacrament is the outer anointing itself; the reality of the sacrament is the inner anointing, which is brought about by the remission of sins and the increase of the virtues" (Peter Lombard, *Sent.*, IV.23.2), while following the Lombard, Radulphus Ardens added that "the sacrament is the exterior anointing, but the thing of this sacrament is the remission of sins and the accumulation of grace" (Radulphus Ardens, *Speculum universale* 92 [ed. Evans, 211]).

Though confirmation and unction were both anointings, an important difference emerged in the fact that the former could be received once, while the latter more than once (though this was debated).

PENANCE

By the end of the twelfth century, private confession of sin to a priest had become standard practice throughout the Latin West, and thinkers during this period paid considerable attention to this, the sacrament of penance (Levy 2003a: 549). Peter Lombard, for example, devoted more distinctions in his *Sentences* to this sacrament than to any other, with the exception of the sacrament of marriage.

At mid-century Peter Lombard named three necessary components to this sacrament: contrition, confession, and works of satisfaction. Opinions varied, though, regarding the relative importance of each. Some, like Peter Abelard, stressed the paramount importance of contrition—genuine heartfelt sorrow for and repugnance of sin, inspired by the awareness of divine love and mercy directed toward the sinner. Other sources, such as Gratian's *Decretum*, stressed the necessity of confession to a priest, who alone possesses the power of the keys, namely, of declaring divine forgiveness, and insisted that sin is not forgiven apart from such confession along with works of satisfaction imposed as penance by the priest (Levy 2003a: 549–550).

These three components of penance were easily accommodated to the threefold eucharistic paradigm. At the very end of Peter Lombard's discussion, without passing judgment, though seeming to concur, he reports the view of "some" who say that:

> the sacrament alone (*sacramentum tantum*) is one thing, namely, outward penance; another is sacrament and reality (*sacramentum et res*), namely inward penance; another is reality and not sacrament (*res tantum*), namely, the remission of sins. For inward penance is both a reality of the sacrament, that is, of the outward penance, and a sacrament of the remission of sin, which it both signifies and brings about. Outward penance is also a sign of both inward penance and the remission of sins. (Peter Lombard, *Sent.*, IV.22.2.5)

In fact, the application of the threefold structure to this sacrament was common. Peter Comestor, Master Martin, Simon of Tournai, and Peter of Poitiers all repeated it, with minor variations (Evans 2010: 262–263). By the end of the century, the wording had changed slightly but the same idea was clearly expressed by Radulphus Ardens: "This sacrament has three parts: exterior satisfaction, interior contrition, and the remission of sins. The first is a sacrament and not a reality; the second is a sacrament and a reality; the third is a reality and not a sacrament. The first signifies the second; the second is signi-fied by the first and signifies the third; the third is signified alone" (*Speculum universale*, 89; ed. Evans, 203).

ORDERS

At the turn of the eleventh century, three issues surrounding the clergy and their orders were hotly contested: clerical celibacy, lay investiture (the control of clerical office by lay rulers), and simony (the buying and selling of clerical office). A quarter way through the century, the issues had been resolved, at least in theory. A compromise on lay investiture was reached with the Concordat of Worms in 1122, while the First Lateran Council of 1123 forbade priests, deacons, and subdeacons to marry and refused to recognize the validity of ordinations tainted by simony (Levy 2003a: 551–552).

As the Lombard efficiently put it, holy "orders are called sacraments, because a sacred thing is conferred in the receiving of them, that is, grace, which the things carried out at ordination signify" (Peter Lombard, *Sent.*, IV.24.13.2). While the Lombard noted seven distinct clerical offices, he accepted the canons of the Beneventan Council of 1091 in conferring the narrower designation "holy orders" on the offices of deacon and priest alone (Levy 2003a: 551).

Importantly, a widespread approach to "sacred ordination," as clearly expressed in the Lombard's *Sentences*, correlated the seven distinct spiritual offices (door-keeper, lector, exorcist, acolyte, subdeacon, deacon, and priest) both with distinct events in Christ's earthly life and at the same time "with the sevenfold grace of the Holy Spirit": "There are seven degrees or orders of spiritual offices … as is shown by the example of our head, namely, Jesus Christ," who "showed forth in himself the offices of all, and he left the same orders to be kept by his body, which is the Church" (Peter Lombard, *Sent.*, IV.24.1.2). Earlier, Peter Damian averred that "the Holy Spirit is received by those who are conse-crated" so that they "might become ministers and dispensers of the ministry of God" and "by the same disposing Spirit that they might generate sons of God …" (Peter Damian: PL 145.102C–D). Geoffrey of Vendôme insisted that "by the invocation of the Holy Spirit" one consecrated to be a bishop becomes "the master and commander of Christians, and is believed to produce a representative of Christ" (Geoffrey of Vendôme: PL 157.218C–D).

By the end of the twelfth century, perhaps as a result of the influence exerted by the threefold eucharistic framework, thinkers began in relation to certain sacraments (including holy orders) to posit the presence of a "mark" or "brand" (*character*) pro-duced in the soul by the sacraments. Already in the Lombard's *Sentences*, this is evident with respect to ordination: An order "is some mark, that is, something sacred, by which spiritual power and office are granted to the one ordained. And so the spiritual charac-ter, when a promotion of power is made, is called an order or degree" (*Sent.*, IV.24.13.1). For these sacraments, the *character* seems to stand in the middle place where the person of Christ himself was located in the Eucharist, in between the *sacramentum* and the *res sacramenti*, to function, so to speak, as the *res et sacramentum*.

MARRIAGE

Surprisingly, some notable twelfth-century sacramentalists—for example, Hugh of St. Victor and Peter Lombard—devoted more attention to marriage than to any other sacrament. It was unique, since it alone had been instituted before the Fall. Most authors in this period, responding to certain dualist groups such as the Cathars who denigrated all aspects of bodily life, including sexual activity, stressed the goodness of marriage, both for its role in procreation and as a remedy for concupiscence (Levy 2003a: 552–553).

Hugh of St. Victor inaugurated an influential train of thought that found sacramental significance in both the spiritual union of wills and a physical union of bodies associated with marriage. Regarding the first, marriage is a sacrament "of the society which exists in the spirit between God and the soul"; regarding the second, it is a sacrament "of the society which was to be in the flesh between Christ and the Church," that is, "that union which was made between Christ and the Church through his assumption of flesh" (Hugh of St. Victor, *Sacr.*, 2.11.3). Influenced by Hugh, Peter Lombard put it thus: "There is a symbol of this twofold joining in marriage: for the consent of the partners signifies the spiritual joining of Christ and the Church, which happens through charity; but the intermingling of the sexes signifies that union which happens through the conformity of nature" (Peter Lombard, *Sent.*, IV.26.6.1). For his part, Hugh tentatively pioneered the application of the threefold structure to the sacrament of marriage:

> And perhaps, to speak more specifically, the very association which is preserved externally in marriage between male and female by a compact is a sacrament (*sacramentum*), and the reality of the sacrament (*res sacramenti*) itself is the mutual love of souls which is guarded in turn by the bond of conjugal society and agreement. And this very love again, by which male and female are united in the sanctity of marriage by their souls, is a sacrament and sign (*sacramentum et signum*) of that love by which God is joined to the rational soul internally through the infusion of His grace and the participation of his Spirit. (Hugh of St. Victor, *Sacr.*, 2.11.3)

Here, quite clearly, though without the exact terminology, is the threefold structure of *sacramentum tantum*, *res et sacramentum*, and *res tantum*. The external marriage compact and agreement (perhaps Hugh has a marriage ceremony in mind) between man and woman is the *sacramentum* of the reality (*res*) of their mutual love, which reality itself in turn is a *sacramentum* of another reality (*res*), namely, the infusion of grace and participation in the Spirit. Admittedly, neither Hugh nor the Lombard places Christ or the Spirit as the active agent of the signified realities in this sacrament (though Hugh does mention a participation of the Spirit). Neither do they suggest that this sacrament actually effects or communicates the grace that it signifies. This may, in fact, be owing to the antiquity of marriage and its origin prior to sin, as Peter of Poitiers suggests at the end of the century. An objection claimed: "Marriage is a sacrament of the new covenant; therefore it effects what it signifies; therefore it effects the unity of Christ and the Church." To which Peter responded: "To this it should be said that this sacrament was celebrated in the old covenant just as in the new, and it is older than all the sacraments; for it was instituted in paradise when the Lord said: *be fruitful and multiply* [Gen 2]" (Peter of Poitiers: PL 211.1257D).

CONCLUSION: THE EUCHARIST
AS SOURCE AND SUMMIT

In these various ways, twelfth-century thinkers developed their understanding of the sacraments as ecclesial participation in the life of Christ through the Spirit, a participation often structured in conformity with the threefold structure of the Eucharist. Throughout this period, though, the Eucharist was not only the paradigm sacrament; it was also the "solar" sacrament around which the others orbited: it was the goal or summit or focal point of all the sacraments. In a sense, nearly all the other sacraments were designed to enable, facilitate, and restore the possibility of eucharistic communion. For the deepest reality of the Eucharist, the *res tantum*—union with Christ and his body—was the goal of the entire Christian life.

In the broadest sense, the deep reality (*res tantum*) of the Eucharist was simply grace. But more precisely, as noted above, it was union with Christ, as Gerhoh Reichersberg said when, after quoting the Johannine words "... *so that we may be in Christ and Christ may be in us*," he observed: "by these words is shown ... what the effect of this sacrament is" (Gerhoh Reichersberg: PL 193.503C). This was union with Christ *the Head*—later scholastics will call it "capital grace"—from which came the source of spiritual life, an "invisible and spiritual participation with Jesus, which is being accomplished within the heart through faith and love" (Hugh of St. Victor, *Sacr.*, 2.8.7). This sacramental unity of the bodily members with their Head was the work of the "vivifying" Holy Spirit, who "now descends upon the sacrament on the altar," just as he had overshadowed Mary at the conception (Peter Damian: PL 145.388B). So this deep reality could also be called "the participation of the Holy Spirit" (Hugh of St. Victor, *Sacr.*, 2.8.7). For, "just as the spirit of a man descends through the mediating head to vivify the members, so the Holy Spirit comes through Christ to Christians." Here was the source and font of the spiritual life: "through His body and blood we are vivified ... we are made participants in vivification (*participes vivificationis*)" (Hugh of St. Victor, *Sacr.*, 2.2.1, PL 176.416A). For "he is Life according to his nature as God, and when he became united to his flesh, he made it also to be life-giving, as also he said to us: *Verily, verily, I say unto you, unless you eat the flesh of the Son of Man and drink his Blood* ..." (Gerhoh of Reichersberg: PL 193.498A). In short, the reality was "every effect of salvation ..." (Wolbero of Cologne: PL 195.1135A).

For all these reasons, finally, this deep reality was the church, since in the Eucharist, "the church is con-sacramentally and con-corporally brought about (*consacramentalis et concorporalis efficitur*) with Christ, the mystery of him and them" (Wolbero of Cologne: PL 195.1134C). As noted above, a Victorine commentator on First Corinthians called the *res tantum* that reality which the Eucharist "signifies but does not contain, namely, the unity of the Church" (Ps-Hugh of St. Victor: PL 175.530B). Christ's sacramental body and blood were thus "sacraments of the unity of the church," for, "just as bread comes from many grains and wine flows from many grapes, so ecclesial unity comes from many persons of faith" (Peter of Poitiers: PL 211.1241D-1242A). This moreover was a union of believers, not only with Christ, but with one another "through this sacrament of intimate unity" (Peter Damian: PL 145.239A), where "all the faithful ... as if present communicating in the faith and charity of the sacrament ... as long as they are joined to one another by the gluten of charity, are like a single person" (Stephanus de Balgiaco: PL172.1289C–D) or "like a single republic of their magnificent emperor (*una respublica hujus magnifici imperatoris*)" (Wolbero of Cologne: PL 195.1134B).

Writing at the end of the century in his *De sacro altaris mysterio*, Pope Innocent III summed up the whole matter succinctly in words that provide an apt conclusion to this brief survey:

> Indeed three things are distinguished in this sacrament, namely, the visible form, the truth of the body, and the spiritual power. The form of the bread and wine, the truth of the flesh and blood, the power of unity and charity. The first is discerned by the eye, the second is believed in the soul, the third is received in the heart. The first is a sacrament, and not a reality; the second is a sacrament and a reality; the third is a reality and not a sacrament. But the first is the sacrament of a twofold reality, while the third is the reality of a double sacrament, and the second is the sacrament of the one and the reality of the other. For the form of bread signifies a double flesh of Christ, that is, the true and the mystical [flesh]. It both contains and signifies the true flesh; while it signifies but does not contain the mystical [flesh]. Just as one bread is confected from many grains and one wine flows together from many grapes, so the body of Christ is composed of many members and the unity of the church consists from diverse [members] ... But what is here called the mystery of faith, in other places it is called spirit and life. For the Spirit is a mystery, according to this: *the letter kills, but the spirit vivifies* (2 Cor. 3). Faith is life, according to this: *the just shall live by faith* (Rom 1). Here therefore the Lord said: *The words which I speak to you, they are spirit and they are life.* (Innocent III: PL 217.879B–880A)

In the twelfth century, the sacraments and the grace they communicated were conceived on the model, not of quantity, nor of production, not as a "thing" to be acquired, but of a pneumatic and ecclesial participation in the very life of Christ.

SUGGESTED READING

Goering (1991); Levy (2003a); Macy (1984).

BIBLIOGRAPHY

Primary Sources

Alger of Liege, *Liber de misericordia et justitia*. Patrologia Latina, vol. 180.857A–968D.

Anselm of Laon, *Ennarationes in evangelium Matthaei*. Patrologia Latina, vol. 162. 1227C–1500B.

Bruno of Segni, Tractatus Tertius. *De sacramentis ecclesiae, mysteriis atque ecclesiasticis ritibus*. Patrologia Latina, vol. 165.1089B–1110A.

Bruno the Carthusian, *In primam epistolam ad Corinthos*. Patrologia Latina, vol. 153.121C–218A.

Bruno the Carthusian, *In epistolam ad Hebraeos*. Patrologia Latina, vol. 153.487D–566C.

Eckebert of Schönau, *Sermo VII contra quartem haeresim de baptism parvulorum*. Patrologia Latina, vol. 195.41D–51B.

Ivo of Chartres, *Panormia*. Patrologia Latina, vol. 161.1041A–1344D.

Geoffrey of Vendôme, *Tractatus de ordinatione episcoporum, et de investitura laici*. Patrologia Latina, vol. 157.281B–290C.

Gerhoh of Reichersberg, *Epistolam VIII*. Patrologia Latina, vol. 193.300B–314B.

Guitmund of Aversa, *De corporis et sanguinis Christi veritate in Eucharistia*. Patrologia Latina, vol. 149.1427–1494.

Hugh of St. Victor, *De sacramentis christianae fidei* (*On the Sacraments of the Christian Faith*). Patrologia Latina, vol. 176.173–618. English translation: Deferrari, Roy, J. (1951), *On the Sacraments of the Christian Faith (De sacramentis)* (Cambridge, MA: The Mediaeval Academy of America).

Honorius of Autun, *Speculum ecclesiae*. Patrologia Latina, vol. 172.807A–1180A.

Innocent III, *De sacro altaris mysterio*. Patrologia Latina, vol. 217.773B–916A.

Master Bandini, *Liber de ecclesiasticis sacramentis*. Patrologia Latina, vol. 192.1089C–1112B.

Otto of Lucca, *Summa sententiarum*. Patrologia Latina, vol. 176.41A–174D.

Peter Abelard, Theologia "Scholarium." Corpus Christianorum Continuatio Mediaevalis, vol. 13.

Peter Damian, *Dissertatio Tertia. Contra clericos intemperantes*. Patrologia Latina, vol. 145. 416A–424A.

Peter Lombard (1971–1981), *Magistri Lombardi Sententiae in IV libris distinctae*, 2 vols. Ed. Collegi S. Bonaventurae ad Claras Aquas. (Grottaferrate [Rome]: Editiones Collegii S. Bonaventurae ad Claras Aquas).

Peter of Poitiers, *Sententiarum Libri Quinque*. Patrologia Latina, vol. 211.783A–1280D.

Ps.-Hugh of St. Victor, *In epistolam I ad Corinthios*. Patrologia Latina, vol. 175.513A–544B.

Ps.-Hugh of St. Victor, *Speculum de mysteriis ecclesiae*. Patrologia Latina, vol. 177.335A–380D.

Radulphus Ardens, *In festo omnium sanctorum*. Patrologia Latina, vol. 155.1470D–1475D.

Radulphus Ardens, *Speculum universale* (ed. Christopher P. Evans).

Stephanus de Balgiaco, *Tractatus de sacramento altaris*. Patrologia Latina, vol. 172.1273C–1308A.

Wolbero of Cologne, *Commentaria vetustissima et profundissima super canticum canticorum Salomonis*. Patrologia Latina, vol. 195.1017A–1272C.

Zachary of Besançon, *In unum ex quatuor sive De Concordia evangelistarum libri quatuor*. Patrologia Latina, vol. 186.11A–620B.

Secondary Sources

Blankenhorn, Bernard (2006), "The Instrumental Causality of the Sacraments: Thomas Aquinas and Louis-Marie Chauvet," *Nova et Vetera* 4: 255–294.

de Ghellinck, Joseph (1924), "Eucharistie au XIIe siècle en Occident," in *Dictionnaire de Théologie Catholique*, vol. 5 (Paris: Letouzey et Ané), 1233–1302.

de Lubac, Henri (1988), *Catholicism: Christ and the Common Destiny of Man* (San Francisco, CA: Ignatius Press).

Evans, Chris (2010), *Radulphus Ardens, The Questions on the Sacraments: Speculum uniuersale 8.31–92* (Toronto: PIMS).

Friedberg, Emil, ed. (1959), *Corpus iuris canonici*, 2 vols. (Graz, Austria: Akademische Druck- u. Verlagsanstalt).

Goering, Joseph (1991), "The Invention of Transubstantiation," *Traditio* 46: 147–170.

Levy, Ian Christopher (2003a), "Sacraments and Sacramental Theology," in William Chester Jordan (ed.), *Dictionary of the Middle Ages*, vol. 14, Supplement 1 (New York: Charles Scribner's Sons), 544–553.

Levy, Ian Christopher (2003b), *John Wyclif: Scriptural Logic, Real Presence, and the Parameters of Orthodoxy* (Milwaukee, WI: Marquette University).

Jackson, Pamela (1999), "Eucharist," in Allan D. Fitzgerald, O.S.A. (ed.), *Augustine through the Ages: An Encyclopedia* (Grand Rapids, MI: Eerdmans), 330–334.

Macy, Gary (1984), *The Theologies of the Eucharist in the Early Scholastic Period: A Study of the Salvific Function of the Sacrament according to the Theologians c. 1080–1220* (Oxford: Clarendon Press).

van den Eynde, Damian (1950), *Les Définitions des sacrements pendant la première période de la théologie scolastique (1050–1235)* (Rome: Antonianum).

van den Eynde, Damian (1952), "The Theory of the Composition of the Sacraments in Early Scholasticism (1125–1240)," *Franciscan Studies* 12: 1–20.

Wawrykow, Joseph P. (2012), "The Heritage of the Late Empire: Influential Theology," in I. Christopher Levy, G. Macy, and K. Van Ausdahl (eds.), *A Companion to the Eucharist in the Middle Ages* (Leiden: Brill), 18–25.

CHAPTER 15

THE SACRAMENTS IN THIRTEENTH-CENTURY THEOLOGY

JOSEPH P. WAWRYKOW

THE sacraments held tremendous significance for Catholic Christians in the thirteenth century. Sacramental practice shaped Catholic Christian identity, and the sacraments offered repeated opportunity for Catholic public performance and expression of faith. Infant baptism was by now long the norm, affirming formal entry into the believing community; and as decreed at Lateran IV (1215), Catholic Christians were expected to confess their sins to a priest and to receive the Eucharist at least once a year (*Constitutiones* c.21/Tanner 1990: I, 245). Ordained clergy officiated at marriage ceremonies, giving God's blessing to newly formed couples embarking on a new stage of life. The sacraments also helped to distinguish Catholic Christianity from other religions, including other claimants to the title of "Christian." Through the use of material elements in many of the sacraments, Catholics expressed their rejection of the Cathar denigration of matter and affirmed the goodness of all of God's creation. God creates all, the visible as well as the invisible, and can employ the material for spiritual ends. In restricting the consecration in the Eucharist and the proclaiming of absolution in penance to ordained ministers (on whom a sacramental power had been bestowed through their ordination), Catholics likewise were rejecting a Waldensian claim that the conveying of grace was in some way dependent on the personal holiness of the celebrant (Lateran IV c.1/Tanner 1990: I, 230; Peters 1980: chs. III, IV; Rubin 1991: chs.1, 5). In this, of course, there is a medieval resumption of the anti-Donatist teaching of Augustine.

Catholic theologians accordingly devoted considerable attention to the sacraments, to how they worked and why, and how they fit into God's plan for human salvation. The present chapter focuses on thirteenth-century scholastic treatments of the sacraments. The chapter falls into two parts. The first is given over to what the scholastics taught in general about the sacraments, observing where there was broad consensus as well as occasional points of disagreement. Here, I consider the teachings on the sacraments in general offered by such representative scholastic authors as William of Auxerre, Alexander of Hales, Bonaventure, Robert Kilwardby, and Thomas Aquinas. The second part of the chapter moves the discussion forward by examining the teaching of Aquinas about the greatest of the sacraments, the Eucharist, with the aim of showing the subtlety of his depiction of the various actors in the Eucharist—God and Christ, the ordained minister, those who receive the Eucharist worthily and contribute to the eucharistic sacrifice. In that analysis, Aquinas has, in a way characteristic of scholastic teaching (but expressive as well of his particular acuity as a theologian), struck a nice balance between sacramental objective efficacy and spiritual disposition, portraying the Eucharist as at once a means of grace and an important opportunity for spiritual expression and growth.

SACRAMENTS IN GENERAL

Important for thirteenth-century discussions was the teaching on sacraments found in the *Sentences* of Peter Lombard. By the end of the first third of the thirteenth century, that mid-twelfth-century writing had attained status as the *de facto* "textbook" on which all budding scholastics were to comment to qualify for taking up university teaching positions. The four books of the *Sentences* aspire to comprehensiveness, presenting the main theological topics along with the sayings of leading authorities on those topics. Through the *Sentences*, novice theologians were exposed to areas of consensus, as well as to disagreement on specific issues. Much of Book IV is devoted to the Christian sacraments in general and then on each of the seven sacraments in particular. In his discussion of the sacraments in general (dd.I–II), Peter announced themes that would remain current in thirteenth-century treatments of the sacraments. He discusses in turn the nature of a sacrament, the purpose of a sacrament, the composition of sacraments, and the difference between the sacraments of the New Law and those of the Old. Thirteenth-century theologians produced writings other than commentaries occasioned by the *Sentences*. Many tried their hand at their own comprehensive presentation and investigation of the truths of the Christian faith, according to other models of organization; works such as William of Auxerre's *Summa aurea*, Bonaventure's *Breviloquium*, and Aquinas' *Summa theologiae* come readily to mind. But, even in such works, what Peter taught about the sacraments, the issues he thought worthy of discrete treatment along with scriptural and patristic citation, all remain in view. The later scholastics by no means simply repeat the Lombard. They add their own ideas and questions, and the investigations can be even more vigorous and pointed, and more philosophically deft. But the Lombard does provide a point of departure for thirteenth-century reflections on the sacraments. With Peter, the later theologians, for example, define a sacrament as both cause and sign of a sacred reality; number the Christian sacraments at seven; and place the sacraments in the broader context of God's saving work through Christ, as the principal, although not exclusive, means of conveying Christ's grace.

Scholastic accounts of the sacraments rest on certain shared convictions about God and about humans. God is loving and good, and acts in a wise way. God calls human beings into existence in order to share God's own life with humans: creation is geared to salvation, to the bringing of human beings into God's own presence in the next life, and to the sharing with humans what belongs to God. The account of human beings is firmly grounded in God's creative and saving plan. To be human means to be made by God, for God; being human involves body (with the senses) as well as soul; realizing the possibilities set for humans by God involves the use of the powers that make a human human—those of knowing and loving—in a way intended by and pleasing to God. Sinning is factored into this account of the human, the sin that is due to the misuse of the will. To sin is to rebel against God, to reject God's plan for humans; it is to set oneself and one's immediate surroundings as one's end, in place of God. Different scholastics can posit a greater or lesser disruption caused by sin, that is, can play up different facets of the "consequences of sin"; but all agree that sin is an obstacle to the successful movement of humans to God as end, one that must be overcome for God's plan for humans to come to fruition. God does not leave sin as the final word; God meets the human condition as marked by sin with grace. The scholastics are thus attentive to the healing or medicinal function of grace: Christ the physician addresses the illness that is sin, and by grace restores the sinner to health. But they are also aware of another function of grace: the God who beatifies is transcendent, beyond natural capabilities; the grace that Christ conveys is thus also elevating.

Presentations of sacraments and their grace and of how sacramental grace works to the good of human beings, in accordance with God's plan in Christ, display a basic dynamism. Different metaphors can be employed to convey this dynamism. For example, in the *Breviloquium* (Part VI, ch.1), Bonaventure, echoing Peter (*Sententiae* Bk.IV, d.I, ch.1), portrays the sacraments as *remedy*, here taking the illness that is sin, with its lingering effects, at full value. Thus, different sacraments are depicted as expelling the disease (baptism), restoring to health those who have relapsed (as in penance), and maintaining health once restored (as in confirmation, and the Eucharist). The characterization of the sacraments as "remedy" is in fact quite common; we meet it too in William of Auxerre (*Summa Aurea*, Bk.IV, Tractatus Quartus/61–64), Alexander of Hales (*Glossa In IV*, Introitus/1–8), and Aquinas (*ST* III, q.61, 1c). Aquinas for his part trades as well on a view of life as a *journey* in his account of the sacraments (*ST* III, q.65, 2c; III, q.73, 1c and 6c). Life in this world is a journey, by which humans are readied for, and become qualified, with God's grace through Christ and his sacraments, for eternal life in the next. This journey, of the affections and behavior, is a spiritual journey, one that testifies to spiritual life. By baptism, someone is reborn, coming to spiritual life for the first time; that life is strengthened in distinctive ways by confirmation and by Eucharist; penance allows those who have strayed to get back on track. The sacraments are an integral part of a process in which God through Christ and Christ's sacraments interacts with those who have been made for God, to their benefit.

As was the Lombard, thirteenth-century scholastic theologians are attentive to the sacraments as both sign and cause. The material elements employed in several of the sacraments have a natural aptitude for pointing to sacred reality; their signification has been determined by God's employment of material elements in the salvific process. The actions of the celebrant in the sacrament are, too, not incidental; by natural aptitude and divine appointment, the washing with water, for example, or anointing with oil proclaim God's actions in Christ for human salvation. Whatever the philosophical affinities of given scholastic theologians (e.g. "Platonizing," "Aristotelian") and their precise episte-mologies, this aspect of scholastic sacramentology speaks to a holistic view of the human person. A person is body and soul, and each contributes to and is involved in spiritual progress. Sacramental signs address the senses, but not just the senses; the whole human perceives and discerns, and learns anew through the sacraments what God has done in Christ for human beings.

Scholastics offer extensive reflections on the causality of the sacraments, concerned to show what sort(s) of causality can be involved, what is caused, and the contributions of the various actors in sacramental celebration. Authors such as Bonaventure can allege a full array of causes in teaching the sacraments. As he writes in the *Breviloquium* (Part VI.ch.1.6), in the sacraments the efficient cause is the divine institution of the sacra-ment; the material cause is their representing by a sensible sign; their formal cause is gratuitous sanctification; and their final cause is the medicinal healing of humankind. The tendency in scholastic discussions, however, is to focus on efficient causality, on the doing that results in the effects of the sacraments. For each of the sacraments, the main effect is grace itself, which takes on a shape appropriate to a given sacrament. What is done, in some sense, results in grace.

But some of the sacraments (baptism, confirmation, holy orders) have character as an additional effect. Character is an indelible imprint on the soul, designating its recipient as marked off as in some particular relationship to God and Christ and for some sort of service to God, Christ, and the church (Alexander, *Glossa in IV*, d.I/14). All those who receive baptism receive the character that makes them members of the church and ordered to God as their end. Confirmation confers an additional character, which strengthens one's membership in the spiritual body that is church, while by ordi-nation, certain men are ordered to sacramental celebration. By their priestly character, they are marked as representatives of Christ, the Priest (for this designation of Jesus see Lateran IV *Constitutiones* c.1/Tanner, I, 230); and to them is entrusted responsibility, and power, for the sacraments. They typically officiate in the sacraments, and by their priestly character, their acting in the sacraments is effective; and some sacraments, not least the Eucharist, are dependent on their involvement. An ordained priest normally officiates in baptism, but the scholastics recognize that in case of emergency, someone who is not ordained (e.g. a lay person, even a non-Christian) can baptize (Lateran IV *Constitutiones* c.1/Tanner I, 230; William of Auxerre, *Summa aurea*, Bk.IV, Tractatus V, cap.III/103–7). All that is required in such an instance is that the baptizer intend with the words and action what the church intends, even if the baptizer does not personally believe.

The Eucharist has its own particular effect, one that fully accounts for its centrality in the sacramental system and in the life of high medieval Christians. When the sacrament is correctly performed, by an ordained priest acting in the person of Christ and with the intention of the church in performing the sacrament, Christ truly and infallibly becomes present. Christ has promised his presence in the Eucharist and keeps that promise, presenting himself anew in eucharistic celebration to those who seek him.

By the thirteenth century, a threefold sacramental formula was in place that displays the scholastic concern for the sacrament as both sign and cause, and which helps to summarize the effects of the sacrament: *sacramentum tantum* (sign only), *res et sacramentum* (thing or reality and sign), and *res tantum* (thing or reality itself) (King 1967). The formula, which in its parts goes back at least to Augustine, was broadly employed to discuss the Eucharist, but could be applied to the other sacraments as well. In the Eucharist, the bread and wine are signs only. They point to the reality that is the Christ truly present; and when they are consecrated by Christ's priestly representative, Christ is really present; and the Christ who is truly present points to and conveys what is *res tantum*, which is variously described as grace, and charity, and the spiritual body that is church. In terms of the sacraments that impart a particular character, that character is identified as *res et sacramentum*: in baptism, for example, the washing with water (*sacramentum tantum*) imprints a character, which itself points to the grace and forgiveness and incorporation into the spiritual body of Christ that is church, which is baptism's *res tantum*.

There are several who are involved in sacramental performance and reception. What does each do, and to what extent, if at all, is their doing efficiently causal of grace? All theologians agreed that the principal agent is God. The sacraments are divinely instituted and bring about grace by the activity of God in the sacraments. The same points can be made in Christological terms, and were. Scholastic Christology is incarnational. The person of Jesus is the second divine person; and in becoming human, the second divine person has not ceased to be fully God. By incarnation, the second divine person is also, and truly, human. Thus, as God Jesus has the authority, and the power, to institute the sacraments and make available their effects, and cause those effects. The sacraments themselves are not the source of grace, in the sense of originating grace or giving rise to this spiritual power. Grace derives from God and the fully divine Christ alone.

Why then do sacraments—created entities—convey grace? The scholastics disagreed about the reason for the effectiveness of the sacraments (Courtenay 1972; Blankenhorn 2010). For some, that the sacraments bring about grace is due simply to the will of God. God has chosen to convey God's grace in conjunction with sacramental performance. There is a *sine qua non* causality at play here. God, of course, could convey grace directly; but God has decided, and made a pact (Kilwardby, *Quaestiones*, q.39/200) to tie God's grace to particular sacramental elements, words, actions. Sacraments are the occasions, rather than the cause, of grace, which God alone causes. Aquinas for his part wants to ascribe an efficient causality itself to the sacraments, without undermining the divine role in the causing of grace. Sacraments are instrumental efficient causes of grace (*ST* III, q.62, 1c). Aquinas' mature teaching about the sacraments as separate, instrumental causes is part of a broader theological account of instrumental causality, one that begins with and has its principal point of reference in Jesus himself. Aquinas distinguishes among several instrumental causes. The humanity of Jesus stands to the divinity as personal, conjoined, animate instrument: personal and conjoined, for the humanity is united to the divinity in the person of the Word who becomes incarnate; animate, for the humanity of Jesus includes both soul and body, and the Word as incarnate possesses full human capacity and acts as truly and fully human, knowing and loving in authentically human fashion. The priest stands to Christ as a separate, not conjoined, instrument; and as acting in Christ's person, and in conformity with Christ's will in celebrating the sacraments, the priest is the instrument through whom God works, to bring about the effects intended by God. And the sacraments too are separate instruments, inanimate however, through which God acts to bring about spiritual good (*ST* III, q.64, a.1). The causality of all these instruments is real, and that causality is thoroughly subordinate to that of the principal efficient cause, the God who is able to work through secondary causes.

Recipients of the sacraments, however, do not exercise any such efficient causality. The grace of the sacrament is not dependent on the faith or love or any act of the recipient; again, grace has its origin in God and Christ, and is brought about, made present, by God. But the disposition and attitude of the recipient are nonetheless pertinent to a discussion of the sacraments; on this, all scholastics are agreed. Sacraments cause grace; but not all who receive a sacrament receive its grace. In asserting the value of correct subjective disposition on the part of recipients, scholastics can at times be content with a minimalist claim: as long as the recipient does not place an obstacle (*obex*; see Alexander of Hales, *Glossa In IV*, d.IV/92) to sacramental grace, it will be received. Here, correct disposition is put negatively, in terms of mortal sin. Mortal sin thwarts, blocks, the infusion of grace. A comparison could be drawn to the sun's rays: the sun may be shining, but the room is not lit when the shades are drawn (Alexander of Hales, *Glossa in IV*, d.IV/73).

But scholastics can also be more positive in stating subjective disposition, insisting on an openness on the part of the recipient to God that testifies to an existing, spiritual relationship with God through Christ. In this more expansive, positive presentation, faith informed by charity is to the fore. By formed faith, a person is a member of Christ's spiritual body; those who are already part of Christ's spiritual body accept, by their formed faith, the offer of grace made by God in the sacraments. This holds in the Eucharist. It holds too for penance, where a person who is repentant seeks to confess to a priest and receive formal absolution. And it holds for adult baptism, where the baptism marks a formal profession of one's living faith. Infant baptism offers only an apparent exception to this insistence on the presence of faith in the recipient to benefit spiritually from sacramental performance. The infant, of course, is incapable of the act of faith; but there is an act of faith even in this baptism, the faith of the church, expressed by the sponsors on the child's behalf. In terms of the threefold sacramental formula, one can put the scholastic consensus as follows: the *sacramentum tantum* is received by all those who receive a sacrament. So too will be the *res et sacramentum*, whatever the subjective disposition of the recipient (this is why the sacraments that offer the indelible mark that is character are not repeatable: character is simply imprinted on the soul). But not all ascend to the *res tantum*, actually get the grace and spiritual benefits of a sacrament. The mortal sinner in effect rejects the *res tantum*. In such sacramental reception, there is a fictive element; the sinner receives *ficte* (William of Auxerre, *Summa Aurea*, Bk.IV, Tractatus V, cap.II, q.1/76–82): the sinful person is only pretending to have the formed faith required for fruitful reception. The person alive in faith and charity, professing truthfully, does accept that grace, and so grows in it.

While all agreed on the need for an appropriate subjective disposition to receive sacramental grace, there was no consensus about how a person attains that disposition. For those who took at face value the *facienti quod in se est* ("to someone doing what lies in him"; "to someone doing his best"), the onus is on the person to take the initiative. The person must take the first step—repent of mortal sin; come to the faith that justifies—and then God will meet the person, as it were, halfway, and give grace. To someone who does her best, God gives grace. In this view, the actual reception of a sacrament involves the completion of a process set in motion by the person. For Scotus, for example, in penance what is needed at the start of the process is attrition on the part of the penitent, a sorrow for sins that may be motivated by fear of punishment. In confessing sins to the priest and receiving absolution, that attrition will be transformed into contrition, true sorrow for sins because of a desire to please God and not be separate from God, and grace is infused. Other theologians, however, placed the initiative in readying a person with God, not the person. By the time of the *Summa* (*ST* I–II, q.112, aa.2–3), Aquinas has rejected a straightforward interpretation of the *facienti*, here influenced by his reading of the very late Augustine (writing against the Massilians) and showing his own progress in refining a teaching on grace (Wawrykow 1995: 210–211). For the reception of habitual grace, the person does need to be prepared, but that preparation is not the human's achievement. It is worked in the person by God, by the operative *auxilium* that readies the person for the infusion of habitual grace. By God's grace of *auxilium*, that person is already set right with God, oriented to God by the faith and charity that accompany and emerge from grace. Such a person receives fruitfully, responding by God's grace to God's offer of new grace and other spiritual gifts.

Aquinas on the Eucharist

Resonance, as well as significant detail, will be added to this account of sacrament by taking a closer look at a particular sacrament, as taught by a particular scholastic theologian: the Eucharist, at the very center of Christian life in this world (*ST* III, q.73, a.3c), as discussed by Aquinas in his *Summa theologiae* (*ST* III, qq.73–83). What has been stated about the sacraments in general—on sacrament as cause and sign, the role of the priest, the importance of proper spiritual disposition in the recipient for fruitful reception—comes to more exact expression in Aquinas' treatise on the Eucharist. Looking at this particular treatise will make more evident that talk of sacrament presupposes and brings to bear certain key convictions about God and Christ, and humans in relation to God through Christ. And by looking at this sacrament, according to Aquinas, the significance of Christ as priest will come into clearer focus, as will the ways in which sacramental performance by the entire church offers members of the church the opportunity for spiritual growth into Christ, precisely through the proclamation of their formed faith.

The point of departure here is a particular passage that falls in the first article of the penultimate question of the *Summa*'s treatise on the Eucharist. *ST* III, q.82, a.1, ad2 reads as follows:

> the just layperson is united to Christ in a spiritual union by faith and charity, but not by sacramental power. And thus the just layperson has a spiritual priesthood (*spirituale sacerdotium*) for offering spiritual sacrifices, about which it is said in Psalm 50 [51]:19, "a sacrifice to God is an afflicted spirit"; and in Romans 12:1, "offer up your bodies as a living sacrifice." Whence it is also written in I Peter 2:5, "a holy priesthood, to offer spiritual offerings." [my translation]

The passage is quite rich, and offers a distinctive access to themes that are important to the treatise on the Eucharist as a whole. It also calls for a closer consideration of the Christology that courses its way through the treatise on the Eucharist, picking up on and expanding upon ideas about Christ, in his person and work, expressed earlier in the *Summa*'s third part, in the *ex professo* treatment of Christ.

ST III, q.82 has as its topic the minister of the sacrament. The first article is concerned with eucharistic consecration: who can consecrate, and on what basis does that one consecrate? The second objection in the article thinks that every Christian can consecrate in the Eucharist. In the response to that objection, Aquinas answers with a distinction, between two priesthoods that are found in the church. The one is the priesthood to which sacramental power *is* attached, and so is involved in eucharistic consecration; Aquinas pursues that point in the rest of the article. The other is what he here calls a "spiritual priesthood," one that involves spiritual union with Christ by faith and charity. This other priesthood, the main focus of this response, is in its own way pertinent to a teaching on the Eucharist.

The treatise on the Eucharist in the *Summa* covers a wide range of topics, from the matter and formulae of the sacrament, through the effects of the sacraments and the recipients of the sacraments, to a concluding series of reflections on the liturgy of the mass. The question in which the passage is found—q.82—turns to the minister of the sacrament; and the greater part of q.82 focuses on the priesthood to which sacramental power is attached.

By the time we reach q.82, on the minister, Aquinas has, however, made several observations about the sacramental priest. Indeed, the core of the teaching about the *sacramental* priest is already in place by the time we get to the article in which this passage is found; q.82 simply adds some coloring to the depiction. And in the teaching thus far about the sacramental priest, *consecration* in fact holds pride of place. The Eucharist is for Aquinas a sacrament, a sign of a sacred reality that causes grace. But it is a distinctive sacrament. The other sacraments come to their perfection in being applied to a recipient. This sacrament, however, has as its "first perfection" the presence of Christ

(*ST* III, q.73, a.1, ad3). By the consecration, what was bread is changed into the substance of Christ's body; what was wine into the substance of Christ's blood. Christ is distinctively and irreducibly present in the sacrament; and Christ becomes present, and unfailingly so, when the sacrament is properly performed. Who then is the priest that consecrates, and what is the nature of his contribution to the change? First, he is the representative of Christ; he acts *in persona Christi*, whose instrument he is (*ST* III, q.78, a.1c). He is designated Christ's representative by his ordination. In his ordination, he receives a priestly character (in addition to that character that all Christians receive in their baptism). By that priestly character, which is stamped on his soul, he is delegated for sacramental service, to represent Christ and on behalf of Christ. In the eucharistic consecration, the words he speaks are not his own, but Christ's (*ST* III, q.78, a.4c). He speaks Christ's words of institution; he is not speaking for himself, but for Christ. Christ has made the promise of his presence, and it is Christ who keeps the promise, by the words of Christ spoken by the priest. The words of consecration are transformative—through them the change is wrought—and descriptive (*ST* III, q.78, a.5c): this *is* Christ's body, Christ's blood.

The spiritual attributes and personal qualities of the sacramental priest, Aquinas notes by contrast, are *not* pertinent to the consideration of the change and the presence that results from the change. Indeed, it may be that a sacramental priest is himself not a believer, or himself a lover of Christ. What *does* matter is the priestly character that the sacramental priest has received, delegating him for this work. Provided the sacramental priest is able to form the intention that the church has in celebrating the sacrament—that is, to follow Christ's command to "do this in memory of me"—that is sufficient. In this rendering, the sacramental priest is viewed as an instrumental cause (as too are the words of consecration). The principal agent in the consecration is Christ, who has instituted the sacrament and promised his presence; the change is worked by the power of Christ's Spirit, the principal efficient cause of the change, acting through the priest and the words of consecration.

In our passage in q.82, however, there is another priesthood that is named, the *spiritual* priesthood; and it is apparent enough that in the present passage it is with that priesthood that Aquinas is especially concerned. This is a priesthood that is based on spiritual union, and spiritual union with Christ, and spiritual union with Christ by faith and charity. The making of the distinction—there is a second priesthood, in addition to the sacramental—and the identification of a priesthood that is "spiritual" may on first reading be a surprise. This is the first mention in the treatise on the Eucharist of a "spiritual priesthood," a priesthood that is distinctive and that has the importance conveyed by the scriptural citations (Ps.50 [51]:19; Rom 12:1; 1 Pet 2:5) that express what is involved in this "spiritual priesthood." And, as a quick search in the *Index thomisticus* confirms, one of the scriptural verses cited in this response—that from 1 Peter—is extremely rare in the Thomistic corpus. Its use here, with the affirmation of a spiritual priesthood, thus calls out for comment.

While the term ("spiritual priesthood") is new, what is conveyed by the term is most definitely not new to the treatise on the Eucharist. Especially in the questions on the effects and recipients of the sacrament (*ST* III, qq.78–79), Aquinas has had consider-able occasion to reflect on spiritual union with Christ through faith and charity and the importance of that spiritual union in an account of this sacrament. Through his com-ments in this vein, Aquinas gives expression to a second theme important in the treatise, alongside the insistence on what amounts to an objective sacramental efficacy (in terms of the change and the presence): proper spiritual disposition, when it comes to the recip-ients of this sacrament, must be given its due.

Christ is the source of grace and charity. The coming to be present of Christ in the Eucharist thus *can* be the occasion for the distribution of grace and charity. Aquinas thematizes this point about the connection between Christ eucharistically present and spiritual benefits by invoking the formula discussed in the first part of this chap-ter: *sacramentum tantum, res et sacramentum*, and *res tantum*. After the consecration, the *sacramentum tantum* is the remaining accidents of the bread and wine; these sig-nify, act as sign, pointing beyond themselves, to both the *res et sacramentum* and the *res tantum*. The *res et sacramentum* is the Christ truly present in the sacrament through the consecration; as signified by the bread and wine, Christ is present as spiritual food and spiritual drink. The eucharistically present Christ is thus *res* (of the signifying bread and wine); the eucharistically present Christ is also *sacramentum*, also sign, pointing to the *res tantum*, to what is provided by spiritual food and drink. By *res tantum*, Aquinas summarizes in various ways the spiritual benefits of the Eucharist. Grace and charity, to be sure; but Aquinas can also refer here to the church, to the mystical body of Christ, the body that has Christ as its head. In that body, many are brought together as one; to invoke the *sacramentum tantum* again, here as pointing as well to the *res tantum*, that body is like one bread, made out of many grains (*ST* III, q.74, a.1c).

The threefold formula is prominent in Aquinas' teaching about sacramental *recep-tion*. Aquinas reflects on several different sorts of possible recipients of the Eucharist. To name a few (*ST* III, q.80, aa.1–4): the non-believer; the person who is in mortal sin, and so is estranged from God; the person who is marked by grace, faith, and charity. What does each receive? For each, there is a "sacramental eating": each receives the *sacramentum tantum*, the remaining accidents of bread and wine, which signify both real presence and spiritual benefits. Each also receives the Christ who is truly present in the sacrament (what was bread is in truth, by virtue of the consecration, the substance of Christ's body). But not all receive the spiritual benefits; for some, there is a block between the *res et sacramentum* and the *res tantum*. Only those who eat in faith and charity, and out of grace, attain the *res tantum*. It is again helpful to think here in terms of the difference between the making of an offer and its acceptance (or rejection). Those who, in their reception, express their faith and charity are in effect open to the offer that Christ, who is present, makes. By their faith and charity, they accept that offer; and so their eating is both sacramental *and* spiritual. And in their sacramental eating that is spiritual, they receive Christ as their spiritual food and spiritual drink, and *grow* in grace and charity, and are *more fully incorporated* into the body of Christ. For others, who lack faith and charity, who lack grace because of mortal sin, there is a sacramental eating, but one that is not spiritual. The offer that the eucharistic Christ makes is rejected; they receive the eucharistically present Christ, but not his benefits. For that further eating, union with Christ through faith and charity is required.

One of Aquinas' favorite designations of the Eucharist in the *Summa* is as the "sacrament of charity" (e.g. *ST* III, q.73, a.3, ad3). That title is indeed apt. It nicely underscores Christ's own love, not least in instituting this sacrament, guaranteeing his sacramental presence when he was about to leave those whom he calls "friends" (this point about the institution of the Eucharist as by a friend for friends is made in the very first question of the treatise; *ST* III, q.73, a.5c). But this designation of the sacrament as the sacrament of charity also reinforces what is called for on the part of the recipients, in their fruitful engagement with the Christ who is truly present.

THE SACRAMENT THAT IS ALSO SACRIFICE

Much of the treatise is devoted to the Eucharist as *sacrament*. Aquinas has woven into the treatise another characterization of Eucharist: the Eucharist is *sacrifice* as well (e.g. *ST* III, q.79, a.5, ad7; q.83, a.1). And in the teaching about eucharistic sacrifice, charity again comes very much to the fore.

Aquinas' comments about the Eucharist as sacrifice gather together and extend others made earlier in the *Summa*—about sacrifice in general, in the second part of the second part (*ST* II–II, q.85); on Christ's priesthood in the third part, q.22; and an article in q.48 that describes the cross in terms of sacrifice (a.3). In all of these discussions of sacrifice, Aquinas explicitly acknowledges his debt to the teaching on sacrifice in Book X of Augustine's *On the City of God* and Book IV of Augustine's *On the Trinity*. Augustine's definition of sacrifice, and application to Christ, following the scriptural witness, shapes Aquinas' own teaching about sacrifice in the *Summa*.

For Augustine, and for Aquinas, a sacrifice is something done that *gives* God the honor due to God and is pleasing to God. In the giving that is sacrifice, four elements need to be discerned, four questions answered: "*to whom* is the sacrifice offered, *by whom* is it offered, *what* is offered, and *for whom* is it offered." In considering the "by whom," it will be especially important to consider the willingness with which the offering is made; the greater the charity, and so the willingness of the act and concern for the object of the giving, the more pleasing the offering will be. And in considering the "for whom," one cannot restrict oneself to the offerer. It may well be that the intention of the offering is not just for oneself or even principally for oneself. The offering can be of more general application, that is, for others to benefit from what the offerer gives to God in doing what the offerer does.

With this understanding of sacrifice, Augustine has no difficulty concluding that in Christ one meets the paradigmatic sacrifice, sacrifice in its most perfect form. Aquinas' discussion of Christ's priesthood, in *ST* III, q.22, shows that Aquinas has made this assessment his own. In the treatment of Christ as priest, sacrifice stands to the fore. Christ the Priest offers himself to God, who is pleased by this offering; and this offering is perfect, done out of perfect charity. Lying behind Aquinas' depiction of the perfection of this sacrifice is his earlier account in *ST* III, q.7 of Christ's personal holiness as rooted in Christ's perfect grace and charity. As is well known, Aquinas advances an incarnational Christology, and in that Christology he wants to take seriously the divine personhood, the full divinity, and the true humanity. The Word, the fully divine second person, has without loss to itself as fully divine person taken up and expressed a second nature and fully instantiated that humanity. The Word incarnate is the subject of that humanity, the agent of the human doings and undergoings ascribed in scripture to Jesus. A fundamental goal of Aquinas in this incarnational Christology is to speak correctly of Christ, to know what is in play, in terms of the Christology, when speaking of Christ. Is a statement made with regard to the divinity? Made with regard to the humanity? In the discussion of Christ and his priesthood and his sacrifice, Aquinas puts the focus where he thinks it should be. The Word incarnate is priest in terms of the humanity that has been taken up and expressed by the Word. The Word incarnate is morally perfect, and so can make the perfect offering, because the human Word is full of grace and charity, has received from God these perfections which allow for fully correct action in relation to God. And so, as in III.22 where Aquinas is contemplating Christ's sacrifice and asserts its perfection, he is in effect able to make the point on two grounds, having to do with two of Augustine's four elements in sacrifice. What is offered—Christ's holy actions and ultimately his holy life—is perfect; Christ offers his actions and life perfectly, in perfect obedience and love and out of the perfection of his grace (*ST* III, q.22, a.2). And to continue this tracing of Christ in terms of perfect sacrifice, and to bring up another element of the Augustinian account of sacrifice: q.7, on Christ's personal holiness, is followed by a question (8) that deals with Christ as head of the mystical body that is the church. That headship is due to grace, due to the same grace that provides for his personal holiness, but now viewed from a different angle, with an eye to the acting out of that grace and charity as *for others*. What we meet in qq.7–8, which undergird the depiction of Christ's priesthood and sacrifice, is in effect the Thomistic gloss on the Johannine point: Jesus was "full of grace and truth; from that grace we have all received" (John 1: 14, 16).

In *ST* III, q.48, Aquinas will reflect on the sacrifice of the cross, employing the Augustinian definition of sacrifice and breaking this sacrifice down in terms of the four Augustinian elements. However, Aquinas will not restrict sacrifice to the death on the cross; nor does he want to suggest that only dying for God is sacrificial. All of Christ's actions can be thought of in terms of sacrifice; and given Aquinas' notion of Christ as model for moral emulation, he thinks that Christian acting, done in imitation of Christ, can be put in sacrificial terms. As Aquinas says, following Augustine, every good work done in charity, by which one comes closer to God, is a true sacrifice. Helpful here is a passage from one of Aquinas' commentaries—that on the Ten Commandments—which gestures at the range of good works that are sacrifice, pleasing to God (*de decem preceptis*, a.5c). The passage, not incidentally, is also notable for its citation, while listing these diverse sacrifices, of two of the scriptures cited in our originating passage from *ST* III, q.82 (the Romans and the Psalms quotes). Sacrifice is owed (in justice) to God daily, and doubly so, Aquinas states in this commentary, on the sabbath. We should offer sacrifice to God from all that we possess. We should offer, first of all, our soul to God, being sorry for our sins (here, our psalm is quoted about the afflicted spirit) and also pray for God's blessings. Secondly, we should offer our body (here, Romans is cited), by mortifying it with fasting, and also by praising God. And thirdly, we should sacrifice our possessions by giving alms. What holds of others, of their sacrificing, holds of Christ. His sacrifice meets, as it were, sin. But it testifies at the same time to the human life well lived, in accordance with what God seeks of beings of such nature and called to the end that is eternal life. He evinces his commitment to God, his devotion to God, his offering to God in his own profound love, giving to God his holy life and actions that are pleasing to God. Aquinas underscores, in fact, this broader scope of sacrifice even in the case of the cross, in the article (a.3) on the Passion as sacrifice in *ST* III q.48. Christ's suffering and death, done in love, please God in their justice and love even as they address the problem of sin.

For two closely related reasons, the Eucharist can rightly be called a "sacrifice." First, in accordance with Christ's institution of the Eucharist, the Eucharist commemorates, recalls, the Passion (which of course for Aquinas is sacrificial). And secondly, Christ is truly present in this sacrament. When Aquinas reflects on the one who is present, a favorite designation of this sacrament's *res et sacramentum* is the "crucified Christ" (e.g. *ST* III, q.73, a.5, ad2), the one who suffers and dies on the cross. In the eucharistic sacrifice, the Christ who offered himself on the cross is offered to God.

The identification of the Eucharist with the crucified Christ and his work on the cross thus allows a prompt answering of at least some of Augustine's four questions about sacrifice. When it comes to the "what" and the "to whom," the same answers are given as for the sacrifice of the Passion, which the eucharistic sacrifice commemorates. The "to whom" is God: the eucharistic sacrifice, rooted in and recalling that on the cross, gives honor to God and is pleasing to God. The "what" that is offered is, also, the same, the Christ whose holy actions and life and dying are pleasing to God.

In those articles in the treatise on the Eucharist devoted to sacrifice, Aquinas teases out at some length the "for whom" of the sacrifice. The analysis of the beneficiaries of the sacrifice follows in the main the teaching about fruitful *reception* of the Eucharist as *sacrament*. For fruitful reception of the Eucharist as sacrament, the one who encounters the Christ truly present must be correctly disposed, marked by grace and faith and charity, to receive Christ's benefits. Those who lack such personal faith and charity receive the Christ truly present but not his benefits. Aquinas expresses the same concern for correct spiritual disposition in discussing the beneficiaries of the Eucharist as *sacrifice*. Christ's self-offering suffices for all, but only those who are joined to Christ by their faith and charity have the benefits of the sacrifice communicated to them (*ST* III, q.79, a.5c; *ST* III, q.79, a.7, ad2). Those who lack formed faith and grace, those who are in mortal sin and so cut off from Christ as head, have placed an obstacle in the way of its sacrificial benefits; this holds as well for the sacramental priest if he is lacking in personal devotion and charity.

The parallel between sacramental and sacrificial benefits is not, however, perfectly exact. The eucharistic sacrifice is offered for the living and the dead, that is, with regard to the latter, also for those in purgatory whose attainment of the end of the journey to God as beatifying end is delayed. *Sacramental* reception of the benefits offered by Christ requires a presence and participation in the sacrament, a reception of the sacrament and so of the Christ truly present and the benefits conveyed through the sacrament. The reception of the *sacrificial* benefits does not require a presence at the liturgy. Here, the intention of the offerer—with a view to the "for whom" the offering is made—in intending the offering for the living and the dead allows a broader distribution of Christ's benefits. But, again, this exception does not detract from Aquinas' main contention, that it does matter that those for whom the offering is intended, whether living or dead, whether at the liturgy or absent, be in fact truly members of Christ to receive the sacrificial benefits.

Only the fourth of Augustine's questions about sacrifice remains, having to do with the "who" of the offering. Aquinas' answer is intricate and layered. Again, as with the question of the beneficiaries, there is a parallel between the Eucharist as sacrifice and as sacrament. *Who* offers the sacrifice? Christ, in the first place; the eucharistic sacrifice commemorates and echoes the offering that Christ made of himself on the cross. The sacramental priest too is an offerer, inasmuch as he is the instrument of Christ, acting *in persona Christi* in the consecration and so involved in the becoming present of the crucified Christ. But the parallel extends only thus far, for as he continues his discussion of the Eucharist as sacrifice, Aquinas limns a role for yet another offerer, one not mentioned in the account of sacramental consecration.

That third offerer makes an appearance in an article, later in q.82 (a.6), that asks about the "worth" of the Mass, with particular attention to the contribution of the sacramental priest. The value of the Mass as sacrifice will, as a reminder, be assessed on two grounds: what is offered, and the spirit (the willingness, the love, the devotion) in which it is offered. In terms of the "what" of the offering, this, Aquinas tells us, is the sacrament (containing Christ) and the prayers offered for the living and the dead. Christ, of course, has an intrinsic worth; he is most pleasing to God. But what about the spirit in which Christ and the prayers are offered? The personal devotion of the *sacramental* priest too may be factored into this assessment of value; and so, Aquinas notes, the mass of a good priest (that is, someone marked by grace, and formed faith, and so devout) will on that score be worth more than that of a sinful or non-personally believing priest.

Aquinas, however, does not leave it at that. He has a further designation of the sacramental priest. For the most part in the treatise on the Eucharist, that priest is described in terms of Christ, as acting *in persona Christi*. But in this article, Aquinas states that the sacramental priest also acts "in the person of the *entire Church*." In offering Christ and the prayers for the living and the dead, the sacramental priest is speaking for all who make up Christ's body; and so the worth of the Mass will be assessed as well according to the *spirit* in which they move towards God as beatifying end and identify with Christ as the way to God as end and offer their prayers to God through Christ—that is, according to the grace out of which *they* act, *their* formed faith, *their* devotion. What we are encountering here, although the identification is left implicit, is the "spiritual priesthood" of *ST* III, q.82, a.1, ad2. The spiritual priesthood is also involved in the offering, and the involvement of spiritual priests adds to the value of the offering, making it even more acceptable to God—a point that Aquinas makes explicitly in the following question (q.83), in an article devoted to the words of the liturgy (*ST* III, q.83, a4, ad8).

The passage with which the second part of the chapter began can now receive its full force. Christ is not an incidental figure in this passage. Thomas's portrayal of each of these priesthoods involves Christ, and each of these priesthoods is to be understood in terms of Christ. The point is clear enough with regards to the sacramental priest, the one who avowedly acts in the consecration "in the person of *Christ*." However, the portrayal of the spiritual priest also, perhaps especially, invokes a deep connection to Christ, positing a resemblance of that priest to Christ. In receiving and in offering, the spiritual priest echoes Christ; Christ provides the model for proper spiritual disposition and action, for receiving in love, for offering in love. However, Christ is here more than a model; as source of grace and charity, this Christ provides the resources out of which imitation of Christ becomes a possibility. Those who are truly members of Christ can love as Christ loves, because Christ has shared with them this love from which they can act. Indeed, when it comes down to it, there would appear to be considerable justification for concluding that the portrayal of the spiritual priest in the treatise on the Eucharist is at the same time a compelling proclamation of Christ in his saving work.

SUGGESTED READING

Blankenhorn (2010); Emery (1999); Finkenzeller (1980); Wawrykow (1993); Walsh (2005).

BIBLIOGRAPHY

Primary

Alexander of Hales (1957), *Glossa in Quatuor Libros Sententiarum*, Bk.IV, Quaracchi, Florence, ed. the Fathers of the College of S. Bonaventure (Bibliotheca Franciscana Scholastica Medii Aevi cura Pp. Collegii S. Bonaventurae), tom. XV.

Bonaventure, *Breviloquium* (1891), in *Opera Omnia* V, studio et cura Pp. Collegio S. Bonaventura (Quarrachi), 199–291.

De causalitate sacramentorum iuxta scholam franciscanam (1931), ed. W. Lampen (Bonn: Peter Hanstein).

De Sacramentorum Efficientia apud Theologos Ord. Praed. Fasc.I: 1229–1276 (1936), ed. H.-D. Simonin, O.P. et G. Meerseman, O.P. (Rome: Pont.Institutum Internationale).

Lateran IV, *Constitutiones*, in N. P. Tanner, S.J. (ed.) (1990), *Decrees of the Ecumenical Councils*, vol. 1 (London: Sheed and Ward), 230–271.

Peter Lombard, *Sententiae in IV Libris Distinctae*. Tomus II. Liber III et IV (1981). Spicilegium Boanventurianum V (Rome: Editiones Collegii S. Bonaventurae ad Claras Aquas).

Robert Kilwardby, *Quaestiones in Librum Quartum Sententiarum* (1993), ed. R. Schenk (Munich: Verlag der Bayerischen Akademie der Wissenschaften).

Thomas Aquinas, *Collationes de decem praeceptis*, in *Opuscula theologica* (1954), vol. 2, ed. R. A. Verardo and R. M. Spiazzi (Turin: Marietti), 245–271.

Thomas Aquinas, *Summa theologiae* (1941–), cura et studio Instituti Studiorum Medievalium Ottaviensis (Ottawa: Commissio Piana).

William of Auxerre, *Summa Aurea*, Bk. IV (1985), ed. Jean Riballier (Paris, Editions du Centre National de la Recherche Scientifique/Rome, Editiones Collegii S. Bonaventurae ad Claras Aquas), Spicilegium Bonaventurianum XIX.

Secondary

Blankenhorn, B., O.P. (2006), "The Instrumental Causality of the Sacraments: Thomas Aquinas and Louis-Marie Chauvet," *Nova et Vetera* (English) 4/2: 255–294.

Blankenhorn, B., O.P. (2010), "The Place of Romans 6 in Aquinas's Doctrine of Sacramental Causality: A Balance of History and Metaphysics," in R. Hütter and M. Levering (eds.), *Ressourcement Thomism: Sacred Doctrine, the Sacraments, and the Moral Life. Essays in Honor of Romanus Cessario, O.P.* (Washington, DC: The Catholic University of America Press), 136–149.

Courtenay, W. J. (1972), "The King and the Leaden Coin: The Economic Background of 'Sine Qua Non' Causality," *Traditio* 28: 185–209.

Emery, G., O.P. (1999), "Le Sacerdoce spiritual des fidèles chez saint Thomas d'Aquin," *Revue Thomiste* 99: 211–243.

Emery, G., O.P. (2004), "The Ecclesial Fruit of the Eucharist in St. Thomas Aquinas," trans. T. C. Scarpelli, *Nova et Vetera* (English) 2: 43–60.

Finkenzeller, J. (1980), *Handbuch der Dogmengeschichte*, Band IV, Faszikel 1a: Die Lehre von den Sakramenten im allgemeinen. Von der Schrift bis zur Scholastik (Freiburg: Herder).

King, R. F. (1967), "The Origin and Evolution of a Sacramental Formula: *Sacramentum tantum, Res et Sacramentum, Res Tantum*," *The Thomist* 31: 21–82.

O'Collins, G., S.J., and Jones, M. K. (2010), *Jesus Our Priest: A Christian Approach to the Priesthood of Christ* (Oxford: Oxford University Press).

Peters, E. (ed.) (1980), *Heresy and Authority in Medieval Europe: Documents in Translation* (Philadelphia: University of Pennsylvania Press).

Rubin, M. (1991), *Corpus Christi: The Eucharist in Late Medieval Culture* (Cambridge: Cambridge University Press).

Scheller, E. J. (1934), *Das Priestertum Christi im Anschluss an den h. Thomas von Aquin: Vom Mysterium des Mittlers in seinem Opfer und unserer Anteilnahme* (Paderborn: Verlag Fredinand Schoeningh).

Schenk, R., O.P. (2010), "*Verum sacrificium* as the Fullness and Limit of Eucharistic Sacrifice in the Sacramental Theology of Thomas Aquinas," in R. Hütter and M. Levering (eds.), *Ressourcement Thomism: Sacred Doctrine, the Sacraments, and the Moral Life. Essays in Honor of Romanus Cessario, O.P.* (Washington, DC: The Catholic University of America Press).

Torrell, J.-P., O.P. (2011), "The Priesthood of Christ in the *Summa theologiae*," in *Christ and Spirituality in St. Thomas Aquinas*, trans. B. Blankenhorn, O.P. (Washington, DC: The Catholic University of America Press).

Torrell, J.-P., O.P. (2013), *A Priestly People: Baptismal Priesthood and Priestly Ministry*, trans. P. Heinegg (New York: Paulist Press).

Van den Eynde, D. (1950), *Les Définitions des sacrements pendant la première période de la théologie scolastique (1050–1240)* (Rome: Antonianum).

Walsh, L., O.P. (1993), "The Divine and the Human in St. Thomas's Theology of Sacraments," in C.-J. Pinto de Oliveira, O.P., *Ordo Sapientiae et Amoris: Hommage au Professeur Jean-Pierre Torrell* (Fribourg: Éditions Universitaires).

Walsh, L., O.P. (2005), 'Sacraments', in R. Van Nieuwenhove and J. P. Wawrykow (eds.), *The Theology of Thomas Aquinas* (Notre Dame, IN: University of Notre Dame Press).

Wawrykow, J. P. (1993), "Luther and the Spirituality of Thomas Aquinas," *Consensus* 19: 77–107.

Wawrykow, J. P. (1995), *God's Grace and Human Action: 'Merit' in the Theology of Thomas Aquinas* (Notre Dame, IN: University of Notre Dame Press).

CHAPTER 16

....

THE EUCHARIST IN THE FOURTEENTH AND FIFTEENTH CENTURIES

....

IAN CHRISTOPHER LEVY

In his textbook of theology, the *Sentences* (*c.* 1155), the Parisian master Peter Lombard named seven sacraments of the New Law, which were to be distinguished from those of the Old Law, because they are signs that actually confer the grace that they signify. The Lombard's list of sacraments included baptism, confirmation, Eucharist, penance, extreme unction, orders, and marriage. The Second Council of Lyons (1274) and the Council of Florence (1439) recognized these seven, which were formally ratified at the Council of Trent (1545–1563). Even as there were skirmishes over the precise institution of some sacraments, the nature or necessity of the impressed sacramental character, and whether sacraments function as instrumental causes of divine grace or are simply occasions for God to bestow grace directly, there was relative peace surrounding most sacraments in the late Middle Ages.

The Eucharist was the exception that dominated late medieval sacramental discourse and generated controversy both within and without university walls. Much of the debate surrounding this sacrament turned on the manner in which Christ is present in the Eucharist. This proved to be the most vexing, and indeed fascinating, sacramental question of the period. How could the one body of Jesus Christ—the very same body that was born of the Virgin Mary and then ascended into heaven—be present in such a small wafer on so many different altars at once? No suitable explanation of this mystery could propose anything less than "real" or "substantial" presence; it is not enough for the consecrated host to function only as a symbol (*sacramentum*) of a non-present reality (*res*). The body of Christ on the altar must be a real thing in itself, which is wholly present to those who receive the consecrated host. That much was agreed upon by the thirteenth century. Precisely how this miracle could be accomplished, however, had not been officially determined by the church.

Looming over all eucharistic discussions by the fourteenth century was the opening statement of faith issued by the Fourth Lateran Council in 1215. This wide-ranging creed, which was intended to shore up Catholic orthodoxy against the threats of Cathar and Waldensian sectarianism, had employed the term "transubstantiation" when affirming the authority of the priesthood in the celebration of the Eucharist (*transsubstantiatis pane in corpus et vino in sanguinem*). The creed was subsequently incorporated—under the title *Firmiter*—into the decretal collection promulgated by Pope Gregory IX in 1234, known as the *Liber extra*, and thereby became established law. One can add to this decree the letter that Pope Innocent III had sent to the Archbishop of Lyons in 1202, which also used the term "transubstantiation" and entered the collection as *Cum Marthae*. In both cases this recently devised term was employed in order to affirm Christ's real presence in the Eucharist against any lurking memorialism; there was no attempt to endorse any single scholastic theory as to how precisely this presence is achieved. In fact, canon lawyers from Johannes Teutonicus to Hostiensis reckoned substantial conversion, annihilation, and consubstantiation as perfectly orthodox theories that could be included under the larger umbrella of "transubstantiation." Many late medieval theologians, on the other hand, concluded that orthodox theological discourse was constrained by an understanding of transubstantiation limited to substantial conversion. Working under such constraints, which were notably absent from canon law, led some of the best theologians of the period into some very tight spots as they attempted to accommodate their own metaphysical insights to this one particular theory.

JOHN DUNS SCOTUS

In the latter part of the thirteenth century the Dominican theologian Thomas Aquinas (d. 1274) had insisted that the process of transubstantiation—understood as substantial conversion—was the only viable means to account for Christ's eucharistic presence. This view was generally contested by Franciscan theologians such as William de la Mare, John Peckham, and Peter John Olivi, who placed the emphasis firmly upon God's power to render Christ's body present, which could be accomplished in various ways apart from substantial conversion. Transubstantiation, therefore, was merely a contingent means of effecting real presence, not a necessary one (Bakker 1999: 1: 40–49). One of the most articulate spokesmen for this Franciscan position was John Duns Scotus (d. 1308), who was confident that real presence could be preserved apart from the substantial conversion of the bread into the body of Christ. Indeed, said Scotus, Christ's body could be truly present along with the remaining substance of the bread, just as it could be with the accidents alone after the bread's substance ceased to exist. In point of fact, the simplest way for Christ to be present would not entail any substantial conversion at all. Hence Scotus thought that consubstantiation offered the more straightforward and scriptural definition of real eucharistic presence. For all that, however, he was convinced that God in his infinite freedom had chosen to effect Christ's real presence by means of substantial conversion. Scotus could be so certain because he believed that Lateran IV had explicitly endorsed this one theory, and thus it must be believed as an article of faith solemnly declared by the Holy Catholic Church (*Sent.* IV, d. 11, q.3).

But even granting transubstantiation as the official teaching of the church, Scotus spotted a metaphysical hurdle that had to be overcome: how is it that the body of Christ comes to exist in some particular place? In answering this question, Scotus was partly indebted to his Franciscan predecessor Peter John Olivi (d. 1298), who had pursued the notion that eucharistic presence could be understood as a relation (*esse relatum*) established between Christ's body and the consecrated host. Scotus picked up this basic principle and ran with it. For Scotus, merely positing a substantial change does not in itself account for how a substance comes to be present in some particular place. This was one of the central faults that he found with Aquinas's doctrine; it could not account for how the substance of Christ's body came to exist here on this altar. To solve this problem Scotus contended that, following the consecration of the host, Christ's body, which is in heaven, acquires a new place relationship (*respectus extrinsicus adveniens*) although without vacating the place it currently inhabits (*Sent.* IV, d. 10, q.1; Bakker 1999: 1: 63–69).

Having thus established how Christ's body can be present on many altars at once without undergoing a substantial change in itself or resorting to local motion, Scotus also sought to maintain the integrity of Christ's body in the consecrated host. For Scotus, this meant that the body had to be quantified in some manner. To that end he distinguished between two sorts of position: intrinsic and extrinsic; the first requires quantification whereas the second does not. Christ's body in the Eucharist would retain the intrinsic order of its parts, and thus be quantified, even as the body is not quantified with respect to the place that it occupies. God can preserve a quantified thing (*quantum*) such that it retains an intrinsic position without having any such extrinsic relationship to a specific place. The body of Christ will retain its natural extension, therefore, even as there are no spatial relations between Christ's body parts and the parts of the host to which his body is present (*Sent.* IV, d.10, q.1; Burr 1972).

WILLIAM OF OCKHAM

Like his confrere Duns Scotus, the Franciscan William of Ockham (d. 1347) reckoned consubstantiation the more satisfying theory, since it is not only free from contradictions but also underscores divine omnipotence. And yet, like Scotus, he rejected consubstantiation on the strength of ecclesiastical authority. Ockham maintained that while it has been clearly conveyed in Holy Scripture that Christ's body is indeed present underneath the accidents of the bread, the bread's substantial conversion has not been so clearly stated in Scripture. When it came to securing the authentic interpretation of Holy Scripture, Ockham appealed to canon law: Gratian's *Decretum* for the canons *Quia corpus* (D. 2 de cons. c. 35) and *Panis est* (D. 2 de cons. c. 55); and the *Liber extra* chapters

Firmiter (X 1.1.1) and *Cum Marthae* (X 3.41.6). On this basis Ockham could declare that the authoritative texts of the saints and doctors all affirm that the bread's substance has been really converted by divine power into the substance of Christ's body (*Opera Theologica* 10: 95–96).

Where Ockham differed from Scotus, however, was on the question of quantity. Like Peter John Olivi before him, Ockham maintained that quantity is not some absolute thing (*res absoluta*) separate from substance and from quality; it is simply a means of connoting that a given substance or quality is extended (*Opera Theologica* 7: 71–72; Buescher 1950: 67–68). What does this mean for the presence of Christ's body in the Eucharist? Ockham contends that Christ's body does not possess the mode of quantity upon the altar, which means that it is not present there circumscriptively. Rather, says Ockham, Christ's body is definitively present on the altar such that the whole body exists underneath the whole host and the whole body under every single part of the host. Christ's body is not extended in the host, therefore, even as it does remain extended in heaven (*Opera Theologica* 7: 80–88). Ockham's position on quantity meant that he also rejected the notion that quantity functioned as the subject in which the rest of the bread's accidents inhered following the conversion of its substance. Instead, said Ockham, accidents such as color and flavor subsist without any subject following consecration. Rather than being upheld by the accident of quantity, therefore, they subsist in their own right through divine power (*Opera Theologica* 10: 61–62).

For all of his demurrals, however, Ockham was intent on retaining the term "transubstantiation" when speaking of eucharistic presence, precisely because he reckoned it Catholic dogma. If consubstantiation was plausible, even preferable, but nevertheless not a viable option, then perhaps one could explain the eucharistic change by positing the bread's annihilation. Unfortunately, that way also seemed blocked by ecclesiastical authority, so Ockham had to find a way around yet another obstacle. To that end, Ockham distinguished between two sorts of annihilation. If one means that the bread is annihilated such that it is reduced to nothing and cannot be converted into something else, then this sort of annihilation must be rejected. Yet there is a second theory of annihilation that Ockham thinks is compatible with transubstantiation, whereby the bread is reduced to the sort of existence it once had in the divine power prior to creation. The substance of the bread can be said to abide within the body of Christ along the same lines that it exists in the creative power of God (*Opera Theologica* 7: 148–149). In this way, then, Ockham believed that he had found a way to reconcile the demands of Catholic orthodoxy with the criteria of coherent metaphysics.

JOHN WYCLIF AND THE WYCLIFFITES

If Ockham pressed his theories to the limit at times—even being called to the papal court at Avignon in 1324 to account for them—the Oxford secular theologian John Wyclif (d. 1384) crossed over the line. After years of reflection Wyclif finally came to the conclusion late in his career that transubstantiation was metaphysically untenable; this is because an accident cannot exist apart from its proper subject. Here Wyclif was clearly swimming against the tide. For whether the bread's accidents following conse-cration inhere within quantity or subsist without a subject by divine power, late medi-eval theologians generally agreed that the substance of the bread no longer supported these accidents. Everyone recognized that this ran contrary to Aristotle's basic concep-tion of the categories, but then the theologians reckoned transubstantiation a miracle in which God circumvents standard procedure. In his outright objection to the prevailing theory, Wyclif was—even if unwittingly—hearkening back to an earlier clash between philosophers and theologians.

When in 1277 Bishop Stephen Tempier condemned some 219 propositions emanat-ing from the University of Paris, four specifically targeted the claim that accidents could not exist apart from their proper subjects. Actually, some members of the Paris arts fac-ulty, such as Boethius of Dacia, had argued that inherence in a subject constitutes the very nature of an accident. The stability of the accident, it was said, depends upon the substance in which it inheres, such that to separate it from that substance would be to bring about its corruption. Thus Siger of Brabant and others contended that, while faith may indeed demand that we believe that the eucharistic accidents exist apart from the bread's substance, this simply cannot be supported by philosophical analysis (Bakker 1999: 1:323–331).

Like those members of the Paris arts faculty before him, John Wyclif insisted that the very point of an accident's existence is to modify a substance. For God to preserve an accident without a subject would be tantamount to preserving something which does not actually exist, since accidents are only real insofar as they inhere in a specific sub-stance (*Sermones* 3: 508). Yet unlike those Parisian masters, Wyclif did not concede the theological viability of transubstantiation as a matter of faith despite the problems it raised for reason. Quite the opposite was the case; Wyclif regarded free-floating acci-dents as a metaphysical absurdity and a hoax that a good God would not perpetrate on faithful Catholics.

Perhaps Wyclif's greatest concern, however, was what became of the bread's substance following consecration. If this substance has been annihilated, as Wyclif believes the doctrine of transubstantiation demands, it would set off a chain reaction resulting in the annihilation of the created universe. This is because each substantial instance of a thing, such as bread, is inexorably connected to a set of eternal causal principles, which lead all the way to God through whom they derive their existence. At all events, that the sub-stance of the bread is not annihilated is proven by the continued existence of the acci-dents, since annihilation would entail the destruction of both accidents and substance (*De potencia productiva dei ad extra* in *De ente librorum duorum excerpta*: 289–290). Actually, Wyclif's opponents were perplexed by his claim that transubstantiation inevi-tably involves annihilation of one substance and its replacement by another, whereas they tended to regard this process as a conversion of the first substance into the second. Wyclif never really explained how he came to equate transubstantiation with annihila-tion, but it may hinge on the fact that he was a temporal atomist who believed that time itself is composed of indivisible instants. Given such a clear divisibility of time, there must be one moment when the bread ceases to exist followed by the next moment when the body of Christ takes its place beneath the accidents. Hence there could be no seamless conversion of one substance into another (Lahey 2009: 118–131). As it was, then, the substantial remanence of the bread formed the mainstay of Wyclif's eucharistic theology. Appealing to basic Christological doctrine offered one way to explain what happens following consecration. Just as Christ is simultaneously God and man, so the sacrament is at once bread and Christ's body—the former naturally and the latter sacramentally. And as Christ's divine nature remains constant despite variations in his human nature, so his body remains constant no matter the changes affecting the bread (*Sermones* 4:15).

The central points of Wyclif's eucharistic theology were formally condemned at the Blackfriars Synod convened by the archbishop of Canterbury William Courtenay in 1382. Among the list of propositions deemed heretical, three dealt directly with Wyclif's denial of transubstantiation: that the substance of the bread and wine remain after consecration; that the accidents of the bread and wine do not abide without their proper subject; and that Christ is not really in the Eucharist in his proper corporeal presence (*Fasciculi Zizaniorum*: 277–282). Wyclif might have effectively skirted heterodox territory had he proposed a doctrine of consubstantiation, thereby affirming—if nothing else—the substantial presence of Christ on the altar. He could not bring himself to do this, however, precisely because he equated substantial presence with materiality and physical extension—the very sort of presence that Christ's body enjoys in heaven, but not in the host. Christ has only one body, and this body is certainly present in the consecrated host, but it is present there in a different manner than in heaven. Wyclif maintained that Christ's presence in the Eucharist is threefold: virtual, spiritual, and sacramental. The first speaks to the manner in which Christ is active throughout his entire dominion; the second by which he is present in the Eucharist and his saints through grace; while the third refers to Christ's unique manner of presence in the consecrated host. Each level builds upon the previous one with the result that Christ's sacramental presence comprises them all. As genuine as this sort of presence in the host is, however, Wyclif said that Christ's body achieves an even greater level of reality in heaven where it exists substantially, corporeally, and dimensionally. These three modes of presence are interdependent and thus are only applicable to the body as it exists in heaven, for only there—not in the host—can it enjoy bodily extension (*Fasciculi Zizaniorum*: 115–117). Christ cannot be present corporeally or dimensionally in the Eucharist, therefore, since that manner of being pertains only to his celestial existence where his body is corporeally situated in a place (*De antichristo* in *Opus Evangelicum*: 2:165). Yet while it is impossible for a single material body to be extended throughout distant locations simultaneously, a body can be extended in one place even as it has spiritual existence in another. So it is that Christ's body is present dimensionally in heaven while also being present by way of its spiritual power in the host (*De eucharistia*: 271).

Wyclif attracted adherents to his eucharistic theology within his own lifetime and beyond. This sometimes amorphous collection of followers were generally referred to as "Wycliffites," or even "Lollards," by their opponents. Although there is no creed by which this movement can be measured precisely, they seem to have been united in their rejection of transubstantiation. One of Wyclif's early confidants John Purvey reckoned this doctrine as a "new article of faith" inflicted on the church with the unloosing of Satan. Contrary to the notion of an accident subsisting without a subject, Christ and his apostles had taught that the Eucharist is equally bread and Christ's body (*Fasciculi Zizaniorum*: 383). One Wycliffite document, *The Twelve Conclusions*, derided transubstantiation as a false miracle that leads people into idolatry. Christ's body is in heaven, but people are led to believe that it is enclosed in the host, which they thereupon worship (*Fasciculi Zizaniorum*: 361–362). While another, *The Sixteen Points*, stated that just as Christ is both God and man, so the Eucharist is at once bread and Christ's body (Hudson (ed.) 1978: 20). One tract went so far as to liken current prelates to Manichees, since they cannot comprehend how the eucharistic host can be both bread and body just as the person of Christ comprises the two natures of humanity and divinity (Hudson (ed.) 2001: 204–205). William Sawtrey, who was burnt for heresy at Smithfield in 1401, declared himself willing to die for the position that the Eucharist is "the true body of Christ in the form of bread." The host, he insisted, does not cease to be bread following consecration even as it does then become sacred and life-giving (*Fasciculi Zizaniorum*: 410). William Thorpe had to answer to Archbishop Thomas Arundel for preaching that the material bread remained following consecration. Evasive as Thorpe could be at times, he managed to blame Thomas Aquinas for reducing the Eucharist to an accident without a subject—a position that Thorpe claimed had no basis in Holy Scripture (Hudson (ed.) 2001: 55–56). And William White considered it sufficient for a Christian to believe that Christ's body is present in one's memory while the true bread is present in its own nature (*Fasciculi Zizaniorum*: 424). It is clear, therefore, that the doctrine of remanence formed the cornerstone of Wycliffite eucharistic theology. Not only was it affirmed in their numerous tracts, but it was also the position most often singled out as heterodox in the works of their opponents, and is overwhelmingly attested to in the trial records (Hornbeck 2010: 68–103).

ANTI-WYCLIFFITES: WILLIAM WOODFORD AND THOMAS NETTER

Having looked at some examples of dissenting eucharistic doctrine at the turn of the fifteenth century, it will be instructive to see how the prevailing theology was defended. In his writings against the Wycliffites, the Franciscan theologian William Woodford (d. 1397) appealed to the decree of Lateran IV, which he reckoned in perfect accord with the patristic tradition. The bread and wine are transubstantiated into the body and blood of Christ, said Woodford, and by "transubstantiation" we mean that there is a real transition of the bread's substance into the substance of Christ's body. It is on account of this decree that the medieval schoolmen state in their *Sentences* commentaries that the bread ceases to exist when consecrated. Woodford presented a list of recent theologians in support of this position: Thomas Aquinas, Albert the Great, Henry of Ghent, Alexander of Hales, Bonaventure, Richard of Middleton, Peter Auriol, and Giles of Rome (*De causis condempnationis articulorum*: 191–193).

Among Wyclif's many arguments against transubstantiation, one hinged more on grammar than metaphysics. He contended that the very force of the proposition *Hoc est corpus meum* demands that the bread substantially remain on the grounds that the demonstrative pronoun (*hoc*) must signify the same thing at the beginning and end of the proposition—namely the bread that Christ had taken in his hands. Wyclif was tapping into a long-standing medieval discussion of just how the words of institution function in the act of consecration—both at the Last Supper itself and then in the course of a daily Mass. For his part, Woodford seemed to reflect the general trend when he determined that Christ took the material bread in his hands and consecrated it by means of his blessing before he spoke the words "*Hoc est corpus meum.*" This means that the bread was fully converted into Christ's body even before the Lord had begun to utter this proposition. Hence the pronoun "*hoc*" is not demonstrating the material bread, but rather the body of Christ, which is now contained underneath the species of the converted bread. In keeping with Pope Innocent III's tract on the canon of the Mass, therefore, Woodford argued that when the priest at the altar today consecrates the host, he is speaking the words "*Hoc est corpus meum*" materially and recitatively, rather than indicatively and assertively. Hence these words are simply conveying the blessing by means of which Christ had converted the bread into his body (*De causis condempnationis articulorum*: 194).

Yet if the substance of the bread and wine no longer exist, how does one account for the fact that a priest can be nourished by consuming the host and inebriated from drinking the wine? Woodford contends that the priest may indeed feel himself to be nourished or inebriated, but this does not mean that the substance of the bread and wine, or even their accidents, must account for this fact. Drawing on the work of fellow Franciscans Peter Auriol and Francis of Mayrone, he notes that it is possible for the sacramental accidents at the end of the alteration to be converted into some other sort of substance that can provide nourishment. Thus the priest can be nourished and fattened, although not by the substance contained in the sacrament nor by its accidents as such, since these accidents have now been converted into some sort of nutritive substance. This does not mean that the sacramental accidents are themselves providing the nutrition, but rather that they have been converted into a substance that is able to nourish the priest (*De causis condempnationis articulorum*: 196).

We noted above that one of Wyclif's chief objections to the doctrine of transubstantiation was that it amounts to a process of annihilation. In his response Woodford seems to have adopted a line similar to his Franciscan predecessor William of Ockham. For he argues that although it is true that no part of the substantial bread remains in an actualized state following consecration, this does not mean it is thereby annihilated. For the annihilation of a thing requires that the annihilated thing does not even remain in proximate potential so that it might later return to being. Yet the bread that is transubstantiated into Christ's body does remain in such proximate potential; hence it is not annihilated. Annihilation, moreover, requires that the end point (*terminus ad quem*) would be nothing rather than something. In the case of the Eucharist, however, the end point of the bread's conversion is the body of Christ, and so this process still amounts to a conversion, not an annihilation (*De causis condempnationis articulorum*: 203).

In his response to the Wycliffites, the Carmelite theologian Thomas Netter (d. 1430) was very keen to emphasize that transubstantiation involves the conversion of one substance into another in a single seamless process. Netter repeatedly argued that transubstantiation is not a case of the bread's substance being annihilated and then succeeded by Christ's body. For Netter, far from being an act of annihilation, this is a "wonderful conversion." The bread cannot be said to lose its being absolutely, therefore, since its total essence undergoes a process of inestimable amelioration. According to Netter: "The Catholic Church maintains and declares that the substance of the bread is converted into the substance of Christ's body by way of a translation of whole into whole without destroying the bread in any way ... No one who has carefully read the books of the Holy Fathers could fail to realize that this is the ancient faith which they taught and that the apostles believed, the very faith that Innocent III also taught some years ago" (*Doctrinale* 2: 413–421).

JAN HUS AND BOHEMIAN REFORM

The Bohemian reformer Jan Hus was burned at the stake for heresy at the Council of Constance on July 6, 1415. Condemned though he may have been for holding various Wycliffite positions, Hus never denied the doctrine of transubstantiation. Indeed, Hus had no qualms about saying that the true body and blood of Christ are consumed under alien species. He also made it clear that the laity do receive both the body and blood under the bread alone in keeping with the doctrine of concomitance. And when it came to wicked clerics celebrating Mass, Hus lined up the standard scholastic authorities to affirm that the presence of Christ's body cannot be jeopardized by the immorality of the celebrating priest (*Super Sent.* 4.8–13). It was not Hus himself, therefore, who stirred up eucharistic controversy in Bohemia so much as those who followed in his wake.

By the fall of 1414 Hus' younger colleague, the Prague master Jakoubek of Stříbro, was advocating that lay people receive the Eucharist under the species of both bread and wine—the practice known as "utraquism"—thereby restoring the chalice to the laity along the lines of the primitive church. On June 15, 1415, however, the assembled fathers at Constance formally ratified the now-established custom of offering communion to the laity solely under the species of the bread to the exclusion of the wine. Their decree freely admitted that Christ had administered this sacrament to his apostles under bread and wine, and that it had been received by the faithful under both species in the early church. Nevertheless, good custom had developed such that only those confecting the sacrament were to receive bread and wine, while the laity would communicate solely under the species of bread. Those who pertinaciously resisted this conciliar enactment were henceforth to be confined as heretics and severely punished (Denzinger-Schönmetzer (ed.) 1976: 1198–1200).

Notwithstanding the Council's decree, lay reception of the chalice was formally approved by the University of Prague on 10 March 1417. And despite the fact that Pope Martin V demanded that the Bohemians put an end to this practice, they would not relent. Frequent lay communication under both species, and even infant communion, were becoming mainstays of Bohemian religious identity. Following negotiations at the Council of Basel, the Bohemians were finally granted the lay chalice according to the Compactata of Prague in 1433, which were later confirmed at the Diet of Iglau in 1436, although subsequently nullified by Pope Pius II in 1462 (Kaminsky 1967: 98–140; Fudge 2010: 154–163).

In a vigorous defense of the utraquist position, Jakoubek of Stříbro insisted that Christ in his infinite wisdom had directly instituted this spiritual and sacramental way of drinking his blood under the species of the wine for the great benefit of souls. And it is because Christ instituted the sacrament in just this way that those who receive only the bread are not consuming Christ's blood in the correct sacramental manner. Jakoubek certainly accepted the doctrine of concomitance, granting therefore that Christ is never present without his own blood. Yet he insisted that this does not mean reception of the bread is thereby tantamount to reception of the blood as spiritual drink. Christ only promised his body as food to those who came to the species of the bread, and his blood as drink to those who received the cup. Simply because the whole living Christ is present in the species of the bread does not mean that his blood is also there in a sacramental manner. Hence the body is only received spiritually and sacramentally in the species of the bread, and the blood spiritually and sacramentally in the chalice. In fact, were this not the case, Christ's dual form of institution would seem superfluous (Hardt (ed.) 1700: 3: 456–457). For Jakoubek, therefore, communion under both kinds is not a custom of the primitive church that later ecclesiastics are free to change. It is a direct precept of Christ for every Christian. This is made clear in the New Testament and throughout the ancient church. Christ willed communion under both kinds for every Christian precisely because this is the best way for the people to be united to their Lord (Hardt (ed.) 1700: 3: 578–580).

Arguments made against lay chalice reception turned less on sacramental theology than on ecclesiological principles, namely the hierarchical church's right to determine and legislate good practice. Two fundamental points made repeatedly by anti-utraquist polemicists were that chalice reception was neither a precept of Christ nor necessary for salvation. Hence this practice can be altered and the laity will not suffer any adverse effects. Writing against the utraquists in 1415, the Vienna theologian Peter Pulka, noted that while it is true that Christ did not leave the church the power to alter anything substantial in relation to the sacrament of the Eucharist, he did grant her the power to determine various uses that are accidental to that immutable substance. Thus when it comes to the rites surrounding the use of this sacrament, the church—precisely under the inspiration of the Holy Spirit—can make certain changes both to increase devotion and avoid impiety. Christ, therefore, had reserved to the apostles and their successors a certain latitude in accidental features. So it is, then, that the church can establish or prohibit such accidental rites for "reasonable causes" (Girgensohn (ed.) 1964: 222–229). Among the various good reasons not to offer the chalice to the laity were the danger of spillage and irreverence, since there are many country folk (*rusticani*) who are bound to make such communication difficult. Add to that the practical problems arising from transportation across great distances, whether by foot or by horse over slippery and muddy terrain, and then finding the right sort of container for the wine (Girgensohn (ed.) 1964: 230–239).

When the Prague theologian Andrew of Brod responded to Jakoubek and the utraquists he contested their reading of John 6:53, "Unless you eat the flesh of the Son of Man and drink his blood, you have no life in you." These words of Christ, said Andrew, cannot be read literally but instead must be interpreted in a spiritual manner: to eat and drink spiritually is to abide in Christ through faith and charity (Hardt (ed.) 1700: 3: 392–394). As it was, then, Andrew maintained that lay communication under both species is "contrary to the will of Christ, contrary to the understanding of the entirety of Holy Scripture, and runs against the canons of the Holy Mother Roman Church." Christ never had any intention of offering the chalice to the laity. When he instructed his disciples, "Drink this all of you" (Matt 26:27), he was speaking only to the twelve apostles as he consecrated them cardinals and bishops. The apostles, in turn, represented future generations of the priesthood who offer up the sacrifice; they did not represent the laity (Hardt (ed.) 1700: 3: 394–397). Any examples the utraquists might point to from the primitive church were dismissed as bad practice soon corrected. The Roman Church, said Andrew, considered the many errors that had arisen and came to realize that in the age of the New Law the laity should receive only under the species of the bread. This decision was henceforth sanctioned and confirmed by canons, decrees, decretals, and good custom over many centuries, such that the faithful priest must observe it under pain of anathema (Hardt (ed.) 1700: 3: 412–413).

In a similar vein, the German churchman Nicholas of Cusa also appealed to the hierarchical church's authority in determining the meaning of biblical texts pertaining to the administration of the sacraments. The Bohemians point to various passages that seem to promote lay reception of the chalice, Cusanus acknowledged, but they have given themselves over to a crudely literalistic reading of Scripture. In these matters, cautioned Cusanus, the Catholic Church cannot be bound to the letter of Holy Scripture, but must follow the spirit. Apart from the church, which draws out the spiritual sense, these texts remain a dead letter. As it is, the practice of the church can interpret the text at different times in different ways; interpretation which conforms with good practice constitutes the life-giving spirit (Izbicki (ed.) 2008: 412–415). So it is, then, with the church's current practice of lay communion under one kind.

DEVOTION TO THE BLOOD OF CHRIST

The blood of Christ can certainly be found in the sacrament of the Eucharist, but could it be found elsewhere on earth? During the fourteenth and fifteenth centuries there was an upsurge in lay devotion to the blood of Christ, perhaps accelerated by lack of access to the chalice. While there were many aspects to this phenomenon, blood relics came to occupy a prominent place—the bleeding hosts of Wilsnack being a prime example. So strong was the emotional power of a direct and palpable encounter with the blood shed by Christ the Lord, the protestations of leading theologians and churchmen most often proved of little consequence. Blood awakened in the faithful a deep sense of their Savior's sacrificial suffering and offered a comforting witness to his mercy. If lay people could not have the sensation of drinking the Lord's blood from the chalice, they would seek it elsewhere (Bynum 2007).

While Jan Hus found himself on the wrong side of ecclesiastical authority in some matters, his position on blood relics was markedly conservative. Hus was one among many theologians in the late Middle Ages who attempted to tamp down the blood relic phenomenon. Relic proponents were arguing that Christ's blood was visible to this day on pieces of the true cross or crown of thorns, which had once been sprinkled with this sacrificial outpouring. Here one could find Christ's blood perceptible to the senses in its unglorified form. In his response to such claims Hus did not deny that these relics had once been reddened by the blood of Christ, and are even red today; but he did deny that Christ's blood still remained on these objects. He drew a comparison with the sacrament of the Eucharist wherein, following the consecration of the host, the accidents of bread and wine remain without the subject in which they once inhered. If that is the case, there is no reason why the (accidental) redness of Christ's blood could not remain upon the relic apart from the (substantial) blood that once served as its subject. Hence a fragment of the true cross may indeed be stained red, but the blood that once stained it is no longer present. To say that these relics were once bloodied does not mean, therefore, that they are still bloody. For the fact is that Christ and his blood are now hidden from the bodily senses. Indeed, it is just such hiddenness that allows for the merit of faith in the reception of the Eucharist, since faith would have no merit were such an encounter with Christ's blood open to sense experience (*De sanguine Christi* in *Opera Omnia* 1: 9–12).

Yet relic supporters had raised the objection that Christ could have willed that some of the blood, which he shed here on earth, would never be glorified, and thus could remain perceptible to the senses. Here the question of divine power enters into the discussion, specifically the distinction between the absolute and ordained powers of God. Hus admitted that, by his absolute power, the Lord could have done whatever he so chose. But as it was, according to his ordained power, he did not wish to leave the blood he shed unglorified, for it was said by the Holy Spirit through the mouth of David: "You will not give your holy one to see corruption" (Ps 15:10). This, argued Hus, has been certified by Scripture, by the revelation of the Holy Spirit made to David, and by the authority of the church. Hence Christ had sufficiently merited that all the blood which flowed from his body would be glorified in that same body (*De sanguine Christi* in *Opera Omnia* 1: 13–14.).

Another objection maintained that just as it is possible for Christ's blood to be present in some place sacramentally even as it exists locally somewhere else, so it also is possible for Christ's blood to be present somewhere naturally in an unglorified state, even as it remains glorified elsewhere. For although the totality of Christ's blood is contained in his body which abides in heaven in a glorified state, it could also be present on earth in a natural state outside of that body and without glorification. To this Hus responded that although Christ, following the resurrection rendered his glorified body palpable and visible in order to strengthen the faith of his disciples, he never left it here in an unglorified state; the same would apply also to his blood (*De sanguine Christi* in *Opera Omnia* 1:14).

Now if Hus is right and such blood sightings really were illusions, how does one account for all the reported miracles they have produced? For it is argued that on the strength of these accounts such miraculous blood must be honored and contemplated with our bodily eyes, and is therefore worthy of the offerings made by pilgrims. In fact, to say otherwise is to dishonor God and render oneself a heretic. Hus responds to this first of all by deploring the obsession with miracle reports, which he reckons typical of a faithless generation (Matt 17:16). Christians no longer seem content with the fact that the true blood of Christ, which is effective for their salvation, is always present in the Eucharist, even as it is hidden from corporeal eyes. Hus makes it quite clear that Christ's body is really present in the Eucharist along with his blood, and thus should not be sought elsewhere in visible form (*De sanguine Christi* in *Opera Omnia* 1: 20–21).

Taking up the Wilsnack miracles directly, Hus denied that the reported miracles (lame walking, blind seeing, captives being set free) have really been caused by this mysterious redness. He is sure that many such publicized reports are driven by greedy priests eager to rake in cash from credulous pilgrims. There is simply no basis in Scripture, faith, divine revelation, experience, or logical argument for the assertion that the blood at Wilsnack is the cause of these supposed miracles. For it does not follow that if a criminal in prison awaiting execution found his chains broken following a pledge made to the Wilsnack blood that he must thereby have been freed by that same blood (*De sanguine Christi* in *Opera Omnia* 1: 26–27). Hus can only lament that many in the name of Christ's blood are now preaching lies and false miracles, which not only do no good, but even positive harm as they lead people away from Christ into the arms of the devil. Thieves and murderers are now comforted by false miracles and thus confirmed in their own evil (*De sanguine Christi* in *Opera Omnia* 1: 29–30).

Some years later, in his effort to implement a sweeping reform program, Nicholas of Cusa likewise warned against fake relics being foisted on the people merely for the sake of turning a profit. Bleeding hosts are regarded by pilgrims as the source of miracles and thus worthy of their offerings. Yet Cusanus, like Hus before him, is convinced that avarice and deception are the real driving factors. Here again, attention is focused back upon the Eucharist. Christian people, says Cusanus, should be content with the fact that they already have Christ truly present in their church within the sacrament of the Holy Eucharist. Surely, that is all they could desire for their salvation (Izbicki (ed.) 2008: 572–573).

Suggested Reading

Bakker (1999); Bynum (2007); Hornbeck (2010). See also Ian Christopher Levy, Gary Macy, and Kristen Van Ausdall (eds.) (2011), *A Companion to the Eucharist in the Middle Ages* (Leiden: Brill).

BIBLIOGRAPHY

Bakker, P. J. J. M. (1999), *La Raison et le miracle: Les Doctrines eucharistiques (c. 1250–c. 1400). Contribution à l'étude des rapports entre philosophie et théologie*, 2 vols. (Katholieke Universiteit Nijmegen).

Brown, E. (ed.) (1690), *Fasciculus rerum expetendarum et fugiendarum prout Orthuino Gratio . . . editus est Coloniae*, A. D. MDXXXV (London: Richard Chiswell).

Buescher, G. (1950), *The Eucharistic Teaching of William of Ockham* (Washington, DC: Catholic University of America Press).

Burr, D. (1972), "Scotus and Transubstantiation," *Mediaeval Studies* 34: 336–360.

Bynum, C. W. (2007), *Wonderful Blood: Theology and Practice in Late Medieval Northern Germany and Beyond* (Philadelphia: University of Pennsylvania Press).

Denzinger-Schönmetzer (1976), *Enchiridion Symbolorum*, 36th ed. (Rome: Herder).

Fudge, T. (2010), *Jan Hus: Religious Reform and Social Revolution in Bohemia* (London: I.B.Tauris).

Girgensohn, D. (ed.) (1964), *Confutatio Iacobi de Misa*, in *Peter von Pulkau und die Wiedereinführung des Laienkelches: Leben und Wirken eines Wiener Theologen in der Zeit des großen Schismas* (Göttingen: Vandehoeck & Ruprecht).

Hardt, H. (1697–1700), *Rerum concilii oecumenici constantiensis*, 6 vols. (Frankfurt and Leipzig).

Hornbeck, J. P. (2010), *What is a Lollard?* (Oxford: Oxford University Press).

Hudson, A. (ed.) (2001), *The Works of a Lollard Preacher* (Oxford: E.E.T.S. o.s. 317).

Hudson, A. (ed.) (1978) *Selections from English Wycliffite Writings* (Cambridge: Cambridge University Press).

Izbicki, T. (ed. and trans.) (2008), *Nicholas of Cusa: Writings on Church and Reform* (Cambridge, MA: Harvard University Press).

Jan Hus (1905), *Magistri Iohannis Hus Opera Omnia*, W. Flašhans and M. Komínková (eds.), 3 vols. (Prague: Josef Vilímek).

John Duns Scotus (1891–95), *Quaestiones in Quartum Librum Sententiarum, Opera Omnia*, 26 vols. (Paris: Vives).

Kaminsky, H. (1967), *The History of the Hussite Revolution* (Berkeley: University of California Press).

Lahey, S. (2009), *John Wyclif* (Oxford: Oxford University Press).

Netter, Thomas (1757–1759), *Doctrinale Antiquitatum Fidei Catholicae Ecclesiae*, ed. B. Blanciotti, 3 vols. (Venice).

Shirley, W. W. (ed.) (1858), *Fasciculi Zizaniorum Magistri Johannis Wyclif cum Tritico*, Rolls Series 5 (London: Longman, Green et al.).

William of Ockham (1967–), *Opera Theologica* (St. Bonaventure, NY: Franciscan Institute Press).

Wyclif, John (1895–6), *Opus Evangelicum*, Johann Loserth and F. D. Matthew (eds.), 2 vols. (London: Wyclif Society).

Wyclif, John (1909), *De ente liborum duorum excerpta*, Michael Henry Dziewicki. (ed.) London: Wyclif Society.

Wyclif, John (1892), *De eucharistia tractatus maior*, Johann Loserth (ed.) (London: Wyclif Society).

Wyclif, John (1887–90), *Sermones*, Johann Loserth (ed.), 4 vols. (London: Wyclif Society).

CHAPTER 17

SACRAMENTAL RITUAL IN MIDDLE AND LATER BYZANTINE THEOLOGY: NINTH–FIFTEENTH CENTURIES

YURY P. AVVAKUMOV

"SACRAMENTAL THEOLOGY" BETWEEN EAST AND WEST

THE title of this volume presents a certain challenge to the one who has the task of writing a chapter on the Byzantine material. The notion of "sacramental theology" does not sound unproblematic for the medieval Greek context; it makes it almost inevitable to treat Byzantine sources against the background of the Western developments of the period. Of course, one would not wish to interpret Eastern Christian thought by dissecting it according to Western theological concepts and employing the terminological apparatus of Latin origin, as was the case with a number of prominent Roman Catholic scholars in the first half of the twentieth century, educated in the intellectual atmosphere of Neo-Scholasticism (Späčil 1926, 1928–1929, 1931, 1937; Jugie 1930; Gordillo 1960, and, to a certain degree, De Vries 1940 and 1948). Even if many of the studies conducted in this manner remain highly valuable and instructive reading, their approach rightly belongs to the past. Even more misleading, and regrettably highly tenacious, have been the attempts to write a history of Christian theology in the categories of the global opposition between "East" and "West," in which the two sides are portrayed as fundamentally irreconcilable "worldviews," each possessing qualities unattainable or unknown to the other (Sherrard 1959; Yannaras 2006; that such attempts are ideologically biased and/or naïvely simplifying has recently been well demonstrated by Plested 2012: esp. 1–5 and 220–228). In our case the problem, however, consists in the fact that the very subject announced by the *Handbook*, that is, "sacramental theology," emerged as a product of Western intellectual development and was formed precisely in the period to be reviewed in this chapter. The first difficulty is that Byzantine theology did not have concepts to function like the Latin *sacramentum*: its Greek prototype, μυστήριον, did not acquire a terminological status in the liturgical sphere in a manner similar to its Latin equivalent in the West (Finkenzeller 1980: 4–37). Secondly, and this is what counts most, the Greek church in the Byzantine Empire did not develop theological schools and academic ("scholastic") theology similar to the university theology of the Latin West. Not that there was no theological education in Byzantium at all, but the church there refrained from taking on the same role in the organization of education that appears in the West (Hussey 1963 [¹1937]: vii and 23). Now, it was the medieval Latin schools that gave rise to the phenomenon and the genre of "sacramental theology," in the form of the treatise *de sacramentis*, that became an indispensable part of theological systematics throughout the later medieval period. Such "sacramental theology" simply did not exist in the Byzantine East. Thus, there arose a notable asymmetry between Latin and Greek theological literature during the time treated in the present chapter. The earlier period had not as yet known such an asymmetry of genre and structure (although, to be sure, even then there had been differences in details and accents). This is why the topic "sacraments" could shed an interesting light on the complicated and lengthy process of the "parting of the ways" (Brown 1976) between the Latin West and the Byzantine East. The Byzantine material could be seen more distinctly if it were explored within the broader East-West context, just as one cannot adequately interpret Western medieval sacramental theology unless one considers its reception of Greek patristic thought and its controversies with contemporary Byzantines.

AFTER ICONOCLASM

The reluctance of Byzantine theologians to engage in constructing an academic sacramentology, their declared adherence to the Fathers, and their resistance to "introducing new things" (καινοτομεῖν; examples are numerous; see, e.g., PG 155: 184A; 208B; 253A–B) may tempt a modern scholar to regard the medieval Greek treatment of sacramental rites as a seamless continuation of patristic thought. Such a view, supported by the Orthodox neo-patristic paradigm, would postulate a contrast between the Western "break" with the authentic patristic tradition and the Eastern "fidelity" to it (Hotz 1979; Papadakis and Meyendorff 1994: 181f.). This would be a misreading of the sources. Discontinuities (as well as continuities, of course) between the late antique and the medieval periods were by no means less present in the East than in the West, even as their dynamics and history might occasionally differ. It is a consensus among the scholars of Byzantium that the era of iconoclasm (ca. 726–843) marked a turning point in the history of the Eastern Roman Empire that separated its late Antique/early Byzantine identity from the medieval era properly speaking (Brubaker and Haldon 2011: 773). In this sense, the entire chronological scope of the present chapter could be seen as "post-iconoclast," and this is valid also for the sacramental area.

For our topic, the stabilization and unification of the liturgy that took place in the middle Byzantine period (ninth to twelfth centuries) is of crucial importance. It was in the post-iconoclast centuries that the complex liturgical system known today as "the Byzantine rite" (Taft 1992) gradually acquired its definitive features as practiced to this day in the Greek Church and other churches belonging to the Byzantine cultural space, such as Bulgarian, Serbian, Romanian, Kyivan (Ukrainian), and Moscovite (Russian). The medieval Byzantine ritual practice was a unique combination of at least two lines of development. One of them was the liturgy of the main church of the Christian Empire (οἰκουμένη)—St. Sophia in Constantinople constructed under Justinian I (527–65)—with its public, stationary, and highly ornate character (Taft 1992: 28–42). The beginning of the post-iconoclast period is marked by an imperial liturgical celebration that determined theological developments in Byzantium for centuries: the "Sunday of orthodoxy," celebrated for the first time in 843 as a sign of the victory over iconoclasm, on which a conciliar definition (συνοδικόν) containing excommunications of heretical teachings was solemnly read. This *Synodicon of Orthodoxy* has several times been expanded in the course of later Byzantine history in response to new teachings condemned as heretical; among other definitions, it contains a series pertaining to the sacramental sphere (critical edition and commentary: Gouillard 1967). Another line of liturgical development represented the traditions of monastic prayer and liturgy formed under the decisive influence of the Stoudion monastery in Constantinople. There is a certain symbolism in the fact that the eve of our period includes a crucial date in Byzantine monastic history: the reorganization of the Stoudion by Theodore the Studite in 799. Later, Mount Athos began its rise in the mid-tenth century with the arrival of Athanasios the Athonite and the founding of the Great Lavra, gradually becoming the most influential center of Byzantine monasticism (Morris 1995: 31–63). Monastic practices, in contrast to the imperial style, promoted greater privatization of the liturgy and sought allegorical re-interpretation of the rites that had outlived their original purpose (Taft 1992: 72) in the spirit of personal piety, which was to become a powerful driving force behind liturgical commentaries.

SOURCES AND LOCI

It makes sense to distinguish two aspects in the Byzantine treatment of sacraments and liturgy—the polemical/apologetic and the exegetical/didactic. First, sacraments were the subject of polemics against heretics/infidels (Muslims, Paulicians, Bogomils; for a helpful anthology of translations see Hamilton and Hamilton 1998), against other ecclesiastical traditions (Latin, Armenian; see Jugie 1930; Avvakumov 2002: 60–116; 199–206; 223–301), and against dissidents within the imperial Greek Church itself. Relevant episodes are the condemnation of Soterichos Panteugenos, who in 1157 allegedly taught that Christ's sacrifice is represented in the Eucharist not in reality, but φανταστικῶς καὶ εἰκονικῶς (Gouillard 1967: 73; PG 140: 137–148; PG 139: 893–897); the schism between Arsenites and Josephites in the late thirteenth century that spurred discussions about clerical ordination (Sinkewicz 1988); and the controversies on Palamite theology in the fourteenth century (on texts related to sacraments: Polemis 1996: 83–7; 110–12; for the basics in general see: Beck 1959: 306–344 and 1980: 174–179, 218–226; Angold 1995: 82–86; Hussey 2010: 142–166). Our sources for this aspect of Byzantine thought are the *Synodicon of Orthodoxy*, polemical treatises, in particular writings κατὰ Λατίνων and κατὰ ᾿Αρμενίων, as well as heresiological compendia (Πανοπλία δογματική of Euthymios Zigabenos, and Θησαυρὸς τῆς ὀρθοδόξου πίστεως of Niketas Choniates) and relevant chapters in canonical collections and commentaries, such as those by Photios, Theodore Balsamon, Joannes Zonaras, Alexios Aristenos, Demetrios Chomatenos, and Matthaios Blastares (Rhalles and Potles 1852–1859; PG 102; 137; 138; 144; for an introduction, see Hartmann and Pennington 2012).

Secondly, sacraments and liturgy were a prominent topic of spiritual instructions, above all liturgical commentaries (Bornert 1966): "Protheoria" known under the names of Nikolaos and/or Theodore of Andida (composed between 1054 and 1067; PG 140: 417–467), the commentary on the Divine Liturgy and "The Life in Christ" of Nikolaos Kabasilas (SC 4bis; 355; 361), a series of commentaries on the church, sacraments, and liturgy of Symeon of Thessalonike (†1429; PG 155 and Hawkes-Teeples 2011). Scholars agree that at least two types of allegorical interpretation of the liturgy are represented in the commentaries: cosmic "anagogical" symbolism of Alexandrian origin, on the one hand, and the "representational historicism" that originated in Antiochene exegetical style, which prefers to see in liturgical rites representations of events in Christ's life (Bornert 1966: 47–82). The former approach would inform the *Mystagogy* of Maximus Confessor, the latter *Ecclesiastical History* attributed to Germanos, Patriarch of Constantinople in 715–730 (Congourdeau 2002: 149–150). Besides commentaries, important treatments pertaining to our topic can be found in a variety of genres, such as the exegetical literature commenting on relevant scriptural passages (e.g. Theophylaktos of Ochrid, PG 123: 444–446; 124: 705–709), and the spiritual and mystical writings that are not connected immediately with commenting on liturgy, such as the discourses, letters, and hymns of Symeon the New Theologian (949–1022; a classical treatment: Krivochéine 1963 and Krivošein 1980; on sacraments: 96–135). Liturgical commentaries are probably the most conservative of all the genres: they are particularly dependent on earlier examples—the works of Dionysius Areopagite, Maximus Confessor, and the *Ecclesiastical History*. Polemical and canonical writings, by contrast, responded more freely to current events, developments, and struggles. In particular, it was in the canonistic literature that the genre of a "Q&A" (ἐρωταποκρίσεις) developed, among which many questions and responses were devoted to the problems connected with sacraments and rites, and displayed apodictic argumentation. If one looks for a formal parallel to Western sacramental theology, Byzantine canon law may, perhaps, come closest.

NAMING AND NUMBERING
SACRAMENTAL RITES

Compared with Latin theology of the scholastic type, medieval Greek thought on sacramental rites might seem elusive. It would have been hardly appropriate to approach it as a coherent and well-structured system based on one particular generic concept (cf. Latin *sacramentum*) that implies a definite number of specific liturgical rites fixed in the doctrinal (e.g. conciliar) tradition. First, there was hardly one single, universally recognized, and unmistakably discernible generic concept. The expression "the mysteries of the church" (τὰ μυστήρια τῆς ἐκκλησίας, e.g. PG 155: 177B; Paris BN Suppl. Grec. 64, fol. 239r) would appear as the closest parallel to Latin *sacramenta*. However, there were other words employed in very similar contexts (such as τελητaί, ἱερουργίαι, ἱεροπραξίαι: the last word was used as translation of Latin *sacramenta* by the unionist Patriarch Joannes Bekkos in 1277, see Theiner and Miklosich 1872: 27, cf. ibid. 10). The list of sacramental rites and their number also vary in different theologians. Thus, in one of his letters from the early ninth century (Fatouros 1992: 719–722), Theodore Studite speaks of six "mysteries" instituted by Christ encompassing the life of a Christian: baptism (περὶ φωτίσματος), eucharistic communion (περὶ συνάξεως εἴτουν κοινωνίας), chrismation (περὶ τελητῆς μύρου), ordination (περὶ ἱερατικῶν τελειώσεων), monastic tonsure (περὶ μοναχικῆς τελειώσεως), and burial (περὶ τῶν ἱερῶς κεκοιμημένων). His enumeration follows the *Ecclesiastical Hierarchy* of Dionysios Areopagite. The number seven appears in the thirteenth century: the standard Western "post-Lombardian" corpus of seven sacraments was accepted by the Greek delegation at the Second Council of Lyons in 1274. The Latin list of seven sacraments became a part of the confession of faith *Credimus Sanctam Trinitatem* prepared for the Greeks in 1267 in the Roman Curia under Pope Clement IV and used repeatedly by the Byzantine unionists (CICO Fontes V/1: No. 23; cf. Theiner and Miklosich 1872: 8–13). The acceptance of the number seven should not be seen, however, exclusively as a Latin influence. Numeric symbolism was in the air throughout both the West and the East, and it seems that the Byzantines were on their own path to a septenarium of sacramental rites. It did not, however, become fixed and rationalized as in Western theology. The monk Job the Sinner, probably identical with Job Jasites (Beck 1959: 677), in a treatise composed most likely in the late thirteenth century (Paris BN Suppl. Grec. 64, fol. 239r–254v), lists the following seven "mysteries of the Church of Christ" (fol. 239r): baptism, chrismation, Eucharist (μετάληψις τῶν ἁγιασμάτων τοῦ ζωοποιοῦ σώματος καὶ αἵματος), ordination, marriage, monastic tonsure, and "anointing of the sick, or penance" (εὐχέλαιον … ἤτοι μετάνοια). Symeon of Thessalonike (PG 155: 177) counts the seven mysteries that are identical with the Latin corpus; however, he makes monastic tonsure (σχῆμα τῶν μοναχῶν) a form of penitence (PG 155: 197), thus elevating it to the status of a "mystery," just as Job does. It is noteworthy, however, that one encounters another septenarium in Symeon: the seven rites (τεληταί) administered by the bishop representing the seven gifts of the Holy Spirit, all of them having basically a sacramental nature: baptism, the consecration of chrism, two minor (lector, subdeacon) and three major (deacon, priest, bishop) ordinations (PG 155: 249D). As late as in the 1430s metropolitan Joasaph of Ephesos (PLP 4: 192) opined that "there are not seven mysteries of the Church, but more," and named baptism, Eucharist, chrism, ordination, consecration of the church, marriage, service of the burial, anointing of the sick, monastic tonsure, and penance (Almazov 1903: 38). Overall, Byzantine theologians seem to have had other preferences when they engaged in dogmatizing the number seven. If Latins were particularly fond of insisting on the seven sacraments as the foundation of the church of Christ, the Byzantines would rather see their Christian oikoumene as "the church of the seven imperial (οἰκουμενικαί) councils" (Photios was probably the first to stress this idea: PG 102: 629–632).

Towards the Idea of Sacramentality

To discern the core of the Byzantine understanding of sacramentality, it might be helpful not to focus too much on lists and numbers, but to proceed from the notion of a holy thing that brings together and unites in itself two aspects—the material/visible/human and the spiritual/invisible/divine. This is how Symeon of Thessalonike expresses it:

> The mysteries that [Christ] gave us, are two-fold: [on the one hand,] they are visible, consisting of [material] elements, because of our body; [on the other,] they are also spiritual (νοητά), hidden (μυστικά) and filled with invisible grace, because of our spirit. Through these mysteries we become purified and illumined both in body and soul, and partake of healing and sanctification. (PG 155: 525A; cf. ibid.: 181A)

The idea that the sacramental sign possesses a dual nature, bringing the material and the spiritual, the human and the divine in harmony and thus exercising a purifying and enlightening power grounded in Christ's salvific act—the understanding that is basically similar to the Western definitions of the period (cf. the famous Berengarian "*invisibilis gratiae visibilis forma*" attributed to Augustine in the medieval West)—enables us better to delimit the area of sacramentality in Byzantium. The sacramental area, essentially, included not only, and even not primarily, the six, seven, or more rituals parallel to the Western septenarium. Of course, the baptismal water, the holy chrism, and the bread and wine that become the body and blood of Christ in the eucharistic consecration were seen as the true and foundational "mysteries of the Church" (cf. the Isidorian "*baptismus et chrisma, corpus et sanguis*" in the West); the churches (temples), in which these mysteries were administered, also belonged to the sacramental reality constantly re-produced with the help of their servants who had been granted by God sacramental power through ordination. Hence, at least four sacramental rites (baptism, chrismation, Eucharist, and ordination) from the classical Western septenarium are addressed; however, the solemn preparation of chrism and the consecration of the temple conducted by the bishop/patriarch are also implied, both thus acquiring sacramental status (cf. Symeon of Thessalonike, PG 155: 249D). And there are more: the holy cross, icons, and relics were sacramental for the Byzantines; their veneration took place as a sacramental act founded on an incarnational Christology just as much as baptism and Eucharist did. This becomes apparent, for instance, in those parts of the *Synodicon of Orthodoxy* that determine the catholic/orthodox teaching (in Byzantine Greek, these words were ecclesiological synonyms, not opposites) against dualist heresies. In its condemnation of the Bogomils, the *Synodicon* speaks in a single breath about baptism, the cross, Eucharist, icons, and holy churches (Gouillard 1967: 67–69; Engl. transl. Hamilton and Hamilton 1998: 138–139). The Bogomils are condemned because they deny the twofold—visible *and* invisible—nature and therefore also the salvific power of the things that play such an important role in the ritual life of the official church: they dare to assert that the holy baptism "is just water" (ὕδωρ εἶναι ψιλόν), that the eucharistic communion "is a communion of mere bread and wine" (ἄρτου ψιλοῦ καὶ οἴνου ἐστὶ μετάληψις), that the holy and life-giving cross is nothing but "a gallows" (φούλκα), and that the churches built to the glory of God and holy icons in them are simply "works of men's hands" (ἔργα χειρῶν).

At first glance, the *Synodicon*'s line of argument might seem predetermined not so much by its inherent "sacramental theology" but rather by the logic of the adversary's teachings. It is interesting, however, that marriage, also rejected by the Bogomils, did not find similar treatment in the *Synodicon*: the author connected the rejection of marriage with refusal to eat meat, and resorted rather, in a quite "old-testamental" way, to the idea of God's disciplinary precept than to the notion of the sacramental duality founded on the incarnation (Gouillard 1967: 67). Such uneasiness about the sacramental status of marriage appears often in Byzantine theology; of course, every theologian knew that marriage is a symbol of the bond of Christ and his church, according to the apostle (Eph 5:32), and therefore likely also a "mystery"; however, it is clear that marriage did not occupy nearly as central a place in Byzantine sacramental theology as holy images did (an almost negligible space devoted by Symeon of Thessalonike to marriage compared with the ubiquity of holy images in his large compendium is an example of this: PG 155: 504–516).

In the iconodule theology that dominated the Byzantine intellectual scene throughout the middle and later period, the cross, icons, and relics enjoyed sacramental status and sometimes even seem to rank with the "classical" Christian μυστήρια such as baptism and the Eucharist by guaranteeing the real presence of Christ's salvific power (the cross) or of a saint (icons and relics) to everyone who venerates them (Brown 1973; Brubaker and Haldon 2011: 786; cf. on the images: Beck 1975 and 1980: 73–74). It is revealing that the iconoclast *Inquiries* of Emperor Constantine V prepared before the council in Hiereia of 754 accused iconodules of undermining the unique sacramental role of the Eucharist as the only true image (τύπος) of Christ (Hennephof 1969: 54–55 [Nos. 165–167]; Gero 1975).

Monastic Approaches and
Byzantine "Ritualism"

The tenacity with which monastic tonsure had been counted among the mysteries of the Church testifies to the contribution of monk-theologians to sacramental theology. There were voices critical of attempts to ascribe sacramental status to monks: thus, Michael Glykas protested in the twelfth century against the claim that σχῆμα τῶν μοναχῶν effects, like baptism, the remission of sins (PG 158: 935–952). The influence of monk-theologians was, however, always especially weighty. Later Byzantine theology to a great extent developed as a legitimation of monastic ascetic experience: this becomes particularly evident in the writings of Gregorios Palamas (c. 1296–1357) and his followers (on a eucharistic topic discussed in connection with Palamite theology: Polemis 1996: 110–112; Meyendorff 1997: 257; cf., however, ibid., 426–427).

The monastic way of doing theology, undoubtedly akin to the monastic method of practicing liturgy, ranged from the charismatic and bold, highly personal style of a Symeon the New Theologian to the calm, didactic, and meticulously descriptive manner of a Symeon of Thessalonike. There was, however, something they all shared: the firm belief in the monastic way of life being the ultimate model for *every* Christian (PG 155:197C–D; 200D), and the unremitting focus on the two main occupations of the monk—ritual and prayer, and concern for their purity. Commentators such as Symeon of Thessalonike were focused more on the formal, "enacted" purity of the ritual, and engaged in detailed allegorical interpretation of liturgical practice. An "enthusiast," such as Symeon the New Theologian, concerned especially with the moral purity of the person immersed in ritual and prayer, was prone to relativize the established, "objectified" sacramental order of the church: hence his strong critique of immoral priests and bishops, his insistence on the right of the non-ordained monks to hear confessions (Turner 2009: 48–49), and his idea of a "second baptism," the baptism in tears, which "is no longer a type [symbol] of the truth," like the baptism in water, "but the truth itself" (SC 51bis: 58–60; transl. McGuckin 1982: 42; this idea appears in earlier monastic theology, in particular in Joannes Klimakos, but never before so explicitly). The sacramental space of Symeon the New Theologian is broader and "freer" than the one fixed in canon law and liturgical books (cf. Golitzin 1996). This led repeatedly to scholarly debates about Symeon's orthodoxy and his alleged proximity to heretical movements (Symeon's orthodoxy indeed came under suspicion during his life; for discussion see: Garsoïan 1971; Holl 1898; cf. Krivošein 1980: 40, n.19; Turner 2009: 65–69).

Both monk-"commentator" and monk-"enthusiast," however, were, above all, "ritualists": ritual occupied the very center of their universe. In such an intellectual atmosphere, even the smallest liturgical detail could, potentially, gain utmost significance, especially if this detail happened to touch upon cultural sensitivities; the borderline between "important" and "unimportant" in ritual tended occasionally to get blurred (Avvakumov 2006). In this sense the monastic approach is different from what could be called the "imperial" line in the theology of those such as Photios or Theodoros Balsamon who viewed rituals in a more instrumental way, as tools for maintaining "orthodoxy" and ecclesiastical order in Christendom. This made promoters of the "imperial" line in theology intellectually closer to Western scholastic thought with its distinction between the "substance" and the "accidents" of a sacrament (Avvakumov 2002: 314–317)—even if many of them hold strongly anti-Latin views.

Overall, there undoubtedly existed a tension between monasticism and empire: monk-theologians reserved for themselves the right to castigate the Empire anytime "orthodoxy" was, in their view, threatened (in particular when the Empire sought a union with the West), but often "imperial" and monastic theologies joined their efforts, mostly for identifying and condemning heresies. In such cases, the degree of intolerance could be extremely high, as we observe in the history of iconoclasm in the ninth century, the attack on dualist heresies in the tenth to twelfth centuries, as well as the persecutions of defenders of the union of Lyons in the thirteenth century, and of adversaries of Gregorios Palamas in the fourteenth century. The Byzantine monastic ethos, a peculiar alloy of humility and pride, conservative yet, to quote George Florovsky, "a permanent 'Resistance Movement' in the Christian Society" (Florovsky 1957: 150), played a momentous role in all those conflicts.

CLASHES WITH OTHER CHRISTIAN TRADITIONS

The Byzantine sacramental practice, as it was shaped in the middle and later period, differed through a series of features both from the Western liturgy and from the liturgies of Oriental pre-Chalcedonian traditions (foundational for the Byzantine liturgy: Hanssens 1930–1932; Taft 1975 and 1991–2008; Schulz 1986 and 2000; for a comparison with pre-Chalcedonians: Dalmais 1980 and 1989). The differences repeatedly gave pretexts for disagreements and controversies between the churches; these controversies, in their turn, spurred theological reflection on sacramental rites.

In our period, the see of Constantinople, being the church of the imperial capital, was pursuing the policy of unification of sacramental rites and liturgy in the entire area accessible to its influence ("byzantinization": Taft 1992: 57 and *passim*). Theodoros Balsamon, canonist and Chalcedonian patriarch of Antioch (fl. 1170s), in his responses to Patriarch Markos of Alexandria, prohibited the use of Alexandrian eucharistic liturgies of St. Jacob and St. Mark and prescribed the Byzantine liturgies of St. John Chrysostom and St. Basil, because "all churches must follow the custom of the New Rome, that is, Constantinople"

(PG 137: 953D). The Armenian Church was repeatedly urged by the Greeks to abolish its eucharistic practices of using unleavened bread and not mixing water into the chalice (e.g. PG 130: 1181–1184; PG 133: 257; Hergenröther 1869: 139–154; Taft 1987).

If the attempts to eliminate the liturgical diversity of the East proved to be ultimately unsuccessful, it was not because of the lack of the unificatory pressure from Constantinople, but because vast parts of the Empire's territory had been conquered by its Muslim neighbors and were outside Byzantine control. On the Western borderline, the policy of liturgical unification, together with political rivalries with Western powers over territories such as South Italy, Dalmatia, and Bulgaria, led to clashes with the Roman papacy. Thus, in the heat of the conflict over the Christianization of Bulgaria in 866–867, Patriarch Photios of Constantinople accused Rome, among other things, of not allowing priests to administer the sacrament of chrismation, and assaulted the celibacy of Latin clerics (Laourdas and Westerink, 1983–88: I, 42–43). Overall, conflicts with other Christian traditions over issues of sacramental ritual became the hallmark of the medieval period. Of course, there were precedents in the earlier era: medieval polemic against Latin and Armenian sacramental practices repeatedly appealed, for instance, to the so-called "anti-Roman" and "anti-Armenian" canons of the council in Trullo of 691–92 (Nedungatt and Featherstone 1995; c. 13; 32; 33; 55; 56; 99). But only in the middle and later Byzantine period did such polemic begin to be systematically applied as a tool of the imperial-ecclesiastical policy of Constantinople.

Controversy over the Eucharistic Bread

One sacramental issue in particular occupied a prominent place in the history of estrangement between Byzantines and Latins—the use of leavened or unleavened bread ("the azymes," τὰ ἄζυμα) in the Eucharist. The controversy originated in the mid-eleventh century and throughout the later medieval period remained the second most important issue of disagreement between Latins and Greeks after the Trinitarian issue of Filioque, generating a great number of polemical writings (for a detailed treatment see: Avvakumov 2002: 29–159; 221–301, and passim; a list of Byzantine anti-azymite works: 91–103). It began with the attack of the Greeks on the Latin use of the "azymes" and a number of other Latin liturgical and disciplinary customs in a letter composed by Archbishop Leo of Ochrid in 1053 (critical edition: Büttner 2007: 176–193). The Byzantine assault did not limit itself to literary polemic: Patriarch Michael Keroularios is reported to have hindered in 1053–1054 the regular functioning of Latin churches and monasteries in Constantinople on the pretext of their eucharistic celebration with unleavened bread (Will 1861: 68; 80–81). A disciple of Symeon the New Theologian and a Studite monk Niketas Stethatos, who was the author of a vita of Symeon (Greenfield 2013), composed several foundational anti-azymite writings.

Among the four main lines of argumentation (Avvakumov 2002: 103–111) brought forward by Niketas and other Byzantine polemicists against unleavened bread, two are especially interesting for our topic. First, Byzantine authors identified the unleavened bread of the Latin Eucharist with the Jewish "azymes" prescribed in Mosaic law (Ex 12:8–20; Deut 16:2–4): Latins were therefore accused of practicing Jewish ritual, "Judaizing," often with a reference to canon 11 of *Trullanum* which prohibited participation in Jewish feasts, and of accepting cultic azymes from them (Niketas Stethatos, Διάλεξις, in Michel 1930: II, 321; Symeon of Jerusalem, Περὶ τῶν ἀζύμων, in Leib 1924: 222; Leo of Pereyaslavl, Πρὸς Ῥωμαίους ἤτοι Λατίνους, in Beneševič 1920: 95; cf. Nedungatt and Featherstone 1995: 81–82). This gave the Greek authors opportunity to engage in reflections about the relation between the Old and the New Testaments and the new character of Christian sacraments (see the second and third letters on the azymes by Leo of Ochrid in Büttner 2007: 202–260). Another objection against unleavened bread proceeded from the concept of ἀντίτυπον ("that which bears an image of something, corresponds symbolically to something," cf. 1 Pet 3:21, with a reference to baptism; the word appears also in the anaphora of St. Basil with reference to the eucharistic bread and wine). Between the material substance of bread and the body of Christ there must be some correspondence and symbolic affinity: bread should be ἀντίτυπος of the body of Christ. Unleavened bread, however, lacks a "soul" because it lacks yeast; yeast "animates" the dough, gives "life" to it; unleavened bread is therefore "dead" and cannot function as an ἀντίτυπον of Christ's body because the Divine Logos took on a human body with a soul; Latins are therefore guilty of the Apollinarian heresy (Niketas Stethatos, Κατὰ Ἀρμενίων καὶ Λατίνων in Hergenröther 1869: 141).

The origins of the idea of yeast as an animating substance must not occupy us here: it has been suggested that it could have come from a medieval treatise on the virtues of plants (Erickson 1970: 162, n. 35); there is also a passage in Albert the Great who reported that contemporary Greeks themselves pointed to Aristotle's Περὶ ζῴων γενέσεως as the source of their views (Avvakumov 2002: 153, n. 178 and 179). What is interesting for our topic, however, is that this argument illuminates the Greek polemicists' way of thinking about the sacramental sign and the differences in theological temperament and style on the Latin and on the Byzantine side. Among all Greek anti-azymite objections, this one made Latins especially annoyed and angry owing to its unscientific, "bizarre," and "crazy" character (Humbert of Silva Candida, *Dialogus*, in Will 1861: 104; later scholastic theologians disregarded this argument entirely, although they engaged enthusiastically in discussing other Greek objections against unleavened bread). The ultimate Latin response to this Greek argument was founded on the idea of the real presence: *before* the eucharistic consecration, it should be of no relevance whether the bread is leavened or unleavened; *after* the consecration, it is no longer bread but the body of Christ (Will 1861: 257; cf. the contemporary definitions against Berengar written, most likely, by Humbert of Silva Candida). Contrary to this, the main Greek promoter of this argument, Niketas Stethatos, seems to never lose sight of the typological aspect of the sacrament. Starting with the accusation that Latins were heretics, the Greek polemic against the azymes ended in a denial of the sacramentality of the Eucharist of the Roman Church: the Latin sacrifice "is dead"; it cannot give life; the Holy Spirit does not come upon the eucharistic substances, and they remain only bread and wine (Feodosij Grek, *Poslanie o vere latinskoi* in Ponyrko 1992: 18; Matthaios Angelos Panaretos, Κατὰ τῶν λατινικῶν ἀζύμων in Risso 1916, 11/12: 156). Regarded by Latins as a second-rate question, the issue of azymes was considered "the summary of the whole Christian religion" (τῆς εὐσεβείας τὸ κεφάλαιον) by a Byzantine theologian of the early twelfth century (Patriarch John Oxeites of Antioch, in Leib 1924: 245 [113]).

A HUMANIST THEOLOGIAN
ON SACRAMENTAL RITUAL

One more point of disagreement with Latins on the Eucharist emerged in the fourteenth century and was debated at the council of Ferrara-Florence in 1438–9: the question of the *epiclesis* (Jugie 1930: 256–301; DThC 5: 194–300). The subject of disagreement was the particular moment at which the eucharistic consecration could be regarded as completed—the moment after which there is no longer bread and wine on the altar, but the true body and blood of Christ. To answer the question about the precise moment of the consecration of the Holy Gifts meant also to determine which part of the eucharistic liturgy possessed sacramental power. In the anaphora of the liturgies of St. John Chrysostom and St. Basil, the words of Jesus ("Take, eat …" and "Drink of it all of you …") are followed by the prayer of ἐπίκλησις, the invocation of the Holy Spirit over the Holy Gifts; this prayer began to be regarded in Byzantine theology, at least from the fourteenth century onwards, as consecratory, by which the change (μεταβολή) of the bread and wine into the body and blood of Christ is consummated. The issue appeared for the first time in the commentary on the Divine Liturgy by Nikolaos Chamaëtos Kabasilas (1322/3–after 1392), who reports an attack of "certain Latins" who "claim that after the words of the Lord *Take and eat* and what follows there is no need of any further prayer to consecrate the offerings" (SC 4bis: 178–198; Hussey and McNulty 2010: 71). In the Latin view, the consecration is completed with the words of Jesus.

Kabasilas' treatment of this issue differs substantially from the way disagreements about sacramental rites had been handled by Byzantine polemicists during at least three previous centuries. First, he demonstrates the logic of the adversaries' argument—truthfully, as far as we can judge today (cf. Hofmann 1955: 238–239; 248–252), and, one would almost say, "sympathetically" (SC 4bis: 178–80). Secondly, in his refutation of Latin arguments, Nikolaos is reluctant to engage himself in a search for one particular "magic moment" in the ritual, refusing the consecratory power to the one and ascribing it fully to another (as sometimes happened later, when the epiclesis issue was discussed in the Early Modern period; cf. Jugie 1930: 290–293). Kabasilas takes an "inclusive" view on the problem by saying that the Greeks "believe that the Lord's words indeed accomplish the mystery, but through the medium of the priest" (SC 4bis: 182; Hussey and McNulty 2010: 72). It is more important for him to safeguard the Christological foundation of the sacrament than to score for himself a "victory" in a ritualistic quarrel. And thirdly, he disarms, in a clever way, his Latin adversary by discerning a prayer of *epiclesis* in the Latin Mass itself: "The point had escaped them, no doubt, because the Latins do not recite this prayer immediately after pronouncing Christ's words, and because they do not ask explicitly for consecration and the transformation of the elements into the Body of the Lord, but use other terms which, however, have exactly the same meaning" (SC 4bis: 190–192; Hussey and McNulty 2010: 76). Behind this standpoint there is a clear ecclesiological recognition of the Latin church and her sacramental life: "[N]ot the whole Latin Church ... condemns the prayer for the offerings after the words of consecration, but only a few innovators, who are causing her harm in other ways" (SC 4bis: 198; Hussey and McNulty 2010: 79).

In his last book, which has not as yet received the attention it deserves, the late Fr. Gerhard Podskalsky SJ (†2013) identified what he called "humanist theology" in Byzantium (Podskalsky 2003). Previously, the notion of "humanism" had been associated almost exclusively with secular learning and classical pagan heritage in Byzantium (see the bibliography in Podskalsky 2003: 13, n. 3). The German scholar convincingly located a humanist element present also in theology, which merits scholarly interest and further study. Among humanist theologians Nikolaos Kabasilas occupies a prominent place. His alleged closeness to Palamite theology (Bobrinskoy 1974; Meyendorff 1979: 107–109) does not withstand a critical test; Kabasilas, on the contrary, was in his early years a sharp critic of Palamas (Demetracopoulos 1998) and also later in his life moved freely between different, sometimes opposing, theological currents of contemporary Byzantium, being both an advocate for his uncle, the pro-Palamite author Neilos Kabasilas, and a close friend of the Unionist and translator of Thomas Aquinas, Demetrios Kydones (Plested 2012: 100–107). Nikolaos' oeuvre represents various genres and touches upon many subjects (Spiteris and Conticello 2002: 322–352); his contribution to sacramental theology, however, is of special value. The treatment of sacraments in his commentary on the Divine Liturgy and in his work on the life in Christ can be deemed a synthesis of the best developments of middle and later Byzantine sacramentology (Congourdeau 2002: 158–159; Spiteris and Conticello 2002: 389). It displays a perfect command of patristic thought and, at the same time, acquaintance with the achievements of the latter period including Thomas Aquinas and other Latin authors; he shows the ability to see the core of the problem and not to lose the sight of the whole, as well as a clear Christological focus and irenic attitude to other Christian traditions. Given the example of Nikolaos Kabasilas, further studies on the contribution of humanist theologians (such as Basileios of Ochrid, Theorianos Philosophos, Joannes Bekkos, Manuel Kalekas, Gennadios Scholarios) to Byzantine thinking about sacramental ritual are highly desirable; they will definitely lead to intriguing discoveries and offer refreshing perspectives on Byzantine theological thought.

Suggested Reading

Bornert (1966); Congourdeau (2002); Jugie (1930); Meyendorff (1979): 191–211; Ware (2005).

Bibliography

Almazov, A. I. (1903), *Kanoničeskie otvety Ioasafa, mitropolita Efesskago: Maloizvestnyi pamiatnik prava grečeskoi cerkvi XV veka* (Odessa).

Beneševič, V. N. (1920), *Pamiatniki drevnerusskogo kanoničeskogo prava*. Part II/1 (Petrograd).

Catanzaro, C. J. de (trans.) (1974), *Nicholas Cabasilas: The Life in Christ* (Crestwood, NY: St. Vladimir's Seminary Press).

CICO Fontes = Tăutu, A. L., et al. (eds.) (1943–75), *Pontificia Commissio ad redigendum Codicem juris canonici orientalis. Fontes*. Series III. 15 vols. Rome: Typis Pont. Universitatis Gregorianae).

Congourdeau, M.-H. (ed.) (1990), *Nicolas Cabasilas. La vie en Christ*. 2 vols. SC 355; 361 (Paris: Cerf).

Darrouzès, J. (ed.) (1980), *Syméon le Nouveau Théologien: Chapitres théologiques, gnostiques et pratiques*. SC 51bis (Paris: Cerf).

Fatouros, G. (ed.) (1992), *Theodori Studitae Epistulae*, vol. 1. Corpus fontium historiae byzantinae, 31 (Berlin and New York: de Gruyter).

Greenfield, R. P. H. (2013), *The Life of Saint Symeon the New Theologian. Niketas Stethatos*. Dumbarton Oaks Medieval Library (Cambridge, MA, and London: Harvard University Press).

Hawkes-Teeples, S. (ed. and trans.) (2011), *Symeon of Thessalonika. The Liturgical Commentaries*. Studies and Texts 168 (Toronto: Pontifical Institute of Mediaeval Studies).

Hennephof, H. (1969), *Textus byzantini ad iconomachiam pertinentes* (Leiden: Brill).

Hergenröther, J. (1869), *Monumenta graeca ad Photium ejusque historiam pertinentia* (Regensburg: Manz).

Hofmann, G. (1955), *Andreas de Santacroce. Acta Latina Concilii Florentini* (Rome: Pont. Inst. Orientalium Studiorum).

Hussey, J. M., and P. A. McNulty (transl.) (2010), *Nicholas Cabasilas. A Commentary on the Divine Liturgy* (Crestwood, NY: St. Vladimir's Seminary Press) [11960: SPCK].

Krivochéine, B., and J. Paramelle (ed.) (1963–65), *Syméon le Nouveau Théologien: Catéchèses*. 3 vols. SC 96; 104; 113 (Paris: Cerf).

Laourdas, B., and L. G. Westerink (eds.) (1983-88), *Photii Epistulae et Amphilochia*. 6 vols (Leipzig: Teubner)

Leib, B. (1924), *Deux inédits byzantins sur les azymes au début du XIIe siècle. Contribution à l'histoire des dicussions theologiques entre grecs et latins*. Orientalia Christiana II–3, No. 9 (Rome: Pont. Inst. Orientalium Studiorum).

McGuckin, P. (trans.) (1982), *Symeon the New Theologian: The Practical and Theological Chapters, and The Three Theological Discourses* (Kalamazoo, MI: Cistercian Publications).

Ponyrko, N. V. (1992), *Epistoliarnoe nasledie Drevnei Rusi XI-XIII vv. Issledovaniia, teksty, perevody* (St. Petersburg: Nauka).

Rhalles, G. A., and M. Potles (1852–1859), Σύνταγμα τῶν θείων καὶ ἱερῶν κανόνων. 6 vols. (Athens, repr. Athens 1966).

Risso, P. (1914–16), "Matteo Angelo Panareto e cinque suoi opuscoli," in *ReO* 8 (1914): 91–105, 162–179, 231–237, 274–290; 9 (1915): 112–120, 202–206; 10 (1915): 63–77, 146–164, 238–251; 11/12 (1916): 28–35, 76–80, 154–160.

Salaville, S. (ed.) (1967), *Nicolas Cabasilas. Explication de la Divine Liturgie.* 2nd ed., munie du texte grec, revue et augmentée par R. Bornert et al. SC 4bis (Paris: Cerf).

Sinkewicz, R. E. (1988), "A Critical Edition of the Anti-Arsenite Discourses of Theoleptos of Philadelphia," in *Mediaeval Studies* 50: 46–95.

Theiner, A., and F. Miklosich (1872), *Monumenta spectantia ad unionem Ecclesiarum Graecae et Romanae* (Vienna: Braumüller).

Turner, H. J. M. (ed. and trans.) (2009), *The Epistles of St Symeon the New Theologian* (Oxford: Oxford University Press).

Will, C. (1861), *Acta et scripta quae de controversiis Ecclesiae graecae et latinae saeculo undecimo composita extant* (Leipzig and Marburg: Elwert).

Secondary Literature

Angold, M. (1995), *Church and Society in Byzantium under the Comneni, 1081–1261* (Cambridge: Cambridge University Press).

Avvakumov, Y. [G.] (2002), *Die Entstehung des Unionsgedankens. Die lateinische Theologie des Mittelalters in der Auseinandersetzung mit dem Ritus der Ostkirche.* Veröffentlichungen des Grabmann-Institutes zur Erforschung der mittelalterlichen Theologie und Philosophie, 47 (Berlin: Akademie-Verlag).

Avvakumov, Y. [G.] (2006), "Die Fragen des Ritus als Streit- und Kontroversgegenstand. Zur Typologie der Kulturkonflikte zwischen dem lateinischen Westen und dem byzantinisch-slawischen Osten im Mittelalter und in der Neuzeit," in Bendel, R. (ed.), *Kirchen- und Kulturgeschichtsschreibung in Nordost- und Ostmitteleuropa. Initiativen, Methoden, Theorien* (Münster: Lit Verlag), 191–233.

Beck, H.-G. (1959), *Kirche und theologische Literatur im byzantinischen Reich* (Munich: C. H. Beck).

Beck, H.-G. (1975), *Von der Fragwürdigkeit der Ikone.* Sitzungsberichte der Bayerischen Akademie der Wissenschaften, Phil.-Hist. Klasse, 7 (Munich: Verlag der Bayersichen Akademie der Wissenschaften).

Beck, H.-G. (1980), *Geschichte der orthodoxen Kirche im byzantinischen Reich.* Die Kirche in ihrer Geschichte, I/D1 (Göttingen: Vandenhoeck & Ruprecht).

Bobrinskoy, B. (1974), "Nicholas Cabasilas: Theology and Spirituality," in C. J. Catanzaro (1974), *Nicholas Cabasilas. The Life in Christ* (Crestwood, NY: St. Vladimir's Seminary Press), 17–42.

Bornert, R. (1966), *Les Commentaires byzantines de la Divine Liturgie du VIIe au XVe siècle.* Archives de l'Orient chrétien, 9 (Paris: Institut français d'études byzantines).

Brown, P. (1973), "A Dark Age Crisis: Aspects of Iconoclastic Controversy," in *English Historical Review* 88: 1–34; reiss. in P. Brown, *Society and the Holy in Late Antiquity* (London: Faber and Faber, 1982), 251–301.

Brown, P. (1975), "Society and the Supernatural: A Medieval Change," in *Daedalus* 104: 133–51; reiss. in P. Brown, *Society and the Holy in Late Antiquity* (London: Faber and Faber, 1982), 302–332.

Brown, P. (1976), "Eastern and Western Christendom in Late Antiquity: A Parting of the Ways," in D. Baker (ed.), *The Orthodox Churches and the West* (Oxford: Blackwell), 1–24; reiss. in P. Brown, *Society and the Holy in Late Antiquity* (London: Faber and Faber, 1982), 166–195.

Brubaker, L., and J. Haldon (2011), *Byzantium in the Iconoclast Era c. 680-850: A History* (Cambridge: Cambridge University Press).

Büttner, E. (2007), *Erzbischof Leon von Ochrid (1037-1056). Leben und Werk (mit Texten seiner bisher unedierten asketischen Schrift und seiner drei Briefe an den Papst* (Bamberg).

Congourdeau, M.-H. (2002), "L'Eucharistie à Byzance du XIe au XVe siècle," in M. Brouard (ed.), *Eucharistia. Encylopédie de l'Eucharistie* (Paris: Cerf), 145-165.

Conticello, C. G., and V. Conticello (eds.) (2002), *La théologie byzantine et sa tradition*, vol. 2: *(XIIIᵉ-XIXᵉ s.)* (Turnhout: Brepols).

Dalmais, I.-H. (1980), *Les liturgies d'Orient* (Paris: Cerf).

Dalmais, I.-H. (1989), "Die Mysterien (Sakramente) im orthodoxen und altorientalischen Christentum. Theologie und liturgischer Vollzug," in W. Nyssen, et al. (eds.), *Handbuch der Ostkirchenkunde*, vol. 2 (Düsseldorf: Patmos), 141-181.

Demetracopoulos, J. D. (1998), "Nicholas Cabasilas' *Quaestio de rationis valore*: An Anti-Palamite Defense of Secular Wisdom," in *BYZANTINA* 19: 53-93.

De Vries, W. (1940), *Sakramententheologie bei den syrischen Monophysiten* (Rome: Pont. Institutum Orientalium Studiorum).

De Vries, W. (1948), *Sakramententheologie bei den Nestorianern* (Rome: Pont. Institutum Orientalium Studiorum).

Erickson, J. H. (1970), "Leavened and Unleavened: Some Theological Implications of the Schism of 1054," in *St. Vladimir's Theological Quarterly* 14: 155-176; reiss. in Erickson (1991), 133-155.

Erickson, J. H. (1991), *The Challenge of Our Past: Studies in Orthodox Canon Law and Church History* (Crestwood, NY: St. Vladimir's Seminary Press).

Finkenzeller, J. (1980), *Die Lehre von den Sakramenten im Allgemeinen. Von der Schrift bis zur Scholastik*. Handbuch der Dogmengeschichte IV:1a (Freiburg etc.: Herder).

Florovsky, G. (1957), "Empire and Desert: Antinomies of Church History," in *Greek Orthodox Theological Review* 3: 133-159.

Gallagher, C. (2002), *Church Law and Church Order in Rome and Byzantium: A Comparative Study* (London: Ashgate).

Garsoïan, N. G. (1971), "Byzantine Heresy. A Reinterpretation," in *Dumbarton Oaks Papers* 25: 85-113.

Gero, S. (1975), "The Eucharistic Doctrine of Byzantine Iconoclasts and Its Sources," in *Byzantinische Zeitschrift* 68: 4-22.

Golitzin, A. (1996), "Hierarchy versus Anarchy? Dionysius Areopagita, Symeon the New Theologian, and Nicetas Stethatos," in B. Nassif (ed.), *New Perspectives on Historical Theology. Essays in Memory of John Meyendorff* (Grand Rapids, MI: Eerdmans), 250-276.

Gordillo, M. (1960), *Theologia Orientalium cum Latinorum comparata. Commentatio historica*, vol. 1: *Ab ortu Nestorianismi usque ad expugantionem Constantinopoleos 431-1453* (Rome: Pont. Institutum Orientalium Studiorum).

Gouillard, J. (1967), "Le Synodikon de l'orthodoxie: Édition et commentaire," in *Travaux et mémoires* 2: 1-316.

Hamilton, J., and B. Hamilton (1998), *Christian Dualist Heresies in the Byzantine World* (Manchester: Manchester University Press).

Hanssens, J. M. (1930-2), *De Missa rituum orientalium*. 2 vols. Institutiones liturgicae de ritibus orientalibus 2-3 (Rome: Pont. Institutum Orientalium Studiorum).

Hartmann, W., and K. Pennington (2012) (eds.), *The History of Byzantine and Eastern Canon Law to 1500* (Washington, DC: Catholic University of America Press).

Holl, K. (1898), *Enthusiasmus und Bussgewalt beim griechischen Mönchtum. Eine Studie zu Symeon dem Neuen Theologen* (Leipzig: Hinrichs).

Hotz, R. (1979), *Sakramente—im Wechselspiel zwischen Ost und West.* Ökumenische Theologie 2 (Zürich: Benziger; Gütersloh: Gerd Mohn).

Hussey, J. M. (1963 [1937]), *Church and Learning in the Byzantine Empire (867–1185)* (New York: Russell & Russell).

Hussey, J. M. (2010), *The Orthodox Church in the Byzantine Empire.* Foreword and updated bibliography by A. Louth (Oxford: Oxford University Press).

Jugie, M. (1930), *Theologia dogmatica Christianorum orientalium ab Ecclesia Catholica dissidentium,* vol. 3: *De sacramentis* (Paris: Letouzey et Ané).

Krivochéine, B. (1963), "Introduction. Ch. I: La peronnalité spirituelle," in B. Krivochéine (ed.), *Syméon le Nouveau Théologien: Catéchèses.* SC 96 (Paris: Cerf), 15–54.

Krivošein, V. (1980), *Prepodobnyi Simeon Novyi Bogoslov (949-1022)* (Paris: YMCA Press).

Meyendorff, I. (1997), *Žizn' I Trudy sviatitelia Grigoriia Palamy. Vvedinie v izučenie* [rev. and enlarged Russ. ed. with commentaries by V. M. Lurie and I. P. Medvedev]. Subsidia byzantinorossica, 2 (St. Petersburg: Byzantinorossica).

Meyendorff, J. (1979), *Byzantine Theology. Historical Trends and Doctrinal Themes* (New York: Fordham University Press).

Michel, A. (1924–1930), *Humbert und Kerullarios.* 2 vols. (Paderborn: Schöningh).

Morris, R. (1995), *Monks and Laymen in Byzantium, 843–1118* (Cambridge: Cambridge University Press).

Nedungatt, G., and M. Featherstone (eds.) (1995), *The Council in Trullo Revisited.* Kanonika, 6 (Rom: Pontificio Istituto Orientale).

Papadakis, A., and J. Meyendorff (1994), *The Christian East and the Rise of the Papacy. The Church AD 1071–1453* (Crestwood, NY: St. Vladimir's Seminary Press).

Plested, M. (2012), *Orthodox Readings of Aquinas* (Oxford: Oxford University Press).

PLP = Trapp, E. (ed.), *Prosopographisches Lexikon der Palaiologenzeit* (Wien: Verlag der Österreichischen Akademie der Wissenschaften, 1976–1996).

Podskalsky, G. (2003), *Von Photios zu Bessarion. Der Vorrang humanistisch geprägter Theologie in Byzanz und deren bleibende Bedeutung.* Schriften zur Geistesgeschichte des östlichen Europa, 25 (Wiesbaden: Harassowitz).

Polemis, I. (1996), *Theophanes of Nicaea: His Life and Works.* Wiener byzantinische Studien, 20 (Wien: Verlag der Österreichschen Akademie der Wissenschaften).

Schulz, H.-J. (1986), *The Byzantine Liturgy. Symbolic Structure and Faith Expression* (New York: Pueblo).

Schulz, H.-J. (2000), *Die Byzantinische Liturgie. Glaubenszeugnis und Symbolgestalt.* Dritte, völlig überarbeitete und aktualisierte Aufl. (Trier: Paulinus).

Sherrard, Ph. (1959), *The Greek East and the Latin West: A Study in the Christian Tradition* (Oxford: Oxford University Press).

Spáčil, Th. (1926), *Doctrina theologiae Orientis separati de sacramento baptismi.* Orientalia Christiana 25 [vol. VI–4] (Rome: Pont. Institutum Orientalium Studiorum).

Spáčil, Th. (1928–1929), *Doctrina theologiae Orientis separati de SS. Eucharistia.* 2 vols. Orientalia Christiana 48 [Vol. XIII–3] (Rome: Pont. Institutum Orientalium Studiorum).

Spáčil, Th. (1931), *Doctrina theologiae Orientis separati de sacra infirmorum unctione.* Orientalia Christiana 74 [Vol. XXIV–2] (Rome: Pont. Institutum Orientalium Studiorum).

Spáčil, Th. (1937), *Doctrina theologiae Orientis separati de sacramentis in genere.* Orientalia Christiana Analecta 113 (Rome: Pont. Institutum Orientalium Studiorum).

Spiteris, Y., and C. G. Conticello (2002), "Nicola Cabasilas Chamaetos," in C. G. Conticello and V. Conticello (eds.), *La théologie byzantine et sa tradition*, vol. 2: *(XIIIe-XIXe s.)* (Turnhout: Brepols), 315–410.

Taft, R. (1992), *The Byzantine Rite. A Short History* (Collegeville, MN: The Liturgical Press).

Taft, R. (1975), *The Great Entrance. A History of the Transfer of Gifts and Other Pre-Anaphoral Rites of the Liturgy of St John Chrysostom*. Orientalia Christiana Analecta 200 (Rome: Institutum Studiorum Orientalium).

Taft, R. (1987), "Water into Wine. The Twice-Mixed Chalice in the Byzantine Eucharist," *Le Muséon* 100: 323–342.

Taft, R. (1991–2008), *A History of the Liturgy of St John Chrysostom*, vol. 4: *The Diptychs* (1991); vol. 5: *The Precommunion Rites* (2000); vol. 6: *The Communion, Thanksgiving, and Concluding Rites* (2008) (Rome: Pont. Institutum Studiorum Orientalium).

Ware, K. (2005), "'Not an Image or a Figure': St Nicholas Cabasilas on the Eucharistic Sacrifice," in J. Getcha and M. Stavrou (eds.), *Le feu sur la terre: Mélanges offerts au Père Boris Bobrinskoy* (Paris: Presses Saint-Serge), 141–153.

Yannaras, Ch. (2006), *Orthodoxy and the West: Hellenic Identity in the Modern Age*, trans. P. Chamberas and N. Russell (Brooklyn, MA: Holy Cross Orthodox Press).

PART IV

FROM THE
REFORMATION
THROUGH TODAY

CHAPTER 18

....

SACRAMENTS IN THE
LUTHERAN REFORMATION

....

MICKEY L. MATTOX

THE Lutheran Reformation transformed all aspects of Christian life and experience in the regions where it was adopted, not least in the area of the sacraments. As opposed to the seven sacraments of the medieval Catholic Church, the Lutheran reformers quickly settled on only two: baptism and the Lord's Supper (Eucharist). Nevertheless, Lutheranism remained very much a sacramental religion in terms of the practices and piety surrounding these two central, Christian rites. Both the change and the continuity one finds in Lutheran sacramentalism have their origins in the life and thought of Martin Luther as it was carried through in the Lutheran confessional writings, in the various Lutheran church orders, and in Lutheran theology.

In spite of the changes brought to sacramental theology by the Lutheran reformers, their church practice was characterized by a vigorous and distinctive commitment to the sacraments as means of grace. Following the lead of Martin Luther, the Lutheran churches emphasized the lifelong validity of baptism, which was in the ordinary course of life to be received as an infant and afterwards persistently reclaimed as the sure ground of the believer's salvation, given from without. The Lutheran reformers also developed a distinctive eucharistic realism, which emphasized the regular reception of Christ's body and blood for the forgiveness of sin, the strengthening of faith, and as mystical participation in the church's risen Lord. Indeed, on the Lutheran account the church itself was instituted for the purpose not only of the right proclamation of the gospel, but also for the proper administration of the life-giving sacraments. If the gospel is about Christ, moreover, then so too are the sacraments. Indeed, Christ himself is the one true sacrament.

The Lutheran Reformation brought with it not only theological but also liturgical reforms. The latter entailed significant changes in the structure of the mass, as well as a new hymnody, much of it devoted to the sacraments, so that congregational singing functioned both to teach Lutheran sacramental theology and to deepen Christian experience (Brown 2008). While the Lutherans rejected five of the traditional sacraments, they nevertheless continued in modified form the practices of confirmation, of private confession, of Christian marriage, of ordination into the Church's ministry of Word and Sacrament, and of ministering the Lord's Supper to the sick and dying. Although these five important ritual actions were not understood as sacraments in the strict sense, orders for their administration were included in Lutheran church regulations and service books. Thus, in the Lutheran churches they remained decisively Christian practices that shaped the lives of countless Lutheran faithful. The Lutheran Reformation's critical reduction of the number of the sacraments did not, therefore, entail a reduction in the scope of Christian experience; still less was it intended as a first step in secularization. To the contrary, it was accompanied by a broad determination to more deeply Christianize both the individual experience of Christian faith and the Christian societies in which the Lutheran reforms were adopted (Hendrix 2004).

BACKGROUND

The Lutheran movement emerged during a difficult period in the church's history, and as a direct consequence of a crisis that was initially centered in the sacrament of penance. This crisis itself had extensive social and political, even military, implications, that multiplied the complexity of an already difficult set of theological questions. It is important, therefore, to recount some of this history in order to make clear the fundamentals of Lutheran sacramental theology and practice. The age during which Lutheranism's formative development occurred, moreover, was marked by a climate of extreme mutual vilification between the Lutherans and their opponents, on both the Catholic and on the Protestant sides. The controversies of these bygone times testify not only to theological division, but to a failure of the bond of Christian charity as well.

The Lutheran Reformation began with Martin Luther's proposal of a series of academic theses for debate concerning the sacrament of penance, and especially the church's practice of offering indulgences, on All Saints' Day in October 1517 (Brecht 1985: 190–202). Scholars have debated for a generation now the question whether the theses were actually posted on the door of Wittenberg's Castle Church, a story and an image that loom large in Lutheran lore (Lohse 1986: 42–4). It now seems likely, however, that Luther did something much less dramatic, and that his "Ninety-Five Theses" became an accidental overnight sensation when, quite without his permission, they were published and news of his objections to the practice of indulgences spread far beyond his native Saxony (Leppin 2007). In any case, the theses posed a series of difficult questions about a practice that was clearly open to abuse, and about which the church's critics, including Luther's later Catholic opponent Cardinal Cajetan, had frequently complained (Bagchi 2006). Is there a danger that indulgences can lead to a false sense of complacency in the Christian life? Does the pope's earthly jurisdiction over the faithful, as well as his exercise of the "office of the keys" (power to forgive sins based on Matthew 16), extend also beyond this life, even to the departed dead suffering in purgatory? Why spend money to buy one's way out of purgatory while the poor are still in need?

The most fundamental of Luther's objections to indulgences was arguably to be found in the first of the theses, where the pious young Augustinian professor of Bible insisted that the entire life of the Christian should be one of repentance. Jesus' exhortation to "repent and believe the gospel," in other words, meant not that the Christian should occasionally go to the sacrament of penance, but rather that the gospel itself should initiate the Christian into a new way of life whose central identifying mark is the humility of daily repentance (*Luther's Works* 31: 25). Luther may also have been motivated by pastoral concern that some simple Christians would be deceived by the benefits attached to some indulgences and so develop a false sense of security, one that would suggest they could afterwards avoid the hard work of this lifelong repentance.

There were good reasons for Luther's concerns. An indulgence being preached that year in nearby territories offered full ("plenary") remission of the punishments owing for sin (and thus from the torments of purgatory) based on a sliding contribution scale with an amount fit for everyone from the poorest peasant to the richest noble. This particular indulgence had been approved by Pope Leo X as a fund-raising program for Archbishop Albrecht of Brandenburg, who had recently added to his titles that of the archbishop of Mainz after he agreed to make a sizable contribution (21,000 ducats, borrowed from the Fugger banking house) to the Roman see based on the proceeds of a special indulgence sale (Brecht 1985: 175–183). Luther was unaware of these financial arrangements, but was deeply concerned with what he saw as the false promises and errant theology associated with indulgences. Again, Luther was hardly the first to express such concerns, but the controversy sparked by his theses soon set off a firestorm and inscribed the rejection of indulgences indelibly on his person.

The debate over indulgences between Luther and his many opponents expanded almost immediately to include the issue of authority, particularly that of the pope. In 1520, after a series of tense and personally threatening encounters with theologians representing, in one way or another, the Roman Church, Luther reached a crucial juncture. In 1517 Ulrich von Hutten (1488–1523), a knight of the lesser German nobility, brought into print for the first time a scandalous exposé written by the Italian scholar, Lorenzo Valla (1407–1457), *On the Donation of Constantine* (Whitford 2008). This work, which Valla himself had considered too dangerous to publish, demonstrated that the so-called "Donation" was, at best, a pious forgery. It purported to document the Emperor Constantine's gift to Pope Sylvester I of the imperial power, including "all provinces, localities and towns in Italy and the western hemisphere." The document, in short, made the papacy a secular power. Luther read Valla in February 1520, and as a consequence he became deeply suspicious of the Roman curia, particularly what he saw as their greed and lust for power. A new and more fundamental critique of the church's sacramental system, suffused with an undercurrent of apocalyptic outrage, soon followed.

In June 1520 Luther was threatened with excommunication in the papal bull *Exsurge Domine* (Brecht 1985: 389–396). He responded with a flurry of treatises. In August, his *Appeal to the Christian Nobility of the German Nation* asked the nobles to take charge of the reform of the churches in their territories on the basis of the priesthood given them in baptism. This appeal seemed in the eyes of representatives of the Roman Church to constitute little less than a handover of the church's own authority to the secular powers. In the light of the long medieval struggle regarding the "two swords" of ecclesiastical and secular power, moreover, it seemed a capitulation to everything the church had been struggling against for the past four centuries.

REFORMING THE SACRAMENTS

In October Luther published the ominously-titled *Prelude on the Babylonian Captivity of the Church*, an explosive and radically revisionist tract that called for a thoroughgoing reconfiguration of sacramental theology and practice, both of which he believed had been corrupted when they were integrated into a broad scheme of ecclesial revenue production in which fees and contributions were connected to sacramental graces. Although the *Babylonian Captivity* was written during a period of distinct religious and existential angst, and under the shadow of a growing apocalypticism, Luther's positions on the sacraments almost immediately became the abiding positions of the Lutheran tradition. Indeed, as one leading scholar puts it, in the *Babylonian Captivity* of 1520 we find the "final formulation of the Reformation understanding of the sacraments" (Brecht 1985: 380). Nevertheless, a good deal of development and controversy still lay ahead for Luther and his Lutheran followers, as they strove to fashion out of his original protest a durable theological and ecclesial tradition.

As reflected in the *Babylonian Captivity*, Luther's first steps were critical, even apocalyptic. Simony, he figured, had become nothing less than regular practice in the church, and the papal curia had given themselves over to unbridled greed. How else, he thought, could the church herself have come to persecute the very gospel for whose sake she had been founded? In the *Babylonian Captivity*, Luther argued for the reduction of the church's traditional seven sacraments, first to three (including penance), but finally to only two: baptism and the Lord's Supper. A crucial criterion for this reduction was institution by the Lord of the church, Jesus Christ, in association with a promise of grace. Wherever God deals graciously with humankind, Luther argued, he attaches a sign to the gift of grace. In the case of the covenant with Abraham, for example, God gave the sign of circumcision, while to the promise not to destroy the world again by a flood God attached the rainbow. Likewise, Jesus instituted both baptism and the Lord's Supper, Luther thought, as external signs of the grace and salvation he had promised through them. There was some theological precedent for Luther's argument for only two sacraments. In the medieval Latin tradition, for example, Peter Lombard's *Sentences* had allowed that one could distinguish the "sacramenta maiora," baptism and Eucharist, from the remaining "sacramenta minora." Even the two "major sacraments" Luther allowed to stand, however, required substantial theological and, eventually, ritual adjustment.

Sacraments Rejected

In the *Babylonian Captivity*, Luther flatly rejected five of the church's traditional sacraments. He did not deny their ritual importance, but he saw the church's elevation of these important rites to sacramental status as motivated by greed and a desire for control. In the case of penance, for example, he found private confession a helpful practice and commended it as such. However, he dismissed mandatory private confession to a priest on grounds that Christ in Matthew 18 had given to the faithful both individually and collectively the duty and power to assure one another of the forgiveness of sins. Confession to a brother or sister in the faith is therefore just as valid as confession to a priest, for by virtue of their baptism all Christians belong to the spiritual priesthood. Similarly he found that ordination had no instituted rite and divine promise. Instead, he found this "sacrament" an invention of the church, which, he argued, as a "creature of the Word," has no power to institute new sacraments. He also rejected arguments for an "indelible mark" on the priest's soul imparted in the rite of ordination. To be sure, Luther himself and the later Lutheran tradition would afterwards take care to underscore the necessity that a priest or pastor should be "rightly called" (*rite vocatus*) and ordained in order to carry out the public functions of the ministry, and even that this ministry was to be exercised "over against" the congregation of believers and not merely in their stead or, still less, at their command. No matter how necessary those functions might be, however, they did not understand installation into the public ministry as a sacrament through which the Lord had promised saving grace. Luther also criticized the "reservation" of the forgiveness of certain grave sins to the papacy, partly on grounds that this practice required the confessor to reveal the confessed sin to a superior.

He found further that confirmation and marriage, though commendable practices, did not have associated with them a divine promise. Hence, they lacked divine institution as a sacrament. Per Ephesians 5, however, he allowed that marriage is a "material allegory" of the love between Christ and the church. Significant adjustments, he thought, needed to be made to the traditional rules concerning proposed marriages between blood relations (i.e. consanguinity). Likewise he found no divine institution or related promise of grace in the prayer of anointing ("Last Rites"). Lutheran Christians would continue to live, and to die, as Christians, but they would not understand the church's ministrations to the dying, important though they surely were, as a sacrament in the strict sense.

Baptism

Baptism, on the other hand, was moved to the center of the Christian life. Already in the *Babylonian Captivity* Luther argued that it should be seen as a sacrament whose grace could never be "sinned away," not even through mortal sin. Its abiding validity meant that those who sinned away the Spirit could be restored to a state of grace through a repentance that led them not beyond baptism—as a "second plank after shipwreck," as Tertullian put it—but back to it, to grasp hold of it again in faith as the very source of their Christian life. The sacrament of penance, therefore, was not done away with but resolved into a return to the grace of baptism, which suggests why the practice of private confession, though no longer understood as a sacrament, remained vital within the Lutheran churches (Rittgers 2004). Luther's teaching in the following years remained remarkably consistent with these early pronounce-ments, but it was extended, applied, and further developed, particularly in his *Small* and *Large Catechisms*, as well as in the Lutheran confessional writings (Kolb and Wengert 2000).

In his own later work, Luther articulated a theology of baptism that made clear its deep continuity with the antecedent theological tradition, albeit with a number of dis-tinctive accents (Trigg 1994). Baptism is valid and effective, on Luther's account, because it is founded on God's own unbreakable word of promise, and it effects the forgiveness of sin. The faith of the Christian community gathered at baptism holds to God's word of promise, such that in the sacrament God conveys new life and regeneration in the Holy Spirit. Luther cites often and with satisfaction the traditional wisdom of Augustine that "when the word is added to the element it becomes a sacrament." Baptism thus has an objective validity in Luther's theology, regardless of his rejection of the medieval notion that the sacraments of the New Testament excel those of the Old Testament because they work not *ex opere operantis* but *ex opere operato*. To be sure, on Luther's account the faith of the baptizing church is necessary for the sacrament, as is the baptizand's own subjective appropriation of the gift of faith. To that extent in Luther's baptismal theol-ogy one finds an element of subjectivity, of cooperation, and even reciprocity. The work that is accomplished in the sacrament itself, however, is strictly divine, which means that the Christian can always look back on his or her own life as having begun and being perpetually established upon the firm ground of God's own word and work, alone. Baptism thus becomes the Christian's strongest bulwark against the dark night of the soul, when the devil tempts one to believe that her sins are too great, and that she will be lost. Against the demonic voices of temptation and despair one can ever turn, and return, to the gift of salvation given, one's present faults and failings notwithstanding, at the baptismal font.

The abiding significance of baptism, therefore, consists in its establishment in the Christian of that life of perpetual repentance mentioned so prominently in the Ninety-Five Theses. The true and daily repentance that marks authentic Christian existence therefore means nothing less than a return to baptism, and *ipso facto* a reappropriation of the grace once given. At the same time, however, baptism in Luther's theology also initiates a life of renewal, which is understood as one's daily putting to death of the "old Adam" in order that, in Christ, the "new Adam" might rise. In this sense, justification in Luther's theology already includes sanctification, as well as a recognition—indeed, an insistence—that the Christian life itself includes a Spirit-led dynamism that moves the believer ever forward toward holiness; toward, that is, the completion of the good work that was begun in one's baptism. This reality as a whole, moreover, is founded upon the sacrament and is therefore fully ecclesial. Consequently, the church with her preaching of the gospel and administration of the sacraments is the *sine qua non* of the Christian life as such. Much as one begins the life of faith in the gathered company of the faithful, so also that life is ever renewed and strengthened there. Return to baptism means return to church; both the church and her sacraments are necessary for salvation, for as Luther writes, "the church is the mother that begets and bears every Christian through the word" (Kolb and Wengert: 436).

In so far as Luther's baptismal theology is ecclesial, then, it is also communal. Indeed, Luther's sense of a communal Christian solidarity in this sacrament includes not only the here and now, but also the long tradition of Christian faith and faithfulness. Thus, in the *Large Catechism* (1529) Luther could look back to the church's own faith and tradition to prove the practice of infant baptism, a practice the Lutheran churches enthusiastically continued. Is infant baptism right and valid? Rather than turning to a series of biblical proof texts to answer this question, Luther instead appealed to the evident faith of those many great saints who were themselves baptized as infants. Can one doubt that, for example, St. Bernard had the Spirit? The Spirit is promised in baptism, moreover, so Bernard's infant baptism, together with those of a great host of other saints, must have been effective, particularly when one takes into account their clear and sometimes even heroic faith.

This aspect of Lutheran baptismal theology reminds us that in an era of rapid ecclesial change Lutheranism soon found itself in between the emerging confessional families, opposed on the one hand by Catholics and on the other hand by a developing array of the new Protestant traditions. The Anabaptists were prominent among the latter, and they generally held that baptism is an external rite that testifies to an internal change of heart, repentance, that can be expected only of those old enough to make a decision for or against faith. The Anabaptists rejected infant baptism, and for that and other reasons, particularly their refusal of oaths, they faced fearsome persecution from both Catholics and Protestants. Luther's continuation of the practice of infant baptism, in defense of which he himself would sometimes appeal to "infant faith" (Huovinen 1997), therefore reflects not only his deep theological satisfaction with the fact that the Christian life begins in utter helplessness, with a word of God that comes from without to claim and transform the believer, but also a hermeneutical approach to the reception of liturgical traditions that does not always ask whether a particular practice is clearly commanded in Scripture, but seeks rather to discern whether that practice coheres well with the faith and sacramental life clearly established in Holy Scripture. To this extent, the approach of the Lutheran Reformation to the broader nexus of ritual life and practice within which the sacraments themselves are embedded differs significantly from what is found in some other Protestant traditions, where, for example, only the psalter is to be sung in church, per scriptural injunction. Luther's more broadly affirming approach, where traditional practices may be retained so long as they are not forbidden by Scripture, alerts us to the fact that the Lutheran Reformation was not iconoclastic, either in its reception of ecclesial art and music or in its approach to sacramental life and practice. The resulting continuities between emerging Lutheran church life and that of the medieval Catholic tradition are striking, even if one recognizes that powerful, life-shaping changes were afoot as well.

The Lord's Supper

In the *Babylonian Captivity*, Luther argued that the Lord's Supper could be properly understood neither as a good work nor as a sacrifice that earned merit before God, but instead as the gracious action through which God offers the benefits of grace to the faithful through this, the last Testament of Christ: *beneficium, sed non sacrificium*. Luther complained, moreover, that the doctrine of transubstantiation purported to explain philosophically what should rather be left a mystery known only to faith, the true presence of Christ in his body and blood in the Lord's Supper. Why add the "miracle" of the annihilation of the bread and wine to the true and essential miracle of Christ's presence in the bread and cup? Nor could he find justification for the church's practice of withholding the cup from the laity. Communion in one kind, distributing the bread only, he argued, is inconsistent with the clear commands of Christ that participants should both "take and eat" and "take and drink." Nor, Luther thought, is it right to describe the mass as an *opus operatum*, because living faith, as in the case of baptism, is necessary for its worthy reception. It is not enough, he thought, to come to the sacrament unburdened by the obstacle of mortal sin. Rather, one ought to come in true and living faith, aware of what is to be offered and received.

In his later work, particularly his two catechisms, however, Luther was pressed not to allow proper subjective preparation for the sacrament to overwhelm its de facto reality, even apart from subjective faith. Thus, he defended the reality and objectivity of the sacramental presence of Christ on the basis of Christ's own words of promise. The sacrament offers and all who participate—the worthy and the unworthy alike—receive the true body and blood of Jesus Christ. Nevertheless, as in the sacrament of baptism he continued to insist on subjective faith, not as the means of making Christ present, but as requisite for "worthy" reception of the sacrament, that is, for life and salvation. Indeed, on Luther's account the "sacrament of the Altar" offers the forgiveness of sins. Just as Christ poured out his body and blood on the cross to effect the forgiveness of sin, so here he does the same. All who receive the sacrament thus receive its benefits. This sacrament, moreover, strengthens faith and in just that way nurtures the life of faith. Luther also urges frequent reception of communion, for only a faith strengthened by the true body and blood is fit to carry on the daily struggle against the old Adam. The life of repentance and renewal depends vitally on the most effective presence of the saving Christ, given in the Lord's Supper.

Luther's understanding of the Lord's Supper met opposition, however, not only from Catholics but also from other church reformers. In April 1521, not long after his excommunication in January 1521, and only a few months after the *Babylonian Captivity*, Luther appeared before the Imperial Congress ("Diet"), meeting under the leadership of the newly crowned emperor, Charles V. A few days afterward, the congress issued the Edict of Worms, which declared Luther an outlaw and heretic and forced him into hiding at the Wartburg Castle under the protection of his prince, Frederick the Wise. Back in Wittenberg, however, church reform continued, now under the leadership of Luther's colleague, the theologian Andreas Bodenstein von Karlstadt (1486–1541). Karlstadt's vision for reform was at once more radical and more spiritualistic than that of Luther, and in that respect he had much in common with the so-called "Zwickau Prophets," three visionary reformers who emphasized the direct inspiration of the Holy Spirit. For his part, Karlstadt thought that massive liturgical reform was mandated by divine law. With the agreement of the city council some of these reforms were instituted, and social unrest, including episodes of iconoclasm, soon resulted. These "radical" approaches to reform helped set Luther on a more moderate path (Brecht 1990: 34–38). In early 1522 he returned to Wittenberg where he took up the mantle of leadership, stilled the social unrest, and instituted a more measured pace of reform in which liturgical change was understood as a matter of evangelical freedom.

Thus Luther found himself throughout the 1520s at the center of sacramental controversies, and for the most part they had to do with church reformers who urged more radical approaches. Luther and most of these other reformers agreed broadly that baptism and the Lord's Supper are the two valid sacraments. Where Luther affirmed the true presence of Christ's body and blood in the Lord's Supper, however, others adopted a spiritualist doctrine derived in different ways from both St. Augustine and the humanist scholar, Desiderius Erasmus of Rotterdam (1466–1536). In a few short years the controversy between Luther and the Swiss exploded into a pamphlet war, primarily between Luther and Zwingli. In a short time, moreover, it became apparent that the controversy over the Lord's Supper had profound and potentially divisive consequences in Christology. Zurich's Ulrich Zwingli was an original and independent church reformer, who had also opposed indulgences. He articulated a spiritual memorialism, which, as noted above, seems to have been derived in roughly equal parts from both St. Augustine ("believe and thou hast eaten") and Erasmus' *philosophia Christi*, which was rather deeply indebted to a broadly Platonist dualism. Luther, on the other hand, defended the reality of the sacrament as Christ's very body and blood. The particulars of the inner-Protestant controversy over this sacrament are important, for they reveal the depth of the Lutheran commitment to "real presence" and, more specifically, the dense network of connections between Lutheran Christology and eucharistic theology.

In this matter, the interpretation of John 6 was crucial. Luther argued that this text could not be understood as applying to the Lord's Supper. Zwingli and his followers, however, seized on Christ's words there that "the flesh profits nothing" to advance their view that what matters in the Supper is that believing hearts together feed on Christ in the Holy Spirit. The presence of Christ as they understood it is brought to the Supper, internally, within the hearts of the faithful rather than received by them, externally, from the hands of the minister. The Zwinglian side in this controversy was also deeply impressed by a letter written by Cornelius Hoen (*c.* 1521), which, borrowing significantly from Hussite eucharistic teaching, offered a thoroughgoing critique of Catholic eucharistic theology (Oberman 1966: 268–278; Burnett 2011: 83–90). Perhaps most importantly, Hoen argued that the verb in the crucial words of institution, the Latin "est" in the phrase *hoc est corpus meum*, should not be taken literally. Instead, it should be understood with the Latin *significat*, as in "this *signifies* my body … my blood." Zwingli was joined in his efforts by the capable humanist and reformer of Basel, Johannes Oecolampadius (1482–1531), who sought through his knowledge of the church fathers to demonstrate that the Zwinglian understanding was consistent with the ancient faith.

In a word, Zwingli and Oecolampadius saw the Lord's Supper as a memorial meal, one that commemorates but does not celebrate. They rejected, in other words, not only eucharistic sacrifice, as per the *Babylonian Captivity*, but also eucharistic presence. A crucial problem here was the humanity of Christ. His true humanity, these reformers argued, requires a body like ours in every way, which includes its finitude in regard to space and time. If Christ's humanity, including his body and blood, is really like our own, then it cannot be in more than one place at one time. These reformers therefore rejected any realistic understanding of the Lord's Supper. There is no elemental change (*metabole*) in the bread and wine of the Lord's Supper, and those who insist that there is come perilously close to the sin of idolatry when and if they venerate the Christ supposedly present in the eucharistic bread and cup (*artolatreia*).

Luther reacted explosively to these claims, so much so that it left observers, then and now, at some pains to understand why. It seems that for Luther, whose spiritual geography had no middle ground, the Swiss were simply "Sacramentarians," that is, unbelievers who denied the efficacy of the external means of grace. Thus, after they met at the failed Marburg Colloquy in 1529 Luther seemed to dismiss Zwingli: "[H]e has another spirit." Luther's point seems to have been that Zwingli and his followers were rationalizers who were unwilling to attend to the plain sense of the Bible. More importantly Luther believed that the status of the sacraments as the external and unique means of saving grace were at stake in this controversy. Put differently, on Luther's understanding Zwinglian spiritualism eventually cuts the believer off from the objective word and promise of grace that comes from "outside us" (*extra nos*), in the external word and sacraments. One is forced, therefore, to turn inward in a subjective search for grace and assurance, which on account of sin must remain ever elusive apart from the external sacraments. Whereas for Zwingli the Holy Spirit needs no means, for Luther the Spirit employs the very means God has ordained, drawing us to Christ's true body and blood, which are to be found precisely where the Lord in his own words has promised them to be: in the church, at the table, and in the bread and the cup. When we add to that, moreover, Luther's clear teaching that the Spirit leads us to Christ in order to show us the Father's heart then we are in a position to appreciate the Trinitarian shape of his theology of the Lord's Supper, which gave due attention to the internal, subjective side of the sacrament even while insisting upon its visible and external side too, where the consecrated elements become the "visible words" of God.

Just one year after Marburg, the Lutheran reformers under the theological leadership of Luther's younger colleague Philip Melanchthon offered a theological explanation of the reforms undertaken in Lutheran territories to the Imperial Congress gathered in the German city of Augsburg. This "Augsburg Confession" of the faith submitted by the reforming Protestant princes subsequently became one of the definitive "confessional" statements of the Lutheran Reformation, even though it was rejected by the congress. The emperor ordered a confutation from the Roman side, which on the subject of the Lord's Supper offered a lukewarm affirmation of the Lutheran teaching that in the bread and cup the body and blood are "truly and substantially present." At the same time, it also criticized the Lutherans for avoiding the doctrine of concomitance, which had been used to defend the Catholic practice of communion in "one kind," that is, the distribution to the faithful of the bread only, with the understanding that the body and blood of Christ are truly and equally present under either of the eucharistic species (Kolb and Nestingen 2001: 112). By the end of 1530, then, the Lutheran reformers found themselves positioned somewhat uncomfortably between the spiritualizing reformers of South Germany and Switzerland, and the Catholic defenders of the "old faith." This situation persisted throughout the Reformation period, and it led eventually to the reification of intra-Protestant theological difference into two competing "magisterial" traditions, the Lutheran and the Reformed.

Returning once again to the argument with the Swiss reformers, Luther found himself in the mid- to later 1520s at pains to explain how it was possible that Christ's body and blood could at the same time be both truly human (per the definition of Chalcedon) and present on many altars at one and the same time. He agreed fully with the biblical and creedal assertion that after the Ascension Jesus Christ is "seated at the right hand of the Father," which Zwingli had urged as proof that the humanity of Christ was locally circumscribed and for that reason could not be present at the altar. Luther rejected that claim, arguing that the Father's "right hand" is clearly a metaphor for a position of power and honor. The Father, after all, has not become enfleshed and therefore has no "right hand." To explain the true presence of Christ's body and blood, however, he made a rather elaborate appeal to Christology, particularly the communication of attributes (*communicatio idiomatum*). Christ's humanity, he argued, takes on certain attributes of divinity by virtue of its union with deity in the one Person, including that of ubiquity. Christ's body and blood, in short, are everywhere after the manner of God's own presence, that is, in a way that is not merely local—as in "that thing over there"—nor even angelic—a spiritual as opposed to a physical presence, or perhaps a multi-presence—but rather "repletive," that is, after the very manner in which God fills all things and yet cannot be reduced to them. The fullness of the divine presence is therefore a property, which although it does not belong properly to Christ's humanity is nevertheless communicated to it by virtue of the union with deity in the one Person, Christ the Lord. As proof for the qualitative changes the union effects in Christ's human body, Luther would appeal to biblical texts that seemed to portray the human body of Christ doing things that would be impossible for any other human body, most notably entering a room without using the door (see John 20).

This very presence is offered and received, in a mystical way, in the Lord's Supper. Pressed to explain why one needed to turn to the Lord's Supper to participate in Christ, since all of him was apparently present everywhere all of the time, Luther had recourse to the divine institution of the sacrament. Although Christ in his body and blood is indeed everywhere, he has promised to be present in a saving way only in and through the sacrament. Luther distinguished, in other words, between a divine omnipresence of Christ's body and blood that remains without saving effect, and the saving presence effected, per God's ordination, only within the Lord's Supper. The Lutheran theological tradition generally embraced Luther's notion that the humanity of Christ shares in the properties of divinity through the personal union, a genus of the communication of attributes that was soon labeled "majestic" (*genus maiestaticum*), because it entailed the humanity's participation in the divine rule over all things. Lutherans never formally committed themselves to Luther's understanding of ubiquity, however, although Lutheran theologians frequently defended it, including, in modified form, both Johannes Brenz and Martin Chemnitz. And in the seventeenth century Christology in relation to the *genus maiestaticum* became the source of the "kenosis controversy" (see Phil 2) in which the Lutheran faculties at Giessen and Tübingen argued over the exercise of Christ's kingly rule in the incarnation. Did Christ merely abstain from the exercise of his kingly rule over the creation in and through his humanity during the period of his humiliation (that is, from Bethlehem to Golgotha), or did he continue to exercise that rule even during that time, but in a hidden way? These questions suggest some of the important trajectories in Christology that would emerge from the Lutheran tradition, forged in its fundamentals in the eucharistic controversies of the early sixteenth century.

To be sure, the possibility of a united Protestant front against Rome did emerge briefly at the time of the Reformation, after a rapprochement between Lutheran and the Swiss and south German reformers on the Lord's Supper was codified in the Wittenberg Concord of 1536. Crafted long after both Zwingli and Oecolampadius were dead, this ecumenical agreement brought Luther's opponents well into the orbit of his eucharistic theology. The signers of the Concord, including Wolfgang Capito and Martin Bucer, agreed that "when the bread is distributed at the same time the body of Christ is present and truly offered" (Kittelson and Schurb: 125). This phraseology was understood to indicate that Christ was truly present in the bread while in the hands of the minister (that is, before its reception in the mouth of the communicant). In addition, the Concord affirmed that the "unworthy" also receive the true body and blood, a point that remained neuralgic among the Swiss. Within a few short years, however, this agreement unraveled under pressure from such opponents as Heinrich Bullinger in Zurich. Ecumenical agreement proved elusive for the Lutheran and the Reformed.

Turning now to the practice of the Lord's Supper, Luther and his followers emphatically rejected the reservation or use of the sacramental elements beyond the sacramental rite itself. Thus, there was to be no "tabernacling" or reservation of the sacrament, still less any monstrances or Corpus Christi processions. Instead, the bread and the wine were to be entirely consumed by those present for the mass. The Lutheran rejection of the so-called "private masses," moreover, where a priest celebrates mass without the congregation present, meant that there should never be consecrated elements without a congregation present to consume them. The Lutheran Reformation thus seemed to restrict sacramental activity rather insistently within the church walls.

Though these ritual changes may seem like a mere footnote to the theological controversies described above, in fact such rules stand at an important intersection between what goes on in the church and what happens elsewhere. This is where church ritual meets the Christian people, that is, outside the church walls. The cultural historian Robert Scribner has drawn attention to the dense connections between "official" and "popular" religion in the region of the church's sacraments and liturgy in the early Reformation (Scribner 1987). In the later Middle Ages, he argued, the lines between the church's liturgy and what he called "folklorised ritual" were quite permeable. The exhibition of the sacrament in ritual processions outside the church bled quite naturally over into the application of sacred objects elsewhere: "Consecrated hosts could be used as love magic, for example, or scattered over a farm field to ensure agricultural fertility" (Scribner 1987: 36). The "sacramentals" (blessed objects such as palm branches and holy water), moreover, reduced even further the distance between the otherworldly power of the church and a magical view of the natural order. Protestant polemics frequently targeted such "superstitions." To the extent that Protestant theology emphasized the theocentric and monergistic elements of eucharistic practice—turning the Mass into a one-way street, understood as a benefit from God, but not a human sacrifice to God—just so, per Scribner, the reformers sometimes seemed intent on desacralizing the natural world. On the other hand, profoundly "Christianizing" trajectories were deeply embedded within Protestant catechesis, hymnody, and church life. Reformers like Luther wanted the average Christian to see her life as more, not less, an arena of divine activity and demonic opposition. The Lutheran Reformation thus brought new ways of understanding how the sacred was manifested in the profane, not a denial of that manifestation. To that extent, the transition between the sacramental religion of the later Middle Ages and that of the Lutheran Reformation is more subtle and elusive than our theological categories would sometimes suggest.

Suggested Reading

H. G. Haile (1978); R. Kolb and T. J. Wengert (2000); E. Schlink (1961); E. W. Zeeden (2012).

Bibliography

Bagchi, D. V. N. (2006), "Luther's *Ninety-Five Theses* and the Contemporary Criticism of Indulgences," in R. N. Swanson (ed.), *Promissory Notes on the Treasury of Merits: Indulgences in Late Medieval Europe* (Leiden: Brill), 331–355.

Brecht, M. (1985) *Martin Luther*, vol. 1: *His Road to Reformation 1483–1521* (Minneapolis, MN: Augsburg Fortress).

Brecht, M. (1990) *Martin Luther*, vol. 2: *Shaping and Defining the Reformation, 1521–1532* (Minneapolis, MN: Augsburg Fortress).

Brown, C. B. (2008), "Devotional Life, in Hymns, Liturgy, Music, and Prayers," in R. Kolb (ed.), *Lutheran Ecclesiastical Culture, 1550–1675* (Leiden: Brill), 205–258.

Burnett, A. N. (2011), *Karlstadt and the Origins of the Eucharistic Controversy: A Study in the Circulation of Ideas* (New York: Oxford University Press).

Haile, H. G. (1978), *Luther: An Experiment in Biography* (New York: Doubleday).

Hendrix, S. H. (2004), *Recultivating the Vineyard: The Reformation Agendas of Christianization* (Louisville, KY: Westminster John Knox).

Huovinen, E. (1997), *Fides Infantium: Martin Luthers Lehre vom Kinderglauben* (Mainz: Philipp von Zabern).

Kittelson, J. M. and K. Schurb (1986), "The Curious Histories of the Wittenberg Concord," *Concordia Theological Quarterly* 50 2: 119–138.

Kolb, R. and J. A. Nestingen (Eds.) (2001), *Sources and Contexts of the Book of Concord* (Minneapolis, MN: Fortress Press).

Kolb, R. and T. J. Wengert (Eds.) (2000), *The Book of Concord: The Confessions of the Evangelical Lutheran Church* (Minneapolis, MN: Fortress Press).

Luther, M. (1955–86), *Luther's Works* (Philadelphia, PA and St. Louis, MO: Fortress Press and Concordia Publishing House). [For the sacraments, see especially vols. 35–38.]

Mattox, M. L. (2003), "Offered and Received: Lutheran Theology and Practice of the Eucharist," *Lutheran Forum* 37 2: 33–44.

Oberman, H. A. (1966), *Forerunners of the Reformation* (New York: Holt, Rinehart & Winston).

Rittgers, R. (2004), *The Reformation of the Keys: Confession, Conscience and Authority in Sixteenth Century Germany* (Cambridge, MA: Harvard University Press).

Schlink, E. (1961), *Theology of the Lutheran Confessions* (Philadelphia, PA: Fortress).

Scribner, R. W. (1987), "Ritual and Popular Belief in Catholic Germany at the Time of the Reformation," in *Popular Culture and Popular Movements in Reformation Germany* (London and Ronceverte: The Hambledon Press), 47–77.

Trigg, J. D. (1994), *Baptism in the Theology of Martin Luther* (Leiden: Brill).

Whitford, D. M. (2004), "*Cura Religionis* or Two Kingdoms: The Late Luther on Religion and the State in the Lectures on Genesis," *Church History* 73 1: 41–62.

Zeeden, E. W. (2012), *Faith and Act: Medieval and Lutheran Practices Compared* (St. Louis, MO: Concordia Publishing House).

CHAPTER 19

....

SACRAMENTS IN
THE REFORMED AND
ANGLICAN REFORMATION

....

MICHAEL ALLEN

WHATEVER else one makes of the Protestant Reformation—and much has been made of it, ranging from political to economic interpretations and back again—it was first and foremost about worship. Luther, Zwingli, and their compatriots confessed that the worship of the Roman Church was not consonant with the gospel of Jesus Christ. When Reformers began to challenge Rome, more often than not they pointed to liturgical deficiencies as their presenting concerns. The Ninety-Five Theses of Luther largely addressed worship and sacramental practices. When Reformers were excommunicated from the Roman Church, their first reforms in Protestant churches were invariably revised liturgies. If the classic formula *lex orandi, lex credendi* holds true, then the realm of reform must also be the realm of prayer. And so it was with the Reformed Reformation: it began and ended with a concern to see worship and the sacramental life of the church, in particular, brought under the discipline of the gospel.

The Reformation has frequently been mischaracterized as a movement toward individual autonomy: removing the authority of the pope and replacing him with a million popes (Gregory 2012). The emphasis upon biblical authority and the priesthood of all believers, of course, can seem to underwrite such charges. Yet the Reformed wing of the Protestant Reformation sought to emphasize its ecclesial character in multiple ways. Reformed theologians made a concerted effort to argue not only on the basis of Holy Scripture, but also through the voices of the Church Fathers (Lane 1999; Chung-Kim 2011). Another method by which the Reformed churches sought to emphasize their ecclesial character was by the frequent preparation of and the constant employment of confessional statements.

Therefore, our analysis of the sacraments in the Reformed and Anglican Reformation will focus not on the theological accounts of their most accomplished pastor-theologians or professors, but will offer commentary upon their confessional statements. It will not be surprising that major theological themes of the Reformation—such as the Word of God, grace, or faith—will be woven through our exposition, precisely because these confessional statements seek to describe the sacramental life of the church amidst the economy of the gospel. Talk of elements, practices, and officers occurs only within the wider context of God's generosity: "the gifts of God for the people of God."

A word about the inclusion of Anglican confessions within this chapter on the Reformed Reformation is in place. The Anglican Communion at present includes various sacramental theologies, which range from the evangelical to the high church Anglo-Catholic. But there is no denying the Reformed character of the sixteenth-century confessional writings of the Church of England. While Anglicanism today may have become broader, the Church of England in the sixteenth century reformed her sacramental practice into a decidedly Reformed approach. Indeed, the very tensions of the Elizabethan period and the Puritan era managed to sustain such a long conversation (filled with both tensions and peace), precisely because they occurred amidst a broader commitment to a Reformed sacramental theology. Debates ensued as to when reform of worship had gone far enough—the Puritans pushing further, Elizabeth settling for a more moderate approach—but no one doubted that the Reformed insistence on disciplining worship according to the gospel was essential for the Church of England.

This chapter makes no normative claims regarding the worship and theology of the present-day Anglican Communion. To do so would require a host of other questions being addressed. Indeed, this chapter does not even directly address the continuing relevance of the Reformed confessions for Reformed churches in the twenty-first century. But it does suggest that renewal of sacramental theology is likely to occur only when genuine retrieval is a lived experience. Reformed and Anglican churches alike would do well to refamiliarize themselves with their Reformational beginnings (as well as, it should be added, with their earlier catholic heritage). For the sake of renewal through retrieval, I will offer commentary on Reformed and Anglican confessional statements as they address the two sacraments: baptism and Eucharist. These contested areas of sacramental theology will be considered following an initial focus upon the question of authority. The chapter will conclude by returning to the material concern of the Reformed Reformation—the doctrine of grace—and an analysis of its operative effect upon sacramental faith and practice. In so doing we will see that the primary concern of the Reformed confessions in the sixteenth century was to realign sacramental practice with the shape of the gospel economy.

Authority

The Reformed and Anglican Reformation was centered upon the Word of God. Indeed, the first of the Ten Theses of Berne states its operative principle well: "The holy, Christian Church, whose only Head is Christ, is born of the Word of God, abides in the same, and does not listen to the voice of a stranger" (Cochrane 2003: 49). There is a corollary that follows: "The Church of Christ makes no laws or commandments without God's Word. Hence all human traditions, which are called ecclesiastical commandments, are binding upon us only in so far as they are based on and commanded by God's Word" (Cochrane 2003: 49; see also the Scottish Confession of Faith [1560], chapter 18, in Cochrane 2003: 177). The Thirty-Nine Articles specifically states in its eighth article that the ecumenical creeds are to be received, but only because "they may be proved by most certain warrants of Holy Scripture" (Leith 1982: 269). Huldrych Zwingli spoke for the Reformed churches when he confessed: "In the Gospel we learn that human doctrines and traditions are of no avail to salvation" (Cochrane 2003: 37). "Human traditions" serves as a marker throughout Reformed confessions for errant innovations that run contrary to scriptural wisdom and Christ's lordship of his church.

Not all tradition was overthrown in such reforms, of course, for much of the catholic heritage of the church was viewed as being entirely consonant with the biblical witness. Heiko Oberman has spoken of two conceptions of tradition—Tradition 1 and Tradition 2—that marked the medieval scene (Oberman 1983: 371–372): according to his scheme, the Reformed confessions strongly endorsed Tradition 1, wherein tradition was an essential and important component of the church's life, though it was always under the final authority of Christ's written Word. While Rome affirmed Tradition 2 and the possibility of conciliar or papal authority in something like a two-source theory of revelation, the Reformers insisted that the church must exercise conciliar or ministerial authority only under biblical authority; hence, ecclesial authority was always termed ministerial rather than magisterial. But such authority and the development of traditions in the church, therefore, must be exercised. Indeed the church had to wisely institute certain practices for her discipline and peace. The Genevan Confession of 1536 addresses such realities in its seventeenth article, on "human traditions": "The ordinances that are necessary for the internal discipline of the Church, and belong solely to the maintenance of peace, honesty and good order in the assembly of Christians, we do not hold to be human traditions at all." These ordinances are then identified with Paul's command to operate decently and in order (1 Cor 14:40). Eventually some Puritans would oppose some of these practices, but they were upheld by many Reformed churches in the sixteenth century (see also the Tetrapolitan Confession of 1530, ch. 14, in Cochrane 2003: 71–72). The Genevan Confession does not treat such ordinances as merely "human traditions" but as necessary and proper extensions of biblical teaching and scriptural wisdom. Yet it does distinguish such good traditioning from its illegitimate child: "all laws and regulations made binding on conscience which oblige the faithful to things not commanded by God, or establish another service of God than that which he demands, thus tending to destroy Christian liberty, we condemn as perverse doctrines of Satan" (Cochrane 2003: 124).

The Reformed approach to faith and practice did not involve a purported return to pristine conditions. While at times various Reformers did refer to more recent eras (and, sometimes, large swathes of the medieval era) as periods of darkness, they did not in so doing suggest that the patristic or even first-century church figured as a pure era to which they should return. According to Amy Plantinga Pauw, "a Reformed narrative of the church has no Eden. The church on earth has always existed 'after the fall,'" so that "Reformed ecclesiology is marked by a stark recognition of the church's fallibility." This is not merely a belief about the present *status quo*, either; rather, "because there is no Edenic church, Reformed theology rejects restorationist wistfulness for pre-Constantinian or premodern forms of ecclesial existence" (Plantinga Pauw 2006: 189, 190). Pauw's reflections surely fit with the accounts found in Luther's *On the Councils and the Church*, Calvin's *Institutes of the Christian Religion*, as well as other notable works by Bucer, Vermigli, and others.

The authority of Scripture, when applied to sacramental theology, first required a renewed focus upon the institution of sacraments. Sacraments required divine mandate. The First Confession of Basel (1534) proclaimed that "we confess that just as no one may require things which Christ has not commanded, so in the same way no one may forbid what He has not forbidden … Still less may anyone permit what God has forbidden" (Cochrane 2003: 95; see also the Lausanne Articles [1536], art. 7, in Cochrane 2003: 116). The crucial issue here and in other confessions is to follow what Christ has pledged. The Scottish Confession of Faith (1560) makes the matter plain in its discussion of the sacraments (ch. 21): "we have two chief sacraments, which alone were instituted by the Lord Jesus and commanded to be used by all who will be counted members of His body, that is, Baptism and the Supper" (Cochrane 2003: 179). Two criteria are highlighted: a sacrament must be (1) expressly instituted by Jesus and (2) commanded of all Christians.

If the institution of sacraments is recalibrated, then it is not surprising that the number of sacraments is rethought as well. The Geneva Confession of 1536 articulates this clearly in its fourteenth article: "Of them there are in the Christian Church only two which are instituted by the authority of our Saviour: Baptism and the Supper of our Lord; for what is held within the realm of the pope concerning seven sacraments, we condemn as fable and lie" (Cochrane 2003: 123). The Belgic Confession of Faith (1561) addresses the number of sacraments in its thirty-third article: "Moreover, we are satisfied with the number of Sacraments which Christ our Lord hath instituted, which are two only, namely, the Sacrament of Baptism, and the Holy Supper of our Lord Jesus Christ" (Cochrane 2003: 213). Note that the confession makes this a spiritual matter: they claim to be "satisfied" with the direction and provision of Jesus in instituting two and no more sacraments. This is a moral and fiduciary claim: those who strive and stretch for further sacramental practices are in so doing failing to trust the Lord.

The Reformed and Anglican churches were not opposed in every respect to the other five purported sacraments of Rome: confirmation, ordination, marriage, anointing of the sick, and penance. They did express concerns about the way in which such practices were performed, such as the sale of indulgences for the remission of sins. About such practices, Zwingli confessed: "Whoever remits sins solely for the sake of money is the partner of Simon and Balaam and is really a messenger of the devil" (Cochrane 2003: 42). And they did dispute the meaning which some were believed to carry. Zwingli insists that "confession which is made to a priest or to a neighbor is not for the remission of sins, but for counselling" and "imposed works of penance stem from human counsel (with the exception of excommunication). They do not remit sin and are imposed to warn others" (Cochrane 2003: 42). The Second Helvetic Confession (1566) makes plain that repentance, ordination, and marriage are "profitable ordinances of God, but not sacraments"; it goes on to deny such "profitable" status to confirmation and extreme unction, instead calling them "human inventions which the Church can dispense with without any loss" (ch. 19 in Cochrane 2003: 277; see also art. 25 in the Thirty-Nine Articles in Leith 1982: 274–275). Yet the Reformed churches continued to marry and ordain, to confess sin, and to minister to ailing and dying saints, as well as to anoint the sick. They did not practice each of these rites in the Roman form, and they did not believe these rites were commanded by Jesus Christ for each and every Christian. The twofold criterion mentioned explicitly in the Scottish Confession of Faith (1560) was upheld: sacraments are (1) explicitly instituted by Christ and (2) commanded for all Christians. Many disciplines and rites are useful in the church, but only two sacraments are given for the people of God.

Baptism

Jesus Christ instituted the sacrament of baptism, as attested in the words of the apostles. The Second Helvetic Confession points to its institution:

> Baptism was instituted and consecrated by God. First John baptized, who dipped Christ in the water in Jordan. From him it came to the apostles, who also baptized with water. The Lord expressly commanded them to preach the Gospel and to baptize "in the name of the Father and of the Son and of the Holy Spirit" (Matt. 28:19). And in the Acts, Peter said to the Jews who inquired what they ought to do: "Be baptized every one of you in the name of Jesus Christ for the forgiveness of your sins; and you shall receive the gift of the Holy Spirit" (Acts 2:37f). (Cochrane 2003: 140–141)

Baptism replaces circumcision. The Second Helvetic Confession states that the "sacraments of the old people are surely abrogated and have ceased," while "in their stead the symbols of the New Testament are placed—Baptism in the place of circumcision" (Cochrane 2003: 279). Replacement terminology can be somewhat misleading when one takes these confessional terms into account. The Reformed churches viewed baptism as the typological fulfillment of circumcision: it summed up circumcision rather than superseding it. Indeed Hughes Old has shown the frequency of typological exegesis of the Old Testament in early defenses of infant baptism; this was a hermeneutical debate between the Reformed and the Anabaptists (Old 1992: 120–122). While Johannes Oecolampadius later marshaled patristic argument on behalf of infant baptism, the initial defense offered by Zwingli was entirely exegetical (employing humanistic literary study) and insisted on reading the Hebrew Scriptures in light of their principle of corporate solidarity (Old 1992: 118, 120).

Baptism was termed "Holy Baptism" precisely because it assures one of their purity in Christ. The Heidelberg Catechism, constantly focused upon the issue of assurance (remember that its first question speaks to our "comfort in life and death"), is indicative of this concern:

> Q. 69. How does holy Baptism remind and assure you that the one sacrifice of Christ on the cross avails for you?
>
> A. In this way: Christ has instituted this external washing with water and by it has promised that I am as certainly washed with his blood and Spirit from the uncleanness of my soul and from all my sins, as I am washed externally with water which is used to remove the dirt from my body. (Cochrane 2003: 317)

The symbolic action presents divine testimony. The Geneva Confession of 1536 attests to this function in its fifteenth chapter: "Baptism is an external sign by which our Lord testifies that he desires to receive us for his children, as members of his Son Jesus. Hence in it there is represented to us the cleansing from sin which we have in the blood of Jesus Christ, the mortification of our flesh which we have by his death that we may live in him by his Spirit" (Cochrane 2003: 123–124). The confession clearly picks up on the Augustinian tendency to identify sacraments as visible words: here an "external sign" is a means through which the "Lord testifies." There is much "represented" as well: of cleansing, of mortification, of our new life in the Spirit.

The meaning of the baptismal rite is regularly tied to adoption and exposited by means of mortification and vivification. As seen above, the Geneva Confession of 1536 declares that baptism "testifies that he [God] desires to receive us for his children, as members of his Son Jesus." Later, under the influence of Calvin, the French Confession of Faith (1559) would highlight the same truth as its governing principle for understanding baptism: "baptism is given as a pledge of our adoption; for by it we are grafted into the body of Christ, so as to be washed and cleansed by his blood, and then renewed in purity of life by his Holy Spirit" (art. 35 in Cochrane 2003: 156). The French Confession links adoption with engrafting to the body of Christ, as does the Geneva Confession (see also the Thirty-Nine Articles, ch. 27, in Leith 1983: 276). Both then also extend this union to mention its two benefits: justification and sanctification. Indeed, the "lasting witness" of baptism that "reaches over our whole lives and to our death," according to the French Confession, is that "Jesus Christ will always be our justification and sanctification."

While some confessions focus largely upon death and justification/forgiveness with respect to baptism (see ch. 21 of the Scottish Confession of Faith [1559] in Cochrane 2003: 179), the confessions regularly look to the wider orbit of the gospel, addressing the experience of death and resurrection/new life in Christ and in light of the twofold description in Acts 2:37, where forgiveness of sins in Christ is paired with the transformative gift of the Holy Spirit. There is an order, of course, but there is also a pairing: while one must die before being raised anew, still such news can only be gospel (that is, good news) if resurrection does follow death. This sort of soteriological reflection is most notably found in Calvin's theology, where he speaks of the "double grace" (*duplex gratia*) enjoyed in union with Christ. Interestingly, it is a fixture of widespread Reformed teaching on baptism (which is not to say necessarily that Calvin is the source or chief influence of all such confessions).

Baptism was not strictly identified with adoption. It was also a sign and seal. There is a coordinated relationship that involves genuine communication without moving into the realm of confusion. Zwingli employed a distinction between the internal and external work of God to affirm this distinction; while he has frequently been taken as beholden to a Platonic philosophy here, he does not wish this distinction to be defined as a spiritual and material dichotomy. Rather, internal and external description is meant to highlight the divine and human agency involved in baptism. God commands human, external action in baptizing a person, and this agency symbolizes and seals God's own agency in uniting them to Christ, though it is strictly speaking a different agency (Zwingli 2006: 131, 137, 154, 163). Others, from the Calvinian tradition or those even further from Zwingli's influence, might employ other means: whereas Zwingli would deny that the "thing signified" is in the sacrament (Zwingli 2006: 131), the Second Helvetic Confession explicitly attests that the sacrament consists of "the word, the sign, and the thing signified" (ch. 19 in Cochrane 2003: 279). Nevertheless, the common concern to distinguish between the physical act and its spiritual concomitant is consistent across the confessions. This distinction helped underwrite polemic against Roman Catholic teaching that baptism remits the guilt of original sin (see ch. 15 of the Belgic Confession of Faith in Cochrane 2003: 199). Regeneration is symbolized in baptism, though it need not necessarily occur at that particular moment.

Debates were brought into the Reformed churches regarding the appropriate recipients of this sacramental rite, as Anabaptist theology proposed limiting its practice to those who make a profession of their own faith. In the 1520s Zwingli was forced to respond to such credobaptist claims. Zwingli did speak of baptism as a pledge of faith, though he insisted that it was a statement of the church's faith, not simply the faith of any given individual (Riggs 2002: 24–25). Indeed, the distinction between the act of water baptism and that of Spirit baptism helps make sense of this occurrence, wherein a child may be baptized physically prior to an expression of faith and union with Christ. The spiritual act of adoption into Christ need not occur at the same temporal moment as the washing with water. Zwingli insisted that a distinction between divine and human agency undergirded the practice of infant baptism (Zwingli 2006: 135).

Over time the Anabaptist threat was viewed with utmost seriousness, as on a par with the errors of Roman Catholic amalgamation of "human tradition." The Second Helvetic Confession draws the lines between the Reformed and the Anabaptist approach clearly:

> We condemn the Anabaptists, who deny that newborn infants of the faithful are to be baptized. For according to evangelical teaching, of such is the Kingdom of God, and they are in the covenant of God. Why, then, should the sign of God's covenant not be given to them? Why should those who belong to God and are in his Church not be initiated by holy baptism? (Cochrane 2003: 283)

Such claims had been made as early as the Tetrapolitan Confession of 1530 (ch. 15 in Cochrane 2003: 74–75). The First Helvetic Confession, in article 22, stated that denial of baptism to infants of the faithful would be "unjust" and would be to "rob" them of their "intended" blessing (Cochrane 2003: 108). Here we see the nature of the Anabaptist threat from a Reformed perspective: a reduction in the subjects of baptism manifested a massively divergent approach to its meaning. Hughes Old has argued that while "opposition to infant baptism arose primarily from an understanding of salvation radically different from that of classical Protestantism … it also shows that the approach to Scripture of the Anabaptists was just as radically different from that of the Reformers." The individual's crisis experience was paramount for salvation and, hence, for baptism, according to the Anabaptists. Therefore, the movement of Balthasar Hubmaier and other Anabaptists was not a "radical reformation in the sense that it took the principles of the Protestant Reformation to their logical conclusions. It is far more a reaction against the Protestant Reformation" (Old 1992: 103, 109).

Interestingly, baptism was not a hot button issue in early Reformed confessions to the same degree as the Eucharist, largely because there were not as many concerns with Roman Catholic practice on this matter (though regular mention was made of the Roman allowance for laywomen to baptize: see, for example, chapter 22 of the Scottish Confession of Faith [1560] in Cochrane 2003: 181). Differences regarding the relationship of the sacrament to faith and original sin were matters of concern, but confessional statements were really forced owing to the Anabaptist threat more than anything else. There were notable concerns about Roman practice (in as much as Latin baptismal rites on the eve of the Reformation were dominated by the language of exorcism, separated from catechetical instruction, and at times included the saying of the creed by the priest rather than the subjects of baptism), but these were largely addressed by renewed liturgical practice and occasional sermons and treatises rather than by lengthy confessional polemics (Old 1992: 7–25).

EUCHARIST

As with baptism, when we come to the Eucharist (otherwise known as "holy communion" or "the Lord's Supper"), we should begin by asking *why this practice*? The Heidelberg Catechism relays the biblical witness in a clear manner:

> Q. 77. Where has Christ promised that he will feed and nourish believers with his body and blood just as surely as they eat of this broken bread and drink of this cup?

> A. In the institution of the holy Supper which reads: The Lord Jesus on the night when he was betrayed took bread, and when he had given thanks, he broke it, and said, 'this is my body which is for you. Do this in remembrance of me'. In the same way also the cup, after supper, saying, 'this cup is the new covenant in my blood. Do this, as often as you drink it, in remembrance of me'. For as often as you eat this bread and drink the cup, you proclaim the Lord's death until he comes.

This promise is also repeated by the apostle Paul: When we bless the 'cup of blessing', is it not a means of sharing in the blood of Christ? When we break the bread, is it not a means of sharing the body of Christ? Because there is one loaf, we, many as we are, are one body; for it is one loaf of which we all partake. (Cochrane 2003: 319)

The Incarnate Son institutes the Supper, and the apostle Paul rehearses the ongoing significance of that singular event wherein the Lord partook of his Last Supper, a meal that Paul shows to have continual significance "until he comes" again. Because the Eucharist is instituted by Christ himself and meant for all Christians to continue to practice, it fits the theological definition of a Christian sacrament.

Nothing was as debated in the sixteenth century as the Eucharist (Elwood 1999: 3–4). Debates centered around two major questions, each relating the Supper to a key theological notion (sacrifice or the presence of Christ). The first major Reformational debate related to the connection of the Eucharist to the sacrifice of Christ. John Calvin distinguishes between two sorts of sacrifices: those of expiation and those of praise, adoration, and thanksgiving. Todd Billings has highlighted the way that these two sacrifices relate to the double grace of the gospel: justification in Christ and sanctification by his Spirit. "The nature of the second sacrifice is gratitude, praise, and thanksgiving, made possible because the first grace is a gratuitous gift, a free pardon" (Billings 2007: 132).

The mode of partaking shows forth the substantive meaning of the sacrament. Hence Reformation era debates swirled around not merely the theology of the meal but also the place where it was served and the person who did the serving. Whereas the Roman Catholic Mass occurred upon an altar, Calvin insisted that "the cross of Christ is overthrown, as soon as the altar is set up" (Calvin 2006: 1431). Reformed confessions also protested the use of priestly language for the minister who served the meal, arguing that it connoted a continuing sacrificial function. Lutheran and Anglican practice maintained a less ardent protest of (by then) traditional language for the clergy, continuing to refer to them as priests.

The second major Reformational debate regarded the presence of Christ in the meal. Over against not only the Roman Catholic approach (transubstantiation) but also the Lutheran approach (consubstantiation), the Reformed churches presented a unique perspective on the matter. First, "[i]t cannot be proved from the Biblical writings that the body and blood of Christ is essentially and corporeally received in the bread of the Eucharist" (Cochrane 2003: 49). The Fourth Thesis of Berne (1528) summarizes well a consistent Reformed concern, namely, that the presence of Christ not be located in the elements. The Heidelberg Catechism addresses this matter as well:

Q. 78. Do the bread and wine become the very body and blood of Christ?

A. No, for as the water in baptism is not changed into the blood of Christ, nor becomes the washing away of sins by itself, but is only a divine sign and confirmation of it, so also in the Lord's Supper the sacred bread does not become the body of Christ itself, although, in accordance with the nature and usage of sacraments, it is called the body of Christ. (Cochrane 2003: 319)

Symbolism remains very much a part of the sacramental reality. These are holy signs, and that symbolic function means that they cannot be identified precisely with the reality as such: the water is not literally Christ's death and resurrection, much less his blood; the bread and wine are not, nor do they become per se the physical body and blood of Jesus. There remains a fundamental difference between the Roman approach and the Reformed analysis of the Supper: whereas the Roman doctrine of transubstantiation involves a claim that the local presence of Christ occurs in multiple eucharistic hosts simultaneously, the Reformed insist that Christ remains in heaven, and this is a decisive difference for understanding the Eucharist (Davis 2008: 130–132; *contra* Ewerszumrode 2012). While the Lutheran approach required attributing ubiquity to the human Jesus, Reformed theologians have retorted that whatever it might mean to be ubiquitous, it cannot mean being human (Vermigli 1995: 23–25).

Second, though, while they were united in opposing a presence in the elements per se, Reformed churches did believe Jesus to be present to his people in the symbolic act. The Scottish Confession of Faith (1560) makes this distinction in a clear way: "Therefore, if anyone slanders us by saying that we affirm or believe the sacraments to be symbols and nothing more, they are libelous and speak against the plain facts. On the other hand we readily admit that we make a distinction between Christ Jesus in His eternal substance and the elements of the sacramental signs" (ch. 21 in Cochrane 2003: 180).

Brian Gerrish has presented a typology of three ways in which Reformed theologians sought to relate the person of Christ with the presentation of his gospel in the Supper (Gerrish 1982: 128). "Symbolic memorialism" was the viewpoint of Zwingli. Zwingli viewed the Supper as a visible word and a prompt for faithful remembrance, but he insisted that his approach was markedly different from Andreas Karlstadt and the sacramentarians, who believed in mere memorialism. Of course, Zwingli was not influenced by Karlstadt, but there were certain noted similarities in their expression: the Supper as a prompt for spiritual remembrance (Burnett 2011: 91–114). The latter two approaches, however, moved from the realm of remembrance into the experience of ongoing grace as well. "Symbolic parallelism" was the approach of Heinrich Bullinger. Bullinger admits the significance of the Holy Spirit, but repeatedly with respect to *faith*, *never* with respect to the media of the sacraments themselves as Calvin does (Rozeboom 2010: 87). The Spirit brings the believer and Christ together by faith, but this occurs alongside rather than through the sacramental media. Indeed, Bullinger "was concerned that Calvin's use of the noun *instrumentum*, the verb *exhibere*, and the preposition *per* ascribes more efficacy to the sacramental signs than to the Holy Spirit" (Bierma 1999: 24). "Symbolic instrumentalism," by contrast, was the proposal of John Calvin (Gerrish 1993: 168 n.33). Indeed Calvin made use of instrumental language by 1539, quite early in his career (Rozeboom 2010: 194 n.138). The Supper and the very partaking of the elements served as a conduit or instrumental means by which Christ and the believer communed in the Spirit. "The sacramental sign has a 'union' with the substance of the sacrament (Christ) such that the substance 'must always be distinguished from the sign, that we may not transfer to the one what belongs to the other'" (Billings 2007: 119). Calvin argued that the fellowship occurred by the Spirit's drawing the believer up to the local presence of Christ in the heavenly places, rather than by the incarnate Son being present to multiple earthly spatialities. He continued to oppose the doctrine of ubiquity even in affirming a real presence through the instrument of the sacrament.

Once we move beyond the work of Zwingli and the confessions marked by his immediate influence in the first two decades of the Reformation, we see the Reformed confessions affirm either "symbolic parallelism" or "symbolic instrumentalism" (Gerrish 1982: 128; Venema 2001: 167–168 n.32). The later Reformed and Anglican confessions were dominated by the theology of Bullinger, Calvin, Bucer, and, to some extent, Vermigli, not by Zwingli and the sacramentarians (who only influenced minor confessions). Paul Rorem clarifies:

> In any case, the two views of the Lord's Supper have managed to live side by side within the Reformed tradition for centuries. Does a given Reformed statement of faith consider the Lord's Supper as a testimony, an analogy, a parallel, even a simultaneous parallel to the internal workings of God's grace in granting communion with Christ? If so, the actual ancestor may be Heinrich Bullinger, Zwingli's successor in Zurich. Or does it explicitly identify the Supper as the very instrument or means through which God offers and confers the grace of full communion with Christ's body? The lineage would then go back to John Calvin (and to Martin Bucer). (Rorem 1994: 90)

The sacrament is viewed not only as a reminder of Christ's past presence or his spiritual presence completely separable from the sacrament, but the sacrament is also an occasion for the contemporaneous presence of the risen Christ.

Some confessions, such as the Heidelberg Catechism, made this point in a rather vague way (Bierma 1999: 21–30). They did so in an effort to maintain confessional unity amidst followers of Bullinger, Calvin, and Melanchthon. Indeed Calvin's own language was flexible in his efforts to present sacramental teaching on the presence of Christ united with Melanchthonians and those from Zurich (during the leadership of Bullinger) and elsewhere (Rozeboom 2010: 90 n.268; Janse 2008: 68–69). Other confessions were much more specific in that they used language that clearly connoted an instrumental view of the sacrament (Rohls 1998: 181–185; *contra* Venema 2000: 77 n.61). All the confessions were clear that the Zwinglian approach was not viable as an alternative to the Roman and Lutheran doctrines of Christ's presence. While the Reformed churches would not affirm transubstantiation or consubstantiation, they would speak of real grace that takes the form of real presence through the means of this sacramental practice.

MEANS OF GRACE: TOWARD A REFORMED SACRAMENTAL THEOLOGY

Having considered the two sacraments individually, what summarizing remarks might we draw about sacraments in the faith and practice of the Reformed and Anglican Reformation?

First, the sacraments are not mere pledges of human faith but truly exhibit divine grace and effectively communicate Christ. The Thirty-Nine Articles speak to their relationship with grace: "Sacraments ordained of Christ be not only badges or tokens of Christian men's profession, but rather they be certain sure witnesses, and effectual signs of grace, and God's good will toward us, by the which he doth work invisibly in us, and doth not only quicken, but also strengthen and confirm our Faith in him" (art. 25 in Leith 1982: 274). The Anglican confession affirms that sacraments do manifest our profession as a "badge" or "token," yet they also serve as a gift of grace.

"These sacraments are significant, holy signs of sublime, secret things. However, they are not mere, empty signs, but consist of the sign and substance." The sacraments do not merely point to grace, according to the First Helvetic Confession (1536), but the sacraments are an instantiation of grace. Further it confesses: "As the signs are bodily received, so these substantial, invisible and spiritual things are received in faith. Moreover, the entire power, efficacy and fruit of the sacraments lies in these spiritual and substantial things" (Cochrane 2003: 107). The Thirty-Nine Articles affirm that the sacraments not only serve as "certain sure witnesses, and effectual signs of grace," but that they actually confer grace (art. 25 in Leith 1982: 274). They do not merely point toward or remind us of past grace or grace found elsewhere, but their proper use becomes an instrument of Christ's generosity.

Second, while they are not mere badges of faith, reflection upon the sacraments must come around to the biblical teaching that grace is to be received in faith. Reformed confessions insist upon the necessity of speaking to the proper use of the sacraments. They are to provide for God's pilgrim people along their journey. Brian Gerrish recounts Calvin's approach to the relationship of baptism and Eucharist: "Calvin liked to sum up the relationship between the two sacraments by describing baptism as the sign of adoption or of entrance to the family, the Supper as the sign of the Father's constant provision of sustenance" (Gerrish 1993: 124). Whether for initiation or for sustaining, we are called to entrust ourselves and our families to God in Christ.

Faith has been the calling of the Christian community, so that it might believe even infant children of believers to be called genuinely children of the Most High King. Further, faith has been the demand of the Christian community, so that it may approach the table of the Lord for regular reminders of the work of the Son. "The presence of Christ is truly (*vere*) offered by God in the sacrament, whether or not received by faith. Yet, without faith the sacrament does not give its benefit" (Billings 2007: 120 n.53). A real presence is given by the Spirit, but it may be a blessing or a curse, depending upon the manner in which it is received (whether or not by faith).

Perfect faith is never the ground for the sacrament: either in the person receiving or in the person ministering the sacrament. While showing grave concern for many "human traditions" that had encircled Roman Catholic sacramental practice, the Hungarian Confession affirmed that baptism remained true and genuine (Müller 1903: 422). The Reformed churches, precisely because they lacked an Edenic notion of any era of church history, did not denigrate the validity of the Roman Catholic sacrament of baptism. This determination manifests the underlying belief regarding the nature of sacraments: they involve divine grace in pursuit of humans before they entail humans in pursuit of still further grace (by grace).

What is a Reformed sacramental theology, as suggested by the sixteenth-century Reformed and Anglican confessions? We can conclude by listening to the Heidelberg Catechism's definition of a sacrament:

Q. 66. What are Sacraments?

A. They are visible holy signs and seals, instituted by God, so that by our use of them, he might make us understand the promise of the gospel better and seal it. This promise of the gospel is that because of Christ's one sacrifice finished on the cross, he will grant us by grace forgiveness of sins and eternal life. (Cochrane 2003: 316)

The language "make us understand ... and seal" is especially refined, drawn from Melanchthon's 1521 *Loci Communes*, Zacharias Ursinus' *Catechismus Minor*, Heinrich Bullinger's *Catechismus*, and Calvin's Genevan Catechism of 1545 (Bierma 1999: 11–12). The language reminds us that the sacraments are visible words (in the Augustinian sense), and they are also efficacious words by the Spirit's wonder-working power through these material practices. They have not merely intellectual effect, but relational force inasmuch as they bring about genuine covenantal commitment and integral covenantal communion. And it is this covenantal closeness which is the center of these practices: reflecting on the eucharistic theology of Peter Martyr Vermigli (who was so influential in the mind of John Calvin and other second and third generation Reformed theologians on the European continent and especially in the Church of England), George Hunsinger has specified: "The primary union and communion in the eucharist were always between Christ and the communicants, not between Christ and the elements" (Hunsinger 2008: 40). Hence we come to the best characterization of the sacraments in early Reformed theology: as means of grace, practices whereby the Spirit enacts genuine fellowship between the communicant and the risen Christ by means of various creaturely media.

SUGGESTED READING

Cochrane (2003); Gerrish (1982); Rohls (1998).

BIBLIOGRAPHY

Bierma, Lyle D. (1999), *The Doctrine of the Sacraments in the Heidelberg Catechism: Melanchthonian, Calvinist, or Zwinglian?*, Studies in Reformed Theology and History NS 4 (Princeton, NJ: Princeton Theological Seminary).

Billings, J. Todd (2007), *Calvin, Participation, and the Gift: The Activity of Believers in Union with Christ*, Changing Paradigms in Historical and Systematic Theology (New York: Oxford University Press).

Burnett, Amy Nelson (2011), *Karlstadt and the Origins of the Eucharistic Controversy: A Study in the Circulation of Ideas*, Oxford Studies in Historical Theology (New York: Oxford University Press).

Calvin, John (2006), *Institutes of the Christian Religion*, John T. McNeill (ed.), trans. Ford Lewis Battles, Library of Christian Classics (Louisville, KY: Westminster John Knox).

Chung-Kim, Esther (2011), *Inventing Authority: The Use of the Church Fathers in Reformation Debates over the Eucharist* (Waco, TX: Baylor University Press).

Cochrane, Arthur C. (2003), *Reformed Confessions of the Sixteenth Century*, rev. ed. (Louisville, KY: Westminster John Knox).

Davis, Thomas J. (2008), *This is My Body: The Presence of Christ in Reformation Thought* (Grand Rapids, MI: Baker Academic).

Elwood, Christopher (1999), *The Body Broken: The Calvinist Doctrine of the Eucharist and the Symbolization of Power in Sixteenth-Century France*, Oxford Studies in Historical Theology (New York: Oxford University Press).

Ewerszumrode, Frank (2012), *Mysterium Christi spiritualis praesentiae: Die Abendmahlslehre des Genfer Reformators Johannes Calvin aus römisch-katholischer Perspektive*, Reformed Historical Theology 19 (Göttingen: Vandenhoeck & Ruprecht).

Gerrish, Brian (1982), "Sign and Reality: The Lord's Supper in the Reformed Confessions," in *The Old Protestantism and the New* (Chicago: University of Chicago Press), 118–130.

Gerrish, Brian (1993), *Grace and Gratitude: The Eucharistic Theology of John Calvin* (Minneapolis, MN: Fortress).

Gregory, Brad S. (2012), *The Unintended Reformation: How a Religious Revolution Secularized Society* (Cambridge, MA: Belknap).

Hunsinger, George (2008), *The Eucharist and Ecumenism: Let Us Keep the Feast*, Current Issues in Theology (Cambridge: Cambridge University Press).

Janse, Wim (2008), "Calvin's Eucharistic Theology: Three Dogma-Historical Observations," in Herman J. Selderhuis (ed.), *Calvinus Sacrarum Literarum Interpres* (Göttingen: Vandenhoeck & Ruprecht), 37–69.

Lane, Anthony N. S. (1999), *John Calvin: Student of the Church Fathers* (Grand Rapids, MI: Baker).

Leith, John H. (1982), *Creeds of the Churches: A Reader in Christian Doctrine from the Bible to the Present*, 3rd ed. (Louisville, KY: John Knox).

Müller, E. F. K. (1903), *Die Bekenntnisschriften der reformierten Kirche* (Leipzig: Deichert).

Oberman, Heiko Augustinus (1983), *The Harvest of Medieval Theology: Gabriel Biel and Late Medieval Nominalism* (Durham, NC: Labyrinth).

Old, Hughes Oliphant (1992), *The Shaping of the Reformed Baptismal Rite in the Sixteenth Century* (Grand Rapids, MI: Eerdmans).

Pauw, Amy Plantinga (2006), "The Graced Infirmity of the Church," in Amy Plantinga Pauw and Serene Jones (eds.), *Feminist and Womanist Essays in Reformed Dogmatics*, Columbia Series in Reformed Theology (Louisville, KY: Westminster John Knox), 189–203.

Riggs, John W. (2002), *Baptism in the Reformed Tradition: An Historical and Practical Theology*, Columbia Series in Reformed Theology (Louisville, KY: Westminster John Knox).

Rohls, Jan (1998), *Reformed Confessions: Theology from Zurich to Barmen*, trans. John Hoffmeyer, Columbia Series in Reformed Theology (Louisville, KY: Westminster John Knox), 177–237.

Rorem, Paul (1994), "The *Consensus Tigurinus* (1549): Did Calvin Compromise?" in Wilhelm H. Neuser (ed.), *Calvinus Sacrae Scripturae Professor: Calvin as Confessor of Holy Scripture* (Grand Rapids, MU: Eerdmans), 72–90.

Rozeboom, Sue A. (2010), "The Provenance of John Calvin's Emphasis on the Role of the Holy Spirit Regarding the Sacrament of the Lord's Supper" (Ph.D. Diss., University of Notre Dame).

Rozeboom, Sue A. (2012), "Doctrine of the Lord's Supper: Calvin's Theology and Its Early Reception," in J. Todd Billings and I. John Hesselink (eds.), *Calvin's Theology and Its Reception: Disputes, Developments, and New Possibilities* (Louisville, KY: Westminster John Knox), 143–165.

Venema, Cornelis P. (2000), "Sacraments and Baptism in the Reformed Confessions," *Mid-America Journal of Theology* 11: 21–86.

Venema, Cornelis P. (2001), "The Doctrine of the Lord's Supper in the Reformed Confessions," *Mid-America Journal of Theology* 12: 135–199.

Vermigli, Peter Martyr (1995), *Dialogue on the Two Natures in Christ*, trans. John Patrick Donnelly (ed.), Peter Martyr Library 2 (Kirksville, MO: Sixteenth Century Essays and Studies).

Zwingli, Huldrych (2006), "Of Baptism," in G. W. Bromiley (ed.), *Zwingli and Bullinger*, Library of Christian Classics (Louisville, KY: Westminster John Knox), 129–175.

CHAPTER 20

SACRAMENTS IN THE RADICAL REFORMATION

JOHN D. REMPEL

INTRODUCTION

INHERENT in the notion of a "sacrament" is the mediation of Spirit by matter. In a symbolic, mysterious way the created order participates in the uncreated order of reality. How can a material symbol represent a spiritual reality? Does it become identical with that reality? The elusiveness of these questions suggests that "mystery," the New Testament term for such things, more adequately allows for this paradoxical reality than the later terms "sacrament" (holy things that represent the gospel), "ceremony" (holy actions), and "ordinance" (ordained by Christ).

The complexity of a seemingly straightforward gesture is already present at the Last Supper, the densest ritual moment in Jesus' ministry. There is a relationship between the Passover bread and the body of Jesus, but what is it? What changes when the two are brought together? Who are the actors? The four accounts of that meal (Matthew, Mark, Luke, Paul) all address these questions differently. (See Willi Marxsen's insightful, if reductionist, treatment of this development [Marxsen 1970: 88–122].) The contribution made to sacramental thought by the Gospel of John consists of its teaching that the Word became flesh; the Infinite One took on finite form. This quickly became a principle that the early church applied to the relationship between the infinite and the finite as a whole.

After Jesus' ascension he was no longer physically accessible to his followers. Yet the church continued to break bread as a sign that Jesus was still present. Other contributors to this volume deal exhaustively with the intricacies of this development; my concern will be to sketch out the story of sacraments from the vantage point of the Radical Reformation.

In the post-apostolic era Gnosticism challenged the claim that the Word had become flesh, that Christ had taken on our nature. In their defense of the Incarnation theologians began to use the analogy of bread and body in the Lord's Supper as part of their argument. Soon the language of symbol was evoked. A symbol was an act that participates in the reality it represents. A few centuries later the terms of reference had changed. One school of thought that emerged is sometimes called "representative symbolism." It emphasized a sign's participation in the reality it signifies. Another school of thought, often called "realism," placed the weight on the oneness of the physical gesture with the spiritual reality. Gradually popular piety and official teaching took the latter interpretation. Even though the thought of Thomas Aquinas sought to keep this teaching from being reduced to a physical presence of Christ in the eucharistic elements, that claim, in fact, became what most Western Christians believed.

Another factor enters the picture in the fourth century. In the following centuries the church became the official religion of the empire. It was less and less a church based on a freely given personal profession of faith than one to which everyone in society belonged. Over time this meant that the church was no longer the body of believers in each place but the clergy who were the agent of the Spirit in making Christ present in worship. Gradually, congregations became spectators of a drama in which they had no active role. There was a second way in which the congregation was displaced. More and more the medium of Christ's presence was not seen to be the body of Christ as the church but the body of Christ as bread and wine.

The recent translation of Henri de Lubac's writings into English has brought the history of this notion to popular attention. De Lubac documents a profound shift in the sacramental thought of the High Middle Ages (de Lubac 2006: 141–180, esp. 162–175). William Crockett's interpretation of this dense text is that in this shift of thought an inversion takes place. The church is no longer primarily the sacramental but the mystical body of Christ; the Eucharist is no longer primarily the mystical but the sacramental body of Christ (Crockett 1989: 107). It goes beyond the scope of this chapter to try to demonstrate a continuity of thought in the Radical Reformation with the older definition, but one could say that an affinity of thought exists in Anabaptism for the notion of the church as the sacramental body of Christ, which de Lubac attributes to the age of the Fathers and the early Middle Ages. Thus the sacramental dimension, that is, the mediation of spirit by matter, was not lost in Anabaptism; it referred not primarily to elements but to the church. It was the tangible worshipping community gathered to break bread that was transformed. Christ's presence in the meal flowed from his presence in the community.

Dissident movements in the High and late Middle Ages had kept the notions of representative symbolism and the congregation as an actor in salvation's drama alive into the sixteenth century, often in small conventicles. Then two decisive changes happened. One was that representative symbolism burst into new life in Protestant sacramental thought as a challenge to Catholic realism. The other change was that, once loosened from Catholic liturgical and dogmatic structures, the spiritualizing corrective to a perceived Catholic materialism became so severe that it led one wing of the Radical Reformation into Spiritualism.

Thus, the church's long battle to hold matter and spirit together without separating or identifying them again became a central struggle. This is the dilemma all parties faced: if you separate spirit from matter as well as if you identify spirit with matter you no longer have a sacrament. That is, if you separate the two, you are asserting that beings of flesh and blood can apprehend spirit without mediation and are in danger of vitiating the meaning of the Incarnation. If you claim an identity between the two you merge the symbol with the reality symbolized and are in danger of idolatry.

In his magisterial treatment of radical religious dissent in the sixteenth century George Williams (1962) identifies three streams of nonconformity: Anabaptists, Spiritualists, and Evangelical Rationalists. The difference among them was not absolute. Anabaptists tended toward the letter of Scripture (the commanding of ritual acts) and a visible church. Spiritualists tended toward Spirit over letter (the inner meaning of ritual acts) and the invisible affinity of true believers. Evangelical Rationalists tended toward mind over Scriptural letter (the implausibility of ritual acts) and belief based on rationality. What united them, according to Williams, was separation from the state, pacifism, a missionary calling, the experience of regeneration (whether in believers' baptism or the unmediated possession of the Spirit), and a wariness of forensic justification and the Augustinian understanding of original sin to the extent that they undercut transformation and discipleship (Williams 1962: xxv).

Anabaptism, Spiritualism, and Evangelical Rationalism gradually differentiated themselves from one another. The most defining difference was Trinitarian belief, and with it, the implications of the Incarnation. There were Trinitarians whose thought and practice included the finality of outward revelation (i.e. the Bible), a visible church, and visible signs of God's saving work. These were the Anabaptists. There were Trinitarians who embraced Spiritualism and the unmediated presence of God in the individual heart. Luminaries such as Caspar Schwenckfeld gathered kindred spirits around themselves. Many of the Evangelical Rationalists, such as Michael Servetus, were non-Trinitarians.

With rare exceptions, such as the Schwenckfelders (contrary to their luminary's intention) and Unitarians, the Spiritualists and Rationalists did not beget enduring communities. Their inwardness and individualism left little room for a visible church with collectively shared beliefs and practices. For those reasons the focus of this study will be on the Anabaptists, especially those who directly shaped the various Mennonite denominations that emerged in Dutch- and German-speaking Europe as well as the Hutterites. In the process of describing Anabaptist doctrine and practice we will encounter their interaction with Spiritualistic Radicals. We will see that the Anabaptists themselves existed on a spectrum from the more spiritualistic to the more sacramentally inclined.

ORIGINS

Anabaptism came into being as a church when it carried out a renegade celebration of baptism and the Lord's Supper in Zurich in January 1525. It became a church not through a political or theological declaration but through a liturgical act. Even though Anabaptists reinterpreted, and in some cases rejected, what medieval tradition had claimed concerning the substance and form of baptism and the Eucharist, they remained for them the primal signs of Christ and the church (Blanke 1966: 21–28; Baylor 1991: 38–41).

The distinctive nature of early Anabaptism has a direct bearing on how its ritual practices developed. It was a charismatic and barely institutionalized type of church. Although the formal beginning of the Swiss Brethren was an outgrowth of Zwingli's reformation in Zurich, radical religion was in the air from Flanders to Poland. Anabaptism emerged in many settings mostly within but also beyond German- and Dutch-speaking Europe. In each of these settings the theology and practice of ceremonies had common as well as distinctive marks. We will look at the Lord's Supper as a case study.

Ecclesiology was the interpretive key to Anabaptist thinking about the "ceremonies," as they most often called them. They believed in a visible and pure church composed of those baptized on their confession of faith in Christ and living a life of mutual forgiveness and faithful discipleship. For them the primary meaning of "body of Christ" was a visible historical community that acted in imitation of its Lord. It was this body that took on form and was transformed in Communion. The gathered community was the human agent of God's work in the world just as the Holy Spirit was the divine agent. In his analysis of this development among the Swiss Brethren, J. F. G. Goeters describes their Supper as a movement from the self-communion of a priest without a congregation to the self-communion of a congregation without a priest (Goeters 1969: 270).

Since the Anabaptists were Trinitarian their picture of God obligated them to take the Incarnation seriously. They placed the existing notion of the church as the prolongation of the Word become flesh in history into a novel ecclesiology shaped by various Christologies. This notion was most fully articulated by Pilgram Marpeck. But it was most completely expressed in the Hutterian practice of holding all things in common, including economics. It was also at work in the Dutch emphasis on the church as the body "without spot or wrinkle" (Ephesians 5:27) that was in the process of being divinized.

At the same time Anabaptists confessed that the church is the broken body of Christ; the church and its members remain sinners in need of forgiveness and restoration. The church had received power from Christ to forgive sins; what it bound or loosed on earth was bound or loosed in heaven (John 20:21–23). The believer is initiated into the church by baptism on the basis of a confession of faith in Christ before the gathered congregation. The church was separated from the world in its loyalty to Christ above its loyalty to nation and ethnicity. This stance expressed itself, among other things, in nonresistance to evil and love of enemy. The church's worship was to be grounded in the commandments of Christ to baptize, break bread, wash feet, call leaders, and anoint the sick. The body of Christ took on outward form as it was led by the Holy Spirit in prayer and song, as well as in reading, proclaiming, and discerning the Bible as exemplified in I Corinthians 11–14.

A second commonality of the movement was its emphasis on discipleship. Its leaders were often autodidacts whose overriding concern was faithful living: that was the point where the church most needed reform. This focus left limited time and talent for comprehensive theologizing. Christological reflection in Anabaptism gener-ally affirmed Nicaea and Chalcedon as necessary boundary markers but focused largely on the life, death, and resurrection of Jesus as described in the New Testament. Nevertheless, the challenges thrown up by contemporary debate concerning the Lord's Supper pressed several Anabaptist authors to move beyond simple biblical reflection to theological formulation. Relating the earthly Jesus to the heavenly Christ, for example, required attention to the tradition's paradoxical claims regarding the Trinity and the two natures of Christ. An excellent compendium of this process in the sixteenth century and theological reflection on it for today is found in Thomas Finger's *A Contemporary Anabaptist Theology* (2004). The standard historical studies of the movement in English are Hans-Juergen Goertz (1996), C. Arnold Snyder (2002), and J. Denny Weaver (2005).

In order to highlight both the commonalities and contrasts within Anabaptist sacra-mental thought and practice we turn to the movement's three most systematic think-ers on the subject, Balthasar Hubmaier, Pilgram Marpeck, and Dirk Philips. Hubmaier, a German, standing between Zwingli and the Swiss Brethren, represented a biblical ethicism. He is the defining figure for Baptists who trace their origin to Anabaptism. Marpeck, an Austrian, stood closest to Catholic tradition, holding together the bibli-cal, mystical, and sacramental strands. Long forgotten, he has become a formative figure again in current Radical Reformation thought. Philips, a Dutchman, was Menno Simons' closest collaborator and systematized their shared theological impulses. He has had an enduring influence on the Amish movement.

MAJOR WRITINGS ON THE CEREMONIES

Balthasar Hubmaier (1480–1528)

Balthasar Hubmaier is the most original and sophisticated thinker associated with the Swiss Brethren, whose influence began in the canton of Zurich and quickly spread into southern Germany and Moravia. Hubmaier was a restless spirit. He received his doctor-ate in theology under Johannes Eck in Ingolstadt, taking a special interest in liturgical studies. He subsequently engaged Lutheran and Reformed thought and finally cast in his lot with the Anabaptists. The theology of Hubmaier, like the person, stands between the fronts of the Reformation. He was unique, for example, in his attempt to fashion a Mass church that was also a believers' church. He brought his training in liturgy to bear on his Anabaptist ministry, particularly in the services he wrote for baptism, the Holy Supper, and the ban (Pipkin 1989: 386–392, 393–408, 409–425).

For Hubmaier the church has been given the role Christ had while he was on earth. It is commissioned to live a Christlike life in his absence from history in his human nature. As was Christ, so is the church now the agent of the Holy Spirit (Pipkin 1898: 352). It has the power of the keys "to remit or to bind sins" (Pipkin 1989: 371, 351). The church has been given the signs or ceremonies "to gather a church, to commit oneself publicly to live according to the Word of Christ in faith and brotherly love" (Pipkin 1989: 384). It is a tangible "community of goods" (Pipkin 1989: 183). Thus, the visible church is the mediator of God's grace; it forgives people in Christ's stead.

Hubmaier's great passion during his time as an Anabaptist was correctly to set forth the relationship between divine initiative and human response. Nowhere is this theme presented as vividly as in his theology of the ceremonies. We will look at his teaching on baptism, the Supper, and the ban.

In his construction of a theology of baptism, most fully articulated in "On the Christian Baptism of Believers," Hubmaier makes much use of New Testament references that suggest sequence rather than simultaneity in the relationship between inward and outward. Through the Holy Spirit we are given a new birth, as described in John 3:1–10. This gift is received through the "yes" of faith, "which the person proclaims publicly in the reception of water baptism" (Pipkin 1989: 100, 118).

In "A Form for Water Baptism" a candidate presents herself to be questioned on teachings that concern newness of life, being able to pray in her own words, and showing that she understands the articles of the Apostles' Creed. Then she is presented to the congregation, which is asked to pray for the candidate to receive the grace and power of the Spirit in order to complete what God has begun in her. This prayer suggests that Hubmaier is still in the process of bringing consistency to his thought. Here baptism is not simply a witness to God's action but a moment in which God is acting. Questions to the candidate follow concerning the creed, the renunciation of the devil, and the willingness to give and receive counsel in the congregation. Then the act of baptism takes place in the name of the Trinity. There is another call for the congregation to pray for the newly baptized and for all the baptized for perseverance, and finally, the laying on of hands with these words:

> I testify to you and give you authority that henceforth you shall be counted among the Christian community, as a member participating in the use of her keys, breaking bread and praying with other Christian sisters and brothers. (Pipkin 1989: 487–489)

For Hubmaier baptism is the basis of the church's mission and thus "more essential than the table of the Lord" (Pipkin 1989: 122–127, esp. 125). The church baptizes only after scrutinizing the candidates, but it acknowledges that ultimately only God knows who is a believer (Pipkin 1989: 117).

Hubmaier's theology of the Supper, like his view of baptism, flows from his understanding of faith and church, free will and covenant, which he had received from his nominalist mentor, Johannes Eck (Moore 1981: 79–83). It is shaped by his extreme reaction against late medieval eucharistic thought and practice as he had experienced them, especially claims for the physical presence of Christ in the sacrament. In order to avoid any notion of a corporeal presence in the bread and cup Hubmaier posited the community's communion with Christ as an inward reality prior to the outward event.

In this move Hubmaier sided with Zwingli in confining the human nature of Christ to heaven. Hubmaier goes further than Zwingli: as regards a divine presence in the Supper it comes not as Christ in his divinity but as Spirit, in Johannine fashion; after the ascension the Spirit replaces the Son on the plane of history. The church and the believer are the outward actors while the Spirit acts inwardly. (Pilgram Marpeck uses this parallelism to heighten the church's union with Christ in the breaking of bread rather than to displace it.) As a consequence the object of baptism becomes the candidate's oath rather than the water, and the object of Communion becomes the community's covenant rather than the elements of bread and wine. For Hubmaier, the breaking of bread as an outward act of the visible church focused on being rather than receiving the body of Christ. Because of this radical reformulation, the exegetical debate concerning "est" or "significat" as the way in which Christ is present had become anachronistic for Hubmaier.

The last of Hubmaier's church-defining ceremonies is fraternal admonition, or the ban, which functions according to Matthew 18. Its intent is for Christians to help one another back onto the path of holiness when they have fallen from it. When members persistently and heedlessly live a life contrary to the command of Christ they are to be publicly separated from the church. The ban is the mirror image of baptism. Acting as Christ's representative, the church wields the keys that bind and loose in the hope of reconciliation (Pipkin 1989: 412–416).

Pilgram Marpeck (1495–1556)

Marpeck was a water engineer in the Austrian mining town of Rattenberg. His religious development was shaped by his radical, but still Catholic, parish priest, Stephan Castenbaur. Soon he opened himself to Lutheran teaching that was spreading through the area. These influences were followed by itinerant Anabaptist ones, especially the preaching of the mystically inclined Leonard Schiemer. By 1528 the Radicals had won Marpeck's loyalty, even though this meant fleeing with his wife Anna to Anabaptist congregations emerging in Moravia. They deputized the Marpecks to give leadership to Anabaptists in the midst of the great theological ferment taking place in Strasbourg (Klaassen and Klassen, *Marpeck* 1990: 39–115).

Most authors explain Marpeck's at once eclectic and original way of thinking with the notion that he was an autodidact. In the course of his career he critically reclaimed Catholic and Lutheran notions in the process of shaping a coherent Anabaptist theology. Marpeck was the most theologically innovative and comprehensive thinker to emerge from urban Anabaptism in the swath of Anabaptist congregations extending from the Alsace across southern Germany to Moravia. His theologizing was increasingly done in a collective of leaders who came to be known as the Marpeck Circle. His dissatisfaction with Catholic sacramental thought was that in his view it lacked a dynamic, relational principle. Very soon he realized that the emerging alternative of Spiritualism, which rejected all mediation between the divine and human, brought an opposite danger with it: that of dispensing with outward signs all together.

An excellent summary of Radical Reformation Spiritualism, centering on Marpeck's chief debating partner, Caspar Schwenckfeld, is found in Emmet McLaughlin (2007); and here one should also see the examination of Spiritualist Anabaptists by Geoffrey Dipple (2007).

As Marpeck saw it, when the Spiritualist corrective to an externalized sacramentalism was made into a first principle, it negated the Incarnation and its prolongation in the church and its signs (Snyder 2002: 305–326). Marpeck's chief debating partner on the subject, Caspar Schwenckfeld, taught that the principle of the Incarnation as "a physical medium" had been superseded (Klaassen, Packull, Rempel 1999: 111).

The alternative Marpeck offered against the tendency to spiritualize Christ's presence, especially in relation to bread and wine, emerged out of the inseparable relationship he posited among Christology, pneumatology, ecclesiology, and sacramentology. (See Boyd 1992: 117–121 for a summary of Schwenckfeld's critique of Marpeck.) The principle that tied these realms together was that God uses matter to convey spirit in such a way that inner and outer cannot be separated.

> We stand by the claim … that the external eating of the above mentioned forms (gestalt) is a true, inward communion of the body and blood of Christ—a true communion of believers to eternal life, including their whole humanity, spirit, soul and body. (Klaassen, Packull, and Rempel 1999: 75, 106)

This bond had to do with the very nature of a sacramental act: it concerned the inseparability of divine initiative and human response. For Marpeck, a ceremony was the point at which grace and faith meet and the point at which God's initiative takes on flesh. It was his attempt to overcome the Catholic notion of *ex opere operato*, in which the sign achieves what it signifies, as long as an obstacle is not put in its way. In Marpeck's mind the principle of *ex opere operato* reduced the Eucharist to a static object. His alternative was to see the ceremonies as actions rather than objects (Klaassen, Packull, and Rempel 1999: 85–86). When a baptismal candidate is immersed or has water poured over her the outward water is united with the inward Spirit for the forgiveness of sins. Similarly, when bread and wine are shared in the power of the Spirit with those who have gathered in faith and love, those who gather are united with Christ and one another.

Once the relational nature of a ceremony was in place Marpeck could speak freely of the church's sacramental participation in Christ and turn to its defence against Spiritualists. In *A Clear Refutation*, Marpeck's first Strasbourg treatise of 1531, he expanded on what he meant by "ceremony." The defining rituals of the gospel are baptism and the Lord's Supper but the list does not end there. "Ceremonies" are all external rites given by Christ to proclaim the gospel, to pass on his teaching and identity. Whatever embodies the gospel counts as a ceremony. The longer, and not always identical, lists Marpeck used include Scripture, footwashing, teaching, separation from the world, prayer, and the example of believers, especially as expressed in love of neighbor (Klassen and Klaassen 1978: 52, 54, 58).

In *A Clear and Useful Instruction*, Marpeck's second Strasbourg treatise of the same year, he introduced the key to his sacramental thought. It is "the humanity of Christ" (Klassen and Klaassen 1978: 76–88; see also Rempel 1993: 108–116). Through Christ's "outwardness" in the Incarnation his "inwardness" was made tangible. The Word becoming flesh was God's act of condescension to meet the creation on its own terms. He summarizes his argument thus: "The Lord Christ became a natural man for natural man" (Klassen and Klaassen 1978: 85). Christ's humanity is prolonged in the church. The church and its ceremonies become extensions of the Incarnation. If the church is the hand of Christ, then the ceremonies are his fingers.

Later on, in the *Admonition of 1542* Marpeck describes this reality in Trinitarian terms.

> For that which the Father does, the Son of Man does simultaneously: the Father, as Spirit, internally; the Son, as Man, externally. Therefore, the external baptism and Lord's Supper are not signs; rather, they are the external work and essence of the Son. (Klassen and Klaassen 1978: 195)

Marpeck explained this reciprocal quality of sacramental reality by the notion of "co-witness." In it two mediums through which God is at work mutually validate God's activity (Klassen and Klaassen 1978: 197, 387, 424). In the Holy Supper, for instance, there are two aspects of co-witnessing. First, the bread and wine bear witness with the Spirit to Christ's presence. Second, when faith responds to the Spirit, the elements become the Spirit's medium to unite believers with Christ. There is a hint here of a metaphysical correlation between bread and wine and body and blood: when the elements are shared in faith and love they participate in the reality they represent.

In Marpeck's breaking of bread we encounter a similar ethical cruciformity of the church to Christ's self-offering as the outcome of true communion that we saw in Hubmaier. "[Christ] offered up his soul, his very life for us in death that we might offer up our bodies in love like his, as an act of true thanksgiving with everything we possess" (Klaassen, Packull, and Rempel 1999: 102, also 100, 105). But in contrast with Hubmaier, Marpeck preserved the sacramental reality of the bread and wine as well as that of the community. For Hubmaier the weight fell almost entirely on becoming the body of Christ. For Marpeck the weight fell equally on receiving and on being the body of Christ. At the same time, Marpeck intensified the ritual expression of Christ's and the church's self-giving beyond the breaking of bread, extending its pledge to live a christomorphic life into the act of footwashing, which Marpeck calls a model of love.

Dirk Philips (1504–68)

All we know of the early life of Philips is that he was the son of a priest and in early life associated with the strict Franciscans in his hometown of Leeuwarden in the Dutch province of Friesland. It is also known that after 1500 there was a Sacramentarian conventicle, a form of Dutch Spiritualism, in Leeuwarden. It is not known whether the influence of Sacramentarianism on his thinking began at that time. He committed himself to the Anabaptist cause in 1533 and was soon ordained as a minister and later a bishop.

At that time Philips also came under the influence of the Spiritualist Anabaptist Melchior Hoffmann. Hoffmann held to a celestial flesh Christology in order to preserve the sinlessness of Christ. In the Incarnation the divine Christ clothed himself in unfallen flesh that he brought with him from heaven; he was born in but not of Mary (Voolstra 1982: 11ff, 137ff).

An enormous tension existed between this rejection of fallen flesh as a potential place of grace and, at the same time, the affirmation of a visible church whose members' flesh was fallen as a place of grace. The task of overcoming this tension in Hoffmann's thought between two contrary understandings of the Incarnation was left to Dirk Philips and Menno Simons, both of whom breathed deeply of the atmosphere Hoffmann inhabited. Simons is the most prominent figure in early Dutch Anabaptism, but his gifts were more pastoral and apologetic than systematic. Philips revealingly grapples with the implications of the Incarnation for doctrine. He wants to hold onto Christ's unfallen flesh but backs off from other aspects of Hoffmann's heterodoxy (Dyck 1992: 137, 145ff, 160). To sustain the link between Christology and ecclesiology he turns to the notion of "divinization." By this he means that the believer receives divine life, "creating life in his heart which penetrates and purifies ... to the origin from which it has sprung, namely, eternal divine life itself" (Dyck 1993: 149).

To begin his argument, Philips asserts Christ's two natures in traditional language (Dyck 1992: 136, 140, 147). But we soon see that there is a difference: Christ's human nature remains different from ours in its unfallenness. Yet there is a bridge between the two. In the new birth we are restored to the image and likeness of Christ; as the Spirit "sanctifies and keeps the new creature in a divine nature" (Dyck 1992: 296) our fallen nature recedes and takes on the character of Christ's unfallen humanity, but never fully in this life (Dyck 1992: 308, 313). The notion of divinization led the Dutch Anabaptists to a uniquely stringent understanding of a pure church. It is noteworthy that this taking on of a divine nature does not lead to a despising of the Lord's commandments concerning outward signs, such as baptism, "the spiritual fellowship of his body and blood," foot-washing, and the ban (Dyck 1992: 301). Contrary to his Spiritualist opponents, Philips asserts that the truly spiritual do not outgrow material signs but find life in them. His breakthrough in overcoming the tension between two expressions of Incarnation he had inherited was that divinization does not mean that we transcend our created nature but that we are restored to it.

This train of thought may be seen in the treatise "The Congregation of God" (Dyck 1992: 350–382), which offers an overview of Philips's view of the ceremonies. The church began in heaven and was present in paradise. Although it became part of the fall, the church was carried forward to the age of the Messiah through God's covenant with Abraham. In Christ the church has been restored as part of God's intended restoration of all things, as described in Colossians 1 (Dyck 1992: 356).

There is a Trinitarian preface to the section on seven "ordinances," Philips's term for "ceremonies," in which the Holy Spirit is described as the agent of creation and sanctification. But what might have been the beginning of a pneumatic theology of ceremonies, and by implication, of the created order, is not developed. The author simply goes on to describe each ordinance. The first one is ordination (Dyck 1992: 363–365). The second one is "the scriptural use of the sacraments of Jesus Christ, namely, baptism and the Lord's Supper." These two primal signs that constitute one ordinance "establish the unspeakable grace of God and his covenant, and us with it, as visible signs" (Dyck 1992: 365). The third ordinance is footwashing. The fourth is visible separation from the world that is signified by the keys of binding and loosing (Dyck 1992: 369). The fifth ordinance is the commandment of love. The sixth is the keeping of all Christ's commandments including the love of enemy (Dyck 1992: 373). The final ordinance is the church's suffering for the sake of the gospel.

"The Baptism of our Lord Jesus Christ" begins with Philips's cardinal concern, that, "the external baptism with water is a witness to spiritual baptism, a proof of true sorrow and a sign of faith" (Dyck 1993: 72). Yet it goes on to weave most of the New Testament images of baptism into a fabric without making a distinction between Spirit baptism and water baptism. One has the sense that for once the author's treatment of a subject is removed from polemics. No one is disputing that saving grace can be received only through the faith of its recipient. Therefore, Philips is free to use New Testament references, such as "You were buried with him through baptism" (Dyck 1993: 75), without polemical qualifications as descriptions of God's use of water baptism as part of his work in the believer.

In the argument against infant baptism that follows, Philips affirmed that "children receive the kingdom of heaven" (Dyck 1993: 91). Although they inherit the guilt of Adam, their condemnation is taken away by the atoning work of Christ. Their salvation is declared by God universally and does not need to be signified by an outward act, such as infant baptism. Philips nowhere accounted for the inconsistency that one of God's saving acts, the salvation of children, requires no visible, outward sign, while another of God's saving acts, the salvation of those who have reached the age of accountability, does require such a sign.

The tension between fallen and restored creation works itself out in Philips's theology of the Lord's Supper. It is presented in summary fashion in "The Supper of Our Lord Jesus Christ" (Dyck 1992: 112–133). There we see that only a "spiritual" understanding allows us to grasp the multiple meanings of the Eucharist: bread and wine, body and blood, fellowship of his body and memorial of his blood (Dyck 1992: 113). In passages reminiscent of John Calvin, Philips asserts that faith is necessary to receive what is offered and that Christ's presence is not physical or localized. The significance of the sacrament lies in the whole action from the initiating role of the Spirit to the response of the people. The parallel continues when Calvin writes that the bread and wine are signs, "which represent for us the invisible food that we receive from the flesh and blood of Christ" (McNeill 1960: 1360).

As he lays out his eucharistic thinking Philips reinforces his exegetical forays into the Synoptics and Paul with increasing reference to the Fourth Gospel. This legitimates the use of realistic language without suggesting that "his natural body and blood" are in the elements (Dyck 1992: 120, 127). With reference to I Corinthians 10:16 the author explains: in that communion Christ unites his divine self with believers, and in the process, divinizes them (Dyck 1992: 121–122), drawing them beyond the limits of the fallen world into the realm of a new creation. At the same time a relationship between "natural bread" and "spiritual body" is hinted at but never unambiguously described.

Toward the end of his life, Philips encountered the writings of Sebastian Franck, the brilliant defender of Spiritualism. In a switch of adversaries, the challenge was coming from the spiritualistic rather than the sacramentalistic side of the Reformation spectrum. It is noticeable in his late writings that the author's language is less guarded than earlier. In water baptism and the laying on of hands believers receive the Spirit (Dyck 1992: 460, 464). First there is a biblical argument. The church breaks bread because Jesus commands it to do so. Then it is followed by a Christological and pneumatic argument. As the Son is the visible image of the Father, so the church and its "sacramental signs" are visible manifestations of the Spirit's work. In making the Spirit the reference point for the church and its signs, Philips thinks like Hubmaier. Both of them stand in contrast to Marpeck for whom the sacramental actor is Christ, "in his humanity." Finally, the ban is important because it purifies the visible church as a sign of the Spirit. As a way of summarizing Philips's fragmentary arguments one might say that the church is the historical manifestation of a restored humanity; its divinization leads to its restored creatureliness (Dyck 1992: 461–466).

CONCLUSIONS

Anabaptist ways of describing the relationship between Spirit and matter, inward and outward, were experiments in biblical exegesis and theological reflection. The commands of Jesus to act in his name by baptizing, breaking bread, and otherwise embodying the gospel were the first line of argument. This was buttressed in varying degrees by reflection on the Incarnation and its continuation in the church. The theologians we have examined were concerned to find an alternative to both Catholic sacramentalism and Radical Reformation Spiritualism. First, they sought to overcome a use of ceremonies in which God's outward signs are received in any other way than by the faith of the recipients. Second, they sought to overcome a view of ceremonies in which God's outward signs are dispensed with.

In all of them the sacramental dimension, that is, the meeting point of spirit and matter, is displaced in varying degrees from the water to the faith of the candidate and from the bread and wine to the love of the congregation. This is most true of Hubmaier's thinking but with a significant qualification. The emphasis on the faith of the candidate does not nullify God's initiative as the final cause of both faith and love. As we have seen in the service of baptism, the Spirit is called upon to act simultaneously with the church and the believer in the moment of baptism.

In Marpeck's thought the shift of the means of grace from the elements to the congregation is not a displacement but an inversion. When it is gathered in faith and love in the presence of the Holy Spirit the congregation takes the elements. Unity with Christ and the church happens in the act of taking, blessing, breaking, and giving bread and wine.

In Philips's thought there is a clear Spiritualist impulse. But it is overwhelmed in the end by his admittedly fragmentary theology of divinization. In becoming a partaker of the unfallen flesh of Christ, our humanity as it was at creation is restored. Salvation consists not in transcending our creaturely nature but in re-inhabiting it.

In the three subjects of our study and in Anabaptism as a whole there remains an unexplored dimension. It concerns the extension of sacramentality beyond baptism and the Supper to additional outward actions that participate in the same inward reality. For example, in their separate lists Marpeck and Philips both claim separation from the world as a tangible expression of the gospel, a place where grace is embodied and visible.

The significance of this concept becomes even clearer when we take an Anabaptist practice that is not on Philips's or Marpeck's list but that was part of almost all early forms of the movement. It is the community of goods (Stayer 1991: 9–11, 112–121, 132; Packull 1995: 51, 128–136, 308–310). The odious example of coerced community in Muenster and contentiousness as various forms of communalism vied with one another in Moravia led to a disavowal of commonly held property but not a disavowal of the underlying covenant of mutual aid. Even in the wake of these developments Menno Simons defends mutual aid, not only among members but with refugees, as a practice without which the church has abandoned the gospel (Wenger 1984: 558–559). It was the distinguishing mark of the Hutterites that they held to common property and a common way of life as the fullest prolongation of the Incarnation, or in their words, the fullest surrender to the gospel (Friesen 1999: 119–123). This novel extension of the sacramental principle parallels the medieval profusion of sacraments before they were limited to seven in number. There is a commonality between these two developments. It is not only in the liturgical acts but also in the ethical practices of the church that Christ is incarnate: they too are sacraments.

Hubmaier, Marpeck, and Philips all struggled to find the right place for profane things in the realm of the holy. On the one hand, they highlighted the sacramental nature of the visible church, flesh and blood mediating the divine. It was a seminal act of creativity for Anabaptism to extend this sacramentality to actions such as love of neighbor. By the same token, it is ironic that the subjects of our study found it so difficult to extend the sacramental nature of the church to other embodiments of flesh and blood, such as water, bread, and wine.

Marpeck's way of thinking came the closest to resolving this struggle in his relational and dynamic understanding of the sacramental moment. For him grace works not only inwardly but simultaneously outwardly. In other words, the meal of Jesus is the offer of grace. As an audacious expansion of this root symbol the love of neighbor and enemy also prolongs the incarnation of grace.

SUGGESTED READING

Armour (1966); Cross and Thompson (2003); Finger (2004); Rempel (1993); Roth and Stayer (2007).

BIBLIOGRAPHY

Armour, R. (1966), *Anabaptist Baptism* (Scottdale, PA: Herald).

Baylor, M. (ed. and trans.) (1991), *The Radical Reformation* (New York: Cambridge).

Blanke, F. (1966), *Brothers in Christ* (Scottdale, PA: Herald).

Boyd, S. (1992), *Pilgram Marpeck: His Life and Social Theology* (Durham, NC: Duke University).

Crockett, W. (1989), *Eucharist: Symbol of Transformation* (New York: Pueblo).

Cross, A. and P. Thompson (eds.) (2003), *Baptist Sacramentalism* (Waynesboro, GA: Paternoster).

de Lubac, H. (2006), *Corpus Mysticum: the Eucharist and the Church in the Middle Ages* (Notre Dame, IN: University of Notre Dame).

Dipple, G. (2007), "The Spiritual Anabaptists," in J. Roth and J. Stayer (eds.), *A Companion to Spiritualism and Anabaptism* (Boston, MA: Brill), 257–298.

Dyck, C., W. Keeney, and A. Beachy (eds.) (1992), *The Writings of Dirk Philips* (Waterloo, ON: Herald).

Finger, T. (2004), *A Contemporary Anabaptist Theology: Biblical, Historical, Constructive* (Downers Grove, IL: InterVarsity).

Friesen, J. (ed.) (1999), *Peter Riedemann's Hutterite Confession of Faith* (Waterloo, ON: Herald).

Goertz, H.-J. (1996), *The Anabaptists* (New York: Routledge).

Goeters, J. F. G. (ed.) (1969), *Studien zur Geschichte und Theologie der Reformation.* (Neukirchen: Neukirchner).

Klaassen, W., and W. Klassen (2008), *Marpeck: A Life of Dissent and Conformity* (Waterloo, ON: Herald).

Klaassen, W., W. Packull, and J. D. Rempel (trans.) (1999), *Later Writings by Pilgram Marpeck and his Circle* (Kitchener: Pandora).

McNeill, J. (ed.) (1960), John Calvin, *The Institutes of the Christian Religion*, vol. II, (Philadelphia, PA: Westminster).

Marxsen, W. (1970), *The Beginnings of Christology together with the Lord's Supper as a Christological Problem* (Philadelphia, PA: Fortress).

McLaughlin, E. (2007), "Spiritualism: Schwenckfeld and Franck and their Early Modern Resonances," in J. Roth and J. Stayer (eds.), *A Companion to Spiritualism and Anabaptism* (Boston, MA: Brill), 119–162.

Moore, W. (1981), "Catholic Teacher and Anabaptist Pupil: the Relationship between John Eck and Balthasar Hubmaier," *Archiv für Reformationsgeschichte*, 72: 68–97.

Packull, W. (1995), *Hutterite Beginnings: Communitarian Experiments during the Reformation* (Baltimore, MD: The Johns Hopkins University Press).

Pipkin, H. Wayne and J. H. Yoder (trans. and eds.) (1989), *Balthasar Hubmaier: Theologian of Anabaptism* (Scottdale, PA: Herald), esp. "A Form for Water Baptism," 386–392; "A Form for Christ's Supper," 393–408; "On the Christian Ban," 409–425.

Rempel, J. D. (1993), *The Lord's Supper in Anabaptism* (Scottdale, PA: Herald).

Roth, J. and J. Stayer (eds.) (2007), *A Companion to Spiritualism and Anabaptism* (Boston, MA: Brill).

Snyder, C. Arnold (2002), *Anabaptist History and Theology* (Kitchener: Pandora).

Stayer, J. (1991), *The German Peasants' War and Anabaptist Community of Goods* (Montreal: McGill-Queen's).

Voolstra, S. (1982), *Het word is flees geworden* (Kampen, Netherlands: J. H. Kok).

Weaver, J. Denny (2005), *Becoming Anabaptist* (Scottdale, PA: Herald).

Wenger, J. C. (ed.) (1984), *The Complete Writings of Menno Simons* (Waterloo, ON: Herald).

Williams, G. (1962), *The Radical Reformation* (Philadelphia, PA: Westminster).

CHAPTER 21

SACRAMENTS IN THE
COUNCIL OF TRENT AND
SIXTEENTH-CENTURY
CATHOLIC THEOLOGY

PETER WALTER,
TRANSLATED BY DAVID L. AUGUSTINE

PRE-TRIDENTINE Catholic sacramental theology largely rests upon the doctrinal statements of the Council of Florence (1439–1443), which, in its Bull of Union for the Armenian Church in 1439, determined the following: the number of the seven sacraments (baptism, confirmation, Eucharist, penance, extreme unction, holy orders, and matrimony); the "matter" for each sacrament (water, anointing oil, bread and wine; actions such as contrition, the confession of sins, and the reparation of the penitent; and the presentation of objects such as the chalice and paten, and the Book of the Gospels, which are typical for the exercise of ordained ministry), the "form" (form of administration), the minister (usually a bishop or priest, except for baptism, which in the case of necessity can even be administered by a non-Christian, and the bridal couple, whose consent brings about matrimony), and the effect of the sacrament (a specific sacramental grace) (DH 1310–1328). In so doing, the council had recourse to the work *De articulis fidei et Ecclesiae sacramentis* of Thomas Aquinas (Aquinas 1927), which applied the Aristotelian teaching on causes to the sacraments. These were thought of more as operating within the framework of a productive action than as a representative action. Concentration on the minimal requirements of a valid administration of the sacraments caused the liturgical context to take a backseat.

The Reformers placed in question the traditional theology and praxis of the sacraments by appealing to sacred Scripture. Thus, since in the Bible an explicit institution by Jesus Christ is demonstrable only for baptism and for Communion, they reduced the number of sacraments to these two and, with the Eucharist, required the administration of the chalice to the laity. Expressly, they excluded only confirmation and extreme unction. Penance, ordination, and the celebration of matrimony were retained as ecclesial ceremonies, even if with a modified theological interpretation. Against this reduction, Catholic controversial theology undertook to establish the traditional sacraments above all with appeal to tradition. One of the first defenses was the *Assertio septem sacramentorum Adversus Martinum Lutherum* (1521), which the theologically educated English king Henry VIII had written with the assistance of several theologians (Heinrich VIII 1992), and for which he received from the pope the title *Fidei Defensor*. King Henry, who follows the structure of Luther's *De captivitate Babylonica* (1520), lays especial emphasis on the Eucharist (the question of the chalice for the laity, transubstantiation, the sacrifice of the Mass) and treats thereafter baptism, penance, confirmation, marriage, holy orders, and extreme unction (Nitti 2005: 259–417).

The Council of Trent (1545–1563) (for a short overview: Walter 2011) devoted the largest part of its dogmatic decrees to questions of sacramental theology and made pronouncements on all seven sacraments. These pronouncements defend the existing ecclesial praxis and the theology underlying it against the challenges put forward by the Reformers, though they do this not always with a Counter-Reformational intent. When, for instance, the Decree on Original Sin of June 17, 1545, mentions baptism as the sole "means of salvation" from original sin (DH 1513), it expresses fundamental agreement with the Reformers. The difference with the Reformation concerns the question of whether concupiscence (*concupiscentia*) remaining in the baptized is sin that is not imputed, as the Reformers claimed, or inclination toward sin, as the council claims (DH 1515). With regard to infant baptism, which was rejected by several currents of the Reformation (the so-called Anabaptists), the council holds on to it, along with the main currents of the Reformation (DH 1514). When the Decree on Justification of January 13, 1547 enumerates in a Scholastic manner the different causes of justification, baptism is referred to as its "instrumental cause," while at the same time it emphatically asserts that without faith justification is not possible (DH 1529). This also brings to the fore a shared position.

This first impression is confirmed when we trace the texts on sacramental theology of the council. The Decree on the Sacraments in general as well as on baptism and confirmation of March 3, 1547 (DH 1600–1630) initiates the council's teaching on the sacraments. The subject of the conciliar debates was a list of "errors," which were supposedly taken from Martin Luther's *De captivitate Babylonica*, the *Confessio Augustana*, and the *Apologia Confessionis Augustanae* of Philipp Melanchthon, as well as from other Reformation writings, but which were mostly derived from the works of Catholic polemical theologians and were, as a result, pointed in their articulation (Pfnür 1990). For the interpretation of the decree, it is important that the papal legates to the council specified that only the errors of heretics be condemned, while controversies between the schools, where there could be differences of opinion, should not be decided. Moreover, clear language was to be used, and scholastic terminology had to be avoided as much as possible (Jedin 2: 318). The Decree on the Sacraments, Baptism and Confirmation restricts itself to condemnations (*Canones*) according to the schema *Si quis dixerit ... anathema sit*. In the decrees on the remaining sacraments, the council placed doctrinal chapters (*Doctrina*) before the condemnations, not least so as to make it easier for pastors to preach on these topics. The dogmatic value of these doctrinal chapters is disputed, since, unlike the canons, they were frequently adopted without much discussion. "Dogmatic relevance belongs to the doctrinal chapters insofar as and to the extent that their text agrees with the doctrinal statements of the canons, inasmuch as they succeed in bringing the teaching of the canons into objective and logical coherence, and as they are indispensable for the hermeneutic of the dogmatic propositions" (Vorgrimler 1978: 172).

The canons are also not all of the same weight. They aim "not only at serious deviations in teaching, but also at purely disciplinary offenses, which were the expression of very serious disobedience against the ecclesial authority" (Vorgrimler 1978: 172). In the following, I mainly use the canons and refer to the doctrinal chapters when they are helpful in interpretation. In assessing the conciliar texts, it is ultimately to be taken into account that the council did not primarily have in view certain books or authors, but rather doctrines that were held to be reprehensible, without always being able to prove in detail their origin from specific authors or texts of the Reformation. Analysis of a great number of the Tridentine as well as of the Reformers' own doctrinal judgments shows "a wide spectrum of differentiated judgments": "a series of condemnatory pronouncements rest on misunderstandings about the opposing position; others no longer apply to the doctrine and praxis of today's partner; in the case of still others new factual insights have led to a large degree of agreement: but where some of the condemnatory pronouncements are concerned, it cannot be said that there is as yet any agreement at the present day" (Lehmann and Pannenberg 1990: 179f.).

With respect to the general teaching on the sacraments (Finkenzeller 1987: 54–67), the Council of Trent bases itself on the Decree for the Armenians of the Council of Florence, but without taking over its scholastic terminology and stereotypical structure. This also explains the absence of a definition of the term "sacrament." It is not until the 1551 Decree on the Eucharist that we find a definition, taken from the *Decretum Gratiani* and ultimately going back to Augustine: a sacrament is "a sign of a sacred thing and the visible form of invisible grace" (DH 1639). Since the Reformers had not questioned the existence and meaning of the sacraments in principle, it did not appear necessary to formulate an abstract articulation of the meaning of a sacrament. Against the Reformation reduction of the number of the sacraments, the council maintains the number seven (DH 1601). Owing to the definition of Florence, the council could not possibly assent to a reduction in number, although it also rejected the compromise proposal formulated on the Reformation side, namely, to broaden the notion of "sacrament" to any signs that in sacred Scripture have a promise attached. For the justification of the number seven, it was thought sufficient in the conciliar debates to review biblical examples of sets of seven. The council was concerned less for the numerical than for the symbolic significance of the number seven. It is only in post-Tridentine theology that the numerical-arithmetic point of view comes to the fore, without which, however, the symbolic aspect would have been entirely forgotten (Seybold 1976).

To be sure, the council does place the seven sacraments of the New Covenant next to one another in an undifferentiated way, but this does not exclude a hierarchy of sacraments. Rather, the council explicitly teaches a hierarchy of sacraments, without, however, explaining what it looks like (DH 1603). This matter should be left to theologians. Therefore, one can by all means think of the traditional distinction between baptism and Eucharist as *sacramenta maiora* and the rest of the *sacramenta minora*, since all Christian confessions deemed the former to have priority (Lehmann and Pannenberg 1990: 73). The Decree on the Eucharist grounds the uniqueness of the Eucharist on the fact that the author of holiness, Jesus Christ, is already present here before its "use," whereas the rest of the sacraments receive their power of sanctification only in the moment of their use (DH 1639).

As for the relation of the sacraments to faith, one can discern in the *sola fide* of the Reformation a supposed exclusivity of faith at the expense of the sacraments (DH 1604f.). By way of contrast, the Council of Trent adheres to the salvific necessity of the sacraments or at least of the desire thereof, though it concedes that not all of the sacraments are necessary in the same way for all Christians (DH 1604). In the strict sense, this salvific necessity is true only of baptism and, in case one of the baptized has grievously sinned, also of penance, as the Decree on Justification teaches (DH 1543).

The council pursues in detail the question of the sacraments' mode of operation. It reaffirms the traditional teaching that the sacraments confer grace to those "who do not place an obstacle in the way" (DH 1606). The council held onto this manner of speaking, which was strongly criticized by the Reformers, since infant baptism was the paradigm for this sacramental understanding: here the personal aspect, in particular the faith required for a fruitful reception of a sacrament, does not apply, since infants are not yet capable of such reception. At the same time, the council rejects the view of the Swiss Reformer Ulrich Zwingli—though he is not explicitly mentioned by name—that the sacraments are only external tokens of remembrance. With this rejection, the council agrees with Article 13 of the *Confessio Augustana*.

In what follows, the council underscores the objective efficacy of the sacraments: from God's point of view, the sacraments are efficacious when they are performed and received in the right way, always and in relation to all (DH 1607f.). With this emphasis on the willingness of God to bestow his grace, Trent is preaching to the converted among the Reformers. When this efficacy, however, is described with the expression *ex opere operato*, which the Reformers opposed, and their view is expressed as *sola fide* (DH 1608), it becomes clear that in unfortunate ways, people in the sixteenth century were speaking past each other. Trent wanted to ward off an error that the Reformers also rejected, namely, the view that divine grace can be merited through prior human works. Whereas the Reformers associated this suspicion with the teaching of *opus operatum*, which they interpreted in the sense of works-righteousness, Trent detected behind the Protestant *sola fide* a subjectivism and performance-orientation. In their appropriate contexts, however, these expressions give voice to the objective givenness of the divine promise prior to human acceptance. The Scholastic term *ex opere operato* denotes both the redemption wrought by Jesus Christ and the performance of a sacrament, while *sola fide* denotes the complete surrender of the believer to the divine promise of salvation (Lehmann and Pannenberg 1990: 77–79). Since the fundamental role of faith does not come up in the doctrinal condemnations and is absent from the corresponding doctrinal chapters, this led to a narrow perspective in post-Tridentine Catholic sacramental theology. The relationship between sacrament and faith was treated more or less exclusively under the negative aspect of the rejection of *sola fide*—though faith was not denied as the basis of the sacraments even on the Catholic side.

With regard to the sacramental character (*character sacramentalis*) conveyed by the sacraments of baptism, confirmation, and holy orders, Trent maintains their reality (DH 1609), as taught by the Council of Florence (DH 1313) but as denied by the Reformers. The theological interpretation of this character, however, was left to the theological schools.

Finally, the council expresses itself on the question of who should administer the sacraments, and with what rites. It denies a general authority of all Christians to proclaim the word and administer the sacraments (DH 1610). It maintains that the minister, in celebrating the sacraments, must have the intention of doing what the church does (DH 1611), but that he need not himself be in the state of grace (DH 1612). With regard to the rites, the minister has to keep to the ones the church has approved. He may neither disregard them nor substitute new ones on his own initiative (DH 1613).

The doctrinal condemnations on baptism and confirmation (Neunheuser 1983: 117–120, 143f.) yield no comprehensive teaching, as they take positions only on particular questions. In accord with the tradition since the ancient church, the council teaches the validity of baptism administered by heretics, when they have the right intention and use the Trinitarian formula (DH 1617, 1624). This allows those baptized in the churches of the Reformation to be received into the Catholic Church. When there are doubts about the validity of someone's baptism, however, the candidate for entrance into the Catholic Church receives a "conditional" baptism. Whereas Pius V recognized as valid the baptism administered by Calvinists despite the fact that their baptismal theology differed from that of Catholics, doubts arose in subsequent centuries (Mangenot 1923: 340). Against those Reformation groups that questioned of the role of the sacraments, the council stresses the salvific necessity of baptism (DH 1618) and defends the practice of infant baptism (DH 1625–7). In this connection, it confirms the view that children, who are not yet able to make their own act of faith, are "baptized solely in the faith of the Church" (DH 1626). The proposal, advocated by Erasmus of Rotterdam (Payne 1970: 171–174) and taken up by some of the Reformers, including Martin Bucer and Zwingli, that those baptized as infants should, upon entry into adulthood, appropriate the baptismal promises given by their godparents—a practice from which (Protestant) "confirmation" developed—is rejected (DH 1627). The council only concerned itself with questions of the legitimacy, validity, and salvific necessity of baptism, without in each case going into the theological considerations. The inclusion of the baptized in Jesus Christ and their incorporation into the church are not addressed. The council had already addressed the connection between baptism and the teaching on original sin in its Decree on Original Sin (DH 1510–1516).

With the condemnation of the Reformation errors concerning confirmation, the council again turns against an idea already rejected in connection with baptism, namely, that this would involve merely a ratification of faith by adolescents; the council reaffirms confirmation as "a true and proper sacrament" (DH 1628). Moreover, the council defends the anointing with oil against the accusation that this would be an offense against the Holy Spirit (DH 1629); it rejects the view that this sacrament could be administered not only by bishops, but by every priest (DH 1630). Trent fails to provide the scriptural proof for this sacrament, which the Reformers demanded.

The council dealt with the question of the Eucharist in three decrees, which correspond in their subject matter to the Reformation critique: (1) "Decree on the Sacrament of the Eucharist," adopted on October 11, 1551 (DH 1635–61); (2) "Doctrine and Canons on Communion under both Species and the Communion of Young Children," adopted on July 16, 1562 (DH 1725–34); and (3) "Doctrine and Canons on the Sacrifice of the Mass," adopted on September 17, 1562 (DH 1738–60).

The Decree on the Eucharist of 1551 includes a doctrinal section and eleven canons. It deals mainly with the acknowledgement of the presence of Jesus Christ in the Eucharist and its theological rationale. The council sets itself against the denial of the real presence of the body and blood of Christ, of his soul and divinity in the sacrament of the Eucharist, and it rejects a merely symbolic, figurative, and virtual presence (*"ut in signo vel figura, aut virtute"*) (DH 1651). The Council Fathers would not and could not thereby address Luther, with whom, despite all their differences, they were agreed on the fundamental affirmation of the real presence of Christ in the Eucharist. Luther had broken with the Swiss Reformers because they taught differently with regard to this question. In rejecting a merely symbolic presence of Christ in the sacrament, the council addressed Zwingli, Johannes Oecolampadius, and the "Sacramentarians," whose position the council critiqued for holding to a purely external relationship between sign and signified reality. Language about a figurative presence was considered ambiguous, since, as the disputes since the ninth century made clear, such language might signify only a hermeneutical category, which does not do justice to the presence of Christ in the Eucharist. If with its third variant (*virtute*) the council intended to address the position of Calvin, with hindsight we must observe that this statement of his eucharistic teaching does not do it justice. Although Calvin certainly does speak of a presence of Christ *virtute*, he has in view the *virtus spiritus sancti*, by virtue of which the personal presence of Christ comes about in the Eucharist (cf. Lehmann and Pannenberg 1990: 89–92).

The council rejects the teaching on consubstantiation as an explanation of the real presence and stresses in its place a "wonderful and unique change" (*conversio*), which the Catholic Church in a highly suitable way (*aptissime*) calls transubstantiation (DH 1652). Traditionally, this has been regarded as the dogmatic articulation (*Dogmatisierung*) of the doctrine of transubstantiation and the condemnation of all other views. Looked at today, however, the situation appears more complex. The council certainly did not have the intention to dogmatically ensconce a philosophical theory. Instead—and in this respect it is of one mind with Luther—it wished to safeguard the mystery of the presence of Christ in the sacrament, to which the first doctrinal chapter refers as a "manner of existence" which, though "we can scarcely express it in words, yet we can, however, by our understanding illuminated by faith conceive to be possible to God, and which we

ought most steadfastly to believe" (DH 1636). Lehmann and Pannenberg rightly conclude from this:

> It emerges from the conciliar documents that in can. 2 the fathers were not con-
> cerned to tie the matter down to a particular kind of philosophical thinking. Their
> purpose was a theological one. They wished to reconcile the once-for-all nature of
> the incarnation with the presence of Christ, "in many other places sacramentally"
> (D[H] 1636), thereby resisting the view of a hypostatic union between the human
> nature of Christ and the substance of bread and wine (a view ascribed to Luther in
> the conciliar drafts of this article). (Lehmann and Pannenberg 1990: 99)

The council rejects so to speak an "'excess' of real presence," which "would have
destroyed its sacramentality" (Wohlmuth 1975: 290). On Christological grounds, that is,
so as to distinguish Christ's "natural way of existing" at the right hand of the Father (DH
1636) from his sacramental presence, the council falls back on the traditional, not philosophically "charged," notion of *conversio* ("transformation"), which is rendered only secondarily with the *terminus technicus* of transubstantiation (DH 1640, 1652). "The idea
of the *conversio*, or transformation ... also tries to preserve the idea of 'sacramentality'
from a falsification which it was feared could arise through notions in the direction of
re-incarnation, impanation, or a repeated hypostatic union" (Lehmann and Pannenberg
1990: 99). An earlier formulation of the canon still claimed patristic origins for the term
"transubstantiation." "Considering the many historical problems," the final text dis-
penses "with a historical derivation of the term and makes it without further ado into
the 'code word' of the Catholic tradition for the present Church" (Wohlmuth 1975: 290).

The subsequent doctrinal condemnations serve mainly to justify the traditional
praxis of the church. Thus, with respect to Communion under only one species, the
presence of the "whole Christ" under each species and in each part of the same is maintained (DH 1653). Another rejected view is that Christ is present in the Eucharist "only
in the use, while it is being received, and not before or after." The council emphasizes
that Christ is present also in the leftover hosts that remain after Communion (DH 1654).
With that, the council reaffirms eucharistic adoration outside the Mass, denounced by
the Reformers as "idolatry", and especially the Corpus Christi processions introduced
in the thirteenth century (DH 1644), which subsequently Catholics used particularly to
express anti-Protestant sentiment. The council stresses that there are also fruits of the
Mass other than the forgiveness of sins emphasized by the Reformers, without of course
naming these fruits (DH 1655). Furthermore, the reservation of the Eucharist and its
administration to the sick are defended (DH 1657). Against a purely spiritual interpretation of the Eucharist, the council teaches that Christ is not eaten merely *spiritualiter*
(spiritually), but also *sacramentaliter ac realiter* (sacramentally and really) (DH 1658).
It inculcates anew the precept of the Fourth Lateran Council (DH 812) with regard to
yearly Communion (DH 1659) and defends the practice of the priest giving himself
Communion at Mass (DH 1660). Finally, the council condemns the view that faith alone
would be sufficient as preparation for the reception of the Eucharist, and it requires,
where possible, prior confession in case of mortal sins (DH 1661).

The document on Communion under both species from 1562 also consists of doctrinal chapters and canons. The council recalls that Communion was originally administered under both species, but that this was modified for significant reasons, which the Church has a right to do, as long as in the process she preserves the "substance" of the sacraments (DH 1728). (In post-Tridentine theology there was discussion about how one was to understand the "substance" of the sacraments. Here, one often had recourse to the distinction between "matter" and "form," and it was thought that they could be traced back to Jesus Christ and were thus not under the church's power of control. Where a historical development of the sacrament could be observed, theologians generally sought to resolve the problem by differentiating between the institution of a sacrament in a specific and in a general way [Finkenzeller 1981: 90–3].) For the defense of existing praxis, the council rejects, on the one hand, the view that all Christians must "by reason of God's command or out of necessity for salvation" communicate under both species (DH 1731), and, on the other hand, those who claim that the church has no serious reasons for the introduction of Communion under one species (DH 1732). Reiterating the claim of the Decree on the Eucharist (DH 1653), the council teaches the presence of the whole Christ under the species of bread alone (DH 1733). Finally, the council rejects the necessity of Communion by children prior to the attainment of the "age of discernment," that is, before age thirteen or fourteen (DH 1734). That the council does not absolutely reject Communion under both species in principle can be seen in the fact that, on September 17, 1562, it places the practical matter of granting the chalice to the laity at the discretion of the pope (DH 1760). By the time Pius IV (1559–65) permitted the use of the chalice to the laity in 1564 in Germany, Austria, Bohemia, and Hungary, this had already become a matter where confessional practices diverged. Therefore, the Catholic population did not make much use of this permission, and various popes revoked it, in 1584 for Germany and Austria, in 1604 for Hungary, and in 1621 for Bohemia (Ganzer 1997).

As the two previously considered documents, so the one dealing with the sacrifice of the Mass includes both doctrinal chapters and canons (Duval 1985: 61–150). The latter treats side by side very different topics, which vary widely also in dogmatic import. The issue of whether the Mass is a sacrifice was a central point of the Reformation critique of the traditional praxis of the church. Not only the understanding of the priestly office, but also the care for the temporal and eternal lives of all the faithful depended on the sacrificial view of the Mass. The vast majority of priests, who did not engage in pastoral care, derived their *raison d'être* as well as their livelihood from the celebration of Masses, which the faithful commissioned so as to bring their requests before God. Mainly, it was about Masses for the dead.

Of special significance are Canons 1 and 3, in which the council defends the sacrificial character of the Mass and, from this perspective, wards off false interpretations of it, such as treating the sacrifice as consisting in the fact that Christ is given to the faithful as food (DH 1751), or that it is "merely offering praise and thanksgiving or that it is a simple commemoration of the sacrifice accomplished on the Cross, but not a propitiatory sacrifice" (DH 1753). Trent meets the Reformation criticism that the sacrifice of the Mass obscures the once-for-all, sufficient character of Christ's sacrifice on the cross by defining "the sacrifice of the mass as a making present (*repraesentatio*) of Jesus Christ's once-for-all sacrifice of himself on the cross" (Lehmann and Pannenberg 1990: 85). The council expresses this primarily in the first of the doctrinal chapters, which comments: Christ has left behind "to his beloved Spouse the Church a visible sacrifice (as the nature of man demands)—by which the bloody (sacrifice) that he was once for all to accomplish on the Cross would be re-presented (*repraesentaretur*), its memory (*memoria*) perpetuated until the end of the world, and its salutary power applied for the forgiveness of the sins that we daily commit" (DH 1740). The Reformation view of the Last Supper as a "commemoration" of the sacrifice of the cross, however, is misunderstood and rejected as a "simple commemoration" (*nuda commemoratio*) (DH 1753). According to the conviction of the council, this renders it a matter of strictly subjective remembrance, a mere commemoration of the sacrifice of the cross, rather than an objective re-presentation of the same, which requires visibility.

The council sees in Christ's mandate to repeat what he did—"Do this in remembrance of me" (Luke 22:19; 1 Cor 11:24)—a commissioning of the apostles as priests, along with the commandment given to them and to all priests, to offer his body and his blood (DH 1752). The latter is done for the living and the dead, for the repayment of sins and the punishment due to sin, for atonement, and for other needs (DH 1753). Finally, the council wards off the Reformation accusation put forward especially by Urbanus Rhegius, that the sacrifice of the Mass is a blasphemy (DH 1754). Further sanctions concern the form of celebration, such as Masses in which only the priest communicates, which is declared to be legitimate (DH 1758). The traditional eucharistic prayer, the Canon of the Mass, is defended against the reproach that it contains errors that make its abolition necessary (DH 1756). Moreover, its recitation in a low voice, especially of the words of institution, as well as the admixture of water in the eucharistic chalice, are declared to be legitimate, and the demand to celebrate Mass only in the vernacular is rejected (DH 1759). Finally, the position is condemned that regards the ceremonies, vestments, and external signs, customary in the Catholic Church for the celebration of Mass, as "incentives to impiety rather than works of piety" (DH 1757).

The council, which in no way closed its eyes to blatant shortcomings, was concerned particularly to ward off Reformation attacks on traditional customs in the celebration of Mass. "This defense initially refers to the ceremonies of the celebration of Mass as a whole. The Council endeavored to prove or at least to show their origins as much as possible in Jesus himself or in the praxis of the Apostles, or at least to make clear they did not contradict the gospel and were not introduced without the working of the Holy Spirit. Finally, time and again, Old Testament prefigurements were pointed out, along with the fact that human nature requires rites" (Meyer 1989: 259). The council at the same time proposed often to explain to the faithful the meaning of the readings and of the eucharistic celebration itself during the celebration of Mass (DH 1749), and it recommended frequent Communion of the faithful (DH 1747). However, preaching was still done outside Mass; moreover, the faithful attended Communion rather infrequently, and it, too, was often administered outside the celebration of the Mass. People had often sensed a certain deficit in this, but nonetheless the rationale given in defence of the celebration of Mass without Communion added to the deficit (DH 1747). "Such Masses were referred to as truly communal celebrations (*vere communes*), since the faithful communicate spiritually and since the priest celebrates them as a 'public minister' (*minister publicus*) of the church, not only for himself, but rather for all the members of the body of Christ" (Meyer 1989: 259). This is true then also for the Masses which the priest celebrates with only one altar server and without the faithful (*missa solitaria*). The communal character of the eucharistic celebration, its form as a meal, thereby retreats wholly into the background. The "growing individualization and privatization of the praxis of celebration and of the devotion to the Mass, especially that of the priest himself" (Meyer 1989: 259) is, of course, a development that Trent did not inaugurate, but rather only further promoted.

Doctrinal chapters and canons for the sacrament of penance and for extreme unction were adopted on November 25, 1551 (DH 1667–1719). Whereas the canons for penance had been discussed in detail, there was hardly any discussion on the doctrinal chapters, which "can be called a document of the Council only in a qualified way" (Vorgrimler 1978: 173). With regard to penance, the council teaches that it is a true sacrament instituted by Christ (DH 1701), which differs from the forgiveness of sins granted in baptism (DH 1702). For biblical justification, the council refers to Jesus' authorization of the apostles to forgive sins or to withhold forgiveness (John 20:22f.), as the Catholic Church has always understood these words "from the beginning" (DH 1703). With regard to penance, the council distinguishes three "acts" of the penitent, or rather, "parts" of penance: contrition, the confession of sins, and satisfaction, which together form the *quasi materia* of the sacrament of penance (DH 1704). The council thereby rejects a Reformation division of these acts into anguish over sin and faith in forgiveness, as it is found, for example, in the *Confessio Augustana* and in the *Apologia Confessionis Augustanae* of Melanchthon, each in the twelfth article.

Moreover, the council contests Luther's suspicion of contrition as hypocrisy, and Melanchthon's allegation that it was not done voluntarily (DH 1705). The council confirms what the Decree on Justification said about the significance of contrition as the right disposition of the sinner for the reception of justification (DH 1554–57, 1559). In the fourth doctrinal chapter, the council distinguishes between perfect and imperfect contrition (*contritio perfecta* and *imperfecta*). Whereas the former can already reconcile one with God before the reception of the sacrament of penance, but not without the desire for the sacrament, the latter, which is also called *attritio*, cannot do this, but it does dispose one for the correct reception of the sacrament, as long as it does not consist simply of fear of punishment (DH 1677f.). Regarding the interpretation of Canons 6–8, there still exists no unanimity in Catholic theology (Vorgrimler 1978: 177–182; Duval 1985: 209–222). The council defends the confession of all mortal sins "to the priest alone" against the accusation of Luther and Calvin that this is a human invention. The council holds that it can be traced back to a mandate of Christ, so that it is declared to be divine law (*ius divinum*). Whereas for Luther, only directives explicitly contained in sacred Scripture could have such a status, according to contemporary Catholic theology, inferences from biblical commands could also claim the authority of divine law. In the present case, the requirement of a confession of sins represents a legitimate inference from the power bestowed by the Risen Lord on the apostles (and their successors) to forgive or to withhold forgiveness (John 20:23). After all, without a confession of sins, a decision about the granting of forgiveness is not possible. It was debated at Trent, however, whether this means that confession as such can be designated as divine law, regardless of whether it is public or secret confession i.e. auricular confession, or whether this holds true explicitly only for auricular confession. With regard to this issue, the council could not make a decision. It defended auricular confession, however, against the Reformation accusation that it had been introduced without a mandate of Christ, and asserted that it had been practiced continuously from the beginning (DH 1706).

In this connection, the council also dealt with the question of the exhaustive character of the confession of sins. Luther, who had a high view of the confession of sins, rejected a full enumeration of all mortal and venial sins, as was usually required by Catholic theology of penance and as was encouraged by confessors through their questioning of the penitent. The council defended the existing praxis (DH 1707f.). There is disagreement, however, whether or not the council, by characterizing it as "divine law," wished to go beyond the preceding canon by positing also secret auricular confession as dogma. Against Reformation criticism, the council declares legitimate the view of priestly absolution as a judicial act, without, however, thereby designating auricular confession strictly as a "penitential tribunal" and without excluding other aspects such as that of healing (DH 1709).

Although the power to forgive sins is reserved to bishops and priests and does not depend on the state of grace of the confessor (DH 1710), the council adheres to the traditional view that certain cases can be reserved to bishops (DH 1711). Finally, the council deals in more detail with the question of satisfaction. It distinguishes between the guilt remitted by God and the punishment to be performed by the penitent, which does not simply consist of faith in the satisfaction accomplished by Christ (DH 1712). The council considers it necessary to bear patiently the punishments imposed by God and pronounced by the priest, and beneficial to take on voluntarily works of penance such as fasting, prayer, and almsgiving (DH 1713). Such penitential works in no way obscure the merits of Christ, but rather constitute acts of worship of God (DH 1714). The language of the "keys" includes not only the confessors' power to loose, but also their power to bind. Hence, it certainly is part to their mandate from Christ to impose penances. "The canons for the doctrine of satisfaction ... safeguard, with their anathemas, the ecclesial principle, practiced from antiquity onward, that the forgiveness of sins, in a baptized person, brings with it a laborious dealing with the guilty past and not only the start of a new life" (Vorgrimler 1978: 186).

We can notice already prior to the Council of Trent an increasing frequency of confession and a reception of Communion beyond the specified minimum of the Fourth Lateran Council (1215). The Fourth Lateran Council prescribed that Christians do penance at least once a year in their parish church and receive Communion (DH 812). However, Trent no longer bound the reception of the sacrament to the parish church. It thus took into consideration that many Christians sought out monastic churches for the reception of the sacraments. Here we can see a sign of a progressive individualization of the reception of the sacraments, as of piety in general.

Following the sacrament of penance, the Council of Trent in the same decree also dealt with extreme unction (*extrema unctio*), a designation we should retain here for historical reasons (as compared with the anointing of the sick [*unctio infirmorum*] taken up again by Vatican II [Vorgrimler 1978: 226–231; Duval 1985: 223–279]). This placement of extreme unction after the sacrament of penance highlights the penitential character of anointing. Following Thomas Aquinas, extreme unction is referred to as "the consummation not only of penance but also of the whole Christian life, which ought to be a continual penance" (DH 1694). The four canons for extreme unction formulate four respective counterpoints to accusations of the Reformers, as they had been presented to the Fathers of Trent: whereas the Reformers regarded extreme unction, if at all, as a rite handed down by the Church Fathers, Trent teaches that it is a sacrament instituted by Jesus Christ, even if it was promulgated by the apostle James (DH 1716). James 5:14 is the classical biblical reference for extreme unction, but the Reformation side rejected it as a foundation for the sacrament (DH 1718f.). For its part, the council rejects the view that regards the healings attested to in the New Testament as simply the result of an extraordinary grace of healing that was restricted to the early church (DH 1717).

Trent disassociated itself from the Reformation understanding of the decisive biblical passages regarding extreme unction by defending the present use of this sacrament as practiced in the Western church. Luther recognized that this practice hardly represented the overall history of the sacrament, and "with his at times remarkable eye for historical developments" (Jedin 3: 62), he critically brought this up for discussion. In its defensive posture, the council was not in a position adequately to appreciate the historical findings.

In the Decree on the Sacrament of Orders of July 15, 1563 (DH 1763–78) (Duval 1985: 327–404; Freitag 1991), the council teaches the institution of this sacrament by Jesus Christ, and it defines the offering of the eucharistic sacrifice as well as the forgiveness of sins as the essential powers conferred by priestly ordination (DH 1771, 1773). It also defends the minor orders (DH 1772), the hierarchical structure of orders (DH 1776), and the superiority of the episcopal office over the priestly (DH 1777f.) (Freitag 1991: 370–376). However, it remains rather vague in its description of the episcopal office, since the fiercely discussed question of the place of the papal office prevented a clear conclusion (Freitag 1991: 368–370). In the Reformation teaching about the common priesthood, the Council of Trent sees an undermining of the hierarchical structure of the church (DH 1767, 1776). Preaching and pastoral activity, referred to in the reform decrees as the main task of bishops and priests (Sessio 24, *Decretum de reformatione*, Canon 4 and 13; DEC 763, 768), show up in the dogmatic decree only in a negative light, when it rejects an understanding of the office that reduces the powers of the office to proclamation (*nudum ministerium verbi*) (DH 1771).

In the Decree on Marriage adopted on November 11, 1563, shortly before the conclusion of the council, Trent defends marriage as being a sacrament (DH 1801) as well the jurisdiction of the church with regard to legal questions on marriage (DH 1812), something that is given expression in numerous individual regulations (DH 1803–11). With regard to the indissolubility of marriage, the council restricts itself to defending the Catholic praxis of denying divorce under all circumstances, without thereby condemning the different praxis of the Greek Orthodox Church, which provides for such on the grounds of adultery (DH 1807)—this with a view to the Greek territories under Venetian governance (Gaudemet 1987: 289f.). Of special significance for the future was the introduction of the so-called canonical form, which was adopted on the same day, after fierce discussion, by the reform decree *Tametsi* (DH 1813–16). According to church teaching, the free consent of the partners sufficed to constitute a valid marriage, a consent that could be expressed without involvement of a clergyman or of witnesses and also without the approval of the parents (*matrimonium clandestinum*: secret marriage). Naturally, this opened up the possibility of abuse. Although the council certainly saw this, it could not bring itself to declare null and void marriages that had been ratified without parental approval. Nevertheless, the council does express its disapproval of this practice. In order to prevent clandestine marriages and to establish legal certainty, the council stipulates a particular form, with which it is adapting to the aspirations of modern social discipline; the form involves a public announcement of the marriage ceremony so that impediments to the marriage can be aired, as well as an inquiry concerning marriage consent by the responsible parish priest (Gaudemet 1987: 290–295). The council does not express itself on the question discussed in contemporary Catholic theology of whether the sacramentality of marriage depends on the participation of a priest in the marriage ceremony (as advocated by Melchior Cano) or on the traditionally recognized unity of marriage consent and sacrament (which a majority of Catholic theologians maintained, above all Robert Bellarmine), though the canonical form prescribed by the council seems to point in the direction of the former (Bricout 2005).

There was no consistent formula used throughout whole church for the administration of the sacraments before Trent encouraged this. The first such formula was published in 1570, the *Missale Romanum* for the celebration of the Eucharist. With the *Rituale Romanum*, published in 1614, a "model book" (Kaczynski 1992: 289) was presented for the first time for the administration of the sacraments and sacramentals, which was intended for the Roman Catholic Church as a whole, though it was in no way stringently prescribed: it was simply characterized by a certain streamlining of the rites.

For the theological rationale and the catechetical mediation of this sacramental teaching, the *Catechismus . . . ad parochos*, called in short the *Catechismus Romanus*, which was intended for pastors, first appeared in 1566 (Rodríguez 1989). This had been commissioned on November 11, 1563, mainly in order to give bishops and priests assistance for the administration of the sacraments (*Sessio* 24, *Decretum de reformatione*, Canon 7; DEC 764). Therefore, it is not surprising that the section on the sacraments is twice as long as those on the Profession of Faith, the Decalogue, and the Lord's Prayer, which are all approximately of the same length (Bellinger 1970: 70). That the section on the sacraments turned out to be so extensive is part of the nature of the document. On account of the Reformers' reduction of the number of the sacraments, a response had to be developed in detail with respect to all of the sacraments, but especially the ones that they disputed. Nevertheless, the characteristic style of the presentation, here as well as in the other parts of the Catechism, conforms to the subject matter and is not determined by anti-Reformation polemics (Bellinger 1970: 250–253). The *Catechismus Romanus*, in its presentation, draws mainly from sacred Scripture, the Church Fathers, and testimonies from conciliar doctrinal tradition (Bellinger 1970: 74–86). Naturally, the Decree for the Armenians of the Council of Florence occupies a privileged place at this point. This is true also for the most influential post-Tridentine Catholic controversialists, the Jesuits and Cardinal Robert Bellarmine, who dedicated the second volume of his *Disputationes de controversiis christianae fidei* to the sacraments (Bellarminus 1588). Against Reformation theology, which emphasizes the promissory character of the sacraments and the role of the sermon in their administration, Bellarmine insists on the consecratory effect of the sacramental form and sees in the sermon, though it is important as a matter of principle, no condition for the completion of a sacrament (Finkenzeller 1981: 71–76). He shares the Reformers' conviction that sacraments must have been directly instituted by Jesus Christ in order to achieve the believed effect. Unlike them, however, he does not regard the lack of scriptural witness for such an institution as reason for exclusion. For example, according to Bellarmine, the communication of the Spirit through the laying on of hands, attested to in the New Testament, entitles us to infer a corresponding commission. He also takes recourse to the distinction used by Trent (DH 1716) between an institution by Christ not recorded in the Bible and a promulgation that is attested in Scripture by an apostle (Finkenzeller 1981: 80–82). On this basis, and taking into account the Church Fathers as well as the ecclesial doctrinal tradition, Bellarmine proves the legitimacy of all seven sacraments (Finkenzeller 1981: 94–98).

It is typical of the post-Tridentine theology of the sacraments that the traditional school controversies—for example, on the mode of operation of the sacraments (Finkenzeller 1981: 105–115) or on the sacrificial character of the Mass—were pursued down well-worn paths, which of course were ever more subtle and differentiated (Daly 2000). On the whole, although Trent did not wish to favor the opinions of any school, the Thomistic perspective prevailed (Finkenzeller 1981: 69). Moreover, "as a result of the focus on the minimal prerequisites and conditions, practiced by Trent itself and then developed always further, sacramental theology ended up under the rubric of Canon Law, where it increasingly ceased to be theology" (Vorgrimler 1987: 79). As a result, the administration of the sacraments in the post-Tridentine era—not only in terms of matrimony and penance—was increasingly subjugated to the church's hierarchy (Prosperi 2001: 114–142). The liturgy itself, above all the celebration of the holy Mass, was surrounded on Sundays and feast days with a certain splendor, which underscores the eschatological character of these celebrations, an interpretation that allows us to resist the (rather narrow-minded!) understanding of this display of splendor as a purely triumphalistic expression of self-aggrandizement.

Abbreviations

DEC = N. P. Tanner (Ed.), *Decrees of the Ecumenical Councils*, 2 vols. (London: Sheed & Ward—Washington, DC: Georgetown University Press, 1990).

DH   = Heinrich Denzinger, *Enchiridion symbolorum definitionum et declarationum de rebus fidei et morum/Compendium of creeds, definitions, and declarations on matters of faith and morals*, ed. by P. Hünermann (San Francisco, CA: Ignatius Press, 43rd edn., 2012).

Suggested Reading

Finkenzeller (1981); Duval (1985); Lehmann and Pannenberg (1990).

Bibliography

Aquinas, Thomas (1927), "De articulis fidei et Ecclesiae sacramentis," in P. Mandonnet (ed.), *S. Thomae Aquinatis Opuscula omnia*, vol. 3 (Paris: Lethielleux), 11–18.

Bellarminus, R. (1588), *Disputationes de controversiis christianae fidei adversus huius temporis haereticos*, vol. 2 (Ingolstadt: Sartorius).

Bellinger, G. (1970), *Der Catechismus Romanus und die Reformation. Die katechetische Antwort des Trienter Konzils auf die Haupt-Katechismen der Reformatoren*, Konfessionskundliche und kontroverstheologische Studien, 27 (Paderborn: Bonifatius).

Bricout, H. (2005), "Le Ministre du sacrement de mariage. Aux origines de la controverse: Melchior Cano et Robert Bellarmin," *La Maison-Dieu* 244: 69–90.

Daly, R. J. (2000), "Robert Bellarmine and post-Tridentine Eucharistic Theology," *Theological Studies* 61: 239–260.

Duval, A. (1985), *Des sacrements au Concile de Trente*, Rites et symboles (Paris: Cerf).

Finkenzeller, J. (1981), *Die Lehre von den Sakramenten im allgemeinen von der Reformation bis zur Gegenwart*, Handbuch der Dogmengeschichte, IV/1b (Freiburg: Herder).

Freitag, J. (1991), *Sacramentum ordinis auf dem Konzil von Trient. Ausgeblendeter Dissens und erreichter Konsens*, Innsbrucker theologische Studien, 32 (Innsbruck and Vienna: Tyrolia).

Ganzer, K. (1997), "Laienkelch I. Historisch-theologisch," in *Lexikon für Theologie und Kirche*, 3rd ed., VI, c. 600.

Gaudemet, J. (1987), *Le Mariage en Occident. Les Mœurs et le droit*, Histoire (Paris: Cerf).

Heinrich VIII. (1992), *Assertio septem sacramentorum adversus Martinum Lutherum*, ed. P. Fraenkel, Corpus Catholicorum, 43 (Münster: Aschendorff).

Jedin, H. (1949–75), *Geschichte des Konzils von Trient*, 4 vols. (Freiburg: Herder).

Kaczynski, R. (1992), "Feier der Krankensalbung," in *Sakramentliche Feiern*, I/2, Gottesdienst der Kirche: Handbuch der Liturgiewissenschaft, 7, 2 (Regensburg: Pustet), 241–343.

Kilmartin, E. J. (1998), *The Eucharist in the West: History and Theology*, J. R. Daly (ed.) (Collegeville, MI: The Liturgical Press, Pueblo).

Kleinheyer, B. (1989), "Die Feiern der Eingliederung in die Kirche," in *Sakramentliche Feiern*, I, Gottesdienst der Kirche: Handbuch der Liturgiewissenschaft 7, 1 (Regensburg: Pustet).

Lehmann, K. and W. Pannenberg (eds.) (1990), *The Condemnations of the Reformation Era: Do They Still Divide?*, trans. Margaret Kohl (Minneapolis, MI: Fortress).

Mangenot, E. (1923), "Valeur du baptême des anglicans et des protestants aux yeux de l'église catholique," in *Dictionnaire de théologie catholique* 2: 337–341.

Meßner, R. and Oberforcher, R. (1992), "Feiern der Umkehr und Versöhnung," in *Sakramentliche Feiern*, I/2, Gottesdienst der Kirche: Handbuch der Liturgiewissenschaft 7, 2 (Regensburg: Pustet), 9–240.

Meyer, H. B. and I. Pahl (1989), *Eucharistie. Geschichte, Theologie, Pastoral*, Gottesdienst der Kirche: Handbuch der Liturgiewissenschaft, 4 (Regensburg: Pustet).

Neunheuser, B. (1983), *Taufe und Firmung*, Handbuch der Dogmengeschichte, IV/2 (Freiburg: Herder).

Nitti, S. (2005), *Auctoritas. L'Assertio di Enrico VIII contro Lutero*, Studi e Testi del Rinascimento Europeo, 27 (Roma: Storia e Letteratura).

Payne, J. B. (1970), *Erasmus and His Theology of the Sacraments*, Research in Theology (Richmond, VA: John Knox Press).

Pfnür, V. (1990), "Verwirft das Konzil von Trient in der Lehre von den Sakramenten die reformatorische Bekenntnisposition? Zur Frage der Kenntnis der reformatorischen Theologie auf dem Konzil von Trient. Untersuchung der Irrtumslisten über die Sakramente," in W. Pannenberg (ed.), *Lehrverurteilungen—kirchentrennend?*, vol. 3 (Freiburg: Herder, Göttingen: Vandenhoeck & Ruprecht), 159–186.

Prosperi, A. (2001), *Il Concilio di Trento: una introduzione storica*, Piccola Biblioteca Einaudi 117 (Torino: Einaudi).

Rodríguez, P. et al. (eds.) (1989), *Catechismus Romanus seu Catechismus ex decreto Concilii Tridentini ad parochos Pii Quinti Pont. Max. iussu editus* (Città del Vaticano: Libreria Editrice Vaticana—Barañain-Pamplona: Ediciones Universidad de Navarra).

Seybold, M. (1976), "Die Siebenzahl der Sakramente (Conc. Trid., sessio VII, can. 1)," *Münchener Theologische Zeitschrift* 27: 113–138.

Vorgrimler, H. (1978), *Buße und Krankensalbung*, Handbuch der Dogmengeschichte, IV/3 (Freiburg: Herder).

Vorgrimler, H. (1987), *Sakramententheologie*, Leitfaden Theologie (Düsseldorf: Patmos).

Walter, P. (2011), "Trienter Konzil," in *Enzyklopädie der Neuzeit* 13: 761–766.

Wohlmuth, J. (1975), *Realpräsenz und Transsubstantiation im Konzil von Trient. Eine historisch-kritische Analyse der Canones 1–4 der Sessio XIII*, 2 vols., Europäische Hochschulschriften, XXIII 37 (Bern and Frankfurt am Main: Lang).

CHAPTER 22

ORTHODOX SACRAMENTAL THEOLOGY: SIXTEENTH–NINETEENTH CENTURIES

BRIAN A. BUTCHER

INTRODUCTION

IN the Orthodox world, the sixteenth to nineteenth centuries witnessed the repercussions of Reformation polemics, and corollary efforts at clarifying and consolidating the Eastern church's position vis-à-vis those of Protestantism and Roman Catholicism. The period's sacramental theology, therefore, is best charted through the primary sources documenting these efforts: principally, Western-style doctrinal "Confessions" of hierarchs and decrees of local councils, which have since obtained ecumenical authority as "Symbolical Books" (Ware 1997: 203). The most significant of these are available in English in *Creeds & Confessions of Faith in the Christian Tradition* (Pelikan 2003), whence they are cited below, unless otherwise noted: the first *Reply* of Jeremias II to the *Augsburg Confession* (1576); the *Confession of Faith* of Metrophanes Critopoulos (1625); the *Eastern Confession of Faith* of Cyril Lucaris (1629); the *Orthodox Confession* of Peter Moghila (1638/42); and the *Confession* of Dositheus and the Synod of Jerusalem (1672). For Moghila, attention is also given to the rubrics and commentary of his liturgical books. Finally, we consider the systematic and canonical legacies of Eugenios and Nicolas Bulgaris, and Nicodemus the Hagiorite, respectively.

Twentieth-century churchman Georges Florovsky decried the centuries in question for their *pseudo-morphosis* of the Orthodox tradition because of the scope of—in his estimation, all but exclusively negative—Western influence. Contemporary Alexander Schmemann could similarly rue the "the Babylonian Captivity of Orthodox theology to Western Scholasticism." Yet a remarkable dynamism is evident: Kallistos Ware acclaims seventeenth-century writers, for example, for their "permanent and constructive contribution to Orthodoxy" inasmuch as "[t]he Reformation controversies raised problems which neither the Ecumenical Councils nor the Church of the later Byzantine Empire was called to face ... Orthodox were forced to think more carefully about the sacraments, and about the nature and authority of the Church" (Ware 1997: 99).

JEREMIAS II, *THE REPLY TO THE AUGSBURG CONFESSION*, 1576

We begin with the so-called "Age of Confessionalism." Philipp Melanchthon had sent a Greek version of the *Augsburg Confession* to Constantinople already in 1559, soliciting support for Lutheran reforms. The response of Jeremias (*c.* 1530–1595) exemplifies how "it was only in response to a Western attack or ... formulation that the East first achieved some conceptual clarity on a doctrine" (Pelikan 1974: 280). In Article 7, the patriarch surveys the sacraments, before discussing each in turn. He affirms the *septinarium*—by then common to East and West—with scholastic precision: "These are also called *mysteria*, because it is understood that the visible symbols have the completed action as well as the mystical effect. Furthermore, each ... has been set down as law by the Scriptures with a definite matter and form, but also a definite productive, or rather, instrumental cause" (Pelikan 2003: 412). As humans are composed of both soul and body, so each sacrament is twofold: God sanctifies our souls intelligibly through the Spirit, and simultaneously through perceptible means.

Noteworthy is the sacraments' dominical origin: "When our Lord ... had completed the entire work of salvation ... he left to us the divine liturgy and the holy sacraments in remembrance of his magnificent condescension for us. He ordained James, the brother of the Lord, to be the first hierarch" (Pelikan 2003: 428). Jeremias' account of this legacy may be summarized thus:

> *Baptism* is rebirth through the Spirit, a cleansing of the sin 'in which we were conceived' (Ps 50:5, LXX).

> *Chrismation* imprints the likeness of God, the grace of the original creation 'which Divinity breathed into man's nostrils'.

> *Communion* unites us with the Lord in a true partaking of his body and blood, inverting the eating of Eden.

> *Ordination* imparts the Maker's authority and power, for 'nothing is sanctified without the priest'.

> *Marriage* displays God's postlapsarian condescension for the sake of procreation. We reproduce like irrational animals, to know to what depths we have fallen: 'For God did not intend an irrational, fluctuating and sordid union to occur among us'.

> *Penance* restores us from sin for 'after baptism there is no other recovery, neither by grace or by gift, nor without struggle or pain, except through conversion and through tears, through confession of iniquities and turning away from evil'.

Unction is similarly therapeutic, granting forgiveness and sanctification but also potentially healing illness. (Pelikan 2003: 412–413)

The patriarch confirms the *Augsburg Confession* on the necessity of baptism, but posits Communion and chrismation as equally requisite. The latter, instituted by Christ at Pentecost, is thereafter to have developed into anointing (Pseudo-Dionysius being marshalled as "apostolic" testimony). Neither should be delayed, since the former, via the latter, is "the end purpose of the entire sacrament [of baptism], that having been freed of error and the filth of sin, and having been cleansed anew and sealed by the holy myrrh, we may have communion ... and be united completely with him" (Pelikan 2003: 401). In this connection emerges a curious criticism of Latin baptism by *single immersion*, instead of the customary three (which number honors the Trinitarian persons as also Christ's sojourn in the tomb): could Jeremias have been unaware that this atypical usage of medieval Spain (Johnson 2007: 234–237) was obsolete, remote from the sixteenth-century Catholic norm of threefold affusion?

Concerning the Eucharist, Jeremias avers the gifts to be not only symbols:

> The catholic church is of the opinion that after the consecration the bread is changed by the Holy Spirit into the very body of Christ and the wine into his very blood ... To be sure, the flesh of the Lord, which he bore, was not at that time given as food to the apostles ... even as now the Lord's body does not descend from heaven in the divine liturgy, for it would be blasphemous to think that! But then and now, having been changed and altered by the epiclesis and grace of the all-powerful Spirit, the source of consecration, through the holy petitions and words of the priest, the bread is the very body of the Lord ... (Pelikan 2003: 420)

As iron in the fire becomes such, not vice versa, so likewise the church, united to Christ, becomes verily his body. The Eucharist is offered for the forgiveness of the departed, following tradition. It is, furthermore, an *oblation* which, together with the other sacraments, effectively conciliates God: "If then, the sacrifice which was offered by Noah, although it was only a typology, predisposed God kindly toward the human race, much more so will the only-begotten Son of God, who was sacrificed for us, reconcile us to the Father when we come with faith to the holy ceremonies" (Pelikan 2003: 428). Jeremias contends that while sacraments certainly do require faith, they are fundamentally divine acts. Man disposes, but God *proposes*: "Thus he baptizes; thus he anoints; thus he receives us and imparts of the awesome table to us" (Pelikan 2003: 429).

Approving the Lutheran retention of confession, the patriarch demands that sins be enumerated, rehearsing the metaphor of the physician who cannot heal without knowledge of the illness. The attendant medicinal remedies (that is, the canonical penances) should accommodate the particulars of the penitent/patient, being dispensable altogether for those *in extremis*—when genuine repentance suffices (with Communion administered to vouchsafe forgiveness). Echoing the Fathers, alms-giving is reckoned an especially praiseworthy penance: "[A]lms alone can do everything. For he who gives alms and who loves the poor for the Lord's sake is set free from the debt of infinite sins as well as from dreadful captivity among the demons" (Pelikan 2003: 425). Penance also frames Jeremias's approbation of monasticism, typically considered in Orthodoxy as a second *baptism*: "[T]here is here included the vow of monks to live in a manner which is a continuing pledge of repentance" (Pelikan 2003: 413).

Most salient in the *Confession* is the appreciation of the Divine Liturgy, even if marred by chauvinism for the rites of Basil and Chrysostom. The patriarch opines that the venerable anaphoras of Mark and James might be corrupt: notwithstanding local custom, all churches must in principle celebrate in the Byzantine manner, given New Rome's primacy as the "head church of Orthodoxy." No interest in Western liturgy is apparent—surprising, perhaps, given Jeremias' readership. Purview aside, he is refreshingly cognizant of the existential thrust of the Liturgy, as both preparing participants for the sacraments, and duly sanctifying them.

Sanctification occurs on two levels: first, we benefit from hymns (propitiating God), prayers (eliciting forgiveness), and readings (proclaiming his character, inducing reverence and love): "All of the above activate within the priest and the people a better and holier soul and make both more susceptible for the reception and retention of the divine gifts, which, indeed, is the purpose of the sacred rites" (Pelikan 2003: 429). Such a clarion endorsement constitutes an implicit critique of received practice, since Byzantine Christians had long been accustomed to infrequent Communion, focusing their piety rather on the Liturgy's illustrative symbolism, to wit, the manner in which the ritual panorama enacts a series of analogies to the salvific economy of the Gospel (Taft 1992). Yet this development, crystallized in the eighth-century *Historia Ecclesiastica* of Germanus of Constantinople, suffers no neglect, being counted the *second* way of sanctification:

> [T]he work of redemption of the Savior is signified in the hymns and in the readings and in all the acts which are performed throughout the entire divine liturgy by the priest … Thus, it is possible, for those who closely observe the above parts of the liturgy to have the whole work of redemption before their very eyes … The entire sacred ceremony, as a picture of one body, portrays, before one's vision, the life of the Savior, bringing into view all of its parts from the beginning to the end … (Pelikan 2003: 429–430)

Jeremias proceeds to modestly reiterate the mystagogy inherited from prior Byzantine masters: the Little Entrance symbolizes Christ's coming into the world, the Great Entrance his burial cortège, and so forth.

Nevertheless, with quasi-modern self-consciousness, the patriarch recognizes the rites' *functionality*, even while crediting their semiotic value. Hence, apropos the Little and Great Entrances: "They are both necessary. The former so the Gospel can be read. And the latter so that the sacrifice can be consummated. Yet, both signify the manifestation and appearance of the Savior. The former signifies the yet dim and incomplete manifestation of Christ, while the latter signifies the total and final manifestation" (Pelikan 2003: 430). If the Great Entrance was, in Jeremias' day, unnecessary *stricto sensu*, the gifts being prepared near the altar itself (rather than in the *skeuophylakion*, as formerly in Hagia Sophia), his pragmatism impresses. Concerning the interaction of the sensorial and the psychological in liturgical experience, he exhorts:

> And for this [that is, for us to approach the Liturgy with 'faith, piety and warm love'], to visualize that which brings about such emotion in us had to be signified in the sacred assembly so that we should not only think about it in our minds, but also see with our eyes the great poverty of him who is rich ... For it is not enough to intend to become this kind of person [who 'communicates with the flame of the sacraments truly and in a proper manner'] and to learn of Christ. But it is necessary that we actually see, we must affix the eye of the mind there, we must reject all rationalizing if we would cultivate our soul to become worthy of the sanctification of which I have spoken. Piety should be discerned not by words alone, but also by works. The divine service brings everything before our view, so to speak, and also implants what is seen in the soul. The imagination is more clearly impressed through the eye, so that we cannot forget such a table. (Pelikan 2003: 431–432)

The *Reply* concludes with an invitation to the Germans to "conform to the holy councils and canons of the apostles and, thus, follow Christ in all things" (Pelikan 2003: 474). Given his desideratum that all churches emulate Constantinople, one wonders whether Jeremias actually envisioned the Lutherans becoming Orthodox *tout court*, or if he might have accorded validity to the Latin Rite per se—aside from the heterodoxy of its adherents.

METROPHANES CRITOPOULOS, *CONFESSION OF FAITH*, 1625

Critopoulos (*c.* 1589–1639) received a cosmopolitan education throughout Europe, prior to becoming resident patriarch of Alexandria. Whether his *Confession* stands as a private account of Orthodox distinctiveness for the benefit of his Western friends, or a doctrinal canon, has been debated (Maloney 1976: 141). Article 5 introduces the sacraments, seemingly a reprise of Jeremias. They are comparably ascribed a dual character: since we are both body and soul, God communicates "through perceptible matter and through the Holy Spirit." But Metrophanes works a Calvinistic twist into this appraisal, namely, that sacraments are proof of predestination:

> [I]t is so that men might have a greater assurance through these pledges which God presented to their senses, that they were foreknown and pre-destined to eternal life by the grace of God ... For otherwise, such men would soon have doubted whether they had already been chosen or not yet, and would have wondered whether they would ever be chosen ... But now all doubt has been dispelled for God's chosen people, by their looking at his pledges, which are like ineradicable royal signatures. It is

these which we call sacraments, holy baptism and holy communion, which are made up of material things and the Holy Spirit. (Pelikan 2003: 507–508)

Having *prima facie* deferred to the Protestant privileging of baptism and Eucharist, the author unexpectedly adds a third sacrament: penance is likewise necessary for salvation, given our proclivity to sin. A sacramental triad is thus established (reflecting the Trinity): baptism signals reconciliation to the Father; Communion, incorporation into the Son; penance, the life of the Spirit in the soul: "For through repentance, however much I have suffered a loss of divine grace, through sinning after having been chosen by God, I regain the divine grace, and am even given much more of it, because having been wounded in the fight, I have triumphed with God's help" (Pelikan 2003: 508–509).

Only after securing this "theological" paradigm, does Critopoulos concede that beyond "these three essential sacraments, there are certain other sacramental rites which are similarly called sacraments by the church, because of their mystical and spiritual content: such as the holy chrism, which we receive immediately after baptism, the order of priests, the first marriage, and unction" (Pelikan 2003: 508–509). Such an unusual schema is, to my knowledge, *sui generis*. *Septinarium* there is, but prioritized idiosyncratically. Note the standard Orthodox take on the sacramentality of marriage: only the *first* is crowned, held to be a "mystery"; a second or third is merely conceded.

Metrophanes's biblical warrant for the mysteries also diverges from Jeremias, in admitting the administration of the sacraments to issue from the "unwritten word of God," the Church's oral tradition. Scripture but commands the sacraments to be celebrated, telling not how; equally arcane are such axial practices as *iconoduleia*, the invocation of the saints, the Lenten fast, and prayer facing east. Yet Scripture and tradition are linked:

> *Inference*: '[T]hose who are baptized must be dipped three times in the water, because our Savior also went down into the water for us'—and spent three days in the tomb.
>
> *Typology*: 'You anoint my head with oil, my cup overflows' (Ps 22:5, LXX)—hence the reception of Communion after Chrismation.
>
> *Analogy (scriptural, contextual & liturgical)*: Chrismation emulates the Spirit's descent at Christ's baptism; it is 'the King's seal' on his treasure chest (to ward off thieves), which 'confirms and ratifies holy baptism, just as the word "Amen" confirms and ratifies the creed'. (Pelikan 2003: 514)

A fascinating excursus ensues on the Orthodox use of leavened bread. The Last Supper narratives have Christ taking "bread" (neither "unleavened" nor "unleavened bread"), a detail corroborated by the Emmaus pericope. And why infer that such bread was leavened? Because, explains the author, Jesus was not actually celebrating Passover together with everyone else—and shame on the Jews for not keeping festival with him! Azymes are also tainted by association with the Apollinarian denial of Christ's full humanity. Moreover, the single, leavened loaf represents the unity that should prevail among the faithful.

All ought to commune in both kinds, including infants, given Jesus' invitation, "Let the little children come to me" (John 6:53). As to the transformation of the elements, Critopoulos displays agnosticism, or better, a kataphatism *that* they are changed, with an apophaticism respecting *how*:

> For the consecrated bread is truly the body of Christ. That which is in the cup is without doubt the blood of Christ. But the manner in which they are changed is unknown to us and cannot be explained. The clarification of such things is reserved for the elect when they enter the kingdom of heaven. For the time being their simple faith and lack of curiosity will win them greater grace from God. (Pelikan 2003: 520–521)

Especially intriguing is the ensuing catalogue of liturgical *varia*: preparation for Communion involves eating only fruit, bread, and water the day before; staying awake all night (napping allowed in a chair, but not a bed!); avoiding sexual relations; being reconciled with all; Confession and almsgiving on the day and eve of communing. Only one Liturgy per day is celebrated, on one altar (since Christ is one): each church is an image of the whole world, each day an image of the whole of time, and since Christ was once crucified, so the sacrifice must likewise be unique (though celebration is not mandatory, since certain days are non-eucharistic). And paralleling the twenty-fifth of the Anglican "Thirty-Nine Articles of Religion," Metrophanes admits that while the Sacrament is reserved for the sick, it is not to be carried about in the streets, being instituted rather for consumption. Incidentally, despite this veiled rebuke of Latin practice, Ware observes that seventeenth-century Roman Catholic and Greek Orthodox relations were, in certain places, so cordial that Orthodox would in fact participate in Catholic processions of the Blessed Sacrament, fully vested and with all due ceremonial (Ware 1997: 98).

Finally, speaking of clergy, Metrophanes explains that a sevenfold order survives in the Eastern church; this is incorrectly attributed to Ignatius of Antioch who, in fact, only mentions the ministry of bishop, priest, and deacon. Aside from these, Metrophanes lists subdeacons and lectors, as well as door-keepers (who prevent the lazy from leaving and the hostile from spying or mocking), and exorcists (who perform pre-baptismal exorcisms and catechesis). One wonders, in this connection, about the extent to which the author relays actual, rather than ideal practice (or even accepted custom). The manuscript history of the Byzantine Rite, for instance, gives no evidence of ordination rites for the offices of door-keeper or exorcist (Parenti 2000), in contrast to their medieval Western development (Bradshaw 1990). Also odd is Metrophanes's omission of acolyte or candle-bearer, an office attested in eleventh-century euchology *Paris Coislin 213*, and perduring in the *textus receptus* alongside that of lector/cantor and subdeacon. Like his taxonomy of the sacraments, Metrophanes's account of Holy Orders thus seems peculiar.

In "On the Rites of Penance" Critopoulos suggestively appears to claim that penitents may confess to a priest *or* a spiritual father. Is he perchance condoning the long-standing Eastern inclination to honor the *charismata* of "spiritual" men (and, on occasion, women) apart from any consideration of ordination? As Tomáš Špidlík observes: "There have undoubtedly been people in the East ... who claimed for spiritual persons as such the power to "bind and loose" whether they were priests or not" (Špidlík 1986: 191). Regarding modes of confession, Metrophanes names two: public and, more commonly, private, with almsgiving particularly commended as penance (should one's wealth allow), to the specific end of redeeming prisoners. Describing the legalized abduction of Christian children by Turkish authorities, Critopoulos explains the imperative to retrieve them through bribery, poignantly linking sacramental and moral theology.

Concerning unction, the author cites both apostolic injunction (Jas 5:14–15) and precedent (Mark 6:13). Sicknesses result not purely from corporeal disorder, but sin as well; sent by God upon the elect, they are a spur to amend one's ways and lessen the temporary punishment of the soul after death, prior to the Judgment. Here we find, as elsewhere in contemporary texts, an analogue to the Latin doctrine of purgatory—the potential legitimacy of which is still disputed by Orthodox today (Ware 1997: 255).

CYRIL LUCARIS, *THE EASTERN CONFESSION OF FAITH*, 1629

Since its original publication in Geneva, this notoriously heterodox document has suffered opprobrium—along with its author, five-time ecumenical patriarch. Sympathizing with the Reformation principle *sola Scriptura*, Lucaris (1572–1638) instructs the "evangelical sacraments in the Church" to be only baptism and Eucharist:

> These consist of the word and the elements, and we believe firmly that they are seals of God's promises and procure grace. But for the mystery to be whole and entire, it is necessary that an earthly substance and an external act concur with the use of that element ordained by Christ our Lord and joined with sincere faith; for when faith is not present in the recipient, the wholeness of the sacrament is not preserved. (Pelikan 2003: 554)

Cyril accentuates the *subjectivity* of the participant in the sacraments, as potentially mitigating their objective efficacy—an efficacy presumed, for instance, by the diaconal admonition following Communion in the Byzantine Divine Liturgy: "Having received the divine, holy, immaculate, immortal, heavenly, and life-giving, awesome Mysteries of Christ, let us rightly give thanks to the Lord" (Galadza 2004: 169).

In article 16, the patriarch asserts the doctrine of baptismal regeneration: it forgives ancestral and actual sin alike. Unlike his predecessors, however, Lucaris ignores chrismation and post-baptismal Communion. Discussing the Eucharist, in turn, he cites both the Gospels and 1 Corinthians to demonstrate the perspicuousness of his teaching: "This is the simple, true and genuine tradition of this wonderful sacrament, in the performance and administration of which we acknowledge and believe in the true and real presence of our Lord Jesus Christ; that, however, which our faith presents and offers unto us, not that which the arbitrarily invented doctrine of transubstantiation teaches." The faithful are said to eat Christ not by mastication but by an inner experience of communion; this body is not that perceived with the senses but that "which faith spiritually apprehends, presents, and bestows to us. From whence it is true that we eat and partake and have communion if we believe" (Pelikan 2003: 555). The fruits of Communion are reconciliation with Christ, and confirmation of the hope of being an heir of the heavenly kingdom.

While this *Confession* has been touted as the *bête noire* of the confessional genre, Pelikan deems Cyril's intention to have been sincere:

> The central content of Eastern Orthodox dogma consisted of the doctrine of the Trinity and the doctrine of the person of Christ ... defined by the ancient councils and restated in subsequent centuries. On many other doctrinal matters, the church had not spoken with equal definiteness ... [Cyril] strove to adhere to official orthodoxy on the two basic dogmas and to use the official silence of the church on other questions as a warrant to graft Protestantism onto his Eastern Orthodoxy. The outcome of the controversy over his confession showed that the East in fact believed and taught much more than it confessed, but it was forced to make its teaching confessionally explicit in response to the challenge. (Pelikan 1974: 283)

PETER MOGHILA, *THE ORTHODOX CONFESSION OF THE CATHOLIC AND APOSTOLIC CHURCH*, 1638/1642

Moghila (1596–1646) had a prominent career in today's Ukraine, as metropolitan of Kiev. While canonized by the Ukrainian Orthodox in 1996, and others since, his legacy has typically been regarded as ambivalent at best, insidious at worst, owing to his introduction of significant Latinizations into Slavic liturgical practice—ironically, in tandem with what has come to be recognized as a prescient pastoral strategy to protect Orthodoxy, in the face of Protestant and Roman Catholic advances (McGuckin 2011: 390). Peter's *Orthodox Confession of Faith*, as edited and ratified by the Synod of Jassy (1642), evinces several important shifts in sacramental theology. After itemizing the liturgical regimen expected of ordinary Christians (dominical/festal worship, i.e. vespers, matins, Eucharist, sermons) and its corollary ascetical obligations (the four traditional fasts; confession monthly or quarterly, or at least annually), Peter turns to sacramentology proper, resuming much of Jeremias' third *Reply* and recommending it by name. "A mystery is a certain rite or ceremony which, under a visible sign, causes and conveys into the soul of the faithful the invisible grace of God, an institution of our Lord, whereby every one of the faithful receiveth the divine grace" (Pelikan 2003: 601). Such were instituted to mark the true children of God, as a pledge of trust in God and remedy for sin; the *septinarium* is further correlated to the sevenfold gifts of the Spirit.

Novel in Peter's *Confession*, however, is a technical, scholastic concern with what *exactly* is necessary for the due celebration of the sacraments: fit matter, a priest/bishop, and the invocation of the Holy Spirit through a solemn formula (including correct *intention* on the minister's part).

Baptism serves to root out ancestral sin, which Peter also calls "original sin"— without thereby explicitly commending the Augustinian anthropology this term might connote (Pelikan 2003: 573). Chrismation is traced to 2 Corinthians 1:21–22, taken to designate literal anointing, though it is granted that the apostles themselves "anointed" through the imposition of hands. Despite his scholastic orientation, favoring respect for the unique imprint of chrismation, Moghila allows it to be *repeated* for repentant apostates (as per the Second Ecumenical Council's seventh canon). A generation later, the *Catechism* of the prolific metropolitan Dmitri Tuptalo of Rostov (1651–1709) will corroborate and extend Peter's concession (sanctioning one further re-chrismation: the anointing of a tsar upon his ascension): "It is not necessary to baptize [apostates], but only to anoint them with oil [i.e. chrism], while they must declare their renunciation of their delusion" (Steeves 1997: 128). Here it is worth clarifying that the reconciliation of apostates has not always and everywhere implied repetition of the post-baptismal rite of chrismation: Arranz, for example, in reconstructing eleventh-century Byzantine practice, cites the use of chrism with another, context-specific formula (Arranz 1996: 292–293).

Dmitri also reiterates Peter's treatment of the Eucharist: both expect a consecrated altar or *antimension*, along with the purest elements: the former, however, allows for rye bread and white wine. The *sine qua non* is the priest's resolve for the substance of bread and wine to be changed into Christ's body and blood, via the epiclesis: "At these words there is wrought a change in the elements ... the species only remaining, which are perceived by the sight" (Pelikan 2003: 604). Or as Dmitri has it: "Do we see the tran-substantiation of the bread and wine into the body and blood of Christ? We do not, but we believe it without question" (Steeves 1997: 128). Here we encounter one of the Jassy Synod's *quaestiones disputatae*. For Peter personally believed in consecration through the *verba Domini* rather than the epiclesis; this is demonstrable from contemporary documents referring to the original, no longer extant, version of his *Confession* (Popivchak 2002–04), as well as surviving editions of his *Sluzhebnik*, or service book (P. Meyendorff 2002).

Surprisingly, Moghila's 1629 *Sluzhebnik* modified the rubrics of previous editions in a conservative direction: the rubrics for Chrysostom's Liturgy direct the priest to merely *point* at the elements with fingers joined to bless, rather than blessing the diskos and chalice manually, as formerly prescribed (a by-product of surreptitious Latin influence on the first printed editions of Byzantine liturgical texts). Even so, later East Slavic practice would ironically become even *more* Latinized: 1) in requiring concelebrants to enunciate the Words of Institution in unison (if not the presider alone) lest disorder enter into the Liturgy by someone pre-empting the consecration, and 2) in more subtle rubrics, such as having a bishop doff his headgear before the institution narrative, rather than the epiclesis (Uspensky 1985: 221–226).

And Peter's 1639 *Sluzhebnik* restores the Latin-style blessing, also highlighting the celebrant's intention to consecrate through the *verba*: "The priest bows his head with compunction and all concentration, thinking how the holy bread is to be changed into the Body of Christ our God crucified. He adds to this his own intention as well, and, raising his right hand, joining together the fingers for a blessing and looking at the holy bread, he points to it, and blesses it, exclaiming and saying: 'Take, eat ...'" (translated in Uspensky 1985: 203). Such was his freighting of the celebrant's mental state, indeed, that Peter regarded the commemorative particles surrounding the Lamb—hitherto revered as blessed, but not consecrated for Communion—as *also* transformed, should the priest so intend. That such minutiae are not "much ado about nothing" is clear from Michael Zheltov's adroit analysis of the variety of transformative "moments" historically proposed in Byzantine sources (Zheltov 2010): not only the epiclesis, but also the *verba Domini*, the prothesis, the Great Entrance—even the elevation of the gifts at "Holy things for the holy!"

Equally portentous were the Petrine rubrics for the Presanctified Liturgy, that is, Lenten vespers with Communion. The Greek tradition had originally accepted, for this rite, a "consecration by contact": before Communion, a particle of the reserved bread was added to the customarily mixed chalice to produce the Precious Blood (Alexopoulos 2009). Influenced by scholasticism, however, the opinion arose among the Slavs that the chalice's transformation required the consecratory prayers of the full Divine Liturgy. This in turn implied that presanctified Communion involved bread alone. Now, while both editions of Moghila's *Sluzhebnik* prescribe the clergy to partake of the chalice as usual, his later, magisterial *Trebnik* (1646)—containing the ordo for all the sacraments and sacramentals—elucidates that the blood is not actually imbibed at this time, but only ordinary wine, "for ceremonial reasons, as for a purification of the mouth" (translated in Uspensky 1985: 221). Hence the received rubric: a priest *may not* drink in the absence of a deacon (ordinarily charged with consuming the gifts remaining after the Liturgy), lest he himself break the eucharistic fast before doing so! Compare this development with the *Confession*, which defends the indispensability of clergy and laity alike communing under both species—undoubtedly a polemic against contemporary Latin convention, and its theoretical justification in terms of the doctrine of concomitance. Unwittingly, perhaps, Moghila ends up effectively validating this very doctrine, inasmuch as his *Trebnik* teaches presanctified Communion to be uniquely, and yet sufficiently, in the Precious Body.

As for the other sacraments, the following merit attention. Article 108 acknowledges the priesthood of all believers alongside that of the ordained. Instituted by Christ, this latter is invoked in the apostolic admonition, "Let a man account of us ... as stewards of the mysteries of God" (1 Cor 4:1). It comprises both the power and permission to absolve, and to teach in Christ's name. Moghila here cites the only New Testament application of the term "liturgy" to the cultic practice of the church, to wit, Acts 13:2: "As they *ministered* unto the Lord [that is, while they offered the unbloody sacrifice to God] and fasted ..." Peter speaks further of the diaconate as one of several orders preceding priesthood (reader, chanter, lampadary, subdeacon), apparently not distinguishing major and minor orders as such. These are all subsumed by the priesthood, though individually equal in stature, and complementary: "For each degree is distinguished from another by its own peculiar duty and habit, and this is to be explained and taught them by the bishop" (Pelikan 2003: 607).

While his *Confession* promotes no novelty concerning penance, his liturgical books import (via Uniate sources), along with a legion of Latin rites or elements thereof, the first-person singular absolution (still standard among Slavs): "May our Lord and God … forgive you, my child (name), all your transgressions. And I, an unworthy priest, through His power given to me, do forgive and absolve you from all your sins, in the name of the Father … " The older, deprecatory prayer nevertheless survived in the order for Confession and Communion of the Sick:

> O Lord our God, who have granted remission [of sins] to Peter and to the sinful woman because of their tears … Receive the confession of your servant (name), and if he has committed a sin willingly or unwillingly, in word, or in deed, or in thought, since You are good, ignore it, since You are the only One who has the power to remit sins. For You are the God of mercy, compassion, and love for mankind … (translated in Getcha 2007: 211)

Concerning marriage, Article 115 accentuates the parties' consent, following both Latin theology and the exigencies of Peter's sociopolitical context under the Polish-Lithuanian commonwealth. Moghila's *Trebnik* gives the role of consent an even sharper profile, by the inclusion of Western-style vows, transmitted in Slavic books and their derivatives to the present.

DOSITHEUS AND THE SYNOD OF JERUSALEM, *CONFESSION* (1672)

The *Confession* of Dositheus (1641–1707) serves as a summation, and evaluation, of the texts treated above; John Meyendorff lauds it as "the most important Orthodox dogmatic text of [the] period" (J. Meyendorff 1981: 96). Noteworthy is its forthright condemnation of Lucaris, and approval of Jeremias. Decree 10 defends the integrality of the episcopate to the sacramental *esse* of the church, an emphasis appreciable in light of the discrete theologies of Christian office and ministry then emergent in Protestant circles. Bishops surpass priests, since the latter's ministry comprises only some sacraments (and those, derivatively):

> [D]eemed worthy of being a bishop as a successor of the apostles, and having received in continuous succession by the laying on of hands and the invocation of the All-holy Spirit the grace that is given to him from the Lord of binding and loosing, he is a living image of God on earth; and by a most ample participation of the operation

of the Holy Spirit, who is the chief functionary, he is a fountain of all the sacraments of the catholic church … (Pelikan 2003: 620)

Decree 15 reaffirms the *septinarium*, with each sacrament again justified by Scripture: baptism follows Christ's command; chrismation announces the Spirit's advent (here 2 Cor 1:21–22 obtains, as with Moghila); the priesthood is inaugurated *ipso facto* by the Last Supper and the mandate to bind and loose (Mt 18:18); marriage issues from the dominical warning for none to put asunder what God has joined, and from correspondence to the nuptial mystery of Christ and the church (Eph 5:32); penance is warranted by John 20:23; and unction from apostolic practice (Mark 6:13) and testimony (Jas 5:14). The synod proceeds to commend the *ex opere operato* efficacy of the mysteries, which "consist of something natural, and of something supernatural. And they are not bare signs of the promise of God, for then they would not differ from circumcision … they are, of necessity, efficacious means of grace to those who receive them. But we reject, as alien to Christian doctrine, the notion that the integrity of the sacrament depends upon its reception" (Pelikan 2003: 625–626).

Despite pretensions to critique Western influence, the synodal text advocates a classically Augustinian interpretation of baptism, as necessary for salvation even for infants, "for they also are subject to original sin and without baptism are not able to obtain its remission" (626). Various Church Fathers, including Augustine, are referenced; it is even insinuated that infants face *damnation* if not baptized. Given this prospect, any Orthodox may baptize, in case of urgency. As with baptism, so the Eucharist: the *Confession*'s polemic concerning Christ's sacramental presence invokes Thomistic terminology with a quasi-Tridentine flair:

> [C]hrist is present, not typologically, nor figuratively, nor by superabundant grace, as in the other sacraments, nor by a bare presence, as some of the fathers have said concerning baptism, nor by impanation, so that the divinity of the Word would be united hypostatically to the bread of the Eucharist that is set forth, as the followers of Luther most ignorantly and wretchedly suppose; but truly and really, so that after the consecration … the bread is transmuted, transubstantiated, converted, and transformed into the true body itself of the Lord, which was born in Bethlehem … there no longer remains the substance of the bread and of the wine, but the very body and blood of the Lord, under the species and form of bread and wine, that is to say, under the accidents … (Pelikan 2003: 628–629)

In addition to transubstantiation (μετουσίωσις), the text effectively approves the doctrine of concomitance; clarifies that particles reserved for the sick are the self-same body and blood; enjoins the elements to be adored with *latria*, as the Trinity; and defends the Eucharist as truly sacrificial. An Orthodox sensibility may be detected, nonetheless, in the description of multiple celebrations (in churches throughout the world) as effecting the assimilation of discrete loaves to the heavenly body of Christ, rather than the descent of the same. Moreover, the Sacrament is comprehensible only by faith, not by the "sophistries of human wisdom, whose vain and foolish curiosity in divine things" is rejected; transubstantiation serves not to explain, but only to bespeak the ineffable mystery.

MANUALS AND CANONS

To do justice to our period, it is necessary to conclude with developments in the eighteenth and nineteenth centuries, as reflected in the genre of theological manuals and collections of Orthodox canon law—though it is impossible within the compass of the present survey to treat all the available sources. Archbishop Eugenios Bulgaris, or Voulgaris (1716–1806), widely regarded as the "outstanding Orthodox theologian of the 18th century" (Maloney 1976: 176), encapsulates its thrust: on the one hand, conservative reiteration of Orthodox distinctiveness (albeit using Western terminology), as elaborated in the debates of the preceding centuries; on the other, a guarded interest in dialogue with, and limited appropriation of, the new knowledge available in the Enlightenment. Known for the dogmatic manual *Theologikon* (before 1785), his *Against the Latins* (1756) may serve as an index of the stringent exclusivism marking contemporary Greek, if not necessarily Slavic, theology.

The author renews the well-worn Eastern objection to azymes, as to other practices which today might count as disciplinary rather than doctrinal: the celebration of multiple Liturgies in a given day on one altar, for example, or the ordination of multiple deacons at once. More gravely, he excoriates the neglect of full immersion in Western baptism, as well as its deferral of chrismation; Catholic (and Protestant) initiation is, in consequence, without grace (Stiernon 2002: 815). Such a verdict mirrors the influential *Horos* of Patriarch Cyril V of Constantinople (1755), normative for the Greek Church into the twentieth century. This text adduces dominical, apostolic, patristic and canonical precedent,

> [W]hich order us to receive as unbaptized those aspirants to Orthodoxy who were not baptized with three immersions and emersions, and in each immersion did not loudly invoke one of the divine hypostaseis [*sic*], but were baptized in some other fashion. We too, therefore … abhor baptisms belonging to heretics … They give no sanctification … nor avail at all to the washing away of sins. (translated in Dragas 1999: 245)

Such sacramental *akribeia* ("rigorism"), however, did not go entirely unchallenged; the complementary principle of *oikonomia* would prevail in the Great Church's *Patriarchal and Synodal Letter* (1875), wherein the alternate Russian practice of reception by chrismation is acknowledged, and the pastoral discretion of local bishops approved—until a future gathering of the Orthodox should attain unanimity on the matter (Dragas 1999: 249).

The *Holy Catechism* of Nicolas Bulgaris (*c.* 1634–1684), arranged in question and answer format, boasts both an introduction to the mysteries and a commentary on the Liturgy, as well as a compendium of moral theology. Although originally published in

1681, it has proven popular to the present day; the 1852 edition treated here, revised to accord with Orthodox tradition as then understood, serves to represent its time. A mystery, for Nicolas, illustrates its etymological ambivalence, the Greek root μύω implying both "to keep the mouth closed" and "to teach divine things." It speaks, as it were, by its very unspeakableness, since it "appears one thing to the eye, and figuratively signified and intends another, showing from material and sensible form the immaterial and spiritual grace which the great God gives to those worthily receive it" (Bulgaris 1893: 3). Originating with Christ, the sacraments emulate by their humble matter the condescension expressed in his Incarnation. Following the now-standard biblical proof-texts, Bulgaris presents an interesting analogy for the sufficiency of the *septinarium*: physical birth, growth, nourishment, and healing, as well as human drives to socialize and reproduce, offer the *raison d'être* for the corresponding mysteries. Each of these may, in turn, be scholastically dissected in terms of matter and species as well as efficient and final causes, and correlated to the gifts of the Spirit (efficient cause of all the sacraments). Significant in Bulgaris' account are a Western-style description of chrismation, as ordered to "give the Christian strength to confess freely Christ's name"; a complex itemization of unlawful marriages arising from natural and spiritual kinship (the latter occasioned by godparenthood or adoption); a rigorous taxonomy for confession (what sin? with whom? by what means? how often? where? to what end? how? when?); acceptance of lay baptism, in case of emergency (even in the form of sprinkling); and recognition of the erstwhile office of deaconess (Bulgaris 1893: 11–21).

The *Pedalion* or "Rudder" (1800), of Athonite monk Nicodemus (1749–1809), comments upon the Orthodox canonical heritage, particularly the ninth-century revision of the seventh-century compilation of ecclesiastical and civil law known as the *Nomokanon in 14 Titles*. Having also co-edited the *Philokalia*, that renowned anthology of Eastern ascetical and mystical literature, the Hagiorite yet demonstrated a surprising attraction toward contemporary Roman Catholic spirituality: for example, his *vademecum* for confession, the *Exomologetarion*, based on the manuals of Italian Jesuit Paolo Segneri (1624–1694) but altered, where necessary, to preserve such Orthodox distinctives as the patristic notion of the eight evil thoughts (*logismoi*) and the deprecatory form of absolution (Citterio 2002: 945–946).

Despite this ostensible "ecumenism," however, Nicodemus firmly espoused the dictum *extra ecclesiam, nulla salus*, reiterating in his *Pedalion* the Cyprianic sacramentology of the 1755 *Horos*. Discussing the "85 Canons" of the fourth-century *Apostolic Constitutions*, for instance, he is unequivocal:

> We declare that the baptism of the Latins is one which falsely is called baptism, and for this reason it is not acceptable or recognizable either on grounds of rigorism or on grounds of economy … [I]t being admitted that the Latins are heretics of long standing, it is evident in the very first place from this fact that they are unbaptized … Because, having become laymen as a result of their having been cut off from the Orthodox Church, they no longer have with them the grace of the Holy Spirit with which Orthodox priests perform the mysteries. (Agapios and Nikodemos 1957: 72)

Moreover, Alkiviadis Calivas shows that the Third Council of Carthage (256), remembered for its rejection of heretical/schismatical baptism, enjoyed Nicodemus' especial esteem as the prototypical sub-apostolic synod, its "limiting concept" that outside the church there can be no grace and, therefore, no valid sacraments, serving as an "undeniable authoritative standard" (Calivas 2009: 19). Nevertheless, the *Rudder* is chronologically comprehensive, and thus ambivalent. Included are other canons subverting the Hagiorite's categorical "anabaptism," even indicting it as a departure from Orthodox tradition writ large (Calivas 2009: 28–29).

Ambivalence also marks Nicodemus' discussion of marriage. The nuptial union is created by God and, therefore, intrinsically good (Agapios and Nikodemos 1957: 77)— not, of course, the view of all the Church Fathers, some of whom saw prelapsarian humanity as unfettered by sexual relations. Mitigating against a benign view of wedlock, however, is the Hagiorite's stance on the defilement incurred by contact with something or someone impure, barring the one defiled from receiving or celebrating the Eucharist. Menstruating women may not receive Communion, nor couples who have not abstained for three days; while a sodomized boy may not be ordained, regardless of his personal innocence, nor a man whose wife commits occult adultery, and subsequently imparts her pollution to him unawares. Invoking Levitical strictures, Nicodemus' casuistry also exhibits inference based on the fundamental premise that purity equals virginity/celibacy/continence (Viscuso 1992: 193–195)—a premise which, historically, served to justify the gradual disqualification of married presbyters from the episcopate, in favor of monastics.

Importantly, the Hagiorite esteems marriage primarily for the spiritual companionship it furnishes, and only secondarily, for the begetting of children (Viscuso 1992: 197). Still, those who re-marry, whether widowed or divorced, are presumed to have carnal motives, and therefore do so according to concession. Such a union is not crowned: "For digamists appear to have been conquered [by pleasure] and on this account have become unworthy of the crowns" (Agapios and Nikodemos 1957: 514). Only a first marriage is sacramental, with clerics bound to uphold its dignity; clemency applies to the laity, however, whose digamy and trigamy are tolerable. Regarding the resultant theology of marriage, one is left with a conundrum: "[T]he fact that divorce and remarriage are permitted leads to the conclusion that marriage is not indissoluble by nature. In apparent contradiction, the denial of remarriage for separated clergy supports the principle of indissolubility. No attempt is made to reconcile the two differing practices" (Viscuso 1992: 204).

CONCLUSION

Do the sixteenth to nineteenth centuries lend themselves to generalizations? Firstly, we observe a consistent use of *Scripture* to justify sacramental theology and practice. That the mysteries can be located in and explicated through the Bible—albeit interpreted by Holy Tradition—opens a space for further dialogue with Christians who do not share that tradition, yet take Holy Writ as the *terminus a quo*. The historical stimulus to Orthodoxy to define itself in contradistinction to the West, may thus be interpreted as providential, bringing the inchoate to light. Secondly, there is the variety claiming Orthodox auspices. Even discounting the controversial Lucaris, given his repudiation by Orthodoxy at large, the different hermeneutics of, for example, Critopoulos and Moghila, display a theological pluralism within the Eastern tradition often missed. In consequence, Orthodox today admit discrete practices: *inter alia*, in confession and crowning. Thirdly, one is struck by the paradox of Orthodox conservatism: aspiring only to galvanize tradition, and presuming upon the sufficiency of the *lex orandi*, our authors sought originality only in the literal sense of fidelity to the *origin*, that is, to the pattern established by the Holy Fathers: *non nova, sed nove*. Yet inasmuch as the Fathers were not themselves compelled to theorize a distinctively Orthodox sacramentology, what emerges in the texts treated above often proves original rather in the sense of *novel*. But how is such novelty to be reckoned? Indeed, the question of what *does* count as authentic Orthodoxy is itself brought into relief. Orthodox today continue to weigh the implications for their own self-understanding (cf. the contemporary rehabilitation of Moghila).

The vast amount of material produced surviving from the period remains fertile ground for further research, especially regarding the complexity of the *lex orandi, lex credendi* rapport. Perhaps Critopoulos' unique view of minor orders, for instance, was informed by a local preservation of offices which had elsewhere fallen into desuetude. Without clarity on which euchological texts he employed, one is left to speculate. The theological cross-pollination of these centuries also merits sustained probing, as it defies reductionistic description. Marcus Plested's *Orthodox Readings of Aquinas*, for example, illustrates the Eastern church's sophisticated and enduring engagement with the Angelic Doctor, refuting caricatures of the Ottoman era as "paltry in achievement and shamefully subject to Western influence" (Plested 2012: 137).

Finally, there is the perennial question of "the meaning of tradition" (Meyendorff 1978). Inasmuch as the elaboration of orthodoxy has frequently been occasioned by heresy, one may perhaps sympathize with the opinion, common among Eastern Christians, that what the West calls the "development of doctrine" is a misnomer—at issue is a prudent *defense* of the deposit of faith, rather than an open-ended progression towards greater understanding of it. Andrew Louth warns, "I know of no Orthodox theologian who calls on the category of authentic development to justify the later doctrine. Development does not seem to be perceived as an available category for Orthodox theology" (Louth 2005: 47). Hence the sacrosanct status of the Seven Ecumenical Councils, and Orthodox reluctance to attribute quite the same value to second-millennium ecclesiastical accomplishments, irrespective of their "ecumenical" import. But is Louth's verdict tenable historically? Or only mystically? Arguably, the authors examined above do evince, *nolens volens*, a veritable development of "right belief"—and, thereby, of the "right glory" by which such is to be handed down.

SUGGESTED READING

Conticello and Conticello (2002); McGuckin (2011).

BIBLIOGRAPHY

Agapios and Nikodemos (1957), *The Rudder (Pedalion) of the Metaphorical Ship*, ed. and trans. D. Cummings (Chicago: The Orthodox Christian Educational Society).

Alexopoulos, S. (2009), *The Presanctified Liturgy in the Byzantine Rite: A Comparative Analysis of Its Origins, Evolution, and Structural Components* (Leuven, Belgium: Peeters).

Arranz, M. (1996) (ed.), *L'eucologio costantinopolitano agli inizi del secolo XI: hagiasmatarion & archieratikon (rituale & pontificale): con l'aggiunta del Leiturgikon (messale)* (Rome: Pontificia Università Gregoriana).

Bradshaw, P. (1990), *Ordination Rites of the Ancient Churches of East and West* (Collegeville, MN: Liturgical Press, Pueblo).

Bulgaris, N. (1893), *The Holy Catechism of Nicholas Bulgaris*, ed. R. Raikes Bromage, trans. W. Daniel (London: J. Masters & Co).

Calivas, A. C. (2009), "Receiving Converts into the Orthodox Church: Lessons from the Canonical and Liturgical Tradition," *Greek Orthodox Theological Review* 54: 1–76.

Citterio, E. (2002), "Nicodemo Agiorita," in C. G. Conticello and V. Conticello (eds.), *La théologie byzantine et sa tradition II (XIIIe–XIXe s.)* (Turnhout: Brepols).

Conticello, C. G., and V. Conticello (eds.) (2002), *La théologie byzantine et sa tradition II (XIIIe–XIXe s.)* (Turnhout: Brepols).

Dragas, G. (1999), "The Manner of Reception of Roman Catholic Converts into the Orthodox Church with Special Reference to the Decisions of the Synods of 1484 (Constantinople), 1755 (Constantinople) and 1667 (Moscow)," *Greek Orthodox Theological Review* 44: 235–271.

Galadza, P. (2004) (ed.), *The Divine Liturgy: An Anthology for Worship* (Ottawa: Metropolitan Andrey Sheptytsky Institute of Eastern Christian Studies).

Getcha, J. (2007), "Confession and Spiritual Direction in the Orthodox Church: Some Modern Questions to a Very Ancient Practice," *Saint Vladimir's Theological Quarterly* 51: 203–220.

Johnson, M. E. (2007), *The Rites of Christian Initiation: Their Evolution and Interpretation* (Collegeville, MN: Liturgical Press, Pueblo).

Louth, A. (2005), "Is Development of Doctrine a Valid Category for Orthodox Theology?" in V. Hotchkiss and P. Henry (eds.), *Orthodoxy and Western Culture: A Collection of Essays Honoring Jaroslav Pelikan on His Eightieth Birthday* (Crestwood, NY: St. Vladimir's Seminary Press), 45–63.

Maloney, G. (1976), *A History of Orthodox Theology since 1453* (Belmont, MA: Nordland Publishing Company).

McGuckin, J. A. (2011) (ed.), *The Encyclopedia of Eastern Orthodox Christianity, Vol. I (A-M)* (Malden, MA: Wiley-Blackwell); see also *Vol. II(N-Z)*.

Meyendorff, J. (1978), *Living Tradition* (Crestwood, NY: St. Vladimir's Seminary Press).

Meyendorff, J. (1981), *The Orthodox Church: Its Past and Its Role in the World Today*, trans. J. Chapin (Crestwood, NY: St. Vladimir's Seminary Press).

Meyendorff, P. (2002), *Russia, Ritual and Reform: The Liturgical Reforms of Nikon in the Seventeenth Century* (Crestwood, NY: St. Vladimir's Seminary Press).

Parenti, S. (2000), "Ordinations in the East," in A. J. Chupungco (ed.), *Handbook for Liturgical Studies*, vol. 4: *Sacraments and Sacramentals* (Collegeville, MN: Liturgical Press, Pueblo), 205–217.

Pelikan, J. (1974), *The Spirit of Eastern Christendom (600–1700)*, vol. 2 of *The Christian Tradition: A History of the Development of Doctrine* (Chicago: The University of Chicago Press).

Pelikan, J. (2003), *Creeds and Confessions of Faith in the Christian Tradition*, vol. 1: *Early, Eastern, Medieval* (New Haven and London: Yale University Press).

Plested, M. (2012), *Orthodox Readings of Aquinas* (Oxford: Oxford University Press).

Popivchak, R. P. (2002–2004), "The Life and Times of Peter Mohyla," *Logos: A Journal of Eastern Christian Studies* 43–45: 339–360.

Špidlík, T. (1986), *The Spirituality of the Christian East* (Kalamazoo, MI: Cistercian Publications).

Steeves, P. D. (ed.) (1997), *The Modern Encyclopedia of Religions in Russia and Eurasia*, vol. 7 (Gulf Breeze, FL: Academic International Press).

Stiernon, D. (2002), "Eugène Bulgaris," in C. G. Conticello and V. Conticello (eds.), *La Théologie Byzantine et Sa Tradition II (XIIIe-XIXe S.)* (Turnhout: Brepols).

Taft, R. F. (1992), *The Byzantine Rite: A Short History*, American Essays in Liturgy Series (Collegeville, MN: Liturgical Press).

Uspensky, N. (1985), *Evening Worship in the Orthodox Church* (Crestwood, NY: St. Vladimir's Seminary Press).

Viscuso, P. (1992), "The Theology of Marriage in the *Rudder* of Nikodemos the Hagiorite," *Ostkirchlichen Studien* 41 (September): 187–207.

Ware, T. (1997), *The Orthodox Church: New Edition* (London: Penguin Books).

Zheltov, M. (2010), "The Moment of Eucharistic Consecration in Byzantine Thought," in M. E. Johnson (ed.), *Issues in Eucharistic Praying East and West: Essays in Liturgical and Theological Analysis* (Collegeville, MN: Liturgical Press, Pueblo), 263–306.

....

CHAPTER 23

POST-TRIDENTINE
SACRAMENTAL THEOLOGY

....

TRENT POMPLUN

MANY of the debates that roiled the Catholic Church for four hundred years after the Council of Trent concerned sacramental theology. The council's canons invigorated the now-traditional schools of scholastic theology with new matters for disputation and led to the systematization of controversial theology as a genre. Increasing historical knowledge of the liturgy led to new considerations of the "form" and "matter" of several sacraments, and the church's expansion in the New World and Asia led to inevitable questions in the theology of the sacrament of matrimony. Not to be forgotten, the sore feud between Jesuits and Jansenists touched on several questions in the practical theology of the Eucharist and penance, just as the controversies that surrounded Molinos, Madame Guyon, and François de Fénelon were driven by worries that the sacraments would be deemed unnecessary for spiritual progress. In fact, with questions about sin and grace, the great majority of papal bulls, letters, interventions, and instructions from this era touched upon the sacraments. And yet, only the faintest outline of post-Tridentine theology can be found in the writings of today's theologians, who are content to summon in their sketches a shadowy ghoul sufficient to scare their students into not reading it at all. Being too modern for *ressourcement*, but too fusty for a fashion-conscious *aggiornamento*, the theology of Suárez, Bellarmine, Punch, or Mastrius—to say nothing of wholly forgotten geniuses such as Juan Vicente Asturiensis or Salvator Montalbanus—serves as little more than a whipping boy for "traditionalist" and "progressive" alike.

Consider the following passage from Robert J. Daly, S.J.: "A notable difference," he writes, "indeed a chasm, appears between what many liturgical scholars today agree is sound eucharistic theology and the eucharistic theology of several official documents of the Roman Catholic magisterium. Historical research suggests that Robert Bellarmine is one of the 'messengers' if indeed not one of the 'villains' of this unhappy story" (Daly 2000: 239). In Daly's telling, the tradition that begins with St. Robert Bellarmine and culminates in Pius XII's *Mediator Dei* (1947) and John Paul

II's *Dominicae cenae* (1980) is at odds with Vatican II's *Sacrosanctum concilium* and the subsequent liturgical reform in the Roman Catholic Church. Echoing his fellow Jesuit Edward Kilmartin, Daly declares the teaching of St. Robert Bellarmine and the post-Tridentine teaching of the Roman Catholic magisterium generally to be "bankrupt" and "without a future" (Daly 2000: 240; cf. Kilmartin 1998). Even allowing for the "prophetic" *hyperbole* in which so many twentieth-century theologians indulged, these charges are overdrawn. To see why, we will need to follow the broad development of sacramental theology from the Council of Trent to the generation of Joseph Kern, Paul Galtier, and Maurice de la Taille, with special attention given to intra-Catholic controversies in eucharistic theology during these four centuries. To do so, I will give a broad bibliographical outline of post-Tridentine sacramental theology and identify a few of its salient features. After that, I will take one example, the so-called "destruction" theories of the eucharistic sacrifice, to illustrate the historical processes by which post-Tridentine sacramental theology came to be sorely and unjustly maligned.

Post-Tridentine Sacramental Theology: Sources and Positions

Like their medieval predecessors, the theologians of the baroque age wrote treatises *De sacramentis* that discussed the sacraments *in genere* before addressing each of the seven sacraments in turn. They treated the definition, division, and number of the sacraments, their manner of operation, and the conditions for their valid and worthy administration and reception, before addressing topics unique to each sacrament. Not to put too fine a point on it, these treatises are often enormous. They make Karl Barth and Hans Urs von Balthasar look like men who rarely put pen to paper. That said, Thomists and Scotists dominated the discussion, with important contributions by Jesuits and Jansenists on questions of sacramental practice, but niche markets in systematic theology also existed for St. Anselm, St. Bernard, St. Bonaventure, Giles of Rome, Henry of Ghent, and John Baconthorpe. In this regard, we can discern a certain "house style" for most of the religious orders. Augustinians, for example, generally affirmed the existence of sacraments in Eden, whereas Dominicans usually denied them. On the other hand, Bonaventureans generally differed from the Thomistic, Scotistic, and Augustinian consensus that Christ instituted the seven sacraments *immediate ac per se ipsum*. Of course, Thomists and Scotists famously disagreed about a whole range of issues in sacramental theology: whether the sacrament of circumcision conferred grace *ex opere operato*; whether the sacramental character of baptism, confirmation, and holy orders resided primarily in the intellect or the will; and whether Christ was present in the eucharistic species *per productionem* or *per adductionem*. Sometimes the theologians of the Society of Jesus look to form a school of thought, as when Suárez, Vásquez, and de Lugo argued that it would not have been fitting for there to be a number of adult sacraments in Eden or when Suárez, Bellarmine, and de Lugo argued that the sacramental character resided in the soul itself rather than in the intellect or in the will, but more often than not, the Jesuits held a wide variety of views.

On any particular topic, unity sometimes crossed the boundaries set by the "schools." On the famous issue of whether the sacraments are efficacious on account of a physical or moral causality, for example, Thomists such as Suárez, Bellarmine, Gonet, and Billuart asserted a physical causality without denying its moral aspects, while those who favored a moral efficacy, such as Melchior Cano, de Lugo, Vásquez, and the Scotists generally, did so because they did not want to subject God's mysteries to mechanical or magical laws. Augustinians were also divided on this issue. Some, such as Gianlorenzo Berti, argued that the Holy Spirit exerted a physical causality on the soul in the presence of an external sign, whereas others supported more traditional formulations of moral efficacy. Some Thomists maintained that the sacramental character itself was a "physical" medium of grace. In much the same way, no unanimity existed on questions of whether the disciples, when they baptized "in the name of Jesus," did so by an extraordinary privilege, or whether the phrase merely referred to Christ's baptism as opposed to John's. A more celebrated example of great diversity in post-Tridentine theology can be found in the voluminous treatises on the relative place of contrition and attrition in the sacrament of penance and, like today, there were seemingly as many positions on the form and matter of the sacrament of matrimony as there were individual theologians. In rare instances, the theologians of the modern era departed from the general medieval consensus. The general tendency of baroque theologians, quite against the grain of the earlier tradition, was to interpret the sacrament of extreme unction as a strengthening, by supernatural grace, that prepared the dying Catholic for purgatory. Aquinas, Bonaventure, and Scotus had each maintained the sacramentality of the minor orders, although Cajetan, following Durandus, was the only major baroque theologian to deny the sacramentality of the diaconate. Jesuits such as Bellarmine and Estius and Dominicans such as Gonet, Gotti, and Billuart maintained the position of Aquinas, while Vásquez affirmed the sacramentality of the diaconate and subdiaconate, but denied the sacramental status of the other minor orders. It might be interesting to note that Jean Morin, when he treated the medieval controversy about the blessing of deaconesses, judged those blessings to be true ordinations, albeit to a minor order. At any rate, most theologians of the nineteenth century discarded both their medieval and baroque traditions, and followed the minority position of Durandus and Cajetan.

This diversity of post-Tridentine sacramental theology is nowhere more apparent than in eucharistic theology. Although Scholastic theologians unanimously affirmed the reality of the eucharistic accidents, some, such as Gregory of Valencia, Suárez, Vásquez, and de Lugo thought that the reality of the eucharistic accidents to be an article of the faith, although most others judged it a theological conclusion. So, too, almost every Catholic theologian of note addressed the sacramental mode of Christ's bodily presence at great length, and such discussions of internal and external quality, impassibility, and aptitudinal extension must be counted among the most technically bewildering discussions of the baroque age. Such discussions ran parallel with the oft-disputed question whether the human eye might be granted the capacity to see the sacramental body of Christ in the beatific vision. Although Aquinas and Suárez denied the possibility, Vásquez and de Lugo affirmed it. Indeed it was for this very reason that Scotists restricted the words of consecration to the cause of the sacrament; they did not believe that the words of consecration were part of its intrinsic form, which consisted rather in the body and the blood of Christ. To these highly speculative issues, we might add the problem of how Christ is simultaneously in heaven and yet present on many altars on earth. One can find extensive treatments of the ongoing debate about circumscriptive and definitive multilocation in Bellarmine, Suárez, Cardinal de Lugo, and the Scotists. Sometimes, speculations about the effects of the glorified Christ upon our own bodies in communion took rather adventurous forms, as in Contenson's claim that the Eucharist gives us a claim upon resurrection by communicating a certain "physical quality" to the body itself.

Nor can we discount the peculiar genius of several individual theologians. De Lugo, for example, maintained several unique views on questions of sacramental theology, arguing, among other things, that the essence of any sacrament must include the intention of the minister in addition to its matter and form. The cardinal also argued that sacramental graces, while not modes of perfection (as per Billuart and Thomists generally), were permanent dispositions that led us to the ends for which God instituted each sacrament in question (against Suárez, however, who maintained that sacramental graces consisted merely of a moral claim to the actual graces of each sacrament). Vásquez, while often fiercely anti-Scotist in his rhetoric, sided with the Scotists against the Thomists in treating the Eucharist as a "permanent sacrament." For this reason, the Jesuit theologian argued that sacraments need not be essentially composed of *res et verbum*, but might simply proceed from them. He also sided with Bonaventurians against both Thomists and Scotists that the *sacramentum naturae* need not be a sign of hope in the future Redeemer. In the same way, the greatest theologians of the era routinely applied the critical distinctions of one theological *locus* to other theological *loci*. Debates about whether the sacraments were physical or moral causes of grace, for example, incorporated material from the more famous debates about physical premotion, the *scientia media*, and congruism, just as debates about the precise relationship of sacramental and sanctifying graces incorporated material from Christology. Scotists, for example, following Anthony Hickey, applied their master's celebrated views on the predestination of Christ to highlight the eschatological significance of baptism and so to argue that God might well grant some a greater grace in particular sacraments than he granted others. If we learn anything from these baroque treatises, it is for all intents and purposes impossible to understand any one issue in isolation from the larger systems of the schools or the individual theologians themselves. More to our purposes, it is frivolous—if not futile—to attempt to reduce these vast systems to an easily dismissible "position."

Baroque Theology of the Eucharistic Sacrifice

No single topic better demonstrates the diversity of post-Tridentine sacramental theology than the sacrificial nature of the Mass, and no aspect of baroque eucharistic theology has attracted more attention from twentieth-century theologians than the so-called "destruction" theories of the eucharistic sacrifice. Daly arranges in his own criticism of post-Tridentine eucharistic theology a number of (mostly Jesuit) theologians according to four theories about the degree to which the eucharistic victim can be said to undergo some change in the Mass: theologians such as Melchior Cano and Alfonso Salmerón argued that Christ did not undergo any actual change during eucharistic sacrifice, since the Mass contains only a figure of his immolation on the cross; Toledo and Suárez locate the change in the act of transubstantiation itself, namely, in the substance of the bread and wine; Gregory de Valencia and Bellarmine see the change in Christ's acquisition (or loss) of a new state of *esse sacramentale*; finally, Vásquez and Lessius located the real change in the absolute sacrifice Christ makes on the cross and a "figurative" or "mystical" change in the act of consecration which constitutes the relative sacrifice on the altar (Daly 2000: 249–257).

It is generally assumed that these "destruction" theories are responses to Melanchton's *Apology for the Augsburg Confession*, which taunted "Romanists" with their failure to give a general definition of sacrifice. And, indeed, after the Council of Trent solemnly defined the Mass to be a sacrifice in 1562, theologians devoted much of their energies to exploring the manifold aspects of the theology of sacrifice: its role in salvation history; its relationship to the Last Supper, Christ's redemptive death on the cross, and presentation of his blood before the Father in heaven; its essential form and its manner of operation; who offers it and who (or what) is offered; whether its merit is infinite or finite; how it is applied for the benefit of the church or individuals thereof; the sense in which it must be propitiatory or immolatory. That said, post-Tridentine theologians still began with definitions from Augustine (*De civitate Dei* X.5) and Isidore (*Etymologies* VI.19.38), with Thomists adding relevant backing from the *Summa contra gentiles* III, ch. 119 or the *Summa theologiae* I-II, q. 102, or III, q. 48 and Bonaventureans and Scotists generally drawing upon the *Summa fratris Alexandri* III, 55, 4, 1. For the purposes of our discussion, the fateful passages are *Summa theologiae* II-II, q. 85, a. 3, ad 3 and II-I, q. 86, a. 1. In the first, Aquinas defines sacrifice as "something done concerning the things offered [to God]" (*circa res oblatas aliquid fit*). In the second, Aquinas further defines sacrifice in contradistinction to oblation: "When something is offered in divine worship to be consumed and become some sacred reality thereby, it is both an oblation and a sacrifice. If it is offered but remains an integral whole, either to be set aside for divine worship or for the use of ministers, it is an oblation, but not a sacrifice." Taken together, it is not hard to see how theologians who wished to provide a definition of "sacrifice" might infer that Aquinas defined sacrifice as something done to the *res oblata* that implies breaking and consumption. Indeed, the examples Aquinas gives in *Summa theologiae* II-II, a. 85, a. 3 include the killing of animals and the roasting of their meat, or the breaking and eating of bread.

Although the Council of Trent made no mention of Aquinas's *aliquid fit*, it became something of a fashion to discuss it in the 1560s, especially at the University of Louvain. It is broadly assumed that Bellarmine, who taught at Louvain from 1569 to 1576, brought the topic to Rome when he accepted the Chair in Controversial Theology at the Collegio Romano, which he held until 1588. Bellarmine interpreted Aquinas's *aliquid fit* as "the consecration and change of some visible and permanent thing by a mystic rite" (*De controversiis*, tom. III, lib. 1, ch. 2), although he later glossed this by noting, "A true and real sacrifice requires the true and real death, or destruction, of the thing offered" (*De controversiis*, tom. III, lib. 1, ch. 27). The saintly cardinal believed that the termination of Christ's *esse sacramentale*, when the priest consumed the eucharistic accidents, was sufficient to fulfill the definition of a "true" and "real" sacrifice. That said, no unanimity existed during the baroque age on the celebrated question about whether the transformation of the *res oblata* necessarily involves the so-called "destruction" of the eucharistic victim. Vásquez, for example, rejected the "destruction" theory altogether, maintaining that the Mass, being a relative sacrifice, need not involve a slaying of Christ at all, but only that his death be represented visibly by the separation of the body and blood on the altar. In Vásquez's view, Christ, being impassible, undergoes no transformation in the double consecration beyond being made present under the eucharistic species. Suárez, on the other hand, hoping to safeguard the Tridentine definition of the Mass as a true and proper sacrifice, argued for a real transformation of the sacrificial victim, but opted to defend the transformation not as a change for the worse (*immutatio deterius sive destructio*) but rather for the better (*immutatio melius*). Lessius argued that the sacramental slaying enacted in the consecration would indeed spill Christ's blood on the altar, were Christ's own impassibility not to render it impossible. In defense of the great number of theologians who favored Lessius' view (among them Hurtado, Billuart, Gonet, and Gotti), it might be said that this is indeed a proper view of Christ's glorified impassibility. De Lugo, accepting the notion that Christ's glorious impassibility, makes a genuine physical slaying impossible, argued that the merely "moral" slaying effected by the double consecration consists in Christ's voluntary self-abasement to the condition of food and drink. Christ's abasement, by which he divests himself of the powers connatural to his glorified body, is akin to the very *kenosis* by which he divested himself of his divine power during the Incarnation. The principal defenders of de Lugo's position in the early modern period were the Jesuits Juan de Ulloa and Domenico Viva, the Scotist Franz Henno, and the Wirceburgenses. A more exotic view was held by Cardinal Cienfuégos, who taught that the "destruction" of the sacrificial victim consisted in the suspension of Christ's senses from the consecration to the mixture of the species, although this view can be traced back to St. Bonaventure.

There is hardly a single baroque position, however exotic, that did not find a defender in the nineteenth or early twentieth century. Matthias Scheeben, while questioning whether such modern approaches to "destruction" agreed with the fathers and great scholastics, might be seen as offering a variant of Suárez's position when he argued that Christ's sacramental mode of existence consists in exaltation rather than abasement. Contenson's theology of the resurrection and the sacrament found a defender in Heimbucher, who argued that eucharistic communion planted a "seed of immortality" in the human body. Johannes Baptist Franzelin revived some of Cardinal Cienfuégos' more exotic speculations. De Lugo's theory, although hardly favored in his lifetime, underwent something of a revival in the late nineteenth century, being adopted by Franzelin, Bernard Tepe, and even Gerard Manley Hopkins. In fact, when theologians such as Giovanni Perrone, Louis Billot, and J. A. de Aldama argue that the sacrifice of the Mass was merely a "mystical immolation" that required no new destruction of the *res oblata*, they might be seen as a return to the position of Vásquez. Truth be told, I cannot see a significant difference between the claims of Charles-Vincent Héris and Charles Journet that the separate consecration of the eucharistic elements, as an efficacious sacramental sign, makes Christ's saving death present to us and the general position found in earlier Dominicans such as Cajetan and Cano, or even later ones who followed Lessius, such as Gonet and Billuart.

Of course, the nineteenth century saw its own theological developments as well. Franzelin, when confronted with such eucharistic miracles, attempted to explain them with certain theses of Leibniz. The sacramental mode of existence, in which Christ's body is present under the eucharistic species, generated similarly exotic speculations in Salvatore Tongiorgi and Domenico Palmieri. Several of the condemned theses taken from the works of Antonio Serbati Rosmini concerned sacramental theology, including the teaching that Christ distributed the Eucharist to the dead when he descended into hell. Since the Holy Office rehabilitated Rosmini in 2001, this strong reading of John 6:54 has become an acceptable—albeit admittedly exotic—*theologoumenon*. At the very end of this tradition, before its abandonment in the generation of Henri de Lubac and Karl Rahner, stands the monumental contribution of Maurice de la Taille's *Mysterium Fidei,* which carefully combines all of the significant trends of post-Tridentine theology, including a renewed interest in the Church Fathers and Eastern liturgical forms, into one coherent whole. The Jesuit theologian also took significant pains to synthesize divergent Thomist and Scotist traditions, a remarkable act of theological charity for which several reviewers duly punished him.

ROBERT DALY, S.J., ON SO-CALLED "DESTRUCTION" THEORIES

Daly faults these theologians on three points: (1) a "narrow" interpretation of the axiom *in persona Christi* that "eliminates" an ecclesiological interpretation in favor of a Christological interpretation; (2) an over-emphasis on the words of institution at the expense of other aspects of the Eucharistic Prayer and accompanying ritual; and (3) an interpretation of eucharistic "action" whose dynamic is expressed as a movement from Christ to the priest to the church (rather than from Christ to the church to the priest), which Daly believes leads to an over-emphasis on "priestly power, position and privilege against which many have protested" (Daly 2000: 240). Although Daly concedes that *Lumen gentium* (n. 10) and *Sacrosanctum concilium* (n. 48) seem to conform to the earlier tradition of Bellarmine that was taken up by the Magisterium, he believes the force of this tradition weakened by Paul VI's addition of the *epiclesis* in the 1969 *Missale Romanum*. Although Paul VI left the "traditional Western overemphasis" on Jesus' words of institution intact, Daly believes that the addition of the explicit *epiclesis* warrants the discarding of the traditional scholastic notion that the words of institution are the "essential form" of the sacrament. To justify this sweeping change, he appeals to Kilmartin, who lays the blame for the "modern average Catholic theology of the Eucharist" on post-Tridentine theologians, who sought to find the visible sacrifice of the Mass in the separate consecration of the elements and proposed a "mystical mactation" of Christ at the level of sacramental signs. "Thus," Kilmartin says, "they espoused the idea of a sacrificial rite, the structure of which was the sacrifice of the self-offering of Christ in the signs of the food. This is a pre-Christian concept which is now generally discarded in current Catholic theology" (Kilmartin 1998: 294–295). In fact, according to Daly, the scholastic tradition exemplified by John Paul II's *Dominicae cenae* "reflects the same kind of confusion as that caused by Trent when it used *offerre* to refer both to the historical sacrifice of the cross and to the phenomenological, history-of-religions liturgical-ritual sacrificial act of the eucharistic celebration, not attending to the fact that sacrifice, in the history-of-religions sense of the word, had been done away with by the Christ event" (Daly 2000: 245). In this confusion, the baroque tradition that stretches from the sixteenth century to John Paul II ultimately neglects the Eucharist's Trinitarian dimensions, its ecclesiological perspective, and its eschatological goal.

Whether they realize it or not, Kilmartin and Daly unwittingly find themselves at the end of a long line of Protestant critics of late medieval and post-Tridentine eucharistic theology. Although its roots sink deeper into older Lutheran histories of philosophy and theology, the modern critique is best known in the Anglican genealogy that purports to unmask the persistence of "medieval errors" in post-Tridentine sacramental theology that begins with A. W. Haddan's *Apostolic Succession in the Church of England* (Haddan 1869), finds its most influential form in B. J. Kidd's *The Later Mediaeval Doctrine of the Eucharistic Sacrifice* (Kidd 1898), and attains a postmodern apotheosis in Catherine Pickstock's *After Writing* (Pickstock 1997). Truth be told, it is somewhat embarrassing that theologians continue to repeat these claims a full fifty years after Francis Clark demolished them in *The Eucharistic Sacrifice and the Reformation* (Clark 1960). All in all, Clark identifies no fewer than sixteen errors that Anglicans claimed were present in late medieval and early modern Catholic theology, and he quite ably refutes each one with a wealth of primary texts. One will see in item thirteen that the equation of sacrifice with death or destruction, which implies that Christ must somehow suffer anew on the altar, was a common feature of Protestant criticisms of Catholicism generally, and a particular favorite of twentieth-century Anglican theologians, such as Gore, Bicknell, Hicks, and E. L. Mascall (Clark 1960: 210–212). In fact, the general trend in late nineteenth- and early twentieth-century theology to emphasize the theology of the heavenly sacrifice and bemoan the allegedly exclusive emphasis of medieval theologians upon Christ's passion and death found purchase in Catholic theologians who felt little compulsion to follow the renewed scholasticism. This genealogy, beyond its ignorance of the particular texts of Aquinas, Scotus, Cajetan, and so forth, over-emphasizes the discontinuity between the medieval and early modern traditions. After all, the scholastic theologians of the post-Tridentine era built their accounts of the eucharistic sacrifice from Peter Lombard's *Sentences*, lib. IV, dist. 12, and repeated the same patristic texts from Lombard and Gratian. Apart from characteristic differences of emphases between Thomists and Scotists, the two most influential theologians before the Council of Trent, Gabriel Biel and Cajetan, agreed (1) that the sacrifice of the Mass was a memorial of Calvary, but not a *mere* memorial; (2) that the Mass is one with Christ's all-sufficient sacrifice on the Cross, although its *manner* of offering is different, because Christ does not suffer or die anew on the altar; and (3) that the eucharistic sacrifice is the means through which the efficacy of the one redemptive sacrifice is mediated and applied to humankind (Clark 1960: 84–94). Of course, it should go without saying, *pace* Protestant accounts, that not one of these modern theologians believed that the grace of the sacrament somehow derived, not from Christ's cross, but from the "destruction" of the *res oblata*.

We may likewise dismiss certain aspects of Daly's rhetorical exaggerations. The "many liturgical scholars" to whom he appeals never make an appearance: He depends almost entirely on two sources for his information, his friend Edward Kilmartin and Maurice Lepin's *L'Idée du sacrifice de la messe* (Lepin 1926). In point of fact, Lepin's classic seems to be the source for much of Kilmartin's knowledge of this tradition. At any rate, neither Daly nor Kilmartin appears to have read Lepin very closely. Although Lepin had his own reasons for arguing against these so-called "destruction" theories of the eucharistic sacrifice, the Sulpician's advocacy for a modern account of Christ's "heavenly sacrifice"— *pace* Daly—gives abundant proof from the Bible, the Church Fathers, and baroque theologians for a "metahistorical" interpretation of Christ's saving acts. More to the point, Lepin's digest of post-Tridentine theologians, even as it reduces sensitive treatments of the eucharistic sacrifice to rehearsed and easily refutable "positions," shows us that post-Tridentine theologies of the eucharistic sacrifice were far richer than Daly allows. First and foremost, almost no one, besides Ysambert and Alphonsus Liguori, followed Bellarmine on this score. Vásquez allowed for an immolation of the *res oblata* in the absolute sacrifice, but for the relative sacrifice all that was needed, strictly speaking, was that the eucharistic species be removed from their ordinary use by humankind. Suárez located the "change" in the transformation of the bread and wine into Christ's body and blood, but this "change" was "perfective," not "destructive." Lessius preferred a merely "virtual immolation" signified by the *separate* presence of Christ's body and blood on the altar. Even de Lugo, the great villain in many twentieth-century accounts, maintained only that Christ condescended to be present without the outward exercise of his vital activity. He made it clear, however, that Christ's *status declivior* was such only "in a moral sense, that is, according to human usage." Although all of these theologians agreed that the commemorative representation of the past immolation includes some "change," they usually saw this change as transformative, not destructive per se. In fact, the very terminology of the baroque theologians clearly demonstrates that they did not believe in any *physical* change in Christ; indeed, the various terms—"mystical," "moral," "virtual," and so forth—stand opposed to the mere "physical" transformation of the *res oblata*. In this respect, it could be argued that post-Tridentine eucharistic theology as a whole decisively rejected Bellarmine's peculiar theory. "None of the theologians in question," says Clark, "not even De Lugo, to whose opinion is meted out the severest criticism of all—ever defended the bizarre notion of a new slaying, or of any real destruction or injury suffered by Christ in the sacrifice of the Mass. On the contrary, all exclude that error" (Clark 1960: 439).

Of course, one cannot doubt the influence of de Lugo and Vásquez on later theologians; still, they are not the only representatives of post-Tridentine theology. In this regard, Daly acts as though the only theologians of the baroque age were Jesuits. More than a few theologians, however, remained faithful to the older Thomist and Scotist traditions, and one cannot discount the historical influence of the newer "oblationist" eucharistic theologies of the French School. Indeed, the writings of Pierre Bérulle, Charles de Condren, and Jean-Jacques Olier provide the chief alternative to these scholastic theologies of the eucharistic sacrifice. These theologians argued that the sacrifice of Calvary and the Mass were identical for the further reason that Christ offers the same "inner oblation" in both. These theologians also tended to interpret "destruction" as "abasement" as well, but in such a way that the Mass, as a relative sacrifice, finds its orientation not merely from the cross, but rather from Christ's "heavenly sacrifice," which is the truly absolute form of the sacrifice. The corresponding emphasis on the "heavenly sacrifice" of the French School might be said to be the chief rival to broadly scholastic theologies of the Eucharist in the baroque age. The notion of the "heavenly sacrifice" also found broad support in Germany, being defended by Johann Adam Möhler, Heinrich Klee, and Albert Stöckl. Perhaps its most interesting formulation is found in the *forma sacrificii* of Valentin Thalhofer. Of course, its most famous defender in the twentieth century was none other than Maurice Lepin himself. Although broadly rejected by scholastic theologians—unfortunately—these baroque theologies of heavenly sacrifice might be seen to stand behind the better-known speculations of Dom Odo Casel, Eugène Masure, and Aloysius van Hove in the early twentieth century. Even Anscar Vonier's speculations about eucharistic time and space can be included in this general trend, even though he rejected the notion of a heavenly sacrifice.

If Daly and Kilmartin fail to do justice to the historical diversity of early modern theology, what does one make of their theological arguments against the so-called "destruction" theories of the eucharistic sacrifice? Frankly, not much. The charge that post-Tridentine eucharistic theology promotes a "narrow" interpretation of the axiom *in persona Christi* that "eliminates" an ecclesiological interpretation in favor of a Christological interpretation depends upon a dichotomy falsely posed between the Christological and the ecclesiological. Of course, it also ignores the fact that the entire Scotist tradition, arguably the most powerful between Trent and the rise of Neo-Thomism in the nineteenth century, maintained the ecclesiological offering of the eucharistic sacrifice. The charge that post-Tridentine eucharistic theology over-emphasized the words of institution at the expense of other aspects of the Eucharistic Prayer and accompanying ritual is, I suppose, a veiled way of claiming that the absence of an *epiclesis* somehow led to a devaluation of the Holy Spirit. This charge, too, ignores a wealth of baroque texts that discussed the role of the Holy Spirit in the Eucharist. Witness, for example, Suárez's profound discussion of the relationship between the mutual eucharistic abiding promised by Christ in John 6:57–58 and the Holy Trinity, or Olier's *Explication des cérémonies de la grande messe de paroisse selon l'usage romain* (Olier 1661). Note, too, that Scotists and many Jesuit theologians such as Vásquez and de Lugo did not define the "essence" of the Eucharist solely in terms of the *res et verbum*. Did these baroque theologians interpret the eucharistic "action" as a "movement" from Christ to the priest to the church, which Daly believes leads to an over-emphasis on "priestly power, position and privilege" against which many have protested? Perhaps they did. Still, apart from an *ad hominem* that might be quickly turned upon its author, this third charge is little more than a variation on the first one. What is more important, it is not clear how any of Daly's three charges relate to the larger tradition of "destruction" theories that allegedly stemmed from Bellarmine. At this point, he seems to have pronounced the *anathema* upon the entire tradition of post-Tridentine Catholicism up to and including Pius XII and John Paul II. As for the "fact" touted by Kilmartin and Daly that a so-called "history-of-religions" notion of sacrifice has been done away with by the Christ "event": it is nothing more substantial than an "interpretation" in the history of religions, namely, the theory of René Girard. Even were Girard right about the "history of religions," such an interpretation of the history of religions does not give one warrant to interpret the sacrifice of the Mass in this manner. After all, everyone agreed that the Mass is an *unbloody* sacrifice, and in this respect it would not fulfill the Girardian definition of a sacrifice. At this point, it is difficult to see (for me at least) how Kilmartin and Daly do not project the highly reductive notion of sacrifice as "destruction" found in the old Anglican genealogies upon their baroque sources and attempt to slander them with the appellation "religion." One might note the irony, too, that after arguing against the "narrow" Christocentrism supposedly manifested in an emphasis on the words of institution, Kilmartin and Daly substitute a quasi-Barthian "Christ event" that denies the role of the Holy Spirit in the *praeparatio evangelica* found in the sacrifices of non-Christian religions. In this, the two Jesuits find themselves quite against both the *text* and the *spirit* of the Second Vatican Council.

EPILOGUE

It could be argued that, of the four primary sources of baroque sacramental theology—scholastic, controversial, mystical, and historical—only liturgical theology truly flowered in the twentieth century. Apart from the final flourish of Neo-Thomism, most of the characteristic positions of baroque sacramental theology had fallen into abeyance by the middle of the twentieth century. Controversial theology gave way to more broadly ecumenical concerns, even as many Protestant theologians intensified their polemic against Catholicism. The distinctive mysticism of the priesthood or the eucharistic sacrifice found in the French School found defenders into the 1950s, but few defend these positions now, at least as *theological* positions. As a rule, twentieth-century theologians such as Romano Guardini, Otto Semmelroth, Karl Rahner, and Edward Schillebeecx began the tradition that finds expression in the work of contemporary theologians such as Louis-Marie Chauvet, Edward Kilmartin, Robert Daly, and Joseph Ratzinger, who attempt to discredit the eucharistic theology of the baroque age as "modern" or "decadent." These contemporary theologians have even attempted to suggest that the saints of the early modern period received no spiritual sustenance from the Tridentine liturgy. Let us accept this Romantic prejudice for the sake of argument. If we are to judge the sacramental theology of an era by the devotion it inspires, I am afraid we must acknowledge that, from St. Ignatius's ecstasies at the altar to the Jansenists' abstinence from the eucharistic meal, Christ present on the altar is the primitive *fact* of the baroque age. More to the point, if we accept this Romantic prejudice, we must also—with an extreme shortage of priestly vocations, a precipitous drop in participation in the sacrament of reconciliation, and young people leaving the church in droves—conclude strongly against today's sacramental theology. Better, I suppose, to jettison the Romantic prejudice altogether and acknowledge that the men and women of the baroque age brought about the conversion of continents with the very sacramental "system" contemporary theologians have tried so desperately to eradicate.

Suggested Reading

I depend largely on Pöhle (1915) for summaries of many of these scholastic controversies. The state of the art for the debates about Eucharistic sacrifice is Clark (1960); Daly (2000); and Kilmartin (1998).

Bibliography

de Aldama, J. A. (1952–1953), *Sacrae theologiae summa* (Madrid: Editorial Católica).

Bellarmine, R. (1873), *Opera Omnia*, vol. 4 (Paris: Vivès).

Berti, G. (1776), *Opus de Theologicis Disciplinis*, vol. 3 (Venice: Remondini).

Bérulle, P. (1623), *Discours de l'estat et les grandeurs de Jésus* (Paris: Antoine Estiene).

Biel, G. (1488 [1963–1976]), *Expositio sacri canonis missae* (Wiesbaden: F. Steiner).

Billot, L. (1931), *De ecclesiae sacramentis*, 7th ed. (Rome: Universitatis Gregorianae)

Billuart, C.-R. (1747), *Cursus Theologiae*, vols. 14–17 (Würzburg: Ioannis Iacobi Stahel).

Cajetan, Thomas de Vio Cardinal (1903), *Commentarium in Tertiam Partem Summae Theologiae in Sancti Thomae Aquinatis Doctoris Angelici Opera Omnia*, vols. 11–12 (Rome: Ex Typogaphia Polyglotta S. C. de Propaganda Fide).

Cano, M. (1577), *Relectio de sacramentis in genere* (Ingolstadt: Ex Officina Weissenhorniana).

Casel, O. (1931), "Die Messopferlehre der Tradition," in *Theologie und Glaube*.

Cienfuégos, A. (1728), Vita abscondita, *seu speciebus eucharisticis velata, per potissimas sensuum operationes de facto à Christo domino ibidem indesinenter exercita circa objecta altari* (Typis Antonii de Rubeis è Foro Rotunda).

Clark, F. (1960), *Eucharistic Sacrifice and the Reformation* (Westminster, MD: Newman Press).

de Condren, C. (1677), *L'idée du sacerdoce et du sacrifice de Jésus-Christ* (Paris: Jean Baptiste Coignard).

Contenson, V. (1687), *Theologia mentis et cordis, seu Speculationes universae doctrinae sacrae* (Cologne: Metternich).

Daly, R. (2000), "Robert Bellarmine and Post-Tridentine Eucharistic Theology," *Theological Studies* 61: 239–260.

Daly, R. (2013), "The Council of Trent," in Lee Palmer Wandel (ed.), *A Companion to the Eucharist in the Reformation* (Leiden: Brill).

Estius, G. (1615–1616), *In quatuor libros sententiarum commentaria* (Douai: Petrus Borremans).

Franzelin, I. B. (1858), *Tractatus de SS. Eucharistiae: de Sacrificio* (Rome: Typis S. Congregationis de Propaganda Fide).

Galtier, P. (1956), *De poenitentia tractatus dogmatico-historicus* (Rome: Universitatis Gregorianae).

Gonet, J.-B. (1671), *Clypeus theologiae Thomisticae contra novos eius impugnatorus*, vol. 5 (Cologne: Sumptibus Joannis Wilhelmi Friessem junioris).

Gotti, V. L. (1750), *Theologia scholastico-dogmatica juxta mentem divi Thomae Aquinatis*, vol. 3 (Venice: Ex Typographia Balleoniana).

Gregory of Valencia (1603), *Commentariorum theologicorum tomi quatuor* (Lyons: Sumptibus Horatii Cardon).

Heimbucher, M. (1884), *Die Wirkungen der heiligen Kommunion* (Regensburg: J. G. Manz).

Henno, F. (1719), *Theologia dogmatica, moralis, et scholastica: de Sacramentis*, vol. 2 (Venice: Apud Antonium Bortoli).

Héris, C.-V. (1952), *Le mystère de l'Eucharistie* (Paris: Éditions Siloë).

Hiquaeus, A., *Commentarius in Ioannis Duns Scoti Opera Omnia*, vol. 9 (Lyons: Sumptibus Laurentii Durand).

Hurtado, G. (1633), *Tractatus de Sacramentis et Censuris* (Antwerp: Moretus).

Journet, C. (1957), *La Messe, Présence du sacrifice de la croix* (Bruges: Desclée de Brouwer).

Kern, J. (1907), *De sacramento extremae unctionis tractatus dogmaticus* (Regensburg: Friedrich Pustet).

Kilmartin, E. (1998), *The Eucharist in the West* (Collegeville, MN: The Liturgical Press).

Klee, H. (1844), *Katholische Dogmatik* (Mainz: Kirchheim, Schott, and Thielmann).

Lepin, M. (1926), *L'Idée du sacrifice de la messe, d'après les théologiens depuis l'origine jusqu'à nos jours* (Paris: Gabriel Beauchesne).

Lessius, L. (1620), *Opuscula in quibus pleraque theologiae mysteria explicantur* (Antwerp: Moretus).

Liguori, A. (1779), *Theologia moralis*, vol. 2 (Venice: Remondini).

de Lugo, J. (1644), *Disputationes Scholasticae et Morales: de Sacramento Eucharistiae* (Lyons: Sumptibus Haered. Petri Prost).

Mastrius, B. (1661), *Disputationes Theologicae in Quartum Librum Sententiarum* (Venice: Apud Valuasensem).

Masure, E. (1957), *Le Sacrifice du Chef*, rev. ed. (Paris: La Colombe)

Möhler, J. A. (1843), *Symbolik, oder Darstellung der dogmatischen Gegensätze der Katholiken und Protestanten nach ihren öffentlichen Bekenntnisschriften* (Mainz: F. Kupferberg).

Morinus, J. (1655), *Commentarius de sacris ecclesiae ordinationibus, secundum antiquos et recentiores Latinos, Graecos, Syros et Babylonios* (Paris: Sumptibus Gaspari Metvras).

Olier, J.-J. (1661), *Explication des cérémonies de la grande messe de paroisse selon l'usage romain* (Paris: Chez Jacques Langlois).

Palmieri, D. (1893), *Opus theologicum morale*, vol. 4 (Prati: Giachetti).

Pasqualigo, Z. (1707), *De sacrificio novae legis* (Venice: P. Balleonium).

Perrone, G. (1842), *Praelectiones theologicae* (Paris: Migne).

Pöhle, J. (1915), *The Sacraments: A Dogmatic Treatise* (St. Louis, MO: B. Herder).

Rosmini-Serbati, A. (1882), *L'introduzione del Vangelo secondo Giovanni* (Turin: Stamperia dell'Unione Tipografico-Editrice).

Sanchez, T. (1669), *De sancto matrimonii sacramento disputationum* (Lyons: Laurentii Anisson).

Scheeben, M. (1903), *Handbuch der katholischen Dogmatik*, vol. 4 (Freiburg im Breisgau: Herder).

Stöckl, A. (1861), *Das Opfer nach seinem Wesen und nach seiner Geschichte* (Mainz: Verlag von Franz Kirckheim).

Suárez, F. (1860–1861), *Opera Omnia*, vols. 20–2 (Paris: Vivès).

de la Taille, M (1921), *Mysterium Fidei: de augustissimo corporis et sanguinis Christi sacrificio atque sacramento* (Paris: Beauchesne).

Tangiorgi, S. (1869), *Institutiones philosophicae* (New York: Collegi Sancti Francisci Xaverii).

Tepe, B. (1896), *Institutiones theologicae in usum scholarum*, vol. 4 (Paris: Lethielleux).

Thalhofer, V. (1883), *Handbuch der Katholischen Liturgik*, 2 vols. (Freiburg: Herder).

de Ulloa, J. (1719), *Theologiae Scholasticae*, vol. 4 (Augsburg: Sumptibus Philippi, Joannis, & Martini Veith).

Vásquez, G. (1612), *Commentariorum ac disputationum in Tertiam Partem S. Thomae*, tom. 2 (Ingolstadt: Andreas Angermarius).

Van Hoye, A. (1941), *Tractatus de sanctissima Eucharistia*, 2nd ed. (Mechlin: H. Dessain)

Viva, D. (1712), *Cursus Theologicus ad usum Tyronum elucubratus* (Padua: Ex Typograpfia Seminarii apud Joannem Manfrè).

Vonier, A. (1925), *A Key to the Doctrine of the Eucharist* (London: Burns, Oates, and Washbourn).

Wirceburgenses [Thomas Holtzclau] (1768 [1880]), *Theologia dogmatica, polemica, scholastica, et moralis: de Sacramentis*, 3rd ed., vol. 9 (Paris: Berche et Tralin).

Ysambert, N. (1639), *Disputationes in Tertiam Partem S. Thomae* (Paris: Denis de La Noüe).

CHAPTER 24

......

LUTHERAN AND REFORMED SACRAMENTAL THEOLOGY: SEVENTEENTH–NINETEENTH CENTURIES

......

SCOTT R. SWAIN

INTRODUCTION

LUTHERAN and Reformed sacramental teaching identifies baptism and the Lord's Supper as divinely instituted means of grace: instruments whereby God communicates Christ and his benefits to creatures through creatures in accordance with his promise (*contra* Gregory 2012: 41–43, 57, *et passim*). Protestant sacramental teaching, initially established in the biblical commentaries, treatises, and commonplace books of the Reformers and codified in the ecclesiastical confessions of the sixteenth and seventeenth centuries, received its most sophisticated exposition in the era of Protestant orthodoxy (*c.* 1560–1790) as theologians benefitting from several generations of Protestant biblical exegesis and trained in the principles of classical Trinitarian and Christological metaphysics applied themselves to the task of contemplating and commending the evangelical sacraments within the context of a fully developed systematic theology. During this period, Lutheran and Reformed sacramental thought flourished in the major universities and seats of learning throughout Europe and the British Isles: Wittenberg, Tübingen, Strasbourg, Leipzig, Jena, Heidelberg, Geneva, Basel, Leiden, Franeker, Groningen, Saumur, Oxford, Cambridge, St. Andrews, Aberdeen, and Edinburgh; and found vital expression in the sermons, liturgies, catechisms, and festal communions of Protestant churches well into the eighteenth century (Kalb 1965; Holifield 1974; Schmidt 2001; Payne 2004; Spinks 2006).

Protestant sacramental teaching was also the occasion for sharp conflict during this period. Theologians of the Lutheran and Reformed churches fiercely disputed the views of Rome, which in their judgment erred *in excessu* by multiplying the sacraments beyond the two that Christ instituted and by exaggerating the metaphysical status and efficacy of these rites, and also the views of Anabaptists, Socinians, and English Baptists, which erred *in defectu* by failing to identify the sacraments as instruments of divine grace, regarding them merely as badges of faith and bonds of ecclesiastical union and communion. Debates raged between Lutheran and Reformed theologians as well, deepening fissures introduced at the time of the Reformation. To be sure, the contentious nature of sacramental theology was regularly lamented: "we cannot behold without grief," Francis Turretin declares, "that those things which were instituted by God to be bonds and symbols of union and concord among Christians, have been made (by the depravity of men) the seed plot of contentions and the apple of discord" (Turretin 1997: 337). Nevertheless, despite numerous attempts, especially on the part of the Reformed, to achieve concord if not consensus on the sacraments (Hotson 2004; Denlinger 2012), aspirations toward sacramental unity between Lutheran and Reformed churches were not realized through theological persuasion but only through Erastian mandate, as most notably in the Prussian Church Union of 1817. Although the latter event in some ways fulfilled longstanding hopes for ecclesiastical harmony, it also gave political impetus to a distinctly modern theological quest to transcend the discrete sacramental theologies of the Protestant confessions by means of a new "evangelical" synthesis (Schleiermacher 1989; Dorner 1896).

The greatest challenge to confessional sacramental teaching between the seventeenth and nineteenth centuries, however, came from the various intellectual and social changes that accompanied the Enlightenment. Philip Schaff, somewhat impressionistically, identified rationalism and "sectarism" as the two agents responsible for birthing a bastardized form of Protestantism (Schaff 1845). Changing theological and metaphysical conceptions of causality (van Ruler 1995; Oliver 2005; Bac 2010), attended by increasingly atomistic modes of theological, historical, and textual analysis (Howard 2006; Schmitz 2007: 3–36), and also changing patterns in piety from the external, public, and mediate to the internal, private, and immediate (Holifield 1974; Heyd 1995; Tanner 2010: 274–301), created a setting that rendered Protestant orthodox sacramental theology implausible, and often times inscrutable, to many eighteenth- and nineteenth-century thinkers. This period thus witnessed significant transition in Lutheran and Reformed sacramental thought: faced with the wide-ranging intellectual, political, and social changes brought about by the Enlightenment, we see a shift from theologies that sought to inherit, elaborate, debate, and apply the doctrine enshrined in the confessions of the Protestant churches to theologies that sought, with varying degrees of self-awareness, to rehabilitate traditional ecclesiastical doctrine within a more or less revisionist theological framework.

In what follows we will survey some of the major themes and thinkers of this rich but understudied period of Protestant sacramental thought, bypassing contemporaneous developments in North American Lutheran and Reformed theology since they are treated within a separate chapter of the present volume. We will first consider Lutheran and Reformed sacramental theology in the era of Protestant orthodoxy. Following a discussion of the ontological and epistemological principles of Protestant orthodox sacramental thought, we will examine three representative topics discussed and debated by Lutheran and Reformed orthodox divines: the nature of sacramental efficacy; the efficacy of infant baptism; and the nature of Christ's presence in the Lord's Supper, and of our feeding upon him. We will then consider developments in Lutheran and Reformed sacramental theology "after orthodoxy" with the rise of a self-consciously modern form of Protestant theology in the nineteenth century. A brief introduction to four representative theologians, Julius August Ludwig Wegscheider, Friedrich Schleiermacher, Isaak Dorner, and William Cunningham, will help us appreciate the status of modern Protestant sacramental theology as a new phase in the reception of Reformation thought.

Lutheran and Reformed Sacramental Theology in the Era of Protestant Orthodoxy

Principles of Sacramental Theology

In the *loci* devoted to the sacraments, we see a clear example of how the doctrines of the Trinity and Scripture function as the twin ontological and cognitive principles of Protestant orthodox dogmatics (on these principles more generally, see Muller 2003: 430–445). As *principia*, these doctrines are not merely foundational topics within the theological system, treated first in the sequence of doctrines only to be left behind when later doctrines are discussed. As *principia*, the doctrines of God and Scripture are materially present *to* each doctrinal locus within the system as productive sources *of* the *loci* that follow from them as *principiata* (Preus 1970: 116; Schmitz 2007: 12, 16). Thus, for example, David Hollaz identifies God, the ontological principle of the sacraments, as the sole *auctor* and *fons* of all sacramental grace, responsible for both the institution and operation of baptism and the Lord's Supper (Hollaz 1763: III.3.iii,qiv). In similar fashion Scripture, the cognitive principle of the sacraments, functions as the sole source from which the dogmatic, polemical, and practical dimensions of the sacraments are derived through biblical exegesis.

The status of the divine Trinity as the ontological principle of sacramental grace explains in part the widespread use of causal language within these theologies. Both Lutheran and Reformed divines regularly identify the triune God in general, and Christ the Mediator in particular, as the principal efficient cause of sacramental grace, while they identify lawfully ordained ministers along with the sacramental elements, distributed in accordance with the word of God, as instrumental and (in the case of Lutherans) less principal causes through which God signifies, seals, and confers evangelical grace to recipients of the sacraments (Wollebius 1655: XXII.v–vii, xv, xvii; XXIII.iii; Baier

1879: III.VIII.iv, vi; Turretin 1997: 365; Gerhard 2000: 82). In each case, the purpose in these identifications is to coordinate the incommunicable action of the Trinity with the media and action of creatures in order to portray the sacraments as true means, and not simply occasions, of divine grace. Far from dissolving the mystery of the sacraments through recourse to Aristotelian philosophy (cf. Raitt 1972: 71–73), causal analysis of the sacraments also enables these theologians to indicate the immediacy of Christ's personal agency in distributing grace to his church in and through these divine institutions (Wollebius 1655: XXII.xv, xvii). Causal analysis, in other words, secures theological understanding of the *opera ad extra* as *opera Dei*. There is no independent doctrine of creation, providence, redemption, or the sacraments in these theologies. Every doctrine is an aspect of the doctrine of the triune God: God creating, God sustaining, God redeeming, and God distributing sacramental grace.

Johann Gerhard's *Ausführliche schriftmäßige Erklärung der beiden Artikel von der heiligen Taufe und dem heiligen Abendmahl*, published in 1610, well illustrates the role of principles within Protestant orthodox sacramental theology. Gerhard's stated aim in this work is to draw "the pure doctrine of holy Baptism and of the holy Lord's Supper singularly and solely from the source of the divine Word" (Gerhard 2000: 6). Accordingly, though it discusses many of the same topics treated in Gerhard's *Loci Theologici* (on which, see Scaer 1999), the focus of the *Erklärung* is on thoroughly establishing the biblical bases of those topics and on refuting the various opinions which contradict Lutheran sacramental teaching through scriptural exegesis. Furthermore, though inattentive by design to dogmatic-historical and philosophical analysis, the *Erklärung* maintains throughout a clear focus on the ontological principle of the sacraments so that its readers may appreciate that baptism "is a powerful means through which the Holy Trinity works powerfully: the Father takes on the one who is baptized as his dear child; the Son washes him of his sins with his blood; the Holy Spirit regenerates and renews him for everlasting life" (Gerhard 2000: 56) and that it is Christ "himself who distributes his true body and blood in this worthy Sacrament" (Gerhard 2000: 222). It is this concern of the *Erklärung* to draw sacramental doctrine solely from its scriptural source and to locate the sacraments in relation to their trinitarian and Christological principle that distinguishes it as a work of Protestant orthodox theological exegesis.

Sacramental Theology Elucidated and Debated

Through the washing of regeneration and the distribution of bread and wine God mercifully communicates evangelical grace to his people in accordance with scriptural promise. This is the object of Protestant orthodox sacramental theology as determined by that theology's twin principles. In commending this object, Lutheran and Reformed theologians employ a variety of dogmatic-theological genres and elucidate a wide range of topics. Representative forms of discourse include the disputations of the *Synopsis Purioris Theologiae*, published by the Leiden theological faculty in 1625, Johannes Wollebius's brief textbook, *Compendium Theologiae Christianae* (1626), whose concise dogmatic propositions summarize Reformed doctrine with learned brevity, and David Hollaz's more extensive *Examen Theologicum Acroamaticum* (1707), which develops various doctrinal topics by means of the *quaestio* method. Through these literary forms and others, Protestant theologians treat a host of topics such as: the range of classical and ecclesiastical senses applied to the term "sacrament," as well as the biblical warrants for retaining and explaining this extrabiblical term, the Augustinian distinction between natural and conventional signs, the requisites that constitute a sacrament, the various causes (efficient, impulsive, instrumental, and final) of the sacraments, the distinction/ relation between the external matter or sign (*signum*) and the internal matter or thing signified (*res significata*), the relationship between Old Testament and New Testament sacraments, and the mode of administration. On the latter, for example, Edward Leigh reports that, for Zanchi and Perkins, immersion is the preferred mode of baptism "in persons of age and hot Countreys" (Leigh 1654: VIII.viii). A number of polemical questions are treated in this literature as well, including: whether the intention of the minister is required to establish the efficacy of the sacraments, whether sacraments work *ex opere operato*, whether the bread and the wine are converted into the body and blood of Christ, and whether laypersons may administer baptism. Each topic, furthermore, is expounded with an impressive degree of dogmatic-historical awareness. Augustine is preeminent among patristic citations; his definition of a sacrament as a visible sign of an invisible grace is ubiquitous in this literature. Lutheran and Reformed theologians also display familiarity with various medieval sacramental theories regarding, for example, the nature of sacramental efficacy, though this is sometimes a familiarity mediated through other sources (e.g. the Roman Catholic polemicist Cardinal Bellarmine). In many instances, patristic and medieval theologians are adduced in support of Protestant teaching, as in the case of Bernard's rule regarding the necessity of the sacraments for salvation: *non privatio, sed contemptus damnat*.

The Nature of Sacramental Efficacy

"The Sacraments are signs to represent, instruments to convey, Seals to confirm the Covenant" (Leigh 1654: VIII.VII.ii). Leigh's description reflects at a formal level the common Protestant orthodox definition of a sacrament: "In defining a sacrament," Turretin asserts, "we follow Paul, who speaking of circumcision, says, it is 'a sign and seal of the righteousness of faith' (Rom 4:11). This is a generic definition and is rightly ascribed to the species" (Turretin 1997: 339). Similarly, Johann Wilhelm Baier describes the sacraments as *signa et media sive organa conferendae et obsignandae gratiae* (Baier 1879: III.VIII.ii). These common definitions nevertheless mask different understandings of the nature of the sacraments. The differences are partly a matter of emphasis: the Reformed stressing the sealing function of the signs and Lutherans stressing the conferring function of the signs. More fundamentally, they concern different understandings of sacramental efficacy. Though both sides reject the Roman Catholic doctrine that sacraments work *ex opere operato* (acknowledging, it should be noted, that this phrase is susceptible to different interpretations), and though both sides contend that sacraments are indeed effectual means of grace, they differ on the status of sacraments as "instruments" by which God communicates grace. Lutheran and Reformed theologians provide diverse answers to the question, "*how* do they exert their efficacy?" (Turretin 1997: 364, emphasis mine).

Without eliding the distinction between sign and thing signified, the Lutheran answer to this question strongly emphasizes the *relation* between the two: "the Holy Spirit is given in and through Baptism," Gerhard states (Gerhard 2000: 91). Consequently, they are willing to describe sacraments as less principal causes or passive agents of divine grace. Again Gerhard: "The water of holy Baptism is not just a sign by which is symbolized rebirth and the washing away of sin; rather, it is an effectual means through which the Holy Spirit washes sin away. The Holy Spirit is and remains at all times the principal cause, the chief cause who works the rebirth and washes from sin. The water in Baptism, since it is combined with the Word of God and thus is no longer base water, is the instrumental cause—the means and passive agent—through which the Holy Spirit performs his gracious work" (Gerhard 2000: 82; Baier 1879: III.VIII.ii). The Reformed for their part worry that, in speaking this way, their Lutheran counterparts are guilty of transferring God's incommunicable power to creatures (Polyander 1881: XLIII.xxviii): "They all sin in excess who hold the sacraments to be vehicles and vessels containing grace or who make them real and less principal causes of grace" (Turretin 1997: 362).

Without denying the relation between sign and thing signified, the Reformed answer to the question nevertheless seeks to preserve the *distinction* between the two. Consequently, they are not willing to describe sacraments as less principal causes or passive agents of grace but only as instruments: "the Spirit," Turretin insists, is "the principal and efficacious cause who uses the word and sacraments as instruments" (Turretin 1997: 353). Referring to the standard proof texts of the Lutheran argument, Turretin goes on to explain: "If the sacraments are said to remit sins, to save and to regenerate (Acts 2:38; 22:16; Eph 5:26; Tit 3:5; 1 Pet 3:21), they do so not by a proper, immediate and internal force (as is evident from 1 Pet 3:21). Rather they do it sacramentally and improperly because they are efficacious signs by which those benefits are signified and sealed and in their legitimate use conferred" (Turretin 1997: 367). Lutheran theologians worry that the interpretation of the "Calvinists" evacuates Holy Scripture of its plain sense and reduces the sacraments to the status of *nuda signa* (Baier 1879: III.VIII.x; Gerhard 2000: 83).

Divergent Lutheran and Reformed views regarding sacramental efficacy undoubtedly reflect the deeper Christological differences that divide the two theological systems, as is readily apparent in interconfessional debates about Christ's presence in the Supper (see below). The differences however are not merely Christological. They also seem to reflect diverse sensibilities regarding the relationship between divine and creaturely causes, sensibilities that are traceable to medieval theological debates on sacramental efficacy (on which, see Courtenay 1984). Protestant orthodox divines are certainly cognizant of these medieval debates (see Turretin 1997: 362–363). Moreover, Reformed theologians such as André Rivet and Herman Witsius seem willing to note similarities between their views and medieval conceptions of "covenant causality" when defending themselves against the charge of promoting *nuda signa* (Polyander 1881: XLIII.xxvi; Witsius 2006: 173; see also Polyander 1881: XLIII.xxvii; Montefortino 1903: 576–581; Turretin

1997: 363; and Witsius 2006: 168–169). Still others employ common medieval analogies associated with this conception of causality in order to illustrate the nature of sacramental efficacy. Thus Benedict Pictet, illustrating the way sacraments function as "exhibitory signs," states: "they do this in the same way, as a man is put into possession of a house by having the keys delivered to him; and as formerly bishops obtained their investiture by the staff and ring given to them. The moment we receive the sacramental symbols in faith, the Holy Spirit, operating in an indescribable manner, strengthens faith; diffuses joy over the soul; gives the sense of sins forgiven, communion with God, adoption, and title to eternal life; increases hope, and adds a new degree of holiness. The sacraments, therefore, do not increase and confirm *faith*, by merely setting before us the objects we are bound to believe; nor *love*, merely by shewing how great is God's love toward us; but because the Holy Spirit accompanies them by his grace in all who rightly use them; hence the sacraments are said to *save* us; and hence baptism is called 'the washing of regeneration'" (Pictet 1847: 475; Turretin 1997: 348–349).

The Efficacy of Infant Baptism

The different views of Protestant theologians regarding the nature of sacramental efficacy come into sharp relief on the topic of infant baptism. Both Lutheran and Reformed divines believe infant baptism to be mandated by Scripture and offer a series of biblical warrants in support of bringing the children of Christians to the baptismal font. Hollaz, for example, commends infant baptism on the basis of: (1) universal necessity: because all infants are born in sin, all infants need to be reborn of water and Spirit (John 3.5–6); (2) Christ's universal mandate: Christ commanded the apostles to baptize all nations; infants are included within all nations (Matt 28:19); (3) universal promise: since the promise of grace and the evangelical covenant belong to infants, they too should be baptized (Acts 2:38–39; Gen 17:7); (4) the equivalence of circumcision and baptism (Col 2:11); (5) the aptitude of infants for the kingdom of heaven (Mark 10:14); and (6) the practice of the early church, which baptized whole households (Acts 16:15; 18:8; 1 Cor 1:16) (Hollaz 1763: III.II.iv, q xi). Reformed writers present similar arguments (e.g. Turretin 1997: 415–418). When it comes to the effects of baptism upon infants, however, we discover different opinions not only between Lutheran and Reformed theologians but also among Reformed theologians themselves.

According to Lutheran orthodox divines, the Spirit makes baptism an effectual means and organ of salvation for infants in two important ways. First, baptism is a *medium exhibitivum*: in baptism the Spirit exhibits the blessings of evangelical grace to infants. These blessings include membership in the covenant of grace, justification, forgiveness, and regeneration. Second, baptism awakens the *medium receptivum*: through baptism the Spirit awakens within infants the instrument whereby the aforementioned blessings are received and embraced, namely, faith (Hollaz 1763: III.II.iii, q xvii; III.II.iv, q xvi). The faith stirred up and kindled in infants through baptism moreover is a living and active faith, not an idle habit (Baier 1879: III.X.x). Lutheran doctors argue that, unlike adults (e.g. Simon the Magician in Acts 8:23), infants are unable to resist the graces offered and awakened in baptism. Consequently, the sacrament of baptism is always effective in their case. This is not because the sacrament works *ex opere operato* but by virtue of Word and Spirit, which always accompany the rite of baptism to make it an effectual means of grace in those who do not resist the Holy Spirit (Hollaz 1763: III.II.iii, q xvii; Gerhard 2000: 75–93).

Reformed teaching on this subject is more difficult to summarize owing to the variety of opinions espoused. In his *De Efficacia et Utilitate Baptismi in Electis Foederatorum Parentum Infantibus*, published in 1693, Herman Witsius identifies and engages several of the major views promoted by Reformed orthodox divines. The first view, articulated by theologians such as David Pareus and John Davenant, argues that baptism brings all infants, regardless of their status vis-à-vis election, into a conditional state of justification and regeneration that may or may not result in final salvation. Witsius considers this position unsound for several reasons: first, by introducing a category of saving benefits that are universally applied to all baptized infants, including those who are not elect, this view separates the application of salvation from "the divine good pleasure" of election; second, by suggesting that remission of original sin is not in every case accompanied by remission of actual sins, this view either severs the connection between Christ's status as surety for the elect and the application of his atoning grace or suggests that Christ made only a partial atonement for sin; third, by introducing a sort of regeneration that might result in eternal death rather than eternal life, this view fails to appreciate the character of the eternal life that Christ introduced through his resurrection from the dead and that he seals, at least in its principle form, to elect infants in baptism: "The life that Christ has merited by his death is everlasting … And it flows from the Spirit of life in Christ risen from the dead, for Christ himself having once died, dies no more, so neither shall the second death reign over anyone who, by the Spirit of life in Christ, is raised from the first" (Witsius 2006: 132–136).

Having dispensed with this view, Witsius proceeds to discuss four other views that directly concern the relationship between infant baptism and regeneration. The second view, espoused by theologians such Jerome Zanchi and William Ames, holds that God may regenerate elect infants before baptism, in the act of baptism, or after baptism. Though Witsius admires the modesty of this view for its refusal to "restrict the freedom of God's actions within no limits that he has not clearly prescribed for himself" (Witsius 2006: 143), he personally ascribes to the third view that he discusses. This view, promoted by Gisbertus Voetius, Cornelius Burges, and the churches of the Belgic Confession, holds that God ordinarily regenerates elect infants before baptism and therefore that, in the case of these infants, baptism functions to seal the regeneration previously granted (Witsius 2006: 149–151). That God can regenerate infants before baptism, producing within them "the initiatory principle of spiritual life," cannot be doubted Witsius contends, given the examples of Jeremiah, John the Baptist, and ultimately Jesus Christ, who received influences of the Spirit as well as the principle of spiritual life from their mothers' wombs (Witsius 2006: 143–147, 154–158). The fourth view, held by Moses Amyraut, argues "that infants are baptized with a view to future sanctification." Witsius finds Amyraut's view a bit confusing and difficult to understand. He also believes it suffers from a failure to appreciate fully the distinction between the presence of spiritual life in the form of a faculty or habit (*in actu primo*) and the presence of spiritual life in the actual exercise of that faculty or habit (*in actu secundo*) (Witsius 2006: 151–158). The fifth and final view, held not only by theologians of the Augsburg Confession but also by many Reformed thinkers, contends that regeneration is granted to elect infants ordinarily in the administration of baptism. Advocates of this opinion appeal to several Reformed liturgies for support, and this requires Witsius to engage in extensive liturgical-interpretive debate. Witsius concludes however that this understanding of baptismal regeneration lacks both liturgical and biblical foundation (Witsius 2006: 158–168).

As he brings his treatise to a conclusion, Witsius argues that, apart from the first and fifth views, great consensus exists among Reformed orthodox theologians on the efficacy of infant baptism. All agree on several points: (1) That the sacraments "are destitute of all physical efficacy." (2) That, notwithstanding the previous point, "the sacraments are not naked and empty signs but the seals of the covenant, possessing, according to the divine appointment, the greatest efficacy in the way of signifying and sealing divine blessings." (3) "That the grace of God is not so connected with any sacrament such that, without the use of a sacrament, God may not confer grace whenever and upon whomever he will, although by his divine freedom he has decreed the use of the sacraments unto the possession and increase of his grace." (4) That infant baptism "is founded upon the Word of God." Because God embraces both believers and their children in his covenant of grace, the sign and seal of the covenant should be applied to both believers and their children. (5) "That the benefit of infant baptism is great not only as respects those who grow up to maturity but also in the case of such as die in infancy." (6) "That parents ought to exert themselves to procure baptism for their children as early as it can be conveniently done." The only differences that exist between Reformed orthodox divines on this topic concern "the manner and the time of its operation" (Witsius 2006: 186–187).

The preceding discussion further illustrates the different emphases placed by Lutheran and Reformed theologians on the sacraments' sealing and conferring functions. It also indicates some of the diverse soteriological, anthropological, and covenant theological principles at work within the two sacramental theological systems. With respect to soteriology, there are discernible links between differing Lutheran and Reformed views of baptismal efficacy and their differing views of election and perseverance. With respect to anthropology, while both sides agree that infants are capable of being brought into vital spiritual union with Christ, and therefore that they are capable of regeneration, Lutheran and Reformed theologians generally disagree on whether this capacity requires faith to be present merely *in actu primo* or also *in actu secundo*, the Reformed being convinced that only the former is required (Pictet 1847: 493–494; Ames 1983: 211), Lutherans being convinced that both are required (Baier 1879: III.X.x). Finally, with respect to covenant theology, different views of baptismal efficacy in the case of infants reveal different understandings of the means whereby God embraces infants within the covenant of grace. Typically for the Reformed, it is God's covenant promise to believers and their children that admits infants into the covenant of grace and baptism that seals their admission (Witsius 2006: 187). For Lutherans, it is God's covenant promise to believers and their children that warrants the baptism of infants but only baptism itself that admits them into the covenant of grace (Hollaz 1763: III.II.iv, q xv).

The Nature of Christ's Presence in the Supper, and of our Feeding upon Him

In the doctrine of the Lord's Supper, we turn from the sacrament of initiation to the sacrament of nurture and nourishment. Thus Johann Gerhard: "just as we are born again through the Sacrament of holy Baptism, so also we are nurtured for eternal life through the sacrament of this holy Supper. Just as we were taken into God's covenant of grace through the former Sacrament, so also through the latter Sacrament we are preserved in the very same covenant of grace. Just as the Holy Spirit awakens faith in us through the former, so also he strengthens and increases it through the latter" (Gerhard 2000: 209). According to Lutheran and Reformed theologians, the sacramental elements of bread and wine minister spiritual nourishment and strength because they enjoy a sacramental "fellowship" with the body and the blood of Christ (1 Cor 10.16), the "true food" and "true drink" of God's children (John 6.55). The Lord's Supper, on such an understanding, functions both as a means of grace and as a mode of Christ's sanctifying presence: in the meal whereby he causes his name to be "remembered," Christ "comes to" his people and "blesses" them in keeping with his promise (Exod 20.24) (Gerhard 2000: 268–269).

That Christ comes to his people in the Supper in order to strengthen and nourish faith constitutes the supreme mystery of sacramental thought in the era of Protestant orthodoxy; how he does so is an abiding source of controversy. The controversy fundamentally concerns two interrelated questions: What is the nature of Christ's presence in the Supper, and what is the nature of our feeding upon him? Protestant orthodox theologians devote considerable attention to disputing Rome's answer to these questions, concluding that its doctrine of transubstantiation is repugnant to Scripture and reason, contrary to the nature of the sacrament, and cause of "manifold superstitions" and "gross idolatries" (Westminster Confession of Faith 29.6 in Schaff 1931: 666). Furthermore, failing to achieve conciliation on these questions during this period, Lutheran and Reformed theologians devote considerable intellectual energy to elaborating and defending their opposing confessional viewpoints regarding the mode of Christ's eucharistic presence. Doing so in a manner true to Scripture and appreciative of much of the Catholic theological tradition requires these theologians to engage a series of sophisticated interpretive and theological issues.

The interpretive crux of Protestant orthodox eucharistic debate is the dominical saying, "this is my body" (Matt 26.26 et par). The Lutheran doctrine of Christ's presence in the Supper arises from a literal interpretation of Christ's words: "The words of institution clearly give the understanding that the Lord Christ ordained—on the strength of his institution and promise—not just simple bread and wine to his holy apostles, but [gave them also] with the bread his body to eat, and with the wine his blood to drink" (Gerhard 2000: 258). Lutheran orthodox divines adduce several arguments in favor of this interpretation. For example: (1) Because all articles of faith rest upon the plain sense of Scripture, rather than figural interpretations, and because the words of institution provide the chief biblical basis for the article of the Lord's Supper, these words must be taken literally. (2) Because the Lord's Supper is Christ's last will and testament, and because we must abide by "the testament of a dying man according to the simple meaning which the words of the testament have," therefore we must interpret these words literally. (3) Because three evangelists, and also the Apostle Paul, recorded the words of institution without indicating the possibility of a nonliteral interpretation, we should read them in their plain sense. (4) Because Christ always provided an explanation for his figures of speech and parables, but left us no explanation of these words, we must therefore take them in their literal sense (Gerhard 2000: 273–276). Those who refuse to receive the plain sense of Christ's saying "in simple and obedient faith" do so, Gerhard explains, because "human reason finds [it] to be strange and unbelievable" (Gerhard 2000: 273; see also 262–264).

Conversely, the Reformed doctrine of Christ's presence in the Supper arises from a figural interpretation of the words of institution. Reformed orthodox theologians argue that a figural interpretation of the relationship between the subject ("this") and the predicate ("my body") of Christ's saying is the most natural way of taking Christ's identification of the body that reclined with his disciples at the table with the bread that sat upon the table. That in fact is how the copula "is" functions when seeking to identify two things that are not the same thing: "Nothing is more common in ordinary discourse," Turretin insists, and "nothing occurs more frequently in the Scriptures of the Old as well as the New Testament" (Turretin 1997: 468; Wollebius 1655: XXII xix). Furthermore, a figural interpretation of the words of institution acknowledges Christ's authorial "design" in the Last Supper, which was "to institute a sacrament of the New Testament" (Turretin 1997: 470). To the Lutheran claim that figural interpretations should not be applied to a last will and testament, Wollebius offers three responses: (1) We should not assume that figurative expressions always obscure meaning; we often use them to illustrate our intended meaning. (2) Figurative expressions are commonly used in wills that are recorded in biblical (e.g. Gen 49; Deut 33; 2 Sam 23) and Jewish literature (e.g. Tobit 4; 1 Macc 2). (3) Christ used at least one figurative expression in the Last Supper when he identified "the cup" with "the New Testament in blood" (Wollebius 1655: XXIV.xiii).

Following from their differing interpretations of Christ's words of institution, Lutheran and Reformed theologians propose differing accounts of the mode whereby Christ gives his body and blood to be eaten and drunk by communicants in the Supper. Hollaz provides a particularly sophisticated Lutheran account. According to Hollaz, Christ is not present with the sacramental elements in a physical, local, or circumscribed manner. Rather he is present in a "hyperphysical" manner that transcends our natural modes of perception. Christ's hyperphysical mode of presence in the sacrament is twofold: (1) Christ is present in the Supper by virtue of a "definitive presence." By this mode of presence, a finite being can be present in a nonlocal, non-circumscribed manner. This mode of presence, Hollaz explains, characterizes spiritual essences, such as angels, who cannot be spatially measured. This mode of presence also characterizes the bodies of the saints in glory. (2) Christ is also present in the Supper by virtue of his "repletive presence." Repletive presence indicates the relationship between God's infinite being and space whereby God "is measured by and circumscribed to no place but penetrates and fills each and every place without multiplication, extension, inclusion, and division of his own essence" (Gerhard 2007: 164). This mode of presence characterizes Christ's divine nature essentially. It also characterizes Christ's human nature, which receives its capacity for repletive presence from the divine nature as a consequence of the hypostatic union (Hollaz 1763: III.II.V, q xii). Consequently, because of the sacramental union that Christ establishes between his body and blood and the sacramental elements through the words of institution, and by virtue of his definitive and repletive presence, Christ is literally but supernaturally present with the bread and the wine and literally but supernaturally consumed with the bread and the wine by all who communicate in the Eucharist, believers and unbelievers alike (Hollaz 1763: III.II.V, q xvi; Baier 1879: III.xi.13; Gerhard 2000: 336–354).

Reformed confessional teaching regarding Christ's eucharistic presence exhibits significant diversity (Gerrish 1982: 118–130). Among Reformed orthodox theologians there is nevertheless a fairly consistent desire to affirm Christ's real presence in the Supper, while denying that this requires a physical or local presence on his part. Leigh thus insists: Christ is truly present in the sacrament, not just in our imaginations; and Christ is effectually present in the sacrament, not simply by means of bare representation. However, Leigh disputes the communication of Christ's divine repletive presence to his human nature on two grounds: (1) Reason teaches us that "the body of one and the same man cannot be present in many places all together, but must needs remain in some definite and certain place." (2) Religion teaches us that "Christ was taken up into heaven, there to abide till the end of the world." Therefore the humanity of Christ is not present in the Supper "according to its essence or natural being" but "according to its subsistence or personal being" (Leigh 1654: VIII.IX). To the mind of the Reformed, Christ's presence in this manner is sufficient to establish the sacramental reality that, in accordance with his promise, Christ truly gives his body and his blood to the faithful when the minister distributes the bread and the wine to them (Wollebius 1655: XXII.xv). Contrary to their Lutheran counterparts, the Reformed argue that Christ's body and blood are only received by believing communicants, and this by "the mouth of faith" rather than by oral manducation (Turretin 1997: 510).

Reformed sacramental theology places special emphasis on the role of the Holy Spirit in the Lord's Supper. Although Reformed teaching on this subject is not uniform, the point of emphasizing the Spirit is not to make him a surrogate for Christ's real presence but rather to indicate the mode whereby Christ, in his theandric person, makes himself present in the eucharist (Turretin 1997: 507). "It is *Christ himself,*" says John Owen in a 1675 communion sermon, who is "the *immediate exhibitor*" of his body and blood to us in the Supper. Consequently, it is our duty to "direct our faith to consider Jesus Christ present among us, *by his Spirit and word*, making this tender or this exhibition unto us. It is Christ that does it; which calls out our faith unto an immediate exercise *on his person*" (Payne 2004: 197–198, italics in the original).

As the preceding discussion demonstrates, the debate between Lutheran and Reformed orthodox theologians regarding the sanctifying presence of Christ in the Supper is not about whether Christ can be physically present in the Lord's Supper, Reformed polemics notwithstanding. Nor is it a debate about whether Christ is present in both his divine and human natures in the Supper, Lutheran polemics notwithstanding. The debate fundamentally concerns the question of how Christ in his theandric—and hence physical—person can be present in the administration of the sacrament despite the fact that he has ascended to the right hand of the Father and therefore rules and relates to his people in a nonlocal manner. For Lutheran theologians, the doctrine of the *genus maiestaticum* provides the answer to this question: Christ's divine nature communicates the power of its repletive presence to his human nature. For Reformed theologians, the answer is provided by pneumatology: by the Spirit Christ gives himself, with his body and his blood, to the faithful through the sacramental elements of bread and wine.

AFTER ORTHODOXY: PROTESTANT SACRAMENTAL THEOLOGY IN THE NINETEENTH CENTURY

The transition from the eighteenth to the nineteenth century witnessed the decline of Protestant orthodoxy and the ascendency of a self-consciously modern form of Protestant theology characterized at once by impulses toward revision and retrieval in relation to its evangelical heritage. Relative to Protestant orthodoxy, modern Protestant theology is revisionist insofar as it relinquishes the task of elucidating and defending Lutheran and Reformed confessional systems of theology qua systems and embraces the task of doing theology under the political, social, and intellectual conditions of the Enlightenment. Relative to the Reformation of the sixteenth century, however, modern Protestant theology exhibits an intentionally more conservative stance, regarding itself as a new phase in the reception history of evangelical thought: "Our lineage can no one take away from us," Friedrich Schleiermacher declares. "We are legitimate sons of the Reformation and not bastards" (Gerrish 1982: 195). This stance of critical receptivity toward its evangelical past explains the emergence of a new style of Protestant sacramental theology in the nineteenth century. Whether in its more rationalist, mediating, or confessionally oriented versions, this theology seeks to commend what it regards as the true essence of evangelical sacramental teaching—conceived in different ways by different thinkers, to an enlightened academic and ecclesiastical public.

We may better appreciate the character of Protestant sacramental thought in the nineteenth century by considering a few examples.

Rationalist Lutheran Theology: Julius August Ludwig Wegscheider

Julius August Ludwig Wegscheider's *Institutiones Theologiae Christianae Dogmaticae*, published in eight editions throughout the nineteenth century, provides an example of the rather drastic sacramental theological revisions that follow when natural reason is elevated to the status of critical principle in Protestant dogmatics. For Wegscheider, the efficacy of the sacraments is moral in nature. By baptism, the individual is received into the Christian society, within which true religion and virtue can be nurtured (Wegscheider 1844: 604–605). In the Lord's Supper, the divine teaching that Christ sealed in his death is signified and exhibited to celebrants. Though he considers the manducation of Christ's flesh and blood an intolerably antiquated concept, Wegscheider nevertheless insists that the Supper may be converted to excellent moral use in promoting Christian discipleship (Wegscheider 1844: 634–635). Given their moral efficacy in relating communicants to the church's ethical teaching and formational activity, the sacraments function in this rationalist Lutheran system of theology as "a means to the means of grace" (Scaer 2011: 19).

Protestant Mediating Theology: Friedrich Schleiermacher and Isaak Dorner

Friedrich Schleiermacher, Wegscheider's erstwhile colleague at Halle, and Isaak Dorner exemplify a "mediating" approach to sacramental theology that is less willing to accommodate traditional Protestant sacramental teaching to the exigencies of modern reason and, consequently, is substantially more robust in its dogmatic claims about the status of the sacraments as means of grace: "The idea of the sacraments held in common by evangelical teachers is, that they are sacred actions instituted by Christ himself, which, under visible signs, offer the invisible grace promised in the words of institution" (Dorner 1896: 270). Accordingly, both Schleiermacher and Dorner devote significant attention to retrieving Reformation era confessional teaching on the sacraments for a modern Protestant church. Where they find themselves unable to resolve longstanding confessional disputes within the orbit of their own constructive theological systems, as for example on the nature of Christ's real presence in the Supper and on the efficacy of infant baptism, they nevertheless express optimism that old divisions will be transcended eventually within a future evangelical synthesis (Dorner 1896: 284–285; Schleiermacher 1989: 650–651).

The sacramental theologies of Schleiermacher and Dorner are not without significant differences. Because he begins with Christian experience of the sacraments and only proceeds thereafter to contemplate "how this experience first originated" (Schleiermacher 1989: 638), Schleiermacher's sacramental thought offers a considerably less developed account of trinitarian and Christological agency than Dorner's, which characteristically offers more detailed attention to the *principium essendi* of the sacraments (Dorner 1888: 169–170). Moreover, whereas the Reformed Schleiermacher suggests that infant baptism might be given up since it retains no "magical powers" to confer grace upon its recipients (Schleiermacher 1989: 637–638), the Lutheran Dorner regards infant baptism as "the right mode of administering baptism" since "God wishes their [i.e. Christian parents'] children brought into the number of Christ's disciples' as "a sign of his grace directed towards children" (Dorner 1896: 294). In arguing that infant baptism is a mode of administration proper to the nature of the sacrament, not merely an allowable concession, Dorner stands contrary to common nineteenth-century Protestant opinion (Scaer 2011).

Confessional Reformed Theology in a Modern Key: William Cunningham

If Wegscheider represents a modern trajectory toward radical revision of Protestant sacramental teaching, while Schleiermacher and Dorner represent a trajectory toward retrieving the Lutheran and Reformed confessional witness within the context of a higher evangelical synthesis, William Cunningham, principal and professor of theology at New College, Edinburgh, represents a trajectory aimed at preserving a distinctly Reformed confessional viewpoint on the sacraments within the modern world. Although his confessional commitments set him apart to some degree from our previous examples, the manner in which Cunningham pursues his task reveals him to be a characteristically modern thinker and thus a curious example of nineteenth-century Protestant sacramental thought.

In his essay, "Zwingli and the Doctrine of the Sacraments," originally published in 1860, Cunningham seeks (1) to trace an alternative but neglected line of Reformation sacramental thought to the one initiated by Luther and (2) to commend the dogmatic value of this line of thought for interpreting the confessional documents produced by the Westminster Assembly and for refuting contemporary challenges to Protestant sacramental teaching, particularly the Puseyite/Tractarian doctrine of baptismal regeneration. According to Cunningham, Zwingli is especially instructive on the sacraments due to his "clear, definite, and practical" thinking on this subject (Cunningham 1862: 229), in contrast to Calvin and later seventeenth-century Protestant divines who tended to magnify "the value and efficacy of the sacraments" to "unsuccessful" and "unintelligible" effect (Cunningham 1862: 240). In order to support his contention that the Westminster Confession of Faith and Catechisms do not support a Tractarian view of baptismal regeneration in the case of infants, Cunningham attempts to demonstrate that the description of baptismal efficacy provided by these documents only applies "fully to adult baptism," where faith can be exercised and expressed, and that it "does not directly and *in terminis* comprehend infant baptism" (Cunningham 1862: 250).

Cunningham arrives at this interpretation by means of a kind of confessional *Sachkritik*, interpreting the confessional documents in light of what he regards as "a fundamental principle in the theology of Protestants," namely: "that the sacraments were instituted and intended for believers, and produce their appropriate beneficial effects, only through the faith which must have previously existed, and which is expressed and exercised in the act of partaking in them" (Cunningham 1862: 244). The irony, of course, is that it would be difficult to find this fundamental principle enunciated in the literature of Protestant orthodoxy. According to Lutheran orthodox theologians, the sacrament of baptism elicits faith. And, according to widespread Reformed orthodox teaching, the sacrament of baptism seals to elect infants all the benefits described in ecclesiastical documents such as the Westminster Confession and Catechisms without requiring the presence of faith in its mature "expression and exercise" but only in its principal form—and, notably, without entailing a Tractarian view of baptismal regeneration.

We thus witness in Cunningham, the confessional Reformed theologian, what Bruce McCormack identifies as a characteristically modern methodological move: the use of a "material norm" (in this case, "a fundamental principle in the theology of Protestants") to interpret traditional sources of theological understanding in a manner that is "disciplined and consistent with his/her approach to other doctrines" (McCormack 2012: 7). Though he does not represent the whole story of confessional sacramental theology in the nineteenth century, it does seem that with Cunningham, as with Wegscheider, Schleiermacher, and Dorner, we have entered a new phase of Protestant sacramental thought.

CONCLUSION

The preceding discussion complicates the narrative that would blame the Reformation and its traditions of reception for desacramentalizing the Western mind (e.g. Gregory 2012). Lutheran and Reformed orthodox sacramental theologies diverge from Tridentine sacramental doctrine at many points. They do not, however, dispute the claim that God ministers grace to creatures through creatures but instead draw upon a wealth of patristic and medieval sacramental resources in order to articulate this claim in a manner consistent with their distinct confessional standpoints. Even the radical changes accompanying the development of modern Protestant sacramental theology in the nineteenth century do not lead in every case to denial of Christ's real presence in the sacraments, as the theologies of Schleiermacher and Dorner attest in different ways. It appears, then, that the decline of sacramental sensibilities in late modern thought requires an alternative explanation. It also appears that the principles of Protestant orthodox sacramental theology may yet have something to offer in the recovery of this sensibility.

Suggested Reading

Dorner (1896); Heppe (1978); Schmid (1961).

Bibliography

Ames, W. (1983), *The Marrow of Theology*, trans. John D. Eusden (Durham, NC: Labyrinth).

Bac, J. M. (2010), *Perfect Will Theology: Divine Agency in Reformed Scholasticism as against Suárez, Episcopius, Descartes, and Spinoza*, Brill Series in Church History, 42 (Leiden: Brill).

Baier, J. W. (1879), *Compendium Theologiae Positivae*, vol. 3, ed. C. F. W. Walther (St. Louis, MO: Concordia).

Courtenay, W. J. (1984), *Covenant and Causality in Medieval Thought* (London: Variorum).

Cunningham, W. (1862), *Collected Works of the Rev. William Cunningham, D.D.*, vol. 1 (Edinburgh: T & T Clark).

Denlinger, A. C. (2012), " 'Men of Gallio's Naughty Faith?': The Aberdeen Doctors on Reformed and Lutheran Concord," *Church History and Religious Culture*, 92: 57–83.

Dorner, I. A. (1888), *A System of Christian Doctrine*, vol. 1., trans. A. Cave (Edinburgh: T & T Clark).

Dorner, I. A. (1896), *A System of Christian Doctrine*, vol. 4, trans. J. S. Banks (Edinburgh: T & T Clark).

Fesko, J. V. (2010), *Word, Water, and Spirit: A Reformed Perspective on Baptism* (Grand Rapids, MI: Reformed Heritage Books).

Gerhard, J. (2000), *A Comprehensive Explanation of Holy Baptism and the Lord's Supper*, trans. E. Hohle (Malone, TX: Repristination).

Gerhard, J. (2007), *On the Nature of God and on the Most Holy Mystery of the Trinity*, Theological Commonplaces, trans. R. J. Dinda (St. Louis, MO: Concordia).

Gerrish, B. A. (1982), *The Old Protestantism and the New: Essays on the Reformation Heritage* (Edinburgh: T & T Clark).

Gregory, B. S. (2012), *The Unintended Reformation: How a Religious Revolution Secularized Society* (Cambridge, MA: Harvard University Press).

Heppe, H. (1978), *Reformed Dogmatics: Set Out and Illustrated from the Sources*, trans. G. T. Thomson (Grand Rapids, MI: Baker).

Heyd, M. (1995), *'Be Sober and Reasonable': The Critique of Enthusiasm in the Seventeenth and Early Eighteenth Centuries*, Brill's Studies in Intellectual History, 63 (Leiden: Brill).

Holifield, E. B. (1974), *The Covenant Sealed: The Development of Puritan Sacramental Theology in Old and New England, 1570–1720* (New Haven, CT: Yale University Press).

Hollaz, D. (1763), *Examen Theologicum Acroamaticum Universam Theologiam Thetico-Polemicam Complectens* (Lipsiae: B. C. Breitkopfii).

Hotson, H. (2004), "Irenicism in the Confessional Age: The Holy Roman Empire, 1563–1648," in H. P. Louthan and R. C. Zachman (eds.), *Conciliation and Confession: The Struggle for Unity in the Age of Reform, 1415–1648* (Notre Dame, IN: University of Notre Dame Press), 228–285.

Howard, T. A. (2006), *Protestant Theology and the Making of the Modern German University* (Oxford: Oxford University Press).

Jerome of Montefortino (1903), *Ven. Ioannis Duns Scoti Summa Theologica* (Rome: Typographia Sallustiana).

Kalb, F. (1965), *Theology of Worship in 17th-Century Lutheranism*, trans. H. P. A. Hamann (St. Louis, MO: Concordia).

Leigh, E. (1654), *A Systeme or Body of Divinity* (London: William Lee).

McCormack, B. L. (2012), "Introduction: On 'Modernity' as a Theological Concept," in B. L. McCormack and K. M. Kapic (eds.), *Mapping Modern Theology: A Thematic and Historical Introduction* (Grand Rapids, MI: Baker), 1–19.

Muller, R. A. (2003), *Post-Reformation Reformed Dogmatics: The Rise and Development of Reformed Orthodoxy, ca. 1520–1725*, vol. 1 (Grand Rapids, MI: Baker).

Oliver, S. (2005), *Philosophy, God and Motion* (London: Routledge).

Payne, J. D. (2004), *John Owen on the Lord's Supper* (Edinburgh: Banner of Truth).

Pictet, B. (1847), *Christian Theology*, trans. Frederick Reyroux (London: Henry G. Bohn).

Polyander, J., A. Rivetus, A. Walaeus, and A. Thysius (1881), *Synopsis Purioris Theologiae*, 6th ed., Herman Bavinck (ed.) (Leiden: Donner).

Preus, R. D. (1970), *The Theology of Post-Reformation Lutheranism*, vol. 1 (St. Louis, MO: Concordia).

Raitt, J. (1972), *The Eucharistic Theology of Theodore Beza: Development of the Reformed Doctrine*, AAR Studies in Religion, 4 (Chambersburg, PA: American Academy of Religion).

Scaer, D. P. (1999), "Johann Gerhard's Doctrine of the Sacraments," in C. R. Trueman and R. S. Clark (ed.), *Protestant Scholasticism: Essays in Reassessment* (Carlisle: Paternoster), 289–306.

Scaer, D. P. (2011), *Infant Baptism in Nineteenth Century Lutheran Theology* (St. Louis, MO: Concordia).

Schaff, P. (1845), *The Principle of Protestantism: As Related to the Present State of the Church*, trans. J. W. Nevin (Chambersburg, PA: German Reformed Church).

Schaff, P. (1931), *The Creeds of Christendom*, vol. 3 (repr. Grand Rapids, MI: Baker, 1996).

Schleiermacher, F. (1989), *The Christian Faith*, H. R. Mackintosh and J. S. Steward (ed.) (Edinburgh: T & T Clark).

Schmid, H. (1961), *The Doctrinal Theology of the Evangelical Lutheran Church*, 3rd ed., trans. C. A. Hay and H. E. Jacobs (Minneapolis, MN: Augsburg).

Schmidt, L. E. (2001), *Holy Fairs: Scotland and the Making of American Revivalism*, 2nd ed. (Grand Rapids, MI: Eerdmans).

Schmitz, K. L. (2007), *The Texture of Being: Essays in First Philosophy*, Studies in Philosophy and the History of Philosophy, ed. P. O'Herron (Washington, DC: Catholic University of America Press).

Spinks, B. D. (2006), *Reformation and Modern Rituals and Theologies of Baptism: From Luther to Contemporary Practices*, Liturgy, Worship and Society (Aldershot: Ashgate).

Tanner, K. (2010), *Christ the Key*, Current Issues in Theology (Cambridge: Cambridge University Press).

Turretin, F. (1997), *Institutes of Elenctic Theology*, vol. 3, trans. George Musgrave Giger (Phillipsburg, NJ: Presbyterian & Reformed).

van Ruler, J. A. (1995), *The Crisis of Causality: Voetius and Descartes on God, Nature and Change*, Brill's Studies in Intellectual History (Leiden: Brill).

Wegscheider, J. A. L. (1844), *Institutiones Theologiae Christianae Dogmaticae*, 8th ed. (Lipsiae).

Witsius, H. (2006), "On the Efficacy and Utility of Baptism in the Case of Elect Infants Whose Parents are Under the Covenant," trans. W. Marshall, J. M. Beach (ed. and rev.) *Mid-America Journal of Theology* 17: 121–190.

Wollebius, J. (1655), *Compendium Theologiae Christianae* (Amstelodami).

CHAPTER 25

···

SACRAMENTAL THEOLOGY IN AMERICA: SEVENTEENTH–NINETEENTH CENTURIES

···

E. BROOKS HOLIFIELD

EUROPEAN clergy and lay settlers imported to colonial America a spectrum of sacramental theologies, ranging from the Catholic view that grace manifested itself through tangible and visible actions and objects to the Quaker conviction that sacraments impeded spiritual inwardness and lacked biblical justification. By the early nineteenth century, a spectrum of possibilities, expanded by a proliferation of denominations, produced increasing conflict. In the later part of the century conflict abated, but sacramental interests did not wane. Sacraments remained the center of worship in Catholic, Anglican, Lutheran, and Disciples of Christ traditions, while they retained an honored status among such groups as Methodists and Presbyterians. In every tradition, however, sacraments embodied not only ancient religious meanings but also layers of cultural, ethnic, and racial significance that complicated their meanings.

Even before the Council of Florence (1439) placed its imprimatur on seven sacraments, Catholics had affirmed that holy baptism, confirmation, the Eucharist, penance, extreme unction, order, and matrimony bore sacramental import as effective signs that Christ mandated for the transmission of grace. After 1549, the missionary priests to America carried these sacraments, except for ordination and confirmation (which required a bishop), to Native Americans on the east coast and in the far West, informing the native population that "if they were baptized and became good Christians, they would go to heaven to enjoy an eternal life" while also teaching them the forms of devotion and behavior, including Christian marriage, appropriate to "the altars where the body and blood of the Son of God may be offered" (Hedge and Lewis 1907: 190; Hammond and Rey 1953: 1, 177). Both in the missions and in early Maryland, Catholics knelt before altars at which the priest enacted the repeated sacrifice of Christ, and they received Christ's body in the consecrated bread which, through the transubstantiation effected by priestly power, offered them the substance of Christ's body and blood. Even when the service had to take place in private homes, as in Maryland after the Glorious Revolution of 1688, the re-enactment of the sacrifice and the offering of the bread (which was deemed to be in substance both the body and blood of Christ) kept alive Catholic traditions.

The missionaries celebrated the Mass, the service that enveloped the eucharistic sacrament, at least twice daily, with frequent special Masses. To the Native Americans, however, the sacraments signified not only participation in the body of the sacrificed Christ and a foretaste of eternal life but also mundane blessings, especially health. They sought sacraments not only for spiritual but also for physical benefits, which led Native American traditionalists to blame illness on baptism. Cultural custom impinged on sacramental celebration; participants brought their own meanings to it (Hodge, Hammond, and Rey 1945: 66).

Colonial Lutherans followed Luther in accepting the validity of only two sacraments, holy baptism and the Eucharist, though they shared with Catholics a belief in the corporeal presence of Christ in the elements of the Eucharist and in baptism as a means of regeneration. They denied, however, transubstantiation, which, they thought, wrongly explained the mystery with philosophical terminology and attributed the change to the power of the priest, and unlike Catholics they located the efficacy of baptism not in the inner working of the sacrament but in the Word that baptism visibly re-presented. Lutherans in New Sweden on the Delaware River (1638) accentuated traditional sacramental doctrine and ritual in order to distinguish their views from the "heresy" of the neighboring Dutch, who were Reformed in doctrine and practice, and one of the earliest Lutheran publications in America was the *Fundamental Instruction* of Justus Falckner (1672–1723), a preacher in New York and New Jersey, who taught how to prepare for receiving the sacrament. The chief organizer of colonial Lutheranism, Henry Melchior Muhlenberg (1711–1787), who had been trained as a Pietist in Halle, collaborated on an edition of Luther's *Small Catechism*, one of several that disseminated Luther's sacramental teaching (Falckner 1708: 1–2, 66–69; Johnson 1930: 33, 150–155, 163).

Muhlenberg's encounter with a woman seeking rebaptism, however, revealed that lay people could bring their own assumptions to the sacraments. Baptized by a Presbyterian, she had become a Baptist, to the dismay of her German Lutheran husband. Both agreed to confer with Muhlenberg, who told her that baptism was a rebirth that had ingrafted her into Christ and that she should not cause offense by implying that her childhood "Holy Baptism" was insufficient. But the religious pluralism of colonial America meant that no singular view of the sacraments could go unchallenged, and the plurality created a context that must have subtly influenced the way Americans thought about both baptism and the Lord's Supper. Nothing could be taken for granted, and divisions even within families, while not frequent, were always a possibility (Tappert and Doberstein 1945: 2:161–163).

Like the Lutherans, colonial Anglicans considered only baptism and the Eucharist as sacraments, and *The Thirty-Nine Articles of Religion* (1563) guided Anglican conceptions of baptism as an "instrument" of the promise of the forgiveness of sins (rather than merely a sign of faith) and of the Eucharist as a "partaking" of the body and blood of Christ, though "only after an heavenly and spiritual manner," through faith. The notion of a real spiritual presence of Christ in the Eucharist, reminiscent of John Calvin, and of baptism as an instrument of forgiveness was mandatory for Anglican priests in the seventeenth century. By the end of the colonial period, however, a group of rationalist clergy, including the future bishop William White (1748–1836), promoted an interpretation of the Eucharist as a memorial of Christ's sacrifice and sought to remove any reference to baptismal regeneration from the proposed new prayer book in order to assure worshippers that their church held no "magical" view of the sacrament. By 1789, the attempted revision failed (Prichard 1991: 96; Temple 1946: 15–19, 39). In its place, some Anglicans moved toward "higher" conceptions of the sacraments. As early as 1696, Thomas Bray (1658–1730), who resided briefly in Maryland, had insisted that baptism did not merely seal a prior covenant but introduced the baptized infant into the covenant of grace (God's promise of salvation to the faithful), where God provided lifelong assistance, mainly through sacramental means (Bray 1696, 1704: 2–3, 39, 50. In New England, Samuel Johnson (1696–1772) taught also that baptism had that function and that the Eucharist, which offered a real spiritual communion with Christ, nurtured members through sacramental grace (Chorley 1946: 136).

The struggle of White and others over the sacraments represented a dispute over the appropriate degree of the church's accommodation to the Enlightenment. It had a cultural subtext. Baptism assumed a quite different cultural meaning for African American slaves who sought the sacrament for their children. Dutch Reformed clergy complained that the Africans sought baptism as a rite that would bring release from slavery, and the Anglican-dominated colonies in the South felt constrained to pass laws as early as 1664 decreeing that the sacrament did not bring earthly freedom to people in bondage. It is also not unlikely that for some Africans the rite retained the aura of water rituals in some indigenous African cultures.

Colonial Presbyterians rarely questioned the sacramental theology of the Westminster Confession of 1647, which defined sacraments as signs and seals of grace, with baptism as a seal of the covenant of grace and the Lord's Supper as the remembrance of Christ's sacrifice and the sealing of its benefits to believers. Some envisioned the Supper as a memorial; others found in the Confession's reference to spiritual nourishment a ground for affirming Calvin's doctrine of a real spiritual presence. More divisive was the question of who should receive the sacraments. Most took the view, popular among the Scotch-Irish, that baptism was open to any believing and non-scandalous adult and to any infant for whom a godly sponsor could be found, even if the parents were scandalous. In this tradition, moreover, the Lord's Supper was available to all believers who led godly lives or repented sincerely. (Thomson 1749: iv, 161, 168). The minority, influenced by English and New English Puritan traditions, limited baptism to faithful adults and their children and restricted the Lord's Supper to the pious who could show evidence of grace (Green 1768: 2–6). Both groups avoided practices that might imply a sacrifice at an altar or adoration of a corporeal Christ, so they refused to kneel to receive the elements, often gathering around a table in imitation of the disciples in the biblical account. Both sides, moreover, often used communion tokens, coin-like wood or metal emblems distributed by the minister to signify worthiness to receive the elements, and both believed that faith was the true "eating" of Christ. Traces of ethnic, geographical, and cultural difference, however, helped determine the party alignments.

In New Amsterdam (later New York), Calvinist views of the sacraments prevailed among the Dutch Reformed churches, but the presence of Lutherans, Presbyterians, Congregationalists, Mennonites, Baptists, and Quakers meant that baptism and the Lord's Supper signified not only religious but cultural disputes despite a decree of 1646 designed to permit only Dutch Reformed worship. The Dutch clergy feared that such "strife in religious matters would produce confusion in political affairs" (Smith, Handy, and Loetscher 1960–1963: 1:72–74). The racial dimension reappeared when Domine Henricus Selyns refused in 1664 to grant baptism to African slaves because he worried that "they wanted nothing else than to deliver their children from bodily slavery" (Hastings 1901: 1:548).

No group wrote more prolifically about sacraments than the Puritan settlers in New England, who gradually evolved a Congregational form of church government and sought a sacramental practice consonant with that of the primitive church of the New Testament. As heirs of a covenantal theology originating in the continental Reformed tradition, they interpreted the sacraments as seals of the covenant of grace, bearing God's promise of salvation, though only to the elect who would persevere in faith. Like the seal on a royal document, a sacrament guaranteed the validity of the Word that it bespoke. As a seal, baptism promised salvation to elect infants, while it sealed an external church membership to all others, though no one knew the spiritual status of the recipient. Most early Congregationalists also agreed, however, that since baptism sealed a covenant, only the infants of the faithful, who stood within the covenant, could receive it. The parents had to be church members whose narrative of conversion had convinced other members that they had, in all probability, received the effectual grace reserved for the elect. They anticipated that their children would also experience God's effectual call as they matured into adulthood.

In fact, many of the children of members failed to have such an experience, though they remained in the church and wished to present their own children for baptism. The dilemma grew so intense that it required a special synod in 1662, which ruled that these unconverted church members could present their children for baptism but could not receive the Lord's Supper until they could testify to the workings of grace in their hearts. Later opponents of this innovation dismissed it as a "half-way covenant" and labeled its beneficiaries as "half-way members". The churches of New England continued dividing over the practice well into the eighteenth century.

Most New England Congregationalists assumed that the Lord's Supper offered the faithful believer the real spiritual body and blood of Christ (though views of it as a memorial were not unknown), and pastors repeated the Pauline warning that it was dangerous to commune unworthily, so by the end of the seventeenth century half-way members often held back from full membership (which brought a right to communion).

They normally declined the elements when the bread and wine were distributed to worshippers as they sat in their pews. As a result, pastors began to urge communion and to reassure the doubtful that even the desire for grace manifested sufficient grace to join the church and to commune. The pastors imported sacramental treatises that helped to stimulate a small sacramental renaissance, but a small number of clergy, led by the Northampton, Connecticut, pastor Solomon Stoddard (1643–1729), decided that New England's sacramental restrictions impeded conversion. Stoddard taught in around 1708 that the Lord's Supper was a converting ordinance and that the unconverted had an obligation to commune as a means to their regeneration. Stoddard's grandson, Jonathan Edwards, later tried to reverse Stoddardean doctrine and practice. On the doctrine of the Lord's Supper, Edwards held traditional Puritan views, wanting to reserve it for those who could testify to a heartfelt desire for grace, but his effort to bar from baptism the children of half-way members, combined with other disputes, led to his dismissal from his pastorate in Northampton (Holifield 1974: 206–224).

One reason for both the half-way covenant and for Stoddard's practice was the desire of families to ensure that their children would receive the benefits of the covenant. The impulse to preserve the wellbeing of the family and to care for children informed innovation. Edwards lost his pulpit in part because sacramental practice impinged on a cultural institution, the family. (Brown and Hall 1997: 41–68).

Baptists believed that the half-way covenant revealed the contradiction at the heart of churches that thought of the church as a community of the faithful and that yet baptized infants, who could not evidence faith. Isaac Backus (1724–1806), a separatist preacher in Middleborough, Massachusetts, argued in the 1750s against Congregationalist and Presbyterian clergy who thought that God's command to Abraham to circumcise his offspring was a warrant for Christians to baptize their children. Using the language of typology—an exegetical method, usually presupposed in debates over the sacraments, according to which events and practices in the Old Testament "typified" or foreshadowed Christian institutions and actions—Backus argued that Abraham typified Christ, Abraham's offspring typified the spiritual children of Christ, and their circumcision was therefore a "type" of rebirth, not of baptism (McLoughlin 1968: 148–157). For Backus and other Baptists, who preferred to speak of "ordinances" (actions ordained by Christ) rather than sacraments, baptism was a sign of rebirth, reserved for faithful believers. They found no evidence in scripture for the contrary position. Baptists, moreover, reserved the Lord's Supper for those deemed truly faithful, and they avoided any implication that the rite was efficacious, seeing it as a memorial of Christ's sacrifice.

Views of baptism, the Lord's Supper, and the church brought Baptists into conflict especially with the state church establishments in much of New England and the South. Because they believed that the church should be separated from the state, their views about the ordinances had political implications that divided them especially from Congregationalists and Anglicans. Occasionally, the implications became explicit, as when the Virginia Baptist John Leland defended a view of churches as "little republics," democracies that valued liberty and equality among faithful members who had freely chosen their baptism. On such grounds, Leland resisted coercive state authority (Leland 1845: 251, 275, 278). Among Baptists, a decision to seek baptism could be, by implication, both a religious and a political statement.

At the far end of the colonial spectrum stood the Quakers, who rejected sacraments on the grounds that the covenant was entirely inward, dependent only on the Inner Light of Christ that enlightened every human being who would recognize it. Francis Daniel Pastorius (1651–c. 1720) of Pennsylvania, who wavered between Anabaptist and Quaker views, argued that worship through the consumption of material food or the practice of baptism was a form of conformity to the Old Testament dispensation, not the New, and that Christ had eclipsed all "figures, types, and shadows," bringing instead a pure religion of the Spirit (Pastorius 1697: 3–15). To other colonists, however, especially in the seventeenth century, Quaker belief was an invitation to religious anarchy and political instability. Even the refusal of sacraments bore cultural meaning.

This spectrum of theologies and practices by no means exhausts the variety of colonial Christianity, which also included Mennonites, who rejected infant baptism; followers of Samuel Gorton (c. 1592–1677) in Rhode Island, who proclaimed a Christianity without sacraments; the Shaker followers of Ann Lee (1736–1784), who joined the Quakers in repudiating traditional sacraments; the devotees of Jemimah Wilkinson (1752?–1819), whose vision of herself as the "Publick Universal Friend" entailed also a Quaker-like avoidance of sacraments; and Universalists such as Judith Sergeant Murray (1751–1820), who contended that baptism was unnecessary and the Lord's Supper merely a symbol for the common humanity of all, or Elhanan Winchester (1751–1797), who maintained his earlier Baptist views (Skemp 2009: 62; Winchester 1791: 18). Sometimes these views accompanied a claim for immediate revelation, at other times a literal reading of the Bible. The frequent appearance of women in this group suggests again that views about sacraments could reflect social positioning in the culture. An assertion about sacraments could be assertive in multiple ways.

DEVOTION AND CONFLICT

Conflict over sacraments, as well as heartfelt sacramental devotion, permeated an increasingly diverse nineteenth-century religious life. The conflicts not only pitted one tradition against another but also divided traditions internally, and a few nineteenth-century clergy agreed with the theologian John Williamson Nevin (1803–1886), who argued that a group's stance on sacramental doctrine would have consequences on "the farthest limits of theology" and that a change in views of the Eucharist could alter the character of "the Christian system as a whole" (Nevin 1846: 52, 106; Yrigoyen and Bricker 1978: 372, 374). The majority would have rejected that assertion, but most recognized that sacramental theology could not be isolated from broader views of the church, Christ, and salvation. This recognition made sacramental debates widespread, even to the extent that public contests could attract large audiences who traveled from long distances to hear experts contend about ancient languages, biblical passages, and patristic exegesis (Holifield 1998: 508–511).

Sacraments were, in the first instance, occasions for devotion, and nowhere more profoundly than in the Eastern Orthodox traditions that entered North America in 1794 when the Russian Orthodox Church established a mission in Alaska. Immigration later brought Carpatho Russians, Romanians, Serbs, Greeks, Ukranians, Ruthenians, Albanians, Syrians, and still others, who accepted the same seven sacraments as the Catholics, though sometimes understanding and administering them differently. They celebrated either the Liturgy of St. John Chrysostom or the Liturgy of St. Basil the Great, so eucharistic worship began with the priest's breaking the bread at the "table of oblation"—an act that recalled the multitude of the saints, who were also attested in the icons—and ended with the distribution of bread and wine in a special spoon after they had been transformed by the invocation of the Holy Spirit into the body and blood of Christ. Practicing the triple immersion of infants in the rite of baptism, the Eastern Orthodox normally followed the act immediately with the confirmation of the child, the anointing with holy chrism, and Holy Communion. Orthodoxy by no means escaped conflict, though it was the ethnic and political issues of the late nineteenth century that produced disputes, not the sacraments (Ware 1997: 12–16).

The significance of the sacraments among Roman Catholics found expression in an 1818 journey of the Jesuit John Grassi into his expansive rural Maryland parish. Carrying sacramental elements and chrism for anointing baptized infants, the sick, and the dying, he heard confessions and pronounced absolution on Sunday morning, celebrated the Mass at noon, preached and catechized after lunch, baptized infants and performed funeral services in the afternoon, and frequently then officiated at holy matrimony. Above all, his ministry was sacramental (Gleason 1978: 238–239). Throughout the nineteenth century, long lines formed in Catholic churches for confession and absolution, and when the priests celebrated the Mass, the elevation of the host, announced by the ringing of a small bell, drew rapt attention from worshippers.

Nonetheless, Catholics had to defend this sacramental piety and its supporting theology. Countering Protestant claims that their sacramental doctrines made salvation mechanical and external, such bishop-theologians as John Joseph Hughes (1797–1864) and Francis Patrick Kenrick (1796–1863) pointed out that the church required right intention and disposition, adding that such criticisms were one more symptom of a rationalistic dismissal of mystery (Kehoe 1840: 2, 295; Kenrick 1841: 127, 139). In response to Protestant charges that transubstantiation defied reason and the evidence of the senses, most Catholics replied that their doctrine was "above reason but not contradictory to it." Bishop John England (1786–1842) of Charleston argued that Catholics simply took seriously the words of Jesus at the last supper: "This is my body" (Luke 22:19) meant what it said (Reynolds 1849: 354). They defended their doctrine of the Eucharist as a sacrifice with similar biblical arguments (Mal 1:2; Gen 14:18; Heb 9:24), but Father Demetrius Augustine Gallitzin (1770–1840), founder of the Catholic colony of Loretto in Pennsylvania, also contended that the Mass stood as a constant rebuke to "all the arguments of human reason" on which Protestants were inclined to rely (Gallitzin 1940: 59).

Every Catholic sacrament came under scrutiny, sometimes with vulgar insinuations about penance and the confessional, sometimes with reasoned argument against the doctrine that baptism was an instrumental cause of justification that conveyed "the pardon of sins and the grace of the Holy Ghost" (Kenrick 1841: 72). Conservatives James Henley Thornwell (1812–1862) and Robert J. Breckinridge (1800–1871) convinced the Presbyterian General Assembly in 1854 to deny the validity of Catholic baptism and pronounce Catholics "outside the visible Church of Christ." The Princeton theologian Charles Hodge (1797–1878) opposed this pronouncement, even though he thought that no doctrine could be more radically opposed to the teaching of the New Testament than the doctrine of baptismal regeneration, but the more extreme Presbyterian decision reflected the opinions of countless Protestants, inside and outside the Presbyterian Church (Palmer 1875: 290).

The most vigorous Lutheran debate occurred when the so-called American Lutherans, led by Samuel Simon Schmucker (1799–1873), professor of theology at Gettysburg seminary in Pennsylvania, called for revision of the Augsburg Confession. Drawn by the practices and piety of American revivalism and convinced by the positions of the eighteenth-century Scottish Common Sense philosophers Thomas Reid and Dugald Stewart, the Americanist group wanted a Lutheranism that assumed its rightful place in an ecumenical Protestant evangelical culture. Among the doctrines subject to revision in Schmucker's proposal were the doctrines of the real presence of Christ in, with, and under the elements of bread and wine, and the doctrine of baptismal regeneration (Wolf 1966: 44). He also wanted to remove the confession's affirmation of private confession and absolution, which he thought sounded Catholic. Schmucker would substitute the view that the Lord's Supper "influenced" the faithful with unusual power and that baptism was simply a symbolic initiation into the church and the covenant (Schmucker 1834, 1st. ed. 1826: 199–218, 246, 251, 255).

When Schmucker distributed, without signing, a *Definite Platform* containing his ideas, the confessionalists, defenders of the *Augsburg Confession* and the *Book of Concord*, coalesced into an opposition. David Henkel (1795–1831) in Tennessee operated a printing press that produced treatises defending the doctrine of baptismal regeneration and the physical presence of Christ in the elements of the Eucharist. The publication of *The Conservative Reformation and its Theology* (1871), by Charles Porterfield Krauth (1823–1883), a pastor in Virginia and Pennsylvania and the leader of the confessionalists, was the most sophisticated historical treatise defending the confessional position on the sacraments. In Missouri, meanwhile, Carl Ferdinand Wilhelm Walther (1811–1887), an immigrant pastor from Saxony, led the formation in 1847 of the Lutheran Church-Missouri Synod, which joined with the confessionalists in defending Luther's original sacramental positions. Other issues entered into the debates, but in 1867 the dispute split the Lutherans into an Americanist General Synod and a confessionalist General Council. Some Lutherans saw the sacraments within a context of revivalist piety; others saw them as alternatives to such a piety.

Additional divisions reminiscent of older sacramental debates further divided Lutheran confessionalists; Walther, for example, held that absolution by a minister imparted forgiveness regardless of the faith of the penitent even though penance was not technically a sacrament, while Swedish-American Lutherans decried this view as "Romanizing," importing a third sacrament into Lutheranism (Tappert 1972: 141–165; Holifield 2003: 402–414). The dispute spilled over the borders of the Lutheran tradition when Krauth defended against Princeton's Charles Hodge the Lutheran doctrine that baptism, as a sacrament of regeneration, was normally necessary for salvation (Krauth 1874: 10, 13, 73; Hodge, *Systematic Theology*, 1871–3: III, 245).

Similar debates wracked the Episcopal tradition. After the formation in 1789 of the Protestant Episcopal Church in the United States, the denomination promptly fell into divisions that reflected factions originating in the seventeenth century. The evangelical party, led by William H. Wilmer (1782–1827), professor of systematic theology in The Theological Seminary of Virginia at Alexandria, and Charles McIlvaine (1799–1873), the bishop of Ohio and president of Kenyon College, could speak of baptism, following the *Book of Common Prayer*, as the means of regeneration, but what was important to them was the experience of adult renewal toward which, they thought, the sacrament pointed (Wilmer 1829: 113, 142–145; McIlvaine 1851: 34). The high church party, who followed John Henry Hobart (1775–1830), bishop of New York after 1816, also accepted the need for adult renewal, but they wanted to protect a view of baptism as the means and pledge of spiritual grace, the rite that translated the baptized into "the Holy Church of God," where they became heirs to the kingdom of heaven (Hobart 1810: IX, 25; Moore 1820: 13). Hobart taught that baptismal "regeneration" was normally the necessary condition of the later adult "renovation". During the mid-1820s the high church party tried to convince the General Convention to restrict the term "regeneration" to a sacramental usage, but the effort was unsuccessful (Prichard 1991: 88). Both parties, however, rejected the baptismal doctrine of the American Tractarians, the admirers of John Henry Newman (1801–1890) in England, some of whom argued that baptismal regeneration made a subsequent "renewal" unnecessary. By 1849, Levi Sullivan Ives (1797–1867), the bishop of North Carolina, contended that baptism conferred on infants "a new and heavenly nature" (Ives 1849: 9, 25). It was also objectionable to evangelicals when some high church theologians linked their sacramental views to the argument that only bishops could convey the authority to baptize (Mullin 1995: 16–25).

In the 1840s the Eucharist moved toward the forefront of contention, especially after the tracts of the Oxford Movement in England persuaded a few American Episcopalians to affirm what John Henry Newman called a "substantial" presence of Christ in the bread and wine (McIlvaine 1841: 392). Such a position was unacceptable even to Hobart's high church party; Hobart urged frequent communion but he held to a Reformed doctrine of a spiritual presence, even though he had once felt the lure of Catholic doctrine, even of eucharistic sacrifice. By the time he became a bishop he spoke of the sacrament's "becoming" the "spiritual body and blood of Christ" to those who received it faithfully. Evangelicals were more inclined to speak of it merely as a "sign" of Christ's body and blood or a vehicle of his "virtual" presence to the faith of the communicant (Hobart 1810: 26; Wilmer 1829: 130). The American Tractarians, however, wanted to emphasize, with the Oxford movement, the "reality" of the presence, even though they displayed some ambiguity in interpreting the term. Some disavowed any belief in transubstantiation, though they did speak of the Eucharist as a "sacrifice," even if it was unclear exactly what they meant. Even some high church theologians, however, suspected that the Tractarians inclined toward Catholic sacramental doctrine, and indeed some converted to Catholicism, while others later affirmed an essentially Catholic doctrine while remaining within the Episcopal Church.

In the Reformed tradition, the most sophisticated sacramental reflection occurred at Mercersburg Seminary in Pennsylvania. In 1840, the Presbyterian theologian John Williamson Nevin (1803–1886) left Western Seminary to accept a teaching position at the German Reformed school at Mercersburg. Even at Western he had thought that John Calvin had taught a real, though spiritual, presence of Christ in the Lord's Supper, but he traced the roots of his developing sacramental views to 1843, when he opposed the revivalism of Charles Grandison Finney (1792–1875) by writing that the catechizing of the baptized rather than the sudden conversion of the sinful offered the best way to nurture the church (Nevin 1843: 29, 52). By 1847 he was convinced that sacramental ideas offered the best clues for deciphering any theological system, and in his own theology, grounded in a view of Incarnation influenced by a conservative Christian reading of Hegelian philosophy and by Isaac Dorner's *History of the Development of the Doctrine of the Person of Christ* (1839), Nevin proposed a Christocentric theology that implied, he thought, a real spiritual presence of Christ in the Lord's Supper and a view of baptism as a "washing of regeneration" for the "remission of sins" that incorporated infants into the incarnate Life of Christ (Nevin 1850: 249–250). In *The Mystical Presence* (1846), he contended that he was merely repeating Calvin's views, but with a different philosophical psychology, making it clear, as Calvin had not, that the presence of Christ in the Eucharist made possible a special mystical union of the faithful with the whole person of Christ, the humanity and the divinity, particularly the human nature. Calvin had not, Nevin thought, sufficiently noted the distinction between Christ's individual and generic life. As generic, the life of Christ could be truly present in a special and extraordinary way in the Lord's Supper (Nevin 1846: 62, 156–162). The German Reformed Church named Nevin in 1849 as the chair of a committee to produce a liturgy that could extend his theology into the local congregations, but the liturgical revision never achieved wide favor. Nevin's *Vindication of the Revised Liturgy* (1867) provided the best short summary of his thought and laid out its practical implications.

Nevin's *Mystical Presence* prompted an extended debate over the sacraments with Hodge at Princeton, who represented the typical sacramental positions of nineteenth-century Presbyterians. Hodge found Nevin "murky" and it took him nearly two years before he could muster sufficient energy to work his way through the book, but he felt a need to defend a Presbyterian view that the Lord's Supper was a memorial and an occasion for communion with the Spirit of Christ. Nevin had erred, he thought, by speaking of union with the divine-human Christ, by making the Lord's Supper a special and extraordinary means of Christ's presence, by overemphasizing the unity of Christ's two natures, and by superimposing philosophical idealism on doctrine (though Hodge's allegiance to Scottish Common Sense Realism influenced his doctrine). He also could not tolerate Nevin's allusions to "regeneration" in connection with baptism, though Nevin had made it clear that he intended neither a Catholic nor a Lutheran interpretation. (Hodge 1848: 230, 238, 247, 267, 272). Nevin attracted few disciples, though the Old School Presbyterian John Adger (1810–1899) did teach some of Nevin's ideas to his students at Columbia Presbyterian Seminary in South Carolina.

To most Presbyterians Charles Hodge was much closer to the truth. Hodge viewed the sacraments in conventional American Reformed terms as seals of the covenant of grace, which meant that baptism confirmed a child's status within the parental covenant with God while the Lord's Supper sealed the covenant by conveying to faithful believers the "virtue and efficacy" of Christ's saving work. Baptism, however, was not necessary for salvation, and the Lord's Supper contained neither a corporeal nor a "mystical" (Nevin) presence of Christ's body and blood. Hodge also disliked the notion that the sacraments conveyed a unique grace, unobtainable elsewhere (Hodge 1838: 86, 105; Hodge 1857: 359–362). The Southern Old School Presbyterian Robert Lewis Dabney (1820–1898) in Virginia worried about John Adger's penchant for Mercersburg's doctrines, insisting that it was important to retain the Reformed accent on the distinction between Christ's divine and human natures and to deny any special union with Christ through the sacrament (Dabney 1878: 615–616, 810). The New School Presbyterians, foes of the Old School on doctrines of sin, rebirth, and the will, had no objections to Hodge's sacramental positions (Nevin 1846: 133–135).

Presbyterians illustrated, however, the point that a revivalist piety need not entail a disregard for the sacraments. The awakenings that began in the eighteenth century and continued in what came to be called the Second Great Awakening, had their origins, at least in their Presbyterian form, partly in the sacramental gatherings of the Scots and Scotch-Irish. Celebration of the Lord's Supper constituted a prominent part of the camp meetings on the frontier, sometimes even among groups such as the Methodists, whose main interest was conversion and the spreading of holiness. Such Protestant groups might not have had a "Catholic" sacramental sensibility, but they did not ignore sacraments even in the midst of their revivalist fervor (Westerkamp 1988; Schmidt 2001).

One offspring of Presbyterian tradition, Alexander Campbell (1788–1866), reacted against Presbyterian theology, briefly allied himself with the Baptists, and then joined with Barton W. Stone (1772–1844), another former Presbyterian, in attempting to build a restorationist movement that would reform the church on the basis of the primitive model in the New Testament epistles. These Christians, or Disciples of Christ (they did not think of themselves as a denomination), debated among themselves about sacramental doctrine, but Campbell's views won widespread assent. He declared infant baptism unscriptural, soon insisted that immersion was the sole valid means of baptizing, and by 1823 declared that the purpose of baptism was the remission of sins. The ordinance brought assurance of favor with God, at least to the extent that it changed the "state" of believers by introducing them into the church and so to a new relation to God and the kingdom. He insisted, however, that he attached no efficacy to the rite itself. The doctrine disturbed some in the Christian movement, since it seemed to require the exclusion of members baptized without immersion from religious fellowship (Campbell 1890, 1st ed.

1835: 204; Hughes and Allen 1988: 115). By 1837 Campbell altered his doctrine to concede that the non-immersed could be forgiven unless they opposed the scriptural truth that immersion was normally necessary for forgiveness (Campbell and Purcell 1914: 61).

Campbell concluded also that the most prominent expression of Christian worship was the Lord's Supper, which he preferred to call the "breaking of the loaf," since the phrase seemed more consonant with the biblical account. He took the Reformed position associated with sixteenth-century Zurich that the elements were "emblematic" of Christ's body and blood and that the rite commemorated Jesus' death. Both he and Stone wanted a weekly celebration because they saw the loaf as the sign of the Christian unity they sought (Stone 1834: 176–177; Campbell 1890, 1835: 268–274).

Nineteenth-century Congregationalists remained, for the most part, within the Reformed tradition as it had existed in the late seventeenth-century colonies. Some still fought the battles that the followers of Jonathan Edwards, the so-called New Divinity theologians, had fought in the eighteenth century, when Joseph Bellamy (1719–1790) and Samuel Hopkins (1721–1803) had continued the battle against the half-way covenant (Bellamy 1769: 5, 7; Conforti 1981: 82). Others stood in an Old Calvinist tradition that either maintained the half-way position or held to Stoddard's view of the Lord's Supper as a converting ordinance (Hemmenway 1792: 8, 51). Most of the representatives of the nineteenth-century "New England theology" also opposed the practice of allowing baptized but unconverted parents to present their children for baptism or to receive the Lord's Supper, and they retained a symbolic, memorialist view of the rite (Tyler 1829: 8; Nevin 1846: 110–113).

Even more than the Congregationalists, the Unitarians who predominated in Massachusetts viewed the sacraments symbolically, baptizing infants not because they bore the stain of original sin but because baptism symbolized God's love for the infant. They celebrated the Lord's Supper as a remembrance of the life and death of Jesus. And yet sacraments became the occasion for conflict within Unitarianism. Ralph Waldo Emerson (1803–1882) resigned as the pastor of Boston's Second Church when his congregation refused to abandon its customary celebration of the Lord's Supper, which he viewed as subversive of a true religion of the spirit but which they still cherished. (Whicher 1953: 39, 21) Unitarians hardly constituted a sacramental tradition, but they continued to celebrate baptism and the Lord's Supper as memorials of Jesus' life and signs of communal harmony and love.

The exception to standard Congregationalist views was the Hartford, Connecticut, pastor Horace Bushnell (1802–1876). On the surface, Bushnell stood in the tradition of Hopkins and the Edwardeans, who had seen baptism as the seal of a covenant that had already been transmitted to children through the faithfulness of their parents. In his *Christian Nurture* (1847), however, he elevated infant baptism and the subsequent nurture of the child to the center of his view of the church. His view of the symbolic nature of theological language meant that he no longer cared much about the minute differences that divided other theologians, but he did believe that his Episcopal critics had an exaggerated view of baptismal efficacy, while the Congregational revivalist tradition failed to value the sacrament highly enough (Bushnell 1967, 1st ed. 1847: 74–101; Smith 1984: 113).

The revivalist tradition also found a home outside Congregationalism, especially among the Methodists and Baptists who by mid-century were becoming the largest American denominations. Neither, in their American forms, could be called a sacramental tradition, even though the Methodist founder John Wesley (1703–1791) in England held high views of both sacraments, and the Baptists argued endlessly about them. American Methodists often denied, despite Wesley's words, that he had ever believed in baptismal rebirth; they preferred to define the sacrament as a seal to a universal but conditional covenant. Believing that every infant came into the world tainted by original sin but also as a beneficiary of the covenant, they insisted that baptism was a "saving ordinance" only in the sense that it gave the baptized title to the salutary influences of the church. It sealed a covenant already made, but since the covenant was conditional, the efficacy of baptism could be realized only by later repentance and faith. The same was true for adult converts who sought baptism after their conversion; if they fell away from the faith, the sacrament no longer benefited them (Rosser 1854: 17, 19; Wakefield 1869, 1st ed. 1862: 431–432).

Wesley had also attempted to transmit, through his revised Anglican liturgy, his strong sense of Christ's real spiritual presence in the Eucharist, but American Methodists tended more toward views of the sacrament as a memorial. It was, however, an efficacious memorial, for the Methodists, like Wesley, thought of it as a converting ordinance that had the power to change the heart. They tended, therefore, to admit repentant "seekers" to the sacrament in the hope that they would find there the grace sufficient for salvation (Ralston 1871, 1st ed. 1847: 999).

Baptists were unified in their rejection of infant baptism and their conviction that the ordinance was a sign of faith on the part of the baptized. They continued to argue against views of Abraham's covenant that had long been used to justify infant baptism as a "seal" of the covenant. The Southern theologian John Dagg (1794–1884) argued that scripture nowhere called it a seal. Since the Bible required profession of faith and appointed baptism for that purpose, the ordinance could be considered indirectly "necessary for salvation," though not as the seal to an efficacious divine promise. Baptist theologians denied even that the rite was the entrance into the church; faith and obedience were the virtues that enabled converts to become church members (Dagg 1858: 73, 79, 195).

Baptist unity on these questions did not preclude conflicts over baptismal practice. No battle was more intense, at least in the South, than the Landmarkist controversy, a label derived from a book entitled *An Old Landmark Reset*. The Landmarkists insisted on a continuous succession of Baptist churches since the era of the New Testament, and their most prominent spokesman, James Robinson Graves (1820–1893) concluded that baptism by immersion was essential to the validity of a church and that the only valid baptism came from an immersed believer acting under the authority of a local congregation, even if this meant that Baptist ministers should re-baptize anyone who had been immersed by unauthorized ministers (Graves 1903, 1st ed. 1858: iii–xi). Graves also thought that members of one congregation should not receive the Lord's Supper in another, since the true church was the local congregation and the ordinance signified its unity. Other Baptists, however, felt no hesitation to accept any faithful, immersed Christian as truly baptized and to open the Lord's Supper to Baptists outside their own congregations (Graves 1855: 415–427, 451–470; Dagg 1858: 286–288).

The frequency of conflict over the sacraments was an indication of the seriousness with which early American Christians took them. Communities could sometimes divide over questions of baptism, and the celebration of the Lord's Supper aroused intense emotions. American denominationalism did not, on the whole, promote a sacramental sensibility, even though Catholics were becoming by 1860 the largest church in the United States. And cultural assumptions continued often to alter sacramental practice. Yet Americans faithfully observed the sacraments as they understood them in their various traditions, defended their doctrines about them, and instructed their children in their meaning. They transmitted those sensibilities to the twentieth century, and the early American heritage still influences Christian practice in the twenty-first.

SUGGESTED READING

Holifield (1974); Holifield (2003); Nevin (1846); Schaff (1966).

BIBLIOGRAPHY

Bellamy, Joseph (1769), *That There is but One Covenant, Whereof Baptism and the Lord's Supper Are the Seals* (New Haven, CT: Green).

Bray, Thomas (1696, 1704), *A Short Discourse upon the Doctrine of our Baptismal Covenant*, 4th ed. (London: S. Hole).

Brown, Anne S. and Hall, David D. (1997), "Family Strategies and Religious Practice: Baptism and the Lord's Supper in Early New England," in David D. Hall (ed.), *Lived Religion in America* (Princeton, NJ: Princeton University Press), 41–68.

Bushnell, Horace (1967, 1st ed., 1847, rev. 1861), *Christian Nurture* (New Haven, CT: Yale University Press).

Campbell, Alexander (1890, 1st ed. 1835), *The Christian System* (St. Louis, MO: Christian Publishing).

Campbell, Alexander and Purcell, John B. (1914), *A Debate on the Roman Catholic Religion* (Nashville, TN: McQuiddy).

Chorley, Clowes E. (1946), *Men and Movements in the Episcopal Church* (New York: Scribner's Sons).

Conforti, Joseph (1981), *Samuel Hopkins and the New Divinity Movement* (Grand Rapids, MI: Christian University Press).

Dabney, Robert Lewis (1878), *Lectures in Systematic Theology* (Grand Rapids, MI: Zondervan).

Dagg, John (1858), *Treatise on Church Order* (Charleston: no publisher named).

Falckner, Justus (1708), *Grondlyche Onderricht* (New York: William Bradford).

Gallitzin, Demetrius A. (1940), *Gallitzin's Letters* (Loretto, PA: Angelmodde).

Gleason, Philip, ed. (1978), *Documentary Reports on Early American Catholicism* (New York: Arno Press).

Graves, James R. (1855), *The Great Iron Wheel* (Nashville, TN: Graves and Marks).

Graves, James R. (1903), "Introduction," *Paedobaptist and Campbellite Immersions* (Louisville, KY: Baptist Book Concern), iii–xi.

Green, Jacob (1768), *An Inquiry into the Constitution and Discipline of the Jewish Church* (New York: Hugh Gaine).

Hammond, George P., and Agapito Rey (eds.) (1953), *Don Juan de Oñate: Colonizer of New Mexico*, 2 vols. (Albuquerque, NM: The University of Mexico Press).

Hastings, Hugh, ed. (1901), *Ecclesiastical Records of New York*, 17 vols. (Albany, NY: J. B. Lyon).

Hemmenway, Moses (1792), *A Discourse Concerning the Church* (Boston, MA: Thomas and Andrews).

Hobart, John Henry (1810), *The Excellence of the Church* (New York: T & J Swords).

Hodge, Charles (1838), "Tracts for the Times," *Biblical Repertory and Princeton Review* 10/1: 84–118.

Hodge, Charles (1848), "Doctrine of the Reformed Church on the Lord's Supper," in *Biblical Repertory and Princeton Review* 20/2: 227–277.

Hodge, Charles (1857), *Essays and Reviews* (New York: R. Carter).

Hodge, Charles (1871–3), *Systematic Theology* (New York: Scribner, Armstrong).

Hodge, Frederick W. and Theodore H. Lewis (1907), *Spanish Explorers in the Southern United States, 1528–1543* (New York: Charles Scribner's Sons).

Hodge, Frederick W., George P. Hammond, and Agapito, Rey (eds.) (1949), *Fray Alonso de Benavides Revised Memorial of 1634* (Albuquerque: University of New Mexico Press).

Holifield, E. Brooks (1974), *The Covenant Sealed: The Development of Puritan Sacramental Theology in Old and New England, 1570–1720* (New Haven, CT: Yale University Press).

Holifield, E. Brooks (1998), "Theology as Entertainment: Oral Debate in American Religion," in *Church History* 67/3: 499–520.

Holifield, E. Brooks (2003), *Theology in America: Christian Thought from the Age of the Puritans to the Civil War* (New Haven, CT: Yale University Press).

Hughes, Richard T. and Leonard, Allen C. (1988), *Illusions of Innocence: Protestant Primitivism in America, 1630–1875* (Chicago, IL: University of Chicago Press).

Ives, L. Sullivan (1849), *The Obedience of Faith* (New York: Stanford and Swords).

Kehoe, Lawrence (ed.) (1865), *Complete Works of the Most Rev. John Hughes*, 2 vols. (New York: Lawrence Kehoe).

Kenrick, Francis Patrick (1843), *A Treatise of Baptism* (Philadelphia, PA: M. Fithian).

Kenrick, Francis Patrick (1841), *The Catholic Doctrine of Justification Explained and Vindicated* (Philadelphia, PA: Cummiskey).

Krauth, Charles P. (1874), *Infant Baptism and Infant Salvation in the Calvinistic System* (Philadelphia, PA: Lutheran Book Store).

Leland, John (1845), *The Writings of the Late Elder John Leland* (New York: G. W. Wood).

McIlvaine, Charles Petit (1841), *Oxford Divinity Compared with that of the Romish and Anglican Churches* (London: Seely and Burnside).

McIlvaine, Charles Petit (1851), *Spiritual Regeneration with Reference to Present Times* (New York: Harper and Brothers).

McLoughlin, William G. (ed.) (1968), *Isaac Backus on Church, State, and Calvinism* (Cambridge, MA: Harvard University Press).

Moore, Richard (1820), *The Doctrine of the Church* (Philadelphia, PA: William Fry).

Mullin, Bruce (1995), *Episcopal Vision, American Reality* (New Haven, CT: Yale University Press).

Nevin, John Williamson (1843), *The Anxious Bench* (Chambersburg, PA: Weekly Messenger).

Nevin, John Williamson (1846), *The Mystical Presence: A Vindication of the Calvinistic Doctrine of the Holy Eucharist* (Philadelphia, PA: J. B. Lippincott).

Nevin, John Williamson (1850), "Noel on Baptism," *Mercersburg Review* 2: 231–266.

Palmer, Benjamin (1875), *The Life and Letters of James Henley Thornwell* (Richmond, VA: Whittet, Shepperson).

Pastorius, Francis Daniel (1697), *Four Boasting Disputes of the World Briefly Rebuked* (New York: William Bradford).

Prichard, Robert (1991), *A History of the Episcopal Church* (Harrisburg, PA: Morehouse-Barlow).

Ralston, Thomas N. (1871), *Elements of Divinity* (Nashville, TN: A. H. Redford).

Reynolds, Ignatius A. (ed.) (1849), *The Works of the Right Rev. John England*, 5 vols. (Baltimore, MD: John Murphy).

Rosser, Leonidas (1854), *Baptism* (Richmond, VA: the Author).

Schaff, Philip (1966, 1st. ed. 1877), *The Creeds of Christendom: Volume III The Evangelical Protestant Creeds with Translations* (Grand Rapids, MI: Baker Book House).

Schmidt, Leigh Eric (2001), *Holy Fairs: Scotland and the Meaning of American Revivalism* (Grand Rapids, MI: Eerdmans).

Schmucker, Samuel S. (1834, 1826), *Elements of Popular Theology* (New York: Leavitt, Lord).

Smith David, ed. (1984), *Horace Bushnell: Selected Writings on Language, Religion, and American Culture* (Chico, CA: Scholars Press).

Smith, H. Shelton, Robert Handy, and Lefferts Loetscher (eds.) (1960–1963), *American Christianity*, 2 vols. (New York: Scribner).

Stone, Barton W. (1834), "The Lord's Supper," in *Christian Messenger* 8/6: 176–177.

Tappert, Theodore G., ed. (1972), *Lutheran Confessional Theology in America, 1840–1880* (New York: Oxford University Press).

Wakefield, Samuel (1869), *A Complete System of Systematic Theology* (Cincinnati, OH: Cranston and Curtis).

Westerkamp, Marilyn (1988), *Triumph of the Laity: Scots-Irish Piety and the Great Awakening, 1625–1760* (New York: Oxford University Press).

Wilmer, William (1829), *The Episcopal Manual* (Baltimore, MD: E. J. Coale).

Tappert, Theodore. G., and J. W. Doberstein (eds.) (1945), *The Journals of Henry Melchior Muhlenberg* (Philadelphia, PA: The Muhlenberg Press).

Temple, Sydney A., ed. (1946), *The Common Sense Theology of Bishop White* (Morningside Heights, NY: King's Crown).

Thomson, John (1749), *An Exposition of the Shorter Catechism* (Williamsburg, VA: William Parks).

Tyler, Bennett (1829), *Strictures on the Review of Dr. Spring's Dissertation* (Portland, ME: Shirley and Hyde).

Ware, Timothy (1997), *The Orthodox Church* (London: Penguin).

Whicher, Stephen (1953), *Freedom and Fate: An Inner Life of Ralph Waldo Emerson* (Philadelphia, PA: University of Pennsylvania Press).

Wolf, Richard C. (ed.) (1966), *Documents of Lutheran Unity* (Philadelphia, PA: Fortress Press)

Yrigoyen, Charles Jr., and George H. Bricker (eds.) (1978), *Reformed and Catholic: Selected Theological Writings of John Williamson Nevin* (Pittsburgh, PA: Pickwick Press).

CHAPTER 26

TWENTIETH-CENTURY AND CONTEMPORARY PROTESTANT SACRAMENTAL THEOLOGY

Part I: Sacraments in General and Baptism in Twentieth-Century and Contemporary Protestant Theology

MARTHA L. MOORE-KEISH

THE first task in describing twentieth-century and contemporary Protestant sacramental theology is to define terms. "Protestant" in this case is construed broadly, to refer to Christians who are neither in full communion with the bishop of Rome nor with any Eastern Orthodox churches. The category thus includes Christians who trace their roots to sixteenth-century reformations (Lutheran, Reformed, Anglican, Anabaptist) as well as those whose defining history is more recent (e.g. Methodist, Baptist, and Pentecostal churches). "Protestantism" includes a wide variety of perspectives, including some which reject the term "sacrament" itself.

Part I of this chapter first briefly addresses general trends in Protestant sacramental theology during the twentieth and early twenty-first centuries. It then considers baptism and Eucharist in particular, the two sacramental practices most generally accepted among Protestant churches. When referring to the Supper, I will use several terms to honor the several ways that Protestant churches name this act, including Eucharist, Lord's Supper, and Holy Communion.

Sacramental Theology

Ecumenical Convergence

One profound shift in Protestantism in the twentieth century is the extent to which Catholic-Protestant polemics of preceding centuries diminished, giving way to a new spirit of ecumenical respect and shared learning. By the last decades of the century, this led to significant mutual influence both in sacramental practice and in theological reflection on the sacraments. Ecumenical convergence in practice can be seen, for instance, by comparing baptismal and eucharistic liturgies in post-Vatican II Roman Catholicism to those of Anglicans, Lutherans, Presbyterians, and Methodists. These liturgical reforms display a shared reclaiming of scriptural imagery and language as well as appreciation for liturgical practices of the first four centuries of Christianity.

This convergence in liturgical practice was accompanied by a common conviction that sacramental theology of more recent centuries, which focused on questions such as how sacraments "cause" grace, and the validity and efficacy of sacraments, failed to take seriously actual sacramental practice (Fahey 2007: 268). Thus, much twentieth- and early twenty-first-century sacramental theology has attended closely to liturgical texts and embodied sacramental practices, as the "primary theology" of sacraments (Wainwright 1983: 99; White 1983; Lathrop 1993). Some major themes in twentieth-century sacramental theology are likewise shared across the Catholic-Protestant divide, rendering problematic any simple division of these traditions one from another.

Beginning in the late twentieth century, the emphasis on common ecumenical sacramental theology and practice was accompanied by a helpful counter-trend, namely, enhanced attention to diversity. Greater recognition of the variety of sacramental theologies and practices in the early church by scholars such as Paul Bradshaw informs recent recognition of the value of diversity, not as a hindrance to unity, but as a source of ecumenical enrichment (Bradshaw 1992, 2009).

Growing Protestant Appreciation for Sacraments

Greater ecumenical openness, significant new biblical and historical research into liturgy and sacraments, and growing appreciation for the formative value of embodied practices all contributed to a surge of interest in sacraments among Protestants over the twentieth and early twenty-first centuries. Paul Tillich in 1948 cautioned that to eliminate completely the "sacramental element" from religion would lead to the dissolution of the visible church. With the help of depth psychology, he later argued that Protestants needed to recover appreciation for the sacraments, rather than only words, as mediators of Spiritual Presence in order to understand human multidimensional unity (Tillich 1948: 94; 1963: 121f). Donald Baillie noted and encouraged a revival of interest in sacraments among Protestants in a series of lectures on "The Theology of the Sacraments" in 1952 (Baillie 1957: 39); three decades later, James White testified to the growing Protestant interest in sacraments and awareness of their role in faith formation (White 1983). And Hans Boersma recently issued a comprehensive call, particularly for evangelical Protestants, to recover a pre-modern worldview in which created things have value only as they participate in heavenly realities—what he calls "a sacramental tapestry" (Boersma 2011). This marks a recent turn among evangelical and other Protestants toward an entire sacramental worldview, not just an appreciation for sacramental actions in worship.

What is a Sacrament?

Protestant (as well as Catholic) theologians since the turn of the twentieth century have frequently begun their sacramental reflections by interpreting the New Testament term *mysterion* and its Latin translation *sacramentum*. With historical-critical exegesis challenging the sixteenth-century Protestant definition of a sacrament as an act expressly instituted by Jesus, theologians sought new ways of defining "sacrament" in Protestant terms.

Some have rejected the term altogether. Many Baptist and Pentecostal Christians, for instance, have long avoided the term "sacrament" in favor of "ordinance," arguing that "sacrament" is a non-biblical word that ascribes semi-mechanical efficacy to certain human actions, independent of the faith of believers (Land 1994: 117; Ellis 1996: 23f). "Ordinance," in contrast, emphasizes Jesus' institution and the obedient response of believers. Baptist theologian James McClendon in the late twentieth century called baptism, proclamation, and Communion "remembering signs," connecting the great narrative of God's salvation history to particular believers and believing communities in the present (McClendon 1994: 382). Some Baptists, however, now acknowledge the historical value of the term "sacrament" to indicate an oath of allegiance, and some have even argued for a kind of "Baptist sacramentalism" (Ellis 1996; Cross and Thompson 2007). Among Reformed theologians, Karl Barth (by the end of the *Church Dogmatics*) and Eberhard Jüngel notably reject the term "sacrament" to refer to anything apart from the mystery of Christ's Incarnation, calling baptism and the Lord's Supper "witnesses" or "signs" (Barth 1967: 55; cf. Pannenberg 1998: 345). Some theologians who reject the term "sacrament" nevertheless believe that baptism and the Lord's Supper are occasions when believers are drawn into unity with Christ in the power of the Spirit—convictions shared by many who continue to use the traditional term.

Others retain the term "sacrament" and attempt to purify it of older medieval meanings. John Howard Yoder, for instance, seeks to use the word "sacrament" without its "magical or instrumental" meanings, to refer to an ordinary human practice about which the New Testament says that when humans do it, God is doing it (Yoder 1992: 44, 71).

Yet others, both Protestant and Catholic, identify a "primal sacrament" underlying the particular sacraments, based in the apostolic usage of the term *mysterion*. For instance, Catholic theologian Karl Rahner described the church (grounded in Christ) as the fundamental sacrament of salvation, while Barth called the Incarnation of Christ (to whom the church attests) the "first sacrament" (Barth 1957: 54) and later, the "one and only sacrament" (Barth 1967: 55). German Reformed theologian Jürgen Moltmann proposed that this divide could be overcome by naming the Spirit as primal sacrament, reflecting the New Testament usage of *mysterion* to name the divine eschatological secret (Moltmann 1977: 202–206). Scottish Reformed theologian T. F. Torrance, like Barth, identified Christ as the primal sacrament, but went beyond Barth to argue that we are incorporated by the Holy Spirit into Christ through the sacraments (Torrance 1975: 82). American Methodist theologian James White approvingly cited Edward Schillebeeckx's statement that Christ is the original "sacrament of the encounter with God" (White 1983: 22). White concurred with the Dutch Catholic scholar that Christ is the source of all individual sacraments that carry on what he initiated.

Finally, many theologians in this century suggested a move away from consideration of "sacraments in general" toward consideration of baptism and Eucharist in particular, not as different species of a common genus, but as two basic practices of Christian faith with distinct shape and implications.

Sacraments, Christ, and the Church

Related to the impulse to identify Christ (or the Spirit) as "primal" sacrament, many Protestant (especially Lutheran, Anglican, and Reformed) theologians during this period emphasized that Christ and the Spirit really act in and through baptism and Eucharist to bind believers to Christ and to one another in the church. This emphasis on the interconnection of sacraments, Christ, and the church constituted an explicit critique of an individualistic focus and an interpretation of sacraments as "mere" symbols, two tendencies which had haunted many forms of Protestant sacramental theology between the seventeenth and nineteenth centuries.

British Congregationalist P. T. Forsyth was one of the first to voice these concerns and offer a strong view of Christ's agency in the sacraments. Central to Forsyth's understanding of sacraments was the conviction that Christ is the actor in baptism and the Lord's Supper: "They are acts of Christ really present by his Holy Spirit in the Church. It is Christ doing something through the Church as His body" (Forsyth 1917: 177). Sacraments, according to Forsyth, are not mere "keepsakes" reminding us of someone now departed. They are real means by which the risen Christ is present, conveying love to believers here and now. Nor are they tokens for separate individuals; sacraments are inherently public, corporate acts of the church.

German Lutheran Peter Brunner shared Forsyth's emphasis on Christ's action by the Spirit in and through the church's sacraments of baptism and Holy Communion. Unlike

Forsyth, however, Brunner's interpretation of the sacraments (and all of worship) was thoroughly eschatological. In Christian worship, the messianic congregation, set apart from the world and integrated into Christ's body, is gathered to await Jesus' return. In this time of waiting, the sacraments (together with proclamation) are the only way that Jesus himself is really, though not visibly, present, in the power of the Spirit (Brunner 1968: 79).

As noted earlier, T. F. Torrance affirmed Barth's interpretation of Christ as the primary sacrament, in whom all particular sacraments are grounded. Christ, in other words, is the one in whom God is truly incarnate in our humanity, and into whose body we are incorporated. This conviction led Torrance to a strong emphasis on the sacraments as Christian worshipers' participation or *koinonia* "in the mystery of Christ and his Church through the *koinonia* or communion of the Holy Spirit" (Torrance 1975: 82). Again, the emphasis on the corporate nature of sacraments is clear, as well as the resistance to any kind of sacramental minimalism.

Sacraments as "Signs"

Many Protestant theologians since the early twentieth century have reacted against the teaching that sacraments are "mere" signs, that the material elements of bread, wine, and water simply point beyond themselves to a reality elsewhere—a view often (perhaps unfairly) attributed to Zwingli. In response, they have proposed fuller understandings of "sign" and "symbol," challenging dualistic presumptions that divide "sign" from "reality."

Several theologians have emphasized that sacramental signs are best understood as modes of personal communication from God to humanity. P. T. Forsyth argued that sacraments are "Christ in a real presence giving anew his redemption." He compared sacraments to wedding rings, love-tokens, compositions, poems given from one lover to another. They are means by which Christ in the Spirit really acts in the church (Forsyth 1917: 176). Donald Baillie likewise emphasized that sacraments are personalized visible symbols through which God communicates with human beings. They are not merely mechanical or material things, but God's personal gifts by which he conveys grace to us (Baillie 1957: 52f). Decades later, James White concurred: "When we speak of sacraments, we are speaking of actions through which God relates to us here and now in establishing or renewing personal relationships" (White 1983: 27).

Others have proposed participatory understandings of sacramental signs, without describing them as personal communication. Tillich, for instance, insisted that sacraments are not "signs" but "symbols." Signs point beyond themselves; symbols participate in the power of what they symbolize. In sacraments, the Spirit uses inherent qualities of symbols (water, bread, wine) to "enter man's spirit" (Tillich 1963: 123). Torrance and Pannenberg likewise insist that sacramental theology has suffered from a rigid separation of "sign" and "thing," stemming from Augustine's definition of sacrament, and that sacramental signs participate in the reality that they signify. Signs do not merely illustrate the thing signified, but establish and re-present it (Torrance 1975: 95–99;

Pannenberg 1998: 292, 348ff). So too Hans Boersma, drawing on the work of Henri de Lubac, evokes a sacramental ontology in which symbol and reality are not separated, but symbols participate in the reality to which they point (Boersma 2011: 111–112).

Sacramental symbols, however, do not mediate the pure presence of Christ, many recent interpreters have insisted. Following the interpretation of Catholic theologian Louis-Marie Chauvet, some Protestants have cautioned that to forget the real absence of Christ in the symbol risks turning sacramental signs into fetishes that we control, rather than signs that shape a paschal people. In sacraments (especially Eucharist), we encounter "the presence of the absence of God," which allows us to recognize the radical otherness of the risen Christ (Pickstock 1998; Farwell 2005: 73–78).

Attention to the material reality of sacraments, together with ecumenical emphasis on liturgical action as primary theology, led some Protestant theologians in the late twentieth century to explore ritual studies as a resource for sacramental theology. Ritual scholars such as Catherine Bell and Ronald Grimes have influenced theologians attentive to the ways in which Christ by the power of the Spirit communicates through embodied human action (Farwell 2005; Bieler and Schottroff 2007; Moore-Keish 2008). Other theologians, however, have raised concerns about too much attention to ritual practices. T. F. Torrance in 1975 already cautioned that too much focus on the church's ritual acts could distract from the main meaning of sacrament, which is the mystery of Christ (Torrance 1975: 82–84).

Sacraments and Ethics

Since the second half of the twentieth century, Protestant theologians have voiced a growing conviction that the church's sacramental acts affect ethical engagement with the world. James White in 1983 lamented the traditional Protestant view that preaching enacts prophetic ministry (and thus ethics), while sacraments have to do with priestly ministry. This dichotomy, he argued, obscured the deep connection of sacraments and ethics (White 1983: 93ff). Baptism, for instance, enacts and reinforces the basic equality of all persons, which should shape our ethical engagements with all human societies. Later he noted that the environmental movement has contributed to a more positive doctrine of creation underlying sacramental theology, and to greater awareness of how sacramental activity shapes engagement with the natural world (Baillie 1957; White 1999: 29).

Gordon W. Lathrop and John Howard Yoder describe how sacramental practices of eating and drinking and washing display and shape Christian ethics. Lathrop notes that in Justin Martyr's second-century liturgy, the Great Thanksgiving led to distribution of food to those present and to those absent, accompanied by collection for the poor. Fundamentally, the dialectic of the one holy God and the "holy people" breaks open the truth that God's holiness in Jesus Christ is given away to outsiders (Lathrop 1993: 46–47). For Yoder, eating together is simply a basic economic act of sharing, and baptism of people from different economic and social groups into one community simply is the egalitarian social act, rooted in the work of Christ on the cross (Yoder 1992: 21, 33, 40).

BAPTISM

Baptismal theology during this period was shaped by several developments: the Pentecostal/charismatic movement, which began at the turn of the twentieth century; the ecumenical movement, with its accompanying attention to apostolic and early church sources; the late twentieth-century growth in numbers of "unchurched" persons in North America and Europe, which has prompted new reflection on baptism and nurture; and growth in numbers of new Christians in the global south, which has prompted new questions on baptism, culture, and the Spirit.

Baptism as Entrance into the Church

As noted earlier, many Protestants during this period came to emphasize the integral connection of Christ, the sacraments, and the church as a reaction against sacramental minimalism and individualism. In discussions of baptism, this led such theologians to a strong view that baptism constitutes entrance into the church, the body of Christ. Focus on the ecclesiological implications of baptism has sometimes been expressed in more personal and practical terms, as with Donald Baillie, who said "baptism brings the child into a new environment, the environment of the Church of Christ" (Baillie 1957: 85). Other theologians have emphasized the objective dimension of baptism as participation in the mystery of Christ and his church through the communion of the Holy Spirit (Cullmann 1950: 30–45; Torrance 1975: 82f; Jenson 1978: 136–142).

Renewed focus on baptism as entrance into the church has often led to emphasis on "one baptism" as a sign of the unity of the worldwide church. In the late twentieth and early twenty-first centuries, this has been a major assumption of the ecumenical movement, including Protestant ecumenical reflection on baptism. The landmark World Council of Churches document *Baptism, Eucharist and Ministry* (1982) clearly states this common conviction: "Through baptism, Christians are brought into union with Christ, with each other, and with the Church of every time and place" (BEM 1982: par. 6). The process of developing BEM itself, along with other recent ecumenical documents on mutual recognition of baptism, emerged from and nurtured the theological conviction that baptism unites Christians into one church, despite the visible institutional divides that obscure that unity. In recent years, focus on baptism as a basis for church unity has begun to supplement the focus on Eucharist as the sacrament that defines and unites the church. Scottish theologian David Wright illustrates and encourages this development: "It has become a commonplace in recent ecumenical discussion to describe the church as a Eucharist community. It would be far truer to the New Testament to describe it as a baptismal community" (Wright, 2007: 363).

While a focus on baptismal ecclesiology has been central to recent ecumenical theological reflection, it has also prompted significant questions about the status of the unbaptized. Are the unbaptized firmly outside the church and its common life? Does celebration of baptism as entrance into the church marginalize people who for a variety of reasons are not baptized? Examples include "churchless Christians" in India, children in communities that practice believer baptism, and adults in North America and Europe who participate in Christian communities without (yet) making the public commitment of baptism. Each of these cases has prompted practical theological reflection on baptism as sign of entrance into God's church without restricting the grace of God to the visible church alone (Kidd 1996; Rowland 1996).

Infant/Believer Baptism

One major debate in Protestant baptismal theology in the twentieth and twenty-first centuries has been this: should infants be baptized? This debate has roots in the sixteenth-century Anabaptist and seventeenth- and eighteenth-century Baptist critiques of the majority practice of infant baptism. Two key issues are the relationship of baptism to the grace of God, and the relationship of baptism to the faith of the recipient. Does baptism confer grace, receive grace, or witness to grace already received? Does baptism presume public profession of faith of the recipient; presume the faith of the wider community, and anticipate the faith of the recipient; or is it not about our own faith, but primarily about the faithfulness of Christ, to whom we are united? Another issue raised by theologians in this period is the relationship of church and nation in areas where infant baptism has constituted the basis of a "Christian society."

Mennonite John Howard Yoder focused on the social and ethical implications of believer baptism, emphasizing that baptism establishes a new community that overcomes all ethnic and economic divisions, marking Christian society as a radical alternative to the world (Yoder 1992: 28–46). Baptist theologians likewise describe baptism as a decisive boundary between the old life and the new, and many in this period sought like Yoder to emphasize the ecclesial, not just the individual, dimension of baptism. In addition, Baptists share the view that baptism signifies repentance and forgiveness of sins, that one who is baptized is following Christ's example, displaying obedience to Christ's command, and making personal profession of faith (George 1993: 243; McClendon 1994: 386–397; Ellis 1996: 23).

In 1948, Karl Barth issued a strong critique of infant baptism, challenging Reformed and other "mainline" infant-baptizing Protestants to rethink their understanding and practice of baptism. Based on his interpretation of the New Testament, Barth argued that baptism is in essence "the representation of a [person's] renewal through ... participation by means of the power of the Holy Spirit in the death and resurrection of Jesus Christ" (Barth 1948: 9). The practice of baptism needs to communicate this clearly. This led him to conclude that while infant baptism may be technically "valid," it fails to communicate the truth of baptism. What is needed, instead, is a recipient who freely and responsibly receives the promise of grace, and can "be party to the pledge of allegiance concerning the grateful service demanded of him" (Barth 1948: 40). Barth is concerned above all that baptism not be construed as a passive act, but the act of a free partner of Jesus Christ.

Protestant theologians since 1948, from Baptists to Anglicans, have responded to Barth's challenge. One of the first major responses came from Oscar Cullmann, who agreed with Barth that baptism is participation in Christ's death and resurrection but disagreed sharply about the role of the recipient at the moment of baptism. According to Cullmann, Jesus' one baptism signifies both death (which brings forgiveness of sins) and resurrection (which brings the gift of the Spirit). When Christians are baptized, they are joined to the one baptism already effected by Jesus. None of this depends on the faith or understanding of the recipient. Cullmann insists that baptism in the New Testament is a passive reception of God's work, which sets the recipient in the body of Christ (Cullmann 1950: 31).

Several theologians have concurred with Cullmann, emphasizing that baptism is primarily Christ's gracious act of forgiveness and renewal, and that the response of the recipient is both secondary and subsequent. Peter Brunner insisted that in baptism, Christ unites people in his body, and that this act is the same regardless of whether the baptized is an infant or an adult (Brunner 1968: 86–87). Many others have similarly emphasized that in baptism we receive what Christ has already done for us, which is not conditioned by anything in us, not even faith. Repentance and reception of forgiveness are also basic to Christian life, but they may follow, rather than precede, baptism. For all of these theologians, the corporate nature of the church is primary; according to T. F. Torrance, baptism is a form of God's word which establishes and renews the church in union with Christ, through his Spirit (Baillie 1957: 80–90; cf. Torrance 1975: 82–138; Pannenberg 1998: 260–265).

Others, however, have heartily agreed with Barth's critique of infant baptism. Notably, Jürgen Moltmann embraced Barth's political critique of infant baptism as the basis of a national church, which obscures baptism's basic character as a call to free and responsible discipleship. Moltmann highlighted the eschatological nature of baptism, as the sign of Christ's resurrection from the dead, and the mark of the messianic community of the Spirit that lives already in light of the new creation. As such, baptism is to be a "public, confessional sign of resistance and hope" (Moltmann 1977: 232; cf. 226–242).

Recognizing the critiques of infant baptism as well as its powerful witness to prevenient grace, some theologians affirmed the importance of retaining both forms of baptism in the church. P. T. Forsyth, for instance, argued for recognition of both forms of baptism, since they exhibit that the church is both a voluntary association (constituted by free human response), and the spiritual body of Christ called into being by God's grace that precedes the individual. A difference in practice, he argued, should not be the basis of church separation (Forsyth 1917: 214–220). Decades later, BEM emphasized that both forms of baptism witness to God's initiative in Christ as well as the response of faith in the believing community (BEM 1982: "Baptism" par. 12, commentary). Even among theologians who continue to defend their opposing positions, ecumenical dialogue has led to significant new appreciation for the insights of the other—as for instance among

Baptists who acknowledge that infant baptism witnesses to valid Christian insights (Wagner 1983: 26; cf. Fiddes 1996: 60), and Reformed theologian David Wright, who concluded shortly before his death: "I am now inclined to regard infant baptism as consistent with scripture but not required by it ... What cannot be claimed for it on credible biblical grounds is that it is normative baptism, whether theologically or practically" (Wright 2007: 372).

Baptism as Event, Process, and Identity

Rather than focusing on baptism as a solitary event, many Protestant theologians and ecumenical documents have turned attention to the water rite of baptism as part of a larger process of initiation, and as the foundation of a lifelong Christian identity. This has raised some ambiguities regarding the term "baptism" itself. As James D. G. Dunn pointed out, "baptism" in recent decades has become a "concertina word," expanding to refer to a whole process, or contracting to refer to the water rite alone (Dunn 1970: 5). Twentieth-century scholarship wrestled with how to understand "baptism" properly in the New Testament; T. F. Torrance and Dunn, for instance, disagreed sharply on this. Nevertheless, Protestant baptismal theology in this period generally expanded attention to the connection of the rite itself to the whole process of conversion-initiation, and to the whole of life.

Attention to baptism as the culmination of a process of initiation—or as the name for that whole process—has been largely due to recognition that in the early church the water rite was embedded in the larger context of baptismal preparation (catechumenate) and included rites of anointing and hand-laying that the Western church later separated out as "confirmation." An emphasis on the "unified rites of initiation" was reaffirmed in the late twentieth century by Lutherans, Reformed, Methodists, and Anglicans, even when they continued to practice "confirmation" as a separate event (Brunner 1968: 86f; Jenson 1978: 152–168; Holeton, 1983: 68–89; White 1983: 49–51; Lathrop 1993: 59–68; Pannenberg 1998: 265–272).

Parallel with this development, some Protestant theologians have placed fresh emphasis on baptism as the basis of a new identity that is lived out over a lifetime. Pannenberg, for instance, argued that baptism constitutes Christian identity, establishing a relation between the individual and Christ. "Baptism is the basis of a new human identity outside the self—an identity that we have then to appropriate and work out in the whole process of our life history" (Pannenberg 1998: 274). T. F. Torrance, while not dismissing the importance of human reception, argued forcefully that baptism in Christ is complete, not the beginning of a process to be finished later. The New Testament Greek *baptisma* refers first to the mystery of Christ crucified and risen, and only secondarily to the church's act by which we are engrafted into Christ. Any description of baptism as process should be viewed with caution, lest it detract from the objective finished work of Christ (Torrance 1975: 90, 97f).

Baptism by Water and the Spirit

Twentieth- and twenty-first-century Protestant theologies of baptism have also focused much attention on the relationship between baptism by water and baptism of the Spirit. This was prompted by several developments, including an outpouring of interest in eschatology (prompted partly by Schweitzer's work at the turn of the twentieth century); the emergence of the Pentecostal/charismatic movement; and reconsideration of confirmation's relationship to baptism, which raised the question of the relationship between water baptism and the reception of the Spirit.

Since the turn of the twentieth century, Pentecostal theologians have preached and written on the significance of Spirit baptism as a gift of power distinct from water baptism. Informed particularly by the preaching of John the Baptizer (who distinguished baptism of repentance from baptism of the Spirit) and the book of Acts, Pentecostal Christians view water baptism not as a converting sacrament, but as public witness to conversion and commitment to Christ. Aimee Semple McPherson, pioneering Pentecostal preacher, described water baptism as a sign of separation from the old life, "the burial of the past and the birth of the new" (McPherson 1931: 90; cf. Land 1993: 114f). Spirit baptism, which is usually a second event, is more closely connected with participation in God, the gift of "divine life," which empowers the believer for the kind of work seen in Jesus' life of healing and teaching. Spirit baptism itself does not "save," but it confirms the Spirit's presence in the believer's life and empowers her for ministry. Speaking in tongues usually evidences the initial gift of baptism in the Spirit. "Spirit baptism" can mean both the initial charismatic event and the ongoing experience of receiving the Spirit in life (Albrecht 1999: 231).

Some non-Pentecostal Protestant theologians have agreed with the distinction between water and Spirit baptism. Barth in his later work saw a significant difference between the two: water baptism was the public ethical response of the believer to the prior reception of the Spirit, which awakened faith and thus marked the actual movement of a person into the Christian life (Barth 1969). In similar fashion, James D. G. Dunn argued that in the New Testament, Spirit baptism was a definite and dramatic experience, distinct from water baptism, which constituted the central event of the process of "conversion-initiation." While he disagreed with the Pentecostal interpretation that Spirit baptism was an entirely separate stage of salvation, he affirmed the significance of this event as the true beginning of the Christian life. In this way, he sharply disagreed with T. F. Torrance that *baptisma* in the New Testament refers to the whole complex of salvation events that must always be held together, with the Spirit working in and through the water rite (Dunn 1970: 4–6).

Others have emphasized the unity of water and Spirit baptism, based on alternate readings of the New Testament witness. Cullmann, for instance, argued that the new element in Christian baptism, which distinguished it from Jewish proselyte baptism or John's baptism of repentance, is the gift of the Spirit. Baptism, which is participation in Christ's death and resurrection brings both forgiveness of sins (immersion) and new life/gift of the Spirit (emergence) (Cullmann 1950: 13–15; cf. Pannenberg 1998: 259–260, 279–280; BEM 1982: par. 14). Peter Brunner and T. F. Torrance both emphasized that Christian baptism has from the beginning been understood to include the Pentecost event, which is connected with the charismatic Spirit (Brunner 1968: 88; Torrance 1975: 82–105). Torrance criticizes Barth for his separation of water and Spirit baptism, and offers his own fully Trinitarian understanding of baptism as an act of God the Father through the Son and in the Spirit—a unified act that cannot be separated into discrete events. Robert Jenson agreed that New Testament baptism included the gift of the Spirit, and pointed out that this did not always mean a particular experience of the baptized, but indicated entrance into a community that included prophets and charismatics (Jenson 1978: 130f).

Critique of the Baptismal Formula

Since the 1970s, North American feminists have raised particular concern about the dissonance between the freedom and new life proclaimed at baptism and the oppression perpetuated by the traditional baptismal formula that uses only language of "Father, Son, and Holy Spirit." Ruth Duck, in particular, has argued that the liberating truth of baptism is undermined by the traditional language, and has proposed alternatives that affirm the triune nature of God without gendered language (Duck 1991; cf. Ramshaw 1994). One amplified baptismal formula that has been used with increasing frequency by many North American Protestant churches in recent years comes from the Riverside Church in New York City: "I baptize you in the name of the Father, and of the Son, and of the Holy Spirit; one God, Mother of us all." The discussion of language used at baptism continues to be central to ecumenical sacramental conversations, and most Protestants engaged in those dialogues seek to honor the long tradition of baptismal practice while also listening to the voices of those who have been harmed by the teaching of the church regarding the Trinitarian name of God.

SUGGESTED READING

Fahey (2007); Spinks (2006).

BIBLIOGRAPHY

Albrecht, Daniel (1999), *Rites in the Spirit: A Ritual Approach to Pentecostal/Charismatic Spirituality* (Sheffield: Sheffield Academic Press, 1999).
Baillie, Donald (1957), *The Theology of the Sacraments and Other Papers* (New York: Charles Scribner's Sons).
Baptism, Eucharist, and Ministry (1982) (Geneva: World Council of Churches).
Barth, Karl (1948), *The Teaching of the Church Regarding Baptism* (London: SCM Press).

Barth, Karl (1957), *Church Dogmatics II.1: The Doctrine of God, Part 1* (Edinburgh: T. & T. Clark).

Barth, Karl (1967), *Church Dogmatics IV:2: The Doctrine of Reconciliation* (Edinburgh: T. & T. Clark), 55.

Barth, Karl (1969), *Church Dogmatics IV.4: The Doctrine of Reconciliation* (Edinburgh: T. & T. Clark).

Bieler, Andrea and Luise Schottroff (2007), *The Eucharist: Bodies, Bread, and Resurrection* (Minneapolis, MN: Fortress Press).

Boersma, Hans (2011), *Heavenly Participation: The Weaving of a Sacramental Tapestry* (Grand Rapids, MI: Eerdmans).

Bradshaw, Paul F. (1992), *The Search for the Origins of Christian Worship: Sources and Methods for the Study of Early Liturgy* (Oxford: Oxford University Press).

Bradshaw, Paul F. (2009), *Reconstructing Early Christian Worship* (London: SPCK).

Brunner, Peter (1968), *Worship in the Name of Jesus* (St. Louis, MI: Concordia Publishing House).

Bultmann, Rudolf (1951), *Theology of the New Testament*, vol. 1, trans. Kendrick Grobel (New York: Charles Scribner's Sons).

Cross, Anthony R. and Philip E. Thompson (eds.) (2007), *Baptist Sacramentalism* (Carlisle: Paternoster Press).

Cullmann, Oscar (1950), *Baptism in the New Testament* (Naperville, IL: Alec R. Allenson, Inc.).

Duck, Ruth (1991), *Gender and the Name of God: The Trinitarian Baptismal Formula* (New York: Pilgrim Press).

Dunn, James D. G. (1970), *Baptism in the Holy Spirit: A Re-examination of the New Testament Teaching on the Gift of the Spirit in Relation to Pentecostalism Today* (Naperville, IL: Alec R. Allenson, Inc.).

Ellis, Christopher (1996), "Baptism and the Sacramental Freedom of God," in Paul Fiddes (ed.), *Reflections on the Water* (Oxford: Regent's Park College), 23–45.

Fahey, Michael A. (2007), "Sacraments," in John Webster, Kathryn Tanner, and Iain Torrance (eds.), *The Oxford Handbook of Systematic Theology* (Oxford: Oxford University Press), 267–284.

Farwell, James (2005), *This Is the Night: Suffering, Salvation, and the Liturgies of Holy Week* (Edinburgh: T. & T. Clark).

Fiddes, Paul S. (ed.) (1996), *Reflections on the Water: Understanding God and the World through the Baptism of Believers* (Oxford: Regent's Park College).

Forsyth, P. T. (1917), *The Church and the Sacraments* (London: Independent Press).

George, Timothy (1993), "The Reformed Doctrine of Believers' Baptism," *Interpretation* 47: 242–254; repr. as "Believers' Baptism: More Than American Individualism," *Modern Reformation* 6 (1997): 41–47.

Holeton, David R. (1983), "Confirmation in the 1980s," in Max Thurian (ed.), *Ecumenical Perspectives on Baptism, Eucharist, and Ministry* (Geneva: World Council of Churches), 68–89.

Hunsinger, George (2008), *The Eucharist and Ecumenism: Let Us Keep the Feast* (Cambridge: Cambridge University Press).

Jenson, Robert (1978), *Visible Words: The Interpretation and Practice of Christian Sacraments* (Philadelphia, PA: Fortress Press).

Johnson, Maxwell (2007), "Christian Initiation in the Churches Today," in *The Rites of Christian Initiation*, revised and expanded ed. (Collegeville, MI: Liturgical Press), 375–450.

Kidd, Richard (1996), "Baptism and the Identity of Christian Communities," in Paul S. Fiddes (ed.), *Reflections on the Water: Understanding God and the World through the Baptism of Believers* (Oxford: Regent's Park College), 85–99.

Land, Stephen Jack (1994), *Pentecostal Spirituality: A Passion for the Kingdom* (Sheffield: Sheffield Academic Press).

Lathrop, Gordon W. (1993), *Holy Things: A Liturgical Theology* (Minneapolis, MN: Fortress Press).

Macchia, Frank D. (2006), *Baptized in the Spirit: A Global Pentecostal Theology* (Grand Rapids, MI: Zondervan Press).

McClendon, James William, Jr. (1994), *Systematic Theology: Doctrine* (Nashville, TN: Abingdon Press), 386–406.

McPherson, Aimee Semple (1931), *The Holy Spirit* (Los Angeles, CA: Challpin Publishing Co.).

Moltmann, Jürgen (1977), *The Church in the Power of the Spirit: A Contribution to Messianic Ecclesiology* (New York: Harper and Row).

Moore-Keish, Martha L. (2008), *Do This in Remembrance of Me: A Ritual Approach to Reformed Eucharistic Theology* (Grand Rapids, MI: Eerdmans Publishing Co.).

Pannenberg, Wolfhart (1998), *Systematic Theology*, vol. 3, trans. Geoffrey W. Bromiley (Grand Rapids, MI: Eerdmans).

Pickstock, Catherine (1998), *After Writing: On the Liturgical Consummation of Philosophy* (Oxford: Blackwell Publishers).

Ramshaw, Gail (1994), *Words Around the Font* (Chicago: Liturgy Training Publications).

Rowland, Christopher (1996), "A Response: Anglican Reflections," in Paul S. Fiddes (ed.), *Reflections on the Water: Understanding God and the World through the Baptism of Believers* (Oxford: Regent's Park College), 117–134.

Spinks, Bryan (2006), *Reformation and Modern Rituals and Theologies of Baptism: From Luther to Contemporary Practices* (Aldershot: Ashgate).

Tillich, Paul (1948), *The Protestant Era* (Chicago: University of Chicago Press).

Tillich, Paul (1963), *Systematic Theology*, vol. 3 (Chicago: University of Chicago Press).

Torrance, T. F. (1975), *Theology in Reconciliation* (London: Chapman).

Wagner, Gunter (1983), "Baptism from Accra to Lima," in Max Thurian (ed.), *Ecumenical Perspectives on Baptism, Eucharist, and Ministry* (Geneva: World Council of Churches), 12–32.

Wainwright, Geoffrey (1983), "Introduction" (Liturgies of the Eucharist), in Max Thurian and Geoffrey Wainwright (eds.), *Baptism and Eucharist: Ecumenical Convergence in Celebration* (Geneva: World Council of Churches), 99–110.

White, James (1983), *Sacraments as God's Self-Giving* (Nashville, TN: Abingdon Press).

Wright, David F. (2007), "Scripture and Evangelical Diversity with Special Reference to the Baptismal Divide" and "*Baptism, Eucharist and Ministry* (the 'Lima Report'): An Evangelical Assessment," in idem (ed.), *Infant Baptism in Historical Perspective: Collected Studies* (Milton Keynes: Paternoster Press), 285–300, 308–326.

Yoder, John Howard (1992), *Body Politics: Five Practices of the Christian Community before the Watching World* (Nashville, TN: Discipleship Resources).

Part II: The Lord's Supper in Twentieth-Century and Contemporary Protestant Theology

GEORGE HUNSINGER

PROTESTANT views of the Lord's Supper during this period ran the gamut from unbending traditionalism to ecumenical innovation, with a variety of gradations in between. "Real presence" and "eucharistic sacrifice"—the traditional sticking points—were addressed in various ways. Particular views of *epiclesis* (the invocation of the Holy Spirit) and *anamnesis* (eucharistic memorial or remembrance) generally depended on these prior questions. How the Lord's Supper could be conceived in a way that would promote Christian unity without falling into unacceptable compromise remained a pressing question.

REAL PRESENCE

As suggested by Brian Gerrish (Gerrish 1966), Protestant views of the Lord's Supper can be categorized under three main headings: "symbolic memorialism," "symbolic parallelism," and "symbolic instrumentalism." These terms point to the diversity that prevails in Protestant understandings of "real presence."

1. Symbolic memorialism. This is the view that the bread and wine in the Lord's Supper are simply signs or reminders of a salvation accomplished by Christ in the past and communicated to believers in the present through the Word of God. The bread and wine are not converted into Christ's body and blood in the Lord's Supper. They serve to recall, confirm, or seal salvation, but not to communicate or transmit it. The "real presence" of Christ to the faithful is not tied to the bread and wine.

A strong representative of this view was Markus Barth, the Swiss Reformed New Testament scholar (Barth 1987). The Lord's Supper was a communal meal linked to Passover and future expectation. The connection with Passover showed that the Supper was a meal in memory of Christ's death, not a sacrifice. It was a celebrative, not a redemptive event; a response to grace, not a means of grace. All should be welcome to participate in the joyful feast, especially Jews (just as Christians may be welcome at a Seder). The only relevant conversion was of the faithful through the Word of God, not of the bread and wine. Christ's "real presence" to the community occurred not only through the Word but also in the form of the poor and needy. Eating and drinking joyfully prefigured eating and drinking in the kingdom of God.

Others who exemplified symbolic memorialism were the American Mennonite John Howard Yoder (Yoder 1992), the Canadian Baptist Stanley Grenz (Grenz 1994), and many "free church" theologians (including Pentecostals and charismatics). By the end of the twentieth century, this view would have been accepted by perhaps 20 percent of world Christianity (Jacobsen 2011).

2. Symbolic parallelism. The key to this view is the syntax of "*as ... so also simultaneously.*" As the bread and wine are received by the faithful, so also does Christ impart himself spiritually at the same time. Christ is present with (but not in) the consecrated elements. The focus is on the sacramental action of eating and drinking, not on the elements themselves. They receive a new sacramental use but not a new metaphysical status. They do not contain and communicate Christ's life-giving flesh, although they do symbolically represent it. Christ's body and blood are received by faith but not by the mouth. Whereas the "memorialist" view is associated with Zwingli, this view is associated with Calvin.

The German Reformed theologian Otto Weber (Weber 1955) exemplified this view. As a form of God's Word, the Lord's Supper was more nearly a temporal than a spatial event. The focus was not on the bread and wine but on the sacramental action. In contrast to the "memorialist" view, Christ was really present sacramentally (not just through the Word), and in the Supper he gave himself to the faithful along with the bread and wine. In receiving them the faithful received a share in Christ's salvation and in the new covenant he introduced. His "real presence" involved a future orientation. It was the presence of the Coming One by whom history would attain its fulfillment in the Heavenly Banquet.

Symbolic parallelism was embraced by other Reformed theologians such as Herman Bavinck (Bavinck 1901), G. C. Berkouwer (Berkouwer 1954), and Thomas F. Torrance (Torrance 1976). Found mainly among the Reformed and those influenced by the Reformed (e.g. some Episcopalians, Methodists, and Baptists), this view would have been present in no more than 5 percent of world Christianity by the century's end (Jacobsen 2011).

3. Symbolic instrumentalism. According to this view the consecrated bread and wine become mediators of Christ's body and blood. As in all Protestant conceptions, the Roman Catholic doctrine of transubstantiation is seen as something studiously to be avoided. The bread and wine do not cease to be bread and wine, yet Christ joins himself to them by a sacramental union to impart his life-giving flesh. Christ is received by faith even as he is received also by the mouth, though he is received by the mouth even when he is not received by faith. His "real presence" is tied firmly to the elements. He is not only present with them, but also in and under them. This view is associated with Luther, though aspects of it appear occasionally in Calvin.

Wolfhart Pannenberg, the German Lutheran theologian, represented this outlook (Pannenberg 1988). Christ was present to the community in the bread and wine under the aspects of his body and blood. His prior presence by the Spirit was the basis of his "real presence" in bread and wine. This presence was not brought about by human action but solely by the Spirit. The change in the elements was "mystical" but not substantial.

Through them Christ's life-giving flesh was orally received. The bread disappeared when eaten but not Christ's body, into which the faithful were spiritually incorporated. The Supper granted fellowship with Christ, the forgiveness of sins, and the hope of his eternal kingdom.

Other exponents of this view were the Danish Lutheran Regin Prenter (Prenter 1958) and the German Lutheran Peter Brunner (Brunner 1954), along with many Anglicans (e.g. Dix 1949; Pickstock 1998) and also many Methodists (e.g. White 1999; Westerfield Tucker 2002).

When one considers world Christianity taken as a whole—with about 65 percent consisting of the high sacramental churches (Roman Catholic and Eastern Orthodox) and perhaps another 10 percent constituted by Protestant churches holding to a high view of the Eucharist (Lutherans, many Anglicans and Episcopalians, also many Methodists)—it would appear that "symbolic instrumentalism"—in one form or another—was not only the most ancient Christian view of "real presence," but also the most widespread at the century's end. (While memorialists and parallelists might claim antiquity for their views, they could not claim unbroken continuity for them prior to the sixteenth century.) (Jacobsen 2011).

Eucharistic Sacrifice

Some important convergences exist ecumenically on the question of eucharistic sacrifice. All churches can agree that the Eucharist involves "a sacrifice of thanks and praise." They can also agree that Christ's sacrifice on the cross was a once-for-all event that cannot be repeated. Finally, there is general agreement that as the faithful give thanks in the Lord's Supper, they also offer themselves as a living sacrifice to God (Rom. 12:1).

Nevertheless, three main divergences remain. First, most Protestants would not agree that the Lord's Supper re-presents Christ's sacrifice sacramentally. Second, they would not agree that the church can offer Christ as a sacrifice to God. Finally, and perhaps most intractably, they would not agree with the Council of Trent that the Eucharist must be seen as a propitiatory sacrifice. Protestants see these divergences as required by the central themes of the Reformation.

In a study of the early Church Fathers, Rowan Williams concluded that the Eucharist was an offering back to God of what was given to the faithful in Christ (Williams 1982). Although the Eucharist memorialized Christ's sacrifice, it neither repeated nor re-presented it. It was not the faithful who took Christ to themselves, but more fundamentally, Christ who took them to himself, in his own self-offering to the Father. This did not involve an active offering by the community of Christ's body and blood in the Eucharist. There was no need for a continual propitiation of the Father's wrath. The faithful rather participated in Christ's completed self-offering in a way that entailed profound personal commitment. "If we are to be fully a gift to the Father, given by ourselves yet also by and through the crucified Jesus, by our association with that prior gift, we must bear the cost—which is the loss of all we do and all we possess to defend ourselves against God" (Williams 1982: 29). As deep as Williams's reflections were, they did not go far in resolving the remaining points of ecumenical divergence.

Wolfhart Pannenberg suggested that the Eucharist could be seen as a sacrifice while still meeting the concerns of the Reformation (Pannenberg 1988). The Eucharist was neither an additional offering to God beyond that of Calvary, nor were the faithful or the celebrant independent actors alongside Christ. In the Eucharist the faithful were drawn into Christ's own self-offering to the Father. "The congregations do in faith what the celebrants depict by their actions and words, and what they depict is the action of Jesus Christ himself as the one who invites us to the Supper but who also sacrifices himself in it" (Pannenberg 1988: 317). It was not the faithful who offered Christ, but Christ who offered them. He brought them to participate in the effects of his perfect self-offering on the cross. By entrusting themselves to Christ, the faithful offered themselves through him in the signs of bread and wine. The Eucharist was not only a sacrifice of thanks and praise, but also a sacrifice in which forgiveness was received and sin was removed. Although Pannenberg made great strides toward ecumenical convergence, important details were left rather vague, and the problem of "propitiation" (the removal of wrath), which remained so important to the Vatican, was unresolved.

A strong doctrine of eucharistic sacrifice was developed by T. F. Torrance (Torrance 1976). His contribution was essentially threefold. First, there could be no "real presence" of Christ in the Eucharist without the presence of his saving work, because his person and his work were one. Second, the indivisible and unrepeatable act of atonement in Jesus Christ assumed two different forms. The constitutive form was the cross while the mediating form was the Eucharist. The Eucharist had no significance in itself that was not derived from the cross and grounded in it. Finally, Christ himself functioned vicariously as our human response to God. It was by grace through faith that the faithful were brought to participate in his perfect self-offering to the Father as it had occurred in their place and on their behalf. With their sacrifice of thanks and praise, the faithful were sanctified by Christ and taken up into the eternal intercession of his one atoning sacrifice. His finished and perpetual self-offering, as sacramentally re-presented in the Eucharist, served as the means of their eternal access to the Father. As his work was made theirs in the Eucharist, there was one sacrifice common to Christ and the church.

Despite this great step forward, Torrance, like Pannenberg, left points of ecumenical divergence unaddressed. In his case it was not clear whether Christ was really present in the consecrated elements under the aspects of his body and blood. Nor was it clear whether the faithful and the celebrant offered Christ to the Father in the bread and wine, even as Christ took them all up and incorporated them into his one indivisible sacrifice. Again, it remained unclear how the Eucharist might have propitiatory significance in a way that could satisfy both the Vatican and the Reformation. Not until after the turn of the twenty-first century would a Protestant proposal appear that attempted to resolve all points of divergence in a way that would accord with both Trent and the Reformation (Hunsinger 2008).

EPICLESIS AND ANAMNESIS

Some issues in the Eucharist pertaining to *epiclesis* (the invocation of the Holy Spirit) and *anamnesis* (memorial or remembrance) include the following:

- Does the Spirit bless only the faithful, making them receptive of grace in the Eucharist, or does the Spirit also bless the bread and wine so that they become Christ's body and blood?
- Is *anamnesis* a mental act of remembrance over and above the eucharistic celebration, or is the celebration itself the *anamnesis* in the form of a communal memorial?
- Does the memorial involve only celebration, reception, and thanksgiving, or does it also have a sacrificial character?
- Are the past events of salvation simply recalled in the Eucharist, or are they actually made present by the Spirit in the memorial?
- Does the Spirit also make present the promised future in an anticipation of the heavenly banquet?

These questions are answered in a way that reflects a theology's basic stance toward the Lord's Supper.

For "symbolic memorialism" the answers are relatively straightforward. The Spirit may perhaps bless the faithful, but does not convert the bread and wine into Christ's body and blood. *Anamnesis* is an act of mental recollection, not the celebration itself. It does not have a sacrificial character apart from being a sacrifice of thanks and praise. The past events of salvation are not made present, just as the future of salvation may be anticipated but not made present. Theologians such as M. Barth, Yoder and Grenz would reflect this basic pattern. They tend to incorporate a strong social and ethical element into their understanding of the Lord's Supper.

For "symbolic parallelism" the answers are slightly different. Along with blessing the faithful, the Spirit may also be thought to bless the bread and wine, but not to convert them into Christ's body and blood. It is Christ himself who is thought to be made present more than saving events, although he is present as the one who has accomplished salvation in the past and who will bring it to fulfillment in the future. The *anamnesis* remains more a matter of mental recollection than of liturgical enactment. Beyond thanks and praise it involves no particular sacrificial element. Weber, Bavinck, and Berkouwer would more or less fit this pattern, while Torrance would be somewhat of an exception because of his convergences with symbolic instrumentalism.

Finally, for "symbolic instrumentalism" the Spirit not only blesses the faithful that they might receive the eucharistic gifts, but also transforms the bread and the wine. In this transformation they do not cease to be bread and wine, but Christ himself enters into sacramental union with the elements, through the Spirit, under the aspects of his body and blood. The *anamnesis* is generally thought to make present, by the power of the Spirit, the saving events of the past and the future. It is more a matter of being a communal memorial than simply a mental recollection. The *anamnesis* is therefore also eschatological, anticipating the Heavenly Banquet, along with being a sacramental re-presentation of Christ's sacrifice. Pannenberg, Dix, Pickstock, and others would exemplify this eucharistic outlook.

SUGGESTED READING

Torrance (1976); Williams (1982); Yoder (1992).

BIBLIOGRAPHY

Barth, Markus (1987), *Das Mahl des Herrn: Gemeinschaft mit Israel, mit Christus und unter den Gästen* (Neukirchen: Neukirchener Verlag) (English: *Rediscovering the Lord's Supper: Communion with Israel, with Christ, and among the Guests* [Atlanta, GA: John Knox Press], 1988 [abridged]).

Bavinck, Herman (1901), *Gereformeerde dogmatiek*, Deel 4 (Kampen: J. H. Bos) (English: *Reformed Dogmatics: Holy Spirit, Church and New Creation* [Grand Rapids, MI: Baker Academic], 2008).

Berkouwer, G. C. (1954), *De Sakramenten* (Kampen: J. H. Kok) (English: *Studies in Dogmatics: The Sacraments* [Grand Rapids, MI: Eerdmans], 1969).

Brunner, Peter (1954), *Zur Lehre vom Gottesdienst der im Namen Jesu versammelten Gemeinde* (Kassel: Johannes Stauda Verlag) (English: *Worship in the name of Jesus* [St. Louis, MI: Concordia Publishing House, 1968]).

Dix, Gregory (1949), *The Shape of the Liturgy* (Westminster: Dacre Press).

Gerrish, Brian (1966), "The Lord's Supper in the Reformed Confessions," *Theology Today* 23/2: 224–243.

Grenz, Stanley J. (1994), *Theology for the Community of God* (Nashville, TN: Broadman & Holman).

Hunsinger, George (2008), *The Eucharist and Ecumenism: Let Us Keep the Feast* (Cambridge: Cambridge University Press).

Jacobsen, Douglas (2011), *The World's Christians* (Oxford: Wiley-Blackwell, 2011).

Pannenberg, Wolfhart (1988), *Systematische Theologie*, Band 3, (Göttingen: Vandenhoeck & Ruprecht) (English: Systematic Theology. vol. 3 [Grand Rapids, MI: Eerdmans], 1993).

Pickstock, Catherine (1998), *After Writing. On the Liturgical Consummation of Philosophy* (Oxford: Blackwell).

Prenter, Regin (1958), *Schöpfung und Erlösung: Dogmatik* (Göttingen: Vandenhoeck & Ruprecht) (English: *Creation and Redemption* [Philadelphia, PA: Fortress Press], 1967).

Torrance, Thomas F. (1976) "The Paschal Mystery of Christ and the Eucharist," in idem, *Theology in Reconciliation* (Grand Rapids, MI: Eerdmans): 106–38.

Weber, Otto (1955), *Grundlagen der Dogmatik*, Band 2 (Neukirchen: Neukirchener Verlag) (English: *Foundations of Dogmatics*, vol. 2 [Grand Rapids: MI: Eerdmans], 1981).

Westerfield Tucker, Karen B. (2002), "'Let Us Thy Mercy Prove': A United Methodist Understanding of the Eucharist," *Quarterly Review* 22/3: 234–47.

White, James F. (1999), *The Sacraments in Protestant Practice and Faith* (Nashville, TN: Abingdon Press).

Williams, Rowan (1982), *Eucharistic Sacrifice: The Roots of a Metaphor*, Grove Liturgical Study, No. 31 (Bramcote: Grove Books).

Yoder, John Howard (1992), *Body Politics* (Scottdale, PA: Herald Press).

CHAPTER 27

....

CATHOLIC SACRAMENTAL THEOLOGY IN THE TWENTIETH CENTURY

....

PETER J. CASARELLA

CHARLES TAYLOR, in reflecting upon the "Enlightened narrative" of modernity proposed by Edward Gibbon, hits upon the idea of the ratchet effect (Taylor 2007: 273). Gibbon realized that modernity would never take hold all at once but could not specify the process whereby modernity's effects would become permanent. As Taylor further narrates, certain effects of the imposition of the fully modern "buffered self" will be sufficiently hardy to prevent any backsliding to pre-modern naiveté while other elements will be subject to a great deal of negotiation. Ratcheting hardens the more dynamic possibility of modern progress as a living, organic process. In fact, the ratchet effect conforms to what Taylor calls the subtractive theory of secularization. In this view, as the new goods of secularism are installed, the old unmodern practices are sent into the oblivion of a conceptual Goodwill store. Here only the hidden underprivileged side of humanity can use them.

In other words, the Catholic experience of the sacraments went through an upheaval in the twentieth century, and that process of transformation was more like a selectively applied ratchet effect than steady, uniform, and linear progress. The metaphor does not speak just to the erratic pace of change. The ratchet also allows one to see in sociocultural terms how the rapid accumulation of new approaches needs to encompass in its view and without dilution the ongoing witness of Christ in the church. To remain with Taylor's metaphor (and give it a new twist), Christ remains the toothed gear that turns. The sacramental experience of God in the church through the encounter with the person of Jesus Christ is the single most recurring leitmotif of twentieth-century Catholic theology. The progressive efforts at rediscovery allow for more active participation in the encounter, but the ratchet *qua ratchet* of liturgical progress can also impede any organic attempt to preserve what is old with what is new. Sociologist Michael Tomasello makes this claim generally about human development and cites as just one example the introduction of processed food in the course of the twentieth century. The parallelism seems apt, for those who favor the unmodern prayer of traditional liturgy today occupy the same cultural space as the slow food movement.

Eucharist and Sacrifice: Spiritual Renewal in the Early Twentieth Century

The century that began with a commercial, technological, and social revolution epitomized by the dissemination of light bulbs, telephones, the mechanical reproduction of images, and world wars also underwent a wave of liturgical renewal. The beginnings of liturgical scholarship had already arisen in the Roman Catholic Church in 1832, when the French Benedictine abbey at Solesmes was refounded under Dom Prosper Guéranger. Benedictines pioneered the restoration of the Roman liturgy to its medieval form. At first Guéranger focused on studying and recovering authentic Gregorian chant and the liturgical forms of the Middle Ages, but their efforts at renewal had a far broader impact. At the end of the nineteenth century, one work of liturgical theology in particular illuminated a path of intensely Christocentric liturgical spirituality informed by the Fathers of the Church that many would follow in the twentieth century, namely, Matthias Scheeben's *The Mysteries of Christianity* (1865–1897). But there were also other liturgical reformers in the early decades who carried forward that spirit of returning to the sources for the purposes of reform: Abbé Lambert Beauduin in Belgium, whose work *La Piété de l'Eglise* (1914) included new principles for liturgical reform; the highly influential Bavarian priest and scholar Romano Guardini, who in 1918 published *Vom Geist der Liturgie* (ET: *The Spirit of the Liturgy*), and the indefatigable and socially engaged monk from Collegeville, Minnesota, Virgil Michel, who in 1926 founded the journal *Orate Fratres* (now known as *Worship*), the same year that the International Eucharistic Congress was hosted by Cardinal George Mundelein at the Seminary of St. Mary of the Lake on the outskirts of Chicago. In other words, multiple currents of renewed piety and theological reflection were making their way through Europe and North America.

This rapidly changing world would be responsible for handing on Pope Leo XIII's encyclical on the Eucharist, *Mirae Caritatis*. Promulgated in 1902 when Leo was already ninety-two and close to the last year of his pontificate, the work's erudite tone masks a fervent desire for social renewal. It lies in the wake of Leo's two masterpieces, *Aeterni Patris* (1879) and *Rerum Novarum* (1891). But neither the former's defense of Thomism nor the latter's elaboration of a new Catholic social principle of subsidiarity (freeing the lowest levels of social structures to combat injustices) serve as the structuring principles of his liturgical theology.

Instead four major themes are articulated: (1) Eucharist as a source of life, (2) Eucharist as a mystery of faith, (3) Eucharist as a bond of charity, (4) The sacrifice of the

Mass. Like the great Catholic reformers of the mid nineteenth century (e.g. John Henry Newman, Johann Adam Möhler, or Scheeben), Pope Leo turns to a biblical and patristic model of sacramental renewal. Speaking to the naturalistic denial of the supernatural, Leo affirms: "Now nothing can be better adapted to promote a renewal of the strength and fervor of faith in the human mind than the mystery of the Eucharist, 'the mystery of faith,' as it has been most appropriately called" (*Mirae caritatis 7*). Leo maintains that the mutual charity awakened by the institution of the sacrament of the Eucharist will promote "Christian brotherhood and social equality" and thus help to bring the class warfare on the streets of Europe to an end (*Mirae caritatis* 11).

Frequent reception of the Eucharist is extolled as a *condicio sine qua non* for the preservation of Christianity's vitality (*Mirae caritatis* 16, 19). This basically means that worthy reception of the Eucharist could take place more than once a year. Leo's successor Pius X issued two decrees, *Sacra Tridentina Synodus* (1905) and *Quam Singulari* (1910), admonishing the faithful in similar terms. As Joseph Dougherty has demonstrated, Leo is responding on this point to an ongoing debate between two Belgian theologians, the Redemptorist François-Xavier Godts and the Jesuit Jules Lintelo, a debate that originated with the fear of Jansenists in the seventeenth century that frequent communion would gradually erode the faith (Dougherty 2010: 45–50).

The methods for moral and spiritual renewal of Leo XIII relied heavily on the promotion of popular piety, namely, eucharistic congresses, adoration sustained by new confraternities, Communion breakfasts, holy name societies and parades, rosary leagues, and the apostolate of prayer. Frequent communion is a good example of a ratchet that moved into place during the late nineteenth and early twentieth century. The appeal was openly debated in the first decade of the century and then affirmed with great approbation by the time of the Second Vatican Council. Ironically, practicing Catholics in areas of the world that offered frequent communion had already begun by the end of the century to take the new ideal for granted.

In the period right after World War I, Catholic theologians intensely debated the meaning of the eucharistic sacrifice. Maurice de la Taille, S.J. published *Mysterium Fidei* (in Latin) in 1921, and the work met with both acclaim and outright rejection. The key distinction in the work is between the sacrificial oblation and immolation (Matthiesen 2013). De la Taille places the essence of sacrifice in the act of oblation. "The supper and the cross are a single sacrifice, with Jesus acting as the priest of his death on the cross in the ritual offering of the Last Supper" (Matthiesen 2013: 25). The church enters mystically into the redemptive self-offering of God when the ritual offering is enacted. De la Taille is drawing from the tradition a new lens for seeing the participation of Christ's followers in the mystery of the Mass as sacrifice.

Abbot Anscar Vonier's *The Key to the Doctrine of the Eucharist* (1st ed., 1925) is a Thomistic counterpoint to de la Taille even though the latter's book is not mentioned therein. For de la Taille the Last Supper was the priestly oblation by Christ of the flesh that, by bloody slaughter, was sacrificed on the cross. The French school, Vonier seems to argue, makes it appear that Calvary was incomplete without the foregoing Supper and what took place there. Vonier also implies that for de la Taille, "the first Mass, which the Lord Himself celebrated in the Upper Room, is more truly the opening phase of the Sacrifice of Christ than it is the sacramental presentation of that Sacrifice" (Nichols 2003). Vonier maintains that the Holy Eucharist is the sacrament of the sacrifice of Christ. He believed that through St. Thomas's approach one could also recognize that "the sacrifice of the Mass is the expression in sign of all that our great high priest in his once-for-all offering on the Cross underwent, did, and was. Calvary and the Mass are the self-same reality, in two utterly different modes" (Nichols 2003). Like de la Taille, Abbot Vonier is offering a profoundly spiritual reading of the sacrifice of the Mass.

The Ratchet in Motion:
Mediator Dei (1947) and the
Growth of Liturgical Renewal

By the middle of the century (in the aftermath of an even more mournful and disorienting world war), theological efforts to renew the tradition by simultaneously returning to the sources and speaking to glaring social disparities were in full gear. The years between the end of World War I and the end of World War II were immensely fecund in the broader field of Catholic liturgy. Two movements coalesced and aided one another: the liturgical movement and the ecumenical movement. The exchange of gifts between East and West and between a Protestant emphasis on the salvific dimension of reading Scripture and a Catholic sense of the sacramentality of the church was also evident. Some of the more noteworthy Roman Catholic works include: Odo Casel, *Das christliche Kultmysterium* (1932, ET: *The Mystery of Christian Worship* [1962]), Henri de Lubac, *Corpus Mysticum: l'eucharistie et l'Église au Moyen âge* (1944, ET: *Corpus mysticum: The Eucharist and the Church in the Middle Ages* [2007]), Louis Bouyer, *Le Mystère Pascal* (1947, ET: *The Paschal Mystery* [1950]), Otto Semmelroth, *Vom Sinn der Sakramente* (1953, ET: *Church and Sacrament* [1965]), Edward Schillebeeckx, *Christus, sacrament van de Godsontmoeting* (1957, ET: *Christ the Sacrament of the Encounter with God* [1963]), and Cipriano Vaggagini, *Il senso teologico della liturgia* (1957, abridged ET: *Theological Dimensions of the Liturgy* [1976]). In different ways, each of these continental European theologians provided a reading of the Catholic tradition that placed the mystery of redemption in the saving work of Jesus Christ at the very center of liturgical spirituality. They emphasized the symbolic and social character of liturgical participation without diminishing the call to inward renewal.

Pius XII's encyclical reflects both enthusiasm for and caution regarding the liturgical reform that had been emerging in recent decades in Europe, above all, in the Benedictine monasteries of Belgium and Germany. But it is more than a papal gloss on these badly needed scholarly advances. It offers penetrating insights into the nature and purpose of the divine liturgy based upon the unifying leitmotif of the analogy between Christ's high priestly sacrifice and the sacrifice offered by the church: "the priesthood of Christ is a living and continuous reality through all the ages to the end of time, since the liturgy is nothing more nor less than the exercise of this priestly function" (*Mediator Dei* 22). The ordained priest represents commemoratively the death of Christ at Calvary and thus through "a true and proper act of sacrifice" leads the faithful in their self-offering into union with the mystical body of Christ (*Mediator Dei* 68; cf. 20, 69–74).

None of this recapitulation of the Tridentine doctrine is meant to exacerbate the focus on the externality of the rite. On the contrary, the unity of body and soul demands that both exterior and interior worship are fostered, but "the chief element of divine worship must be interior" (*Mediator Dei* 24, cf. 23). In this manner, the goal of worship is not just to develop a rhythm of thanksgiving both within and outside the celebration of the church's liturgy but is more antecedently the encounter with the person of Christ: "This result is, in fact, achieved when Christ lives and thrives, as it were, in the hearts of men (*sic*), and when men's hearts are in turn fashioned and expanded as though by Christ" (*Mediator Dei* 20). This explicitly "theocentric" vision of the liturgy allows for principles of active participation and a truly liturgical criteriology for the promotion of popular devotions, all of which elements would be expanded in the liturgical decree of Vatican II (*Mediator Dei* 33, cf. 172–185). Moreover, Pius XII presciently expresses a concern regarding exaggerations in the area of liturgical pragmatism, noting that the profession of the creed in the liturgy demonstrates that liturgy is at the service of doctrine as much, if not more so, than, the inverse principle (*Mediator Dei*, 46–48). In sum, Pius XII maps out a program for a theological interpretation of the liturgical life of the church that not only prepares for but undergirds the enactment of principles of liturgical reform that will follow in the subsequent decades.

Liturgical Piety after a Conciliar Awakening: *Mysterium Fidei* (1965)

Several dramatic events took place in the 1960s and early 1970s, including much heralded changes in the liturgy itself. The narratives of these epochal events already fill multiple shelves of any decent theological library. Let me focus on the underlying theological developments. First, there was intense work being done in liturgical renewal right up to the beginning of Vatican II. Major theological innovations came from Karl Rahner. His compilation from 1960, *Kirche und Sacrament*, was preceded by highly technical but still enduring studies of the notion of the symbol as well as research into the presence of Christ in the sacrament of the Lord's Supper (Rahner 1982: 221–320). Other German theologians such as Joseph Ratzinger (the future Pope Benedict XVI) and Johann Auer, author of *Das Mysterium der Eucharistie* (1971), were also making worthy contributions in this period.

The theological developments were critical but even then were overshadowed by the breathtaking news of the council itself. The Second Vatican Council began its teaching in 1963 with a document on the liturgy that allowed for a revision of the Roman rite, and the *Mass of Paul VI* came six years later. Not to be overlooked is the *Order of Christian Initiation for Adults* (1972), which today plays a decisive role in the mystagogical incorporation of the new faithful into the life of the church.

The council's lead document, *Sacrosanctum Concilium*, offered a new theological orientation to Roman Catholic liturgy. As such, it also gave impetus to the overall ecclesiological shift that was taking place in the council itself (cf. Faggioli 2010). It was the first document of the council and is the only proper lens for grasping the elusive and sometimes ideologically charged notion of "the spirit of Vatican II." I have already demonstrated that the gears for this development had been turning since the time of the liturgical reform in the nineteenth century. At its core the bishops in *Sacrosanctum Concilium* located the principle of active participation in the baptismal vocation of the lay faithful (*Sacrosanctum Concilium* 14). This is not so much a democratic takeover of institutional Catholicism as an ecclesial examination of conscience of the reason for existing as a Christian in the contemporary world. Without the portal of baptism and the sacramental grace of a baptismal faith, Catholic Christians are existentially homeless in the world. Without God there cannot be a people of God. Formation and reformation of the liturgy had to follow from this dynamic, situated, and theocentric principle of being.

What theological principles did Paul VI articulate in his encyclical of 1965, *Mysterium Fidei*, to accompany, undergird, and allow for the correct interpretation of these new practices? He is quite clear about the need to maintain a thoughtful equilibrium between tradition and innovation. He begins with a reaffirmation of what was said in the Second Vatican Council about the convergence of sacrament and sacrifice. But he still sees reason to caution errant reformers by pinpointing recent theological positions not in line with the tradition. In the very opening of *Mysterium Fidei* (11), for example, he criticizes the following ideas: (1) "to emphasize what is called the "communal" Mass to the disparagement of Masses celebrated in private"; (2) "to exaggerate the element of sacramental sign as if the symbolism, which all certainly admit in the Eucharist, expresses fully and exhausts completely the mode of Christ's presence in this sacrament"; (3) "to discuss the mystery of transubstantiation without mentioning … the marvelous conversion of the whole substance of the bread into the Body and of the whole substance of the wine into the Blood of Christ, speaking rather only of what is called 'transignification' and 'transfinalization'"; and (4) "to propose and act upon the opinion according to which, in the Consecrated Hosts which remain after the celebration of the Sacrifice of the Mass, Christ Our Lord is no longer present." His strong criticism is not meant to stifle all discussion: "We certainly do not deny that those who are spreading these strange opinions are making a praiseworthy effort to investigate this lofty Mystery and to set forth its inexhaustible riches and to make it more understandable to the men of today; rather, We acknowledge this and We approve of it" (*Mysterium Fidei* 14).

His warning to the faithful is much like that of Leo XIII at the turn of the century; he reclaims the supernatural element of the faith that is called into question by these tendencies that lead to a domestication of the mystery and its transcendence. The very idea of mystery in Paul VI's encyclical is taken from Pope Leo: "It contains within it, as Leo XIII, Our predecessor of happy memory, very wisely remarked, 'all supernatural realities in a remarkable richness and variety of miracles'" (*Mysterium Fidei* 15, citing *Mirae Caritatis* 122).

At the heart of *Mysterium Fidei* is an ancient doctrine that is already present in *Mediator Dei* and *Sacrosanctum Concilium*, namely, the teaching on the multiple presences of Christ in the Eucharist (*Mysterium Fidei* 35–39). Christ is accordingly present in the presider and in the assembly, in the offering of the sacrifice through the presider's headship and in the entire body. Most of all, he is substantially present as "a kind of consummation of the spiritual life, and in a sense the goal of all the sacraments" (*Mysterium Fidei* 38). The expanded teaching on the multiple presences of Christ in the Eucharist responds to the errors presented in the first part of the encyclical. Although based on the Fathers of the Church, it is a more modern presentation of the teaching on real presence. As articulated in the encyclical, the ratcheting is being accomplished by the activity of the incarnate Word as a response to secular modernity rather than as a necessary unfolding of the very concept of progress. The pope wants to clarify, moreover, that there is a proper use of symbolism in liturgical theology, namely, one that does not stand in opposition to real presence. He concludes that the Eucharist is a sign and cause of unity (*Mysterium Fidei* 70).

A New Pentecost: *Ecclesia de Eucharistia* (2003)

A virtual explosion of new paths to understanding the doctrinal foundations of sacramental theology were proposed during the long pontificate of John Paul II (1978–2005). For example, a lengthy survey by theologians in the United States that treated Catholic sacramental theology written in the 1980s and early 1990s concluded that "sacramental theology can no longer be done without an interdisciplinary approach" (Duffy et al. 1994: 705). They cite the Istituto de Liturgia Pastorale of Padua, founded in 1966 by the Benedictines in Santa Giustina, as a paradigm for interdisciplinary work that will promote a new approach to sacramental *praxis*. Interestingly, these authors allied the adoption of interdisciplinary methods into new thinking about sacrament in terms of a "post-Rahnerian Formulation" (Duffy et al. 1994: 665–670). While not all the methodologies, particularly those from the global South, derived from that source, Rahner's conception of *Realsymbol* and symbolic causality were assumed to be the most comprehensive benchmark. Rahnerian theological anthropology continued to play a decisive role in the Catholic sacramental imagination in this period, but the following list of contemporary works also includes phenomenology, theology of liberation, and some other non-Rahnerian approaches: Aidan

Kavanaugh, *On Liturgical Theology* (1984); Edward Kilmartin, *Christian Liturgy: Theology and Practice 1: Systematic Theology of Liturgy* (1988); Arno Schilson, *Theologie als Sakramententheologie: Die Mysterienlehre Odo Casels* (1992); Jean-Yves Lacoste, *Expérience et Absolu* (1994); Francisco Taborda, *Sacramentos, práxis e festa: para uma teologia latino-americana dos sacramentos* (1994); and Paul McPartlan, *Sacrament of Salvation: An Introduction to Eucharistic Theology* (1995).

John Paul II's encyclical *Ecclesia de Eucharistia* begins by picturing vividly two scenes, linking the image of the birth of the church at Pentecost with the institution of the Eucharist in the upper room (*Ecclesia de Eucharistia* 5). Contemporaneity is the overarching theme, allowing the pope to ponder whether the olive trees in Gethsemane were the same ones present at his Passion. These two images, one of mission into the world and another of the memorializing of the death and resurrection of the Lord, form the core of the encyclical, which comes at the end of St. John Paul's strenuous efforts at a renewal of global Catholic faith in a secularized age. It is organized around the aging pontiff's desire to renew a sense of amazement (*Ecclesia de Eucharistia* 6) in the Eucharist as well as offer a personal reflection after his own pilgrimage as bishop of Rome on the catholicity and cosmic dimension of the eucharistic prayer (*Ecclesia de Eucharistia* 7).

The first chapter, "The Mystery of Faith," explains that the celebration of the Eucharist is not a repetition of Christ's sacrifice. The pope reminds believers of their responsibility for the present earth, in which the weak, the most powerless, and the poorest await help from those who, by their solidarity, can give them reason for hope. In the second chapter, "The Eucharist Builds the Church," the consecrated bread and wine are the force that generates the church's unity. The church is united to her Lord who, veiled by the eucharistic species, dwells within her and builds her up. The third chapter is a reflection on "The Apostolicity of the Eucharist and of the Church." Following the Dogmatic Constitution on the Church at Vatican II, there is no true Eucharist without the bishop (*Lumen Gentium* 23). The priest who celebrates the Eucharist acts in the person of Christ the Head; he is its servant for the benefit of the community of the saved. It follows that the Christian community does not "possess" the Eucharist, but receives it as a gift. In the fourth chapter, he addresses "The Eucharist and Ecclesial Communion." The Eucharist cannot be "used" as a means of communion; rather it presupposes communion as already existing and strengthens it. In this context emphasis needs to be given to the commitment to ecumenism which must mark all the Lord's followers. "The Dignity of the Eucharistic Celebration" is the subject of the fifth chapter. The celebration of the "Mass" is marked by outward signs aimed at emphasizing the joy which assembles the community around the incomparable gift of the Eucharist. The final chapter, "At the School of Mary, 'Woman of the Eucharist,'" is an original reflection on the analogy between the Mother of God, who by bearing the body of Jesus in her womb became the first "tabernacle," and the church, who in her heart preserves and offers to the world Christ's body and blood. The Eucharist, he says, is given to believers so that their lives may become a continuous *Magnificat* in honor of the Most Holy Trinity.

This encyclical ties together themes of the latter years of St. John Paul's pontificate: the call for a New Evangelization, the extension of the celebration of the Jubilee Year into a spirituality of communion for the new millennium, and the presentation of the new luminous mysteries of the rosary. Although it introduces timeless themes such as the dignity and beauty of the Eucharist, it is also offered as a corrective to the shadows of postconciliar reform (*Ecclesia de Eucharistia* 10). More fundamentally, St. John Paul wants to link the theology of the Eucharist to a renewed appreciation of the mystery of the church: "The Church draws her life from the Eucharist. This truth does not simply express a daily experience of faith, but recapitulates *the heart of the mystery of the Church*" (*Ecclesia de Eucharistia* 1). Accordingly, the pervading spiritual motifs are the oneness in time between Eucharist and Passion (*Ecclesia de Eucharistia* 5) and the retrieval of the spiritual fecundity of the paschal mystery. In that light, the main response to the academic issue of interdisciplinarity is not to lose sight of the cosmic and eschatological horizon of eucharistic practice. The pope does not disparage academic creativity, but he nonetheless admonishes liturgical theologians not to confuse thanksgiving to an eternal Creator with ritualized social activism.

ECCLESIAL COMMUNION AND SOCIAL SOLIDARITY: *SACRAMENTUM CARITATIS* (2007)

Sacramentum Caritatis was promulgated in 2007 by Pope Benedict XVI. It was only the second year of his pontificate but already an opportunity to reiterate the German pontiff's long-standing interest in promoting a hermeneutic of continuity with respect to the liturgical reforms initiated by the Second Vatican Council. It overlaps in doctrinal content with his encyclical *Deus Caritas Est* and thus merits being considered alongside the other papal encyclicals we have reviewed.

In the Eucharist we are fed the "food of truth," writes Pope Benedict (*Sacramentum Caritatis* 2, cf. 91). The contemplative and aesthetic retrieval of the tradition, including "traditional" aspects of everyday life such as eating, is also evident in the more noteworthy contributions to scholarship in this period: David W. Fagerberg, *Theologia Prima: What is Liturgical Theology?* (2004); Matthew Levering, *Sacrifice and Community: Jewish Offering and Christian Eucharist* (2005); Alejandro García-Rivera and Tom Scirghi, *Living Beauty: The Art of Liturgy* (2008); and Angel F. Méndez-Montoya, *Theology of Food: Eating and the Eucharist* (2009). Paradoxically, the twenty-first century is thus simultaneously more open than its predecessor to the spiritual content of an unratcheted tradition *and* more focused than before on the unfiltered, everyday aspects of contemporary life. The theologians just enumerated attempt what seemed *least* possible according to the bifurcating, Gnostic logic of the ratchet of progress, namely, that there could be direct cross-fertilization between pre-modern liturgical materiality and late modern spiritual conditioning of human experience.

The principal aim of *Sacramentum Caritatis* is to encourage "the Christian people to deepen their understanding of the relationship between the eucharistic mystery, the liturgical action, and the new spiritual worship which derives from the Eucharist as the sacrament of charity" (*Sacramentum Caritatis* 5). In fact, Christ himself is this sacrament: "The sacrament of charity, the Holy Eucharist is the gift that Jesus Christ makes of himself, thus revealing to us God's infinite love for every man and woman" (*Sacramentum Caritatis* 1). Other themes such as the nuptial mystery in the Eucharist as a form of renewal of the sacrament of marriage revolve around this central claim. Following in the footsteps of the liturgical reform movement, Pope Benedict shows that the Eucharist is a gift from the Trinity that is celebrated as an ecclesial event.

In the light of a recent synod, Pope Benedict reclaims many of the central insights of *Sacrosanctum Concilium*: the bishop as the principal presider in every liturgy, the sacramentality of the church seen in and through each of its sacraments, active participation of the faithful in the eucharistic sacrifice, the revival of mystagogy as a practice of liturgical renewal, and the placement of practices such as eucharistic adoration within the liturgical rhythms of the church. The most central teaching of the council, the active participation (*actuosa participatio*) of all the laity, is also subjected to a lengthy analysis (*Sacramentum Caritatis* 52–63). Basically, he critiques any subjective and individualistic excesses that have been attached to this doctrine in order to bring it back to the idea that Christ is the food of truth. Hunger for the Eucharist presupposes and is reinforced by formation in the mystagogical dimensions of the new rite and even more basically into the proper eucharistic sense of participation in the entire, globally inculturated mission of Christian existence. Alongside personal reconciliation with the Lord, "the faithful need to be reminded that there can be no *actuosa participatio* in the sacred mysteries without an accompanying effort to participate actively in the life of the Church as a whole, including a missionary commitment to bring Christ's love into the life of society" (*Sacramentum Caritatis* 55).

The exhortation closes with a fervent call to connect the celebration of the pascal mystery in the Eucharist with social concerns:

> The union with Christ brought about by the Eucharist also brings a newness to our social relations: 'this sacramental "mysticism" is social in character'. . . . The relationship between the eucharistic mystery and social commitment must be made explicit. (*Sacramentum Caritatis* 89)

Pope Benedict famously repudiated all attempts to confuse Jesus' message of the Kingdom with a social utopia. The church, he states, cannot adopt the role of fashioning the most perfect political utopia possible (*Sacramentum Caritatis* 89). At the same time, he rules out altogether the laissez-faire attitude of standing on the sidelines. The strengthening of our communion with our neighbors is accomplished in the sacramental mystery by God. Given the grace-filled gift that infuses our being and acting, Christians cannot remain indifferent to unjust social structures.

FOUR CONTESTED ISSUES

After Heidegger: Presence and Gift

The publication of Martin Heidegger's *Being and Time* in 1927 was a watershed event in the history of philosophy. In that work Heidegger envisioned a positive destructuring of the metaphysical tradition that had centered around the idea of presence. Without even mentioning the idea of a sacrament, Heidegger nonetheless gave license to Catholic thinkers in the second half of the century to re-imagine the idea of real presence in terms of a post-metaphysical activity of gift-giving (Chauvet and Power, among others). Rather than making himself present in a substantial mode of self-communication, the symbolic figuring of Christ's nearness to the recipient of the grace of the sacrament is better understood as an event eventing itself. Dynamic categories replace static ones; a metaphysics of being is outstripped and internally refashioned by the semiotics or play of material signifiers of radical self-giving, praise of the unnameable One, and unanticipated patterns of utopian social bonding.

Can the substance of the sacramental gift still be represented in terms of "presence"? This is the question posed by the post-Heideggerian deconstruction of sacramental theology. At the center of the sacramental mystery is the paschal mystery, so we are told by multiple Roman pontiffs in the twentieth century. But is this mystery not itself a form of destructuring of the very notion of being as presence? The cry of forsakenness uttered on the cross bespeaks alienation on behalf of sinful humanity, a split between a recognition of distance from God and the hope for union in love with the divine Other. Where this approach differs from the path outlined in Heidegger's *Being and Time* is that the final projecting of human self-realization in the world does not end in finitude. The sacramental refiguration of the world takes seriously the temporal and sociocultural shape of worldliness but ultimately makes present a vision of the infinite possibilities of reintegration intersecting with finite brokenness. Pope Benedict was not unaware of the Heideggerian challenge and writes in *Sacramentum Caritatis* 11: "The substantial conversion of bread and wine into his body and blood introduces within creation the principle of a radical change, a sort of 'nuclear fission,' to use an image familiar to us today, which penetrates to the heart of all being, a change meant to set off a process which transforms reality, a process leading ultimately to the transfiguration of the entire world, to the point where God will be all in all" (cf. 1 Cor 15:28). In sum, the critique of metaphysics can play a salutary role in the future of Catholic sacramentalism in terms of reclaiming biblical and liturgical motifs that were obscured by certain philosophical categories in the past, but the category of real presence is still an essential part of Catholic language and thought.

Liturgy and Social Justice

From Leo XIII to the present, Roman pontiffs have underscored the connection between interior celebration and exterior realization. In a recent Wednesday Audience Pope Francis states: "So too the Eucharist brings us together with others—young and old, poor and affluent, neighbors and visitors. The Eucharist calls us to see all of them as our brothers and sisters, and to see in them the face of Christ" (Wednesday Audience, Feb. 12, 2014).

U.S. Catholicism has made its distinctive contribution in this area. In the first half of the twentieth century in the United States, liturgist Virgil Michel, sociologist Paul Hanley Furfey, and social activist Dorothy Day reflected on how the liturgical renewal offered a new understanding of the connection between the dismissal and social justice. More recently, the same theme has been taken up by Keith Pecklers, Catherine Vincie, Michael Baxter, and William Cavanaugh. All of these efforts reinforce the idea that being in eucharistic communion entails a form of solidarity with the poor, the marginalized, the undocumented, the disabled, and all those to whom the Word of God shared his own ministry of peace, justice, and reconciliation. This solidarity can be separated from the everyday existence of individuals or communities only at our own peril. Stated more positively, the worshipping community that is sent into the world will be the body of Christ by sharing his bread in their daily life and in their prophetic incarnation of more gratuitous economies of communion. Thanksgiving that begins in the Mass ends in social responsibility (and vice versa).

The interrelationship of liturgy and justice is evident in the dismissal. The actual words of dismissal spoken by the celebrant now take multiple forms in English, including: "Ite missa est. Go forth. The Mass is ended." Pope Benedict approved three new formulae in 2008, which in English read as follows: "Go forth and announce the Gospel of the Lord," "Go in peace, glorifying the Lord by your life," and "Go in peace." The rite, while short, is of great importance because it bridges the time we spend at Mass with everyday life. It includes the sign of the cross, a Trinitarian blessing, and the exchange of Christ's presence in his Spirit between the presider and the congregation. Driscoll underscores its deeply spiritual meaning: "The entire rite is about our sharing in our bodies in the mystery of the cross, and this sharing reveals to us the mystery of the Trinity" (Driscoll 2005: 129). This spiritual framework shows why the rite is not about "It's over, you can go home now. I hope you didn't get a parking ticket." The dismissal is a sending of the church into the world that is simultaneously a self-emptying of the individual and the community. Through communion in the body and blood of Christ, the whole church and each member become for the world what Christ is for the world: "life-giving Spirit" (1 Cor 15:45).

Gender and Sacramentality

No issue has been more contentious than gender. On the one hand, the scholastic tradition of sacramental theology takes embodiment and gender seriously on multiple levels. But the interpretation of that important legacy has been interpreted anew, even by recent popes. Then in 1976 the Congregation for the Doctrine of the Faith issued a declaration, *Inter Insignores*, reaffirming the reservation of the ordained priesthood to men on the basis of the teaching of Jesus Christ. Many (but not all) feminist theologians objected to both the conclusion and the line of reasoning used to support it.

These kinds of discussions in contemporary Catholic theology are nothing if not charged with polemic and fear. A few brief points may illustrate the challenge of addressing the nature of the disputed question. The first step would be to isolate the nature of the question: "What is the fundamental difference between revisionist feminism and the magisterium on the relationship between engendered embodiment and sacramentality?" This question must be approached with caution. For example, feminist theologian Susan Ross decries liberalism (for its avoidance of the problem), naturalism (for its equation of anatomy with destiny), and constructivism (for its disconnection from stable categories), and then proceeds to unfold a notion of family as the embodied context for sacramentality (Ross 1998: 125–136). Her account of female agency in the family claims to depart from the nuptial symbolism favored by St. John Paul II and his successors in that it shows that "as mothers, women take actives roles in rearing and nurturing children, as do their partners" (Ross 1998: 132). The problem is essentially one of theological anthropology. Maintaining creative female agency in both "private" and "public" spheres and an agency of genuinely female receptivity within a spirituality of engendered sacramentality remains an unfinished task in contemporary theology. Paul's words in 1 Corinthians 11:11–12 occur in the middle of a debate about women's roles in the ancient liturgies (and his admonition that they cover their hair), but despite that obvious anachronism they still seem to express the current scope of the question: "Woman is not independent of man or man of woman in the Lord. For just as woman came from man, so man is born from woman; but all things are from God."

Recently, noted historians of Christianity have drawn attention to a model of eucharistic mysticism among high medieval and colonial Latin American female writers. A careful study of these authors could perhaps shed new light on the controverted issue of engendered sacramentality. Teresa Berger opines in the middle of a feminist reconstruction of the feast of the Annunciation: "In many ways, the Middle Ages, with their shrine and tabernacle Madonnas, had a much more profound sense of these links between woman, bodiliness, and the body of God than most of us have today" (Berger 2005: 182). The theme of love as eating and being eaten runs throughout the poetic words of these women even though these pious thoughts were often accompanied by the most rigorous of ascetical practices. Walker Bynum argues that the attention paid to eucharistic union or ecstasy was a distinctively female concern in the thirteenth century (Walker Bynum 1991: 122–125). At the very least these women model a hungering for frequent communion that is today seen as the hallmark of renewal in the twentieth century. They also break "new" ground in linking spiritual senses, erotic love for Christ's humanity, and a theology of self-renunciatory freedom. Catarina Adorna (d. 1510), a remarkable

Genoese saint who selflessly served victims of the plague in her city, brings these elements together in her spirituality:

> I offer myself to [God], and make Him a gift of my body and all that I have and may have, so that He may do with me what I do with the bread … Our happiness is a contentment that God is doing with us what He pleases. (Catherine of Genoa 1964: 123–124)

The novelty and spiritual depth of these women merit further scrutiny as the people of God move forward in their God-centered imitation of Christ (Astell 2006: 136–189).

Inculturation

In his Apostolic Exhortation of 1979, *Catechesi Tradendae*, St. John Paul II expressed the new dynamic of cultural awareness that had been opened up in *Sacrosanctum Concilium* with respect to the need for the "adaptation" and "accommodation" of the liturgy (37–40. Cf. *Ad gentes* 22):

> the Gospel message … does not spring spontaneously from any cultural soil; it has always been transmitted by means of an apostolic dialogue which inevitably becomes part of a certain dialogue of cultures. (*Catechesi Tradendae* 53)

The year 1979 marked a turning point in the magisterial treatment of the question of inculturation and in fact the first official use of the term by a Roman pontiff (Chupungco 1992: 26). Theologians such as Anscar Chupungco, O.S.B., Virgilio Elizondo, Raúl Gómez-Ruiz, S.D.S., and Eduardo Fernández, S.J. have carried this banner over the last few decades, and the fruits of their labor are now evident in the greater awareness of the need for teaching the principles of liturgical inculturation in seminaries, universities, diocesan centers, and parishes.

What is this process? The dialogue of cultures lies at the center of a proper inculturation of the liturgy, and the process of inculturation will thus bring to light the genius of a particular culture as a living, organic member of the Catholic communion of faith. The question arises with respect to the production, translation, and catechetical transmission of any particular liturgical text or event. Inculturation is also part of the process of learning from the popular wisdom in a culture so that the liturgy in that culture reflects that wisdom and guides the people of God to Christ by means of that wisdom. When the Conference of Latin American Bishops met at Puebla, they promoted the "cross-fertilization" (*la mutua fecundación*) between liturgy and popular piety "in order to be able to channel with lucidity and prudence the deep desire for prayer and charismatic vitality that is today being experienced in our countries" (Third General Conference of CELAM, Puebla, 1979, #465, translation my own). Interculturated liturgies promote the deep desire for prayer and the charismatic vitality that is indigenous to believing Catholics around the globe. It is a necessary part of any effort at a new evangelization for the twenty-first century.

CONCLUSION

We have followed over a century of developments in the sacramental life and thought of Roman Catholicism. Where does all of this movement bring us in the end? Pope Francis reminds us that the genuine result of turning the church around the ratchet of Christ is neither to revise doctrine nor to revert to what came before. This is the genuine mystery of the ratchet that eluded modernist historian Edward Gibbon. The ratchet must keep turning in an *ecclesia semper reformanda*. In *Evangelii Gaudium* Pope Francis depicts genuine ecclesial reform not as the ratchet of progress but rather as the launch pad of missionary discipleship. Christ instituted the sacraments for personal as well as social reform. Francis articulates this simple truth with characteristic passion and clarity:

> The Church is called to be the house of the Father, with doors always wide open. One concrete sign of such openness is that our church doors should always be open, so that if someone, moved by the Spirit, comes there looking for God, he or she will not find a closed door ... Everyone can share in some way in the life of the Church; everyone can be part of the community, nor should the doors of the sacraments be closed for simply any reason ... [The] Church is not a tollhouse; it is the house of the Father, where there is a place for everyone, with all their problems. (*Evangelii Gaudium* 47)

SUGGESTED READING

Cavanaugh (1998); Gómez Ruiz (2004); Guardini (1998); McPartlan (1993).

BIBLIOGRAPHY

Astell, A. W. (2006), *Eating Beauty: The Eucharist and the Spiritual Arts of the Middle Ages* (Ithaca, NY: Cornell).

Auer, J. (1971), *Das Mysterium der Eucharistie* (Regensburg: Friedrich Pustet).

Berger, T. (2005), *Fragments of Real Presence: Liturgical Traditions in the Hands of Women* (New York: Crossroad).

Catherine of Genoa (1964), *The Life and Sayings of Catherine of Genoa*, tr. Paul Garvin (Staten Island, NY: Alba).

Cavanaugh, W. T. (1998), *Torture and Eucharist: Theology, Politics, and the Body of Christ* (Oxford: Blackwell).

Chauvet, J.-M. (1987), *Symbole et sacrament. Une relecture sacramentelle de l'existence chrétienne* (Paris: du Cerf), ET: *Symbol and Sacrament* (Collegeville, MN: Liturgical Press, 1995).

Chupungco, A. (1992), *Liturgical Inculturation: Sacramentals, Religiosity, Catechesis* (Collegeville, MN: Liturgical Press).

Dougherty, J. (2010), *From Altar-Throne to Table: The Campaign for Frequent Holy Communion in the Catholic Church* (Lanham, MD: Scarecrow Press).

Driscoll, J. (2005), *What Happens at Mass?* Revised ed. (Chicago: Liturgical Training Publications).

Duffy, R. A., Irwin, K. W., and Power, D. N. (1994), "Sacramental Theology: A Review of the Literature," *Theological Studies* 4: 657–705.

Fagerberg, D. W. (2004), *Theologia Prima: What is Liturgical Theology?*, 2nd ed. (Chicago: Liturgical Training Publications).

Faggioli, M. (2010), "Quaestio Disputata: *Sacrosanctum Concilium* and the Meaning of Vatican II," *Theological Studies* 71: 437–452.

García-Rivera, A., and T. Scirghi (2008), *Living Beauty: The Art of Liturgy* (Lanham, MD: Rowman & Littlefield).

Gómez-Ruiz, R. (2004), *Languages of Worship/Lenguaje de la Fe* (Chicago: Liturgy Training Publications).

Guardini, R. (1998), *The Spirit of the Liturgy* (New York: Crossroad).

Kavanaugh, A. (1984), *On Liturgical Theology* (Collegeville, MN: Liturgical Press).

Kilmartin, E. (1988), *Christian Liturgy: Theology and Practice 1: Systematic Theology of Liturgy* (Kansas City, MO: Sheed and Ward).

Lacoste, J.-Y. (1994), *Expérience et Absolu* (Paris: Presses Universitaires de France).

Levering, M. (2005), *Sacrifice and Community: Jewish Offering and Christian Eucharist* (Oxford: Blackwell).

McPartlan, P. (1993), *The Eucharist Makes the Church: Henri de Lubac and John Zizioulas in Dialogue* (Edinburgh: T&T Clark).

McPartlan, P. (1995), *Sacrament of Salvation: An Introduction to Eucharistic Theology* (Edinburgh: T&T Clark).

Matthieson, M. M. (2013), *Sacrifice as Gift: Eucharist, Grace, and Contemplative Prayer in Maurice de la Taille* (Washington, DC: Catholic University of America Press).

Méndez-Montoya, A. F. (2009), *Theology of Food: Eating and the Eucharist* (Oxford: Wiley-Blackwell).

Nichols, A. (2003), "Introduction," to Anscar Vonier, *Key to the Doctrine of the Eucharist* (Bethesda, MD: Zacchaeus Press), <http://www.ignatiusinsight.com/features2007/anichols_introvonier_aug07.asp>.

Power, D. N. (1999), *Sacrament: The Language of God's Giving* (New York: Herder).

Rahner, K. (1960), *Kirche und Sacrament* (Freiburg: Herder), ET: *Church and Sacrament* (New York: Herder, 1963).

Rahner, K. (1982) *Theological Investigations*, vol. 4 (New York: Crossroad).

Ross, S. (1998), *Extravagant Affections: A Feminist Sacramental Theology* (New York: Continuum).

Schilson, A. (1992), *Theologie als Sakramententheologie: Die Mysterienlehre Odo Casels* (Mainz: Grünewald).

Taborda, F. (1994), *Sacramentos, práxis e festa: para uma teologia latino-americana dos sacramentos* (Petrópolis: Voces).

Taylor, C. (2007), *A Secular Age* (Cambridge, MA: Harvard University Press).

Tomasello, M. (1999), *The Cultural Origins of Human Cognition* (Cambridge, MA: Harvard University Press).

Walker Bynum, C. (1991), "Women Mystics and Eucharistic Devotion in the Thirteenth Century," in *Fragmentation and Redemption: Essays on Gender and the Human Body in Medieval Religion* (New York: Zone Books), 119–150.

....

CHAPTER 28

TWENTIETH-CENTURY AND CONTEMPORARY ORTHODOX SACRAMENTAL THEOLOGY

....

PETER GALADZA

NEAR the chronological midpoint of this chapter's focus stand two works that symbolize the past and the present of Orthodox sacramental theology. The former is volume 3 of Panagiotis Trembelas's Δογματικὴ τῆς Ὀρθοδόξου Καθολικῆς Ἐκκλησίας (1961). The latter is Alexander Schmemann's *For the Life of the World: Sacraments and Orthodoxy* (1963). Trembelas epitomizes the past that survives in some Orthodox sacramentology; Schmemann the past and present dynamically guiding its future. (Both will be treated below.) The appearance of two such different works within two years of each other hints at the field's polyvalence during the twentieth century. The present chapter will survey these two works, along with certain others, in order to indicate the main lines of modern Orthodoxy's sacramentological profile.

PAVEL FLORENSKY'S *Философия культа* (THE PHILOSOPHY OF CULT)

....

The first, truly creative Orthodox sacramentology of the twentieth century derives from a collection of texts prepared between 1908 and 1922 by Pavel Florensky (1882–1937). Some of these were delivered as lectures in 1918. They only appeared in print in 1977 (and except for several pages have not been translated into any Western language). Published under the title "From the Theological Heritage of the Priest Pavel Florensky," the folio-size 161-page work is also cited as "The Philosophy of Cult." The work as published in 1977 is divided into nine sections (though only sections 1–8 are numbered as such).

Sections 5 and 9, that is, "The Deduction of the Seven Sacraments" and "The Philosophy of Cult," will be our focus.

The title of section 5, "The Deduction of the Seven Sacraments," could also be translated "Deducing the *Septinarium*," without, of course, implying that Florensky held to everything that Roman Catholic doctrine at the time taught about the sevenfold nature of sacramentality. Nonetheless, at the end of this section he will twice repeat: "The number of (sacramental) Mysteries is seven, and it must be seven—neither more, nor less" (Florensky 1977: 147). By Florensky's day the sevenfold enumeration had become firmly entrenched within Russian Orthodox thought—even after scholasticism had begun to wane. The enumeration had been given added authority by A. L. Katansky's formidable study, *The Dogmatic Teaching Concerning the Church's Seven Mysteries*, published (in Russian) in 1877. Reviewing the sub-apostolic and pre-Nicene fathers up to Origen, Katansky argued that while the (then) Roman Catholic doctrine was too ambitious in its claims that the matter and form of the seven were instituted by Christ, the early church nonetheless held to a sevenfold sacramental economy. Liturgical history not being one of Florensky's concerns, he was not about to nuance or gainsay Katansky's assertions. In any case, in addition to feeling bound by the Russian Church's doctrine, Florensky would have found a sevenfold delimitation congenial. Numerology fascinated him, and in this case the number seven enabled him to deduce a comprehensive logical system applying Hegelian dialectics.

Florensky builds on the significance of *ousia* and *hypostasis*, announced at the end of section 4. The former is "thesis," the latter "antithesis." *Ousia* is "individuation"; *hypostasis* is "community." The synthesis is the dynamic integration of the individual and community—a thoroughly harmonious balance of the two.

The next thesis and antithesis involve "body" and "speech" (or "meaning"). The synthesis of these two is "marriage." Eventually, Florensky will postulate "thesis sacraments," that is, those related more to the physical, and "antithesis sacraments," those more related to communication, community, and meaning The former are communion, baptism, and chrismation; the latter anointing of the sick, repentance (confession), and priesthood. Their "synthesis" is marriage.

Within these triads, Florensky postulates more theses and antitheses. Communion (as feeding) is "thesis," baptism (as cleansing) is "antithesis." Their "synthesis" is chrismation, "the warming of the body." All of these relate to *ousia*. On the *hypostasis* side, which in his schema requires these sacraments to be related to communication, and so on, we find anointing of the sick as "thesis" (it involves the hearing of the rite's many Scripture readings), juxtaposed to repentance, which involves speech (the disclosure of one's sins), as "antithesis." Priesthood is the "synthesis." The latter's synthetic role pertains to the realm of authority. Authority exists in order to safeguard the relationship of individual and community. This (priestly) authority is a "binding link, into which words enter, and from which they emerge. Words are the currents of mutual understanding among members of the community" (Florensky 1977: 145).

Florensky writes: "Thus are established and arranged the seven basic functions of human existence; and only the immutability of all of them, confirmed and strengthened by cult, is the guarantee of human equilibrium. This immutability is achieved by the maximum sanctification of [human] functions—in the (sacramental) Mysteries. There are **seven** (sacramental) Mysteries because there are **seven** foundations of the human person [or personal identity]. And not only **are** there seven, there **must** be seven—neither more nor less" (145).

As noted above, this assertion will be repeated at the end of section 5. There Florensky will state: "The essence of our transcendental deduction lies in the fact that in their totality—as a whole—the (sacramental) Mysteries express the make-up of the human being [or, the composition of man]" (Florensky 1977: 147). Florensky thus falls on the side of those sacramentologists who believe that a *septinarium* is uniquely appropriate to a divine "recapitulation" of everything human.

In section 9, Florensky stresses the interconnectedness of all the sacraments—in fact, all of the church's liturgical action. "The (sacramental) Mysteries are performed/completed/celebrated [совершаются] mutually/jointly/reciprocally [взаимно] each through the other" (Florensky 1977: 222). He illustrates the interdependence of several of them. Florensky also pulls together every imaginable object and rite found within the Orthodox liturgical tradition. Water, chrism, fragrances, incense (and its smoke), relics, buildings, utensils, vesture (even the *kamilavkion*), wine, honey, wheat, and salt: all of these are analyzed with unique acumen. Thus, Florensky passionately argues for the radical materiality of the holy, and for the awesome holiness of the material. He repeats his disapproval of "Kantian dualism." He adds denunciations of utilitarian materialism and even takes a swipe at Alexei Khomiakov, who had refused to believe in the "incorruptibility" of water blessed at Theophany. All of this, for Florensky, is redolent of "intellectualized religion" (Florensky 1977: 200). And the problem is not confined to newer trends, but extends to scholasticism as well. These approaches are dubbed "the disease of a diminished ontology ... that leads to spiritual infirmity" (Florensky 1977: 230).

Section 9 includes some of the more idiosyncratic parts of the work. Florensky opines, for example, that the unity between the living and the dead is such that when the living pray for the deceased, the latter are able to inhabit the former in order to offer their own prayers. "The living, as it were, temporarily provide the deceased their lips, their hands, their vital faculties and even their hearts and minds, in sum, their vital energy, actively revealed and created. Thus, satisfying their spiritual intention, they enable them [the deceased] to temporarily and partially incarnate themselves ..." (Florensky 1977: 234). Florensky even provides a personal example to buttress his conviction that the souls of forgotten deceased can inhabit bees. During worship the latter can pester the clergy to remind them to commemorate the deceased (237). (Occultists were frequently drawn to Florensky, even though he spurned them.)

Nowhere in this last section, devoted extensively to what is known in the West as "sacramentals," does Florensky suggest a distinction between "the seven" and these other rites. This in spite of his insistence that there can only be seven sacraments. The 1977 edition of Florensky's "Philosophy of Cult" ends with a lengthy reflection on the liturgical year. The sacramentality of time concludes a work that Florensky, unfortunately, never had time to edit.

Pregnant Insights in Sergius
Bulgakov's Thought

Sergius Bulgakov (1871–1944) is frequently considered the twentieth-century's greatest Orthodox theologian. However, as regards sacramentology his legacy is modest. His introductory work, *The Orthodox Church* (1935), includes a six-page overview of the sacraments. More significant reflection appears in several articles. "Евхаристическая жертва" (The Eucharistic Sacrifice), published only in 2005 and still not translated, sees sacrificial love as inhering in the inner life of the Trinity. Sacrifice thus possesses a primordial quality that transcends the crucifixion. The Word's very Incarnation is already sacrificial—along with the rest of Christ's life. And because sacrifice "defines" the Trinity, sacrificial *offering* on the one hand and *communion* on the other (another "defining" aspect of the Three) cannot be separated.

In another article, "Евхаристический догмат" (The Eucharistic Dogma) (1930), Bulgakov rejects "transubstantiation." The doctrine severs the salvific nexus between the divine and the human. He argues for a return to the earlier Greek term μεταβολή.

Two other works gleam with possibilities for a theology of the sacraments. A focused, if brief, reflection forms part of his tome, *The Bride of the Lamb* (1945). There Bulgakov (1) grounds the sacraments in the "all-sacrament" (всетаинство), that is, the church, (2) challenges "the dogmatic fiction imposed on the Catholic Church by the Council of Trent and later adopted by Eastern theology: the fiction that all the sacraments had been instituted personally and directly by Christ" (Bulgakov 2002: 273), (3) insists on the work of the Spirit beyond "the seven," (4) notes how *sobornicity* requires the laity to cultivate their baptismal priesthood, (5) stresses the hierarchy's *ministerial* role *within* the church, and the fact that the "hierarchy arises only on the basis of the universal priesthood" (Bulgakov 2002: 281), (6) provides a nuanced analysis of the laying-on of hands in the New Testament and sub-apostolic period, (7) asserts that "hierarchy comes into being as a function of the regular celebration of the sacraments" (Bulgakov 2002: 285)—which makes "koinonic" life, rather than "dominical dicta," primordial, (8) sees the Eucharist as the basis of all the sacraments, and (9) emphasizes that the synergy of divine giving *and its appropriation*, that is, the flowering of grace, counters the sense that sacraments are "magic."

Bulgakov applies even greater critical acumen in the next section, "The Limits of Sacramentalism." An expansive reading of 1 Corinthians 12 compels him to relativize the "institutional" and hierarchical. And his sophiology grounds his conviction that the Incarnation and Pentecost are ongoing events—"noumenal" realities that inhere in sacramental celebrations, though far transcending these "phenomena."

Of all the authors treated here, Bulgakov is the only one who approaches sacramental origins in the New Testament and early church with a modern critical lens. His indebtedness to solid Protestant scholarship is obvious.

Another work pregnant with possibilities, Bulgakov's *The Comforter* (1936), hints at a fundamental sacramentology, establishing the "conditions for the possibility" of sacraments. The Spirit descends kenotically into creation, and the latter, which sophi-anically bears spirit, is able to receive the Holy Spirit. "The similar receives the similar" (Bulgakov 2004: 221). Creation ontologically remains itself, but because of its transparence to the Spirit is able to commune with God and be deified. Bulgakov's very last work, the *Apocalypse of John*, where he interprets Revelation's liturgical imagery, returns to the theme of the "all-sacrament."

Panagiotis Trembelas's *Dogmatics*

As noted above, 1961 saw the publication of Panagiotis N. Trembelas's (1886–1977) Δογματική της Ορθοδόξου Καθολικής Εκκλησίας. Seven years later the Benedictines of Chevetogne co-published a three-volume French translation, *Dogmatique de l'Église Orthodoxe Catholique*. The last volume of the Athenian professor's magnum opus comprises 638 pages, of which the first 384 are devoted to sacramentology. For all its faults, this tour de force provides:

1) an accurate and comprehensive compilation of Orthodox scholasticism (Androutsos, etc.) as well as the so-called Symbolic Books and Catechisms;
2) an extensive compilation of patristic quotations (though frequently deployed as proof texts);
3) an irenic engagement with Roman Catholic sacramentology;
4) a summary of distinctive Orthodox formulations on individual points (e.g. institution of several of the sacraments by the *Apostles*; and an elucidation of the strict Cyprianic stress on the invalidity of sacraments outside the visible boundaries of the Orthodox Church); and
5) a compendium of canonical history, decisions, and opinions.

But Trembelas's work remains in some ways an Orthodox gloss and supplement to Roman Catholic manuals. This latter tradition of inquiry guides his questions. Bernard Leeming figures in the footnotes more frequently than one might expect, and Augustine is among the Fathers quoted most. One could insist, à la Florovsky, that this is a pseudomorphosis of Orthodox theology, but on the positive side one might argue that Trembelas was not obsessed with Orthodox identity, and that a proto-ecumenism guides his thought. Thus, Trent and even Florence are sometimes cited. In any case, Trembelas's style conforms to the kind of inquiry that was being pursued at many Western universities. Not surprisingly, the work won an award from the Royal Academy of Greece.

The very first four sentences of the first chapter ("The Sacraments: Channels of Grace"), read:

> The action of grace is accomplished in each sinner who does not oppose the means instituted by the Saviour and the Apostles, means that constitute the channels

by which the Holy Spirit is given to those who receive them. This action provides encouragement and supernatural power, which is indispensable for re-birth and the new creation, as well as for the increase of the new life in Christ [in the people receiving them]. Without ignoring the power and necessity of prayer and of the preaching of the word of God, we do not rank them among the specific means that confer grace. Only the sacraments divinely instituted are listed among these. (Trembelas 1968: 9)

This signals the overall tone and content of the next 380 pages. We see a characteristic instrumentalism ("means," and "supernatural *power*"), a reification ("channels"), and a paraphrase of the Latin formulation *non ponens obicem*. A Latin flavor is also discernible in the use of the term "supernatural." The last of the three sentences then leads into a polemic against Protestant sacramentology. Elsewhere Trembelas makes clear that Lutherans and Calvinists are the target.

As regards the paschal mystery, Trembelas writes: "The sacraments draw their saving power from the Saviour's death on the cross" (Trembelas 1968: 9). He leaves it at that— without referencing the resurrection—though later he will correlate Christ's death to the giving of the Spirit.

Concerning Old Testament rites, Trembelas maintains that these were "deprived of grace, and of all supernatural content" (Trembelas 1968: 9). Romans 8ff. is ignored. Trembelas relies on several patristic authors, among them Chrysostom and Cyril of Jerusalem, who argued that these rites only affected the *body*. Trembelas then writes: "Sacraments possess within themselves a power which renders them active and efficacious when they do not find opposition among those who receive them" (Trembelas 1968: 9). The stress on the intrinsic efficacy of the sacraments places him on the "Catholic side" of the Catholic-Protestant debate.

Five of the seven sacraments "were transmitted to the church by the apostles, but their institution nonetheless derives indirectly from the Saviour" (Trembelas 1968: 10). This distinction between apostolic and dominical institution permeates much of Orthodox sacramentology. It has helped the Orthodox avoid some of the mental contortions previously required of Roman Catholic theologians.

As regards necessity, Trembelas comments: "Use of the sacraments is indispensable and absolutely necessary" (Trembelas 1968: 11). He immediately admits that the Holy Spirit can ultimately work wherever he wills, but he does not reflect on this possibility. Later, however, he will cite approvingly the Latin *non defectus, sed contemptus sacramenti damnat*.

Because he has placed prayer and preaching within the category of the non-sacramental, Trembelas concludes this section thus: "These means [i.e. the sacraments] are by their very essence channels and providers of grace; it is only in a very general way that we could list prayer and the Word of God among them" (Trembelas 1968: 11). For Trembelas the latter are "secondary channels" of grace.

Trembelas alludes in passing to the terms "type" and "anti-type" in reference to the Eucharist, but does not reflect on the significance of these important patristic and liturgical terms. Curiously, he also nearly avoids reflecting on the fact that the Byzantine tradition uses the word *mysterion* to refer to a sacramental rite. He almost spends more time discussing the original use of "sacramentum." In spite of the number of references to *mysterion* in the Pauline corpus, Trembelas only cites two—from Romans. Throughout the work, the French translator always uses "sacrament" without any allowance for *mystère* or *mystère sacramentel*. This weakens the connection between the fundamental reality of salvation (referred to as *mysterion* by Paul) and its celebration in specific rites. This connection is central to any authentic Eastern sacramentology.

Trembelas turns to the patristic teaching about the sacraments' inner—spiritual—effects (e.g. "Water is poured over the body, but it is the soul that is cleansed"). But while helping the reader understand that the rites compel us to look beyond the physical, the constant dichotomizing of inner/outer, or spiritual/physical, impair biblical anthropology's stress on the total person's salvation.

He then devotes two pages to tracing the history of the use of the terms "matter" and "form." A certain sympathy for the aims of hylomorphism is expressed, but the Orthodox, according to Trembelas, should still avoid such terminology: it is not traditional, and in Roman Catholicism it has created problems (e.g. what is the form of the sacrament of orders?).

"The sacraments have supernatural power" not because of the one who celebrates them, but "because of their own holiness and truth, owing to the One who instituted them" (Trembelas 1968: 29). In line with the tradition of cosmic sacramental realism—which we find in the actual liturgical texts—Trembelas quotes Cyril of Alexandria, who wrote that baptismal water changes in the same way that bread and wine change. Cyril of Jerusalem had said the same about chrism: oil changes because of the epicletic prayer.

Regarding *ex opere operato* Trembelas insists it is identical to the Greek διὰ τοῦ εἰργασμένου ἔργου (Trembelas 1968: 31). As is often the case, he does not cite the source for the Greek text. Throughout the discussion of *ex opere operato* Trembelas does something typical of the entire volume: he outlines the Roman Catholic approach, defends its substance—or most of it—but then indicates that the actual term is not derived from Orthodox (more exactly, early Christian) usage. He concludes this section: "In any case, the abundance of the harvest [of grace] depends on the receptivity and the will of the person receiving the sacrament" (Trembelas 1968: 33). This suggests the classical distinction between "fruitfulness" and "validity."

Regarding "indelible character," Trembelas asserts that while the Greek Fathers do not employ the term, they use analogous phrases ("a seal not made by hands"—Cyril of Jerusalem; "a branded sheep"—Gregory the Theologian). A lengthy footnote indicates reliance on Leeming. In such notes Trembelas sometimes takes up the more nuanced discussions typical of Latin scholasticism. Following Leeming he discusses whether the "character" is "natural," "ontological," or simply "moral." Citing Leeming he notes that according to the Fathers, there is "certainly a real change that occurs in the soul"), and "the character consequently creates a relationship, but grounded in a real change in the person" (Trembelas 1968: 35n3). Trembelas is legitimately concerned to defend sacramental efficacy: "In a general manner, one can say with regards to all the sacraments that the action of grace is truly generative, and it establishes in the person a new creation" (Tembelas 1968: 37). He is also attempting to deal with the fact that certain sacraments are never repeated.

Chapter 3 is devoted to the "Celebration of the Sacraments." But "celebration" here does not refer to the actual rites, texts, or their environment. Rather, canonical prescriptions and requirements are the focus. This then is not a mystagogy. It is typical of a scholasticism that abstracts from the actual reality of worship in order to organize "data" according to preconceived schemes.

Baptism can be performed by a layperson only in the case of approaching death. (Orthodox, incidentally, do not accept that a non-believer, having the intention to do what the church does, can baptize.) To stress that it is Christ who actually bestows the grace, the formulae are in the third person, for example, "The servant of God *is* baptized …," not "*I* baptize you …" Chrysostom says that the priest lends his tongue, his hand, and so on. It is standard patristic teaching that the clergy are only conduits and instruments. Trembelas cites Augustine, who says that even Judas could baptize, because it is ultimately Christ who performs the action. He does not reflect on the significance of the various—paradoxical—prayers of apologia in the Byzantine tradition, in which the priest prays that his sins not prevent the grace of the Holy Spirit. Androutsos was aware of the debate among Roman Catholics regarding *interior* intention, and Trembelas suggests that it is risky to begin reflecting on this. How could one ever be sure about the individual's intention?

As regards the status of sacraments in heretical communities, Trembelas asserts that Orthodoxy takes a different approach from Catholicism. It is a strict Cyprianic approach: outside the visible boundaries of the "institutional" church there is no salvation, and thus there are no sacraments. He provides a list of heretics who must be baptized and a list of those who must not. And while the *baptism* celebrated in a non-Orthodox church (in particular a heretical body) *might* be recognized according to the principle of *oikonomia* (a derogation from the strict application of canon law for the good of souls), the other sacraments are not. ("Monophysites" are traditionally re-ordained.) Trembelas discusses how such baptisms would require [re-]chrismation. Pope Stephen had asserted that while the baptizand received Christ, he did not receive the Spirit.

Trembelas accepts the strict Cyprianic approach that if a "priest" has not been validly ordained, the baptism administered by him must be repeated. (He does not treat the implications for relations with non-Orthodox.) Any derogation from such strictness involves some form of "economy." Several metaphors are adduced to describe the celebration of sacraments outside the church. If a hand is separated from the body, it can do nothing. Thus, baptism outside the church is not just illicit, it is ἀνίσχυρα—without power (Trembelas 1968: 55). He insists, however, that in the case of Roman Catholics and those Protestants who recite the Symbol of Faith, their sacraments are not without significance. But they are "imperfect" and "deformed" (Trembelas 1968: 58).

Trembelas then provides a string of metaphors and analogies to explain "Economy and the Extent of Its Application." For example, "The Church sacrifices a part in order to save the whole" (Trembelas 1968: 60). "The door is opened temporarily." Or, "the Church fills an empty vessel from her valid contents" (Trembelas 1968: 61). And it does so for *specific* situations.

Regarding the number of sacraments, Trembelas unquestioningly accepts the *septinarium* and repeats the Orthodox decisions confirming it. Aware of the doctrine's complexities, he asserts that "the Lord's ways are inscrutable" (Trembelas 1968: 70). In his opinion, those who would argue for only two sacraments (baptism and the Eucharist) have to admit that in the Scriptures the word *mysterion* is not applied to them either. Trembelas describes the evolution of diverse enumerations and calmly recounts the history of the migration of the sevenfold list from the Latin West. He even relies on Aquinas's explanation that five of the sacraments provide "individual" healing and sanctification, and two relate to man's need for "governance" and "propagation." And while noting that the parallelism with the Spirit's seven gifts is quite appropriate, the *septinarium* remains a mystery of divine wisdom.

AN EXISTENTIALIST TURN: ALEXANDER SCHMEMANN'S *FOR THE LIFE OF THE WORLD*

As already noted, in 1963 Alexander Schmemann (1921–1983), Dean of St. Vladimir's Orthodox Theological Seminary in suburban New York, issued the first version of what would become a twentieth-century classic, *For the Life of the World*. (Another title, added as a subtitle to the most recent edition, is *Sacraments and Orthodoxy*.) Originally written as a study guide for the mainly Protestant Student Conference on Christian World Mission in Athens, Ohio, it has been translated into almost twenty languages. An expanded edition appeared in 1973 (and is cited here). Two seminal chapters were added to the 1973 edition: "Worship in a Secular Age," and "Sacrament and Symbol." The latter in particular demonstrates Schmemann's acumen as a scholar, and not just spiritual writer. Owing to the availability of his works in English, our treatment here will be more cursory.

For the Life of the World takes a decidedly existentialist turn. Schmemann was as well versed in modern French and Russian literature as in theology. Thus, the categories of fear, hunger, meaning, death, joy, loneliness, and so on guide his thought. As for his style, it is evocative rather than discursive. Schmemann explains: "This is not a treatise of systematic theology" (Schmemann 1973: 20).

Schmemann was also thoroughly familiar with the *nouvelle théologie* and the classics of the Roman Catholic liturgical movement. Thus, for him reflection on the sacraments means first and foremost reflection on their actual rites and texts. His is a modern mystagogical approach. His indebtedness to contemporary Roman Catholic thought is acknowledged in the 1965 Herder and Herder edition (an acknowledgement subsequently omitted from Orthodox editions). There, Schmemann mentions Casel,

Beauduin, Jungmann, Bouyer, Guardini, and Reinhold, and writes: "Their writings were and still are as significant for us Orthodox as they are for our Western brothers" (Schmemann 1965: 8). The influence has become reciprocal. The Catholic liturgist, David W. Fagerberg, for example, has made Schmemann the exemplar of his own seminal approach to liturgical theology (Fagerberg 2004: 73–105). And one should clarify immediately that while even among Orthodox theologians of Schmemann's orientation a certain distinction between "liturgy" and "sacraments" remains, it is far less significant than for many Western authors. Thus, *For the Life of the World: Sacraments and Orthodoxy* includes substantial reflection on vespers and matins, as well as the liturgical year. These form part of his thinking on the sacramentality of time. Nowhere does the work treat the number of sacraments, though all seven are discussed—even if, in some cases, very briefly.

Schmemann begins *For the Life of the World* announcing his opposition to both secularizing and "spiritualizing" tendencies within the church: "Both attitudes distort ... the wholeness, the *catholicity* of the genuine Orthodox tradition which has always affirmed both the goodness of the world for whose life God has given his only-begotten Son, and the *wickedness* in which the world lies." He continues: "[This tradition] has always proclaimed and keeps proclaiming every Sunday that 'by the Cross joy has entered the world,' yet tells those who believe in Christ that they 'are dead and their life is hid with Christ in God' " (Col 3:3) (Schmemann 1973: 8).

All of Schmemann's writing revels in the "tension" between the incarnational and the eschatological, though it is the latter that became his trademark. "In this world Christ was rejected. He was the perfect expression of life as God intended it. The fragmentary life of the world was gathered into His life; He was the heartbeat of the world and the world killed Him. But in that murder the world itself died. It lost its last chance to become the paradise God created it to be" (Schmemann 1973: 23). Thus Schmemann begins his reflection on the Eucharist.

The French-American churchman of Russian extraction was gaining prominence just as "death-of-God" and "secular-city" theologies were emerging, and his own experience with the failed experiments of the Bolshevik Revolution, not to mention his commitment to tradition, caused him to bristle at such theologies. But nowhere does Schmemann allow his eschatology to become dour or world-denying. The whole point of Christian eschatology is that it is in *this* world—in the concrete realities of eating, embracing, gathering, and singing—that the Kingdom of God comes in power.

Thus, underlying his approach to the individual sacraments is Schmemann's belief in the sacramentality *of the world*, as well as *the Church as primal sacrament*. "The purpose of this book ... is to remind its readers that in Christ, life—life in all its totality—was returned to man, given again as sacrament and communion, made Eucharist" (Schmemann 1973: 20). He then introduces a critique of classical academic sacramentology, insisting that the church as such—in all her dimensions—is *the* sacrament of Christ's presence and action. Sacraments are not parts or institutions *of* or *within* the church, but realizations of her essence.

Because Christian mission was the theme of the student conference for which the book had been written, Schmemann indicates that while this theme is usually associated with "the word," rather than with "sacrament," the dichotomy is specious. Mission involves witnessing to what one has experienced. For an Orthodox Christian that experience is bound up with the sacraments—and the word that comes to life during liturgy. Schmemann was also concerned to reject any approach to worship that would remove it from the realm of everyday life. Orthodoxy had come to be associated with the "mystical" and "spiritual" and risked having its sacraments viewed as "exotica." He considered this especially detrimental as Christianity was intended to be the end of religion, of everything that would relegate divine–human communion to a segregated realm. Man was intended to be the priest of creation, "standing *in the centre of the world*" (Schmemann 1973: 15) in order to receive and offer it to God.

Schmemann's theology of the Eucharist, as hinted above, is a mystagogy of the actual celebration. For him—as for the Fathers—the meaning of the sacrament is not "behind," "above," or "beyond" the rite, but *in* it and *through* it. We are thus treated to insights on gathering, entering, listening, and praising. And nowhere does he allow reflection on the elements to be divorced from the service as a whole. As for the consecration, while stressing the *epiclesis*, he insists that for too long theologians reduced their thinking to the categories of this world. Because the liturgical assembly ascends on high—finds itself where Christ reigns—the food it consumes shares in this eschatological quality.

Turning to baptism-chrismation, Schmemann begins by refocusing on the cosmic. For too long the significance of water was ignored. Its sanctification is not a rubrical necessity, but the restoration of matter. He then stresses the dying and rising themes embedded in the rite. As for chrismation, it is never separated from baptism. It is a personal Pentecost, vital to Christian identity, as the Holy Spirit constitutes the church's true life. Within this context Schmemann discusses (briefly) the sacrament of penance. The latter is the power of baptism as it lives in the church—not a "juridical power."

Speaking to a predominantly Protestant audience, Schmemann had to explain why marriage is considered a sacrament. He invokes the paschal mystery: Christian marriage involves a dying to self that is graciously crowned and subsumed into the Kingdom. That Kingdom is fundamentally the reality enacted in the sacraments.

The final chapter of *For the Life of the World* is "Sacrament and Symbol," the second of two articles added to the original edition. Schmemann outlines the patristic epistemology undergirding pre-scholastic participatory ontology. The breakdown in sacramental experience and thought occurred once the passion for knowledge *about* triumphed over knowledge *of*. The patristic approach to symbol enables bread, for example, to bear another reality—the Body of Christ. During the Reformation this will later be dubbed "impanation," but the accusation is arguably a function of linear philosophical categories foreign to the patristic mindset.

In addition to *For the Life of the World*, Schmemann published two other book-length studies on sacraments: *Of Water and the Spirit* and *The Eucharist: Sacrament of the Kingdom*. They generally flesh out—with more extensive historical and mystagogical material—the approach taken in *For the Life of the World*. However, Schmemann can be weak in the area of liturgical history. Thus, some of his comments regarding liturgical reform miss the mark (Galadza 2007: 20–23).

DUMITRU STANILOAE'S DOGMATICS AND
THE SANCTIFYING MYSTERIES

In 1978, the premier Romanian Orthodox theologian, Dumitru Staniloae (1903–93), published the Romanian version of his three-volume *Teologia dogmatică ortodoxă*. The first half of volume 3 is entirely devoted to the sacraments. In 2012 this section of his dogmatics appeared in English as *The Experience of God: Orthodox Dogmatic Theology*, vol. 5: *The Sanctifying Mysteries*. Writing in the foreword to the 219-page English text, Alkiviadis Calivas asserts: "[*The Sanctifying Mysteries*] constitutes the first comprehensive treatment in the English language of the holy mysteries from an Orthodox doctrinal perspective" (Staniloae 2012: xii). Calivas' assertion is not entirely true, as the American, Frank Gavin, had produced such a work in 1923. But the mistake is very instructive. Gavin's treatment, while comprehensive, Orthodox, and doctrinal—and in English—is thoroughly scholastic and manualist. Staniloae's sacramentology, on the other hand, reflects the neo-patristic synthesis espoused by Florovsky and Lossky.

Staniloae became immersed in patristics as editor of the Romanian edition of the *Philokalia* (1946–1976). Trained in Orthodox manualism, he had already begun his turn to the Eastern Fathers with his study of Gregory Palamas (1938). A manualist tone remains discernable in *The Sanctifying Mysteries*. And while the predominantly patristic orientation of his sacramentology makes the text an invaluable contribution to Orthodox theology, a modern reader not used to thinking in the categories of *Logos* and *logoi*, "recapitulation" and "microcosm," "divine energies" and "economy," will find parts of his theology remote.

Perceptions and "genealogies" aside, the first four chapters of *The Sanctifying Mysteries* yield absorbing insights. Chapter 1, "Christ's Saving Mysteries: Creation Unified and Made New in the Church," provides an original "fundamental sacramentology." The "possibility" of sacraments is elucidated:

> The general basis of the mysteries of the Church is the faith that God can operate upon the creature in his visible reality. In this sense the general meaning of the mysteries is the union of God with the creature and the most comprehensive mystery is the union of God with the whole creation. This is a mystery that contains everything, and there is absolutely no part of reality not contained within it. This union begins with the very act of creation and is destined to find its fulfillment through the movement of creation toward that state in which 'God is all in all'. (1 Cor. 15:28) (Staniloae 2012: 3)

Note that in authentic Eastern fashion Staniloae *promotes* the "ambiguity" between "sacramental mystery" and "salvific mystery." He also relies on Maximus the Confessor—a favorite of Staniloae's—for his stress on deifying cosmic and human unification. In fact, the words "union," "communion," "encounter," and their synonyms appear several hundred times in the space of this first chapter's twenty-five pages. Finally, the "all-encompassing mystery that is the union of God with creation" is for Staniloae the first of three underlying mysteries that ground those "visible actions of the Church [that] have the character and name of mysteries"—the sacraments (Staniloae 2012: 8). The other two are "the mystery of Christ" and "the mystery called Church."

As for grace, "it is nothing other than the activity of Christ" (Staniloae 2012: 11). Elsewhere he expresses the usual Orthodox reservations toward "created grace," even though some of his own formulations about the graces received through particular sacraments hint at such an approach. In any case, Christ's resurrected and ascended flesh enables humanity's bodily participation now in all that Christ experienced during his earthly sojourn.

Finally, "there is no need to envisage any kind of separation between the matter of the sacrament and the grace or power of Christ that is imparted through it" (Staniloae 2012: 13). Staniloae asserts that "such a dualistic conception" is the product of Western scholasticism. It became possible once the intimate bond that links the Logos and "His activity in the natural world" had been forgotten (Staniloae 2012: 13). "Matter is not merely a symbol, separate from grace, that occasions and intuitively interprets the unseen activity of grace; matter itself is filled with the power of God" (Staniloae 2012: 13).

In a section entitled, "The Christological and Ecclesial Character of the Mysteries," Staniloae displays one of his more egregious misreadings of Roman Catholic theology. This might not merit consideration except that a shallow anti-Catholicism characterizes several sections of this volume (cf. Staniloae 2012: 96, 108, 196). (A misreading of Protestantism is also evident.) Staniloae polemicizes against Karl Rahner for writing that the *church* "instituted" the sacraments. Rahner was contending with the Tridentine doctrine that had Christ's "institution" determining each sacrament's matter and form. In the face of this clearly untenable doctrine, Rahner proposed to retain the connection to Christ by suggesting that to the extent that Christ instituted the church, he instituted the sacraments. For Staniloae this entails a diminution of the Christic grounding for the sacraments. "Christ alone, not the Church, was able to establish the forms and stages of His relationship to believers through the mysteries" (Staniloae 2012: 18). Throughout the volume, Staniloae repeats that the sacraments were instituted by Christ. Obviously a clear statement of the difference between "grounding" and "institution" would have obviated the problem.

As regards a priest's (potentially scandalous) unworthiness, Staniloae notes that his prayer and invocation of the Holy Spirit are in fact "the prayer and invocation of the whole Church" (Staniloae 2012: 21).

Curiously, neither in the introductory chapter nor anywhere else in the book does Staniloae reflect on the number of the sacraments. He only asserts that the first three complete one's union with Christ; penance and unction bring renewed strength in Christ; and the remaining two (orders and marriage) give "the power of fulfilling" a "special mission" or "special duties" (Staniloae 2012: 25). The lack of attention to this question is in part a function of Staniloae's neglect of historical evolution. He also does not discuss any of the "sacramentals."

Turning to the individual sacraments, Staniloae's treatment tends to combine patristic thought with references to the actual rites, elements of biblical exegesis, as well as canon law and catechesis. Moral application is weaved into the last category.

Regarding baptism, Staniloae unpacks the existential transformation effected by the first sacrament. Death and rebirth, restoration of the image, illumination, entrance into a relationship with the entire Trinity—all these are highlighted. Staniloae beautifully articulates baptism's cosmic dimension in a section entitled "The Unity between Water and the Holy Spirit as Womb of the New Man." He writes: "[M]atter itself, brought back to the condition of spiritual mobility, becomes a milieu for the creator Spirit, who is free and ever new in all His acts" (Staniloae 2012: 31).

Ironically, most of Staniloae's reflection—and the patristic sources inspiring it—presume adult baptism. Of course, the prayers of the Orthodox rite also presume it. But as the vast majority of baptizands for a millennium and a half have been children or infants, focusing on an existential dynamic that actually applies to adults is frustrating.

In the last four pages of this chapter Staniloae finally takes up the problem of infant baptism. In "The Absolute Necessity of Baptism for Salvation" we read: "Children too clearly share in this stain [of sin], not through their own personal sin but through their birth" (Staniloae 2012: 51). Considering that he has couched the discussion in terms of "obligation," as well as "the wages of sin," it is hard to imagine how Staniloae can avoid the Augustinian notion of inherited guilt. In any case, he asserts that the family's faith provides the basis for baptizing infants.

Regarding chrismation, Staniloae rightly elucidates how "the second sacrament" is "a kind of continuation of baptism" (Staniloae 2012: 57). The recipient's name is not stated during the recitation of the "formula" ("The seal of the gift of the Holy Spirit"). This is as if to indicate that a single sacrament is celebrated in two parts. Quoting Schmemann, Staniloae notes that baptism and chrismation can be distinguished only to the extent that birth and life can be.

While naïve in his insistence that Christ "instituted" chrismation, Staniloae adroitly weaves New Testament passages concerning anointing, fragrance, sealing, and empowerment into his reflection. Chrismation also imparts priesthood, kingship, and prophecy, a theme he inherits from patristic writings (not Calvin, as some have suggested). Finally, he draws out the implications of the Spirit's role in guaranteeing unity and diversity. The chrism (in some Orthodox churches) is consecrated by the *whole episcopate together*—symbolizing that "the Spirit of the whole Church descends on each of the faithful" (Staniloae 2012: 72). This one Spirit fructifies each individual's unique gifts.

Staniloae does not treat the question of re-chrismation, except to say that chrismation is not celebrated a second time owing to its close relationship to baptism (Staniloae 2012: 72). He also avoids discussing whether the Spirit is given already in baptism—as the New Testament asserts. This not only impacts ecumenical discussions about the status of the "second sacrament," but also the problem of millions of Orthodox baptized in the former Eastern Bloc by lay grandparents. These Orthodox were rarely chrismated.

Staniloae's chapter on the Eucharist is thoroughly patristic. He balances a focus on the elements (but devoid of all fetishism) with a stress on Eucharist as dynamic process. The eucharistic body and blood interpenetrate human flesh, divinizing it. "His body and blood have given our own body and blood their divine qualities" (Staniloae 2012: 80). Simultaneously, the actual celebration of the Eucharist orients one towards the resurrection: "The foretaste of the resurrection grows out of the process by which the dynamic state of resurrection is being imprinted, really and gradually, upon our inner man, and this dynamic state stems from the fact that the risen Christ is united with us" (Staniloae 2012: 79).

All of this is guided and effected by the Spirit, and it all leads to σύσσωμα—becoming fellow members of the same body (Eph. 3:6). As with chrismation, unity and individuality are uniquely fused: "In their common sensation of dissolving within God experienced as a kind of mystical death with Christ, as also in their anticipation of the risen state, no one distinguishes himself any longer from the others, although by the very fact that each one has his own experience of this sensation, even this anticipation proves that the personal existence of each one endures" (Staniloae 2012: 81).

Finally, Staniloae's eucharistic thought achieves a rare feat. He is able to seamlessly weave reflection on the transformation of the gifts, sacrifice, mystery, pneumatization, ritual act, Word and words, thanksgiving and ecclesial unity—not to mention scriptural narrative—in the same way that an actual liturgy does. One senses something happening—in this case conceptually—without any compulsion to stop and "dissect" the formulations.

Regarding repentance (confession), much of Staniloae's thought is an engaging reflection on spiritual fatherhood. Orthodoxy's tendency to join theology and "spirituality" is evident.

Telegraphically summarizing the import of the remaining three chapters, we may say that Staniloae—typically for him—focuses on the *unifying* role of the priesthood; stresses how marriage reveals authentic humanity ("each forgets the self, making him or herself the 'I' of the other") (Staniloae 2012: 178); and emphasizes the unity wrought by anointing. "The Church makes a maximum effort to prepare a sick person for communion with Christ and to open him up to communion with his brothers and sisters ... to this end the Church uses many priests, many prayers and many fellow believers" (200). Staniloae is here referring to the presence of seven priests and as many sets of readings in the Byzantine anointing service.

CONSTANTIN ANDRONIKOF'S *DES MYSTÈRES SACRAMENTELS*

Arguably the most satisfying and comprehensive treatment of the sacraments by a modern Orthodox theologian is from the pen of a far less renowned author, Constantin Andronikof (1916–1997). In 1944 he completed studies at the Institut Saint-Serge, where he later taught and served as Dean from 1991 to 1993. But the Russian-born Frenchman spent much of his life as a civil servant.

This last of the five larger works under consideration here comprises a kind of synthesis of the approaches found in the previous four. But this 1998 work is not only synthetic; it is also apologetic. Andronikof begins by posing the question: how are sacraments possible? In typically Greek patristic fashion he answers that the union of the divine and human is actually the most natural. Anything else is perverted and corrupt. As for the goal of the mysteries, it is holiness. The classic Eastern invitation to communion, "Holy things for the holy," evokes this. This movement is realized *in time*—by acts of faith and expressions of piety—instantiated as uncreated energies of God. These manifest the intersection of eternity and time, of the transcendent and immanent.

Andronikof then asks, "But is it possible to analyze such realities? Or is it rather the case that we can only study the sacraments' *effects*?" (Andronikof 1998: 9). Any study of the *reality* of faith without the faith *that grounds it* seems impossible. He summarizes pithily the insights of an initial chapter of Florensky's *The Pillar and Ground of Truth*: "The criterion of truth is truth itself" (Andronikof 1998: 10). Realities of faith require an appropriate method, and that "method" can only be allegorical, symbolic, and apophatic. These are "broad enough" to include imponderables.

Thus, the mystery itself (and prayer) is not penetrable. But its *expression* is. The theologian's task is to reflect on the coupling of the Spirit's *ineffable sighs* (Rom 8:26), on the one hand, with the actual *expressions thereof* in the sacraments. Andronikof cites this passage from Romans several times. He thereby emphasizes the *sacramental* nature of prayer. (Ironically, Trembelas had begun his treatise disavowing this notion.)

As sacraments inaugurate man's ordinary existence, they actualize the life that God had always intended for him. But this (re)new(ed) existence extends to all of creation. The human is at the centre of creation, and the effects of the sacraments radiate from man's sacramental experience. The goal of the new reality—which is ultimately social and cosmic—is described in the Apocalypse, the great vision of the heavenly city.

As regards cultic action, it is what *we* do. Grace, however, is what *God* "does." Andronikof displays a profound appreciation for the biblical drama of the mystery. The events of the New Testament, celebrated as liturgical feasts, are sacramental. And these narratives take on a cultic/liturgical form in order to make the New Testament realities present now, bringing salvation to all. Sacraments are thus "the practical application of the Christian religion," the good news put into effect.

Andronikof then provides a page-long definition of "sacrament." Its most significant elements are (1) divine-human union through an action of the Church, (2) the making present of God's Son through the Spirit according to the Father's good will, (3) the Trinity as source, and the promise to "two or three" gathered in Christ's name as well as the promise of another paraclete, (4) the motivation as well as efficacy of the sacrament derived from the church's nature as body and spouse of Christ, along with her identity as a sacerdotal community, and (5) an outpouring of grace for purposes of "purification, exorcism, healing, sanctification, illumination, adoption" (Andronikof 1998: 14)—in sum, making redemption a reality here and now.

Later Andronikof will provide a more succinct "definition": a sacrament is anything that signifies and causes (*provoque*) the encounter between the human and divine, that is, the movement of God towards humans and vice versa. This dynamic is summarized in the anaphoral phrase: "Yours of Your own, we offer You in behalf of all and for all ..." Theandrism, or the theanthropic, is thus invoked. Later Andronikof will cite Scripture to note how Christians are *synergoi*. From humanity's side it is a matter of making *epiclesis*. But this is not a matter of "forcing" God to act. God, however, has commanded that the request be made.

Andronikof then provides a list of twenty-two rites or other realities that were considered sacraments in the past. Among them are the consecration of chrism and the dedication of a church and/or altar. Later he cites the Theophany blessing of water and monastic tonsure. He concludes the book with a chapter on funerals—another service listed among the sacraments *in the past*. This indicates the relative status that he accords "the seven."

Andronikof argues that once Peter Lombard and Aquinas began to develop Augustine's "sign of an invisible grace"—a diminution of "mystery" and the "secret" in reflections on the sacraments ensued. The way Westerners conceive of "sacrament" is similar to what comes to mind when a Byzantine thinks of ἀκολουθία (послѣдованіе). In Andronikof's (debatable) view, the "ordo"—that which is visible—ends up predominating. But he approvingly notes Ambrose's and Isidore of Seville's pre-scholastic emphasis on "mystery" and "secret."

As regards "causation," the scholastics—owing to their intellectual milieu—elaborated the categories of formal, material, and final causality. Our milieu inspires other approaches. In any case, fundamental to the sacraments is their orientation towards the Kingdom. They are eschatological. That which Christ has promised from on high and for the future breaks into the present. By its nature, then, a sacrament is an instance of sanctification and deification. And far more than the "soul" is implicated. The Frenchman develops the importance of the *spoken* word, along with gestures, light, and music. The aesthetic is not a cosmetic supplement! It is an environment that is created—not an "atmosphere." Numbers and liturgical seasons also bear sacramental significance. All of this serves to highlight how "mysterion" is a "technical" term for *all* liturgical actions.

We then find a description of a foundational *typos* of the church—Acts 1:14ff. The Pentecost narrative indicates the context of her sacramental nature. Unity in Christ is caused and permeated by the Holy Spirit according to the good will of the Father. The mystery of the Trinity—as revealed at Pentecost—becomes the foundation of all sacraments.

According to Andronikof, Western "sign theology," compared to classical Eastern symbol theology, is impoverished. In the past, a symbol *was* that which it symbolizes. He cites Ps.-Denys and Cabasilas—and then von Harnack. "The symbol was a mystery and the mystery was inconceivable without the symbol" (Andronikof 1998: 25). The sacrament relies on the symbol—and not as something extrinsic to it. For the sacramental to be real, it must be symbol. This is because of the symbol's polyvalence, "indeterminacy," "transcendence." Besides, God can be conceived only symbolically.

While cognizant of the methodological rationale for hylomorphism, Andronikof is concerned that it diminishes the symbolic. Water is a symbol of baptism; chrism a symbol of chrismation. And the words (that is, the "form") are a *sensible* ("material") expression of an invisible essence. The sound quality of words makes them *material*. Thus the phenomenology expresses an ontology. The rites of a sacrament are like the colors and forms of an icon—intrinsic to them. As regards hylomorophism, he also notes the problem of trying to determine the "matter" of marriage, ordination, and confession.

Turning to *ex opere operato*, while a sacrament may thus be "valid," it is nonetheless received unto judgment and condemnation. Human synergy with the divine is required. Andronikof, however, cautions against soteriological pessimism (one might say Jansenism), insisting that Christians must simply continue celebrating the sacraments in spite of "the risks." When humans consciously refuse the sacraments, one cannot begin to imagine what God has in store for them. (Andronikof turns Paul's "indescribable delights" of 1 Cor 2:9 on its head.) But God alone remains the ultimate judge. Antinomically, though, the church does excommunicate, and according to Christ's mandate, it binds and looses even "in heaven."

Andronikof returns to the question of other sacraments—beyond "the seven." Only the perceived need to combat Protestantism at the time of Loukaris compelled Patriarch Jeremiah and the Council of Constantinople in 1638 to proclaim the seven. Because the church experienced a far broader sacramental life long before anyone attempted to limit it, and because the *lex orandi* is the *lex credendi*, the *septinarium* must be relativized. Besides, according to the classical definition, several other rites have all the qualities of a sacrament. But regardless of all enumerations, baptism and Eucharist retain a unique status, as even John Damascene had insisted.

CONCLUSION

Twentieth-century Orthodox sacramentology displays a rich variety of approaches, and even beliefs. Nonetheless, in spite of the absence of a "magisterium" à la Roman Catholicism, one finds a cohesion derived from reverence for tradition (though to what extent this is conditioned by sociology cannot be discussed here). No Orthodox theologian questions the centrality of sacramental experience, or the sacraments' "objective efficacy" (to use a term derived from Catholic-Protestant debates). Nor for that matter do they question the basic ordo prescribed by the Eastern churches.

But in other areas Orthodox are willing to live with ambiguity. (See, for example, the responses of the Eastern Orthodox Churches to BEM.) This is not only because patristic theology—Orthodoxy's privileged authority—leaves us with such uncertainties, but also because Orthodoxy's "de-centralized" structure permits each autocephalous church to resolve certain questions on their own. Whether it is the number of sacraments, terminology for eucharistic consecration, "re-baptism," or more generally the status of rites celebrated outside Orthodoxy, one finds a diversity ironically very congenial to contemporary Western sensibilities.

Suggested Reading

A. Schmemann (1974 and 1988); P. Sherrard (1964); J. D. Zizioulas (1985); Михаил Желтов [Mikhail Zheltov, ed.] (2009).

Bibliography

Afanasiev, N. (2007), *The Church of the Holy Spirit*, trans. Vitaly Permiakov (Notre Dame, IN: University of Notre Dame Press).

Andronikof, C. (1998), *Des mystères sacramentels* (Paris: Cerf).

Bulgakov, S. (2002), *The Bride of the Lamb*, trans. Boris Jakim (Grand Rapids, MI: Eerdmans).

Bulgakov, S. (2004), *The Comforter*, trans. Boris Jakim (Grand Rapids, MI: Eerdmans).

Bulgakov, S. (1935), *The Orthodox Church* (London: Centenary Press).

Булгаков, С. [Bulgakov, S.] (2005), "Евхаристическая жертва" [The Eucharistic Sacrifice] and "Евхаристический догмат" [Eucharistic Dogma], in *Евхаристия* [The Eucharist] (Москва-Париж [Moscow-Paris]: YMCA Press). An English translation of the second article is available in Bulgakov, S. *The Holy Grail and the Eucharist*, trans. Boris Jakim (Hudson, NY: Lindisfarne Books, 1997).

Fagerberg, D. W. (2004), *Theologia Prima: What is Liturgical Theology?* (Chicago and Mundelein, IL: Hillenbrand Books).

Флоренский, П. [Florensky, P.] 1977, "Из богословского наследия ('Философия культа')" [From the theological heritage ("The Philosophy of Cult")] in *Богословские труды* 17 (1977): 85–248.

Galadza, P. (2007), "Schmemann between Fagerberg and Reality: Towards an Agenda for Byzantine Christian Pastoral Liturgy," *Bollettino della Badia Greca di Grottaferrata, terza serie* 4: 7–32.

Gavin, F. (1923), *Some Aspects of Contemporary Greek Orthodox Thought* (New York: Morehouse).

Schmemann, A. (1965), *Sacraments and Orthodoxy* (New York: Herder and Herder).

Schmemann, A. (1973), *For the Life of the World: Sacraments and Orthodoxy* (Crestwood, NY: St. Vladimir's Seminary Press).

Schmemann, A. (1974), *Of Water and the Spirit: A Liturgical Study of Baptism* (Crestwood, NY: St. Vladimir's Seminary Press).

Schmemann, A. (1988), *The Eucharist: Sacrament of the Kingdom* (Crestwood, NY: St. Vladimir's Seminary Press).

Sherrard, P. (1964), "The Sacrament," in A. J. Philippou (ed.), *The Orthodox Ethos, Studies in Orthodoxy*, vol. 1 (Oxford: Holywell Press), 133–139.

Staniloae, D. (2012), *The Experience of God, Orthodox Dogmatic Theology*, vol. 5, *The Sanctifying Mysteries*, trans. Ioan Ionita and Robert Barringer (Brookline, MA: Holy Cross Orthodox Press).

Trembelas, P. (1968), *Dogmatique de l'Église Orthodoxe Catholique*, Tome 3. Traduction française par l'Archimandrite Pierre Dumont, OSB (Éditions de Chevetogne—Desclée de Brouwer), translation of Δογματική της Ορθοδόξου Καθολικής Εκκλησίας (Athens: Sotir, 1961).

World Council of Churches (1986–1988), *Churches Respond to BEM: Official Responses to the 'Baptism, Eucharist and Ministry' Text*, vols. 1–6, ed. Max Thurian (Geneva: World Council of Churches).

Желтов, Михаил, ред. [Mikhail Zheltov, ed.] (2009), *Православное учение о церковных таинствах* [The Orthodox teaching concerning the Church's sacraments], том 1–3 [vols. 1–3] (Москва: Синодальная библейско-богословская комиссия [Moscow: The Synodal biblical and theological commission]). Serviceable English translations of some of these articles are available online.

Zizioulas, J. D. (1985), *Being as Communion: Studies in Personhood and the Church*, Contemporary Greek Theologians, 4 (Crestwood, NY: St. Vladimir's Seminary Press).

PART V

DOGMATIC APPROACHES

CHAPTER 29

LITURGY, SIGNS, AND SACRAMENTS

DAVID W. FAGERBERG

That life which was with the Father became visible, and has appeared to us.
—Communion antiphon, Weekdays of Christmas Time, Roman missal

PART V of this volume is concerned with dogmatic approaches to sacramental theology, and each of the chapters following this one will focus upon an individual sacrament. Therefore, I will give pride of place to liturgy in this preliminary chapter, making it the hermeneutical keyhole through which we peek at the sacramental life of the church. What could liturgical theology say about signs and sacraments? In the Christian life the two dimensions of liturgy and sacraments are integrated in fact, but maybe not so well integrated in our thinking. Without a necessary connection, the relationship between liturgy and sacrament will be thought to be only accidental: for example, sacraments are usually done in a liturgical format, and liturgies are occasionally interrupted by special sacraments. But surely they have more to do with each other than that.

This chapter will therefore first argue for a thicker definition of liturgy, one that understands liturgy as immersion in the eighth day. Second, it will propose that liturgy is sacramental. And third, it will propose that sacraments are liturgical.

A THICKER DEFINITION OF LITURGY

On one occasion, I was standing in ceremonial cap and gown waiting with my fellow faculty to march into our annual commencement exercises, when the colleague behind me said, from out of the blue, "You must like this sort of thing." He knew that I was in liturgical studies, so naturally he thought I was enamored of hoary tradition, meaningless repetition, useless formality, and extravagant ceremony. All too frequently, this is all that people think liturgy is: the rubrical rules for running the Jesus club. But I find this much too thin a definition. Rubrics are important for the ceremony, that is true, but liturgy itself has a theological and supernatural dimension deeper than what thin, horizontal, and natural definitions allow. What we want is a definition that is theological in nature, biblical in foundation, cosmic in function, eschatological in orientation, and ecclesiological in depth. In my efforts to make such a capacious definition, I have arrived at this: *liturgy is the perichoresis of the Trinity kenotically extended to invite our synergistic ascent into deification.* Four comments are in order, before integrating sacraments into it.

First, if liturgy is communion with God, remember that this God is himself a community of love. The mutual indwelling of Father and Son and Holy Spirit turns outward toward other creatures and invites them to participate in divine, eternal life. One of the pioneers of the liturgical renewal, Virgil Michel, O.S.B., saw the activity of the Trinity in the church's liturgy:

> The liturgy, through Christ, comes from the Father, the eternal source of the divine life in the Trinity. It in turn addresses itself in a special way to the Father, rendering him the homage and the glory of which it is capable through the power of Christ. The flow of divine life between the eternal Father and of the Church is achieved and completed through the operation of the Holy Ghost.
>
> The liturgy, reaching from God to man, and connecting man to the fullness of the Godhead, is the action of the Trinity in the Church. The Church in her liturgy partakes of the life of the divine society of the three persons in God. (Michel 1937: 40)

The first out-turning of God was creation itself, which brought into being non-divine creatures who could receive and return love. God created the world for the sake of this communion, which is why the early Christians said the world was created for the sake of the church. This was the plan of creation from the very beginning, although no one could have known it, not even the highest angels, until the mystery was revealed by the Incarnation (Eph 3). Liturgy and sacraments are the celebration of the Christian mystery that the Pasch of Christ brought to fulfillment, but that mystery was prepared for by Israel, and it predates Abraham by being a plan in the will of the Father from the very beginning.

This is summarized in paragraph 1066 of the *Catechism of the Catholic Church*, which is the first paragraph in the section concerning liturgy:

> In the Symbol of the faith the Church confesses the mystery of the Holy Trinity and of the plan of God's "good pleasure" for all creation: the Father accomplishes the "mystery of his will" by giving his beloved Son and his Holy Spirit for the salvation of the world and the glory of his name. Such is the mystery of Christ, revealed and fulfilled in history according to the wisely ordered plan that St. Paul calls the "plan of the mystery" and the patristic tradition will call the "economy of the Word incarnate" for the "economy of salvation."

Apparently, we join a liturgy already in progress, one begun in a place where we do not normally look. This liturgical activity stretches from creation, itself a protological cosmic liturgy, across the motion of the Logos in the divine economy, through Israel's typological foreshadowing, to the apostolic church, and arriving at the parousia, which is an eschatological liturgy of the heavenly Jerusalem. When the church celebrates her liturgy, she knows it is with cosmic and eschatological consequences.

Second, this definition assumes bidirectional traffic on the mystical ladder going from heaven to earth, and from earth to heaven. The name for this golden ladder is *hierarchy*. Calling liturgy hierarchical is not a reference to clerical domination; instead it refers to the fact that the church, in her ministers, mediates a powerful liturgy, which has its origin (*arche*) in God. Dionysius says, "In my opinion a hierarchy is a sacred order, a state of understanding and an activity approximating as closely as possible to the divine" (Pseudo-Dionysius 1987: ch. 3). Agape graciously descends across this golden ladder with its creative power to enlighten and enliven, and eucharistia gratefully ascends in thanksgiving and worship. Here is how Louis Bouyer pictures it:

> Across this continuous chain of creation, in which the triune fellowship of the divine persons has, as it were, extended and propagated itself, moves the ebb and flow of the creating Agape and of the created eucharistia ... Thus this immense choir of which we have spoken, basing ourselves on the Fathers, finally seems like an infinitely generous heart, beating with an unceasing diastole and systole, first diffusing the divine glory in paternal love, then continually gathering it up again to its immutable source in filial love. (Bouyer 1955: 28–29)

But a dissonance has been introduced. Lucifer, the morning star and the Prince of this tangible world, has broken the hierarchy and set himself up as a competing center. Sin is an-archy. Nothing could prevent the diastole of agape, but Satan's fall disrupted the systole of eucharistia. And Satan furthermore sought to draw man and woman into his rebellion. Original sin was the forfeiture of Adam and Eve's liturgical career. Alexander Schmemann says, "The only real fall of man is his noneucharistic life in a noneucharistic world" (Schmemann 1963: 34–35), and so he concludes that our redemption will require a liturgical reconstruction of our eucharistic life. This has happened in Christ, "For He Himself was the perfect Eucharist; He offered Himself in total obedience, love and thanksgiving to God. God was His very life. And he gave this perfect and eucharistic life to us. In Him God became our life ... [This Eucharist] is the movement that Adam failed to perform, and that in Christ has become the very life of man" (Schmemann 1963: 34–35). Liturgy is not one of the religions of the old Adam (human history is littered with them); it is the cult of the new Adam. Liturgy is not the religion of Christians; liturgy is the religion of Christ perpetuated in Christians. It is the praise of Christ passing through the lips of his church. That is why Christ is the mediator of all things in liturgy and sacrament, and everything must pass through the hypostatic union before it is of any use to us. The liturgy on earth is the visible enactment of the invisible cosmos gathered round the throne of God, and the two are united. There are not two liturgies, one in heaven and one on earth; there is one liturgy, in heaven and on earth. Liturgy is an action of the whole Christ, and "those who even now celebrate it without signs are already in the heavenly liturgy, where celebration is wholly communion and feast" (*Catechism of the Catholic Church* §1136). On earth we celebrate it with sign and sacrament.

Third, our ascent cannot be forced; it must have our cooperation. In Greek, it is called synergy: the working together of two energies that are unequal in power but equal in necessity. "The incorporation of man into Christ and his union with God requires the co-operation of two unequal, but equally necessary, forces: divine grace and human will" (Gillet 1987: 23). The human being has been created in the image of God, indeed, created with such a full image of the Sovereign One that free will is operative on every level of our lives, even our religion. There is one corner of the cosmos that God has placed off limits even to his own omnipotence, and that is the human heart. He shelves his power in deference to our free will. Therefore, to enter into the life-giving stream of liturgy that flows from heaven to earth, and back up again, requires conversion. Christ finally and fully does the cosmic priesthood that Adam and Eve failed to do, and now invites and empowers the members of his body to assist at his worship. Christ is the premier liturgist, and we apprentice ourselves to him in a process that must take up our whole life. Placing our entire life in his hands requires a progressive conformation to him, involving a constant death to sin. There is an ascetical cost to celebrating liturgy.

Fourth, and finally, the teleological end of liturgy is deification—*theosis*—which is union with God. Our human nature does not change into a divine nature, as some ideas of pantheism would have it. Rather, we can be plunged into God's energies and be filled with divine light and heat—the fathers used the illustration of an iron bar being plunged into fire and glowing hot. "His divine power has bestowed on us everything that makes for life and devotion, through the knowledge of him who called us by his own glory and power. Through these, he has bestowed on us the precious and very great promises, so that through them you may come to share in the divine nature ..." (2 Peter 1:3–4). This is possible because the Son has first plunged himself into humanity in the womb of the Virgin. The Incarnation of God is the inverse of the deification of man; the descent to Bethlehem is the mirror of our ascent to the heavenly Jerusalem. More than a moral code or doctrinal system, Christianity is the transfiguration of a person into a liturgical being who, like the spiritual powers, praises God in every act and thought. This is the final glory of a man and woman. The person schooled by the liturgical life becomes a theologian, that is, someone who is in "a personal communion with *Theos*, the Father, through the Logos, Christ, in the Holy Spirit—an experience lived in a state of prayer" (Spidlik 1986: 1). Our deification is the reason for the church and her sacraments.

In summary, the Trinity's circulation of love turns itself outward, and in humility the Son and Spirit work the Father's good pleasure for all creation, which is to invite our ascent to participate in the very life of God; however, this cannot be forced, it must be done with our cooperation. Such a definition leads me to two assertions regarding the integration of liturgy and sacrament: the liturgy itself is a sacrament, and each individual sacrament is best understood as equipping us for this liturgical life.

LITURGY IS SACRAMENTAL

A more familiar definition of liturgy might simply say that it is the celebration of the paschal mystery of Christ. We would not disagree. But the thicker definition above has attempted to put the scale of that paschal mystery before our eyes, as Jean Daniélou does here:

> The Christian faith has only one object, the mystery of Christ dead and risen. But this unique mystery subsists under different modes: it is prefigured in the Old Testament, it is accomplished historically in the earthly life of Christ, it is contained in mystery in the sacraments, it is lived mystically in souls, it is accomplished socially in the Church, it is consummated eschatologically in the heavenly kingdom. Thus the Christian has at his disposition several registers, a multi-dimensional symbolism, to express this unique reality. (Taft 1997: 28–29; citing Daniélou 1945: 17)

The paschal mystery saturates God's creation, and to step into liturgy is to step into the storm center of God's economy. This is the mystery that was made flesh in the Incarnate One (which is why Christ is the primordial sacrament of God), but Calvary is not the only place at which this mystery is found at work. Like an underground aquifer whose springs break surface in various locations, the work of salvation has been under way since Eden, breaking surface in human history in order to bring creation to its fulfillment.

> Through its sacred signs the liturgy celebrates the work of salvation that God the Father accomplished through Christ in the Holy Spirit. This salvation is a work that God the Father has carried on through the ages. This is the salvation announced by the patriarchs and prophets ... This is the salvation that was fully revealed in Christ Jesus ... This is the salvation that comes to pass in the 'age of the Church' ... This is the salvation that will reach its consummation in Christ's glorious Second Coming. (*Collection of Masses* 1988: §4)

The work of salvation we celebrate through the sacred signs of every liturgy has a connection to the multiple registers or modes under which the mystery of Christ subsists. The liturgy itself can therefore be understood as sacrament for making the activity of the Trinity present in efficacious signs.

By defining liturgy as sacrament, we are moving from a thin, phenomenological definition to a thick, theological definition. A sacramental liturgy, in its entirety, is a visualization (making visible) and symbolization (making sacrament) of the mystical work of God. The eye of the body is too small to see all that is going on, so an eye of faith has been given. As the fathers said, in a sacrament one thing seen while another is understood, and where the eye of the sociologist sees an assembly, a theologian is able to see the body of Christ; where the eye of the anthropologist sees a festive ceremony, the liturgy is immersion in the eighth day; where the eye of the ritologist sees a ritual, it is actually a liturgy. The liturgy celebrates, sacramentally, the saving work of God carried on through the ages; the liturgy celebrates, sacramentally, the invisible liturgy of heaven; the liturgy celebrates, sacramentally, the perpetual presence of the Incarnate One, who, by uniting the divine and the human in his own person, makes possible the deification of those with whom this same form of life is shared by grace. The outstretched perichoresis of the Trinity brings us to deification.

If a sacrament is an efficacious sign that makes visible an invisible grace, then what does the liturgy make visible? That is an appropriate question for liturgical theology. Alexander Schmemann attempted an answer in his book *The Eucharist* when he deliberately included the word "sacrament" in each of the twelve chapters: the Sacrament of the Assembly, the Sacrament of the Kingdom, the Sacrament of Entrance, the Sacrament of the Word, the Faithful, Offering, Unity, Anaphora, Thanksgiving, Remembrance, the Holy Spirit, and Communion. It is 160 pages before Schmemann reveals his reasoning:

> Therefore it was not to sound more solemn but perfectly consciously and responsibly that I have entitled each of the chapters devoted to the first parts of the liturgy ... with the word *sacrament*. For I see the entire task at hand in demonstrating as fully as possible that the divine liturgy is a single, though also 'multifaceted,' sacred rite, a single sacrament, in which all its 'parts,' their entire sequence and structure, their coordination with each other, the necessity of each for all and all for each, manifests to us the inexhaustible, eternal, universal and truly divine meaning of what has been and what is being accomplished. (Schmemann 1987: 160–161)

What does the liturgy sacramentalize? It assembles a people of God and knits Jew and Gentile, male and female, slave and free into one mystical body; they submit themselves to the rule of God, otherwise known as the Kingdom; they enter into a sacred time and sacred space, where they find the first rung of the ladder that ascends to the heavenly throne; they listen to God's word which stirs a response in new hearts cracking out of stone into flesh; the faithful don their baptismal robes of priesthood and intercede on behalf of the world; continuing their ascending gesture they offer their first fruits, the work of human hands, bringing creation to its Creator to be sanctified; they exchange a kiss of unity that overcomes the alienation that divides human beings; and the Holy Spirit descends upon what they lift up, and a sacrifice is perfected by becoming the body and blood of Christ, who alone is the perfect sacrifice; we participate in his action by prayer and communion. One thing is seen, but all this invisible activity is understood to be operating in a sacramental liturgy. The temple is experienced and perceived as a gathering together of heaven and earth, and from the altar in the church shines the light of Mount Tabor upon our world, a transfiguring light for our daily lives. The ritual liturgy expands into a constantly lived liturgy.

The modern understanding of symbol wrongly places a ditch between symbol and the thing symbolized, but the etymology of the word means the opposite: *sym + ballo* means to throw together. An object was broken in half (a coin or bone in ancient practice), and at a later date the two contracting partners would "symbolize them." In a symbolic liturgical act, what is thrown together? God's life and ours, heaven and earth, form and matter, grace and sacramental rite. We do not celebrate the liturgy; rather, liturgy is the organ by which we celebrate the Kingdom of God. The liturgy symbolizes the divine kingdom. With her symbols the church does not represent or illustrate or call to mind or denote the kingdom; with her symbols she epiphanizes the kingdom in her activity. The sacramental liturgy is a symbol of the kingdom, made possible because Christ shares with his church his symbolic capacity:

> In Christ the world is joined together again in symbol, in a profusion of symbols. The invisible part appears in the visible: the visible draws its meaning from the invisible. Each symbolizes the other in the 'house of the world', of which God is the 'eccentric centre', being radically transcendent. God transcends the intelligible as well as the visible, but through the incarnation of the Logos he penetrates them both, transfigures and unites them. The world is a vast incarnation which the fall of the human race tries to contradict. The *diabolos*, the opposite of the *symbolon*, is continually trying to keep apart the separated halves of the ring; but they come together in Christ. Christian symbolism expresses nothing less than the union in Christ of the divine and the human—of which the cosmos becomes the dialogue—displaying the circulation in Christ of glory between 'earth' and 'heaven', between the visible and the invisible. (Clement 1996: 219)

SACRAMENTS ARE LITURGICAL

Sacramental theology has aided us in dilating the definition of liturgy, and provided it a more sure theological footing. Now it is time for liturgy to return the favor. What can liturgy add to our understanding of sacraments?

Sacrosanctum Concilium is the Catholic Church's Constitution on the sacred liturgy, but it has some remarks to make about sacraments, and it will prove illuminating to notice what they are. It also begins, as we did above in our definition of liturgy, at the point where the divine economy pours forth from the heart of God and directs itself toward our salvation. God wills all people to be saved (I Tim 2:4), and he spoke in many and various ways by the prophets (Heb 1:1), but these works of God were but a prelude to the work of Christ in redeeming mankind and giving perfect glory to God. The salvation history that was ripening under the care of Israel climaxed in Christ's paschal mystery, wherein Christ destroyed our death by dying and restored our life by rising. This gave birth to the church. "It was from the side of Christ as He slept the sleep of death upon the cross that there came forth 'the wondrous Sacrament of the Church'" (*Sacrosanctum Concilium* §5). Thus, the whole church, in her entirety, is to be considered a sacrament; the church not only has sacraments, she is a sacrament. Christ is a sacrament of the Father and makes him present; the church is a sacrament of Christ and makes him present, and the seven mysteries are a sacrament of the church and makes her present in each one. The church is a visible communion in grace; she is a visible realization of God's economy of salvation in history; she is an efficacious sign that already contains the redemptive reality.

Only under this light can the apostolic mission and foundation of the church be properly understood. "Just as Christ was sent by the Father, so also He sent the apostles, filled with the Holy Spirit" (*Sacrosanctum Concilium* §6). Why did he do that? Two answers are given. First, the apostles are sent so that "by preaching the gospel to every creature, they might proclaim that the Son of God, by His death and resurrection, had freed us from the power of Satan and from death, and brought us into the kingdom of His Father" (*Sacrosanctum Concilium* §6). But that is not enough; there is a second, intricately connected reason why the apostles were sent. "His purpose also was that they might accomplish the work of salvation which they had proclaimed, by means of sacrifice and sacraments, around which the entire liturgical life revolves" (*Sacrosanctum Concilium* §6). Proclaim it, yes, but accomplish it too. Because the thing the apostles were to accomplish was beyond natural human powers, it is done by sacrifice and sacrament. "To accomplish so great a work, Christ is always present in His Church, especially in her liturgical celebrations" (*Sacrosanctum Concilium* §7). From that time forward the church has lived her liturgical life by proclaiming the gospel and celebrating the sacraments.

To restate: our liturgical life revolves around the sacrifice and sacraments because they accomplish the work of salvation that Jesus achieved, which he then built into the apostolic foundation of his church. When the Constitution later speaks about a *liturgy of the sacraments*, it is not referring to the liturgical format for performing sacraments; it is saying that the sacraments give access to the font of sanctification from which the church lives her liturgical life. "Thus, for well-disposed members of the faithful, the Liturgy of the Sacraments and sacramentals sanctifies almost every event in their lives; they are given access to the stream of Divine Grace which flows from the Paschal Mystery of the passion, death, the resurrection of Christ, the font from which all Sacraments and sacramentals draw their power" (*Sacrosanctum Concilium* §61). If anyone thinks that liturgy can exist separate from sacraments, or vice versa, because liturgy is our act of worship and sacrament is God's application of grace, then one can already sense this barrier crumbling. Tradition has customarily identified two ends of liturgy, namely, the sanctification of human beings and the glorification of God. (Pairings of these two can be found in *Sacrosanctum Concilium* at §10 "the sanctification of men in Christ and the glorification of God"; §61 "the sanctification of men in the praise of God"; §112 "which is the glory of God in the sanctification of the faithful.") These two purposes are twinned, because the latter happens when the former occurs: God is glorified when human beings are sanctified. The liturgy of the sacraments sanctifies men and women, which builds up the body of Christ, and thereby gives worship to God: we could easily say they capacitate us for liturgy by divinizing us.

From this viewpoint, our definition of sacrament can be thickened. Sometimes the sacraments seem to be treated as band-aids for sin, intended to repair a damaged good, go back to an earlier state, erase a debit. But a recuperative cure is for the sake of health, and likewise the medicinal sacrament is for the sake of transformation. Not merely medicinal, sacraments are also transformative; not merely therapeutic, they are also constructive. In his book on deification, Nellas expresses it nicely: "The Church is creation reassembled and restructured sacramentally. It is higher than the first creation. The world is no longer the house of man only, but the house of the living God" (Nellas 1987: 145). Sacraments reassemble and restructure matter toward its liturgical end, as seen in the book of Revelation, and they capacitate us in our liturgical identity as cosmic priests. Vladimir Lossky writes, "After the Fall, human history is a long shipwreck awaiting rescue: but the port of salvation is not the goal; it is the possibility for the shipwrecked to resume his journey whose sole goal is union with God" (Lossky 1978: 84). Yes, the sacraments patch sinful holes in our lives, but they do so for the purpose of rigging us for our journey to deification. In his book *The Wellspring of Worship* Jean Corbon emphasizes this thought:

> What we call the sacraments are in fact the divinizing actions of the body of Christ in our own very humanity ... During his earthly life Jesus could not attain to the full development of his power to divinize; he was limited in his relationships, not by his body as such but by its mortality. Once he had conquered death, these limitations were transcended and abolished. In this sense, the body of Christ became fully 'sacramental' as a result of the cross and resurrection. (Corbon 1988: 173)

The Christian is on a liturgical journey from exile to the New Jerusalem, and the sacraments accompany the Christian at every stage.

The sacraments communicate divine life: they inaugurate it, nourish it, heal it, and order it. This is how the sacraments are categorized: sacraments of initiation (baptism, confirmation, Eucharist), sacraments of healing (anointing the sick and reconciliation), and sacraments in the service of communion (holy orders and marriage). These accompany the faithful from the cradle to the grave, giving a foretaste of the heavenly liturgy. Baptism inaugurates the pilgrimage through the narrow gate of conversion by placing our life under the Holy Spirit, and bestowing a character (spiritual power) that enables the baptized to participate in the church's own worship; an additional character is bestowed in confirmation to strengthen that grace which further conforms the Christian to the ministry of Christ, and places the Christian in a new order of ministerial service; the wages of sin are death and as embodied persons we battle with death in the form of illness, so require from the sacrament of anointing strength, peace, and courage that comes from being united to the passion of Christ; the struggle with sin in the Spirit is aided by the sacrament which reconciles both with God and with the Church, and remits the eternal punishment incurred by mortal sins; for the ministry at the altar certain men are configured to Christ by a special grace of the Holy Spirit, so that they may serve as Christ's instrument for his church; the natural order of marriage is raised up in faith to be a sacrament of Christ's own union with the church in a covenant ordered to the good of the couple and the generation of children; and the Eucharist stands as queen at the center of this array of sacraments, with all others leading to it or coming from it. In the others we receive a gift of grace, and in this one we receive the giver himself. Communion in the sacramental Christ makes us over into new persons, and by our communion in his body and blood we participate in his own communion with God.

Conclusion

That life which was with the Father became visible, and has appeared to us. A stable outside Bethlehem holds the tabernacle who holds in her womb the one who holds the cosmos in his hand. An eternal life enters the temporal realm; the uncircumscribable is circumscribed; the one before whom angels fall allows himself to be touched; the glorious light is veiled (except when it peeks out on Mount Tabor) in order to invite us to draw nearer; the immortal one descends into Sheol to rescue our father and mother who are responsible for our mortality. Water and blood were released from Christ's side by the soldier's spear and thus poured forth baptism and Eucharist. The sacraments do not stand between us and Jesus, like a wall, they extend from Jesus to us, like a bridge, and the faithful can swim up as they flow to the very heart of Christ and put their lips to his blood. Christ's life of sacrificial obedience to his Father received full expression on the cross, but it was active throughout his life, which involved giving himself over to the Father. A Christian is a eucharistic person in the making, being conformed to Christ by the Holy Spirit, who spiritualizes our worship by breathing in us with sighs too deep for words and equipping us with sevenfold charismatic gifts. Our liturgical life is lived around sacrifice and sacrament.

Suggested Reading

Corbon (1988); Schmemann (1963 and 1987). See also Cabasilas (1974); Fagerberg (2003 and 2013).

Bibliography

Bouyer, L. (1955), *The Meaning of the Monastic Life* (London: Burns & Oates).
Cabasilas, N. (1974), *The Life in Christ* (Crestwood, NY: St. Vladimir's Seminary Press).
Clement, O. (1996), *The Roots of Christian Mysticism* (New York: New York City Press).
Collection of Masses of the Blessed Virgin Mary (1988), the General Introduction (New York: Catholic Book Publishing Co.).
Corbon, J. (1988), *The Wellspring of Worship* (New York: Paulist Press).
Daniélou, J. "Le Symbolisme des rites baptismaux." *Dieu vivant* 1 (1945): 15–43.
Fagerberg, D. W. (2003), *Theologia Prima: What is Liturgical Theology?* (Chicago: Liturgy Training Publications, Hillenbrand Books).

Fagerberg, D. W. (2013), *On Liturgical Asceticism* (Washington, DC: Catholic University of America Press).

Gillet, L. (1987), *Orthodox Spirituality* (Crestwood, NY: St. Vladimir's Seminary Press).

Lossky, V. (1978), *Orthodox Theology, An Introduction* (Crestwood, NY: St. Vladimir's Seminary Press).

Michel, V. (1937), *The Liturgy of the Church, According to the Roman Rite* (New York: Macmillan).

Nellas, P. (1987), *Deification in Christ: The Nature of the Human Person* (Crestwood, NY: St. Vladimir's Seminary Press).

Pseudo-Dionysius (1987), *The Celestial Hierarchy*, in Pseudo-Dionysius, *The Complete Works*, trans. Colm Luibheid with Paul Rorem (New York: Paulist Press).

Schmemann, A. (1963), *For the Life of the World* (Crestwood, NY: St. Vladimir's Seminary Press).

Schmemann, A. (1987), *The Eucharist* (Crestwood, NY: St. Vladimir's Seminary Press).

Spidlik, T. (1986), *The Spirituality of the Christian East* (Kalamazoo, MI: Cistercian Press).

Taft, R. (1997), "Toward a Theology of the Christian Feast," in his *Beyond East and West: Problems in Liturgical Understanding* (Rome: Pontifical Oriental Institute), 15–29.

CHAPTER 30

ONE BAPTISM, ONE CHURCH?

GEOFFREY WAINWRIGHT

AGREEMENTS, DIFFERENCES, RESOLUTIONS

PHENOMENOLOGICALLY, baptism is readily described as application of water to the body of a person under invocation of the Triune Name of God: "N., I baptize you in the name of the Father and of the Son and of the Holy Spirit"; "The servant of God, N., is being baptized in the name of the Father and of the Son and of the Holy Spirit." Theologically, the questions quickly arise as to the meaning and effect of that act, and as to who may properly perform and who may properly receive it. Ecclesiologically, the issue concerns the nature and location of the church, its character, and composition—its identity. Ecumenically, the engaging topic is that of the existing or envisaged recognition of baptism across the boundaries of variously divided communities making ecclesial claims and the possible role of such recognized baptisms in the achievement or restoration of unity among them. The dogmatic interplay between baptism and church will recur throughout our record and reflections.

BAPTISM, EUCHARIST, AND MINISTRY: THE LIMA TEXT OF 1982

Eventually we shall have to revert to earlier Christian history, and then in turn we shall have to move a little further forward into the most recent developments; but we may appropriately begin with what became known as "the Lima text" of the World Council of Churches (WCC). Decades in the making, the text received its final formulation by the WCC Commission on Faith and Order at its plenary meeting in Lima, Peru, in January 1982, where the document was unanimously approved as ready or mature for submission to "all churches" under the title *Baptism, Eucharist and Ministry* (Faith and Order

Paper No. 111). It was accompanied by a respectful invitation for attention and response on the part of the churches. No claims were made of full consensus, but the text certainly underwent wide discussion among its addressees and justified its aim to register and promote "convergence." Our own chief concern here will be with baptism, but incidences will be registered with Eucharist and ministry.

The approach in *Baptism* is strongly Christological, which does not in any way demean the Trinitarian range:

> Christian baptism is rooted in the ministry of Jesus of Nazareth, in his death and in his resurrection. It is incorporation into Christ, who is the crucified and risen Lord; it is entry into the New Covenant between God and God's people. Baptism is a gift of God, and is administered in the name of the Father, the Son, and the Holy Spirit. St Matthew records that the risen Lord, when sending his disciples into the world, commanded them to baptize. The universal practice of baptism by the apostolic Church from its earliest days is attested in letters of the New Testament, the Acts of the Apostles, and the writings of the Fathers. The churches today continue this practice as a rite of commitment to the Lord who bestows his grace upon his people. (n. 1)

The New Testament offers "various images" to "unfold the meaning of baptism," some of them "linked with the symbolic uses of water in the Old Testament":

> Baptism is participation in Christ's death and resurrection (Rom. 6:3–5; Col. 2:12); a washing away of sin (1 Cor. 6:11); a new birth (John 3:5); an enlightenment by Christ (Eph. 5:14); a reclothing in Christ (Gal. 3:27); a renewal by the Spirit (Titus 3:5); the experience of salvation from the flood (1 Peter 3:20–21); an exodus from bondage (1 Cor. 10:1–2); and a liberation into a new humanity in which barriers of division whether of sex or race or social status are transcended (Gal. 3:27–28; 1 Cor. 12:13). The images are many but the reality is one (n. 2).

Baptism then goes on to expound in a more systematic way "The Meaning of Baptism," which might also be termed its benefits: "Participation in Christ's Death and Resurrection"; "Conversion, Pardoning and Cleansing"; "The Gift of the Spirit"; "Incorporation into the Body of Christ"; and "The Sign of the Kingdom."

When the text arrives at "Baptism and Faith," the way is still open to a broad agreement on the principles, which will nevertheless find theological understanding and practical embodiment in divisive ways. In principle, "Baptism is both God's gift and our human response. It looks towards growth into the measure of the stature of the fullness of Christ (Eph. 4:13). The necessity of faith for the reception of the salvation embodied and set forth in baptism is acknowledged by all churches. Personal commitment is necessary for responsible membership in the body of Christ" (n. 8).

Already, however, the Lima text has hinted at the ecumenical, indeed ecclesiological, issues that underlie the (recognizably limited) measure of agreement concerning baptism, and which call for resolution in the cause of ecclesial unity. Thus, already paragraph 6 under the headline "Incorporation into the Body of Christ":

> Administered in obedience to our Lord, baptism is the sign and seal of our common discipleship. Christians are brought into union with Christ, with each other and with the Church of every time and place. Our common baptism, which unites us to Christ in faith, is thus a basic bond of unity. We are one people and are called to confess and serve one Lord in each place and in all the world. The union with Christ which we share through baptism has important implications for Christian unity. 'There is ... one baptism, one God and Father of us all ...' (Eph 4:4–6). When baptismal unity is realized in one holy, catholic, apostolic Church, a genuine Christian witness can be made to the healing and reconciling love of God. Therefore, our one baptism into Christ constitutes a call to the churches to overcome their divisions and visibly manifest their fellowship.

The "commentary" to paragraph 6 needed immediately to add this:

> The inability of the churches to recognize their various practices of baptism as sharing in the one baptism, and their actual dividedness in spite of mutual baptismal recognition, have given dramatic visibility to the broken witness of the Church ... The need to recover baptismal unity is at the heart of the ecumenical task as it is central for the realization of genuine partnership within the Christian communities.

THREE ISSUES NEEDING RESOLUTION

At the level of dogma and liturgy we ourselves may formulate the following issues as needing resolution: first, who may properly receive baptism? Second, in what does the ritual of baptism properly consist? Third, and perhaps the most difficult: who, or what community or communities, has or have the right and responsibility to bestow baptism?

The Lima text has declared agreement as to "the necessity of faith for the reception of the salvation embodied and set forth in baptism" (n. 8). When the text arrives at "Baptismal Practice," the—perhaps relatively modern—question of "adult-believers" and "infants" has to be faced:

> While the possibility that infant baptism was also practised in the apostolic age cannot be excluded, baptism upon personal profession of faith is the most clearly attested pattern in the New Testament documents.
>
> In the course of history, the practice of baptism has developed in a variety of forms. Some churches baptize infants brought by parents or guardians who are ready, in and with the Church, to bring up the children in the Christian faith. Other churches practise exclusively the baptism of believers who are able to make a personal profession of faith ...
>
> All churches baptize believers coming from other religions or from unbelief who accept the Christian faith and participate in catechetical instruction. (n.11)

Both the baptism of believers and the baptism of infants take place in the Church as the community of faith. When one who can answer for himself or herself is baptized, a personal confession of faith will be an integral part of the baptismal service. When an infant is baptized, the personal response will be offered at a later moment in life. In both cases, the baptized person will have to grow in the understanding of faith ... At every baptism the whole congregation reaffirms its faith in God and pledges itself to provide an environment of witness and service. Baptism should, therefore, always be celebrated and developed in the setting of the Christian community. (n. 12)

The commentary to paragraph 12 provides a hint as to how the practices of "infant baptism" and "believers' baptism" may be beneficially accommodated within an ecumenically construed church: "In some churches which unite both infant-baptist and believer-baptist traditions, it has been possible to regard as equivalent alternatives for entry into the church both a pattern whereby baptism in infancy is followed by later profession and a pattern whereby believers' baptism follows upon a presentation and blessing in infancy. This example invites other churches to decide whether they, too, could not recognize equivalent alternatives in their reciprocal relationships and in church union negotiations." Paragraph 13 firmly declares that "Baptism is an unrepeatable act. Any practice which might be interpreted as 're-baptism' must be avoided."

We may thus arrive more directly at our second type of question: in what does the ritual of baptism consist? What are its words, its gestures, its material substance(s)? The Lima text declares straightforwardly: "Baptism is administered with water in the name of the Father, the Son and the Holy Spirit" (*Baptism*, 17). The trinitarian dimension is thus unambiguously affirmed, which may come to verbal expression both in the minister's pronouncement and in the profession of faith by recipient, sponsors, and the worshiping assembly. As to the "symbolic" quality of the water and the performative act: "In the celebration of baptism the symbolic dimension of water should be taken seriously and not minimalized. The act of immersion can vividly express the reality that in baptism the Christian participates in the death, burial and resurrection of Christ" (n. 18), which of course leaves possible the perhaps lesser gesture of pouring, while some would question the propriety of mere sprinkling.

Still under the heading of "Baptismal Practice," the Lima text arrives at another point where liturgical, and even dogmatic, variety exists between, and even within, the churches: namely, the moment and the agency of the Spirit's gift. The sub-heading "Baptism—Chrismation—Confirmation" covers the following exposition in paragraph 14:

In God's work of salvation, the paschal mystery of Christ's death and resurrection is inseparably linked with the pentecostal gift of the Holy Spirit. Similarly, participation in Christ's death and resurrection is inseparably linked with the receiving of the Spirit. Baptism in its full meaning signifies and effects both.

Christians differ in their understanding as to where the sign of the gift of the Spirit is to be found. Different actions have become associated with the giving of the Spirit. For some it is the water rite itself. For others, it is the anointing with chrism and/or the imposition of hands, which many churches call confirmation. For still others it is all three, as they see the Spirit operative throughout the rite. All agree that Christian baptism is in water and the Holy Spirit.

Unmentioned here is the sometimes debated matter of the minister of confirmation, especially if confirmation is viewed as a distinct sacrament in which bishops have had (historically varied) parts to play.

The responses of the churches to the Lima document display no agreed resolution as to "the relation between baptism and confirmation" (*Baptism*, 14), yet the issue may be moving towards some kind of dogmatic accommodation within the broader liturgical frame of a complex and temporally variable process of "Christian initiation":

> The responses to BEM reveal remarkable agreement on the conviction that God gives the Holy Spirit to those who die and rise with Christ in baptism. They show lack of agreement about how the anointing and sealing of the Spirit is to be expressed in the baptismal rite, and how it relates to confirmation and participation in the eucharist.
>
> The churches, in fact, demonstrate changing attitudes and actions concerning confirmation in accordance within an increasing awareness that originally there was one complex rite of Christian initiation. Confirmation is still seen to be serving two different purposes. Some churches see confirmation as the special sign of the gift of the Spirit in the total process of initiation; others take confirmation above all as the occasion for a personal profession of faith by those baptized at an earlier age. All are agreed that the first sign in the process of initiation into the body of Christ is the rite of water baptism; all are agreed that the goal of initiation is nourishment in the eucharist. Whichever emphasis is made in the understanding of confirmation, each is related to baptism and holy communion. This might be taken as a hopeful sign that the churches are coming to an understanding of initiation as a unitary and comprehensive process, even if its different elements are spread over a period of time. The total process vividly embodies the coherence of God's gracious initiative in eliciting our faith.[1]

Holy communion as that to which baptism gives access—"nourishment in the eucharist" as "the goal of initiation"—comes to expression early in the Lima text's *Eucharist*. Under "The Meaning of the Eucharist," paragraph 2 immediately reads thus:

> The eucharist is essentially the sacrament of the gift which God makes to us in Christ through the power of the Holy Spirit. Every Christian receives this gift of salvation through communion in the body and blood of Christ. In the eucharistic meal, in the eating and drinking of the bread and wine, Christ gives communion with himself. God himself acts, giving life to the body of Christ and renewing each member. In accordance with Christ's promise, each baptized member of the body receives in the eucharist the assurance of the forgiveness of sins (Matt 26:28) and the pledge of eternal life. (John 6:51–58)

We may wonder whether baptism can have been *recognizably* performed *without* giving access to Holy Communion. The historic and continuing existence of *rival* eucharistic

---

[1] *Baptism, Eucharist and Ministry 1982–1990* (1990: 112 esp.).

communities calls the celebration of baptism into question. If now, in an ecumenical situation, mutual recognition of baptism starts to take place, the possible implication for eucharistic admission across ecclesiastical lines must at least be investigated—and therewith the question of mutual ecclesial recognition gets further opened up and the solution of churchly reconciliation perhaps brought closer.

With that, we have arrived back at the third, and perhaps the most delicate and difficult of our baptismal questions: who, or what community or communities, has or have the right and responsibility to bestow baptism? For that right and responsibility implies ecclesial status and identity: it is "the church" that, as God's minister, gives baptism. In the matter of baptismal recognition, ecclesial identity is at stake. When mutual baptismal recognition comes into prospect, each partner must determine what ecclesial elements it claims for itself and what ecclesial elements it looks to find in its prospective partners. Before looking at those questions in an ecumenical age, we must first dig deeper into history and encounter the phenomenon of schism in various shapes and forms. It is in relation to the overcoming of schisms of various kinds and degrees that the possibility, achievement, purpose, and result of mutual recognition of baptism has come into prominence.

THE EARLIER HISTORY

It must be noted at the outset that in the early Christian centuries the question of baptismal recognition usually arose in connection with the transfer—or conversion—of people from a putatively false community to membership in a body claiming (sole) authenticity for itself. In the third century the scene of the major controversy shifted between North Africa and Rome. It arose when persons already baptized by the (schismatic) Novatianists sought admission to what what became known as the continuing Catholic Church. Did their baptism by the Novatianists count as true baptism, or should they now receive baptism at Catholic hands? Cyprian of Carthage, with epistolary support from Firmilian of Caesarea, held that Novatianist baptism was "no baptism," being administered outside the community of the church in which alone the Holy Spirit dwelt. But Stephen of Rome contended that the African Catholics should not *re*-baptize, for "whoever is baptized in the name of Christ, no matter where, immediately obtains the grace of Christ." Hands were to be laid on the converts, apparently in penance.[2] The Council of Arles (314) pronounced thus: "Concerning the Africans who use their own laws and rebaptize, the decision is that if anyone should come to the Church from heresy, they should ask him the creed and if they see that he was baptized in the Father and the Son and the Holy Spirit, let a hand only be imposed upon him so that he may receive the Holy Spirit. But if he should respond negatively to the question about

---

[2] All the material for the controversy about Novatianist baptism is found in Cyprian's Letters 69–75 (Vienna Corpus numbering), and in the anonymous *De rebaptismate*.

the Trinity, let him be baptized." Augustine's solution to the problem of baptism administered by the Donatists amounted to saying, in later "Roman" terminology, that it was "valid" but not—unless perhaps momentarily—"efficacious" until the baptized person was reconciled to the Catholic Church, where alone the Holy Spirit is found to remit sins.[3]

As the centuries rolled by, schisms continued to occur, often with connection to mutual suspicions or accusations of heresy. (Doctrinal) questions were often in the air regarding the "baptisms" performed by "the other party."

A focus in the massive split of 1054 fell on the judgment of Constantinople that Rome, by its insertion of the *filioque* clause into its confession of the Holy Spirit's essential procession, had inserted a dogmatic error into the creedal faith and so rendered its baptisms objectionable. We shall come later to the variety in Eastern Orthodox Churches as to their manners of receiving converts from other churches.

At the time of the Reformation, the Roman Council of Trent, doubtless with conversions in mind, declared anathema upon anyone who should say that "Baptism—even though conferred by heretics in the name of the Father and of the Son and of the Holy Ghost and with the intention of doing what the Church does—is not true Baptism" (Trent, session 7, canon 4; Denzinger-Hünermann, *Enchiridion symbolorum* 1617). "By baptism we are clothed in Christ and are made a new creature" (Trent, session 14; Denzinger-Hünermann 1671).

Those historic Protestant churches that baptize infants as well as baptizing persons upon personal profession have generally shown little difficulty in accepting any intended baptism performed in water in the name of the Holy Trinity.

THE ECUMENICAL MOVEMENT

With the coming of the modern ecumenical movement, the language of heresy and schism softened to that of "faith and order."

The First World Conference on Faith and Order, held at Lausanne in 1927, chastely declared: "We believe that in Baptism administered with water in the name of the Father, the Son and the Holy Spirit, for the remission of sins, we are baptised by one Spirit into one body. By this statement it is not meant to ignore the differences in conception, interpretation and mode which exist among us" (Report of Section VI). The Second World Conference on Faith and Order, held at Edinburgh in 1937, went slightly further: "Baptism is a gift of God's redeeming love to the Church; and, administered with water in the name of the Father, the Son, and the Holy Spirit, is a sign and seal of Christian discipleship in obedience to our Lord's command. It is generally agreed

---

[3] See Augustine, *De Baptismo contra Donatistas*, I, 11–12, and III, 13 (PL 43, 118–120 and 146); cf. *Serm.* 8, 11 (PL 38, 72–73), *Serm.* 71, 17–23 (PL 38, 460–466), and *Serm.* 269 (PL 38, 1234–1237).

that the united Church will observe the rule that all members of the visible Church are admitted by Baptism" (Final Report: "The Church of Christ—Ministry and Sacraments").

Around 1960, WCC Faith and Order studies on "One Lord, One Baptism: The Divine Trinity and the Unity of the Church" and "The Meaning of Baptism" (all in Faith and Order Commission Paper No. 29; London: SCM Press) eased the way towards the start in the mid-1960s on the process that would eventually produce the Faith and Order Commission's tripartite *Baptism, Eucharist and Ministry* (the "Lima Text" of 1982); and to that we shall soon return.[4]

VATICAN II: *LUMEN GENTIUM* AND *UNITATIS REDINTEGRATIO*

Meanwhile the Second Vatican Council took place. Already in its first constitution—that on the sacred liturgy—the Second Vatican Council located the "preeminent manifestation of the Church (*praecipua manifestatio Ecclesiae*)" in the eucharistic celebration under the presidency of the bishop (*Sacrosanctum Concilium*, 41–42). Arriving at its dogmatic constitution on the church, the Second Vatican Council resumed the sacramental theme in order to expound the nature of the church as a communion in Christ (*Lumen Gentium*, 7). In its very next paragraph the dogmatic constitution goes on to make an ontological identification between the one church of which it has been speaking and the Roman Catholic Church, while nevertheless opening the door—by at least a crack—to the presence of some ecclesial elements beyond the visible confines of the latter, which may thus eventually make for an integration of other Christian communities into "Catholic unity."

In the simultaneously issued decree *Unitatis Redintegratio* it was declared that "the restoration of unity among all Christians is one of the principal concerns of the Second Vatican Council"; and it was recognized that "in recent times the Lord of the Ages has begun to bestow more generously upon divided Christians remorse over their divisions and longing for unity":

> Taking part in this movement, which is called ecumenical, are those who invoke the Triune God and confess Jesus as Lord and Saviour. They do this not merely as individuals but also as members of corporate groups in which they have heard the Gospel, and which each regards as his Church and indeed, God's. And yet, almost everyone, though in different ways, longs for the one visible Church of God, a Church

---

[4] At this point we may already mention a booklet published by the WCC Department on the Laity, authored by Lukas Vischer, the Swiss Reformed theologian who was to play a major part in the construction of *BEM: Ye are Baptized: A Study of Baptism and Confirmation: Liturgies as the Initiation to the Ministry of the Laity* (1961).

truly universal and sent forth to the whole world that the world may be converted to the Gospel and so be saved, to the glory of God. (*Unitatis Redintegratio*, 1)

The decree then moves fairly quickly to consider the ecclesial status of the "separated brethren," both as individuals (baptized and believing) and in their own professedly churchly communities:

> One cannot charge with the sin of separation those who at present are born into these [dissentient] communities and in them are brought up in the faith of Christ, and the Catholic Church accepts them with respect and affection as brothers. For men who believe in Christ and have been properly baptized are put in some, though imperfect, communion with the Catholic Church (*in quadam cum Ecclesia catholica communione, etsi non perfecta, constituuntur*). (*Unitatis Redintegratio*, 3)

The ecumenical decree of Vatican II immediately goes on to give positive appreciation, in a nuanced way, to the worship practices of the separated communities:

> The brethren divided from us also carry out many liturgical actions of the Christian religion. In ways that vary according to the condition of each Church or community, these liturgical actions most certainly can truly engender a life of grace, and, one must say, can aptly give access to the communion of salvation . . .
>
> Little by little, as the obstacles to perfect ecclesiastical communion are overcome, all Christians will be gathered, in a common celebration of the Eucharist, into the unity of the one and only Church, which Christ bestowed on his Church from the beginning. This unity, we believe, subsists in the Catholic Church as something she can never lose, and we hope that it will continue to increase until the end of time. (*Unitatis Redintegratio*, 3–4)

But, to insist: what meanwhile of the Eucharist within and between the separated communities, and even in relation to the Catholic Church? The cases vary. The Eastern and Oriental Orthodox churches occupy a "special position" by virtue of their love for the liturgy and the sacramental validity of their ministries. The case of "the separated churches and ecclesial communities in the West" is historically and theologically different. Limiting our attention to recognizably Protestant churches (which include the Methodists, to which I belong):

> We rejoice that our separated brethren look to Christ as the source and centre of ecclesiastical communion . . . Although the ecclesial communities separated from us lack the fullness of unity with us that flows from Baptism, and although we believe they have not preserved the proper reality of the eucharistic mystery in its fullness, especially because of the sacrament of Orders, nevertheless when they commemorate the Lord's death and resurrection in the Holy Supper, they profess that it signifies life in communion with Christ and await his coming in glory. (*Unitatis Redintegratio*, 20–22)

The Roman Catholic Response to *BEM*

Since 1968 the Roman Catholic Church has been consistently represented in the WCC Faith and Order Commission by a dozen officially designated members, and its theologians played significant parts in the composition of the Lima text, *Baptism, Eucharist and Ministry*, to which that same church also made an official response. While offering various criticisms of detail, the Catholic response is generally positive in tone. A consistent feature is the call for greater attention by Faith and Order to the broader and deeper ecclesiological locus and dimensions of the themes treated, and especially to the nature, location, and exercise of authority in the church.[5]

With regard to the basic sacrament, the Roman response to *BEM* says this:

> We find the text on baptism to be grounded in the apostolic faith received and professed by the Catholic Church. It draws in a balanced way from the major New Testament areas of teaching about baptism; it gives an important place to the witness of the early church. While it does not discuss all major doctrinal issues that have arisen about baptism, it is sensitive to the effect that they have had on the development of the understanding of this sacrament and to the positive values of differing solutions that emerged; it appreciates the normative force that some forms of liturgical celebration may have and the significance of pastoral practice; within the ecumenical scope it sets for itself, it articulates the development of the Christian understanding of baptism with a coherent theological method. It has many affinities, both of style and of content, with the way the faith of the church about baptism is stated in the Second Vatican Council and in the *Liturgy of Christian Initiation* promulgated by Pope Paul VI. (Thurian [ed.], pp. 9–10)

While *Baptism* in paragraph 6 "does not give adequate attention to the implications of the fact that a person is baptized within a particular ecclesial fellowship in a divided Christianity," says the Roman response, "it rightly emphasizes that, in uniting people to Christ, baptism establishes a bond between them that is deeper than anything that divides them," and so "calls for an overcoming of division and a visible manifestation of baptismal fellowship" (Thurian [ed.], p. 11).

In its next paragraph, the Roman response notes that in speaking of the "dynamic of baptism which embraces the whole of life, extends to all nations, and anticipates the day when every tongue will confess that Jesus Christ is Lord to the glory of God," the Lima text "touches the question of the relation between baptism and salvation of all humankind—a question which is also connected with the necessity of the church for salvation"; yet, says the Roman response, it does not seem to deal adequately with "the doctrine of original

---

[5] Thurian (1988: 1–40) ('Roman Catholic Church'). References to pagination are given in the course of the ensuing paragraphs.

sin" and that doctrine's "understanding in faith about universal human sinfulness, about the universal need for salvation, about Christ as universal Saviour, and about the necessity of baptism for salvation"—all of which needs to be "explicitly incorporated into the discussion on the meaning and effects of baptism." Moreover, the language used in paragraphs 8–10 of *BEM*'s *Baptism* in reference to the church seems "less than adequate to express the ecclesiological dimension of baptismal grace." What Lima says about the celebration of baptism "is liturgically rich and includes all of the classical elements related to that celebration. An acceptance of it by ecclesial communities would certainly contribute greatly towards the process of mutual recognition of baptism" (Thurian [ed.], pp. 11–15).

The Lima text is praised by Rome for its statement that "baptism, as incorporation into the body of Christ, points by its very nature to the eucharistic sharing of Christ's body and blood" (*Baptism*, comm. 14b; cf. *Unitatis Redintegratio*, 22); but more could have been made of this, says the Roman response, in order to clarify particularly the ecclesiological dimension of baptism: "Christian initiation begun in baptism is completed by participation in the eucharist, which is the sacrament that engages and manifests the full reality of the church." As to eucharistic sharing: "For Catholics, it is unity in the profession of faith that constitutes the core of ecclesial communion. Because the eucharistic celebration is by its very nature a profession of the faith of the church, it is impossible for the Catholic Church presently to engage in general eucharistic sharing. For in our view we cannot share in the eucharist unless we share fully in that faith" (Thurian [ed.], p. 25). This, of course, is where the teaching authority of the ordained ministry comes into play, at all levels and times.

Not surprisingly—and indeed gratifyingly—the Catholic response to *BEM* concludes that the Lima text in each of its three areas "concentrates on those aspects of the theme that relate in some way to problems of mutual recognition leading to unity. Thus the development of the text leads to the need to work for 'mutual recognition of baptism' (*Baptism*, 15), and towards 'unity in eucharistic celebration and communion' (*Eucharist*, 28), and for 'mutual recognition of the ordained ministries' (*Ministry*, 51ff). Though the notion of visible unity still needs to be clarified from an ecumenical point of view, *BEM* is a reminder to us that the ecumenical movement aims not only at a renewal of attitudes of Christians, but also at a rethinking of relationships between divided Christian communities" (Thurian [ed.], p. 37).

BAPTISM, EUCHARIST AND MINISTRY 1982–1990[6]

Study of the responses to *BEM* from the churches (some 200 of them) noted the widespread recognition of "the text's stress on baptism as the primary and fundamental sacrament of unity" and the approval shown—amid the remaining ecclesiological tensions

---

[6] A thematized gathering of the churches' responses to *BEM* was made in *Baptism, Eucharist and Ministry 1982–1990* (1990).

and ecclesiastical claims—to the final sentence of *Baptism*, 6: "Our one baptism into Christ constitutes a call to the churches to overcome their divisions and visibly manifest their fellowship."

As to *Baptism* as a whole, in general, there is welcome for the text's firm grounding in holy scripture; the recognition of a fundamental relation that exists between God's gift and the human response of faith; the insistence on the priority of God's initiative; the setting of the individual's response of faith within the context of the faith of the believing community; the emphasis upon initiation as a process; the stress on the ethical implications of baptism; and the relation between a common baptism and the imperative to witness to that in unity.

The Orthodox Church in America called for an explanation of the implications of "the recognition of authentic and acceptable baptisms in divided churches for the unity of Christians in the one church of Christ" and a clarification of what is implied about "the ecclesial reality of those communities in which these baptisms, so recognized, are performed." For, indeed, the "implications" of this recognition are at the very heart of the churches' self-understanding in their search for visible unity. The same Orthodox Church in America asked about the creed used in baptism: "For the Orthodox, the content of the credal confession of faith made at baptism is of crucial importance" (*Baptism, Eucharist and Ministry 1982–1990*, pp. 52–53).

Following such study of the churches' responses to *BEM*, the WCC Faith and Order Commission—at its meeting in Budapest (Hungary) in 1989—determined three "major issues demanding further study": "Scripture and Tradition; Sacraments and Sacramentality; The Search for Common Perspectives on Ecclesiology." Particularly interesting is the prominence suggested for the notion of *koinonia* (communion, participation, fellowship), which was "currently being given serious attention by many churches" and might be "pursued seriously in Faith and Order work towards a convergent vision on ecclesiology":

> *Koinonia* in the life of the Father, the Son and the Holy Spirit … is the centre of all who confess Jesus Christ as Lord and Saviour. They share and participate in the gospel and in the apostolic faith, in suffering and in service … This *koinonia* is lived in Christ through baptism (Rom. 6) and the eucharist (1 Cor. 11) and in the community with its pastors and guides (Heb. 13). *Koinonia* means in addition participation in the holy things of God and the communion of the saints of all times and places (*communio sanctorum* in the double sense of the word). Each local Christian community is related in *koinonia* with all other local Christian communities with whom it shares the same faith. In this *koinonia* they live the catholicity of the church.[7]

Koinonia, in fact, became the title theme of the Fifth World Conference on Faith and Order, held at Santiago de Compostela (Spain), in 1993: *On the Way to Fuller Koinonia*.[8]

---

[7] See *Baptism, Eucharist and Ministry 1982–1990* (1990: 131–151; esp. 150).

[8] Thus the title of the official report, *On the Way to Fuller Koinonia*, ed. Thomas F. Best and Günther Gassmann, Faith and Order Paper No. 166 (Geneva: WCC Publications, 1994).

Section III of the Conference was devoted to *BEM*. Its report figured under "Sharing a Common Life in Christ" (pp. 245–252).

As to baptism:

> A common baptism among the churches highlights the place of the sacrament in the appropriation of salvation. While all human creatures have in common their creation at God's hand, God's providential care for them, and certain social and cultural institutions which preserve human life, it is as they hear the Gospel and respond in faith that they are baptized and enter into the koinonia of Christ's body (1 Cor. 12:13), receive that share of the Holy Spirit which is the privilege of God's adopted children (Rom. 8:15f.), and so enjoy by anticipation that participation in the divine life which God promises and proposes for humankind (2 Pet. 1:4). (n. 13, p. 247)

Noting the increase in mutual recognition of baptisms, the report asks: "If the baptism celebrated by a community is recognized, then what else in the life of that community may already be recognized as ecclesial? Insofar as they recognize each other's baptisms, the churches may be at the start of developing a baptismal ecclesiology in which to locate other elements of shared belief and life. Meantime, mutual recognition of baptism may be attested, as is happening in some regions and among some churches, by the issuance of a common certificate of baptism and by presence and participation in each other's baptisms" (n. 12, p. 247). Section III at Santiago de Compostela, in fact, made the following recommendations:

- that Faith and Order put in process for consideration by the churches a way for mutual recognition of each other's *baptism* by the churches;
- that, where this is possible but not already done, the churches develop a common baptismal certificate;
- that the churches invite neighbour churches to participate in baptism in appropriate ways. (p. 252)

We might (at last!) come to a concrete example of the mutual recognition of baptism.

MAGDEBURG, APRIL 2007

In April 2007, at a service in Magdeburg cathedral, the mutual recognition of baptisms performed in their respective communities was declared and enacted by the Roman Catholic Bishops' Conference of Germany, the main Lutheran, Reformed, United, and Methodist churches in Germany, and, quite remarkably, the Orthodox Church and the Ethiopian and Armenian churches in Germany. The agreed statement on "Christian Baptism" ran thus:

> Jesus Christ is our salvation. Through him God has overcome the sinner's distance from God (Romans 5:10), in order to make us sons and daughters of God. As

participation in the mystery of Christ's death and resurrection, baptism means new birth into Christ. Whoever receives this sacrament and in faith affirms God's love is united with Christ and also with Christ's people from every time and place. As a sign of the unity of all Christians, baptism binds us to Jesus Christ, the foundation of this unity. Despite our different understandings of the Church, we share a basic common understanding of baptism.

Therefore we recognize every baptism performed in accordance with Jesus' command in the name of the Father and the Son and Holy Spirit through the sign of immersion in water or affusion with water, and we rejoice over every person who is baptized. The mutual recognition of baptism is an expression of the bond of unity that is grounded in Jesus Christ (Ephesians 4:4–6). Baptism thus performed is unique and unrepeatable.

We confess with the Lima Document: 'Our one baptism into Christ is a call to the churches to overcome their divisions and visibly manifest their fellowship' (*Baptism, Eucharist and Ministry*, B6).

In fact, "different understandings of the Church" point to the unavoidable questions of ecclesiology that we have been examining in this chapter: what is the church? What is the church for? And, Where is the church concretely to be found? What, ecumenically, are the necessary and sufficient conditions of its unity? What is the proper form of that unity?

The principal question is that of the body which claims the privilege and the responsibility of administering baptism, and the matter presents itself first in an "Orthodox" guise. Thus, for example, the "Basic Principles of the Attitude of the Russian Orthodox Church toward the Other Christian Confessions," issued from the Bishops' Council in the jubilee year 2000,[9] begins by declaring (1.1):

The Orthodox Church is the true Church of Christ established by our Lord and Saviour Himself, the Church confirmed and sustained by the Holy Spirit, the Church about which the Saviour Himself has said: 'I will build my church; and the gates of hell shall not prevail against it' (Mt. 16:18). She is the One, Holy, Catholic and Apostolic Church, the keeper and provider of the Holy Sacraments throughout the world, 'the pillar and ground of the truth' (1 Tim. 3:15). She bears full responsibility for the proclamation of the truth of Christ's Gospel, as well as full power to witness to 'the faith which was once delivered unto the saints' (Jude 3).

While the Orthodox Church, as "the true Church," considers itself the true steward of the sacraments, it treats in nuanced ways those who may "return to unity in the Church." The document of 2000 continues:

The ecclesial status of those who have separated themselves from the Church does not lend itself to simple definition. In a divided Christendom, there are still certain characteristics which make it one: the Word of God, faith in Christ as God and

---

[9] The text is available on the website of the Moscow patriarchate: www.mospat/ru/index.php?mid=91. It can be found in print in, for instance, *One in Christ* 41/2 (April 2006): 88–100.

Saviour come in the flesh (1 John 1:1–2; 4:2, 9), and sincere devotion. The existence of various rites of reception (through Baptism, through Chrismation, through Repentance) shows that the Orthodox Church relates to the different non-Orthodox confessions in different ways. The criterion is the degree to which the faith and order of the Church, as well as the norms of Christian spiritual life, are preserved in a particular confession. By establishing various rites of reception, however, the Orthodox Church does not assess the extent to which grace-filled life has either been preserved intact or distorted in a non-Orthodox confession, considering this to be a mystery of God's providence and judgement ("Basic Principles," 1.15–17).[10]

The Joint Working Group: "Ecclesiological and Ecumenical Implications of a Common Baptism"

According to the "study document" contained in the "Eighth Report (1999–2005)" from the Joint Working Group (JWG) between the Roman Catholic Church and the World Council of Churches,[11] baptism is an "expression and icon of the Church's very nature" (para. 14).

The JWG study document brings together in a noteworthy way the doctrinal, the liturgical, the cultural, and the ecumenical aspects of our question:

> 51. In the Latin tradition infant baptism received strong support in the theology of Augustine and his reaction against Pelagian views. This view gave expression to the fear of exposing infants to the danger of dying without being rescued from [original] sin by the saving work of Christ, as well as to the positive advantages of initiation into life in Christ and his Church that baptism brings. A restored theology of baptism and a critical re-evaluation of certain explanations of the consequences of original sin for children would give increased weight to the christological and ecclesiological

---

[10] In admitting converts, the Orthodox churches do—with some historical and geographical variety—compensate for what they apparently judge to have been lacking or mistaken in the faith and ritual of other would-be ecclesial bodies. See, for instance, Merja Merras, "Baptismal Recognition and the Orthodox Churches," in *Baptism and the Unity of the Church*, ed. Michael Root and Risto Saarinen (Grand Rapids, MI: Eerdmans; Geneva: WCC Publications, 1998) 138–149; John H. Erickson, "The Problem of the Sacramental Economy," in his *The Challenge of Our Past: Studies in Orthodox Canon Law and Church History* (Crestwood, NY: St. Vladimir's Seminary Press, 1991), 115–132; idem, "The Reception of Non-Orthodox into the Orthodox Church: Contemporary Practice," *St. Vladimir's Theological Quarterly* 41 (1997): 1–17.

[11] *Joint Working Group between the Roman Catholic Church and the World Council of Churches: Eighth Report 1999–2005: Geneva-Rome 2005* (Geneva: WCC Publications, 2005), 45–72 ("Ecclesiological and Ecumenical Implications of a Common Baptism: A JWG Study"). Accessible also in *Pontifical Council for Promoting Christian Unity Information Service* No. 117 (2004/iv) 188–204.

reality of baptism. These churches also recognize that there are risks of mishandling the gifts of God in baptizing children. The promises of Christian nurture given by parents and sponsors may not be kept and the sacrament may be profaned. In fact, these churches have, theoretically if not always in practice, required that baptism be delayed until the child is old enough to speak for him/herself when there is not a reasonable guarantee that the child will be nurtured in the faith. While these concerns, which must surely be intensified in our post-Christian world, do not amount to identifying with the position of churches that practise only believer's baptism, they certainly indicate a belief that the full pattern of Christian initiation must be respected. In this they affirm something that can serve as an important ground for recognition of baptism between them and churches that practise only believer's baptism.

52. We have proposed that the pattern of baptismal initiation has three elements: formation in faith, baptism in water, and participation in the life of the community. These three elements are present in the rite of water baptism itself for every church, though not in the same way. Likewise all three elements are present in the life-long process of Christian discipleship, with its continual formation in faith, recollection of baptismal grace and promise, and deepening participation in the life of the Church. If we ask about the relation of faith to baptism in reference to the water rite alone, the differences among the churches remain substantial. When we compare instead the wider pattern of baptismal initiation and formation in Christ, more extensive convergence emerges. It is a convergence that is compatible with, and even enriched by, the fact that different traditions emphasise one or other element of the pattern and put them together in different ways.

53. The convergence is grounded on the fact that churches recognize a paradigmatic and normative quality of baptism performed upon personal profession of faith, illustrated in the New Testament and practised by all churches, as the most explicit sign of the character of baptism. Those traditions that practise only this form of baptism in their pattern of initiation maintain a living witness to the reality of baptism the churches affirm together, and express powerfully the shared conviction that baptism is inherently oriented to personal conversion. Those traditions that practise infant baptism as part of their pattern of initiation maintain a living witness to the initiating call and grace from God that the churches agree enable human response, and express powerfully the shared convictions that infants and children are nurtured and received within the community of Christ's Church prior to any explicit confession.

54. It is being suggested that each church, even as it retains its own baptismal tradition, recognize in others the one baptism into Jesus Christ by affirming the similarity of wider patterns of initiation and formation in Christ present in every community...

The acknowledgement, in paragraph 53, of the "paradigmatic and normative quality" of "baptism performed upon personal profession of faith" becomes particularly poignant in "our post-Christian world." The achievement of the post-Vatican II "Rite for Christian Initiation of Adults"—and its adaptive imitation in other Western churches—is particularly to be welcomed.

Especially in connection with divergences over infant baptism—although the areas of dispute are wider—the JWG report recognizes among the issues needing resolution "the questions of the nature and purposes of the Church and its role in the economy of salvation" (n. 57); and it notes soberly that "the mutual recognition of baptism implies an acknowledgment of each other's baptism, but in itself is only a step toward full recognition of the apostolicity of the church involved" (n. 98). The question must be put in any constellation of presently divided "churches" among which mutual recognition of baptism exists: what more do you require of the partners—and of yourself—before you can discern "church"? Meanwhile, the JWG report offers a solemn admonition: "Through the ecumenical movement, separated Christians have come to acknowledge a significant degree of *koinonia*. In light of this we ask churches not to allow practices to develop, which threaten the unity they now share in respect of the *ordo*, theology and administration of baptism. One example is the replacement of the traditional Trinitarian baptismal formula (Father, Son, Holy Spirit) with alternative wording. Another example is the admission of persons to the eucharist before baptism" (n. 109). Programmatic admission of the unbaptized to the Lord's Table in fact downplays the ecclesiological significance of both sacraments.

It will be observed that the JWG study document does not yet speak of "our" common baptism but rather of "the growing acknowledgment of a common baptism"—so that "one can speak of a 'common' baptism in a legitimate, though qualified, sense" (n. 8). Looking at the widest ecumenical scene, there is still only a "convergence" of understanding and practice, and not the full consensus that would be necessary for full mutual recognition in the matter across the board. Nevertheless, some churches have already recognized as "Christian baptism" the rite as performed in some other ecclesial communities than their own. The time has perhaps come—among willing partners—to solidify that recognition in a formal doctrinal and canonical statement that sets out their common doctrine and practice. Such might even be concisely formulated in a common baptismal certificate as the Fifth World Conference on Faith and Order recommended from Santiago de Compostela in 1993. I could envisage a text as simple as: "At such a place, on such a date, N. was baptized in water, in the name of the Father and of the Son and of the Holy Spirit, for the remission of sins and for rebirth into the life in Christ"—signed by the minister, with specification of ecclesial allegiance; though a little elaboration might be possible.[12]

FAITH AND ORDER'S RECENT WORK ON BAPTISM AND CHURCH

In the last two decades, WCC Faith and Order has been paid sustained attention to ecclesiology and to baptism, in close collocation. In 1998 WCC Faith and Order produced a text under the title *The Nature and Purpose of the Church: A Stage on the Way to*

---

[12] The echo to the Nicene-Constantinopolitan Creed is deliberate, and liturgical historians will remember the formula from parts of the early medieval West: "Ego te baptizo ... in remissionem peccatorum."

a Common Statement (Faith and Order Paper No. 181), and seven years later this draft appeared in revised form in 2005 as *The Nature and Mission of the Church* (Faith and Order Paper No. 198). For ecclesiological purposes, the greatest progress in *The Nature and Mission of the Church* over the Lima text has been made by integrating into the picture of Lima's *Eucharist* 19 the other properly constitutive elements of the eucharistic community and communion:

> The communion of the Church is expressed in the communion between local churches, in each of which the fullness of the Church resides. The communion of the Church embraces local churches in each place and all places at all times. Local churches are held in the communion of the Church by the one Gospel, the one baptism and the one Lord's Supper, served by a common ministry.[13]

Springing from a 1997 consultation among "some twenty Christians—liturgists, theologians, church musicians, pastors," Faith and Order published a short collection of essays that looked at baptism particularly from a variety of cultural angles: *Becoming a Christian: The Implications of our Common Baptism* (eds. Thomas F. Best and Dagmar Heller, Faith and Order Paper No. 184 [Geneva: 1999]). This was followed by a much fuller anthology showing the current baptismal situation among the churches: *Baptism Today: Understanding, Practice, Ecumenical Implications* (Faith and Order Paper No. 207, ed. Thomas F. Best [Geneva: 2008]). A resultant "study text" appeared as *One Baptism: Towards Mutual Recognition* (Faith and Order Paper No. 210 [Geneva: 2011]). Signed by the director (Canon John Gibaut) and the moderator (Metropolitan Vasilios of Constantia-Ammichostos) of the WCC Commission on Faith and Order, it calls upon the churches to face positively the multiple questions involved in the "paradox" that "Baptism occurs in a particular church (with its own history of ecclesial relations and divisions), but brings persons into the unity of Christ's body, which is one" (n. 85; cf. n. 58).

Finally, the WCC Commission on Faith and Order arrived in 2012 at what was intended as a broad-ranging "convergence text" on ecclesiology, published in Geneva in 2013 as *The Church: Towards a Common Vision* (Faith and Order Paper No. 214). Signed again by the director and the moderator of the Commission on Faith and Order, it was to be sent—after the manner of *Baptism, Eucharist and Ministry* three decades earlier—to all the churches for their study and responses. In their preface the officers say, "Just as the convergence on baptism in the responses to *Baptism, Eucharist and Ministry* gave rise to a fresh impetus toward mutual recognition of baptism, similar ecclesial convergence on ecclesiology will play a vital role in the mutual recognition between the churches as they call on one another to visible unity in one faith and one eucharistic fellowship."

Of particular interest from the viewpoint of our own present chapter—"One Baptism, One Church?"—is the claim that the new text "addresses what many consider to be the

---

[13] So *Nature and Mission of the Church*, text of 2005, para. 65; cf. also 66.

main issues facing the churches in overcoming any remaining obstacles to their living out the Lord's gift of communion: our understanding of the nature of the Church itself." *The Church: Towards a Common Vision* continues thus: at "the initiative of God the Father, the Son and the Holy Spirit" the Church is at heart a participation in the *koinonia* of the Triune God. Baptism is a sign of union and unity in Christ and is one of several vehicles in the transmission of the Church's apostolicity:

> Each of the four gospels closes with a missionary mandate ... This command by Jesus already hints at what he wanted his Church to be in order to carry out this mission. It was to be a community of witness, proclaiming the kingdom which Jesus had first proclaimed, inviting human beings from all nations to saving faith. It was to be a community of worship, initiating new members by baptism in the name of the Holy Trinity. It was to be a community of discipleship, in which the apostles, by proclaiming the Word, baptizing and celebrating the Lord's Supper, were to guide new believers to observe all that Jesus himself had commanded. (n. 2)

> Most Christians agree that the local church is 'a community of baptized believers in which the word of God is preached, the apostolic faith confessed, the sacraments are celebrated, the redemptive work of Christ for the world is witnessed to, and a ministry of *episkopé* exercised by bishops or other ministers in the community' (n. 31, quoting from the Joint Working Group's study document of 1990, 'The Church: Local and Universal').

As to the Church "growing in communion," in the tension between the "already" and the "not yet," the document comments: "On the one hand, as the communion of believers held in personal relationship with God, the Church is already the eschatological community God wills. Visible and tangible signs which express that this new life of communion has been effectively realized are: receiving and sharing the faith of the apostles, baptising, breaking and sharing the eucharistic bread, praying with and for one another and for the needs of the world, participating in each other's joys and sorrows, giving material aid, proclaiming and witnessing to the good news and working together for justice and peace" (n. 34).

As to "sacraments," Faith and Order's ecclesiological text of 2012 registers, with tribute to Lima's *BEM*, "the growing convergence among churches in their understanding of baptism": "Through Baptism with water in the name of the Triune God, the Father, the Son and the Holy Spirit, Christians are united with Christ and with each other in the Church of every time and place ... Baptism is thus a basic bond of unity ... The general agreement about baptism has led some who are involved in the ecumenical movement to call for the mutual recognition of baptism" (n. 41). Moreover, "there is a dynamic and profound relation between baptism and the eucharist. The communion into which the newly initiated Christian enters is brought to fuller expression and nourished in the eucharist, which reaffirms baptismal faith and gives grace for the faithful living out of the Christian calling" (n. 42). The two sacraments are said to be "both *instrumental* (in that God uses them to bring about a new reality), and *expressive* (of an already existing reality) ... They are visible, effective actions instituted by Christ and, at the same time, are made effective by the action of the Holy Spirit who, by means of them, equips those who receive the sacraments with a variety of gifts for the edification of the Church and its mission in and for the world" (n. 44).

The convergence text issues a final challenge: "We ... invite churches to consider ... closer convergence about who may receive baptism and who may preside at the Church's liturgical celebrations?" (n. 44).

One baptism, one Church?

Towards one baptism, towards one church....

SUGGESTED READING

Baptism, Eucharist and Ministry (1982); *Baptism, Eucharist and Ministry: Report on the Process and Responses* (1990); Heller (2012).

BIBLIOGRAPHY

Baptism, Eucharist and Ministry (1982), (Faith and Order Paper No. 111) (Geneva: WCC Publications).

Baptism, Eucharist and Ministry 1982–1990: Report on the Process and Responses (1990), (Faith and Order Paper No. 149) (Geneva: WCC Publications).

Best, Thomas F. (ed.) (2008), *Baptism Today: Understanding, Practice, Ecumenical Implications* (Faith and Order Paper No. 207) (Geneva: WCC Publications).

Best, Thomas F., and Günther Gassmann (eds.) (1994), *On the Way to Fuller Koinonia: Official Report of the Fifth World Conference on Faith and Order, Santiago de Compostela 1993*. Faith and Order Paper No. 166. (Geneva: WCC Publications).

Best, Thomas F., and Dagmar Heller (1999), *Becoming a Christian: The Implications of Our Common Baptism* (Faith and Order Paper No. 184) (Geneva: WCC Publications).

The Church: Towards a Common Vision (2013), (Faith and Order Paper No. 214) (Geneva: WCC Publications).

Ferguson, E. (2009), *Baptism in the Early Church: History, Theology, and Liturgy in the First Five Centuries* (Grand Rapids, MI: Eerdmans).

Heller, D. (2012), *Baptized into Christ: A Guide to the Ecumenical Discussion on Baptism* (Geneva: WCC Publications).

Joint Working Group between the Roman Catholic Church and the World Council of Churches, Eighth Report (1998), *Ecclesiological and Ecumenical Implications of a Common Baptism* (Geneva: WCC Publications).

One Baptism: Towards Mutual Recognition. A Study Text (2011), (Faith and Order Paper No. 210) (Geneva: WCC Publications).

The Nature and Purpose of the Church: A Stage on the Way to a Common Statement (1998), (Faith and Order Paper No. 181) (Geneva: WCC Publications).

The Nature and Mission of the Church (2005), (Faith and Order Paper No. 198) (Geneva: WCC Publications).

Thurian, M. (ed.) (1988), *Churches Respond to BEM*, vol. VI (Faith and Order Paper No. 144) (Geneva: WCC Publications).

Wainwright, G. (1969), *Christian Initiation* (London: Lutterworth Press; Richmond, Virginia: John Knox Press); reprint with minor typographical corrections: Cambridge, England: James Clarke, 2002.

Wood, S. K. (2009), *One Baptism: Ecumenical Dimensions of the Doctrine of Baptism* (Collegeville, MN: Liturgical Press).

CHAPTER 31

···

CONFIRMATION

···

CHAD C. PECKNOLD AND
LUCAS LABORDE, S.S.J.

> *That which was visible of our Redeemer passed to the sacraments [of the Church].*
>
> —Pope St. Leo the Great, *Sermon 74.2*

In these fifth-century words of Pope St. Leo the Great, we can see the essential connection between the mystery of Christ and the mystery of the church. This continuity can be seen in retrospect, by the ancient patterns of the church's mysterious pilgrimage through the ages, and guided by the virtue of hope, we have faith that what the disciples saw with their own eyes, we now see by faith: Christ himself communicated to us through the sacraments of his holy church. The sacraments are not merely "structures" or "ordinances" of power or assembly; they are visible instruments of Christ's saving grace that he personally instituted for those who would freely believe in him and enter into communion with himself.

When it comes to the sacrament of confirmation, one may wonder what has in fact "passed" to us from what the disciples saw. "When the Apostles who were in Jerusalem had heard that Samaria had received the Word of God they sent unto them Peter and John, who, when they were come, prayed for them that they might receive the Holy Ghost; for He was not yet come upon any of them, but they were only baptized in the name of the Lord Jesus. Then they laid their hands on them, and they received the Holy Ghost" (Acts 8:14–17). What an extraordinary sight! The laying on of hands, the reception of the Holy Spirit! And yet how many have come to see the sacrament of confirmation as something much less than this? How many have seen in their confirmation something more analogous to high school graduation than the setting ablaze of the tongue with the gift of the Holy Spirit? The apostle Paul talks about being confirmed, being pledged, being sealed, being anointed with oil in the name of the Lord. This sacred oil of anointing is no mere sign, however. St. Cyril of Jerusalem compares anointing of confirmation to the Eucharist. He writes:

> You were anointed with oil, being made sharers and partners of Christ. And see well that you regard it not as mere ointment; for, as the bread of the Eucharist, after the

invocation of the Holy Ghost, is no longer mere bread but the body of Christ, so likewise this holy ointment is no longer common ointment after the invocation, but the gift of Christ and of the Holy Ghost, being rendered efficient by His Divinity. You were anointed on the forehead, that you might be delivered from the shame which the first transgressor always experienced, and that you might contemplate the glory of God with an unveiled countenance . . . As Christ, after His baptism and the descent of the Holy Ghost upon Him, going forth overcame the adversary, so you likewise, after holy baptism and the mysterious unction, clothed with the panoply of the Holy Ghost, stand against the adverse power and subdue it, saying: 'I can do all things in Christ, who strengtheneth me'. (*Mystagogical Catechesis*, 3)

Again, if one clings to the principle of either St. Cyril of Jerusalem or St. Leo the Great, a striking aspect becomes crystal clear: the sacrament of confirmation communicates to the disciple an enormous spiritual power that is intimately tied to communicating the Gospel. Through a brief examination of the apostles, Augustine, and Aquinas, and the teaching of the Catechism and Pope St. John Paul II, this chapter will examine why the sacrament of confirmation should be understood as central to Christian faith.

The Acts of the Apostles

An attentive reading of the Acts of the Apostles shows that sacraments and faith always go together—and this was true for the apostles before it was so for us. The link between faith and sacraments might first be thought about in terms of Christ's expectation that those to be healed had to evidence sufficient faith (cf. Acts 2:36–38; 8:35–38; 16:30–33; 18:8; 19:1–7). How would the apostles have understood this connection? As the Gospels note, there were times when Christ could not heal people in a certain place because of their lack of faith (cf. Mark 6:5–6; Mt 13:58). St. Augustine understood this connection between the offer of redemption and the response of faith well when he wrote: "The God who created you without you, will not save you without you" (*Sermon* 169, 13). Faith and sacraments are two elements that call for one another because the grace given in the sacrament is one that needs to be freely accepted. The very initial grace—the *initium fidei*, the grace of conversion or the grace of our first turning towards God—is effected by what St. Augustine would call "operative" grace. It is a motion in our faculties caused only by the power of God. But in order for this initial motion to bear fruit, it requires that the recipient accept it and cooperate with it. Actions that are subsequent to that initial grace—listening to preaching, reading certain books, turning away from sin, and so on—are also the effect of subsequent graces, but each of those "graced" actions build upon prior ones. One would not receive the words of preaching with an open heart if one had not heeded the Holy Spirit's motion to reject one's past sins. The journey towards sacraments of initiation is usually a long sequence of received graces with which one has cooperated. The very first grace is purely God's initiative, but all the subsequent ones are the joint action of grace and freedom (cooperative grace). Each of those actions enlarges the scope of the soul's understanding and freedom, enabling it to take further steps.

The series of initial graces that lead an unbaptized person towards Christ are of a transient character. They are graces that move one to specific acts. But God's wisdom has established that there be sacramental actions through which a *stable principle* of supernatural life is infused in the soul. The reception of the sacraments of initiation is the culmination of that conversion process. Through the infusion of sacramental grace, the action of grace in the soul is not of a merely transient nature, like the rains and the dew that fall from above, but becomes a wellspring in the heart of the believer, as Christ promised: "Let anyone who thirsts come to me and drink. Whoever believes in me, as scripture says: 'Rivers of living water will flow from within him'" (John 7:37b–38).

In this fashion, the sacraments of initiation provide the foundational, stable graces on which the whole of Christian life is built. Christian initiation is not the completion of the work, but the laying of the foundations of the building. Precisely because the construction of the building needs to continue after initiation, the role of preparation towards the sacraments consists in providing the context in which one learns how to cooperate with divine grace. It constitutes a privileged time in which the one to be initiated learns to listen to the Father and respond to the promptings of the Holy Spirit. This learning functions as a guarantee that this cooperation will continue after the reception of the sacraments of initiation.

Returning now to the exploration of the sacramental elements in the New Testament, we can see that the time of Christ's public ministry was for the disciples a time of growth and preparation that was oriented to their "initiation" in the events of Holy Week. Sharing in the Lord's public ministry was for the disciples a time in which, through the interaction of grace and free cooperation, their faith grew in depth and understanding.

To proceed further on this analogy, one should note that the kind of initiation that Christ's disciples underwent corresponds to the case of adult Christian initiation. The adult reception of sacraments of initiation is preceded by a free decision to follow Christ; a time of preparation and catechesis follows, and finally the sacraments are administered to them. But what could be the New Testament parallel to the very common case of infant baptism? In this case, there is no possibility of preparation. All the steps that in adult initiation precede the sacraments must be moved to the time that follows the reception of the sacraments. Arguably, a model for this could well be St. Paul's conversion. St. Paul was initiated at once, through his encounter with the risen Christ on the way to Damascus and his baptism a few days later (Acts 9:1–9). Note that the similitude with the paschal events is highlighted in that narrative: Saul spends three days in darkness, just as Jesus had spent three days in the tomb, the resurrection corresponding to his baptism when Ananias is sent to him. But St. Paul received sacramental initiation without having had significant time of preparation. It was a sudden and formidable change. Yet, the combination of faith and sacraments is always needed. In St. Paul's case, one in which the time of preparation was almost non-existent, a certain distension of time would be introduced afterwards in mystagogical fashion. The letter to the Galatians tells us that St. Paul spent three years in Arabia, and then went back to Damascus

(Gal 1:17–18). Not much is known about what happened through that time, but it may be presumed that this time constituted for St. Paul a time of inner growth and assimilation of the grace he received in his sudden conversion. Only after that time did he reach the full stature of Christ and was he summoned to serve the church.

The model of St. Paul's conversion opens the possibility of considering the introduction of a period of time between baptism and the time in which the Christian is ready to assume an active role in the church. This could be, precisely, the reason for delaying the reception of confirmation to a later age, when the subject of baptism is an infant. This "stretching-out" or distension of time is meant to allow for the gradual assimilation of the effects of baptism through the child's free acceptance of Christian revelation and through docility to God's commandments.

St. Augustine's Theology of Grace

Even when a distension of time is introduced, baptism and confirmation remain closely connected. As a matter of fact, in the early church they were always administered together. Catechumens were led to the baptismal font by a deacon or priest, and after being baptized, the bishop would confirm them (cf. Hippolytus, *Apost. Trad.*, 21–22). As Christianity continued to spread and, especially from the fourth century on, large numbers joined the church, it was no longer possible to confine the celebration of baptism to the liturgy presided over by the bishop. Baptismal liturgies took place simultaneously at various churches. While in the East this necessity led to the administration of all three sacraments of initiation by priests, in the West the anointing with holy chrism was reserved to the bishop in order to highlight the unity of sacramental dispensation with the apostolic origins of the church. Thus, the rite of confirmation, which was initially seamlessly united with the baptismal liturgy, became a separate rite, and it was eventually presented as a different sacrament, though closely connected to baptism. The custom soon became extended in the West: baptism would be administered at churches where the bishop could not be present, and the visit of the bishop to each place would provide the occasion for those who were baptized to be confirmed. The rationale for this development was to highlight the role of the bishop in Christian initiation, rather than any concern for the age of the candidate. This can be noticed in the response of Pope Innocent I to a bishop in the early fifth century: "But in regard to the signing of little children (*de consignandis vero infantibus*), it is evident that it may not be done by any other than a bishop. For the presbyters, although they are in the second order, nevertheless do not possess the crown of the pontificate" ("Letter to Bishop Decentius of Gubbio," 3). In the beginning, even little children were confirmed as soon as the bishop came. The main concern was to maintain the link between Christian initiation and the *apostolicity* and *unity* of the church. But once the separation had been introduced, other theological and pastoral reasons would also be entertained as the grounds for this practice.

The teaching of St. Augustine provided the foundations to understanding the development of confirmation in the West from a different perspective. The development of the theology of grace by St. Augustine introduced further considerations that would justify a distension of time between baptism and confirmation, particularly in the case of infants.

St. Augustine had to contend with three battlefronts. Against Manicheans, he affirmed the goodness of creation and of matter in particular, and averred that human nature had not been totally corrupted by sin. Against Donatists, he emphasized that the power of sacraments was not owed to the holiness of the minister; the effectiveness of the sacraments was the result of Christ's agency. Against Pelagians, he asserted the absolute need for grace in order to obtain salvation and the insufficiency of human nature alone to perform works of justice. These converging polemical contexts forced St. Augustine to achieve a nuanced expression of the manner in which divine grace, human will, and sacraments interact.

On the one hand, St. Augustine underscored that human actions can be meritorious, that is, worthy of eternal life, only when preceded and elevated by God's grace. Without the healing influence of antecedent grace, no human action can be called just. Thus, he writes:

> This question, then, seems to me to be by no means capable of solution, unless we understand that even those good works of ours, which are recompensed with eternal life, belong to the grace of God, because of what is said by the Lord Jesus: 'Without me you can do nothing.' (John 15:5) … Now, hear and understand. 'Not of works' (Eph 2:9) is spoken of the works which you suppose have their origin in yourself alone; but you have to think of works for which God has moulded (that is, has formed and created) you. (*On Grace and Free Will*, 20)

The remarkable aspect of this passage is St. Augustine's ability to show that, once elevated by grace, human works themselves are "graced." They become "living" works. Christians can produce actions that are meritorious because they are standing on the foundation of divine grace, in such a way that God is cooperating with them, and they are cooperating with God. The merit is joint because it is a genuine participation in the operative grace of God, which has justified us through Jesus Christ. We can merit grace only by cooperating in the operative grace of God. That means that the works of Christians cannot be thought of as an achievement that they could attain without God. It is precisely because the Holy Spirit is working within them that their works become just—and not only "just" through external declaration, but truly made just and holy by the power of God infusing supernatural charity and opening the possibility of works that are intrinsically holy.

Besides declaring the importance of a grace that precedes human action, St. Augustine is also aware of the need to build upon the grace that has been received. This is done in such a way that, in their spiritual growth, Christians are capable of walking towards greater perfection because they stand on prior graces and also upon their own prior works, which are themselves the fruit of grace. In this fashion, subsequent steps of Christian perfection stand both on the foundation of divine grace and free will. Commenting on St. Peter's progress, St. Augustine writes:

> But yet, however small and imperfect [St. Peter's] love was, it was not wholly wanting when he said to the Lord, "I will lay down my life for Your sake;" (John 13:37) for he supposed himself able to effect what he felt himself willing to do. And who was it that had begun to give him his love, however small, but He who prepares the will, and perfects by His co-operation what He initiates by His operation? Forasmuch as in beginning He works in us that we may have the will, and in perfecting works with us when we have the will. (*On Grace and Free Will*, 33)

In this passage, St. Augustine describes God's cooperative grace as an aid by which he brings to perfection what he has begun by operative grace. It should be noted that bringing to perfection does presuppose not only a prior grace that was given, but also the fact that "we have the will." The latter is a will that has already been moved to consent with grace. In doing so, the will has not been deprived of its freedom. On the contrary, grace has truly opened the field of freedom which had been robbed by sin so that, standing on the foundation of grace, the human will can truly work according to its nature. It is through the joint action of grace and the human will that freedom is restored. St. Augustine observes elsewhere that this free "graced" action of the will is a prerequisite for the bestowal of subsequent graces: "Now no man is assisted unless he also himself does something; assisted, however, he is, if he prays, if he believes, if he is 'called according to God's purpose' (Rom 8:28)" (*On Man's Perfection in Righteousness*, 20.43).

It can be now observed how this development would provide an expanded view to understand the distension of time introduced between baptism and confirmation. As noted in the prior section, when adults are prepared for the sacraments of initiation, they have the opportunity to journey for some time, so that the initial grace of conversion is followed up by a process of spiritual development, in which the convert learns how to receive the promptings of the Holy Spirit and respond to them in docility. When the Scriptures refer to the correlation between faith and sacraments, it is envisioned that faith normally involves a time of discipleship in which the cooperation between grace and free response can take place. This interaction will naturally continue after baptism, but it has always proved to be a prudent practice to verify how a candidate walks in faithful response to actual graces before being admitted to the sacraments. A person's fidelity "in small matters" is a guarantee of his or her fidelity in "great ones" (Luke 16.10). Clearly, this process of gradual assimilation of the Christian lifestyle, which proved to be so fruitful for catechumens, could not take place in the case of the baptism of infants. An analogous process would have to take place for those baptized in infancy once they reached the age of reason. It was natural to perceive that the sacrament of confirmation could have the function of perfecting what baptism had begun.

An important reason for the distension of time between baptism and confirmation, which can be drawn from St. Augustine's theology of grace, is that further steps are possible for Christians once an initial grace has been accepted and a path of cooperation with grace has been pursued to some extent. There is a further suitability to receive grace, once the subject has cooperated with it, particularly in the case in which a free acceptance of the gift of faith was not possible before baptism.

St. Thomas Aquinas's
Synthesis in the *Summa*

Despite the theological foundations that Augustine and other Church Fathers provide, it must be admitted that the Fathers did not develop a comprehensive treatise on this sacrament. This could hardly have been otherwise when the sacrament of confirmation was not actually celebrated separately from baptism until the fourth century in the West. But they did shape the foundational elements of sacramental theology, the building blocks that would be used by scholastic theologians to develop a systematic presentation on the subject. St. Thomas Aquinas was one of the theologians who most decisively contributed to organizing those various building blocks in an architectonic manner. As Colman O'Neill writes, "St. Thomas's genius as a theologian lay in his ability to organize coherently the scattered elements of Christian truth revealed in piecemeal fashion in the course of history and preserved in the Church" (O'Neill 2010: 147).

The question that opens St. Thomas's treatment of confirmation is that of the institution of this sacrament. This issue involves a particular difficulty in light of the scant explicit biblical references to confirmation. Other theologians, because of the lack of clear scriptural evidence, attributed the institution of confirmation to the apostles (Pierre de Tarentaise) or to the church (Alexander of Hales, St. Bonaventure). Aquinas argues, instead, that only Christ has the authority to institute a sacrament. Although Scripture contains no explicit text pointing to the institution of confirmation, St. Thomas explains, "Christ instituted this sacrament not by bestowing, but by promising it, according to John 16:7: 'If I go not, the Paraclete will not come to you, but if I go, I will send Him to you'" (*ST* III, q.72, a.1, ad1). The reason why Christ promised the sacrament instead of instituting it was that the Holy Spirit could only be bestowed upon the disciples after the resurrection and Ascension.

It is illustrative to notice how St. Thomas gradually builds, piece by piece, a complete theological blueprint for the sacrament of confirmation. He does not limit himself to one or two texts, but extracts insights from many texts in Scripture and Tradition, and then combines them into an original synthesis. Besides the passage just quoted, he also references John 7:37, "As yet the Spirit was not given, because Jesus was not yet glorified." He points to the most explicit scriptural reference to confirmation that occurs in the book of Acts, when John and Peter go to Samaria and lay their hands on those who have been baptized (Acts 8:4–25); a parallel case in which Paul administers the sacrament is found in Acts 19:1–7. But St. Thomas does not limit himself to these explicit indications.

He also includes texts that contain a more generic resemblance to confirmation. Two of these references are particularly significant, since they allow St. Thomas to connect this sacrament with the divine missions.

The first of those references is the baptism of Christ at the Jordan River. After his baptism, the Holy Spirit descended upon Jesus in the form of a dove. This visible manifestation revealed an invisible reality, the anointing of the Holy Spirit, which filled Jesus' soul. Even when Christ was filled with the Holy Spirit from the moment of his conception, St. Thomas notes, "this fulness was made known at His Baptism, when 'the Holy Ghost descended in a bodily shape ... upon Him' (Luke 3:22)" (*ST* III, q.72, a.1, ad4). The manifestation of the Holy Spirit descending upon the humanity of Christ signified that the promises of the messianic age had arrived. What the prophets had foretold regarding the outpouring of the Spirit over all flesh and the knowledge of the Lord filling the earth was coming to pass. In his treatment of the Lord's baptism, St. Thomas indicates that what took place in the person of Christ had a salvific meaning: "Wherefore, though He needed not baptism for His own sake, yet carnal nature in others had need thereof" (*ST* III, q.39, a.1, quoting St. John Chrysostom). The baptism of Jesus and the descent of the Holy Spirit upon him was a prefiguration of Christian baptism, through which the Holy Spirit would be poured upon the disciples. The particular reason why the baptism at the Jordan is connected with confirmation, however, is that it points to an overflowing of the Spirit. The fullness of the Spirit, which Christ possessed from the moment of the Incarnation, served, in a sense, his personal sanctification. At the baptism, instead, Christ received a new effusion of the Spirit precisely when his public ministry was about to begin: he then received the Spirit for the sanctification of others. He was filled in order to become a living fountain of grace. This is a parallel to what takes place in the sacrament of confirmation.

A second biblical passage that contains a resemblance to confirmation is that of Pentecost (cf. *ST* III, q.72, a.7). The outpouring of the Spirit then took place upon the nascent church. The apostles received the Holy Spirit, St. Thomas explains, *in order to be strengthened for their mission*. In this same article—responses to the second and third objections—St. Thomas notes that the grace that the apostles received at Pentecost presupposed the reception of prior graces—a parallel to baptism and penance in the Christian. This resumes the theme of subsequent grace that St. Augustine had articulated, and provides biblical support for the distension of time introduced between infant baptism and confirmation. The special effect of grace given in this sacrament, Aquinas explains, is *to be strengthened for bearing public witness to Christ, even in the face of visible opposition*. From this perspective, it becomes clearer why a time of consolidation and growth between baptism and confirmation is fitting. The fidelity to Christ's call to become his disciples must first be tested in peaceful circumstances. The first enemies to be resisted are the invisible ones: the resistance of the flesh, the temptations of the devil (cf. *ST* III, q.72, a.5, ad1). Once the roots of faith have been strengthened, and the Christian has responded well "in small matters," greater challenges can be faced.

St. Thomas places the special grace that is the effect of confirmation in the intersection of these two mysteries: the baptism of the Lord and Pentecost. The specific grace that the *confirmandi* receive is the attainment of perfect age in the spiritual life (*ST* III, q.72, a.1). Perfect age does not mean in this case a psychological phenomenon or a natural call to responsibility. It refers to a certain excellence and vigor in the life of the Spirit, which can be obtained, according to Aquinas, even at a very young age. "[E]ven in childhood," he writes, "man can attain to the perfection of spiritual age ... And hence it is that many children, by reason of the strength of the Holy Ghost which they had received, fought bravely for Christ even to the shedding of their blood" (*ST* III, q.72, a.8, ad2).

Interestingly, it is not that confirmation is bestowed when the candidates evidence this readiness, but rather, they are "spiritually advanced *by* this sacrament to perfect age" (*ST* III, q.72, a.8, emphasis added). There ought to be, naturally, a certain correspondence between the preparation and the special grace of the sacrament. That is why a degree of progress in the Christian path should be observed prior to the reception of the sacrament. But it is *not* that their preparation makes them ready. Fundamentally, it is the grace of the sacrament itself that which will make them strong and spiritually mature.

It might not be easy to understand what this "perfect age" implies, since it is not to be understood of psychological age. For St. Thomas, the "perfect age" is connected in Christ's life with the moment of his baptism in the Jordan and the beginning of his public ministry (*ST* III, q.39, a.3). It was the time at which he became engaged in the salvation of others. That is precisely the sign that one has passed from childhood to the perfect age: one begins to be *actively involved in the life of others*. A similar observation can be made with regard to the change that took place at Pentecost, as O'Neill writes:

> Whereas before Pentecost the apostles were concerned only with their personal relations with Christ, afterwards their attention was also turned outwards to their fellowmen. And is not this, asks St. Thomas, just what we understand by attaining adult age? The child lives for himself; his whole activity is directed towards his own development. The adult, on the contrary, is involved in the give and take of social relations; he contributes something to the life of others; he '*communicates his actions to others*' (*ST* III, q.72, a.2). (O'Neill 2010: 152, emphasis added)

St. Thomas refers this active involvement in social relations to the symbolism of chrism, the matter of confirmation: "Christ is said to be anointed 'with the oil of gladness' (Ps. 44:8)" (*ST* III, q.72, a.2). Correspondingly, the one who is sealed with chrism and receives the anointing of the Holy Spirit becomes "the good odor of Christ" (2 Cor 2:15), as St. Paul says.

In virtue of the attainment of perfect age, the confirmed Christian receives official adult status in the visible body of the church (see O'Neill 2010: 150). The church is the "sacrament" of Christ, inasmuch as through its visible manifestations, she extends the visibility of Christ—his proclamation of the Kingdom, his saving actions, especially the paschal mystery—throughout the centuries. What St. Thomas is stating is that, through confirmation, Christians are empowered to become part of the church's sacramental dimension. Confirmation bestows the grace through which believers have the privilege and the responsibility of contributing to the sacramental visibility of Christ in the world. Through their words and actions, through their choices, their works of mercy, their interaction with others, confirmed Christians are enabled to radiate the light of Christ and become for those around them an occasion of grace.

The power that confirmed Christians receive to radiate the light of Christ is the scope of the character received in confirmation. For St. Thomas, the sacramental character is a "spiritual power," which deputizes one to divine worship. "Now the worship of God," he explains, "consists either in receiving Divine gifts, or in bestowing them on others. And for both these purposes some power is needed; for to bestow something on others, active power is necessary; and in order to receive, we need a passive power" (*ST* III, q.63, a.2). The character of the sacrament of Holy Orders consists of an active power: the instrumental power to sanctify others through the celebration of the sacraments, and through the teaching and guidance that prepares for, and results from, the reception of the sacraments. The character of baptism involves a power to participate in divine worship as recipients of the grace that is bestowed in it. The character of confirmation is an extension of this same passive power (*ST* III, q.63, ad6). If one integrates this presentation of the character of confirmation with the idea that Aquinas presents in other texts of the Christian being *deputized to bear public witness*, it may be argued that the character of confirmation is situated halfway between the character of baptism and that of holy orders. By the reception of a new sacramental character, the confirmed are not only capable of participating more profoundly in divine worship as recipients of their sanctifying effects, but the character of confirmation also qualifies them, in some way, to dispose others to divine worship. Their public witness to Christ cannot operate the *res sacramenti*—as the character of holy orders does—but it can become a certain extension of the *signum* that the sacraments are. The transforming effects of sacramental grace are part of the signs that constitute the visibility of the church, the sacrament of Christ. Thus, the life of exemplary Christians, and the example of martyrs in particular, are part of that visibility that can be an occasion of grace: the grace of conversion for those who are outside, and of growth for those who have been already justified. In summary, the public witness for which one is deputized by the character of confirmation can be understood as a *dispositive cause* or as a *propaedeutic element* that draws others to the sources of divine life and illustrate for them the transforming power of Christ's grace.

Something particularly noteworthy in St. Thomas's synthesis on the sacrament of confirmation is the way in which the understanding of the effect of this sacrament is made to depend upon the visible missions of the Son and of the Holy Spirit. The references to these mysteries provide St. Thomas with the fundamental insights that will characterize his theological treatment of confirmation. The invisible missions of the Son and the Holy Spirit is nothing but the indwelling of the Divine Persons in the just through sanctifying grace (*ST* I, q.43, a.3). The actual final goal of the entire economy of salvation is directed to this end: that the Blessed Trinity may dwell in those who have accepted the Son (see John 1:12) and that in this way they may have eternal life in his Name (see John 20:31). But since the invisible divine realities are better made known to human beings through visible means, it was fitting that the invisible missions should be manifested through the visible missions of the Son (Incarnation) and of the Holy Spirit (Pentecost) (*ST* I, q.43, a.7). The visibility of the church and its sacraments, as Pope Leo the Great observed, was an extension of the visible missions of the Divine Persons.

St. Thomas's presentation of the effect of confirmation contains a reference to both the *invisible* and the *visible* divine missions. As is the case with any other sacrament, confirmation aims at an increase of sanctifying grace, in which the invisible divine mission consists (*ST* III, q.72, a.7). In other words, *this sacrament deepens the grace of baptism*: "it roots us more deeply in the divine filiation ... it unites us more firmly to Christ; it increases the gifts of the Holy Spirit in us; it renders our bond with the Church more perfect" (*Catechism of the Catholic Church*, 1303). But in a certain way, the effect of this sacrament, as is particularly manifested in its sacramental character, is also connected with the visible divine missions. The sacramental character that the confirmed Christian receives is a power that deputizes him or her to bear public witness to Christ. This witness, because of the official character of the deputizing, is no longer an individual performance or the outward manifestation of the inward effects of baptismal grace (cf. *ST* III, q.72, a.5, ad2; *ST* III, q.72, a.9, ad3). It is a commissioning, and therefore it elevates the life of the confirmed Christian to a certain degree of sacramentality—they receive the power to become the "good odor of Christ." Of course, they do not stand on a par with the signs of public revelation—the life of Christ, the testimony of the apostles, sacred Scripture—but they are now assimilated and conformed to the elements that comprise the visibility of the church. As Colman O'Neill observes, the sacrament of confirmation

> makes [the confirmed Christian's] external professions of faith different from those of a person who has not received the sacrament. It makes these actions objectively part of the fabric of the visible Church ... Christ uses the actions of the confirmed, as he uses the sacraments, but in a different way, for bringing grace into the world. (O'Neill 2010: 158)

The way in which Christ uses the actions of Christians is particularly eloquent in the lives of the saints, especially when one notes the impact that the example of the saints has in bringing others to conversion. Learning about the life of St. Anthony was an important milestone in St. Augustine's spiritual journey towards the church. A similar phenomenon can be observed in countless cases: St. Francis Xavier was inspired by St. Ignatius of Loyola's example, St. Theresa Benedicta of the Cross by reading the life of St. Theresa of Avila. It is clear that the lives of Christians that have been profoundly shaped by sacramental grace become powerful signs, which, in a manner different than that of the sacraments, constitute channels of grace for those who come in contact with them.

Epilogue: Confirmation as Sacrament of the New Evangelization?

In our study of Augustine and Aquinas, we have stressed how the sacrament of confirmation *deepens* the grace of baptism and *deputizes* the Christian at "the perfect age" for bearing public witness to Christ. This brings us to examine the connection between the sacrament of confirmation and what Pope St. John Paul II has called "the new evangelization." Since the early years of his pontificate, John Paul II perceived the need for the church to engage in what he called a "new evangelization":

> The commemoration of the half millennium of evangelization will gain its full meaning if it is a commitment on your part as bishops, together with your priests and faithful: a commitment, not to re-evangelization, but to a new evangelization, new in its ardor, in its methods, in its expression. (Pope St. John Paul II, "Speech to the Assembly of CELAM" in Port-au-Prince, Haiti, March 9, 1983)

This call for a new evangelization was based on the realization that the ardor of Christianity had been declining in countries with a long Catholic tradition, particularly in the West. John Paul II noted that this challenge was to be met not only by the bishops whom he was addressing, but also by the laity.

The sacrament of confirmation has not often been the first sacrament that comes to mind in discussions of the new evangelization. This is largely because too many Catholics have come to think of the sacrament of confirmation as something like the culmination of their religious education (i.e. Confraternity of Christian Doctrine) rather than the deepening of the grace of baptism and the deputizing of the Christian for bearing public witness to Christ. There is nothing more important for young Catholics than to see the sacrament of confirmation not as a diploma, but as a deputizing to proclaim the Gospel.

The sacrament of confirmation is an ecumenical bridge in the new evangelization. Every baptized Christian who comes to "the perfect age" and desires to come into full communion with the Catholic Church will be received through the sacrament of confirmation. This is an occasion of great joy for the church and for those Christians being received and confirmed. If the new evangelization is to be truly effective in our lifetimes, then we will see the first fruits of the church's renewed evangelical mission precisely through the door of the sacrament of confirmation. Christ himself renews his church through this sacrament.

Whether raised up in the church or newly initiated, everyone receives the sacrament of confirmation as a *conversion*. Or rather, it is a deepening and deputizing of those who have furthered their conversion to Christ and who seek to conform their whole lives to this conversion to Christ's body. They themselves now become signs of that body for others. They radiate the light of Christ through their love for the Lord, their options of faith, their works of mercy, a new way of relating to others, a new sense of purpose. It is in this way that deepening our understanding of the sacrament of confirmation is central to our understanding of the Christian faith itself.

SUGGESTED READING

Aquinas (1981); O'Neill (2010).

BIBLIOGRAPHY

Aquinas, Thomas (1981), *Summa Theologica*, trans. the Fathers of the English Dominican Province (1948, repr.) (Westminster, MD: Christian Classics).

Augustine (1992), "Sermon 169," in *Sermons, (148–183) on the New Testament*, Vol. III/5, trans. Edmund Hill, ed. John E. Rotelle, 169–177. (New Rochelle, NY: New City Press).

Augustine (1994), *On Grace and Free Will*, in *Augustin: Anti-Pelagian Writings*, Vol. I/5 of *Nicene and Post-Nicene Fathers*, trans. Peter Holmes et al., ed. Philip Schaff (1887, repr.) (Peabody, MS: Hendrickson).

Augustine (1994), *On Man's Perfection in Righteousness*, in *Augustin: Anti-Pelagian Writings*, Vol. I/5 of *Nicene and Post-Nicene Fathers*, trans. Peter Holmes et al., ed. Philip Schaff (1887, repr.) (Peabody, MS: Hendrickson).

Catechism of the Catholic Church (1997), 2nd ed. (Vatican City: Libreria Editrice Vaticana).

Cyril of Jerusalem (1986), *Lectures on the Christian Sacraments: The Procatechesis and the Five Mystagogical Catecheses*, trans. R. W. Church, ed. F. L. Cross (Crestwood, NY: St Vladimir's Seminary Press).

Haffner, Paul (1999), *The Sacramental Mystery* (Leominster: Gracewing).

Hippolytus (2001), *On the Apostolic Tradition*, ed. Alistair Stewart-Sykes (Crestwood, NY: St Vladimir's Seminary Press).

O'Neill, Colman E. (2010), *Meeting Christ in the Sacraments* (New York: Alba House).

Pope John Paul II (1983), "Speech to the Assembly of CELAM in Port-au-Prince, Haiti, March 9." <http://verbatimetapothegm.blogspot.ca/2009_03_01_archive.html>, accessed September 27, 2014.

Pope Innocent I (2002), "Letter to Bishop Decentius of Gubbio," in *The Sources of Catholic Dogma*, trans. Roy J. Deferrari from the 30th ed. of Henry Denzinger, *Enchiridion Symbolorum* (Fitzwilliam, NH: Loreto). No. 98.

CHAPTER 32

WHAT IS THE EUCHARIST? A DOGMATIC OUTLINE

BRUCE D. MARSHALL

SYMBOL AND EUCHARIST

THE question that forms this chapter's title has fallen out of favor in recent theology, though it was long considered the requisite starting point for a coherent theological treatment of the Eucharist. Rather than taking as basic an answer to the question, "What is it?" current sacramental theology, Catholic and Protestant alike, is apt to focus primarily on what the Eucharist, or any of the sacraments, means to us. This guiding question about the relevance, importance, or meaning the Eucharist has for us can take many different forms. In one way or another, though, understanding how and what the Eucharist "signifies" is usually taken as fundamental for reflection on the question. Or as it is often put, an adequately rich understanding of the Eucharist as a "symbol" is now seen as the most basic task of eucharistic theology, as of sacramental theology in general.

Talk of the signification or symbolic function of the Eucharist typically looks in two different directions at once. On the one hand, the Eucharist, like each of the sacraments in its own way, points to inherently meaningful realities that are in some way distinct from it. So the Eucharist may be held to signify the body and blood of Christ, the paschal mystery of his suffering, death, and resurrection, the saving presence of God, the bond of love among those who receive it, and much else besides. In less traditional language, the Eucharist might be taken as the symbol that effectively explodes, overturns, or transgresses our ordinary symbolic universe, so disclosing the radical immanence of the divine mystery that always eludes our grasp.

Whatever symbolic content it assigns to the Eucharist, the kind of sacramental theology that thinks in these terms is naturally concerned to claim that the Eucharist "signifies" in a distinctive way. The Eucharist (again like each of the other sacraments) is not simply one among many equally useful symbols for whatever it signifies or brings to mind. In some way it is a peculiarly efficacious symbol of, say, Christ's intimate presence with us, perhaps the supremely efficacious symbol. We need truly potent symbols, on this view, for mind and heart to have access to what is most meaningful to us, which as such eludes our ordinary cognitive apprehension. In this assumption lies much of the attraction in seeing the Eucharist as a symbol in the first place.

On the other hand, the Eucharist, seen in these terms, points not simply to realities that require some kind of symbolic access, but also to us who seek those realities, and long to be affected by them. Signifiers and symbols, in other words, are bound up not only with what they signify or disclose, but also with those for whom they come to have symbolic and disclosive power. So the Eucharist might signify not only Christ's body and blood, but also our joy at being redeemed by them; not only the paschal mystery, but also our experience of sharing in it; not only the bond among us who receive it, but also our fellow-feeling, our communal sense of togetherness.

Symbolically understood in this way, the Eucharist thus has two sides or aspects, which the symbol itself draws together. The Eucharist is an effective sign of realities or states of affairs in some way distinct both from the sign itself and from us for whom the sign is our way of access to these realities. At the same time it is the needed sign of our own experience of these realities, whether in the sense that it evokes that experience or expresses an experience already had. To employ familiar terms of modern philosophy, we could say that the eucharistic symbol has both an "objective" and a "subjective" dimension. Sacramental theology that thinks in these terms usually insists that these two dimensions of the Eucharist are distinct but inseparable. There is no presence of the paschal mystery (for example) in the Eucharist without our sense of being taken up into the mystery. Equally, though, there is no sense of being taken up into the paschal mystery without the symbolic presence of that mystery in the Eucharist.

No doubt sacramental theology of this kind has sometimes been tempted to play off the subjective, experiential dimension of the Eucharist against its objective side, to the intended detriment of the latter. Or, with much the same result, talk of the Eucharist as a symbol has sometimes seemed willing virtually to identify the two sides of the sacrament, again in favor of the subjective. Thus to say that the Eucharist is symbolic of Christ's body and blood, or of their very presence, is sometimes taken to mean simply that it is a token of our joy at being redeemed by Christ or loved by God. Perhaps it was this degenerate, purely subjective understanding of the Eucharist as a symbol that provoked Flannery O'Connor memorably to say, "Well, if it's a symbol, to hell with it" (in a letter of December 16, 1955. She added: "[T]his is all I will ever be able to say about it, outside of a story, except that it is the center of existence for me; all the rest of life is expendable" [O'Connor 1988: 977]). Granted, though, the potential problems in talking about the Eucharist as a "signifier" or "symbol," there is nothing inherent in these notions that requires, or inevitably leads, to a subjective reduction of the sacrament to a mere expression of our experiences or beliefs. The more telling question is whether this way of thinking about the sacraments is adequate to the Eucharist, or indeed to any of the sacraments.

There is good reason to think that we cannot be content with a description of the Eucharist's symbolic significance. However richly detailed and evocative our description, whether of the Eucharist or anything else, it still makes perfectly good sense to ask *what* we are describing. Any account of the symbolic meaning the sacraments have for us, even the most studiously non-reductionist, still leaves us with the question, "What *is* a sacrament?" The same goes for each of the individual sacraments in turn. The Eucharist, we may be told, is a symbol so rich that it exceeds even the most successful attempts to describe it. So it surely is, but it remains quite in order to ask just what it is that possesses these remarkable properties.

The long theological habit of looking for the *res* of the Eucharist and the other sacraments is a way of putting just this question. We rightly want to identify, as much as we can, the properties of the Eucharist, symbolic and otherwise. But in the process we seek the reality, the *res*, that has these properties. A sense of what the Eucharist does and what it means to us, important as these are, is not enough. We want to know the being of the Eucharist—what it is. Asking after this not only makes sense to us; it seems inevitable, a basic feature of the way we think about the world. In fact the more important the matter is, the more it means to us, the more pressing the question seems, and the less likely we are to be content with mere descriptions of the meaning it has for us. Addressing a different doctrinal matter, John Courtney Murray effectively generalizes the point, not without a polemical edge: "When it functions without any bias induced by faulty or prejudicial training, the mind moves inevitably from the question of what things are to us (the phenomenological question) to the deeper question of what things are in themselves (the ontological question). The human mind moves from description to definition" (Murray 1964: 41).

Eucharistic theology surely has much to gain from symbolic, phenomenological, and anthropological descriptions of the sacraments, together with countless other matters these approaches may help us describe. Still, even the fullest and most perceptive phenomenology or anthropology of the Eucharist will not suffice for a theology of the Eucharist, at least to the extent that it confines itself to description and declines to move on to definition. Its theological usefulness will end, more precisely, at the point where it stops short of asking—and offering an answer to—the question, "What is the Eucharist?"

This theological claim might prompt a theological objection. The Eucharist is a mystery, on a par with the supreme mysteries of the Trinity and the Incarnation. As the Eastern Liturgy of St. James has it, even the angels, "the many-eyed Cherubim and the six-winged Seraphim," veil their faces as "the King of kings and Lord of lords advances to be slain and given as food to the faithful" (from "Let All Mortal Flesh Keep Silence," an ancient hymn used at the offertory of the Liturgy of St. James: <http://www.anastasis.org.uk/lit-james.htm>). All the more the mystery of the Eucharist will exceed our earthbound comprehension. "What is the Eucharist?" is not a question to which we should expect to give an adequate answer. For just this reason, it seems, the Greek term for "sacrament" is *mysterion*, mystery. Trying to give a definition of the Eucharist is at best fruitless, and worse, may mislead us into thinking that we have mastered the mystery, when all we have really grasped is our own rationalized domestication of it.

The Eucharist is surely a supreme mystery of Christian faith. Our proper insistence on the unfathomable mystery of the Eucharist should not, however, be confused with an inability to say what it is. In order to be able to claim the Eucharist as a mystery in the first place, we need to be able to locate the mystery—to say what it is that presents us with unfathomable depths akin to those of God himself. To locate the Eucharist, and thus the mystery that exceeds our comprehension, we need to define it. Defining it is simply saying what is necessary for an act, object, or event to be the Eucharist, and which of these necessary conditions are together sufficient for us to say correctly, "What we have here is the Eucharist—here is the mystery." We need not offer, or be able to offer, a complete or exhaustive definition of the Eucharist. It will be enough to offer an adequate one. Our task is to identify the essential properties of the Eucharist, but we need not claim to have spotted them all. It will suffice to locate enough of them to say when we are dealing with the Eucharist and not something else, and with just what we thereby have to do.

About this there is, alas, deep and wide disagreement among Christians. Disagreement extends even to what the thing should be called; Catholics and Orthodox normally speak of "the Eucharist," while Protestants tend to prefer the designation "Lord's Supper." The ecumenical labors of the last fifty years have overcome many misunderstandings and to some extent ameliorated the conflicts over the Eucharist that have characterized a good deal of Christian history, especially over the last half millennium. But the disagreements remain, the misery of them perhaps sharpened by our presently unsuccessful efforts to get beyond them. And this means that there is no ecclesially or theologically neutral location from which to answer the question, "What is the Eucharist?" The doctrines of the Trinity and the Incarnation have certainly been sites of conflict in the Christian tradition, but the conflicts long ago yielded widely accepted settlements on essential teaching in both areas. So far conflict over the Eucharist has not given way to a similarly broad settlement. Since the late sixteenth century this conflict has, in fact, been deeply institutionalized, not only in the separation between Protestants and Catholics, but in historic doctrinal disagreements among various Protestant communities. Eastern Orthodox teaching and practice, moreover, is identical with that of neither main Western tradition.

In this situation it is best for even the most irenic reflection on what the Eucharist is to be clear about its own ecclesial and theological assumptions. I write as a Catholic, which for present purposes means two things. First, the liturgical and theological examples I will introduce to illustrate various points will usually be Catholic ones. Second, I will follow a Catholic line in pursuing the question as to what the Eucharist is. At even the most basic phenomenological level, as we will soon see, attempting to offer an adequate definition of the Eucharist confronts us with differences, and often disagreements, among Christians about what we should believe and do. At these manifold decision points in saying what the Eucharist is, I will follow a Catholic line not in the sense that I will defend Catholic teaching (for which there is hardly room here, even if the occasion called for it), but in the sense that I will try to show what follows from making a Catholic decision at each of these points. This will have the effect of carrying us farther in reflection on the nature of the Eucharist than would otherwise be the case. To a greater or lesser degree other Christian traditions are inclined to say "no" at major decision points where the Catholic tradition says "yes," seeing a need to go on where other traditions want to bring their definition of the Eucharist to an end.

SIGN

We can begin where symbolic and phenomenological accounts of the Eucharist do, with the Eucharist as it appears to us. Whatever else the Eucharist may be, it is clearly a Christian ritual, a public liturgical practice. While the celebration of the Eucharist goes back to the very beginnings of Christianity (see, e.g., 1 Cor 10:14–22; 11:17–34), the New Testament itself offers few details as to what this practice looked like during the first generation or two of Christians. Writing between 150–160 AD, however, Justin Martyr offers a succinct description of the Eucharist as he knew it, at the end of his *Apology for the Christians* (or "First Apology"). He gives us a reasonably detailed picture, and as this is the earliest such account of the Eucharist we have, it has naturally attracted much attention. What Justin describes remains easily recognizable in contemporary Christian practice, close to 1,900 years later.

"To the president of the brethren are brought," Justin observes, "bread and a cup of wine mixed with water" (*Apology*, ch. 65; cf. ch. 67; my translation from the Greek text in Marcovich 2005). Here three elements of the Eucharist come into view, each still regarded as essential by virtually all Christian communities: bread, wine, and a president, or presider.

(1) Bread. The Eucharist is a ritual in which things are done with bread and wine. These elements having been brought forward from the midst of the community, the president takes them and speaks words over them, as Justin goes on to describe (see below). What sort of bread is appropriate to the Eucharist—what can count as "bread" in this ritual context—has sometimes been controversial, and Christian practice today is not uniform. The basic question has been whether the bread should be leavened or unleavened. The Orthodox churches have long used leavened bread, a small loaf baked especially for the purpose. The Western Catholic Church has long used unleavened bread, wafers of various sizes likewise prepared for just this use. Protestant churches typically use leavened bread, the type depending mainly on denominational tradition and local custom.

In the Middle Ages serious theological dispute arose between Western and Eastern Christians over what sort of bread ought to be used in the celebration of the Eucharist (the so-called "azyme" controversy). The Western church held that the Last Supper, at which Christ instituted the Eucharist for us, was a Jewish Passover meal. This meant that in instituting the Eucharist Christ used unleavened bread, an act which must be regarded as part of his command to celebrate the Eucharist ("Do *this*"), and not as a matter subject to alteration by us. The Eastern church insisted that as Christ was instituting the new covenant at the Last Supper, the Eucharist should be celebrated with leavened bread, as a sign that the old has passed away and the new has come.

This may seem on both sides like a divisive rationalization of trivial differences in practice, disagreement of a kind all too common in religious controversy. At least two matters basic to grasping what the Eucharist is are, however, in play. One is the foundation of the Eucharist in the Last Supper. Christians have traditionally seen in Jesus' words and deeds with his apostles in the upper room, as presented to us by the evangelists, his deliberate institution of the Eucharist, a command to "celebrate these mysteries" (in the language of the Roman Catholic rite) until the end of time. Conformity to his words and deeds, doing what he did, is not a matter of mere historical accuracy or obsessive primitivism, but of grateful submission to the design of God for our salvation. The interpretation of Jesus' words and deeds in the upper room thereby becomes a matter of the utmost importance, where no disagreement can be lightly dismissed as trivial. However we decide these interpretive questions, the foundation of the Eucharist in the Last Supper limits its malleability.

Differences over what kind of bread to use in the Eucharist also bring to the fore a basic feature common to all the sacraments: they are signs. Among the features of these sacramental signs, a basic aspect of their "sign character," is that they make present what they signify. In this case, the bread brought forth to the presider at the Eucharist will, in the total context of the ritual, signify, and so make present, what Christ did in the upper room (celebrate the Passover, institute the Eucharist, establish the new covenant). Like everything else about the Eucharist, the bread has more than one signification. Its sign character is complex, and difficult, perhaps impossible, to capture in an exhaustive way. But the sign is not on that account arbitrary, or subject to being manufactured at will. The capacity of the bread to make present what Jesus did in the upper room depends on more than just the bread itself (in particular on the words Jesus spoke there), but is nonetheless tied to the kind of thing the bread is, even to what kind of bread it is.

(2) Wine. The wine used in the Eucharist likewise bears with it a rich sign character. It is an apt natural sign of blood, though by itself (that is, outside the context of the Eucharist) there is no necessity of seeing wine this way (in contrast, for example, with smoke, which we can hardly avoid taking to be a sign of fire). The sign character of the wine brought forward to the presider extends even to the mixture of water into it, already mentioned by Justin. This has long been taken, for example, to signify both the inseparable union of the divine and human natures in Christ and our deification through union with Christ in the Eucharist. So in the Catholic liturgy the priest (or deacon) says *sotto voce*, while pouring water into the chalice, "By the mystery of this water and wine may we come to share in the divinity of Christ, who humbled himself to share in our humanity."

What kind of wine to use in the Eucharist has never been a subject of significant controversy among Christians. In modern Protestantism, however, the practice has become widespread of foregoing wine altogether, and using unfermented grape juice instead. The idea originally behind this practice was that alcohol is a poison, and therefore cannot possibly be used in a ritual that is meant to contribute to our salvation, that is, to our spiritual health. (I owe this point, though not the use I make of it, to Woodruff Tait 2011.) To the use of grape juice has been joined the practice of distributing it to the congregation in small individual glasses, thereby avoiding the possible spread of disease from sharing the same cup.

These practices provide a striking case study in what is now called the "enculturation" of the gospel, and its limits. While few would argue that grape juice offered in individual glasses exactly conforms to the pattern established by Jesus in his institution of the Eucharist, many Protestants since the nineteenth century would say that it conforms closely enough to convey the meaning that the Eucharist ought to have for us, a meaning we can only apprehend in light of our own sensibilities (in this case, modern scientific ones). For Christians beyond the orbit of Protestantism, however, this practice seems to sever the Eucharist from its foundation in the Last Supper, and suggests that we can manufacture sacramental signs at will. Substituting grape juice for wine and many glasses for the one cup departs too far from what Jesus said and did in the upper room to count as a genuine enculturation of the gospel. In Catholic and Orthodox eyes, indeed, it is enough to invalidate the sacrament altogether: this ritual may have meaning and value, but it is not the Eucharist.

(3) Presider. Who can celebrate the Eucharist has sometimes been a matter of deep disagreement among Christians. In fourth-century Roman North Africa, the Christian community was split in two over who could exercise a valid and effective sacramental ministry. Baptism was at the center of the conflict, but it naturally extended to sacramental practice as a whole, including the Eucharist. The Donatists held that the holiness of the minister (whether bishop or priest) was requisite for any valid and effective sacrament. This was to embrace not only his personal holiness (though that was certainly included), but the public holiness of those who had baptized and ordained him—in particular whether they or their predecessors were implicated in collaboration with the Romans during the intense persecution of the North African church in the early fourth century. Since the Catholic Church included clergy whose personal holiness and sacramental lineage from the time of persecution was at best in doubt, the Donatists argued that there was no real baptism and sacramental life, and thus no salvation, in the Catholic Church.

On behalf of the Catholics Augustine argued that since Christ himself is the chief minister of every sacrament, and the bishop or priest only his servant (or, as it would later be put, his instrument), the validity of the sacraments cannot depend on the holiness of the minister, whether personal or sacramentally acquired. The Donatists have valid sacraments—real baptism, real Eucharist—which Catholics recognize as such. But, Augustine argued, since they take place in schism, and thus outside the bond of love (*caritas*) that unites the church, they are ineffective. Lack of love blocks them from having the effects in the recipient that Christ intends.

This was a momentous debate. The basics of Augustine's outlook came to be universally accepted in the Western church, with the result that for a full millennium there was virtually no dispute about who could preside at the Eucharist. The president could be anyone whom Christ had chosen and designated as his instrument for that purpose, with the mark of designation being valid priestly ordination at the hands of a bishop. This consensus held until the sixteenth century, when with more or less reluctance

Protestant communities in Switzerland and Germany began to ordain their own pastors without the consent or participation of the local bishop, and thus outside the historic episcopal structure that in both East and West had long been seen as necessary for valid sacramental ministry.

In the sixteenth century the Protestant churches overwhelmingly insisted, in traditional fashion, on the necessity of ordination for presiding at the Eucharist within their own communities. Most still do. The Catholic and Orthodox churches have found it impossible, however, to recognize the validity, and with that the full genuineness or reality, of these ordinations. They take place apart from the succession and communion of bishops that constitutes one way—not the only way, but still a necessary and indispensable way—by which Christ makes his church, spread throughout the world today, one and the same community with the apostolic band that awaited the Spirit on the day of Pentecost. This "deficiency with respect to the sacrament of orders" (*sacramenti ordinis defectum*), as Vatican II calls it, need not be taken to render Protestant eucharistic celebrations simply null and void (*Unitatis redintegratio* 22, in Tanner 1990: 919. *Defectus* here can be translated in a strong sense as "absence" or "lack," but also in a weaker sense as "deficiency" or "defect"). But it leaves their status at best unclear.

This disagreement about what constitutes valid presbyteral ordination, and thus when one of the necessary conditions for the Eucharist can be regarded as met, has proven to be among the most intractable problems confronting modern ecumenical dialogue. In fact, ecumenical theology has made more progress on the doctrine of the Eucharist itself (on the nature of Christ's presence in the sacrament, for example) than on the question of who may preside. Everyone involved sees the irony in this. No one thinks the presider is the most important aspect of the Eucharist. But mutual efforts toward a common Eucharist or "full communion," especially across the Catholic-Protestant divide, have repeatedly run aground at this point, despite much good will on all sides. That many Protestant churches now ordain women as presbyters or priests and bishops, while the Catholic and Orthodox churches continue to reserve priestly ordination to men alone, has not created the present impasse over legitimate eucharistic presidency, but has surely made it more obvious.

REALITY

That the sacraments, including the Eucharist, are signs is not a discovery of recent theories of symbolic meaning applied in sacramental theology. It was basic to much traditional sacramental theology that the sacraments not only have a sign character, but that they are signs first of all. Thomas Aquinas, for example, begins the *Summa theologiae*'s many questions on the sacraments by observing that we can correctly class an object or an action as a "sacrament" in different ways and for various reasons, but that "we are here speaking of the sacraments in a particular way, namely insofar as they have the character of signs. In this respect a sacrament belongs in the genus 'sign'" (*ST* III, q,60, a.1, c [my translation]). In fact to each sacrament belongs an aspect in which it is purely a sign (the *sacramentum tantum*, in medieval terminology), indicating and making present a reality distinct from itself.

As we have already seen, the eucharistic elements are multivalent signs, indeed, potentially open-ended signifiers. In order to specify what the Eucharist signifies in an adequately precise way, we need to consider not only the material objects and human gestures needed for the sacrament, but also the words without which these objects would never come to be the matter of a sacrament. Here Justin is again helpful. Having received the bread and cup, he relates, the eucharistic president offers "at great length" a prayer of praise and thanksgiving "to the Father of the universe, in the name of the Son and the Holy Spirit," to which the gathered faithful assent with their unanimous "Amen" (*Apology*, ch. 65). About the content of the presider's prayer Justin tells us nothing, save at one point. In the Gospels the apostles "have delivered to us what was enjoined upon them," and, *a fortiori*, on us. "Jesus took bread, and when he had given thanks, said, 'Do this in remembrance of me, this is my body', and after the same manner, having taken the cup and given thanks, he said, 'This is my blood', and gave it to them alone" (*Apology*, ch. 66). Already in Justin we can see a precise pattern, virtually universal among Christians ever since, and founded, of course, in the institution narratives of the New Testament. The Christian Eucharist is an offering of thanks to the Father, in remembrance of the Son Jesus, with the invocation of the Holy Spirit ("eucharist," of course, is Greek for "thanksgiving"). The verbal content of this prayer has varied widely through Christian history, and still does. At the heart of it, though, are words that hardly vary at all, and with remarkable unanimity have been seen by Christians of every time and place as necessary for the Eucharist. The celebrant recalls and repeats the precise words of Jesus at the Last Supper. As Justin puts it, "the food has been blessed"—literally "eucharistized" or "made Eucharist"—"by the prayer of the word that originates from him", that is, from Christ speaking to his apostles in the upper room (*Apology*, ch. 66). Without these words, there is no Eucharist.

What happens when Christ's minister utters these words? To begin with, these utterances fix the referent or signification of the bread and wine before the presider and the congregation. These material objects are now signs of Christ's body and blood. The consecrated elements signify other things as well, but all these other referents depend on, and must be tied to, the primary signification imparted to them by the words. It is important to see that the presider's utterance of Christ's words *gives* the bread and wine this precise signification, which they do not naturally have. When the eucharistic president, following Christ's command, says "This is my body" over the bread, he is not simply describing a state of affairs that already obtains. He is not, in other words, pointing to a sign feature the bread already has, as I might point to smoke and observe, "That's a sign of fire." His utterance is, in current terminology, performative rather than descriptive or indicative. It brings about a state of affairs that did not previously obtain, rather than noting one that already exists. The celebrant's utterances make the bread and wine a sacrament, in the first place a sign of Christ's body and blood.

This is an ancient idea. In words that would become central to later Western sacramental theology, Augustine said, "Accedit verbum ad elementum, et fit sacramentum"—when the word comes upon the element, a sacrament happens (*Tractatus in Ioannis Evangelium* 80.3 [CCL 36]: 529; see Augustine 1994: 117). We are familiar with parallel cases. Take, for example, the utterance of marriage vows at a wedding (even if marriage is not thought of as a sacrament), or a declaration of innocence spoken at the conclusion of a trial. Before the man and woman spoke the vows to each other, they were not married; now they are. Before the judge declared the defendant to be innocent, he did not have the rights of a person guiltless before the law of the crime of which he accused; now he does. Along with the other sacraments, the Eucharist is like this. It brings about the very state of affairs of which it speaks.

The Eucharist, the bread and wine consecrated by the words of Christ, is a sign of his body and blood. But in what way? What is the relationship of the sign to the thing signified here? How to answer this question has been openly controversial in Western Christianity. A considerable array of positions has been offered, but the basic disagreement is between those who hold that the Eucharist is only a sign of Christ's body and blood, and those who hold that the Eucharist, while it surely is a sign, actually is Christ's body and blood.

In order to think about how to answer the question, it may be helpful to reflect on parallels the Eucharist has with baptism, since the latter has proven to be a far less divisive matter in the West. Like the Eucharist, the sacrament of baptism requires a specific material element and a particular form of words. The celebrant pours water over the person being baptized, invoking the persons of the Holy Trinity one by one as the name in which the baptism is taking place. The ritual act of baptism signifies many things, but the washing away of sins is fundamental. The use of water to wash is close to being a natural sign for human beings, and the words make this act of washing signify the triune God's act of complete washing from sin and the gift of new life for which the washing opens the way—nothing less than a share in the very life of God.

However, the sacrament of baptism—the poured water plus the words—does not simply signify God's forgiving nature, or the fact that the triune God fully forgives sins by his own action. Baptism actually brings about, or effects, the washing from sin that it visibly enacts; the triune God here actually accomplishes what we invoke his name to do, in obedience to his command. The words spoken at the font do more than turn the everyday act of washing into a sacramental sign of God's forgiveness. A sign as such can point to an object or person that is absent rather than present, or to a state of affairs that already obtains apart from the sign, or to one that does not presently obtain, but may obtain at some other time and place. Baptism is not that kind of sign. A person's baptism does not just point to, or remind her and us of, a fact about her relationship with God that already obtained before she was baptized, or might come to obtain in some other time and place. Baptism is a sign of a qualitatively different kind, namely one that effects what it signifies, or more precisely, that effects here and now what the words make it to be a sign of. The act of baptism is performative not only in that the words make signs, but in that the signs cause or bring about the reality that they signify. The Western Catholic tradition captured this thought by arguing that the sacraments are first of all signs, indeed, but they are signs of a distinctive kind, namely, those that cause what they signify. And within the species of causal or performative signs they are unique, in that what they signify and so bring about can be accomplished by divine power alone, of which they are the created means or instruments. In the case of baptism, this is the forgiveness of sins and a share in the life of the Holy Trinity. When it comes to baptism, then, the relationship of sign to signified is chiefly that of (divine) cause to (created) effect.

The same should be true of the Eucharist as well. The Eucharist is a sign of Christ's body and blood. Since it is not, however, an ordinary sign but a sacramental sign, it effects what it signifies, what the words speak of, namely, Christ's body and blood. The body and blood of Christ, of course, already exist: born of Mary, offered in the upper room, pierced and poured out on the cross, risen and ascended to the right hand of the Father, alive forever at the heart of God. It cannot be the case, therefore, that the consecration of bread and wine by the words of Jesus cause his body and blood to be without qualification, as though they were inexistent prior to his words being spoken at the altar. That cannot be the sense in which the Eucharist is an effective sign.

Rather, Jesus' words spoken at the altar cause his body and blood to be precisely where the material signs of them are. The words of Christ do not change Christ's body; they change what is on the altar. What was brought to the altar was simply bread and wine. When the president has finished speaking the words of Christ over the bread, it is the body of Christ, and so also for the wine, now his blood. The presider's utterances give a sign-value to the material objects on the altar that they did not previously have. But unlike ordinary signs, sacraments make present the reality they signify. In the Eucharist what the material objects signify is not a power or an act (such as God's forgiveness, in the case of baptism) but two quite different objects, also material, now fully present where they are. If they are to be genuinely effective signs of Christ's body and blood, the material objects on the altar must become Christ's body and blood. This change is truly radical; it extends all the way to what these objects on the altar actually are. They were bread and wine, now they are the body and blood of Christ. In Catholic teaching the quasi-technical word for the change effected by Christ's words is "transubstantiation," but the idea is an ancient one, more commonly expressed simply by the ideas of "change" or "conversion." So Ambrose, writing in the late fourth century, asks his catechumens, "Cannot the word of Christ, which was able to make what was not from nothing, change (*mutare*) those things that are into what they were not?" (*De Mysteriis* 9.52, in Ambrose 1963: 25 [altered]). Or as Justin had already said two centuries before, "We have been taught that the food that has been blessed ['made Eucharist'] by the prayer of the word that originates from him ... is the flesh and blood of the incarnate Jesus" (*Apology*, ch. 66).

What the Eucharist effects or brings about, we could say, is simply what is needed to make the words of Christ, spoken by his minister, true. "This is my body," once uttered by Christ's representative, is a true statement: "this"—what is on the altar—is Christ's body. The same goes for "This is the chalice of my blood." The truth of these statements is not obvious from what appears to us. Yet we may, indeed must, take them to be true, since the representative who utters them does not speak his own words and does not act in his own power, but acts merely as the servant of Jesus, God almighty in the flesh. Of course what is now on the altar still retains the appearance of bread and wine. This is neither an illusion nor an obstacle to be surmounted. The sensible qualities of bread and wine are real, and serve as the needed sign of the body that hung on the cross and the blood that flowed there, now fully present where these material signs are—as much present as they were on the cross and are at the right hand of the Father, though in a quite different manner.

The question "What is the Eucharist?" has here its most basic answer. The Eucharist is the body and blood of Christ. This is what awaits discovery when we move from description to definition, from what the Eucharist means to us, and appears to us to be, to what it is in itself. Sacraments are signs that effect, rather than simply pointing to, what they signify, and the Eucharist is unique even among signs of this kind. Alone among the sacraments it fully contains the reality it signifies. In this sacrament, the words bring it about that the material things they make to be signs contain without remainder the reality they signify: the body and blood of Jesus, and thereby, naturally inseparable from these, the total reality of Jesus Christ himself. In the language of Catholic teaching, "Our Lord Jesus Christ, true God and man, is truly, really, and substantially contained under the appearance of these sensible things" (The Council of Trent's Decree on the Eucharist, ch. 1; text in DH 1636 [my translation]. On the uniqueness of the Eucharist among the sacraments—that "in an absolute sense it contains something sacred, namely Christ himself"—see Aquinas, *ST* III, q.73, a.1, ad 3).

The Eucharist is the body and blood of Christ; it is also food. At the Last Supper Jesus commanded his apostles to eat and drink his body and blood. As Justin describes the early Eucharist, the deacons distribute the eucharistized bread and wine to those present, to be consumed by them or taken to their homes and distributed to those who are absent from the eucharistic liturgy. The distribution is not indiscriminate. The Eucharist is given only to the faithful (those who "believe that the things we teach are true"), and among the faithful only to those who are baptized, and who "live in the way Christ handed down to us" (*Apology*, chs. 65–66). This threefold condition for eating the Eucharist is required by the fact that the Eucharist is food, indeed, but no ordinary food. "We do not receive these," Justin notes, "as common bread or common drink," since this food "is the flesh and blood of the incarnate Jesus" (*Apology*, ch. 66).

The common teaching of churches descended from the Protestant Reformation has been that the only right use of the Eucharist is communion, eating and drinking, since that is what Christ commanded us to do with it. This is true even of those Protestant communities that have sought to maintain a strong view of Christ's real presence in the Eucharist (Lutherans and Anglicans, for example, at various points in their histories).

This effort to exclude any use of the Eucharist directed not to its consumption but to the adoration of Christ present in it (such as elevation of the consecrated host in the liturgy, its reservation afterwards, services of benediction, processions, and so forth) is difficult to square with the conviction that this is not ordinary food. We eat and drink the Eucharist, after all, precisely because we believe that what we receive is the saving body and blood of Christ, and not ordinary bread and wine. Our very practice of eating assumes that what we eat is the body and blood of Christ before, and thus apart from, our eating it. We are commanded to eat the Eucharist, but this sacrament should be treated as Christ's body and blood wherever it is present to us, not only in eating it, but before and apart from eating it. Augustine comments: Christ "has given us the flesh he received from Mary to eat for our salvation; but no one eats this flesh unless he has first adored it ... and not only do we not sin in thus adoring it, but we would sin if we did not adore it" (*Ennarationes in Psalmos* 98.9; see Augustine 2002: 474–475 [altered]).

Restricting the use of the Eucharist to the commanded eating and drinking fails, moreover, to embody or express our belief that the Eucharist is not ordinary food. Eating and drinking is just what we do with ordinary food, so if that is all we do with the Eucharist, if it is the only way we treat this sacrament, we will not exhibit to ourselves or to others our belief that this is food of the most extraordinary kind. In order for us to receive it as extraordinary food, we have to treat it as we would never treat mere food of any sort: by kneeling before it, worshiping and praying to it, and the like. It is possible, no doubt, to hold a belief that we never express in any embodied way. But we are embodied creatures, and beliefs held in this entirely interior way are likely, over time, increasingly to seem arbitrary, ephemeral, and unreal. (I owe this point to the English philosopher and committed Catholic Michael Dummett: Dummett 1987.)

SACRIFICE

From the first the Eucharist was regarded not only as a sacrament or mystery, but treated also as a sacrifice. Until the sixteenth century this feature of the Eucharist was obvious and uncontroversial, and as a result attracted relatively little theological attention. Augustine and other patristic writers were concerned to distinguish the Eucharist, as the life-giving sacrifice of Christians, from the demonic and death-dealing sacrifices of the pagans (especially in his seminal treatment of sacrifice in *The City of God*, bk. 10). Beyond this, though, the formative patristic and medieval discussions of eucharistic sacrifice focused on the clear articulation of a few basic principles. Perhaps the most important of these principles was influentially captured by Peter Lombard in book IV of his *Sentences*, based on patristic antecedents: "From these [patristic texts] we gather that what is done on the altar is, and is called, a sacrifice. Christ both was offered once for all, and is offered daily, but in one way then, and in another way now" (*Sentences* IV, dist. 12, ch. 5; Lombard 2010: 65).

Early on Protestantism polemicized vehemently against the tradition of treating the Eucharist as a sacrifice, fearing that any idea of the Eucharist as our offering to God turns the sacrament into an act of works righteousness, and worse, demeans the saving sacrifice of Christ. The once-for-all cross of Jesus needs no supplementation by any sacrifice we could possibly make, but is more than sufficient for the salvation of the world. The liturgy, practice, and theology of the Eucharist or Lord's Supper must therefore be purified of all insinuations of sacrifice. This was no small task, given the degree to which the liturgical tradition of the Church, both East and West, was saturated with sacrificial language, injunction, and allusion. Much of the reform of worship in Protestantism was aimed at making this rejection of eucharistic sacrifice a reality, and resistance to this break with liturgical and devotional tradition accounts for much of the vehemence of the polemic against sacrifice in the sixteenth century and beyond.

The eventual result was a Lord's Supper seen strictly as a gift that comes down from God to us, a pledge of the forgiveness of sins and other gracious benefits, and in no sense as an offering that goes up from us to God. Thus the preference of the designations "Lord's Supper" or "Holy Communion" over "Eucharist." We do offer God a sacrifice of praise and thanksgiving, to be sure, but this is not part of the sacrament itself, rightly understood. Our thanksgiving responds in gratitude to the gift that has come down from God, but must not be confused in any way with the gift itself. Luther gives a particularly clear and forceful version of this outlook on the Eucharist (tied, in his case, to a high doctrine of the real presence), but many who were not Lutherans have agreed with him on this.

The Catholic response to this developing rejection of eucharistic sacrifice was swift—since changes in worship, and not simply in theology, were at stake—and equally forceful. Many issues were in play, including the practice of masses for the dead and for other intentions of the faithful, which underwent considerable expansion in the late Middle Ages. In Catholic eyes the Protestant attack on eucharistic sacrifice seemed, at bottom, to be based on a premise that was not only theologically mistaken, but damaging to the worship and religious life of ordinary Christians. There is no need, or warrant, for playing off the sacrifice Christ made on the cross against the sacrifice we make in the Eucharist, or conversely. As the Fathers had taught, the Lombard had succinctly expressed, and many subsequent commentators had explained, both are true: Christ offered himself once for all on Calvary, and is offered daily in the Eucharist.

Precisely because the sacrifice Christ made, once for all, to the Father on Calvary more than suffices for the salvation of the world, the sacrifice we make to the Father daily in the Eucharist cannot be another and different offering from that made once by Christ. The Eucharist must, rather, be one and the same sacrifice as that offered by Christ on Calvary, now made by us in a different, that is, sacramental, way. Since the Eucharist is no other sacrifice than the one sacrifice of Christ, it must in reality be offered by him, though now with our participation, as it was not in the upper room and on Calvary. The Eucharist is, in other words, Christ's way of giving us a share in his once-for-all sacrifice.

By the sixteenth century the primary concept for expressing this continuity over time of the Eucharist with the cross was "representation," understood in the sense of "making present (again)." As often as it is celebrated, the Eucharist is a true sacrifice for the forgiveness of sins (in the language of the sixteenth century debates, a "propitiatory" sacrifice as well as a sacrifice of praise and thanksgiving). The Eucharist has this character, however, only because it effectively represents or makes present the one sacrifice of Christ—more exactly because Christ, eternal high priest, makes the full reality of his once for all sacrifice present in the hands of his ministers. In the nature of the case, the eucharistic sacrifice does not, and cannot, repeat or add to the once-for-all sacrifice of

Christ; notions of this sort are wholly absent from Catholic doctrine on this subject. The Council of Trent, laying down (in 1562) the first full-orbed church doctrine on the Eucharist as sacrifice in the Western tradition, spells this point out with particular care. Acting as our high priest, Jesus Christ instituted the Eucharist "so that he might leave to his beloved bride the Church a visible sacrifice, as human nature requires, by which the sacrifice accomplished in blood once for all on the cross might be made present (*repraesentaretur*), and the memory of it abide, until the end of the world" (Decree on the Sacrifice of the Mass, ch. 1, DH 1740; my translation).

From the Reformation to Vatican II the sacrificial dimension of the Eucharist was a standard topic in Catholic theology, and generated a vast literature offering an array of nuanced and sometimes conflicting positions on how the eucharistic sacrifice should properly be understood. Since the council, many traditional topics of theological concern have been largely ignored, but sacrifice is not one of them. Catholic theologians themselves have sometimes subjected church teaching on this topic to criticism that goes markedly beyond the classic Protestant rejection of eucharistic sacrifice. Traditional Protestantism held that the cross is a sacrifice but the Eucharist is not; indeed, precisely because the cross is a sacrifice the Eucharist cannot be. Post-conciliar Catholic theology sometimes argues, in effect, that this fails to get to the root of the problem. The cross itself is not a sacrifice—in particular not what was traditionally called a "propitiatory" sacrifice, offered to take away sin—so *a fortiori* the Eucharist cannot be thought of as a sacrifice.

In part the argument seems to be that traditional notions of sacrifice are now outmoded. Discoveries in biblical and liturgical studies have simply rendered established Catholic teaching on eucharistic sacrifice untenable, the way Galileo's discoveries rendered a geocentric universe untenable. But current objections to sacrifice are also rooted in morally tinged arguments from philosophy and cultural anthropology. Traditional teaching on sacrifice (especially that developed in Catholic theology following the Council of Trent) is regarded as enshrining a debased idea both of God and of human beings. The Christian God is not a master demanding tribute from his subjects, least of all tribute paid in blood. God is a giver of gifts who asks nothing in return. The cross, and therefore the Eucharist, is God's gift to us, not a blood sacrifice we offer to God. To think otherwise is to exalt violence and victimization, to see them inscribed in the very nature of things. Liturgical, devotional, and theological language of sacrifice must be, if not expunged, then sweepingly reinterpreted to bring it into line with morally acceptable ideas of God and human flourishing.

As in the case of cross and Eucharist, so in the case of gift and sacrifice, playing one element of Christian faith off against another proves not only to be unnecessary, but to deform both of the things it needlessly opposes. The Christian theology of sacrifice never held that God stood in need, let alone in bloodthirsty want, of our sacrifice. "Do I eat the flesh of bulls, or drink the blood of goats?" (Ps 50:13 RSV). The sacrifice of Jesus accomplished on the cross, and thereby our sacrifice in the Eucharist, is itself the triune God's supreme gift to us, given for our good. That God delivers us from evil by sacrifice when he was entirely free to do so without it (or not to do so at all) might prompt us to reconsider not our idea of God's infinite goodness, but our ideas of sacrifice, and their application to the cross and the Eucharist of God incarnate (see Marshall 2011).

In any event it would likely be impossible to take sacrifice out of Christianity, or to domesticate the scandal of its sacrificial elements, without distorting the whole beyond recognition. This is a religion, after all, whose central symbol is a dying man, nailed to a cross, and whose central ritual is meant to evoke the presence of that man, and that cross. Sacrifice is pervasive in Christian scripture, culminating in the Christian savior's willing acceptance of the lot of a sacrificial victim, a place marked out by the effusion of his blood (referred or alluded to more than fifty times in the New Testament alone).

It would be especially difficult to square any sweeping repudiation of sacrifice with the foundation of the Eucharist in the Last Supper. At the heart of the church's worship and faith stand the words of Jesus, "This is my body, which will be given up"—to death—"for you"; "this is the chalice of my blood, the blood of the new and eternal covenant, which will be poured out for you and for many for the forgiveness of sins." In the upper room Jesus evidently makes an oblation. He offers a sacrifice, namely his own body and blood, to God for our salvation. The sacrifice he offers in the upper room is to be realized or accomplished on the cross. In traditional terms the cross is the immolation, the giving over to death, of the sacrificial victim offered and consecrated as such at the Last Supper—offered, of course, by himself, as priest who himself accepts the lot of victim. At the Last Supper, in other words, Jesus interprets his cross to come as a sacrifice, in the most solemn ritual terms. And he commands us to do likewise. "Do this in memory of me": make, at my command, the oblation I made in the upper room, and perfected once for all on the cross. Without the oblation the cross would not be a sacrifice at all, but simply the unjust killing of an innocent man. Without the cross, the oblation would remain empty and unfulfilled, the pledge of an offering no one was actually able to make. (The distinction between oblation and immolation was long considered basic to the theology of sacrifice. Its nuanced application to the Last Supper and Calvary, and so to the Eucharist, was a contribution of Maurice de la Taille, S.J., especially in his *Mysterium Fidei* [3rd ed., 1931]; for a summary see de la Taille 1930: 3–37. After Vatican II de la Taille's work vanished from sight, along with the rest of the lively debate about eucharistic sacrifice prior to the council. But a retrieval is underway. See Matthiesen 2013.)

CONCLUSION: THE WORK AHEAD

This modest sketch of a theology of the Eucharist raises, no doubt, countless questions. How, for example, should we understand the human being Jesus to be present in his total reality just where realities of a quite different kind, the consecrated bread and wine, are present, without lapsing into absurdity or contradiction? How shall we understand what we offer to the Father in the Eucharist to be precisely the one who offered himself to the Father in the upper room and on the cross, and indeed our offering to be the same as his once-for-all act of self-giving to the Father and to us? (For further reflection on these two questions in particular, see Marshall 2014; also, Marshall 2009.) Questions such as these have attracted relatively little interest in recent sacramental theology. They are questions of just the kind, however, that come to the fore when we persistently seek an answer to the question, "What is the Eucharist?"

Suggested Reading

Augustine (2002); Marshall (2009 and 2014); Matthiesen (2013).

Bibliography

Ambrose (1963), *De Mysteriis,* in *Saint Ambrose: Theological and Dogmatic Works,* trans. R. J. Deferrari (Washington, DC: Catholic University of America Press).

Augustine (2002), *Expositions of the Psalms 73–98,* trans. M. Boulding (Hyde Park, NY: New City Press).

Augustine (1994), *Tractates on the Gospel of John 55–111,* trans. J. W. Retting (Washington, DC: Catholic University of America Press).

Augustine (1954), *Tractatus in Ioannis Evangelium* 80, in CCL 36.

De la Taille, M. (1931) *Mysterium Fidei,* 3rd ed. (Paris: Beauchesne).

De la Taille, M. (1930), *The Mystery of Faith and Human Opinion: Contrasted and Defined* (London: Longmans, Green, & Co.).

Dummett, M. (1987), "The Intelligibility of Eucharistic Doctrine," in *The Rationality of Religious Belief,* W. J. Abraham and S. W. Holzer (eds.) (Oxford: Clarendon Press), 231–261.

Justin, Martyr (1953), "First Apology," in *Early Christian Fathers,* ed. Cyril Richardson (Philadelphia, PA: Westminster), 242–289.

Justin, Martyr (1997), *St. Justin Martyr: The First and Second Apologies,* ed. and trans. L. William Barnard (Mahwah, NJ: Paulist Press).

Justin, Martyr (2005), *Iustini Martyris Apologiae pro Christianis/Dialogus cum Tryphone,* ed. Miroslav Marcovich (Berlin: Walter de Gruyter).

Lombard, Peter (2010), *The Sentences,* Book 4: *On the Doctrine of Signs,* trans. Giulio Silano (Toronto: Pontifical Institute of Mediaeval Studies).

Martyr, Justin (1953), "First Apology," in *Early Christian Fathers,* ed. Cyril Richardson (Philadelphia, PA: Westminster), 242–289.

Marshall, B. D. (2009), "The Whole Mystery of Our Salvation: St. Thomas on the Eucharist as Sacrifice," in *Sacraments in Aquinas,* ed. M. Dauphinais and M. Levering (Chicago: Hillenbrand Books), 39–64.

Marshall, B. D. (2011), "Debt, Punishment, and Payment: A Meditation on the Cross, in Light of St. Anselm," *Nova et Vetera* (English ed.) 9: 163–181.

Marshall, B. D. (2014), "The Eucharistic Presence of Christ," in *What Does it Mean to "Do This"?,* ed. J. J. Buckley and M. Root (Eugene, OR: Cascade Books), 47–73.

Martyr, Justin (1997), *St. Justin Martyr: The First and Second Apologies,* ed. and trans. L. William Barnard (Mahwah, NJ: Paulist Press).

Martyr, Justin (2005), *Iustini Martyris Apologiae pro Christianis/Dialogus cum Tryphone,* ed. Miroslav Marcovich (Berlin: Walter de Gruyter).

Matthiesen, M. M. (2013), *Sacrifice as Gift: Eucharist, Grace, and Contemplative Prayer in Maurice de la Taille* (Washington, DC: Catholic University of America Press).

Murray, J. C. (1964), *The Problem of God* (New Haven, CT: Yale University Press).

O'Connor, F. (1988), *Collected Works* (New York: The Library of America).

Tanner, N. P. (ed.) (1990), *Unitatis redintegratio,* in *Decrees of the Ecumenical Councils,* vol. 2 (London: Sheed & Ward).

Woodruff Tait, J. L. (2011), *The Poisoned Chalice: Eucharistic Grape Juice and Common-Sense Realism in Victorian Methodism* (Tuscaloosa: University of Alabama Press).

CHAPTER 33

··

MARRIAGE

··

BRENT WATERS

Marriage has always been affirmed within the Christian tradition. The strength of and reasons for this affirmation, however, have varied over time, often in response to changing ecclesial, social, and political circumstances. This ferment continues to the present, particularly in response to purportedly shifting public mores regarding the normative status of marriage and to regulatory policies reflecting these changing perceptions. This chapter provides a brief overview of some of the more significant historical shifts in Christian thought and practice, and summarizes selected contemporary theological and moral issues.

Early Christians inherited from their Jewish forbears the belief that marriage was part of a good created or natural order. Adam and Eve were not only a man and a woman, but also husband and wife. It is within the marital household that many of the goods of creation are enjoyed. Moreover, it is through lineage that familial identities, and more broadly the identity of Israel as a people, are maintained over time. Although the Hebrew Scriptures are replete with stories of polygamous marriages, it had fallen into disfavor coinciding with the Diaspora. Indeed, the petty bickering, jealousies, and intrigues of the polygamous households of the patriarchs and monarchs are almost always subjected to moral disapproval, and Christians inherited the presumption of monogamy as the exclusive moral foundation of marriage.

There is, nonetheless, a profound ambivalence about marriage in the New Testament. Jesus, for instance, reaffirms the one-flesh unity of marriage and upholds it through his condemnation of divorce. Yet he warns his disciples that marital and familial bonds may need to be forsaken in following him. St. Paul prefers singleness because it enables a fuller devotion to Christ and the work of his church, but nonetheless permits marriage for those who would otherwise succumb to lust and fornication.

How may we account for this ambivalence? The formation of early Christian thought and practice must be understood against a dominant pagan cultural and political background. The greatest threat to the security of the Roman Empire was not the barbarians at its gates, but the need to produce offspring within its borders. Given high infant mortality rates, it is estimated that each woman had to give birth to at least five children in order to maintain a stable population (Brown 1989: 5–7). But it was not simply a matter of encouraging haphazard breeding, but also of preserving and passing on a cultural legacy. This twofold task fell predominantly upon private households that were based upon monogamous marriage. In this respect marriage and parenthood were civic duties that could not be casually ignored.

Given this key role that households were expected to play, early Christian ambivalence toward marriage becomes more explicable. Although Jesus does not formally condemn or disparage marriage, he also makes it clear that his brothers and sisters are not those who share biological kinship, but those who follow him. It should be kept in mind that the synoptic Gospels were compiled shortly after the Jewish revolt of AD 66–74. Rome crushed the revolt through a series of military campaigns that devastated the region, and the consequent seizure of property and occupational policies destroyed many urban and rural households. These circumstances required itinerants unencumbered by marital and familial responsibilities who could move easily among a displaced, impoverished, and often homeless population to conduct the ministry of the fledging church. The teachings against marriage and family are harsh only to those who have placed their hope and confidence in household stability, but they are a message of hope to those who cannot presume such stability (Waters 2007: 8–10). The Kingdom of God proclaimed by Jesus is not based on flesh and blood, but on water and the Spirit.

In contrast, Paul wrote his letters, roughly twenty years earlier, to predominantly Gentile churches located in relatively stable cities. His criticism of marriage is much less severe, marked more by indifference than admonition. He does not claim that a disciple of Jesus may be required to leave an unbelieving spouse, and marriage is permitted though not encouraged. In addition, Paul's missionary efforts often depended upon affluent benefactors who opened their homes as a place for converts to meet and worship. Despite Paul's indifference, many of the congregations he established drew upon the strength of supportive households, and it is not coincidental that the so-called "household codes" appear in the Deutero-Pauline literature (Dunn 1996: 43–63).

Nevertheless, Paul's perception of married Christians as at best half-hearted believers was only thinly disguised as subsequent theologians more clearly professed. With a few notable exceptions, such as St. Clement of Alexandria, the patristic writers lionized continent singleness often at the expense of denigrating marriage. This created two problems for the early church. On the one hand, the implicit superiority of singleness tended to confirm the suspicions of pagan critics that Christians were untrustworthy if not subversive. Was not a refusal to marry tantamount to shirking a civil duty to produce children for the empire? This suspicion was particularly telling in light of imperial edicts that fined men if they did not marry by a certain age and rewarded them if they sired five legitimate offspring within a specified period of time. On the other hand, as the church grew over time, its membership increasingly comprised married couples, and their children in turn became the principal source of new generations of Christians as opposed to adult converts. How could the church continue to denigrate, both explicitly and implicitly, an institution that had become its mainstay? This issue became particularly acute following the Edict of Milan in 313, which in establishing legal toleration for the church also afforded greater opportunities for Christians to participate in the governance of the empire (Leithart 2010).

St. Augustine tried to resolve this tension by portraying the intrinsic value of marriage in a manner that did not challenge the superiority of continent singleness as exhibited in Jesus' life and ministry and propounded in Pauline and patristic precepts. His strategy was to emphasize how marriage and singleness were related. Instead of contrasting the superiority of singleness over the inferior life of marriage, he compared them as greater and lesser goods; somewhat similar to comparing a mountain with a hill. Both are praiseworthy vocations, but continent singleness entails a more difficult and demanding way of life. Marriage is the lesser good because of its association with sexual intercourse and procreation that had become disfigured in the fall. These acts, however, are not inherently evil, for Adam and Eve had been created as a married couple with bodies capable of producing offspring. It was the will and desire, not the body, which had been corrupted in the Fall. Humans can still pursue this good, albeit in a diminished or "limping" manner given the corrupting influence of original sin (Ramsey 1988: 66).

According to Augustine, marriage is based upon three goods: offspring (*proles*), faith, and sacrament. Faith directs lust in assisting a married couple to pursue propagation. A faithful couple help restore the rightful place of sexual intercourse in God's created order, a way of guiding desire and anatomy more in keeping with what God intends. Fidelity presupposes mutual charity (*caritas*), which in turn provides the basis of the sacramental bond that carries most of the weight of Augustine's argument. He does not advocate lifelong marriage because it enables procreation and faith, but on the grounds that marital permanence is inherently good. Marriage based on friendship and concord provides a foundation for the task of ordering creation in anticipation of Christ's Kingdom.

Since Augustine held marriage in relatively high regard, why did he continue to insist on the pre-eminence of continent singleness? In the Incarnation the significance of procreation diminished while the importance of singleness increased. Before Jesus' birth procreation was needed to prepare the time when the Word would be made flesh, and that purpose has now been fulfilled. History is separated into the eras of marriage and continence, and Christians are living in the latter. Although marriage is good because it bears witness to a good created order, it nevertheless retains a compromised relationship with a fallen world. Continent singleness is thereby superior because it provides an indication of creation's destiny in Christ. Augustine's legacy in this respect is that he effectively establishes marriage and singleness two complementary vocations. Marriage is naturally oriented toward temporal concerns, so its three goods affirm an ordering of human life that accords, however imperfectly, with God's created order. Singleness, however, is a reminder that the world's destiny transcends temporal concerns as it is drawn toward its transformation in Christ. In short, marriage bears a providential witness while singleness is an eschatological witness, and both are needed to give a singular witness to the providential unfolding of creation over time and until the end of time.

This essentially Augustinian framework was subsequently refined, particularly in the works of such medieval theologians as Gratian, Hugh of St. Victor, Peter Lombard, and St. Thomas Aquinas. Although codification in canon law was a gradual and often contentious process, three definitional themes emerged that guided its progression (Waters 2007: 23–28; Witte 2012: 81–96). First, marriage is a natural association governed by the laws of nature. Men and women are naturally drawn to one another, and this attraction is in part sexual. Although the urgency of the procreative mandate to be fruitful and multiply had been eased with Jesus' birth, it was still in force. Consequently, the purpose of sexual intercourse was not pleasure but to produce offspring, so marriage should be ordered to promote this outcome. Marriage is therefore a "monogamous, exclusive, and indissoluble union" (Witte 2012: 83). Given this definition, such acts as fornication, adultery, and bigamy are condemned as violations of natural law.

Second, marriage is a contract governed by civil law. Stable households promote the common good, so marriage should be a publicly regulated institution. In this respect, marriage is a contractual agreement that a man and woman accept freely and without coercion. In order to protect marriage as a civil institution a number of legal impediments, such as consanguinity, affinity, age of consent, and disability were identified and explicated, often in excruciating detail.

Third, marriage is a sacrament governed by spiritual laws. Although marriage was still a means of controlling sexual desire, friendship between spouses received greater and more positive attention. Marriage was not only an antidote to lust, but also a way of receiving grace. This sacramental emphasis was subtle but decisive, for a couple's one-flesh unity mirrored the relationship between Christ and his church. For instance, Augustine had used "sacrament" to demonstrate marital stability, whereas thirteenth-century theologians used the same term to designate the "spiritual efficacy" of marriage (Witte 2012: 96). This more pronounced Pauline emphasis is seen in the indissolubility of marriage, for the spiritual bond between wife and husband could no more be broken than could the relationship between Christ and the church. Previous generations had assumed that a marriage ought not be dissolved; it was now asserted that it could not be dissolved.

As was noted above, this refinement of an Augustinian framework was a slow, painstaking process that can be said to have concluded with the Council of Trent (1545–64). It is not coincidental that the council coincided with the growing Protestant movement, for its purpose was to consolidate Catholic doctrine and practice in reaction to the Reformers' criticisms and teaching. This was particularly the case in respect to marriage, for the Reformers had argued that marriage was a predominantly secular rather than ecclesial concern. In short, jurisdiction for ordering the earthly household should be entrusted to the civil magistrates rather than a priest or bishops. Consequently, Protestants stripped marriage of its formal status as a sacrament, recovering to some extent Augustine's more limited understanding. In doing so, however, divorce was permitted, most often on the grounds of adultery, abuse, or abandonment. In addition, the Protestant churches disbanded monastic orders, rejected celibacy as a requisite clerical practice, and continued requiring single persons to refrain from sexual intercourse until married.

The Reformation, however, was itself a fractured movement, and the Protestant churches differed in respect to their theological understanding of marriage and how it should be regulated. Some of these key differences are summarized below. Lutherans portrayed marriage as a *social estate* (Waters 2007: 28–30; Witte 2012: 113–158). Martin Luther argued that marriage is a duty stemming from divine commands derived from scripture. All Christians have a presumptive obligation to marry and raise children fit to serve God, not only for their own sake but also for the good of society. The principal theological claim undergirding this duty is that marriage is part of God's created order, providing the foundation of the family as one of the chief estates, alongside church and state.

In contrast to Luther's account of marriage as a natural institution, John Calvin emphasized *covenant* as the primary foundation of marriage (Waters 2007: 31–38; Witte 2012: 159–215). Marriage was not merely a private contract, but a public component of the overlapping covenants comprising civil society. The marriage ceremony, for instance, symbolized this covenantal emphasis. In addition to the couple, parents, witnesses, minister, and magistrate must all be present in a church during public worship to form a valid marriage. Moreover, these parties did not perform cursory roles in the ceremony, but "represented different dimensions of God's involvement in the marriage covenant. They were essential to the legitimacy of the marriage itself" (Witte 2012: 186–187). Their absence would be tantamount to excluding God from the marital covenant. The Puritans, drawing upon Calvin, placed even more prominence upon the civil significance of marriage, portraying civil society as a collection of households rather than individuals. In the Massachusetts Bay colony, for example, single persons were assigned to households, and the magistrate, rather than the minister, presided over weddings (Morgan 1980).

The Anglican tradition carved a middle way among contending Catholic, Lutheran, and Calvinist parties, eventually settling upon an understanding of marriage that may be characterized as *commonwealth* (Witte 2012: 217–285). The household is a domestic commonwealth governed by the husband-father as its head. His power, however, was limited by both natural law and biblical teaching; his rule should be just and loving, and not tyrannous. Arriving at this middle position, however, was the culmination of a long and arduous process, often reflecting the bitter political and ecclesiastical conflicts between Catholics and Protestants. At varying times marriage wavered "from the Anglo-Catholic to the Anglo-Puritan, from the sacramental to the contractarian" (Witte 2012: 220). Both parties, however, eventually agreed that marriage was not a formal sacrament alongside baptism and Holy Communion. Consequently, marital permanence was of little theological significance, and divorce was permissible. Subsequent proposals for regulating marriage ranged from very modest reforms of canon law to John Milton's scheme of what amounted to no-fault divorce (Milton 1645). Successive laws that changed over time reflected this tension, and often wavered between these two poles.

Although Milton's radical proposal was never enacted by Parliament, his basic idea is that marriage is a contract between a husband and wife, and if the peace of their domestic commonwealth suffers from the tyranny of unhappiness, it can be dissolved. This basic idea prompted further reflection by future generations of philosophers. John Locke, Thomas Hobbes, and Immanuel Kant, for instance, effectively reduced marriage to nothing more than a contract entailing the subjective desires of the contracting parties (Waters 2007: 65–74). Later liberal refinements spurred the secularization of marriage (Waters 2007: 74–82; Witte 2012: 287–323), effectively paving the way for contemporary mores and policies in respect to cohabitation, easy divorce, and single-parent households. Theological and political reactions to this trend have ranged from staunch opposition to cozy accommodation (Waters 2007: 74–130).

The reason for the preceding overview of a developing Christian understanding and practice of marriage is to note two important themes. First, marriage is *not* a Christian invention. Early Christians largely adopted the forms and practices of their pagan neighbors, and their descendants throughout the following centuries altered what they inherited in response to changing cultural circumstances. The tripartite household of early Christian literature consisting of husbands and wives, parents and children, and masters and servants, for example, has all but disappeared from contemporary theological, moral, and pastoral discourse; Friedrich Schleiermacher is the last prominent theologian to assume that this triadic structure is the Christian norm (Schleiermacher 1991). When guardians and assailants declare "traditional" Christian marriage as the object of their respective defense or attack, it is often not clear what either has (or should have) in mind.

Second, although a Christian account of marriage has evolved over time, the process has not been undertaken randomly or haphazardly. There has been a continuous thread portraying Christian marriage as a monogamous relationship between a man and a woman, and that marriage in turn is the preferred social setting for the procreation and nurture of children. Consequently, there is a tension between the poles of adaptation and continuity, and in the remainder of this chapter I suggest some ways in which Christian theology and ethics might draw upon this tension in engaging some selected issues that are presently commanding ecclesial and public attention, as well as often acrimonious debate, in respect to marriage.

Sacramentality. Although Protestant churches, unlike Catholic and Orthodox churches, do not regard marriage as a sacrament, many retain what may be characterized as an implicit sacramentality. Marriage is something more than a contract or special friendship. This is reflected in the wedding vows that are exchanged, and the imagery of the relationship between Christ and the church that is often invoked. More importantly, marriage is affirmed as an institution that was created and ordained by God. Since it is not a sacrament, however, lifelong marriage is an ideal rather than an inviolable status, and divorce and remarriage are therefore permissible, options that are not open to Catholics, Orthodox, and (at least officially) Anglicans. It should be noted in passing that the ease with which some, but certainly not all, Protestant churches embrace divorce and remarriage is a matter of concern, for it diminishes the theological significance of marriage. Affirming the good of marriage is diminished when the divorce and remarriage rates of Protestants are nearly identical to those of the general population, at times appearing to implicitly sanction serial polygamy and polyandry.

Common convictions about marriage among the Catholic, Orthodox, and Protestant churches, however, are, at least potentially, more striking than the differences separating them over its formal sacramental status. They are bound together by a theological tradition, which insists that marriage is not a mere human contrivance but an institution established and ordained by God as part of a good created order. Consequently, it is a basic form of human association whose regulation and ordering is entrusted to the church and secular government. As addressed below, this divine origin raises the question of the extent to which church and state have the authority to redefine what marriage is since neither created it.

Family. The Christian theological tradition has always affirmed marriage as the normative foundation of the family. As Augustine recognized, it is an institution well suited for pursuing the good of offspring in an orderly fashion. But more deeply, children can deepen and help fulfill the marital bond that is, in part, driven by both physical and affiliative desires. This recognition has been further developed in modern Catholic encyclical teaching (Waters 2007: 105–116), and among Protestant theologians, Paul Ramsey portrayed children as the end or *telos* of a couple's one-flesh unity (Ramsey 1975). In this respect, it may be said that a married couple is oriented toward becoming parents, or should at least be open to the prospect.

This parental orientation instantiates the providential witness of marriage and family (Waters 2007: 192–229). The intergenerational relationship between parents and offspring bears witness to a good creation that perpetuates itself over time. But this perpetuation is not accomplished through haphazard breeding. Rather, it is undertaken within social bonds ordering affinity, kinship, and affection. A person is born into given social structures and relationships that predates her and will continue after her death (O'Donovan 2013: 1–6). Humans are therefore situated in and dependent upon a series of overlapping associations that enable both their survival and flourishing. Theologically we may say that family is a basic association in which humans are provided mutual and timely belonging in an intense and intimate manner. Through bonds of affinity and kinship family members are drawn toward each other in satisfying mutual needs and desires in both reciprocal and asymmetrical ways. Since humans are also finite and mortal creatures these bonds change over time and eventually come to an end. More expansively, we may characterize family as a series of concentric circles of mutual affection or love. An initial marital love expands into parental love, which in turn unfolds into familial love. In short, spouses, parents, and children belong with each other within a family ordered to and by mutual love.

The family described above is admittedly an ideal, one that sadly often fails to be honored. In addition, lifting up this ideal of marriage and family should not be understood as an explicit or implicit denigration of singleness, single parents, or childless couples. To the contrary, early Christians, for instance, were repeatedly enjoined to care for widows and orphans. This support, however, presupposes an ideal or given standard that makes the provision of such care necessary as well as guiding its pursuit. Adoption, for example, is not solely a means for satisfying frustrated parental desire. Rather, it provides a child who would otherwise have none with a place of mutual and timely belonging. Consequently, adoption has never been confined to childless couples, but is undertaken by a variety of couples and single persons. Adoptive parents, however, nonetheless represent to children a place or space of belonging that is normed by an ideal standard of marriage and family; even in single parent households there is an absent parent. Familial roles and structures are to a large extent malleable and synthetic, but the bonds of affinity and kinship from which they are derived can never be dismissed as entirely irrelevant, and the groundwork of these bonds are embodied in the ideal of the one-flesh unity of marriage.

This significance is diminished, however, if marriage is understood as a self-contained and isolated relationship. When marriage, and more broadly family, is regarded as a self-sufficient association, it degenerates into a secluded enclave or private haven (Lasch 1995) that in turn diminishes its important moral and social contributions to the good of civil community. Some of the more troubling consequences of this diminishment are examined below in the discussions of the relation between marriage and singleness, followed by that of households and strangers.

Singleness. To appreciate more fully the theological significance of marriage requires some inquiry into how it is or should be related to singleness. As noted above, marriage bears a providential witness to the goodness of creation while singleness bears witness to the end of creation in Christ. Both are needed to offer a complete witness, and when one is ignored or accentuated to the detriment of the other, the complementary character of their respective witness is lost. Creation without eschatology distorts a penultimate good into an ultimate good, and eschatology without creation is little more than a Gnostic fantasy. Or in more prosaic terms, marriage without singleness serves no greater purpose, and singleness without marriage has no purpose. Consequently, a more robust account of vocational singleness is needed in order to have a richer understanding of marriage.

Protestants are at a loss in undertaking this task, for there is no tradition affirming singleness as a calling or vocation. Indeed, the implicit duty to marry has often been accompanied by a perception of singleness as, at best, a perplexing aberration. In short, singles tend to be viewed as persons who are presently not married. This perception effectively negates the providential witness of marriage. Marriage can continue to bear witness to a good created order, but since there is no contrast with a calling to singleness, there is no vocational witness to the end or *telos* of creation that orients its providential unfolding over time. Ultimately, marriage bears witness to itself rather than to the greater goods it should be anticipating. Some Protestant authors have tried to recover a sense of vocational singleness. Rodney Clapp, for example, contrasts the "missionary" advantage of singles with the "hospitality" centers afforded by married households (Clapp 1993). Together, singleness and marriage offer a more complete ministry of the church. The Catholic, and to a much lesser extent Orthodox and Anglican churches have retained a stronger sense of vocational singleness through both ordination and monastic communities. Yet some writers have urged a broader embrace of singleness, as a temporary calling that does not involve formal vows (Bennett 2008).

Such attempts to restore a theological relationship between marriage and singleness on the part of Protestants and to expand the concept among Catholics are to be welcomed, but they often have a tendency to collapse both vocations into ecclesiological categories. The church is often portrayed as the first family, and families in turn as small, domestic churches. Although familial imagery has been employed to describe ecclesial fellowship—the church, for example as the bride of Christ, and its members as sisters and brothers in Christ—their conflation diminishes their respective significance. If the family is the church writ small and the church a family writ large, then the distinctive and complementary witness each bears is effectively negated. Since marriage is an institution grounded in the order of creation its providential witness is predicated upon a first birth of flesh and blood, whereas the church as a witness to the end or *telos* of creation is based upon a second birth of water and the Spirit. People are born into families where they are provided places of mutual and timely belonging. In contrast, people are baptized into the church where they embrace and affirm the end and hope of that belonging. Conceptually blurring these respective modes of admission and subsequent forms of association serves to confuse the distinctive roles that should be pursued and confined to church and household respectively. When, for instance, a family is at the Lord's Table they properly regard each other as sisters and brothers, and treat each other accordingly. But at the household table they are spouses, parents, and children and, again, should treat each other accordingly. Although these two forms of association are different, they are complementary rather than mutually exclusive; second births do not deny or destroy first births. This complementarity serves as a reminder that although forms of human association overlap, in this case the ecclesial with the marital and familial, their moral and social ordering remains distinctive rather than uniform. The church cannot be ordered as a family, nor can a family be ordered as a church. The need for maintaining such distinctions is reinforced in turning our attention to the relation between households and strangers.

Households and strangers. As argued above, marriage should not be fixated exclusively upon itself but should be oriented toward promoting broader spheres of human association such as the familial and ecclesial. This orientation was captured in the New Testament's "household codes" and throughout the greater part of subsequent Christian tradition. Until fairly recently the "normative" Christian household was based upon marriage and family, but also included the presence of strangers as domestic servants. The household was a means of relating marriage and family to broader public spheres while also protecting their privacy. In this respect, we may say that marriage and family have both private and public poles that are determinative features in their moral and social ordering.

This polar tension has been largely lost in most late modern societies. To a great extent, households are regarded as bulwarks protecting the privacy of its members from unwanted public contact or scrutiny. Such contact is limited to contractual arrangements designed to procure goods or services to maintain a household, effectively reducing a household to a secluded enclave. This reduction, however, produces three problematic consequences. First, it reinforces the perception that individuals enter and participate in the public square as autonomous and unaffiliated individuals. Any other social spheres to which an individual might be related are seen as idiosyncratic and therefore irrelevant to questions of political ordering. The resulting civil society consists of an asymmetrical relationship between an organized and powerful state and its weak and isolated citizens. Second, when a household is perceived exclusively as a bulwark of privacy with little or no recognized public importance, it becomes defensive and embattled in fending off intrusions by the state. Consequently, its status and welfare are precarious since the household is subjected to shifting political priorities and fortunes. As argued below, this emphasis upon the household as a secluded enclave has diminished its public value, thereby effectively weakening the privacy of marriage and family. Before examining some selected implications of these two consequences, however, we must first turn our attention to the third.

The third consequence is that when a household is reduced to a secluded enclave, strangers are largely regarded as threats. In order to protect its privacy, a household becomes a closed and opaque association, related to a broader civil community in a highly selective and tenuous manner. Yet this emphasis upon privacy fails to acknowledge a household's dependence upon broader social and political spheres. Particularly in late modern societies no household can be self-sufficient, and its survival and flourishing depends upon a wide variety of supportive educational, medical, cultural, commercial, and governmental institutions. When a household becomes fixated solely on its private pole, it collapses in upon itself, in turn distorting its dependent relationship with broader spheres of human association. In this respect, we may say that a household is or should be simultaneously an openly sequestered *and* intimately open space in order to provide a timely place of mutual belonging for its members (Waters 2007: 202). Without this tension the privacy of a household becomes a matter of public indifference. Ironically, as households grow increasingly secluded the public urgency for protecting their privacy is diminished. Married couples and families are effectively perceived as autonomous individuals who happen to be residing together for a time. As a result, there is no compelling reason to publicly support marital and parental bonds.

As noted above, the presumed inclusion of strangers in the household within the Christian tradition captured the necessary tension between its private and public poles. With its relatively recent demise, at least within many affluent societies, nothing has emerged to fill the void, and a revival of household servants seems both unlikely and unwanted. In short, if households, and thereby marriage and family, requires sustained relationships with strangers, how should that relationship be ordered? There are some recent theological attempts to address this question. There is, for example, a growing body of literature proposing intentional Christian communities comprising married couples, families, and singles that live together or in close proximity, and share common household practices (Janzen 2013). These communities prevent marital bonds or kinship from imploding by creating social settings comprising both families and strangers. Or in theological terms, they recognize the priority of water and the Spirit over flesh and blood as well as the fact that households can, and perhaps should, be based on second rather than first births. Proposals are also on offer to replace the nuclear family with the household as the principal social setting for ordering marriage, procreation, and childrearing (Waters 2007: 126–130). David Matzko McCarthy, for example, envisions networks of "open households" that create neighborhood economies in which certain goods are held in common, services are exchanged, and childrearing responsibilities are shared (McCarthy 2001).

These attempts have made some important contributions toward restoring both the public importance and theological significance of the household, but they nonetheless suffer some acute liabilities, particularly in respect to marriage. An intentional community may resemble a household, but it is not the household that Christian theology has traditionally affirmed. Such households were centered upon a particular marriage and family, and were not coalitions of married couples, families, and singles. Intentional communities tend to blur the lines demarcating families and strangers rather than defining their distinctive complementarity and how they should be related. In addition, intentional communities at the same time resemble monastic communities that again serve to conflate, and therefore diminish, the distinctive but complementary providential and eschatological witness. In trying to be both household and monastery, the resulting community ends up being neither. The confusing consequences of such a hybrid are captured rather nicely and entertainingly in Iris Murdoch's novel *The Bell* (Murdoch 1958).

McCarthy certainly relates the household to a broader public, but at the expense of marriage and parenthood. He contends that marriage promotes mutuality between a particular man and woman but that it cannot meet all of their respective needs; a larger network of friends is required. More importantly, marriage is too fragile a foundation to undertake the important task of childrearing on its own. A neighborhood, and more extensively the church, is needed in which all adults take on parenting responsibilities. If McCarthy is correct, however, then he begs a crucial question: does marriage carry any social and theological weight? Marriage presumably enjoys a privileged position in a network of friendships, but little else since it is not the basis of the family. Friendship is certainly a good of marriage but only a partial good, for marriage is also ordered toward the good of offspring. What McCarthy fails to acknowledge is that particular children are entrusted to the care of particular parents; *these* children belong with *those* parents and *not* to a neighborhood. Neighborhoods can support parents in undertaking their childrearing, but cannot replace them, for when every adult is regarded as a parent, then effectively no one is.

Despite the weaknesses noted above, these attempts at recovering theological accounts of the household will hopefully spark further reflection on how marriage might be promoted and what role it should play in civil society. Such sustained reflection is needed if marriage is to retain broad public and political support, especially in light of current disputes over who has the authority to define and regulate marriage.

Authority. For over two millennia the church has affirmed marriage as an institution established by God and grounded in the created order. This affirmation, however, did not imply that marriage may be entered into by any two (or more) consenting individuals. Certain restrictions, such as physical disability, consanguinity, and divorce have been seen as legitimate impediments that serve to protect the moral and social substance of marriage. Over time these impediments have variously been narrowly or broadly defined. To a large extent governments embedded, at least initially, in the so-called Judeo-Christian tradition have tended to mirror these constraints, though increasingly in terms of contractual relationships that are permitted, protected, and enforced through the state's coercive power (Witte 2012: 315–323).

It should be emphasized that it has been traditionally presumed that both church and state exercise a *limited* authority in respect to marriage. Moreover, this authority is regulatory rather than definitional, for marriage was not invented by either church or state but is a divinely instituted estate entrusted to their care. Admittedly, this care has not been uniform, and has been performed both well and badly over time. But the limit of regulation has largely been honored—until now. Christians and many civil societies are embroiled in acrimonious disputes over whether or not marriage can and should be redefined by church and state to include same-sex couples. Unfortunately, most of these debates have tended to fixate on either questions of sexual morality or the pursuit of individual self-fulfillment and happiness. These are important issues, but what has received inadequate attention is the potential ecclesial and political consequences, should church and state exceed their limited authority. In other words, is there reason to be concerned if church and state redefine rather than merely regulate marriage?

In respect to the church, the task of theology is not to create but to interpret the object of faith that is revealed by God in Christ. Subsequently, the task of moral theology is to help the church to discern how particular acts and practices embody such interpretive beliefs, and to order its life and witness accordingly. Admittedly, particular interpretations have often been wrong, requiring amendment. Arguably the most egregious examples are those that have also been the most inventive, as when novel expressions of love have been used to justify and promote inquisitions and crusades. In a similar vein, for the sake of inclusion, baptism and the Eucharist could presumably be theologically redefined in a way that would preclude the necessity of any profession of faith. But what, then, would be the point of these sacraments if there were no difference between believers and nonbelievers? Similarly, marriage could also be redefined to include same-sex couples, but would such an innovation further erode the theological significance of marriage and singleness, in turn weakening their complementary providential and eschatological witness? Moreover, is such inclusion a faithful interpretation of what marriage is and of who may pursue this vocation? To raise these questions is not to suggest that gays and lesbians should be forbidden from participating in the life and ministry of the church; nor does it foreclose the possibility of some formal recognition of same-sex unions. Rather, it is simply to challenge the necessity and wisdom of theologically redefining marriage in addressing these concerns.

In respect to the state, legally redefining marriage to include same-sex couples could unwittingly weaken civil society. As a broader range of claimants petition for legal recognition (e.g. polygamous and multiple partner marriages) the state may eventually refuse to recognize any relationships other than highly specified contracts among consenting individuals. But this would effectively further isolate citizens as autonomous individuals while weakening the private associations mediating their relationship with the state. As individuals become increasingly isolated, bound together only through contracts enforced by the coercive power of the state, conditions become ripe for ubiquitous governmental intrusions and potentially totalitarian control (Arendt 1968). In restricting the authority of the state to regulate but not define marriage, it serves, along with the many other private associations comprising civil society, as a bulwark against the unwarranted encroachment of the "homogenous and universal state" (Strauss 2000). Again, this restriction of the state's authority does not suggest that the civil rights and liberties of gays and lesbians should be restricted, or that some legal recognition or registration of same-sex couples is unwarranted. Rather, it is simply to challenge the necessity and wisdom of legally redefining marriage in order to achieve these goals in a just manner.

Since the church's inception it has frequently needed to revisit and refine its theological understanding of marriage, often in response to changing cultural, social, and political circumstances. Throughout these centuries of intermittent scrutiny punctuated by periods of indifference or neglect by both church and state, marriage has proven to be a remarkably resilient institution. It is therefore incumbent upon the church to promote careful and sustained theological reflection upon marriage as a providential witness to the goodness of creation. Such reflection should aspire to clarify what Christians are and are not defending in lifting up this witness both within the church and to the broader civil community.

Suggested Reading

Brown (1989); Waters (2007); Witte (2012).

Bibliography

Arendt, H. (1968), *The Origins of Totalitarianism* (San Diego, CA: Harvest Book).

Bennett, J. (2008), *Water is Thicker than Blood: An Augustinian Theology of Marriage and Singleness* (Oxford and New York: Oxford University Press).

Brown, P. (1989), *The Body and Society: Men, Women, and Sexual Renunciation in Early Christianity* (London: Faber & Faber).

Clapp, R. (1993), *Families at the Crossroads: Beyond Traditional and Modern Options* (Downers Grove, IL and Leicester, UK: Inter-Varsity Press).

Dunn, J. (1996), "The Household Rules in the New Testament," in S. Barton (ed.), *The Family in Theological Perspective* (Edinburgh: T & T Clark), 43–63.

Janzen, D. (2013), *The Intentional Christian Community Handbook: For Idealists, Hypocrites, and Wannabe Disciples of Jesus* (Brewster, MA: Paraclete Press).

Lasch, C. (1995), *Haven in a Heartless World: The Family Besieged* (New York and London: Norton).

Leithart, P. J. (2010), *Defending Constantine: The Twilight of an Empire and Dawn of Christendom* (Downers Grove, IL: Inter-Varsity Press).

McCarthy, D. (2001), *Sex and Love in the Home: A Theology of the Household* (London: SCM).

Milton, J. (1645), *The Doctrine and Discipline of Divorce* (London).

Morgan, E. (1980), *The Puritan Family: Religion and Domestic Relations in Seventeenth Century New England* (Westport, CT: Greenwood Press).

Murdoch, I. (1958), *The Bell* (London: Chatto & Windus).

O'Donovan, O. (2013), *Self, World, and Time: Ethics as Theology 1, An Induction* (Grand Rapids, MI and Cambridge, UK: Eerdmans).

Ramsey, P. (1975), *One Flesh: A Christian View of Sex Within, Outside and Before Marriage* (Bramcote: Grove Books).

Ramsey, P. (1988), "Human Sexuality in the History of Redemption," *Journal of Religious Ethics* 16: 56–86.

Schleiermacher, F. (1991), *The Christian Household: A Sermonic Treatise* (Lewiston, NY: Edwin Mellon Press).

Strauss, L. (2000), *On Tyranny* (Chicago and London: University of Chicago Press).

Waters, B. (2007), *The Family in Christian Social and Political Thought* (Oxford: Oxford University Press).

Witte, J. (2012), *From Sacrament to Contract: Marriage, Religion, and Law in the Western Tradition*, 2nd ed. (Louisville, KY: Westminster John Knox Press).

CHAPTER 34

THE SACRAMENT OF ORDERS DOGMATICALLY UNDERSTOOD

ADAM A. J. DEVILLE

INTRODUCTION

WHEN I teach my introductory course on Eastern Christianity to a classroom of students for whom invariably the Christian East is a completely foreign "other," I take pains to stress—without polemics, apologetics, or romantic treatments—both the similarities and the differences in sacramental practices between Protestant, Catholic, and Orthodox Christians, the latter being by far the most "mysterious" and "exotic" group to my students, who almost uniformly have no idea Orthodoxy even exists or is Christian. When it comes to the sacrament of ordination, we watch brief clips of a Southern Baptist ordination in Florida, a priestly ordination in the Vatican basilica, and a diaconal ordination in the Orthodox Church of America. In all three I point out the unmistakable similarities: a prayer for the Holy Spirit to descend on the kneeling man, on whose head hands have been laid by the other clergy. There is, then, a commonality of ritual gesture employed liturgically in both Eastern and Western Christian celebrations.

That common ritual, however, belies a commonality of dogmatic meaning. While outwardly most Christian ordinations may generally employ the same manual gestures, and while Christians in the last half-century have come a long way in ecumenical dialogue and search for unity on many questions, including sacraments and ministry (see World Council of Churches 1982), there is no universal consensus on the dogmatic import of orders. Indeed, there is not even consensus on whether holy orders is in fact a sacrament or not. Some Anglicans would say it is, but officially most Protestants, even while recognizing its importance and celebrating it liturgically, do not count it as a sacrament, at least not on the same level as the so-called dominical (or "great" or "major" sacraments of baptism and Eucharist). For these Christians, "holy orders" is purely an administrative necessity for organizing the church on earth and does not say anything dogmatic about the church, the faith, or perforce God. (Some, of course—e.g. Quakers, and Salvation Army—eschew the whole notion of *any* sacraments.) Catholics definitively count it as a sacrament, as do both Oriental and Byzantine Orthodox, though unlike Catholics following the "canonization" of the sacramental septinarium at Trent (Congar 1976), Eastern Christians have never definitively limited the sacraments to seven, and today, as we shall see, there is one very considerable exception (the Assyrian Church of the East) to an otherwise de facto Orthodox consensus on the nature and number of sacraments. Nevertheless, Catholics and all Eastern Christians are united in understanding orders to have dogmatic significance beyond the merely pragmatic-pastoral benefits of ordering the life of the earthly church.

This chapter will confine itself to an examination of the dogmatic and "proto-dogmatic" understandings of ordination in the Catholic, Orthodox, and Assyrian traditions, the three which definitively count it as a sacrament of importance, not so much in itself as for its constitutive links to the dogma of the *church* understood as herself the sacrament of communion with God. "Orders," then, through a long development not atypical of many sacramental and liturgical acts, is first seen as a more "practical-pastoral" arrangement for the earthly church to conduct her life "decently and in order" (1 Cor 14:40) and only later, via an "anabatic" and mystogogical ascent, finds fuller dogmatic meaning in ecclesiology, and ecclesiology ultimately in Triadology or Trinitarian theology. (The two best recent treatments linking priesthood and orders in particular, and ecclesiology in general, to the Trinity are Levering 2010 and Bordeianu 2011.)

The "method" of this chapter is inspired by the 1937 essay "Dogma and Dogmatic Theology" of Sergius Bulgakov, widely regarded as the greatest Russian Orthodox theologian of the twentieth century (Bulgakov 2003). Here Bulgakov very carefully tries to distinguish between dogmatic declarations as such—which have been very few and usually very restrained—and the larger, more expansive category of "dogmatic theology" which, using Scripture, the Fathers, the councils, and history (inter alia) for its basis, attempts to understand more deeply the faith of the church as articulated in categories appropriate to whatever context in which she finds herself. Sometimes, though, such "dogmatic theology" smuggles in what Bulgakov calls "quasi-dogmas" or even disguised personal opinions that do not in fact accurately reflect the mind of the church. Bulgakov explicitly notes that this is a danger with "the theology of the sacraments," which, together with the Theotokos, have only very rarely, at least in the East, been subject to official dogmatic declarations, none exhaustive by any means. The task of the dogmatic theologian, then, is to clarify what has and has not been taught officially and dogmatically by the church, and also to show the "mutual transparence" of dogmas, not as an "inventory" but as "internally organically tied, so that in the light of one dogma the content and strength of the other is revealed" (Bulgakov, 2003: 78). What follows aims to show the organic links of a theology of orders to the other sacraments and above all to the dogma of the church because, as Emmanuel Clapsis said nearly three decades ago, "ministry must be seen in the greater context of ecclesiology from which it cannot be separated" (1985: 421).

The sacrament of orders, moreover, must be understood not only ecclesiologically, but also liturgically, and we begin first with liturgy because, as David W. Fagerberg (2007) has shown (building on Prosper of Aquitaine's famous adage *lex orandi, lex credendi*), it is *theologia prima*. When we look at the liturgies of ordination, especially in the West, it is clear that there has been a great deal of diversity and change, a process that was renewed by widespread reforms in Latin liturgy following Vatican II (Fink 1982). We can, in fact, document several periods of significant change in the liturgical practices of ordination (Santantoni 2000a), and such relative "instability" in practice has shaped, and to a considerable degree altered, the meaning of the sacrament (Barkley 1956; Hinson 1981; and especially Mitchell 1982). Indeed, as Antonio Santantoni has said, "no other sacrament, with the exception of the Eucharist and baptism, has known the spectacular flowering of new gestures and new symbols as has the rite of episcopal ordination" (Santantoni 2000b: 227). As a result, there is no one "dogmatic meaning" good for all time. As Peter Fink has shown, every change in the liturgies of ordination over the last two millennia has resulted in an alteration of "the images we form of ourselves as church ... As the images change, a new theological understanding is called forth" (1982: 483). Today, as we shall see, thanks not only to the Second Vatican Council but also to the groundwork laid before it was convened, in the *ressourcement* movement, both Catholic and Orthodox, and in the ecumenical movement, the sacrament of orders is inextricably linked not to the new but to the newly recovered and greatly deepened dogmatic understanding of the church as *communion*.

ORDERS IN ROMAN CATHOLICISM

A clear instance of a change in both liturgical practice and theological reflection may be found in the reforms of the Latin Church following Vatican II, a council whose most central document, *Lumen Gentium* (LG), is a profound ecclesiological "charter," which changed Catholic practice and understanding as to the ordination of a bishop and his sacramental character. (The council also treated priestly orders in the important decree, *Presbyterorum Ordinis* and reflected on the "Pastoral Office of Bishop" in *Christus Dominus*, both issued in October 1965.) Before this point, it had been fairly common in the West to see the priesthood as the highest of the "major orders." It was, from the time of late scholasticism until at least the Council of Trent, commonplace to consider the priesthood as the highest "order" with the episcopate being almost an afterthought, held to be scarcely different sacramentally from the priesthood save that the former had "jurisdiction" while the latter did not. Thus the episcopate was seen not as a higher order but as consisting simply of priests to whom a grant of "jurisdiction" was given, a manifestly juridical notion in which the ordination of the bishop was downplayed and his sacramental role attenuated. By contrast, the council insisted stoutly that "by episcopal consecration the fullness of the sacrament of Orders is conferred, that fullness of power, namely, which both in the Church's liturgical practice and in the language of the Fathers of the Church is called the high priesthood, the supreme power of the sacred ministry" (LG 21).

The Second Vatican Council further solidified the new understanding of the essential "form" and "matter" of the sacrament of orders, a change begun under Pope Pius XII in 1947, and altering nearly a millennium of widespread thought and ritual practice from early scholasticism onward (and confirmed by the Council of Florence), that held that orders were definitively given in ordination not through the laying on of hands, but through the passing on of the "instruments" typical of an office—for example, a chalice and paten for a priest, since his most important work was celebrating the Eucharist. Pius XII definitively clarified this in the apostolic constitution (the most authoritative of papal documents) *Sacramentum Ordinis*, insisting that the laying on of hands was indeed the "matter" that "confected" the sacrament, drawing, for support, on the example of the Eastern Churches: "everyone knows that the Roman Church has always held as valid ordinations conferred according to the Greek rite without the *traditio instrumentorum*" (no. 3). As a result, it was no longer permitted to hold any other view than that which recognized that "the matter, and the only matter, of the Sacred Orders of the Diaconate, the Priesthood, and the Episcopacy is the imposition of hands; and that the form, and the only form, is the words which determine the application of this matter, which univocally signify the sacramental effects—namely the power of Order and the grace of the Holy Spirit" (no. 4). This change in 1947 would be given even clearer reflection in the revised Latin ordinal issued after Vatican II, where the laying on of hands is clearly the "high point" and the giving of instruments has a secondary character. Such a renewed emphasis underscores the theme of communion, for the laying on of hands is done (at least with presbyteral and episcopal ordinations) by many people: the principal consecrator and his co-consecrators (in the case of a bishop being ordained), or the bishop and fellow presbyters in the case of a priestly ordination (whereas the giving of instruments was almost a "private exchange" between bishop and soon-to-be priest alone).

These changes, together with other even more dramatic and far-reaching conciliar changes in liturgy, ecumenism, and ecclesiology, were all animated and united by a deep sense of the sacramental nature of the church as a communion and as a means for communion between earth and heaven, a theme made clear in the very opening paragraph of *Lumen Gentium*: "the Church is in Christ like a sacrament or as a sign and instrument both of a very closely knit union with God and of the unity of the whole human race" (no. 1). These changes would be reflected in revised liturgical forms for ordination and in the 1992 universal *Catechism of the Catholic Church (CCC)*, which offers a number of reflections on the dogmatic import of ordination, noting that "this sacrament configures the recipient to Christ by a special grace of the Holy Spirit, so that he may serve as Christ's instrument for his Church. By ordination one is enabled to act as a representative of Christ, Head of the Church, in his triple office of priest, prophet, and king" (*CCC* 1581).

Christ's priesthood is not, however, limited exclusively to those in orders. *All* Christians are called to exercise priestly ministry every day by virtue of their baptism—a notion given perhaps its deepest explication in the ecclesiology of Nicholas Afanasiev (Afanasiev 2007), an Orthodox observer at Vatican II whose influence on his own communion, and on the drafting of *Lumen Gentium*, was enormous and well known. (Attention should be paid also to the council's document on the "Apostolate of the Laity," *Apostolicam Actuositatem*.) It would be a mistake—a common mistake, and one with often deleterious consequences for all concerned—to continue what has often been called a "clericalist" mindset, which sees only those in orders as having any kind of "official" role in the church, as being, *alone*, constituted as the "vicars of Christ."

Pope Paul VI, sensitive to the role of the laity, abolished the minor orders in 1972 in *Ministeria Quaedam*, arguing that restricting the tasks of those in minor orders to celibate men en route to the priesthood was unnecessary. Instead, those roles now to be called simply "lector" and "acolyte," both conveyed not by an ordination but an "installation," could and should be exercised by "lay Christians" (no. 3), which, de facto, some have since interpreted as including women, but which the pope, in article 7, explicitly excludes: "in accordance with the ancient tradition of the Church, institution to the ministries of reader and acolyte is reserved to men." Later, during the papacy of John Paul II, girls and women would be explicitly approved to function as lectors and acolytes, and in many other newly created pastoral roles.

The universal catechism, building on conciliar and papal decisions, would go on to insist on the distinction between what is often called the "royal" priesthood of all the baptized, and the "ministerial" or "hierarchical" priesthood of those in orders, who are at the service of, and not the lords over, the faithful living their priesthood:

> Christ, high priest and unique mediator, has made of the Church 'a kingdom, priests for his God and Father.' The whole community of believers is, as such, priestly. The faithful exercise their baptismal priesthood through their participation, each according to his own vocation, in Christ's mission as priest, prophet, and king. Through the sacraments of Baptism and Confirmation the faithful are 'consecrated to be . . . a holy priesthood'. (*CCC* 1546)

Why have orders at all? As suggested earlier, the answer is deeply ecclesiological: "Holy Orders is the sacrament through which the mission entrusted by Christ to his apostles continues to be exercised in the Church until the end of time: thus it is the sacrament of apostolic ministry" (*CCC* 1536). Thus is established a clear link between orders and the constitution of the church as the sacrament of communion between the past (the apostles) and the present (the bishops). But indisputably the most important reason for the existence of orders is so that communion may exist between the church on earth and her heavenly Father. In making this argument the catechism turns rightly to one of the earliest patristic sources: "Through the ordained ministry, especially that of bishops and priests, the presence of Christ as head of the Church is made visible in the midst of the community of believers. In the beautiful expression of St. Ignatius of Antioch, the bishop is *typos tou Patros*: he is like the living image of God the Father" (*CCC* 1549).

ORDERS IN BYZANTINE AND ORIENTAL ORTHODOXY

This stress on sacramental communion, newly recovered in the West, is also the most central theme in understanding orders in the Christian East, every celebration of which (for the "major" orders) must take place during the Eucharist and only during the Eucharist: ordinations remain "inseparably united with the Divine Liturgy" (Foundoulis 2010: 435). For deeper understanding of this, we must of course look to the liturgy primarily not only because it has pride of place as *theologia prima* (Taft 2011) in the East but also because the East has not often resorted to catechisms (though there are clear counter-Reformation examples of them, some rather controverted) and has only rarely—as Bulgakov noted—felt it necessary to "dogmatize" as the West has. Instruments for authoritative teaching are therefore fewer, and there is no universal consensus on what such instruments would be or on the authority to give to those extant statements purporting to offer dogmatic clarity (see a list of such statements in McGuckin 2011). As a result of its political situation, first under Islam and more recently under communism, most of the Orthodox world has not been able to gather in councils and indeed has not felt the need to do so: few doctrinal doubts existed in churches that were concerned almost entirely with fighting for their very survival. Only in our times, as Orthodoxy has been freed from the communist yoke, and as it has developed in the West, has it come to face greater doctrinal questioning about orders, particularly over the question of the ordination of women (about which see below).

To understand, then, how orders may be viewed dogmatically, we find the clearest articulation in various liturgical texts, brief surveys of which may be found in Parry (Parry 2007) and Pettis (Pettis 2011). Unlike in the West, the Byzantine rite of ordination has, as Nicholas Denysenko recently demonstrated, "remained remarkably stable since the eighth century" (Denysenko 2011: 12). Denysenko's careful analysis of this rite unpacks often overlooked aspects of Orthodox ecclesiology, all suggestive of an overriding emphasis on communion. His analysis has demonstrated several themes—the importance of "synodality and collegiality," the role of the "gathered assembly," and the responsibility of the "laity." Moreover, the central prayer for the ordination of a bishop "expounds a theology that includes the apostolic, prophetic, and teaching ministries" (Denysenko 2011: 22).

In general, the dogmatic meaning that emerges from all Eastern liturgical rites of ordination—whether from the Alexandrian, Armenian, Byzantine, or Syrian traditions—is that of *communion* (Dragas 2010), a theme that none has made clearer in recent ecclesiology than the most important Greek theologian alive today, Metropolitan

John Zizioulas (Zizioulas 1971, 1985, 2006, 2010, and 2011): communion understood both among members of the church, and between the church and God. This notion of communion is understood (if sometimes inconsistently) to be less hierarchical or "pyramidal" than in the Latin West, with the latter's overriding stress on communion with (some would say "communion *under*") the pope of Rome (cf. DeVille 2011). Zizioulas has stated the central connection between orders and communion most clearly: all "orders," all gifts, all "charismata distributed by the Holy Spirit in the Church … are defined … not in themselves but as *absolutely relational notions*," which must be understood as nothing less than expressions of, and means for, love (Zizioulas 2010: 184).

Such an Eastern understanding of communion is seen in four distinct aspects of a theology of orders: the first is the fact that the actual prayers for ordination explicitly mention the place (church and city) in and for which a man is being ordained. The second follows closely from this: as Zizioulas has said, "it is impossible to have ordination *in absoluto*. Ordination in the context of communion means necessarily *commitment to a community*. One cannot love *in absoluto* and cannot claim commitment but to concrete human beings" (Zizioulas 2010: 185). One is always therefore ordained for, and thus enters into a lifelong commitment to, a particular church (parish or diocese) in a particular place, and never as a "freelancer" or a vagrant. (Early canons very strictly and repeatedly forbid clergy from moving from town to town without first gaining permission of their home bishop and also the bishop whose territory they wish to visit, even briefly, never mind reside in permanently.) As a result of this, a bishop is often described as living a quasi-sacramental "marriage" to his diocese, and bishops are not, therefore, to be moved from diocese to diocese as this—continuing the marital metaphor—would require a virtual "divorce" from his original diocese. Moreover, there should not be any "titular" bishops who function without a concrete community—a much more rampant problem in the Roman Church (e.g. nuncios, and bishops in the Roman curia), though a problem, albeit on a smaller scale, not unheard of in Orthodoxy.

The third is the emphasis on each order having an integrity in its own right, and not being a mere "stepping-stone" to a "higher" order. As a result, it is not uncommon to find those in minor orders remaining thus for life, and those in the diaconate remaining thus for life also—even if they might be "eligible" for "promotion" to a higher order. (Most Eastern churches still maintain at least two "minor" orders—lector and subdeacon, with some adding acolyte—and all Eastern churches maintain the three "major" orders of deacon, priest, and bishop found in the West. The minor orders are conferred outside the altar usually but not always during the Eucharist and are referred to as *cheirothesia*, while the major orders, *cheirotonia*, may be conferred only during the Divine Liturgy, and the ordained is inside the altar, indeed resting his head on the altar table.)

The fourth aspect is tied closely to the third and consists in the general (though by no means universal) proscription on *athroon* ordinations, a term that is usually understood today to forbid such things as rapidly sequential or "compacted" ordinations in a short period of time—for example, making a man a deacon one day, priest the next, and bishop on the third day. (This practice is known to have occurred in both East and West. Famous examples in the latter would include Pope Constantine Nepi in 767, who went from being a layman to bishop in just over a day. An even more famous earlier example would be Ambrose of Milan, who went from being unbaptized to being ordained bishop in eight days.) Such a compacted ordination seems to be a later development in order to comply with the increasingly widespread notion of a *cursus honorum* probably begun under Pope Gaius (r. 283–293) and borrowed from an extant tendency in early imperial Rome's political offices, whereby a man must first be passed through each minor order en route to his ultimate major order without bypassing any along the way (Gibaut 1996). But early liturgical sources, both East and West, would seem to suggest that such a *cursus* was not the original practice. Rather, men could indeed be ordained directly to a given order without passing through, or being required to spend some time in, the "lower" orders. Thus, in this earliest practice, a layman elected a bishop might be ordained a bishop directly without ever having been made a deacon or priest, still less an acolyte or subdeacon. Such a practice of direct ordination, according to contemporary Greek Orthodox liturgical scholar Philip Zymaris, protects the "roles of lesser clergy ... involving lifelong commitment for the serving of specific ecclesial needs" from being viewed merely as "temporary, transitional roles, mere rungs on a ladder and thus indeed 'lesser' " (Zymaris 2010: 787).

Zymaris goes on to argue that ordinations in which a man is rushed through the "lower" to the "higher" orders run the risk that we may suffer "theologically from a loss of the concept of communion in the Church. This ultimately points to the loss of the theology of the *person* as seen in the relations of communion of the Persons of the Holy Trinity. This loss allowed for the development of a pyramidal (rather than horizontal-communion based) ecclesiology" (Zymaris 2010: 797). Such an ecclesiology is thought to undermine the Church as communion in favor of an "hierarchical interpretation of Church ministry ... in the sense of higher and lower functions" (Zymaris 2010: 785) rather than as one collective-communal effort of all the baptized in their "diverse *leitourgemata*-functions, each having specific duties and prerogatives ... to make the local church the complete expression of the body of Christ" (Zymaris 2010: 783).

ORDERS IN THE ASSYRIAN CHURCH OF THE EAST

We come to the Assyrian Church last not only because it is unique, but also because it is arguable that in her sacramental theology the theme noted above, of the apostolic nature of orders as a means of communion in the church and between the church and God, is most highly developed. As one of her bishops has recently written, "the priesthood of the ... Assyrian Church ... is grounded in ... God the Father through the Only-Begotten Son" (Royel 2011: 80).

The Assyrian Church of the East is, even in the diverse world of Eastern Christianity, unique and, for a time in her history, especially misunderstood. She was once the largest church in the world, with communities spread from Mesopotamia to as far east as China and Korea. She was once derided as "Nestorian," a pejorative term, which was neither accurate in the fifth century nor today. (Recent good overviews of her history may be found in Baumer 2008; Soro 2007).

The Assyrian Church maintains today a unique sacramental practice similar to, but also significantly different from, Oriental and Byzantine Orthodox churches, as well as the Catholic churches in both number and kind (the most succinct discussion of this is Baumer 2008: 121; and for a longer history, including etymological history, see Arangassery 2009). The Assyrian tradition has its own preferred vocabulary distinct from both Latin notions of "sacrament" and Greek notions of "mystery": the Persian-derived term of *Raza*, which refers to "something concealed or hidden" (Royel 2011: 33). Her most well-known, if controverted, theologian, Theodore of Mopsuestia, defined "sacraments" in a way instantly recognizable to other Eastern and Western Christians: "Every sacrament consists in [its] representation of unseen and unspeakable things through signs and emblems" (Baumer 2008: 119).

In her early history, the Assyrian Church, like others, recognized those sacraments explicitly "celebrated" by Jesus Christ: baptism and Eucharist. Later, she would recognize others and, as with many Christians both East and West, be unsure how many those are: some lists will suggest anywhere from two to seven to eleven to as many as thirty (Baumer 2008: 120). Today, the consensus is that neither marriage nor anointing of the sick are sacraments (Baumer 2008: 121) but that "priesthood" is because of its links to the other sacraments: "priestly ordination represent[s] the precondition for the conferring of sacraments upon the faithful" (Baumer 2008: 120). Thus, according to a recent treatment by an Assyrian bishop bearing the *imprimatur* of his catholicos-patriarch, "the sacraments, as defined by Mar Abdisho of Nisibis (d. AD 1318) ... are ... : 1) Priesthood 2) Baptism 3) Oil of the Apostles 4) Eucharist 5) Absolution 6) Holy Leaven (Malka) and 7) Sign of the Cross" (Royel 2011: 44).

Of these, most sources agree that orders is paramount because without it none of the other sacraments can be given: "the main sacraments in the Church of the East ... Baptism and Eucharist ... presupposed the existence of the Sacrament of Ordained Priesthood ... the foundation and source of every sacramental act in the Church" (Soro 2007: 201). Holy orders, then, comes to an important place of recognition in the Assyrian Church, though once again there are significant differences from other Christians. Early synods (until the sixth century) refused all requirements for celibacy, even for patriarchs and bishops, many of whom were married. (Later, reflecting a change earlier in Greek Christianity, the Assyrians began from the mid-sixth century onward to choose bishops from celibate monks alone.) Today, priests can marry and, in contrast to the position in the Orthodox and Catholic churches, Assyrian priests are free to marry even after ordination.

Orders is crucial also because of its links to, and indeed expression of, the apostolic nature of the church, which the Assyrian Church has been at pains to stress historically and currently—if at times rather defensively in the face of charges from other Eastern and Western Christians of being "heterodox" and in the face of her own internal

Table 34.1 The Nine Orders of the Assyrian Church

Earthly Order	Heavenly Order
Highest Rank	
1) Patriarch	Cherubim
2) Metropolitan	Seraphim
3) Bishop	Thrones
Middle Rank	
4) Archdeacon	Dominions
5) Chor-Bishop	Authorities
6) Priest	Powers
Lowest Rank	
7) Deacon	Principalities
8) Subdeacon	Archangels
9) Reader	Angels

upheaval thanks to internal schisms and fights over her head (some details of which are discussed in DeVille 2007), as well as the warfare and politics of her Iraqi homeland.

The structure of the sacrament of orders in the Assyrian Church is arguably the clearest and most highly developed of all the apostolic churches, and likely goes back to the early fourth century and the rule of her Catholicos Mar Shimun bar Sabba'e (d. 340/1), who argued that there are in fact nine "orders" and that each is explicitly linked to the heavenly hierarchy in its proximity to the throne of God (cf. Royel 2011: 90; and especially Arangassery 2009: 94–96). See Table 34.1 for the breakdown of each order.

Each of these orders has its own detailed responsibilities, and each is given sacramentally through a unique "ordination" or ritual of blessing and installation involving the ordaining prelate's right hand only. Even the patriarch-catholicos undergoes an ordination even if already a bishop, the prayer for such reading in part: "Lift up your minds to the heights and seek mercy from God the compassionate for N. the bishop (or, bishop-metropolitan) … is ordained, ordered, and confirmed catholicos-patriarch for the Mother Church of all the East" (Royel 2011: 117).

New Challenges

The practice of ordaining men married to women is common to all Christian traditions, especially in the East. But in the last half of the twentieth century, and in the first two decades of the twenty-first, two new challenges have arisen connected precisely to the sacrament of orders: ordaining women, and ordaining those in same-sex relationships.

Some Christians, under wartime strains, began as early as the 1940s (as happened in the Anglican Communion) to consider the possibility that women could be ordained if no men were available. Matters quickly accelerated in the mid-1970s in both Canada and the United States when Anglicans in both countries went ahead and ordained women to the presbyterate, an enormously controversial move at the time that has since been regularized and is now commonplace. Indeed, women in some places constitute the majority of ordained clergy in numerous Protestant traditions. This move brought considerable pressure to bear on the Catholic Church and on some Orthodox churches to do likewise.

Anglicans felt that their doctrine of ordination, and their operative theological anthropology, not only allowed but in fact required that women be ordained. The response from the Catholic and Orthodox churches was swift: ordination of women was not only impossible, but such action by Anglicans destroyed any prospects of full communion between the Anglican Communion and the Catholic and Orthodox churches. Such ordinations also finally answered the longstanding controversy over whether Anglican ordinations were "valid" in the first place, and whether "apostolic succession" was lost permanently at the Anglican Reformation in the sixteenth century. As Walter Cardinal Kasper said in addressing Anglican bishops in 2008, the Catholic Church now considers that Anglicans have firmly entered the "Protestant" side of the divide, and any claim to their being a legitimate part of the "reformed church catholic" in England is otiose.

Most Catholics and most Orthodox thus consider it impossible that women can be priests, though some very prominent Orthodox theologians (e.g. Kallistos Ware, a widely published metropolitan of the Greek Orthodox Church who spent his career teaching at Oxford) say, unofficially, that it is in fact an open question—a minority view among Orthodox notwithstanding the fact that the patristic literature is clear (see Harrison 1990, 1996, 1998) that the male sex of Christ is irrelevant to his being high priest of the new covenant. Officially it is a closed question for Catholics after Pope John Paul II's decree (1994).

Many Orthodox, however, view the possibility of ordaining women as *deacons* not only as a very real one, but as one having ample historical precedent (Fitzgerald 1998; McDowell 2011)—so much so that some churches today (e.g. Armenian, Coptic, and Greek) have recently been planning publicly to undertake precisely such ordinations at least in some parts of the world. Here too debate remains open as to whether, historically at least, women ordained as "deaconesses" were the sacramental and liturgical equivalent of male deacons; most historians would suggest they were (Vagaggini 1974; Elm 1991; Taft 1998; Karras 2004; Mavrichi 2009).

A yet more recent controversy, again driven in part by Anglican developments though with wider analogues, has been the possibility of ordaining openly practicing, and sometimes "married," homosexuals. This has generated massive controversy and schism in Anglicanism. Once again most other Christians, especially Catholics and Orthodox, have said that these are theologically incoherent and impossible developments to countenance, and have deepened the divide between Christians. Once more, the central issue here—as with the ordination of women—is not about the sacrament of orders as such: it is, rather, a deeper statement about theological anthropology (Reiss 1999; Wilson 2010) and ultimately about how Christians understand the *imago Dei* and God's purpose in creating the human person as sexually differentiated.

SUMMARY

In reviewing Roman Catholic, Byzantine, and Oriental Orthodox, and Assyrian understandings of orders, what emerges clearly is that orders have far deeper dogmatic meaning beyond the pastoral or practical necessity of "ordering" the life of the church. We may, in sum, discover that orders are inextricably tied to the other sacraments and embody in powerful ways several dogmatic claims by and about the church and ultimately about God. What are they? We may discern four, each reflecting one of the hallmarks of the church as articulated in the Niceno-Constantinopolitan symbol of faith.

First, Western and Eastern traditions are clear that orders are the paramount expression of the dogmatic belief in the *apostolic* nature of the church. The church was founded on the apostles, and the connection to the apostles is a necessary constitutive of the church's life and is maintained through the succession of bishops, each of whose episcopal lineages could be traced back to the original twelve in some fashion. This apostolic succession is perpetuated precisely through the sacrament of orders in pre-eminent fashion.

Second, the apostolic foundation of the church is necessary if the church is to be *one*. The most important role above all of him who expresses the fullness of orders, namely the bishop, is to maintain the unity of the church. Christ prayed (John 17:21ff.) precisely for this unity in his apostles to whose unifying role the bishops succeed.

Third, the role of the bishop is not only to maintain unity, but also to do so in a way that prevents uniformity. He, and all who receive orders, is to extend the *catholicity* of the church by ensuring that the gospel is preached to all the ends of the earth so that every creature may know the salvation of God.

Fourth and arguably most important, holy orders exist precisely so that the church may be and become like unto God: that is, to be *holy*. The ultimate purpose of orders, then, is *theosis*: those in orders lead the church so that every Christian can become like God, who became man for our sake.

SUGGESTED READING

Bradshaw (1990); Chupungco (2000); Royel (2011); Schmemann (2000).

BIBLIOGRAPHY

Afanasiev, N. (2007), *The Church of the Holy Spirit*, ed. Michael Plekon (Notre Dame, IN: University of Notre Dame Press).

Arangassery, L. (2009), "East Syrian Perspectives on the Fullness of Priesthood," *Christian Orient* 30: 82–101.

Barkley, J. M. (1956), "The Meaning of Ordination," *Scottish Journal of Theology* 9: 135–160.

Baumer, C. (2008), *The Church of the East: An Illustrated History of Assyrian Christianity* (London: I.B.Tauris).

Bordeianu, R. (2011), *Dumitru Staniloae: An Ecumenical Ecclesiology* (London and New York: T&T Clark).

Bradshaw, P. F. (1990), *Ordination Rites of the Ancient Churches of East and West* (New York: Pueblo).

Bulgakov, S. (2003), "Dogma and Dogmatic Theology," in Michael Plekon (ed.), *Tradition Alive: On the Church and Christian Life in our Time* (Lanham, MD: Sheed and Ward).

Chupungco, A. J. (2000), *Handbook for Liturgical Studies IV: Sacraments and Sacramentals* (Collegeville, MN: Liturgical Press).

Clapsis, E. (1985), "The Sacramentality of Ordination and Apostolic Succession: an Orthodox-Ecumenical View," *Greek Orthodox Theological Review* 3: 412–432.

Congar, Y. (1976), "The Notion of 'Major' or 'Principal' Sacraments," *Concilium* 31: 21–32.

Denysenko, N. E. (2011), "Primacy, Synodality, and Collegiality in Orthodoxy: a Liturgical Model" (unpublished paper).

DeVille, A. A. J. (2007), "Eastern Ecclesial Polity: A Review Essay," *Logos: A Journal of Eastern Christian Studies* 48: 243–265.

DeVille, A. A. J. (2011), *Orthodoxy and the Roman Papacy: Ut Unum Sint and the Prospects of East-West Unity* (Notre Dame, IN: University of Notre Dame Press).

Dragas, G. D. (2010), "The Church as Communion: An Approach to Ecclesiology with Special Reference to the Catholicity of the Church," in G. D. Dragas (ed.), *Legacy of Achievement: Metropolitan Methodios of Boston: Festal Volume on the 25th Anniversary of his Consecration to the Episcopate* (Columbus, MO: Newrome Press), 357–369.

Elm, S. (1991), "Vergini, vedove, diaconesse: Alcuni osservazioni sullo sviluppo dei cosidetti 'ordini femminili' nel quarto secolo in Oriente," *Codex Aquilarensis* 5: 77–90.

Fagerberg, D. W. (2007), *Theologia Prima: What is Liturgical Theology* (Chicago and Mundelein, IL: Hillenbrand).

Fink, P. E. (1982), "The Sacrament of Orders: Some Liturgical Reflections," *Worship* 56: 482–502.

Fitzgerald, K. (1998), *Women Deacons in the Orthodox Church: Called to Holiness and Ministry* (Brookline, MA: Holy Cross Press).

Foundoulis, I. (2010), "Historical Development of Ordinations," in G. D. Dragas (ed.), *Legacy of Achievement: Metropolitan Methodios of Boston: Festal Volume on the 25th Anniversary of his Consecration to the Episcopate* (Columbia, MO: Newrome Press), 432–445.

Gibaut, J. St. H. (1996), "The *Cursus Honorum* and the Western Case Against Photios," *Logos: A Journal of Eastern Christian Studies* 37: 35–73.

Harrison, V. (1990), "Male and Female in Cappadocian Theology," *Journal of Theological Studies* 41: 441–471.

Harrison, V. (1996), "Gender, Generation, and Cappadocian Theology," *Journal of Theological Studies* 47 (1996): 38–68.

Harrison, V. (1998), "The Maleness of Christ," *St. Vladimir's Theological Quarterly* 42: 111–151.

Hinson, E. G. (1981), "Ordination in Christian History," *Review and Expositor* 79: 485–496.

Karras, V. (2004), "Female Deacons in the Byzantine Church," *Church History* 73: 272–316.

Levering, M. (2010), *Christ and the Catholic Priesthood: Ecclesial Hierarchy and the Pattern of the Trinity* (Chicago and Mundelein, IL: Hillenbrand).

McDowell, M. G. (2011), "Deaconesses," in John McGuckin (ed.), *The Encyclopedia of Eastern Orthodox Christianity* (Oxford: Wiley-Blackwell), 178–180.

McGuckin, J. (2011), "Foundational Documents of Orthodox Theology," in *idem* (ed.), *The Encyclopedia of Eastern Orthodox Christianity* (Oxford: Wiley-Blackwell), 647–671.

Mavrichi, I. (2009), "The Ordination of the Deaconess in the Barberini gr. 366 Euchologion," *The Selected Works of Ionut Mavrichi*, <http://works.bepress.com/ionut_mavrichi/1>.

Mitchell, N. (1982), *Mission and Ministry: History and Theology in the Sacrament of Order* (Collegeville, MN: Michael Glazier).

Parry, K. (2007) (ed.), *Blackwell Companion to Eastern Christianity* (Oxford: Wiley-Blackwell).

Pettis, J. B. (2011), "Ordination," in John McGuckin (ed.), *The Encyclopedia of Eastern Orthodox Christianity* (Oxford: Wiley-Blackwell), 425–427.

Pope John Paul II (1994), *Ordinatio Sacerdotalis*: <http://www.vatican.va/holy_father/john_paul_ii/apost_letters/documents/hf_jp-ii_apl_22051994_ordinatio-sacerdotalis_en.html>.

Reiss, W. (1999), "Dogma, Theology, and the Ordination of Women," *Ecumenical Review* 51: 401–404.

Royel, Bishop Mar Awa (2011), *Mysteries of the Kingdom: the Sacraments of the Assyrian Church of the East* (Commission in Interchurch Relations and Education Development).

Santantoni, A. (2000a), "Orders and Ministries in the First Four Centuries," in Anscar J. Chupungco (ed.), *Handbook for Liturgical Studies IV: Sacraments and Sacramentals* (Collegeville, MN: Liturgical Press, A Pueblo Book), 193–203.

Santantoni, A. (2000b), "Ordination and Ministries in the West," in Anscar J. Chupungco (ed.), *Handbook for Liturgical Studies IV: Sacraments and Sacramentals* (Collegeville, MN: Liturgical Press, A Pueblo Book), 217–252.

Schmemann, A. (2000), *For the Life of the World: Sacraments and Orthodoxy* (New York: SVS Press).

Soro, Mar Bawai (2007), *The Church of the East: Apostolic and Orthodox* (San Jose, CA: Adiabene Publications).

Taft, R. (1998), "Women at Church in Byzantium: Where, When—And Why?" *Dumbarton Oaks Papers* 52: 27–87.

Taft, R. (2011), "Mrs Murphy Goes to Moscow: Kavanagh, Schmemann, and 'the Byzantine Synthesis,'" *Worship* 85: 386–407.

Vagaggini, C. (1974), "L'ordinazione delle diaconesse nella tradizione greca e bizantina," *OCP* 40: 145–189.

Wilson, S. H. (2010), "Tradition, Priesthood, and Personhood in the Trinitarian Theology of Elisabeth Behr-Sigel," *Pro Ecclesia* 19: 129–150.

World Council of Churches (1982), "Baptism, Eucharist, and Ministry" (Faith and Order Paper 111, "Lima Text").

Zizioulas, J. (1971), "Ordination et Communion," *Istina* 16: 5–12.

Zizioulas, J. (1985), *Being as Communion* (Crestwood, NY: St. Vladimir Seminary Press).

Zizioulas, J. (2006), *Communion and Otherness*, ed. Paul McPartlan (London: T&T Clark).

Zizioulas, J. (2010), *The One and the Many: Studies on God, Man, the Church, and the World Today*, ed. Gregory Edwards (Alhambra, CA: Sebastian Press).

Zizioulas, J. (2011), *The Eucharistic Communion and the World*, ed. Luke Ben Tallon (London: T&T Clark).

Zymaris, P. (2010), '"Athroon" Ordinations in the Traditions of the Church', in G. D. Dragas (ed.), *Legacy of Achievement: Metropolitan Methodios of Boston: Festal Volume on the 25th Anniversary of his Consecration to the Episcopate*, (Columbia, MO: Newrome Press), 782–798.

CHAPTER 35

·····································

RECONCILIATION

·····································

ANTHONY AKINWALE, O.P.

In an age of individualism, the human person is reduced to a self-sufficient and unrelated entity in the midst of other self-sufficient and unrelated entities. He is the one who stands apart and alone and who can accomplish anything he wills without the assistance of any other person. This manner of conceiving of the human person has implications in matters of religion. Individualism facilitates the conception of religion as a purely private affair. Religion then is between me and my God. By extension, sin is an offence against God, and reconciliation is between me and my God. Unable to understand that religion is not a private but a personal act, individualism finds it difficult to accommodate a ritual of reconciliation that involves confession of sins. If sin is a private affair, why does one need the mediation of a priest (cf. Akinwale 2002, 2008)? A theology of reconciliation needs to respond to this challenge today, and one can begin to weave this together using the teaching of the Second Vatican Council on the church in Christ.

At the beginning of the landmark conciliar document on the church, *Lumen Gentium*, we read that the church, in Christ, is in the nature of a sacrament, "a sign and instrument, that is, of communion with God and of communion among all men" (*Lumen Gentium* 1). In this conciliar affirmation can be found a launchpad for reflection on the theology of sacramental reconciliation. This conciliar self-understanding of the church, which sums up the ecclesiology of the New Testament and of the patristic era, is an invitation and challenge to venture out of an exclusive conception and practice of reconciliation as nothing but a ritual in personal piety, a private affair between the sinner and God. Such a conception would have been adequate if sin were merely an affair between the sinner and God without consequences on others.

This modest chapter, however, intends to show that the goal of sacramental reception and celebration of reconciliation is to bring the sinner back into communion with God and into unity with all men and women, into the reconciliation of all with God, and of all with all, that is, the reconciliation of all with and in Christ as Head.

A theology of reconciliation involves many other theological issues, each of which merits a treatise in itself. In concrete terms, there is need for prior theological reflection on creation, on sin, on Christ, and on the nature of a sacrament. It is when the beauty of creation is appreciated that one can come to grips with the damage inflicted by sin. And, as Thomas Aquinas argues, although Christ could have come even if Adam and Eve had not sinned, there is a sense in which the Incarnation, redemption, and the sacraments are better understood when the damage of sin is kept in view, just as a physically indisposed person is in a good position to appreciate the work of the physician (cf. *ST* III q.1, a.3). Finally, having reflected on these matters, an adequate theological analysis cannot fail to show us that the ordinary way to this reconciliation necessarily passes through the church.

This chapter will be divided into four parts. The first is a reflection on the departure from the original harmony of creation; the second observes that the fourfold alienation of sin requires a fourfold reconciliation; the third focuses on Christ as the primary agent of reconciliation; and the fourth considers the church as its instrumental agent.

FROM HARMONY TO CONFLICT

In words that serve as a fitting commentary on the two creation narratives in the book of Genesis, the council states: "The eternal Father, in accordance with the utterly gratuitous and mysterious design of his wisdom and goodness, created the whole universe, and chose to raise human beings to share in his own divine life" (*Lumen Gentium* 2). In other words, the purpose of creation is communion between God and human beings.

To avoid theologically embarrassing conclusions of biblical positivism, we should make clear that neither of the two narratives of creation (Gen 1:1–2:4a; Gen 2:4b–25) represents an eyewitness report given by the correspondent of a modern media outlet. Instead, both represent a myth born of an etiological inquiry embarked upon by the Hebrew people. According to the historical consciousness of the Hebrew people informed and formed by faith in the one true God who made a covenant with Israel on Mount Sinai, God created a beautiful world. The refrain of the priestly narrator in the first chapter of the book of Genesis sums up this faith-filled conviction: God said, "Let there be... And there was... and God saw that it was good" (cf. Gen 1:10, 13, 19, 22, 25, 31).

By the mere fact that God brought creatures into being he conferred goodness on them. St. Thomas Aquinas expresses the intelligibility of this biblical teaching when he writes that "Goodness and being are really the same, and differ only in idea" (*ST* I, q.5, a.1). In the identification of being and goodness, the goodness of creation is depicted in the bringing forth of order from the primeval chaos at the beginning of the book of Genesis. The Greek word *kosmos* signifies order. As pointed out by John Scullion, "Creation is order; 'before creation' is the opposite of order; it is *tohu wa bohu*, a formless waste or chaos" (Scullion 1992: 15). Creation is order, and order is beauty. The creative utterance of God conferred existence, beauty, and harmony on the work of God. The beauty and harmony of creatures consist in their subjection to human beings and in the subjection of human beings to the Creator. God is the perfect agent to whom creation owes its origin and its purpose. Contrary to the position Origen advanced, to the effect that creation proceeds from divine punishment, and contrary to the position of the Gnostics that creation is the result of an error, it should be maintained that creatures proceed from God's goodness and perfection, and find their own goodness in tending to God's goodness. As a perfect agent, his work can only be good. The goodness in the creature comes from God, is sustained when the creature is ordered to God, and is attained when the creature returns to God. The creature is bereft of internal harmony when, by deliberate choice, it is no longer ordered to God.

The priestly narrative emphasizes that, of all the creatures made by God, the human being alone—in its maleness and in its femaleness—is created in the image and likeness of God. It is endowed with an intellect that is capable of knowing truth, and with a will that is capable of choosing good. Human beings, like all creatures, desire their own goodness. But in addition to what they have in common with other creatures, they tend to their goodness through operations that are rational and deliberate. They find their goodness in tending to God, not apart from being-with-others, and not apart from being-loved-and-loving-others—for the God to whom the individual must tend to find his or her goodness is a God who is found in the experience of loving and being loved.

Although like the priestly narrator the Yahwist does not furnish us with a literal description of how man and woman were created, the theological significance of his rather graphic "description" of the creation of the woman brings to our attention the divine intention of interpersonal harmony between the man and the woman. When the Yahwist paints the portrait of a God who saw that it was not good for *ha adam* to be alone (Gen 2:18), he points out that the being and the operation of human beings find their authenticity and efficacy in cooperation within modes of collectivity: family, society, the state, and community of worship. According to Scullion, God's observation as reported in the Yahwist narrative, points out the fact that the human being is created to live in community and that the origin of all human beings is to be traced to the community of man and woman (Scullion 1992: 37). In this regard, the Judeo-Christian tradition has a precedent and an ally in the Greek philosopher, Aristotle, who, in his *Nicomachean Ethics* postulates that human beings cannot achieve their ultimate goal, which is happiness, if they do not enter into friendship. For Aristotle, happiness is attained through virtue. Virtue, the mean between excess and deficiency, is not in us by nature. Moreover, for him, virtue is not infused. It is acquired in friendship.

According to the Yahwist account, God said, "It is not good for *ha adam* to be alone" (Gen 2:18). In other words, God was speaking of a natural yearning found in every man and woman, an innate quest for communion, a natural desire to be with other human beings. Every animal has a natural habitat in which it was conceived, in which it is nurtured, and in which it conceives and nurtures. The same is true of the human being. Its natural habitat is love in a network of relationships. To be truly human is to have been conceived in love, nurtured in love, and to conceive and nurture in love, within a network of relationships constituted by modes of collectivity. Consequently, there can be no pursuit of real goodness in isolation. The man or woman who seeks his or her own good outside the natural habitat of love embarks on a path of destruction of the self and of others, in self-victimization and in the victimization of other selves. Human relationship is the *locus caritatis*, the privileged place where human subjects encounter each other because God has loved them first. This divine impulse of love, when it is not resisted by sin, communicates to them the desire to love, a desire that brings them together. God's love confers the capacity to love God and to love one's neighbor.

The writer of the first letter of John wrote down inspired words when he said: "God is love. He who abides in love abides in God, and God in him" (1 John 4:16). To be in communion is to abide in love, to abide in love is to abide in God, and to abide in God is to share in the very life of God. The harmony between God and human beings necessarily finds expression in harmony among human beings. The one who really loves God will love the creatures of God. Where this obtains, the goodness of creation is intact; where it does not, there is sin, conflict, and the need for reconciliation.

Sin is in conflict with order, that is, with the harmony that ought to exist between God and the human being, among human beings, and within the human being. I will further comment on this later in the chapter. Suffice it to say at this point that the fact that sin is conflict reflects in the type of disposition that sin is. It is not a disposition in the sense of something that inclines a power to act, as is the case with science and virtue. Rather, it is a disposition in the sense of something that disposes a nature to the extent that the disposition becomes like a second nature, as is the case with sickness or health. Hence, sin is a disposition in conflict with human nature. The sin of origin "is an inordinate disposition, arising from the destruction of the harmony which was essential to original justice, even as bodily sickness is an inordinate disposition of the body, by reason of the destruction of that equilibrium which is essential to health. Hence it is that original sin is called *languor of nature*" (*ST* I–II, q.82, a.1). This inordinate disposition affects every dimension of human existence because, as St. Thomas Aquinas says, it "infects the different parts of the soul, in so far as they are the parts together in one" (*ST* I–II, q.82, a.2, ad3).

Sin does not destroy the good of nature. Sin corrupts it by diminishing its beauty and power. The beauty communicated to human beings by the Creator cannot be taken away but is diminished when they turn away from the beauty of divine light. After all, it is when the radiance of divine light touches the human being that his or her beauty becomes manifest. Despite sin, the human being's natural desire for the truth remains, even as the human intellect is weakened by ignorance and prejudice that produce conflicts. Again, despite sin, the natural desire for goodness remains, even as the will, in its inordinate appetites, mistakes the apparent good for the real good. Its inclination to virtue—a prerequisite for common good—is diminished (*ST* I–II, q.85, a.1). But when love and pursuit of common good is no longer a concern, the love and pursuit of competing and conflicting interests become the order of the day. Then the power to love is replaced by the love of power in the pursuit of selfish interests.

FOURFOLD ALIENATION

Let us keep in mind that the book of Genesis is to be read on its own terms, that is, in terms of its symbolic character. While the aetiological narrative in the first two chapters of the book of Genesis sings the refrain of beauty and harmony—"God saw that it was good"—that of the third chapter of the book of Genesis sees the origin of all conflicts in the Fall. Before the Fall, the undiminished beauty in creation was a fourfold harmony, that is, between the human being and God, between the man and the woman, between the human being and the universe, and within the human being. The Fall was the disruption of this fourfold harmony.

A conversation started it all. Human beings ceased to converse with God and entered into a fatal conversation with the Tempter. A conversation was opened. A promise was made. And the promise was kept. The first couple ate of the fruit of that tree. We do not know what the fruit was. Was it greed, pride, worship of self? Whatever it was, it made them feel good at first; afterward they felt bad. To feel good is not the same as to do good. They acquired the knowledge of good and evil as the Tempter promised them. The acquisition of knowledge by human beings is not merely an intellectual operation; it is also an experience of the truth. At creation they experienced harmony in the knowledge of good. After the Fall, in the knowledge of good and evil, they would experience a conflict—the conflict between good and evil. It is this conflict that is at the origin of all conflicts: conflict within the human person, conflict among human beings, conflict between human person and the cosmos, conflicts of gender, conflict between the races in our world, conflicts of philosophies, of religion, of culture, and conflicts of interests.

The fourfold harmony that was in creation now gives way to a fourfold alienation, and each dimension of the alienation is, at the same time, cause and symptom of other dimensions. First, when human beings are not at peace with God, they become afraid of God. We find an illustration in the myth of the Fall. When the communion between God and human beings was broken by the disruption of cosmic order that human disobedience is, the man and the woman hid from God upon hearing his voice (Gen 3:8–10). But breaking communion with God is not merely a private affair. It has dire consequences for interpersonal relationships. Sin is injurious to the person and to the community because the person it wounds lives within a community. Every sin is an assault on the common good.

Secondly, that the common good is assaulted is seen in alienation within the human family. The will of God, expressed in his creative command, "let there be," communicates goodness to the whole of the created order. The order is altered when human beings act against the will of God. As a result of sin, the first man, who at the first sight of the first woman exclaimed in joyous ecstasy: "This one at last is bone of my bones and flesh of my flesh" (Gen 2:23), will no longer be at peace with the woman. Instead, he will lord it over her (Gen 3:16). Such domination, which has made victims of millions of women and men, cannot be said to have been intended by the Creator. The verse does not prescribe what the relationship between man and woman should be. Rather, it tells us what it ought not to be precisely by pointing to the fact that the communion between man and woman, having been sundered by the sin of the man and the woman, results in male domination and all embarrassing forms of gender conflicts. In other words, the verse is pointing out that male domination is not something promoted by the book of Genesis. Rather, it is a sin that is symptomatic of the wound inflicted on nature by the sin of origin. To have overcome this sin of seeing and using the woman as inferior to man is to have had one's gender bias healed by the grace of Christ in whom there is no male or female (Gal 3:28).

There is a further indication that all is not well in the community of the man and the woman. Before the Fall, both were naked but felt no shame before each other. There was mutual trust between the man and the woman. Neither was afraid that the other would exploit his or her vulnerability. After the Fall they felt the need to clothe themselves. Since the community of the man and the woman is the origin of all human community, conflict within the community of the man and the woman will turn out to be the origin of conflict within the human family itself.

Thirdly, deprived of peace with God and with one another, human beings can no longer live in harmony with the rest of the created order. Again, the words of the book of Genesis provide an illustration: "Accursed be the soil because of you! Painfully will you get your food from it as long as you live. It will yield you brambles and thistles, as you eat the produce of the land" (Gen 3:17–18).

Fourthly, alienated from God, from the community, and from the rest of creation, the human being can not be at peace within himself. This loss of inner peace is, at the same time, cause and symptom of the loss of peace with God, with the community, and with the cosmos. The man and the woman were afraid of God, and no one who fears God can experience interior peace.

Aquinas's reflection on the cause of sin is more explicit in the emphasis he lays on this inner disequilibrium. For him, sin is an inordinate act which, accordingly, "has a cause, in the same way as a negation or privation can have a cause" (*ST* I–II, q.75, a.1). In the inordinateness of sin, that which naturally is and ought to be in human nature is lacking. The will rebels against the direction of the rule of reason and of the divine law and, in this absence of direction and right order, it turns toward a mutable good. It mistakes what feels good for what is valuable. The fact that this self-alienation is, at the same time, cause and result of other alienation is lucidly expressed in the teaching of the Second Vatican Council:

> The dichotomy affecting the modern world is, in fact, a symptom of the deeper dichotomy that is in man himself. He is the meeting point of many conflicting forces. In his condition as a created being he is subject to a thousand shortcomings, but feels untrammeled in his inclinations and destined for a higher form of life. Torn by a welter of anxieties he is compelled to choose between them and repudiate some among them. Worse still, feeble and sinful as he is, he often does the very thing he hates and does not do what he wants. And so he feels himself divided, and the result is a host of discords in social life. (*Gaudium et Spes* 10)

The fourfold alienation so described comes from the knowledge of good and evil, which is knowledge of the pain of schisms, of the painful experience of disharmony. But the Tempter came to suggest that there was nothing evil in acquiring it, nothing evil in experiencing conflicts in the universe. Human beings have always had to do battle with the temptation to conceive of the best way to live as the desire, acquisition, and utilization of what is good in a way that is evil, that is to say, apart from the Creator of all that is good. This not only affects the relationship of the human subject with God, but it also affects interpersonal relationships inasmuch as it manifests itself in disregard for the image of God in other human beings, for God himself.

The Tempter was able to convince the first man that living in the world can be more beautiful without God. Hence, after God created a beautiful world, human beings, persuaded by the Tempter, distorted its beauty and, by so doing, set in motion a chain of evil reactions. One man struck the chord of hostility towards God, and it continues to echo throughout the universe. Hostility to God is hostility to life. And the consequence of hostility to life is death. The many iniquities of the history of our world, our own iniquities, and the iniquities of others; the many forms of alienation and hostility that the human race has witnessed and continues to witness; the times we have been victims and the times we have been perpetrators of evil deeds: all can be traced to an act of disobedience. Ever since human beings succumbed to the Tempter's attractive but deadly proposition to construct a universe without God, ever since the decision to marginalize God, the original cosmic equilibrium has been disturbed.

The existence of a fourfold alienation, which I have described, is an indication that a privatized notion of sin does not deal with the effects of sin in our lives. It is a wrong diagnosis, which can lead only to a bad therapy. One must go beyond this privatized notion in order to move beyond the privatized notion of reconciliation that it begets. The conciliar ecclesiology of communion enables such a move. Christ is the primary agent of reconciliation, and the church in Christ is his instrumental agent.

CHRIST AS PRIMARY AGENT OF RECONCILIATION

"Christus innocens Patri reconciliavit peccatores." These words of the Easter Sequence depict the mystery of reconciliation in and through the crucified and risen Christ. Christ is the sinless reconciler who brings sinners back to communion with the Father. The Second Vatican Council, echoing this, states that when human beings had fallen in Adam, "God did not abandon them, but at all times held out to them the means of salvation, bestowed in consideration of Christ, the Redeemer" (*Lumen Gentium* 2). Taking his cue from Hebrews 5:1, Thomas Aquinas explains this. Christ, says Aquinas, achieved this reconciliation through his office as priest (*ST* III, q.22, a.1). Going to the root of the word *sacerdos*, that is, one who gives sacred things (*sacra dans*), Aquinas explains that a priest is a mediator between God and the people, bestowing divine things on the people. The priest carries out this office by using the law of God to instruct the people, by offering up their prayers, and by making satisfaction for their sins.

Christ, continues Aquinas, fits into this "job description" of the priest because through him God has bestowed gifts on us, and, more specifically, has reconciled the human race to God. He illustrates this by quoting from Colossians 1:19–20: "In him [Christ] it has well pleased the Father that all fulness should dwell, and through him to reconcile all things unto Himself" (*ST* III, q.22, a.1). But Christ was not only priest, the one who offered sacrifice; he was also victim, that is, the one who is offered. In a nutshell, he is the priest who offers himself as the sacrifice that reconciles us with the Father (*ST* III, q.22, a.2). A sacrifice is whatever is offered to God to raise the human spirit to God. It serves three purposes: firstly, it is offered for the remission of sins by which we are turned away from God; secondly, it is for preservation in the state of grace by which we adhere to God; and thirdly, a sacrifice is offered to order the human spirit to perfect union with God, a perfection that will be realized in glory. By offering himself on the cross, Christ in his humanity conferred the effects so enumerated on us by removing our sins, conferring grace on us, and acquiring for us the perfection of glory.

But when the death of Christ is considered from the purely human point of view, it is almost inevitable, perhaps impossible, to avoid drawing the conclusion that it was a tragedy. Just what was in the death of Christ the Sinless that brought reconciliation of sinners to the Father? The answer lies in the love and obedience with which he freely offered himself to suffering (*ST* III, q.49, a.3). The paradox of reconciliation is that the suffering and death of the Sinless in the hands of sinners offers the possibility of reconciliation to the whole universe. But this paradox of the Christian faith is predicated on the fact that the God Christianity proclaims is not a God who is handicapped by evil in the course of the realization of his plan of salvation. In Jesus, this God became human, like us in all things but sin. The paradox is resolved by the obedience of Christ: "Christ's voluntary suffering was such a good act that, because of its being found in human nature, God was appeased for every offence of the human race with regard to those who are made one with the crucified Christ" (*ST* III, q.49, a.5). It was not as if God suspended his love for the human race until Christ's passion assuaged his anger. Rather, out of love for us, a love that he did not withhold at any moment, God sent his Son to reconcile sinners to him. The love between the Father and the Son, which is the Holy Spirit, inspired the Son to offer himself in obedience in a reconciling sacrifice. Christ's passion delivered us from sins because he endured it out of love and obedience. By his obedience to the Father, he subjected himself to the injustice of sin to dissipate the power of the injustice of sin.

Irenaeus' doctrine of recapitulation contains and offers a further explanation of this obedience. According to Irenaeus, Christ summed up in his life all the stages of Adam's life and, by so doing, identified himself with every stage of human existence from birth to death. But unlike Adam, in this recapitulation, he did everything right because he did not sin. He summed up all things but broke the cycle of disobedience initiated by the first disobedience. His obedience unto death put an end to the rebellion against God that manifests itself in social conflicts and cruelty. Like Adam, who contained all his descendants in himself, Christ sums up in himself all the divided peoples of the universe from the time of Adam until now (Irenaeus, *Adversus Haereses* 3.21.10).

It was Christ's obedience unto death that made the difference, for the Holy Spirit inspired him to accept the death of an innocent on the cross, thus making it possible for the cycle of disobedience to be broken. This cycle of disobedience to God's will was the obstacle standing in the way of reconciliation of all with God and of all with all. His love for the Father and for us made him accept an unjust death. He knew it was an unjust death, but his Father willed that he accept this unjust death, and he freely consented. The union of his human will with the divine will during the course of his life, and in particular, at this decisive moment of his passion and death, changed the course of history for good. This obedience in the union of his human will with the divine will was the absolute negation of the Adamic rebellion that triggered the fourfold alienation explained earlier. Adam made a difference by pretending to be God. Christ made a difference by becoming obedient to God to the point of death. While the first man struck the chord of hostility, Christ, by his obedience unto death, neutralized its effect by striking the chord of forgiveness. Hence, whereas sin is knowing good as evil, desiring good as evil, acquiring good as evil, and using good as evil, forgiveness is knowing evil as occasion for good. That forgiveness is knowing evil as occasion for good is what Christ proclaimed on the cross when he prayed: "Father, forgive them, for they know not what they do." Plunged into the darkness of conflicts, Christ obediently and lovingly entered into the darkness of death and so also into the kingdom of his wonderful light. It was an obedience and love that turned an occasion of evil into an occasion for good.

THE CHURCH AS INSTRUMENTAL AGENT OF RECONCILIATION

A sacrament is a sign and instrument of grace. It not only signifies grace, but it also makes grace really present. When the Second Vatican Council described the church as sacrament of communion with God and of unity among peoples, the council was presenting the church in Christ as agent of reconciliation. As remarked by the council, when human beings fell in Adam, not only did God send his Christ to redeem the world, "he determined to call together in a holy Church those who should believe in Christ" (*Lumen Gentium* 2). If, therefore, Christ is the primary agent of reconciliation, the church is its instrumental agent. The sacrament of reconciliation is what the church is and what the church offers. She is the assembly of the reconciled, comprising men and women of every age, place, and race. By virtue of the theory of recapitulation according to which Christ saved us by summing up in himself all men and women of every age, place, and race, the efficacity of the redemptive work accomplished in the paschal event is not restricted by any boundary of race, nation, gender, religion, language, or culture. The work of recapitulation is the work of God in and through his Christ. Being the work of God in person, it is the work of one who is omnipotent, and who, in his omnipotence, is not restricted by any boundary. In God's providence, care of the universal and care of the particular are neither in tension nor in opposition. This comes true in the church, where men and women of every race, culture, place, and social status are called and constituted as the assembly of the reconciled.

In and through the sacrament of reconciliation, the church is the actualization in space and time of the reconciling effects of Christ's death on the cross. In other words, what took place over 2,000 years ago can be felt through the grace of the sacrament of reconciliation in which Christ's forgiving love is not merely present in symbol but is really present. At the same time, while this and all other sacraments remain the ordinary means of salvation, nothing prevents God from providing extraordinary means.

That reconciliation is a fruit of the paschal mystery, and that the church is the privileged place of sharing this fruit, is succinctly stated in the words of the prayer of absolution in the current Catholic Rite of Penance. According to the words of this prayer:

> God, the father of mercies, through the death and resurrection of his Son has reconciled the world to himself, and sent the Holy Spirit among us for the remission of sins. Through the ministry of the Church may God give you pardon and peace. And I absolve you from your sins; In the name of the Father, and of the Son, and of the Holy Spirit.

The link between three themes of capital importance in Christian theology is visibly expressed in the words of this prayer. Reconciliation is presented in its indissoluble relationship with the death and resurrection of Christ, with the gift of the Holy Spirit, and with the ministry of the church. God chose to reconcile the world to himself through the death and resurrection of his Son. Remission of sins was effected through the mission of the Holy Spirit. And the work of reconciliation is brought into the here and now of our existence through the ministry of the church. A careful celebration of the church's Easter liturgy serves as an invaluable pointer to the fact that the death and resurrection of Christ and the mission of the Holy Spirit at Pentecost are not three separate events but form one Easter event that took place in three moments. In this respect, it is not out of place to recall that in the Johannine account of the Easter event, the death, resurrection, and ascension of Christ, and the emission of the Holy Spirit on the disciples all took place on the same "day."

The Gospel of John supports this understanding. First, the repeated reference to the "hour" of Jesus by the author of the fourth Gospel directs his audience to the fact that the hour of Jesus' passion is also the hour of his exaltation. As Jesus became conscious of the imminence of the hour of his death, he recognized the same hour as the hour of his glorification. "Now the hour has come for the Son of man to be glorified" (John 12:23). Yet, the approach of this hour troubled him (John 12:27). Second, when Jesus appeared to Mary of Magdala as she stood weeping by the empty tomb, Jesus told her: "Do not cling to me, because I have not yet ascended to the Father. But go and find my brothers and tell them: I am ascending to my Father and your father ..." (John 20:17). Third, the same Jesus would later appear to the disciples, "in the evening of that same day," according to the Johannine paschal chronology, to offer them peace, and to pour out the Spirit on them in view of their mission to forgive sins (John 20:19–23).

These Johannine indications are grounds to affirm that the summary statement of the theology of reconciliation in the prayer of absolution finds its inspiration in the Johannine chronology of Easter. Reconciliation is the gift from God the Father of mercies to his church through his Son, the risen Christ's outpouring of the Holy Spirit on the disciples, who not only receive this gift, but are to continue to dispense it to the world.

The church as communion of the reconciled is a place where the wounds that sin, hatred, and division have inflicted on humanity are healed. Augustine's allegorical exegesis of the parable of the Good Samaritan is to be recalled here (cf. St. Augustine, *Quaest Evang.* 2, 19). According to Augustine, the man who fell into the hands of robbers signifies Adam, the representative of humanity. He fell from the heavenly city, signified by Jerusalem. He was on his way to Jericho, signifying his descent into mortality. The robbers, into whose hands he fell, are the devil and his angels. The near-death situation in which they left him signifies the wounds inflicted on the human condition by sin. The priest and the Levite who did not stop to assist him but passed by signify the shortcomings of the official representatives of the old covenant. The Good Samaritan signifies Christ. And the inn into which the Samaritan took the wounded man signifies the church.

Christ has brought us into the inn of the church through the sacrament of baptism. Baptism washes away original sin and incorporates the Christian into Christ and his body, the church. Again, as Augustine would say in another version of the allegorical exegesis of the same parable of the Good Samaritan, through baptism, iniquity was blotted out but infirmity was not brought to an end. We are still weak and sinful (cf. St. Augustine, *Serm lxxxi*, 6).

Sin affects our common life by wounding the body of Christ. The church instituted for the reconciliation of the world experiences sin and division among her members. The sacrament of reconciliation heals the church by re-incorporating the penitent into Christ, the one Mediator, through the ministry of the church. The church is thus a reconciled and reconciling church. This re-incorporation into Christ is not a private affair, for in Christ, there is reconciliation not just with God but also with others. If our sins wound others, they wound Christ. In the same way, if we reconcile with others, we reconcile with Christ. There can be no person without community: what affects the person affects the community; what the person does affects the community.

The reconciliation effected through the ministry of the church responds to the imperatives of a fourfold reconciliation. I shall support this argument with three points. *First, reconciliation with the church, represented by the priest, fulfils the social or communal dimension of reconciliation insofar as reconciliation with the church is our re-insertion into a humanity renewed in communion, a reconciled humanity willed by God.* The restoration of our relationship with the ecclesial *koinonia* is our re-entry into the church in which the chord of hatred and hostility is broken, and the walls of division crumble (cf. Eph 3). Love, the natural habitat of human beings, is damaged by sin. However, using the allegorized reading of the parable of the Good Samaritan by Augustine, in the church, the inn in which the wound of human nature is healed, our damaged natural habitat is rehabilitated and transformed into a supernatural habitat where reconciliation in and with community re-establishes a new humanity. How this reconciliation with the church fulfils the demands of the social dimension of reconciliation is a point that is so important to grasp that I should give further clarification.

The church as communion is God's offer of reconciliation of all things in Christ prolonged in history. She is not just God's offer to Christians; she is God's offer to the whole world. If she is to be true to her identity and mission as God's irrevocable offer of *reconciliation-in-Christ prolonged in history*, she must open up to embrace our separated brethren as well as adherents of other religions. She becomes a truly reconciling church when she undertakes ecumenical and inter-religious dialogue. In other words, she lives up to the spirit of Vatican II when she enters into dialogue and collaboration with all men and women of goodwill. In this respect, one who is reconciled with the church in Christ through the sacrament of reconciliation is transformed by the grace of this sacrament into a peacemaker in a world torn apart by innumerable latent and open conflicts.

Second, reconciliation with the church is reconciliation in Christ, since the church, as has been said repeatedly, is the communion in Christ of all those reconciled with God and with one another in Christ. According to the fundamental intuition of Paul, reconciliation with the church and reconciliation with Christ are inseparable insofar as there is a mysterious identification between the eucharistic body of Christ and his ecclesial body, the church. This aspect of Pauline theology is a reflection of the common faith of the early apostolic communities. One is saved by being in Christ and in his Spirit, and one is in Christ by being member of his body in communion with other members of the same body. Reconciliation is the restoration of communion, and the Christian existence, which ecclesial life is, is the absolute negation of all forms of self-sufficiency. Living in Christ is inseparable from relationship with others. The reconciliation in Christ that constitutes salvation is reconciliation of all with God and of all with all—for, as the Christological canticle of the letter to the Colossians teaches: "God wanted all fullness to be found in him and through him to reconcile all things to him, everything in heaven and on earth, by making peace through his death on the cross" (Col 1:19–20). God made peace with the world in his Son's death on the cross, and the peace dividend is brought into the here and now of our existence through the sacraments—in this specific instance, through the sacrament of reconciliation.

Thirdly, since alienation from God and from others was at the root of the fourfold alienation described in the first part of this chapter, it follows that to have dealt with alienation from God is to have dealt with alienation at its roots. Consequently, really to have dealt with alienation from God necessarily demands and manifests the resolution of conflicts with one's fellow human beings. It is to have dealt with the self and with the alienation from the cosmos. One who is at peace with God will live in harmony with the rest of creation and with him- or herself.

SUGGESTED READING

Flannery (1996); Scullion (1992).

BIBLIOGRAPHY

Akinwale, Anthony (2002), "The Human Victim: A Portrait of the Priest," *The Nigerian Journal of Theology* 16: 91–104.
Akinwale, Anthony (2008), "The Decree on Priestly Formation: *Optatam Totius*," in *Vatican II: Renewal within Tradition*, ed. Matthew Lamb and Matthew Levering (Oxford: Oxford University Press), 229–250.

Aquinas, Thomas (1981), *Summa Theologica*, 5 vols. (Westminster, MD: Christian Classics).

Augustine (1980), *Quaestiones evangeliorum*. In Corpus Christianorum, Series Latina, vol. 44B (Turnhout: Brepols).

Augustine (1991), *Sermons 51–94*, trans. Edmund Hill (Brooklyn, NY: New City Press).

Flannery, Austin (1996), *Vatican Council II*, vol. 1: *The Conciliar and Post Conciliar Documents* (Northport, NY: Costello).

Irenaeus (1994), *Against Heresies*, in *The Apostolic Fathers with Justin Martyr and Irenaeus*, ed. A. Cleveland Coxe (Peabody, MA: Hendrickson).

Scullion, John J. (1992), *Genesis: A Commentary for Students, Teachers, and Preachers* (Wilmington, DE: Michael Glazier).

CHAPTER 36

··

ANOINTING OF THE SICK

··

JOHN C. KASZA

ONE of the least understood of the sacraments is the sacrament of the sick. Although the practice of anointing the sick with oil by a presbyter is found in the Letter of James and presumably was used by the early Christian community, in the twenty-first century, it is still viewed as the "sacrament of last resort." Despite over forty years of catechesis concerning sacramental anointing, there is still confusion regarding how the sacrament should be used. However, the church plays an important role in health and healing, as it has for two thousand years. Yet, there are some who dismiss the church's rites and ministry to the sick as merely a placebo when "real" medicine fails to cure. For others, however, one's religious faith is part and parcel of the healing process, sometimes to the exclusion of all other forms of medicine. They eschew modern medical techniques and prefer to rely on prayer alone as the means of healing. When the patient's condition worsens (or when the patient dies), the reason given is: "It was God's will." In the face of these two extremes, the church and its ministers need to cooperate with the medical community in providing a holistic approach to health and healing.

This article concerns the relationship between three areas: anthropology, medicine, and theology. The sacramental healing ministry of the church must appeal to and work with all three areas in order to be viable and effective in the twenty-first century. Anthropology offers a glimpse of how society conceives of the human person. In particular, it can shed light on how sick members of that society are treated. When examining medical practices, one must consider how modern medicine perceives sick persons. Unfortunately, the patient is sometimes viewed as an object of medical research rather than a subjective person who has relationships. Finally, any discussion of healing from a theological perspective cannot fail to include one's relationship with God. In examining the issue of the church's role in healing, especially sacramentally, it is important to recognize how God heals and restores his people.

There are several books that cover the history of healing that is found in Scripture. The reader is encouraged to consult the works of John J. Pilch and John Wilkinson for a more in-depth treatment of this subject (Wilkinson 1998; Pilch 2000, 2004). For the past two thousand years, Christianity has often been ambivalent toward the healing arts and medicine. In the early church, for example, traditional medicinal remedies were dismissed because they often involved entering pagan temples and offering sacrifice to gods. In the early Christian community, the preference was to call for the elders of the community to pray over the sick person whose prayer of faith would save and raise him up (Jas 5:14–15). Over time, this practice came to be seen as sacramental. In addition to the church's official practice, the faithful often visited shrines or persons noted for their curative powers, especially when traditional medicine failed to heal. This practice still continues in the twenty-first century. Roman Catholics continue to visit Lourdes in France or Fatima in Portugal seeking healing and intercession from the Blessed Mother.

As time passed and the church continued to grow, the theological tradition came to view the healing role of the church as merely a preparation for eternal glory rather than as a method of healing for the present. While homeopathic medicinal practices were still the norm, gradually professional healers came to play an important role in the community. Especially during times of plague and pestilence, doctors and those with healing gifts came to the fore. On the other hand, the church, especially through the work of Scholastic theologians, shifted its focus regarding the sacrament of the sick. What had been seen previously as a means of healing, came to be seen as a last anointing prior to death.

This view prevailed and was concretized at the Council of Trent. Although the prayers still referred to the healing aspect of the sacrament, in reality, the sacrament was given only near death and in some cases following death. A real paradigm shift had occurred: instead of helping to heal the person by joining his or her sufferings to Christ, the attitude of the church was that sick persons needed to be forgiven of their sins before entering into eternal life. This led to some ambiguity as people were unsure when to call the priest who would then administer "last rites." In the popular mind, the priest had to be at the deathbed just before the patient expired rather than a few days or even weeks earlier.

To further cement this paradigm shift, the church developed rituals for the various kinds of priestly visitations that could occur: visits to the sick (in which the sacrament was not offered, although Communion might be given), visits to a sick child, visits to a patient on his or her deathbed (in which they would receive sacramental anointing), and visits after death (in which they still might receive anointing if the duration between expiration and the priestly visit was not too long).

As a result of advances in medical science during the nineteenth and twentieth centuries, theologians began to reflect on the role that the church could play in assisting the healing process. The liturgical movement with such luminaries as Bernard Botte, Dom Prosper Gueranger, Odo Casel, and Romano Guardini was an impetus for studying how the church might better utilize the rites and rituals of the liturgy to promote a more active, conscious participation in the church's life. These reflections brought about the study weeks of the early twentieth century in which theologians and medical professionals began to collaborate on how the church might better serve the needs of the sick.

As a result of the tumultuous events of the twentieth century as well as rapid advances in technology, anthropology, and science, Pope John XXIII called for the Second Vatican

Council to examine the role of the church in the modern world. The council invited the church to engage in a paradigm shift which resulted in a great number of liturgical and sacramental changes. This major shift in thinking was most noticeable in the promulgation of the *Pastoral Care of the Sick* in 1972.

In that document, the church restored the sacrament to its earlier focus of being for the sick, rather than a sacrament for the dying. Yet, because of the ambiguity of the earlier tradition and the predominance of the medieval and Scholastic viewpoint, in the popular mind of both priest and parishioner alike, the sacrament of the sick was still seen as a preparation for death, rather than as a healing for continued life. Even today, the sacrament is seen as one received *in extremis* rather than *in infirmoris*. This is especially true among certain ethnic populations and age groups. Despite the catechesis of the past fifty years, there is still much confusion over the meaning and role of the sacrament.

In addition, perhaps owing to the increasing success of medical technology, the church has downplayed its own role in the healing process. While not denying the effects of prayer in promoting health, the church has allowed the medical arts to take precedence. The church, if its presence is felt at all, is usually seen in the last days of a person's life.

There is simply too much extant information to do justice to the topic of healing in the church's tradition in a brief article. Other authors have written histories and theological reflections on the subject of healing in the Christian tradition (Gusmer 1989, 1978; Dudley and Rowell 1993; Florez 1993; Glen 2003; Larson-Miller 2005; Meyendorff 2009). Suffice it to say, the church has had a long-standing practice of ministry to the sick. While the practice was not called "sacramental" until the Second Council of Lyons (1274), the custom of commending the sick to the care and mercy of God through the use of prayer, the laying on of hands and anointing with blessed oil was part and parcel of the religious traditions of Christianity and Judaism. The New Testament scriptural basis for the tradition of ministry to the sick is Jesus' own ministry to the suffering and marginalized. In addition, the apostles continued his healing ministry as they evangelized the known world.

The classic text which is the scriptural basis for the church's sacramental ministry to the sick and dying is the Letter of James:

> Is anyone among you suffering? He should pray. Is anyone in good spirits? He should sing praise. Is anyone among you sick? He should summon the presbyters of the church, and they should pray over him and anoint [him] with oil in the name of the Lord, and the prayer of faith will save the sick person, and the Lord will raise him up. If he has committed any sins, he will be forgiven. (James 5:13–15 NAB)

A brief exegesis of the text reveals several interesting distinctions. First, the sick summon the presbyters who will pray over them and anoint them. The fact that the presbyters were summoned strongly suggests that the sickness was of a more serious nature. The prayer made in faith saves and raises the person up while forgiving any sins that may be present. The Greek term used to refer to the sick in this passage may be translated as either "to be weak [or] to be sick" (Rienecker 1980: 395). These weaknesses could include bodily weakness, sicknesses, incapacity to understand, ethical-religious weakness, and the term may also refer to the economically weak, the poor (Balz and Schneider 1993: 170–171). Gerhard Kittel offers this explanation of the term and its cognates: "In the NT the words are hardly ever used of a purely physical weakness, but frequently in the comprehensive sense of the whole man" (Kittel 1964: 491). However, the word used to refer to the sick person in verse 15 has a much stronger meaning: "Its fundamental sense is that of physical exhaustion or debility, but it was also widely used to mean 'sick beyond hope, withering away', and it may even mean 'dead'" (Dudley and Rowell 1993: 58). Finally, it is worthwhile to note that some ambiguity still exists among commentators on this passage. Most agree that the passage seems to suggest that the person is "sick enough to be confined to bed, but not yet *in extremis*" (*Jerome Biblical Commentary*, section 35).

Ambroise Verheul offers the following observation: "For James and Mark (6:7–13) ... the purpose of the anointing of the sick is not purely medicinal; it is salvific as well. The letter of James speaks of 'saving' and 'raising up'. In Mark, the anointing is connected with the expulsion of demons and the coming of the kingdom of God" (Verheul 1983: 251). In short, one could make a case that the author of James is recommending anointing only for those who are seriously ill and possibly in danger of death (see Dudley and Rowell 1993: 57–58). In the final analysis, the passage accounts for both the possibilities of healing the sick person from their illness and preparing the mortally ill person for entrance into God's kingdom.

Furthermore, there is a strong association between sickness and sin in both the Jewish and Christian traditions. In his ministry Jesus heals both physical sickness and moral deficiency; however, there is some ambiguity as to the connection between the two (John 1993: 56). In many of the healing passages of the Gospels, sickness was associated with sin. When Jesus healed, it was done in the context of forgiving sins. As Bo Reicke notes, "In order to terminate a sickness it was necessary to confess one's sins and to receive forgiveness for them" (Reicke 1964: 60). However, in the Fourth Gospel, "Jesus rejects the view that all sickness springs from sin (see John 9:3)" (Williams 1965: 139). Needless to say, because sickness was often attributed to sin, it posed a particular problem for the early church community (Reicke 1964: 58). The writer of James retained the ambiguous connection between sickness and sin in order to show that the Lord both heals *and* forgives. In short, "the act of healing and the act of forgiving are indistinguishable in James' thinking here; and presumably the 'prayer of faith' would have included a request for both" (John 1993: 57).

The history of the calling of the Second Vatican Council and its far-reaching effects is well known. One of the most significant areas of reflection and change was that of liturgy and the sacraments (Sefański 1987: 88–127; Gutierrez 1982: 269–314). In *Sacrosanctum concilium*, the Council Fathers, simply but definitively, encouraged the reform of the rites associated with the sick and the dying (*Sacrosanctum concilium* 73; hereafter SC). One significant adaptation was to change the name of the sacrament to reflect its primary use with those who are sick rather than those who are in their last moments of life.

Furthermore, the council defined the subject for anointing as "one of the faithful (that is, a baptized Christian), who is *beginning* to be in danger of death, due to sickness or old age" (SC 73). In this brief paragraph, one sees a convergence of the ancient tradition (found in the Letter of James) with the Tridentine reform (restricting the use of the sacrament to those who were dying, or in some cases, already dead). In addition, there is a suggestion for the possibility of further adaptation. The use of the verb "beginning to be" allows for a more liberal use of the sacrament.

The council also called for new rituals to be written (SC 74). The Council Fathers urged for a distinction to be made between the sacrament of the sick and the rites of the dying: "The number of anointings is to be adapted to the occasion, and the prayers accompanying the rite of anointing are to be revised so as to correspond with the varying conditions of the sick who receive the sacrament" (SC 75). In the history of the sacrament, this distinction blurred over time. By the time of the Council of Trent, the rites for the sick and the rites for the dying were almost synonymous. Furthermore, the sick only received the sacrament when they were at the point of death. The Tridentine ritual envisioned three possibilities: a rite for the sick person, a rite for a person who was near death, and a rite for the person who was in the process of dying in which death was imminent but not immediate.

In the discussions that followed the promulgation of the Vatican II documents, the consilium concerned itself with the subject of anointing. As noted several times previous, the council saw the subject as one who was *infirmus*, not *moriens* (Gutierrez 1982: 300). Yet, as Carlos Gutierrez notes, it was necessary to clarify "danger of death" as meaning both proximate and remote (Gutierrez 1982: 301–302).

Since the promulgation of the new *Pastoral Care of the Sick*, there have been five successors of Peter: Paul VI, John Paul I, John Paul II, Benedict XVI, and Francis. However, while the popes have written about sickness in general or about sick persons, their focus has not been specifically on the sick person in relation to the use of the sacrament of the sick. Rather, they have restated the church's commitment to ministry to the sick and dying. In addition, the popes have commended the work of health care professionals and those who are the primary caregivers of the sick. While there is little in the way of papal pronouncements regarding the sacrament of the sick per se, through papal writings one is able to discern an ever-broadening definition of who the sick person is.

While Paul VI promulgated the new *Pastoral Care of the Sick* (PCS) in 1972, in the remaining years of his pontificate, he did not make many significant pronouncements on the role of the sick person in society. However, two events are noteworthy. The Holy Father held a special Jubilee Mass for the Sick during the Holy Year of 1975, during which fifty pilgrims were anointed. In his homily, the pope noted that "[w]e recently authorized a reform of the rite for anointing the sick, so that its complete finality might be made more evident and its administration might be facilitated and extended (within just limits) even to cases where *the illness is not mortal*" (Pope Paul VI 1975: 276; emphasis added). The pope continued by saying that human suffering has value because it is transformed by the mystery of Christ, which enables the whole church to profit (Pope Paul VI 1975: 278). In a particular way, the sick have direct contact with Christ

(Pope Paul VI 1975: 278–279). In a homily delivered on World Leprosy Day, Paul VI noted that throughout the centuries, missionaries have been in solidarity with lepers in whom the missionaries saw the image of the suffering Christ (Pope Paul VI 1978: 171). In addition, the pope specifically mentioned that those who suffer from alcoholism or drug addiction also find themselves marginalized. They also bear the image of the suffering Christ. While Paul VI did not specifically mention who the recipients of the sacrament of the sick could be, he did display a particular compassion for those who were on the margins of society. He was clearly interested in broadening the recipient of the sick to those who were not in a state of mortal danger (see especially his homily on "The Value of Christian Suffering").

John Paul II, who reigned from 1978 to 2005, was by far one of the most prolific popes in terms of his writing and speaking. He had been one of the most consistent in speaking out about the rights of the sick and the elderly. In a general audience given in 1992, the Holy Father spoke directly about the sacrament of the sick. He noted that "the Sacrament of Anointing is thus an effective presence of Christ in every instance of serious illness or physical weakness due to advanced age ..." (Pope John Paul II 1992: 366). Furthermore, "experience also shows that the sacrament gives a spiritual strength which changes the way the sick person feels and gives him relief even in his physical condition" (Pope John Paul II 1992: 366). John Paul II reminded the church that the mentally ill should also be considered in the image and likeness of God: "[W]hoever suffers from mental illness 'always' bears God's image and likeness in himself, as does every human being" (Pope John Paul II 1997: n. 8).

Continuing the tradition begun by his predecessor, in his message written for the twentieth World Day of the Sick, Pope Benedict XVI gave particular attention to the "sacraments of healing" which have "their natural completion in Eucharistic Communion" (Pope Benedict XVI 2012: n. 1). He noted that the sacrament of the sick is "God's medicine ... which now assures us of his goodness, offering us strength and consolation, yet at the same time points beyond the moment of the illness towards the definitive healing, the resurrection" (Pope Benedict XVI 2012: n. 3). Moreover, the sacrament is both a "sign of God's tenderness towards those who are suffering" and "brings spiritual advantage to priests and the whole Christian Community as well" (Pope Benedict XVI 2012: n. 3).

In his first Chrism Mass homily as supreme pontiff, Pope Francis reflected upon the role of the priest as "anointed ones." He reminded priests to be generous with the anointing they received at ordination: "The Lord will say this clearly: his anointing is meant for the poor, prisoners and the sick, for those who are sorrowing and alone" (Pope Francis 2013).

In summary, since the promulgation of the *Pastoral Care of the Sick* in 1972, one sees that the definition of sickness has become broader. Rather than localizing the illness to a specific part of the body, we now have a more holistic approach, recognizing that sickness as well as health affects the mind, body, and spirit of the patient. Therefore, the whole person, taken as a psychosomatic unity, is to be accorded dignity and pastoral care. Our knowledge of the human person tells us that men and women are holistic beings. An illness affects all parts of one's being. Moreover, the sickness of one of its members affects the whole community as well. As St. Paul notes in his famous description of the body: "If [one] part suffers, all the parts suffer with it; if one part is honored, all the parts share its joy" (1 Cor 12:26). Any illness, no matter how inconsequential, has ramifications that affect all our human dimensions and relationships.

On the anthropological level, when a person is affected with disease or an illness, his or her relationships are affected. Sickness, especially of the serious variety, causes depression or anxiety and alienates the person from society, from himself and even from God.

While sickness is seen as alienating, this alienation can be transformed by the paschal mystery. The *Pastoral Care of the Sick* and sacramental anointing may assist in this transformation. Sickness may become a time for self-evaluation and analysis. It is an opportunity to assess one's relationships. This introspection can be an opportunity for realizing change. If the person is restored to health and wholeness, the reflection which has taken place can result in a new way of living. However, if the patient began to decline further and moved closer to death, their meditation could perhaps lead them to a conversion and a deeper relationship with God in order to prepare for eternal glory.

In the theological sphere, a person can never be totally alone as a result of their illness. God is always present. The community of faith commends the sufferings of one of its members to the crucified and risen Lord. On the ecclesial level, the community should reach out to its suffering members in order to draw them out from a condition of alienation. The community needs to ask itself, "What is God saying to us about life, death, sickness, suffering and resurrection through the illness of this particular member? How does God want us to approach illness and death? What are we being taught by this particular illness?" (Kasza 2007: 9).

While everyone has an experience of illness, not all people suffer from a serious illness. The concept of "grave" or "serious" illness has changed over time. In the church's mind, serious means "danger of death." To physicians and psychiatrists, "serious" takes on the connotation of an "incapacitation," which impairs the ability to function normally in society or within oneself. A serious illness or disorder represents a severe dysfunction of the balance in one's psycho-physiological make-up.

In today's society, many people suffer from dysfunction. Certainly, many physical ailments incapacitate a person or place the person in danger of death. However, many disorders also have both psychological and physical components. Addictions and mental disorders are two such examples. While persons with a mental disorder may appear to be physically fit, mentally and emotionally, they are unable to function in society. Moreover, those who suffer from addictions may have a genetic or chemical attraction for the substance (such as food, alcohol, or drugs) which is compounded by the mental attractiveness of or need for that same substance. When the physical and the psychic attractions interact, exacerbated by situations or events, the addictive cycle begins. Finally, a serious illness may be caused by a person's lifestyle or choices. Again, many mitigating factors cause a person to contract a serious illness or disorder.

Despite the fallen condition of humanity, God in his mercy sent Jesus to restore relationship and order in the world. Through his Passion, death, and resurrection Jesus Christ redeemed creation. The result of this redemption was transformation. No longer is death the end, but we may have hope for eternal life. Sickness does not need to end in sorrow. When the patient joins his or her sufferings to the sufferings of Christ, illness can become redemptive and transformative. The human condition, once seen as an example of evil, because of the redemption of Christ is the occasion of humanity being restored back to God. In short, because of the paschal mystery, human beings once again have a relationship with God. "Sickness and sin, because of the Paschal Mystery, are beginnings rather than ends of existence. Both allow us to 'start again' after 'missing the mark' or after failing to live up to our potential as human beings. Ultimately, the goal in both sickness and sin is healing and growth in order to conform us more closely to the person of Christ" (Kasza 2007: 13).

There are several effects of the sacrament. For the first eight centuries, the primary effect was healing. In the following twelve centuries, the effect was preparation for death. At the beginning of the third millennium, all of the effects of the sacrament must be explored. Moreover, these effects must be seen in balance with one another. One effect is not more important than another: all have value and importance, although at times one effect may be more noticeable.

The *Catechism of the Catholic Church* lists five primary effects of sacramental anointing:

- the uniting of the sick person to the passion of Christ, for his own good and that of the whole Church;
- the strengthening, peace, and courage to endure in a Christian manner the sufferings of illness or old age;
- the forgiveness of sins, if the sick person was not able to obtain it through the sacrament of Penance;
- the restoration of health, if it is conducive to the salvation of his soul;
- the preparation for passing over to eternal life. (*Catechism of the Catholic Church*, n. 1532)

In order more fully to appreciate the nuances of the sacrament of the sick, it is necessary to review the *praenotanda* (or introduction) to the ritual itself. Contained in these often-overlooked pages is a wealth of information about the essence of the sacrament.

Concerning the recipient of the sacrament, the *Pastoral Care of the Sick* notes that those "whose health is seriously impaired by sickness or old age" should receive the sacrament (PCS no. 8). The ritual further defines those who are seriously impaired as potentially including those preparing for surgery, the elderly, sick children, and even the mentally ill (PCS nos. 10–11, 53). Moreover, even those who have lost consciousness or the use of reason may also receive sacramental anointing (PCS no. 14). Finally, non-Catholic Christians may also receive the anointing of the sick, provided that they fall under the criteria given in the *Ecumenical Directory* (Kasza 2007: 180). In recent years, some theologians have explored the use of the sacrament of the sick with those who have addictions of various kinds, citing number 53 in the *Pastoral Care of the Sick* as the rationale. In short, most Catholic Christians and even certain non-Catholic Christians are viable candidates for sacramental anointing. The only persons who are precluded from receiving the sacrament of the sick are those who remain "obdurately in open and serious sin" (PCS no. 15).

The minister of anointing is a priest (or bishop). Deacons may not anoint because they lack the capacity to act as an instrument of sacramental absolution. Because the sacrament is linked to the forgiveness of sin, only those having priestly ordination may confer sacramental anointing. However, others (such as deacons, religious, medical personnel, caregivers, and family members) may act as ancillary ministers of healing and may participate in the ritual by reading the scripture, by responding to the priest-celebrant, by joining their prayers to those of the priest, and by their presence and support.

The sacrament is conferred by the laying on of hands and anointing with the oil of the sick on the forehead and hands. However, "it is sufficient that a single anointing be given on the forehead or, because of the particular condition of the sick person, on another suitable part of the body, while the whole sacramental form is said" (PCS no. 23). Such "particular conditions" could include accident victims, those who have intravenous tubes inserted into their hands, and highly contagious persons.

The ritual allows for a variety of situations, ranging from a visit to a sick person to a continuous rite in which the sick person is initiated into the church. While the *Pastoral Care of the Sick* has been primarily used by priests or hospital chaplains, all who minister to the sick should have a copy of the ritual at hand. Chapters 1 to 3 and 5 to 7 are especially useful in giving direction for non-sacramental celebrations pertaining to the sick.

A brief word about viaticum is in order. In the history of the sacrament, the priest was often called at the moment of death to administer anointing. However, the primary "last sacrament" is the Eucharist. As the word *viaticum* suggests, Eucharist in this context is "food for the journey." Literally, the word could be translated as *via te cum*: "go on the way with you." Jesus (under the form of the Eucharist) goes with the patient as he or she passes from this world to the next. The ordinary ministers of viaticum are pastors and chaplains; however, any priest, deacon, or "member of the faithful who has been duly appointed" may give viaticum (PCS no. 29). So, in essence, the "last rites," as the term is used in common parlance, should not be thought of as anointing of the sick, but rather, Holy Communion as viaticum. Moreover, the minister of "last rites" does not have to be a priest or even an ordained minister. As the *Pastoral Care of the Sick* has clarified, and theologians after the Second Vatican Council have elucidated, sacramental anointing is for the living and to offer healing. While the ritual still retains the Tridentine focus of preparing one for death, ideally, the patient should receive Eucharist, not the anointing of the sick, as the last sacrament before death.

In the twenty-first century, a misunderstanding still exists as to the use of the sacrament of the sick. Despite over forty years of catechesis, people still call the priest to administer "last rites." Some parishioners fail to see the blessings that can be received from sacramental anointing while the patient is still lucid and coherent. Moreover, there is a fear of "letting go" of the one who is sick. Delaying anointing, in some people's minds, delays death; their rationale is, "If the priest comes to anoint, Mom will surely die." Unfortunately, some families wait too long, and the patient dies without having received any kind of ministry from the church.

There are several ways in which the church and its ministers may better utilize the sacrament of the sick. One way is for more catechesis about the sacrament. Priests and ministers of the sick should acquaint themselves with all the documents associated with ministry to the sick. Furthermore, those who work with the sick should learn from one another about the nature of illness and how it affects patient, family, physician, and caregiver alike. In addition, pastoral ministers and medical personnel should have a cooperative relationship in which they share ideas about how better to serve the sick. Priests and ministers, in turn, should catechize their parishioners. This may be done through parish bulletin articles and websites, workshops, and through carefully prepared and delivered homilies.

Another area to assist in better celebration is personal prayer. Those who seek to minister to others should first ground themselves in a relationship with Jesus Christ. Their own ministry should flow from their experience of being ministered to by Christ. Moreover, their own faith life needs to be nurtured by frequent meditation on the scriptures and the assiduous use of the sacraments of the Eucharist and penance. Those who exercise a ministry of healing must themselves have recognition of the healing that God has done in their own lives or in the lives of those around them.

A good celebration of the sacrament of the sick, whether done in the hospital room or in the church building, results from careful and prayerful planning. Those who are charged with the arranging of liturgies for the sick (especially priests) should enlist the help of others in the parish to ensure that the celebrations will be prayerful, joy-filled, and well-executed. Too often, the celebration of the sacrament of the sick is haphazard and rushed. This is especially problematic when it is done in the context of a parish liturgy. While unintended, the impression given is that the sick are a "bother" or that "they're taking up Father's valuable time." Rather, the impression that the sick as well as their caregivers should be given is: "those who are sick among us are the most valuable because they teach us about God and how much God wants to be a part of our lives."

Another area of interest is that of the celebration itself. The sick persons as well as their family, friends, and caregivers should be made to feel welcome. Their alienation, resulting from the sickness, should be diminished, not enhanced by the ritual. They should feel that the community desires their presence and truly wants to celebrate their restoration to health. Many individuals from the parish ought to be present to assist the sick and their caregivers. The presider (the priest in sacramental celebrations, the deacon, or another member of the community in non-sacramental celebrations) should be attentive to the generous use of symbols. Moreover, presiders should convey the presence of Christ not only in their actions, but in their attitudes, expressions, and body language as well. Finally, all of those who participate, both the sick and the healthy, should experience the healing touch of Christ through their participation in the ritual action, prayers, and song. Everyone should leave the celebration believing that some kind of healing has taken place, both in themselves and in those who care for the sick, but especially in the sick.

Finally, there needs to be a clearer articulation of the relationship between the sacrament of the sick and the forgiveness of sins (see Kilker 1926; Kryger 1949; Brzana 1953; Renati 1961). In the Jacobean text, the phrase is in the conditional: "and *if* he has committed any sins ..." Does every illness require that a person be forgiven from sin? While we may say that sickness is a consequence of sin *in genere*, we need to be very careful in attributing a particular sickness to a person's personal sinful behavior. For example, the baby born with leukemia or with fetal alcohol syndrome is certainly not sick because of their sin. Moreover, what is the relationship between sickness and sin? This question needs to be addressed not only from a moral perspective, but from a sacramental and liturgical one as well.

It should be noted that the *Book of Blessings* offers several non-sacramental blessings for those who suffer: Orders for the Blessing of Elderly People Confined to their Homes (*Book of Blessings*: 149 ff.; hereafter BB), Orders for the Blessing of the Sick (BB: 163 ff.), the Order for the Blessing of a Person Suffering from Addiction or from Substance Abuse (BB: 177 ff.), and the Order for the Blessing of a Victim of Crime or Oppression (BB: 186 ff.). These rituals may be used by both ordained and non-ordained ministers of healing. Moreover, the *Pastoral Care of the Sick* also allows for the non-ordained to preside at certain rituals that do not involve the laying on of hands or the anointing with oil.

By way of conclusion to this chapter, it might serve best to offer a summary of where we are currently, at the beginning of the twenty-first century: Clearly, the recipient of sacramental anointing is one who is seriously ill owing to age or condition. The definition has broadened over time to include those who suffer from mental illness, which may include addictive behavior as well. Moreover, children who suffer serious illness may also benefit from the sacrament. The minister of sacramental anointing is always a priest (or bishop). Because the sacrament may also forgive sins, the minister may not be a deacon or a non-ordained person.

The sacrament may be administered anywhere at any time, provided that the patient would have wanted to receive sacramental anointing. This also includes situations in which the patient is unable to articulate his or her wishes because of a comatose state. This provision also extends to non-Catholic Christians, provided that they do not have access to a minister of their own faith and that they believe what the church believes about the sacrament.

The effects of sacramental anointing include the strengthening of the person, the joining of the patient's sufferings to those of Christ, the healing of their ailment if it is conducive to the healing of their soul, the forgiveness of sins, and the preparation for the passing from this life to the next. The sacrament may be repeated, especially if the patient's condition worsens. While the priest is the primary minister of sacramental anointing, other persons, including the patient's family, friends, and caregivers, the medical professionals, the ecclesial community, and even the patient himself, participate in the healing process by their prayers and presence. Ultimately, the goal of the sacrament is to draw the person out of alienation and into communion with Christ himself.

At the beginning of this article it was noted that there is still some confusion regarding the use of the sacrament of the sick in the present day. Hopefully, as healing practitioners explore the myriad of options available to them, the ritual of the church (and the church's ministers) will be considered a vital part of their ministry. Rather than medical professionals and pastoral ministers being at odds or in competition with one another, perhaps they may see themselves as collaborators in bringing about healing.

In addition, continued catechesis of both the faithful and the ministers (both ordained and non-ordained) needs to happen. When someone becomes ill, the faithful usually ask for prayers, but not for a sacramental presence. The ritual of the church (either the *Pastoral Care of the Sick* or the *Book of Blessings*) is rich with prayer texts and symbolism that help to convey the church's vision of the ill patient as being in the arms of a loving God. In short, there needs to be more integration of the work of the pastoral minister with that of the medical professional.

Finally, as the church's presence in the world is furthered, it is imperative that its concept of the human person be promoted. The patient is not an object for experimentation; nor is the patient's value diminished simply because they cannot function at one hundred percent capacity. Furthermore, the patient is not to be viewed as a "thing." Instead, the human person, whether completely healthy or living in a vegetative state, is always to be seen as a child of God, redeemed by Jesus Christ through the blood of the cross. In their suffering, they are configured to the suffering of Christ on the cross. In their dying, they die with Christ. And in their burial, they have the hope of resurrection and eternal life.

The more that the sacrament of the sick can be promoted and celebrated, the more will society begin to see the intrinsic value and importance of the sick person in the world. By using the rituals contained in the *Pastoral Care of the Sick* and the *Book of Blessings* more effectively, the ministers of the church will help to draw the patient out of alienation back into community. Moreover, each person will see how all of us are both minister and patient. We learn from our experiences, which hopefully configures us more closely to Christ himself.

SUGGESTED READING

Dudley and Rowell (1993); Gusmer (1990); Meyendorff (2009); Pilch (2000).

BIBLIOGRAPHY

Balz, H., and G. Schneider (1993), *Exegetical Dictionary of the New Testament* (Grand Rapids, MI: Eerdmans).

Book of Blessings (1989) (New York: Catholic Book Publishing Co.).

Brown, R., J. Fitzmyer, and R. Murphy (1990), *The New Jerome Biblical Commentary* (Englewood Cliffs, NJ: Prentice-Hall).

Brzana, S. (1953), *Remains of Sin and Extreme Unction according to Theologians after Trent* (Romae: Officium Libri Catholici).

Catechism of the Catholic Church, 2nd ed. (1997) (Washington, DC: United States Catholic Conference).

Dudley, M., and G. Rowell (1993), *The Oil of Gladness* (London: Society for Promoting Christian Knowledge).

Flórez García, G. (1993), *Penitencia y unción de enfermos* (Madrid: Biblioteca de Autores Cristianos).

Gusmer, C. (1990), *And You Visited Me* (Collegeville, MN: Liturgical Press).

Gusmer, C. (1974), *The Ministry of Healing in the Church of England: An Ecumenical-Liturgical Study*. (Great Wakering, Essex: Mayhew-McCrimmon).

Guttierrez, C. (1982), El Sentido Teologico de la Uncion de los Enfermos en La Teologia Contemporanea (1940–80) (Bogota: Typis Pontificiae Universitatis Xaverianae).

John, J. (1993), "Anointing in the New Testament," in Martin Dudley and Geoffrey Rowell (eds.), *The Oil of Gladness: Anointing in the Christian Tradition* (London: SPCK).

Kasza, J. (2007), *Understanding Sacramental Healing* (Chicago: Hillenbrand Books).

Kilker, A. (1926), *Extreme Unction* (Washington, DC: Catholic University of America).

Kittel, G., and G. Bromiley (1964), *Theological Dictionary of the New Testament* (Grand Rapids, MI: Eerdmans).

Kryger, H. (1949), *The Doctrine of the Effects of Extreme Unction in Its Historical Development* (Washington, DC: Catholic University of America Press).

Larson-Miller, L. (2005), *The Sacrament of Anointing of the Sick* (Collegeville, MN: Liturgical Press).

Meyendorff, P. (2009), *The Anointing of the Sick* (Crestwood, NY: St. Vladimir's Seminary Press).

Pastoral Care of the Sick: Rites of Anointing and Viaticum (1983) (New York: Catholic Book Publishing Co).

Pilch, J. (2000), *Healing in the New Testament* (Minneapolis, MN: Fortress Press).

Pilch, J. (2004), *Visions and Healing in the Acts of the Apostles* (Collegeville, MN: Liturgical Press).

Pope Benedict XVI (2012), "Message of the Holy Father on the occasion of the Twentieth World Day of the Sick" (11 February 2012).

Pope Francis (2013), Homily of Pope Francis, Chrism Mass, Holy Thursday, 28 March 2013.

Pope John Paul II (1987), "Defending Human Dignity," *The Pope Speaks* 32.

Pope John Paul II (1992), "Anointing of the Sick," *The Pope Speaks* 37.

Pope John Paul II (1997), "The Image of God in People with Mental Illnesses," *Origins* 26 (January 16): 495–497.

Pope Paul VI (1975), "The Value of Christian Suffering: Homily of Pope Paul VI at a Jubilee Mass for the Sick," *The Pope Speaks* 20.

Pope Paul VI (1978), "Leprosy in Our Time: Homily of Pope Paul VI during Mass for World Leprosy Day" (January 29), *The Pope Speaks* 23.

Reicke, B. (1964), *The Gospel of Luke* (Richmond, VA: John Knox Press).

Renati, C. (1961), *The Recipient of Extreme Unction* (Washington, DC: Catholic University of America Press).

Rienecker, F., and Rogers, C. (1980), *A Linguistic Key to the Greek New Testament* (Grand Rapids, MI: Zondervan).

Second Vatican Council (1966), *Sacrosanctum concilium*, in Walter M. Abbott (ed.), *The Documents of Vatican II* (New York: The America Press).

Stefański, J. (1987), "Das Krankensakrament in den Arbeiten des II. Vatikanischen Konsils," *Notitiae* 23: 88–127.

Tripp, K. and G. Glen (2002), *Recovering the Riches of Anointing* (Collegeville, MN: Liturgical Press).

Verheul, A. (1983), "The Paschal Character of the Sacrament of the Sick: Exegesis of James 5:14–15 and the New Rite for the Sacrament of the Sick," in M. O'Connell (ed.), *Temple of the Holy Spirit* (New York: Pueblo).

Wilkinson, J. (1998), *The Bible and Healing* (Edinburgh: Handsel Press).

Williams, R. (1965), *The Letters of John and James* (Cambridge: Cambridge University Press).

PART VI

PHILOSOPHICAL
AND THEOLOGICAL
ISSUES IN
SACRAMENTAL
DOCTRINE

CHAPTER 37

....

SACRAMENTS AND
PHILOSOPHY

....

THOMAS JOSEPH WHITE, O.P.

A typical way to consider the sacraments philosophically is to ask in what way diverse philosophical traditions allow us to analyze sacramental practices and articulate sacramental faith. What advantages might Aristotelian ontology have for our understanding of the "substance" or "accidental properties" of the Eucharist? Does a phenomenological description of baptism help us either to bypass or to enrich various traditional accounts of this sacrament that remain controversial among diverse Christian confessions?

Without denying the value of this approach, I take in this chapter a different tack, one that is more idiosyncratic but I hope at least equally constructive. Here I want to consider two classical questions that touch directly upon the "philosophy" of the sacraments. First, in what way are sacramental actions "natural," pertaining to the virtue of religion? Second, what does it mean to say that the sacraments are "causes" of grace? Both these are subjects that remain highly disputed. The first topic invites us to examine the natural intelligibility or philosophical rationality of Christian sacramental activity. In doing so, we can think more deeply about the relationship between nature and grace in the Christian life. The second question allows us to consider how Christian realism regarding the sacraments as instrumental causes of grace fits into a broader realistic vision of causality in creation more generally. Here we can see the ways that the causality of sacramental grace is both like and unlike the natural causality of the cosmos.

These two subjects converge thematically in important ways. As I will argue below, Christian theology should affirm that it is only through the effects of grace caused by the sacraments that human beings can recover an authentic sense of what it means to be genuinely religious. The grace of the sacramental life acts in fallen human history so as to heal the natural religious dimension of the human person. The sacraments, then, are a privileged locus of reflection on the mystery of nature and grace, and show forth in a particular way the harmony of philosophical reason and divine revelation.

NATURE, GRACE, AND
THE VIRTUE OF RELIGION

Sacraments are acts of religion. The church invokes the Father, Son, and Holy Spirit in order to confect the sacraments. They are instruments or channels through which God's grace descends into the world. However, while celebrating the sacraments, the church simultaneously acts in distinctively religious ways. Christians pray in the course of the sacraments of baptism, confirmation, marriage, confession, ordination, the Eucharist, or holy anointing. They make inward acts of devotion, and adore outwardly in physical posture. They offer sacrifice (both interior and eucharistic), make vows or promises to God, or pose acts of repentance for wrongdoing. They pledge care for other human beings for the sake of God, and offer tithes to God on behalf of others, or on behalf of the various activities of the church. These are all acts of religion, both sublime and ordinary.

Is religion, however, natural to rational animals? Religious behavior is, after all, relatively common in human culture. Is it natural to pray, for instance? Is it of the essence of what it means to be a human person to do penance once one has done something wrong? Why, for example, is sacrifice a common feature of virtually all pre-modern societies? Decreasing rates of religious practice can signal a loss of *supernatural faith*. Is decreased attendance at the Christian liturgy also somehow *unnatural* on the part of modern European and American society, or is it more natural?

There are a number of ways to answer such difficult questions. Here I would like to delineate briefly a Thomistic treatment of the subject, which will necessarily be partial and mostly suggestive. I begin by identifying two extremes that should be avoided in responding to the above-mentioned queries. One extreme would privilege the necessity of grace to the detriment of the integrity of nature. The other extreme would underscore the integrity of nature in such a way as to obscure a true recognition of the necessity of grace.

The first extreme stems from a certain reading of the Augustinian tradition. In the *De Civitate Dei contra Paganos* (Books I–X) St. Augustine wishes to underscore the inherently fallen character of human religion in non-Christian civilization. Pagan religion, he argues, is unnatural and idolatrous. He presents Christianity, by contrast, as the one true religion, a form of worship that is made possible only because of grace (II.28; VII.32; X.1). The charity of Christ brings forth in human persons a unique form of inward devotion and sacrifice—that present in the sacramental life of Christians (X.3.6).

In subsequent theological tradition, this idea would give rise (in a thinker such as St. Bonaventure) to the claim that the virtue of religion is inwardly determined *essentially* or *formally* by grace. At heart, religious activity simply is the activity of charity as such, expressed outwardly through the sacramental life (Bonaventure *III Sent.*, d.9, a.2, q.3). Note the ambiguity that results from this point of view. Such a claim seeks to make charity the very essence of religious activity, which is attractive on the surface. This claim, however, requires that we posit a corollary thesis: that religious activity, formally considered, is alien to the nature of human beings as such. One must distinguish nature and grace precisely insofar as the "true religion" of charity *is a grace*, that is to say, a gift of Christ, and not a possession of our human nature. But in this case, the substrate to which the gift is given (our human nature) is formally non-religious. Karl Barth takes this point of view to its logical extreme: our human nature has no inherent potency for religious behavior, and the gift of prayer and devotion made to God is a grace that therefore remains entirely extrinsic. We only ever respond to God in prayer through the actualistic impulses of the grace of Christ (Barth *Church Dogmatics* I.1.198–227). Ironically, from the attempt to "build charity in" to the very essence of religious behavior, Augustinianism in an extreme form leads to an acute grace–nature extrinsicism.

The other extreme is logically contrary to the first. Instead of emphasizing grace in such a way as to ignore a natural religious dimension in human beings, this view would underscore the integrity of our religious nature in such a way as to ignore the necessity of grace *for a right exercise* of that natural capacity. Historically this position originates with the fifth-century theologian Pelagius, and it has an influential modern proponent in the person of Luis de Molina, the sixteenth-century Jesuit. A doctrinally nuanced version of the idea can be found in the early writings of Matthias Scheeben. Here the idea is to underscore the natural essence of religion. Human beings as rational animals are inherently capable of *natural* knowledge of God and of the *natural* love of God above all things. As embodied agents they are prone to a holistic form of religious behavior when they acknowledge the truth about God and the ethical love of God in the form of outward religious actions. It is natural to be religious. Even after the Fall, so these thinkers claim, it is possible for human beings to rise to the level of a natural love of God above all things, in accordance with the natural law inscribed in human nature. The virtue of religion, then, derives not from charity as such, but from natural knowledge and love of God. It is essential to the human person in a fallen world, even despite the consequences of original and personal sin. In this vision of things, religion is certainly not extrinsic to human nature, in contrast to the first view. However, the grace that makes authentic religiosity possible in a fallen world *does* appear as something extrinsic to the needs of human nature as such, at least in the domain of religion. Arguably, another problematic form of grace–nature extrinsicism results.

What each of these positions fails to recognize sufficiently is that religious virtue in the human person derives from a complex origin. On the one hand, the capacity for religious actions derives from something formally inherent to human nature: our rational power to know God the Creator and to love God above all things. It is the case that human beings are naturally religious, or more precisely, they are naturally capable of being religious. They *tend* toward religion by a natural potency that is proper to rational animals. On the other hand, *in its fallen state* human nature is wounded and deprived of grace. This being the case, it is not possible for the human beings acting *by inherent natural powers alone* to orient their lives toward God in an authentically healthy, religious way. Human beings without grace remain intrinsically religious rational animals, but all their attempts at a coherent, theoretically true, and ethically sound form of religiosity remain wounded and partially frustrated.

On this view, Barth is correct: the history of human religion is a murky one, subject to potential irrationality, superstition, and unethical practices. Scheeben is correct, also, however, in asserting that religious behavior is proper to the nature of human beings. Sin wounds deeply but does not destroy man's inherent religiosity. Consequently, philosophical investigation of what is essential to human religiosity as such is possible, but it is best realized when it considers religious activity conducted under the exercise of grace. Philosophy, then, can attempt to consider the *natural anthropological substrate* of human religious practice as it unfolds within the context of the supernatural life of the sacraments. Charity elevates human nature, but it also heals human nature. This thesis preserves the Augustinian vision of Christianity as the true religion, yet it also allows that religion is in some way endemic to human beings, and that even elements of sacramental religion can be anticipated or foreshadowed within the tangled history of human religious behavior.

Toward this end, let us consider a number of Thomistic ideas regarding the virtue of religion, which should help indicate a way forward in view of the theory that is being proposed. First, Aquinas affirms that the human person is naturally capable of knowing God as the Creator of all things, indirectly by means of his effects (*ST* I, q.2, a.3). This knowledge is difficult and rare, but a capacity for it resides structurally within the intellect of the rational animal (*ST* I, q.1, a.1). Therefore, man is inherently capable of taking on a religious intellectual orientation toward the world. It is reasonable to believe that God exists, and that he is good and provident toward his creatures. Likewise, it possible for human beings *naturally* to love God above all things (*ST* I–II, q.109, a.3). Indeed, the human will is naturally inclined toward God as the sovereign good who is the uncreated source of all other goods. Consequently, the human will can find no ultimate natural rest in anything less than God himself. Even when man's religious life remains *morally* impeded by the effects of sin, his will remains structurally or metaphysically made for God (*ST* I, q.105, a.4).

Second, it follows from this that the human person should seek to acknowledge and serve God as a matter of justice. The virtue of religion is a potential part of the virtue of justice, a virtue according to which each one renders to others what is rightly due to them (*ST* II–II, q.81, a.5, ad3). Speaking according to an analogy, then, it is truly just to acknowledge God as the author of one's being and as one's ultimate final end. The justice of religion is embodied in diverse internal and external acts that are natural to the human being, by which he or she recognizes the Creator and renders to him what is his due (*ST* II–II, q.81, a.4). Correspondingly, failure to worship God constitutes an objectively grave injustice, whether human beings commonly recognize this or not. Irreligiosity is profoundly unnatural (*ST* II–II, q.92). The form of justice we are speaking of, however, is not contractual. The absence of human religious practice can in no way diminish the majesty and goodness of God (or his perennial mercy). But it does impede the fulfillment of the human creature. The justice of religious practice Aquinas indicates is not mechanical but deeply personal, as the human being is made for God and so comes into his or her own perfect internal order and fulfillment only by being turned outward theocentrically toward God. With respect to man's natural capacities and end, it is the good who is God who alone can fulfill the human heart in all justice.

Third, the human being in the fallen condition is incapable of keeping the entirety of the natural moral law. In particular, he is incapable of loving God naturally above all things, owing to the inclination toward egotism that resides in man's heart as a consequence of sin. Aquinas posits that the inclination toward God as the final natural end of the human person is not eradicated by this contrary inclination to sin, but it is weakened and wounded. Consequently, the human person is naturally religious essentially, but functionally (morally) incapable of the deepest and most necessary form of religious practice (*ST* I–II, q.109, a.3). In addition, knowledge of God in the fallen condition is extremely fragile, limited, and subject to aggressive forms of misinformation, both religious and areligious alike. Consequently, phenomenologically speaking, the world of religion in the sphere of human history is often filled with questionable beliefs and practices, violence, mind-numbing ignorance, and intellectual obscurantism. These kinds of dangers are also pervasive, however, in the non-religious world of human beings, and the culture of atheism. Arguably they are present there even more so.

Fourth, this religious dimension of the human person is intrinsically open to an elevation to the higher form of divine life that derives from supernatural grace. In other words, human religiosity is inherently capable of being elevated "passively" or "obedientially" so as to enter into a life of *graced* religiosity. No matter how religiously disoriented fallen human beings have become, then, the grace of Christ is not something wholly alien to them, and it can address them in their hidden religious core, wherein they are inherently capable of receiving the life of God. The corollary to this claim is important: grace and infused charity cannot operate in the human person *in depth* without the personal subject under grace becoming himself actively religious in regard to God the Holy Trinity. Grace does not destroy nature, then, but reclaims the religious dimension of the human person for Christ. This occurs principally through the practice of the sacraments. By the power of Christ and fidelity to the sacraments, any human person can progressively transcend the unnatural vice of secularity or the erroneous practices and beliefs of religious error and superstition.

Fifth, natural religious actions are manifold (as is manifest in the complexities of religious liturgy). Such actions have a diversity of natural objects. For example, the inward acts of religion are prayer (an act of the intellect as it is raised up to the consideration of God) and devotion (worship and submission of the will to God). Outward actions flow forth from prayer and devotion as physical expressions and signs of the human community in relation to God, so human beings assume postures of worship (physical adoration). They perform outward gestures as actions of praise and thanksgiving, reparation, and penance. This occurs particularly through the offering of external objects to God as in the case of sacrifices, oblations, and tithes. Human beings also make vows and oaths to God, both in public and in private (*ST* II–II, qq.82–89).

What is important to underscore in this context is that the specific objects being noted are formally natural as such. Consequently, there are non-Christian forms of liturgy, prayer, devotion, sacrifice, vows, tithes, and so on. Aquinas underscores that every moral action is constituted by both an object and an end (*ST* II–II, q.81, a.5; q.82, a.2). Religious actions, then, can be quite similar as to their material content and formal object, and yet be directed to very different and even incompatible ends. For example, one can sacrifice an animal to the Lord God of Israel or to Moloch or Baal. Here, then, Aquinas affirms the essentially natural character of religious acts (with their own formal objects) while maintaining the Augustinian insistence on the distinctly Christian character of "true religion." Grace assimilates the formal objects of human religious life into a deeper set of objects and practices. These are the objects of the theological virtues: faith, hope, and love, and sacramental practices that accompany them. Faith, hope, and love are supernatural, infused virtues that incline the human person to know Jesus Christ as the God-Man and to hope in him and love him. The sacraments are formally of divine institution and are meant to accompany the practice of the theological virtues. Catholic doctrine holds that all seven sacraments were instituted by Christ whether explicitly (as clearly is the case with baptism, holy orders or the Eucharist) or implicitly (for example, marriage is contained implicitly within baptism). Even while the sacraments are of divine institution, the supernatural "objects" and "ends" of these rites can and should assimilate the "objects" of human religious practice, orienting them toward the end proper to the life of grace. Sacramental life creates a vast and complex form of religious culture, then, that extends down through ages across the various local rites and liturgies of the church.

A good example pertains to the sacrament of baptism. Anthropologists rightly note that purification rites through washing exist in a great variety of religious cultures. There is something natural about the practice, since water can readily symbolize moral or spiritual purification. Nevertheless, this material practice is given a new objective specificity in the Old Testament where passing through the Red Sea is seen to signify a new relationship of Israel with the Lord (YHWH) (Exod 14:22, 29). The New Testament affirms that the waters of baptism not only signify but also communicate effectively the grace of Christ (1 Cor 10:1–2; Rom 6:4). Baptism is therefore a rite of divine institution, but it has a remote historical and ontological foundation in natural human religiosity. This is not odd, since any religious rite of washing can take on its deeper formal intelligibility only in light of the verbal significations and symbols used in the act of washing. This intelligibility is established only within a larger context of theoretical interpretation, giving the act its ultimate meaning or deepest inner sense. What is different in this particular case is that the natural form has been assumed or assimilated into a specifically supernatural practice. Pouring water three times over the forehead of a human being while pronouncing "I baptize you in the name of the Father, Son and Holy Spirit" is objectively sacramental, and it communicates supernatural grace *ex opere operato*, which no other form of purification by water can do. And yet baptism is *also* at the same time an act of the virtue of religion. It is simultaneously a supernatural and a deeply human religious act.

Sixth, if we distinguish between objects and ends, as we have just done, then there are two ways that religious practices can go wrong (*ST* II–II, q.92, a.1). One pertains to the end. Religious practices can be directed to what is not truly God, or toward metaphysically problematic conceptions of the divine or the absolute. Idolatry is a real possibility for human beings and is commonplace in human history. (Aquinas thinks idolatry is never a pure evil, for it always includes some partially accurate notion of the divine. Otherwise it would simply fail to be idolatry, which consists precisely in the ascription of divine features to that which is not God: see *ST* II–II, q.94.) Human beings can also fail to live up to this proposed end by being irreligious. They can simply live for a final end that is unworthy of themselves.

Likewise, religious practices can err by way of the mode in which one pursues religious objectives. One can offer to God what one should not, or offer something to him in a way that is not morally fitting. A classic example is found in the attempt to approach the sacred through inherently evil practices (divination or human sacrifice, both of which are quite common in human history). Sacrilege is another example, which occurs through the misuse of objects, persons, or institutions consecrated for sacred worship. The persecution of a true religion can often take the form of sacrilege. This occurs, for example, when the state makes priestly ordination illegal, or tries to oblige by law the misuse of church institutions and persons in view of what is contrary to the natural law. Sacrilege can also stem from the wrong practice of a true religion by its own adherents. This is why Catholic theology traditionally insists on the disciplines of canon law so as to encourage the ethical use of the sacraments of the Eucharist and confession, as well as the right exercise of holy orders.

Seventh, based on what has been said above, there must be some real if limited capacity of philosophy *as such* to evaluate the truth or falsehood of religious practices. Why is this the case? Because religious practices have a firm foundation in human nature. Ancient philosophers such as Xenophon, Socrates, Plato, Aristotle, and Plotinus were critical of various forms of Greco-Roman religious myth and practice based on their respective appeals to philosophical reason. The Fathers of the Church (figures such as Justin, Clement, and Augustine) did not claim that these criticisms were unwarranted. They did not accuse the philosophers of a rationalism that was overstepping its legitimate boundaries. Rather, they embraced many aspects of the philosophical critique of non-Christian religion and argued *both* philosophically and theologically (from Scripture) that there are legitimate grounds for receiving Christian revelation as "the true religion" or "the true philosophy."

Take again the example of baptism. The philosopher as such can in principle observe that there exist profound tendencies in human beings toward moral weakness such that they "do the evil that they know they ought not to do" (Rom 7:19). Aristotle observes something of this state in the *Nicomachean Ethics* VII.2-8, as Aquinas point outs (*ST* I–II, q.77, a.2). What the philosopher cannot demonstrate, however, is the ontological and historical reality of a human fall from grace, or the existence of grace as such. He cannot say, therefore, from a speculative point of view, whether the sacrament of baptism is warranted as an act of religious practice. He can observe that baptism entails no action that is contrary to human dignity, in contrast to, say, the practice of human sacrifice. He cannot (qua philosopher) argue that the supposed graces of sacramental regeneration have a positive effect upon the human person. So while the sacramental life cannot be ruled out by natural human reason, it cannot be demonstratively proven to be real or useful either. This may seem like a modest claim, but it is significant if one also believes (as we should) that human reason *can* rule out as inherently irrational or morally problematic a high percentage of human religious beliefs and customs. Furthermore, it provides a philosophical basis for the natural right of the religious practice of the sacraments within a modern, secular political setting.

As this last comment suggests, however, a chief difficulty pertains to which philosophical criteria we employ for a diagnosis of true religious practice. The Christian philosopher can be accused of circularity. To justify the practice of the Christian religion, he might appeal to metaphysical arguments or arguments of the natural law that were developed within the Christian theological tradition. At the same time, when these arguments are not recognized as being universally legitimate by philosophers who do not share his philosophical premises, he can also claim that this incapacity to perceive the truth may stem from the effects of original sin and personal sin; or that it derives from the cultural influences of religious ignorance, as well as the problematic philosophical traditions that blind human beings to what is best and most profound in the patrimony of human philosophical wisdom.

This is not a circular argument, however. The acceptance of grace and the study of theology in its historically most sound instances helps steady the philosophical regard of the human person, both speculatively and ethically. Likewise, a profound formation in the perennial philosophical tradition of Christianity allows one to perceive more readily the profound harmony between supernatural faith and philosophical reason that exists in the Catholic Christian tradition. The interplay between sacramental theology and the theory and practice of the virtue of religion is a key instance of this harmony between grace and nature, faith and reason. It is also one that is rarely studied or even considered in our own time. This is all the more reason why a renewed reflection on the theology of the sacraments would do well to give greater attention to the virtue of religion.

Sacramental Causality

A second, related theme has to do with the sacraments as *causes* of grace. Here we are insisting not so much on the naturally human dimension of the sacraments as on their divine element. The Council of Trent teaches that a sacrament is "a sign of sacred reality and the visible form of invisible grace ... *[having] the force of sanctifying ...* " (Sess. XIII, ch. 3; trans. N. Tanner). Each of the seven sacraments is said to work *ex opere operato*, by the very performing of the action, independently of the merits of the minister (Sess. VII, can. 8, 12). What does it mean, however, to say that the sacraments confer grace? How might we make this claim most intelligible theologically, by recourse to analogies drawn from the realm of philosophy and natural reason?

Traditionally, there has arisen within Catholic theology a variety of theories regarding sacramental efficacy. No one of them has been adopted by the Catholic Magisterium in the form of a universal dogmatic definition or doctrinal norm. The Council of Trent was composed deliberately in sufficiently indeterminate language so as to permit some diversity of theological interpretation in this regard. Some theories, however, have traditionally been favored over others by the majority of theologians.

The first thing to be said in this respect is that the notion of an "instrumental causality" of grace enters theology historically not in the considerations of the sacrament, but in reflection on the humanity of Jesus Christ. Athanasius spoke of the human body of Christ as an instrument (*organon*) of the Logos (*De Incarn.* 44–45), and this language became commonplace within the traditional theology of the Eastern church. It was from this tradition (principally via John Damascene) that the notion of instrumentality entered into western medieval theology. It was Aquinas, above all, who developed the notion analogically so as to extend it to the sacraments. The human nature of Jesus is the "hypostatically conjoined" instrument of the activity of the Word. The sacraments are the "separated" instruments through which the grace of Christ operates effectively in the lives of Christian people (*ST* III, q.62, a.5).

Grace can be said, however, to derive from the sacred humanity of Jesus in a twofold way (*ST* III, q.48, aa.1, 6). In one way it is derived from him "morally," that is to say, through the moral impetration of the will of Christ. Jesus prays and intercedes on behalf of human beings, and in this way he merits grace on behalf of human beings. Christ crucified prays to the Father in Luke 23:34: "Father, forgive them; for they know not what they do." We might call this Christ's "ascending mediation" in the order of grace. In another way, grace is derived from Christ acting as the Word and Son *in and through* his human nature. He gives grace not only as God but also as one who is human, thinking and willing, feeling with a human heart, expressing himself through human gestures. So Christ crucified says to the thief in Luke 23:43: "Today you will be with me in paradise." He is understood effectively, instrumentally, to give grace to the repentant sinner. We might call this the "descending mediation" of Christ's humanity in the order of grace.

When we consider the sacraments as "instrumental causes" of grace, it is by analogy to this second form of Christological mediation. What does it mean to say that grace "descends" into the human heart through the celebration of the sacraments? More to the point, how can a physical element employed by a priest and accompanied by gestures and words be the medium through which spiritual grace operates?

Traditionally, three prominent theories have been developed in Catholic theology. Each has been influential historically, though little attention is paid to them in more recent sacramental theology. My presentation in what follows is indebted in part to the mid-twentieth-century theologian Bernard Leeming. There are several subdivisions of these various views, but one is obliged in this context to paint with very broad brushstrokes.

The first theory is that which has classically been termed "sacramental occasionalism." This view is traditionally associated with St. Bonaventure, Duns Scotus (though some Scotists dispute that he held this view), and William of Ockham. In this view, God alone is the author of grace in every sacramental action while the visible aspects of the rite are merely external signs of the invisible grace that is given. The pouring of water and pronouncement of the baptismal formula, for instance, are the occasion for the giving of grace, and God has assured the giving of grace whenever this solemn rite is correctly performed. In this case, the physical action of the sacrament is not a true efficient cause of grace, but only the mere *occasion* for that action on the part of God. Bonaventure makes the following comparison:

> the king decrees that whoever has a certain token [*signum*] shall have a hundred marks. After that institution the token has no more absolute qualities than it had before; but it is ordained to something to which it was not before. And because it has the effective ordination, it is said to have power to make people have a hundred marks, and nevertheless it has no more goodness in it now than before. If you ask what power is in that token, [theologians] say nothing absolute, but towards something, i.e. a relation … [T]he sacrament disposes a man to receive grace because it efficaciously orders him to receive and have grace. (*In IV Sent.*, d.1, p.1, a.1, q.4; trans. Leeming)

The "relation" in question seems to be one of signification. Baptism itself does not cause the sacramental regeneration that results from the sacrament, even instrumentally. It is a mere *relational sign* of the grace that is *occasioned* by the outward performance of the rite.

This understanding is difficult to square with the teachings of the Council of Trent. There the following doctrine is affirmed: the sacraments of the New Law differ from those of the Old Law because they "contain the grace which they signify" (Sess. VII, can. 6). That is to say, the sacraments of the Old Law merely symbolize the grace that is given by God for the sake of faith in the covenant, but they do not confer that grace themselves. The sacraments of the New Law, by contrast, instrumentally confer the very graces that they signify. This is what it means to say that grace is conferred *ex opere operato* "by the very working of the sacrament." (Sess. VII, can. 8). "By Baptism we put on Christ and become in him an entirely new creature" (Sess. XIV, ch. 2). "The fruit of [the sacrament of penance] … its force and efficacy … is reconciliation with God" (Sess. XIV, ch. 3). "Grace is conferred in sacred ordination …" (Sess. XXIII, ch. 3). "By the consecration of bread … there takes place the change of the whole substance of the bread into the whole substance of the body of Christ our Lord" (Sess. XIII, ch. 4). "If anyone say that they are slighting the Holy Spirit who assign some special power [*virtutem*] to the holy chrism of Confirmation, let him be anathema" (Sess. VII, can. 2).

When Aquinas considers the occasionalist position he gives the same example as Bonaventure (the token of the king). He then points out two problems. First, this view obscures the notion of a sacrament as a cause of grace. Second, therefore, this view understands the sacraments of the New Law in a way that merely equates them in one important respect with the sacraments of the Old Law. The Old Testament sacraments were signs of grace and indicated the redemption that was to come about fully only through the merits of Christ. The sacraments of Christ, however, derive their power from the Passion of Christ, and consequently are not merely signs of grace but also true causes of grace. An occasionalist theory of the sacraments is unable to recognize this distinction:

> According to this opinion the sacraments of the New Law would be mere signs of grace; whereas we have it on the authority of many saints that the sacraments of the New Law not only signify, but also cause grace. We must say therefore otherwise, that an efficient cause is two-fold, principal and instrumental. The principal cause works by the power of its form … just as fire by its own heat makes something hot. In this way none but God can cause grace since grace is nothing else than a participated likeness of the divine nature (2 Pet. 1:4).… But the instrumental cause works not by the power of its form, but only by the motion whereby it is moved by the principal agent, so that the effect is not likened to the instrument but to the principal agent. For instance the couch is not like the axe, but like the art which is in the craftsman's mind. And it is thus that the sacraments of the New Law cause grace: for they are instituted by God to be employed for the purposes of conferring grace. (*ST* III, q.62, a.1; trans. English Dominican Province)

Notice that this theory has a relation to our earlier remarks about the instrumentality of the sacred humanity of Christ. Aquinas thinks that the human nature of Jesus is integral to the personal actions by which he, as the Son of God, confers grace to others. To the leper who asks to be clean, Jesus speaks with his voice, "I will it, be cleaned" (Mt 8:3). Consequently, his human desires, thoughts, actions, words, and physical gestures are associated instrumentally with the giving of grace. If this is the case for his human nature, then it is fitting also for the sacraments of the New Law instituted by Christ. They are true causes of grace, albeit in an instrumental fashion.

However, the contrary is potentially true as well. If one adopts an occasionalist theory of sacramental causality, it is typically in order to safeguard a sense of the divine transcendence. God alone is the author of grace. However, by this same purist principle, one ought also to dissociate the humanity of Christ from the divine activity of the eternal Logos. If God is the principal author of grace, then the humanity of Jesus is not a true *organon* of divine life, as the Eastern church has typically held. Rather, the humanity of Christ is a mere sign or symbol of the presence of God acting in the world. In this case, we can see how an occasionalist sacramental logic can be employed to push theology toward an anti-incarnational stance. Because all of the mysteries of the faith are interrelated, the view we take of sacramental causality can impact deeply the view we take of the reality of the Incarnation. And the inverse is the case as well, as we see in the coherent reflection of Aquinas, itself influenced greatly by John Damascene, Cyril, and Athanasius.

The second theory can be treated more succinctly. This is the view of the sacraments that is traditionally denoted as the theory of "moral causality." It is a view developed by the Dominican Melchior Cano, and held in turn by influential Jesuit theologians such as Gabriel Vásquez and Johann Baptist Franzelin. On this view, the sacraments are said to "contain" and cause grace. They do so, however, by the inherent power of a moral pledge.

The sacraments are signs and tokens of the Passion of Christ, and therefore signify the power of his Passion to redeem humanity and cause grace. They are like promises or commands, instituted by Christ, of the grace that is given by God. By the very fact that they bear within themselves this moral pledge of grace, the sacraments can also bring it about or realize it as the effective gift of God for those who practice the sacraments. Franzelin distinguishes this "moral causality" from occasional causality in the following way: "A moral cause properly speaking differs from a mere condition without which the effect does not occur, in that a moral cause is accompanied by some power, dignity, and excellence which—although it does not physically influence and work toward the very being of the effect produced—does nevertheless present a reason to the physical cause. By contrast, in that which is a mere condition *sine qua non*, there is no such dignity or power" (Franzelin 1868: 109; my trans.). "Physicality" here denotes not a material reality, but the concrete, real ontological cause of grace. Franzelin is saying that there is an inherent moral power in the sacraments that is mysterious, and that this power is akin to a persuasive act, itself turned toward someone else (God himself) who is the unique ontological source of the grace of the sacraments.

Notice that in this view the sacraments can be instruments of grace in one respect. They are moral causes in much the same way that human *requests* or *petitions* are causes. We may ask a friend to do something for the sake of friendship, and he may do it. But if he does do so, the concrete action of efficient causality is his, not ours. The moral power of intercession is more in keeping with the order of final causality (sending a message to someone) rather than efficient causality (being the source of an action). Consequently, this form of sacramental causality claims that the sacraments participate in some mysterious way in the *merits* of Christ, or the power of his *intercession* on behalf of the world.

The difficulty with this view is that it conflates the instrumental efficacy of the sacraments as such with the sacrifice of Christ. The efficacy of the sacraments does indeed *derive originally* from the merits of Christ crucified (the charity, obedience, and intercession of Christ in his Passion). The sacrifice of the Passion is therefore the moral cause of the grace of all the sacraments. The sacraments, however, apply this grace to the lives of human persons. The question then is: how does the power of the cross act instrumentally in and through the visible rites of the sacraments, which themselves signify that power? The theory of moral causality seems to evade rather than answer this important question.

Analogously, we can note that this theory also runs into problems if we seek to apply it within the domain of Christology. The human actions of Jesus (his moral choices stemming from charity and obedience) are true causes of grace, owing to their moral value. This is what I have termed above the "ascending mediation" of Christ. However, if we reduce all instrumental causality to this species of causality, then it is no longer possible to maintain a plenary realism regarding the theandric actions of Jesus. When Christ says at the tomb of Lazarus, "Come out!" (John 11:43) the command is not a mere moral impetration made to God, who in turn effectively answers the prayer of Christ. Rather, the command is given by God the Word in his own human voice, with his own human mind and heart. The Son of God acts principally here by virtue of his divine power, but he also acts instrumentally in and through his free human decisions as a man. The humanity of Jesus is the effective *organon* of his person.

This leads us to the last of the theories, which is denoted in early modern scholastic parlance under the title of "physical causality." This theory originates with Roland of Cremona and Thomas Aquinas and was rearticulated (accurately in my opinion) by thinkers such as Thomas de Vio Cajetan and Domingo Bañez. Here again, the term "physical" does not mean "material" but "ontological and instrumental." The sacraments are true effective causes of grace by the power of God working in and through them.

The core thesis of this theory was noted in the citation of Aquinas given above. God uses the sacraments of the New Law as instruments of grace. "[However,] the instrumental cause works not by the power of its form, but only by the motion whereby it is moved by the principal agent, so that the effect is not likened to the instrument but to the principal agent" (*ST* III, q.62, a.1). A key term in this context is "motion." Material realities such as water and oil are created entities that have in themselves no *natural* potency for the communication of grace. They do have, however, what Aquinas calls an "obediential potency" as creatures (*In IV Sent.*, d.8, q.2, a.3, ad4). They are subject to God as the Creator, such that God can employ them at his discretion so as to make them signs and instruments of the presence and activity of his grace. There is no logical contradiction in the idea of God using physical things in order to transmit spiritual grace, just as there is no logical contradiction in the idea of God becoming a human being.

We should note that this last view of sacramental causality bears a greater similarity to the theology of the hypostatic union, but only by way of analogical likeness. The human nature of Christ is an instrumental cause of grace *internal* to the source of grace, since that humanity subsists hypostatically in the person of the Word. The human voice or the human touch of Christ is the voice and touch of the person of the Son of God made man. The sacraments, meanwhile, are separated instruments that are not united with God and that provide only a virtual presence or a temporary presence of God, acting through the celebration of the sacraments.

Aquinas underscores that the power at work in the sacraments is something "transitory and incomplete as to its natural being" (*ST* III, q.62, aa.3–4). In other words, the sacraments differ in an important way from the mystery of the Incarnation. They transmit grace because of the transient activity of God at work in them and possess no inherent power to do so *of themselves*. The sacraments do effectively transmit grace *ex opere operato* if they are celebrated validly (in accord with their divinely instituted form and/or matter). Accordingly they provide a stable presence of the gift of grace in the church down through time, independently of the moral merits of the ministers of the sacraments. This view does not entail the view that the sacraments should have an automatic effect upon the lives of those who *receive* them. The fruitfulness of the sacramental life depends in great part upon the internal dispositions of the subject, and this is in turn itself related to the internal work of God in the human soul preparing it for the sacraments. The promised effects of sacramental grace can be better welcomed, diminished, or even blocked altogether depending upon the subjective dispositions of the recipient.

There is an important exception to these general rules, as Aquinas notes, with regard to the Eucharist. Here there is a change of the whole substance of bread into the body of Christ and a change of the whole substance of wine into the blood of Christ. Consequently, there is a substantial presence of the body, blood, soul, and divinity of Christ that remains in the church so long as the sacramental species endure. In this case, the priest who consecrated the elements is an instrumental cause of the real presence of Christ, but the consecrated host and the precious blood are not themselves *mere instruments* of the presence of Christ. They are the sacramental species *in which* Christ *is* truly present. The host on the altar simply is Christ, ontologically present in a sacramental mode. "The sacrament of the Eucharist is the greatest of all the sacraments ... because it contains Christ Himself ... whereas the other sacraments contain a certain instrumental power which is a share of Christ's power. Now that which is essentially such is always of more account than that which is such by participation" (*ST* III, q.65, a.3). I am not making this last point in order to roil any ecumenical sensibilities. It is important to note, simply, that there is a hierarchical order among the seven sacraments. They are each true causes of distinct kinds of graces, but they are also each ordered teleologically toward the Eucharist as the source and summit of the life of the church. This sacrament alone provides a substantial presence of Christ who is in perpetual communion with the church. Accordingly, it nourishes the growth of charity in the faithful in a particular way. Communion in the body and blood of Christ engenders already in this life an inchoate participation in the eternal life of God the Holy Trinity.

CONCLUSION

In the first section of this chapter we underscored the fact that the sacraments are acts of religion in which the full human subject is meant to be engaged. In the second section, we observed that God makes use of created things employed by human beings in order to communicate the grace of Christ. The two ideas are deeply interconnected. In the sacred liturgy, God is the cause of grace *in and through* the sacraments, even as the sacraments are themselves *acts of religion* of the human community. What should we infer from this connection? Just as the sacraments are the loci of the "descent" of grace, they are also the place of religious "ascent" of human beings toward God under grace. Owing to the divine institution of the sacraments, human religious life can be redeemed under the grace-filled effects of the sacraments, and the sacraments engender a life-giving form of religious worship. (There is a firm basis here for Augustine's notion of Christianity as the true religion.) Simultaneously, human beings can participate in the active impartation of God's grace by administering the sacraments faithfully and reverently. The whole of this process culminates, however, in the celebration of the Eucharist, the real presence of the body and blood of Christ. Here there is a kind of plenitude of the presence of the grace of God descending into the life of the church in sacramental form. Here the church is offered a form of religious activity that is no longer instrumental, a means to an end. Rather, she encounters under the veil of faith the presence of that which is final and most ultimate. The study of philosophy cannot give us any power to obtain knowledge of the sacramental mysteries. Philosophy can be employed, however, in the service of theological faith so as to permit us to understand more profoundly how Christ is truly present and active in the church's sacramental life, and how we as human persons might best respond to the presence of his grace, as beings religiously alive in Christ.

SUGGESTED READING

Aquinas (1947); Augustine (1972); Leeming (1960).

BIBLIOGRAPHY

Aquinas, Thomas (1947), *Summa Theologica*, English Dominican Province Translation (New York: Benziger).

Augustine (1972), *Concerning the City of God against the Pagans*, trans. Henry Bettensen (London: Penguin).

Barth, Karl (1936–1975), *Church Dogmatics*, trans. G. W. Bromiley and T. F. Torrance, *Church Dogmatics*, 4 vols. in 13 parts (Edinburgh: T&T Clark).

Bonaventure (1882–1902), *Doctoris Seraphici S. Bonaventurae. Opera Omnia. Collegii Sancti Bonaventurae*, 10 vols. (*Ad Aquas, Quaracchi*: Collegium Sancti Bonaventurae).

Ciappi, Aloisius M. (1957), *De Sacramentis in Communi: Commentarius in Tertiam Partem S. Thomae (qq. LX–LXV)*, Pontificum Institutum Internationale Angelicum (Turin: R. Berruti & co.).

Decrees of the Ecumenical Councils (1990), trans. N. Tanner (ed.) (London and Washington, DC: Sheed and Ward and Georgetown University Press).

Franzelin, Johannes Baptist (1868), *Tractatus de sacramentis in genere* (Romae: S.C. de Propag. Fide; Taurini: Marietti).

Leeming, Bernard (1960), *Principles of Sacramental Theology*, 2nd ed. (London and Westminster, MD: Longmans and The Newman Press).

Lynch, Reginald, "The Sacraments as Causes of Sanctification," *Nova et Vetera*, English ed., 12: 2014, 791–836.

Scheeben, Matthias (2009), *Nature and Grace*, trans. Cyril Vollert (Eugene, OR: Wipf & Stock).

Serry, Jacques-Hyacinthe (1700), *Historia Congregationum De Auxiliis Diviniae Gratiae: Libri Quinque* (Louvain).

CHAPTER 38

....

THE SACRAMENTS AND THE DEVELOPMENT OF DOCTRINE

....

BENOÎT-DOMINIQUE DE LA SOUJEOLE, O.P.,
TRANSLATED BY DOMINIC M. LANGEVIN, O.P.

THE seven sacraments enter into the development of doctrine in two principal ways. On the one hand, concerning the sacraments in the strict sense of the term, the essence of a sacrament was gradually recognized by the distinction and the close relationship between what is a sign and what is a cause in sacramental liturgical acts (first section, "The Definition of the Sacraments"). Furthermore, the content of sacramental grace has been better perceived both from the theocentric angle and from the anthropocentric one (second section, "The Complexity of the Effects of the Sacraments"). On the other hand, reflection upon the sacramentality of salvation has permitted us to make the connection between the mystery of Christ (the fundamental sacrament), the mystery of the church (the sacrament founded upon Christ), and the mystery celebrated liturgically (final section, "The Sacramentality of Salvation"). The following contribution will explore and explain these three areas.

THE DEFINITION OF THE SACRAMENTS

....

At the heart of the Christian understanding of the sacraments, there is—in continuity with their Old Testament origins—the conviction that the relationship of salvation between God and men is expressed through sacred rites. The sacraments are the distinct expression of an even larger relationship—the covenant—by which God constitutes his people, this people being the principal manifestation of his plan of salvation (Vatican II, *Lumen gentium*, ch. 2, "De populo Dei").

The patristic era expressed this through the words *mystērion* and *sacramentum*. The chief intuition of the first thousand years consisted in what can be called Christian *realism*: there is a *mystery* or *sacrament* when the ontological reality of the grace of salvation is said and is given by and in the words and actions that express and realize the divine intention to save man (Schillebeeckx 2004: 47–92). There is, in consequence, an inseparability between the *sign* that makes known this will for salvation and the *signified reality* that is the actual gift of grace. Whether in Greek culture (Origen, *Commentaria in Epistolam B. Pauli ad Romanos* 4.2; PG 14, 968) or in Latin culture (Augustine, his expression "sacramentum, id est sacrum signum" ["a sacrament is a sacred sign"] in *De Civitate Dei* 10.5; PL 41, 282), the notion of sign is primary. The sign "contains" in a certain way the signified reality, the *virtus sacramenti*, the power of the sacrament (Augustine, *Enarratio in Psalmum* 77, 2; PL 36, 983–984). For the Fathers, the link between the sign and the signified reality is, in a certain way, patent. The reality that occurs when the sign is performed occurs, in a certain way, by the sign.

In our day, the attention of our contemporaries, especially in Western culture, often seems to limit itself to the efficacy of the sacraments, which is seen too often still in acts of liturgical nonchalance that weaken the sacramental sign (the sign is incomplete, but the rite remains "valid"). In contrast, the Middle Ages successfully made the effort to demonstrate the unity between what pertains to the signification and what pertains to the efficacy of a sacrament. We need to retrieve that today.

The Scholastic era desired to surpass the Fathers in the understanding of the connection between the functions of understanding (sign) and real efficiency (what it would call the *res sacramenti*: the grace). This was not an easy question. In itself, a sign can generate only signification, that is to say, only a piece of knowledge. How thus to explain the typically Christian connection that holds that the reality of grace occurs *through* and *in* the sign?

The early Scholastic period thought it sufficient to add the mention of efficacy to the Augustinian definition: "In sacramento autem non sola significatio est, sed etiam efficacia" ("In a sacrament there is not only signification, but also efficacy") (Hugh of St. Victor, *Dialogus de sacramentis legis naturalis et scriptae*; PL 176, 35). Thus it is that the notion of cause became current in sacramental theology, permitting us to distinguish more clearly the Christian sacraments from the Jewish sacraments, and to distinguish in a strict sense, within the Christian symbolic economy, seven sacramental signs: "Strictissime, sacramenta Novae Legis, quae efficiunt quod figurant; quae sunt signa et causae gratiae invisibilis" ("Most strictly, the sacraments of the New Law are those that effect what they symbolize, those that are the signs and causes of invisible grace") (Alexander of Hales 1957: 4, d. 1, 1).

St. Thomas Aquinas, reaping this heritage, would propose, at the zenith of his teaching career in the *Summa theologiae*, an understanding of the connection between the sign and cause that entails a decisive advance. Beginning from the Augustinian definition in *De Civitate Dei* (*sacrum signum* [*ST* III, q.60, a.1, sed c.]), St. Thomas added the specificity of a Christian sacrament ("signum rei sacrae inquantum est sanctificans homines" ["the sign of a sacred thing insofar as it is sanctifying men"]; *ST* III, q.60, a.2): what is signified is a sacred reality in the act of sanctification, that is to say, the sign of a cause at work. Having thus united in a coherent order the notions of sign and cause, it remained for Thomas to demonstrate that the signification and efficacy are conjoined not only on the outside, but are also intrinsically united. Thomas achieved this by proposing the presence of instrumental causality. Let us take the example of a pianist who uses a piano to perform a sonata of Chopin. What is proper to the intermediate cause (the piano) between the principal agent (the pianist) and the produced final effect (the sonata of Chopin) is that, in being moved toward its own act (a piano emits sounds), this act is assumed by the principal author in order to effect an act of which he is the true author (the pianist brings about a sonata of Chopin). We must distinguish thus between that which the instrument brings about *ut res* (the sounds) and that which it brings about *ut instrumentum* (the sonata). By analogy, God, the only possible principal cause of grace, wished to give his grace by instituting the sacraments. These latter, intermediate causes, in bringing about their proper acts as determined by divine institution (in other words, precisely in signifying), state that, in them and by them, God gives grace here and now. That which the sacraments realize *ut res* is the signification, and that which they realize *ut instrumentum* is the gift of grace (Aquinas, *De Veritate* q.27, a.4, ad2). God has thus arranged that his grace comes to us by being signified to us. A sacrament, in the image of the humanity of Christ and dependent upon him, is a mediation of the gift of grace. This mediation is an action (the washing of water, an anointing, the imposition of hands, etc.) whose meaning is provided by the words. This divine work of salvation is fulfilled at the moment when the sign operation is performed, and, indeed, the divine work is fulfilled by this sign.

This doctrine of a sacrament as a *sign of a present divine efficiency* is now a general principle of the church. It has been set forth not only in response to Protestant objections (the Council of Trent, *DS* §1605 and 1606), but also for itself (*Catechism of the Catholic Church*, hereafter *CCC*, §1127). Even if St. Thomas's elaboration of the relationship between sign and cause through recourse to instrumentality has not been officially "canonized," one should nonetheless note that magisterial statements seem to refer to it implicitly. For example, the affirmation concerning a sacrament that "the power of Christ and his Spirit acts in and through it" (*CCC* §1128) is explained extremely well by instrumentality. One can even go further by speaking of an *efficacious sign*. While the efficacy of a sign normally is its signification only at the level of knowledge, this limitation binding a sign to the order of knowledge alone can be transcended when the situation involves the *word* of Christ, whose human word is the sign and instrument of the Divine Word. In fact, the Word of God truly present *in* and *through* the human word effects what it signifies. A sacrament thus appears as the highest manifestation of the Word of God. The sign thus signifies that which it itself effects.

THE COMPLEXITY OF THE
EFFECTS OF THE SACRAMENTS

What is liturgically manifested by and in the sacraments is a reality that is always complex. Let us look at some examples. The grace of baptism, according to common doctrine, is at the same time the gift of filial adoption and the remission of sins and their related penalties (*CCC* §1262–66). The Eucharist is celebrated for the glory of God and the salvation of men (*CCC* §1407). The effect of the sacrament of holy orders (to the episcopal and presbyteral degrees) is to render a man apt to act *in persona Christi* and *in nomine Ecclesiae* (*CCC* §1548–52). In the sacrament of reconciliation, the minister gives God's forgiveness, which is both just and merciful (*CCC* §1455).

The understanding of a complex reality requires principally two things: a correct understanding of each of the elements and a correct understanding of the relation (*ordo*) that manifests their profound unity. History shows rather clearly that, in different time periods, the accent has been placed with greater emphasis on one aspect or the other. For example, in the context of the Catholic Counter-Reformation initiated by the Council of Trent, baptismal grace was presented first of all as a purification from sin. The eucharistic liturgy emphasized sacrifice for the glory of God. The priest was above all *vice Christi gerens* (acting in the role of Christ). Confession accentuated the aspect of justice (satisfaction). These were only matters of accent, but they were strong ones, for they involved affirming clearly what Protestants were denying. In our day, filial adoption, the paschal banquet where Christ is our food, the priest expressing the response of the Bride to the Bridegroom, reconciliation through mercy—these are more easily proposed. Here as well, it is only a question of accent, but such emphases are indeed found.

These diverse sacramental elements should be solidly tied together, for they are all essential. The perception of the connection between these aspects is decisive not only for a correct understanding of the sacraments, but also in order to live more and more in the grace bestowed by them.

The *Ordo* of Sacramental Elements

The essential relationship ought to be delineated for each sacrament. For baptism, one finds that Vatican II mentions first—and sometimes alone—filial adoption (*Lumen gentium* §10, 21, etc.), while the *Catechism* places the remission of sins first (*CCC* §1263–64) and then the grace of adoptive sonship (*CCC* §1265). Studying with St. Thomas Aquinas, we can say that "the effect of baptism is twofold: one being essential (per se) and the other accidental. Indeed, per se, the effect of baptism is that for which baptism was instituted, namely, for generating men in the spiritual life ... The accidental effect of baptism" is the wiping away of sins (*ST* III, q.69, a.8). Aquinas seems to affirm that the baptismal order places first the gift of divine life and second the remission of sins. Now, the same St. Thomas seems to situate the wiping away of sins before the gift of divine life when he presents the effects of baptism (*ST* III, q.69, a.1). Basing himself on Romans 6:3 ("Do you not know that all of us who have been baptized into Christ Jesus were baptized into his death?" [RSV]) and on Romans 6:11 ("So you also must consider yourselves dead to sin and alive to God in Christ Jesus"), St. Thomas says, "through baptism, man dies to the old life of sin and begins to live for the newness of grace."

In order to understand the order of the two aspects of baptismal grace, one can use-fully consider the issue from two vantage points (*ST* I–II, q.113, a.8). From the point of view of God—he who bestows grace—baptismal grace is the communicated divine life that drives away sin, as the sun drives away the night. But from the point of view of this action's effect in man, what we have here is a movement from death toward life, that is to say, a movement by which the subject separates himself from one extremity (*a quo*: spiritual death) in order to move to the opposite extremity (*ad quem*: spiritual life). From this point of view, the abandonment of the state of sin possesses a prior-ity over the acquisition of life, even though both take place at the same time (one sole movement), as the forest passes from night into day with the rising of the sun.

This clarification permits us to understand that, when the *Catechism of the Catholic Church* starts with the remission of sins in its presentation of baptismal grace, it is adopt-ing the point of view of the baptized person. This perspective is existentially important insofar as it underlines first of all the radical purifying action of God, the permanence of the inclination to sin (the Augustinian *concupiscence*), and finally the necessary coop-eration of man in his own salvation.

For the Eucharist, there arises the question as to how to order the glory of God and the salvation of the world. With the other six sacraments, their finality is to sanc-tify man (their immediate end) in order to render man capable of glorifying God by the entirety of his life (their mediate and ultimate end). In contrast, in the case of the Eucharist, because it is first of all the sacrifice of Christ to the Father, its immediate end is the perfect worship rendered to God, and its mediate and ultimate end is the sanctifi-cation of man so that man, in his turn, may glorify God in his works. Concerning this, one need only see that in the Eucharist the sacramental reality exists first of all in the consecrated species and independently in the persons who participate in the celebra-tion. The sacrament is first of all the sacrament of the sacrifice of Christ to his Father. The invisible reality visibly signified is Christ in his Passion. Therein we find the central point for understanding the Eucharist: that which is sacramentally signified (Christ in his Passion) allows us to perceive the sacrifice of Christ as offered to the Father, and, received in Communion, allows us to embrace the finality of life "in Christ," that is, to be an offering to the praise of God.

This clarification indicates that it is disastrous to separate the sacrifice and the sacra-ment, for the heart of the sacrament is the sacrifice of Christ. Therefore, that which is manifested as central in this sacrament is not first of all God's gift of grace to men, as in the six other sacraments, but the presence and offering of Christ to his Father. As such, we may herein place the eucharistic Communion that inserts the faithful into the eccle-sial body of Christ that precedes them. This Communion is the communion of the faith-ful with God and with each other "in Christ."

The sacrament of holy orders configures the man who receives it both to Christ and to the church. It is necessary to demonstrate correctly the relationship between these two configurations. This relationship can be seen in the eucharistic celebration. Whereas the priest is configured to Christ as head so that he (i.e. the priest) can realize the consecra-tion of the bread and wine, so the priest can also act in the name of the entire church as a body, the church that offers Christ to the Father, the church that offers herself in Christ. The unity between Christ and the church expressed in the singularity of the priest is what serves as the basis for his capacity to represent Christ and the church (*CCC* §1553).

This perspective allows us, first of all, to leave aside the idea that the minister is the delegate of the community. The church does not "face" Christ like an autonomous partner capable of entering into a relationship with Christ. Instead, she is continuously issued from the open side of Christ on the cross (John 19:34). Furthermore, this perspective allows for a correct understanding of the liturgy, which is the one voice of the Bridegroom and the Bride. When the minister acts in the name of the church, such can only be a response to Christ, an unconditional "fiat," using the same words of Christ taken from sacred Scripture or the *lex orandi*. Finally, this perspective permits us to situate more correctly the participation of the faithful, the members of the body of Christ, who are not in an autonomous or private "activity," but in a *cooperative act* signifying the union of the Bridegroom to his Bride, expressing their bond with and dynamic adherence to what the minister is accomplishing (Vatican II, *Sacrosanctum Concilium* §30).

With the sacrament of reconciliation, we come to the difficult question concerning the moral unity within the distinction between the virtues of justice and charity (mercy). With a guilty person—which is what a sinner is—justice seeks his punishment, while mercy seeks his pardon. How is it possible to appreciate that, in this sacrament, the minister is simultaneously judge and doctor (*Code of Canon Law*, c. 978 §1)? The celebration of the sacrament consists essentially in the actions of the penitent (contrition, confession of sins, satisfaction) and of the minister (determination of the penance, absolution). The liturgical rite of reconciliation demonstrates an order that gives first place to justice: the penitent is to truly recognize his sins and sincerely regret them. Now, the decisive criterion for the penitent's sincerity is in the offer to repair all that can be repaired (e.g. to return the stolen object). This is on the level of justice, which must be honored (*CCC* §1459). However, the sinner cannot completely satisfy this justice, especially with respect to God, for, whereas the gravity of the offense varies relative to the offended person, an infinite satisfaction would be required. The sinner cannot perform such infinite satisfaction; only Christ satisfied perfectly. This is why mercy completes the process of reconciliation by granting forgiveness, while the penitent's act of reparation is always only partial (*CCC* §1460).

Nonetheless, this *ordo* that places justice first and mercy last is not the full story. Indeed, the sinner, by the very fact of his sin, becomes blind to his own state. This is why "the movement of a 'contrite heart'" is the fruit of the attraction and the motion of grace (*CCC* §1428, quoting Ps 51:17). After his previous denials, the conversion of St. Peter was begun through the mercy of Christ (*CCC* §1429). We find here the Lord's prevenient mercy that gives direction and an end to the repentance that should assume justice, with the final mercy completing the process. The exact *ordo* is thus the following: prevenient mercy, justice, final mercy.

In a general fashion, St. Thomas teaches, "in any work of God, so far as its first source is concerned, mercy is evident" (*ST* I, q.21, a.4). Always willing the good in what he causes to exist, God always wills to remove evil from everything, particularly man. It is this constant will of God that leads the sinner, as an expression of his dignity, to satisfy justice insofar as he is able. It is this constant divine will that completes the process, thanks to God's final act of mercy. The perfect illustration of all this is the mystery of redemption. The very gift of the Savior is an act of mercy from God, for man could not rectify sin. Christ, through the satisfaction accomplished on the cross, accomplished a work of justice. The most abundant mercy completes this process by giving life to us (*ST* III, q.46, a.1, ad3).

Reflections on the Different Types of *Ordo*

The development of sacramental doctrine is the development of the understanding of the content of sacramental grace through knowledge of the complexity of its elements and of the relations between these various aspects, while respecting that this grace is always a unified reality. While it may be legitimate from a pastoral point of view to emphasize—depending upon the circumstances—one aspect rather than another, it is also necessary to demonstrate the full richness of sacramental grace.

There are two principal conceptions of a sacrament: as a remedy and as life. These two conceptions contribute to knowledge of sacramental grace. We can clearly see that the "remedy" aspect is primary according to the point of view of the subject receiving a sacrament. This involves the remedy for an imperfection (baptism, penance). But the true remedy is in the infusion of divine life. From the point of view of God, who gives grace, this infusion is first of all the offer of a real participation in his life, this being the true response to human deficiency. The distinction between these two points of view is necessary in order to manifest the cooperation that grace permits man to honor: God, through the communication of his life, permits man to participate in his own salvation, by conferring a real value to human acts done under the movement of grace. It is in this way that grace restores human dignity.

Nonetheless, the distinct place of the Eucharist ought to be noted, for its place furthermore permits us to locate the exact place of the minister instituted to celebrate this sacrament. Whereas the Eucharist is above all the sacrifice of Christ to the Father, the ministerial priesthood is first of all a particular configuration to Christ in order to perform this sacrifice. Whereas the ultimate perfection of the Eucharist is to be the sacrifice of "the total Christ," head and body, the ministerial priesthood is also a configuration to the mystery of the church in order to express liturgically this "total" sacrifice. Here, it seems indeed that the "life" aspect comes first (the life offered by Christ and by the church as the communion of saints), while the "remedy" aspect comes second and depends upon the spiritual condition of each participant.

Finally, it is good to remember—as the doctrinal history shows—that, if sacramentality in the strict sense occurs in the seven sacraments, it does so in an analogical fashion. There is a great difference here between the Eucharist and the other six sacraments. These latter have their finality in the Eucharist. These six sacraments sanctify people so that they may glorify God by the gift of their lives, a gift that attains its perfection in being united to the sacrifice of Christ.

These precisions permit us fittingly to articulate the *theocentric* aspect and the *anthropocentric* aspect in the sacrament. The Eucharist's *ordo* places the *theocentric* dimension first. The Eucharist is celebrated above all in order to glorify God, for it is really the sacrifice of Christ. As for the spiritual sacrifice of the Christian who participates in the celebration and in which resides the Christian's salvation, this sacrifice follows after Christ's sacrifice as its fruit. The *anthropological* dimension is a consequence. This explains the *ordo* of the two aspects of the ministerial priesthood, which has its principal *raison d'être* in the Eucharist: to act firstly *in persona Christi capitis* and to express secondly the response *in nomine ecclesiae*.

For the other six sacraments, the *ordo* is inversed. They are celebrated in order to communicate to man the grace of salvation according to the modality that is proper to each sacrament. In this, the anthropological dimension comes first. The sacrament begins by transforming man so that he becomes capable of glorifying God through his entire life. Herein, the theocentric dimension comes second.

From the perspective of efficiency, it is always God who, in Christ, communicates a participation in his life. From the perspective of finality, it is always God who, through Christ, ought to be glorified. All the same, man's necessary participation in his own salvation is not diminished, but rather is clearly indicated. Continually dependent on the saving plan of God, man ought to make this his own through a God-centered moral life, the cause of which is sacramental grace. *Theocentrism* and *anthropocentrism* do not exclude each other, but rather mutually call for each other.

THE SACRAMENTALITY OF SALVATION

One can say that the properly Christian perfection offered by Christ resides in the fullness of revelation and in the seven sacramental actions that truly offer what revelation makes known. It contains acts (God speaks, God gives grace) that are similarly constituted by two co-essential aspects. There is a divine aspect, namely, what is said (a supernatural truth) or what is done (a participation in the divine life). And there is a human aspect, namely, the word of the preacher or the instituted sign-instrument. This divine–human "alliance" is the mode chosen by God to save the world. It was already present, announced, and prepared in the Old Testament, and it finds its fulfillment in Christ.

The Fathers of the Church displayed profound wisdom when they elaborated their teaching on *mystērion* in order to explain this economy of salvation (Schillebeeckx 2004: 47–92). The Fathers of Vatican II rediscovered this fundamental understanding, leading them to entitle the first chapter of *Lumen gentium* "De Ecclesiae mysterio." As the council's doctrinal commission stated: "The word 'mystery' not only indicates something unknowable or hidden, but, as now today is recognized by many, designates a divine, transcendent, salvific *reality* that is *revealed* [i.e. known] and *manifested* [i.e. really present] in some visible way. Whence this word, which is above all biblical, appears particularly apt for designating the Church" (*Acta synodalia sacrosancti concilii oecumenici Vaticani II* 1970–2000: vol. 3/1, p. 170; with emphasis and bracketed clarifications added). This sense is found in the chapter in an important place that describes the relation between the church and the Kingdom of God on earth: "The Church, or, in other words, the kingdom of Christ now present in mystery (*iam praesens in mysterio*), grows visibly in the world through the power of God" (*Lumen gentium* §3; translation from Abbott 1966: 16).

This *economy of the mystery* (Eph 3:9) has Christ as its central realization. In him, the divine plan of salvation is fully realized. In a preeminent way, he is the mystery or *sacrament*. He is God the Word revealed and manifested through his humanity. This latter is the sign (that which makes known) and the instrument (that which gives what is known) of the divinity. We have here a central insight of the Greek Fathers of the Church (Tschipke 2003: 35–85) that the Latin tradition, thanks to St. Thomas, assumed and has handed down to our day (Vatican II, *Sacrosanctum Concilium* §5; *CCC* §515). We are speaking about a mystery-sacrament that designates first of all a sacramental *being*, that is, the union without confusion or separation of a divine reality (the eternal Son) and a human reality (the son of Mary), so that the divine reality may be revealed and manifested through the human reality. It is in his identity as a mystery-sacrament that Christ acts: his preaching (his human word being the sign and instrument of the divine Word) and his actions (his words and physical movements being the signs and instruments of the gift of grace), especially his miracles, are the proper acts of the Savior who saves the persons that he encounters. The sacramentality of Christ arranges that his humanity is the conjoined sign and instrument of the divinity.

The church as well has been presented as a mystery and a sacrament in the Tradition (La Soujeole 2006: 306–330). Vatican II is the culmination of an invaluable rediscovery on this point, a rediscovery rooted in the patristic revival (*Lumen gentium* §1, 9, and 48). As the body or Bride of Christ, the church is in some way coordinated to him, in the sense that the church's union to Christ forms the human ecclesial community as the Savior's sign and instrument for the communication of salvation to all mankind (*Lumen gentium* §8.1). In consequence, it is the entire church, as a sacrament, that, "in her whole being and in all her members ... is sent to announce, bear witness, make present, and spread the mystery of the communion of the Holy Trinity" (*CCC* §738). What we have here is a sacrament that sets forth, in a certain way, first a being and then an action. On account of the mystical union (i.e. *in mysterio*) of the community of believers to Christ and his Spirit, this ecclesial human community is constituted so as to act sacramentally through the preaching of the gospel and the celebration of saving actions (*CCC* §775–76). Founded upon Christ—the fundamental sacramental—the *ratio* of a *sign* and that of an *instrument* are found analogically realized in a primary, very close participation: the ecclesial mystery. The church can be called the adjunct sign or instrument (or sacrament) of Christ.

This communion in being and therefore in action between Christ and the church entails that this "sacramental couple" Christ-church (Eph 5:25–27; "the nuptial union of Christ and the Church" [*CCC* §772]; *CCC* §796) is present and active for the salvation of the world. In consequence, the "concrete" expression of this union between the Savior and his Bride—the expression of this union acting to reveal and to give divine life to men—takes place through an apostolic ministry that is itself also sacramental (*CCC* §876–879), rendering Christ present in his headship and expressing itself in the name of the church (*CCC* §1548 and 1553). Through ordination, the minister receives a genuine consecration that expresses the selection of Christ through his church (*CCC* §1538). He is constituted a *minister*, which is to say that Christ has confided to him the Word and the grace that come from God. For this, he ought to signify personally the gifts of God that he will provide instrumentally (Vatican II, *Presbyterorum ordinis* §12). Nonetheless, one cannot speak of the minister as a sacramental being who acts sacramentally in the same fashion as one speaks about Christ and the church. Indeed, while Christ and the church sanctify because they are personally holy (*CCC* §823–824), the same is not true for ministers, who transmit a Word and grace independently of their personal sanctity. We have here a sacramentality of a mode of action that is founded on a personal aptitude conferred by ordination, an aptitude distinct from sanctity. This sacramentality is of a charismatic order. It makes the minister a *separated* sign and instrument of Christ and the church, a *sacramental link* between Christ and men (*CCC* §1120).

We may add a further word about the conjoined acts of Christ and the church, which are the preaching of the gospel and the celebration of the saving mysteries. These purely sacramental acts are signs and instruments that, in order to be authentic, ought to express and realize what the church believes about them, for the church received them from Christ (*CCC* §1114–1120).

The manifestation of this sacramental "chain," which is founded in the very mystery of Christ and is completed in the "concrete" act that touches man today, permits us to discern a profound coherence in the economy of salvation. What took place once for all through the mystery of the Incarnation—that covenant between the Word of God and a human nature like our own—spreads to others beyond the Incarnate Word so that the perfect economy of salvation as found in Christ reaches out to all people of all times and places. At its source, the *raison d'être* of the Incarnation is the goodness of God, who did not give up the idea of communicating his life to sinners. The first, decisive expression of this goodness is seen in the choice of the mode of salvation: God became man so that, in and through his assumed humanity, all may have access to the Father through the Spirit. To this first reason for the Incarnation, one must add its great anthropological fittingness, namely, that in accordance with man's nature as incarnate spirit or animated flesh, man is met by a divine manifestation of humanly perceptible salvation. Here and now, the divine Word is heard through and in a human word. Here and now, the gift of divine grace is received through and in a religious rite.

What has been described above can be summarized in visual form through figure 38.1 (originally published in La Soujeole 2011: 553).

God, the sole principal cause of grace. (Grace here is the divine power that heals and elevates nature, i.e., grace as an accident.)

in the Word Incarnate:

- hypostatic union

full of grace (*plérôme*): holy

Humanity ↗ an animated, conjoined instrument – sanctifying

⊤ the Eucharistic sacrament

{ an entitative sacrament leads to an operative one

- mystical union

Church ↗ full of grace (*plérôme*): holy

↗ an animated, adjunct instrument – sanctifying

{ an entitative sacrament leads to an operative one

- *in persona Christi*
and
- *in persona Ecclesiae*

Ministers ↗ character: power

↗ an animated, separated instrument: sanctifying

{ an entitative sacrament leads to an operative one
acts of Christ and the Church

⇧ preaching

⇧ sacraments

{ Operative sacramentality - inanimate, separated sacraments

→ the receiving subject

- authentic reception: if the instrumental chain is intact
- fruitful reception: if the virtue of faith is present

- The divine power is conveyed by the instruments.
- The capacity to be the instrument of this divine power flows from:
  o the hypostatic union for the animated, conjoined instrument;
  o the mystical union for the animated, adjunct instrument;
  o character for the animated, separated instrument;
  o the divine institution for the inanimate, separated instruments [the institution intended here entails the *signification*].

FIG. 38.1   The Chain of Sacramentality.

CONCLUSION

The three subjects that we have discussed demonstrate clearly, in our opinion, how reflection on the essence of a sacrament (*the sign of a present cause*) was able gradually to clarify the complexity of sacramental grace. This more profound understanding of the sacramentality of the seven saving acts permitted us to situate this mode of salvation in a larger ensemble that includes the mysteries of Christ and the church. The sacramentality of salvation emerges thus as being solidly founded upon the careful considerations of the Church Fathers. This sacramentality was explained and expanded during the theological renewal that preceded and enabled Vatican II. We find ourselves now at a privileged moment for soteriology, one that should permit and facilitate new theological syntheses. Benefitting from the broad picture provided by the *Catechism of the Catholic Church*, such new syntheses, we hope, will be one of the foremost services that the twenty-first century can render to us.

ABBREVIATIONS

CCC   *Catechism of the Catholic Church* (2000), 2nd ed. (Washington, DC: Libreria Editrice Vaticana/United States Catholic Conference).

DS   Denzinger-Schönmetzer, *Enchiridion Symbolorum, definitionum et declaratio-num de rebus fidei et morum* (1973), 36th ed. (Freiburg im Breisgau: Herder).

PG   Migne's Patrologia Graeca

PL   Migne's Patrologia Latina

RSV   The Bible, Revised Standard Version

SUGGESTED READING

La Soujeole (2006 and 2011); O'Neill (1983); Revel (2004 and 2005); Schillebeeckx (2004).

BIBLIOGRAPHY

Abbott, Walter M. (ed.) (1966), *The Documents of Vatican II* (London: Geoffrey Chapman).

Acta synodalia sacrosancti concilii oecumenici Vaticani II (1970–2000) (Vatican City State: Typis Polyglottis Vaticanis).

Alexander of Hales (1957), *Glossa in quatuor libros Sententiarum Petri Lombardi*, vol. 4 (Quaracchi, Florence, Italy: Editiones Collegii S. Bonaventurae).

Aquinas, Thomas (1999), *Summa theologiae*, 3rd ed. (Turin: Edizioni San Paolo).

Blankenhorn, Bernhard (2006), "The Instrumental Causality of the Sacraments: Thomas Aquinas and Louis-Marie Chauvet," *Nova et Vetera*, English edition, 4: 255–293.

Bourgeois, Daniel (2007), *Le Champ du signe: Structure de la sacramentalité comme significa-tion chez saint Augustin et saint Thomas d'Aquin* (Doctoral thesis, University of Fribourg, Switzerland, <http://ethesis.unifr.ch>).

La Soujeole, Benoît-Dominique de (2006), *Introduction au mystère de l'Église* (Paris: Parole et Silence).

La Soujeole, Benoît-Dominique de (2008), "Réflexions sur la causalité du salut," *Annales theo-logici* 22: 369–383.

La Soujeole, Benoît-Dominique de (2011), "The Economy of Salvation: Entitative Sacra-mentality and Operative Sacramentality," *The Thomist* 75: 537–553.

O'Neill, Colman (1964), *Meeting Christ in the Sacraments* (New York: Alba House).

O'Neill, Colman (1983), *Sacramental Realism: A General Theory of the Sacraments* (Dublin: Dominican Publications).

Revel, Jean-Philippe (2004), *Traité des sacrements, I: Baptême et sacramentalité; 1. Origine et signification du baptême* (Paris: Cerf).

Revel, Jean-Philippe (2005), *Traité des sacrements, I: Baptême et sacramentalité; 2. Don et récep-tion de la grâce baptismale* (Paris: Cerf).

Schillebeeckx, Edward (2004), *L'Économie sacramentelle du salut* (Fribourg, Switzerland: Academic Press Fribourg), French translation of *De sacramentele heilseconomie* (Antwerpen and Bilthoven: 't Groeit and H. Nelissen, 1952).

Sicard, Patrice (2008), *Théologies victorines: Études d'histoire doctrinale médiévale et contempo-raine* (Paris: Parole et Silence).

Tschipke, Theophil (2003), *L'humanité du Christ comme instrument de salut de la divinité*, trans. Philibert Secrétan (Fribourg, Switzerland: Academic Press Fribourg), French translation of *Die Menschheit Christi als Heilsorgan der Gottheit* (Freiburg im Breisgau: Herder, 1940).

CHAPTER 39

....

A SACRAMENTAL
WORLD: WHY IT MATTERS

....

DAVID BROWN

INTRODUCTION

....

THE year 2013 marked the fiftieth anniversary of the publication of John Robinson's *Honest to God*, Britain's bestselling work on theology in the twentieth century, achieving over one million sales of the short paperback. Initially it might seem an odd place to begin a discussion of the significance of treating the world as sacramental, but Robinson's book did draw attention to one dangerous feature of the Christianity of the time that continues into our own day and is in part to blame for the decline of sacramental attitudes toward the world. This is the practice of taking metaphors over-literally. Since Scripture and subsequent tradition had constantly used the image of God up in heaven, Robinson observed a tendency among his fellow Christians to suppose that the deity was in fact far distant from us. His own preferred solution was to substitute the imagery of Paul Tillich and speak of God as "the ground of our being" (Robinson 1963: 45–63). But that equally carries dangers, of supposing God to be merely a larger version of ourselves.

Instead, we need a range of metaphors, including those that follow neither of the two options so far mentioned, among them one from John Henry Newman who in a sermon for St. Michael and All Angels' day speaks of how "every breath of air and ray of light and heat, every beautiful prospect is, as it were, the waving of the robes of those whose faces see God in heaven" (Newman 1891: 2.29, p. 453). Far from any point about angels' wings literally brushing our faces, his intention was to underline how close the reality of heaven is to us: neither in the far distance, nor buried in the depths of ourselves, but, as it were, just behind a thin veil alongside us. After all, heaven is by definition where God is, and God is, again by definition, omnipresent, and so present everywhere, all around us. It is this kind of sacramental attitude that Newman espouses, of an earthly reality enabling participation in a heavenly one, that I wish to defend in this chapter. In the remainder of the introduction some attention will be given to reasons why such attitudes are now less common in modern Western society. Thereafter, three arguments will be offered for insisting that such sacramentality must nonetheless lie at the foundation of all theology.

First, then, it will be appropriate to explore briefly some of the main reasons why such attitudes are in fact much less common today than they were in the past. Among sociologists reference is frequently made to one of their founding fathers, Max Weber (d. 1920), who spoke of "the disenchantment of the world"—that is, the way in which modern society tends to value only what is a means to something else, and so turns aside from what appears mystical or magical, and thus without further purpose (Weber 1948: 129–156, esp. 155). Although Weber had no explicit religious belief himself, it was not a direction in human thought that he himself liked, despite the fact that he believed the continuing advance of such secular notions to be inevitable (D. Brown 2004: 16–19). In that belief he is probably still followed by most sociologists, but among specialists in the sociology of religion judgments are more mixed. Thus, in Britain, while Steve Bruce continues to advance such a secularization thesis (Bruce 2002), others offer more nuanced accounts that suggest that part of the problem lies within Christianity itself, in a mismatch between what it proclaims and ordinary people's experience. So, for example, Grace Davie talks of continuing deep-seated spiritual aspirations in the population at large but expressed in what she calls a "believing without belonging" (Davie 1994); Callum Brown identifies the problem as the failure of Christianity to come to terms with the changed status of women in the 1960s (C. G. Brown 2001); while the historian Hugh McLeod postulates factors that vary from society to society but are often heavily bound up with an inadequate response to industrialization (McLeod's ideas are discussed in C. G. Brown and M. Snape 2010).

As these various responses indicate, sociologists tend to point to practical behavior and attitudes as the prime cause whereas intellectual historians on the whole find their answer in the structure of the belief system itself. Three significant books in this connection are Michael Buckley's *At the Origin of Modern Atheism* (1987), Charles Taylor's *A Secular Age* (2007), and Michael Gillespie's *The Theological Origins of Modernity* (2008). Although they differ greatly over when precisely change set in, their common contention is that the problem begins when religious belief comes to be seen as an *inference* from something else rather than itself directly experienced as part of the air we breathe, as it were. Charles Taylor wants to blame the Reformation when there ceased to be a common culture, but one might equally well go back as far as Aquinas with his five proofs for God's existence. Although modern attempts to disengage him from later neo-Thomism and also to stress continuing influence from Platonism are largely correct (e.g. Kerr, Hankey), it still seems to me that the new influence from Aristotle did also have its impact, in generating a rational structure whereby God in effect became an inference rather than part of immediate human experience.

Despite modern attacks on the other-worldly character of the Platonism that Aquinas's use of Aristotle began to supplant, it did have one obvious advantage over the newcomer. Its primary metaphors of participation and imitation did suggest nature and humanity already in some sense bridging the two domains of earthly and heavenly realities, and it is precisely this same aim that talk of the sacramentality of the world is intended to reflect in more explicitly theological terms. So far from being an inno-vation as some allege, it can be seen as a return to the wider sense of sacramentality that dominated the first millennium of the Christian church before the narrowing of the High Middle Ages, which came to confine talk of sacraments to the seven adopted by the Fourth Lateran Council in 1215. To explain such narrowing one need look no further than various philosophical and juridical considerations—the characteristically philo-sophical and legal desire for precise definition—that, while entirely legitimate in their proper place, obfuscated a larger vision to which the Second Vatican Council (1962–1965) invited a return. This return was already anticipated within Anglicanism thanks in large part to Charles Gore, the leader of the Anglo-Catholic movement in the first quarter of the twentieth century. In an influential essay "The Sacramental Principle," he argued that the foundations for explicitly Christian sacraments were laid in "natu-ral sacraments" such as the handshake of friendship and the kiss of love (Gore 1901). Significantly, if the Hegelianism of the time was one of the influences on Gore, no less prominent was Plato, an integral element in the Oxford syllabus.

Yet in much more recent writing on this wider sense of sacramentality, indeed per-haps most, the story is told almost entirely from the inside out as it were, that is, with the assumption that such a reading of the world has validity only if it starts with Christ and his church. For example, one can see such an assumption running through what Alexander Schmemann has to say in his influential essay on *The World as Sacrament* (1966). But the problem then becomes that there is no easy way of dialoguing with all those who in some sense "believe without belonging" or for Christians themselves to comprehend how sac-ramentality might effectively bridge the gap between the two worlds, the earth that is ours, and heaven, God's space, since on this analysis the latter seems to belong firmly on the other side of a great divide. So in the rest of this chapter I want to posit three key ways in which the world understood as sacramental—even without appeal to revealed theology—might effectively bridge that gap. As will become clear, it is my contention that, so far from this involving a simple reversion to Platonism, such an understanding can deliver answers to some of the principal dilemmas in contemporary theology. I con-sider first the collapse of traditional proofs of God's existence, then the dismantling of the dualist conception of human beings as two entities (body and soul), before finally turn-ing to the challenge to revelation itself in the socially conditioned character of all human thought. In each case the role played by the imagination will prove crucial.

THE COLLAPSE OF THEISTIC ARGUMENTS AND SACRAMENTAL EXPERIENCE

Perhaps from as early as the Aristotelian revolution in European thought that began with Aquinas, but certainly more clearly from the seventeenth century onwards, dis-cussion of God's existence outside revelation has been dominated by the so-called proofs: formal arguments such as the cosmological, teleological, and ontological, to which the moral and experiential were in due course added. While these arguments are not without value, they did distort the actual situation by implying that belief in God must either arise through such a process of rational reflection or else find some such retrospective justification. Surprisingly, such a view even became part of the official teaching of the Roman Catholic Church in the nineteenth century (Denzinger-Schönmetzer: 3026). Yet most Christian philosophers would now concede that the contention was overblown.

Characteristic of approaches today is the more modest reinterpretation of such arguments that has been offered by the American philosopher, C. Stephen Evans in his 2010 book, *Natural Signs and Knowledge of God*. He suggests that they function more as signs rather than proofs, hints that stimulate reflection rather than compelling belief as such. The cosmological argument is, for example, interpreted in terms of "cosmic wonder." However, such an interpretation still leaves those signs at a distance, requiring an inference before what they imply can be appropriated. Contrast the attitude of Gerard Manley Hopkins:

> The world is charged with the grandeur of God.
> It will flame out, like shining from shook foil;
> It gathers to a greatness, like the ooze of oil
> Crushed. (opening lines of *God's Grandeur*)

Admittedly, the poet goes on to query why all human beings do not have such experience, and somewhat oddly blames this on the advance of trade (possibly a reference to trees being valued only for their timber, and so on). However that may be, there remains no doubt in his mind that the perception can sometimes still be very much more than an inference, functioning instead as direct experience. Such experiences would then be appropriately described as sacramental because we have now moved beyond the realm of signs into symbols that themselves always participate in the reality to which they point. The philosopher and former priest Anthony Kenny, however, objects that this is not the right use of the term for, to quote him specifically in relation to this poem, the sacramental must "relate to God not as designer but as redeemer of the world" (Kenny 1988: 118). Again, that seems to me to put the sacramental on the wrong side of the divide, for even sacraments in the narrow sense are concerned not just with transformation but also with affirmation, with reassuring individuals of their valued status in the eyes of God. So my inclination would be to identify any experience of the natural world that involves an encounter with God as itself inherently sacramental, whether or not it is redemptive and whether or not the terminology as such is employed. To see the legitimacy of the point, one could scarcely do better than turn to John Ruskin who, despite the Calvinism of his formation, seems to advance well beyond it in his account of experience of God through nature.

Although primarily an art critic, and indeed Britain's greatest art critic of the nineteenth century, Ruskin also wrote extensively on the natural world and its capacity to yield experience of the divine. In part he did so because of his belief that human art was at its best when imitating nature, but he also wanted to register the claim that through the way the world is made God is somehow brought closer to us. But, whereas for Calvin all this meant was that the natural world could be experienced by those of faith as divine effects (Calvin 1960: I, 16), for Ruskin (Ruskin 1906: II, 3, v–x) much more was entailed, in some sense an experience of divinity itself. So, for example, a seascape stretching to infinity is said not just to point to the possibility of a similar infinity in God, it allows us the actual possibility to experience such infinity as one of the divine's own distinctive attributes. In Ruskin's own words, "light receding in the distance is of all visible things the least material, the least finite, the farthest withdrawn from the earth … the most typical of the nature of God, the most suggestive of the glory of his dwelling place" (Ruskin 1906: II, 3, v, 45). In all, six different "types" of beauty are distinguished, each of which has the capacity, he suggests, to mediate a particular divine attribute: infinity or incomprehensibility, unity or comprehensiveness, repose or permanence, symmetry or justice, purity or energy, and moderation or restraint.

There is not the space here to explore these types in any detail. All that can be done is to indicate Ruskin's general thrust by some specific examples. With purity or energy he mentions the vitality of flowing water, and in that respect it is salutary to remember Christ's own appeal to living water in John's Gospel (4.10). Again, the psalmists' appeal to God being like the repose of the everlasting mountains (Ps 36:6; 65:6; 90:2; 125) can also be indicated by the way in which God's presence was sought on mountains such as Sinai and Carmel. Not that repose need be found only in this form. Ruskin quotes from Wordsworth's poem *The Excursion*:

> Earth quiet and unchanged; the human soul
> Consistent in self-rule; and heaven revealed
> To meditation, in that quietness. (Wordsworth 1836: 3.402–3.405)

Yet, important though these insights of Ruskin are, in my view they still stop well short of the range of human experience to which appeal might be made. To give a rather different example, consider the various ways in which we experience the world as gift, as the product of factors well beyond our own personal control: the birth of a child, for example, or the daily provision of food. Although for significant numbers in the modern Western world such events amount to no more than that to which they are entitled, for most people through most of history the experience was one of "grace," the provision of a blessing to which they felt they had no entitlement. As my use of that term "grace" is intended to imply, it went with a sense of being caught up into a relation with the divine, however understood: gratitude for a graced life (D. Brown: 2007: 121–135). Of course, the legitimacy of such a framework could be challenged, but it is open to the religious believer to observe that this is part and parcel of the way God has made the world, with religious belief in some sense natural as the product of the way human beings are situated in their world or, put more theologically, of the fact that both human beings and the world they inhabit are divine creations.

Although the strength of Ruskin's certainty of such an intimate connection between nature and God was severely tested by Darwin's new theories, it is by no means clear why this should have been so. Strange creatures that had anticipated human beings were already known to the biblical authors in the form of Behemoth and Leviathan, and, so far from finding them repulsive, an author such as Job can detect God's delight in such variety of forms (Job 40:15–41:34). Again, "nature red in tooth and claw" could be said to count against a sacramental reading of the world, but that it is possible to read and experience the apparent evidence in more than one way is well illustrated by the particularly sensitive approach adopted by Annie Dillard in her classic meditation of 1976, *Pilgrim at Tinker Creek*. Dillard's work is in effect a poet's reflection on her experience of nature and of the divine through nature. But, although scarcely structured as a formal argument, it does indicate how an "answer" to the problem of natural evil might be mediated through experience. Thus, although she is adamant that her readers must face up to nature at its most brutal and wasteful, as with the giant water bug and praying mantis (Dillard 1976: 18–20, 60–67), rather than allowing such facts to undermine belief in God, she is insistent on holding such experience in creative tension with how nature appears elsewhere, not least because there is no easy way of assessing overall significance given that what we attend to varies greatly from individual to individual. There are plenty of indicators of both "spendthrift genius" and "extravagance of care," with "the shadow" sometimes "resolving into beauty," but otherwise always with the remembrance that "grotesques and horrors bloom from that same free growth, that intricate scramble and twine up and down the conditions of time" (Dillard 1976: 70, 117, 133). Purely negative features should thus not be allowed to outweigh direct experience of a graced world, because there are simply no common scales in terms of which one can be weighed against the other.

THE COLLAPSE OF DUALISM AND THE SACRAMENTAL IMAGINATION

A second issue that the modern world raises for bridging the gap between God and ourselves—that is, apart from the collapse of the proofs of God's existence just mentioned—is the fact that few now believe in the conception of ourselves that has dominated most of Christian history and which we inherited from Platonism, and that is the sense of us already inhabiting the two worlds. Technically known as dualism, it spoke of human beings as consisting of two substances, mortal bodies and immortal souls, and thus of us inhabiting the visible earth as the home of matter and an invisible reality that is the home of minds, ours and God's. Instead we have been returned to a more biblical picture, of us as psychosomatic unities, mind and body entirely interdependent, with us only surviving death thanks to divine action and not because of anything inherent in the way we have been made.

But, if such a conclusion excludes any sense of us already linked to heaven, the invisible world that is God's, there still remains an alternative way of making the connection, and that is through appeal to the sacramental imagination, that is, an appeal no longer to the fundamental nature of our minds but rather to how those minds work. Human beings learn the use of words in application to the sensible world. So clearly, if the jump to the divine is to be made, language will need to be stretched in analogies, images, and metaphors, what are in effect the common tools of the imagination. Perhaps the relevance of the point to all the imaginative arts can be expressed most clearly by making explicit the parallel between symbol in action, metaphor in writing, and image in the visual arts, and how the theological notion of sacramentality is based on a similar structure. Consider first the traditional sacraments. Each involves an action that by doing one thing intends another: the consecration of bread and wine to become the body and blood of Christ, the exchange of rings to establish a permanent relation between two individuals, the anointing of a dying person's body to prepare for life in another world, and so on. Works of the imagination, irrespective of the medium, appear very similarly founded. The metaphors of the poet are intended to take us from one sphere of discourse to another, the images of the artist from one visual image to another (whether it be a mental idea or an actual scene), while a medium such as ballet is full of symbolic acts under which gestures of the body are intended to imply acts performed quite differently in ordinary life.

Even prior to his conversion to Anglo-Catholicism in 1927, T. S. Eliot had already detected the importance of metaphor in helping to interconnect what might otherwise seem an unintegrated, uncreated world. Thus in a famous essay on "The Metaphysical Poets" he observes: "When a poet's mind is perfectly equipped for its work, it is constantly amalgamating disparate experiences; the ordinary man's experience is chaotic, irregular, fragmentary. The latter fails in love, or reads Spinoza, and these two experiences have nothing to do with each other, or with the noise of the typewriter or the smell of cooking; in the mind of the poet these experiences are always forming new wholes" (Eliot 1975: 59–67, esp. 64).

In other words, as symbol is to action, metaphor to language, and image to art, so sacrament is to religion. Each is trying to move us analogically, to take us to a different place. Of course in most uses of the imagination, that other place remains firmly in our present world. Nonetheless, the imagination has already accepted the principle of a move elsewhere, and so it may well be asked, why not then to a vastly different world? As Jesus' use of parables illustrates, or some of the extraordinary imagery and word play found in the prophets, similes and metaphors when well used can draw us from the material world into quite a different order of existence. As already noted, this is not at all to claim that every exercise of the imagination even implicitly evokes God, but it is to observe that the imagination is deploying precisely the same kind of tools that make talk of God possible. So, however hostile to faith individual artists may be, they are at least moving humanity onto the same terrain that legitimates talk of God. While my approach thus presupposes the need to listen to the imagination, none of this is to suggest that everything produced by the imagination will be of value, only that imaginative searchings, however negative their connotations, can at least open our eyes to other possibilities of a more transcendent kind.

The sacramental can thus be seen to build upon the symbolic and metaphorical inasmuch as, though the latter are not sacramental as such, it is not hard to see how the process that they utilize might extend to the more explicitly sacramental participation of one thing in another where too there is both similarity and difference, as in earthly light and heavenly light, running water and living water, and so on. Indeed, that very fact of difference that is opened up in analogical language and action helps identify another key contribution that the imagination can make towards an encounter with the divine, and that is in the essentially open-ended character of all imagery and symbol. That is to say, the interpretation of such devices can be pulled in quite a number of different directions, and so the question of an alternative religious world can be raised even when such a thought was far removed from the intention of artist or speaker. This is because once we move beyond the literal, the multivalent character of possible comparative allusions cannot be strictly controlled, and indeed one might argue that it is the mark of a great poet or artist to welcome such allusive richness. So the transition to the immaterial can sometimes be imaginatively made even where such thoughts were far from the Creator's mind and perhaps even from most of his audience or viewers.

To some this might suggest a purely "subjective" interpretation but, while obviously some interpretations might be "strained," this is hardly to concede that this inevitably happens whenever there is deviation from the majority view. Perhaps one might be allowed to use a poem on the relation between *Poetry and Religion* to itself express this view, one by the contemporary Australian poet Les Murray:

Full religion is the large poem in loving repetition . . .
and God is the poetry caught in any religion,
caught, not imprisoned. Caught as in a mirror
that is attracted, being in the world as poetry
is in the poem, a law against closure. (Murray 1991: 272–273)

Perhaps a couple of examples will make the point clearer. Take the painter Francis Bacon. Of his atheism there is not a shadow of doubt, nor of the sheer awfulness and meaninglessness of suffering that he intended to convey through his paintings. The religious imagery he frequently employed was meant to enhance that sense of pointlessness, not to provide any kind of answer. Yet viewing a picture such as *Fragment of a Crucifixion* (1950, Stedelijk Van Abbemuseum, Eindhoven), where the figure above the cross seems powerless to help, may inadvertently make a Christian more conscious of what it means to say that Christ has entered into the full reality of human suffering. Again, the triptych (in the Steinberg Collection) he produced in 1973 in honor of his lover George Dyer (whom Bacon had driven to suicide) may be seen to contain an implicit hint against Bacon's own general message of despair, in the centrality he has given to the glowing light bulb. It could suggest that despite all that has happened

Bacon's love for Dyer will continue, and so, in spite of himself, the painting after all conveys an implicitly Christian message about the possibility of forgiveness and of love redeeming loss.

Or, to take a poetic example this time, A. E. Houseman's *Easter Hymn* ("If in that Syrian garden ..." e.g. Gardner 1972: 294) reflects the author's atheism. Thus the first verse assumes that Christ remains in his grave, while the second ends with the injunction that, if he has risen, he needs to "bow hither out of heaven and see and save." Yet it is now quite commonly set as part of the liturgy for Holy Saturday, with believers entering into the same doubts as the first disciples had and which, unlike Housman, they have overcome. In other words, the openness of the language allows the possibility for the poem to be experienced quite differently from the undermining of belief that was intended.

So recent proposals to restore the right hemisphere of the brain to the more central place that is its by nature, as in the neurologist Iain McGilchrist's influential book, *The Master and his Emissary* (2009), might suggest something quite deep about how God has made us, with the poetic and the imaginative at the heart of who we are because it makes possible this strong link with the non-material world. It would also endorse the speculations of child psychologists such as Bettelheim, Piaget, and Yardley, who make the imagination central to child development, and thus pick up on the thought of eighteenth-century philosophers such as Herder and Hamann, for whom poetry is "the native tongue of the human race" (Hamann 1957: II, 197).

SOCIAL CONDITIONING, INCARNATION, AND EUCHARIST

Finally, there is the whole issue of cultural conditioning, not only of us ourselves caught up in the cultural assumptions of our time but also of Christ himself. Throughout most of the twentieth century the dominant response had been the Barthian one, echoed on the Catholic side by Hans Urs von Balthasar, in a very strong emphasis on the distinctiveness, indeed uniqueness, of Christianity, of Christ's message being, as in the language of the early Barth, "like a flash of lightning ... as the dissolution of all relativity" (Barth 1933: 331). But the problem with such an answer is twofold. First, it flies in the face of the facts. Human life begins with a long period of dependence on others prior to full adulthood. But even when adulthood arrives, a system of interdependency continues rather than anything like complete autonomy. Acceptance of such a pattern in the Bible can be seen in the way in which the primary address in the Hebrew Scriptures is to one particular social grouping, the nation, while in the New Testament it is to another, the body of Christ. One way of reading this feature of Scripture is the Bible's and thus God's recognition of the fact that what becomes a pertinent topic at one particular moment of history often has as much to do with the nature of the society at the time as with prayerful searching. But, secondly, in any case unless the Incarnation builds on the way human beings are actually situated, it is hard to see why its message should be relevant to socially conditioned beings such as ourselves.

To say this is not to endorse some form of absolute determinism, but it is to accept social conditioning: that thoughts and reflections always have a particular social context, and that responses to God and Scripture therefore operate within a similar frame. Such conditioning does not mean that human beings cannot take any steps beyond the times in which they live (otherwise how would new ideas be possible?), but it does mean that any such overstepping must bear some relation to where the society as a whole has already reached in its reflections.

But to focus exclusively, or even mainly, on the limitations of such conditioning would be, I suggest, to present the matter in altogether too negative a light. Being born into a particular culture and time was also for Jesus full of creative possibilities, not least in the whole inheritance from Judaism. So a whole host of imaginative ideas were available to Jesus as he was growing up, which would not have been present or not present to the same degree in earlier generations and in other parts of the world, among them, for example, the suffering servant, the Kingdom of God, the Passover lamb, and so on. Austin Farrer rightly stressed the possibilities for development that this opened up for Jesus; indeed so much so that he suggests in *The Glass of Vision* (Farrer 1948; MacSwain 2013) that such imagery became the primary vehicle of revelation. In saying this, it is important to note that Jesus does not then simply transmit ideas he has inherited from the past: he meditates on them and creatively shapes them to his own unique sense of mission. Most frequently, this was in prayerful relation to his Father, but sometimes, as in our own case, it is the minds of others that helped shape Jesus' own mind. As well as his parents and disciples, Farrer includes the influence of the local village rabbi. But there may be more controversial examples, for it seems to me not impossible that the encounter with the Syro-Phoenician woman (Mark 7:24–30) provided the requisite stimulus for Jesus to move beyond the common attitudes of his own time, under which Jews saw Gentiles as holding an inferior place in God's designs: "dogs" not spoken of as household pets, as some commentators suggest (e.g. Cranfield 1977: 248), but instead functioning as a diminutive of contempt. Yet those same Gentiles were now to be fully incorporated into God's purposes.

So to talk of Christ as sacrament involves rather more than just indicating him as the source of the Christian sacraments: it is to speak of him assuming human life as it is, sometimes endorsing it and sometimes transforming it, but always with a view to enabling it to engage better with that other world to which the divine reality belongs. So the incarnation was not simply a thunderbolt out of the blue; it was a deep enmeshing in the ordinary conditions of human existence, our dependence on others, and in particular the culture within which we are set. And that is what gives his life an explicitly sacramental dimension. Christ draws on the images and metaphors of his time that were already helping to bridge the two worlds in a way that allows them to be brought even closer in a real creative participation. So, although the essential building blocks of his life and teaching were no different from those of any other great artist or thinker, as an imagination set within a particular social tradition, it was an imagination and life that embodied the bridge and so made available such participation to those who came after him as the images acquired new resonances and meaning.

Nowhere is this more evident than in the Eucharist, which is why it is so important to stress not only universal features of Jesus' existence, his joy in food and drink and in human friendship, but also the more culture-specific features of meals that helped determine the shape he gave to this central act of Christian worship. At one level, that might seem conspicuously obvious. So, for example, it is based not only on a meal that speaks of the endorsement of a graced world where human sharing and a sense of being graced by God come together but also on the Passover, and so speaks of redemptive transformation. But there are other aspects that are less easily incorporated into modern thought, such as the whole notion of sacrifice, with not just Passover but every meal that involved meat, including at least some token sacrificial element, as indeed was true of the ancient world generally. This is not the place to explore the various theories of meaning behind sacrifice except to observe that even pagan sacrifice can be seen to be sacramental in intention, in the use of the victim to draw human and divine into a common purpose. Of course, no doubt sometimes, perhaps often, underlying intentions were base, but there are no grounds for universalizing the claim. Instead, we may see Jewish sacrifice building on pagan and Jesus in turn on Jewish, to create a reality in which his own body becomes the vehicle for our incorporation into his new resurrected life. The Eucharist thus nicely encapsulates the power of symbol, metaphor, and image that I have emphasized throughout this chapter, the power the human imagination gives us, thanks to the way God has made us, to move from one world to the other, the most material of realities, through their symbolism enabling us to participate in the place where Christ now is, in the heaven that exists alongside us.

Lest this stress on continuities be thought to preclude any real form of distinctiveness, let me end with one instance of this in respect of the Eucharist. Relevant to that drawing of ourselves into the divine life is a major change that occurs in how those key symbols are applied from Old Testament to New. In Jewish rites of sacrifice, while some flesh was eaten and some burnt as an offering to God, the life-blood had been viewed as essentially a divine possession, and so worshippers were required to pour it on the altar or on the ground (Lev 3:8, 13), with anyone drinking blood cut off from the people of Israel (Lev 17:10). Here, however, that same life-blood is given to us to consume, as is most explicitly asserted in John's Gospel (D. Brown 1995: 146–150). We are thus made partakers in what is no longer a purely human rite but one that also involves us in receiving what had once been seen as an exclusive prerogative of God. Christ thus allows us to participate in both his human and divine life through a sacramental symbol that effectively bridges the two worlds, the reality of this life in which he once shared and his present life in heaven as both human and divine.

SUGGESTED READINGS

Brown, D. (2007); Farrer (1948)—see also the critical edition in MacSwain (2013); McGilchrist (2009). Also:

Boersma, H. (2011), *Heavenly Participation: The Weaving of a Sacramental Tapestry* (Grand Rapids, MI: Eerdmans).

Brown, D. (2008), *God and Mystery in Words* (Oxford: Oxford University Press).

BIBLIOGRAPHY

Barth, K. (1933), *The Epistle to the Romans* (London: Oxford University Press).

Brown, C. G. (2001), *The Death of Christian Britain* (London: Routledge).

Brown, C. G., and M. Snape (2010), *Secularisation in the Christian World: Essays in Honour of Hugh McLeod* (Farnham: Ashgate).

Brown, D. (1995), *The Word To Set You Free: Living Faith and Biblical Criticism* (London: SPCK).

Brown, D. (2004), *God and Enchantment of Place: Reclaiming Human Experience* (Oxford: Oxford University Press).

Brown, D. (2007), *God and Grace of Body: Sacrament in Ordinary* (Oxford: Oxford University Press).

Bruce, Steve (2002), *God is Dead: Secularization in the West* (Oxford: Blackwell).

Buckley, M. J. (1987), *At the Origins of Modern Atheism* (New Haven, CT: Yale University Press).

Calvin, J. (1960), *Institutes of the Christian Religion* (Philadelphia, PA: Westminster Press).

Cranfield, C. E. B. (1977), *The Gospel According to St Mark* (Cambridge: Cambridge University Press).

Davie, G. (1994), *Religion in Britain since 1945* (Oxford: Blackwell).

Dillard, A. (1976), *Pilgrim at Tinker Creek* (London: Picador).

Denzinger-Schönmetzer (1976), *Echiridion symbolorum* 36th ed. (Freiburg: Herder).

Elliot, T. S. (1975), "Metaphysical Poets," in F. Kermode (ed.), *T. S. Eliot, Selected Prose* (London: Faber & Faber).

Evans, C. S. (2010), *Natural Signs and Knowledge of God* (Oxford: Oxford University Press).

Farrer, A. (1948), *The Glass of Vision* (London: Dacre Press).

Gardner, H. ed. (1972), *The Faber Book of Religious Verse* (London: Faber and Faber).

Gillespie, M. A. (2008), *The Theological Origins of Modernity* (Chicago, IL: University of Chicago Press).

Gore, C. (1901), *The Body of Christ* (London: John Murray), 36–47.

Hamann, J. G. (1957), *Sämtliche Werken*, ed. J. Nadler (Vienna: Verlag Herder).

Hankey, W. (1987), *God in Himself: Aquinas' Doctrine of God* (Oxford: Oxford University Press).

Kenny, A. (1988), *God and Two Poets* (London: Sidgwick & Jackson).

Kerr, F. (2002), *After Aquinas: Versions of Thomism* (Oxford: Blackwell).

MacSwain, R. (2013), *Scripture, Metaphysics and Poetry: Austin Farrer's* The Glass of Vision *with Critical Commentary* (Farnham: Ashgate).

McGilchrist, I. (2009), *The Master and His Emissary* (New Haven: Yale University Press).

Murray, L. (1991), *Collected Poems* (Manchester: Carcanet).

Newman, J. H. (1891), *Parochial and Plain Sermons* (London: Longmans, Green & Co.).

Robinson, J. A. T. (1963), *Honest to God* (London: SCM).

Ruskin, J. (1906), *Modern Painters* (London: George Allen).

Schmemann, A. (1966), *The World as Sacrament* (London: Darton, Longman & Todd).

Taylor, C. (2007), *A Secular Age* (Cambridge, MA: Belknap Press).

Weber, M. (1948), "Science as a Vocation," in H. H. Gerth and C. W. Mills (eds.), *From Max Weber* (London: Routledge & Kegan Paul), 129–156.

Wordsworth, W. (1836), *The Poetical Works of William Wordsworth* (London: Edward Moxon).

....

CHAPTER 40

CHRIST, THE TRINITY, AND THE SACRAMENTS

....

FRANCESCA ARAN MURPHY

WHAT IS A SACRAMENT?

"IF it's just a symbol," Flannery O'Connor famously observed of the consecrated host, "to hell with it" (O'Connor 1979: 124–125). But it is easy to see why people think of the sacraments simply as symbols or signs of Christ. And it is easy to see why they think the signpost says that he is some degree of distance from us. All human signs, symbols, and words are different and irredeemably distant from the things which they signify. The word for a fact or an event belongs to the dimension of thought, the fact or event to the dimension of reality. The realm of language as we experience it is a human creation, whereas we do not experience reality purely as a human artifact. It seems as if sacraments should rightfully belong to the realm of signs rather than that of things and events. Certainly it seems as if they must be one or the other, because everything else is either a communication *about* things or a thing itself.

Beginning from God's actions in history helps us to see the sacraments. The Bible is both a story told by the Triune God, in language, the words given in Scripture, and a string of events, which match the words. It is, according to Thomas Aquinas, "peculiar to the sacred writings and no others" that their "signification is twofold: one ... through words; the other through the things signified by the words." The point is that, whereas human authorship consists solely in communicating through words, divine authorship also takes in communicating through things: "since" the "author" of Scripture is "God in whose power it lies not only to employ words to signify (which man can also do), but things as well." God can "write" both the history which is "in" the Bible and the history itself, which the Bible depicts: so things can "speak," and become the voice of God, while remaining things, indeed, redemptive things and events (Aquinas 1966: ch. 4, lect. 7).

This compenetration of word and event from the beginning of the biblical history reaches its intended culmination when the Word of God becomes incarnate in history.

The Incarnation unites the two ways God was present to the people of Israel: through the Prophetic Word and in the blood sacrifice. Christ the Incarnation of God is both Word event and sacrifice (von Balthasar 1991: 402–14, von Balthasar 1989: 33–40). Understanding the sacraments on analogy with the Scriptures, as being not merely words, but words which somehow present Christ and his sacrifice is an implication of the historical Incarnation of the Word. Both in the Incarnation and in the sacraments which Christ instituted, the sign becomes the signified, through the power of the divine author. All the sacraments, from baptism to matrimony, are both word and deed: they point or refer to the sanctification of the persons who undergo them (word), and they actually sanctify (in deed). The sacraments are liturgical gestures in which the grace of God is shown to be communicated, and is communicated.

Thomas Aquinas draws the analogy between Scripture and sacraments when he writes:

> Though the same thing can be signified by divers signs, yet to determine which sign must be used belongs to the signifier. Yet it is God Who signifies spiritual things to us by means of the sensible things in the sacraments, and of similitudes in the Scriptures ... just as the Holy Ghost decides by what similitudes spiritual things are to be signified in certain passages of Scripture, so also must it be determined by Divine institution what things are to be employed for the purpose of signification in this or that sacrament. (*ST* III, q.60, a.5, ad1)

One can envisage the sacraments as the continuation of what Lutherans have called "salvation history." In this salvation history, God speaks and acts not only through words but also through things and culminatively in the Word made flesh and blood sacrifice.

If the sacraments can be understood by analogy with the sacred history told by Scripture, and are the divinely intended aftermath of that history, what is the difference between the biblical events which initiate the sacraments and the sacrament as it occurs in the Christian liturgy? The sacramental event channels the efficacity of the original historical events without repeating the historical events. The sacramental event is a liturgical event, not a historical event. God acts in both the historical event and the liturgical event, but the second, sacramental, event as such leaves no mark on history. The baptisms of Clovis and of other kings who converted to Christianity had historical repercussions, but in the act of baptism itself God authors a sacramental event, not an historical action: in the vocal witness of the liturgical action baptismal grace is silently given to sanctify the baptized.

Sacraments are defined as "sensible signs of invisible things whereby man is made holy" (*ST* III, q.61, a.3). Many experiences make your "gypsy soul fly into the mystic" (Van Morrison, "Into the Mystic," *Moondance*). Listening to music, walking in the countryside, the sight of a beautiful moon in the sky, and most of all a stroll in the moonlight with our beloved may seem to us to fit the definition of a sacrament: a physical act which is so redolent with "invisible" significance that it lifts us up to God. Why limit the "sacraments" to liturgical acts when so many acts in human life seem to be signs of the invisible, and to raise our hearts to God? Doesn't God act and speak through these events just as much as through liturgical acts such as confirmation or matrimony? One reply to this question would be that a sacrament is *about* worshipping God, so that non-liturgical actions, actions which are not literally part of the worship of God, are not literally sacramental.

Historically, the seven sacraments upon which Orthodox and Catholics agree, were not all dogmatically defined in the primitive church. It could be argued that the church does many things which look liturgical but which are not taken to be literally sacramental. Matrimony was not defined as a sacrament until the High Middle Ages, and it had a close competitor in the coronation of kings for inclusion as seventh sacrament. The coronation of kings is accompanied by magnificent liturgy or at least ritual. Many patriots feel as uplifted by coronations, and presidential inaugurations, as they do by marriages. Is it not excessively exclusive and dogmatically arbitrary to treat marriage and not coronation as sacraments? Both seem to meet the qualification of occurring within a liturgical act.

What makes a sacrament sanctify is that the sacrament unites the persons who undergo it with the sacrifice of Christ. Many human acts uplift our hearts to God, and very many are used by God to do so, but "the sacraments of the church derive their power specifically from Christ's passion" (*ST* III, q.61, a.3). It's difficult to see how one could connect coronation to the Passion of Christ, in the way that Paul directly linked marriage to union with Christ's Passion (Eph 5). Certainly the implements of kingship are present at the Passion, and Christ does indeed reign from the cross, crowned with thorns. But as Scripture describes it, the Passion overturns the human meaning of kingship (John 19:1–22).

The grace the sacraments give overflows from the sacrifice of Christ at Calvary. This sacrifice satisfies for sin, makes penal reparation for sin, merits our justification, and earns our redemption and divinization. We access this grace by means of faith in the saving efficacy of the sacrifice of Christ: "the power of the sacraments which is ordained unto the remission of sins is derived principally from faith in Christ's sacrifice" (*ST* III, q.61, a.3, ad2). There are only seven sacraments, because only seven liturgical events qualify as means by which the power of the sacrifice of Christ is channeled to a faithful human being. This act of sacrifice by Christ, on the cross, is the supreme act of divine worship. This is why the seven sacraments are liturgical acts: not because a sacrament is arbitrarily restricted to an action performed by clerics inside a church, but because a sacramental act draws its meaning and power from Christ's historical act of worship of the Father, in his self-offering on the cross.

Those delightful moments when we intuit the meaning of the moonlight as a grace of God or a coronation as the sign of God's good pleasure are essentially private, whether to one or two people or to a single nation. The sacraments, on the other hand, always involve the whole church: the whole church is engaged every time holy orders are conferred, a couple is wedded in Christ, the Eucharist broken and shared out (and so on): the sacraments exhibit the love of God for the church in its entirety. As Adrienne von Speyr puts it,

There is, indeed, no single sacrament in the Church that is wholly private; they are all means and occasions for unity. Each of them binds together all believers that have any connection with the sacraments, whether they directly receive them or not. The sacraments are among the most powerful forces of unity, for they act in a most mysterious way to lead Christians to the unity of the Church. This unity does not consist in a community and harmony of outlook. The unity of the Church is, essentially, love, and those who are sacramentally incorporated are led into this love, receive the sacraments ... with a sense of the communion of saints. (von Speyr 1985: 67)

Because the church's sacramental liturgy is engendered by Christ's sacrifice, "The liturgy is the *fons et culmen* of the very life of the Church. It is at the liturgy that the church is principally the church. In each liturgical action the church continuously reveals and communicates her universal inner essence and identifies herself with it again and again. The liturgy is where the church gives herself completely to God, like the bride to the bridegroom" (Dobzsay 2010: 64). One may describe the church as "sacrament" without devising an eighth sacrament.

It is through the sacraments that the "door" between heaven and earth which was built by Christ's incarnation remains standing: "through these sacred Mysteries," says Nicholas Cabasilas,

as through windows the Sun of Righteousness enters this dark world ... and introduces the abiding and immortal life into a mortal body which is subject to change ... This way the Lord traced by coming to us, this gate He opened by entering into the world. When He returned to the Father He suffered it not to be closed, but from Him He comes through it to sojourn among men, or rather, He is constantly present with us ... Therefore, as the patriarch said, "... this is the gate of heaven" (Gen 28.17). By it not only the angels descend to the earth ... but even the very Lord of the angels Himself.

The church is the keeper of what Cabasilas calls "The Gates of the Mysteries" (Cabasilas 1974: 50–1, 53).

In the nineteenth century, Adam Möhler spoke of the church as the continuation of the Incarnation (Möhler 1997: 259). The thought was developed by Matthias Scheeben whose ecclesiology exudes nuptial mysticism:

The Fathers view the Incarnation itself as a marriage with the human race ... But the relationship of unity it sets up comes to full fruition only in the Church. Man is to attach himself to his divine bridegroom by faith; and the bridegroom seals His union with man in baptism, as with a wedding ring. But both faith and baptism are mere preliminaries for the coming together of man and the God-man in one flesh by a real Communion of flesh and blood in the Eucharist, and hence for the perfect fructifying of man with the energising grace of his head. By entering the Church every soul becomes a real bride of God's Son, so truly that the Son of God is able ... to compare His love and union with the Church and her members with the unity achieved in matrimony ... In the Son and through the Son the Holy Spirit dwells there also, personally and essentially. His is the very Spirit and, as it were, the soul of the Church. Thus the great mystery of the Eucharistic Christ is the center around which is grouped the noble community of Christ's faithful. (Scheeben 2006: 543–545)

The documents of Vatican II several times describe the church as the sacrament of Christ. *Sacrosanctam Concilium* says that "it was from the side of Christ as He slept the sleep of death upon the cross that there came forth 'the wondrous sacrament of the whole church'" (*SC* 11.5). *Lumen Gentium* states that "the Church is in Christ like a sacrament or as a sign and instrument both of a very closely knit union with God and of the unity of the whole human race" (*LG* 1). It is fair to define the church as sacrament in so far as by the church one means the church as the bride of Christ, celebrating her liturgical union with him. One may then, by means of this definition, somewhat extend the range of the term "sacrament" beyond the seven dogmatically defined sacraments of the church. *Sacrosanctam Concilium* does this when it claims that the mission of the church is achieved by using the sacramental powers which God invests in or through her:

> Just as Christ was sent by the Father, so also He sent the Apostles, filled with the Holy Spirit. This he did that, by preaching the gospel ... they might proclaim that the Son of God, by his death and resurrection, had freed us from the power of Satan and from death, and brought us into the kingdom of His Father. His purpose also was that they might accomplish the work of salvation which they had proclaimed by means of sacrifice and sacraments, around which the entire liturgical life revolves. Thus by baptism men are plunged into the paschal mystery of Christ: they die with Him, are buried with Him, and rise with Him; they receive the spirit of adoption as sons "in which we cry Abba, Father" (Rom 8.15), and thus become true adorers whom the Father seeks ... To accomplish so great a work, Christ is always present in His Church, especially in her liturgical celebrations. He is present in the sacrifice of the Mass, not only in the person of His minister, "the same now offering, through the ministry of priests, who formerly offered himself on the cross", but especially under the Eucharistic species. By his power He is present in the sacraments, so that when a man baptizes it is really Christ Himself who baptizes. He is present in His word, since it is He Himself who speaks when the holy scriptures are read in the Church. He is present, lastly, when the Church prays and sings, for He promises, "Where two or three are gathered together in my name, there am I in the midst of them" (Matt 18.20). (*SC* 6–7)

As the sacrament of Christ, the church is the Mystical Body of Christ. Christ is the active agent within the life of the church. As Pius XII expressed it in *Mystici Corporis Christi* (1943), "Our Savior is continually pouring out his gifts of counsel, fortitude, fear and piety, especially on the leading members of his Body ... When the Sacraments of the Church are administered by external rite, it is He who produces their effect in souls" (*MCC* 51). The encyclical depicts the effects of the seven sacraments, the clearest expression of the continuation of the Incarnation in the life of the church (*MCC* 18–20).

The whole of creation is a living language which expresses the self-giving love of the Trinity. The moon itself can be to us a sign of the blessed sacrament:

Do you see there stands the moon?—
It is but half in view
And yet it is round and beautiful!
So too are many things
We lightly laugh to scorn,
Because our eyes fail to see. (From Matthias Claudius's "Abendlied")

The gift quality of a sudden glimpse of a full moon evokes the gift of God himself in the Eucharist: "For the first thing about Christianity is that it is a gift of God to men, and, because God is not a mean giver, it is the most beautiful gift possible ... [T]he gift is indeed truly the crystallized ... love of the giver: God in the form of his given-ness" (von Balthasar 1975: 11–15). But the fact that all creation is a sign of the Passion does not mean that the Eucharist is itself just a sign. Rather, it is the "crystallized ... love of the giver."

EXTREME UNCTION

Mystici Corporis Christi notes that, just as a human body "is given the proper means to provide for its own life, health and growth, and for that of all its members," so "the Savior of mankind ... has provided ... for His Mystical Body, endowing it with sacraments, so that, as through an uninterrupted series of graces, its members should be sustained from birth to death" (*MCC* 18). The encyclical conceives of the sacrament of extreme unction as being administered at death: "like a devoted mother, the Church is at the bedside of those who are sick unto death; and if it be not always God's will that by the holy anointing she restore health to the mortal body, nevertheless she administers spiritual medicine to the wounded soul and sends new citizens to heaven" (*MCC* 19). The image of Christ the healer is primitive, deriving its force from the early patristic conception of the power and scope of baptism. The sacrament of extreme unction could be taken as redistributing some of the powers which were originally concentrated in the baptismal event, reapportioning some of the medicinal efficacy of baptism to the needs of those in mortal illness. Extreme unction, or the sacrament of the sick, as it came to be designated after Vatican II (cf. *SC* 73–75), is a personal encounter with Christ in the capacity so vividly attested in his earthly ministry, as healer.

HOLY ORDERS

All baptized Christians are incorporated into the priesthood of Christ. Thomas Aquinas notes that "the whole rite of the Christian religion is derived from Christ's priesthood. Consequently, it is clear that the sacramental character is specially the character of

Christ, to Whose character the faithful are likened by reason of the sacramental characters, which are nothing else than certain participations of Christ's priesthood, flowing from Christ himself" (*ST* III, q.63, a.3). The sacramental character (which Thomas Aquinas compares to a tattoo) is the mark left on the human soul by the sacraments. This mark is a badge enabling us to worship God rightly: "in a sacramental character Christ's faithful have a share in his Priesthood; in the sense that as Christ has the full power of a spiritual priesthood, so his faithful are likened to him by sharing a certain spiritual power with regard to the sacraments and to things pertaining to divine worship" (*ST* III, q.63, a.5). All Christians share in Christ's priesthood, and are "priests" in the broad sense of the term, of "God-worshippers," liturgants.

Those who receive the sacrament of holy orders are given in addition to the common priesthood the capacity to represent Christ as his ministers. Holy orders is the sacramental means whereby the priesthood of Christ is extended and transmitted within the human race. This priesthood is at the service of all the baptized, enabling the sacramental character instilled in them at baptism and confirmation to grow and bear fruit. Those anointed with the Holy Spirit in the sacrament of holy orders encounter Christ the High Priest, and are integrated into this divine priesthood. This integration enables them to sow the seed of grace, to confect and administer the sacraments, whether or not they are humanly worthy to do so. Scheeben notes that the cleric's capacity to nourish the faithful through the Eucharist and to guide them into all truth "presupposes that the priesthood of the Church is truly the bride of Christ and the organ of the Holy Spirit" (Scheeben 2006: 550). The clergy exhibit the motherhood of the church. Charles Journet compared the Holy Spirit's spiritual "siring" of Christ in Mary to the way in which the Spirit gives ordained priests the power to "create" the sacraments:

> the power of order, the priesthood ... as a mere instrument indeed of the divine omnipotence, brings forth children at Baptism, prepares them for the struggle of life at Confirmation, nourishes them with eucharistic Bread, cleanses them of their stains and heals their infirmities by Penance and Extreme Unction; and finally renews and perpetuates itself by the conferring of Orders. On the day of the Annunciation the Holy Spirit gave a mysterious fecundity to Our Lady, making her the Mother of Christ and consequently the Mother of all men. This fecundity he now communicates, in a different and analogical manner ... to the power of order, to the priesthood, so that it may bring the eucharistic Christ into the world and generate the Church which is His Body. (Journet 1955: 95)

The point of comparison is the Virgin Mary's miraculous fertility, her conceiving Christ, and the priest's making the bread of the Mass into the body of Christ. Both happen through the power of the Holy Spirit.

There are three degrees of holy orders: episcopal being the top notch for bishops, presbyterial for priests, and diaconal for deacons. The sacrament of holy orders can only be conferred by a bishop, that is, one of the successors of the apostles. Holy orders is genealogically tied to Christ's choosing of the twelve during his earthly ministry.

MATRIMONY

Marriage is a sacrament because the relation between Christ and his body the church is that between a bridegroom and a bride. As a *sign* matrimony represents the bond between Christ and his church; as an instrument of sanctification, marriage supplies the grace of union between man and wife. This symbolism has a wide-ranging biblical basis, beginning with Hosea and Ezekiel's conception of Israel as the—often errant—spouse of the Lord, and culminating in St. Paul's "nuptial mysticism":

> Be subject to one another out of reverence for Christ. Wives, be subject to your husbands, as to the Lord. For the husband is the head of the wife as Christ is the head of the church, his body, and is himself its Savior. As the church is subject to Christ, so let wives also be subject in everything to their husbands. Husbands, love your wives, as Christ loved the church and gave himself up for her, that he might sanctify her, having cleansed her by the washing of water with the word, that he might present the church to himself in splendor, without spot or wrinkle or any such thing, that she might be holy, and without blemish. Even so husbands should love their wives as their own bodies. He who loves his wife loves himself. For no man ever hates his own flesh, but nourishes and cherishes it, as Christ does the Church, because we are members of his body. "For this reason a man shall leave his father and mother and be joined to his wife, and the two shall become one flesh." This mystery is a profound one, and I am saying that it refers to Christ and the church; however, let each one of you love his wife as himself, and let the wife see that she respects her husband. (Eph 5:21–33).

St. Paul's ecclesial and Christological midrash on Adam's exhortation to Eve in Genesis 2 led after a millennium to the formal inclusion of matrimony amongst the sacraments of the church. Alongside Paul, there is also the Johannine witness to the bridal form of the church. In John's Gospel, the wedding at Cana is Jesus' first miracle, and Revelation 22:17 refers to the bride. When Jesus lays peculiar emphasis on the indissolubility of marriage (Mt 19:8) that is because of what matrimony means.

The Council of Trent stated that,

> The first parent of the human race, under the influence of the divine Spirit, pronounced the bond of matrimony perpetual and indissoluble, when he said; "This now is bone of my bones, and flesh of my flesh. Wherefore a man shall leave father and mother, and shall cleave to his wife, and they shall be two in one flesh." But, that by this bond two only are united and joined together, our Lord taught more plainly, when … He … confirmed the firmness of that tie, proclaimed so long before by Adam, by these words; "What therefore God hath joined together, let no man put asunder." But, the grace which might perfect that natural love, and confirm that indissoluble union, and sanctify the married, Christ Himself, the institutor and perfecter of the venerable sacraments, merited for us by His passion; as the Apostle

Paul intimates, saying: "Husbands love your wives, as Christ also loved the Church, and delivered himself up for it"; adding shortly after, "This is a great sacrament, but I speak in Christ and in the Church." ... [T]herefore matrimony ... is to be numbered amongst the sacraments of the new law. (Trent, Session 24)

PENANCE

The normal term for the sacrament of penance is "confession": no-one has ever said, "I'm off to the sacrament of penance." Confession differs from the other sacraments in that, like an appendectomy, or a *Marathon Man*-type encounter with a dentist, it surgically extracts toxic material, rather than elevating or consecrating a material thing. In the sacrament of confession, sins confessed to a priest are forgiven and the chain of the penitent to his sin is removed. This occurs by "the power of Christ's passion," which "operates through the priest's absolution and the acts of the penitent, who co-operates with grace unto the destruction of his sin" (Aquinas, *ST* III, q.84, a.5). This sacrament signifies and brings about absolution from sins. The author of the grace of penance is God, acting through his human clerical representatives: "God alone absolves from sins and forgives sins authoritatively; yet priests do both ministerially, because the words of the priest in the sacrament work as instruments of the divine power ... because it is the divine power that works inwardly in all the sacramental signs" (*ST* III, q.84, a.3, ad3).

St. Thomas argued that all the sacraments were instituted by Christ (so the sacraments say and do what Christ intended them to say and do). But he traced the institution of confession to the episode in which Jesus gives Peter the keys of the kingdom, to bind and to loose (Mt 16:19: see *ST* III, q.84, a.3, ad1, and q.84, a.7). Thomas says the "form" of the sacrament of confession comes from Jesus' empowerment of Peter with the "keys." He also mentions the scene in Luke 24:47, when the resurrected Christ teaches that "penance and remission of sins should be preached in his name unto all nations." It seems more plausible to connect the institution to a command of the resurrected Christ than to Peter's installation, at Caesarea Philippi. In the latter, Jesus seems to be conferring a jurisdictional office on Peter, not giving him the power to expunge sins.

Adrienne von Speyr traces the origin of the sacrament of confession to the upper room, when the risen Jesus said to the disciples, "'As the Father has sent me, even so I send you.' And when he had said this, he breathed on them, and said to them, 'Receive the Holy Spirit. If you forgive the sins of any, they are forgiven; if you retain the sins of any, they are retained'" (John 20:22–23). It makes sense to think of the resurrected Christ as instituting the sacrament of confession because his doing so is an exegesis of his Passion, which naturally occurs after and not before it, and in answer to the question the gathered disciples must have for him:

The risen Christ owed the apostles ... an explanation why he had died and was once more alive, why he had utterly failed and yet conquered, why he had suffered and was now rejoicing, why he had left them and was back among them ... There was no question to be put to the Lord ... which was not already answered ... by his words of institution ... [T]he words of institution illuminated the Passion from within, revealed its central meaning and purpose, so central that the faith of the apostles was required for the disclosure of the inner connection between the Passion and confession ... [T]he words of institution point back to [the Passion] ... and cannot be explained apart from it. Conversely, too, the Passion can only be explained through these words. (von Speyr 1985: 83–84)

The penitent has to lay himself open for the priest's surgical operation. An entire anthropology could rest on the sacrament of confession, so well does this act of self-revelation exhibit our humanity:

The Lord became man to manifest to us the intense life of the Trinity ... [A]s his living intercourse with the Father in the Spirit does not prevent the Son from being fully man, but ... makes him perfectly so, the Christian in confessing is not thereby less a man, but rather more mature and responsible. The act in which he participates to receive absolution is ... of divine ordinance and so pertains to the sphere of the institutional Church. It is nonetheless, something personal, a matter of individual responsibility, and thus fully human. (von Speyr 1985: 97)

For the Thomist Charles Journet, the priest who performs the sacraments acts purely as a transparent instrument or transmitter through which the power of God passes. Outside the sacraments, exercising his jurisdictional functions within the church, the priest may exercise "second causality," and use his own wits, but not in the exercise of his liturgical office (Journet 1955: 124–126).

Adrienne von Speyr offers a somewhat different picture. She suggests that, in confession, the priest has to assess and decide whether to forgive the sins of the penitent ("If you forgive the sins of any, they are forgiven; if you retain the sins of any, they are retained," John 20:22–23; von Speyr 1985: 63). When the priest says the words of institution at the Mass, he "does as he was told," in pure obedience. He "quotes" Christ's words, and they achieve their effect (Sokolowski 1993: 14–15, 91–94). But when the priest remits sins, he must have some inner grasp and comprehension of what he and the penitent are up to. The power to forgive sins relies on the Holy Spirit ("Receive the Holy Spirit"!). But the apostles (and their descendants) "were required" here "to serve ... as persons having insight of their own. Their understanding and will were used as tools for the Spirit's action and in union with him" (von Speyr 1985: 63–64). This seems phenomenologically accurate. St. Thomas may have been aware of the need for nuance here, to indicate the surgical probing incumbent upon the priest in order to cut out and destroy the toxic material of sin: perhaps that is why he cites the episode at Caesarea Philippi as the institution of this sacrament. There is something "jurisdictional" about the act of absolving sins.

Just as the priest is empowered at confession, so Christ is empowered to send the Holy Spirit on the disciples at his own volition:

> After Easter the conqueror of sin had the fulness of power which he could impart to the apostles. He had come back to them with a new experience, that of having suffered and died for sinners. The experience of redemption he had acquired in his own person for God and man ... It was as Redeemer that he gave to his apostles the gift of the Holy Spirit; there is no mention of any request to the Father or any permission from him. He gave them the Spirit entirely on his own, and yet, in so doing, he made over to them a mystery of the Trinity in God; for the Holy Spirit must have been ready and in agreement to be sent by him into his Church. The Son made use of the Spirit for the purpose of the redemption, and the apostles had a share in this power of the Son's, applying it as they saw fit. It was as if the Son, who before his death was the servant of the Father, now wished to make more evident his independent domination; but the independence of a divine Person, when emphasized, often serves to show more clearly the unity of mind and will of all three. The will of the Son is the same as that of the Spirit, and since the Son's will is always the revelation of the Father's will, the latter is also the will of the Spirit. In what the Son spoke on this occasion, there is no mention of the Father; he was as if hidden in the Son and the Spirit, and yet revealed along with them in the will of both. But what the Father willed to reveal through being thus hidden was the mission of the Son. The Son is not just a servant or instrument; he shares explicitly in the Father's power, communicated to him by the Father without restriction. The disposition made by the Son on this occasion shows clearly that nothing, not even his Passion and death, happened through weakness or limitation. Had the Son said: "I have asked the Father that I may give you the Spirit ... " he would indeed have been an emissary, but not the eternal Son. When he was on the cross, he handed over all to the Father, even his Spirit, so unreservedly that now it was the Father's will to manifest in all its splendour the power inherent in the Son. (von Speyr 1985: 64–65)

Confession is an overtly Trinitarian sacrament, because whereas "Communion is what Christ is," confession is "what he does," in the Spirit and for the Father (von Speyr 1985: 96).

Confirmation

Adam Möhler described the visible manifestation of the Spirit at Pentecost in tongues of flames as being in keeping with the tangible and visible character of the Incarnation (Möhler 1997: 260). Pentecost was the last liturgical gesture of the historical Jesus, a kind of backhand wave after the Ascension. The outpouring of the Spirit which Christ promised, in John 16:7 ("If I go not, the Paraclete will not come to you, but if I go, I will send him to you"), comes about on Pentecost. He instituted the sacrament by anticipation and in promissory form. Confirmation is the "charismatic sacrament, the reception of the Holy Spirit, and it could not come about until after the ascension: 'As yet the Spirit was not given, because Jesus was not yet glorified'" (*ST* III, q.72, a.1, citing John 7:39). The purpose of this charismatic sacrament is the reception of the Spirit "for strength in the spiritual combat."

> Wherefore in this sacrament three things are necessary ... The first of these is the cause conferring fulness of spiritual strength which cause is the Blessed Trinity: and this is expressed in the words, "In the name of the Father," etc. The second is the spiritual strength bestowed on man unto salvation by the sacrament of visible matter; and this is referred to in the words, "I confirm thee with the chrism of salvation." The third is the sign which is given to the combatant, as in a bodily combat: thus are soldiers marked with the sign of their leaders. And to this refer the words, "I sign thee with the sign of the cross," in which sign, to wit, our King triumphed (cf. Col 2:15). (*ST* III, q.72, a.4)

Confirmation is a mark of sanctifying grace: "In this sacrament ... the Holy Ghost is given to the baptized for strength: just as he was given to the apostles on the day of Pentecost ... and just as he was given to the baptized by the imposition of the apostles' hands, as related in Acts 8:17 ... [T]he Holy Ghost is not sent or given except with sanctifying grace" (*ST* III, q.72, a.7).

BAPTISM

Baptism is "the sacrament of faith," the sacrament by which one signifies one's faith and is initiated into the life of faith (*ST* III, q.69, a.5; q.66, a.1, ad1; q.68, a.9, obj.1). In the waters of baptism, sins are washed away, whilst the believer is incorporated into the death of Christ which baptism symbolizes (Rom 6:3–4). Baptism re-enacts the death and resurrection of Christ, and thereby makes the believer a member of this once dead but now eternally living body. The believer's act of faith that Christ died and rose again after three days is not an autonomous act of faith or belief in Christ. Rather, the believer has faith in and through other members of the body. As the belief of one who is incorporated into the whole body of Christ, baptismal faith is a communal, ecclesial act. In entering the body of Christ, the believer puts on the mind of Christ. At baptism, believers "receive salvation not by their own act, but by the act of the Church" (*ST* III, q.68, a.8, ad1). And so, in a sense, the church believes for them or on their behalf. The entirety of what any one believer has faith in is believed by the church as a whole, not by numerous individuals as such.

Baptism is the "door of the sacraments," and the sacraments were created "for a remedy against sins, and for the perfecting of the soul in things pertaining to the divine worship" (*ST* III, q.69, a.5; q.63, a.3). Thus it is through baptism that we begin to worship God in the right way. So baptism initiates us into the "common priesthood" of the church, instilling in us the "character" or mark of Christ the high priest who worshipped the Father perfectly. "Baptism operates by the power of Christ's passion, which is the universal remedy of all sins" (*ST* III, q.69, a.1, ad2); "by Baptism man is incorporated into the very death of Christ," and "Christ's death satisfied sufficiently for sins" (*ST* III, q.68, a.5).

Maximus the Confessor reminds us that calling God "Father" is a grace, and not simply a human right: "through the prayer which grants us the right to address God as 'Father,' we learn of our very genuine adoption through the grace of the Holy Spirit" (Maximus 1982: 103). This grace is given to us at baptism.

Eucharist

Henri de Lubac had a well-known phrase which was often cited by John Paul II and by Benedict XVI: "The Eucharist makes the Church." The Eucharist makes the church by unifying its members with Christ and thus with one another: "Because there is one bread, we who are many are one body, for we all partake of the one bread" (1 Cor 10:17). Thus, the eleventh century author Placidus wrote, "*Ecclesia, corpus Christi effecta*" (de Lubac 1949: 103–104). Thomas Aquinas says that "the Eucharist is a figure" of "the union of Christ with the Church" (*ST* III, q.65, a.3).

For Thomas, the Eucharist is the greatest sacrament, because, whereas Christ works *through* the other sacraments, the Eucharistic sacrament *is* "Christ himself substantially" (*ST* III, q.65, a.3). The *form* of the other sacraments derives from *words* spoken by Christ in his earthly ministry; the form of the Eucharist *is* Christ himself, the Word in person. Although not all theologians concur about the preeminence of the Eucharist, the use of speech tends to favor St. Thomas's opinion: Catholics habitually refer to the Eucharist as "the sacrament." The Eucharist resonates with all the sacraments, containing the healing force of extreme unction, the unitive force of matrimony, the "adoptive" element of baptism.

The Eucharist *is* Christ and means the church, "Christ's mystical body, which is the fellowship of the saints." So "whoever receives this sacrament, expresses thereby that he is made one with Christ, and incorporated in his members; and this is done by faith" (*ST* III, q.79, a.4). In a prayer which is used today in preparation for "the sacrament," Thomas asks,

> Grant … that I may receive not only the sacrament of the Body and Blood of our Lord, but also its full grace and power. Give me the grace, most merciful God, to receive the body of your only Son, our Lord Jesus Christ … in such a manner that I may deserve to be intimately united with His mystical body and to be numbered among his members. Most loving Father, grant that I may behold for all eternity face to face your beloved Son, whom now … I am about to receive under the sacramental veil. (*Latin-English Booklet Missal* 1998)

Incorporation into the mystical body is not automatically consequent upon reception of the Eucharist, but depends on the Eucharist being received with pure and fervent grace (itself a grace of God).

This prayer is directed to the Father. The whole eucharistic liturgy of the Mass is directed to the Father (von Balthasar 1982: 575). As an iconic channeling of the Passion at Calvary, the eucharistic sacrifice is a death offered by the Son to the Father. "The gift of his love and obedience to the point of giving his life … is in the first place a gift to his Father. Certainly it is a gift given for our sake … Yet it is *first and foremost a gift to the Father*." The Father accepted this gift and " 'gave … in return for this total self-giving by his Son … his own paternal gift, that is to say the grant of new immortal life in the resurrection' " (John Paul II, *Ecclesia de Eucharistia* 13 citing *Redemptor Hominis* 20). The resurrection of Christ is evidence that, as a result of his sacrifice, the power of sin is overthrown, and we are no longer in thrall to death. Christ gave his body and poured out his blood in order to respond to the Father's absolute rejection of sin with an act of absolute loving obedience: Christ "overcame through his action that which provokes the anger" of the Father, that is, the sin which puts us at a distance from God. Christ's

> charity conquered the malevolence in which we are caught. "The wrath of God toward the denial of divine love encounters a divine love, that of the Son, that exposes itself to this wrath and disarms it and, literally renders it objectless. Jesus took upon himself the greatest alienation, the greatest distance there could be between God and his creatures, and extinguished it through his obedience. This was … his conquest, and it was revealed and confirmed by his Resurrection from the dead." (Sokolowski 1993: 61, citing von Balthasar 1992: 326)

The sacramental life is a process of filiation to God. Nicholas Cabasilas claims that, unlike "slaves" or "hirelings," "sons are the ones who neither under fear of threats nor out of desire for the promises, but through the character and habit of the soul's voluntary tendency and disposition toward goodness, are never cut off from God: like that son, to whom it was said, 'Son, thou art ever with me, and all that I have is thine.' For by their state in grace they may really be what God is believed to be and is both as the author of goodness, and by His nature" (Cabasilas 1974: 110).

Suggested Reading

Aquinas (1981); Dobzsay (2010); von Speyr (1985).

Bibliography

Aquinas, Thomas (1966), *Commentary on Galatians*, trans. F. R. Larcher (Albany, NY: Magi Books).

Aquinas, Thomas (1981), *Summa Theologica*, 5 vols., trans. Dominicans of the English Province (Westminster, MD: Christian Classics).

Cabasilas, Nicholas (1974), *The Life in Christ*, trans. Carmino J. DeCatanzaro (Crestwood, NY: St. Vladimir's Seminary Press).

de Lubac, Henri (1949), *Corpus Mysticum: L'Eucharistie et l'église au moyen âge* (Paris: Aubier).

Dobzsay, Lázló (2010), *The Restoration and Organic Development of the Roman Rite*, ed. Laurence Paul Hemming (London: T&T Clark).

John Paul II, *Ecclesia de Eucharistia*, 2003.

Journet, Charles (1955), *The Church of the Word Incarnate: An Essay in Speculative Theology. Volume One: The Apostolic Hierarchy*, trans. A. H. C. Downes (London: Sheed & Ward).

Latin-English Booklet Missal (1998) (Glenview, IL: Coalition in Support of Ecclesia Dei).

Levering, Matthew (2005), *Sacrifice and Community: Jewish Offering and Christian Eucharist* (Oxford: Blackwell).

Maximus the Confessor (1982), *The Church, the Liturgy and the Soul of Man: The Mystagogia of St. Maximus the Confessor*, trans. Dom Julian Stead, O.S.B. (Still River, MA: St. Bede's). von Balthasar, Hans Urs (1975), *Elucidations*, trans. John Riches (San Francisco, CA: Ignatius Press).

Möhler, Johann Adam (1997), *Symbolism: Exposition of the Doctrinal Differences between Catholics and Protestants as Evidenced by their Symbolical Writings*, trans. James Burton Robertson (New York: Crossroad).

O'Connor, Flannery (1979), *Letters of Flannery O'Connor: The Habit of Being*, edited Sally Fitzgerald (New York: Farrar, Straus and Giroux).

Scheeben, Matthias Joseph (2006), *The Mysteries of Christianity*, trans. Cyril Vollert (New York: Crossroad).

Sokolowski, Robert (1993), *Eucharistic Presence: A Study in the Theology of Disclosure* (Washington, DC: Catholic University of America).

von Balthasar, Hans Urs (1982), *Glory of the Lord: A Theological Aesthetics*, vol. 1: *Seeing the Form*, trans. Erasmo Leiva-Merikakis (Edinburgh: T&T Clark).

von Balthasar, Hans Urs (1991), *Glory of the Lord: A Theological Aesthetics*, vol. 6, *The Old Covenant*, trans. Brian McNeil and Erasmo Leiva-Merikakis (Edinburgh: T&T Clark).

von Balthasar, Hans Urs (1989), *Glory of the Lord: A Theological Aesthetics*, vol. 7, *The New Covenant*, trans. Brian McNeil (Edinburgh: T&T Clark).

von Balthasar, Hans Urs (1992), *Theo-Drama: Theological Dramatic Theory*, vol. 3, *The Dramatis Personae: The Person in Christ*, trans. Graham Harrison (San Francisco: Ignatius Press).

von Speyr, Adrienne (1985), *Confession*, trans. Douglas W. Stott (San Francisco, CA: Ignatius Press).

....

CHAPTER 41

SIGNS OF THE ESCHATOLOGICAL EKKLESIA: THE SACRAMENTS, THE CHURCH, AND ESCHATOLOGY

....

PETER J. LEITHART

KEEP it concrete, I tell my students. Theologians are tempted to drift about in vehicles constructed from grand abstractions, forgetting that all Christian theology is pastoral theology. Even the most arcane investigation aims to serve the church's life and mission. So: keep it concrete.

This counsel might seem relatively easy to observe in sacramental theology, since sacraments are, by definition, created materials and cultural products actively used in the liturgy and life of embodied humans who assemble in actual communities. Yet a cursory glance at the history of sacramental disputes reviewed elsewhere in this book shows that sacramental theology has been drawn away again and again from the concrete occasions of sacramental performance. Eucharistic debates raise questions about substance and accidents, modes of presence, the nature of bodies, the theory of signs, the relation of heaven and earth, the crossover of divine and human attributes in Christ. Disputes about baptism have been fewer, and less philosophical. Post-Reformation disputes have often focused on details about the rite itself (immersion v. some other mode) or the proper subjects of baptism (infants v. professing believers). In the early church, though, baptism was implicated in the Donatist and Pelagian controversies, which entwined baptismal theology with questions about primary and secondary causality, the nature of sin and its transmission, the distinction of validity and efficacy, and the precise nature of sacramental grace.

Such efforts to fill in the scaffolding of sacramental theology are necessary, especially when the church has to deal with deviant teachers. But scaffolding is not a building, and fundamental sacramental theology should be worked out not from the philosophical supports for the gospel, but from the gospel itself.

In this chapter, I strive to heed my own advice. I propose to do so by framing sacramental theology within an eschatological ecclesiology that is, I argue, inherent in the Christian gospel. To maintain a pastoral focus, I draw mainly from the universal source of Christian theology, the Bible, and particularly from the apostle Paul. Paul did not formulate sacramental theology in the leisure of a faculty office or a library reading room, but in the rough bustle of planting and leading churches. From Paul, it emerges that baptism and the Lord's Supper are signs of the new community that the Christian church is, and hence also criteria by which the lives of the members and communities are measured (Williams 1987; 1996).

Making Peace

In the beginning, the Creator created the world and humanity very good. Because of Adam's sin, the human race was excluded from the garden of God's presence and from the tree of life. When mankind filled the earth with violence, the Creator decreated and selected a new Adam, Noah, to reboot humanity. Postdiluvian humanity fell into Adamic hubris at Babel, and Yahweh scattered the nations and confused their languages.

This is the setting in which Israel's history began, when Yahweh called Abram from Ur and promised him a land and a great seed. Abram's family was to be a restored human race and the Creator's instrument for renewing the rest of humanity and the creation (cf. Wright 2013: 456–537). Throughout Israel's often rebellious history, Yahweh never deviated from his plan to reunite the human race at the last, to accomplish a reversal of Babel through the seed of Abraham, to form a community of table companions (cf. Wells 2006). The prophets reiterated Yahweh's purpose to gather the Gentiles to form one human race who will praise him with one lip (e.g. Isa 2:2–4). Over time, Israel became a mirror of the divided world, as much in need of healing and reunion as the Gentiles. So long as humanity, and Israel, remained divided, the one God's work could not be finished.

Under Torah, Israel had "sacraments," known in medieval Christian theology as the "sacraments of the Old Law." Those signs simultaneously symbolized Israel's privileged status before Yahweh and communicated the provisionality of the Torah. Circumcision was a sign of Yahweh's covenant with Israel, but the cut in the flesh signified the division between Jew and Gentile in the body of humanity. Purity regulations repetitively reenacted the division of circumcision. Yahweh dwelt within Israel and, as hospitable host, invited his people to his home and his altar table. Still, he hid, first behind tent curtains and later the walls and doors of the temple. Only priests entered, and only under specified conditions. Israel gathered in the Lord's court to worship and feast, but even the circumcised were not given full access to the presence of Yahweh and his life-giving food. They crossed the threshold of Yahweh's house only through representative animals that were turned to smoke on the altar. Israel's "sacraments" were *effective* signs, creating and maintaining the welcome and purification, as well as the exclusions and separations that they signified. Israel's "sacraments" also served as criteria for judging Israel's faithfulness to Yahweh. Intermarriage with idolatrous Gentiles, for example, was an offense against the special status signified by circumcision. Sacrificing to the Baals violated the covenant and the covenant-renewal effected by Israel's offerings at the temple.

Israel's signs were prophetic of better things to come. The repetitive nature of the sacrifices, and the fact that Israel stood at a distance from Yahweh, were signs that the Abrahamic promise awaited fulfillment. Torah's "sacramental system" was a system of exclusion and distance, instituted until Yahweh fulfilled his promise to Abraham and the nations. When that day came, the signs of Israel would give way to effective signs of union and welcome.

The gospel announces the fulfillment of the promises to Abraham (cf. Luke 1:54–55, 70–73). Raised from the dead, Jesus is the eschatological Adam (ἔσχατος Ἀδάμ, 1 Cor 15:45), the last man and the head of the promised new humanity. Jesus tears the curtain that separated God from Israel, bringing many sons to glory, and in uniting his disciples to his Father he also forms a renewed, *unified* humanity. By the cross, he breaks down the dividing wall between Jew and Gentile (Eph 2:11–22), and after his ascension he sends the Spirit who transforms the disciples into an anti-Babel, speaking a language understood by *all* nations (Acts 2). Jesus will return to judge, but *already* the eschatological form of the human race has been established on earth, in concrete reality, as the *ekklesia*, an assembly from every tribe and tongue and nation. As last Adam, Jesus revolutionizes the sacramental order that organizes the people of God. In place of sacraments of exclusion and division, he establishes effective signs of reconciliation and intimate communion, and he fulfills the promise inherent in the old sacraments of distance by instituting sacraments of hospitality. The signs of provisionality yield to eschatological signs of finality. As Augustine put it, the sacraments of the old law were promises of things to come, while the sacraments of the new are proofs of their fulfillment (Augustine 2007). Christian sacraments are signs that the eschatological *ekklesia* has now arrived though the Son and Spirit, signs that make what they announce and do what they signify. Humanity is social, and the salvation of humanity must thus take a social form. That social form of salvation is the church (de Lubac 1998).

In what follows, I show in detail that Paul's teaching on baptism and the Lord's Supper follows this eschatological ecclesio-logic.

Is Christ Divided?

The New Testament's most elaborate treatment of what we, anachronistically, call "sacramental theology" appears in Paul's first letter to the Corinthians. It is also, significantly, the letter that focuses most deliberately on the problem of schism and "heresy." Christian signs and schism are radically contrasted at the beginning of the epistle. He chides the

Corinthians for the σχίσματα and ἔριδες among the members (1:10–11). Factions have attached themselves to a favored teacher, Paul, Peter, Apollos, of Christ (v. 12). Paul can barely contain his outrage at the sacrilege: "Is Christ divided into parts (μεμέρισται ὁ Χριστός)? Was Paul crucified for you?" If Paul had suffered for the Corinthians, it would make sense for them to baptize in the name of Paul, for baptism is the rite that joins the baptized to the crucified. In reality, baptism is into the name of Jesus, and that means that all the baptized are members of one body, joined to one another because joined to Christ. Because it is applied equally to all, baptism is the effective sign of this one-bodiness, a ritual announcement of the fulfillment of Abrahamic promise. It is also a criterion of faithfulness: Paul weighs the Corinthians in the balance of baptism and finds them wanting.

It is worth pausing over baptism "in the name" (εἰς τὸ ὄνομα), which appears regularly in baptismal formulae (Matt 28:19; Acts 2:38; 8:16; 10:48; 19:5). At the most superficial level, this indicates that baptism confers a new name, and, Paul stresses, it is a surname rather than a given name. Each of the baptized says, "I am Christ, I am Christ, I am Christ," like the "Je suis Jacques, Je suis Jacques" of Dickens's *sans culottes*. In common Greek, "in the name" has a financial and commercial connotation, indicating a transfer of money or property from one person's account "into the name" of another (Hartman 2000: 38). Had the Corinthians been baptized into the name of Paul, they would be Paul's slaves. This Paul vehemently denies: those sealed by baptism belong to Jesus as his flock, field, land, servants, family, army (cf. Lampe 1951). Later in 1 Corinthians, Paul say that since the Corinthians have been "washed ... in the name of the Lord Jesus and in the Spirit," they are "sanctified and justified," judged just and claimed as holy ones (6:11). As holy things, they are the holy God's personal property. Baptism "in the name" authorizes the baptized to say, with the bride of the Song of Songs, "I am his, he is mine."

Paul's question about a divided "Christ" highlights the deep Christological link between church and sign. Instead of asking about divisions within the "*body* of Christ," Paul uses *Christ* to describe the community associated with Jesus, anticipating Augustine's later concept of the head-and-body *totus Christus*. Admittedly, Paul's point may be somewhat indirect: it is possible that Paul does not identify the community *itself* as "Christ," but rather stresses that division in the community is tantamount to a division of Christ because all who are in the community are in Christ. Whatever we make of Paul's question in chapter 1, the notion of *totus Christus* is clearly present in chapter 12, where Paul directly compares the one-body-and-many-member nature of the human body to "Christ" (v. 12). *Christ*, not "Christ's body," is one body with many members. Importantly, Paul immediately brings up baptism again as a sign of the unification of the one body by the one Spirit (ἐν ἑνὶ πνεύματι ἡμεῖς πάντες εἰς ἓν σῶμα ἐβαπτίσθημεν, v. 13).

In chapter 12, baptism signifies the unified community forged from the ethnic, religious, and social diversity of humanity. Jews and Greeks, slave and free, are all baptized by the Spirit into the one body that is Christ, and so are incorporated—bodied together—as members of Christ. As in Galatians 3:29, baptism is the solvent of *natural* social, ethnic, religious, and sexual differences. Within the body, however, there are *pneumatic* differences, as the Spirit distributes gifts in varying proportions to each member baptized into the body (vv. 4–11). Baptism does not signify an undifferentiated unity or a chaos of disorder, but a complexly ordered community. As a sign of *this* ecclesial form, it is a sign of inaugurated eschatology. Baptism is a flood (cf. 1 Pet 3:20–21). When it has washed away the old, what emerges is a new social *cosmos*.

Baptism is mentioned only once in 1 Corinthians 12, but the entire chapter contributes to baptismal theology. As the Spirit's instrument, baptism joins diverse people into a unified body and gives that body its shape and vitality. Because each is grafted in as a member of the body, each is necessary. Feet should not indulge low self-esteem because they are not hands, nor should eyes preen themselves on their superiority to ears (vv. 15–21). In Christ's body, there are no vestigial organs. Paul's vision of community is dramatically new, undreamt by the democrats of Athens, for whom distinctions between citizen and non-citizens and between freeman and slave were immutable foundations of social order. Paul is even more revolutionary in what follows. The weaker and more shameful members are not despised, isolated, or marginalized, but rather "those members of the body, which we deem less honorable, on those we bestow more abundant honor" (v. 23). The fact that Paul roots this in sartorial custom (i.e. we "honor" unseemly members by covering them with clothing, while we display the more seemly members) should not obscure the novelty of the social idea he advocates: Not *Achilles* but his slave receives the abundant honor. In the eschatological *ekklesia*, the weakest are the subject of the focused care of the strong, and, even more radically, the weak are recognized as essential members of the community. So bound together are the members that each one's fortunes reverberate through the entire body (v. 26). Of this social vision, baptism is the ritual dramatization and the standard according to which the *ekklesia*'s performance is judged.

Paul's declaration in Ephesians 4:4–5 that there is "one baptism" makes the same point. Ephesians 2 ends with one of the New Testament's clearest and most exhilarating summaries of eschatological ecclesiology (vv. 11–22). In the cross, the excluded are brought near, strangers made citizens, the dividing wall is broken down, and the two halves of humanity bound into one new man, one human body. Gentiles are now co-citizens with the ἅγιοι, so that together with Jews they can form a single holy household, a temple of the Spirit (2:11–22). Paul begins an exhortation based on this good news (3:1), but it is aborted by a digression on Paul's own stewardship of the mystery (Eph 3). The exhortation from 2:11–22 does not arrive in full until 4:1: because Gentiles and Jews are one new humanity, they must "walk in a manner worthy of the calling with which you have been called," the call to unity (4:1). That walk requires "humility and gentleness, with patience ... forbearance ... love," diligence to "preserve the unity of the Spirit in the bond of peace" (4:2–3). The sevenfold unity that Paul declares in 4:4-6 shows the facets of the "one new man" whose birth from the cross was announced in chapter 2. In this new humanity, the unity of body and Spirit, of hope and faith, the submission to one Lord and Father, is signified by the rite of baptism. Baptism is "one" because it signifies and effects the newborn unified humanity. As in 1 Corinthians, Paul moves from a stress on the unity of the body to a discussion of the diverse gifts and roles within the church, affirming, with a combination of architectural and organic imagery, that each contributes to the *progress* of the body. Only as each member edifies the whole does the church grow up in love, strain toward her *telos*, and mature into her head, Christ. Baptism calls each to share in this construction project.

What baptism signifies as a one-time transition, the Lord's Supper reiterates as ongoing practice. Those baptized to constitute one body are *made* one as they share the bread of the Supper: "We are one because we all partake of the one loaf" (1 Cor 10:17). As with baptism, this unity among the members of the body is grounded in the common unity each member has with the head of the body in the Spirit. Because the blessed cup is participation (κοινωνία) in the blood of Christ, because the bread broken a participation (κοινωνία) in the body of Christ, the bread and wine feast forms the companions into a single body (v. 16). As believers eat together week after week, the Spirit tunes their bodies to the common life they share as one body.

The ecclesiological accent in Paul's treatment of the Lord's Supper clarifies Paul's later exhortations about the divisions at the Corinthian table and discerning the body. As at the beginning of the letter, Paul rebukes the Corinthians for their σχίσματα (11:18) that have become manifest at the very table that is supposed to be a sign of the church's unity in the one bread from heaven, Jesus. The Corinthians had conformed their eucharistic feasts to common pagan practice, in which the food and drink was distributed in proportion to social status (Detienne and Vernant 1998; Smith 2003). Nobles got more, slaves less; some gorged and got drunk, while others went away hungry. Such an inequitable distribution is so perverse that the Corinthian meal is no longer the Supper of the Lord (v. 20); it might as well be a feast of Bacchus. In this context, Paul urges the Corinthians to "discern the body" (διακρίνων τὸ σῶμα, 11:29). In some Christian traditions, this means that any participant who fails to grasp the mode of Christ's presence in the Supper becomes sick and weak, and may die (v. 30). As a result, in such traditions, the feeble, untutored, senile, and immature are barred from the table, lest they suffer God's judgment. Nothing in the context suggests that the real presence is remotely an issue for Paul. Here as elsewhere in 1 Corinthians, the problem is a concrete, pastoral, ecclesial one—division, discord, and factionalism. "Judging the body" rightly means living in accord with the unity of the body that Paul emphasizes throughout this letter, and all his others. It means living in accord with the reality of the eschatological *ekklesia* that assembles and is unified at the table. Like baptism, the Supper is a criterion to measure the church's performance.

An ecclesiological understanding of the Supper also clarifies another somewhat puzzling statement: "as often as you eat this bread and drink this cup, you proclaim the Lord's death until He comes" (11:26). Eating bread and drinking wine is a natural sign of an eschatological feast, as the Church Fathers insisted (Wainwright 2002). But Paul says that the meal shows forth the death of Jesus. How does a meal represent a *crucifixion*? The answer lies in Paul's claim that the crucifixion is the act by which God breaks down the barriers dividing Jew and Gentile, so as to form a new human being and a new race (Eph 2:11–22). When the church keeps the Supper without division or schism, when each member "judges the body" rightly, showing in empirical reality that the church is a unified body, she proves that Christ's death was effective in bursting through all barriers that divided human beings from God and one another. The church's common eating and drinking proclaims the death of Jesus in the same sense that it anticipates the eschaton when God's companions from all peoples, tribes, tongues, and nations celebrate the feast of the Lamb.

TABLE OF THE LORD, TABLE OF DEMONS

All this emphasis on the unity of the body threatens to turn Paul into an apostle of tolerant getting-along and letting-live. Paul's evangelical sacramental theology, his sacramental ecclesiology, has a double edge. Because it announces a new human race, united in Christ, it simultaneously rejects the way the world goes. Baptism and the Lord's table do not merely portray the outlines of the new community, but effectively mark off this new community from perverse anti-communities outside. Baptism incorporates, and so baptism also cuts a chasm between what used to be and what is, cutting as thoroughly but more deeply than circumcision. This surgery is essential to Paul's gospel. A unified humanity cannot be created without separation from the separated humanity that is the result of sin. Humanity can only be renewed if it first dies. The good news is that it has, in the cross of Jesus.

Baptism is a sign of this death. Paul's brief reference to the "washing ... in the name of Jesus" (1 Cor 6:11) is part of a contrast between "once" and "now": some of the Corinthians were formerly fornicators, idolaters, adulterers, drunks, homosexuals, but now, by the sanctifying wash of baptism, they have become God's precious possession (6:9–11). The imagery comes from Numbers, where plunder from conquered cities was purified with fire or water before it was added to Israel's store of treasure (Num 31:21–24). The Corinthians are Jesus' plunder, purified from the world into the kingdom. They are heirs of the kingdom only because they have been extracted from their idols and adulteries and given a share in the eschatological *ekklesia*.

Romans 6 makes a similar point. Romans 6, as the exegetes have observed, follows Romans 5. In the second half of the latter chapter, Paul surveys the history of the human race under the two "heads," Adam and Christ. By his disobedience, the first man condemned humanity to the dominion of Sin and Death. Life according to the flesh expresses itself in an Adamic form of human society—economic systems built on greed and oppression, politics dominated by the *libido dominandi*, social orders divided between the exploiting patricians and the exploited plebs. By the obedience of the last man (implicitly, on the cross), the reign of Death and Sin has given way to the reign in life of "those who receive the abundance of grace and the gift of righteousness" (5:17). The transition from the kingdom of Sin and Death to the kingdom of life and righteousness is effected by the death and resurrection of Jesus, a transition replicated in an individual life through baptism: "Do you not know that all of us who have been baptized into Christ have been baptized into His death?" (6:3). Those buried with Christ walk in newness of life by the power of Jesus' resurrection (6:4). Thus, the baptized should consider themselves dead to death and dead to sin (6:11), dead to the world of Adam dominated by flesh. The new humanity of the last Adam is formed through a baptismal break from the world of Adam.

In this sense too, baptism serves as a criterion of faithfulness. After the exodus of baptism (1 Cor 10:1–4), there ought to be no going back. Returning to Adam was the Corinthian apostasy: having died and risen in Christ, they reconstructed the divisions of the old, Babelic world. They committed an offense against Christ and his baptism, which called them to walk in unity and to cultivate the virtues of peace.

Paul's theology of the Supper likewise has a divisive aspect as well as a unitive aspect. His most elaborate treatment of the Eucharist belongs to a discussion of "things sacrificed to idols" (περὶ δὲ τῶν εἰδωλοθύτων, 8:1). Paul begins addressing that question at the beginning of 1 Corinthians 8, and he does not turn to χαρίσματα until the beginning of chapter 12 (περὶ δὲ τῶν πνευματικῶν). All Paul's teachings concerning the Supper—participation in the body and blood, becoming one body by partaking of one loaf, discerning the body and overcoming factionalism—are nestled within his answer to the pastoral question of the legitimacy of Christians eating meat offered to idols.

Shedding blood was serious business for the ancients, and there was no secular butchery (Detienne and Vernant 1998). The meat offered at Corinthian meat markets would have been prepared in sacred ceremonies at a pagan temple, and the meat market was likely in a temple complex. Converts who had only recently left pagan worship behind would understandably have scruples about eating food from gods they had renounced. Jewish Christians would have even more serious and long-standing qualms. Food sacrificed to idols had obvious potential to combust into conflict, pitting scrupulous Jews against omnivorous, pork-loving Greco-Romans. Galatians is proof enough that Jews and Gentiles could descend to food fights.

Even bigger questions are at stake. The question of meat sacrificed to idols is implicitly about the church's stance toward the pagan world in general. On the one hand, Christians might have decided to follow the lead of some philosophical sects and refrain from meat as a protest against a world dominated by idols. Refusing sacrificial meat would have been a political decision. Citizens shared in the festivities of the *polis*, which *was* connected with the religious politics of the city. Christians who refused to eat meat would renounce full participation in the civic life of the Greco-Roman world. On the other hand, if Christians were free to eat meat sacrificed to idols, they could blend smoothly into Greco-Roman civic life much more seamlessly than Jews had done.

Paul's complex response to this dilemma traces a nuanced paradigm of the church's relationship to the world, rooted in the church's own food practices. He begins with a thoroughly Jewish dismissal: echoing the *shema*, he declares that "there is no such thing as an idol in the world, and there is no God but one" (8:4). Since there are no idols, there cannot be meat sacrificed to idols. What is sold on the market has been offered to *nothings*, and therefore Christians are free to receive it as a gift from the giver of all gifts. Those who eat without qualms of conscience Paul characterizes as the "strong".

The church, though, is not a community of the strong. Some do not have the same knowledge that Paul has. Some "accustomed to the idol until now, eat food as if it were sacrificed to an idol; and their conscience being weak is defiled" (8:7). Because the church is called to walk in the unity signified by baptism and the loaf, because the strong and weak are members of one another by water, Spirit, and food, they must defer to one another. The strong are not to flaunt their strength but to accommodate to the weak: "If someone sees you, who have knowledge, dining in an idol's temple, will not his conscience, if he is weak, be strengthened to eat things sacrificed to idols?" (8:10). If he eats against his conscience, the weak man's conscience is defiled. Thus the strong can ruin the weak. Knowledge without love destroys the ignorant (v. 11). So, Paul counsels, the strong ought to refrain even from feasts they know to be allowable, so as to preserve unity and love within the body.

Later, Paul seems to do an about-face: "The things which the Gentiles sacrificed they sacrifice to demons, and not to God; and I do not want you to become sharers in demons. You cannot drink the cup of the Lord and the cup of demons; you cannot partake of the table of the Lord and the table of demons" (10:20–21). Where he originally had declared pagan gods non-existent, he here views them as demonic powers. Where he had allowed the strong to eat without question, he now appears to forbid it. But the two chapters address subtly different questions. In chapter 8, Paul discusses consumption of meat purchased in the public meat markets at Corinthian temples. In chapter 10, he refers to the sacrificial festivals that take place *within* pagan temples. Eating meat prepared in a sacred ceremony is licit. *Participating* in that sacred ceremony is not.

Paul's paraenesis emerges from the sacramental ecclesio-logic we have been examining. Christians who participate in the cup and loaf of the Lord's Supper have communion with the body and blood of the Lord and share together with other participants in a rite that makes them one body. Because the Christian shares in Christ at the Lord's table, he is prohibited from celebrating meals at the table of other lords. If he tries to feast at both tables, he provokes the Lord of the Lord's Table to jealousy (10:22). Communion with Christ in the Eucharist joins and divides; it divides from idols *because* it joins to Christ.

For Paul, baptism and the Lord's Supper are signs of the unity of the *ekklesia*, constituted from the union of Jew and Gentile in the one body of the eschatological Man, who broke the dividing wall. Through these signs the Spirit unifies the church in Christ. But they are equally signs of the separation of the church from the world. The sacraments display too the mission of the church, to *be* the eschatological humanity over against the old, divided humanity, but also to be the new humanity *on behalf of* Jew and Gentile, to invite all to cross the water into the fellowship at the Lord's table.

Dogmatic and Practical Implications.

Few sacramental theologies have been constructed precisely as I have suggested here, but the elements of this structure are accepted in all branches of the church. An ecclesial sacramental theology is deeply embedded in the Christian tradition. In his reply to Faustus the Manichean, Augustine defended both the presence of sacraments in the church and the change of signs that came with the gospel. Sacraments, he insisted, are necessary to the church because "people could not be gathered together under the name of any religion, whether true or false, if they were not bound together (*coagulari*) by some sharing of visible signs or sacraments" (Augustine 2007: 19.11). Thomas quoted this passage in answer to the question, "whether sacraments are necessary for man's salvation?" (*ST* III, q.61, a.1; cf. Dittoe 1946), though in the *respondeo* Thomas focuses on the way corporeal sacraments accommodate to human weakness to raise us to contemplate God, rather than on the communal dimension highlighted by Augustine. Medieval uses of the distinction of *sacramentum* and *res* also pushed toward an ecclesial sacramentology. The Eucharist has a triple structure: the *sacramentum tantum*, the *res et sacramentum*, and the *res tantum*, which correspond to the triple body of Christ. The eucharistic body is solely sacrament, pointing to the historical body; the historical body is the thing to which the sacrament points, but it is itself a *sacramentum* of the third form of Christ's body, the church. At the "apex" of the structure, as it were, is the church, the body unified in love, the *res* signified directly and indirectly by the other forms of Christ's body (Bauerschmidt 1997; de Lubac 2007). For the Reformers, the ecclesial inclusiveness of the Eucharist was a key point in their condemnation of the late medieval Mass. "All the baptized are clerics," Luther cried against the Catholic exclusion of the laity from the cup (Luther 1959 [1520]), and if they are clerics then they are table companions of the Lord who should be free to share in the full meal. The form of the Eucharist should reflect the evangelical announcement of the church's unity. For all his anti-sacramentalism, Zwingli agreed on this point, stressing the presence of Christ in and as the covenant community of the church (Davis 2006; on Calvin, Gerrish 1993). In the Anabaptist tradition, egalitarian communion is an effective sign of the church's non-hierarchical communion.

Orthodox theology also affirms the ecclesial character of the Eucharist. John Zizioulas writes that the early Christians "so identified the Eucharist with the Church herself that the terms 'Eucharist' and 'Church' are interchangeable" (Zizioulas 2011: 15; cf. McPartlan 2006). Following the lead of the Church Fathers (Wainwright 2002), Schmemann (1973) stresses the eschatological dimension of the Eucharist. In the eucharistic liturgy, the church journeys to the kingdom that is to come to enjoy the first fruits of the new creation. The church thereby discovers the kingdom is not some other, spiritual world, but *this* world of eating and drinking transfigured in resurrection life. By its participation in the Eucharist, the church becomes a sign of the coming kingdom, a real-life preview of what the world will be.

This framework for sacramental theology is, I suggest, able to illumine all sorts of traditional sacramental puzzles. Here I discuss three: the grace of the sacraments; the participants in the Eucharist; and the number of sacraments. My aim is ecumenical as well as dogmatic. I know full well that my brief forays leave many important questions unanswered. My observations are offered in the hope that they fruitfully reframe debates that have divided Christians for far too long and that they provide some material for advancing ecumenical dialogue and, as the Lord wills, agreement.

What grace does the baptized person receive? From the perspective of ecclesial sacramental theology, the answer is, simply enough, a share in the body of Christ. This is not a reduction of grace to the "merely social," since the body of Christ *is* the human community joined by the Spirit to the incarnate Son who is one with the Father (Leithart 2000). Since the body of Christ is the eschatological humanity, the gift of membership in that body is an eschatological gift, a "taste of the powers of the age to come" (Hebrews 6:5). Sacramental theology has been distracted seeking a deeper, more secretive and hidden grace, but the gift of baptism is the gift evident on the surface: it is given by the Holy Spirit (1 Cor 12:12–13), but the gift itself is membership in the Spirit-enlivened body of Christ.

On this basis, one can formulate an ecumenically viable and dogmatically rich understanding of baptismal regeneration (Leithart 2000). For Paul and the other New Testament writers, life outside Christ is living death: "Who shall deliver me from the body of this death?" Paul asks at the end of a passage describing his schizophrenic reaction to the Law (Rom 7:24). Jesus delivers from death in his death (Romans 8:1-4), and by baptism individuals are "co-crucified" with Jesus, dying to sin so that they might live to God and his righteousness (Rom 6). Baptism "regenerates" not because it infuses spiritual power into a person but because it extracts him or her from the dead world and plants him in the church, the people of the risen Last Adam.

On this basis, one can also clarify and simplify the question of whether baptism is a "cause" of grace or a "mere sign," and cut through interminable debates about whether the grace is conferred by the performance of the sacrament per se. Nearly every branch of the church acknowledges that baptism is the ritual entry into the Christian community. Baptism *confers* and does not merely signify membership, but since membership in the eschatological humanity *is* the gift, baptism confers the grace it signifies. By virtue of its performance (*ex opere operato*), baptism adds members to the body of Christ, enlarging the eschatological humanity that is the *poiema* of the Son and Spirit. By its very performance, baptism forms a new community out of an old, transforming Jew and Palestinian, Serb and Croat, Tutsi and Hutu into brothers. By its very performance, baptism fulfills the promise of God to reverse Babel through the seed of Abraham.

One can follow similar reasoning in the theology of the Eucharist. The social and communal gifts of the Eucharist depend entirely on the self-gift of Christ in the Spirit through bread and wine, about which Christians will continue to debate. If Christ is not given and received, those who feast at the table are not sharing in the body and blood of the Lord and so are not formed into the one body signified by the one loaf. Yet the eucharistic gift is plain to the most casual observer of a eucharistic celebration: it is the gift of participation in the feast of the Lord. The unity of the church is the *res* of the sacrament, a *res* evident in the *sacramentum*. The gift of the Supper is precisely what the Supper empirically *is*: the union of all nations as table companions of the Creator God.

Questions about the participants and recipients of the sacraments may also be answered from the viewpoint of an eschatological ecclesiology. If the church is the body in which the least honorable are given more abundant honor (1 Cor 12:22–25), if the church is made up of disciples of Jesus who welcomed little children, and if the sacraments signify the character of the new covenant, then the water and the feast are *especially* for the weak, vulnerable, needy, poor, childish. Baptism should be performed in a way that manifests Jesus' welcome of little children. The centuries-long exclusion of children from the Eucharist in Protestant and Catholic churches is, by the same token, a standing repudiation of the character of the church.

Throughout this chapter, I have focused on the two sacraments acknowledged in all Christian traditions. Because Protestants define sacraments as markers of the *church*, they do not consider marriage, a universal and natural institution, as a sacrament. Most Protestants acknowledge that ordination and anointing are biblically warranted rites, but do not consider them sacraments because they are not shared by all members of the church. Even Protestant churches that practice confirmation do not consider it a sacrament because it does not have clear biblical support, and for the same reason Protestants do not consider confession a sacrament.

An eschatological ecclesiology makes "sacrament" a more supple term, and in that flexibility there is some hope of dogmatic and ecumenical advance. What Protestants consider *non*-sacramental rites of the church *do* function like the acknowledged sacraments. Ordination comes with a divine promise of grace (1 Tim 4:14). Following the reasoning above, in fact, one can say that ordination *is* the gift conferred, *ex opere operato*, in the rite. Leadership in the church is, after all, an undeserved gift. Like baptism and the Eucharist, ordination displays the nature of the new humanity that is the church by articulating the internal structure of the baptized community. By ordination, a previously baptized member of the eucharistic community is deputized to a specific form of service in the body, and each "ordained office" offers a perspective on the ministry of the church as a whole. Anointing the sick is also a biblical rite (James 5:13–18), and comes with a promise of physical healing. As a rite of the eschatological humanity, it is an effective indicator of the kind of community the church is—a community of healing but also a community of triumphant suffering in union with the Suffering Anointed One.

Marriage is not a sacrament in the same sense as baptism and the Eucharist, but it too can be understood as a rite that effectively articulates the body of Christ and manifests the nature of the eschatological humanity. Paul is explicit about the latter: a man and woman united in marriage symbolize the "great mystery" that is Christ and the church (Eph 522–33). The marriage ceremony "ordains" every married couple to be a living icon of the *totus Christus*, Christ unified in one body with his bride. As the baptized live out of the rite of baptism, so the lifelong sacrificial love and mutual respect of a husband and wife is a living out of the rite of matrimony. Penance too, though not a sacrament in the same sense as baptism and the Eucharist, is sacramental in the sense I am using the term. John promises that those who confess will find mercy (1 John 1:9–10). Confession in the weekly liturgy and in private pastoral counseling displays the eschatological humanity as a people of truth, humility, contrition, forgiveness, and reconciliation. Public absolution of sins and private assurance of forgiveness are concrete practices in which the church signifies what she is, and *becomes* what she is. Confirmation has no obvious biblical warrant or divine promise, and a shady history (Fisher 2005). Yet as a tradition within the church it has pastoral value and can serve as a quasi-sacrament displaying the church's nature as an intergenerational family and mission.

The Spirit uses baptism and the Supper to constitute and grow the eschatological *ekklesia*. But we see in Paul that baptism and the Supper are not guarantees of faithfulness. They are witnesses to the church's nature, vocation, and mission, but may become witnesses testifying against the church's infidelities. Sacraments gauge even as they give. And so I cannot but end soberly. If Israel was a mirror of Babel, the splintered church is infinitely more so. Paul's rebuke to the contemporary church should electrify: In whose name were you baptized? At whose table do you feast? Do you *dare* return to a world from which Jesus died to deliver you?

SUGGESTED READING

Cavanaugh (1998); de Lubac (2007); Schmemann (1973); Wainwright (2002).

BIBLIOGRAPHY

Augustine (2007), *Answer to Faustus, A Manichean*, trans. Boniface Ramsey (Hyde Park, NY: New City Press).

Bauerschmidt, F. Christian (1997), "The Threefold Body: Theology After Suspicion," Christian Theological Research Fellowship, <http://evans-experientialism.freewebspace.com/bauer-schmidt.htm>.

Cavanaugh, W. (1998), *Torture and Eucharist: Theology, Politics, and the Body of Christ* (London: Wiley-Blackwell).

Davis, T. (2006), "Discerning the Body: The Eucharist and the Christian Social Body in Sixteenth Century Protestant Exegesis," *Fides et Historia* 38: 67–81.

De Lubac, H. (2007), *Corpus Mysticum: the Eucharist and the Church in the Middle Ages* (Notre Dame, IN: Notre Dame University Press).

De Lubac, H. (1998), *Catholicism: Christ and the Common Destiny of Man* (San Francisco, CA: Ignatius).

Detienne, M. and J. Vernant (1998). *The Cuisine of Sacrifice Among the Greeks* (Chicago: University of Chicago Press).

Dittoe, J. T. (1946), "Sacramental Incorporation into the Mystical Body," *The Thomist* 9: 469–514.

Fisher, J. D. C. (2005), *Christian Initiation: Confirmation Then and Now* (Chicago: Hillenbrand Books).

Gerrish, B. A. (1993), *Grace & Gratitude: The Eucharistic Theology of John Calvin* (Minneapolis, MN: Fortress).

Hartman, L. (2000), *Into the Name of the Lord Jesus: Baptism in the Early Church* (London: T&T Clark).

Hauerwas, S. (1991), *The Peaceable Kingdom: A Primer in Christian Ethics* (Notre Dame, IN: University of Notre Dame Press).

Holifield, E. Brooks (1974), *The Covenant Sealed: The Development of Puritan Sacramental Theology in Old and New England, 1570–1720* (New Haven, CT: Yale University Press).

Lampe, G. W. H. (1967), *The Seal of the Spirit: A Study in the Doctrine of Baptism and Confirmation in the New Testament and the Fathers* (London: SPCK).

Leithart, P. J. (2000), "Modernity and the 'Merely Social': Toward a Socio-Theological Account of Baptismal Regeneration," *Pro Ecclesia* 9: 319–30.

Luther, M. (1959 (1520)), "The Babylonian Captivity of the Church," in Helmut T. Lehmann (gen. ed.), *Luther's Works*, 55 vols., trans. A. T. W. Steinhäuser (Philadelphia: Muhlenberg Press), vol. 36.

MacGregor, G. (2004), *Corpus Christi: The Nature of the Church According to the Reformed Tradition* (Eugene, OR: Wipf & Stock).

McPartlan, P. (2006), *The Eucharist Makes the Church*, 2nd ed. (Fairfax, VA: Eastern Christian Publications).

McPartlan, P. (2000), *Sacrament of Salvation: An Introduction to Eucharistic Ecclesiology* (London: Bloomsbury T&T Clark).

Oliver, S. (1999), "The Eucharist Before Nature and Culture," *Modern Theology* 15: 331–353.

Schmemann, A. (1973), *For the Life of the World: Sacraments and Orthodoxy* (Crestwood, NY: St. Vladimir's Seminary Press).

Smith, D. (2003). *From Symposium to Eucharist: The Banquet in the Early Christian World* (Minneapolis, MN: Fortress).

Wainwright, G. (2002), *Eucharist and Eschatology* (Memphis, TN: Order of Saint Luke Publications).

Wallace, R. S. (1982), *Calvin's Doctrine of Word and Sacrament* (Tyler, TX: Geneva Divinity School).

Wells, S. (2006), *God's Companions: Reimaging Christian Ethics* (London: Wiley-Blackwell).

Williams, R. (1987), "The Nature of a Sacrament," in John Greenhalgh and Elizabeth Russell (eds.), *Signs of Faith, Hope, and Love: The Christian Sacraments Today* (London: St. Mary's Bourne Street).

Williams, R. (1996), "Sacraments of the New Society," in David Brown and Ann Loades (eds.), *Christ: The Sacramental Word* (London: SPCK).

Wright, N. T. (2013), *Paul and the Faithfulness of God*, 2 vols. (Minneapolis, MN: Fortress).

Zizioulas, J. D. (2011), *The Eucharistic Communion and the World* (London: T&T Clark).

CHAPTER 42

··

LITURGY, PREACHING, AND THE SACRAMENTS

··

GORDON W. LATHROP

THE sacraments take place in a Christian assembly. They involve communal action and participation, communal ritual activity. This assertion certainly holds true for baptism and Eucharist, those Christian events most widely and centrally called "sacraments" in the diverse churches—in Orthodox and Oriental, Roman Catholic, and most Protestant churches. These events should happen "in church"; indeed, among most Christians they are seen to *constitute* church. This essential ecclesial-communal character of baptism and Eucharist has come to strong practical expression in our day. Most of the churches have been encouraging baptisms to be held in the full assembly rather than simply in family groups. Even "emergency baptisms" or baptisms in the face of death are to be in some way announced or remembered or confirmed in the full assembly. Furthermore, many Roman Catholics—joining long-held Orthodox and Protestant convictions—have also come to regard "private masses" as odd, exceptional, even malformed. Eucharist creates church and most properly takes place in an assembly that can be seen as church.

But the assertion of the communal character of the sacraments also holds true for the others of the customary seven, whether or not they are called "sacraments" by a church where they are being practiced. A participating community also forms the locus for confirmation or chrismation, for ordination, for the celebration of marriage, and even for anointing the sick and for reconciliation. Although in the latter two cases the ritualizing assembly may be a small one, the outreach of the larger Sunday assembly toward someone who is ill or the reconciliation to the Sunday assembly of someone who has been alienated from it make up part of the deepest intention of these rituals. Even these more personal events express and lean toward assembly.

Such, at least, has been the insight of the ecumenical liturgical movement of the twentieth and twenty-first centuries. For liturgists involved in this movement, Christian sacraments are not static objects or private matters of individual religious consumption distributed by sacred specialists. They are communal, bodily events.

They involve ritual process and participation. The sacraments make up a large part of the core of Christian liturgy, the public ritual work that Christian communities do. And their continually renewed practice today should express the basic insights of the liturgical movement: that faithful liturgy is always corporate; that the assembly is the "celebrant" of the sacraments; that priests or pastors preside and serve, rather than dominate, in the assembly's celebration; that "full, conscious, and active participation" of all the baptized in the mystery of Christ—and so in the sacraments—is a goal of renewal (*Sacrosanct Consilium* 14); and that in such celebration "the authentic liturgical act must involve our bodies and our senses—our hearts as well as our minds" (Weil 2013: 52–53).

From this point of view, reflection on sacramental meaning today has needed to become, at the same time, reflection on liturgical practice (Garrigan 2004). Sacramental theology and liturgical theology—the consideration of liturgical meaning as theological meaning (see Lathrop 2013)—have needed to merge. Indeed, in many places, they have so merged. Basic works of sacramental theology have also become important reflections on liturgical practice (e.g. already Jenson 1978, and then, more recently, Chauvet 2001). Ecumenical statements on sacramental meaning have included liturgical proposals (BEM Baptism 17–23 and Eucharist 27–33). This shift can also be observed in many articles in this book, in which counsel for liturgical practice and reflection on liturgical process are seriously present. Furthermore, seminal works of liturgical theology have extensively reflected on sacramental meaning (e.g. Schmemann 1973 and 1975, Kavanagh 1978 and 1984, and, more recently, Bieler and Schottroff 2007). Where this merger has continued to occur, at least two tasks have emerged: we have learned that we need "to avoid … an exclusively cognitive analysis of the phenomenon of sign and symbolic activity" (Schillebeeckx 2005: 20). Discussion of *signum* and *res* will not be enough if the *signum* is not seen to include the actual celebrating, participating, bodily assembly. And, at the same time, we have seen that the very liturgies of that assembly will need to come under an ongoing reforming criticism so that those liturgies clearly serve the gospel of which the sacraments are meant to be ritual expressions. When sacramental theology and liturgical theology merge they become together a new liturgical criticism (see Lathrop 1993: 161–179).

SACRAMENTAL ASSEMBLY, SACRAMENTAL PREACHING, OLD CONTROVERSIES RELATIVIZED

If these insights of the liturgical movement are granted, several corollaries follow. For one thing, it becomes possible to urge that the assembly itself, in doing its liturgy, be seen as sacramental. That urging can mean several things. Many liturgists have noted that the basic *ordo* of Christian Sunday liturgy in most of the churches revolves around the sacraments (e.g. see Lathrop 1993: 33–83). The entrance rite recalls baptism, perhaps by means of an act of confession and forgiveness—what Martin Luther would call "a return and approach to baptism" (*Large Catechism* 4:79)—perhaps by means of the ministers leading the opening rite from the font or by means of a sprinkling of the whole assembly, perhaps simply by the use of the triune name from Matthew 28:19. Then the full service involves a juxtaposition of the reading and preaching of Scripture, together with responsive singing and praying, to the setting out of the Lord's Supper, with its thanksgiving and Communion and sending to a needy world. Indeed, what we customarily call "the Eucharist" is not simply the ritual meal but the full weaving together of word and sacrament. Others of the traditional seven rites—ordination or marriage, for example—may then also find their place within this flow between word and table.

Then reflection on the assembly itself as sacramental has brought us all to continued efforts to make this sacramental center clear. Protestant liturgists have engaged in inviting congregations to recover the full service of word and sacrament—the service focused around what Lutherans, Anglicans, Methodists, and Presbyterians call "the means of grace"—as the principal liturgy of every Sunday. Among many Protestants, Eucharist every Sunday has returned as a norm. Roman Catholic and Orthodox liturgists have urged that nothing be allowed to obscure the central matters of word and sacrament in the liturgy. In many places, devotional exercises have yielded to more frequent Communion, priests have become presiders in a participating assembly rather than performers before an observing audience, and iconostases have become permeable or have been removed. Some Roman Catholic ecclesiologists have read *Sacrosanctum Concilium* (the Constitution of the Sacred Liturgy of the Second Vatican Council) as proposing, indeed, that the basic idea of "church"—an idea that operates throughout the decisions of that council and not simply in the Liturgy Constitution—is the idea of a concrete local assembly around Christ in word and sacrament (Faggioli 2012: 1, 4). And some ecumenical documents have argued that Christians may affirm and admonish each other, even across denominational boundaries, toward a recovery of the centrality of word and sacrament in balance (e.g. *Ditchingham Statement* 7). "Sacramental assembly" may then mean an assembly centered on the enacted, church-making, communally practiced sacraments. Martin Luther's old idea has new currency as a liturgical proposal among us now: one can tell that a gathering is church, he wrote, by the presence of the "marks of the church," baptism, preaching, the holy supper, the absolution of sins, and an ordained ministry being chief among them (Lathrop and Wengert 2005: 39–40).

But the "sacramental assembly" can also mean that the assembly itself, in its meeting around word and sacrament, is to be seen as a sacrament, that is as a symbol that, by the promise of God, actually participates in and makes available for communal participation the heart of the thing symbolized. Thus, the celebrating assembly may be seen as a primary locus for the presence of Christ—in the reading and preaching of the Scriptures and in the intercessions, but also in the very gathering of the baptized themselves, as well as in the holy supper. To support this idea *Sacrosanctum Concilium* 7 quotes Matthew 18:20: "For where two or three are gathered in my name, I am there among them." Or, if we were to quote Paul and Augustine, the expression "sacramental assembly" might be taken to mean that the gathering itself is what it eats—"you are the Body of Christ" (1 Cor 12:27) and "you are the mystery that is on the table" (Sermon 227)—and is sent to be given away as that body amidst the needs of the world. Or, the church-as-assembly, when it shows the marks of being church, is to be seen as a sacrament of the reign of God (Chauvet 2001: xxii). Thus, the faithful assembly may be said to be the sacrament of the presence of Jesus Christ or of the body of Christ or of the reign of God. None of these ideas of the sacramentality of the assembly is mutually exclusive.

Another corollary follows: preaching ought to be considered sacramental. Again, several things may be meant, none of them mutually exclusive. Preaching can be seen (as proposed by Brilioth 1965) as being not only exegetical and prophetic, but also liturgical. That is, a sermon occurs within a liturgical order, with responsibility to bring the meaning of that order, its readings and its sacraments, to expression (see Rice 1990; Lathrop 2006: 41–58; and Quivik 2009). Preaching is part of the liturgy. It is, however, that part which bears responsibility to articulate in the present what the whole liturgical meeting is about. Preaching thus ought to speak the meaning of the sacraments being practiced in the assembly.

That idea can be expressed even more strongly. If, as Augustine says (*In Johannis Evangelium* 80:40), "the word comes to the element and so there is a sacrament," for liturgists that word is not simply a consecratory formula, not simply the "words of the institution" of the Lord's Supper or the words of baptism taken from Matthew 28. The word that "comes to the element" is rather all the words of the church woven into sacramental practice and its processes, all the catechesis and liturgical texts and hymnody and teaching. The word of preaching is also part of the word that comes to water, bread, and wine, articulating the gifts of baptism and the holy supper to create and hold us in faith and being part of the very word of God that creates the sacraments (see Willimon 1992). Preaching belongs to the event of the sacraments. The Sunday assembly, where preaching occurs, begins with a remembrance or return to baptism; the Sunday assembly gathers as a baptismal assembly. Preaching should thus say, in the terms of the texts of the day, what the baptismal bath gives and has given. More, preaching should also say to its hearers, in alternative terms, what the meal it accompanies will say: "my body … my blood … given for you." The word of God, also in preaching, comes like a life-giving meal.

Indeed, the deepest word that comes to "the element," of course, is the word that is our Lord Jesus Christ. Preaching may also be called "sacramental" because it bears witness to him, to the crucified and risen one who is himself our bath and our meal and the Word of life in our ears. Furthermore, this risen one can also be seen as actually present in the word of preaching. As the Fourth Gospel has it, where his Word is "kept" the Advocate will enliven that Word and the Father and the Son will come to dwell (John 14:23–26). To say the matter in other, Pauline terms: a faithful sermon, set in the heart of a sacramental assembly and bringing the meaning of that assembly and its Scriptures to expression, will, like the apostolic greeting itself, be engaged in actually giving the grace, love, and communion of the Holy Trinity to its hearers (2 Cor 13:13). Such is sacramental preaching.

Thus, many liturgists who have reflected upon sacramental meaning from the context of communal practice and many sacramental theologians who have moved toward doing liturgical theology have found some of the classic Christian sacramental controversies to be relativized. Of course, liturgists might say, Christ is really present in the Eucharist. Our liturgies—in virtually all of the diverse churches, at least as these are renewed liturgies—say so. The metaphysics of that presence is less important. Of course the churches that baptize those who cannot answer for themselves bear a responsibility to call and form those who are so baptized toward mature discipleship. But then catechesis and continued learning and regular gathering with the assembly that sends us again to a needy world all belong to the life-long process of baptism, at least to baptism as it has been renewed in those churches. And of course those churches that baptize only those who do answer for themselves also need to listen again and again to the Word of grace, seeing and proclaiming that God acts in baptism. Their renewed liturgies say so, as well. One possibility is that the people of such churches will be raising their children to know this promise of grace as if these children were—to use the language of the old Christian tradition—in a kind of extended catechumenate. Recent ecumenical statements have helped us on this point (see BEM Baptism 16 and the *Ditchingham Statement* 10–11).

But there is more. From the point of view of liturgy, our arguments about the number of the sacraments ought not be church-dividing. For all of us—at least as we experience the matter in assemblies—baptism and Eucharist live at the heart of a sacramental economy (see Schillebeeckx 1963 and 2005: 20). When baptism is seen to include catechesis and Eucharist is seen to include Scripture reading, preaching, prayer, and sending—when these sacraments are indeed communal events and processes—then these indeed are the primary sacraments, forming and marking a church. All the other sacramental events flow into and out of this church. Indeed, if assembly itself and preaching are sacramental, if prayer and blessing and visiting those in need and sitting silently with someone in grief might be called "sacramental" as well, then perhaps there are fourteen sacraments or forty, as some medieval theologians proposed, all of them focussed around and flowing from an assembly gathered in Jesus Christ and knowing him in word and bath and meal. Christ himself is the "sacrament of the encounter with God" (Schillebeeckx 1963) and all other sacraments, however we number them, are meant to bring him to expression.

Nor, from the point of view of many liturgical theologians, ought we argue about what is necessary to consecrate a sacrament by building our arguments on historical reconstructions of "institution." We certainly can join in asking the increasingly complex questions of sacramental history, finding many old assertions of obvious beginnings and clear and uniform development to be no longer tenable (Bradshaw 2002). But then, as we have said from a liturgical theological point of view, the word that founds the sacraments is the whole range of faithful words alive in the rites and preaching of the current church. And, to faith, the "founder" of the sacraments is the risen Christ, continually acting in the church to break our rituals into bearers of his grace (Lathrop 2012: 49–50, 170–171, 201–202). As Edward Schillebeeckx says, "where religious faith exists, it will express itself spontaneously, anthropologically, in ritual, so that searching for the actual 'founder' of these rituals (from a Christian point of view, sacraments) is not an issue of primary importance" (Schillebeeckx 2005: 18). On the other hand, the issue of the presence of the crucified and risen one and the issue of the continual reforming of our rituals toward the expression of his meaning in our sacramental practice—these are such primary matters.

LITURGICAL-SACRAMENTAL RESPONSE TO A CURRENT ISSUE: COMMUNION OF THE BAPTIZED

Still, the current liturgical practice of the sacraments has also raised new questions, some of those questions leading to new controversies. One of the most urgent has been the question of whether it is necessary to be baptized in order to receive Holy Communion. The increasing practice of weekly Eucharist in Protestant communities and the unclouded centrality of Eucharist in Roman Catholic assemblies have combined with devotion to the ideas of openness and hospitality in both communities to raise the issue sharply. What follows here is one liturgical theologian's attempt to respond to the issue through a liturgically formed conception of the sacraments.

One might say it this way: baptism and Eucharist are the gospel of Jesus Christ by the power of the Spirit made into a continually recalled initiatory bath and a regularly recurring communal meal. Through this bath and meal, God identifies us with the death and resurrection of Jesus, gathers us together with Jesus into the astonishing new age, brings us again and again to faith, makes of us a community witnessing to God's mercy for the life of the world, continually renews and forgives us, and constantly turns us together toward our neighbors and toward the care of the earth itself. Baptism and Holy Communion are essentially communal events. Together with the read, preached, and sung word of God, they continually create and mark the church.

But, as we have seen, it is not wise to spend too much energy on enumerating or distinguishing the sacraments. In many ways, baptism and Holy Communion make up a single sacrament or a single sacramental economy. In terms of the human material out of which they are created—in Augustinian terms, the "element" to which the word comes—they are like washing up before a festal meal and then the meal itself. But because they bear witness to the arriving new age, the "washing up" occurs once for all and involves an immersion into the death and resurrection of Jesus, an introduction into the community around him, and an identification with those—the outsiders, the needy, the sinful, the dying, and the earth itself—with whom he identifies. Baptism is thus a "new birth." The meal is continually repeated, the end-time banquet available now in the death and resurrection of Jesus, the food for the new-born. Catechesis, the echoing and deepening word that accompanies baptism, is also continually repeated in age-appropriate form (see *The Use of the Means of Grace* 19 and 37). One could say that the baptismal process—call it *baptisma*—is the basic sacrament. It is as if the Holy Supper is one extended and repeatable part of the baptismal process. The word that accompanies baptism and the announcement of the forgiveness of sins are yet others that extend into our whole life. And the preached word of God in the assembly must constantly be announcing to us, in the terms of the texts of the day, what this *baptisma* means.

In truth, however, the basic sacrament is Jesus Christ, God in the flesh and in the material of our world, immersed in our alienation and death, changing everything. This is what we mean by "new age." The word of God in assembly, baptism as the introduction to that assembly, and the supper as the assembly's meal are faithfully seen as concrete means whereby the Spirit of God draws us into that one sacrament and so into the life of the Holy Trinity. Thus, "Jesus Christ is the living and abiding Word of God. By the power of the Spirit, this very Word of God, which is Jesus Christ, is read in the Scriptures, proclaimed in preaching, announced in the forgiveness of sins, eaten and drunk in the Holy Communion, and encountered in the bodily presence of the Christian community. By the power of the Spirit active in Holy Baptism, this Word washes a people to be Christ's own Body in the world. We have called this gift of Word and Sacrament by the name 'the means of grace.' The living heart of all these means is the presence of Jesus Christ through the power of the Spirit as the gift of the Father" (*The Use of the Means of Grace* 1).

The understanding and practice of this sacramental economy can be minimized and endangered in our times both by a kind of religious consumerism and by a certain sacramental legalism. The reception of Communion ought not be seen as the reception of an individual religious product, implying no communal involvement and no continuing commitment. Such reception is not a "right" nor a religious "work." It is not an occasionally nice thing for an individual to do. Similarly, having baptism "done" ought not be seen as the satisfaction of a divine demand or the meeting of a vague social or religious requirement, also without ongoing communal significance other than familial interest in a ceremony. On the other hand, the sacraments ought not be protected, as if they were religious rituals meted out only under clergy control, without reference to the heart of the sacraments, the basic sacrament that is Jesus Christ, nor to his gracious identification with outsiders and sinners. Both of these misuses call upon our assemblies to teach the meaning of the sacraments and continually renew the practice of the sacramental economy—of *baptisma*—in all of our contexts.

Paul's admonitions to the congregation in 1 Corinthians 11:17–34 have been misunderstood and misused when they have been taken to mean that only those with a certain level of religious knowledge and discernment should be admitted to the Lord's Supper. On the contrary, Paul urges the current participants in the meal at Corinth to "discern the body," that is to see the poor members of the community whom they are excluding by their practice. By this act of exclusion, they risk sickness and death. It is toward the stopping of exclusion that Paul urges the participants to "examine themselves." Still, the excluded here were most likely *baptized* members of the community. And the goal of Paul included the establishment of a truly *communal* meal: not "each of you goes ahead with your own supper," but "wait for one another." More: for Paul, the grounds of this inclusion was that the meal is to proclaim the cross, Jesus' identification with all in their need.

On the other hand, Jesus' meals with outsiders have also been misinterpreted when they have been taken to imply that baptism is not needed or that participation in the Supper has no consequences. To read the stories of Jesus without thinking of the context of the churches in which they were told is naive and misleading. The stories of Jesus' meals were probably indeed recounted in the Gospels with the intention of reforming the meal-practice of the communities of the late first and early second century, among other things the intention of urging the inclusion of Gentiles and other outsiders (Lathrop 2012: 39–59). But, for example, the Markan Jesus has compassion on the crowd and urges the disciples to feed them after "they have been with me now for three days" (Mark 8:2), an old symbolic shorthand for being with Christ in his death and resurrection, the very content of baptism. In the time of the church, these outsiders and Gentiles are of course to be baptized and so gathered into the community of the cross and resurrection, so brought to be with Jesus for the three days. Just so, the young man who is stripped at the outset of the Passion in Mark (Mark 14:51–52)—stripped like an ancient candidate for baptism—three days later seems to appear as witness to the resurrection for the community, clothed in a white robe (Mark 16:5). And throughout Mark, Jesus being with the sinners and outsiders is a down payment on and image of the cross (e.g. 3:6 at the end of the stories of chapters 1 and 2) as well as a promise to them of the resurrection. The Lukan Jesus finds the outsiders included in both a kind of Eucharist, with the widow at Zarephath, and a kind of baptism, with Naaman at the Jordan (Luke 4:25–27). Then too, the Markan Jesus says to the disciples, "Are you able to drink the cup that I drink or be baptized with the baptism that I am baptized with?" (Mark 10:38). Both cup and baptism are to be full of the cross, and they belong together. Similarly, the Johannine Jesus says, in the footwashing that stands for both baptism and supper, "Do you know what I have done to you? ... you also ought to wash one another's feet" (John 13:12–14).

Participation in the meal has consequences, draws us into the way of the cross, raises us up with the resurrection, and turns us toward the needs of our neighbor, even when we do not initially see those consequences, even when we easily say with James and John, "We are able" (Mark 10:39). *Baptisma* means to begin to make clear those meanings and those consequences in our lives. The Holy Supper is always intended as grace, never a work. But it is not cheap grace. Nor is "grace" easily understood in our cultural moment without profound catechesis. Anyone who eats and drinks inevitably belongs to the way of *baptisma*. They need to have that way made continually available to them. This is true for all of us. All of us need the catechesis and the way of *baptisma*.

Holy things are indeed for holy people. But only one is holy. While the Markan Jesus calls the Gentile woman a "dog" (Mark 7:27), she willingly becomes the dog under the table who eats the children's crumbs. While the Matthean Jesus says, "Do not give what is holy to dogs" (Matt 7:6) and the *Didache* uses that very passage to warn the unbaptized and the unrepentant against participation in the Eucharist (*Didache* 9:5), the liturgies of the Christian East have legitimately developed a response not unlike that of the Syrophoenician woman, now in the mouth of the assembly: "Only one is holy, Jesus Christ," they sing as they then come to Communion. Admission to Communion is always a paradoxical matter of warning and contradiction. Pastors, teachers, and liturgical leaders have a responsibility to guard and heighten this paradox, not flatten it into either legalistic refusal or easy, consumerist admission. "Yes, you are welcome. Absolutely. But also, it will cost you your life." "Yes, this is for you. Absolutely. But also, this will turn you toward your neighbor's and the earth's need." "Here is the food of the great and free new banquet. It is the body and blood of the crucified, risen one, and it will make you hungrier for justice for all."

One denominational statement has it right and something like this should be taught and practiced in the diverse churches: "When an unbaptized person comes to the table seeking Christ's presence and is inadvertently communed, neither that person nor the ministers of Communion need be ashamed. Rather, Christ's gift of love and mercy to all is praised. That person is invited to learn the faith of the Church, be baptized, and thereafter faithfully receive Holy Communion" (*The Use of the Means of Grace* 37). Sometimes, it is indeed true that someone comes first to the single sacrament that is Jesus Christ through the means of the Eucharist. That may be increasingly so in our congregations as Eucharist continues to become the principal service of every congregation, every Sunday or as Eucharist is the unobscured center of our liturgies, as good eucharistic preaching occurs, and as our congregations practice "strong center and open door" (Lathrop 2012: 204) in all of our mission lands, amid many people who have known nothing of authentic Christianity. Eucharist does indeed proclaim the gospel. People who hear and eat and drink the gospel first in this way ought not be presented with baptism as if baptism were a requirement or a demand rather than a gift. Baptism is always gift and grace, never demand or grounds to achieve self-righteousness. But one who eats and drinks with the community is bound to the community and the community to her or to him. The way of *baptisma* must be made available, even if it is approached first in this way. The community cannot simply let such a person go, unconnected, as a solitary consumer. Still, that same denominational statement also asserts a matter that remains unresolved between the churches: ordinarily, eucharistic hospitality ought to be extended to all baptized Christians of whatever church—indeed, like James and John, of whatever conviction about the supper (*The Use of the Means of Grace* 49). In any case, the ordinary, classic, and meaningful order of washing and festal meal ought to be maintained and made clear as the norm for our practice. Ordinarily, we should welcome the seeker first to catechesis and baptism. While these proposals together do not make up a consequent and logical legal decision, they can have the value of maintaining the pastoral paradox: "Holy things for holy people." Yet, "only one is holy."

Some communities may be called to a "catholic exception" in their practice (Lathrop 1993: 158), so that their open table and later baptismal process may stand as a challenge to us all to recover the deep anchor of the sacraments in the single sacrament of Jesus Christ. In such places, all are welcome to the table. Baptism and its catechesis may follow, as the way to come into deeper identity with the church and its mission. Examples of communities engaged in such a catholic exception might include the Episcopal

congregation of St. Gregory of Nyssa in San Francisco and many Methodist congregations (Stamm 2006). It is important to note, however, that John Wesley's understanding
of Holy Communion as a "converting ordinance" is to be understood within the context of eighteenth-century revivalism: those to be "converted" were the already baptized
but inactive or inattentive members of the church. Still, such communities of the open
table in our own time have a responsibility to understand their practice as an intentional
exception (Stamm 2006: 19–40) and also a responsibility to maintain a dialogue with the
larger church, a serious baptismal process, a constant reference to the Trinitarian and
Christological center of the sacraments, a profound engagement with the needs of the
world, and a critique of their own practice (for a fine example of the latter, see Stamm
2006: 119–159).

Current Christian congregations, thus, need to make clear the grace and open mercy
that is available for all people in baptism, and they need to place a congregationally
based baptismal/catechumenal process at the center of their life. The baptismal process
should be seen as important, beautiful, existentially powerful, desirable, highly valued
by the Christian community, challenging, life-changing, and yet utterly open and free.
Baptism is always gospel, and that gospel needs to be seen and heard. A recovery of
immersion pools, of a baptismally focused Lenten observance, and of the liturgy of the
Three Days can assist in this seeing and hearing in our time. On the other hand, pastors
deceive themselves if they think that baptism without catechesis and formation are easily perceived by people as "grace," instead of as a thing they ought to have done. Pastors
are also misled if they think that reception of the Holy Communion apart from the
word of the cross and the mystery of the Trinity, the words that fill a faithful baptismal
process, is perceived as "grace." Pastors may think—as they may have been catechized
to believe—that they are forgiving sins by the free distribution of Holy Communion.
Many communicants, however, may themselves see no particular need for the forgiveness of sins and may altogether miss the many other meanings of the Supper. In our cultural moment, God's grace and these many meanings need to be taught. The danger also
exists that while baptism without sponsors, catechists, and catechesis, and Eucharist
without baptism may seem to congregations to be the most hospitable or "gracious"
choices, these practices may have actually come into existence largely as the easiest
and most culture-conforming way, requiring the least effort by the congregation or the
pastor.

The communal meanings of the supper will be much clearer to us all with a renewed
eucharistic practice. The continued use of medieval hosts and of individual glasses in
the distribution of Communion tends to support the individualist and consumerist
approach to religious meaning. So does the "eastward" celebration of the thanksgiving,
the absence of a full thanksgiving prayer, and the kneeling congregation. A shared loaf
of bread and a shared cup of wine need to be widely recovered, and the latter needs to
be clearly taught as the most communally hygienic mode available. The celebration of
eucharistia should be at a table, with the presider facing a participating assembly that
is standing together—as they have been raised up with Christ so to stand—around the
holy gifts. For a visitor to see that assembly, that sign of the body of Christ enlivened by

the Spirit and standing before God and the world, will also be for her or him to see the gospel, into which we all are being continually invited.

The consequences of receiving Holy Communion may best be taught in our day with the words of Martin Luther's 1519 sermon on "The Blessed Sacrament of the Holy and True Body of Christ." This sermon makes clear to all of us how receiving Communion is always a communal matter, gathering us together into God's going out in care for the life of the world, inserting each of us into a fellowship of beggars. *Baptisma* exists to gather us into this fellowship and form us in this mission:

> When you have partaken of this sacrament, therefore, or desire to partake of it, you must in turn share the misfortunes of the fellowship ... Here your heart must go out in love and learn that this is a sacrament of love. As love and support are given to you, you in turn must render love and support to Christ in his needy ones. You must feel with sorrow all the dishonor done to Christ in his holy Word, all the misery of Christendom, all the unjust suffering of the innocent, with which the world is everywhere filled to overflowing. You must fight, work, pray, and—if you cannot do more—have heartfelt sympathy ... It is Christ's will, then, that we partake of it frequently, in order that we may remember him and exercise ourselves in this fellowship according to his example. (*Luther's Works* 35: 54, 56)

Sacramental and liturgical theologians, together with pastors and church leaders, may respond to this current question in quite another way than that indicated here. But it remains true: in one way or another, sacramental-liturgical reflection on the unified economy of the sacraments can assist churches to respond to this issue with both grace and theological integrity.

SUGGESTED READING

Chauvet (2001); Kavanagh (1984); Schillebeeckx (2005). See also G. W. Lathrop, *Holy Ground: A Liturgical Cosmology* (Minneapolis, MN: Fortress, 2003), 97–152.

BIBLIOGRAPHY

BEM (1982), *Baptism, Eucharist and Ministry*, Faith and Order Paper 111 (Geneva: World Council of Churches).

Bieler, A., and L. Schottroff (2007), *The Eucharist: Bodies, Bread, Resurrection* (Minneapolis, MN: Fortress Press).

Bradshaw, P. (2002), *The Search for the Origins of Christian Worship*, 2nd ed. (New York: Oxford University Press).

Brilioth, Y. (1965), *A Brief History of Preaching* (Philadelphia, PA: Fortress Press).

Chauvet, L.-M. (2001), *The Sacraments: The Word of God at the Mercy of the Body* (Collegeville, MN: The Liturgical Press).

Constitution on the Sacred Liturgy (1963) (Collegeville, MN: The Liturgical Press).

Ditchingham Statement (1995), "Towards Koinonia in Worship: Report of the Consultation," in T. Best and D. Heller (eds.), *So We Believe, So We Pray: Towards Koinonia in Worship*, Faith and Order Paper 171 (Geneva: World Council of Churches), 4–26.

Faggioli, M. (2012), *True Reform: Liturgy and Ecclesiology in Sacrosanctum Concilium* (Collegeville, MN: The Liturgical Press).

Garrigan, S. (2004), *Beyond Ritual: Sacramental Theology after Habermas* (Aldershot: Ashgate).

Jenson, R. (1978), *Visible Words: The Interpretation and Practice of Christian Sacraments* (Philadelphia, PA: Fortress Press).

Kavanagh, A. (1978), *The Shape of Baptism: The Rite of Christian Initiation* (New York: Pueblo).

Kavanagh, A. (1984), *On Liturgical Theology* (New York: Pueblo).

Lathrop, G. W. (1993), *Holy Things: A Liturgical Theology* (Minneapolis, MN: Fortress Press).

Lathrop, G. W. (2006), *The Pastor: A Spirituality* (Minneapolis, MN: Fortress Press).

Lathrop, G. W. (2012), *The Four Gospels on Sunday: The New Testament and the Reform of Christian Worship* (Minneapolis, MN: Fortress Press).

Lathrop, G. W. (2013), "What is Liturgical Theology," *Worship* 87 (January 2013), 45–63.

Lathrop, G. W. and T. Wengert (2004), *Christian Assembly: Marks of the Church in a Pluralistic Age* (Minneapolis, MN: Fortress Press).

Luther, M. (1960), "The Blessed Sacrament of the Holy and True Body of Christ, and the Brotherhoods," in T. Bachmann (ed.), *Luther's Works 35: Word and Sacrament I* (Philadelphia, PA: Fortress Press).

Luther, M. (2000) "The Large Catechism," in R. Kolb and T. Wengert (eds.), *The Book of Concord: The Confessions of the Evangelical Lutheran Church* (Minneapolis, MN: Fortress Press), 377–480.

Quivik, M. (2009), *Serving the Word: Preaching in Worship* (Minneapolis, MN: Fortress Press).

Rice, C. (1990), *The Embodied Word: Preaching as Art and Liturgy* (Minneapolis, MN: Fortress Press).

Schillebeeckx, E. (1963), *Christ the Sacrament of the Encounter with God* (New York: Sheed and Ward).

Schillebeeckx, E. (2005), "Towards a Rediscovery of the Christian Sacraments: Ritualizing Religious Elements in Daily Life," in D. Lange and D. Vogel (eds.), *Ordo: Bath, Word, Prayer, Table* (Akron, OH: OSL Publications), 6–34.

Schmemann, A. (1973), *For the Life of the World: Sacraments and Orthodoxy*, 2nd rev. and exp. ed. (New York: St. Vladimir's Seminary Press).

Schmemann, A. (1975), *Introduction to Liturgical Theology*, 2nd ed. (New York: St. Vladimir's Seminary Press).

Stamm, M. (2006), *Let Every Soul Be Jesus' Guest: A Theology of the Open Table* (Nashville, TN: Abingdon).

The Use of the Means of Grace: A Statement on the Practice of Word and Sacrament (1997) (Minneapolis, MN: Evangelical Lutheran Church in America).

Weil, L. (2013), *Liturgical Sense: The Logic of Rite* (New York: Seabury Books).

Willimon, W. (1992), *Peculiar Speech: Preaching to the Baptized* (Grand Rapids, MI: Eerdmans).

CHAPTER 43

....

SENSE AND SACRAMENT*

....

CATHERINE PICKSTOCK

In his essay "Art and Sacrament," the twentieth-century Catholic poet David Jones contrasted the *utile*, the useful, with that which has its point within itself, the gratuitous, whose meaning is intrinsic and inseparable from just what it is (Jones 1959: 143–179). He suggested that modernist art, by rebelling against art as both mimetic and instructive, had regained a certain religious dimension. For the modern artwork might be compared with sacrament for a Catholic view, which operates either as effective sign or as a means to salvation if it is first and last something mysteriously in itself *and* uniquely valuable just for that reason. A sacrament can be a gift to us only if it rests on the rock of "gratuity-ness," as Jones humorously put it (Jones 153–154). The Eucharist, to take the supreme example, is an effective sign of Christ's body, and a means of *effecting* this body *as* the church, because it truly *is* this body, mysteriously under the modes of bread and wine. Since God is all-powerful and never without effect, he can only, as Jones put it in the closing lines of "Art and Sacrament" and in the epigraph to *Epoch and Artist*, "place himself in the order of signs," if here, uniquely, signifier is made to coincide with signified. In order to be anything else, to represent or to bring about, the Eucharist must be just what it is, unfathomably.

To some degree, all human ritual has this element about it. Human beings do "what has always been done," "in the manner that it has always been done," to cite the closing stanza of Jones's long poem, *The Anathemata*. They never quite know why they are doing it. Thus, Jones's Catholic contemporary, the historian Christopher Dawson, considered that a Christian view of history should learn from some then considered eccentric ethnographers, such as A. M. Hocart, in making ritual or liturgy the driving motor of history, and not either material utility or abstract ideas. Consciously invoking the eighteenth-century Catholic philosopher Giambattista Vico, and in coincidence with his near-contemporary, and also Vico-influenced, German Catholic meta-historian Eric Voegelin, Dawson proposed that over-rational civilizations, which forget that only

* I am grateful to the late John Hughes, in whose honor I offer the present chapter; also thanks to John Robb, Paul Vitebsky, Don Cupitt, and Julius Lipner, and to the audience of the Cleaver Ordinands' Study Day, Pusey House, Oxford (March 1, 2014), for comments on the following arguments.

mysterious myth and ritual bind them together, are liable to collapse (Dawson 1998; Hocart 1933). Ritual is both material and ideal; like every sacrament, it fuses both, but is less transparent than either utility or reason.

At the time, anthropology was moving away from a Darwinian legacy, which traced human development to the utility of survival. Likewise, archaeology, as it dealt in material remains, obtained to a natural bias toward material causation, often linking it with Marxist theory. Yet Jones, like Dawson, suggested that without gratuity-ness, there would be no human culture, and we would remain beasts. So when it comes to human history, the fundamental determining point is the seemingly pointless.

Today, however, the views of these Catholic (or Catholic-inclined) thinkers seem less eccentric. Anthropologists now conjecture that agriculture and the taming of animals may have begun as ritual practices even before their utility was grasped, rather than as useful practices being later ritualized once a society's material resources had become sedimented. Evolutionary theorists surmise that play came before work, and if they go on to say that this is for more basic reasons of adaptation, they are being inconsistent, since this cannot be proven, as Aristotle knew. In the pre-human world, it seems likely that change is at first random and then proves useful or is made to be so. Equally, modern archaeology is inclined to read ancient sites and practices as religious rather than practical. Why did prehistoric man invent mining by delving for flint in Norfolk when it was strewn all around them? Grime's Graves are now reinterpreted as initiation chambers or resources for more sacred as more deeply buried flint stones. The rings that surround hill forts may be to ward off demons as much as or more than mortal enemies; and so on. The material bias of the archaeologist's trade now suggests ritual gratuity and no longer stark utility to be located in the buried and concealed foundations beneath us.

The same applies to the origins of religion. Burial seems to be as old or perhaps older than language. Recent archaeological excavations in south-eastern Turkey and elsewhere suggest that it was not that sedimentation led to priesthood, but rather the reverse, for at Göbekli Tepe, we seem to have a temple to high gods built by hunter-gatherers (Cauvin 2000; Hodder 2001; Rollefson 2001).

So maybe gratuity is basic, and the unnecessary precedes the necessary. Maybe ritual is first, basic, and last, just because it is more than basic, and yet less than reflectively transparent. Maybe we are naturally religious creatures because we have a certain kind of body, just as much as because we have a certain type of mind.

It is still not so common in anthropological circles to take Western Christian forms as ethnographical source material, and yet, if we find that the impulse to worship is a universal, transhistorical one, without wishing to unify it as a uniform act or set of actions, it may be salutary to consider the logic of Western Christian liturgical forms, as conceived by its speculative and theological origins, as well as by the assumptions of its participants, as a starting point to further understandings of ritual enactment more generally. It may also be the case that, in doing this, we may understand in new ways certain aspects of these apparently well-understood ritual practices. Although I am examining the relationship between form and content in a particular set of religious practices and texts, I propose from these examples to suggest that ritual enactment of this kind may have a specific role to play in the production of human meaning as such. I will return to these questions of meaning and ritual below.

Liturgy is generally situated within the broader category of ritual. The Greek denotation of "work of the people" (*leitourgia*) tends to be condensed in usage to refer to a specific rite or ritual enactment. Christian liturgical enactment emplots the lineaments of specific social memories, anticipated by the originary, founding command to "do this in remembrance of me": a command that pre-contains all future instantiations.

In line with the foregoing, recent study of premodern monastic and liturgical ritual has emphasized that such operations do not encode hidden messages remote from ordinary activity, nor divide inner purpose from outward gesture. Rather, they seek to realign inner motive and outer shape via the formation of virtues through the exercise of certain disciplines that are embedded within, and constitutive of, a way of life. Indeed, rather than appending ritual activity to the normative instrumental activity of the everyday, it is implied that, if anything, it is the other way around.

Giorgio Agamben has recently argued that Christianity, especially in the religious orders, sought to bring the ritual character of human life to a new height of intensity by merging liturgy with life. One sees this in the unceasing round of Cluniac prayer, the Benedictine integration of labor into liturgy, the attempt of the orders of friars to extend this coincidence to everyday life. Being, life, and prayer by aspiration come to coincide (Agamben 2012). On this view, Christianity is the most religious of religions, if ritual is central to them all. And one could say that there is a special reason for studying its "total" liturgy, cosmic as well as human, leaving not a sliver of interval between action and symbolic meaning. It could be then that the examination of Christian liturgy offers certain unique keys to ritual theory in general.

But in what ways does Christian ritual bring together bodily activity on the one hand with sense or meaning on the other?

Liturgy as Mystery and *Kenosis*

For the Christian tradition, human beings are mixed creatures, neither quite beast nor quite angel, as Blaise Pascal expressed it (Pascal 1897: §329). This apparently grotesque hybridity is our miniature dignity. Unlike angels, as human beings, we combine in our persons every level of the created order, from the inorganic, through the organic and the animally psychic, to the angelically intellectual. And so God must communicate to human beings through their bodies and senses as a tilting of his sublime thought toward their particular mode of understanding. But this does not denote merely condescension and economic adaptation. This is because human beings, unlike angels, have privileged access to the mute language of physical reality (St. Thomas Aquinas, *ST* I, q.77, a.3 resp). The latter is an essential part of God's creation for a biblical outlook, part of the plenitude of divine self-expression, and so in this respect, human beings enjoy a certain advantage as compared with angelic spiritual confinement. For even if material reality is lower in metaphysical status than angelic or human rational being, it must, as part of the pleni-tude of creation as a whole, be an essential part, and so reveal something of God hidden even from the angels themselves, just as the angels (according to the New Testament) could not comprehend the mystery of the Incarnation. The dumb simplicity and lack of reflexivity in physical things, or the spontaneity of animals, show aspects of the divine simplicity and spontaneity itself, which cannot be evident to the somewhat reflective, discursive, and abstracting operation of limited human or angelic minds.

This is why sacramental signs have, for Christian theology, a heuristic function; they are not just illustrative or metaphorical. They prompt human beings to new thought and provide guidance into deeper modes of meditation because they contain a surplus that thought can never fully anticipate or fathom. It is also the case, as Aquinas elaborates in his discussion of analogical language (in *ST* I, q.13), that when we harness a metaphor, or hazard an analogy, we cannot comprehensively survey its meaning, but only tenta-tively move in the direction of its meaning, or hurl ourselves into it—for the source of its meaning lies pre-eminently in God, and only, as it were, derivatively, by dint of the metaphysics of participation, in the world at hand; that this is the case in theological dis-course, which only intensifies what pertains in the case of all language.

Liturgy is therefore seen not simply as a public duty relating to collective concerns (often today expressed in the political focus of petitionary prayers) that stand in contrast to inner spiritual formation. Rather, it is itself the primary way in which the Christian, throughout her life, from baptism to extreme unction, is gradually inducted into the mystery of revelation and transformed by it.

"Mystery" for St. Paul names the primal secret shown through Christ's life and the liturgical participation in that secret: "the wisdom shown in mystery that was once hid-den," as one might translate the phrase in 1 Corinthians 2:7 (see also 1 Cor 5:51; Col 1:27; and Matt 13:11). It is an ancient Greek term whose early context was the mystery reli-gions, especially those of the cults of Eleusis, Ilion, Thebes, and Arcadia, and the oracular cult of Boeotia. While such rites had initially been seen as local fertility cults (Mikalson 2005: 85–87), and have been described as more fragile and human-orientated than the mysteries of Christianity (Burkert 1987), some later commentators have observed a metaphysical and sometimes Pythagorean element in the cults, associated with an induction into immortal life for the participants' souls (Cosmopoulos 2003; Mikalson 2005: 90). The word *musterion* referred to the rite itself, which revealed and yet preserved a secret. Its Eleusinian context, indeed, thematized the withholding of secrets: "the awful mysteries [are] not to be transgressed, violated, or divulged, because the tongue is restrained by reverence for the gods" (*Hymn to Demeter*, Athanassakis 1976).

One can suggest that Paul's later use of the term, whilst retaining a resonance of mys-tery, presents the withheld quality of divine secrecy as compatible with, and not contra-dicted by, revealedness. The revelation in Christ as perpetuated by the church implies that Paul regarded the historical drama of Christ's life (which indeed began with his obscurely liturgical baptism by John in the Jordan) as itself a liturgy, the perfect wor-ship of the Father, which could be performed by the Son alone. However, Paul implic-itly saw the liturgy of the church as a making present again, a showing forth, and even continuation of, the original salvific drama. These human contributions to the mystery are a crucial part of its secret, new stages in its unfolding, showing forth what is at the same time, and by the same gesture, held back.

It follows that, within the Christian mysteries, humanity is thought to be redeemed through participation in the liturgical process; this is at once a speaking, acting, sensorial and contemplative process, as the twentieth-century German liturgist, Dom Odo Casel, emphasized, even if the etiology and full entailments of words and actions are not commanded, or even known or understood (Casel 1963; Bouyer 1978; Louth 2007). The Christian mystery, like the pagan mysteries, concerns an induction into things shown, said and done, but not exhaustively interpreted. Otherwise, Christ would be a human example, and not the God-Man who infused into humanity a new sharing in the divine life by conjoining his own body with the body of the church. However, the Christian mystery, unlike pagan mysteries, is an initiation offered to all, to slaves and metics as well as to freemen, women, and children. It brings together initiation with universal citizenship and an entering of all into a school of wisdom, so synthesizing mystical, political, and philosophical elements that classical antiquity had tended to keep apart (Blumenfeld 2001).

But the "logic" of Christian liturgy is not seen as a means to transform the consciousness of the worshipper by a vivid appeal to his imagination, even if this is indeed one of its aspects. Rather, as the early twentieth-century German Catholic philosopher and priest Romano Guardini emphasized, liturgy is a kind of play, something which is carried through like a game for its own sake, and not for the sake of anything else (Guardini 1934: 176–184). The only reason for performing a liturgy is that there might be more liturgies, and that its participants might eventually offer themselves in the eschatological liturgy. That ultimate worship, like all preceding worship, enacts and celebrates the outgoing of all things from God and the return of all things to God, including the rejection of God by created things through the perverse will of human beings and fallen angels, and the divine overcoming of this rejection through the "mystery" of the divine descent and human elevation.

But liturgy is also seen as a play more serious than any seriousness. It incorporates the cosmic drama of divine descent and human elevation; to be fallen means to be without the capacity of rising by one's own account. For Christian understanding, once Adam had asserted himself against God and so ceased to offer all back to God in worship, it was not possible for him to recover himself by recovering a true concept of the divine. This concept was available only through the right orientation of the human person—in her spirit, soul, and body—in worship. In order to restore human worship of God, God must himself descend in person to offer again through the human being such true human worship.

Liturgy and Embodiment

The kenotic movement that is central to Christian liturgy is repeated within the ordering of the individual human economy itself. Even though the body and the senses can teach the mind something that the mind does not know, requiring the mind's humble submission to the body, it is nonetheless the case that the mind should govern the body on account of its greater capacity to abstract, judge, and comprehend. But when Adam and Eve yielded to temptation, they allowed their greedy and power-seeking passions to overrule their intellects. In this way, the natural government of the mind over the passions, the senses, and the body was overthrown.

However, Augustine, other Church Fathers, and Aquinas taught that this natural order is paradoxically to be restored through a further humiliation of the mind. The body, the senses, and the passions are relatively innocent; they have simply been given undue weight. The mind, on the other hand, is submitted to a more distinct perversity. So the senses must now be deployed, liturgically, to re-instruct the mind.

The logic behind this is as follows. Because the means deployed was in the first instance the incarnation of the Logos, and this involved, beyond instrumentality, the eternal elevation of Christ's human nature, including his body, to unity with the godhead, all human sensation is likewise eternally raised higher than its originally created dignity. As the Eastern Orthodox tradition has emphasized, matter—and particularly the human body—is now, after the Incarnation, more porous to the passage of the divine light (Boulnois 2008: 133–185). The play of the liturgy is therefore a play of the newly transformed and heightened or intensified senses, beckoning the intellect to follow them back into the divine ludic economy.

Since the passions and the sensations have now become ontologically heightened, the tradition also intermittently recognized a subtle transformation in the ontological order of gender relations: a man, Christ, stands still highest amongst humanity, yet only as more than human, as divine reason incarnate. But within the ranks of human beings, a woman now stands in the highest place: Mary the Mother of God. Since the supposedly weaker sex first fell victim to temptation, it is the weaker sex that must reverse this temptation and be raised to the status of first amongst mortals, more elevated even than the cherubim. As certain medieval writers suggested, whilst it was Eve who seized the fruit of the knowledge of good and evil from the tree, so it is Mary who through a passionate yielding to the Holy Spirit now bears in her womb the living fruit of the Word of God itself, and this is later transformed into the fruit of the Eucharist, which all may eat for their salvation (Astell 2006: 27 ff). The liturgical action is not only primarily a sensory affair; it is also a movement of active receptivity on the part of the church, which is identified with Mary as the bride as well as the mother of Christ. As passionate bride, she is conjoined to the bridegroom of true reason in order once more to engender the bridegroom as human son in the new form of a sacramental food that is nourishing to our entire person—body, senses, imagination, and intellect.

Finally, liturgy is cast as neither passive contemplation nor merely a human work of art. Rather, it is held to exceed this contrast. The liturgy is not thought to be entirely a human artifact, but is somewhat given to us, because the life of Christ is, as we have seen, the first liturgy and continuing inner reality of all Christian liturgies. This is the way in which it is thought that the full grace of Christ comes to human beings—liturgically, in baptism, the Eucharist, and other sacraments. But because it comes liturgically, it is not something in which participants must simply passively believe, and so be "justified" by extrinsic imputation, as for certain Protestant readings of St. Paul (Casel 1963: 9). Rather, because grace is liturgical in character, the transmission of a mystery through a sharing in that mystery, the reception of grace has from the outset also a practical dimension. In order to receive the action of the liturgy, human beings must also perform it, and in this respect it is a "human work of art." The *Opus Dei* of the liturgy, as it was known to the Benedictine order, could not be "work" at all unless it were also a human work (Clark 2011: 60 ff.). David Jones's idea of the modernist work of art, as exceeding human experience and intention, thereby becoming a quasi-liturgical thing in itself, can be connected with this tradition.

Guardini, in line with the medieval attempt to render all of life liturgical, suggested that liturgy overcomes this duality between life's pathos and art's idealization of life because here the contrast between "real" history and artistic representation is foregone. Within liturgical time and space, participants borrow liturgical roles that they put on more intensely than those they inhabit in their quotidian runnels. Just as liturgical symbols and objects are hyperreal, more real than everyday instrumental things or words, so the worshipers become themselves, as being works of art. In this way, one can see how liturgy could be seen to fulfill the purposes of art as imaging according to the modern Russian filmmaker and photographer, Andrei Tarkovsky. The image should displace the original because the original thereby becomes more itself, if what a created thing and especially the human creature is, is after all "image," the image of God. So when in the course of liturgy, the participants are transformed into a wholly signifying—because worshipping—body, they are at that moment closest to their fulfillment as human beings.

In these four aspects we find a context for thinking about liturgy and the senses: (1) sacraments are heuristic, not metaphoric; (2) the physical and sensorial liturgical enactment is itself the work of saving mystery; (3) liturgy involves a redemptive heightening of the senses into the playing of the divine game; and (4) liturgy exceeds the contrast of art and life, transforming the human body into transparent image.

THE SPIRITUAL SENSES

These aspects must be borne simultaneously in mind in our further reflection on the innate logic of Christian liturgy.

Sensation, in a liturgical context, has both a passive and an active dimension, in accordance with the principle that liturgy is a divine-human work because it is a Christological work. In liturgy the participants *undergo* sensory experiences, but they—collectively—*produce* this sensory experience, along with the natural materials that they deploy.

First, let us consider the sensing, spectatory aspect, remembering that this cannot readily be divided from the sensation-forming, acting aspect. Sensory experience in liturgy is not a prompt or cue for the intellect to speak the real lines of the drama in its higher, interior chamber. It is not an instrumental pedagogy of the mind. Indeed, insofar as the sensory and aesthetic experience of the Mass is a manner of instruction adapted to the mode of humanity, as Thomas Aquinas emphasized, it incites the participants' spiritual desire to penetrate further into the secret, and worship ever more ardently (Pickstock 2001). Were the smell of incense or the sight of the procession or the savor of the elements mere triggers for the recollection of concepts, held aloft, they might do their work on one single occasion, once and for all. But they must be repeated and returned to, and this suggests that they are vehicles for the forward moving of human spiritual desire, which can never entirely be disincarnate and so separated from these physical allurements.

This point can appear to be contradicted by the long Christian tradition of "the spiritual senses." This tradition was linked with meditation upon Solomon's *Song of Songs,* an erotic poem about the love between an unidentified man and woman which the church has read allegorically to refer both to the love between God and the soul and between Christ and his bride, the church. Since this poem involves an active catalogue of bodily parts and sensations, a luxuriant *allegoresis* sought to find both spiritual and ecclesial equivalents for each one of these physical aspects. It spoke, for example, following certain beginnings with St. Paul, of "the eyes of faith," of the neck as representing steadfastness, of hair which cannot suffer even when cut as representing spiritual endurance, of the ears as actively obedient to God's Word, of the lips as pouring forth the honey of divine praise, of the feet as the heart's following in the footsteps of previous saints and hastening to welcome Christ the bridegroom (Chrétien 2005).

This might seem to reduce to the operation of a rather mechanical sort of metaphor: the senses as they function within the liturgy being harnessed as natural symbols for an inner attentiveness and responsiveness to divine meaning. However, the sacraments are *heuristic* rather than metaphorical. If sensations are essential lures for our true thinking, and all the more so in the order of redemption after the Fall, can it be that the "spiritual" sensations are all that really matter?

The French philosopher Jean-Louis Chrétien has shown in his discussion of the tradition of commentary upon the *Canticles* why this is not so. First, the idea of the "spiritual senses," or the notion that there are psychic equivalents for physical sensations and even parts of the body, is traceable to Origen, as earlier thinkers such as Karl Rahner and Hans Urs von Balthasar have pointed out. This holds a biblical rather than Greek lineage, since the Bible spoke of "the heart" of a human being in a way that was both physical and spiritual, and included both thinking and willing, as well as suggesting a concentration of the whole human personality (Webb 2005: 2010). This sense is preserved today in the liturgical *sursum corda:* "lift up your hearts." It is, however, the Christian reading of the *Canticles* as referring to our love for Christ who is God incarnate, which seems to have suggested a kind of physicalization and diversification of the biblical heart, which, for Origen, was more commonly thought of in terms of the soul or *anima,* though Augustine often reverts to heart or *cor.* One should not read this, Chrétien argues, as simply many analogues for the essential unity of the heart or soul: only in God is it the case that the diversity of the spiritual senses is mysteriously "one" in pure simplicity.

Rather, there is a real diversity in the human soul, on account of its close link with the body of which it is the form, in Greek philosophical terms. The soul "hears," for example, in its imaginative recollection or in its mental attention to God, because it is primarily conjoined with the hearing function of the physical body (Chrétien 2005: 15–44).

However, as Chrétien implies, the point just made may be reversed. It is not that, via a secondary move, sensation is metaphorically transferred from body to soul; rather, it is the case that sensing has a double aspect, outer and inner, from the very outset, in accordance with the double biblical meaning of the term "heart." And here one can reiterate the point that liturgy can be seen as the best guide to the double aspects of *all* sensation, which they instantiate in an intensified manner. Here Christian liturgy points to the primacy for humanity and history, of ritual over both material utility and ideal intention, as Dawson argued. For, as has been discussed, the core gesture of ritual is simultaneously externalizing and interiorizing. This is because the ritual object "interrupts" and "stands out," because a normally taken for granted exterior process is here stalled through reflection and so pleated or folded in upon itself both as artefact and as mental awareness. Without this exterior and interior duality, it could not occur.

A related point is that if one sees with the outer as well as with the inner eye, then one relates one mode of sensation to another. Our seeing dark trees against the background of the setting sun is affected by our awareness that we can touch the one and not the other. And were it not for our sense of hearing, we would never be able to see the organ in a church as an organ, a musical instrument, at all. The mental operation of synesthesia is in play whenever just one of our physical senses is activated (Chrétien 2005: 35). The Church Fathers sometimes spoke in synesthetic terms when they suggested that our eyes should listen, our ears see, or our lips attend like ears to the word of God through a spiritual kiss, suggesting that for our inner sense, contemplation is also active obedience and vice versa, while all our speaking to and of God must remain an active attention to his presence. But this kind of language does not remove us from our literal bodies: rather, an inner and a synesthetic response pervades our bodily surface in the course of our original sensitive responses.

What this implies for liturgical practice is that worshippers are regarded as making a response of incarnate souls—a response of the heart—to the incarnate God. This response is immediately inscribed in their bodies and requires no interpretation. In liturgical terms, worshippers are invited to adopt diverse stances appropriate to the various phases of worship and the various positions that should be assumed before God. Sometimes they stand before God, alert and ready as his militant troops, as Guardini suggests (Guardini 1993: 21–23). Sometimes they kneel before him, adopting a posture that, according to some writers in the Christian tradition, rehearses both corporeally and psychically the fetal situation of a baby in the womb. Here the worshippers express their birth from Mother Church as well as their dependence upon God. The drawing closer together of the knees and the cheeks suggests for some sources a concentration around the eyes, the source of tears which should constantly be shed by the Christian soul, both for sorrow and for joy. This suffering includes a constant spiritual shedding of blood. According to a "synorganic" logic, psychic blood was regarded as blood that is clear with the luminosity of tears that are transparent to the divine light (Chrétien 2005: 42–43). At other times, such as in processionals, the soul and body should be in movement towards God, towards other members of the congregation, or outwards towards the world.

As for the feet, so for the hands. Sometimes they are tightly clasped together as though guarding psychic or bodily integrity. At other times, they are placed palm to palm in serene self-meeting through self-touching that allows the beginning of psychic reflexivity. Equally, however, as every Christian child used to be taught, this gesture expresses microcosmic identity with the church and its attentive pointing towards God. Hands may also be raised in supplication or openly uplifted by the priest in a gesture of triumphant saturation by the divine. Finally, the priestly hand is often raised in blessing, which is an acknowledgement of what is there, and what has been done, which is a conferring of grace, and which allows what is there fully to be at all—echoing the divine benediction, "and God saw that it was good," in his act of creation (Guardini 1956: 15–18, 81–84).

The Eucharist without Hegel

If, as we have seen, bodily postures are also inward, then conversely inner sensation has an outward aspect. Because sensation has an interior aspect from the beginning, it becomes possible for this interior aspect to be deepened, and so for the sight of material things to turn into the sight of spiritual things. However, the possibility of this deepening is paradoxically connected with the *excess of material things* over rational thought. The mind can exceed abstract reflection in the direction of mystical encounter (the inward absorption of the liturgical mysteries) only through the constantly renewed prompting of corporeal sensing of the sacramental realities. The distance of material things from us is a vehicle for conveying the infinite "distance" of God from us. And because of the Incarnation, in the eucharistic liturgy, these two distances become one and the same.

For Christian practice, the Eucharist can become an object of contemplation that extends beyond the eucharistic liturgy itself. Here, nevertheless, the tradition underwent changes in terms of the subtle complexity of the original logic. The reserved sacrament or the exposed and paraded elements carried in a Corpus Christi procession brought an emphatic sacralization of matter out into the streets (de Lubac 2006), by emphasizing the physical manifestation of God within inhabited time and space and the Christian worshiper's need to dwell upon this wonder.

If the Eucharist renders the distance of matter from us also the distance of God from us, then, when the participants receive the eucharistic elements, it is assumed that God comes to be as close to them as food and drink entering their stomach. Hegel suggested that human religion began when people stopped seeing nature as simply something to be eaten and started to contemplate it instead. But this would suggest that specific sacramentality began with the reservation of nature and the simplistic move from the utile to the conceptual (Hegel 1977: §109; Hammacher 1998). It is rather the case that human eating has always had a ritual dimension, in accordance with the new evidence, mentioned above, from Turkey and elsewhere, that religion preceded the birth of agriculture. Religion began with a sacred doing and not a sacred looking, even though the latter is an aspect of the former. Thus, the monumental findings at Göbekli Tepe suggest the primacy of ritual but not the Hegelian primacy of ideas in human formation. On the contrary, it indicates ways in which human religion remains firmly rooted in material reality.

And ritual eating has always been at the heart of most religion, conjoined with sacrificial practices (Detienne and Vernant 1989). Eucharistic worship sustains this human universality, but with the radical emphasis that the supreme Creator God has been sacrificed for humanity and offers himself more than humanity can offer itself to him, since he sustains humanity through a spiritual feeding (Astell 2006: 227–253).

In the eucharistic rite, moreover, one finds a combining of spectacle with feasting. Not merely is the sacred food accompanied by ritual; it is itself the supreme ritual object and the very thing that is most displayed, in the elevation by the priest. Albert the Great spoke of the supreme beauty of the eucharistic host in terms which combine inner and outward aspects. The elements, like the crocus flower, exhibit *claritas*, *subtilitas*, and *agilitas*, since they show the splendor of the fullness of grace, penetrate to the height of deity, and flow with the fragrant odor of the virtues (Astell 2006: 54–61). There may seem to be something shocking in the idea that the participants then proceed to "eat beauty," but, as the historian Ann Astell has shown, this idea was thematized in the Middle Ages. Whereas under ordinary circumstances, to eat beauty would be to destroy it, here the eaters are partially assumed by the very beauty they consume, and their own beings are transfigured and shine with a new inward and outer light. By a further process of synesthesia, the participants are called upon in the Mass to "taste and see," not first to see and then to taste, but through tasting seemingly to see further (Astell 2006: 1–26).

But this is not to suggest that the Middle Ages neglected the ugliness of the crucified Christ or the sorrows of Mary, which had distorted the appearance of a woman whose beauty was held to exceed even that of Helen of Troy. Far from it; the Christ of the Eucharist is the Christ of the Passion, a grotesquely wounded divine-human form. However, by grace even this grotesqueness is transfigured into beauty, just as the destruction visited upon Christ on the cross is transformed into a positive voluntary self-destruction of the body of Christ through our eating, which permits him to nourish the church as his body (Astell 2006: 54–61). Hegel saw in the Passion of Christ the source of "romantic" art, one which combines the symbolism of the monstrous found in most pagan art with the beauty of divinized human form found in Greek art. But for Hegel this heralded the "end" of art and its displacement into philosophy and politics, since the sacred was shown in the ordinary, the ugly, the discarded, the sufferings of the human subject through which it develops—and which exceed—the idea of beauty (Hegel 1975). But for a traditional Christian viewpoint, the perspective of art is infinitely opened up and cannot be superseded. In the light of the cross, the ugly is not discarded, but integrated into the divine beauty itself. God is not identified with the abandoned ordinary by which we come to an abstract self-realization; rather, all our specific human narratives of suffering become suffused with a significance that allows them in their specificity to mediate the divine. Instead of Christ abandoning his broken body for internal consolation, he appears as the resurrected Christ whose wounds are now glorious. And instead of Christian people abandoning the bread and wine as only that, in order to fulfill human unity in the political state, they must again and again find the source of this unity in the transubstantiated physical elements themselves.

The specifically Christian logic at work here is that of paradox rather than of dialectic. The latter never exceeds a merely negative relation between opposites (*contra* Žižek 2006: 68–123), whereas for a paradoxical perspective, God is also Man—not God as mere manhood, but both God and Man at the same time. By analogy, body and blood are also bread and wine, and our inner senses remain conjoined with our outer ones. It is this very outerness that allows our interior being to be exalted through a spiritual diversification.

The Body as Ritual Mediator

The sensory aspect of the liturgy is, however, not merely something passively *received* by the individual worshiper; it is also actively and collectively *produced*. Altogether, the participants pray, sing, process, look forward, and exchange the *pax* through mutual touch. The resultant sensory experience can to some degree be received by an individual worshipper, but it presumably exists more fundamentally for an angelic and a divine gaze.

The collective body of the congregation is nonetheless made up of individual bodies. It is the individual body that stands as the gatekeeper between the two different allegorical senses for the bodies of the lovers in the *Canticles*—by allusion to the soul, on the one hand, and to the church, on the other. The parts of these bodies and their sensations have spiritual aspects as the spiritual senses. Thereby, as we have seen, Christianity diversified the unity of the soul. Bodies and their sensations, following St. Paul, represent offices in the church, since the latter, more emphatically than the soul, is taken to be the "bride" of the *Canticles*. And so Christianity unified the human social community in a very specific manner (Chrétien 2005: 15–72).

The relationship between the inner soul and the collective body as mediated by the individual body is crucial to a deepened grasp of the liturgical action that dramatizes the relationship between Christ and his bride. In doing so, it draws, like Christianity itself, upon a certain fluidity within the *Canticles*, a book that Chrétien suggests the church effectively raised to the status of a kind of "Bible within the Bible," a hermeneutic key to the relationship between the two testaments (Chrétien 2005: 291–295).

It was such a key despite or perhaps because of its own obscurity and need or call for interpretation. Chrétien observes that we do not know who its protagonists are at a literal level, and their status as lover and beloved is not exhausted by any conceptual equivalence. They are God and Israel, Christ and the church, Christ and the soul, but also human marriage partners (given the Pauline signification of Christ and the church) as the supreme model of natural inter-human love, and so by extension they represent any human loving relationship. We can see a pattern here: a sensory image elevates the participants' perceptions, but it does so because and not despite the fact that it is a sensory image. It can further elevate them only if it is constantly returned to, just as the human worshiper can grow in love for God only if she is constantly re-confronted with the challenge of her human neighbor.

In the liturgy, all these relationships are at stake. And the individual, sensing physical body is their pivot. Just how are we to understand its mediating role? One can start with the earlier observation that while Christianity diversifies the soul, it also grants organic unity to the human collectivity. Instead of the *polis* being compared with the hierarchy of the soul, as for Plato, St. Paul compares the church polity to the co-operation of the various functions of the human body. However, this is no more a metaphor than was the case with the relationship of the physical with the spiritual senses. If anything, as Chrétien points out, metaphoricity runs from the collective to the individual body. This is because St. Paul speaks of eye and hand, head and feet announcing their need for one another, like holders of different offices within the church (1 Cor 12:21). Yet this is to compare eye and hand, which in reality are mute, with individual Christians, who are not, rather than the other way around (Chrétien 2005: 45–72). Similarly, one might expect a metaphoric transference of the unity of the physical body to the unity of the Christian people. However, the "bodiliness" of a social body is not a fiction; it is literally the case that human beings physically and culturally depend upon one another, and one could argue that this is our primary source for our understanding of embodied unity.

The parts of the soul-body remain as parts, however, and might be regarded as merely apparent diversifications on the surface of something more fundamentally one. It is rather through the comparison of the eye and the hand and other bodily parts to members of the church that this possibility is interpretatively avoided, and so the body, and in consequence the soul, are dramatically diversified. Only the collective body of the church possesses decisively distinct parts, since these are independent persons with independent wills, even though they are diversified according to specifically defined offices—priesthood, prophecy, the diaconate, and so forth—rather than according to their biological individuality. For this reason, the church, unified through the Holy Spirit, uniquely possesses a fully organic or bodily unity, a unification of genuinely independent parts that nonetheless exceeds their sum.

This reflection suggests the priority that traditional theologians have given to the church-reference over the soul-reference with respect to the import of the bride in the *Canticles*. Our bodies and souls are to be conformed to the church more than the other way around. This is why there can be no Christian non-liturgical spirituality. For the rich potential of diversity specific to the Christian soul is opened up through participation in collective worship, just as the unity of individual character is given as a mirroring of the collective character of the church. When participants lose themselves in the liturgical process, they *find* themselves, whereas when they cleave to a supposedly natural unity of soul and body, they will find that this hysterically dissolves (Chrétien 2005: 45–72, 294–295).

At the same time, the individual is not absorbed into the congregation as though into a modern undifferentiated mass or "crowd," which represents an anti-congregation (Canetti 1984). Individual rumination within and upon the liturgy is crucial, and this is shown especially with respect to the traditional *Canticles* imagery of the teeth. Collectively speaking, the teeth guard the church, but they also allow entrance of the divine word and a mastication of this word by church doctors in order that they further utter through their mouths truths appropriate to time, place, and circumstance. But this digestive process can only be consummated within the individual person, the organic unity of soul and body (Chrétien 2005: 73–88).

Individual and Corporate Bodies in Tension

One can observe in Christian practice a liturgical tension between the priority of a congregational construction of sensation on the one hand, and a private sensory meditation on the other. This tension is benign and perhaps never resolved, since it derives from the originally liminal and oneiric character of all ritual action. All the same, one might suggest that three rites in particular hold this tension in balance. The first is the "solemnization" of matrimony, a "sacrament of the natural law" and not a sacrament of the gospel, in which bridegroom and bride are directly personified, returning both the collective and the psychic allegory to their literal base through their performative utterance of vows. Here the inward and the outer sensory responses are at one, since the private is immediately the communal when two bodies become one.

However, in the second place, the rite of the anointing of monarchs also suggests a certain synthesis (Chrétien 2005: 294–295). Here, the unity of the Christian body depends both upon a continuous invisible collective body, associated with the eternal church in heaven, and upon the actual personal authority of one man. This dual requirement was theologically thematized in the Middle Ages by the idea of the king's two bodies, his literal body and his fictional undying one, which came to be associated with the mystical body of the church, once this term had migrated from denoting the body of the eucharistic elements to the body of the church itself. Here, the "inward" spiritual aspect of the body now belongs to the collective body, and the outward physical aspect to the individual body of the king.

And yet the same modification occurs with respect to the sacrament of ordination. Christ as the one high priest is conjoined with the church but is also in excess of it, as represented by the bishop and his representative, the priest. Christ in his concrete person constitutes the church in its spiritual collectivity. Imperfectly to extend this, we need both the collective lay body and the individual episcopal representative. Action belongs more to the former, symbolism to the latter, as with coronation. But because of this, marriage achieves the more perfect ritual and eucharistic synthesis of life and liturgy.

The synthesis achieved by coronation and ordination is not as complete as that achieved in marriage: for here active concreteness and mystical symbolism stand equally on either side of a dual relationship. Here the bride is more fully deified than is the political or ecclesial populace as united with the bridegroom. But, inversely, the bridegroom, representing Christ, only is such by the equal active reception of the bride, just as the Son is only born of the Father eternally through the desire of the Spirit and this is perfectly echoed on earth by Mary's yes to the Incarnation. She only says yes in obedience to the Logos being born within her, yet were she not, as the Thomist Dominican Louis Chardon taught, the uniquely highest yet not divine human being by virtue of her perfect yes that coincides with the eternal yes of the Spirit to the Father, Christ could not have been born on earth (Chardon 2004 [1657]: 407–429). This yes is already the yes of the collective church, and this suggests, following Matthias Scheeben, the incarnation of the Spirit in the church and so a new equality of bride with bridegroom, which is shown if one thinks of the sacraments of marriage and the eucharist together (Scheeben 2006: 539–610). Balthasar echoed this, but evaded the feminist implication of this extended but orthodox Trinitarian logic. The actively receptive feminine is no longer subordinate but paradoxically equal to the initiator.

By the examples of coronation and ordination, we are reminded nevertheless that the church is a hierarchical organism. Since hierarchy is, following Pseudo-Dionysius, a matter of instruction and elevation of person by person, not of fixed positions, we can see how hierarchy can lend itself to a fusion or coordination of the individual with the collective. The hierarchical offices of the church are provided liturgically and are reproduced through liturgical performance, which is sensory in character. They concern the relative verbal activity of the priesthood and the relative verbal passivity of the laity. Yet they also concern the relatively contemplative vocation of the clergy and the relatively active vocation of laypeople (Chrétien 2005: 65–68).

The liturgical participants never leave their senses behind, and they must work together to produce a collective "sensation," which fuses life with art. But with respect to questions of government and human relationship, we can see how liturgy opens out beyond what happens inside church buildings. The redemption of the world is understood to evolve the increasing absorption and fulfillment of human and cosmic life within liturgical celebration.

THE END OF THE BODY

In the foregoing ways, Christian liturgy exemplifies the logic of ritual process. But more specifically, it inflects this logic with an emphasis upon the body as the mediator between inner and outer, which ritual experience must hold in balance. This insistence upon the body as a crucial pivot helps to perfect this balance.

Such corporeal focus arises because of Christian incarnationalism, and the mediation of the sacred through an economy (*oikonomia*) of the physical and the corporeal.

Moreover, beyond the economic perspective, the doctrine of the resurrection exalts the body to an eternal finality. In consequence, as we have seen, the intensification of bodily experience in Christian liturgy is often regarded as being in harmony with, and not opposed to, a spiritual intensification.

When the more iconoclastic aspect of the Reformation tended to qualify the logic of this incarnationalism, the eventual consequence was a weakening of the Christian hold upon the Western imagination. However, the consequence in turn of this weakening was not the vanishing of economism and corporo-centrism, but rather their seculariza-tion (Gregory 2012). Thus, as Giorgio Agamben implies after Foucault, Western moder-nity diverts the ancient Christian *oikonomia* by promoting an ever-more wide-reaching economism, which seeks to maintain social and political order by flexible adapta-tion to supposed "needs," which in reality it engenders and manipulates (Agamben 2008: 41–87). Equally, as Hervé Juvin has contended, bodily self-gratification, longevity, and the sustaining of eternal youth have become utopian market substitutes for tran-scendent goods and traditional self-transcending values (Juvin 2010).

Such a secularization of resurrection surpasses the secularization of the *oikonomia*, by usurping finality as well as redemption, because, as mentioned, the need for an econ-omy ceases at the eschaton. At that point, as Agamben points out, the hierarchical gov-erning function of the angels becomes coterminous with that of praise and no longer with that of a celestial Byzantine administration. At this point, liturgy becomes imme-diate and loses its mediating economic aspect. Accordingly, the role of the resurrected body becomes one of glorification, along with the glorified soul. Its "economic" role as mediator of redemption here lapses. In this way, the doctrine of the resurrection of the body would appear to affirm the eternal worth and mystery of matter beyond its neces-sary ministering function for the duration of time. Something, it would seem, for this outlook, is supposed to be said in matter, and something is said by matter, although this dark discourse cannot properly be articulated at all.

This vision accords with the logic of ritual, because, as we have seen, the inherently ritual birth of language suggests that in this threshold of sense resides the very possibil-ity of meaning. In the light of the doctrine of resurrection, the existence of a material creation and its derivation from God would seem to suggest that, for Christianity, this material and oneiric mystery of language persists at the very heart of the Godhead in the eternal "birth" of the Son as Logos from the paternal origin.

Christian Ritual
as Hyper-Corporeality

From this perspective, one can approach Christian liturgy not simply as the claimed worship of the triune God and of the Logos incarnate, but as a complex and collective attempt performatively to meditate upon the character of the pre-human Logos, which calls us within the dream of the body out of our merely corporeal state. In this respect, Christian liturgy performs a function that all cultural rituals perform to a degree; and, one might argue, in excess of the normal reach of philosophy.

However, I have suggested that one peculiar mark of Christian practical reflection upon the pre-human Logos is that the waking of mind from the corporeal dream is seen paradoxically as a further descent into the dream and the darkness of the corporeal: as an always incomplete deciphering of the dream logic of human bodily dwelling within the world. For this reason, it could be suggested that the Christian example of ritual is disclosive of the logic of ritual as such, because, in the typical act of deriving from ritual meaning, it reaches back into ritual depths. One aspect of the specificity of Christian liturgy and its hyperbolically ritual character as tending to subsume life into liturgy, might be its kenotic self-surrender to the oneiric darkness of ritual in general and the primordial beginnings of worship, which contemporary human beings are newly unearthing.

SUGGESTED READING

Asad (1993); Astell (2006); Bouyer (1978); Chrétien (2005); Guardini (1956); Hughes (2007); Jones (1959).

BIBLIOGRAPHY

Agamben, G. (1993 [1978]), *History and Infancy: Essays on the Destruction of Experience*, trans. L. Heron (London: Verso).

Agamben, G. (2008), *Le Règne et la Gloire*, trans. J. Gayraud and M. Rueff (Paris: Seuil).

Agamben, G. (2012), *Opus Dei: archeologia dell'ufficio: Homo sacer* II, 5 (Torino: Bollati Boringhieri).

Asad, T. (1993), *Genealogies of Religion: Disciplines and Reasons of Power in Christianity and Islam* (Baltimore, MD: The Johns Hopkins University Press).

Astell, A. W. (2006), *Eating Beauty: The Eucharist and the Spiritual Arts of the Middle Ages* (Ithaca, NY: Cornell University Press).

Athanassakis, A. N. (1976), *The Homeric Hymns* (Baltimore, MD: The Johns Hopkins University Press).

Blumenfeld, B. (2001), *The Political Paul; Justice, Democracy and Kingship in a Hellenistic Framework* (Sheffield: Sheffield Academic Press).

Boulnois, O. (2008), *Au-delà de l'image* (Paris: Seuil), 133–185.

Bouyer, L. (1978), *Life and Liturgy* (London: Sheed and Ward).

Burkert, W. (1987), *Ancient Mystery Cults* (Harvard, MA: Harvard University Press).

Canetti, E. (1984), *Crowds and Power*, trans. C. Stewart (New York: Farrar, Strauss and Giroux).

Casel, O. (1963), *The Mystery of Christian Worship*, trans. B. Neunhauser, O.S.B. (London: D. L. T.).

Cauvin, J. (2000), *The Birth of the Gods and the Origins of Agriculture*, trans. T. Watkins (Cambridge: Cambridge University Press).

Chardon, L. (2004), *La Croix du Jésus, où les plus belles vérités de la théologie mystique et de la grace sanctifiante sont étables* (first published 1657) (Paris: Cerf).

Chrétien, J. (2005), *Symbolique du Corps: La tradition chrétienne du Cantiques des Cantiques* (Paris: Presses Universitaires de France).

Clark, J. G. (2011), *The Benedictines in the Middle Ages* (London: Boydell).

Cosmopoulos, M. B. (ed.) (2003), *Greek Mysteries: The Archaeology and Ritual of Ancient Greek Secret Cults* (London: Routledge).

Dawson, C. (1998), *Christianity and European Culture*, ed. G. J. Russello (Washington, DC: Catholic University of America Press).

De Lubac, H. (2006), *Corpus Mysticum: The Eucharist and the Church in the Middle Ages*, trans. G. Simmonds et al. (London: SCM).

Detienne, M., and Vernant, J. P. (1989), *The Cuisine of Sacrifice Among the Greeks*, trans. P. Wistig (Chicago: Chicago University Press).

Gregory, B. S. (2012), *The Unintended Reformation: How a Religious Revolution Secularised Society* (Cambridge, MA: Harvard University Press).

Guardini, R. (1956), *Sacred Signs*, trans. G. Banham (St. Louis, MO: Pio Decimo).

Hamacher, W. (1998), *Pleroma: Reading in Hegel*, trans. N. Walker and S. Jarvis (London: Athlone Press).

Hegel, G. W. F. (1975), *Aesthetics: Lectures on Fine Art*, trans. T. M. Knox (Oxford: Oxford University Press).

Hegel, G. W. F. (1977), *Phenomenology of Spirit*, trans. A. V. Miller (Oxford: Oxford University Press).

Hervé, J. (2010), *The Coming of the Body*, trans. J. Howe (London: Verso).

Hocart, A. M. (1933), *The Progress of Man: A Short Survey of His Evolution, His Customs, and His Works* (London: Methuen and Co.).

Hodder, I. (2001), "Symbolism and the Origins of Agriculture in the Near East," *Cambridge Archaeological Journal* 11: 105–122.

Hughes, J. M. D. H. (2007), *The End of Work: Theological Critiques of Capitalism* (Oxford: Wiley-Blackwell).

Jones, D. (1959), *Epoch and Artist*, ed. H. Grisewood (London: Faber and Faber).

Louth, A. (2007), "Afterword: Mysticism: Name and Thing," *The Origins of the Christian Mystical Tradition*, 2nd ed. (Oxford: Oxford University Press).

Mikalson, J. D. (2005), *Ancient Greek Religion* (Oxford: Blackwell).

Pascal, B. (1897), *Pensées* (Paris: Delagrave).

Pickstock, C. J. C. (2001), *Thomas d'Aquin et la quête eucharistique* (Paris: Ad Solem).

Rollefson, G. O. (2001), "2001: An Archaeological Odyssey," *Cambridge Archaeological Journal* 11: 112–114.

Scheeben, M. J. (2006), *The Mysteries of Christianity*, trans. Cyril Vollert, S.J. (New York: Herder and Herder).

Tarkovskij, A. (2002), *Luce istantanea; Fotografie* (Milan: Ultreya).

Webb, H. (2005), "Catherine of Siena's Heart," *Speculum* 80: 802–817.

Webb, H. (2010), *The Medieval Heart* (New Haven, CT: Yale University Press).

Žižek, S. (2006), *The Parallax View* (Cambridge, MA: MIT Press).

CHAPTER 44

....

THE SACRAMENTS IN ECUMENICAL DIALOGUE

....

JORGE A. SCAMPINI, O.P.

A KEY AND COMPLEX ISSUE

THE sacraments are a key and complex issue, which is part of the agenda of the theological dialogues between Christian churches, and whose consideration demands that historical, disciplinary, liturgical, and pastoral aspects not be neglected. In fact, the divisions among Christians have had, as one of their causes and results, differences over the understanding and practice of the sacraments.

This is a key issue, first and foremost, because baptism and Eucharist play a central role in the life of faith and worship of a great many of the Christian communities, evidence of this being given by confessional texts, ritual books, and ecclesiastical praxis. In this way, at least recognized convergences (if not full consensus) are expressed, which evidence the degree of communion already existing among Christians, although it is true that it is in the celebration of the sacraments, especially the Eucharist, that the wound of disunity becomes painful.

It is a key issue also because the entire understanding of the Christian mystery converges in the notion of sacrament. Actually, the various forms of consensus, convergence, and divergence that exist in other realms of Christian doctrine have their expression here as in a neuralgic point: the understanding of the unique salvific mediation of Christ; the recognition or not of subordinated mediations and, if recognized, how to understand them without undermining the unique role of Christ; the relationship between the salvation gratuitously given by God in Christ and the free acceptance by human beings; and, lastly, the way of understanding the relationship between the testimony of the Scriptures and that which the church has interpreted throughout the centuries based on that testimony, where we find another open theme in ecumenical dialogue: the relationship between Scripture and Tradition.

At the same time, when faced with the challenge of overcoming the divergences that have caused and justified the divisions, sacraments appear as a complex issue because, when contemplating the spectrum of Christian churches, no homogenous doctrinal and liturgical-sacramental positions can be observed among them. A realistic vision resists our ability to reduce these positions to a few "models," although it is true that, in a schematic way and for pedagogical purposes, usually three major currents are mentioned:

a) A "Catholic" current that views sacraments as constituent elements of the church representing the apex of its liturgical life. These churches (Oriental Orthodox, Assyrian Church of the East, Eastern Orthodox, Roman Catholic, and Old Catholic), in their various ritual and theological traditions, recognize that the community of the faithful, redeemed by the blood of Christ and incorporated in him, is progressively led by means of sacraments towards transfiguration and divinization. Herein lies the profound life and reality of the church.

b) A second current would be represented by "Protestant" churches directly identified with the magisterial Reformation of the sixteenth century and, specifically, with the seventh article of the Confession of Augsburg (1530), received in practically all of the subsequent Protestant confessional texts (Anglicans, Lutherans, Reformed, and Methodist). These churches have preserved the two sacraments unquestionably attested to in Scriptures (baptism and Lord's Supper). When conceiving the relationship between Word and sacrament, this current, unlike the first, has placed the emphasis on the Word proclaimed, which is invested with sacramental significance. It is true that differences have arisen within this second current: while Lutherans have asserted that sacraments confer grace at the same level as the Word, the Reformed churches have at times seen in them a word of testimony that expresses the work of God in the believer.

c) Lastly, there is a third current, whose roots are found in the Anabaptist movement condemned by Martin Luther, which has carried the postulates of the Reformation to an extreme, emphasizing the role of personal faith, as commitment, over ecclesiastical faith (Mennonites, Baptists, and Pentecostals). According to this current, if a sacrament, or, better said, an "ordinance" of the Lord is recognized, it would be considered exclusively a response of the believer that "confirms the faith" that God has already given him.

This schematic vision, useful for pedagogical purposes, is in some sense overly simple, as there are authors who recognize at least five different positions with regard to ritual within Protestantism (Gisel 1995: 1341–1352). In addition, attention should be paid to the developments that have occurred, especially over the last century, in the different churches and confessional traditions at the level of ritual practices and theological reflection. At the same time, between interlocutors about whom no doubts exist that they have preserved the same faith and the same sacraments, as is the case of the Roman Catholic Church and the Eastern Orthodox churches, difficulties arise in another realm, that of sacramental practice, where both parties do not necessarily attribute the same weight to the differences.

If we take into account the preceding discussion, it seems clear that it is not easy to present the topic of sacraments in ecumenical dialogue while attempting to be synthetic and at the same time exhaustive. This calls for certain methodological options:

a) The first option is to determine whether it is best to focus only on the treatment of particular sacraments or, instead, assuming such treatments and taking them for granted, to attempt to identify the elements pertaining to a general theology of the sacraments. The advantage of this second possibility is that it enables us to approach the core of the divergences (notion and number; institution; "instrumentality" and "efficacy"; the relationship between Word and sacrament, as well as between faith and sacraments) that are expressed later when understanding each sacrament. If we observe the path followed by theological dialogues, we note that they have first of all taken the time to study one or some of the sacraments, and only in few instances have they moved on to themes pertaining to a general theory. This path seems logical because reflection on baptism and Eucharist was the step prior to an elaboration of a general theory about sacraments, something which not all confessional traditions have engaged in. To the extent possible, I will attempt to reconcile both options.

b) The main source for any presentation of the theme should be the documents that set out the results achieved in the different multilateral and bilateral theological dialogues celebrated between the different Christian churches in the last forty years. This involves dealing with a vast literature contained mostly in the three volumes entitled *Growth in Agreement* (*GiA*). These are texts of a diverse nature, with different scope and authority, not easily reducible to a single discourse. For the purpose of following a certain order, and respectful of the nature of the documents, I shall give priority to international dialogues without disregarding those local dialogues that, in my view, have made valuable contributions to the subject.

PARTICULAR SACRAMENTS
IN BILATERAL DIALOGUES

These dialogues have been established after the closure of Vatican Council II and, at present, constitute a dense network of relationships among churches of different confessional traditions. A criterion for my presentation will be the degree of affinity between the parties.

In the Eastern Orthodox–Roman Catholic dialogue, sacraments have since the beginning been considered as a solid basis that could be taken as the starting point to focus subsequently on possible divergences in the ecclesiological realm, as pointed out in the "Plan to set underway the theological dialogue between the Roman Catholic Church and the Orthodox Churches" (Borelli and Ericksson 1996: 47–52). Therefore, in the first stage, the commission assumed that the study of the sacraments was propitious for an in-depth and positive examination of the problems of the dialogue, because sacramental experience and theology express themselves in interrelated ways. That consensus was reflected in the treatment of the Eucharist and its ecclesiological implications ("The Mystery of the Church and of the Eucharist in the Light of the Mystery of the Holy Trinity, 1982" [*GiA II* 2000: 652–659]), of sacraments in general, and of sacraments of initiation ("Faith, Sacraments and the Unity of the Church, 1987" [*GiA II* 2000: 660–668]), and, finally, when considering the place that the sacrament of order occupies in the sacramental structure of the church ("The Sacrament of Order in the Sacramental Structure of the Church, 1988" [*GiA II* 2000: 671–679]).

However, the stage that concluded with the publication of the second of the documents just mentioned encountered a difficult moment: the discussions surrounding the scope of the differences existing in the liturgical practice of the sacraments of initiation and surrounding the question of whether or not it was possible to have a formal reciprocal recognition of baptism. Without relativizing these difficulties, which the dialogue attempted to overcome, it is important to recall some of the questions that guided the theological reflection: in which sense does the true faith have a relationship with the sacraments of the church? Do the sacraments of the church presuppose the faith? Or is the true faith the result of sacramental communion? Several principles were used as key criteria in the elaboration of the text: (a) Every sacrament presupposes and expresses the faith of the church that celebrates it. Indeed, in a sacrament, the church does more than profess and express her faith: she makes present the mystery that the sacrament celebrates. In this sense, Roman Catholics and Eastern Orthodox consider that the liturgical tradition is an authentic interpreter of revelation and the criterion for the expression of the true faith. (b) The profession of the same faith is necessary for the con-celebration of the sacraments. This is possible only among the members of churches that have a common faith and that recognize reciprocally the priesthood and the sacraments. (c) The gift of faith exists in the local churches in their concrete historical situations, determined by a particular context and time, and in each one of the believers under the guidance of their pastors. The need always to remain faithful to the authority of faith does not exclude a variety of cultural and historical expressions. A good example of this can be found in differences that coexisted during the first millennium. Thus, the affirmation of the principle of "unity in diversity" was considered essential for the reestablishment of ecclesial communion between the Eastern churches and the Roman Catholic Church.

In view of their respective positions, it is possible to relate this dialogue to the Eastern Orthodox–Old Catholic dialogue ("Sacramental Teaching, 1985–1987" [*GiA II* 2000: 254–263]). In this case, the final text does not offer a great deal of theological development, since it remains at the level of clear and simple statements, but it does provide a panoramic view of the entire sacramental issue, because in addition to presenting the seven sacraments (the only dialogue that accomplished this), the exposition starts off with a discussion of the development of the nature of the sacraments or "mysteries of the Church." At this point, a difference among the churches of the Catholic tradition should be noted: the two parties express consensus on two issues where they differ from the position of the Roman Catholic Church. First, they affirm that marriage is a life-long union and indissoluble; but that it can nonetheless be dissolved because of adultery and other analogous reasons, as for example, when the church, out of forbearance and love, acknowledges that a marriage has failed owing to human shortcomings. Second, according to the ancient church, marriage and ordination are not mutually exclusive, and the ordinand is allowed a free choice between marriage and celibacy. At the same time, after ordination, according to the tradition of the ancient church, the "promise of celibacy" at ordination becomes an impediment to marriage. With regard to the latter issue, the difference concerns the discipline in force in the Latin rite.

In the dialogues between the Roman Catholic Church and some pre-Chalcedonian churches, after the Christological divergences were resolved, the sacraments became the topic of dialogue in view of the pastoral care of the faithful who coexist in the midst of non-Christian majorities or in the Diaspora. On the Roman Catholic side, such dialogue helps to apply what is already expressed in its canonical legislation (*CIC* can. 844, §§2–3; *CCEO* can. 671, §§2–3). The "Pastoral Guidelines on Marriages, 1993" (*GiA II* 2000: 703–706), approved by the Roman Catholic Church and the Malankara Syrian Orthodox Church, are the first example. These guidelines observe that on the occasion of mixed marriages, the couple and any members of their families who belong to the couple's respective churches are allowed to participate in the Holy Eucharist in the church where the sacrament of matrimony is being celebrated. The "Guidelines for the Admission to the Eucharist, 2001" (*GiA III* 2007: 197–205), approved by the Roman Catholic Church and the Assyrian Church of the East for the purpose of ensuring that nobody is deprived of the help of the sacraments (*'rāzā*), are the second example. This joint text presents a novelty with regard to what has been an aspect of the understanding of the Eucharist in the Catholic realm since the Middle Ages. In effect, the guidelines recognize the validity of the Eucharist celebrated by the Assyrian Church, even when it is celebrated according to the anaphora of the Apostles Addai and Mari, which, from time immemorial, has been used without a recitation of the institution narrative. It is recognized that the words of the Eucharistic institution are present in that anaphora, not in a coherent narrative fashion and *ad litteram*, but rather in a dispersed euchological way, that is, integrated in successive prayers of thanksgiving, praise, and intercession. A challenge, in the Catholic realm, is to overcome reductive theological and canonical interpretations with regard to what is essential in the celebration of sacraments.

In the dialogues of the Roman Catholic Church with the Anglican Communion (ARCIC) on the one hand, and the Lutheran World Federation on the other, where the goal is full ecclesial communion, the starting point has been the study of the Eucharist, after which the ministries became the topic of discussion. This order reflects, in a certain way, the themes pointed out by Vatican Council II (*UR* §22c). With respect to the results obtained from these two dialogues (as well as from those with the World Alliance of Reformed Churches and the World Methodist Council), the Roman Catholic Church has provided a thorough assessment and has pointed out the issues that are still pending (Kasper 2009: 159–195).

Having overcome the stage of mutual clarifications very quickly, ARCIC considered it had reached "substantial agreement" on essential points of the doctrine of the Eucharist, consonant with biblical teaching and with the tradition of the inheritance common to both communions ("Windsor Statement, 1971"; "Elucidation, 1979" [GiA 1984: 68–77]). After the text was evaluated by the respective ecclesial hierarchies and ARCIC II clarified the points that, according to the official response of the Roman Catholic Church, required greater precision, it was agreed that, at the present stage, a supplementary study was not necessary. In the process of achieving this result, the rediscovery of the biblical notion of ἀνάμνησις/anamnesis made it possible to express the integrity of eucharistic faith without using the vocabulary consolidated during the times of the controversies. This has been a methodological option that proposes to discover, at a deeper level than that of the diverse and polemical expressions, the common "tradition" (that is, what Roman Catholics and Anglicans affirmed together before the division), so as to use the common vocabulary in use before the shift, and to express the agreements in using this vocabulary rather than that of the polemical disputes. In the case of the Lutheran–Roman Catholic dialogue ("The Eucharist, 1978" [GiA 1984: 190–214]) and of the Reformed–Roman Catholic dialogue ("The presence of Christ in Church and World, 1976," §§67–92 [GiA 1984: 449–56]) notable convergences have been observed, although several issues are still open, such as the doctrinal formulation and the duration of the eucharistic presence of the Lord, and the explanation of the sacrificial dimension.

The study of the ecclesial ministry had to face the historical divergences pertaining to the nature of that ministry and the sacramental nature of the rite of ordination. ARCIC considered that a "consensus" had been reached even about this second aspect ("Canterbury Statement, 1973"; "Elucidation, 1979" [GiA 1984: 78–87]). This created expectations about a possible recognition of Anglican ordinations by the Roman Catholic Church. These expectations, however, were soon frustrated by the new situation created in bilateral relations due to the progressive admission of women to the ministerial priesthood and to the episcopate in the Anglican Communion. This issue, as such, had not been discussed by ARCIC, although it was the subject of a letter exchange between Rome and Canterbury. This new situation has exposed other more fundamental issues that need greater theological clarification, such as the nature of Tradition and the point at which and the manner in which we should refer to it in order to discern what belongs to it. Here, something that the Roman Catholic Church considers as belonging to the Tradition, and which she therefore has no authority to modify, the Anglican Communion considers a disciplinary matter.

The Lutheran–Roman Catholic dialogue has achieved certain convergences with regard to ecclesial ministry ("The Ministry in the Church, 1981" [GiA 1984: 248–275]; "The Apostolicity of the Church, 2006," §§165–293 [Lutheran–Roman Catholic Commission on Unity 2006: 73–134]), while still acknowledging divergences, especially with regard to the sacramental nature of ordination and the recognition of the episcopate as an essential element in the structure of the church. A parallel can be drawn between this and the Reformed–Roman Catholic dialogue ("The presence of Christ in Church and World, 1976," §§93–110 [*GiA* 1984: 456–461]), where perhaps more profound divergences remain.

In these dialogues, where the interlocutors have remained faithful to the understanding of baptism initially forged by St. Augustine, this sacrament was initially considered a common element that did not present difficulties with regard to doctrine or ecclesial praxis (Kasper 2009, §82: 164–168). However, it has become increasingly necessary to explore the effects that this one baptism has. This is the purpose of the current round of Lutheran–Roman Catholic dialogue, which, under the global theme of "Baptism and Growth in Communion," is focusing on baptism from an ecclesiological perspective.

Finally, marriage was discussed in "ad hoc" commissions with a pastoral purpose and as a way to respond to the issues raised by mixed marriages. Such was the case of the Anglican–Roman Catholic International Commission on the Theology of Marriage and Its Application to Mixed Marriage ("The Report, 1976" [Anglican–Roman Catholic International Commission 1976]) and of the Lutheran–Reformed–Roman Catholic Trilateral dialogue ("The Theology of Marriage and the Problem of Mixed Marriages, 1976" [*GiA* 1984: 277–306]).

Even though the Methodists do not date back to the sixteenth century, the Catholic–Methodist dialogue can be compared to these other dialogues with their progress, convergences, and divergences. This dialogue, after discussing on different occasions certain aspects of baptism ("The Apostolic Tradition, 1991," §§63–66 [*GiA II* 2000: 610–11]), Eucharist ("Denver Report, 1971," §§79–83 [*GiA* 1984: 325–328]; "Dublin Report, 1976," §§47–74 [*GiA* 1984: 351–356]), and ministry ("The Apostolic Tradition, 1991," §§78–98 [*GiA II* 2000: 613–616]), centered its reflections on sacraments in a more systematic way ("Encountering Christ the Saviour: Church and Sacraments, 2011," §§28–188 [International Commission for dialogue between the Roman Catholic Church and the World Methodist Council 2011: 23–97]). A common understanding of baptism and its ecclesiological and missiological implications emerged, even if different emphases remain in the way the two communions conceive of the relationship between faith and baptism and the effectiveness of baptismal grace. The study on the Eucharist focuses on the sacrificial character and the real presence of Christ in the Eucharist. The notions of "sacrament" and "memorial" helped to clarify historical misunderstandings and express some real convergences on both topics. At the same time, the commission concluded that some important aspects of the Eucharist as sacrifice require further discussion. Finally, through this dialogue, Catholics and Methodists were able to affirm their full agreement on the sacramental nature of ordination, as a rite that contains and confers the grace it signifies; and on the distinction between the ministerial priesthood and the common priesthood of the faithful, both participating in distinct but related ways in the priesthood of Christ.

The dialogues between the Oriental Churches and these Protestant churches have not undergone such an extensive development. However, the Lutheran–Orthodox Joint Commission may be mentioned, which, in the framework of the study about "The Mystery of the Church," discussed baptism, confirmation, and Eucharist ("Baptism and

Chrismation, 2004" [*GiA* III 2007: 29–32]; "The Holy Eucharist in the Life of the Church, 2006"; and "The Holy Eucharist in the Life of the Church. Preparation, Ecological and Social Implications, 2008").

In the dialogues among Anglicans, Lutherans, Reformed, and Methodists the study of the sacraments has been a way of asserting the content of the seventh article of the Confession of Augsburg. In some cases, discussions also dealt with the ecclesial ministry, although not all interlocutors agree on its sacramental nature. Here, we need to mention the Anglican–Lutheran dialogue: baptism, confirmation, Lord's Supper, and ministry ("Pullach Report, 1977," §§64–69.73–82 [*GiA* 1984: 22–25]); the Anglican–Reformed dialogue: baptism, Eucharist, and ministry ("God's Reign and Our Unity, 1984," §§47–104 [*GiA II* 2000: 128–144]); the Lutheran–Methodist dialogue: baptism and Eucharist ("The Church: Community of Grace, 1984," §§44–56 [*GiA II* 2000: 209–212]); and the Anglican–Methodist dialogue: baptism and Eucharist ("Sharing in the Apostolic Communion, 1996," §§87–92 [*GiA II* 2000: 75–76]).

By allowing for greater confessional and ritual diversity, Protestant traditions do not regard differences among the respective positions as impeding the habitual practice of eucharistic hospitality, or even full Communion agreements among churches of different confessions (Leuenberg Church Fellowship; Meissen Agreement; Porvoo Communion; Reuilly Agreement, etc.).

In the dialogues between the Roman Catholic Church and the Christian communities that administer baptism only to "believers," that is, those who are able to make a personal confession of faith, it has been necessary to discuss basic issues pertaining to the sacramental character and the place of baptism in the respective churches. Thus far, several of these dialogues have remained at the comparative level, clarifying misunderstandings and recognizing some convergences. This is expressed in the concluding documents of the Pentecostal–Roman Catholic dialogue ("Final Report, 1976," §§11–27 [*GiA* 1984: 424–427]; "Perspectives on Koinonia, 1989," §§39–69 [*GiA II* 2000: 740–745]); the Evangelical–Roman Catholic dialogue on mission, 1984 (*GiA II* 2000: 422–423); and the Mennonite–Roman Catholic dialogue ("Called Together to Be Peace-Makers, 2003," §§111–144 [*GiA III* 2007: 235–243]). In the dialogue with Pentecostals, it has been necessary to clarify, in addition, the nature of the "Baptism of the Spirit" and how it relates to the sacrament of baptism. Rather different was the process followed by the Disciples of Christ–Roman Catholic dialogue. In fact, this dialogue began with a study on baptism, where, in spite of the differences in theological understanding and ritual practices, it was possible to affirm a mutual recognition of baptism ("Report, 1981," IV [*GiA* 1984: 158–160]). Later, the dialogue made genuine progress: after studying some aspects of the Eucharist ("The Church as Communion in Christ, 1992," §§25–32 [*GiA II* 2000: 391–393]), efforts were concentrated in a more systematic study of that sacrament (the presence of Christ, the sacrificial character, and the ecclesiological implications), and of the priesthood of Christ and his ministers ("The Presence of Christ in the Church, with special reference to the Eucharist, 2003–2009," §§ 26–72 [Disciples of Christ-Roman Catholic International Commission for dialogue 2012: 9–23]). Finally, the Baptist–Roman Catholic conversations, after the first clarifications on baptism ("Summons to Witness to Christ in Today's World, 1988," §§49–51 [*GiA II* 2000: 383–384]), studied the notions of "sacrament" and/or "ordinance" (nature, effects, and ecclesiological implications) to provide a theological context for a more comprehensive presentation of baptism and Eucharist, trying to formulate some convergences ("The Word of God in the Life of the Church, 2006–2010," §§72–131 [International Conversations between the Catholic Church and the Baptist World Alliance 2012: 61–81]).

The dialogues of these communities with Anglicans, Lutherans, and Reformed have followed the same path. Although there have been significant convergences, it is not possible to assert that a consensus has been reached yet with regard to the understanding of the relation between faith and baptism. The reports published attest to this: Anglican–Baptist conversations ("Conversations around the World, 2005," §§83–90 [*GiA III* 2007: 359–362]); Baptist–Lutheran conversations ("A Message to our Churches, 1990," §§35–48 [*GiA II* 2000: 161–164]); and Baptist–Reformed conversations ("Report, 1977," §§9–29 [*GiA* 1984: 138–147]). Up to now, of these three dialogues, only the Anglican–Baptist conversations discussed the Lord's Supper ("Conversations around the World, 2005," §§62–68 [*GiA III* 2007: 351–354]). The results attained by the Disciples of Christ–Reformed dialogue have been rather different: it was possible to reach agreement on central theological convictions concerning baptism, basic agreement on the sacramental character of Lord's Supper considered as a "means of grace," and fundamental agreement on the theology of ministry ("No Doctrinal Obstacles, 1987," §§12–15.23–36 [*GiA II* 2000: 180–185]).

In December 2012, an international trilateral dialogue was established between Mennonites, Catholics, and Lutherans. The overall theme of this five-year process is "Baptism and Incorporation into the Body of Christ, the Church." This trilateral forum will allow the dialogue to take up questions surrounding the theology and practice of baptism in the respective communions, such as God's grace in Christ and human sin; communicating grace and faith; and living out of baptism.

PARTICULAR SACRAMENTS IN MULTILATERAL DIALOGUES

The only international realm of multilateral dialogue is the Faith and Order Commission (WCC), the aim of which is to proclaim the oneness of the Church of Jesus Christ and to call the churches to the goal of visible unity and one eucharistic fellowship, expressed in worship and in common life in Christ. As "order" alludes to matters of discipline with regard to ministry and the sacraments, the concern over the sacraments has been present in Faith and Order since its inception. This study was conducted in a more specific way, however, between 1963 and 1982. The process concluded with the publication of the document "Baptism, Eucharist and Ministry" (*BEM*), the so-called "Document of Lima" (*GiA* 1984: 465–503). *BEM* brings together the convergences arrived at with regard to the three sacraments mentioned, pointing out a common basis for all participating churches, which has contributed to its being interpreted as a sort of ecumenical *kairos*. The document was translated into almost forty languages and became an inspiration for liturgical renewal movements in local churches. It was considered a sufficient basis for subsequent communion agreements between churches, and elsewhere was received as a point of reference for bilateral dialogues, particularly those carried on among Anglicans, Lutherans, and Roman Catholics, as well as dialogues of these communions with other ecumenical partners. After more than thirty years since its publication, the reception of *BEM* is a task that the churches still have not fully completed. The churches' official responses to *BEM*, which are very useful as a presentation of a *status quaestionis*, have shown that resolution of the remaining differences over the interpretation of the sacramental acts of baptism, Eucharist, and ministerial ordination must await agreement regarding the nature of sacramentality in general (Faith and Order Commission 1990: 142).

In 1994, Faith and Order resumed the theme of baptism with three aims in mind: (a) to explore to what extent an emerging consensus among the churches on *BEM*'s teaching on baptism implies a mutual baptismal and ecclesial recognition; and what are the implications when Christians can, or cannot, recognize as authentic baptisms celebrated in divided churches; (b) to consider the ecumenical baptismal praxis that has emerged since 1982 and may be identified as an instance of a practical reception of *BEM*; and (c) to focus on the ongoing challenges to mutual recognition as well as new issues (such as the increasing use of non-traditional Trinitarian formulae) that equally impede recognition, and that can, in fact, reverse previous agreements on the mutual recognition of baptism.

Faith and Order has thus undertaken a challenge already recognized in the following comment to *BEM*: "The inability of the churches to recognize mutually their various practices of Baptism as sharing in the one baptism, and their actual dividedness in spite of mutual baptismal recognition, have given dramatic visibility to the broken witness of the Church . . . The need to recover baptismal unity is at the heart of the ecumenical task as it is central for the realization of genuine partnership within Christian communities" (Faith and Order Commission 1982: 3). After a long process, the results were published in 2011 as a study document entitled *One Baptism: Towards Mutual Recognition* (Faith and Order 2011).

Almost simultaneously, the Joint Working Group between the WCC and the Roman Catholic Church also studied baptism, trying to respond practically to the same issues as Faith and Order, and adding a fourth issue: the challenge posed to the ecumenical movement by the growing Pentecostal and Evangelical Christian communities that do not see baptism itself as the point of entry into the body of Christ ("Ecclesiological and Ecumenical Implications of a Common Baptism, 2004" [*GiA III* 2007: 559–586]).

The two studies mentioned, which contain many similarities, constitute valuable material that extends and deepens the convergences reported in *BEM*, contributing new elements about the effects of baptism and its ecclesiological consequences. This is important at a time when, as a positive sign, theological essays about a "baptismal ecclesiology" are presented. It should be pointed out in this regard that though for the churches of the "Catholic" tradition baptism may be a constituent element of the church, it cannot be considered as the sole element.

QUESTIONS RELATED TO A GENERAL THEORY OF THE SACRAMENTS

As already pointed out, sacraments have been considered as a shared basis for Eastern Orthodox–Roman Catholic dialogue. It has not been possible to claim the same for the dialogues between those same churches and Protestant churches, because various aspects of the understanding of the sacraments needed clarification, as they constituted historical divergences that occupied an important place in the origins of the divisions.

In the Lutheran–Roman Catholic dialogue, these questions were studied as a corollary of the treatment of the Eucharist and the ecclesial ministry and in view of the broader process that should lead to full communion between Catholics and Lutherans ("Ways to Community, 1980," §§16–19.66–69 [GiA 1984: 218; 228–229]; "Facing Unity, 1984," §§70–85 [GiA II 2000: 460–464]; and "Church and Justification, 1993," §§66–71 [GiA II 2000: 503–504]). The treatment in the Methodist–Roman Catholic dialogue was more diffuse ("Towards a Statement on the Church, 1986," §§11–16 [GiA II 2000: 586]); "The Word of Life: A Statement on Revelation and Faith, 1996," §§94–107 [GiA II 2000: 638–641]); and "Speaking the Truth on Love: Teaching Authority among Catholics and Methodist, 2001," §§52–61 [GiA III 2007: 155–157]). In both cases, however, it would be important to revisit these themes, applying now, as hermeneutical criterion, the "differentiated consensus" on the doctrine of justification. Some theological essays have already reflected this (Genre and Grillo 2003).

Within the framework of a broader study, the Lutheran–Orthodox Joint Commission focused on matters inherent to the sacraments in general, pointing out convergences. Particularly relevant in this regard are "Word and Sacraments, 2000" and "Mysteria/Sacraments as Means of Salvation, 2002" (GiA III 2007: 23–28). Something similar was undertaken in the Oriental Orthodox–Reformed dialogue, although this was more modest in scope, since it remains at the comparative level only ("Report, 2001," §§67–80 [GiA III 2007: 51–53]).

Different in scope (since they recognize common roots) are the dialogues between Protestant churches: Anglican–Lutheran conversations ("Pullach Report, 1977," §§61–63; §§70–72 [GiA 1984: 22–23]); Lutheran–Methodist dialogue ("The Church: Community of Grace, 1984" §§40–43 [GiA II 2000: 209]); and Lutheran–Reformed dialogue ("Towards Church Fellowship, 1989," §§55–62 [GiA II 2000: 242]), discussed themes such as the relation between Word and sacraments and the notion of sacrament and confirmed clear convergences in this respect.

The second phase of Baptist–Roman Catholic conversations has also studied different themes in relation to the sacraments, such as the meaning of sacrament and ordinance, the relation between sacraments and the church, and the link between sacraments and the Word of God, in the process attaining important convergences ("The Word of God in the Life of the Church, 2006–2010," §§72–92).

Numerous local dialogues have dealt with the particular sacraments and with themes inherent in an overall theology of sacraments. A presentation of those results exceeds our purpose. However, I would like to mention two local dialogues that have dealt with questions pertaining to the sacraments in general:

1) The first dialogue is the study of the Ecumenical Working Group of Protestant and Catholic theologians in Germany investigating whether or not the anathemas of the sixteenth century continued to apply to the present dialogue partners. After a thorough study, the results were published under the title "Lehrverurteilungen— Kirchentrennend?" (Lehmann and Pannenberg 1985: 77–88; 89–124). Here, in addition to Eucharist, confirmation, anointing of the sick, and matrimony, questions pertaining to the sacraments in general are treated, clarifying the constituent characteristics of sacraments; the efficacy of sacraments by virtue of their realization (*ex opere operato*) and the importance of faith (*sola fide*). Also discussed are the character imprinted by some sacraments; the priesthood of all the baptized and the power to administer the sacraments; and, lastly, the variability of liturgical forms. The study has shed new light on the historic positions, placing them in context and revealing that fundamental problems pertain both to the way the essence of grace is understood and to the way it is communicated, which is reflected in the different ways in which word and sacrament, faith and word/sacrament, as well as church and sacrament are related.

2) The second dialogue is the Group of Les Dombes, which brought together French-speaking Catholic, Reformed and Lutheran theologians. This group, after studying Eucharist and ministry, focused its reflection on sacramentality as such, considered as the only way of overcoming certain divergences that had appeared when treating the sacraments in particular. After three years of work, the group published the study "The Holy Spirit, the Church and the Sacraments, 1979" (Groupe des Dombes 1988: 115–156). The presentation consists of three sections: (1) a clarification of the terminology habitually used, a proper appreciation of the difficulties inherent in the number of the sacraments and in their significance, and an attempt to elucidate the contemporary mentality; (2) the witness of the Scriptures to God's covenant with his people, seeing that the covenant is the constitutive basic point of reference that enables us to understand the link between the Spirit and the celebrations that the Christian tradition has called "sacraments"; and (3) a doctrinal outline describing in more detail the link between the Spirit, the Word, and the sacraments in the church's life. The value of this text, which originates from a non-official group of dialogue partners, lies not only in going beyond the comparative level by arriving at mutually shared results, but also in succeeding in defining the sacrament in a manner acceptable to all three parties, taking into account, at the same time, the pastoral needs.

Some Conclusions

Although theological dialogues have not yet resolved all the divergences existing in the sacramental realm, they have succeeded in shedding new light on the path to overcoming those divergences. This has been possible thanks to significant developments in sacramental theology and in the sacramental rites of the different churches, as is expressed in certain characteristics common to the different confessional traditions. The first of these is the acknowledgement of the Christological roots of the sacraments. The second is the recognition that the unique and unrepeatable event of Jesus Christ presents itself in his church through the Word proclaimed and the sacrament celebrated. The third is the increasing assumption within the Protestant realm of the ecclesial dimension of worship and, consequently, of the value of sacramental rites for the life of the church. Finally, our theological-doctrinal understanding has been enriched by a greater awareness of the anthropological and cultural foundations underlying the sacramental event, brought to the fore by contemporary researches into symbolism, semiotics, and linguistics. With these common elements in mind, it may be helpful to revisit the unresolved issues. I will present these issues by pointing out a tension between two general positions because, even though we cannot reduce confessional positions to just a few "models," it is nonetheless possible to recognize certain theological "nuclei" present in all of the dialogues, as Max Thurian has clearly shown upon the conclusion of the process of *BEM* (Thurian 1983: 404).

The number of rites to be recognized depends upon our understanding of the notion of "sacrament." For this reason, there is still no full convergence on the number of sacraments. Some criteria have been proposed in order to overcome the divergences: a distinction between the two "scriptural sacraments" and five "commonly so-called sacraments"; or two "sacraments" and five "sacramental signs"; or two "sacraments" and five "sacramental acts"; and finally, a recognition of the analogical character of the notion of sacrament. Such affirmations are in harmony with the classic vision of the Roman Catholic Church, which traditionally has recognized the prominent significance of baptism and Eucharist as *sacramenta maiora*, in contrast to the five *sacramenta minora*. The recognition of the analogical character of sacraments legitimizes both a broader and a narrower usage of the term "sacrament," applying it to Christ and to the church. It is true that this broad use of the term, at least when it is applied to the church, has met with strong objections from many of the Protestant churches.

Historical research has offered an important contribution clarifying the meaning of the "institution" of the sacraments. Among Scholastic authors, this was an "etiological" issue, and they would give a "theological" response: a sacrament can only be "instituted" by him who has the power to produce its effect (grace as participation in salvation). The process of "institution" was considered to have been different with each one of the sacraments. Among the Reformers, the point was to look for "historical" grounds, that is, for them the question was when, during Christ's life, according to testimony in the Scriptures, can we find concrete proof of the institution of each sacrament?

Contemporary Roman Catholic theology, as well as the Magisterium, have overcome the problem of trying to locate the "literal words for the institution." Roman Catholic theologians refer to Christ as the "founder" and "source" of sacraments; or, with the patristic and liturgical title, as their "author" or "origin." The *Catechism of the Catholic Church* (1114–1117), after referring to the doctrine defined by the Council of Trent, affirms that the sources of sacraments are the words and actions of Christ, which were salvific in themselves. Only gradually did the church recognize the treasure received by Christ, as centuries went by before the church discovered or recognized the seven sacraments instituted by the Lord. The role of the church in recognizing and dispensing the sacraments is comparable to its role in establishing the biblical canon. It is the Spirit who has made this possible, leading the church to the fullness of truth.

Many churches affirm that sacraments are "means of grace"; however, a difference arises when explaining the nature of that "means." This is the historical controversy about the efficacy of sacraments. Contemporary theology, with different resources, explains this same topic in different ways and with different expressions. However, in view of the role that it played in the controversies at the time, the historical issue does demand an explanation. Medieval theology affirmed that sacraments confer grace *ex opere operato*, which was a way to explain the sacrament as an act that accomplishes what it signifies. The Council of Trent (Cf. Dz-H 1608) adopted this view to show that each human being, in his own circumstances and through ecclesial mediation, receives the justification that comes only from Christ.

Roman Catholics have the impression that Protestant disapproval of the notion of *ex opere operato* revolved around a distorted understanding of sacramental efficacy—an absolutization of the sacrament—rather than around what the church was really teaching. The notion was not meant to point to the automatic nature of the sacramental act, but to enhance the grace of God signified and communicated in a visible way. The sacraments effect grace by being a certain kind of "instrument" in Christ's hands, their real minister. Their power is owed to the fact that they are "moved instrumentally" by *another*, that is, by Christ, the only one who justifies. Only Christ elevates the sacramental rites and gives them their instrumental power, as he acts through them. The difference between the work of Christ and the work of his instrument is irreducible. Therefore, and in order to avoid the danger of understanding the expression in a distorted way, we should emphasize that affirming the *ex opere operato* efficacy means being sure of God's sovereign and gratuitous intervention in the sacraments.

Speaking of God's intervention in the sacraments brings to mind, however, another point: the sacrament is an action. As such, it communicates a gift from God, and what is offered demands a response. Sacraments are not outside the scope of what we know about every relationship between divine gratuitousness, which grants the gift, and human freedom, which accepts it. It is impossible to think about justification without a personal act on the part of the human being: conversion, which includes the rejection of sin; reaching to God through faith, hope, and charity; and the will to live according to Christ. This attitude manifests a willingness without which the salvific action cannot be operated in the person receiving the sacrament. Thus, the final effect of the sacraments in each person is always the result of a harmonic exchange between the gift of God and one's personal attitude.

Faith and sacraments are closely related; they are two ways through whose unified action man receives the gift of God. By responding to the nature of human beings and to the mystery of the Incarnation, sacraments remind us that faith needs to be visibly expressed through public profession and through the cult celebrated by the community. The adage *lex orandi-lex credendi* pointed to the connection between the celebration of the mysteries and ecclesial faith. Thus, the celebration of the mysteries was based on the professed faith but also represented the living expression of that faith. The liturgical celebration, therefore, had a crucial role: to be a testimony of orthodoxy.

In Scholastic theology, Thomas Aquinas established a close connection between faith and sacraments: for him, sacraments are signs of faith that give evidence to the faith through which man is justified (*ST* III, q.62, a.5 ad2; q.61, a.4). Post-Tridentine theology, prone to distrust anything that could mean siding with the Reformers' doctrine, refrained from delving deeper into this truth. This led to a certain separation between the efficacy of faith and the efficacy of the sacrament, favoring the latter. Vatican II tried to overcome this polarization: "[Sacraments] not only presuppose faith, but by words and objects they also nourish, strengthen, and express it; that is why they are called 'sacraments of faith'" (*SC* 59). We may add to this that contemporary Roman Catholic theology considers the sacramental act itself to have real efficacy of faith, which is necessarily related to the celebration of the rite. The entity and efficacy of the sacrament are conferred by the Word of God, believed and professed, which finds its expression in sacramental form.

If we consider the liturgical forms of each one of the sacraments, we may note that they all express acceptance of God's Word and, at the same time, are a profession of faith. This allows us to return to the more vigorous sense of the traditional expression, *sacramenta sunt sacramenta fidei*. And this on two levels: first, the sacramental rite is a proclamation of God's plan of salvation and grace for the faithful in his church; in this sense, the sacraments are the word of God, objective proclamation of the faith; second, this proclamation of the faith demands a subjective answer: it is necessary for man to accept God's proposal. There can be no gift of grace without faith, without a free acceptance of God's gift. No salvation event is fully complete without the free and amorous entrance of the believer into the covenant God proposes in his church.

The old confessional characterization of the Roman Catholic Church as the church of the sacraments as opposed to the Protestant communities as churches of the Word has been overcome. It has become possible to see a convergence: the church plays a ministerial and instrumental role in the proclamation of the Word and the celebration of the sacraments. Word and sacrament alike are of the very essence of the church. It is true that they also provide us with two different frameworks for understanding the church and the way in which she fulfills her ministerial and instrumental role. The church existing as a community in history has been understood and described in the Protestant tradition as *creatura verbi*; in Roman Catholic teaching the church is described as a "sacrament." In both expressions it is possible to recognize the radical dependence of the church in receiving the transcendental gift that God conveys to her and to acknowledge that gift as the basis of the church's activity of service for the salvation of humanity. Even if it has not yet become possible for the two traditions to understand the nature of this salutary activity in the same way, the two conceptions of church as *creatura verbi* and as "sacrament of grace" can in fact be seen as expressing the same instrumental reality from different angles, as complementary to each other or as two sides of the same coin.

ABBREVIATIONS

ARCIC   Anglican–Roman Catholic International Commission
BEM   Faith and Order Commission, *Baptism, Eucharist and Ministry* (1982)
CCEO   Roman Catholic Church, *Codex Canonum Ecclesiarum Orientalium* (1990)
CIC   Roman Catholic Church, *Codex Iuris Canonici* (1983)
Dz-H   H. Denzinger (2012), *Enchiridion Symbolorum: A Compendium of Creeds, Definitions, and Declarations of the Catholic Church*, ed. P. Hünermann (San Francisco, CA: Ignatius Press)
ET   English Translation
GiA   *Growth in Agreement*
SC   Second Vatican Council, Conciliar Constitution *Sacrosanctum Concilium* (1963)
UR   Second Vatican Council, Decree on Ecumenism *Unitatis redintegratio* (1964)
WCC   World Council of Churches

SUGGESTED READING

Genre and Grillo (2003); Hotz (1979); Kasper (2009); Lehmann and Pannenberg (1985).

BIBLIOGRAPHY

Anglican–Roman Catholic International Commission (1976), "Theology of Marriage and its Application to Mixed Marriage," *Information Service* 32: 12–27.

Borelli, J., and J. H. Ericksson (eds.) (1996), *The Quest of Unity: Orthodox and Catholics in Dialogue* (Crestwood, NY: St Vladimir's Seminary/Washington DC: USCC).

Disciples of Christ-Roman Catholic International Commission for Dialogue (2012), Fourth Agreed Statement "The Presence of Christ in the Church, with special reference to the Eucharist, 2003–2009" (<http://ccu.disciples.org/Portals/CCU/Fourth%20Agreed%20Statement%20-%20Final%20June%202012.pdf>).

Faith and Order Commission (1982), *Baptism, Eucharist and Ministry* (Geneva: WCC).

Faith and Order Commission (1990), *BEM 1982-1990: Report on the Process and Responses* (Geneva: WCC).

Faith and Order Commission (2011), *One Baptism: Towards Mutual Recognition: A Study Text* (Geneva: WCC).

Genre, E., and A. Grillo (2003), *Giustificazione, Chiese, Sacramenti. Prospettive dopo la Dichiarazione cattolico-luterana*. Atti del convegno internazionale di teologia, Roma, 29–31 ottobre 2001 (Rome: Studia Anselmiana).

Gros. J., H. Meyer, and W. Rusch (eds.) (2000), *Growth in Agreement II: Reports and Agreed Statements of Ecumenical Conversations on a World Level 1982–1998* (Geneva: WCC/Grand Rapids, MI: Eerdmans).

Gros, J, Th. Best, and L. Fuchs (eds.) (2007), *Growth in Agreement III: International Dialogue Texts and Agreed Statements, 1998–2005* (Geneva: WCC/Grand Rapids, MI: Eerdmans).

Groupe des Dombes (1988), *Pour la communion des Eglises. L'apport du Groupe des Dombes* (Paris: Le Centurion) [ET: The Group of Les Dombes (2010), *For the Communion of the Churches. The Contribution of the Groupe des Dombes* (Grand Rapids, MI: Eerdmans)].

Henpelmann, R. (1992), *Sakrament als Ort des Vermittlung des Heils. Sakramententheologie in evangelisch-Katholischen Dialog* (Göttingen: Vandenhoeck & Ruprecht).

Hotz, R. (1979), *Sakramente im Wechselspiel zwischen Ost und West* (Zurich: Benzinger).

International Conversations between the Catholic Church and the Baptist World Alliance (2012), "The Word of God in the Life of the Church," *American Baptist Quarterly* 31: 28–122.

International Commission for Dialogue between the Roman Catholic Church and the World Methodist Council (2011), *Encountering Christ the Saviour: Church and Sacraments* (Lake Junaluska, NC: World Methodist Council).

Kasper, W. (2009), *Harvesting the Fruits: Basic Aspects of Christian Faith in Ecumenical Dialogue* (London: Continuum).

Lehmann, K., and W. Pannenberg (Hrsg.) (1985): *Lehrverurteilungen—kirchentrennend?* Band 1: *Rechtfertigung, Sakramente und Amt im Zeitalter der Reformation und heute* (Freiburg im Breisgau: Herder/Göttingen: Vandenhoeck & Ruprecht) [ET: Lehmann, K., and W. Pannenberg (eds.) (1990), *The Condemnations of the Reformation Era: Do They Still Divide?* (Minneapolis, MN: Fortress Press)].

Lehmann, K. and W. Pannenberg (Hrsg.) (1990), *Lehrverurteilungen—kirchentrennend?* Band 3: *Materialien zur Lehre von den Sakramenten und vom kirchlichen Amt* (Freiburg i. Br.: Herder/Göttingen: Vandenhoeck & Ruprecht).

Lyons, P. (ed.) (1997), *Parola e sacramento*. Atti del Simposio presso la Facoltà di Teologia del Pontificio Ateneo S. Anselmo, Roma, 4-5 maggio 1995 (Rome: Pontificio Ateneo S. Anselmo).

Lutheran–Orthodox Joint Commission (2006), "Common Statement: The Mystery of the Church: D. The Holy Eucharist in the Life of the Church" (<http://www.helsinki.fi/~risaarin/lutortjointtext.html#impl>).

Lutheran–Orthodox Joint Commission (2008), "The Holy Eucharist in the Life of the Church. Preparation, Ecological and Social Implications" (<http://www.helsinki.fi/~risaarin/lutortjointtext.html#impl>).

Lutheran–Roman Catholic Commission on Unity (2008), "The Apostolicity of the Church: Study Document," *Information Service* 128/2: 60–134.

Meyer, H., and L. Vischer (eds.) (1984), *Growth in Agreement: Reports and Agreed Statements of Ecumenical Conversations on a World Level* (Mahwah, NY: Paulist Press/Geneva: WCC).

Mottu, H. (1995), "Rites," in P. Gisel (dir.), *Encyclopédie du protestantisme* (Paris: Cerf/Geneva: Labor et Fides), 1338–1354.

Pontifical Council for Promoting Christian Unity (1993), *Directory for the Application of Principles and Norms on Ecumenism* (Vatican City).

Thurian, M. (1983), "Wie steht es mit der Ökumene? Theologische Konvergenzen, Kirchen in Gemeinschaft," *Ökumenische Rundschau* 32: 399–417.

INDEX

Lightning Source UK Ltd.
Milton Keynes UK
UKHW030249160919
349855UK00002B/4/P